10
YOU M

Zack, *if* *any*
do this, you *ca*

Grandpa, *Gran*

XMAS

1001 WHISKIES
YOU MUST TASTE BEFORE YOU DIE

GENERAL EDITOR **DOMINIC ROSKROW**

FOREWORD BY **JIM MURRAY**

UNIVERSE

A Quintessence Book

First published in the United States of America in 2012 by
UNIVERSE PUBLISHING
A Division of Rizzoli International Publications, Inc.
300 Park Avenue South
New York, NY 10010
www.rizzoliusa.com

Fifth Printing, 2015
2015 2016 2017 / 10 9 8 7 6 5

ISBN: 978-0-7893-2487-0

Library of Congress Control Number: 2011938896

QSS.WHSK

This book was designed and produced by
Quintessence Editions Ltd.
The Old Brewery
6 Blundell Street
London N7 9BH
www.1001beforeyoudie.com

Project Editor	Simon Ward
Editors	Frank Ritter, Ben Way
Editorial Assistant	Olivia Young
Designers	Alison Hau, Tom Howey
Editorial Director	Jane Laing
Publisher	Mark Fletcher

Color reproduction by Chroma Graphics Pte Ltd., Singapore
Printed in China by Midas Printing International Ltd.

CONTENTS

FOREWORD

By Jim Murray

It is little surprise the world is in love with whisky. For we are, each and every one of us, the tellers of tales and the listeners of stories. So it has always been.

And when we sit down with a glass a fifth-full of a golden yarn, we listen to the story that unfolds with each sniff and then mouthful. And our natural instinct is to share that story with others. Especially the spellbinding ones, or those that touch a chord with our soul.

Within these pages are 1,001 stories, ranging from the serene and gentle to raging passion and smoke-framed wars, each an interpretation or translation of an eight, or maybe an eighteen- or perhaps a fifty-year-old text. Each translator will give the story a slightly different slant than another might have done: that is human nature and points to just why we find whisky so fascinating. It is just in the same way that two people sitting side by side may watch a football game and rate the performance of a particular player with a quite dissimilar set of values, one marking him the best technician on the field, his neighbor the worst. The story of the quarterback, for instance, might be told in 15,000 different ways by those who saw him play; so the story of a whisky can be viewed in the same manner. Because how much we enjoy the story, or how closely we listen to it, how it thrills or fires our imaginations may well depend on just what kind of tale we had wanted to hear.

What is beyond question is that never before have we had so many liquid stories to read at any one time—so many players in the whisky league. Not only has there been an extraordinary explosion of new distilleries around the world, thrusting at us names like Mackmyra, Penderyn, and King Car, but the advent of single cask bottlings has changed the boundaries of whisky not just on the world map, but also in the taste profiles available to discover. The output from Scotland and the United States in particular means that each year the industry seemingly grows a new skin, the old one shed as the 200 or so bottles from a single cask are bought and then emptied.

Every year I tell over 1,000 new stories in my *Jim Murray's Whisky Bible*, grading them from good to bad. That is on top of the standard brands, some having been around since the days of Queen Victoria; others very much newer, taking advantage of new maturation techniques such as cask finishing or a growth in demand of a particular type of whisky, be it rye-rich or smoke-infused. But of those 1,000, by no means are all worth dying for.

Not everyone agrees with my views of the whiskies I taste and, for certain, the readers of this book will take issue with the conclusions drawn by the writers. But that is how it should be: it is a guide only, the views of professionals in their field and ones that may and sometimes may not resonate with the beholder of a particular whisky of which they are very fond. Likewise, some readers will flick through this book with the single purpose of waging war against those who are heaping praise on a whisky they feel is an affront to the great spirit.

The majority, though, will be looking for an insight, a gentle guidance toward something they have missed: a malt or bourbon or Japanese or Irish that had sneaked beneath their radar or simply one worth fishing for on the Internet with the hope of landing when it can be afforded.

It is possible, however, that the reader may hold back as he might not recognize the name of the judge of the whisky that has caught his eye. That is a natural instinct and understandable, but General Editor Dominic Roskrow is not just a champion of whisky, but also of whisky writing. He shares with me the deep concern for the quality or, rather, lack of it foisted upon us seemingly daily by an unnaturally cozy inner sanctum of ubiquitous scribes.

To this end, Dominic has brought together a team of relatively fresh faces and lively minds to present their views on 1,001 whiskies that may, or may not, win your hearts. Some, I hope, will go on to form the nucleus of a new wave of whisky writing; and one that is desperately needed. However, it must be remembered by both reader and writer alike that the discovery and understanding of whisky is not something that happens overnight. It requires open mouths, open hearts, and open minds. And time. Essentially, though, the realization that having your name in print does not an expert make. I tasted my first whisky in 1974 and dared not express my opinion in public for another sixteen years.

However the Age of Instant, with the Internet and Twitter, means that no writer dare hold back his views so long. So just as we can watch a whisky mature, changing in character, depth, color, and richness as it passes its years in the barrel, so now can we watch writers, like barley or rye, grow in their field and fatten on the stem.

It was all so different twenty years ago when, in 1992, I gave up my job as a journalist for a British national newspaper to become the world's first full-time whisky writer. In those days of comparative famine, a book such as this would have been impossible: I doubt you would have been able to find 1,001 different whiskies, let alone that number representing the very cream. Just twenty years ago it would have demanded the most gigantic leap of the imagination to think that the industry could travel so far in such a comparatively short time.

Back then there was barely a visitors' center, nor a whisky club. Brand ambassadors were an unknown species as there were no whisky fairs. Master blenders and master distillers were just blenders and distillers. The entire terrain of whisky was one unrecognizable to that which we see today. When I turned up at a distillery at some place or other around the world, the manager was often shocked anyone would have an interest in what happened during his working day.

So it warms my heart that, two decades on, a new wave of writers are able to give their views on a new wave of whiskies. And, perhaps above all, that the public has a seemingly insatiable thirst to learn just what makes a whisky tick. As I write this, having just given a tasting in Portland, where they had to change the venue to accommodate demand, I am about to drive through the snow to Seattle to share some of the world's finest whiskies at another full house. And then Vancouver tomorrow, followed by the Whisky Festival in Victoria, where tickets trade like currency. Then later, tastings and appearances in Israel, Taiwan, Germany, and Africa—all points north, south, east, and west.

For the world is in love with whisky. And, with the 1,001 stories as told by Dominic and his team, I hope that love deepens a little further.

INTRODUCTION

By Dominic Roskrow, General Editor

If I had a dollar for every time I have been asked whether there really are 1,001 whiskies, I would have, well, about 1,001 dollars. Truth be told, in every single week my team of whisky writers was putting together this tome, another ten to twenty new whiskies were being released. This book describes the tastiest tip of a very large proverbial iceberg, and I guarantee that, by the time you have read your way through this book, let alone attempted to try even a fraction of the whiskies contained within its pages, another truckload of releases will have appeared. It is like the painting of the Golden Gate Bridge— by the time you get to the end, it is all ready to be done again.

And we are not just talking about whisky from the obvious countries, such as Scotland, Ireland, the United States, Japan, and Canada, either. There is a worldwide whisky revolution going on, and we are seeing the emergence of good-quality spirits from Sweden and Finland in the north to Australia and New Zealand in the south, and from Taiwan and India in the east to Brazil and Argentina in the west. While the original big five, and particularly Scotland, continue to dominate the world of whisky, both in terms of quality and quantity, new nations are making their mark and are proving themselves capable of producing world-class spirits.

So what is whisky? That is a very good question, because people distributed around the world have a variety of ideas about it, and there are several "whiskies" made on the margins of the industry that are blurring definitions. Some big Indian whisky brands, for example, are not permitted to be sold in Europe as whisky. Different countries define whisky in different ways, some do not bother at all, but most recognize whisky as a distilled spirit made from just grain, yeast, and water. That does not sound very much, does it? And yet there are countless different ways of making whisky from this starting point, and countless flavors to discover. It is because of this simplicity that whisky is so ubiquitous, and it is because it offers so many tastes and flavors that it enjoys such popularity. Indeed, whisky enthusiasts would equate a person who claims not to like whisky with someone claiming not to like food. Of course they do; it is just that they may not yet have tried the one they like.

As you would expect, this book is dominated by Scotland, a country that has been distilling grain for more than a thousand years and is very good at it. There are more than a hundred operating distilleries in the country, and, with a bit of effort, you could write a book called *1001 Scotches You Must Taste Before You Die*. It is unsurprising, therefore, that much of the whisky of the world is modeled on the Scottish example. For a drink that enjoys such a high profile, however, it is amazing how little is known about it. There are lots of myths and misunderstandings about whisky, many assumptions and prejudices. How often do you hear, for instance, that you should not add water to Scotch? Well, very often you can. Or that single malts are better than blended whiskies? Nope. That older is better, perhaps? Not in every case. Scotland makes all the best whisky? Negative. And while everyone talks up single malts, are you aware that more than 90 percent of the world's Scotch whisky sales are of blended whisky, a fact that is unlikely to change anytime soon?

Scottish single-malt whisky attracts the headlines because, not to put too fine a point on it, it is a miracle in a glass, a piece of perfectly tuned molecular engineering that never ceases to surprise and delight. The wonder of single-malt whisky is how something made with only malted barley, yeast, and water can produce a drink capable of myriad different flavors. You can dedicate a lifetime to working out how that is the case, and the fun of doing so comes from exploring those flavors for yourself.

Single-malt whisky is simple to make but notoriously difficult to get right. You need to trick the barley grain into growing for a few days by immersing it in water, then halt that process by drying the barley. This is the malting process, and once it is done the grain can be ground into flour, or grist. The malting process releases the sugars and enzymes necessary to make alcohol. The flour is submersed in hot water, and all its goodness is released. The empty husks are then removed, yielding a warm, brown, sweet liquid. Adding yeast to the liquid converts it into alcohol and carbon dioxide. Effectively, what you have created is a rough and strong beer, sour to drink because it has been made in nonsterile conditions.

From here, the beer is put into a copper pot still, which is essentially a giant kettle, and the liquid is heated. Distillation is merely the act of separating alcohol from water. As the beer is heated, the alcohols begin to evaporate, rising inside the copper still until they reach an exit point, a pipe called a lyne arm. The piping to which this leads is subjected to a flow of cold water that causes the vapor to recondense. Often, the first time this process is done, the recondensed liquid is returned to the still and the process is repeated.

In Scotland, distillation normally, but not always, takes place twice. During the second distillation, only part of the run is collected and made into whisky. The distiller rejects the very early part of the run because the volatile alcohols are at their strongest and potentially most dangerous. He also rejects the end of the run because these alcohols are the weakest and taste bad. The middle section, known as the "cut," is stored as "new-make spirit."

How the spirit is turned into whisky can vary in its details. In Scotland, the new spirit must go into oak casks and be stored for a minimum of three years to be called whisky, although the length of time is often far greater. Scottish malt spirit has delicate flavors that normally would be masked by heavy, spicy flavors passed on to it by the oak, and so "secondhand" casks that previously contained sherry or, more commonly, bourbon are used for maturation.

Given that whisky making is pretty much the same at every malt-whisky distillery, why do malt whiskies taste so different from one another? How the malted barley is dried is one big influence; barley dried over a peat fire, for example, makes for smoky, phenolic whisky. Mainly, though, the differences are due to production variables: the length of time the wash or beer is fermented, the size and shape of the copper pot still, where the cut is made, and how fast the spirit passes through the stills. Most important, though, is what happens in the oak cask. Whisky spirit enters the cask as a clear liquid and takes its color from the wood, and more than two-thirds of the flavor will come from the oak.

What the cask contained previously and the time the whisky is left in the cask both affect the eventual spirit's character, but so do more subtle influences. The size of the cask and where it is stored play a part, and all sorts of still-unexplained events within the cask can take the whisky on its own unique journey. Place two identical casks together in a maturation warehouse, fill them with the same liquid, and leave them for the same period of time, and they will not produce the same whisky. That is the miracle, or black magic, of malt.

While single malt plays frontman in Scotland, it accounts for only a fraction of the country's whisky output. In fact, Scotland produces four types of whisky: single malt, which is whisky made using malted barley from one distillery; grain whisky, which is made using other grains and a different production process; blended whisky, which is a mixture of single malts and grain whisky; and blended malt whisky, also called vatted whisky, which is a mixture of malts from different distilleries, and which contains no grain.

While the template of Scotch single-malt whisky is the one that has been most copied, there are other ways to make whisky. Grain whisky, Irish whiskey, and American bourbon whiskey are created primarily on a still that is very different from the pot still used for single malt. The pot-still method produces spirit in batches, but spirit may also be produced by a still that operates continually, called a continuous still, column still, or Coffey still. Under this system, the distillery wash or beer is forced through columns where it meets pressurized stream at extremely high temperatures. Compared to single malt, the resulting spirit has a less distinct taste, but it is able to capture flavors provided from elsewhere, primarily from wood during maturation.

What makes whisky so exciting right now is that a whole new wave of distillers, from Wales to West Virginia and from Austria to Australia, are innovating, prodding at the margins, and experimenting with cask sizes, casks previously used for different drinks, different grains, different woods, different ways of drying the barley, and different maturation methods. There are whiskies made with grains from different continents, whiskies blended at birth rather than shortly before bottling, whiskies matured for different periods in different parts of the world, and whiskies made on unique stills. Whisky is even being made with unusual ingredients such as buckwheat and chestnut.

For this book I brought together more than twenty writers, some of whom will be known to whisky enthusiasts, but many not. The backbone of the team is built around some of the world's most experienced whisky writers, but I have also brought in a new generation of whisky men and women. Some of these are whisky writers specializing in certain regions, and these have made the same journey as many of the readers of this book will do. Others are whisky bloggers I have met through Twitter; some have never published anything before, but I put my trust in them because I have been reading their musings over the last eighteen months or so and have learned from them.

This book has had a long and difficult birth, and no doubt was a painful and uneasy experience for the Quintessence Editions team headed by Simon Ward. But it has been a labor of love and as pleasurable an experience as I have had, both as a newspaper journalist and a whisky editor. Finding somewhere nice to sit with a drink, I would read proofs about Canada or Japan, and immerse myself in this book. I was actually being paid to read about a subject I love, months before anyone else, and I'm not sure it gets much better than that.

I hope you get as much pleasure from this book as I have. If you are new to whisky, then I hope it gives you a fine start in the quest to find the perfect whisky. If you are a seasoned connoisseur, I hope that it reveals some nice new surprises. And whoever you are, I hope it encourages you to explore and experiment. One thousand and one and counting . . .

Index of Whiskies by Name

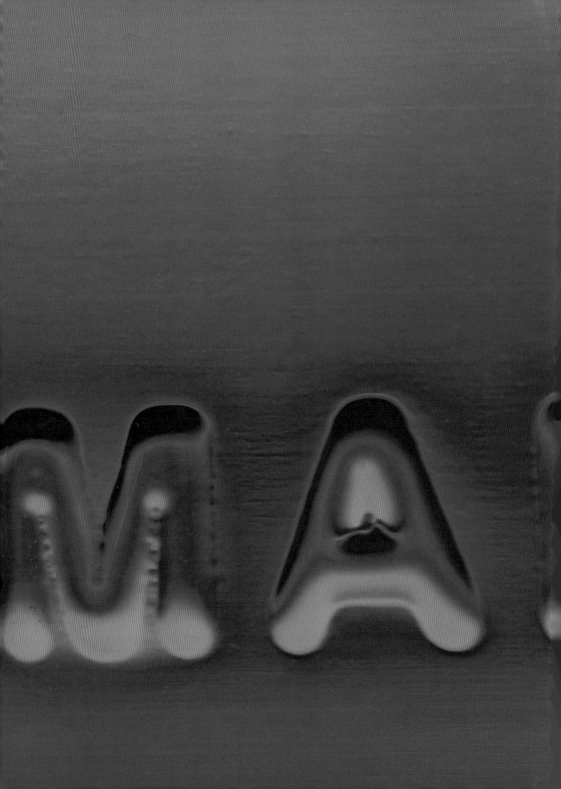

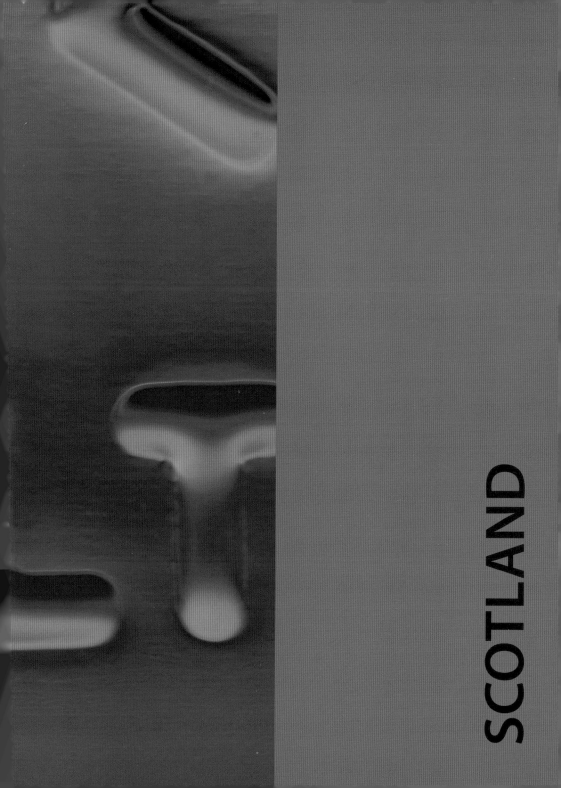

SCOTLAND

Aberfeldy
12-Year-Old

Dewar's (Bacardi)
www.dewars.com

Region and country of origin Highlands, Scotland
Distillery Aberfeldy, Aberfeldy, Perthshire
Alcohol content 40% abv
Style Single malt

Only a small percentage of the 660,500 gallons (2.5 million liters) of whisky produced at Aberfeldy distillery every year is released as a single malt under the Aberfeldy name. The majority goes into the blending of Dewar's White Label, one of the world's best-selling blended whiskies, with Aberfeldy itself marketed as "the spiritual home of Dewar's whisky." There are only two current releases of Aberfeldy single malt: this 12-Year-Old and the 21-Year-Old.

Independent bottlings are relatively hard to find. Perhaps it is fitting, then, that the malt has adopted an association with Scotland's indigenous red squirrel, which appears on its label. Once plentiful and thriving, red squirrels are now rare and endangered. Perthshire is home to many, and a colony resides in the tranquil woodlands bordering Aberfeldy distillery. The strong link between Scotch whisky and the natural environment from which it comes is often overlooked, but the red squirrel icon on the label is deeply significant to Dewar's. Here, in the heart of Perthshire, the endangered red squirrel represents nature in perfect equilibrium—a reminder of the delicate balance and harmony that is as essential for fine whisky as it is for the rare red squirrels. **SR**

Tasting notes

Heather, honey, notes of sweet pineapple, butter toffee, toast, cereal, and vanilla. Great depth. Sweet golden syrup and honey followed by spices and orange.

Aberfeldy
14-Year-Old Single Cask

Dewar's (Bacardi)
www.dewars.com

Region and country of origin Highlands, Scotland
Distillery Aberfeldy, Aberfeldy, Perthshire
Alcohol content 58.1% abv
Style Single malt

Aberfeldy has always been a wonderful single malt—comfortable, soft, pleasant, and noted for its rich, honeyed style—but it is not very well known and has never been given the sort of push it perhaps deserves. This may be because parent company Dewar's, which in turn is part of the Bacardi empire, has established its reputation through blends.

But this whisky, snapped up on its release and therefore extremely rare, is a case in point. Whoever decided to put it on the market obviously wanted to stir things up a bit. Just one cask was emptied for the bottling, in June 2011, and initially there were only 185 bottles of it. On the label there is talk of elder leaves, green apples, and fragrant gorse bushes, but this is altogether a more bruising and heavy-hitting whisky. The Aberfeldy trademark honeyed and toffee notes are here, but the cask strength and the combination of oak from the extra years in wood and the influence of sherry ensure that this is an unforgettable experience.

Hopefully, this whisky's success should encourage the company to release other single-cask Aberfeldy bottlings, so if you cannot find this one, watch out for an equivalent release. Aberfeldy is definitely a distillery worthy of more attention. **DR**

Tasting notes

Dusty dry sherry, cocoa, and hazelnut milk chocolate on the nose, then a rich wallop of sherry, treacle, and dark chocolate fruit and nut on the palate. Wonderful.

← Peat is used to heat containers at Aberfeldy distillery in 1962.

Aberfeldy 18-Year-Old Single Cask

Dewar's (Bacardi) | www.dewars.com

Region and country of origin Highlands, Scotland
Distillery Aberfeldy, Aberfeldy, Perthshire
Alcohol content 54.9% abv
Style Single malt

This 18-Year-Old is a single-cask edition and only a handful of eighteen- and nineteen-year-olds have been released. Being some of the most outstanding Aberfeldy casks that have been found, some display typical Aberfeldy notes; others are totally different.

In 2010, 248 bottles of a new Aberfeldy 18-Year-Old single-cask bottling were made available for sale. Distilled in 1991, the bottling marked the retirement of Dewar's long-serving distilleries manager, Chris Anderson, after forty years in the industry. The whisky is just as it was in the cask: 54.9 percent abv, no chill-filtration, and natural color. Chris Anderson's Cask, as it is named on the label, was specially selected by Dewar's master blender for having the honey and floral notes typical of Aberfeldy single malt. Mr. Anderson took home bottle number one.

Anderson had started working at Caol Ila in March 1968, stenciling casks. After the rebuilt distillery opened in January 1974, he moved on to mashing and then distilling; he was made brewer in 1986. In 1990 he was promoted to assistant manager at Caol Ila and Lagavulin. After becoming manager in 1998 at Brackla, near Nairn, he joined Dewar's at Aberfeldy in 1999. Bacardi had purchased Dewar's in 1998, acquiring the Dewar brands and adding the Aberfeldy, Craigellachie, Royal Brackla, and Aultmore distilleries to its existing Macduff distillery near Banff. Islay-born Anderson was distilleries manager of all five sites.

By 2002, world sales of Dewar's whiskies had doubled. Their White Label is now the best-selling Scotch whisky brand in the United States. **SR**

Tasting notes

Honeyed sweetness and floral notes, with malt and polished wood. Soft spice, malt, and vanilla on the smooth and rounded palate. The addition of water teases out more citrus notes, along with a whiff of smoke. Quite dry and nutty in the lengthy finish.

Aberfeldy 21-Year-Old

Dewar's (Bacardi) | www.dewars.com

Region and country of origin Highlands, Scotland
Distillery Aberfeldy, Aberfeldy, Perthshire
Alcohol content 40% abv
Style Single malt

Aberfeldy 21-Year-Old has really unusual vitality for its age. It could be described as a big bag of orange peel, uncommon in a whisky of this vintage. The distillery works with a team of coopers to source interesting wood of excellent quality from far and wide. Hogsheads, sherry butts, marsala casks, and port pipes all help to create distinctive flavors and colors.

Distillery founder John Dewar established a reputation for quality that still holds good today. He was one of the pioneers of blending, and his sons, John and Tommy, clearly understood the standards they had to live up to. The company pioneered the art of marrying, or double-aging as it is now known, after blending to achieve whiskies with fuller flavors, smoother mouthfeel, and longer finishes. After blending, the Scotch is returned to oak casks, where the flavor improves, becoming smoother and creamier with a longer, lingering finish. The distillery first started double-aging over a hundred years ago.

The double-aging process is explained in great detail at Dewar's World of Whisky at Aberfeldy, an interactive visitor center packed with fascinating whisky information as well as detailed accounts of the distillery's history and the famous Dewar brothers, sons of the distillery founder. Visitors can explore the Dewar brands through an innovative and interactive five-star exhibition that educates and entertains. The experience includes a guided distillery tour that offers a chance to see the Aberfeldy spirit being produced and, afterward, an opportunity to taste a selection of whiskies in the nosing and tasting bar. **SR**

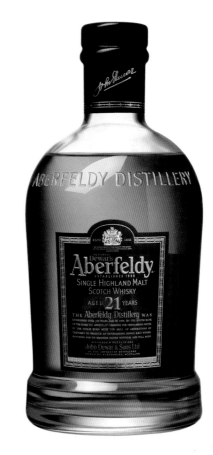

Tasting notes

Richly textured, honeyed nose with sweet, creamy intensity. Dried fruits, floral heather notes, and toasted coconut. Both sweet and full with lashings of Scottish honey and an abundance of orange peel, with notes of cream, vanilla, and oak. Long, spicy, dry finish.

Aberlour 10-Year-Old

Chivas Brothers (Pernod Ricard) | www.aberlour.com

Region of origin Speyside, Scotland
Distillery Aberlour, Aberlour, Banffshire
Alcohol content 43% abv
Type Single malt

Introduced in the 1980s, Aberlour 10-Year-Old replaced the Aberlour 12-year-old as the distillery's benchmark expression. Following the repackaging of the twelve-, sixteen-, and eighteen-year-old versions, the 10-Year-Old retains the old tall bottle and displays distillery founder James Fleming's family motto, "Let the Deed Show" to "reflect the philosophy behind Aberlour and its exceptional malt whisky." Fleming was the son of a tenant farmer, working as a successful grain dealer before he acquired the land at Aberlour and built the distillery. Designing the original buildings and much of the machinery himself, he personally supervised the construction.

Aberlour is a Gaelic word meaning "mouth of the chattering burn," and the pure and clear spring water in the Lour Valley has been famous since ancient times, when a Druid community occupied the distillery site. Water is very important in making whisky, and this high-quality water is still used today to produce Aberlour single-malt whisky.

Aberlour 10-Year-Old is big, rich, and full-bodied. It is a wonderful introduction to Aberlour single malt and makes a great everyday dram. It is also the leading single malt in France, one of the world's largest consumer nations of this type of whisky. Top-quality ex-sherry butts and ex-American oak casks are selected by Douglas Cruickshank, who has managed both spirit and cask selection for the past fifteen years. He takes personal responsibility for buying the very best casks from Spain and the United States, and is supported by chief blender David Boyd. **WM**

Tasting notes

Warm and appealing, with hints of red apple, cinnamon, vanilla, and apple cobbler. The whisky is moderately full-bodied, slightly oily, bright, and fruity, with ample notes of spice and vanilla that linger on the finish.

Aberlour 12-Year-Old

Chivas Brothers (Pernod Ricard) | www.aberlour.com

Region of origin Speyside, Scotland
Distillery Aberlour, Aberlour, Banffshire
Alcohol content 43% abv
Type Single malt

Aberlour 12-Year-Old is the younger of Aberlour's two double-cask-matured expressions; the other is the 16-Year-Old. Double-casking is the process whereby some of the whisky is matured in ex-bourbon casks, and some is matured in ex-sherry butts. The contents are then vatted together prior to bottling in order to add "greater depth of character as well as balanced notes of fruits and spices."

In the mid-2000s Aberlour reassessed its cask selection, as well as the cask composition of its various expressions. Aberlour 12-Year-Old was the "first of this new generation of single malts from the distillery that plays with the delicate balance between the signature ex-bourbon and ex-sherry casks from the Aberlour inventory." Not as bright as the 10-Year-Old, the 12-Year-Old demonstrates more time in the wood. Some of the bright fruitiness is replaced by oak and heavier spices, perhaps due to the higher percentage of ex-sherry butts used. The ex-bourbon casks provide ample toffee and vanilla to balance out the rich, but not overstated, sherry influence.

Vintage bottlings of Aberlour 12-Year-Old can be found in square bottles bearing the name Aberlour-Glenlivet—that distillery was so incorporated in 1950. Prior to the proliferation of single malts, several Speyside distilleries bore the name Glenlivet as part of their name to designate their provenance—as a type of *terroir* designation, or *appellation*. Litigation in the 1980s led to this designation being dropped, with the result being that only spirits distilled at the Glenlivet distillery now bear the name of Glenlivet. **WM**

Tasting notes

Noticeably heavier than the 10-year-old, this is well balanced, with cinnamon, nutmeg, and vanilla. Apple and toffee are also present, along with oak and malt. Further examination produces a hint of mint. The finish is drier than the 10-year-old and fades softly.

Aberlour 16-Year-Old

Chivas Brothers (Pernod Ricard) | www.aberlour.com

Region of origin Speyside, Scotland
Distillery Aberlour, Aberlour, Banffshire
Alcohol content 43% abv
Type Single malt

Aberlour 16-Year-Old, launched in 2003, is the older of Aberlour's two double-cask-matured expressions, the other being the 12-Year-Old.

Following a makeover of sorts in the mid-2000s, when Aberlour reexamined its cask selection and reconsidered the cask composition of the different Aberlour expressions, the resulting double-cask maturation was initially introduced as a twelve-year-old expression. Aberlour 16-Year-Old followed on a limited basis as stock became available.

Building on the double-cask-matured profile of the 12-Year-Old, Aberlour 16-Year-Old is more polished, balancing the rich fruit and spice of the extra-matured ex-sherry casks, which are more prominent than in the 12-Year-Old, with notes of vanilla, honey, and toffee from the older ex-bourbon casks. A very well-made whisky, Aberlour 16-Year-Old retains the distillery characteristics in full.

Aberlour 10-Year-Old is bright and fruity, and the double-cask-matured Aberlour 12-Year-Old demonstrates the benefits of blending ex-bourbon casks (which contribute notes of vanilla and honey) with ex-sherry casks (which add dark fruits and spices). With Aberlour 16-Year-Old, the additional four years in selected ex-bourbon and ex-sherry casks contribute extra complexities and nuances, amplifying those notes of rich vanilla, honey, fruit, and spice while maintaining a wonderful balance. Both of the double-cask-matured expressions of Aberlour have been well received, helping to propel Aberlour to become the world's number seven single malt. **WM**

Tasting notes

Richer, heavier, and more polished than the 12-year-old, with more intense cinnamon, nutmeg, and vanilla. Hints of orange, red apple, plum, and caramel emerge, with spices on the finish joined by hints of nuts. A wonderful expression from this fabled distillery.

Aberlour 18-Year-Old

Chivas Brothers (Pernod Ricard) | www.aberlour.com

Region of origin Speyside, Scotland
Distillery Aberlour, Aberlour, Banffshire
Alcohol content 43% abv
Type Single malt

Released initially in France and internationally in 2010, Aberlour 18-Year-Old is similar to the 12-Year-Old and 16-Year-Old, but is far more refined. The exceptional mouthfeel is attributed to the use of older ex-bourbon casks. "Aberlour 18-Year-Old is considered by many to be the most indulgent of the Aberlour expressions," commented Troy Gorczyca, brand manager of single malts for Pernod Ricard in the United States. "Like all Aberlour whiskies, Aberlour 18-Year-Old utilizes double-cask maturation to create a rich and harmonious balance of flavors with layers of complexity that reveal themselves over time. Our new packaging more accurately reflects the quality and core values of the brand—honesty, pride, discretion, depth, and shared pleasure—in an elegant and more contemporary way."

Although it is easily recognizable as coming from the same distillery as the ten-, twelve-, and sixteen-year-old expressions, Aberlour 18-Year-Old is a cut above and is perfectly balanced. This indulgent single malt exudes a richer, creamier, and more elegant and developed palate, which may result from casks older than eighteen years being incorporated in the expression. Distilleries are allowed to use older casks, as long as every cask in the expression meets the minimum age statement on the label. Aberlour 18-Year-Old is significantly more refined than Aberlour 16-Year-Old because any rough edges have been polished away. The additional two years' maturation makes a remarkable difference, with perhaps some older Aberlours having been blended in. **WM**

Tasting notes

Rich and decadent, with cinnamon, nutmeg, vanilla, and cloves. Big sherry influence, but not so much as to hide the distillery characteristics. Moderately oily, creamy mouth coating, with notes of toffee, red fruit, and a hint of candied orange. The finish is luxurious.

Aberlour A'bunadh

Chivas Brothers (Pernod Ricard)
www.aberlour.com

Region of origin Speyside, Scotland
Distillery Aberlour, Aberlour, Banffshire
Alcohol content Around 60.3% abv (batches vary)
Type Single malt

Aberlour A'bunadh was originally developed by chief blender David Boyd in the 1990s for the duty-free market. *A'bunadh* means "of the origin" in Gaelic, and it is a throwback to a time when people would bring any bottle they could find, such as an apothecary bottle, to the distillery or local grocer to be filled. The whisky would have been bottled at cask strength and not chill-filtered at natural color. For these reasons, A'bunadh is bottled in a replica apothecary bottle, at cask strength, natural color, and sealed with wax.

A'bunadh is aged exclusively in oloroso sherry butts, which are dumped and vatted to be bottled in batches, as designated on the labels. Each batch has a slightly different taste, color, and proof strength. The first five batches had no specific batch designation, which explains why the earliest batch designation is Batch 6. The individual batch number and proof is now included on each bottle.

According to brand director Neil Macdonald, "The casks are selected on merit . . . we tend in our selection to use younger first-fill sherry casks that bring a lot of powerful sherry character and mediate this with older refill sherry casks that allow the Aberlour distillery character to come through." **WM**

Tasting notes

Rich and mouth coating, with huge notes of cloves, cardamom, and cinnamon. Dark vanilla, baked apple, raisin, and date are perfectly balanced.

Aberlour Warehouse No. 1 Single Cask

Chivas Brothers (Pernod Ricard)
www.aberlour.com

Region of origin Speyside, Scotland
Distillery Aberlour, Aberlour, Banffshire
Alcohol content Cask 1684, 63.5% abv; varies by cask
Type Single malt

Upon completion of the full visitor center, the Warehouse No. 1 Single Cask Selections were created to allow those fortunate enough to attend a distillery tour the extraspecial treat of filling their own bottle of Aberlour to take away with them. Warehouse No. 1 is continuously supplied with an ex-bourbon and ex-sherry cask around fourteen years of age. Visitors literally fill 23 fluid ounces (70 centiliters) from the cask into a glass tube, which is then closed off and poured directly into their bottle. Guests complete the bottle labels in their own hand with the cask-specific information, such as cask number, date filled, date bottled, and cask type.

The casks vary between first- and second-fill barrels. Warehouse No. 1 Single Cask Selections are the only way to purchase entirely ex-bourbon cask Aberlour, with the exception of the 1967 Aberlour released in 2010 at $12,480 (£7,862) a bottle. Obtaining cask-strength, single-cask expressions from distilleries is often difficult, and such expressions, when available, are typically quite expensive, in part due to elaborate packaging. However, the Aberlour Warehouse No. 1 expressions cost $95 (£60) and range from very good to exceptional. **WM**

Tasting notes

Big notes of apple and vanilla, complemented by light notes of violets, lemongrass, and straw. Incredibly complex, with features resembling a Lowland malt.

Allt a'Bhainne
11-Year-Old Sherry Cask

Douglas Laing & Co.
www.douglaslaing.com

Region and country of origin Speyside, Scotland
Distillery Allt a'Bhainne, Glenrinnes, Banffshire
Alcohol content 46% abv abv
Style Single malt

Very little Allt a'Bhainne reaches the single-malt market as owners Pernod Ricard use the vast majority in the Chivas Regal and 100 Pipers blends. It has never had an official bottling—the distillery was purpose built in 1975 to supply the blended market—but several independent expressions have been made available, including this newly released sherried finish in the Old Malt Cask range, bottled at a young eleven years. Even though this is the one of the youngest expressions so far bottled, it was actually distilled under Seagram's ownership before Pernod Ricard took over in 2001. It will be interesting to see in a few years' time if more recent distillations have changed significantly; they are all still maturing in the wood.

The almost unpronounceable Gaelic name (Alt-a-varnee) means "burn of milk," but the flavors are classic Speyside, though generally less refined than most single malts. This bottling is very young for a sherry finish and the wood has yet to play a significant part in the flavor. None of the casks are matured on site but are tankered away to warehouses at Keith. On the whole, the distillery management has not needed to play with different wood finishes, so this is something of a rarity from a rare distillery. **AN**

Slightly spiced nose, like peppered limes. Quite hot and forward spice initially with a burst of alcohol, leaving a smooth, lightly sherried but quite short finish.

anCnoc
12-Year-Old

International Beverage
www.ancnoc.com

Region and country of origin Speyside, Scotland
Distillery Knockdhu, Knock, Banffshire
Alcohol content 40% abv abv
Style Single malt

According to the anCnoc brand Web site, the 12-Year-Old is a must-have in any whisky drinker's collection. Well, here is a funny thing: once you have tried the whisky, it is really hard to argue with that statement.

Clean packaging design helps to make anCnoc 12-Year-Old stand out on the shelf. It sits comfortably in the most fashionable bars of Stockholm, Tokyo, or Cape Town. But while the product looks very twenty-first century, the production has changed little since the distillery opened in October 1894. The only piece of modern electronic equipment that goes anywhere near the process is a big blue calculator in the still room. The spirit is still condensed in traditional worm tubs because consecutive owners resisted the temptation to equip the site with modern condensers. While arguably imperfect and most definitely cost-ineffective, the process of condensing low wines and spirit in copper worms immersed in tubs of water often adds to the body and complexity of whisky.

While anCnoc is often described as a fresh, bright, zesty, and fruity dram, all of which are correct, it is worth digging deeper and uncovering its mellow, creamy heart. The 12-Year-Old, despite appearances, is a rustic, full-blooded, burly Speysider. **LD**

First lemon peel and honeycomb, then fresh pear and red apple, with white chocolate mousse. Fresh and sweet, with malty and creamy character. Good body.

anCnoc 16-Year-Old

International Beverage | www.ancnoc.com

Region and country of origin Speyside, Scotland
Distillery Knockdhu, Knock, Banffshire
Alcohol content 46% abv
Style Single malt

All recently released young and old whiskies from Knockdhu are great, but this midrange expression is anCnoc as it was always meant to be. The universe wanted this spirit to be sixteen years old.

When it first joined the portfolio in 2008, great cosmic events were observed. Men all over the world went missing for many hours only to come home disheveled, not remembering what had happened to them. If you are willing to risk such a mysterious abduction, pick up a bottle, hold it close to your chest, and feel pure energy running through your body.

Unlike anCnoc 12-year-old, the 16-year-old is matured exclusively in second-refill ex-bourbon casks. Understated vanilla and gentle spice characteristics complement this citric, fruity, honeyed, and slightly oily spirit. Sixteen years in casks is just enough time for the whisky to develop full, rounded, and complex flavor without being overpowered by oaky bitterness. Distillery staff fondly recall walking past those maturing casks almost every day for many years.

While spirit for blending is transported to a central storage facility in Airdrie, all spirit destined to become anCnoc is poured into casks and kept in dunnage and racked warehouses at the distillery. Sadly, two of the five warehouses collapsed under the weight of snow during the winter of 2009/10. Most of the affected casks were moved to other locations, but a dozen or so, including rare barrels from the 1980s, were lost. A curveball indeed, but life goes on in Knockdhu. New warehouses soon will replace the collapsed ones, and the great cosmic balance will be restored. **LD**

Tasting notes

Lime and apple cider on the nose, with fresh vanilla and cinnamon overtones. It smells like it means business, a very well-balanced, broad aroma. On the palate it delivers even more, with runny caramel, crushed black pepper, and basswood honey. Lingering finish.

anCnoc 1996

International Beverage | www.ancnoc.com

Region and country of origin Speyside, Scotland
Distillery Knockdhu, Knock, Banffshire
Alcohol content 46% abv
Style Single malt

Whisky from Knockdhu was at first named after the distillery, but has been known as anCnoc since its relaunch as single malt under the ownership of International Beverage at the beginning of the millennium. The change of moniker aimed to set the product firmly apart from its near namesake, Knockando—a whisky much more established as a single malt and better known to international drinkers. Manager Gordon Bruce, whenever asked about the name situation, is quick to mention that "the other Knock" is in fact younger. It is all in good spirit. Gordon knows that anCnoc is now widely recognized as an important single malt with its own distinct character and rich heritage. The distillery is slowly starting to showcase the treasures it has stored.

Between 2005 and 2011, anCnoc released six vintage expressions, and it has become a tradition for the company to bottle one or so annually. The limited releases of a few hundred to a few thousand cases tend to fly off the shelves rapidly. But as hard to come by as they may be, some of them are well worth seeking out and sourcing on the secondary market. At the time of writing, perhaps the most interesting of them so far—anCnoc 1996—is still available from specialist retailers in Europe. The vintage bottling consists of whisky matured in ex-bourbon and ex-sherry casks, with some emphasis on the latter. Usually described as light and citrusy, spirit of Knockdhu is in this case showing its darker side—a seriously moody dram to help you set the world to rights on that long winter night. **LW**

Tasting notes

Cocoa and toffee, caramel shortbread, prune, and honey. A hint of elderflower lurking at the back. The taste is full and satisfying, with sweet dried fruit, slight smokiness, and green banana prominent. Full-bodied. Finishes medium long, sweet, and finally slightly drying.

anCnoc 1975

International Beverage
www.ancnoc.com

Region and country of origin Speyside, Scotland
Distillery Knockdhu, Knock, Banffshire
Alcohol content 50% abv abv
Style Single malt

Beg, steal, reason, or charm—do whatever it takes to get your hands on this dram. AnCnoc 1975 was released in 2005. Despite its scarcity and high (but not prohibitive) price, it sent the right message and put the relatively little-known anCnoc on the whisky aficionado's radar. The expression was critically acclaimed, but the real hype started after it was gone.

AnCnoc 1975 comprises whisky from both ex-bourbon white oak casks and ex-sherry red oak. Over thirty years in dunnage warehouses, the spirit squeezed out every bit of aroma and flavor the casks had to offer, and the result is a truly special experience. Rich amber color, eye-watering aroma, smooth yet intense taste, and oily texture—all aspects of this malt make you want to laugh out loud, call your mom just to make her happy, or dance with a stranger.

Despite its age, the whisky retained the anCnoc house style—zingy citrus and honeycomb are still there, as is the signature mouth-coating presence and a touch of sulfur. This last characteristic is present in Knockdhu's new-make spirit due to traditional worm tub condensation. Sulfur-derived aromas have been much stigmatized over the years but are making a welcome comeback. **LW**

Tasting notes

The nose has a rumlike sweetness on the outside and a rich, dark, fruit heart. Rye bread with marmalade; Greek salted lemon and honey are also here. Leave water out.

The Antiquary 12-Year-Old

Tomatin (Marubeni Group)
www.tomatin.com

Region and country of origin Scotland
Distilleries Various
Alcohol content 40% abv abv
Style Blend

Owned by John and William Hardie and named in reference to the novel by Sir Walter Scott, the Antiquary was introduced to the market in 1889/90. At the height of its popularity, the blend was handled by the highly respected William Sanderson and considered one of the very finest of its time. Over the years, however, this fame faded and the brand made its way into the hands of Tomatin Distillery Company, being itself a subsidiary of Takara Shuzo. It has now been repackaged in a distinctive cut-glass bottle and, with a high malt-to-grain ratio of between 45 and 55 percent, it is finding its way into the glasses—and hearts—of whisky lovers once more.

The Antiquary features whiskies from the Highlands, Lowlands, Speyside, and the Islands, and there is little doubt that Tomatin itself plays a role in the personality of this rather light, fragrant blend. The Speyside whiskies are key components and add sweetness to the mix, but it isn't all subtlety, as the Islay whiskies add depth and complexity. The grain whiskies should not be overlooked, of course, and as any skilled blender will attest, it is what these ultimately fresh, delicate distillates do to the malts that helps to make the art of blending so special. **StuR**

Tasting notes

A grassy, vibrant blend with notes of green apple, pear, and melon. Light honey adds sweetness before a herbal mix of dill, tarragon, and green mint develops.

An illustration from Sir Walter Scott's romantic novel *The Antiquary*. ➡

The Antiquary 21-Year-Old

Tomatin (Marubeni Group) | www.tomatin.com

Region and country of origin Scotland
Distilleries Various
Alcohol content 43% abv abv
Style Blend

Older blends such as this can be a tricky balancing act for their creators. There is both the need to add something extra with regard to complexity and overall interest while still adhering to the house style and intrinsic qualities of the other, younger expressions within the range. If the different variations of the blend fail to strike this balance, then the range risks becoming incoherent and even unapproachable to what could be its regular consumers. With this sense of cohesion in the 21-Year-Old, drinkers of the younger example of Antiquary who may wish to purchase a whisky with all of the extra maturity that greater age can bring, will not be disappointed.

The Antiquary 21-Year-Old was introduced in 2001 and quickly found recognition among well-known tasters as a fitting addition to the well-regarded Antiquary 12-Year-Old. Again, malts from the Highlands, Lowlands, and Islands are all represented. Tomatin, of course, provides an integral component, and there is a splash of peated Islay malt that adds a distinctive whisper of smoke. Lowland distilleries, such as Port Dundas, provide the grain whiskies involved and further contribute to the consistency of character found within the range.

The extra years of maturation really shine through, adding additional layers of complexity but without removing any of the attractive freshness and key characteristics of the Antiquary 12-Year-Old. It is a blend that displays so much of what can be gained from the extra years of maturation in wood, while avoiding the possible drawbacks. **StuR**

Tasting notes

A complex blend with notes of canned pineapple, apricot jam, cocoa, and spice. Orange oil and a whisper of dry coal smoke develop with time, alongside herbal tea and a hint of damp moss. The finish is medium length on soft spice, dried herbs, and faint citrus.

Ardbeg 10-Year-Old

Glenmorangie Co. (LVMH) | www.ardbeg.com

Region and country of origin Islay, Scotland
Distillery Ardbeg, Port Ellen, Argyll
Alcohol content 46% abv
Style Single malt

Ardbeg is widely recognized as one of the world's great single malts. Although the term "iconic" tends to be overused, it is surely appropriate in the case of this whisky. In terms of character, Ardbeg is regarded as one of the most extreme Islay whiskies, and with a peating level of around 54 phenol parts per million (ppm), it is the most heavily peated of all regularly available single malts.

The "standard" expression is aged for ten years, and the present version of Ardbeg 10-Year-Old was introduced in 2008, just over a decade after the Glenmorangie company purchased the Ardbeg distillery. The significance of the 2008 relaunch is that, for the first time, the entry-level Ardbeg bottling could be made entirely of spirit produced under Glenmorangie's ownership. Glenmorangie had first introduced a ten-year-old expression of Ardbeg in 2000, although this had followed on from a number of ten-year-old expressions previously issued by former owner Allied Distillers and its predecessor, Hiram Walker & Sons.

Dr. Bill Lumsden, Glenmorangie's head of distilling and whisky creation, has some interesting comments to make about this particular whisky: "For all our bottlings of Ardbeg 10-Year-Old, since its introduction in 2000, I have tried as hard as I can to maintain consistency against our ideal benchmark standard. However, I would point out that we inherited a very erratic stock profile, which from time to time necessitated an element of overaging in some of our earlier ten-year-old bottlings." **GS**

Tasting notes

Relatively sweet on the nose, with soft peat, carbolic soap, and Arbroath smokies. Intense yet quite delicate on the palate, with burning peats and dried fruit, malt, and a touch of licorice. Long and smoky in the finish, with a balance of cereal sweetness and dry peat notes.

Ardbeg 17-Year-Old

Glenmorangie Co. (LVMH) | www.ardbeg.com

Region and country of origin Islay, Scotland
Distillery Ardbeg, Port Ellen, Argyll
Alcohol content 40% abv
Style Single malt

During the past few years, there has been an increase in "non-age-specific" expressions from a number of distillers. This practice tends to suit whisky makers, as it allows them far greater flexibility with their inventories. It is also extremely valuable for distilleries like Ardbeg, where previous periods of "silence" have left major holes in stock inventories. Hence expressions such as Blasda and Supernova. However, back in 1997, when they had just taken over the Ardbeg distillery, Glenmorangie launched a seventeen-year-old variant of Ardbeg some three years before the 10-Year-Old was introduced.

The 17-Year-Old was marketed principally because Ardbeg had not made whisky for most of the 1980s, and there was therefore no ten- or twelve-year-old whisky, for example, available at the time. Distiller Bill Lumsden declares that "overall, it's been a real challenge to eke out the stocks, to maintain quality and quantity, given the bizarre stock situation we had inherited. The level of peating was all over the place, particularly in the older stock."

The spirit used in the new Ardbeg 17-Year-Old bottling had been distilled under the old Hiram Walker and Allied Distillers regimes, and between 1978 and 1981 the distillery produced batches of what was known as "Kildalton" spirit, which was made from malted barley with a range of peating levels below the usual Ardbeg peating formula. Accordingly, the 17-Year-Old launched by Glenmorangie was somewhat less peaty than "standard" Ardbeg, but it offers plenty of flavors nevertheless. **GS**

Tasting notes

Seaweed, tarry rope, brine, and restrained peat on the nose, with oak, oranges, and developing maltiness. Quite sweet in the mouth, with a bigger peat presence, more malt and some milk chocolate. Oily in the finish, with oak, sweet peat, lemon, and pepper. Intriguing.

Ardbeg 1977

Glenmorangie Co. (LVMH) | www.ardbeg.com

Region and country of origin Islay, Scotland
Distillery Ardbeg, Port Ellen, Argyll
Alcohol content 46% abv
Style Single malt

Distilled in 1977 and bottled in 2001, the Ardbeg 1977 was a release of 2,400 bottles. This "vintage" was one of several to be issued by the distillery, and, in addition, a number of highly regarded and now extremely collectable single-cask bottlings from the 1970s have also been marketed.

The 1977 vintage has received its fair share of plaudits, with Bill Lumsden—head of whisky creation—declaring that "I really can't find enough superlatives to describe this fantastic whisky! It's far and away the best peaty whisky I've had the privilege to drink. Some Ardbeg consumers love the 1974, and some love the 1978. Personally, I can't see past the 1977." Peat is indeed evident throughout—rich and smoky on the nose, smoothly chewy in the mouth, lasting through the lengthy finish.

Bill goes on to add that "the actual year of distillation is seldom the sole reason why whiskies are good or otherwise; rather, it is more to do with finding particularly interesting parcels of stock within any one year. Our vintage releases to date have been 1978, 1975, 1977, and 1990 [Airigh Nam Beist]. Whether or not there will be more depends on our view of the maturing stock profile."

Hiram Walker took over total control of Ardbeg distillery in 1977, and even more significantly, this was the year in which the traditional floor maltings were closed, though malt was already being brought in from external sources to supplement the distillery's own output. This is why 1974 is often considered to be the last "old-fashioned" peaty Ardbeg vintage. **GS**

Tasting notes

Rich and creamy on the comparatively delicate, smooth nose. Soft fudge, peat smoke, and cloves. The palate offers more cloves, spicy peat, a touch of iodine, lemon, and steaks cooking on a barbecue. The finish is lengthy, with more medicinal notes and drying smoke.

Ardbeg Airigh Nam Beist

Glenmorangie Co. (LVMH) | www.ardbeg.com

Region and country of origin Islay, Scotland
Distillery Ardbeg, Port Ellen, Argyll
Alcohol content 46% abv
Style Single malt

Along with Uigeadail, Airigh Nam Beist probably deserves an award as one of the most difficult single malt whisky expressions to pronounce. The correct version is "Arry Nam Baysht," and the name is a translation of the Gaelic for "shelter of the beast." Airigh Nam Beist is the second loch down from Uigeadail, and therefore performs a balancing role in supplying the distillery with Loch Uigeadail's water.

According to local folklore perpetuated by the distillers, "no more fitting name could have been bestowed on such an eerie place; this is where—legend has it—something otherworldly lurks, lying in wait. So what measures can be taken to protect local and visitor alike? If you find yourself straying this way, then pray equip yourself with that traditionally reliable antidote to sheer terror—the stiff drink!"

Ardbeg is proudly marketed as the "peatiest and smokiest of all the Islay malts." This expression was introduced in 2007 and is part of a strategy of offering different styles of Ardbeg within the permanent range, rather than age-specific variants. Distillery owner Bill Lumsden declares that "Airigh Nam Beist was my homage to the much loved, but sadly departed, seventeen-year-old Ardbeg, and my use of a very high proportion of first-fill American oak ex-bourbon wood gave a softer, creamier style of Ardbeg." **GS**

Tasting notes

A soft, creamy nose. Big and brooding on the palate, with burning peat and seaweed. Oily, peppery, with ripe fruit characteristics, licorice, and plain chocolate.

Ardbeg Alligator

Glenmorangie Co. (LVMH) | www.ardbeg.com

Region and country of origin Islay, Scotland
Distillery Ardbeg, Port Ellen, Argyll
Alcohol content 51.2% abv
Style Single malt

Introduced in 2011, Ardbeg Alligator takes its unusual name from the deepest style of cask charring, which lends a distinctive scalelike pattern to the surface of the wood. Alligator charring is more common in the making of bourbon than single-malt whisky. Master distiller Bill Lumsden comments, "Ardbeg Alligator was able to be created thanks to a frantic period of experimentation in 1998/99 and 2000, during which I laid down new-make spirit in many different cask types—for example, French oak for Ardbeg Corryvreckan. The particular barrels that form the heart of the Alligator recipe were given an ultradeep 'number four' char. As with Corryvreckan, I felt the straight whisky from these casks was too intense, hence them being mixed with 'classic' Ardbeg."

Whereas the relatively delicate style of Glenmorangie single malt has lent itself well to cask finishing and various other innovations, the heavily peated, assertive nature of Ardbeg means that such practices are much harder to pull off with the company's sister Islay malt. Experimentation has been more limited, although the distillery warehouses do contain small numbers of new oak, toasted oak, and ex-wine casks. Ardbeg Alligator represents one of the more unusual maturation variants to see the light of day so far, and is well worth seeking out. **GS**

Tasting notes

Peat, citrus fruit, and char on the nose. Reminiscent of a barbecue by the sea, with smoldering wood chip notes. Leather, wood smoke, ginger, and savory meat flavors.

Ardbeg Almost There

Glenmorangie Co. (LVMH) | www.ardbeg.com

Region and country of origin Islay, Scotland
Distillery Ardbeg, Port Ellen, Argyll
Alcohol content 54.1% abv
Style Single malt

Ardbeg Almost There was the final release in a series dubbed by the distillers "the Peaty Path to Maturity." This peaty path commenced in 2003 with the release of Very Young Ardbeg—For Discussion. This was an Ardbeg Committee–exclusive offering of whisky distilled in 1997, shortly after Glenmorangie took over the distillery. It allowed makers and aficionados the opportunity to sample and assess the progress of the youthful, maturing spirit.

Subsequently, Still Young appeared in 2006, followed by Almost There in 2007, and together this trio of Committee bottlings presented consumers with an extremely rare opportunity to find out for themselves how increasing time spent in the cask affected the character of whisky distilled and filled all in the same year. The Peaty Path to Maturity culminated in the release of the Renaissance ten-year-old expression during 2008.

Bill Lumsden says that "the key premise of Very Young right through to Renaissance was simply to let our loyal Ardbeg fans see that we were carefully trying to make 'our' ten-year-old as delicious as possible, but also as close as we could make it to the old ten-year-old. Additionally, it was to challenge a few conventions, especially the whole age debate, and to show that 'youth' can also be good!" **GS**

Tasting notes

Initially quite cerealy on the nose. Sweet and smoothly intense on the palate, where lemon can be detected. The finish is long, and peaty, with a peppery prickle.

Ardbeg Blasda

Glenmorangie Co. (LVMH) | www.ardbeg.com

Region and country of origin Islay, Scotland
Distillery Ardbeg, Port Ellen, Argyll
Alcohol content 40% abv
Style Single malt

Of all Ardbeg's recent releases during Glenmorangie's stewardship of the brand, Blasda has been the most controversial. It is only peated to approximately one-third of the distillery's usual level, giving rise to comments that this is really a type of "Ardbeg Lite." It is also chill-filtered, unlike most of the Ardbeg range. Critics argue that chill-filtration strips out elements of flavor and has a particularly adverse effect on the texture of the whisky in the mouth.

Hard-core Ardbeg fans, who tend to be passionate and vociferous about their beloved single malt, have been puzzled by the purpose of Blasda— the Gaelic word for "sweet and delicious"—arguing that it effectively falls between two stools, not being unpeated, but lacking the whisky's characteristic heavily peated character.

"This expression was somewhat misunderstood," laments distiller Bill Lumsden. "It was introduced by brand director Hamish Torrie and me as a bit of daring fun, and we were primarily looking to offer consumers the opportunity to experience more of the fruity and floral flavor congeners in the underlying Ardbeg spirit, and to show that Ardbeg is not just about peat. We were certainly not looking to convert new consumers to this style, rather simply to offer existing fans another facet of Ardbeg's personality." **GS**

Tasting notes

The nose is light and gently peated, with a hint of lemon. The body is less oily and rounded than many Ardbegs. Sweet peat and canned peach on the palate.

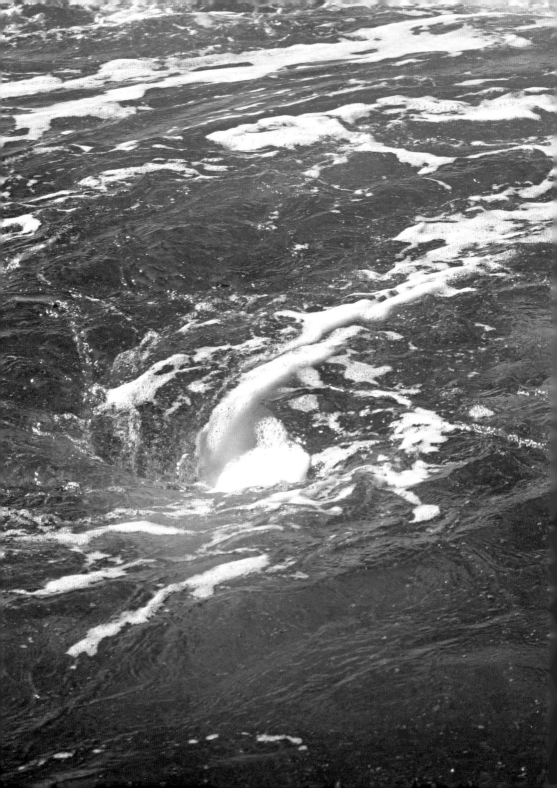

Ardbeg Corryvreckan

Glenmorangie Co. (LVMH) | www.ardbeg.com

Region and country of origin Islay, Scotland
Distillery Ardbeg, Port Ellen, Argyll
Alcohol content 51.7% abv
Style Single malt

One of several new expressions introduced to the Ardbeg lineup in 2008, Corryvreckan is named after the world's third-largest whirlpool, situated off the coast of the island of Jura. Like a number of other Ardbeg variants, it was initially produced as an exclusive bottling for members of the Ardbeg Committee, a 50,000-strong band of international Ardbeg aficionados, but subsequently became available on general release. As part of the permanent core range, along with the 10-Year-Old and Uigeadail, Corryvreckan carries no age statement.

Bill Lumsden explains that "Corryvreckan was introduced as the best possible way of utilizing spirit I had lain down in new French oak casks. It is no secret that Corryvreckan stepped into the gap left by the dwindling stocks of 1990 vintage whiskies used for Airigh Nam Beist.

"The heart of Corryvreckan uses whiskies distilled in 1998/99 and 2000, married with some slightly younger 'classic' Ardbeg whiskies. The whisky from the French oak casks has particularly tarry, spicy, leathery characteristics, which I felt, on their own, were too intense to bottle. I have sporadically filled such casks with new spirit, which should give us the opportunity to keep Corryvreckan going as part of the core range." **GS**

Tasting notes

A classic nose of peat smoke, tar, and freshly dug soil. Mouth-coating and silky on the palate, with rich, sweet peat notes. The finish is long, with peppery peat.

Ardbeg Feis Ile 2011

Glenmorangie Co. (LVMH) | www.ardbeg.com

Region and country of origin Islay, Scotland
Distillery Ardbeg, Port Ellen, Argyll
Alcohol content 55.1% abv
Style Single malt

One of the big debates between whisky aficionados addresses the relative rights and wrongs of buying whisky as an investment. Many argue that the collectors are creating a demand for whisky that affects prices and makes many malts unavailable to "the masses." Whisky lovers who collect claim that this is rubbish, pointing out that many of the whiskies are limited editions anyway, and when there is a big demand, price has to be a determining factor. They may also defend their purchases on the grounds that collectible whisky provides a source of income for the whisky makers.

Undoubtedly, though, the whisky companies are making hay, and never more so than through the Islay Festival, an eight-day whisky and music festival held in May. In recent years it has become a tradition for distillers to release a festival bottling, and such bottles have become extremely collectible. So what to do? Limit the release and sell during the Feis Ile on a first-come, first-serve basis? Or do a much larger bottling so that many more can take advantage? There's no right or wrong solution to the problem, and it has all got a little out of hand. If you want to sample this whisky, try speaking to the distillery directly—you might be able to get it at a price considerably better than those currently listed on eBay. **DR**

Tasting notes

Tries to pull off the very difficult trick of marrying big heavily peated whisky with rich fruity winey notes you get from sherry, port, or red. Fascinating.

 The Corryvreckan whirlpool. The name means "cauldron of the speckled seas."

Ardbeg Kildalton

Glenmorangie Co. (LVMH) | www.ardbeg.com

Region and country of origin Islay, Scotland
Distillery Ardbeg, Port Ellen, Argyll
Alcohol content 57.6% abv
Style Single malt

A limited release of just 1,300 bottles of Kildalton appeared on the market during 2004. This whisky had been distilled in 1980 at a time when there was a significant degree of experimentation with peating levels at the Ardbeg distillery. Although it is difficult to comprehend in these days when heavily peated whiskies are ultrafashionable, during the 1970s and 1980s, Islays had very little cachet as single malts, and when it came to using them as components of blended Scotch, a little went a long way.

Accordingly, during the Hiram Walker era of Ardbeg ownership (from 1977 to 1987, at which point it was purchased by Allied Lyons), lightly peated variants were produced, with the premise that larger quantities of these could be utilized for blending. In theory, this could maximize distillery production in the longer term.

The name Kildalton was chosen for the lightly peated Ardbeg spirit, as Kildalton is the parish within which Ardbeg distillery is situated. Bill Lumsden notes that "Kildalton was not completely unpeated, but as near as damn it. If you assume that bottled 'standard' Ardbeg has about twenty-five to thirty parts per million phenol in it, or approximately half of what is originally in the malted barley, then Kildalton had around four parts per million."

Experimentation with the Kildalton style of Ardbeg lasted from 1978 until the end of 1980 and took the form of making spirit using malt from a variety of different sources and with peating levels varying from zero to the Ardbeg "norm." **GS**

Tasting notes

Fragrant and floral on the nose, nutty, with pine, lemon, and acetone balancing discreet vanilla. Oily on the palate, with more vanilla, malt, and oranges. The finish is lively, with licorice, drinking chocolate notes, peppery peat, and a hint of red wine.

Ardbeg Lord of the Isles 25-Year-Old

Glenmorangie Co. (LVMH) | www.ardbeg.com

Region and country of origin Islay, Scotland
Distillery Ardbeg, Port Ellen, Argyll
Alcohol content 46% abv
Style Single malt

The Ardbeg Lord of the Isles first appeared in 2001, and was named after the chiefs of Gaelic and Viking descent who wielded immense power in the western Highlands and Hebrides during the Middle Ages. According to Hamish Torrie, Ardbeg's brand director, "We owned the Lord of the Isles trademark, and if you've got something as distinctive as that, you've really got to use it!"

Although marketed and sold as a twenty-five-year-old single malt, most of the component whiskies in the mix in fact date from the mid-1970s, making it effectively well in excess of thirty years old. "This expression has not been bottled for several years now," notes Ardbeg's Bill Lumsden, "but I can confirm the last few bottlings were substantially older than twenty-five years."

Bill continues, "The Lord of the Isles used some of our more delicate whiskies, and people loved it. When we've opened a bottle at whisky events, people have congregated to taste it, like bees round a honey pot. Some people have even wanted the empty bottle! I believe that the delicacy of flavor was primarily due to the fact that in older peated whiskies, the peat smoke character is often substantially toned down by the influence of the oak."

Considered by many connoisseurs to be one of the great Ardbegs, this complex and yet beautifully balanced whisky is nicely packaged in a presentation box that includes a collectable scroll. Lord of the Isles is proving increasingly difficult to find but is well worth the search. **GS**

Tasting notes

The nose is sophisticated and rich, with black cherries, apricots, and milk chocolate, plus sweet peat and honey. Sweet in the mouth, with vanilla, toffee, more peat, and a pinch of salt. Long in the drying finish, with chocolate notes turning from milk to dark.

Ardbeg Renaissance

Glenmorangie Co. (LVMH) | www.ardbeg.com

Region and country of origin Islay, Scotland
Distillery Ardbeg, Port Ellen, Argyll
Alcohol content 56% abv
Style Single malt

The final stage in Ardbeg's so-called "Peaty Path to Maturity" was reached in 2008, with the appearance of Renaissance. This cask-strength offering was distilled in 1998 and was the forerunner of the "standard" 10-Year-Old introduced later the same year at a reduced strength of 46 percent. "Renaissance employed a higher percentage of first-fill ex-bourbon casks than is currently possible in the ten-year-old recipe," explains Bill Lumsden.

The Renaissance bottle proudly proclaims, "We've Arrived!" and the name Renaissance was appropriate, as the bottling of ten-year-old whisky exclusively distilled under Glenmorangie's ownership of the distillery set the seal on the distillery's restoration to security and consistency. Prior to Glenmorangie's acquisition of Ardbeg, the distillery had endured several periods of "silence," and owners Allied Distillers had closed the plant and placed it on the market in 1996. Glenmorangie purchased Ardbeg for £7 million ($11 million), including £5.5 million ($8.6 million) for stocks of maturing spirit, and production resumed in June 1997. Apart from periods when maintenance work has been carried out and routine shutdowns, Ardbeg has been making whisky ever since.

"After our acquisition of Ardbeg, we immediately implemented a far superior wood policy, and this has undoubtedly contributed to a definite improvement in quality," says Bill Lumsden. "The distillation regime was set up according to our requirements, but we are essentially trying to re-create the classic style of Ardbeg spirit." **GS**

Tasting notes

Sweet peat, marzipan, and floral notes on the nose, with some salt and spice also making a late appearance. The palate is big, full-bodied, sweet, and fruity. Ginger and spicy peat develop. Lingering fruit, peat, spice, and a slight hint of antiseptic make up the lengthy finish.

Ardbeg Rollercoaster

Glenmorangie Co. (LVMH) | www.ardbeg.com

Region and country of origin Islay, Scotland
Distillery Ardbeg, Port Ellen, Argyll
Alcohol content 57.3% abv
Style Single malt

Along with Supernova, Rollercoaster was one of a brace of 2010 Ardbeg releases. It was marketed to celebrate ten years of the Ardbeg Committee of enthusiasts and was exclusively available to Committee members. This is a youthful Ardbeg, ideal for fans of the younger, bolder, and less "well-mannered" Islay single malts.

There is a story behind the name, as Mickey Heads, distillery manager and chairman of the Ardbeg Committee, explains: "We thought 'rollercoaster' aptly reflected the tumultuous ride we have had over the last ten years at Ardbeg as we have brought the distillery back to life! The whisky itself was created by taking spirit from casks from each year since the distillery's reopening in 1997, right up to 2006—the youngest Ardbeg able to be bottled by law!"

This multivintage Ardbeg expression brings together one cask of each of the following: a 1997 second-fill barrel; a 1998 refill hogshead; a 1999 first-fill barrel; a 2000 first-fill barrel; a 2001 refill barrel; a 2002 refill barrel; a 2003 first-fill barrel; a 2004 first-fill barrel; a 2005 second-fill sherry butt; and lastly a 2006 refill hogshead. That is ten different casks from ten different years. Bill Lumsden says that "in terms of what I was looking for, essentially something just a little bit different; nothing more specific than that, but it was also great fun to do!"

There was considerable marketing hype at the time of release, which inevitably led to disappointed expectations in some quarters, but this is worth trying if only to make up your own mind. **GS**

Tasting notes

A gutsy yet complex nose of printer's ink, sweet peat, bonfire smoke, pine, kippers, and damp tweed. With time, more buttery notes appear. The palate is smooth and buttery, with intense fruitiness and peat, spice, and rock salt. The finish is long and peaty.

Ardbeg Supernova

Glenmorangie Co. (LVMH) | www.ardbeg.com

Region and country of origin Islay, Scotland
Distillery Ardbeg, Port Ellen, Argyll
Alcohol content 60.1% abv
Style Single malt

Initially issued as a limited release during 2009, Ardbeg Supernova—named for its "stellar explosion of flavors"—went on general release a year later. It sits at the opposite extreme to Blasda, being peated to an immense 100 parts per million. Supernova can be seen as part of a tendency for some distillers to try to "outpeat" the opposition, but the Ardbeg team vehemently denies that Supernova is crudely about "my phenol is bigger than your phenol."

Bill Lumsden says that "like Blasda, this was simply an attempt to let Ardbeg fans taste something different, and in this case, there were even more of the chewy, peat-smoke flavors." Ardbeg has created a compelling whisky, one that Lumsden explains "will both delight and challenge those looking for an out-of-this-world whisky experience. With its hot, sizzling, and gristy sensations that effervesce and explode on the tongue, followed by a powerful peaty punch, this is truly yet another galactic explosion of aromas. The intensity of flavors is Ardbeg at its most powerful and peaty, and yet we always have that delightful layered, sweet complexity that makes Ardbeg such a sensational dram!"

The 3,000 first edition bottles all sold in a record 112 minutes, making Supernova the fastest-selling whisky in Ardbeg's 196-year history. **GS**

Tasting notes

Blatant damp soil, peat smoke, tar, and resin on the nose. The palate features spices, tobacco, sea salt, and citrus fruit. The finish is long and includes root ginger.

Ardbeg Uigeadail

Glenmorangie Co. (LVMH) | www.ardbeg.com

Region and country of origin Islay, Scotland
Distillery Ardbeg, Port Ellen, Argyll
Alcohol content 54.2% abv
Style Single malt

Ardbeg Uigeadail—pronounced "Oog-a-dall"—was launched in 2003 as a cask-strength addition to the existing range. It takes its name from Gaelic, which roughly translates as "dark and mysterious place." It is also the name of one of the lochs that supply the distillery with its distinctive, peaty water used in the processes of whisky making.

Uigeadail carries no age statement, but contains a proportion of relatively youthful spirit, distilled under the Glenmorangie regime at Ardbeg and matured in ex-bourbon casks, together with older, sherry-wood-matured whisky that Glenmorangie inherited in 1997.

Distiller Bill Lumsden recalls that the origins of Uigeadail lie in a comment made by the late, lamented drinks writer Michael Jackson at the launch of the Ardbeg Lord of the Isles expression in 2001. "Michael came up to me and said, 'It's very nice, Bill, but I like my Ardbegs mucky and dirty.'

"Uigeadail was a response to that, but I wanted to create something that was different to the other Ardbegs that we had. We are typically looking at around 35 to 45 percent sherry-cask-matured whisky, along with ex-bourbon-cask-matured stock, and the ex-oloroso sherry shipping casks—the very best available—that add rich, sweet, raisiny, and nutty characteristics to the Ardbeg spirit." **GS**

Tasting notes

Fresh, maritime, and heathery on the nose, with vanilla, marzipan, salted butter, and peat smoke. Full-bodied and oily, with a malty sweetness. Complex, satisfying.

The striking centerpiece of an Ardbeg release party in 2006. ➡

Ardmore 25-Year-Old

Beam Global | www.ardmorewhisky.com

Region and country of origin Highlands, Scotland
Distillery Ardmore, Huntly, Aberdeenshire
Alcohol content 51.4% abv
Style Single malt

Although Ardmore has been producing large quantities of whisky for the blending market, the team responsible for the daily running of the distillery takes considerable pride in maintaining its legacy. Old wage records, advertising posters, and century-old staff photos have been lovingly preserved, and old equipment long consigned to the recycling plant at most distilleries has been stored on upstairs floors, making a tour of the distillery akin to a step back in time. It's almost as if the distillery team is hanging on to the hope that one day the public will be admitted and the history and heritage of the distillery will be there, ready and waiting for them.

That day is just about upon us, and if you ever get the chance to visit this distillery, take it. It gives a perfect insight into the way whisky was once made, and it reinforces the point that today the best of the old methods are still in use and well to the fore. Best of all for the whisky lover, though, is the fact that at least some of the distillery's output has been held back and allowed to mature into old age. Few distilleries have quite as much experimentation going on, either, and there are all sorts of unusual casks working their magic on this wonderful spirit. Hopefully we'll see some very special bottlings from the distillery in the future—that's if any of the liquid makes it past the rigorous quality-control tastings the whisky makers insist on putting them through.

The Ardmore 25-Year-Old is bottled at cask strength and offers a very different view of Ardmore but a very pleasant one. **DR**

Tasting notes

A surprisingly delicate and sweet malt, with clean, sweet barley, pineapple candy, and incense-like spices. Less savory notes than the Traditional, but a liberal dose of sweet peat makes sure this doesn't drift into Speyside territory. The peat holds out until the end.

Ardmore 1992 Single Malts of Scotland 19-Year-Old

Speciality Drinks | www.whiskyexchange.com

Region and country of origin Highlands, Scotland
Distillery Ardmore, Huntly, Aberdeenshire
Alcohol content 49.3%
Style Single malt

Whisky writers should not have favorites. Just as parents should treat all their offspring in the same way, whisky writers should not be drawn into debating which is their favorite whisky. In most cases, whisky writers will say that it depends on the occasion, and that they have several favorites from different countries. But for this writer, Ardmore occupies a very special place indeed.

Ardmore is the ultimate forgotten and hidden gem. A Highland distillery providing whisky mainly for the Teacher's blend, it has started to make a name for itself in recent years. It has always had a loyal following among those in the know, and acclaimed whisky writer Jim Murray, for one, raves about it.

Generally, though, Ardmore flies under the radar and is not a recognizable name. The attraction lies in the fact that the distillery is staffed by passionate and dedicated people from the distillery manager down, who make every customer feel welcome. Traditional in the true sense of the word, the distillery itself is a fascinating place, one in which visitors always enjoy rooting around.

There are warehouses at Ardmore where the owner (previously Allied Domecq and now Jim Beam Global) experiments with new flavors and styles. There are unusual cask finishes, many of which won't ever see the light of day, as well as smaller quarter casks, which have proved to be immensely successful for the standard Ardmore Traditional bottling.

This is a great and surprising bottle of Ardmore and one that is definitely worth seeking out. **DR**

Tasting notes

Scuzzy, dirty, earthy, and savory nose but an absolute treat on the palate, with lots of rootsy malt, deep peat, and woody resins. Cutting through all of this is a sharpness that can only come from a whisky distilled in the Highlands. A long and satisfying finish.

Ardmore 100th Anniversary

Beam Global | www.ardmorewhisky.com

Region and country of origin Highlands, Scotland
Distillery Ardmore, Huntly, Aberdeenshire
Alcohol content 40% abv
Style Single malt

Ardmore's link with the world-famous Teacher's blend stretches back to its very beginning. The distillery—located on the edge of the Grampian mountains—was founded in 1898 by Adam Teacher, son of Teacher's founder William Teacher, making it the first Teacher's distillery. But before production started, Adam died. Help was sought from nearby GlenDronach, and so began the special relationship between the two distilleries and the Teacher's brand.

That marriage came to an end when Allied Domecq was broken up and GlenDronach went first to Pernod Ricard, where it was largely ignored and considered surplus to requirements, and then to Billie Walker and the BenRiach team, who have loved and nurtured it ... but that's another story.

Ardmore originally started producing whisky in 1899, and this twenty-one-year-old was released in 1999 to mark the centenary. That any of it is still available is truly remarkable, all the more so in the light of the wonderful smoky taste of this whisky. It has remained on sale at the distillery, however, and some specialist shops still stock it.

Bottled at 40 percent, a little less than other commemorative bottlings, and with a traditional and uninspiring label, the Ardmore 100th Anniversary stands in stark contrast to some of the flashy bottlings commonly seen today. But it is like the distillery—a traditional slice of heritage and history, so if you have the chance to buy a bottle of this, snap it up immediately—the price is rising rapidly and bottles are becoming harder and harder to find. **DR**

Tasting notes

With slightly less body and without the benefit of the intense maturation of the Traditional and the age of the 25-year-old, this is a delicate, soft, sweet ride through the delights of Ardmore, with little to challenge. Peat skips across the tongue and taste buds throughout.

Ardmore Traditional

Beam Global | www.ardmorewhisky.com

Region and country of origin Highlands, Scotland
Distillery Ardmore, Huntly, Aberdeenshire
Alcohol content 46% abv
Style Single malt

With blends accounting for more than 90 percent of the world's Scotch sales, it is unsurprising that many single malts are almost exclusively destined for the blended sector and are rarely bottled in their own right. There are notable exceptions, however, and the whiskies of Ardmore are among them.

Ardmore is a large Highland distillery that produces the core malt for Teacher's and until relatively recently, its malts were known only to aficionados. When drinks giant Allied Domecq combusted a few years back, Beam Global picked up both Teacher's and Ardmore, as well as Islay giant Laphroaig. And it just so happens that the two malts were the only ones in their portfolio that benefited from a traditional quarter-cask maturation process.

The team at Allied wanted to re-create the malts of yesteryear, when smaller casks capable of being carried by pony were used. Smaller casks mean faster maturation, and in most cases the dominance of the wood was too much for the whisky. But with the heavier, peatier styles of Ardmore and Laphroaig the smaller casks made for exceptional whisky.

Ardmore isn't as peated as Laphroaig, but this is a full and rich Highland whisky. Don't be put off by the lack of age statement—this is part of the quarter-cask magic. The malt starts life in bourbon barrels and is transferred to quarter casks for the final part of the maturation process. Very reasonably priced and packed with flavor, it is the starting point for what looks certain to be one of the great whisky success stories going forward. Nicely packaged, too. **DR**

Tasting notes

A swirling, whirling maelstrom of a malt, with delicatessen flavors of salted meat, olives, and sweet pickles delivered with an oily, toffeed, and vanilla-punctuated heart. Fall in love with it, and it'll be a loyal companion for life. Sublime.

Arran 10-Year-Old

Isle of Arran Distillers | www.arranwhisky.com

Region and country of origin Islands, Scotland
Distillery Isle of Arran, Lochranza, Isle of Arran, North
Ayrshire **Alcohol content** 46% abv
Style Single malt

The Isle of Arran, across the Firth of Clyde to the west of the Scottish mainland, got its first legal distillery in 150 years when Arran distillery was founded in 1995.

The ten-year-old variant of Arran single malt was first released in 2006. Arran managing director Euan Mitchell explains, "We couldn't bring it out in 2005 because there hadn't been enough production in that initial year of operation to do it. We needed 1996 stock. It was the first time we had put an age statement on a bottle, so it was very important for us.

"Some people had a prejudice against our whiskies when they carried no age statements, feeling that Arran was a young whisky because it was a young distillery. However, when they tried it, they were pleasantly surprised. Actually, the 10-Year-Old effectively raised people's expectations!"

Arran 10-Year-Old is made using approximately 70 percent second-fill sherry casks; the balance is a mixture of ex-bourbon casks and some first-fill sherry casks. "At ten years, it has more sweet fruit and is rounded, with baked apples and brown sugar," says Mitchell. "You lose the sharper citrus edges, and the sweetness is rounded out."

Mitchell identifies the release of the ten-year-old expression of Arran as being "the start of us setting up a core range that would allow us to compete on a level playing field with our competitors. We have spent a lot of time making sure the vattings are really up to scratch, and with the 10-Year-Old, there was a real feeling that Arran was starting to hit its stride in terms of age and quality." **GS**

Tasting notes

Fig, citrusy notes, and brittle toffee on the nose. Complex, elegant, and poised on the palate but with a full body. Mixed spices, hazelnut, traces of vanilla fudge. The finish is medium in length, with quite sweet and malty notes, followed by a late-arriving nuttiness.

Arran 12-Year-Old

Isle of Arran Distillers | www.arranwhisky.com

Region and country of origin Islands, Scotland
Distillery Isle of Arran, Lochranza, Isle of Arran, North
Ayrshire **Alcohol content** 46% abv
Style Single malt

In 2008, two years after Arran distillery released the Arran 10-Year-Old, its first single malt, the whisky was joined by a twelve-year-old bottling. However, there was never a long-term plan to have both ten- and twelve-year-old variants of the same whisky in the marketplace at the same time. "We felt they were too close together in terms of age for that," explains Arran managing director Euan Mitchell. "We were effectively testing the water to see if the 12-Year-Old really took off, in which case we could well have allowed the 10-Year-Old to disappear. But although the 12-Year-Old did well, we found people still had a real affinity with the 10-Year-Old. Arran 10-Year-Old continued to be the main seller, and feedback from visitors to the distillery was that most people preferred it to Arran 12-Year-Old."

Arran 12-Year-Old displays a sherry influence significantly greater than that of its younger sibling, principally due to the fact that much of the stock that went into it had been reracked from second-fill sherry casks and first-fill bourbon barrels into fresh oloroso sherry hogsheads. The whisky was finished in the sherry wood for some nine months.

"The extra degree of sherry influence pleased some consumers, but others felt we had lost the subtle nuances of Arran," notes Mitchell. "We let the 10- and 12-Year-Olds both run free, as it were, and let natural selection take over. Then we started to look at the evolution, deciding to push the twelve up to fourteen, and eventually release an eighteen-year-old when the stock is of age to do that." **GS**

Tasting notes

Floral, sweet, and spicy on the nose, with a hint of worn leather. Sweet and honeyed in the mouth, with caramel, nuts, and malt merging nicely with apricot and citrusy fruit notes. Medium to long in the finish, with sherry, spices, and a final hint of leather.

Arran 14-Year-Old

Isle of Arran Distillers | www.arranwhisky.com

Region and country of origin Islands, Scotland
Distillery Isle of Arran, Lochranza, Isle of Arran, North
Ayrshire **Alcohol content** 46% abv
Style Single malt

The fourteen-year-old expression of Arran single malt appeared in 2010. This time, the influence of sherry wood that had prevailed in the twelve-year-old variant of 2008 was much more muted.

Arran managing director Euan Mitchell explains that "primarily, the stock we had was in second- and third-fill sherry casks. Distillery manager James MacTaggart was keen that Arran should have more of a bourbon influence. He felt the sherry was masking the spirit a bit, and we had sampled some very good older bourbon-matured stock. For a while we had been filling new-make spirit into lots of bourbon wood, so that was always going to be our ultimate house style."

Arran 14-Year-Old turned out to be a classically fruity Arran, with depth and resonance. Euan Mitchell has this to say: "For the 14-Year-Old, we reracked whisky into first-fill bourbon barrels for a couple of years, so you get lots more spicy vanilla character coming through. You see a more natural progression from the 10- to the 14-Year-Old than you did with the 12-Year-Old. We now ship Arran to China, and they take the 10-Year-Old, but they won't take the 14- because in China four is not a lucky number. Eight is a very lucky number there, and if we had stuck to doing a twelve-year-old we would have been fine!"

While an eight-year-old is not in the cards, Arran's ultimate aim is to finalize its core range as comprising ten-, fourteen-, and eighteen-year-old single malts. The eighteen-year-old Arran is due to complete the sequence in 2014. **GS**

Tasting notes

Very fragrant and perfumed on the nose, with peach, brandy, and gingersnaps, plus vanilla and mild oak. Smooth and creamy on the palate, with spicy summer fruits, apricot, and hazelnut. The lingering finish is spicy, biscuity, and slowly drying with just a hint of salt.

This stone circle on Machrie Moor appears on the 14-Year-Old's label.

Arran Amarone Cask Finish

Isle of Arran Distillers | www.arranwhisky.com

Region and country of origin Islands, Scotland
Distillery Isle of Arran, Lochranza, Isle of Arran, North Ayrshire **Alcohol content** 50% abv
Style Single malt

With cask finishing having played such a significant part in the evolution of the Arran single-malt brand, it is not surprising that the core range includes a trio of disparate finishes. One of these is Amarone, a highly regarded and full-bodied Italian red wine produced near Verona. After spending eight years in bourbon casks, the Arran whisky is transferred into 225-liter (59-gallon) Amarone barriques for a finishing period in the region of nine months.

According to Euan Mitchell, "This stood out as a finish that worked very well. It didn't just taste like Arran from a red wine cask. The sum was definitely greater than the parts. With finishes, the whisky will usually spend from six to nine months in the cask, and sometimes up to twelve months. We reckon on six to nine months for both the Amarone and port finishes. After six months, [Arran distillery manager] James MacTaggart takes samples and carefully monitors their progress because there is always a precise 'tipping point,' when you suddenly lose some of that essential distillery character."

As you might expect, only traditional methods of distilling are used, including wooden washbacks made by Brown & Sons of Dufftown and custom copper stills. The distillery claims that the water from nearby Loch na Davie is the "purest in all of Scotland," but it is of course the Amarone casks that imbue the whisky with a red hue that marks it out from the crowd. Like many of the Arran single malts, this expression is non-chill-filtered, so be prepared for a cloudy, pinkish liquid if you add water. **GS**

Tasting notes

The nose is fragrant, with obvious red wine influence, plus cinnamon, pepper, plums, and raspberries. Behind the big wine "front," this is a relatively straightforward whisky on the palate, with grape pulp, oak, fudge, and spice. The finish is medium in length, with cloves.

Arran Icons of Arran "Peacock" 1996

Isle of Arran Distillers | www.arranwhisky.com

Region and country of origin Islands, Scotland
Distillery Isle of Arran, Lochranza, Isle of Arran, North Ayrshire **Alcohol content** 46% abv
Style Single malt

Creating the Icons of Arran series was a part of the long-term strategy of Isle of Arran Distillers, along with developing a credible range of aged whiskies. The company's intention was to focus on elements unique to the Isle of Arran and emphasize the fact that theirs was the only distillery operating on the island.

"Peacock" was the nickname of the first of the Icons of Arran series, which was released in 2009. The nickname was inspired by the enduring presence of peacocks in the distillery grounds. "The idea was that we were proudly showing off our whisky, like a peacock proudly displaying its feathers," says managing director Euan Mitchell. The Peacock issue was presented in notably splendid and standout packaging, and consisted of 6,000 bottles from 1996 casks, thirteen of which were ex-bourbon while seven were ex-sherry hogsheads.

Mitchell declares, "By the time we were in the final stages of planning Peacock, there was only one of the birds left at the distillery, and just before the launch, it jumped onto the draff lorry as it left the distillery, and soon after we got it back, it died. It had to be replaced pretty quickly, but the replacement hasn't really settled and keeps eating the plants in people's gardens in Lochranza!"

Following the success of Peacock, the Icons of Arran series was continued with Rowan Tree in 2010 and Westie in 2011, the latter celebrating distillery manager James MacTaggart's West Highland terrier, which answers to the name of Ruaraidh. Each of the Icons of Arran bottlings is twelve years old. **GS**

Tasting notes

The nose is soft and pleasing, with honey, vanilla, ripe orange, stewed apple, and coconut. The palate is sweet, with malt, more orange and apple, vanilla, spice, and a hint of oak. The medium-length finish remains sweet to the end. Well-mannered, rounded, and sophisticated.

Arran Machrie Moor

Isle of Arran Distillers | www.arranwhisky.com

Region and country of origin Islands, Scotland
Distillery Isle of Arran, Lochranza, Isle of Arran, North Ayrshire **Alcohol content** 46% abv
Style Single malt

A number of distilleries not usually associated with peated single malts have released peated variants in recent years. Prominent among them was this limited issue in 2010 of 9,000 bottles of a peated Arran expression under the Machrie Moor name. Machrie Moor is named for a peat bog on the west coast of the Isle of Arran, a bog that boasts a number of Bronze Age stone circles and standing stones.

The whisky in question was distilled in 2004 and 2005 and peated to 14 parts per million (ppm). According to managing director Euan Mitchell, "We first produced peated Arran back in 2004, and it has been distilled in small quantities each year since. Originally only 10,000 liters [2,600 gallons] per annum were produced, but we doubled that in 2010 and plan to continue at this level." The peat content has since been increased, as it proved popular. Mitchell commented, "Initially, the peating level was 14 ppm, but more recently we have pushed this up to 20 ppm."

Aware that the degree of peating in Scottish single malts is always a matter of hot debate, Mitchell is quick to point out that the use of peated malt does not alter the essential Arran character, but rather enhances it. "We deliberately went for a medium peating level to ensure the Arran character was not obliterated in the process," he says. "Unlike several other distillers—no names supplied!—we have not gone down the road of the big peat guns where all other flavor characteristics have been sacrificed at the altar of peat smoke. Machrie Moor is classic Arran but with a peaty twist in the tail." **GS**

Tasting notes

Nutty peat, spicy malt, and lemon on the slightly savory nose, with hints of toffee and vanilla. Vibrant on the palate, with lots of citrus fruit. A bonfire smokiness develops steadily, with spice, nuts, and plain chocolate through to the long, spicy, citrusy finish.

Arran Madeira Cask Finish

Isle of Arran Distillers | www.arranwhisky.com

Region and country of origin Islands, Scotland
Distillery Isle of Arran, Lochranza, Isle of Arran, North Ayrshire **Alcohol content** 50% abv
Style Single malt

The practice of cask finishing, or "secondary maturation," is one that divides the Scotch whisky community, with adherents insisting that it allows distillers to present new facets of their single malts, while opponents claim that all too often, it is a way of masking poor or indifferent quality whisky.

In common with several other "young" distilleries, Arran went down the route of cask finishing, starting a program of finished releases in 2003. "Finishes did us a huge favor at the time," insists managing director Euan Mitchell. "They opened the brand up to a lot of people who perhaps thought Arran was too young to take seriously."

For one such cask finish, which was bottled in 2008, Madeira was chosen, mainly because it is one of the more "traditional" and indeed widely used cask types for Scotch malt whisky finishes. "Previously, we had done some quite exotic ones," notes Mitchell, "and Madeira worked really well. Logically, if port works, then Madeira should work with your style of Scotch whisky, too."

Fortified Madeira wine, from the eponymous island southwest of Portugal, was matured in 59-gallon (225-liter) oak barriques for five years before the emptied barriques were transported to Scotland. Arran single malt, which had been matured for eight years in conventional casks, was deposited into the barriques for a final maturation period of ten months. The end result was 5,760 bottles of a whisky described by the distiller as being "a sensational single malt with a rich, brooding character." **GS**

Tasting notes

The nose is rich and inviting, featuring Christmas cake and thick-cut orange marmalade. Full-bodied, mouth-coating, notably sweet, with just a slight citric fruit tang cutting through to add balance. The finish is medium in length, with citrus fruit notes, toffee, and mixed spices.

Arran Open Day Single Cask Release 2011

Isle of Arran Distillers | www.arranwhisky.com

Region and country of origin Islands, Scotland
Distillery Isle of Arran, Lochranza, Isle of Arran, North Ayrshire **Alcohol content** 52% abv
Style Single malt

Arran distillery's annual open days have become very popular, and at the fifteenth anniversary event in 2010, distillery manager James MacTaggart presented a selection of Arran cask samples to the masterclass he held and invited participants to vote on which they would most like to see bottled. The sample that won was subsequently offered as the Open Day release for 2011. All the names of the people who took part were printed on the back label of the bottle.

The cask in question was a 1995 bourbon barrel, filled the year the distillery opened. It was cask number 104, and it yielded just 200 bottles. Euan Mitchell noted at the time that "in future, single-cask bourbon bottlings will be of this sort of vintage."

Reflecting the Scotch whisky industry as a whole, where more than 90 percent of all new-make spirit is filled into ex-bourbon casks rather than the vastly more expensive sherry casks, some 80 percent of Arran spirit is now filled into new bourbon barrels, with the rest going into a mixture of casks, many of which are second-fill sherry casks. "We've filled mainly bourbon casks since 2005," notes Mitchell. As a generalization, ex-bourbon casks give spicy, buttery, vanilla notes to the new spirit as it matures. **GS**

Tasting notes

Soft and sweet on the nose, with maple syrup, banana split, ginger, and canned cherries. The palate shows rich, exotic fruit flavors, with lively spice and oak notes.

Arran Original

Isle of Arran Distillers | www.arranwhisky.com

Region and country of origin Islands, Scotland
Distillery Isle of Arran, Lochranza, Isle of Arran, North Ayrshire **Alcohol content** 43% abv
Style Single malt

Arran Original predominantly contains five-year-old spirit, with some slightly older whisky in the mix, all matured in ex-bourbon casks. Arran Original was created initially for the French market and is targeted toward volume listings with supermarket chains across mainland Europe. According to managing director Euan Mitchell, "At this sort of age, Arran is light, and you tend to get citrus notes, apples, lemon sherbet, and lime. It's an easygoing whisky, and the name Original comes from the fact that it harks back to the first distillery bottlings at five years old."

Arran distillery, located at the north of the picturesque island, came on stream in the summer of 1995, reigniting a legal whisky-making tradition on Arran that had lain dormant for more than one and a half centuries. The distillery was the brainchild of former Chivas Brothers managing director Harold Currie. A one-year-old spirit was released during 1996 to showcase the distiller's art, and some Arran single malt was used at three years old in the Lochranza blend. Euan Mitchell notes that "it was first released as a single-cask bottling at four years of age, in 1999, and was then bottled as the Arran Malt in 2000, at four and five years old." **GS**

Tasting notes

Fresh and fruity on the light nose, with lemon and lime. Barley and hay on the relatively simplistic palate. A hint of digestive biscuit and vanilla with oak notes.

Arran Port Cask Finish

Isle of Arran Distillers | www.arranwhisky.com

Region and country of origin Islands, Scotland
Distillery Isle of Arran, Lochranza, Isle of Arran, North Ayrshire **Alcohol content** 50% abv
Style Single malt

Virtually every distiller who has embraced the concept of cask finishing has at some time or another issued a port wood finish, due to its widespread popularity.

Port is a fortified wine produced exclusively in the Douro Valley of northern Portugal, and tawny ports are made from red grapes aged in wooden barrels using a solera process. The solera is a way of aging the liquid by using fractional blending of the component parts so that the finished product is a mixture of ages. A resulting nutty flavor is characteristic of tawny port, which can be sweet or medium dry and is usually drunk as a dessert wine.

In the past, when Isle of Arran Distillers was experimenting broadly with the process of cask finishing, "secondary maturation" took place in the casks used for Lepanto PX Spanish brandy and Montepulciano d'Abruzzo "Villa Gemma," along with marsala, Château Margaux, Pomerol Bordeaux, Tokaji, and rum. As the company concentrates on consolidating its reputation for high-quality, aged single malts, expect to see less experimentation in this arena, though whether the Arran team will be able to resist future one-off cask finishes if a fascinating opportunity presents itself is another matter. **GS**

Tasting notes

On the nose, vanilla, dried fruits, hazelnut, and orange, plus notes of honey and fudge. Spicy in the mouth, with cereal, apple pie with cinnamon, sultana, and plum.

Arran Premium Cask Selection

Isle of Arran Distillers | www.arranwhisky.com

Region and country of origin Islands, Scotland
Distillery Isle of Arran, Lochranza, Isle of Arran, North Ayrshire **Alcohol content** 54.1% abv
Style Single malt

Launched during 2011, the first release in this new series was a twelve-year-old single-cask, cask-strength bottling (264 bottles) from first-fill sherry hogshead number 1973. It showed the way ahead for Arran's well-established single-cask bottling program, with the emphasis now being on older and rarer casks.

Both sherry and bourbon single casks feature in the lineup, and Euan Mitchell notes, "Bottling single casks was another way for us to get beyond the image of being a young distillery. Single casks are always handpicked by the manager as the true essence of Arran single malt, either from an ex-bourbon or ex-sherry cask. We make handwritten labels to add to the sense of handcrafting.

"The first ones were done in 1999, and we have actually done quite a lot in the past. In fact, we began to find ourselves doing too many. It became a bit less special, so we are now bottling fewer of them. In total, we must have done around fifty, though around half of those were specifically for Norway," Mitchell adds. Arran single malt was first listed by the Norwegian drinks monopoly in 2009, and it is a remarkable fact that after just five months, it had become the second-best-selling malt in the country after Glenfiddich. **GS**

Tasting notes

Vanilla and milk chocolate on the rich, spicy nose. The palate features full-on sweet sherry, with figs, oranges, and cinnamon. A lengthy finish, with dark chocolate.

Spirit Still
4300 Litres

Arran St. Emilion Cask Finish

Isle of Arran Distillers | www.arranwhisky.com

Region and country of origin Islands, Scotland
Distillery Isle of Arran, Lochranza, Isle of Arran, North Ayrshire **Alcohol content** 50% abv
Style Single malt

In 2008, Isle of Arran Distillers launched four finishes, including a St. Emilion finish. This used casks sourced from Château Fonplégade, near St. Emilion in Bordeaux. The vineyard in question produces a Grand Cru Classé that is aged in new French oak barrels for two years. According to managing director Euan Mitchell, "As a slightly softer style of Bordeaux, we found this didn't overwhelm the Arran spirit." The finishing period lasted for twelve months and resulted in 6,636 bottles. The distiller notes that "The new flavors added to the Arran malt by these casks are in perfect harmony with the intrinsic distillery character."

Mitchell adds, "For a couple of years, we did up to six Arran cask finishes each year, then we released four per year for a further four years. It was a more structured program. Some of those releases comprised between 1,200 and 2,000 bottles, though more recently we have released up to 6,000 bottles each time. Every finish we did totally presold before bottling, so we had a good reason to keep going. With a young brand, it allowed us to expand our range significantly. We bought casks directly from producers, and there was a good 'selling' story behind each bottling we did." **GS**

Tasting notes

An intriguing nose that boasts oak, orange, ripe plum, and maraschino cherry, with a hint of milk chocolate. Full-bodied in the mouth, with a lively palate.

Arran Sauternes Cask Finish

Isle of Arran Distillers | www.arranwhisky.com

Region and country of origin Islands, Scotland
Distillery Isle of Arran, Lochranza, Isle of Arran, North Ayrshire **Alcohol content** 50% abv
Style Single malt

Along with amarone and port, Sauternes—the sweet white wine from the Sauternais region of Bordeaux in southwest France—is the third cask finish in the permanent Arran lineup. "We try to keep the core three finished expressions always available, but there are sometimes gaps between batches," explains managing director Euan Mitchell, who adds that "St. Emilion is a sweet white wine, and lots of the sweet notes in Arran are accentuated by the Sauternes casks. With all the casks we source, we are looking for small, 'high-end' producers with the same ethos as ourselves. Stylistically, Sauternes gives us a real contrast with the amarone finish and the port finish."

Reflecting on the early days, Mitchell recalls, "The first finish we did was using calvados casks. The whisky was about six years old, and we chose the calvados to experiment with, in effect. Sometimes people used to detect a calvados note in the nose of Arran when it was quite young, so it seemed logical to use calvados casks."

Among the more unusual cask finishes tried by Isle of Arran's experimental distillers were a German pinot noir finish and a "Champagne" finish whose influence actually came from Argonne Forest oak. **GS**

Tasting notes

Grassy on the nose, with lemon, melon, and a sweet, marzipan note, plus nuts and spices. Mouth-coating, with a palate of baked apple tart, honey, and vanilla.

⬅ One of the pair of stills at Isle of Arran distillery, which opened in 1995.

Auchentoshan 12-Year-Old

Morrison Bowmore Distillers (Suntory) | www.auchentoshan.com

Region and country of origin Lowlands, Scotland
Distillery Auchentoshan, Dalmuir, Dunbartonshire
Alcohol content 40% abv
Style Single malt

As you might expect, there's a great deal of debate in the industry on the merits of triple-distillation, and people's views are often largely dependant on whom they work for or indeed which country they come from. So while most Irish folk will praise the third pass through the still with evangelical zeal, the Scots for the most part see little (or no) merit in the process.

The one thing you can say with all certainty is that the spirit produced at the end of the triple-distillation process is more alcoholic than that produced by double-distillation. Roughly 80-plus percent abv versus 68 percent abv, but again how that relates to taste is a sore point. It certainly means that with double-distillation, more of the congeners are kept in the spirit, and congeners are where some of the flavors lie, so by triple-distilling, you are producing a spirit that is either "less flavorsome" or "more delicate." Take your pick.

Most people will also agree that there's a certain affinity between whisky and sherry butts, but with triple-distillation, that relationship is more complex. Here Auchentoshan has taken on the sherry very well; it really complements the spirit, and the intertwining of flavors is magnificently showcased.

The Auchentoshan 12-Year-Old replaces the now extinct but very popular 10-Year-Old and fills its shoes nicely. The extra two years of interplay between whisky and cask has filled out the flavor, resulting in a more complex, satisfying drink. There are, however, reports of a variable aspect to this malt, with some bottles being smokier than others. **PM**

Tasting notes

Initially sweet, but then some lime notes creep in. The sherry supports the spirit nicely, and the experience is smooth and very pleasant. Fresh green grass and sweet fruit notes in the mouth. Strangely, this whisky also works with a single ice cube.

Auchentoshan 18-Year-Old

Morrison Bowmore Distillers (Suntory) | www.auchentoshan.com

Region and country of origin Lowlands, Scotland
Distillery Auchentoshan, Dalmuir, Dunbartonshire
Alcohol content 43% abv
Style Single malt

Time is a curious thing. Once the Auchentoshan distillery sat in rich farmland on the banks of the River Clyde. Glasgow was nearby, so there were plenty of potential customers for its whisky.

Nowadays Glasgow has all but swallowed up much of the surrounding countryside, and time hasn't been kind to the Lowland distillers. Even though there are more people in the Lowlands than ever, there are fewer distilleries—five Lowland plants have fallen cold and silent within living memory. Indeed, as recently as the mid-1990s, many thought that Auchentoshen would go the same way as Interleven, Littlemill, Kinclaith, St. Magdalene, and Rosebank.

Time has affected Auchentoshan in other ways, too. When production was ramped up, stock had to be put aside for older expressions, and this reduced cash flow. Whisky may only be sold as whisky after it has spent at least three years maturing in oak, but in many cases it is only after seven or even ten years that the stuff gets bottled.

This 18-Year-Old comes from Auchentoshan's troubled period. Eighteen years is quite an age for a light, triple-distilled dram, but the good news is that this whisky has aged very gracefully and is as subtle and as fresh as ever. The color hints at sherry maturation, but this whisky has been aged in North American bourbon oak for at least eighteen years. It was bottled at an inspired 43 percent abv, which means that you get quite a lot for your money. Unsurprisingly, this whisky has started to pick up some major awards. Expect more to come. **PM**

Tasting notes

This whisky is a curious and very pleasant mix of light, almost floral cereal, cut with toasted pine nuts and fine tobacco. The distillery's signature twist of lemon is now a darker marmalade, and there is a very addictive peppery rumble at the end.

Auchentoshan 21-Year-Old

Morrison Bowmore Distillers (Suntory)
www.auchentoshan.com

Region and country of origin Lowlands, Scotland
Distillery Auchentoshan, Dalmuir, Dunbartonshire
Alcohol content 43% abv
Style Single malt

Auchentoshan distillery has numerous distinctions, not least of which is a cooling water supply stored in the crater made by a German bomb during a World War II raid on the nearby Clydeside shipyards.

The distillery is also one of relatively few Scottish whisky makers that still practice triple distillation. Today, Auchentoshan is the only whisky maker in the Lowlands that still employs it. The use at Auchentoshan of a third, or intermediate, still in the preparation of unpeated malt—which has been matured mainly in ex-bourbon barrels and butts that formerly contained oloroso or Pedro Ximénez sherry—gives the finished product a notably sweeter and more delicate flavor than many rival drams.

However, these features, unusual as they are, might be scarcely worthy of mention were it not for the distinctive and, in the view of many, unsurpassed quality of Auchentoshan single malts. Among the most highly regarded by experts is this limited edition. The famously rigorous *Jim Murray's Whisky Bible* is unstinting in its praise, dubbing it "one of the finest Lowland distillery bottlings of our time. A near faultless masterpiece of astonishing complexity to be cherished and discussed with deserved reverence." **GL**

Tasting notes

The nose is soft and supple, producing an aroma of dry grass edged by honey and citrus. The finish evokes apricot jam on whole-grain toast with citrus notes.

Auchentoshan 200th Anniversary

Morrison Bowmore Distillers (Suntory)
www.auchentoshan.com

Region and country of origin Lowlands, Scotland
Distillery Auchentoshan, Dalmuir, Dunbartonshire
Alcohol content 57.5%
Style Single malt

Auchentoshan is an oddball distillery in many ways, a whisky loner and one of the last distilleries in the Lowland region of Scotland. It is described as Glasgow's distillery, but ask the average person in Sauciehall Street, and chances are they won't have heard of it, let alone visited it. Perhaps the distillery was a little overshadowed by Islay sibling Bowmore, which produced a more flavorful whisky than the subtle, rounded, floral, and light Auchentoshan.

The distillery's fortunes under Japanese drinks giant Suntory, owner of Morrison Bowmore, have taken a major turn for the better of late, thanks to a series of special, top-quality bottlings, including some single-cask offerings that show new aspects of the distillery. The parent company has invested heavily, too, repackaging the core range and changing the ten-year-old expression to a twelve-year-old one.

This special anniversary bottling contains a range of aged Auchentoshan whiskies. If you tend to dismiss Auchentoshan as light and floral, the assertiveness of this malt will make you think again. Well received on its release, it is well packaged and comes with a certificate of authentication. A whisky that presents you with a dilemma: drink or save? Drink it. **DR**

Tasting notes

The light and easygoing vanilla and yellow fruit flavors are spiced up. The malt is rich and much more oily, coating the mouth.

Auchentoshan Classic

Morrison Bowmore Distillers (Suntory)
www.auchentoshan.com

Region and country of origin Lowlands, Scotland
Distillery Auchentoshan, Dalmuir, Dunbartonshire
Alcohol content 40% abv
Style Single malt

Auchentoshan is the only distillery in Scotland that triple-distills each and every drop of whisky they make. No one is quite sure just how this came to be, for the practice makes the production of whisky here more costly and time-consuming. It might have something to do with the many Irish workers who moved to the Glasgow area after the famine, during the latter part of the nineteenth century. They would have been used to triple-distilled Irish, and we know that until the middle of the nineteenth century, this distillery had just the two stills. So it's quite possible the distillery was simply meeting customer demand.

Nowadays the addition of a third still does several things. For a start, it produces a lighter, more fragrant whisky, because the spirit is more alcoholic. The three-step process works like this: spirit is at 18 percent abv leaving the wash still, 54 percent abv after the intermediate still, and finally 81 percent abv after the spirit still. This makes Auchentoshan's new spirit the highest abv distillate of any Scottish distillery.

Auchentoshan Classic is the entry-level whisky, and if all that went before isn't different enough, there's not a whiff of peat to it. This is one for those who think that all Scotch tastes the same. **PM**

Tasting notes

This is a delicate and fragrant whisky with hints of toasted coconut and a twist of citrus. It is very clean, refreshing, and approachable.

Auchentoshan Three Wood

Morrison Bowmore Distillers (Suntory)
www.auchentoshan.com

Region and country of origin Lowlands, Scotland
Distillery Auchentoshan, Dalmuir, Dunbartonshire
Alcohol content 43% abv
Style Single malt

Wood has more effect on the end flavor of a whisky than barley, water, and yeast combined. It even has a greater impact than the malting, mashing, and distilling. In a clean, peat-free whisky such as Three Wood, up to 80 percent of the end taste will have come from the casks in which it matured.

In this expression of Auchentoshan, the whisky is aged in American oak barrels that once contained bourbon, and is finished in European oak sherry butts. In other words, the whisky is recasked when mature and left in sherry wood until the men in white coats are happy with it. There is nothing new in the use of oloroso butts for whisky maturation, but here it is the third wood that is interesting: the Auchentoshan makers have chosen Pedro Ximénez casks.

Pedro Ximénez is a sherry made from the juice of grapes that have been dried under the hot Spanish sun. It is a pungent, viscous, fortified wine, and there are certainly notes in this whisky that are darker than you might expect. The demand for fine sherry casks far outstrips supply, so a whisky like this is only as good as the sherry casks that have been used. You can tell on the nose: good sherry wood has a clean, candied-fruit, Christmas-cake kind of scent. **PM**

Tasting notes

A spicy, festive nose. Generous dried fruit, and there is even marzipan and a hint of marshmallow. A very fine whisky that sparkles on the back of the tongue.

Auchentoshan Valinch

Morrison Bowmore Distillers (Suntory) | www.auchentoshan.com

Region and country of origin Lowlands, Scotland
Distillery Auchentoshan, Dalmuir, Dunbartonshire
Alcohol content 57.5% abv
Style Single malt

Sometimes the simple ideas are the best. Here Auchentoshan Classic has been taken pretty much straight from the cask and bottled. Sometimes less, indeed, is more. So this whisky hasn't had caramel added, or been reduced to 40 percent abv or chill-filtered. They've just strained it (who likes bits of cask in their drink?) and given it a name: Valinch—which, as every schoolboy knows, is the metal pipette used to draw samples of whisky from the cask.

Distillers chill-filter their whisky so that it doesn't go cloudy in the cold, or when water or ice cubes are added. The vast majority of blended Scotch is chill-filtered, and a frustrating number of single malts are too. The filtration process removes the guilty fatty acids, but these are the very elements that give whisky some of its flavor. So this bottling is for those who want to experience maximum flavor, in other words, those who are into a more extreme expression of the Auchentoshan signature crème brûlée.

Auchentoshan claims that this whisky came about through consumer demand, so the distillers clearly think that the people who will buy Valinch are not going to stick it in the fridge, add ice, and complain that the whisky has "gone off" because it is hazy.

As for caramel, it is added to give a uniformity of color to a brand. Here the color is derived from maturation solely in ex-bourbon wood. Small quantities of Valinch are released annually, so it should be possible to track subtle changes over time. As this is a cask-strength edition, a small drop of water is required to wake this beauty. **PM**

Tasting notes

This is a creamy, almost citrus whisky—as you would imagine, it's very like Auchentoshan Classic, just cleaner. There's not as much cask influence on show, so the flavors come from the distillate. The crisp, almost tart, finish is wonderful.

Auchroisk 10-Year-Old

Diageo | www.malts.com

Region and country of origin Speyside, Scotland
Distillery Auchroisk, Mulben, Banffshire
Alcohol content 43% abv
Style Single malt

Some distillery names in Scotland are straightforward and create no problem to pronounce, for instance Macallan. Others demand a little more attention, like Glenfiddich. Finally there are some names that seem to be absolutely impossible to get right, and even the locals are divided. Auchroisk is one of them. Some of the suggestions are "auchroysk," "achrask," and "athrusk." With a distillery name like that, it became pretty clear that the whisky had to be called something that the customer could actually pronounce, and the owners came up with Singleton.

Today Auchroisk distillery has been forced to give up the Singleton name to three other Diageo distilleries, and the name of the whisky is back to Auchroisk. The change will probably not affect sales, as this is and has been one of the most obscure single malts of Scotland. Nearly 100 percent of the output is destined to become a part of Johnnie Walker or the other big blends of Diageo. The size of the distillery (producing 1 million gallons/4 million liters per year) makes it an important contributor.

Part of the final whisky's flavor is determined already during the mashing stage. If you decide to produce a cloudy wort, with some solids from the grain still present, you get a slightly nutty character, which is precisely what happens with Auchroisk. This, together with a combination of short (45-hour) and very long (130-hour) fermentations, creates a whisky with sweetness and depth. The only Auchroisk single malt that is bottled on a regular basis by Diageo is this 10-Year-Old in the Flora & Fauna range. **IR**

Tasting notes

A nose to love: a pleasant combination of honey and toffee and with a buttery touch. The cereals come through on the palate but also red berries (raspberry). The finish is quite long and sweet. A gentle lullaby of a finish, with soothing soft spice.

Auchroisk
Managers' Choice

Diageo | www.malts.com

Region and country of origin Speyside, Scotland
Distillery Auchroisk, Mulben, Banffshire
Alcohol content 60.6% abv
Style Single malt

Auchroisk is one of the newest distilleries in Scotland. While most of the sites were established in the 1800s, it dates back to 1974. The huge complex, situated between Keith and Craigellachie, can produce 818,933 gallons (3,100,000 liters) of spirits a year, and acts not only as a production plant but also as a center for maturation and blending. The ten warehouses hold no fewer than 250,000 casks, many of them coming from other distilleries in the Diageo portfolio. A couple of years ago, the spacious still house, and its four pairs of stills, served as a model for Diageo's newest distillery, built at Roseisle in Speyside, near the Moray Firth.

It is very rare that Diageo should release single-cask bottlings from any of their twenty-eight distilleries in Scotland. However, in fall of 2009, something really unusual was announced: within the next twelve months, there would be single-cask releases from every one of the distilleries, with the exception, of course, of Roseisle, where the spirit had not reached the legal age of three years.

Three casks from each distillery were chosen and then a nosing panel assessed all the casks and finally chose one to represent each distillery. In 2009, Auchroisk's time had come; a bodega ex-sherry cask from 1999 was chosen, with only 642 bottles being filled. The choice presented a rare chance to taste a sherry-matured Auchroisk, as it is usually the distillery's bourbon-matured malt that is marketed. **IR**

Tasting notes

Lots of butterscotch, almost like going into a candy store. With water, green notes (grass and meadows) appear, together with zesty orange. Powerful on the palate and now more herbal than fruity. Long and sweet finish. Impressive.

Aultmore Provenance 13-Year-Old Douglas of Drumlanrig Sherry Butt

Douglas Laing & Co. | www.douglaslaing.com

Region and country of origin Speyside, Scotland
Distillery Aultmore, Keith, Banffshire
Alcohol content 46% abv
Style Single malt

While the outside of this distillery will win no awards for looks, this bottling shows that incredible alchemy is taking place inside. Most Aultmore is destined to cross the Atlantic as a component of Dewar's blends, as parent company Bacardi bought the distillery in 1998. There have been a very few official bottlings of the single malt but none that match this single cask sherry butt for its amazing light, tinder-dry taste.

Most sherried whiskies are first matured in ex-bourbon casks before being finished for a few years in a sherry cask, but this one has spent all of its thirteen years soaking up grapey flavors, and the result is quite surprising. The underlay of wood and vanilla that comes from the bourbon oak is absent, replaced by a bone-dry, slightly salty edge. This is no after-dinner drink to complement a rich fruitcake, as with so many sherried whiskies, and neither is there any hint of rubbery sulfur, which sometimes spoils them. Instead it is a clean fresh drink to enjoy in the summer sunshine after work with something savory.

A frequent debate among whisky lovers is whether one can taste the sea saltiness in certain coastal distilleries and, if so, how the sea air gets into the maturing cask. Aultmore is well inland, so we must look for another explanation. Curiously enough, Alexander Edwards, who set up the distillery in 1895, bought the Oban distillery three years later, so we can only wonder and hope that he would have approved of this delightful drink. **AA**

Tasting notes

One of a kind—a light floral salty nose gives way to a very dry tangy zesty experience like a more alcoholic version of Tio Pepe sherry, with a lengthy finish of salted hazelnut. Absolutely fantastic, and lovely as an aperitif with a bowl of olives.

Bailie Nicol Jarvie

Glenmorangie & Co. (LVMH) | www.glenmorangie.com

Region and country of origin Scotland
Distilleries Various
Alcohol content 40% abv
Style Blend

Bailie Nicol Jarvie is named after a character in Sir Walter Scott's novel *Rob Roy*, and there are a few things we can learn about the liquid simply from its name. In the book, Bailie Nicol Jarvie is a Glaswegian bailiff who helps the lead character, a chap called Frank Osbaldistone, on his journey to the Highlands in pursuit of a thief. In many respects, Bailie Nicol Jarvie is Osbaldistone's adviser, speaking in a rich Scottish dialect about his ambivalent relationship with the Highlands—a place with which he feels a natural kinship tempered by a sense of distance. Perhaps the eponymous whisky has some of the same qualities, having its heritage firmly embedded in Scotland and yet being a blend from a scattering of distilleries.

In one famed scene from *Rob Roy*, rather than get embroiled in a one-sided sword fight, Bailie Nicol Jarvie deals with a particularly troublesome barroom brawl by cannily setting his armed opponent's kilt on fire with a hot poker, showing that skill and wit can often outrank superior swordsmanship.

The label of Bailie Nicol Jarvie boasts that the whisky has the highest malt content of any blended Scotch whisky: the proportions are understood to be 60 percent single malt and 40 percent grain whisky. The single malts are from the Highlands, the Isle of Islay, and Speyside, and are blended together with grain whisky from the Girvan distillery in Ayrshire before being matured in a cask for a minimum of six years. This unique style of blending a large number of malts from a relatively small area is really what gives this whisky its well-crafted flavor. **JH**

Tasting notes

A well-balanced and full-flavored blend with a slight hint of smokiness and nuttiness. Deep and rich in color with notes of toffee, vanilla, and pear, while its maltiness and grain flavor are subtly underlying and delicate. A long finish that leaves you wanting more.

Balblair 2000

Inver House (International Beverage) | www.balblair.com

Region and country of origin Highlands, Scotland
Distillery Balblair, Edderton, Tain, Ross-shire
Alcohol content 43% abv
Style Single malt

At the time of writing, Balblair 2000 vintage is the most recent addition to the Balblair range of whiskies. It was presented for the first time to a wider audience at Whisky Live Paris in 2010 where it became an instant hit and a firm favorite for many fans of this coziest of Highland distilleries.

Does that success mean that Balblair 2000 will become a permanent addition to the range? No. The nature of vintage releases is such that no expression can be around forever, no matter how deep the stock pool; its predecessor, vintage 1997, was replaced by the 2000 after only three years on the market.

Every vintage has its own unique character. Balblair 2000 is pale for a ten-year-old and draws some of its key characteristics from second-fill American oak casks. The 1997 vintage was a touch darker and richer but not quite as clean and fresh. What is the next one going to be like? The only person who knows is Stuart Harvey, master blender at Inver House Distillers (International Beverage). This uncertainty, as well as a relatively high vintage turnover—a couple of new ones appear across the range every year—makes Balblair one of the most interesting distilleries in Scotland. That is, if the spirit is to your liking, of course.

How can you determine if you're a potential fan or not if you have never tried it? Simple. If the idea of a roasted banana stuffed with runny toffee and topped with chocolate sauce makes you smile and gives you a funny fuzzy feeling in the roots of your teeth, you will be hooked at the first sip—and will be looking forward to vintage 2051, 2052, 2053. **LD**

Tasting notes

On the nose, pineapple and apricot reign supreme, but intense toffee and chocolate cookie are not far behind. The palate shows even more character typical of the distillery, with a more citrusy feel and lots of green banana. The finish is spicy and fresh.

Balblair 1997

Inver House (International Beverage)
www.balblair.com

Region and country of origin Highlands, Scotland
Distillery Balblair, Edderton, Tain, Ross-shire
Alcohol content 43% abv
Style Single malt

When Balblair received an extreme makeover and relaunched as a range of vintage expressions in designer oval bottles, the whisky world gasped, held its breath, and then clapped its hands raw. That was in 2007, and many are still applauding.

The new Balblair was radical and brilliant—a truly modern brand that reconnected and rediscovered itself by simply taking a step back. What started in the 1790s as a family-run operation in the village of Edderton was once again receiving all the love and attention it deserved from its owners. Of the three vintages released initially, 1997 was the youngest and most accessible and therefore reached the widest audience. The 1997 vintage is the daddy of all the Balblair vintage releases in that it truly whet whisky enthusiasts' appetites for this northern Highland malt.

Balblair's new-make spirit is ridiculously fruity and citrusy but also heavy and sulfury. Short, squat stills are at the heart of it; their shape, the level to which they are filled, and the way the spirit is cut are all important contributors to the Balblair style. Balblair's chunky spirit "talks" to oak like no other, but because of its weight and meatiness, it may need extra time to develop. What other whisky makers might perceive as a hindrance, distillers at Balblair do not mind at all. "The spirit is ready when it's ready" is their mantra. **LD**

Tasting notes

Vanilla custard meets pineapple chunks in syrup on the nose. The palate is bursting with spices, and its ginger heart is wrapped in oaky bitterness. Finishes fruity.

Balblair 1989

Inver House (International Beverage)
www.balblair.com

Region and country of origin Highlands, Scotland
Distillery Balblair, Edderton, Tain, Ross-shire
Alcohol content 43% abv
Style Single malt

Vintage 1989 was one of the three original vintages released in 2007 as part of the relaunch of Balblair single malt. There has since been a second release in 2010. The more recent one is a touch oakier, but blink and you'll miss the difference. Think of them as twins—identical at first glance but easy to distinguish when you get to know them. Both versions share fruity aromas so pronounced that even untrained noses are able to pick them up. Banana and pineapple. Where did they come from? It is the result of various factors, but rest assured, no real tropical fruits were anywhere near the production process.

Balblair uses a deep-bed mash tun that produces very clear, yellowish, aromatic wort. It smells like a good German Hefeweizen (unfiltered wheat beer) and tastes like one, too. Production of big, aromatic, banana/clove and citrusy/floral esters is encouraged at this stage, and some of those flavors carry through the distillation and are very much present in the new make. Another factor in the flavor is the yeast cells that burst during distillation in the peculiar, pear-shaped stills. Open yeast cells release flavor compounds that are captured and condensed with the spirit.

Whether the minutiae of the production process stir the imagination or not, be sure to give the 1989 vintage a try. It is the perfect after-dinner whisky. **LD**

Tasting notes

Creamy, overripe, chocolaty banana. Also fresh pineapple, lemon, sticky toffee, orange peel, raisin, vanilla, and spice.. Layers of complexity.

Balblair 1978

Inver House (International Beverage)
www.balblair.com

Region and country of origin Highlands, Scotland
Distillery Balblair, Edderton, Tain, Ross-shire
Alcohol content 46% abv
Style Single malt

Balblair releases new vintages every year, and this frequency of changes in the lineup may cause some confusion. However, the range follows a set pattern. At any given time, there is a young, a mature, and a very old expression available, and they simply rotate as the years go by. But in the 1970s, a slight disturbance occurred in the cycle.

The initial release in that age bracket was a 1979 vintage. This was soon followed by a 1975 aged in sherry casks and then, in 2010, Balblair 1978 saw the light of day. Not only were the vintages not released in an ascending order, but the later two, the 1975 and 1978, are at the time of writing both available on the primary market. Why should that be? The answer is that they are substantially different. While the 1975 comes from ex-sherry casks, this 1978 is unmistakably a classic refill ex-bourbon American oak expression.

White oak, once completely unknown in Europe, is now found at the heart of the Scotch whisky industry. It lent its sweet vanilla-type flavors to the 1978 and helped to turn the heavy, meaty, and sulfury side of Balblair new-make spirit into the butterscotch heaven found in the younger expressions. But then it gave it more and more of the character, and kept giving generously for thirty-two years. The dram is nothing short of sublime. **LD**

A great intensity of manuka honey, spices, rum and raisin chocolate, blood orange, and vanilla. Signature banana and butterscotch aromas underpin it all.

Balblair 1975

Inver House (International Beverage)
www.balblair.com

Region and country of origin Highlands, Scotland
Distillery Balblair, Edderton, Tain, Ross-shire
Alcohol content 46% abv
Style Single malt

Balblair 1975 vintage was bottled in 2007 but was then kept under lock and key for a year to follow the quickly depleted 1979 vintage in 2008. It offered something different, a Spanish sherry oak punch packed by no other current Balblair. No wonder that when Balblair 1978 was introduced in 2010, the 1975 vintage was still attracting much interest. If you love Balblair in general for its fruity bonanza character, richness, roundness, and great body, prepare for the treat of your life. The 1975 is bursting with all those Balblair characteristics, but also delivers sherry oak spiciness and fantastic dried-fruit overtones. Curiously, the European oak, rather than getting in the way of the house style, leaves room for lightness.

Balblair is the only distillery in the Inver House stable to use condensers (installed by Allied Distillers) rather than worm tubs. Their short, pear-shaped stills with large boiling pots produce a spirit that is on the meaty/sulfury side, but it can be safely assumed that the condensers strip off some of the most waxy and oily character. Is that where the bright sparkle in the 1975 comes from? Such things cannot be known for sure because distillers around the world have only recently started to use scientific methods to analyze their complex craft. So, for now, what makes whisky great has to remain as mysterious as ever. **LD**

Pear and creamy toffee, with spicy raisin and dried plum overtones. The taste surprises with a fizzy hard candy start that quickly transforms into fruit compote. Sultry.

Balblair 1965

Inver House (International Beverage)
www.balblair.com

Region and country of origin Highlands, Scotland
Distillery Balblair, Edderton, Tain, Ross-shire
Alcohol content 52.3% abv
Style Single malt

Only 350 bottles of Balblair 1965 were released, each costing in excess of $1,500 (£1,000). The whisky came from a single cask—an American oak ex-sherry butt said to have been used previously for Ardbeg. Butts are traditionally used for aging sherry in Spain and hold an equivalent of two hogsheads or four barrels: up to 130 gallons (500 liters). In such a huge container, the area of contact between spirit and wood is, by comparison to a standard whisky barrel, limited. This means less interaction with wood and uniquely slow flavor development.

The butt was filled on March 23, 1965, when the distillery belonged to Robert Cumming, long before Allied Distillers replaced traditional worm tubs with modern condensers. Back then, distillers had a much more relaxed approach to controlling malt peating levels. This means that new-make spirit from Balblair was a very different animal in 1965 from what is made at the distillery now. And does it show in the whisky? No question about it.

Peat smoke is there, as is the leathery, waxy scent of an old country house. Four decades in wood make a small dram of this feel like ten pounds of lead in the glass. But make no mistake, Balblair is alive and kicking underneath that with ripe orchard fruits and a distinctly citrusy character. **LD**

Tasting notes

Raisin and date at first, with peat smoke, pipe tobacco, orange peel, and ripe pear emerging. On the palate the texture is creamy and oily, with just a hint of smoke.

Ballantine's 12-Year-Old

Chivas Brothers (Pernod Ricard)
www.ballantines.com

Region and country of origin Scotland
Distillery Various
Alcohol content 40% abv
Style Blend

Following Ballantine's Finest, the 12-Year-Old is the second-youngest expression in the Ballantine's line, established in 1827 when founder George Ballantine opened a grocery store in Edinburgh. At that time, grocers often sold whisky, and George experimented with creating blends. Like the rest of the Ballantine's line, the 12-Year-Old, introduced in the 1960s, is composed of whiskies mostly aged in American oak.

Although the primary single malts in Ballantine's are Glenburgie and Miltonduff, Ballantine's blends are composed of many different malts and grains. They vary by batch, but master blender Sandy Hyslop uses his skill and trained nose to ensure uniformity.

Glenburgie is a rich, fruity, oily malt; Miltonduff, also from Speyside, is a flowery, fragrant single malt. The two have been primary ingredients in Ballantine's blends since 1936, when both distilleries were acquired by Hiram Walker. They are now owned by Chivas Brothers, who took control of Ballantine's when parent company Pernod Ricard acquired Allied Domecq in 2005. Glenburgie has added a pair of stills, increasing capacity by 50 percent to meet demand.

Although it is the least dry of the Ballantine's range, the 12-Year-Old is still drier and more floral than Pernod Ricard's other blended Scotch of the same age, the Chivas Regal 12-Year-Old. **WM**

Tasting notes

On the nose, floral with honey and straw. The palate is dry and floral, with notes of butterscotch, malt, dried flowers, vanilla, and oak. A longer finish than expected.

← This smart Balblair box includes a CD-like tray to hold an information booklet..

Ballantine's 17-Year-Old

Chivas Brothers (Pernod Ricard) | www.ballantines.com

Region and country of origin Scotland
Distillery Various
Alcohol content 43% abv
Style Blend

Introduced in 1937 as "the Scotch," Ballantine's 17-Year-Old was created by George Robertson, master blender for Hiram Walker, James Barclay, and James Horn. "The Scotch" began to be shipped to the United States and the U.S. Virgin Islands in 1938. "This product was different simply because it was so distinctive," says Richard Puddephatt of Ballantine's Brand Integrity Department. "At the time, there was not another seventeen-year-old blend anywhere on the market. It was quite unique." To differentiate the 17-Year-Old from other Ballantine's expressions, a green glass bottle with a squat neck "reminiscent of a malt whisky pot still" was selected for the blend.

George's formula, which has remained largely unchanged, employed what the Scotch Whisky Association described as "Ballantine's magnificent seven": Ardbeg, Balblair, Glenburgie, Glencadam, Miltonduff, Pulteney, and Scapa. While some of these malts may be absent from a particular vatting, each represents a particular taste profile needed for the expression. But companies merge, their ability to source different malts is affected, and substitutions are made. The master blender accommodates these changes by emptying approximately 400 barrels, or 20,000 gallons (76,000 liters) of whisky into each vatting. Up to forty different malts are blended to create the 17-Year-Old.

Of the Ballantine's dry, floral blends, the 17-Year-Old is the most herbaceous, with complex flavors mixing with fruits and spices. A truly unique blend that offers new flavors on each subsequent sip. **WM**

Tasting notes

An herbal nose, with a whiff of smoke, like smelling a peat brick. Allspice, basil, thyme, and spices run through this blend, showing notes of banana, straw, and light vanilla. The finish is dry and herbal, less so than those of Ballantine's 21-Year-Old and 30-Year-Old.

A 1970s U.S. advertisement for Ballantine's is aimed at women. ➜

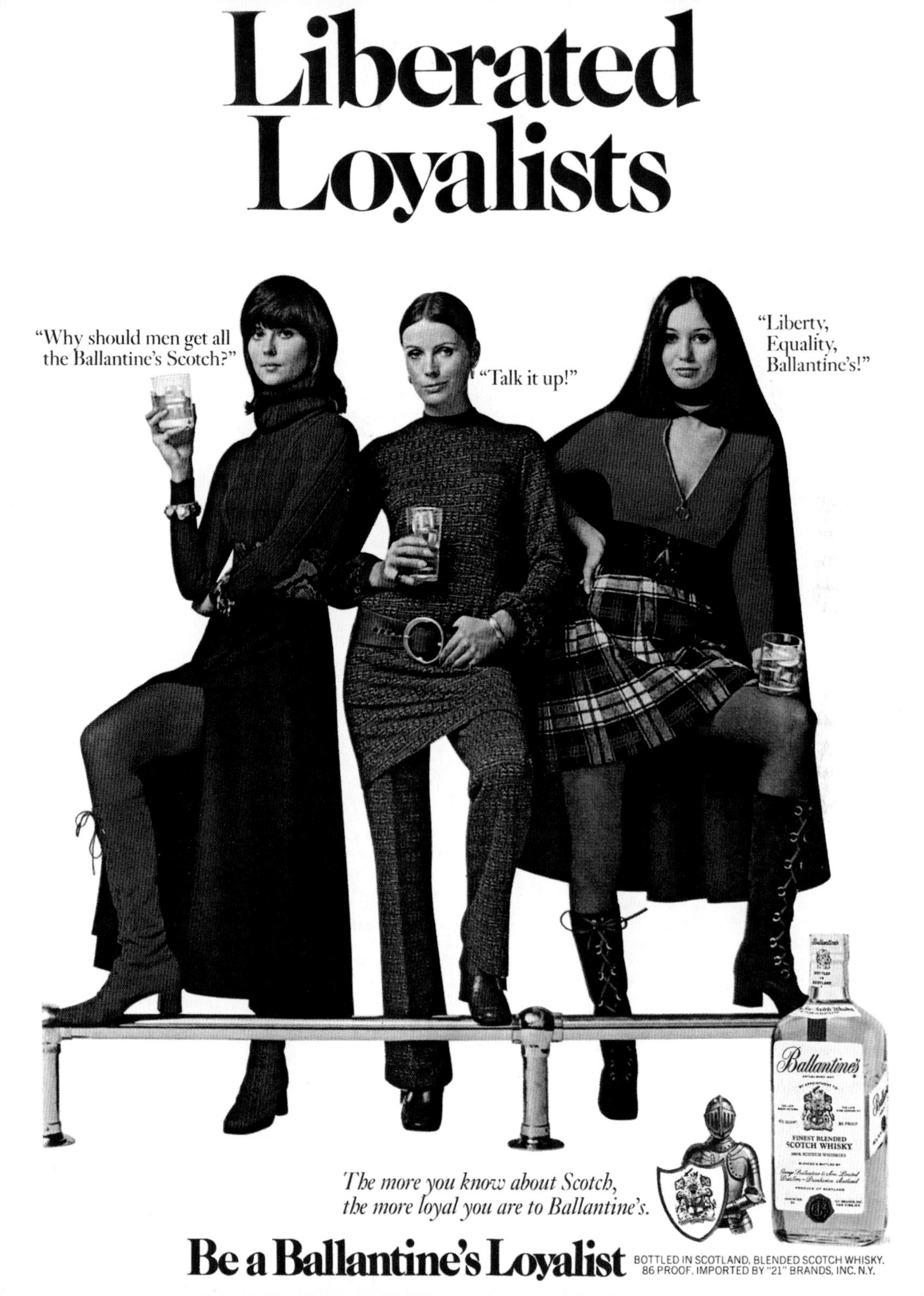

Liberated Loyalists
"Why should men get all the Ballantine's Scotch?"
"Talk it up!"
"Liberty, Equality, Ballantine's!"
The more you know about Scotch, the more loyal you are to Ballantine's.
Be a Ballantine's Loyalist
BOTTLED IN SCOTLAND, BLENDED SCOTCH WHISKY. 86 PROOF. IMPORTED BY "21" BRANDS, INC. N.Y.

Ballantine's 21-Year-Old

Chivas Brothers (Pernod Ricard) | www.ballantines.com

Region and country of origin Scotland
Distillery Various
Alcohol content 43% abv
Style Blend

Introduced in 1993, Ballantine's 21-Year-Old blend is aged in predominantly ex-bourbon American oak, but with a higher percentage of ex-sherry casks to develop its flavor profile. According to master blender Sandy Hyslop, "the supreme reputation of Ballantine's has been achieved by selecting the finest quality single malt and grain whiskies from the four corners of Scotland—the Islands, Highlands, Speyside, and the Lowlands—to create a soft and round whisky with an elegant smoothness on the palate."

Blends such as Ballantine's draw various flavors from different single malts and grain whiskies to create a whole greater than the sum of its parts. Ballantine's previous master blender Robert Hicks compares the creation of a Ballantine's blend to a painter building up a masterpiece, layer by layer. Grain whiskies establish the base coat. "Grain whiskies may lack the strength of character of the single malts, but they play a vital role in holding the whole blend together. My sketching is done with Highland whiskies to create the broad outline of the style I am looking for. Later, the colors will be filled with the Speysides, the Islays, and the Islands." Backgrounds rely on Glenburgie and Miltonduff; bolder colors include Ardbeg, Laphroaig, Balblair, and Glencadam; these are contoured with malts like Tormore and Glentauchers.

If honey describes Ballantine's 12-Year-Old, herbs the 17-Year-Old, and fruit the 30-Year-Old, Ballantine's 21-Year-Old would be described as spice. This is a refined blend that will keep you guessing at what the next sip will reveal. **WM**

Tasting notes

Abundant floral notes, spices, and herbs tempt the nose. The driest of the Ballantine's blends. Oak, anise, and a variety of spices emerge on the palate. Hints of vanilla sneak out but are overpowered by the aged spices. The finish is dry and spicy, with a hint of smoke.

Ballantine's 30-Year-Old

Chivas Brothers (Pernod Ricard) | www.ballantines.com

Region and country of origin Scotland
Distillery Various
Alcohol content 43% abv
Style Blend

When Ballantine's 30-Year-Old was released in the 1930s, it created a benchmark as the first permanent thirty-year-old whisky expression. The feat required great forethought—stocks of whisky had to be selected for maturing before the turn of the twentieth century. Even today, demand exceeds supply and the 30-Year-Old is available only in limited quantities.

Master blender Sandy Hyslop says, "In order to be a blender, you have to be passionate about Scotch whisky. You need to see the entire cycle from distilled spirit to the final blend. You need to devote careful attention to aging whisky, which for Ballantine's, can mean the monitoring of aged malt whiskies that are up to thirty-five years old."

Both the malt and grain components of Ballantine's 30-Year-Old must be aged for thirty years in oak casks. While not as flavorful as malt whisky, grain whiskies are not simply neutral, according to previous master blender Robert Hicks. The grain "has flavor in just the right amount. If it were too strong, it would not be the flavor we are looking for."

When single malts and grains approach and exceed thirty years of aging in oak casks, they develop a rich complexity, like an aromatic patina, which can become overly woody. However, when carefully monitored and blended, combinations of American oak with the occasional European oak create a wonderful flavor. Ripe fruit and spices combine with a smoothness resulting from so many years in the cask. Ballantine's 30-Year-Old is such a whisky, which explains why it is perpetually in short supply. **WM**

Tasting notes

The nose is inviting, with subtle fruit and hints of herbs. The palate reveals fruit, peach, and vanilla, with hints of herbs, just as a chef would add a pinch of allspice to a peach pie to counter the sweetness of the peach and vanilla. Floral notes return on the finish.

Ballantine's Christmas Reserve

Chivas Brothers (Pernod Ricard)
www.chivasbrothers.com

Region and country of origin Scotland
Distillery Various
Alcohol content 40% abv abv
Style Blend

Ballantine's is a big-hitting blended whisky for Chivas Brothers, one capable of taking on company rival Diageo and its ubiquitous street-fighting brand Johnnie Walker shot for shot. With so many emerging markets to play for, the stakes are high, and with everything dependent on maintaining the very highest standards, the pressure is on, particularly so because in many territories the traditional evolution from blended whisky to single malt has broken down.

Ballantine's, with a reputation for quality and a number of expressions to go through the gears with, is ideally placed. But the Christmas Reserve is a chance to have fun. It's recognizably Ballantine's, and there has been no compromise in quality, but it twists the Ballantine's theme. There is an emphasis on those flavors from sherry and bourbon oak that are associated with Christmas cake. The result is a blend that you can not only drink on its own but that actually makes you feel a little guilty about mixing.

The whisky comes in an attractive dark bottle and pretty white box, and is decorated with snowflakes and gold foil to give it a seasonal theme. It was only on sale in selected countries and for a limited Christmas period, so you may struggle to find it. **DR**

Tasting notes

Rich, smooth, rounded, and fruity, this is a stimulating blend with an emphasis on orange, red berries, sherry, cinnamon, nutmeg, and vanilla. Not just for Christmas.

Balmenach 18-Year-Old Malt Cask

Douglas Laing & Co.
www.douglaslaing.com

Region and country of origin Speyside, Scotland
Distillery Balmenach, Cromdale, Morayshire
Alcohol content 50% abv abv
Style Single malt

If you want to understand the variations of taste that a cask can impart, look no further than this unusual whisky from Douglas Laing. In a lineup of whiskies, it's frequently the darker ones that are older, as the oak has had longer to interact with the spirit—this can be a good method of picking the most expensive whisky in a bar when someone offers to buy you a drink!

This Balmenach is, however, one of the palest looking eighteen-year-old whiskies around and makes most twelve-year-old expressions look positively suntanned by comparison. It has been matured in a hogshead—larger than the usual bourbon cask, and a "refill" one—that has held at least two maturing whiskies before this. Both the larger internal surface of the hogshead and the fact that it has probably had whisky in it for twenty-five years before seeing the Balmenach means that very little flavor or coloring is imparted by the oak.

The basic spirit from Balmenach has a reputation for being quite intense and meaty, so the choice of wood will "tame" the more stringent notes. In this case, though, after eighteen years, we have a whisky that has been polished of any rough edges but still has youthful barley and fruity zest at its heart. **AN**

Tasting notes

The pale straw color and citrusy nose, with hints of hard candy, give way to a clean fresh mix of barley and green fruits. Water brings out a certain creaminess.

← The reined-in festive finery of Ballantine's Christmas Reserve.

Balvenie 12-Year-Old DoubleWood

William Grant & Sons | www.thebalvenie.com

Region and country of origin Speyside, Scotland
Distillery Balvenie, Dufftown, Banffshire
Alcohol content 40% abv
Style Single malt

The best of both worlds. Have your cake and eat it with this single malt. The Balvenie DoubleWood is a twelve-year-old single malt, which gets its character from being matured in (funnily enough) two woods: a traditional oak whisky cask and a first-fill European oak sherry cask. While the traditional cask adds character to the whisky, the sherry wood stage brings depth and a certain roundness to its flavor.

That's what makes this a definitive dram—because it volunteers the very best elements from each stage of its maturation. All in all, this makes for a great malt. And, as a result of the Balvenie's efforts here, the DoubleWood is nicely complex and certainly not overpriced in any way, shape, or form.

The Balvenie distillery was founded by the Grant family in 1892 in the Highlands. The family also started the Glenfiddich distillery and the Kininvie distillery. Over at the Balvenie, the makers claim to be the only single-malt Scotch whisky distillery that grows and malts its own barley. Could this be its trump card? Indeed, it seems plausible. After all, this is certainly a plus point. But let's not forget that there are two separate processes at work here. Perhaps its "best of both worlds" quality is really all about the different woods and stages of maturation that they offer.

Imagine that the traditional casks are like an education—or rather, the basis of maturation in general. While the sherry casks are the personality aspect, the quirks and the skills are the elements that steer things in the right direction to make this whisky really fulfill its potential. **JH**

Tasting notes

A layered whisky. On the nose, the DoubleWood is fruity and pleasant, with a touch of honey and hints of sweet sherry and vanilla beneath the surface. On the palate, it is smooth, sweet, warming, and lightly spiced in flavor. The finish is long and satisfying.

Balvenie 14-Year-Old Roasted Malt

William Grant & Sons | www.thebalvenie.com

Region and country of origin Speyside, Scotland
Distillery Balvenie, Dufftown, Banffshire
Alcohol content 47.1% abv
Style Single malt

Balvenie was established in 1893 on land adjacent to the Glenfiddich distillery, the success of which inspired a host of Speyside whisky makers to set up nearby. Although Balvenie has always been one of the smaller of the major Scottish distilleries, it has grown steadily throughout its history. The main period of expansion began in 1957, the year after the business was acquired by the family of William Grant.

Unusually, Balvenie conducts nearly the whole of its production process on its own premises—it grows all its own barley, and has a coppersmith and bottling plant on-site. It also has its own floor maltings, but these can accommodate only 10 percent of Balvenie's current production demands, so the remainder of the requirement is now outsourced to nearby works.

The limited-edition 14-Year-Old Roasted Malt was first bottled in 2006. It was made with barley of a type more commonly used for stout, germinated over twenty-four hours rather than the normal 120, and roasted in a drum at 392°F (200°C) before mashing. Production was restricted to thirty-four casks.

In 2007, William Grant & Sons launched a new initiative known as "Bottle Your Own Balvenie." Visitors to the distillery could make their own blends from three casks, extracting whisky with copper tubes that were sealed at one end with a coin and attached to a length of string that they held in their hands. In the past, such a device was used surreptitiously by distillery workers to steal whisky for their own use; it was known as a "dog" because, according to the most popular etymology, a dog is man's best friend. **GL**

Tasting notes

Although mainly a rush of barley, the nose is oddly suggestive of wet cardboard in clouds of smoke and incense. The taste is predominantly oaky, with a marmalade overlay that is characteristic of Balvenie. The finish is dry and nutty, with hints of mocha.

Balvenie 15-Year-Old Single Barrel

William Grant & Sons | www.thebalvenie.com

Region and country of origin Speyside, Scotland
Distillery Balvenie, Dufftown, Banffshire
Alcohol content 47.8% abv
Style Single malt

In 1993, William Grant & Sons decided to release three very different examples of the Balvenie: the Founder's Reserve 10-Year-Old, a traditional vatting; the Balvenie DoubleWood, a finished expression; and the Balvenie 15-Year-Old Single Barrel. According to Balvenie malt master David Stewart, "Balvenie 15-Year-Old Single Barrel allows our whisky lovers to taste Balvenie straight from the barrel and at a higher-than-normal strength. It allows them to see the differences from cask to cask, and being American oak, it doesn't overpower the whisky and lets the honey, fruit, and vanilla notes shine through." The whisky was originally released at 50.4 percent abv, but the strength was reduced to 47.8 percent abv in 2000.

Balvenie 15-Year-Old Single Barrel contains only spirits from first- and second-fill American oak barrels and hogsheads; no butts are bottled under the name. Written by hand on the label are the bottle number, the specific cask number, and the dates on which the cask was filled and emptied. David Stewart is looking for a specific taste profile in the expression and is less concerned about the malt's age, so, although the label specifies fifteen years of age, the whisky may actually be more than twenty years old. **WM**

Tasting notes

Rich vanilla, honey, and cinnamon hit the nose with notes of oak. The palate is buttery, with an oily mouthfeel and notes of toffee and caramel.

Balvenie 17-Year-Old Peated Cask

William Grant & Sons | www.thebalvenie.com

Region and country of origin Speyside, Scotland
Distillery Balvenie, Dufftown, Banffshire
Alcohol content 43% abv
Style Single malt

In 2001, the Balvenie released what was to become the first of its annual seventeen-year-old expressions. The Balvenie 17-Year-Old Islay was aged in casks that previously held Islay single-malt Scotch. However, the Scotch Whisky Association later disallowed regional demarcations as product descriptors—as in "Islay cask"—for products originating outside the region.

For this expression, Balvenie malt master David Stewart first produced and matured his own heavily peated Balvenie. The distillery has its own malting floors, and this malt was peated to much the same level as malt used in Islay. The heavily peated Balvenie went into casks that absorbed its flavor. Stewart subsequently refilled these casks with Balvenie that had matured for seventeen years in traditional oak barrels. The spirit spent an additional six months in the "heavily peated Balvenie-seasoned" casks.

Stewart then married the contents of these heavily peated casks with Balvenie matured for seventeen years in traditional barrels followed by four to six months in new American oak barrels. The final vatting consisted of roughly 60 percent peated Balvenie casks with 40 percent new-oak casks. The result is an unusual and unforgettable creation. **WM**

Tasting notes

Big notes of orange and vanilla on the nose, but the palate reveals notes of smoked cedar and sandalwood embers, with more smoke on the finish.

Balvenie distillery dries its barley using its own peat-fired kiln. →

Balvenie 17-Year-Old RumCask

William Grant & Sons | www.thebalvenie.com

Region and country of origin Speyside, Scotland
Distillery Balvenie, Dufftown, Banffshire
Alcohol content 43% abv
Style Single malt

This is a sexy malt. It's pretty damn cool, too, and maybe the malt that could get the next generation interested. Soft and smooth, but with a lot of flavors, the Balvenie RumCask is also an acquired taste. Many fans of rum-cask whiskies will already be interested, while others may prefer peat- or port-matured offerings and let this one pass them by. But this is a whisky that should be tried because it can change a person's perception of what whisky is. A previous rum expression from Balvenie, issued three years prior to this 2008 release, saw fans flocking to try it.

The Balvenie RumCask has been matured for seventeen years in butts that originally held Jamaican rum. In the cask, the richness and sweetness of the rum gives the whisky a rich, molasses, sugar-cane flavor. It offers a great way for rum drinkers to trade across to the world of malt whisky, hence its attraction to younger generations. A great whisky to get people who think they know their whiskies to assess—it's such a joy to watch them figuring it out. This is largely because it rewrites the rulebook for what you might expect from a whisky matured for this amount of time. Or a rum, for that matter.

Some may describe it as a bit of a love-it-or-hate-it dram and this, in truth, is because many people already have preconceptions about what to expect in terms of flavor and depth as well as sweetness. All of these elements get people talking. Naturally, there's only one way to know whether it's for you, and that's to try it for yourself. Stay open-minded: the Balvenie RumCask has a lot to offer. **JH**

Tasting notes

Balvenie RumCask offers a varied mix of brown sugar flavors and soft, round, honeyed notes with added spice, notably ginger. Then, tropical fruits and freshly made fudge. Best consumed on a beach, naturally, this whisky has a youthful dexterous energy to it.

Balvenie 21-Year-Old PortWood Finish

William Grant & Sons | www.thebalvenie.com

Region and country of origin Speyside, Scotland
Distillery Balvenie, Dufftown, Banffshire
Alcohol content 40% abv
Style Single malt

Just as St. Paul, while traveling from Jerusalem to Damascus, famously encountered a bright light that made him see the world with new eyes, everyone has moments of revelation on their journey of discovery through the wonderful world of whisky—moments when sampling a whisky turns on a light in the mind and opens a new door toward a fuller understanding of the subject. This writer had one such moment at a whisky and cheese tasting, a professional duty undertaken as the fledgling editor of *Whisky Magazine*.

Among the whiskies on that occasion was this Balvenie PortWood Finish, which was paired so perfectly with a cheese that it became a favorite and has remained so ever since. Particularly astounding were the parallels between this whisky and a good cognac. Among the guests at the tasting was French whisky writer Martine Nouet, who explained in depth how the port wood released the fruity notes into the malt, infusing it in the same way as a good cognac would be laced with fruit. With whisky, that is a hard thing to achieve, because the elements often don't meld properly. Among countless wine and fortified-wine finishes, nothing comes close to this one in its flavors, with the possible exception of some whiskies of the Glenmorangie range.

At twenty-one years, Balvenie is at its absolute peak. There is only one quibble with this whisky: at 40 percent abv, it is a tad too light; a bottling at 46 percent would be wonderful. But that is nitpicking. This is a fantastic whisky by anyone's standards and a must-try even in a list of fifty, let alone one of 1,001. **DR**

Tasting notes

A whisky with the symbiotic character of a fruit-and-nut cake, with the flavors and textures complementary and perfectly balanced. Crisp, unobtrusive oak gives the clean, crisp malt its definite shape and character. The finish is of medium length.

Balvenie Signature 12-Year-Old

William Grant & Sons
www.thebalvenie.com

Region and country of origin Speyside, Scotland
Distillery Balvenie, Dufftown, Banffshire
Alcohol content 40% abv
Style Single malt

Whisky enthusiasts have a tendency to gallop through their journey of discovery and are always looking ahead to the next, better, rarer, older, and more expansive dram. Many overlook the Balvenie altogether, but its whiskies are among the best.

This dram is a case in point. A few years ago, my daughter wouldn't go to sleep without someone sitting at the end of the bed, and so for one long summer, I would take a glass of whisky and a Nintendo DS, and for forty-five minutes, I would linger over a single whisky. In the quiet, I was able to explore great whiskies such as Glenmorangie Original, the Glenfiddich and Glenlivet twelve-year-olds, and this one. The Balvenie nestles behind its sister, Glenfiddich, in the Speyside region, and although it pretends to be a small, handcrafted malt maker, it is actually sizable. And it certainly produces skillfully made malts.

This one is called Signature because it has been lovingly created by malt master David Stewart. It is an entry-level whisky, twelve years old; it doesn't shout, preen, or boast, but spend time with it, and you will discover a thoughtful, complex, and engaging whisky with plenty to say about whisky making in general and Balvenie whisky making in particular. **DR**

Tasting notes

The nose is understated, but on the palate the whisky is fresh and citrusy, with a fruit bowl of flavors, including orange. It doesn't shout, but there's plenty going on.

Balvenie Vintage Cask 1974

William Grant & Sons
www.thebalvenie.com

Region and country of origin Speyside, Scotland
Distillery Balvenie, Dufftown, Banffshire
Alcohol content 47.8% abv
Style Single malt

In the late 1990s, William Grant & Sons, which owns Balvenie distillery, began releasing single-cask, cask-strength expressions of casks over thirty years of age. Balvenie malt master David Stewart has managed to find some amazing single casks, of which around fifty have been released in the past fifteen years. The casks can yield anything from six to 320 bottles.

In selecting this expression, David Stewart was assisted by three members of the Balvenie Club (since renamed Warehouse 24), who had won a competition by describing their favorite Balvenie in up to 100 words.

Cask No. 17893 yielded only 186 bottles. Distilled on December 17, 1974, and bottled on June 1, 2007, Vintage Cask 1974 represented the Vintage Casks' tenth anniversary. According to Stewart, "We generally had six samples drawn from different casks and ages for the panel to select from. I chose these six samples from a larger number of samples from our vintage stocks in order to give the panel samples from six top-quality casks with different styles and characteristics."

The Balvenie's Vintage Casks have consisted of all types of casks, ranging from first-fill ex-bourbon barrels, refill barrels, and hogsheads to first- and second-fill sherry butts. **WM**

Tasting notes

An incredibly complex nose, with notes of spice, fruits, bergamot, and pipe tobacco. The palate is creamy, with vanilla and toffee balanced by apple, orange, and pear.

Balvenie
Vintage Cask 1964

William Grant & Sons
www.thebalvenie.com

Region and country of origin Speyside, Scotland
Distillery Balvenie, Dufftown, Banffshire
Alcohol content 46.9% abv
Style Single malt

Balvenie is among the handful of distilleries that realized the potential of single-malt Scotch as a drink to market alongside the more traditional blended Scotches of the pre-1990s era. In 1987 it released 500 bottles of a very old vintage whisky, the 1937 50-Year-Old. Assisted by whisky author Wallace Milroy's vision for the future of Scotch as a single malt, all 500 bottles sold out within the blink of an eye, instantly catapulting the release into whisky legend. From memory, the 1937 50-Year-Old was released at an original retail cost of $160 (£100). It now sells at auction for well in excess of $5,500 (£3,500).

In 2008, Balvenie's Vintage Cask release (at Hong Kong's international airport) consisted of 151 bottles of a forty-three-year-old whisky distilled in 1964—a testament to the great age this whisky can acquire. Vintage releases such as this are now highly sought after by collectors and investors worldwide. Such is the demand for these rare and old Balvenies, their prices at auction have roughly doubled since 2008.

Balvenie's house style of a light- to medium-bodied, sweet, honey-and-heather Highlander carries through, in varying degrees, to each release. Every vintage distinctly defines the Balvenie. **AS**

Tasting notes

A sweet, honeyed nose, with spiced oak and a hint of dark marmalade give way to lighter fruit aromas of peach, dried orange peel, and caramel or fudge.

Banff 1975
Berry Bros. & Rudd

Berry Bros. & Rudd
www.bbr.com

Region and country of origin Speyside, Scotland
Distillery Banff (closed 1983), Inverboyndie, Banffshire
Alcohol content 46% abv
Style Single malt

Banff distillery earned the reputation of being Scotland's most accident-prone distillery. The first Banff plant burned to the ground, and a new distillery was built, only to burn down subsequently. The distillery was again rebuilt and, from 1932, it enjoyed a few accident-free years of distilling under new ownership. During World War II, the distillery was bombed by a reported lone enemy aircraft, and spirit from a multitude of broken casks apparently poured into the watercourses of local farmers, causing drunkenness in the local cattle for quite some time.

After a routine repair to one of the copper stills went badly wrong, another explosion temporarily closed the distillery in 1959. Another rebuild followed, but in 1983, in a bitter conclusion, Banff was eventually laid to rest, not by fire and brimstone, but by a downturn in the economy. A final twist of fate burned down the remnants of the last warehouse in 1991.

Banff single malts are both rare and inconsistent. Some bottles are still available through specialist retailers, but retail and auction prices are going up fast. Some bottles from Banff have come under criticism for their quality, but find the right bottle, and this distillery can yield an absolute gem. **AS**

Tasting notes

Steely, almost metallic, with very little sweetness. Chewing tobacco and leather add to the appeal. Bitter (not fresh) lemon is present, as is a dusty quality.

Banff Old & Rare Platinum Selection 38-Year-Old

Douglas Laing & Co. | www.douglaslaing.com

Region and country of origin Speyside, Scotland
Distillery Banff (closed 1983), Inverboyndie, Banffshire
Alcohol content 53.4% abv abv
Style Single malt

This is whisky with a sad tale to tell. The first distillery at Banff was built in 1824, at the same time as the one at Glenlivet, and was rebuilt several times over the following 150 years, falling victim to fires and explosions on several occasions. There was even a bombing raid during World War II that led to the intoxication of the local animal population. This bottle was distilled in 1973, only three years after the stills had been converted from coal to oil, and it had been maturing quietly in a sherry butt for the past thirty-eight years before it was decided to bottle it at the original cask strength.

The distillery struggled through the 1970s and '80s with the high cost of fuel, eventually closing in 1983 when the oil crisis caused demand to fall and prices to rise. Many other makers shared the same fate during these difficult times, some of the darkest years in the world of Scottish malts. None of this would matter if the whisky had been mediocre—rarity in itself is no recommendation. But the moment you twist the cork from the 38-Year-Old, you realize what we have lost and what can never be re-created.

The pale straw color—quite translucent for such an old whisky—indicates that this sherry butt was most likely a refill and had been used before. To leave a whisky like this in a new cask for thirty-eight years would have been quite irresponsible. The wood has merged together the smoky and yet fruity flavors with the lightest of touches. Extremely rare and limited, it's hard not to weep when you think what has gone in the name of progress. **AN**

Tasting notes

Pale gold in color. The nose is initially of zesty tropical fruits, followed by a light smokiness, like a fall bonfire in an orchard. The merest hint of sherry and oak but very dry and smooth. Water brings out the spice and some peat, but all are in balance to the end.

Bell's Original

Diageo | www.bells.co.uk

Region and country of origin Scotland
Distilleries Various
Alcohol content 40% abv
Style Vatted blend

There's no denying that Bell's Original is the most popular kid in class. Its fresh-herby, cereal sweetness makes its character pretty distinguishable. With a mix of around thirty-five different malt and grain whiskies all matured between five and twelve years, getting its flavor consistent can't be any easy feat, either—but still, this is all fairly manageable when working with a broad range of whiskies from a number of different distilleries. The key malt comes from Blair Athol distillery in the town of Pitlochry in the Scottish Highlands, but much of the underlying Bell's Original flavor comes from some of the sweet malts from Speyside and the smoky sea salt of the Islands. The whiskies are all matured in oak casks, which adds to the blend's rich and full flavor too.

Bell's Original has begun to push its heritage of late with advertising featuring the brand's founder Arthur Bell much more prominently—reminding one a little of how representative the liquid can be of a man's legacy and craft. This image has not just propelled the brand, but also anchored it slightly too, giving it additional meaning and appeal.

More recently, Bell's Original has also been pushed as a base for cocktails or a spirit that's an ideal partner for a mixer. This has largely been its owner Diageo's attempt to entice a younger audience to the brand. Even though the jury is still out on whether that particular message has been got across, it is unlikely that older fans will be alienated. This much we know because Bell's Original continues to be a top choice on the back bar of many a British pub. **JH**

Tasting notes

Rich but soft. Spiced but gentle. Nutty but smooth. Bell's Original is a bit like ginger cake because you can taste all of the ingredients, but they harmonize together well and none is too overpowering. The result is a distinctive and well-rounded whisky.

Ben Nevis 10-Year-Old

Nikka (Asahi Breweries) | www.bennevisdistillery.com

Region and country of origin Highlands, Scotland
Distillery Ben Nevis, Lochy Bridge, Fort William, Highland
Alcohol content 46% abv
Style Single malt

Ben Nevis is one of the very few distilleries on Scotland's rugged west coast, standing in the shadow of the eponymous mountain—the highest in the British Isles. The whisky has never been one of the well-known single malts. One reason for this might be the confusion caused by the distillery producing blends also called Ben Nevis. It is also not helped by its packaging, which looks as though it has come straight from the 1960s. But get past both of these issues, and you will find an excellent whisky, with a robustly fruity and slight smoky character.

Its nearest distillery neighbor is Oban, some 30 miles (48 km) away down a scenic road that hugs a sparsely populated west coast. Although it is situated some way from sea at the head of Loch Linnhe, the distillery manager Colin Ross regards it as a "coastal" distillery. For over eighty years, Ben Nevis enjoyed the company of the Glenlochy distillery in its hometown of Fort William. Unfortunately, Glenlochy closed in 1983 and is now a hotel and restaurant. Ben Nevis's recent history has also seen it closed and reopened a couple of times, but, even when closed, it has been put to good use, with several Scottish-themed Hollywood films using its warehouses for sets. Happily, thanks to Nikka's ownership, it has now been running continuously since 1990.

This multiple-award-winning ten-year-old entry-level offering was introduced in 1996, and although reviewed here in its 46 percent guise, it has also been available at 40 percent and 43 percent in various international markets. **PB**

Tasting notes

Soft, with grape skins and overripe pears on the nose. On the palate, baked apple and licorice root, with exotic fruit and a distinct tinge of orange-flavored chocolate. Coffee and oak notes persist throughout, and the finish is pleasant and malty.

The distillery's home of Fort William, with Ben Nevis looming in the background. ➡

Ben Nevis 12-Year-Old Douglas of Drumlanrig

Douglas Laing & Co. | www.douglaslaing.com/
www.bennevisdistillery.com

Region and country of origin Highlands, Scotland
Distillery Ben Nevis, Lochy Bridge, Fort William, Highland
Alcohol content 46% abv
Style Single malt

The Japanese company Nikka currently owns the Ben Nevis distillery, but it has passed through a few hands over the years. One former proprietor was a six-and-a-half-foot-tall giant called Long John McDonald, and that was quite some height in 1830s Scotland. Ben Nevis was later owned by an enterprising American called Joseph Hobbs who installed a Coffey still in 1955 to make grain whisky alongside the malt, creating at a stroke the potential to make a "single-blend" whisky—a category that sadly no longer exists, as Nikka removed the grain stills when they took over.

The influence of the new owners, has been significant, and although hard to find in the United Kingdom, Ben Nevis Single Malt was number seven in the Japanese best-seller list in 2010. Most of the whisky goes for blending, including their own Ben Nevis blend, which means you have to be very careful indeed when looking for the malt.

They use a mix of bourbon and sherry casks for maturation, and there are several distillery bottlings as well as the independents. This one from Douglas Laing at twelve years is a typical old-fashioned West Highland style—a rare taste in itself and well worth tracking down. **ANH**

Tasting notes

A pale gold dram, with toffee and pear on the nose and lots of complexity behind it. Oily and rugged in the mouth. The spices fade smoothly to a sweet finish.

Ben Nevis 15-Year-Old Glenkeir Treasures

Glenkeir Treasures
www.thewhiskyshop.com

Region and country of origin Highlands, Scotland
Distillery Ben Nevis, Lochy Bridge, Fort William, Highland
Alcohol content 40% abv
Style Single malt

The Whisky Shop is the United Kingdom's only national whisky retail chain, with about twenty stores dotted across England and Scotland. It has made a huge contribution to bringing quality whisky to the High Street customer, and its approach to retailing is to make buying whisky as straightforward and attractive as possible.

Many whiskies, and certainly the standard Glenkeir Treasures range, are available to "try before you die." The standard in this range is particularly high, and it would be very unusual to find a complaint about any of them. This Ben Nevis is, like all the Glenkeir range, very different from the official bottlings. Ben Nevis is something of a curiosity as a distillery anyway, because it is one of very few that bottles a blend and a single malt under the same name. Much of the output of the distillery goes to Japan for inclusion in blends there, too.

The fifteen years of age has given this Ben Nevis Glenkeir Treasure a lush richness that the official bottling simply doesn't have. It is quite possibly the best of all the standard Treasures range because it is a complete all-rounder and genuinely different from any other malt. **DR**

Tasting notes

Peat and spice more than offset by a big milk-chocolate orange, kumquat, and soft nut cluster. Richer and fuller than you might expect from a whisky of this strength.

Ben Nevis 34-Year-Old Adelphi Blend

Adelphi
www.adelphidistillery.com

Region and country of origin Highlands, Scotland
Distillery Ben Nevis, Lochy Bridge, Fort William, Highland
Alcohol content 50.3% abv
Style Blend

Ben Nevis is one of the few distilleries in Scotland that produced both malt and grain whisky on the same site. Installing a Coffey still in 1955, it produced both styles of whisky, mainly for blending, although no grain has been made since the 1980s. Blending its grain and malt whisky together would produce a mix that, coming from the same distillery, would be referred to as a single blend. Such whiskies are quite rare; only a few distilleries were able to produce them.

Sometimes you get a whisky that's one stage rarer than just a regular single blend—a single-cask single blend. Rather than blend the whiskies together after they have matured, a cask is filled with a mixture of new-make grain and malt spirits and then left to mature. This whisky is one of those, distilled in 1970 and bottled at cask strength from one cask after thirty-four years in the barrel.

The whisky picked up the Best Blended or Vatted Whisky award from the Malt Maniacs in 2005, but despite the small number of bottles—186 in total—it still appears in shops from time to time, as the rarity of its category makes it an unknown quantity. It's definitely worth seeking out for a taste—interesting and different from what you might expect. **BA**

Tasting notes

A gluey nose of paste and acetone, with pine. It has a strong lemon element in the middle of the palate, surrounded by sweet pineapple. A dry, lingering finish.

Ben Nevis 40-Year-Old "Blended at Birth"

Nikka (Asahi Breweries)
www.bennevisdistillery.com

Region and country of origin Highlands, Scotland
Distillery Ben Nevis, Lochy Bridge, Fort William, Highland
Alcohol content 40% abv
Style Blend

Nikka's ownership has given Ben Nevis a greater degree of stability, allowing more consistent production (it was closed for a total of nine years between 1978 and 1990) and a new and improved wood policy, which has gone a long way to boosting the quality of the distillery's whisky.

The Ben Nevis 40-Year-Old "Blended at Birth" whisky is something of an unusual beast that contrasts dramatically with the usual process of creating a blend. Normally, malt whisky and grain whiskies are blended after they have enjoyed their own separate periods of maturation, before being married for a further marrying period in casks. Here, however, the different grains are blended before they have been distilled, a practice that is better known in Ireland in the creation of its pot-still whiskeys.

However, Ben Nevis is not unique in Scotland for making whisky in this way. The now dismantled Lochside distillery from Montrose, Angus, also produced a so-called "single blend." If you can get hold of a bottle of that, good luck. If you are not so fortunate, try to locate a bottle of this forty-year-old beauty instead. This is one purchase it would be almost impossible to regret. **PB**

Tasting notes

Faint smoke on the nose, with soft fruits. Sweet, juicy fruitiness on the palate before chocolate steps in. More chocolate on the finish gives way to oak.

BenRiach 10-Year-Old Curiositas

The BenRiach Distillery Co. | www.benriachdistillery.co.uk

Region and country of origin Speyside, Scotland
Distillery BenRiach, Longmorn, Elgin, Morayshire
Alcohol content 40% abv
Style Single malt

When BenRiach launched its first expressions in 2004, the most remarkable was a ten-year-old heavily peated single malt named Curiositas. To keep stock available to bottle as Curiositas, Chivas Brothers pushed distilling boundaries during their stewardship of BenRiach. As BenRiach owner Billy Walker says, "They made their first peated whisky in 1972, and they distilled it in cycles, though not every year."

The BenRiach distillery itself was "silent" from 1900 until 1965, but its floor maltings remained open. Walker believes that "they probably made the peated malt in their own floor maltings because at that time it would have been very hard to find a mainland commercial maltster geared up to produce peated malt. Basically, they used as much peat as the barley could absorb, and it came out around 35 to 38 parts per million in the actual spirit."

BenRiach bottled Curiositas as a ten-year-old to capitalize on its peatiness. "There is a point at which phenols in a peated whisky are at their most powerful," explains Walker, "and it's usually between eight and twelve years of age. That's a good drinking point. After that, they become more delicate and refined. If you want a really ballsy expression, ten is ideal."

Walker also says that "BenRiach is one of around fifty Speyside distilleries, and Curiositas gave us a real point of difference. Additionally, when it is ten years old, the price is reasonable and you can sell volume, you get it out there. Without the peated whisky, it would have been much harder for us to achieve what we did. Curiositas gave us profile." **GS**

Tasting notes

Initially medicinal on the nose, with tarmac and overt peat. Typical BenRiach honey, fruit, and oak emerge with time. Sweet and smoky on the palate, with a touch of iodine, nuts, dried fruits, and lots of spicy oak. The finish features wood preservative and sweeter notes.

BenRiach 12-Year-Old

The BenRiach Distillery Co. | www.benriachdistillery.co.uk

Region and country of origin Speyside, Scotland
Distillery BenRiach, Longmorn, Elgin, Morayshire
Alcohol content 40% abv
Style Single malt

While some distillers present a core single-malts range that varies from expression to expression purely in terms of an age variable, the BenRiach team set out to offer a portfolio of permanently available whiskies with distinct personalities.

Accordingly, while BenRiach's Heart of Speyside variant is matured entirely in ex-bourbon casks, 40 percent of the 12-Year-Old started its life in ex-bourbon casks and was then transferred to oloroso sherry casks for a final maturation period of four to five years. According to company managing director Billy Walker, "it also has 60 percent whisky from ex-bourbon wood, quite a lot of which is second-fill. This means that the sherry notes are altogether more dominant in the 12-Year-Old than in its core siblings."

Until Walker and his associates came along, the only expression of Benriach (subsequently restyled with that quirky capitalized middle R) was a less than earth-shattering ten-year-old bottling from Chivas Brothers, introduced in 1994. Thus consumers had no preconceived idea of what BenRiach should be like as a single malt. As Walker says, "It was a blank canvas in terms of perception." Billy Walker's son Alistair adds, "Right from the start, we determined not to sell into the major multiple retailers such as Tesco and other supermarkets." This meant that independent traders enjoyed a degree of exclusivity with the BenRiach range and received a better reward for stocking the whiskies, as they were not competing with supermarkets that could undercut their prices by squeezing producers' margins. **GS**

Tasting notes

A floral, fruity nose, with ripe orange and pineapple, plus vanilla, malt, and honey notes. Malt and caramel on the immediate palate, with developing vanilla, milk chocolate, more honey, and bourbon cask-influenced spice. The finish has nutmeg and some drying oak.

BenRiach 12-Year-Old Heredotus Fumosus

The BenRiach Distillery Co.
www.benriachdistillery.co.uk

Region and country of origin Speyside, Scotland
Distillery BenRiach, Longmorn, Elgin, Morayshire
Alcohol content 46% abv
Style Single malt

The success of BenRiach Curiositas and Authenticus spurred the BenRiach team to do something new with their peated whisky. Hence the introduction in May 2007 of a trio of twelve-year-old peated single malts finished in a variety of different casks. Single-malt expressions are often given hard-to-pronounce Gaelic names, but BenRiach chose Latin names for its peated whiskies in homage to their "classic beauty."

Heredotus Fumosus—or "smoky sherry"—was finished in Pedro Ximénez sherry butts. "We chose this because people tend to find sherry less intimidating than some of the more exotic finishes," says managing director Billy Walker. As devotees of the Islay malt Lagavulin know very well, sherry can be an extremely attractive partner for peated whiskies, and Lagavulin's fellow distilleries in the south of Islay—Ardbeg and Laphroaig—have also offered some very well-received sherry-influenced whiskies.

Walker adds, "When it comes to finishing the peated BenRiach, we find with Pedro Ximénez sherry casks that the whisky needs a long time in the cask—upward of three years—in order to get the balance right." Here, as is so often the case in whisky making, a good thing comes to those who wait. **GS**

Tasting notes

Sherry, raisin, clove, oak, and a background of sweet, smoldering peat on the nose. Mellow on the palate, with raisin, sherry, and more soft, muted peat.

BenRiach 12-Year-Old Sherry Matured

The BenRiach Distillery Co.
www.benriachdistillery.co.uk

Region and country of origin Speyside, Scotland
Distillery BenRiach, Longmorn, Elgin, Morayshire
Alcohol content 46% abv
Style Single malt

Following its purchase by Billy Walker and partners in 2004, BenRiach distillery has probably become more associated with wood finishes than any other Scottish distillery. A bewildering variety of secondary cask types have been tried, and with limited bottling runs a number of finished expressions have come and gone, though a core range remains. "We've tried most things!" admits sales and marketing director Alistair Walker. "And one significant point is that we allow the whisky to remain in the secondary cask for longer than most other people do."

Using sherry wood as a finish for Scotch whisky is an obvious starting point, since most drinkers already associate sherry wood maturation with whisky. Accordingly, BenRiach launched a twelve-year-old expression, created by marrying together whiskies ultimately matured in oloroso and Pedro Ximénez sherry butts.

"We introduced this expression because of market demand from Asia," says Alistair Walker. "It's principally Pedro Ximénez with a hint of oloroso. While this one is a twelve-year-old, we have a variety of ages for our BenRiach finishes because they are ready when they are ready, rather than being price-point specific." **GS**

Tasting notes

Warm spices, raisin, nutmeg, sherry, and caramel on the nose. Well balanced, with overt sweet sherry notes on the palate. Plain chocolate in the medium finish.

BenRiach 13-Year-Old Maderensis Fumosus

The BenRiach Distillery Co.
www.benriachdistillery.co.uk

Region and country of origin Speyside, Scotland
Distillery BenRiach, Longmorn, Elgin, Morayshire
Alcohol content 46% abv
Style Single malt

In July 2008, an existing trio of heavily peated, finished BenRiachs was joined by Maderensis Fumosus—"smoky Madeira"—which had been aged for a total of thirteen years. "Madeira casks—whether for peated or unpeated BenRiach—always work well," says Billy Walker. "You get fruit, nuts, molasses, and sugars. Overall, when it comes to choosing casks to finish the peated BenRiachs in, you've got to be careful not to select ones that have had anything relatively light in them previously, or the peated BenRiach just runs over the top of them and totally dominates.

"So what we have are casks that previously held fortified wines, which means you have lots of sugar and high alcohol levels. It's also important to give the whisky long enough in those casks. It's all very experimental—you might find the cask and the peated BenRiach pull in opposite directions. Ideally, you get a good 'sweet and sour' combination."

Peated BenRiach sells well in Sweden, Holland, Denmark, and Germany, which are classic markets for peated Scotch whiskies. "Basically, they sell anywhere that experiences cold weather," reports Alistair Walker. "You can't sell them in Spain or Greece, and the Asian markets tend to go for older, sweeter whiskies." **GS**

A powerful, even medicinal nose of peat and coal, with citrus and then tropical fruits developing. Soft peat on the palate and a slightly rubbery and tannic finish.

BenRiach 15-Year-Old Dark Rum Wood Finish

The BenRiach Distillery Co.
www.benriachdistillery.co.uk

Region and country of origin Speyside, Scotland
Distillery BenRiach, Longmorn, Elgin, Morayshire
Alcohol content 46% abv
Style Single malt

Dark rum cask finishing is common to both BenRiach's peated and nonpeated finish ranges, with the whisky first being matured in ex-bourbon barrels before undergoing their secondary maturation period. Sales director Alistair Walker notes that "rum finishes are popular with younger consumers, with their sweet vanilla and molasses style. Rum in cask is about 80 percent abv, so any residual rum in the cask when it is reused for whisky means that the strength increases rather than decreases during the finishing process."

BenRiach Dark Rum Wood Finish was introduced to the portfolio in November 2006, along with Pedro Ximénez, Madeira, and aged tawny port finishes. The dark rum barrels used by BenRiach are sourced from the Caribbean island of Jamaica.

Although the BenRiach team puts much time, effort, and integrity into making its finished whiskies, there are, inevitably, some that do not turn out as well as might be hoped. "We tried Tokaji, but it didn't work for us," says Billy Walker. "There was an overdominant character of pear drops to it. Perhaps the casks were too fresh. It didn't work with younger whiskies, though it wasn't so bad with older ones, but it certainly won't appear on the market." **GS**

Tasting notes

Unsurprisingly, rum is to the fore on the sweet, spicy nose, with ripe banana and custard. Milk chocolate, toffee, dark and golden raisins on the vibrant palate.

BenRiach 15-Year-Old Madeira Wood Finish

The BenRiach Distillery Co. | www.benriachdistillery.co.uk

Region and country of origin Speyside, Scotland
Distillery BenRiach, Longmorn, Elgin, Morayshire
Alcohol content 46% abv
Style Single malt

Introduced in 2006 at the same time as the Dark Rum Finish, the BenRiach Madeira Wood Finish was initially matured in ex-bourbon barrels before being transferred into Madeira barrels of the company Henriques and Henriques, sourced from the semitropical Portuguese island of Madeira, 250 miles (400 km) north of Tenerife in the Atlantic Ocean.

In the case of the Madeira Wood Finish, BenRiach would be happy to supply specific provenance details of the casks in question. However, the individual companies supplying casks for finishing do not always appreciate having their cherished reputations associated with other products over which they have no control, so the BenRiach team cannot always divulge the suppliers' names.

"Sherry and port were the most obvious finishes," says Alistair Walker, "and while rum and Madeira were more of a risk, they do sell well. We were introducing our finishes just as Glenmorangie were dropping lots of theirs. Their Madeira went out as ours came in, which I think helped us quite a lot."

Company managing director Billy Walker notes that "with all finishes you have to audit progress very carefully. There's no point in doing it for three or six months. For us eighteen months is a minimum, and three years is usually the maximum. Obviously it depends on the casks, and the distiller will be looking at these every month. It is totally bespoke. It's a case of capturing it when it's right. That might, on occasions, mean taking it out of the finishing cask and putting it back into a second-fill bourbon cask." **GS**

Tasting notes

The nose offers wood polish, peach, vanilla, nougat, and popcorn, with Madeira and oak providing a solid platform. Warming, mouth-coating, buttery, and spicy on the palate, with butterscotch, peach cobbler, hazelnut, and Madeira in abundance.

BenRiach 15-Year-Old Solstice

The BenRiach Distillery Co. | www.benriachdistillery.co.uk

Region and country of origin Speyside, Scotland
Distillery BenRiach, Longmorn, Elgin, Morayshire
Alcohol content 50% abv
Style Single malt

Solstice follows firmly in the footsteps of its younger peated Pedro Ximénez, Jamaican dark rum, tawny port, and Madeira finished siblings. Finished in aged tawny port pipes sourced from Portugal's Douro region, the initial batch of Solstice was matured for a total of fifteen years. A second batch was subsequently released at seventeen years of age.

BenRiach Solstice was launched on the shortest day of 2010. Billy Walker declares that "Solstice, with its connotations of rebirth and celebration, is a perfect malt for the midwinter." However, it is also an ideal after-dinner whisky for any time of year, a great accompaniment to a fully flavored Havana cigar.

Billy Walker says, "Solstice is effectively part of the peated finishes family, and tawny port works well with whisky. We had some casks that were head and shoulders above most of the others. What we had were ten port pipes that were behaving in a way that was totally different to the others. They were fantastic. The whisky was being enriched by the casks more than we could imagine. These hand-selected casks were just superb, so we bottled them. The challenge is always to repeat the success of the previous release."

To ensure supplies of peated spirit for future releases, both plain and finished, BenRiach now distills around 53,000 gallons (200,000 liters) of peated spirit a year, with production taking place over six or seven weeks in January and February. A peated expression carrying no age statement and called Birnie Moss was released in 2009 and comprises peated spirit distilled entirely under the current BenRiach regime. **GS**

Tasting notes

A rich, spicy nose of ripe berries and soft peat. Full-bodied and bold on the palate, with intense soft fruit flavors and cinnamon developing in front of relatively dry peat smoke. Slowly and languorously fading, with subtle spices, port wine, and enduring smokiness.

BenRiach
16-Year-Old

The BenRiach Distillery Co.
www.benriachdistillery.co.uk

Region and country of origin Speyside, Scotland
Distillery BenRiach, Longmorn, Elgin, Morayshire
Alcohol content 40% abv
Style Single malt

Following the policy of giving each expression in the BenRiach core range its own unique personality, the 16-Year-Old, which was released in 2004, differs in cask composition from its younger and older compatriots.

Billy Walker says, "The 16-Year-Old captures the essential spirit of the BenRiach Speyside style of single malt, with its use of European and American oak. It contains 40 percent whisky finished for four or five years in ex-oloroso sherry casks." The remaining 60 percent of the whisky has been matured in ex-bourbon casks. Sales director Alistair Walker notes that "quite a bit of the whisky in the BenRiach 16-Year-Old is actually around eighteen years old. . . . You will get more oak tannins coming through in the 16-Year-Old than you do in the 12-Year-Old."

When Chivas Brothers operated the BenRiach site, they were notably experimental and innovative. "Chivas had quietly tried lots of interesting and imaginative things at Benriach," says Billy Walker. "For example, making richly peated spirit and triple-distilled spirit. I think the view was taken that, as Benriach wasn't a 'brand' as such, Benriach distillery was a safe place to experiment and innovate. They wouldn't have done it at Glenlivet, for example." **GS**

Tasting notes

Cereal notes on the slightly reticent nose, with hazelnut, vanilla, and signature BenRiach honey. Creamy in the mouth, with more honey and vanilla.

BenRiach 16-Year-Old
Sauternes Wood Finish

The BenRiach Distillery Co.
www.benriachdistillery.co.uk

Region and country of origin Speyside, Scotland
Distillery BenRiach, Longmorn, Elgin, Morayshire
Alcohol content 46% abv
Style Single malt

Introduced to the BenRiach series of wood finishes in 2008 as a fifteen-year-old and subsequently issued at sixteen, Sauternes Wood Finish has proved a popular addition to the lineup. "We could sell what we produce ten times over if we could get the casks," says managing director Billy Walker, "but they are difficult to source and expensive. But as with so many things in life, you get what you pay for."

Sauternes is a French sweet wine produced in the Bordeaux region, and BenRiach uses *premier cru* casks previously employed to mature Sauternes from Château d'Yquem. Walker notes, "The Sauternes contributes magnificently to classic Speyside-style BenRiach maturation. It's delicate, and so the whisky needs to be in for a long time. At three to three and a half years, it is one of our longer finishes."

More recently, BenRiach has used rioja, burgundy, and claret casks. Alistair Walker remarks, "We have slowed down significantly on our program of core releases, but we will continue to offer lots of single-cask bottlings. We've done a total of around 150 BenRiach single-cask releases. We do twenty-five to thirty a year, and we screen the casks being selected very carefully to ensure that they really are the best." **GS**

Tasting notes

Almond, cereal notes, butterscotch, and a hint of sherry on the nose. The palate is full and sweet, supple and rich, with fig, dessert wine, tropical fruits, and vanilla.

Benriach was built in 1898 by John Duff, who had built the Longmorn distillery the year before. ➡

BenRiach 20-Year-Old

The BenRiach Distillery Co. | www.benriachdistillery.co.uk

Region and country of origin Speyside, Scotland
Distillery BenRiach, Longmorn, Elgin, Morayshire
Alcohol content 43% abv
Style Single malt

The twenty-year-old variant of BenRiach contains around 50 percent whisky from first-fill bourbon casks, some of which are up to twenty-three years old, leading to a major impact of honey, vanilla, and oak. The ex-bourbon barrels are notably influential here because the casks in question have not previously been filled with Scotch whisky before being used by BenRiach. A previous Scotch whisky fill would inevitably blunt the bourbon influence.

Managing director Billy Walker notes, "You have to be sure not to have 100 percent from first-fill bourbon casks, so that the bourbon effect doesn't dominate. Therefore we include 15 to 20 percent Pedro Ximénez sherry casks. We use those rather than oloroso casks because with Pedro Ximénez you've gone to the next sherry level, if you like. The final 35 percent or so tends to come from third- or fourth-fill hogsheads, which helps to balance the big vanilla character of the first-fill ex-bourbons. Everything in the 20-Year-Old is weightier and fuller than in the younger expressions. I like to think that the 20-Year-Old is a cousin rather than the big brother."

Back in the late 1980s, when much of the whisky included in BenRiach 20-Year-Old was made, the distillery was under the ownership of the giant Canadian organization the Seagram Company Ltd., through its Chivas Brothers Scottish subsidiary. While many distilleries were mothballed or permanently closed as a result of past overproduction during the turbulent 1980s, Chivas actually doubled capacity to four stills at BenRiach in 1985. **GS**

Tasting notes

Vanilla, milk chocolate, honey, and fresh fruits—peach and pineapple—on the nose, plus soft peat. A little earthy midpalate, with brief acidic notes, becoming spicy and honeyed through the bourbon oak-influenced finish, with just a whiff of wood smoke.

BenRiach 21-Year-Old Authenticus

The BenRiach Distillery Co. | www.benriachdistillery.co.uk

Region and country of origin Speyside, Scotland
Distillery BenRiach, Longmorn, Elgin, Morayshire
Alcohol content 46% abv
Style Single malt

Such was the success of BenRiach Curiositas that a year after its launch, the heavily peated 21-Year-Old appeared, this time named Authenticus. "We couldn't be accused of jumping on the bandwagon and copying the popular Islay style, because we were producing peated BenRiach long before Islays became fashionable," says sales manager Alistair Walker.

Explaining the difference in character between Curiositas and Authenticus, Alistair's father, Billy, says, "At twenty-one years of age, the phenols are calmer, and they have interacted with the wood more thoroughly, too. Although it's diminished with time, I think originally Authenticus would probably have had the same level of peating as Laphroaig. For me, this is a spectacular expression. It invades every part of your senses. You get vanilla, fruit, and smoke. You don't get the medicinal, oily character that you do with Islays; you get a very different character—principally because it is made using northeast mainland peat, which varies in composition and effect when you burn it in a kiln. If you were going to compare our peated whisky to an Islay, it would probably be Caol Ila. But Chivas did limited production of peated spirit, so there is obviously limited stock of Authenticus—at least until our own peated spirit gets to be twenty-one."

Billy Walker says that, far from being a departure from the stylistic Speyside norm, peated BenRiachs are a return to an older profile of Speyside whisky. "The gentle, mild Speysides of today don't really represent how they were 100 years ago, for example, when distilleries used their own floor maltings." **GS**

Tasting notes

Fruity peat smoke on the nose, with apple, peach, and cucumber in the mix, plus underlying honey and oak. Peat soon makes its major presence felt, along with fresh earth allied to apple, orange, honey, and cinnamon. Spicy in the finish, with smoldering peat.

BenRiach 25-Year-Old

The BenRiach Distillery Co.
www.benriachdistillery.co.uk

Region and country of origin Speyside, Scotland
Distillery BenRiach, Longmorn, Elgin, Morayshire
Alcohol content 50% abv
Style Single malt

While the initial BenRiach expressions embraced an age spread from the youthful Heart of Speyside to a twenty-year-old single malt, by the summer of 2006, the new company was sufficiently well established and confident to offer an older expression, namely this 25-Year-Old, which was bottled in limited quantities at the higher strength of 50 percent abv.

"The 25-Year-Old has a different footprint to the 20-year-old," explains managing director Billy Walker. "Eighty percent of the whisky in this expression has been finished in oloroso sherry casks, and 20 percent was initially matured in ex-bourbon barrels before being reracked into virgin oak casks at the age of twelve years. That is the unusual component here.

"Using virgin oak was virtually unheard of; it's an example of how innovative Chivas was with BenRiach when it owned the distillery. We have also bottled some of the virgin oak whisky as single casks, as it has been extremely well received. As whiskies get older, more unpredictability creeps in, so you do get slight variables from batch to batch, and this is effectively pretty close to cask strength. The use of virgin oak casks makes the whisky sweeter and spicier, with more vanilla, and brings it closer to American-style whiskey. The 20 percent from the virgin oak definitely makes its presence felt here." **GS**

Tasting notes

The nose offers typical BenRiach notes of honey and vanilla with lively spices. Sherry, dark chocolate, and citrus fruits. Peat and oak in the relatively long finish.

BenRiach 30-Year-Old

The BenRiach Distillery Co.
www.benriachdistillery.co.uk

Region and country of origin Speyside, Scotland
Distillery BenRiach, Longmorn, Elgin, Morayshire
Alcohol content 50% abv
Style Single malt

BenRiach 30-Year-Old arrived in 2006 as a limited edition of just 3,000 bottles. It comprises a fifty/fifty split of whisky originally filled into ex-bourbon barrels and finished in oloroso sherry butts, and whisky matured in Gomez fino sherry butts. As owner Billy Walker explains, "Fino has a much more subtle effect than oloroso or other, bigger sherries, so it takes longer in the cask for the influence to come through."

Sales director Alistair Walker adds, "Having older whiskies like the 25- and 30-Year-Olds helps to give the brand credibility. They underline the fact that BenRiach has been around for a long time and is a well-established distillery. European markets favor the 12- and 16-Year-Olds, while Asia likes older single-cask bottlings and also the 25- and 30-Year-Olds. In time, China will become a big market for older whiskies."

BenRiach can offer single malts of these vintages because of the stocks they acquired from Chivas Brothers when the distillery was purchased in 2004. Billy Walker declares, "The inventory was fantastic, going back to 1966, and with not many missing years. We acquired 40,000 casks, or some 1.3 million gallons (5 million liters). Having this inventory meant that when we bought the distillery, we could have product on the market in a matter of a few months, which was obviously important to generate income." **GS**

Tasting notes

Slightly oily on the complex nose, with sherry, raisin, coconut, and lots of spice. Full-bodied, with honey, oak, smoke, and ginger. Toffee and malt in the lengthy finish.

← Sherry barrels are highly sought after for finishing aged whisky.

BenRiach Heart of Speyside

The BenRiach Distillery Co. | www.benriachdistillery.co.uk

Region and country of origin Speyside, Scotland
Distillery BenRiach, Longmorn, Elgin, Morayshire
Alcohol content 40% abv
Style Single malt

BenRiach distillery is located to the south of Elgin, county town of Moray, and this entry-level BenRiach single-malt expression, which carries no age statement, takes its name from the distillery's geographical location in the "heart of Speyside." It was one of the first range of expressions issued by BenRiach's new consortium of owners when it took over in 2004. The BenRiach Distillery Co. is headed by Billy Walker, a former director of Burn Stewart Distillers, while his son Alistair is the company's sales and marketing director.

"Our first releases in August 2004 were Heart of Speyside, 12-, 16-, and 20-Year-Olds, and the ten-year-old Curiositas," says Alistair Walker. "We ran with those five for about a year before we introduced any others. We acknowledged that in some markets there is an appetite for a single malt without an age statement, offered at a good price. It went well in markets such as Estonia and Lithuania, but it also enjoys good sales in the United Kingdom. Our four top sellers are the 12, 16, Curiositas, and Heart of Speyside.

"For some people, Heart of Speyside is a step up from blends to malts, sort of dipping a toe in the water, if you like. It's the only expression in the core range that comprises 100 percent whisky matured in ex-bourbon wood. All other expressions in the core lineup contain a percentage of whisky that has been matured in former sherry casks. In a way, you can see Heart of Speyside as the 'purest' form of BenRiach in that respect. Some of the component whiskies will be up to twelve years old." **GS**

Tasting notes

Fresh on the nose, quite straightforward, with hay, honey, nuts, and spicy oak. Smooth on the palate, with honey and spice carrying over from the nose, together with orange marmalade and black pepper. The finish is longer than might be expected, with a hint of pepper.

BenRiach Horizons

The BenRiach Distillery Co. | www.benriachdistillery.co.uk

Region and country of origin Speyside, Scotland
Distillery BenRiach, Longmorn, Elgin, Morayshire
Alcohol content 50% abv
Style Single malt

Of all the innovative products released by BenRiach, nothing compares to Horizons in terms of originality. It hit the shelves during December 2010, and managing director Billy Walker declares it to be "potentially the most special whisky in our list. It's the only triple-distilled whisky on Speyside, and just Auchentoshan and Hazelburn are genuinely triple-distilled single malts. Chivas made it during 1998, just for one year, as an experiment."

Not only is Horizons triple-distilled, but after maturing for a dozen years in ex-bourbon barrels, it has been finished for three years in ex-oloroso sherry casks. "Triple-distilled means the raw spirit produced comes off the still at a higher alcohol strength," explains Billy Walker. "The whisky is more fruity and floral than a traditional double-distilled BenRiach. It's quite different in character, and certainly a rarity among single-malt whiskies."

Having initially bottled Horizons at twelve years of age, future batches will be released at fourteen and sixteen years, and Walker notes that "we are currently triple-distilling batches of spirit every two years." The spirit from the second distillation is redistilled in one of the pair of spirit stills, and comes off the still at 80 percent abv. "Chivas had a fifth still, which they used for triple-distillation," says Billy Walker. "It's now acting as an ornament in Ontario, Canada. In time we will replace it, because it is a challenge technically for us to triple-distill with the current regime. Triple-distilled BenRiach is a lot lighter than our double-distilled spirit, but the flavors are more intense." **GS**

Tasting notes

Vibrant fruits, dough, nuts, a hint of honey, acetone, and sweet red wine on the nose. Very fresh in the mouth, with a carryover of nuts and honey from the nose, along with intense fruits, toffee, and lots of spice. Nutty in the relatively long, pleasingly oaky finish.

BenRiach
Single Cask Bottling

The BenRiach Distillery Co.
www.benriachdistillery.co.uk

Region and country of origin Speyside, Scotland
Distillery BenRiach, Longmorn, Elgin, Morayshire
Alcohol content Various
Style Single malt

If ever the advice "try before you buy" applied, it is with the special bottling from the BenRiach and GlenDronach distilleries. The two distilleries are owned by a three-person consortium made up of three African whisky importers, who take a good proportion of the distilleries' stock overseas, and Billy Walker. It's something of an industry joke that Billy spends his days clambering through his warehouse in search of unusual casks to bottle, and as his warehouses contain just about every style of whisky imaginable, you're never sure what's coming next.

In 2011 Billy Walker released a selection of single-cask bottlings. The range included big grungy and earthy sherry whiskies to light vanilla ice cream ones and everything in between. If you get the chance to try even just a couple of them, they provide an insight into just how varied malt from one distillery can be. Normally we don't get to see casks in such a naked way—they're combined to create the official bottling taste profile—and the diversity puts a big question mark over the relevance of having taste descriptors for entire regions. Some claim distilleries are moving to offering customers a portfolio to choose from so that all tastes are catered for in a "one stop shop." **DR**

Tasting notes

Take your pick from the rich, earthy, red-berried-fruit notes in the first-fill sherry offerings, to the light candy and cream delights of the bourbon cask offerings.

Benrinnes
13-Year-Old

Harris Whisky Co.
www.harriswhisky.com

Region and country of origin Speyside, Scotland
Distillery Benrinnes, Aberlour, Banffshire
Alcohol content 55% abv
Style Single malt

Harris Whisky Co. is based in the English county of Gloucestershire and is run by Mark Harris. Harris specializes in selecting high-quality casks from lower-profile Scottish distilleries and bottling the result uncolored, unfiltered, at cask strength, and in single-cask format. "The front labels of our bottles are unique and eye-catching," says Harris, "and the surprise comes upon the inspection of the back label and its simple points system, rating smoke, peat, sweetness, dryness, spice, fruit, and complexity with marks out of five."

This example is from the Diageo-owned distillery of Benrinnes, the make of which is nearly all destined for the blending vats of Crawford's, Johnnie Walker, and J&B. It actually deserves to be much better known as a dram in its own right, as it is a very distinctive style of whisky, due in part to a complex system of partial triple-distillation.

The Harris Whisky bottling of Benrinnes comes from cask number 7014 and was distilled in September 1992 and bottled in January 2006. The notably pale color of the whisky is in line with maturation in a refill hogshead that once contained bourbon, but has also previously received at least one filling of single-malt Scotch whisky. **GS**

Tasting notes

Don't be fooled by the color, as this is anything but bland. A grassy, fruity nose with spice, light peat smoke, and orange. Smoke and cereal notes on the palate.

Benromach 10-Year-Old

Gordon & MacPhail
www.benromach.com

Region of origin Speyside, Scotland
Distillery Benromach, Forres, Morayshire
Alcohol content 43% abv
Type Single malt

It is odd to think of a ten-year-old being a "milestone" whisky; that is a tag associated with older malts. However, for Benromach, under the stewardship of independent bottler Gordon & MacPhail, this 10-Year-Old represents the first bottling of whisky entirely distilled on its watch.

Benromach is the smallest working distillery in the Speyside region, located to the north of the town of Forres, not far from Findhorn Bay. Gordon & MacPhail bought the closed and neglected premises in 1993 and rebuilt it from the ground up. It was officially reopened by Prince Charles in 1998, and shortly afterward, Gordon & MacPhail embarked on an innovative production program. This included a range of wine casks for finishing, heavy peating of some of the malted barley, and production of the world's first truly organic Scottish single-malt whisky.

With this production program in mind, the 10-Year-Old is created from 80 percent whisky that has been matured for nine years in ex-bourbon casks and 20 percent whisky from former sherry wood. The two whiskies are allowed to marry together for a final twelve months in ex-sherry casks, and the result is a complex and well-integrated dram. **AA**

Tasting notes

Mellow on the nose, with cinder toffee and fresh wood shavings. The palate shows slightly bitter wood at first, then bursts of spice. A long and warming finish.

Benromach 21-Year-Old

Gordon & MacPhail
www.benromach.com

Region of origin Speyside, Scotland
Distillery Benromach, Forres, Morayshire
Alcohol content 43% abv
Type Single malt

There is a view in the whisky world that if you change a still, you must duplicate all the bumps and dents in the replacement, or your spirit will change. Gordon & MacPhail had a desire to return to a Speyside style of whisky from earlier years, but when reequipping the Benromach distillery the company put in stills that were different shapes from the originals. Effectively, this change was a marker in the sand—a statement that, although the distillers wanted an older style of whisky, they were going to create it in their own way and not be beholden to the past.

After an extensive refit, Gordon & MacPhail fired up the new stills and opened the distillery doors in 1998, its centenary year. It remains Speyside's smallest working distillery, and the comprehensive refurbishment meant that many of the production processes could be streamlined in a way that maintained the traditional handcrafted edge. Whiskies such as this 21-Year-Old are "living" examples of the style of whisky the distillery was producing before its last closure. This spirit, dating from the time when Distillers Company Limited was in charge, was matured in sherry butts—both first- and second-fill—giving a warming, mellow, fruit whisky. **AA**

Tasting notes

Hints of green grass and an old-fashioned apothecary aroma. The palate develops into a rich, coating dram with masses of spices. The finish is long, with caramel.

Benromach 25-Year-Old

Gordon & MacPhail | www.benromach.com

Region of origin Speyside, Scotland
Distillery Benromach, Forres, Morayshire
Alcohol content 43% abv
Style Single malt

Benromach distillery was one of more than twenty distilleries closed by the Distillers Company Ltd. (DCL) during the 1980s, in order to reduce malt whisky capacity at a time of serious overproduction. While many of those distilleries are now lost forever, Benromach has a happier story under independent bottlers and retailers Gordon & MacPhail.

The aim of the new owners was to produce spirit in the style of early-twentieth-century Speysides, and subsequent releases of whisky distilled since 1998 have been relatively robust, with a significant, though subtle, influence of peat. It follows that the 25-Year-Old, distilled under the previous DCL regime, should be entirely different in style from younger expressions. However, associate director and supply manager Ewen Mackintosh says, "Remarkably, we feel there is a common thread, or fingerprint, that connects vintages distilled by the previous owners and spirit distilled by Gordon & MacPhail.

"When the distillery was purchased, we were fortunate to obtain a sample of the new-make spirit from the previous owners. When we analyzed this sample against our distillations, we noticed this common thread. This is despite that fact that we reequipped Benromach with new apparatus. The only constant that remains is the water source."

Unusually for the Benromach range, the 25-Year-Old contains spirit that has all been matured in refill American oak hogsheads, with no sherry cask input at all. The distillers describe it as "fresh and mellow, full of Speyside character." **GS**

Tasting notes

Sweet on the nose, with banoffee pie, soft fruits, toffee, and developing coconut notes. A fruit basket in the mouth, majoring on eating apple, apricot, and raisin, with cinnamon, allspice, and a suggestion of peat smoke. The finish is spicy and sweet, with lingering fruit.

Benromach 1968

Gordon & MacPhail | www.benromach.com

Region of origin Speyside, Scotland
Distillery Benromach, Forres, Morayshire
Alcohol content 45.4% abv
Type Single malt

One of the great pleasures of Scotch whisky is that it's pretty much impossible to taste everything, and there is always something new to discover. Even a book as big as this one cannot do the country justice. For Scotland, then, this book is a sort of "greatest hits" package, and there are a lot of distilleries that make not particularly exciting malt whisky aimed at the blended market, which still accounts for more than 90 percent of Scotland's output. There are many "me too" malts that didn't make the cut. The Benromach 1968, however, isn't one of them.

Benromach 1968 is very special indeed for two reasons: one, its age and, two, because of the distillery it's from. Very few whiskies make it past thirty years before the wood takes over; hardly any make it to fifty, and chances are you're going to pay $8,000 (£5,100) or considerably more if they do. This makes the 1968 one of the oldest malts money can buy. But Benromach is an amazing distillery anyway. It is one of a group of what might be described as "hidden gem" Highland distilleries—distilleries that perhaps don't get the attention that the internationally backed ones get.

Benromach is owned by independent bottlers Gordon & MacPhail, who know more than most about good wood policy. Since their takeover in 1998, the company has released a wide array of exciting and varied malts, including organic, very oak, and heavily peated ones. But this might just be the jewel in the crown, the full-bodied and rich whisky proving itself capable of holding off the effects of the wood. Unsurprisingly, there's not much of it around. **DR**

Tasting notes

Christmas cake drizzled in sweet spicy sherry and served alongside chunky orange marmalade. As you'd expect, there is plenty of oak, with hints of wood smoke and licorice, plus apple. The finish is long, laced with sherry and more of the Christmas cake.

Benromach Classic 55-Year-Old 1949

Benromach Distillery | www.benromach.com

Region of origin Speyside, Scotland
Distillery Benromach, Forres, Morayshire
Alcohol content 42.4% abv
Style Single malt

Just seventy bottles of this ultraold whisky were yielded from cask number 706. For a cask to give so few bottles means the greedy angels have had more than their fair share. It is amazing that the alcoholic strength is above the legal minimum of 40 percent when a whisky of this age is released. The assumption is that mainly the alcohol will be taken by the angels, leaving the water behind, as alcohol evaporates far quicker than water. But this really isn't the case all the time, as in some instances—such as in some areas of a bonded warehouse and in some (mainly warmer) countries—the exact opposite happens, with the water evaporating faster than the alcohol, resulting in an increase in strength.

With the 55-Year-Old, it looks like both water and alcohol have evaporated at broadly the same rate. Amazingly, the whisky isn't overoaked at this age, evidence that good wood management by a distillery really does underpin the industry. Whenever just seventy bottles are released of any whisky, you can assume that it's incredibly rare and carries a premium price. This is most definitely the case here, as a bottle will set you back $10,200 (£6,500). On the face of it, this looks to be a hefty price tag; however, in comparison with other similar aged bottles (sometimes even younger ones), it is not a steep as it could have been. For the investors out there, this will take some time to increase in value, but it wasn't bottled with the intention of sitting on a shelf—it was bottled to be opened and savored next to a log fire, with a blanket of snow outside, and in good company. **AS**

Tasting notes

Huge. Rich, sweet fruits come to the fore. A floral element that belies the whisky's age is also present. A sumptuously velvety affair with chocolate, hints of nut, almost marzipan, and plum jam. Flavors compete for dominance, layer after layer of complexity. Stunning.

Benromach Organic

Gordon & MacPhail | www.benromach.com

Region of origin Speyside, Scotland
Distillery Benromach, Forres, Morayshire
Alcohol content 43% abv
Type Single malt

Once Gordon & MacPhail had refurbished the Benromach distillery, laid lines of communication to the market and its intended customers, and designed a snazzy new livery for its bottles and packaging, all that remained was to find a way to stand out from its competitors. This is an issue that every distiller faces when launching a product: the need to find a wow factor, ultimately the pull that is going to place its whisky in the shopping basket ahead of someone else's. One way of achieving this is to attempt something novel or cutting-edge. But trying to be progressive in the whisky world can prove tough.

Gordon & MacPhail is a company that does not shy away from an interesting task, and it decided to tackle the organic market. An increasing number of people are determined to stretch their green credentials, and how better than with an organic dram? There had been a few organic whiskies before Benromach Organic, but none had such a stringent approach: this whisky is organic from field to bottle. The entire production process passed the rigorous standards of the Soil Association, and it even used Scottish organic barley—significant because not all barley used to make Scotch is from Scotland.

The spirit was matured in virgin American oak. This was taking a bit of a risk because it is generally held that fresh oak can overpower a whisky, hence the normal use of seasoned casks. However, under the watchful eye of the distiller, Benromach Organic seems to carry it off; while the wood is certainly there, the whisky is well balanced. **AA**

Tasting notes

The wonderful virgin oak gives a big hit up front, like diving into a box of pencil shavings and boiled sweets. Eventually a little puff of smoke develops. It is deeply creamy on the palate, with some soft fruit, peach, and nectarine. The wood is still here, too. The finish is toffee.

Benromach Origins Batches 1–3

Gordon & MacPhail
www.benromach.com

Region of origin Speyside, Scotland
Distillery Benromach, Forres, Morayshire
Alcohol content 50% abv
Style Single malt

Gordon & MacPhail's Origins series was designed to show off what can be achieved by tinkering with parts of the production or maturation process. Origins Batch 1, launched in 2008, was produced using Golden Promise barley, which was once the preferred grain in the industry but came to be spurned by distillers looking for higher-yielding varieties. It remains much prized in some quarters—the Macallan is one big consumer, using it in its apparently improved flavor profile. The first bottling of Benromach Origins was matured in first- and second-fill sherry casks.

Origins Batch 2 showcased what could be done by varying cask woods. For Batch 2, distilled in 1999, Gordon & MacPhail chose to mature the spirit in port pipes. This was the first expression to be aged in wine casks. Origins Batch 3 was distilled using a different barley variety, this time Optic, after which the spirit was matured in sherry casks.

Areas ripe for experimentation remain plentiful: alternative wood types (Scotch matured in Japanese oak is one possibility); different yeast varieties (many people say yeast does not have much of an effect, but nothing has been proved); and, of course, other grain varieties. The list is endless. **AA**

Tasting notes

Batch 1 has a dominant toasted malt note that follows to the palate. Batch 2 is rich with toffee and dark fruits. Batch 3 has Christmas cake, dried fig, prune, and toffee.

Benromach Peat Smoke Batch 3

Gordon & MacPhail
www.benromach.com

Region of origin Speyside, Scotland
Distillery Benromach, Forres, Morayshire
Alcohol content 46% abv
Type Single malt

Peated Speyside whisky is surely a departure from the assumption that Speyside should be honeyed apple and pear in flavor. However, it may be that it was another change in tastes and the blenders' dominance that originally reduced the amount of peat in Speyside whisky—that and cheap coal, railroads, and the desire to make a profit.

A decade or so ago, the influence of peat was found in all sorts of whiskies, including Glen Garioch, Glenfiddich, and Brora. Today the peated Speysiders and Highlanders are sparse: they include Ardmore, Benriach, and Old Ballantruan. So the innovative Gordon & MacPhail company decided to experiment. True to form, they did not go for a modest peating— this was a hairs-on-your-chest Laphroaigian level.

This Batch 3 expression was distilled in 2000 and matured in first-fill ex-bourbon casks. While Benromach Traditional's barley has a phenol content of 10 to 12 parts per million (ppm), Benromach Peat Smoke uses barley malted to 55 ppm. The result is a single malt with a seriously smoky character and a lush fruit edge. With the possible exception of the Benromach 10-Year-Old, it is the crowning glory in the distillery's expanding repertoire. **AA**

Tasting notes

Plenty of fresh juicy fruit notes: peach, apple, and apricot. This carries through to the full-bodied palate, which is well balanced between the smoke and fruit.

A kilted Highlander surmounts a weathervane at Benromach distillery. →

Benromach Traditional

Gordon & MacPhail | www.benromach.com

Region of origin Speyside, Scotland
Distillery Benromach, Forres, Morayshire
Alcohol content 40% abv
Type Single malt

The problem with buying a distillery is that, before long, the venture needs to start making money. Most established distilleries come with at least some stock, however, which makes the process of kick-starting an income stream a little easier. This was the case for Scottish independent bottler Gordon & MacPhail when it purchased Benromach Distillery.

The distillery had been silent for fifteen years before the company bought it in 1993. Gordon & MacPhail decided that it wanted to stamp its mark on the site and rebuilt the distillery almost entirely. In addition to refreshing the still house, it took a new approach to the whisky, creating a new range, new packaging, and, eventually, a new liquid. The Benromach Traditional expression is the first new bottling since the distillery doors were reopened in 1998 after its layoff.

This single malt marks the welcome return of one of Speyside's smallest operations. The whisky may be young, but it has a wonderful whiff of peat and has taken a great deal of flavor from the oak casks. The Traditional tag also underlines the importance that Gordon & MacPhail has placed on the techniques used to create its newly acquired whisky. It wants the provenance of fine craftsmanship to go with its liquid, and therefore many of the processes are done by hand with no real automation involved. Once the whisky is laid down to mature, it is checked regularly. The lack of an age statement might mean that it is young, but Benromach Traditional is not released until it is ready. **AA**

Tasting notes

Very light to start. Quite biscuity, with a slight ginger note, too. After a while, it starts getting a little fruity. The palate is very creamy but has great depth with some sweetness and a touch of cracked black pepper. Sweet, gentle fruits return for the finish.

Big Peat

Douglas Laing & Co. | www.douglaslaing.com

Region and country of origin Islay, Scotland
Distilleries Various
Alcohol content 46% abv
Style Blended malt

Whiskies from Port Ellen on Islay were the favorite of distiller Douglas Laing. His son Fred, now a distiller himself, recalls fondly how his father would return from work and wake him to ask about his day at school or his rugby practice, ruffling his hair while breathing whisky fumes over him. Many years later, Fred recognized the distinctive aroma of Port Ellen.

Douglas Laing's excellent stocks of Port Ellen arguably set his company apart from competing independent bottlers. In 2009 it was decided to marry some young Islay stocks with a little old Port Ellen, and the result is Big Peat; there is not much Port Ellen in this blended malt, but it is there nevertheless, along with some Ardbeg, Caol Ila, and Bowmore; other unnamed Islay malts are also included. The youngest constituent malts are five or six years old.

There is something subversive about the company's approach that is epitomized by Big Peat. Conservative whisky enthusiasts say the packaging is too informal, and Fred calls the back label "an indication of what we think of the new blended malt terminology—we still prefer vatted malt." An initial batch of 3,000 bottles was expected to last from September 2009 to the following summer, but the whole lot sold out before the end of November.

Of Douglas Laing & Co.'s current portfolio, this whisky is probably closest to the business's early blends. Vatting sizes are now reaching 3,900 bottles and, at the time of writing, the eighteenth batch of Big Peat had already been released, with increased stocks being laid down for the future. **MM**

Tasting notes

Big and spicy on the nose. The palate is like a Scottish wind in your face, at once sweet and seaweedy. The finish goes on and on—like a sidestepping running back, this is an elegant monster. Islay impetuosity is reined in by Port Ellen's more venerable influence.

The Big Smoke 40 Islay Malt

Duncan Taylor & Co. | www.duncantaylor.com

Region and country of origin Islay, Scotland
Distilleries Various
Alcohol content 40% abv
Style Blended malt

Reacting to a name like the Big Smoke, whisky lovers could be forgiven for thinking that one sip would be like having their head ripped off by a large school bully, kicked around like a sack for an hour, and then used to scour the inside of their assailant's chimney. Thankfully, this 40 percent abv version of the Big Smoke is a far more refined experience than its name might suggest.

The blend shows off a lighter side of Islay while still showcasing some of the flavors for which it is so justly famous—less a punch in the mouth followed by a mouthful of soot, and more kicking over the traces of a smoldering peat fire while receiving a gust of sea spray in the face. This is no poor man's peated whisky, but an excellent introduction to the Islay style for someone who wonders what all the fuss is about.

This blended malt from independent bottlers Duncan Taylor is the younger brother of their ten-year-old, Auld Reekie, and cousin to the muscular and bruising Big Smoke 60. Like several blended malts, the Big Smoke 40 has no age statement, proving that more years in the cask is no guarantee of better quality and that, when a whisky tastes this good, age statements really don't matter. When it comes to peated whiskies, youth is often a positive advantage, providing a vibrant and intense experience for those seeking pungent phenolic and coastal flavors. The Big Smoke 40 successfully combines these elements of Islay malts without losing the softer and fruitier flavors that, in less capable hands, are sometimes obliterated by the intensity of the peat. **PB**

Tasting notes

Chocolate and nut spread on burnt toast on the nose, followed by chardonnay, citrus, and, at the end, a hint of lily. On the palate, it is light and fudgy at first, then the smoke makes a restrained and citrusy appearance, with a vanilla hit beautifully rounding off the finish.

The Big Smoke 60 Islay Malt

Duncan Taylor & Co. | www.duncantaylor.com

Region and country of origin Islay, Scotland
Distilleries Various
Alcohol content 60% abv
Style Blended malt

Unlike its cousin the Big Smoke 40, which is partial to a couple of cigarettes after school before heading home to hide the fact unsuccessfully from its parents, the Big Smoke 60 is an unapologetic sixty-a-day chain-smoking bruiser. Although on the surface the whisky may be all about smoke, scratch a little deeper, and you'll find that it has other, hidden dimensions that are at odds with its outward appearance. Imagine Lemmy from Motörhead simultaneously smoking a Cuban cigar, reading a Jane Austen novel, and making a fresh fruit salad, and there you have the Big Smoke 60.

The "60" refers to the whisky's alcohol-by-volume content, making it an in-your-face, mind-blowing blended malt for those who like the volume on their whisky turned up to Spinal Tap levels. Like the Big Smoke 40, it carries no age statement, nor is there any indication of which whiskies go into making it. None of that matters, because for drinkers who like the intensity of the big-hitting south coast Islay distilleries, this is one hell of a ride, full of the iodine and peat reek of the Laphroaigs and Ardbegs but displaying the fruit and lightness of touch of some of the distilleries from the north and west of Islay.

Duncan Taylor has one of the largest privately held collections of rare Scotch whisky casks, and the company offers premium bottlings of single malts, blended malts, and blends. In the Big Smoke 60, they have produced a whisky that is less a love letter to the god of hellfire and smoke and more an ode to Islay as a whole, showing that the island has plenty more to offer than just peat. **PB**

Tasting notes

Chewy toffee on the nose. Water brings out green fruits, banana, peach skin, and gingersnap, but the smoke is still relatively shy. On the palate, the smoke fills every corner, with fruit cake, marzipan, and polished wood. The finish is spicy, with pepper and vanilla.

Black Bottle

Burn Stewart Distillers | www.blackbottle.com

Region and country of origin Scotland
Distilleries Various
Alcohol content 40% abv
Style Blend

Black Bottle blend was created by Gordon Graham, a grocer and tea blender from Aberdeen. In the 1870s grocers often blended their own whiskies. Gordon's concoction was so fine that his family and customers persuaded him to give up the tea and concentrate on whisky. In 1879 he and his two brothers went into business blending and selling Black Bottle whisky. At that time, many of the malts of Speyside and the Northeast would have been peated.

The origins of the blend may lie in the Northeast but Black Bottle is now strongly associated with Islay. The owners have claimed that all the Islay malts are featured (at the moment, that means seven Islay malts; Kilchoman is too young and Port Ellen too rare). The key malt is Bunnahabhain, which was acquired together with the blend by the current owners, Burn Stewart. Speyside and Highland malts provide sweetness to balance the smoky Islay drams. Further sweetness comes from grain whiskies, although the proportion in Black Bottle is smaller than in most standard blends.

Scotland currently represents Black Bottle's biggest market, while 70 percent of all Black Bottle sales are in the United Kingdom. That will probably change soon, as Burn Stewart Distillers is promoting the brand abroad more vigorously. **RL**

Tasting notes

First sweetness, then smoke on the nose, with honey, candy floss, and toffee apple. On the palate, barley sugar sweetness balanced by nut, licorice, and cinnamon.

Black Bottle 10-Year-Old

Burn Stewart Distillers | www.blackbottle.com

Region and country of origin Islay, Scotland
Distilleries Various
Alcohol content 40% abv
Style Blend

The Black Bottle brand suffered a period in the doldrums after the death of its inheritor, the redoubtable Granny Graham, in 1958. It was not until the 1990s and an Allied Lyons takeover that the brand regained some of its previous status. The decade saw an increase in the use of good Islay malts in the recipe, and only Islay malts go into the 10-Year-Old.

Black Bottle 10-Year-Old was released in 1998 and really is in a black bottle—the regular Black Bottle is actually in green glass. The Black Bottle name comes from the northeast of Scotland, where the fishermen would always take "a wee black bottle" when they went to sea in case of sickness, lack of wind, a successful catch, or any excuse to take a wee dram.

Burn Stewart Distillers bought Black Bottle and Bunnahabhain from the Edrington Group back in 2003. Edrington had been selling the 10-Year-Old relatively cheaply, and Burn Stewart found that the sales volumes were low and the component malts were not that easy to come by; it was discontinued around 2006. The 10-Year-Old can still be found but is becoming increasingly rare. There are no plans to resurrect it, which is understandable but slightly sad, as it was a blend that won a number of awards and medals. At one point in the past, there was also a Black Bottle 15-year-old, but that is now extremely rare. **RL**

Tasting notes

Sweet tobacco, cinder toffee, muted smoke, apricot, and a mix of tar and unpolished wood. On the palate, treacle toffee, licorice, warm aniseed, and clove.

A poster refers to Bunnahabhain, Black Bottle's spiritual home.

Black Bull 12-Year-Old

Duncan Taylor & Co. | www.duncantaylor.com

Region and country of origin Speyside, Scotland
Distilleries Various
Alcohol content 50% abv
Style Blend

The original Black Bull whisky brand was founded in 1933 by George Willshire & Co. of Dundee, a subsidiary of Duncan Taylor. By the 1960s and 1970s, it had become a top-selling blend, especially in Italy and the United States. Perhaps its success was due to the fact that it was a fifty/fifty combination of malts and grains and was the first 100 proof blended whisky sold in the United States. Back in those days, Black Bull had no age statement on the bottle.

Duncan Taylor & Co. resurrected the Black Bull brand in 2007 with the release of a "blended at birth" thirty-year-old, which won at least three major awards. This 12-Year-Old, introduced the following year, was intended to be the core blend of the Black Bull range. It followed the fifty/fifty/fifty precedent of the original by being bottled at 50 percent abv and combining equal measures of malt and grain whiskies. The malt whisky component, which mostly consists of Speyside malts, has a relatively high proportion of sherry-matured whisky.

The very impressive and rather menacing black bull on the bottle is a Highland beast, chanced upon in a field near Aboyne and later painted by Insch artist Angela Davidson. Commissioned by Duncan Taylor, the original painting hangs on the wall of their office in Huntly—very much a product of the Northeast. Prints of the diabolical bovine are available.

Black Bull 12-Year-Old was voted the best blended Scotch whisky in the world, in the class of twelve years or less, at the 2011 World Whisky awards. Of course it is neither chill-filtered nor colored. **RL**

Tasting notes

On the nose, sweet sherry, toffee, vanilla, chocolate, lemon sherbet, and crystallized ginger. The palate is a rich, deep cello suite of a dram; it could be a single malt, with its flavors of treacle toffee, toasted oat, dark chocolate, fig, date, and an espresso's sugary dregs.

Black Bull 40-Year-Old Batch 1

Duncan Taylor & Co. | www.duncantaylor.com

Region and country of origin Speyside, Scotland
Distilleries Various
Alcohol content 41.9% abv
Style Blend

While still far from common, "vintage" Scotch whisky blends are becoming increasingly popular, with a growing number of consumers appreciating the skill that goes into creating a fine blend from an array of elderly and often increasingly unpredictable whiskies.

One of the oldest and most impressive blends on the market is Black Bull 40-Year-Old, created by Duncan Taylor & Co., which operates from the Aberdeenshire market town of Huntly. The Black Bull blended whisky brand was originally trademarked in 1933 by George Willshire & Co. Ltd. of Dundee, and the name refers to the world-famous Aberdeen Angus breed of cattle in the northeast of Scotland.

The first Black Bull blend produced by Duncan Taylor, which acquired the brand in 2001, was a thirty-year-old. The blend was highly unusual in that the component whiskies were vatted together during the 1970s, just after distillation, and subsequently matured in sherry casks for a minimum of thirty years.

Inevitably, stocks of such a blend were finite, and after it was received with great acclaim, Duncan Taylor chose to follow up with twelve-year-old and forty-year-old variants. This first batch of the 40-Year-Old contained 90 percent malt and 10 percent grain whisky, with 80 percent of the contents having been matured in ex-bourbon casks and 20 percent in sherry wood. The blend contains whiskies aged between forty and forty-four years old from the following distilleries: Bunnahabhain, Glenfarclas, Glenlivet, Glenburgie, Highland Park, Miltonduff, Springbank, Tamdhu, and Invergordon. **GS**

Tasting notes

Mellow and mature on the nose; sherried, with old leather, candied fruit, orange marmalade, and developing vanilla notes. Full-bodied, rich, smooth, and spicy, with cinnamon stick, dark fruits, raisin, and vanilla. Finishes slowly, with ginger and licorice.

Black Bull
40-Year-Old Batch 2

Duncan Taylor & Co.
www.duncantaylor.com

Region and country of origin Scotland
Distillery Various
Alcohol content 41.9% abv
Style Blend

Black Bull is an important brand for Duncan Taylor & Co. and the 40-Year-Old is the alpha male in the ring. You can buy an T-shirt from their Web site with a message that declares "No Bull, just whisky," and that's certainly true of the 40-Year-Old—certainly no chill-filtration or added coloring. And the blend, at 41.9 percent abv, has an extremely attractive price tag.

The 40-Year-Old is 90 percent single malts and 10 percent grain whisky. The grain component may be small, but the company claims that it provides the sweetness essential to holding the whole blend together (not to mention the advantage of having a higher percentage of alcohol than the malts).

Black Bull 40-Year-Old is a batch whisky. Unusually for a blend, the label states what its contents are. Batch 2, consisting of only 957 bottles, contains malts from Bunnahabhain, Glenlivet, Tamdhu (all aged between forty-one and forty-four years), while the whisky's 10 percent grain is forty-five-year-old Invergordon. Batch 2 has fewer different malts than Batch 1, and subsequent batches may be different again. Black Bull's component whiskies come mainly from hogsheads and butts; sherry butts are used to marry the blend for a final eight months. **RL**

Tasting notes

The nose is a delightful cascade of exotic fruits, with tobacco coming later. On the palate, the wood is surprisingly restrained, lots of fruit, flowers, and spice.

Bladnoch 8-Year-Old
Belted Galloway Label

Bladnoch
www.bladnoch.co.uk

Region and country of origin Lowlands, Scotland
Distillery Bladnoch, Bladnoch, Dumfries and Galloway
Alcohol content 55% abv
Style Single malt

Although this whisky is made in the Scottish county of Dumfries and Galloway, you might be relieved to learn that a belted Galloway isn't something that Bladnoch owner Raymond Armstrong uses to stop his kilt from falling down. A "beltie" is, in fact, a rare breed of cow from southwest Scotland, and if you ever drive past Bladnoch distillery, you might well see one.

The Belted Galloway "brand" itself predates Armstrong, and there are some quite ancient "beltie" whiskies out there, sired by earlier owners. Tasting and comparing old and new "belties" side by side is an interesting way to spend an hour, and it confirms that, under new management, the standards set by the last owners are being upheld. Armstrong's spirit is possibly more fragrant, but that may be explained simply by its comparative youth.

Bladnoch is one of the few Scottish distilleries that will sell you an entire cask of whisky. The spirit is yours when it is eight years old, although bear in mind that a 53-gallon (200-liter) bourbon cask might yield 380 bottles—enough for one hell of a party. However, if that is too much, you can purchase one tenth of a cask, a more discreet share that will be much kinder on the wallet, and on the head. **PM**

Tasting notes

Rounder and more unctuous than the nine-year-old. Sweetness suggests jam or syrup, but the whole thing is undercut with meadows of grass and wildflowers.

A display of whisky-barrel stencils at Bladnoch distillery. ➡

Bladnoch 9-Year-Old Lightly Peated

Bladnoch | www.bladnoch.co.uk

Region and country of origin Lowlands, Scotland
Distillery Bladnoch, Bladnoch, Dumfries and Galloway
Alcohol content Around 53.4% abv
Style Single malt

This malt, like many other lowland offerings, was once triple-distilled. No one is sure when this practice started, but it stopped in the 1960s when Bladnoch's three stills were sold to a whisky distillery in, of all places, Sweden. With new stills came a new way of working. The owners at the time were in the blended Scotch business so they had no time for triple-distillation. Bladnoch therefore fell in step with the rest of Scotland, leaving neighboring Auchentoshen as Scotland's last outpost of triple- distillation.

Under the leadership of Raymond Armstrong, Bladnoch continues to double-distill, but the distillery is embracing change. This particular whisky is a lightly peated malt, so it's a move away from the traditional flavor of unpeated lowland malt. Distilled on November 19, 2001, and bottled on June 23, 2011, this curious beast is very different from every other lowland whisky, yet it retains the lightness of touch that has long made Bladnoch so appealing.

The layer of peat here works incredibly well, as this is a fragrant peating, not a blanket to smother everything. It's a delicate dram and not for those who ask for the hottest vindaloo on the menu or those who like to chew their malt. **PM**

Tasting notes

Clean washing on a spring day. The rumble of peat is unmistakable, but it's soft, like distant pipe smoke. Fruit and nut chocolate at the end, fading to a gentle glow.

Bladnoch 20-Year-Old (Cask Strength)

Bladnoch | www.bladnoch.co.uk

Region and country of origin Lowlands, Scotland
Distillery Bladnoch, Bladnoch, Dumfries and Galloway
Alcohol content Around 52.4% abv
Style Single malt

Bladnoch is one of the three remaining Lowland malt whisky distilleries in Scotland. Raymond Armstrong bought the picture postcard distillery on the banks of the river Bladnoch from United Distillers in 1995. Armstrong, whose background is in construction, didn't have any previous distilling experience, and initially his idea was to convert the place into apartments. So it didn't bother him that United Distillers had a clause in the sale that forbade distilling from ever happening at Bladnoch again.

But Bladnoch is a stubborn kind of place. For a start it's in the thinly populated far southwest of Scotland, which has few tourists. So when the holiday apartments didn't happen, Armstrong—despite his lack of experience—decided to resurrect the distillery. It took five long years to get Bladnoch ready for production, and nothing could begin until the clause forbidding distillation was painfully renegotiated.

Today Bladnoch is home to a fully functioning distillery, a whisky school, and a rather good café. What's more, it has once again taken its place at the heart of the community. And of course there's also plenty of whisky. This is from Hogshead 136, distilled on January 24, 1990. **PM**

Tasting notes

Pepper in the mouth followed by an intense bite of clove. The wood is very well mannered, and the long finish has a lingering taste of apple strudel.

Bladnoch Distiller's Choice Younger Vatting

Bladnoch | www.bladnoch.co.uk

Region and country of origin Lowlands, Scotland
Distillery Bladnoch, Bladnoch, Dumfries and Galloway
Alcohol content 46% abv
Style Single malt

In a single glass of Bladnoch Distiller's Choice Younger Vatting, you'll see and taste everything there is to know about the differences between large multinational drink corporations and smaller boutique operations. For a start, this vatting isn't fixed; it's an ever-changing canvas, and sometimes it alters on a monthly basis. So there's no corporate template, no color reference to match, and no vast order to fill, with all the blandness that can come with that.

What you get here is a vatting of selected malts with no age statement—whatever Raymond Armstrong feels fits the bill on that particular day. It's not as anarchic as it sounds. Bladnoch has only been back on its feet since late 2001, and it takes a long time to work out the optimum age to sell a whisky. There's also the element of stock control. Whisky can be sold once it's at least three years and a day old, but it might be another decade before it falls into shape. In the meantime, friends need to be made, and cash needs to flow. Armstrong, then, is experimenting, trying different things, innovating with distillate, maturation, and age. If you take the same attitude when you approach this, then you too can be part of the rebirth of this truly indestructible distillery. **PM**

Tasting notes

This is a whisky that builds and builds. Crisp, grassy flavor profile, becoming honied as the younger and older components elbow each other out of the way.

Blair Athol 12-Year-Old Flora & Fauna

Blair Athol

Region and country of origin Highlands, Scotland
Distillery Blair Athol, Pitlochry, Perthshire
Alcohol content 43% abv
Style Single malt

The Blair Athol distillery is of medium capacity, with around 90 to 95 percent of its output being matured in ex-bourbon barrels and destined for blending; much of the bourbon-matured stock is used in the well-known Bell's blend. The remaining 5 to10 percent is casked into sherry wood and set aside for special releases and the Flora & Fauna series—this 12-Year-Old is the only consistently available proprietary bottling currently on the market.

The whisky produced at Blair Athol is particularly heavy in style. The employment of cloudy worts and short fermentation times—typically lasting for forty-eight hours—leads to a new make of considerable weight and pungency. Spirit of this dense, richly malty character tends to respond well to the influence of European or American oak sherry casks. The distinct nature of the whisky finds a common ally in these types of woods as they impart their own nutty, toasted flavors while combining with the spirit to produce fruitiness, balance, and complexity.

This 12-Year-Old is an excellent example of the harmonious interplay between spirit and cask, but it seems, without greater exposure, that Blair Athol will remain largely overlooked as a single malt. **StuR**

Tasting notes

The nose is nutty, creamy, slightly peaty. The smooth, full-bodied taste features fruit cake and candied lemon peel, leading to a finish that is both smoky and treacly.

Blair Athol Old & Rare Platinum Selection

Douglas Laing & Co. | www.douglaslaing.com

Region and country of origin Highlands, Scotland
Distillery Blair Athol, Pitlochry, Perthshire
Alcohol content 58.2% abv
Style Single malt

Many tourists have visited the charming distillery at Blair Athol and discovered the contribution made by its whisky to blends, especially Bell's. Out of every ten casks filled from the stills here, that is where nine of them will end up, probably mixed with ginger ale. Making large and consistent quantities of malt that can survive such treatment requires skill in itself, and you may be forgiven for thinking the story stops there. But there is another hidden side to Blair Athol, exemplified by this Douglas Laing cask-strength bottling.

While the output for blending is matured for a few years in ex-bourbon casks to provide an economical yet fulfilling and rounded component, a small portion is laid down in sherry casks. This largely finds its way into the independent market, because in-house bottlings have been rare.

The Blair Athol Old & Rare Platinum Selection is a full, creamy dessert of a whisky at the perfect age of fifteen years. It is quite unlike that large, inverted bottle of blend found in your local bar, and it is amazing that the whiskies share the same parentage. When a teenager becomes this refined and charming, it shows the difference made by a careful and skilled upbringing. A hidden gem, indeed. **AN**

Tasting notes

Nutmeg and vanilla on the nose. Smooth and full body, reminiscent of "floating island" meringue pudding in a pool of fresh egg custard. A long and warming finish.

Blue Hanger 25-Year-Old (1st Limited Release)

Berry Bros. & Rudd | www.bbr.com

Region of origin Speyside, Scotland
Distilleries Various
Alcohol content 45.6% abv
Style Blended malt

Blue Hanger has become a highly regarded vatted malt from Berry Bros. & Rudd, London's oldest and most prestigious wine and spirits merchant. According to Doug McIvor, the man who blends it, "The First Release was a bit of experimentation that turned out to be quite delicious."

When McIvor joined the company, it had a large inventory of aged casks of Glen Grant and Glenlivet. One evening, he decided to experiment: "Glenlivet has a buttery, sinewy texture to it—whisky is a lot about texture as well as the flavor—and Glen Grant has a slightly more rugged, outgoing style, with more outcrops of flavor going on, so I mixed some samples together just to see what would happen . . ."

The first release ran to only about 700 bottles, made available in November 2003. Blue Hanger was an elegant, well-dressed, twenty-five-year-old whisky bottled at a strength of 45.6 percent abv. The blend contained only two malts, Glen Grant and Glenlivet, with two hogsheads of one and one of the other. This whisky was the first blended malt that McIvor put together and that also went on to be bottled commercially. More bottlings were to follow as Blue Hanger developed a devoted following. **MM**

Tasting notes

Sherry, mixed peel, and tropical fruit on the nose. Warming on the palate, with chocolate-covered orange peel from the sherry influence. A medium-long finish.

← Rampant ivy frames the name of Blair Athol distillery.

Blue Hanger 25-Year-Old (2nd Limited Release)

Berry Bros. & Rudd | www.bbr.com

Region of origin Speyside, Scotland
Distilleries Various
Alcohol content 45.6% abv
Type Blended malt

Blue Hanger was the name of a Berry Bros. & Rudd blend originally introduced in 1934, initially for the diplomatic export market. The blend had become obsolete a few years before spirits buyer Doug McIvor reexamined it in 2003, so McIvor decided to reuse the name. William "Blue" Hanger, the Third Lord Coleraine, was a loyal customer of Berry Bros. & Rudd in the 1790s. Reputedly the best-dressed man of his age, he was known by the soubriquet "Blue Hanger" because of his expensive blue clothing.

McIvor's first release was an instant success and sold out within a few months. The Blue Hanger name was kept alive by the second release, in August 2004, of 1,757 bottles carrying a twenty-five-year age statement. As with the first release, the blend contained only two malts: Glenlivet (four hogsheads from 1974 and a butt from the same year) and Glen Grant (two hogsheads from 1974). Again, McIvor's objective was to create the best blended malt from the stocks available at the time. The blend is a snapshot of the inventory of Berry Bros. & Rudd, as well as a demonstration of which single malts work best together. There is much to discover in this fine alliance of two venerable Speyside malts.

The strength—as with every expression of Blue Hanger—is 45.6 percent, a nod to the original Berry Bros. & Rudd blend, which was always bottled at twenty below proof. Traditionally, all whiskies were sold at this strength until regulations following World War I required spirits to be reduced to thirty under proof in order to prolong stocks. **MM**

Tasting notes

Very rich and mature nose, with alluring notes of ginger and spiced honey cake. The palate is nicely balanced, with mouthwatering satsuma and damson. A drop of water enhances the citrus notes. There is warming spice in the finish, with residual citrus notes gently fading.

Blue Hanger 30-Year-Old (3rd Limited Release)

Berry Bros. & Rudd | www.bbr.com

Region of origin Speyside, Scotland
Distilleries Various
Alcohol content 45.6% abv
Style Blended malt

The first two releases of Blue Hanger were both blended malts—or what we used to call vatted malts—in which the youngest whisky was twenty-five years old. This third release was created from the very same stocks which, by the time of bottling, had matured sufficiently for Blue Hanger to proclaim itself as a thirty-year-old for the first time.

This third release was again a blend of only two single malts, the same two used in previous incarnations of this top-notch blended malt, both from Speyside and distilled less than 15 miles (24 km) apart. The 30-year-old comprised a butt of Glenlivet from 1975, three Glenlivet hogsheads from 1975, and a Glenlivet hogshead from 1973, together with a hogshead of Glen Grant from 1973.

Launched in October 2007, Blue Hanger third release was limited to 1,485 bottles. It won its first competition, being crowned Best Blended Malt at the 2008 World Whiskies Awards. On retasting it for this book, it is easy to see why. Blue Hanger is always an astounding blended malt, and this is the finest expression of them all. It has a particularly rich nose, terrific mouthfeel, and a long and sophisticated finish with the balance of a tightrope walker.

What else could any whisky enthusiast possibly want? Well, you could want for it to be available to buy, but it appears Blue Hanger has something of a cult following and the bottles do not hang around for long. If you are ever offered the opportunity to taste this edition, put on "Mount Harissa" by Duke Ellington, take a sip, then close your eyes and relax. **MM**

Tasting notes

Sherry on the nose, then red berries developing into dried fig. On the palate there is more dried fruit but with lovely spiciness and nuts, too. The finish has a supreme, warming length. Is there is a better blended malt in the world? This really takes some beating.

Blue Hanger 4th Limited Release

Berry Bros. & Rudd | www.bbr.com

Region of origin Speyside, Scotland
Distilleries Various
Alcohol content 45.6% abv
Type Blended malt

The first three releases of Blue Hanger were all made up of only two single malts. This fourth release goes a step further. The whiskies used were Mortlach (two hogsheads from 1992 and a butt from 1991), Glen Elgin (a butt from 1991), and Glenlivet (a hogshead from 1974 and two butts from 1975 and 1976).

Doug McIvor of Berry Bros. & Rudd, the man behind Blue Hanger, relates that the company's stocks of aged malts had dwindled when it came to the fourth release. He wanted to keep a certain style and was adamant that Blue Hanger should stick to the original philosophy of creating the best blended malt possible from existing stocks: "It was quite refreshing to be able to use some younger whiskies—they are more youthful and vibrant."

Of course, stock profiles change all the time, and that is part of the challenge. This fourth release made a virtue of a necessity; the introduction of different malts, required by the change in inventory, resulted in a whisky of great complexity and balance. Using only two malts is a restriction, as is a reliance on older malts only. The freedom to introduce more, younger malts while keeping to the original ethos resulted in a perfectly expressed whisky. It earned Best Scotch Blended Malt at the 2011 World Whiskies Awards.

Rich and luxurious, it shows good complexity with a nose of restrained sherry and mince pie. The relatively high strength ensures a robust presence balanced with a harmonious palate of mixed fruit and nuts. Blue Hanger fourth release has no age statement and is limited to 3,256 bottles. **MM**

Tasting notes

Apricot and white peach (in a mature dessert wine) on the nose. Then rum and raisin followed by white chocolate. A lovely, rich mouthfeel, with lots of sherry, some tropical fruit—honey mango—and hazelnut. The finish is long, spicy, and peppery; smoked chile.

Blue Hanger 5th Limited Release

Berry Bros. & Rudd | www.bbr.com

Region of origin Speyside, Scotland
Distilleries Various
Alcohol content 45.6% abv
Style Blended malt

Released in October 2010, this Blue Hanger was democratically elected. Doug McIvor of Berry Bros. & Rudd presented three prototype blends at Whisky Live Paris, France's premier whisky-tasting event. The public was invited to taste the variations and pick a favorite; truly, this is the people's blended malt. From this evidence, the French know their whisky, choosing extremely well from three very different options; one even had some Islay in it, unlike all previous Blue Hanger incarnations.

Clearly, the flavor profile really suited McIvor's taste: "I like the fifth release a hell of a lot, as I think there is greater balance achieved than in earlier versions. It's got the sherry note, but it isn't too heavy. I've always tried to rein in the sherry influence in Blue Hanger, but in the fifth, an introduction of Clynelish worked well, as it gave the whisky spice and extra complexity."

Blue Hanger fifth release is made up of four casks: a hogshead of Clynelish (No. 4704) distilled in 1997, which was spicy and a little salty with yellow fruit; a hogshead of Dufftown (No. 18584) from 1982, nutty, creamy, and toasty with grape skin and licorice; a Glenlivet hogshead (No. 13510) from 1978, polished oak, apple skin, and sherry trifle; and finally, a sherry butt of Mortlach (No. 5141) from 1991, which was sherry-driven and redolent of dried fruit and orange. As is true of all the best blended malts, the whisky is greater than the sum of its parts. It may even deserve the accolade of best Blue Hanger of them all.

Blue Hanger fifth release has no age statement and is limited to 1,155 bottles. **MM**

Tasting notes

The nose is herbaceous, with ripe fruit and spicy, nutty, creamy notes. Orange and tea—this has terrific depth and maturity. Tastewise, this is well balanced, with a creamy texture, dark cherry, and brazil nut. The finish is long, with lots of fruit embraced by drying oak tannin.

Bowmore 12-Year-Old

Morrison Bowmore Distillers (Suntory)
www.bowmore.co.uk

Region and country of origin Islay, Scotland
Distillery Bowmore, Loch Indaal, Argyll
Alcohol content 40% abv
Style Single malt

In 1837, William Mutter of Glasgow became the proud owner of Bowmore distillery. He kept the distillery for fifty-five years and paid for extensive construction work, expanding the capacity. In 1892 a group of English businessmen took over and held the distillery for the next thirty-three years. J. B. Sheriff and Co. bought Bowmore in 1925, to hold it for only four years before the Distillers Company Ltd. (DCL, a forerunner of Diageo) acquired the distillery in 1929.

This was not the end of changing hands for Bowmore. In 1950 William Grigor & Son took over, managing the distillery for thirteen years. In 1963 Stanley P. Morrison paid the then princely sum of £117,000 for lock, stock, and barrel. He ran Bowmore for more than a quarter century. The Japanese drinks giant Suntory became a 35 percent shareholder in 1989 and acquired the remaining 65 percent in 1994.

Bowmore's malting floor, one of the few in the trade, is still intact and provides 38 percent of the malted barley used by the distillery. The rest comes from Port Ellen Maltings at the southern tip of Islay, a former distillery that was closed in the 1980s and converted to a mechanized malting plant. All but one of the distilleries on the island purchase malted barley from Port Ellen, with each master distiller specifying exactly the peat level desired in the barley. **HO**

Tasting notes

On the nose, simmering root vegetables, burning leaves, and apple pie mingle with briny ropes. The rounded flavors are informed by dark peat.

Bowmore 16-Year-Old

Morrison Bowmore Distillers (Suntory)
www.bowmore.co.uk

Region and country of origin Islay, Scotland
Distillery Bowmore, Loch Indaal, Argyll
Alcohol content Around 53% abv, depending on year
Style Single malt

Two whiskies: sweet sixteen and ready to be kissed. Not by a prince to wake them from slumbering in the wood, but by whisky lovers wishing to know the difference between an expression that matured sixteen years in an ex-bourbon barrel, and one that rested the same amount of years in an ex-sherry cask.

Ex-bourbon barrels are plentiful in Scotland because, by law, bourbon may only mature in virgin oak. Bourbon producers therefore traditionally ship their used barrels to Scotland, where they can be used to mature whisky for another forty to fifty years.

Sherry casks, on the other hand, are now less abundant. Sherry used to be shipped in casks from Spain to Britain, where the contents were bottled in places such as Bristol, Cardiff, London, and Leith, the old harbor serving Edinburgh. The Scots could get their hands on reusable casks for a reasonable price. However, in the 1970s, the Spanish decided to bottle sherry themselves to generate more local work. Sherry casks became scarce and more expensive.

Now, additional ex-bourbon barrels are imported. That is why one of these sixteen-year-old twins might be more easily found in stores than the other one. If you find both, don't hesitate to buy and compare them. Born and bred at the same time, in the same house, they are fraternal twins, not identical ones. **HO**

Tasting notes

A delicious floral scent. Mango and pineapple over peat smoke. The body adds weight and the taste develops into perfumed notes, almost soapy but not obtrusive.

← A portrait of the coastal distillery graces Bowmore's copper Wash Still No. 2.

Bowmore 17-Year-Old

Morrison Bowmore Distillers (Suntory) | www.bowmore.co.uk

Region and country of origin Islay, Scotland
Distillery Bowmore, Loch Indaal, Argyll
Alcohol content 43% abv
Style Single malt

Whereas members of the Bowmore core range are easily obtainable in good liquor stores, some expressions are more likely to be found in the necessarily restricted market of travel retail. They include Surf, Enigma, Mariner 15-Year-Old, and this 17-Year-Old single malt, as well as a cask-strength version of it. Independent bottlings of Bowmore whiskies are also on offer, from suppliers such as Duncan Taylor, Douglas Laing, and Cadenhead.

If it seems that there are enough varieties of Bowmore to take a swim in them, that would be no exaggeration, especially as it is really possible take a dive at the Bowmore distillery, situated on the shore of Loch Indaal in the heart of the town. One of the distillery warehouses was converted into the MacTaggart Leisure Centre for the inhabitants of Bowmore village; opened 29 June, 1990, the center features a swimming pool heated with recycled hot water from the distilling process, giving a new meaning to the expression "water of life."

Within the extensive Bowmore range, the 17-Year-Old single malt in particular has always had a special attraction. It has that rare quality that lifts up a whisky from among its brethren, notwithstanding that the rest of the Bowmore family is very palatable as well. Many consider it their favorite Bowmore expression, possibly because it manages to be so many things in one glass—an Islay whisky, sweet with a touch of fruit yet simultaneously full of smoke, peat, and sea salt, all wonderfully integrated and superbly balanced. At around $160 (£100), it is well worth seeking out. **HO**

Tasting notes

An attractive bronze colored dram with a very aromatic nose. The smooth but firm body develops into a malty taste with a dry, slightly spicy, and somewhat creamy overlay. It finishes ferny, sandy, smoky. Beautifully integrated flavors.

Bowmore 18-Year-Old

Morrison Bowmore Distillers (Suntory) | www.bowmore.co.uk

Region and country of origin Islay, Scotland
Distillery Bowmore, Loch Indaal, Argyll
Alcohol content 43% abv
Style Single malt

Bowmore is more than two centuries old. That is just a drop in a vast whisky sea when compared to the life span of the island whereupon the distillery is built. Islay was formed some sixty million years ago after a long series of volcanic eruptions, and some surface stones date back to half the age of the Earth.

The first traces of human habitation on Islay originated 10,000 years ago when Mesolithic hunters and fisherman settled. Due to the climate change between 2500 and 1500 BC, it became wetter and colder. Moorlands developed and the heavy rainfall caused the peat bogs that provide the fuel now so much in demand in the kiln. Around 400 AD, Christianity came to Islay, brought by Irish monks. In their wake, distilling entered the Scottish Isles.

Eventually, the Macdonalds became lords of the Isles until 1524. Lord Donald Dubh lost a battle, and the Campbells of Cawdor seized power. Two centuries later, Islay passed into the hands of their relative Daniel, who was from the Shawfield branch of the Campbells. Had Donald won the battle, Daniel Campbell might never have built Bowmore, and you would not have been able to taste this 18-Year-Old. It proves there is loss in victory, and victory in loss.

This expression, belonging to the current core range, was launched in January of 2007, so it is comparatively new. That same year, it won Best in Show Whisky at the San Francisco Spirits Competition and also picked up the IWSC Gold Medal Best in Class. At around $120 (£75) a bottle, it is well worth finding out what all the fuss is about. **HO**

Tasting notes

This delicate refined dram does not need water. Dried grass, jasmine tea, and toffee tones open up into praline pecans and soft smokiness. Here, at eighteen years old, Bowmore has come of age, but its younger siblings are very interesting characters, too.

Bowmore
25-Year-Old

Morrison Bowmore Distillers (Suntory)
www.bowmore.co.uk

Region and country of origin Islay, Scotland
Distillery Bowmore, Loch Indaal, Argyll
Alcohol content 43% abv
Style Single malt

At the turn of the eighteenth century, Bowmore distillery was prospering. So was the population of Islay, which grew from 8,000 in 1802 to an impressive 15,000 by 1845. No wonder the distillery did well, supplying so many extra mouths with a fine dram.

However, the Isle of Islay had become vastly overpopulated. The Highland Clearances, the forced eviction of crofters, were copied in the Hebrides and many an Ileach—the name for a person from Islay—was forced off the island. Many traveled to the other side of the Atlantic, taking their distilling knowledge and equipment with them, and it is likely that some of the early employees at Bowmore produced children who grew up to work in a U.S. bourbon distillery.

In 1853 Islay was sold to a wealthy businessman in a transaction that ended the tenure of the Campbells as landowners on the island. Over the next 150 years, the population slowly declined; it is estimated that residents of Islay now number some 3,500 people.

Well, every disadvantage brings with it an advantage. Currently there is more Bowmore to share beyond the island's shores than there was in the mid-1800s. The 25-Year-Old has won awards worldwide, so why not taste a winning dram? **HO**

Tasting notes

With a little added water, vanilla custard and raisin give way to perfumed black tea. A suggestion rum-and-raisin ice cream enjoyed near a seaside hotel's peat fire.

Bowmore 1990
20-Year-Old

Dewar Rattray
www.dewarrattray.com

Region and country of origin Islay, Scotland
Distillery Bowmore, Loch Indaal, Argyll
Alcohol content 50.2% abv
Style Single malt

Ayrshire-based independent bottler Dewar Rattray Ltd. has bottled a number of single casks from Bowmore distillery on Islay. This is not surprising, since company owner Tim Morrison formerly worked with Morrison Bowmore Distillers Ltd. before starting to develop a range of single-cask whiskies under the A. D. Rattray Ltd. Cask Collection banner in 2004.

According to a spokesperson for the firm, "Today the company's principal purpose is to bottle unusual and exclusive casks of Scotch whisky, with each one chosen to reflect the different styles of the six individual whisky regions of Scotland."

Dewar Rattray has bottled Bowmores from 1989, 1990, 1991, and 1996 at varying ages, and from a variety of cask types. First-fill and refill sherry casks have been used, as have first and refill ex-bourbon barrels, giving the opportunity to sample Bowmore in a number of stylistic guises.

This 1990 20-Year-Old expression was distilled in February 1990 and bottled in October 2010, having been matured in a first-fill ex-bourbon cask, No. 272. The output was 204 bottles. It is interesting to compare this bottling with Bowmore's "official" first-fill bourbon cask offering, Tempest. **GS**

Tasting notes

Soft smokiness on the nose, with a hint of freshly squeezed orange. Smooth and silky in the mouth, with sweetness provided by the flavor of vanilla pods.

Bowmore 1968 50th Anniversary Bottle

Morrison Bowmore Distillers (Suntory)
www.bowmore.co.uk

Region and country of origin Islay, Scotland
Distillery Bowmore, Loch Indaal, Argyll
Alcohol content 45.5% abv
Style Single malt

This limited edition of 1,860 bottles was produced to celebrate the fiftieth anniversary of the Stanley P. Morrison Co., which owned Bowmore before Suntory took over. The casks were selected by Brian Morrison, son of Stanley, for their "maturity and sweetness."

This whisky, distilled on November 19, 1968, was some of the last Bowmore distilled by James McColl, who retired as Bowmore distillery manager in 1968 after more than thirty years. The spirit was matured in North American oak, likely ex-bourbon casks, for thirty-two years. Each bottle is hand numbered and bears the signature of Brian Morrison. According to Iain McCallum, master of malts at Morrison Bowmore Distillers, the casks were "hand selected by the legendary Brian Morrison. Complex, vibrant, and balanced. This commemoratory dram retains the traditional Bowmore fruitiness and the might of Islay."

Many Islay malts tend to be fruity at younger ages, but lose their vibrant fruity notes as they mature in the wood. Interestingly, Bowmore has the unique ability to retain these bright, often tropical fruit notes into its twenties and thirties. The other unique quality found in older Bowmores, usually over thirty years of age, is a musty quality, akin to an unattended gym locker. **WM**

Tasting notes

Incredibly fruity with apricot, tangerine, and tropical fruits—a fruit salad with a Bowmore pungency. Sweet fruit and dry smoke go on and on as the finish lingers.

Bowmore Darkest 15-Year-Old

Morrison Bowmore Distillers (Suntory)
www.bowmore.co.uk

Region and country of origin Islay, Scotland
Distillery Bowmore, Loch Indaal, Argyll
Alcohol content 43% abv
Style Single malt

Bowmore is a favorite of aficionados and collectors. The late Dutch liquor specialist Harry Verhaar left an impressive collection of Bowmore paraphernalia to his son Marcel, who continues to take care of his father's legacy in a beautiful shop near Utrecht in the center of the Netherlands. Another collector, Dutchman Hans Sommer, sold his collection to the distillery in 2004. It consists of more than 200 different expressions, one of them being the famous Black Bowmore bottlings (1993, 1994, and 1995).

At the end of 2007, this cult edition was rereleased in a very limited amount, a forty-three-year-old from 1964. Bowmore has always had an impressive range of expressions but decided in 2006 to concentrate on fewer versions.

The current output consists of two different series for regular retail and travel retail. The lineup of the core range is Legend, the 12-Year-Old, the Darkest 15-Year-Old, the 18-Year-Old, and the 25-Year-Old. Most Bowmore whisky matures in ex-bourbon casks, but this 15-Year-Old has had an extra finish in ex-oloroso sherry casks, giving it a beautiful dark hue and the name "Darkest." This different and enjoyable Bowmore has more than a touch of sherry. **HO**

Tasting notes

Spicy sandalwood and cedar cigar box open up to dried tobacco leaf, dark chocolate, and a splash of rich raisin. Give this one time to unfold.

Bowmore Legend

Morrison Bowmore Distillers (Suntory)
www.bowmore.co.uk

Region and country of origin Islay, Scotland
Distillery Bowmore, Loch Indaal, Argyll
Alcohol content 40% abv
Style Single malt

The village of Bowmore on Islay was founded in 1768, although a pier already existed in 1750. The man who constructed it was Daniel Campbell of Shawfield, a visionary with a mission. Some farming methods introduced by the Shawfield branch of the Campbells are still used today. Since those early days, the clan has done much to improve the living conditions on Islay.

Bowmore village was designed on a rectangular grid, with its main street leading up to the famous round church, built without any corners to prevent the devil from hiding in them. A local legend tells that Satan did attempt to sneak in, but to no avail. Instead, he was chased by Bowmore parishioners into the streets, from where he ran inside the distillery, never to be found. However, it was whispered that he made his escape in a cask that was shipped to the mainland shortly thereafter.

Hopping from legend to fact, it may be said with certainty that the Bowmore distillery is the oldest on Islay. Eleven years after Bowmore village was founded, the distillery was started in 1779 by John Simpson, who would own it for nearly sixty years. To turn folklore into a tangible experience, you should pour some Bowmore Legend and raise a toast to him. **HO**

Tasting notes

Tobacco, old leather, and white chocolate notes combine with a hint of wet tea leaf. Creamy on the palate, it has a sweet, smoky, and slightly sandy finish.

Bowmore Tempest Small Batch Release 1

Morrison Bowmore Distillers (Suntory)
www.bowmore.co.uk

Region and country of origin Islay, Scotland
Distillery Bowmore, Loch Indaal, Argyll
Alcohol content 55.3% abv
Style Single malt

Back in the day, older Bowmores had a curious perfumey and floral nose to them, apparently from a fault in the distillation process, but attractive nevertheless. The range included a stunning seventeen-year-old, and the distillery had an awesome reputation for older whiskies. However, the whiskies were rebranded and the seventeen-year-old ended up in travel retail, but it wasn't the same; some of its qualities seemed to fade. Other makers on Islay upped their games, and in comparison, Bowmore started to look a trifle bland. Then the Tempest came out—and, boy, is the distillery back on form!

Tempest is an agitated, vibrant, heavy-hitting storm of a whisky bottled at cask strength. It is released in batches—check what you're buying because at the time of writing they were up to batch three, and the third one is a very different beast. This release and the one that followed it are note-perfect renditions of what a peated Islay whisky should be, with the added attractiveness of some distinctive distillery flavors. While batch two might be sweeter and sharper, batch one has the element of surprise, its strength and peatiness showing it can match the anything produced by the island's big boys. **DR**

Tasting notes

The nose is a delicious invitation to dive in, with smoke, oily citrus, and some floral notes. A busy palate, with salt and pepper, rich citrus, and an abundance of peat.

The seagulls of Loch Indaal dominate a plaque fixed to a Bowmore distillery ➡

Bowmore Tempest Small Batch Release 3

Morrison Bowmore Distillers (Suntory) | www.bowmore.co.uk

Region and country of origin Islay, Scotland
Distillery Bowmore, Loch Indaal, Argyll
Alcohol content Around 53% abv, depending on year
Style Single malt

Both of my favorite whisky places are on Islay. One is by the sea at Laphroaig, looking out at a perfect, rough and wild, rocky view that has remained unchanged for thousands of years. The other is on the seawall at Bowmore, tasting the sea salt in the air and looking across Loch Indaal toward a Bruichladdich lit by the sun—it does happen.

Many is the time that I have been taken down to the warehouse at Bowmore—where you can taste the sea salt in the air—to be treated to a sample of ten- or eleven-year-old Bowmore straight from the cask. Sometimes the samples have been salty, oily, peaty, and intense—a long way from what one normally expects from Bowmore.

This third batch of Bowmore Tempest, bottled at cask strength, is in that category. You need to be prepared for what you're getting, because this is nothing like the sweet, fruity, and lightly peated 12-Year-Old. It is a growling pit-bull terrier of a malt that has to be approached with great caution. Make friends with it, though, and you've got a friend for life.

The Tempest series was a deliberate attempt to change the popular misconception that Bowmore is a peat-lite whisky. This batch is possibly the last of the Tempest series because, in the past, Morrison Bowmore Distillers has tended to do special projects in batches of three. However, the distillery has strongly hinted that more cask-strength, challenging, and exciting expressions similar to the Tempest trio are in the offing. On the strength of this whisky, that is a mouthwatering prospect. **DR**

Tasting notes

There is some peat on the nose, but no real hint of what is to come. On the palate, it is oily, salty, savory, sharp, peaty, and mouth-coating. A tasty, tangy, peat feast. The Bowmore lemon and fruit are there, but only as the backing musicians supporting a rampant frontline.

Braes of Glenlivet 1975 Connoisseurs Choice

Gordon & MacPhail | www.gordonandmacphail.com

Region and country of origin Speyside, Scotland
Distillery Braeval, Chapeltown, Banffshire
Alcohol content 43% abv
Style Single malt

As a relative newcomer to the industry, Braes of Glenlivet was established in 1973 as a workhorse to produce single malt for the Chivas blends. A change of name in 1995 made it the Braeval distillery (this was done to avoid confusion with Glenlivet distillery). Braeval was upgraded in 1997 to make it possible to run the entire distillery with just one person—an impressive prospect, although perhaps one that lacks the team spirit of "twelve good men and true."

Braeval was mothballed in 2002, and production restarted in 2008. As the whisky from Braeval has never been released as an official bottling, it is something of a rarity in itself, with the only route to trying this as a single malt being through the very few independent bottles released. There are collectors and investors who won't buy anything other than distilleries' own releases, but independent bottlers should not be ignored—without them, some wonderful bottles and releases from long-lost distilleries would never have been made available.

Whereas the rarity of the whisky would be expected to result in sky-high prices, this is not the case for Braeval. As a collectible or an investment-grade whisky, it doesn't hit the mark—which is no bad thing, as its relatively low price provides some fantastic drams. The bottle in question is from the iconic Connoisseurs Choice range by Gordon & MacPhail and is a bottling from 1975. This can still be purchased from specialist retailers for around $90 to $110 (£60 to £70), which seems rather a bargain for a thirty-something-year-old whisky. **AS**

Tasting notes

Immediately light, almost refreshing. Cereal notes, with a mildly tannic floral element. Over time, sweeter summer fruits develop to accompany oaky undertones. Slightly resinous, this balances extremely well on the palate. Too easy to drink way too much of.

Brora 22-Year-Old Rare Malts Selection 1972

Diageo | www.diageo.com

Region and country of origin Highlands, Scotland
Distillery Brora, Clynelish, Sutherland
Alcohol content 58.7% abv
Style Single malt

When you combine Brora and the Rare Malts Selection (RMS) bottles, you really do have something very special. RMS bottles are among the most sought-after collectibles ever released. They were started in 1995 by United Distillers and Vintners Ltd., the owners at the time (now Diageo), and discontinued in 2005. There were 111 different bottles released (if you include all the different alcohol percent variants), covering a portfolio of releases from thirty-six distilleries, many of which have long fallen silent.

A phenomenon known as "Rare Malts Madness" is sweeping the collectors and investors market, with virtually every RMS release experiencing steep increases in value over the past few years. Some bottles have increased tenfold. The 22-Year-Old 1972 is one of them. Most of these bottles were released at around $90 to $110 (£60 to £70) and represented incredible value, given that they contained some of the rarest whisky in Diageo's warehouses.

The RMS bottles don't just represent a potentially sound investment, they are also among the best drams money can, or rather could, buy. The Brora 22-Year-Old is very definitely one of those bottles. It's an all-time great. **AS**

Tasting notes

Peat smoke and sea air, sharp and pure. Citrus aromas percolate through the cacophony of smoky brine. A real sour heat with salt and chile attacking the palate.

Brora 24-Year-Old

Ian Macleod Distillers | www.ianmacleod.com

Region and country of origin Highlands, Scotland
Distillery Brora, Clynelish, Sutherland
Alcohol content 46% abv
Style Single malt

Standing on the outskirts of the east Sutherland port and holiday resort of Brora, northeast of Inverness, Brora was founded as Clynelish distillery in 1819. Ownership passed through several hands before John Walker & Sons Ltd. bought into Clynelish Distillery Co. Ltd. in 1916. Walker's became part of the Distillers Company Ltd. (DCL) in 1925, and within five years, DCL owned the entire share capital of Clynelish.

During 1967, a new distillery was constructed and the Clynelish name was transferred. The old distillery was briefly silent before being rechristened Brora, and it operated until 1983. The traditional, stone-built distillery is externally intact, and its two stills remain.

During the 1970s, DCL was concerned about a shortage of Islay-style malts for blending, so Brora was tasked to produce spirit that could replicate the role of Islays in the company's blends. Heavy peating at the distillery dates principally from the period 1969 to 1973, though later batches were also produced.

This twenty-four-year-old example of Brora appears in its Chieftain's Range of limited-edition, rare single malts. It was distilled in December 1981, matured in a cream sherry butt (No. 1522), and bottled in August 2006, when 750 bottles were released. **GS**

Tasting notes

Delicate brine and peat smoke on the nose, sherry and freshly sliced Madeira cake. Waxy and peppery in the mouth, with peat, dried fruit, honey, and toffee.

Brora
30-Year-Old 2010

Diageo | www.diageo.com

Region and country of origin Highlands, Scotland
Distillery Brora, Clynelish, Sutherland
Alcohol content 54.3% abv
Style Single malt

The Brora distillery, founded in 1819 as a philanthropic initiative by the first Duke of Sutherland in order to provide work on his estate, was closed in May of 1968 but reopened the following year, surviving until 1983, when it became a victim of a dramatic round of closures by Distillers Co. Ltd. No fewer than eleven of the organization's forty-five malt-whisky-making facilities fell silent; ten more followed two years later.

Although it has stood silent for almost three decades, the stone-built distillery of Brora, with its distinctive malt kiln pagoda, can still be seen. In addition, a number of its warehouses are still used for the maturation of spirit, and visitors to the neighboring Clynelish distillery can participate in a "Taste of Brora" tour. This extended, private trip around the site embraces both distilleries and includes the opportunity to sample both the Brora 30-Year-Old Special Release 2009 and the 2010 version, which makes it well worth a visit.

Brora is one of the most popular closed distilleries to feature in what is now Diageo's annual Special Release program. The first bottling appeared in 2002, and the 2011 expression—at thirty-two years of age— was the tenth to be bottled in this series. **GS**

Tasting notes

Mellow on the nose, with prunes and a whiff of graphite. Peat, pineapple, and fudgy malt mesh beautifully on the rounded, confident palate. The finish is lengthy.

Brora
32-Year-Old

Diageo | www.diageo.com

Region and country of origin Highlands, Scotland
Distillery Brora, Clynelish, Sutherland
Alcohol content 54.7% abv
Style Single malt

Brora, which occupied the same site as Clynelish distillery in Clynelish village, enjoys iconic status among fans. That reputation has been boosted by the fact that the distillery is closed and Diageo has released excellent bottlings from it before. So when this was released in stellar company by Diageo as part of its 2011 Limited Edition program, it was one of the main attractions. Several people were disappointed. It's possible that their expectations were far too high, combined with the fact that the two or three thirty-year-old releases were so incredibly good.

The trouble with having such an impressive back catalogue of work like this is that expectations are *always* too high, and you end up in that "damned if you do, damned if you don't" situation where you either do what's expected and people get indifferent to you, or you do something radically different and people are appalled.

The 32-Year-Old is actually an all but classic version of the whisky and a worthy addition to the range. Bottlings aren't cheap but still tend to sell out fast, so if you see one—and if you have the cash— don't hesitate. Not the best-ever Brora, but still streets ahead of 90 percent of the competition. **DR**

Tasting notes

Gentle smokiness, dry woodiness, barley on the nose, a soft peated carpet on the palate, with oaky tannins and clean barley. If it has a fault, it is that it's a tad flat.

Brora Old & Rare Platinum Selection

Douglas Laing & Co.
www.douglaslaing.com

Region and country of origin Highlands, Scotland
Distillery Brora, Clynelish, Sutherland
Alcohol content 58.1% abv
Style Single malt

Brora distillery was originally named Clynelish, and was founded in 1819 by the Marquis of Stafford, later the first Duke of Sutherland, to provide an outlet for barley grown by the tenants on his estate, theoretically removing the temptation for them to sell their crops to the many illegal distillers in the area.

Clynelish ultimately came into the possession of the Distillers Co. Ltd. (DCL), who built a new, larger distillery next to the original in 1967. This was given the Clynelish name, and the old plant was rechristened Brora after the nearby east coast port town, which boasted one of the earliest coal mines in Scotland and provided fuel for the distillery.

This expression was distilled in 1981, two years before the Brora distillery closed down, and was matured in a sherry cask before being bottled at twenty-eight years of age. It is presented in Glasgow-based independent bottler Douglas Laing & Co.'s Old & Rare Platinum series and the output was just 120 bottles. The firm considers Port Ellen to be its best-selling single malt from a closed distillery, but Brora is not far behind in terms of popularity. The most highly prized Broras are the smokiest, and the fashion for peaty whiskies shows no sign of abating. **GS**

Tasting notes

Initial nose is quite dry, green, and grassy. With time, there is a touch of gunpowder, tea, and damp soil. Herbal on the palate; the finish is long and peppery.

Bruichladdich 10-Year-Old

Bruichladdich Distillery Co.
www.bruichladdich.com

Region and country of origin Islay, Scotland
Distillery Bruichladdich, Bruichladdich, Argyll
Alcohol content 46% abv
Style Single malt

Bruichladdich distillery, closed in 1994, was bought in 2000 by private investors. Right from the outset, they got on with producing a raft of core expressions, the standard one being this ten-year-old single malt (as it had been under the previous regime). The packaging and philosophy were different, but the whisky stocks had all been made by the previous owners.

The intention with the 10-Year-Old was to make it the benchmark whisky of the range, emulating the style of the old Bruichladdich. Production director Jim McEwan was careful to select casks that gave the spirit the chance to speak for itself—it was citrus zesty, subtly floral, and youthful, with ozone freshness and sweet succulence: an *aperitif cuvée*. It was drawn from both bourbon casks (40 percent) and sherry casks (60 percent) and was complex and multidimensional.

A gap in stock between 1994 and 2001 meant that the 10-Year-Old could not continue beyond 2004; a two-year extension probably contained older whisky. Other ten-year-old expressions became possible in 2008, but this original 10-Year-Old was eventually phased out, to be replaced by the 12-year-old. All this changed in September 2011 when the first "new regime" ten-year-old came on stream. **RL**

Tasting notes

Young and fresh on the nose, with honeysuckle, apple, pear, and green grape. On the palate, fudge, toasted barley, and honey, with lots of citrus. Subtle and refined.

← The first Duke of Sutherland (1758–1833), founder of Clynelish (later Brora) distillery.

Bruichladdich 12-Year-Old Second Edition

Bruichladdich Distillery Co. | www.bruichladdich.com

Region and country of origin Islay, Scotland
Distillery Bruichladdich, Bruichladdich, Argyll
Alcohol content 46% abv
Style Single malt

This 12-Year-Old Second Edition explicitly replaced the Bruichladdich 10-Year-Old as the distillery's "aperitif dram," although that might change as stocks of a new ten-year-old (made after 2011) become plentiful. This 12-Year-Old is a "second edition" because it replaces an earlier twelve-year-old that combined bourbon and sherry-matured malt.

Described as "traditional," the 12-Year-Old marks a "back to basics" approach for Bruichladdich—which, of course, is quite appropriate for a member of the core range. "Traditional" in this context refers only to recent traditions, say from the 1960s, suggesting maturation in bourbon wood and an unpeated style.

It is quite refreshing, in among the plethora of Bruichladdich experiments and wood expressions, to find a product that allows the Bruichladdich style to speak for itself. Bruichladdich, with its generously tall stills and its unhurried distillation regime (only single malts are made), tends to produce crisp and fruity malt that, with nothing to hide or cover up, lends itself to maturation in bourbon barrels. Mostly refill bourbon casks were used, but these were exposed to first-fill bourbon wood to give it "a good boost." The 12-Year-Old has the characteristics of Bruichladdich in a presentation that is delightfully honest and simple.

This 12-Year-Old is a good introduction both to the Bruichladdich range and Islay whiskies in general, especially for anyone who thinks they are all highly peated. The whisky is described as a limited production, rather than limited edition, meaning that it will be produced until stocks run out. **RL**

Tasting notes

On the nose, pear, apple, passion fruit, and gooseberry; bourbon notes, sweet vanilla, gorse, and primrose, with barley sugar and butterscotch sweetness. On the palate, beautiful, syrupy, viscous textures; sweet malt, a kiss of oak, succulent fruits, and perfumed flowers.

Bruichladdich 16-Year-Old Bourbon Cask Aged

Bruichladdich Distillery Co. | www.bruichladdich.com

Region and country of origin Islay, Scotland
Distillery Bruichladdich, Bruichladdich, Argyll
Alcohol content 46% abv
Style Single malt

This is the basic whisky of the "Sixteens" series, the blank canvas to which the finishes of the others, including some called First Growths, were applied. The benchmark against which those can be compared, this natural maturation in 100 percent American white oak bourbon casks holds its ground.

The bottle notes make much of the "symbiotic cycle" between the Scotch whisky industry and the bourbon makers of the United States: "We gave them distilling, so they can sell us cheap casks." The date of release was designed to coincide with the seventy-fifth anniversary of the end of Prohibition in America (December 5, 2008). Since the passing of a law stipulating that bourbon makers can only use fresh oak, and as sherry casks become rarer (they can easily cost ten times as much as bourbon casks), the situation has come about that 95 percent of Scotch whisky is bourbon-matured. White oak (*Quercus alba*), with its tighter, less porous, and easily machine-workable grain and delicious vanilla flavors, has become popular even among sherry makers. Different from European oak, it is certainly not inferior for some whiskies—including Bruichladdich.

This was a limited-release whisky, intended to last two years, depending on sales. It replaced the previous fifteen-year-old. Even with this apparently straightforward release, with no fancy wine finishes, the company could not resist enhancing it in superior first-fill Buffalo Trace bourbon casks "to take it to another level." This 16-Year-Old has been described as "one of the best Bruichladdichs ever." **RL**

Tasting notes

Sweet but crisp barley and lots of fresh fruit on the nose: guava, melon, grape, and peach, then some vanilla and warm spice. On the palate, mellow oakiness encapsulates butterscotch, nougat, honey, vanilla fudge, apple, and pear with peppery, gingery spice.

Bruichladdich 18-Year-Old Second Edition

Bruichladdich Distillery Co. | www.bruichladdich.com

Region and country of origin Islay, Scotland
Distillery Bruichladdich, Bruichladdich, Argyll
Alcohol content 46% abv
Style Single malt

Where does Bruichladdich get such amazing casks? The previous, first-edition bottling of the 18-Year-Old was finished in casks from Willi Opitz used for sweet wine (Trockenbeerenauslese, meaning "selected harvest of dried berries"); this second edition continues the theme by using casks previously filled with sweet Jurançon from the Clos Uroulat vineyard in the southwest of France.

Jurançon is a decadently rich wine made from the Petit Manseng grape. Warm sea breezes cause "noble" mold to form on the grapes, resulting in intensely sweet wines. Jurançon wine from this vineyard was used in the baptism of Henri IV of France in 1553. The first Bourbon king, he was raised as a Calvinist by his mother despite having been baptized a Catholic. The Petit Manseng grape was a favorite of French novelist, poet, and lady of scandal Colette, who described it thus: "I was a girl when I met this Prince; aroused, imperious, treacherous, as all great seducers are." Using this quotation, producers of Jurançon began to market their wines with the slogan "Manseng means Jurançon, means sex."

Production director Jim McEwan says that the Jurançon cask "added a sophistication and style to the shy, sensitive side of this island beauty." Certainly, the relatively unpeated style of the spirit, carefully crafted in the traditional fashion, the eighteen years in ex-bourbon wood, and the sweet white wine finish are strands that combine to make a deliciously complex lover's knot of a whisky. McEwan calls it "voluptuous, absolutely flawless, and unbelievable." **RL**

Tasting notes

Lots of fresh fruit on the nose: lemon, passion fruit, papaya, ripe melon, perfumed pear, and pineapple; biscuit, mellow oak, honey, and grass. On the palate there's pineapple, citrus, rum and raisin fudge, honey, tea, and some nuttiness—almond and macadamia.

Bruichladdich 20-Year-Old Third Edition

Bruichladdich Distillery Co. | www.bruichladdich.com

Region and country of origin Islay, Scotland
Distillery Bruichladdich, Bruichladdich, Argyll
Alcohol content 46% abv
Style Single malt

When Mark Reynier's team from bottlers Murray McDavid acquired Bruichladdich distillery in 2001, they gained enough stock to produce a handful of core malts and a few specials. The new production director Jim McEwan was given the job of creating these various bottlings from the casks in the warehouses. The first core expressions included a ten-year-old, a fifteen-year-old, and a twenty-year-old.

The 20-Year-Old was released in September 2001 and won the Best Whisky in the World award. It sold out very quickly. In 2004, the second-edition twenty-year-old was released; this was the infamous "Flirtation," a whisky tinged with pink, thanks to being finished in mourvèdre red wine casks; this also won awards and quickly sold out.

This Bruichladdich 20-Year-Old, the third edition, is from casks laid down in 1985; it has spent nearly all its life in ex-bourbon wood. The finish is malmsey European oak casks from Madeira. Bruichladdich prefers the term ACE-ing to finishing (ACE stands for "additional cask evolution"). The distillery uses this technique a lot, partly because of McEwan's natural tendency to experiment (he is an alchemist of single malts), but also because much of the stock they acquired had been filled into somewhat tired casks.

The use of malmsey Madeira hogsheads in this case has led to this third edition of the twenty-year-old bloodline being given the nickname "Islands," celebrating what Bruichladdich chose to call the "perfect fusion of two Atlantic islands, one wild and windswept, the other soft and warm." **RL**

Tasting notes

Sweet malt and zesty green fruits on the nose, then rich, dark raisin and cherry; finally nutty toffee, vanilla, pepper, and nutmeg. The short time in Madeira wood has bestowed rich intensity: cherry, date, plum, toasted nut, treacle toffee, and slightly burnt fruit cake.

Bruichladdich 21-Year-Old

Bruichladdich Distillery Co. | www.bruichladdich.com

Region and country of origin Islay, Scotland
Distillery Bruichladdich, Bruichladdich, Argyll
Alcohol content 46% abv
Style Single malt

This expression of Bruichladdich spent its entire twenty-one years in sherry butts. Such casks are relatively rare because Spain put a stop to exporting sherry in casks, and they are expensive— approximately ten times the price of a bourbon barrel. This explains why nearly all Scotch whisky is matured in bourbon wood these days. Most distilleries have a few sherry casks in the warehouse, but it is very unusual to see bottlings like this. Mostly the casks would be used to give color and depth to bourbon-matured whisky in a vatting for a given age release.

Fashions are changing, and fewer people still like the big sherry flavors, but those who do will find this dram to be right up their street. Production director Jim McEwan describes it as "delicate and easily bruised; don't add water" and suggests that it is the right kind of whisky for a nightcap. It could also be fairly described as a reflective whisky or a digestif. At moments like this, big, sherry whiskies come into their own. They are ideal for aiding digestion and conversation after a meal, and can accompany coffee and chocolate with ease. The big, lip-smacking flavors also lend themselves to quieter moments of pleasant self-indulgence. Both in age and in style, this is a backward-looking dram, in the best possible way— perfect for evoking memories and emotions.

This 21-Year-Old expression filled the gap left by the disappearance of the three editions of the Bruichladdich 20-Year-Old. The whisky has the same pedigree and cask provenance as the Blacker Still, though with one more year in the cask. **RL**

Tasting notes

Typical oloroso notes on the nose: hazelnut, raisin, prune, butterscotch, date, and fig; port or marsala. Decadent and rich on the palate, raisiny sweet, dark chocolate, cinnamon, orange, and Brazil nut. A fine marriage of Spain and Islay.

Four copper pot stills are in operation at Bruichladdich distillery. →

Bruichladdich 40-Year-Old

Bruichladdich Distillery Co. | www.bruichladdich.com

Region and country of origin Islay, Scotland
Distillery Bruichladdich, Bruichladdich, Argyll
Alcohol content 43.1% abv
Style Single malt

Tasting notes

Sensuous fragrances of butterscotch, maple syrup, melon, flowers, candied almond, vanilla, and cinnamon; time brings out mandarin and zesty sherbet. Mellow and magical on the palate with toasted oak, fudge, lime, and grapefruit. A lingering, lip-smacking finish.

When the team at bottler Murray McDavid acquired Bruichladdich distillery in 2001, Jim McEwan (distillery manager at Bowmore) was asked to join them as production director. Almost certainly, one of the first things Jim did was to look around the warehouses and see what stock he had inherited, and this may well have been the sexiest package in the place.

Imagine McEwan, an emotional man, coming face-to-face, in some dark corner of a dunnage warehouse, with whisky casked in October 1964. He had started as an apprentice cooper at Bowmore distillery in August of 1963. He probably stood alone, revolving thoughts and memories of all the years that had passed since. Old whisky has the power to evoke emotions; it makes us think back over years, reliving the feelings that accompanied moments in our lives. This is what might inspire people to buy old whiskies, although the cost of the privilege can be high.

Only 500 bottles of the Bruichladdich 40-Year-Old were made available worldwide (100 of them to the United Kingdom). There must have been at least two casks. We know that it came from ex-bourbon wood, and it seems to be the gentle caress of American oak that best stands the test of time. Of the 500 bottles, some have undoubtedly been consumed, hopefully with due ceremony and reverence. Many owners, one suspects, will be afraid to open it, waiting for the right moment. In the movie *Morning Glory*, Mike Pomeroy, played by Harrison Ford, takes a shot of Bruichladdich 40-Year-Old with the words, "I only drink it on special occasions." Well, you would hope so. **RL**

Bruichladdich 1998 Sherry Edition Manzanilla

Bruichladdich Distillery Co. | www.bruichladdich.com

Region and country of origin Islay, Scotland
Distillery Bruichladdich, Bruichladdich, Argyll
Alcohol content 46% abv
Style Single malt

Bruichladdich was actually closed from the end of 1994 until 2001, but for about six weeks in the summer of 1998, it was briefly put back into action by the team at Isle of Jura distillery in order to check that the equipment was in working order. Some of that short run was put into various sherry casks. Subsequently, the new Bruichladdich team created a very limited edition to compare and contrast a pair of single malts, some from oloroso casks and some from manzanilla.

Manzanilla is a Spanish dry white sherry, similar to fino, made at Sanlúcar de Barrameda, where the Guadalquivir river runs into the Atlantic. The wine is very popular further upriver in Seville; here, especially during the fantastic April Fair (Feria), it is the drink of choice for late-night revelers. It is definitely saltier than fino sherry, perhaps because of Sanlúcar's sea air. *Manzanilla* means "little apple," as well as "chamomile": the latter flavor is found in the wine.

Between the Atlantic influence on the maturing spirit at Bruichladdich and the vestigial briny notes from the manzanilla cask, the character of this whisky should be fresh and tangy; indeed, Bruichladdich's notes suggest it be drunk as an aperitif.

The bottle carries a specially commissioned image of a Spanish bull, a "tribute to Picasso" by Brian Grimwood; the oloroso carries a picador. Both are suggestive of the bull ring. The two whiskies can stand independently, of course, but it is interesting to compare "the two wonderful extremes of sherry wood influence." The oloroso, as expected is slightly sweeter; the manzanilla is fresher and saltier. **RL**

Tasting notes

Quite a lot of sherry on the nose, also melon, apricot, apple, and orange marmalade. With walnut, marzipan, brandy snap, and vanilla, it all hangs together well. Butterscotch, honey, and crème brûlée on the palate; juicy fruits and a pleasant chamomile freshness.

Bruichladdich 3D The Peat Proposal

Bruichladdich Distillery Co.
www.bruichladdich.com

Region and country of origin Islay, Scotland
Distillery Bruichladdich, Bruichladdich, Argyll
Alcohol content 46% abv
Style Single malt

Now discontinued, this was the first peated whisky produced at Bruichladdich after its 2001 takeover. A limited run of 12,000 bottles, it was proclaimed as containing three different peating levels, from three separate warehouses, and from three successive eras—hence the 3D of its name.

The Peat Proposal expression contained some of Bruichladdich's new 2001 Port Charlotte at 40 parts per million (ppm) phenolic, some 1989 (old regime) Bruichladdich at less than 5 ppm, and some rather unusual malt distilled in 1998 when the distillery was effectively closed but some whisky was made to test its equipment. The malted barley for that run was the same as Bowmore at 25 ppm. That accounts for the different peating levels and the different ages; effects of the warehousing are hard to determine. Three different woods—sherry butts, refill, and first-fill bourbon casks—added further complexity.

The Peat Proposal was highly popular and quickly sold out. It was followed by 3D Moine Mhor (meaning "The Big Peat") and 3D3 (Norrie Campbell). The latter whisky was named for the last man to cut peat by hand for the distilleries, acknowledged to be one of the great characters of Islay in the 1960s and 1970s. **RL**

Tasting notes

Peat smoke wrestles with soft-scented lemon blossom and carnations; on the palate, vanilla, pear, honeyed gingerbread, demerara sugar, and cinnamon.

Bruichladdich Black Art Second Edition

Bruichladdich Distillery Co.
www.bruichladdich.com

Region and country of origin Islay, Scotland
Distillery Bruichladdich, Bruichladdich, Argyll
Alcohol content 49.7% abv
Style Single malt

The provenance of Jim McEwan's Black Art is a secret; unusually, detailed information about the cask history is missing. Apparently, the whisky spent most of its time in ex-bourbon casks before being introduced to "assorted wine casks." Given the color of the whisky, which is definitely on the pink side, the casks previously must have contained red wine. But it seems that the mischievous Jim has had some fun here and he won't even tell colleagues at Bruichladdich what the recipe is. The "Black Art" name is also playful—certain God-fearing inhabitants of Islay once claimed that distillers were practicing black arts and making potions capable of altering people's minds.

The first edition, nineteen years old at 51.7 percent abv, is no longer available. It has gained the patina of nostalgia and rarity and most people imagine it was even better than this twenty-one-year-old second edition. Bruichladdich, describing the Black Art as bewitching, sensuous, and decadent, links it to a dark, dreamy quotation from Edgar Allan Poe's gothic poem "The Raven"—a suitable accompaniment for what is fast becoming a cult (if not occult) whisky. A third edition, not yet released at the time of writing, waits to emerge from under the raven's wings. **RL**

Tasting notes

Malt, brown sugar, and oaky vanilla are balanced by fruity wine aromas, such as crème de cassis and balsamic strawberry. Hints of honey, spice, and hay.

Bruichladdich Blacker Still 1986

Bruichladdich Distillery Co.
www.bruichladdich.com

Region and country of origin Islay, Scotland
Distillery Bruichladdich, Bruichladdich, Argyll
Alcohol content 50.7% abv
Style Single malt

After Bruichladdich was reopened in 2001, it soon became clear that a proportion of the stock resting in the traditional, lochside warehouses had been filled into tired wood. Managing director Mark Rainier's connections to the wine trade were employed, and much of this stock was reracked into a wide variety of wine barrels. The bewildering array of extramatured bottlings that hit the shelves afterward found favor with some, but questions over consistency of quality, and the team's self-promotion, polarized opinion.

Throughout the turbulent period that was spent reestablishing Bruichladdich, the team's commitment to Islay, to its people, and to producing top-quality spirit should never have been in doubt. It is certain that the last ten years have seen some outstanding whiskies from Bruichladdich, and this first release, in what was to become a small series of such bottlings, is one notable example. Named after an old distillers' myth that "the blacker the still, the better the whisky," this 1986 vintage saw a departure from the excellent bourbon-cask-matured bottlings such as the original seventeen- and twenty-year-olds. The exclusive use of rich, oloroso sherry casks for maturation certainly had a profound impact on the spirit. **StuR**

Tasting notes

On the nose, cold coffee, prune, kirsch, tangerine, and dark chocolate. Hints of rubber, clove, and faint licorice on the palate. The finish is long on nutmeg and brine.

Bruichladdich Golder Still 1984

Bruichladdich Distillery Co.
www.bruichladdich.com

Region and country of origin Islay, Scotland
Distillery Bruichladdich, Bruichladdich, Argyll
Alcohol content 51% abv
Style Single malt

Independent distilleries, free of both the constraints and securities of multinational corporations, are now the exception rather than the rule in Scotland. Bruichladdich represents just such a rarity, and while the difficulties associated with this independence are clear, those owning and running this small distillery on the Rhinns of Islay would not have it any other way.

The distillery blends traditional methods and equipment, much of it dating back to the late 1800s, with a fierce sense of individuality and a desire to be progressive. A wide variety of distillates—including a range of peating levels, Islay-grown barley, and quadruple-distilled spirit—have been produced from the two pairs of stills over the last decade. Visitors find the sheer sense of place and the importance of the distillery to the local community to be undeniable. The stills turn out a spirit that, at its best, is supremely evocative of where it is produced; the coastal breeze almost seems captured within the glass.

The Golder Still 1984 bottling, the most recent in this series, is a vatting from a batch of unusual squat bourbon hogsheads. These casks provide a greater wood-to-spirit ratio, and so emphasize the classic characteristics associated with American oak. **StuR**

Tasting notes

Complex, half-fruity, half-oaky, starting on notes of heady vanilla, kumquat, and beeswax. The oak comes to the fore in time, with eucalyptus and pine resin.

Bruichladdich Laddie Classic

Bruichladdich Distillery Co. | www.bruichladdich.com

Region and country of origin Islay, Scotland
Distillery Bruichladdich, Bruichladdich, Argyll
Alcohol content 46% abv
Style Single malt

Just as many of us approach wine lists with trepidation in case our pronunciation of French or Italian classics is not up to scratch, so whisky novices are sometimes understandably nervous about Gaelic, or Gaelic-derived, distillery names. After all, Gaelic is acknowledged as being one of the most difficult European languages to write and speak. So it has come to pass that Bunnahabhain distillery on Islay, where Gaelic is still spoken, is frequently known as "Bunny," while on the west side of the island, Bruichladdich has long been known as "Laddie."

In 2009 the Laddie abbreviation was formally acknowledged in the name on a new bottling, the Laddie Classic, which carries no age statement. As the distillery's supremo Mark Reynier explains, "While we are famous, some say infamous, for pushing the boundaries of distilling, coopering, and maturation, we know a classic spirit when we make one. This dram has been designed by [production director] Jim McEwan to showcase the classic, floral, and elegant Bruichladdich style; matured purely in American oak bourbon. An Audrey Hepburn rather than a Marilyn Monroe, a natural elegance beyond fad and fashion—truly a classic Bruichladdich!"

Mark Reynier's tongue-in-cheek reference to his distillery's infamy derives from the team's passion for innovation and for releasing a somewhat bewildering array of expressions each year. The distillery is also credited with producing the "world's strongest whisky," a quadruple-distilled dram by the name of X4, although this is bottled at 63.5 percent abv. **GS**

Tasting notes

Crisp, briny, barley notes on the early nose, becoming fruitier and more profound. Honey and developing caramel and bourbon. Smooth on the palate with a fusion of sweet and salt. Quite full-bodied, with more citrus fruits in time. A mellow and gentle oaky finish.

Bruichladdich The Organic

Bruichladdich Distillery Co. | www.bruichladdich.com

Region and country of origin Islay, Scotland
Distillery Bruichladdich, Bruichladdich, Argyll
Alcohol content 46% abv
Style Single malt

The Bruichladdich team are experimenters—no idea is shied away from, no matter how odd or outlandish. They distilled whisky from ancient bere barley; they asked their local farmers to grow specific crops; they triple- or quadruple-distilled; and they played around with peating levels and wine cask finishes. Producing an organic whisky was therefore only a matter of time.

At Bruichladdich they are concerned with honesty, tradition, and terroir, summed up for this whisky as "unparalleled Scottish provenance and quality." While other companies care primarily about yield, Bruichladdich cares about the soul of the whiskies. This one, distilled in 2003 from organic Chalice barley grown at the farms of Mains of Tullibardine, Mid Coul, and Coulmore, links the farmer and the distiller in a way not seen since the Victorian days, when Bruichladdich was built.

The whisky's can bears a depiction of Brighde, the Celts' pagan goddess of fertility, harvest, and home, mother of the Isles and life force of wise Hebridean women. This particular life force is bottled at 46 percent abv and is, of course, certified by the Biodynamic Association. It is a limited edition, matured in both new and used American oak.

While not the first organic single malt, it is the first from Islay. Previous makers of organic malt whisky said that the obstacle to certification was the provenance of the cask. As both new and used oak are employed, Bruichladdich must have found a way around that. All said, Bruichladdich's fight against blandness and sameness in the industry is commendable. **RL**

Tasting notes

Organic barley is all over the dram. Honey, toffee, vanilla, and iced cakes; also sharp, fragrant fruits: lemon, apple, pear, papaya, kiwi, and gooseberry. Elegant and dynamic on the palate—barley sugar, toasted rye bread, popcorn, honeyed lemon, and jelly beans.

Bruichladdich Peat

Bruichladdich Distillery Co. | www.bruichladdich.com

Region and country of origin Islay, Scotland
Distillery Bruichladdich, Bruichladdich, Argyll
Alcohol content 46% abv
Style Single malt

Heavy on the peat and soft on the nose, this is one schmokey whisky. Bruichladdich Peat—or simply "Pete" to "his" constantly growing band of friends and admirers—has been created for two good reasons. First, to display the maker's versatility—the distillery has always had a reputation for the maltiness of its products and wants to avoid being typecast. Second, to demonstrate that, contrary to popular belief, decent drams can emit considerable smokiness without being overpowering or harsh.

Pete may be a lively fella on the surface, but he still has a sweet nature at heart. Sure, there's always room for plenty of camaraderie once he's been invited in to the fireside, but what shines through most luminously is his subtle confidence, which tempers any underlying intensity and hints at a well-rounded maturity that many other whiskies lack. In his youth, he was known as Sweet Pete. By the time college came around, the adolescent malt had acquired a swagger in his step and become Street Pete. These days, he's better known as Neat Pete—a tidy chap, pleasant to be around and great company, one who enjoys a night out but isn't too cocky.

The question, though, in the absence of any age statement, is whether Pete is mature or simply wise beyond his years. Most drinkers of discernment would bet on the latter, and they'd be right on the money: the smokiness mixed with the sweet gives him away every time. In appearance, Pete is now a distinguished gent. But underneath, he's playful and much more adventurous than he looks. **JH**

Tasting notes

A sweet young smoker with a nose for fun and a mature counterpoint of Madeira. The peat remains evident on the palate, where it moves among sherry, raisin, oak, and vanilla. By the time it has finished it has painted the town red, but it can be relied on to clean up afterward.

Testing the water in Bruichladdich's Islay home.

Bruichladdich Redder Still

Bruichladdich Distillery Co.
www.bruichladdich.com

Region and country of origin Islay, Scotland
Distillery Bruichladdich, Bruichladdich, Argyll
Alcohol content 50.4% abv
Style Single malt

Bruichladdich Blacker Still started it all. Sure, it was a dark dram, matured in bourbon sherry casks, but the color reference was actually to the old stillman's adage that "blacker stills make better whisky." Then came Redder Still, and finally, to complete the trilogy, Golder Still, matured in unusual "squat hoggies." The latter two certainly had colors to match their names, and all three were in unusual, eye-catching packages, with color-coated, screen-printed bottles and cans.

An opaque bottle obscures the color of its contents, so the names in this series tease and tempt the buyer to see what is inside. In the case of Redder Still, the whisky's color has been variously described as Turkish Delight, rubescent, garnet, deep red, and antique copper. Some people love a pink whisky; others hate the very idea, but no one can deny that the color gains Redder Still a lot of attention.

The red color comes not from the twenty-two years in bourbon wood but from nine months in rare Bordeaux wine casks from Château Lafleur Pomerol—made from European oak from the Forest of Tronçais, planted in the days of Louis XIV to provide wood for the French navy. Only 4,080 bottles were released, so this malt is becoming as rare as hens' teeth. **RL**

Tasting notes

The nose starts with floral intensity, then fruit, followed by nougat and leather. On the palate, red berry fruits, also marshmallow, Madeira, cocoa bean, and vanilla.

Bruichladdich Waves

Bruichladdich Distillery Co.
www.bruichladdich.com

Region and country of origin Islay, Scotland
Distillery Bruichladdich, Bruichladdich, Argyll
Alcohol content 46% abv
Style Single malt

This single malt is named for its coastal qualities, its maritime magic. But it's not all at sea: in close-up, it reveals a confectionery shop of flavor. More than that, it's a dram whose staying power will have you thinking about it long after the final mouthful. Part of the distillery's Peat/Waves/Rocks series, this medium-peated whisky is aged first in ex-bourbon casks and then in Madeira casks, and the combination gives the whisky a hint of wine and a subtle undertone of sweetness. The nose and palate evoke specialty fudge, but not that alone: buttery vanilla, raspberry, honey, and a range of spice scents are also remarkable.

Incidentally, the presentation case is something to behold, decorated with a monochrome photograph of breakers against an aquamarine background. The packaging never should be all-important, but it definitely adds extra shelf-appeal. Those who fall for the packaging's superficial charms will be drawn happily beneath the Waves. Although the nose is briny, there is scarcely a hint of saltiness on the palate, which is all red licorice and berries, shadowed by flavors of mint and grasses. The tide recedes from the picture, leaving a summer of fun, handfuls of cheap candies, and a carefree mindset. **JH**

Tasting notes

If whiskies could skip, this one would. It has a young sensibility but has you second-guessing its age. Richly influenced by its elders, it is respected by its peers.

Islay's Bruichladdich distillery overlooks Loch Indaal.

Bruichladdich WMD-II The Yellow Submarine

Bruichladdich Distillery Co. | www.bruichladdich.com

Region and country of origin Islay, Scotland
Distillery Bruichladdich, Bruichladdich, Argyll
Alcohol content 46% abv
Style Single malt

The enigmatic WMD-II in this whisky's name refers to a previous "Whisky of Mass Distinction" released after Bruichladdich managing director Mark Reynier discovered that the U.S. government's Defence Threat Reduction Agency had checked out the distillery equipment for chemical-weapon-making capacity.

In an unrelated incident in June 2005, Islay fisherman John Baker chanced upon a yellow submarine floating on the sea. The letters *MOD* on the side suggested it belonged to the British Ministry of Defence, but the Royal Navy denied all knowledge. The submarine was taken ashore and stashed away in a backyard. Three months later, the mine hunter HMS *Blyth* sailed in at dawn to recover the carelessly lost property, a remotely operated vehicle used for detecting mines. Bruichladdich hastily created this bottling and presented a case to the captain of HMS *Blyth* before the ship could sneak off.

Great story; the question is whether the whisky is any good. Actually, many people loved it. Although it sold out some time ago, production director Jim McEwan served the last of it at his master class in May 2011 "as a reminder," and it stood up remarkably well among the other "special" drams. It was a fourteen-year-old whisky matured in American oak and finished in rioja casks. As is usual with non-chill-filtered drams from Bruichladdich, it is bottled at 46 percent abv (below that strength, non-chill-filtered whisky tends to go cloudy). Meanwhile, John Baker has not yet received any reward from the navy, although he did get a wee reward from Bruichladdich. **RL**

Tasting notes

Fruity on the nose—melon, apple, peach, strawberry, cranberry, pineapple, perfumed pear, and orange marmalade. Hints of rose petal, vanilla, and sweet malt. On the palate, syrupy, toffee sweetness mingles with soft fruits, later joined by licorice and peppery spices.

Bruichladdich X4+3

Bruichladdich Distillery Co. | www.bruichladdich.com

Region and country of origin Islay, Scotland
Distillery Bruichladdich, Bruichladdich, Argyll
Alcohol content 63.5% abv
Style Single malt

This experimental, quadruple-distilled whisky was first made in March 2006, shortly after the company had created a triple-distilled whisky called Trestarig. The first quadruple-distilled spirit in Scotland for at least 300 years, it came off the still at 90 percent abv.

At that time, it was called Uisquebaugh Baul ("perilous whisky"), a name taken from Martin Martin's book, *A Description of the Western Islands of Scotland Circa 1695*. Martin had said that "the first taste affects all the members of the body: two spoonfuls of this last liquor is a sufficient dose; and if any man should exceed this, it would presently stop his breath, and endanger his life." The difficult-to-pronounce Gaelic name was later consigned to the small print and the punchier title of X4 was used.

Bottling at 90 percent abv could be considered irresponsible, and an early release of X4, aimed at mixologists, had the new spirit bottled at 50 percent abv. At one year old, called X4+1 Deliverance, it was bottled during the Islay Festival at 65.4 percent abv. When the spirit came of the legal age of three years, it was bottled as X4+3, this time at 63.5 percent abv.

Production director Jim McEwan claims that the high alcoholic strength of the spirit in the cask enhances its extractive qualities and draws out flavors from the oak much more quickly than usual. Certainly, the X4+1 was remarkably drinkable. X4+3 has been matured in a combination of virgin American oak and some traditional ex-bourbon casks. This is the youngest Bruichladdich whisky available; in theory, it could survive in the cask for seventy years. **RL**

Tasting notes

Very spirity on the nose, with pear, gooseberry, lemon, lychee, apple, pineapple, and flowery notes; natural sweetness from the casks and malt: toffee, nougat, and macaroon. Fizzy, citrusy, and hot on the palate. Water opens hazelnut, licorice, coconut, ginger, and vanilla.

Buchanan's 12-Year-Old

Diageo | www.diageo.com

Region and country of origin Scotland
Distillery Various
Alcohol content 40% abv
Style Blend

James Buchanan (1849–1935) was born in Canada of parents who had not long immigrated from Scotland. While he was still a child, his family moved back east again, to Northern Ireland. At the age of fifteen, he moved first to Glasgow, where he worked as a shipping clerk, and later to London, where he took a job as a sales representative for a whisky trader. In 1884, realizing that there was a vast untapped market for blended whiskies, he founded the merchant company that still bears his name today.

The Buchanan Blend soon became synonymous with quality; in 1898, it was granted one of the most coveted accolades in British business: a Royal Warrant to supply whiskies to Queen Victoria. In 1925, Buchanan & Co. was subsumed by the Distillers Company. In 1986, Distillers was purchased by Guinness, and in 1997, Guinness merged with Grand Metropolitan to form drinks giant Diageo.

Throughout all these changes, the various owners have been careful to preserve the Buchanan name: the hard-won reputation as market leader in blended whisky has now been safeguarded for more than a century. This 12-Year-Old is a midrange whisky. It has several ingredients, but its main component is single malt from Dalwhinnie, one of the numerous Scottish distilleries that now also belong to Diageo. **GL**

Tasting notes

An aroma of salted butter-roasted almond, toasted grain, and cocoa. On the palate, it starts silkily before revealing a dryish and substantial body that lingers.

Buchanan's Aged

Diageo | www.diageo.com

Region and country of origin Scotland
Distillery Various
Alcohol content 40% abv
Style Blend

The artistry that goes into the preparation of blended whiskies, and the challenges of combining subtly different flavors to produce medleys of depth and smoothness, will always remain a mystery to some seasoned bibbers, who decry the whole process as against nature. But the beauty of blending was not lost on James Buchanan, who saw not only the attraction but also the commercial possibilities in his early twenties while he was working as the London agent for Charles Mackinlay & Co.

Following this epiphany, Buchanan set up on his own. His first customer was the wine and cigar merchant Dolamore Ltd. His blends soon became popular with the English palate, and it was not long before he was supplying a range of customers— including restaurants, music halls, and even the House of Commons. He later expanded his business into Europe, North America, and ultimately across the southern hemisphere.

In the twenty-first century, some people maintain that anything other than a single malt is not fit to be called a proper whisky. The market takes a different view: nine out of every ten bottles of whisky sold worldwide are made from carefully prepared combinations of various distilleries' products, and Buchanan's Aged is one of the most sought after. **GL**

Tasting notes

A clean, pleasant, and mild blend, with a fresh, grassy palate that is complemented by a light sweetness. The finish is smooth and fruity without any frills.

← James Buchanan & Co.'s grand office in Holborn, London, portrayed in 1914.

Bunnahabhain 12-Year-Old

Burn Stewart Distillers | www.bunnahabhain.com

Region and country of origin Islay, Scotland
Distillery Bunnahabhain, Port Askaig, Argyll
Alcohol content 46.3% abv
Style Single malt

Bunnahabhain is the lightest of the Islay drams, with hardly a trace of peat. The distillery's name translates from Gaelic as "the mouth of the river," and prior to its creation, the site was wild and uninhabited wasteland. The building of the distillery in 1881 brought about a lively little self-supporting community of workers, their wives, and children, which led to the need for a school. The village is now gone, and, although the warehouses look grim, Bunnahabhain is a lovely distillery where time stands still. The buildings overlook the Sound of Islay, a wild and windy sea passage between Islay and the Isle of Jura, once used for bringing in supplies and taking away barrels of whisky. Nowadays that is done by tankers along the narrow and winding road that leads to Port Askaig.

The founders, William Robertson and William and James Greenlees, were well connected in the whisky business. Robertson, from Robertson & Baxter, was a wine and liquor merchant and once an agent for Laphroaig on the southeast side of Islay. The Greenlees brothers were two of the founding fathers of the Islay Distillery Company, which would later merge with William Grant & Sons into Highland Distillers around 1887, taking Bunnahabhain with them. From 1930 until 1937, Bunnahabhain fell silent.

After Highland Distillers reopened the distillery, the two stills arduously worked in unison to make up for the lost years; a second pair were installed in 1963. In the 1970s, Bunnahabhain was introduced for the first time as single malt, in a limited amount, probably tasting very much like this 12-Year-Old. **HO**

Tasting notes

Meatiness on the nose, as though honey-glazed pork aromas are gently drifting over a field of freshly mown sweet grass. On the palate, the aroma is joined by a splash of grapefruit juice and vanilla as it reaches the far horizon. Finishes tight and short, ready for the next sip.

Bunnahabhain 18-Year-Old

Burn Stewart Distillers | www.bunnahabhain.com

Region and country of origin Islay, Scotland
Distillery Bunnahabhain, Port Askaig, Argyll
Alcohol content 46.3% abv
Style Single malt

Bunnahabhain distillery closed in 1982, a result of declining sales, but was reopened in 1984. It was decided to celebrate the hundredth anniversary of the distillery, and a twenty-one-year-old was released, probably the first run from the four stills. Bunnahabhain was actually founded in 1881, but Highland Distillers elected to begin counting from 1883, the year in which production started.

In 1999 the Edrington Group took up the challenge and acquired Bunnahabhain, only to mothball the distillery again almost immediately. Over the next four years, spirit was made for only a couple of weeks per year, mainly for the Famous Grouse blend. Bunnahabhain's water is piped from streams in the hills and does not flow through peat. The resulting whisky, made with unpeated malted barley, is very light and has virtually no peaty influence.

Just before selling Bunnahabhain to Edrington, Highland Distillers experimented with a peaty version. This was under the management of long-serving distillery manager John MacLellan, who moved to Islay's Kilchoman distillery in 2010. Peaty Moine was introduced in 2004 as a six-year-old, but not by Edrington, who had sold the distillery in 2003, with famous blend Black Bottle, to Burn Stewart Distillers.

Throughout its life, Bunnahabhain's output has gone mostly to the blenders. Only a small percentage matures on-site, to end up either in one of the single-malt expressions or in Black Bottle, which contains all Islay malts. There might be some of this 18-Year-Old in that blend, but try it neat on its own first. **HO**

Tasting notes

On the nose, this whisky begins with tones of toffee and vanilla, through which clear hints of green banana, orange, and chocolate-covered cherry are soon detected. On the palate, the whisky is creamy and mouth-coating. The finish is slightly astringent.

Bunnahabhain 25-Year-Old

Burn Stewart Distillers | www.bunnahabhain.com

Region and country of origin Islay, Scotland
Distillery Bunnahabhain, Port Askaig, Argyll
Alcohol content 46.3% abv
Style Single malt

Bunnahabhain 25-Year-Old is part of the distillery's core range, together with the 12-Year-Old and the much-appreciated 18-Year-Old. Various limited editions from the distillery supplement the core range, and several independent bottlers, among them Signatory, release Bunnahabhain at various ages.

The distinctive labels on the distillery's own bottlings feature a sailor behind the captain's wheel, sometimes with the caption "Westering Home." This is the title of a Scottish song by Hugh S. Robertson (1874–1952). The tune somewhat resembles that of "Bonny Strathyre" and has been performed by many artists. Here is a popular version of the first verse: "Westering home and a song in the air, Light in the eye and it's good-bye to care, Laughter o' love and a welcoming there, Isle o' my heart, my own one." There are more verses, but this a whisky tome, not a songbook. But if you are interested, the complete lyrics are easily found on the Web.

The Bunnahabhain distillery, which is 130 years old, produces 660,400 gallons (2,500,000 liters) each year. Located on the northern shore of Islay, it can be reached by a winding, single-track road signposted "nowhere"—well, almost nowhere. When you leave, a painted cask alongside the road kindly tells you the direction: "other places." But the view of the distillery is even better when one approaches Bunna by boat, via the Sound of Islay. The quoted song above then makes all the more sense. It might even make you want to go to Islay yourself and savor the dram at the source. And if you think about it, that's not a bad idea at all. **HO**

Tasting notes

Gentle, fruity tones of pear coupled with Waldorf salad mingled with lily and honeysuckle before merging into orange marmalade on buttered toast. While this creamy, delicate whisky has no lingering finish, it will keep you coming back for more.

Bunnahabhain Manzanilla Sherry Wood Finish

Burn Stewart Distillers | www.bunnahabhain.com

Region and country of origin Islay, Scotland
Distillery Bunnahabhain, Port Askaig, Argyll
Alcohol content 53.2% abv
Style Single malt

For many years, Bunnahabhain distillery has launched limited bottlings such as this one. The whisky's character brings to mind the annual week-long Islay Jazz Festival held every September, with which Bunnahabhain has been heavily involved, along with other distilleries on the small Hebridean island that also participate in the festival.

This version is a limited expression with an age statement of sixteen years, having had an extra maturation in casks that previously contained manzanilla sherry. Like jazz, it is an improvisation on a basic theme. The two belong together: whisky and jazz are acquired tastes—both are products created by professional and dedicated craftsmen. Just as a bandleader picks the right musician for the right solo on a particular tune, a distiller chooses from the resources in his warehouse for the flavors of his limited bottlings. Here, a single-malt whisky benefits from the performance of a manzanilla wood finish.

The music of trumpet player and singer Chet Baker goes very well with this single malt. Pour yourself a generous dram, pick a favorite tune, sit back, sip, listen, and relax. A good solo and a good dram create true pleasure to the ear and the palate. And the pairing works fine with the other Bunnas, too.

Both whisky and jazz have proven to be survivors, no matter what drink or what style of music has risen to become the dominant fad of the day. And these two survivors meet, time and again. Jazz clarinetist Artie Shaw got it just right when he said, "Jazz was born in a whiskey barrel." **HO**

Tasting notes

Fruity on the nose from the sherry finish. Hot buttered popcorn blends with honey-baked ham, turning to orange, caramel, toffee, and then maple syrup. On the palate, the whisky is slightly oily. The finish is short, spicy, and salty, with raisin, chocolate, and leather.

Bunnahabhain Toiteach

Burn Stewart Distillers
www.bunnahabhain.com

Region and country of origin Islay, Scotland
Distillery Bunnahabhain, Port Askaig, Argyll
Alcohol content 46% abv
Style Single malt

Let's improvise some more. Let's make an expression of Bunnahabhain that will stun and surprise the whisky world. Let's do it entirely differently this time. This is Toiteach, which is Gaelic for "smoky." The barley from which this single malt is made is heavily peated—very unusual for this distillery. There is no age statement on the bottle, which is an indication of youth—unbridled powerful youth, bottled as a limited edition. You will be tasting a non-chill-filtered expression, like raw jazz. Picture a smoky jazz lounge; the audience is waiting for the appearance on stage of the mystery guest. The glasses are filled with this heavily peated version of an Islay single malt that is known to be virtually unpeated. The first musician to appear is the percussionist, settling himself quietly behind the drum kit. He is followed by the pianist, taking his place behind the keys. Then, in the background, a figure appears, slowly walking to the double bass. He carefully puts the instrument in its upright position. The tension grows while the three musicians set the pace of the rhythm. Suddenly a saxophone player enters the stage and blows the first tunes of "Smoking Gun"—setting fire to the house. Is this blues or is this jazz? Probably both. Is this Bunna or not? Yes and no. Either way, you're in for a good time. A very atypical Bunnahabhain indeed. **HO**

Tasting notes

The hot, wet ashes of a just-doused campfire reveal a lemony grapefruit salad, toasted marshmallow, and earthy, damp dunnage warehouse aromas.

Campbeltown Loch

J. & A. Mitchell Co.
www.springbankdistillers.com

Region and country of origin Highlands, Scotland
Distillery Springbank, Campbeltown, Argyll
Alcohol content 40% abv
Style Blend

As the name suggests, this blend is produced in the eponymous Kintyre town by the owners of Springbank distillery. Aged for five years, Campbeltown Loch contains both Springbank and its peatier cousin Longrow in its composition and boasts a relatively high malt content of 40 percent abv.

In addition to the "standard" expression, there are twenty-one-, twenty-five-, and thirty-year-old variants of Campbeltown Loch, all of them great value for those drinkers who like to savor a vintage blend.

The physical feature of Campbeltown Loch, after which this whisky is named, is a sea loch toward the southern end of the Kintyre peninsula, facing east toward the Firth of Clyde. The safe and sheltered natural harbor that it created encouraged the development of the settlement that grew into Campbeltown, once a center for herring fishing and still home to a small commercial fleet. During Campbeltown's nineteenth-century heyday as a distilling center, many thousands of casks of whisky were exported from the loch by sea to the Scottish mainland and to export markets abroad.

The 1960s saw Campbeltown Loch popularized in song by the Scottish entertainer Andy Stewart, who sang about his love for the dram: "Campbeltown Loch I wish you were whisky/I would drink you dry..." **GS**

Tasting notes

Well-balanced, with a nose that is initially fresh and fruity. Leather, brine, and mild peat, floral with time. Sweet on the palate, with apricots and gentle spice.

← Bunnahabhain's pier, used for shipping whisky from the distillery.

Caol Ila 8-Year-Old

Diageo | www.malts.com

Region and country of origin Islay, Scotland
Distillery Caol Ila, Port Askaig, Argyll
Alcohol content 64.9% abv
Style Single malt

When you think of single malts from Islay, you think of smoky flavors created by the peat used to dry the barley. This character has been the hallmark for whiskies from the island for so long that people tend to forget that two of the eight distilleries, Bruichladdich and Bunnahabhain, are more known for their unpeated style, even though they produce peated whiskies from time to time. Caol Ila, on the other hand, is a typical representative of Islay.

Although not as peated as the Kildalton trio (Ardbeg, Lagavulin, and Laphroaig), this is heavy stuff with a lot of impact. That is why this particular version, the 8-Year-Old, is so interesting. It is only slightly peated. In the 1980s, trials with more or less unpeated Caol Ila were conducted, but it wasn't until 2006 that the first bottling appeared. There have been a few since then, but the actual production of unpeated Caol Ila (which is sometimes called Caol Ila Highland) has more or less come to a halt.

The main task of Caol Ila is to produce peated whisky for the many blends in the range of its owner (Diageo), and as the demand for Johnnie Walker and the others increase, there is no room for unpeated experiments anymore. Since 2005, only the traditional smoky whisky has been produced at the distillery. Distilling unpeated Caol Ila is a bit different compared to producing the peated version. Both fermentation and distillation are run at a slower speed, and you must also make certain the copper is properly rejuvenated by making sure the main doors are opened for some time after every distillation. **IR**

Tasting notes

Cherry or perhaps cherry pie on the nose. Dry on the palate, with more cherry and cheesecake. A hint of licorice and milk chocolate. Rather long finish, with some spice. A drop of water releases sweeter notes and a trace of smoke.

Caol Ila 12-Year-Old

Diageo | www.malts.com

Region and country of origin Islay, Scotland
Distillery Caol Ila, Port Askaig, Argyll
Alcohol content 43% abv
Style Single malt

The origins of Caol Ila (Gaelic meaning "Sound of Islay," pronounced "Cull–eela") are obscured by the mists of time. It first came into clear view in 1857, when it was purchased by Bulloch Lade, a Glasgow blending company who built a pier capable of withstanding the tidal range in the narrow sound alongside the distillery, an addition that enabled large quantities of coal and barley to be brought in from the mainland on small ships known locally as puffers. The most famous such vessel was the *Pibroch*, which entered service in the 1930s and plied its way around all Islay's distilleries.

In 1972, most of the original Caol Ila distillery was demolished to make way for a larger, more efficient structure: the addition of four new stills brought Caol Ila's total to six, all of which are now encased in glass with windows that can be opened to provide workers and visitors with wonderful views of the Sound.

In 2011, the Scottish parliament announced plans to harness the powerful force of seawater through the channel that separates Islay from Jura through the installation of ten submarine turbines. The £40 million ($62.7 million) project will be the most powerful tidal array in the world and is expected to generate sufficient electricity to power more than 5,000 homes, as well as the adjacent distillery itself.

Released in 2002, the Caol Ila 12-Year-Old is matured in ex-bourbon refill hogsheads. The water—drawn from nearby Loch nam Ban—is rich in limestone and relatively short on peat, a combination that makes the finished product noticeably lighter and less smoky than most Islay malts. **GL**

Tasting notes

The nose is a combination of sweet flowers and lemon or lychees. The body is light, firm, and smooth. The palate gives a sweet, malty start, then develops into a long finish that is simultaneously smoky, treacly, and slightly sour. Water brings out light acidity and saltiness.

Caol Ila 18-Year-Old

Diageo | www.malts.com

Region and country of origin Islay, Scotland
Distillery Caol Ila, Port Askaig, Argyll
Alcohol content 43% abv
Style Single malt

Sometimes you hear whisky drinkers claiming that part of the character you find in Islay whiskies comes from the fact that the whisky has matured in warehouses on the island situated very close to the sea. In truth, the vast majority of spirit distilled on Islay today is transported to the mainland for maturation. In the case of Caol Ila, it was quite rare to have the whisky maturing at the distillery even in the older days—today the entire output is tankered away to any of Diageo's sites on the mainland.

The special flavor in a Caol Ila single malt that distinguishes it from other Islay whiskies lies in the distilling regime and then, of course, in the selection of casks. To compare it with Lagavulin, for example: both distilleries use barley malted at a phenol specification of 35 parts per million (ppm), yet the two whiskies taste very different. At Caol Ila, the middle part of the second distillation (the part you collect for filling into casks) starts when the spirit has an alcoholic strength of 75 percent (compared to Lagavulin's 72 percent), because the makers want to collect the fine, fruity esters in the beginning.

The middle cut stops at 65 percent (at Lagavulin it's 59 percent) so that they do not get too much of the heavy phenols in the new make. On an average, the phenol content (which provides the typical smoky Islay style) from the malted barley is reduced during distillation by some 50 to 60 percent in new-make spirit. In Caol Ila single malt, it's even more, and for every year it is maturing in the cask, it diminishes, as for example in this 18-Year-Old. **IR**

Tasting notes

Buttery, cured ham and some coconut. More fruit on the palate (banana and pear), mellow and soft, with gentle smoke. The contribution from the cask is obvious. Long finish, with some pepper and the peat coming through at the end.

Caol Ila 25-Year-Old

Diageo | www.malts.com

Region and country of origin Islay, Scotland
Distillery Caol Ila, Port Askaig, Argyll
Alcohol content 43% abv
Style Single malt

Caol Ila is the biggest distillery on Islay by a long way. After the refurbishing conducted in 2011, its three wash stills and three spirit stills produces some 1.5 million gallons (5.8 million liters) each year—more than three times as much as, for example, Ardbeg. Although mainly a contributor to blended whiskies, the owners realized a decade ago that the interest in peated single malts was here to stay and that Caol Ila single malt could very well have a place of its own in the market.

At first Caol Ila appeared in a special series called Hidden Malts (together with Clynelish and Glen Elgin, for instance), and the name was well chosen. Geographically, Caol Ila is definitely the most hidden of all the Islay distilleries. It lies at the end of a narrow road leading down to the shores of the Sound of Islay, that body of water that separates the island from Jura. After a few years, though, the owners decided the single malt from Caol Ila deserved a label of its own and its days of being hidden were over. Several new bottlings were launched, including some really old ones where the smoke is more subdued due to the longer maturation. This has also allowed some very nice herbal and fruity notes to play a greater part in the overall character.

The 25-Year-Old was introduced for the first time in 2003, but at that time, it was a limited release and it was bottled at cask strength. It wasn't until 2010 that the more widely available 25-Year-Old bottled at 43 percent was released, and this is now a part of the Caol Ila core range. **IR**

Tasting notes

Sweet, fresh, and quite subtle on the nose, green and grassy. Like soft velvet coating your mouth, sweet but not honey, more like peach in heavy syrup. Medium finish with the peat being very much in the background. Roasted almond toward the end.

Caol Ila Cask Strength

Diageo | www.malts.com

Region and country of origin Islay, Scotland
Distillery Caol Ila, Port Askaig, Argyll
Alcohol content 61.6% abv
Style Single malt

Sometimes a good way of understanding the character of a certain whisky brand is to try a cask-strength version. This one from Caol Ila was first introduced in 2002, and here you get the whisky undiluted and unaltered, straight from the cask. It is high in alcohol, but try it first without water so that you can compare your impressions with what you get when it has been watered down a bit.

New batches of Caol Ila Cask Strength will have different alcohol strength and will also be of different ages, probably around ten to twelve years old. One of the good things about Caol Ila is that you get both the peaty, smoky flavors and also some fresh grassy notes. A lot of work goes into shaping this style. For example, a lower temperature than usual in the wash that goes into the washbacks for fermentation will help create this. Also, during distillation, the stills are only filled to 50 percent. This gives the copper a lot of room to interact with the spirit, and a lot of copper contact during the distillation removes some of the heavy and robust congeners and brings out softer notes.

Caol Ila single malt has not only become popular with customers; the blenders love it, and the independent bottlers seem to be absolutely crazy about it—as evidenced by the vast number of bottlings with labels other than the distillery's own. **IR**

Tasting notes

Sharp on the nose. Not very smoky (bonfire) in spite of its relative youth. Quite sweet on the palate, with some fruit. Slightly minty in the well-balanced medium finish.

Caol Ila Unpeated 1999

Diageo | www.malts.com

Region and country of origin Islay, Scotland
Distillery Caol Ila, Port Askaig, Argyll
Alcohol content 64% abv
Style Single malt

Each year the drinks giant Diageo releases a selection of diverse, unusual, and often rare stock. It normally holds a special evening for retailers, whisky writers, and bloggers, and in 2011, it received a record number of replies and unveiled several big hitters. This wasn't one of them—but it might just have stolen the show on the night.

Caol Ila is the biggest malt distillery on Islay, and in 2011, it reinforced that position by closing for expansion. Islay is known for its peaty whiskies, but if you added up the total amount of unpeated malt that the island produces, it's probably well over half. Why? Because most of Caol Ila's output goes into blends, and certainly very little of its unpeated malt finds its way into the single-malt market. In fact, Caol Ila wasn't known at all as a single malt until stock shortages of its sister whisky, Lagavulin, forced the company to look for some substitute.

The peated version, with its barbecued fish and smoky bacon note and its oily texture, has been a real hit. The Caol Ila Unpeated 1999 is a fantastic version of the whisky, all sherbety fruit, and at this strength and at only around $85 (£55) a bottle, this is a snip. It's actually the sixth Diageo release of unpeated Caol Ila, and it's a great one. It may become very hard to find very quickly. **DR**

Tasting notes

Toffee and vanilla on the nose with some green fruit. On the palate, this is strawberry and raspberry sherbet with some honey. With water, it's a smooth fruit mousse.

The "Bar Caol Ila" in Tokyo, Japan, offers Caol Ila whisky from the barrel. ➡

Caperdonich 1970

Adelphi Distillery
www.adelphidistillery.com

Region and country of origin Speyside, Scotland
Distillery Caperdonich (closed), Rothes, Morayshire
Alcohol content 47.1% abv
Style Single malt

A veteran Speysider, this thirty-eight-year-old Caperdonich was matured in cask no. 4378, which yielded just 184 bottles. It was released by the independent bottler Adelphi Distillery, a company revived in 1992 by Jamie Walker, great-great-grandson of the last owner of Glasgow's Adelphi distillery. In 2004 Adelphi was sold to Donald Houston and Keith Falconer, and today operates from the grand setting of Glenborrodale Castle in Argyll.

Caperdonich distillery was established in the distilling center of Rothes during 1897, and was built by J. & G. Grant of nearby Glen Grant distillery, being designed to supplement the output of Glen Grant. Indeed, it was originally named "Glen Grant No. 2 Distillery" and was connected to Glen Grant by what was known locally as "the whisky pipe," which carried new-make spirit across the main road for filling into casks. However, when boom turned to bust, the plant was closed in 1902. Then, after more than six decades of silence, the distillery was resurrected under the Caperdonich name in 1965, being rebuilt and mechanized. The distillery was mothballed in 2002, and it was finally demolished in late 2010.

Even when the distillery was in production, single-malt bottlings of Caperdonich were very rare. Almost all its output was destined for blending. **GS**

Tasting notes

A very fruity nose, featuring kiwi, gooseberry, and freshly squeezed orange juice. The palate is quite oily, with menthol, eucalyptus, linseed, and smoke.

Cardhu 12-Year-Old

Diageo
www.malts.com

Region and country of origin Speyside, Scotland
Distillery Cardhu, Knockando, Aberlour, Banffshire
Alcohol content 40% abv
Style Single malt

Cardhu distillery is the spiritual home of Johnnie Walker—the world's top-selling Scotch. However, Cardhu is also Diageo's best-selling single malt. It has been extremely popular in Spain and Greece for decades, and ten years ago it was even in fourth place of all the single malts in the world.

Its popularity created some problems for the owners, though. There was not enough Cardhu single malt to go around, so Diageo decided to make a new Cardhu, called Cardhu Pure Malt, which included single malts from other distilleries. The expedient was met with vigorous protests, especially from competitors who claimed that this course of action might damage the reputation of Scotch as a category. After a year, Diageo caved in. Today, there is nothing but single malt from Cardhu in the bottle.

Cardhu single malt is light in style with some nice grassy notes. The undemanding character makes it perfect as a blending malt, but it also appeals to the general taste in Spain, where the hot climate calls for a whisky that is not too heavy on the palate. Many young people also find it perfect to mix with Coke—a common way of enjoying whisky in Spain. The most common expression is the Cardhu 12-Year-Old, but there is also a version called Special Cask Reserve that is exclusive to the Spanish market. **IR**

Tasting notes

Green apple, with some minty notes and cereals. Sweet honey on the palate, with the oak and heather coming through. Slightly oily. An easy-drinking whisky.

Glenborrodale Castle, Adelphi Distillery's imposing headquarters.

Carsebridge 1979

Duncan Taylor & Co.
www.duncantaylor.com

Region and country of origin Lowlands, Scotland
Distillery Carsebridge, Carsebridge, Clackmannanshire
(closed) **Alcohol content** 55.7% abv
Style Single grain

A single-cask, cask-strength expression of Carsebridge single grain was matured in cask no. 33044 and bottled at thirty-one years of age by Huntly-based Duncan Taylor & Co. in their Rare Auld Collection.

Carsebridge distillery was closed by the Distillers Co. Ltd. in 1983 as a result of falling demand. The distillery, located close to the noted brewing center of Alloa in Clackmannanshire, had been founded between 1799 and 1804 by members of the Bald family, who ran it for several generations. After initially making pot-still malt whisky, Carsebridge distillery switched to grain spirit production with the installation of a Coffey still in 1851/52.

Carsebridge was one of the founding distilleries of the Distillers Co. in 1877. By the time distillery chronicler Alfred Barnard visited Carsebridge in the mid-1880s, its initial Coffey still had been augmented by a second. In terms of output, Caresbridge had become the second- or third-largest distillery in Scotland. A third Coffey still was installed during the 1960s, but Carsebridge's large capacity could not save it when the time came to cut back production of both malt and grain spirit. Nine other malt distilleries in the same ownership were also to fall silent. **GS**

Tasting notes

A rich, fruity nose (canned peach in syrup), with spicy vanilla and brittle toffee. Sweet fruits (banana) on the palate, plus digestive biscuits and a hint of marzipan.

Catto's 25-Year-Old

Inver House (International Beverage)
www.cattos.com

Region and country of origin Scotland
Distilleries Various
Alcohol content 40% abv
Style Blend

The Catto's brand of blended Scotch whiskies has its origins in the city of Aberdeen, where one James Catto set up in business as a grocer during the mid-nineteenth century. In 1861 he began to blend the high-quality local Highland malt whiskies that he sold in his grocery store with several Lowland grain whiskies to create a fine blended Scotch.

Although other figures, such as Edinburgh-based Andrew Usher, are credited with being the earliest whisky blenders, James Catto was also in at the start of the blending revolution that changed Scotch whisky from a predominantly Highland beverage of variable palatability to a drink celebrated the world over.

James Catto had attended Aberdeen Grammar School with the men who went on to found the P&O and White Star shipping lines. As a result of this personal connection, his blended Scotch whiskies were soon being shipped globally from Scotland. Before long, Catto's whiskies had become established in clubs and officers' messes around the world.

The latest addition to the Catto's lineup is the 25-Year-Old, which was offered in a limited edition of 2,400 crystal decanters to celebrate the brand's 150th anniversary in 2011. **GS**

Tasting notes

Toffee, spice, and something slightly savory on the fruity nose. Sweet and full-bodied, with spicy toffee and caramel, plus soft fruits, coconut, and vanilla.

Catto's Deluxe 12-Year-Old

Inver House (International Beverage)
www.cattos.com

Region and country of origin Scotland
Distilleries Various
Alcohol content 40% abv
Style Blend

In addition to the standard Catto's Rare Old Scottish blend, twelve- and twenty-five-year-old aged variants have been introduced to the range. Through a series of takeovers and acquisitions, the Catto's blend has lost contact with its Aberdonian origins. Being a thriving port, close to the eastern extremities of the Speyside whisky region, Aberdeen had inevitably developed extensive interests in the whisky trade, and the city also boasted its own distilling base.

Three Aberdonian distilleries survived into the twentieth century. The oldest and smallest of these went by the name of Strathdee, and was established in 1821; it finally closed during World War II, never to reopen. Devanha distillery was constructed by the Devanha brewery in 1837 on an extension of its existing site, on the banks of the River Dee. Devanha finally closed in 1910. Aberdeen's third distillery, Bon Accord, came into existence in 1856, and was based in renovated and upgraded premises on Hardgate, formerly occupied by the Union Glen distillery and an adjacent brewery. Bon Accord closed following a devastating fire in 1904.

All three distilleries once contributed locally distinctive whiskies to the Catto's family of blends. **GS**

The fresh, spring aromas of the Rare Old Scottish variant are apparent here, too, along with more citrus fruit, malt, and a hint of damp earth. Quite complex.

Catto's Rare Old Scottish

Inver House (International Beverage)
www.cattos.com

Region and country of origin Scotland
Distilleries Various
Alcohol content 40% abv
Style Blend

Around the turn of nineteenth century, James Catto passed control of his growing whisky business to his son, Robert, who was to die while fighting in France in World War I. The company was subsequently sold to London-based W. & A. Gilbey Ltd., which already had significant Scottish interests due to its ownership of Glen Spey and Knockando distilleries on Speyside.

The Catto's blend is now significantly influenced by malts produced within current owner Inver House Distillers' Balblair, Balmenach, Knockdhu, Pulteney, and Speyburn distilleries. According to brand manager Lynn Buckley, "It's not the old combination of component whiskies, but the Inver House team did its best to replicate the former style. However, I think the brand as it was when we got it had been 'diluted' somewhat from its heyday. We've won lots of awards with it, so I think we've obviously managed to get it back to its best."

The expression now marketed as Catto's Rare Old Scottish blend, containing no age statement, was formerly known as Catto's Rare Old Scottish Highland Whisky, due to the preponderance of component malts from the Highland region. It was known to aficionados of the brand by the acronym "ROSH." **GS**

Aromatic on the light nose, grassy, and springlike, with honey. On the palate, delicate spices join the honey and grassy notes, with an additional a touch of vanilla.

Chivas The Century of Malts

Chivas Brothers (Pernod Ricard) | www.chivas.com

Region and country of origin Scotland
Distilleries Various
Alcohol content 40% abv
Style Blended malt

Released in 1996, Chivas The Century of Malts is so-called for containing spirit from a hundred single-malt Scotch distilleries. It is packaged with a small book, *The One Hundred Malts*, containing a list of the component malts and a brief description of each distillery, authored by Jim Murray in 1995.

Chivas The Century of Malts includes whiskies from the following distilleries: Aberfeldy, Aberlour, Allt-á-Bhainne, Ardbeg, Auchentoshan, Auchroisk, Aultmote, Balblair, Balmenach, Balvenie, Banff, Ben Nevis, BenRiach, Benrinnes, Benromach, Blair Athol, Bowmore, Braeval, Brechin, Bunnahabhain, Caol Ila, Caperdonich, Clynelish, Convalmore, Cragganmore, Craigduff, Craigellachie, Dailuaine, Dallas Dhu, Dalmore, Dalwhinnie, Deanston, Dufftown, Fettercairn, Glen Albyn, Glenallachie, Glenburgie, Glencadam, Glen Craig, Glen Elgin, Glen Esk, Glenfarclas, Glenfiddich, Glen Garioch, Glenglassaugh, Glen Grant, Glengoyne, Glenisla, Glen Keith, Glenkinchie, the Glenlivet, Glenlochy, Glenlossie, Glen Mhor, Glen Moray, Glenrothes, Glen Scotia, Glen Spey, Glentauchers, Glenturret, Glenugie, Glenury Royal, Highland Park, Imperial, Inchgower, Inchmurrin, Inverleven, Isle of Jura, Kinclaith, Knockando, Ladyburn, Lagavulin, Laphroaig, Ledaig, Linkwood, Littlemill, Longmorn, Macallan, Macduff, Mannochmore, Miltonduff, Mortlach, Mosstowie, Ord, Pittyvaich, Pulteney, Rhosdhu, Royal Brackla, Scapa, Speyburn, Springbank, Strathisla, Strathmill, Tamdhu, Tamnavulin, Teaninich, Tomatin, Tomintoul, Tormore, and Tullibardine. **WM**

Tasting notes

Full bodied with light smoke in the background. Notes of fruit try to peek around the edges of the malt character. The smoke is a dry smoke, without the medicinal Islay characteristics. Nutty notes also lurk in the background, with plenty of malt.

Chivas Regal 12-Year-Old

Chivas Brothers (Pernod Ricard) | www.chivas.com

Region and country of origin Scotland
Distillery Various
Alcohol content 40% abv
Style Blend

Chivas Regal 12-Year-Old dates back to 1938, when it first appeared in the United States; by 1949, the expression had become a global brand. Blends like this contain a mixture of various single malts and grain whiskies to create a unique marriage, taking the best flavors and properties from each.

Many years ago, Chivas Brothers began the practice of blending the malt and grain components separately. The malt portion is blended in Speyside, where Chivas Brothers matures the majority of its single malts. Once the twelve-year-old malt blending is complete, this component is transported to the Chivas Brothers headquarters and bottling plant in Paisley, near Glasgow, which is also where the majority of the grain whisky is matured. Here, the malt is combined with the grain whisky component.

According to Chivas Brothers master blender Colin Scott, "Each stage is carefully quality checked and compared to control samples to ensure that the high quality and luxurious taste of Chivas Regal 12-Year-Old remains consistent year on year. Chivas Regal 18 and Chivas Regal 25 do not follow this route, but are blended and bottled as required."

As each cask is unique, the master blender must constantly adapt each vatting according to the flavors of the component casks. Scott compares what he does to the work of an artist. "As with painting, where you can choose any color or combination of colors to create the work of art, I start off with a picture in my mind of what I want, and I can select from all the finest whiskies in the Chivas Brothers inventory." **WM**

Tasting notes

Notes of butterscotch, vanilla, apricot, and orange appear on the nose, and become more vibrant on the creamy, almost buttery, fruity palate. Butterscotch and light fruit linger on the finish. Further examination reveals hints of heather and malt.

Chivas Regal 18-Year-Old

Chivas Brothers (Pernod Ricard) | www.chivas.com

Region and country of origin Scotland
Distillery Various
Alcohol content 40% abv
Style Blend

Chivas Regal 18-Year-Old was created by Chivas Brothers master blender Colin Scott. It was released in 1997 in response to increased demand and a desire to expand the Chivas Regal lineup of blended Scotch.

The component single malts and grains, which are quite different from those of the 12- and 25-Year-Olds, are married together prior to vatting for bottling. Scott attempted to create a blend in the Chivas Regal tradition, one that would live up to the expectations of consumers accustomed to the 12-Year-Old but be more than simply that blend aged for another six years. The heart of all the Chivas Regal blends is Strathisla, but in the case of the 18-Year-Old, the eighteen-year-old Strathisla is joined by eighteen-year-old Longmorn—another Speyside distillery.

"Making a great whisky takes experience, inspiration, and patience," says Scott. "When I hand-select the casks for Chivas 18-Year-Old, my quest is for superb whiskies to create a blend of exceptional richness. The result is unique and I am therefore proud to put my initials and signature on every bottle."

Scott continues, "Chivas has always represented luxury in Scotch whisky, and it was a great opportunity to be able to extend this reputation by introducing an eighteen-year-old to meet ever increasing demand for more exclusive and special whiskies—and, of course, to add to the legend. As a blender, you are often asked to maintain a recipe handed down through generations, which is a huge responsibility, so this was an opportunity for me as a blender to create my own blend, albeit in the Chivas style. A true privilege." **WM**

Tasting notes

Vanilla, toffee, and honey are immediately apparent. Silky, with a mouth coating like melted vanilla ice cream and more oak evident, adding structure and body. Cinnamon, peach, orange, and a hint of cocoa gradually appear.

A philosophical approach to Chivas in this 1970s advertisement. →

This bottle is ½ empty.

This bottle is ½ full.

If it happens to be your bottle of Chivas that reaches the halfway mark, you'll probably feel it's half empty.

Whereas, if you're visiting a friend and his bottle reaches the same point, you can relax, knowing that it's still half full.

Chivas Regal 25-Year-Old

Chivas Brothers (Pernod Ricard) | www.chivas.com

Region and country of origin Scotland
Distillery Various
Alcohol content 40% abv
Style Blend

Chivas Regal 25-Year-Old, released in New York City in September 2007, is actually a rebirth of the original Chivas Regal. Intended as a luxury blend for the sophisticated palates of American high society, Chivas's Superb Liqueur Whisky "Regal" 25 Years Old, as the whisky blend was originally called, had made its debut in New York in 1909.

Charles Stewart Howard, Chivas Brothers' third master blender, had sought to create the "perfect blend" and eventually achieved the Chivas Regal, a twenty-five-year-old blend of the finest whiskies from their stocks, which were distilled in 1884 or before. Colin Scott, Chivas Brothers' current master blender, picks up the story. "As well as the honor of being asked to re-create Chivas Regal 25-Year-Old, the challenge of re-creating [it] was to live up to the legend of Charles Howard. Just as he used the blending traditions and house style pioneered by James Chivas, I followed the same path. Those traditions had been passed down from one master blender to the next."

Scott sought to maintain the same smooth, rich, Chivas Regal style, but used a totally different selection of single malts and grain whiskies for the 25-Year-Old, ensuring it would provide "its own unique taste experience." The one single malt they all have in common is Strathisla, which lies at the heart of every Chivas Regal blend. Prior to the final vatting, some of the older whiskies are married, or vatted and reracked into different casks, to allow those whiskies to settle. The Chivas Regal 25-Year-Old is considerably drier than both the 12- and the 18-Year-Olds. **WM**

Tasting notes

Rich and creamy, with notes of Longmorn and Strathisla. Honey, heather, spice, and a whiff of smoke. Noticeably dryer than the younger Chivas Regal expressions, the palate shows buttery notes of vanilla and toffee. Full-bodied, especially for a 40-percent-abv whisky.

Clan Campbell

Pernod Ricard | www.pernod-ricard.com

Region of origin Scotland
Distilleries Various
Alcohol content 40% abv
Type Blend

The Campbell Clan has had some bad press over the years, accused by its bitter rivals, the MacDonalds, of any number of crimes, including collusion with the hated English, on whose behalf they slaughtered the MacDonalds in their own homes in the forbidding surrounds of Glencoe in 1692. Naming a whisky after them, then, is a divisive action in itself.

This is a relative newcomer to the world of blends, having been launched in the 1980s, and is both youthful and packed with fruity and sweet Speyside whiskies including Aberlour, but not the big sherried Aberlours so much as the lighter green, fruity ones. It may be that it was launched specifically for a younger, less whisky-savvy consumer, or perhaps into territories where younger and lighter drams are preferred among whisky drinkers. Whatever the case, it's now part of the Pernod Ricard stable, where heavy hitting blends Ballantine's, Chivas Regal, and Royal Salute all find their homes.

Clan Campbell is not a major contender in the world of blended whisky, and it isn't packaged as nicely as its sibling blends. That said, though, it's a well-made blend with a distinctive flavor, and the recent moves toward serving whisky in cocktails and in longer, more refreshing drinks have done it no harm whatsoever. Perhaps it is better off doing well in markets that do not associate it with the negative image of the clan it is named after. It tastes good over ice, too, and could just be the perfect early evening snifter after a long hot summer's day and before the barbecue is fully fired up. **HO**

Tasting notes

A Speyside greatest hits in a glass. Perhaps not groundbreaking, but still welcomingly familiar. A fruit bowl of flavors, with apple, orange, and banana, some honeyed barley in the center and a rounded but somewhat disappointingly short finish.

Clan Denny 30-Year-Old

Douglas Laing & Co. | www.douglaslaing.com / www.northbritish.co.uk

Region and country of origin Lowlands, Scotland
Distillery North British, Edinburgh
Alcohol content 54.2% abv
Style Single grain

Many whisky lovers look with disdain on grain whisky because it was originally developed as a cheap filler for the malts in blended whisky. The process used is easily scaled up, and although the number of distilleries continues to shrink, the total output is increasing every year. Single-grain whisky is now emerging as a popular drink through independent bottlers and, very rarely, distillery bottlings.

This 30-Year-Old, from Douglas Laing's Clan Denny range, was made from a mix of green (undried) malted barley and French corn by the North British distillery, the last remaining in Edinburgh. This huge facility makes vast quantities of whisky for J&B, Famous Grouse, Chivas Regal, Langs, and Cutty Sark, as well as producing spirit for gin and vodka. This diversity is one of the keys to understanding grain whisky; the spirit is less characterful than malt spirit straight off the stills, and much of its flavor comes later.

In this particular example, the refill hogshead has had a big influence on the taste, much more so than it would on a more dominant malt of similar age. The resulting taste is a curious hybrid of malt whisky and bourbon, though it is less sweet than most bourbon. The corn in the mix is unusual for the United Kingdom, where most grain distilleries use unmalted wheat as the main ingredient. The corn provides a softer mellowness, but after thirty years, its influences have diminished. The spirit comes off the stills at more than 95 percent abv and is casked at almost 69 percent; it remains at a high 54.2 percent in this example. Adding water really does shift the flavors around. **AN**

Tasting notes

The nose is aromatic and sweet. Nutty wood and spice at first, on a full, oily body, then waves of subtle vanilla and butterscotch. A short finish for a whisky of this age, with tannins at the end. Water brings the oak into the nose and enhances the sweetness.

Clan Denny Islay

Douglas Laing & Co. | www.douglaslaing.com

Region of origin Islay, Scotland
Distilleries Various
Alcohol content 46% abv
Type Blended malt

Launched in 2008, this whisky, like its stablemate Big Peat, is relatively uncontrolled in its overall style. Granted, the formula is the same every time, and the blend always uses a cask from each of several named—and some unnamed—distilleries. But, as every whisky aficionado knows, each cask is different. It follows that every batch of Clan Denny Islay will be different from the previous batch. Furthermore, the volume of whisky in each cask—expressed in the trade as liters of pure alcohol, or lpa—will differ, too, so no batch will be precisely the same size.

This is blending on a genuinely small-batch scale. A cask is used from each of the following list of illustrious Islays: Ardbeg, Bowmore, Bruichladdich, Bunnahabhain, and Caol Ila—which makes for quite a lineup. Two additional casks are from unnamed distilleries, presumably for legal reasons. It is unlikely that one of these is Kilchoman—the new kid on the Islay block—nor will there be any Port Ellen in there. That leaves only two distilleries on Islay; both are close to Kildalton and begin with the letter L, which is probably more than enough information.

As with its Speyside sibling, Clan Denny Islay is non-chill-filtered, adding to the creamy mouthfeel, and is bottled at 46 percent abv, which makes it robust. Those who know single malts will get exactly what they would expect from a blend made exclusively of Islay malts: something arresting and phenolic, like a smack in the face with a smoked haddock. However, Clan Denny has more elegance to it than Big Peat or several other Islay blended malts. **MM**

Tasting notes

A maritime bonfire with background sweetness on the nose. It is damp and salty on the palate—like a sailor's beard. Sweet licorice, then black pepper, with a salty and distinctly smoky finish. Nice texture and satisfying length, straightforward and distinctly unpretentious.

Clan Denny Speyside

Douglas Laing & Co.
www.douglaslaing.com

Region of origin Speyside, Scotland
Distilleries Various
Alcohol content 46% abv
Type Blended malt

Clan Denny is bottled under the name Hunter Hamilton Company, which is part of Douglas Laing & Co. The birth of the brand can be traced back to Taiwan. In the days when the Asian market was awash with ceramic bottles and aged blends, Douglas Laing had a potential importer—who never actually represented the business—by the name of Dennis. He wanted to have a whisky named after him, so Fred Laing and his team surveyed the various options: "MacDennis" did not really work, but the place name Denny (in Stirlingshire, Scotland) added an element of authenticity. The Laing brothers took the brand name to a local design agency for it to create an identity for Clan Denny; it went well, especially in Holland.

Of the two blended malts in the Clan Denny range, the Speyside is company director Fred Laing's favorite: "It's a lovely wee drink." It comprises a cask of the following notable malts: Macallan, Glenrothes, Glen Grant, Mortlach, and Longmorn, all of which are stalwarts of the blender's art, as well as one each from two distilleries that are unspecified (for legal reasons, one assumes). It is unusual for a blender to state on the packaging which malts are used therein. Some of the components are real heavyweights, both in terms of provenance and style. The whisky is non-chill-filtered and is bottled as 46 percent abv. **MM**

Tasting notes

Fresh apple on the nose, zesty, with very clear vanilla notes. A fruity sweetness on the palate, with pear and toffee, and a nutty texture. A drying, spicy finish.

Claymore

Whyte & Mackay
www.whyteandmackay.co.uk

Region and country of origin Scotland
Distilleries Various
Alcohol content 40% abv
Style Blend

Although in Gaelic *claymore* means "great sword," in warfare the word has at least three meanings. First of all, in late medieval times the claymore was a broad two-handed sword eagerly used by Scots to finish off Englishmen in many a border fight. Men had to be strong to wield it, since it weighed up to 6 pounds (2.7 kg) with a total length of 55 inches (140 cm), including 45 inches (114 cm) of blade. It might be that William Wallace—aka Braveheart—wielded such a deadly weapon. It reportedly fell out of fashion around 1700.

The second claymore is also a sword, albeit not as long, fitted with an intricately forged, basketlike handguard. Officers of the Royal Regiment of Scotland still bear it as an ornamental weapon as part of their ceremonial attire. The third claymore is an even more gruesome weapon. The M18 Claymore is a directional fragmentation mine that projects a fan-shaped pattern of steel balls in a 60-degree horizontal arc, at a height not exceeding 6 feet (1.8 m)—unpleasant.

Although the Claymore blend sports two basket-hilted swords crossed over an ancient-looking shield, it is a peaceful dram, created by Alexander Ferguson in 1882. Coincidentally, the current owner of this brand, Whyte & Mackay, was also founded in 1882. The latter company was purchased in 2007 by a famous Indian business tycoon, Mr. Vijay Mallya. **HO**

Tasting notes

Gutsy, characterful, and tasty blended whisky. Toffee apple, burnt sugar, baked apricot, peach, cream, cinnamon, nutmeg, and spice are all in the mix.

A newsboy figurine eternally promotes the Claymore brand. ➡

Clynelish 12-Year-Old

Diageo | www.whisky.co.uk

Region and country of origin Highlands, Scotland
Distillery Clynelish, Brora, Sutherland
Alcohol content 46% abv
Style Single malt

Clynelish has been a quiet workhorse distillery for many years, but thankfully in more recent times it is being noticed by the whisky community. This 12-Year-Old was originally released in 2009 as part of a continuing range of malts specifically bottled for members of the Diageo whisky fan club, the Friends of the Classic Malts. At first it was only accessible to members, or those who agreed to sign up as members, but over time it has become available from many more retailers. The 12-Year-Old is now seen by many as a mainstay in the distillery's lineup.

The bottling is two years younger than the regular release from the distillery, the 14-Year-Old, which is gradually making its way from the shelves of specialist retailers to the wider supermarket audience. Being younger, it loses a little of the complexity of its older sibling, while still keeping the trademark distillery character of sweet fruit and candlewax. It is matured in ex-sherry casks made from European oak, which adds a rounded sherry influence to the whisky, enhancing the fruity nature of the spirit to produce an easy-drinking and approachable dram.

Add to that the fact that it is generally listed at a very reasonable price when you can find it in stock, and you end up with a must-try Clynelish that makes a perfect introduction to the distillery. **BA**

Tasting notes

A sweet honeyed nose, with hints of heathery meadows leads into mixed fruit and candlewax, edged with some woody spice, chewy fruit candy, and rich sherry wood.

Clynelish 14-Year-Old

Diageo | www.malts.com

Region and country of origin Highlands, Scotland
Distillery Clynelish, Brora, Sutherland
Alcohol content 46% abv
Style Single malt

Being established in 1967, Clynelish is a relative youngster in whisky terms. The distillery's huge, glass-fronted still house sits prominently on a Sutherland hillside, just opposite the legendary closed Brora distillery. The 14-Year-Old is Clynelish's house malt, but is nevertheless a bit of a rarity, as 99 percent of production goes into Johnnie Walker blends.

The remaining 1 percent of single malt is an outstandingly good dram, favored by locals and connoisseurs alike. An old man who was once very dear to this writer used to buy two cases of the now discontinued Clynelish fourteen-year-old Flora & Fauna bottles every year (these have now become collectors' items). I recall sitting in wide-eyed anticipation with every bottle we opened, and there were many. I remember the sound of the wooden box being opened, the rapid *tick, tick, tick*, as the seal was torn away, and the light squeak and *thunk* as the cork stopper was removed for the first time.

While the Clynelish 14-Year-Old isn't broadly available, it is stocked by specialists. Older official bottles from Clynelish have been released, however, as part of Diageo's now discontinued "Rare Malts Selection" series; these sell for many hundreds of pounds. But stick with this luscious easy-drinker and you won't go far wrong. **AS**

Tasting notes

Zesty lemon and greengage with white chocolate. Evocative of a spring tide, with a hint of seaweed. A wisp of smoke is present through to the finish.

 A presumptuous red chimney vies with Clynelish's traditional pagoda.

Clynelish 28-Year-Old 1982

Speciality Drinks | www.thewhiskyexchange.com

Region and country of origin Highlands, Scotland
Distillery Clynelish, Brora, Sutherland
Alcohol content 43.1% abv
Style Single malt

In many ways, Clynelish has managed to combine the best of both worlds, having the backing of a major company in the form of Diageo on the one hand, and maintaining its reputation for off-piste whiskies on the other. Part of the reason for that is the fact that the distillery shares a history with one of the most revered and sought-after closed distilleries of them all; Clynelish is in the village of Brora and survived when the eponymous distillery was closed down.

The whisky from this distillery has always been very good, and Diageo has cleverly drip-fed consumers with a selection of varied but consistently excellent whiskies. The two distilleries at Brora produced a wide range of different versions of Highland whiskies, and Diageo has played its hand magnificently in recent years, intermittently releasing wonderful, swampy, fishy, and peaty thirty-year-old Broras while letting the odd very sweet Clynelish out of the bag for purposes of comparison.

Even in its most common form—at a significant fourteen years old—Clynelish has always been one of the best examples of a solid Highland malt. But this is an absolute revelation. First, it shows that Clynelish is another of the many Highland distilleries capable of maintaining its character into old age. Second, it shows that Clynelish can be every bit as big and peaty as its deceased sister. And finally, it shows that the quality that we admire in Brora has a place here, too. This bottling is one of the Single Malts of Scotland series from Speciality Drinks, and is unlike any Clynelish you've ever had. That should be enough. **DR**

Tasting notes

On the nose, slightly dusty, musky, and woody. The wood is dominant on the palate but with additional flavors of paprika, peat, and banana. The wood is partly restrained by an oily richness. Very rich and full-flavored for such a venerable whisky.

Clynelish Distillers Edition 1992

Diageo | www.whisky.co.uk

Region and country of origin Highlands, Scotland
Distillery Clynelish, Brora, Sutherland
Alcohol content 46% abv
Style Single malt

Bottled in 2007, this is the second Distillers Edition bottling from this Highland distillery, following the 1991 vintage. Historically, the distillery hasn't had much exposure outside of independent bottlings and its major release as part of Diageo's Flora & Fauna range. The Distillers Edition expressions follow on from the initial Flora & Fauna release, adding both age and double-maturation as points of interest. Distillers Edition whiskies are all finished by aging for a number of months in a different type of cask.

This expression has much in common with the later-appearing Clynelish 14-Year-Old. It was aged in ex-bourbon casks before being transferred to dry oloroso sherry butts for a final four months of finishing. The amount of time for which an oloroso barrel is used to mature sherry can vary. Older barrels soak up more of the rich but dry oloroso flavors, while younger barrels retain more of their oak character; each adds different elements to the mix. In addition, the solera method of sherry maturation creates further variations—sherries of differing ages having been filled into each barrel also affects the whisky in different ways during the finishing process. After finishing, the cask contents are married together to create the final bottling, with the characteristics from all of the differing casks mingling thoroughly.

The initial bourbon-cask maturation brings out the expected notes of tropical fruit and accentuates the trademark Clynelish candle wax and brine flavors, while the oloroso casks add depth, richness, and dark fruit flavors, as well as some deeper coloring. **BA**

Tasting notes

A nose of rich, dried vine fruit, backed up by candle wax, pineapple, banana, and glacé cherry. This leads to a big, spicy body, with more fruit, salt, and pepper, and a hint of smoky wood. The finish lingers, with damp wood and sparkly lemon sherbet.

Clynelish The Managers' Choice 1997

Diageo | www.whisky.co.uk

Region and country of origin Highlands, Scotland
Distillery Clynelish, Brora, Sutherland
Alcohol content 58.5% abv
Style Single malt

This whisky appeared in 2009 to the happy appreciation of Clynelish fans, who had been waiting eagerly for the fourth and final set of whiskies of the Managers' Choice series. The range had been an opportunity for Diageo's distillery managers to get together and build a set of twelve whiskies that each exemplified one of their distilleries, the intention being to achieve a consensus rather than have each manager choose their own distillery's entry. Bottled from single casks and at cask strength, the twelve whiskies were chosen only after thorough debate.

The one chosen by the managers for Clynelish is quite simple: cask no. 4341. The spirit was distilled on April 10, 1997, poured into a first-fill bourbon cask, and left to mature for about twelve years before bottling, in 2009. Filling into bourbon casks of various ages is fairly typical for Clynelish, being their stock in trade, but this bottling departed a little from the assumed brief of showing the distillery's primary characteristics. It is subdued when it comes to waxiness, the flavor note that has come to typify Clynelish's output.

Unfortunately, this release was a limited run of only 216 bottles. They were hard to find, which caused general annoyance, but also collectors found them very appealing, causing a climb in price; this applied to all the Managers' Choice releases. Further, because the bottles were of a European size, they could not be made available in the United States.

This is a hard-to-find whisky that, sadly, is more likely to be found gathering dust on a collector's shelf than being poured and enjoyed. **BA**

Tasting notes

Hints of the sea on the nose, with a touch of the traditional Clynelish wax as well as vanilla and sweet spice. The taste is big and rich, with sweet fruit, citrus, and spice mingling with warming wood. The finish is long and fruity.

Compass Box Asyla

Compass Box | www.compassboxwhisky.com

Region and country of origin Scotland
Distilleries Various
Alcohol content 40% abv
Style Blend

Compass Box Asyla is a blend of malt and grain whisky. Its name is the plural of "asylum" and refers to sanctuaries, retreats, and safe places. This seems appropriate since Asyla has a rather unintimidating character, combining the rich, the sweet, and the soft with an approachable, likable, unaffectedness. Asyla has all the comfort of a homecoming.

But Asyla is also a multi-award-winning blend, and, without a doubt, an important expression within Compass Box's core range. It may be a soft blanket, but it's not woolly. If anything, it's a more complex weave, perhaps a tapestry. Its place in the Compass Box story is an important one. It was an early offering from founder John Glaser, and its clutch of awards put the world of whisky on notice that Compass Box was capable of very great things.

In creation, Asyla is made up of single malts from Glen Elgin, Linkwood, and Teaninich distilleries, as well as a grain whisky from Cameronbridge. They are all matured separately in ex-bourbon casks and then blended together one year before bottling.

The blend is incredibly elegant for a non-chill-filtered whisky, but still manages to boast the very high quality and flavor characteristics that whisky buffs crave from small-production whisky bottlings. Could this be an expression that has something for everyone? After all, Asyla plays a trump card for new drinkers, too—it has a relatively malty, fruity, and vanilla character that gives it balance and a distinctly addictive edge. So, easy-drinking with myriad complexities: classic Compass Box whisky. **JH**

Tasting notes

Asyla is as simple as English breakfast tea taken with a thick slice of Battenberg cake, but as complex as spiced eggnog and lemon soufflé. The whisky has a fairly dry finish that leaves the palate begging for a second dram. This, however, is no cause for concern.

Compass Box Double Single

Compass Box | www.compassboxwhisky.com

Region and country of origin Scotland
Distilleries Glen Elgin, Morayshire; Port Dundas, Glasgow
Alcohol content 53.3% abv
Style Blend

Compass Box has excelled at thinking outside of the conventional box. Normally, a blended whisky consists of many different malts with grain whisky, but it doesn't have to. One grain and one single malt will do. This was released to celebrate the Compass Box Whisky Company's tenth anniversary. Founder John Glaser brought back a small-batch whisky he made in 2003. The result was Double Single: a marriage of two single whiskies: one single malt and one single grain.

By Glaser's own confession, he wanted to match one single-malt whisky perfectly with one single-grain whisky, in just the right proportions to create a blended Scotch whisky with only two components, rather than several. That is the true test of a great blender, and it was a challenge suggested by his friends Duncan Elphick and Tatsuya Minagawa of the Highlander Inn at Craigellachie on Speyside. It was too enticing not to try. Double Single is exactly what it purports to be: a couple of singles, one malt, one grain, so complementary to one another that nothing else needs to be added.

Double Single is, in fact, an eighteen-year-old single-malt whisky from Glen Elgin distillery combined with a single cask of twenty-one-year-old grain whisky distilled at Port Dundas, both aged in American oak. The combination mixes pear fruit, maltiness, vanilla, and crème brûlée, and testifies to the virtues of combining grain whisky with malt whisky. It is hard to find because it was launched as a limited release of 876 bottles. Well worth the effort, though, because it is superb. **JH**

Tasting notes

The scent of a walk in wet woods, with honey sandwiches followed by a child's paper bag filled with pear candy and peanut brittle candy. Double Single is a pale lemon-yellow color and smells of fresh picnics, springtime, and the last dessert before bedtime.

Compass Box Flaming Heart

Compass Box | www.compassboxwhisky.com

Region and country of origin Highlands, Scotland
Distilleries Primarily from Port Askaig, Islay, and Brora
Alcohol content 48.9% abv
Style Blended malt

Perhaps the greatest trick a whisky maker can pull off is that of combining big fruit notes with peat. It is rarely done well but, like a great movie stunt, when it comes off, the results are highly impressive.

Compass Box Flaming Heart is a big, peaty malt whisky that combines rich smokiness with the elegance of French oak aging. It is the Vincent Cassel of whiskies: a smooth-talking tough guy with great style who comes from first-class stock.

Flaming Heart is made by racking small quantities of malt whisky—aged between ten and sixteen years in first-fill and refill American oak casks—into new French oak casks for a secondary maturation of approximately eighteen months. The lack of chill-filtering gives it a big flavor and a forthright peatiness that shows you who's boss. But it is the second stage in French oak that really butters up the package.

Compass Box's Limited Release range is based on the philosophy that producing small-lot, single-batch Scotch whiskies from extraordinary casks creates an eclectic array of flavors and styles. The collection ranges from the hearty to the subtle, but every whisky in this range is trying to say something, whether by shouting or whispering. And Flaming Heart, as its name would suggest, is certainly not a quiet beast.

There are just 717 cases of Flaming Heart in existence, and each contains just six bottles. Flaming Heart is bold in style and full flavored, with a punchy but complex delivery. With this blended malt, Compass Box deservedly won its fourth Innovator of the Year Award from *Whisky Magazine*. **JH**

Tasting notes

Flaming Heart is an unprincipled cad of a whisky. It is dapper in appearance, but still a bit rugged, smelling of expensive suits and French cigarettes. On the palate, it is big, rich, and peaty, with sweet clove undertones from aging in new French oak.

Compass Box Flaming Heart 10th Anniversary

Compass Box | www.compassboxwhisky.com

Region and country of origin Scotland
Distilleries Various
Alcohol content 48.9% abv
Style Blended malt

The reputation of the original Compass Box Flaming Heart generated a huge demand, and a second batch was snapped up in record time. When founder John Glaser looked to celebrate his company's tenth anniversary, Flaming Heart was always going to have a role. Great-tasting whisky with a cool image to go with it: what's not to like?

This is Flaming Heart's third limited edition and is a whisky inspired by a rock song. It has a new label illustrated by Alex Machin and an übercool clear Perspex case, and the liquid in the bottle expertly combines Highland, Islay, and Island single malts. These have been aged in a combination of American and French oak casks to create a smoky-sweet flavor profile that doesn't seem like it is trying too hard. The whisky is markedly different from previous versions but no worse for that, being even growlier, peatier, and earthier than the previous two releases.

Flaming Heart 10th Anniversary is a rebel, a socialite, an artist, and a musician. It is the Clash's Paul Simonon smashing his white Fender on the stage; it's a rebellious Casanova, getting its own way against the odds. And in essence, Flaming Heart 10th Anniversary whisky is a crafted example of what can be achieved when you ignore the boundaries of tradition and simply create—to show that you can.

The whisky is enticing yet complicated in flavor; big, bold, rich, sweet, and smoky, it knows what you want and it delivers. Flaming Heart 10th Anniversary is non-chill-filtered and has a big, full flavor. The limited release consisted of 4,186 bottles. **JH**

Tasting notes

A complex and smoky malt whisky, with a rich, sweet, spice-laden fruitiness. There is vanilla here and cinnamon. Beneath the spicy kick, there is a comforting, and generous helping of tobacco. With its long, lingering finish, this is a whisky to relax into.

Compass Box Great King St.

Compass Box | www.compassboxwhisky.com

Region and country of origin Scotland
Distilleries Various
Alcohol content 43% abv
Style Blend

Described as an artisanal whisky maker, and recognized as the most innovative company in the world of whisky, John Glaser's Compass Box has the reputation for pursuing somewhat esoteric and highbrow concepts. Some of the creations produced by the company over the years have been expensive and out of many people's reach. Not this one, though. Compass Box is known for using top-quality whisky in its creations, but on this occasion the priority was to provide a whisky available to everyone.

Was quality sacrificed? Not a bit of it. This is a good, old-fashioned blended whisky made with Scottish malts and grain. It may be pitched at the lower end of the budget scale, but it is right up there with the best when it comes to fine whisky making. Glaser has very clear objectives with Great King St.— to reinvent blended whisky for a new generation, and to bring to the table a whisky that is not overly expensive but has all the quality consumers expect from Compass Box products.

Great King St. is designed to be mixed, of course, and Compass Box has been talking up using the blend as a core ingredient in a highball, which is, says Glaser, how many people were choosing to take their whisky when it first became popular throughout the British Empire. Should you want to sip it neat, however, it proves to be a fine-tasting drink in its own right.

As ever with Compass Box, the packaging is exquisite, while the smaller 50-cl bottle ensures that the price stays in the basement. A worthy addition to the Compass Box range. **DR**

Tasting notes

The nose is light and delicate, with some sweet candy notes. On the palate, it is also sweet, with vanilla and chewy grain dominating, some caramel and toffee notes, and lashings of ginger. A flurry of unexpected, late spice dominates the finish.

Compass Box Hedonism

Compass Box | www.compassboxwhisky.com

Region and country of origin Lowlands, Scotland
Distilleries Cambus, Caledonian, and Cameronbridge
Alcohol content 43% abv
Style Blended grain

Grain, often regarded as malt whisky's poor relation, is unfairly dismissed as less flavorsome and of inferior quality. But there are aficionados who point to grain whisky older than thirty years as evidence that this is nonsense, and Compass Box goes one further with this mixture of different old grain whiskies.

Hedonism is a limited-release vatting of rare old grain whiskies that can boast an average age of around twenty years. Matured in American oak casks, the grains come from two Lowland distilleries. Such a blend is a rarity in Scotland, where fewer than ten grain-whisky distilleries remain in operation.

For the first release, Compass Box used grain whiskies from the Cambus distillery, which closed its doors in the early 1990s, and the Caledonian distillery. The latest expression brings together a little grain whisky from Cambus and a blend of some twelve- and thirteen-year-old Cameronbridge distillery grain whiskies, along with other whiskies nearing the age of twenty-eight or twenty-nine years.

All the grains have been matured in 100-percent first-fill ex-bourbon barrels. With 400 cases available and a bottle price of $60 (£40), this whisky is rare for sure, but it is also accessible. **JH**

Tasting notes

Vanilla, spice, coconut, fudge, and cream are found swinging from the chandeliers within this beautifully balanced, smooth, and indulgent whisky.

Compass Box Lady Luck

Compass Box | www.compassboxwhisky.com

Region and country of origin Islay and Speyside, Scotland **Distilleries** Caol Ila, Islay; Imperial, Carron by Aberlour, Banffshire **Alcohol content** 46% abv
Style Blended malt

Compass Box founder John Glaser admits that one part of him cannot resist the temptation to do something esoteric and indulgent. Lady Luck is a case in point, a one-off vatted malt whisky that tastes wonderful. Its name, after a Bob Dylan song, was also inspired by what is known as a "lucky blend"—a whisky made of both young and very old Islay malt whisky. A Lucky Blend brand was released by a well-known independent bottler many years ago, and Lady Luck pays homage to it in an elegant curtsy.

Like many Compass Box whiskies, Lady Luck was born out of experimentation, passion, and verve. This is a vatting of three casks in total. They comprise two from Caol Ila distillery on Islay, a twenty-five- and a twenty-nine-year old from 1984 and 1980, and some fourteen-year-old Imperial single malt from 1995. The whisky is matured in American white oak hogsheads and is incredibly well-structured.

Lady Luck is as much an innovation as it is a tribute to the malts. While the older whiskies bring depth and complexity, the Imperial has lots of zest and fruitiness, which has helped to balance things out. In all, this is yet another shining example of a vatted malt that really is as good as a single malt. **JH**

Tasting notes

A whisky with subtle smoke in the forefront and fruitiness in the background. The finish keeps on giving fruit and peat flavors long after each sip.

Compass Box
Oak Cross

Compass Box | www.compassboxwhisky.com

Region and country of origin Scotland
Distilleries Various
Alcohol content 43% abv
Style Blended malt

Compass Box's intention with Oak Cross was to bring spice from European oak to the creamy vanilla notes from American bourbon casks. The whisky's name refers to the special casks—with heads of new French sessile oak and bodies of American white oak—used in its creation. The casks were an experiment to find a perfect balance, so it seems fitting that the resulting whisky was named after them.

Oak Cross is made from Highland malt whiskies that are aged for a minimum of ten years before being vatted/blended together and put into bespoke "oak cross" casks to marry and mature for several months. The resulting whisky is well structured with a subtle richness. The contents of the casks are blended together to achieve a complementary balance of flavors: variously elegant, subtle, and complex.

Highland malt whiskies distilled at Teaninich, in the village of Alness, have a lightly malty but delicate nature. These are balanced with whiskies from other distilleries in the villages of Brora and Carron, adding both fruit and weight to the mix. In all, Oak Cross is a testament to the art of whisky blending. Finely tuned, complex flavors are evident, masked within a dram that is approachable, soft, and honeyed. **JH**

Tasting notes

A softly-softly blend of vanilla, clove, and fruit, as well as butterscotch, ginger, and golden syrup. Its true charm is that it is accessible without being pretentious.

Compass Box
The Peat Monster

Compass Box | www.compassboxwhisky.com

Region and country of origin Scotland
Distilleries Various
Alcohol content 46% abv
Style Blend

Some critics say that this whisky is not as monstrous in peat terms as many other releases, which suggests that it doesn't live up to its name. However, to dismiss it as a fraud is to miss the point. Peat is only one of the monstrous tastes on offer here. Furthermore, to call a whisky a monster goes some way to describing its fullness of flavor, but does it go far enough to illustrate its complexity, too? This whisky is big, multilayered, rich, and peaty. And yes, it is certainly a smoky malt whisky to be reckoned with—a colossus of deep smokiness, even a bottle of dragon's sighs, perfectly balanced in richness and subtleness of character.

Single mats from Islay (Port Askaig), the Isle of Mull, and Speyside are combined to make up 50 percent of the blend and give the whisky a smoky character. These peaty malts are married with 30 percent Highland and 20 percent Island single malt to achieve extra earthiness and depth.

The blend of single malts is aged in a range of first-fill and refill American oak casks. The result is a real fiend of a whisky. With a finish that is as luscious as fresh fruit mixed with the earthy scent of bonfire smoke, Peat Monster has an amazing balance of subtle softness too, which surprises, but in a good way. **JH**

Tasting notes

This is not only a peaty, smoky, and big, brash whisky, it also has hidden depths and many complex layers that evoke hints of fruit and slightly sweet spice.

Compass Box
The Spice Tree

Compass Box | www.compassboxwhisky.com

Region and country of origin Highlands, Scotland
Distilleries Various
Alcohol content 46% abv
Style Blended malt

The Scotch Whisky Association (SWA) maintains strict rules as to what is and isn't Scotch whisky in order to protect it from imitation and fraud. When Compass Box Spice Tree was originally launched in 2005, the SWA took issue because French oak staves were placed inside bourbon casks to add the spice. (Even though replacing broken staves or cask heads with new ones is okay, and the end result is the same.) Fortunately, Compass Box developed a maturation process that yielded similar results to the original while also being acceptable to the SWA. Phew!

The Spice Tree is a 100-percent malt whisky sourced from northern Highland distilleries, mainly Clynelish. The primary maturation includes a mix of first-fill and refill American oak. For the secondary maturation, which lasts as long as two years, Compass Box now racks the whisky into barrels with toasted new French oak heads. This imparts a flavor profile similar to that created by the flat staves used for the original Spice Tree. The barrel heads are subjected to three different levels of toasting, which produces whiskies that can be blended to create additional layers of complexity. The Spice Tree is a very rich malt whisky, non-chill-filtered, and it tastes exceptional. **JH**

Tasting notes

A round and rich, well-balanced whisky. The spice and vanilla character on the nose and palate continue through in a long, satisfying finish.

Cragganmore
12-Year-Old

Diageo | www.malts.com

Region and country of origin Speyside, Scotland
Distillery Cragganmore, Ballindalloch, Banffshire
Alcohol content 40% abv
Style Single malt

Cragganmore's whisky has a distinguished reputation as a prominent ingredient in blends. (Old Parr is one, virtually unknown in the United Kingdom but very popular in South America, Venezuela in particular.) Only 5 percent of the distillery's production is released as single malt; it is one of the Classic Malts series, but only a few other official expressions exist.

The distillery has experimented with fourteen- and seventeen-year-old malts but has settled for the industry norm of twelve years. Cragganmore 12-Year-Old is famed for its complexity: smoke, wood, and sulfur are there, but none of them to excess.

Cragganmore uses lightly smoked malt, and the new make is designed to be sulfury—Diageo chooses to run the stills hard to minimize the spirit's contact with copper. At various stages of production, the distillery favors the interaction of wood with the barley. Wooden malt bins keep the malt fresh and don't allow it to sweat as much as other options do. The six washbacks are wooden too, made from European larch; the oldest of them is sixty years old. Finally, the spirit is poured into American oak casks (normally refills, but they vary), so the wood influence does not overtake the gentle spirit. **IGY**

Tasting notes

A gasp of smoke, followed by fresh and then dried flowers. Chewy, malty granola and vanilla pod from the wood. Smoke, cigar box, and flowers in the finish.

New, memorable packaging accompanied the 2009 relaunch of the Spice Tree.

Cragganmore Distillers Edition

Diageo | www.malts.com

Region and country of origin Speyside, Scotland
Distillery Cragganmore, Ballindalloch, Banffshire
Alcohol content 40% abv
Style Single malt

The Distillers Edition of Cragganmore starts out in the same way as its benchmark brother, Cragganmore 12-Year-Old, being aged primarily in refilled American oak casks for the first twelve years. Its transformation into this densely perfumed expression occurs when the spirit is transferred from the ex-bourbon casks to port casks, called "pipes," where it receives an additional or second maturation, or finish. Diageo refers to this process as a double maturation.

The purpose of the finish in port pipes is to introduce intense fruit characteristics. The port itself has rich, full-bodied, fruity flavors, full of raspberry, plum, and spices, with notable sweetness. The finish also serves to enhance or increase existing flavors such as the whisky's natural smokiness.

Although the Distillers Edition of Cragganmore is produced to a prescribed style, each batch has its own natural characteristics. It is thus necessary for each of the vintages to be aged for its own specific length of time in the port pipes. A whisky enthusiast's idle moments may be wiled away in many instructive ways; here, the dates on the label may be read and twelve years subtracted to calculate the number of years the whisky has spent in port pipes.

The differences between the whiskies aged in each of the individual casks can be remarkable. For instance, the more a cask has been charred before use, the more the liquid port will have been absorbed into the wood, ultimately to be passed back into the whisky. Anything from 0.3 to 0.7 of a gallon (1 to 3 liters) of port can be left sleeping in the barrel. **IGY**

Tasting notes

Decant into a glass, add a drop of water, position the glass in dappled sunlight, and wait half an hour. Densely perfumed with ripe fruit and some smoke, and sweet with malt. Flavors of hard candy and wine gums, but the palate is dry, with an oaky, smoky maltiness.

Cutty Sark 12-Year-Old

Edrington Group | www.cutty-sark.com

Region and country of origin Scotland
Distilleries Various
Alcohol content 40% abv
Style Blend

Even today, when spirit bottles are made in a remarkable variety of shapes and sizes, a bottle of Cutty Sark stands out as unusual and nonconformist. It must have had an extraordinary impact when the blend was first released, in 1923.

Cutty Sark was created as a light, peat-free alternative drink for wine-consuming customers of Berry Bros. & Rudd who wanted to try the new Scotch spirit without subjecting their taste buds to too much hardship. The decision to avoid using a name with a reference to the Scottish Highlands, or to put a family name on the label, was a brave one. Further, taking a Scottish term (from Robert Burns's poem "Tam O' Shanter") and linking it with the eponymous speedy tea clipper rather than the original poem was truly inspired. The label was originally white, and the story goes that its yellowing happened by accident and had to be left for reasons of cost and time. Whatever the case, taken as a whole, the innovative blend took the world of whisky by storm

During Prohibition, Cutty Sark was widely exported to the United States, where it was firmly established. Any advantage it had in that market is now long gone, although Edrington has placed its distribution under the control of Rémy once more, so older expressions such as this should be more readily available. While the Original is a perfectly polite and well-made blend, Cutty Sark gets more wind in its sails with this one. The body has extra weight from the increased age in oak, and there would seem to be a hefty amount of sherried Glenrothes. **DR**

Tasting notes

The smooth, soft, and rounded fruity taste of the Cutty Sark Original blend is still present here, but on the palate this whisky is altogether more brash, with some early notes that are fuller, more oily, and closer to sulfur. The finish is oaky and honeyed.

Cutty Sark 15-Year-Old

Edrington Group | www.cutty-sark.com

Region and country of origin Scotland
Distilleries Various
Alcohol content 40% abv
Style Blend

What goes around comes around. A glance along the shelves of a whisky shop today reveals all sorts of modern, eye-friendly, and progressive bottle shapes and packaging. Some distilleries are putting out what seem like scores of new bottlings, bamboozling the hapless consumer, and there has never been greater choice in all areas of whisky retail.

For Cutty Sark, though, planning for the years ahead would seem to be about less being more. As Edrington attempts to reinvent the brand for a new generation, some expressions are set to be deleted from the range, and this is one of them. Although at the time of writing no final decision had been made, it looked as though the Cutty Sark 15-Year-Old would be discontinued. That possibility alone is enough to make it well worth seeking out.

The vast majority of Cutty Sark whisky is sold in bars rather than being made available for the take-home market, and most of that is Cutty Sark Original. Having another eight expressions sharing a tiny slice of the market made no sense, so there was an argument that, to reduce the number of expressions, the logical progression was from the Original to the 12-Year-Old, and from the 12-Year-Old to the 18-Year-Old. It makes sense. The extra three years of the 15-Year-Old add more wood but do not necessarily take the whisky to a better place. And on the other hand, the 15-Year-Old does not quite cut it as a premium blend in the way that the 18-Year-Old does. That said, it is included here because it is a palatable and rare example of a fifteen-year-old blend. **DR**

Tasting notes

Full flavored, rich in red berry and green fruits, with a center of toffee and honey. The landing is soft and gentle, with honey and oak in attendance. But, in the final analysis, it is not really meaty, beaty, big, and bouncy enough to reach Champions League status.

The *Cutty Sark* was raced from China to London to deliver the first tea of the year.

Cutty Sark 18-Year-Old

Edrington Group | www.cutty-sark.com

Region and country of origin Scotland
Distilleries Various
Alcohol content 43% abv
Style Blend

Cutty Sark 18-Year-Old was introduced during the mid-1990s under the Discovery name by previous brand owner Berry Bros. & Rudd. It wished to augment the existing range of younger expressions at a time when aged blends were becoming progressively more popular in export markets.

Since 2010, the Cutty Sark brand has belonged to the Edrington Group, which has enjoyed a long and fruitful relationship with Berry Bros, supplying malt for the blend from its Glenrothes, Macallan, Highland Park, Tamdhu, and Bunnahbhain distilleries. Ownership of the Glenrothes single-malt brand, though not of the distillery, has now transferred to Berry Bros & Rudd; Bunnahbhain is now owned by Burn Stewart Distillers, and Tamdhu by Ian Macleod Distillers. However, the same malts still play their part in all aged variants of Cutty Sark.

Kirsteen Campbell, master blender for Cutty Sark, says, "Additional aging [is used] to create the differences between the various expressions, rather than any conscious changes in component malts or cask types. . . . You wouldn't want first-fills to dominate the flavor, which they would do over a twenty-five-year timescale. I find that there's a soft vanilla note through the range, which really comes on to the palate in the 18-Year-Old.

"The Cutty Sark blend is quite light. While the older expressions, like the 18-Year-Old, are richer in character, you have to be careful to make sure they aren't dominated by heavy sherry notes. They have to remain true to the Cutty Sark house style." **GS**

Tasting notes

The nose is soft and elegant, with malt, sherry, and a hint of sweet wood smoke. With time, caramel and discreet licorice notes emerge. The palate displays good integration of malts and grains, being sweet, fruity, and sherried, with chewy toffee. A lingering, sweet finish.

Cutty Sark 25-Year-Old

Edrington Group | www.cutty-sark.com

Region and country of origin Scotland
Distilleries Various
Alcohol content 45.7% abv
Style Blend

According to Cutty Sark brand controller Jason Craig, "The 25-Year-Old was launched at the end of 1998/ early 1999, and along with the 18-Year-Old it was intended as a top-end extension to the existing portfolio. The deluxe range, which includes the 25-Year-Old, tends to sell well in the Middle East, Greece, Japan, and Portugal." Master blender Kirsteen Campbell observes that, "While you get soft vanilla characteristics across the range, when you come to the 25-Year-Old you are getting more mature notes— dried fruits mask the vanilla to an extent."

Both American oak ex-bourbon barrels and American and European oak ex-sherry casks are used in the maturation of Cutty Sark. Some 15 percent of the component single malts in Cutty Sark Original have been matured in first-fill ex-sherry casks, but the proportion for the 25-Year-Old tends to be higher.

In 2003, Cutty Sark 25-Year-Old was named "Best blended Scotch whisky in the world" by *Whisky Magazine* in its annual Icons of Whisky awards. Campbell notes that, "After it won that award, there was huge demand for the 25-Year-Old, and the challenge for the blenders was to provide the volumes required but also maintain the consistency, which is quite difficult when using whiskies of that age."

In 2012, the Cutty Sark Tam O'Shanter 25-Year-Old special edition commemorated the Robert Burns poem of that name, in which Cutty Sark is a fleet-footed witch. "It's Cutty Sark with a peatier note to it," says Campbell. "We've used two different components to give a sweet smokiness to the blend." **GS**

Tasting notes

The nose offers a blend of exotic spices, including sandalwood and jasmine, along with a hint of orange, coffee, sweet sherry, and moist Christmas cake. The palate is rich, ripe, and spicy, with some smoke and eucalyptus notes. The finish is rich, fruity, and sweet.

Cutty Sark 30-Year-Old

Edrington Group | www.cutty-sark.com

Region and country of origin Scotland
Distilleries Various
Alcohol content 43% abv
Style Blend

Few brands have the class, style, history, and heritage of Cutty Sark, and it is fitting that the oldest expression of this mighty blend should have become the 30-Year-Old in 2012. Cutty Sark was a whisky that was exported to the United States during Prohibition, and it is said to be the whisky that a liquor runner, Captain William McCoy, supplied to the speakeasies. As far as those drinkers were concerned, it was "the real McCoy."

Cutty Sark has drifted in recent years but owner Edrington has taken full control of it once more and invested heavily in it. The common view is that new and emerging markets will first import blended Scotch and then move to single malts. But there is also a pattern of moving from standard Scotch blends to aged ones, so Cutty Sark drinkers may stay with the brand but move to premium and super-premium expressions, such as this one. While older markets may distrust blends, emerging markets embrace them.

Like many other great aged blends, the 30-Year-Old justifies its price tag because of the brilliant marriage of flavors on show. Edrington owns Highland Park and Macallan as well as Glenturret, and has had access to fine aged Glenrothes, too. The age statement means that the very youngest is at least thirty years old. That this whisky is an all-round beauty should come as a surprise to no one. **DR**

Tasting notes

The perfect mix of full, rich, fruity, and oaky malt and soft, cushionlike grain. Orange and red fruits mix with toffee and milk chocolate; oaky spice holds it together.

Dailuaine 10-Year-Old

Harris Whisky Co. | www.harriswhisky.com

Region and country of origin Speyside, Scotland
Distillery Daiuaine, Aberlour, Banffshire
Alcohol content 46% abv
Style Single malt

In 2010, the Gloucestershire-based bottler Harris Whisky Co. unveiled a new series of releases under its Bright Young Things label. According to the company, this range will include "fine examples of some of the best young malts to be found, all specially selected by Mark Harris for their excellent characteristics."

The Dailuaine 10-Year-Old is described by Harris as "the first in our new range of younger, yet delicious single malts. This whisky from the Dailuaine distillery shows just how good a young whisky can be. A wonderful, fragrant, fruity dram, full of life and vigor, this whisky is truly a Bright Young Thing!"

Like nearby Benrinnes, also bottled by Harris Whisky Co., Dailuaine is one of Diageo's lower-profile distilleries, turning out comparatively large quantities of spirit destined for blending purposes. The distillery's main single malt is a sixteen-year-old expression in the Flora & Fauna series. Like Benrinnes, Dailuaine deserves to be better known, particularly as it is one of the rare Speyside single malts offered by Diageo after maturation in ex-sherry casks.

This Harris Whisky Co. Dailuaine, distilled in May 2000 and bottled in July 2010, is in the distillery's classic sulfury house style, in an uncolored, non-chill-filtered, cask-strength, single-cask format. Hogshead cask no. 000090 yielded 400 bottles. **GS**

Tasting notes

Barley, malt, and fresh fruit on the nose, with a hint of lime and a developing herbal note. Fruit punch on the smooth palate, with barley, delicate smoke, and spice.

Cutty Sark distances itself from darker, heavier, whisky blends.

Dallas Dhu
27-Year-Old

Wm Cadenhead & Co.
www.wmcadenhead.com

Region and country of origin Speyside, Scotland
Distillery Dallas Dhu (closed), Forres, Morayshire
Alcohol content 59.2% abv
Style Single malt

The firm of Wm Cadenhead & Co. dates back to 1842. Along with Gordon & MacPhail, it persisted in offering a range of independently bottled single malts through the decades when very few malt distillers released their own brands. The company bottles whiskies in several ranges, including Chairman's Stock, which showcases cask-strength variants of old and scarce single malts.

This Dallas Dhu expression was distilled in 1979 and matured in an ex-bourbon hogshead before being bottled in May 2007. Like so many of its Speyside neighbors, Dallas Dhu was a product of the whisky boom that reached its height during the 1890s; Dallas Dhu, located near Forres, came on stream in 1899. Ultimately, the plant ended up in the distillery portfolio of Distillers Company Ltd. (DCL). Expansion was not possible due to the limited water supply provided by the Altyre Burn. Unsurprisingly, with the downturn in demand in the early 1980s, Dallas Dhu found itself on the company's hit list; its last cask was filled on March 16, 1983.

The distillery is internally quite intact and serves as Scotland's only dedicated whisky museum, having been acquired by Historic Scotland in 1988. **GS**

Tasting notes

Pineapple, peach, and pear, plus a slightly mashy note and a hint of licorice. Elegant in the mouth, smooth and sweet, with mango, olive, white pepper, and spice.

Dallas Dhu Old Malt
Cask 36-Year-Old 1982

Douglas Laing & Co.
www.douglaslaing.com

Region and country of origin Speyside, Scotland
Distillery Dallas Dhu (closed), Forres, Morayshire
Alcohol content 46.2% abv
Style Single malt

The communists among us should be proud—Dallas Dhu is a state-run distillery. Except that it produces no whisky, nor anything else. Along with scores of other equally good distilleries, Dallas Dhu closed as a working concern in 1983. It is lucky that, at the same time distilleries were starting to close in response to waning demand for whisky, the state was looking for one to preserve for the public. Dallas Dhu, being small, complete, and fairly easy to maintain, was saved. It is now a working museum with protected status.

Among the pleasures of visiting a working distillery are the various noises and smells that assault the senses. You won't get that here, of course, but at least you can wander around out of harm's way.

As with all the distilleries that closed in the 1980s, stocks of Dallas Dhu are disappearing fast, so grab a bottle while you can. As anyone who is lucky enough to find a bottle of this Douglas Laing Old Malt Cask 36-Year-Old will find out, Dallas Dhu embraces old age better than many of its fellow Speysiders, with the oak complementing the fruits rather than hammering them out into submission. With only 151 bottles of this expression released from a single hogshead cask, this is a particularly enjoyable piece of history. **PB**

Tasting notes

Light, juicy fruit on the nose, with a sheen of dusty oak. On the palate, the oak never overpowers, leaving the vanillas and fruits to weave their magic.

The Dalmore 12-Year-Old

Whyte & Mackay
www.thedalmore.com

Region of origin Highlands, Scotland
Distillery Dalmore, Alness, Ross-shire
Alcohol content 40% abv
Type Single malt

The Northern Highlands are the home of robust whiskies that demand much more than the legal minimum of three years in cask to reach maturity. At twelve years, this is the very youngest malt that the Dalmore distillery would consider bottling. To cope with the weight and body of Dalmore's spirit, American white oak is first used to age the whisky for at least eight to ten years. Then—and this is where things begin to take shape—the whisky is transferred to first-fill Matusalem oloroso sherry butts. These are deemed compatible because Matusalem sherry is full, rich, and sweet, with 25 percent Pedro Ximénez content. The butts will have held this for thirty years.

Dalmore specifies that 1.3 gallons (5 liters) of sherry be left in each 158-gallon (600-liter) cask. During the transit from Spain to Scotland, half a gallon (2 liters) of the liquid infuses into the cask along the way, and the remaining three-quarters of a gallon (3 liters) must then be removed. Once the Dalmore is put into the sherry casks, it is left for about three years.

The 12-Year-Old originally was aged in 30 percent sherry butts and 70 percent American oak casks. Now the balance is closer to fifty-fifty, which in part justifies the whisky's notable price. **IGY**

Tasting notes

Oloroso sherry, with a warmth on the tongue, a mouthful of exotically spiced almonds, certainly, and some dark chocolate and marmalade, too.

The Dalmore 15-Year-Old

Whyte & Mackay
www.thedalmore.com

Region of origin Highlands, Scotland
Distillery Dalmore, Alness, Ross-shire
Alcohol content 40% abv
Type Single malt

Instead of maturing the Dalmore 15-Year-Old in one type of sherry wood, three different styles of sherry are used. After coming off the stills, the spirit is first aged in American white oak. After twelve years, the whisky is split into thirds and transferred into the three different types of 158-gallon (600-liter) sherry butts, all of them sourced from Gonzalez Byass in Jerez.

One third of the whisky is put into butts that were previously used to age rich, sweet Matusalem sherry for thirty years. Another third is transferred into twenty-five- to thirty-year-old Apostoles sherry casks, which is still a heavy sherry but softer than the Matusalem. The final third goes into casks used for amoroso sherry, a sweetened oloroso with a rich, raisiny, nutty character. The three batches are left to mature for a further three years before being married together for a final three or four months—the marrying time being mainly dependent on demand.

This is an expression that has softer, more elegant notes than the 12-Year-Old. The aged Matusalem, Apostoles, and amoroso oloroso butts have a marked effect on the resultant taste. They certainly add some flesh to the whisky's muscle, and while there remains a firmness, there is a silkiness, too. **IGY**

Tasting notes

The rich, deep mahogany color is a clue to the intensity. Orange, marmalade, and spices appear on the nose and continue to evolve on the palate. A Highlander in silk.

The Dalmore 18-Year-Old

Whyte & Mackay | www.thedalmore.com

Region of origin Highlands, Scotland
Distillery Dalmore, Alness, Ross-shire
Alcohol content 43% abv
Type Single malt

The Dalmore 18-Year-Old was originally launched in 2009/10 to fill the gap between the 15-Year-Old and the now delisted 21- and 30-Year-Olds. The whisky is different in style from the younger expressions, not only because of its great age, but also because it is matured differently. In this expression, the spirit is first aged in plain American white oak casks for at least the first fourteen years (although it can be as many as seventeen years). Then, rather than being split between different types of casks, like the 15-Year-Old, it spends the next four years aging entirely in oloroso sherry butts.

The persistence of time is keenly felt in this expression. This is a fireside dram with a big, impactful palate. According to Whyte & Mackay's master distiller Richard Paterson, when the original new spirit comes off the stills at Dalmore it is, "full, rich, with hints of lemongrass and a tang of citrus." Then, in the early years, when the spirit begins to interact with the air, characteristics such as sea spray emerge. However, after eighteen years, this is a whisky that has had extensive time in cask, and the influences from the wood are strong enough to introduce new and prominent top notes of marzipan and licorice.

As with the release of any very mature whisky, great emphasis is placed on its age. In this instance, Whyte & Mackay has positioned it at the beginning of the luxury end of the Dalmore range. As many as 5,000 to 10,000 cases are produced each year, and most of these are destined for the United States, the brand's biggest market. **IGY**

Tasting notes

Gutsy in hue and dignified in tone, intense on the nose, and opulent on the palate. Heavy, with the intensity of an after-dinner selection of petit four, chocolate truffle, walnut, and vanilla pod, followed by violet, rosemary, and jasmine—and a dark espresso hit.

The Dalmore 40-Year-Old Astrum

Whyte & Mackay | www.thedalmore.com

Region of origin Highlands, Scotland
Distillery Dalmore, Alness, Ross-shire
Alcohol content 42% abv
Type Single malt

The Dalmore 40-Year-Old was distilled in 1966. There are two editions, bottled four years apart, although originally only 1,000 bottles were released. Both editions were matured entirely in butts previously used for the maturation of Matusalem sherry.

The first 40-Year-Old was launched in Paris on October 26, 2006, and was dedicated to Drew Sinclair, who worked at the distillery for forty years. It was introduced as one of Whyte & Mackay's Rare & Prestige collection, which also included Whyte & Mackay 40-Year-Old, Jura 40-Year-Old, and a 1973 Dalmore aged in cabernet sauvignon barriques.

At the time, Whyte & Mackay's Rare & Prestige was the most expensive collection to be launched all at once. The bottles of Dalmore 40-Year-Old, sold at $2,000 (£1,300), marked a boom period in luxury whisky, coupled with a scarcity of very old casks. Indeed, in the last few years, stock levels have been quite critical for a lot of distilleries. Dalmore is among only a handful (with perhaps Macallan, Glenfiddich, Glenfarclas, Bowmore, and Balblair) that possess casks old enough to allow production of such an old whisky.

The second edition was described as a forty-year-old, but was in fact distilled on December 31, 1966, making it forty-four years of age before its launch in 2011. This edition was named Astrum 1966 (an astrum being a brilliantly bright star). While the first 40-Year-Old was bottled at the legal minimum alcohol by volume of 40 percent, it is significant that 40 percent was its natural cask strength. Astrum was also bottled at natural strength, this time at 42 percent abv. **IGY**

Tasting notes

A punch-bowl fragrance of orange, apple, pear, and melon, with a hint of something indescribably meaty and cadaverous. Chewy, creamy, and treaclelike on the palate; the original fruit remains, but becomes more exotic and ripe, preserved with ginger and licorice.

The Dalmore 45-Year-Old Aurora 1964

Whyte & Mackay | www.thedalmore.com

Region of origin Highlands, Scotland
Distillery Dalmore, Alness, Ross-shire
Alcohol content 45% abv
Type Single malt

When it comes to rare and old Dalmores like this one, forget "buy to try before you die," and consider "buy to sell before you die." Dalmore has recently become something of an investor's icon. When the distillery released twelve bottles of its 62-Year-Old (all of them individually named) in 2002, one sold at auction for $35,000 (£22,000, hammer price). In 2005 a bottle sold for $50,000 (£32,000) to a wealthy individual in a London hotel; he promptly cracked it open and drank the lot with friends (leaving just enough to give the barman a dram—a nice tip!). The final bottle (named Drew Sinclair after an ex-distillery manager) was recently sold for $196,000 (£125,000) to an anonymous Chinese businessman in Singapore airport. In just under ten years, that equates to a 468 percent increase in value.

At such a price, can the whisky increase in value much more? It probably will. Take, for example, Dalmore's other big hitter, Trinitas: two of the three bottles immediately sold for $157,000 (£100,000), with the final bottle selling for $188,000 (£120,000) a scant six months later. Not even the best fund managers would sniff at a 20 percent increase in six months.

The Dalmore Aurora will cost you rather less than a six-figure sum, at $4,400 (£2,800) per bottle. Most people planning to spend that amount of money on a bottle of Scotch would want to try it first. Be cheeky and ask for a sample; the very worst that can happen is you hear the word no. The best that can happen is that you get a sample, so you can "try before you die *and* sell before you die." Problem solved! **AS**

Tasting notes

Huge, powerful nose, with oak and menthol, then a dynamic fusion of rich, dark fruit, dried cranberry, sweet orange, blackberry, and mango, all interlaced with undertones of wood. Hints of dark chocolate and freshly ground coffee. An incredible experience.

The Dalmore Age of Exploration 1995

Whyte & Mackay | www.whyteandmackay.com

Region of origin Highlands, Scotland
Distillery Dalmore, Alness, Ross-shire
Alcohol content 40% abv
Type Single malt

Some people have accused Glasgow distiller Whyte & Mackay of attempting to gatecrash the iconic and collectable world of "premier cru" whiskies by launching a series of hyperexpensive malts. But they are wrong. The Whisky Highland Index monitors all Scotch whiskies for price changes, both at auction and through private sales, so it can track how they perform as an investment. The index showed that, for all twelve months of 2011, only the Macallan performed better. Dalmore is a highly collectable whisky, and one of the reasons is that it produces bottles of the quality of this one.

David Robertson, Whyte & Mackay's director for rare malts, is an astute, driven, and competitive person determined to hit the top spot; for Robertson, it is personal. He was the distiller at the Macallan before he joined Whyte & Mackay, and there isn't much he doesn't know about this area of the market. He would love to take the Dalmore to the top of the league. He also believes that distilleries selling high-end investment whiskies gain respect that inevitably benefits the entry-level whiskies it sells also.

This 1995 Dalmore is not at entry level, but it is nearer that end of the market. Bottled in 2011, so probably sixteen years old, it comes in a dinky little bag. As a limited release, it is a collector's item. It is available exclusively through the Whisky Shop retail chain, which has about twenty outlets across England and Scotland. The whisky is the result of one of several special partnerships established between the Dalmore distillery and the Whisky Shop. **DR**

Tasting notes

On the nose, this whisky has rose, hops, Seville blood orange, crushed leaves in fall, toffee, and brittle, burnt nuts. On the palate, distinctive oaky notes mix freely with burnt peach and baked orange crumble, milk chocolate, and toffee.

The Dalmore Castle Leod

Whyte & Mackay | www.thedalmore.com

Region of origin Highlands, Scotland
Distillery Dalmore, Alness, Ross-shire
Alcohol content 46% abv
Type Single malt

This limited-edition release is the follow-up to the Dalmore Mackenzie and has been named after that clan's home: Castle Leod. But it is not simply a sequel. If anything, it is a reminder that great things can emerge from the same location. Indeed, Castle Leod pays homage to the role the Mackenzie clan has played in the creation of the brand's image, and also celebrates the clan's ethos: "I Shine, Not Burn."

In terms of its namesake heritage, the residence of Castle Leod, which was built in 1606, nestles in the Scottish Highlands just 14 miles (23 km) from the Dalmore distillery. Sadly, despite continuing to be the seat of the clan, it is much in need of repair. Like its sibling brand, the Mackenzie, Castle Leod helps to raise funds to restore the Scottish castle. But this whisky is not simply a catalyst for fund-raising; it is more a tribute to the Dalmore's heritage.

Castle Leod was first distilled in 1995, before being matured in ex-sherry and bourbon casks and then finished in Bordeaux casks for eighteen months to give it an extra level of luxury and a smooth finish. In total there are 5,000 bottles of Dalmore Castle Leod; each retails at $160 (£100), giving plenty of opportunity for the castle to be fully restored. **JH**

Tasting notes

Scents of springtime on the nose. The cabernet sauvignon casks lend flavors of bread-and-butter pudding, fudge, and almond croissant.

The Dalmore Gran Reserva/Cigar Reserve

Whyte & Mackay | www.thedalmore.com

Region of origin Highlands, Scotland
Distillery Dalmore, Alness, Ross-shire
Alcohol content 40% abv
Type Single malt

This is whisky with a history. Originally named Cigar Malt, it was renamed Gran Reserva, only to have its name changed once again to Cigar Reserve in 2011.

The Cigar Malt, first created in the late 1990s, was aimed primarily at the American market. It had no age statement and was great value for money. It was aged eight to ten years in American white oak casks. After the first maturation, 60 percent was transferred to Matusalem oloroso butts for two, sometimes three, years, while the other 40 percent remained in American white oak. It was designed to be a strong, distinguished dram, compatible with cigars.

However, the name led some Americans to think that the whisky was aged in tobacco leaf, while others thought it would taste of cigars. At the same time, there was a feeling that anything associated with smoking was bad for your health. The new Gran Reserva, launched in 2007, was a slightly altered whisky with the sherry influence increased from 60 to 70 percent. But it did not have the same appeal, the name change generated confusion, and it was not as popular as before. Whyte & Mackay decided that it should not have bowed to "this sort of pressure," and the name was changed again in 2011. **IGY**

Tasting notes

An entire kitchen cupboard tipped into a bottle, with marmalade, fruit cake, ground coffee, chunks of dark chocolate, dried orange, and lemon peel.

← The watercolor painting of Castle Leod that features on the whisky's box.

The Dalmore
King Alexander III 1263

Whyte & Mackay | www.thedalmore.com

Region of origin Highlands, Scotland
Distillery Dalmore, Alness, Ross-shire
Alcohol content 40% abv
Type Single malt

When Alexander III of Scotland was rescued from the fury of a charging stag by the intrepidity of Colin Fitzgerald in 1263, the king was grateful enough to grant Fitzgerald's family not only the lands of Kintail but also the use of a stag emblem as its crest—the same emblem that adorns every bottle of Dalmore.

King Alexander III 1263 was the second release without an age statement after Gran Reserva. Released in 2009, the spirit was distilled in around 1992 and matured for at least fifteen years in American white oak casks. The whisky was then racked into six different batches, with as many as fifty casks in each.

The details of component parts are as follows: port pipes for between three and five years, Madeira drums also for three to five years, marsala barrels for three years, cabernet sauvignon barriques for one and a half years, small-batch bourbon barrels for three to five years, and Matusalem sherry butts for three years. Once matured, there is a strict formulation to assemble all the component parts, after which it depends on how the fusion of these different styles of casks are progressing over the years. In general, amoroso, port, and marsala casks are used for 50 percent, and the rest comes from the others. **IGY**

Tasting notes

Rose and lemon Turkish delight and Jujubes, with honey caramel, cocoa-dusted almond, chocolate orange, sherbet, and white chocolate. Parma violet, too.

The Dalmore
Mackenzie

Whyte & Mackay | www.thedalmore.com

Region of origin Highlands, Scotland
Distillery Dalmore, Alness, Ross-shire
Alcohol content 46% abv
Type Single malt

The Dalmore Mackenzie takes its name from the Clan Mackenzie, previous owners of the Dalmore distillery before Whyte & Mackay took the helm. In 1263 an ancestor of Clan Mackenzie once saved King Alexander III from being gored by a stag. In the 1780s the Mackenzies commissioned artist Benjamin West to depict the scene, and his painting, *Fury of the Stag* (1786), now hangs in the Scottish National Gallery.

Globally, there are just 3,000 bottles of the Dalmore Mackenzie. The spirit was distilled in 1992 and held in American white oak casks for eleven years before getting a six-year secondary maturation in fresh port pipes. This gives it a lovely amber color that has been likened to the color of a stag's blood.

But rather than fixate on the gore, there are significant merits for buying a bottle of Dalmore Mackenzie. A notable proportion of the profits from sales go toward maintaining and refurbishing Castle Leod, which, even today, continues to be the seat of the Clan Mackenzie. Also, each individually numbered bottle entitles the owner to claim a limited-edition print of West's painting, *Fury of the Stag*, signed by the head of the clan, thus securing their place in Scottish history. Can't say fairer than that. **JH**

Tasting notes

An intensely flavorsome single malt with scents of vanilla, red fruits, and spices amid notes of orange—the trademark of the Dalmore distillery.

The Dalmore Matusalem 1974

Whyte & Mackay | www.thedalmore.com

Region of origin Highlands, Scotland
Distillery Dalmore, Alness, Ross-shire
Alcohol content 42% abv
Type Single malt

Released in 2009 as part of the Dalmore Rare & Prestige range in a limited edition of only 124 cases, the Dalmore Matusalem 1974 Sherry Finesse was distilled on April 15, 1974. The spirit was filled into sherry butts that had held Apostoles Palo Cortado. The whisky was then transferred to sherry butts previously used for Matusalem thirty-year-old oloroso, to be aged for a final five years.

According to master blender Richard Paterson, "To fully experience [Dalmore 1974's] rare attributes, time must be given on the palate. Allow the spirit to sensually drift over the center of the tongue, underneath, and then finally back to the center again. The warmth of the mouth will help to release the very soul of the spirit . . . in particular, the Matusalem thirty-year-old oloroso sherry, which is steeped in the pores of the wood, has made an invaluable contribution to the spirit's outstanding quality."

The Dalmore Matusalem 1974 is not to be confused with a thirty-two-year-old produced in 2006 for French whisky specialist La Maison du Whisky, nor with a slightly younger 1974 launched in 2002 for the Japanese market. Both of those were issued in white cardboard packaging. **GS**

Tasting notes

Intense ginger and orange—bittersweet orange, marmalade, orange peel and zest, and chocolate orange, all heightened by mulling spices aplenty.

The Dalmore Rivers Collection

Whyte & Mackay | www.thedalmore.com

Region of origin Highlands, Scotland
Distillery Dalmore, Alness, Ross-shire
Alcohol content 40% abv
Type Single malt

The Dalmore Rivers Collection celebrates Scotland's great salmon-fishing rivers in the form of four expressions—the Dee Dram, Spey Dram, Tay Dram, and Tweed Dram. Each whisky was launched in partnership with the corresponding regional river's trust to support Scottish sport and tourist attractions. Every bottle sold results in a generous donation to the trusts to assist them in continuing their important conservation work.

The individual whiskies are created differently. Dalmore Dee is laid down in 50 percent oloroso sherry wood to 50 percent American white oak; Dalmore Spey uses 36 percent sherry wood and 64 percent American white oak for its casks; Dalmore Tay is matured in 100 percent oloroso sherry wood; Dalmore Tweed is a whisky matured in 80 percent American white oak to 20 percent oloroso sherry wood.

Dalmore Dee came first and raised $55,000 (£35,000) in nine weeks; the Rivers Collection followed to do more good for the local environment. Each bottle is 40 percent abv and sells for $60 (£40) with a minimum donation of $6 (£4) per bottle going to the river trust or foundation. The whole project has a nice ring to it and results in funds for a great cause. **JH**

Tasting notes

Dee: Cinnamon, coffee, ginger, licorice. Spey: Christmas cake, mixed peel, syrup sponge, cherry. Tweed: Orange, apple tart, and ginger. Tay: orange, lime, and caramel.

The Dalmore Sirius

Whyte & Mackay | www.thedalmore.com

Region of origin Highlands, Scotland
Distillery Dalmore, Alness, Ross-shire
Alcohol content 45% abv
Type Single malt

The Dalmore Sirius is taken from a single-vintage distillation, from a single cask that was filled from the still in June 1951. The spirit was then aged in a butt (no. 1781) that is thought to have contained oloroso sherry; however, the exact style of the sherry is unknown because of the age of the whisky. The limited expression was bottled at cask strength, which in this case was 45 percent abv. The name, Sirius, refers to a particularly bright star and is derived from the ancient Greek for "scorcher." Sirius is visible from almost every inhabited region on Earth, and the star has long been a guiding light for navigators.

Only a dozen decanters of Sirius were released by the distillery for worldwide distribution, and these were only made available to private clients and in travel retail. Before its launch, the first sale was made to a tourist who was walking around on the Dalmore distillery tour. The cask was about to be bottled and, seeing its date in 1951, she said "That's my birthday!" and prebought the first decanter.

Sirius was launched at London Heathrow's Terminal 5 in November 2009. Despite its price being set at $16,000 (£10,000) per decanter, all twelve sold out in just two days. Today, there is apparently no shortage of demand; in 2012, one Web site was quoting $47,000 (£30,000) for a single decanter. **GS**

Tasting notes

Marmalade, licorice, coffee, toffee, nuts, and mulling spices, expanding imperceptibly rather than exploding, then ebbing unhurriedly. With age has come maturity.

The Dalmore Zenith

Whyte & Mackay | www.thedalmore.com

Region of origin Highlands, Scotland
Distillery Dalmore, Alness, Ross-shire
Alcohol content Undisclosed
Type Single malt

The Dalmore Zenith is one of the rarest whiskies—in fact, there is only one bottle. "Zenith" is a term used in astronomy to refer to an imaginary point directly above a particular location, and here it suggests the whisky's quality. In November 2011, Dalmore gave the bottle to the Whisky Shop, a major whisky retail chain in the United Kingdom, who sent it on a five-month tour of its nineteen stores, ending in March 2012.

This unique whisky represents history in a glass. There are three Dalmore single malts in the mix: valuable whiskies from 1951 and 1964, and a historic fifty-two-year-old whisky distilled in 1926—three years before the great Wall Street crash—and bottled in 1978, a year before Margaret Thatcher was elected prime minister of the United Kingdom.

The Whisky Shop invited sealed bids for the single bottle, the minimum being set at $78,500 (£50,000). With a closing date of March 30, 2012, bids were received from around the world—only Macallan is a better investment than Dalmore. Part of the proceeds were donated to the British Red Cross charity.

The minimum bid alone was a lot of money, so what did it buy? Principally, the right of owning the only bottle in the world, just as an art connoisseur would be proud to own a rare painting. But that in itself isn't enough. The whisky has to play a part. **DR**

Tasting notes

On the nose, black cherry, raisin, fig cake, and caramelized citrus fruits. On the palate, nuts give way to coffee, coconut, cracked black pepper, and banana.

← The Sirius prismatic decanter is adorned by a stag's head in solid silver.

Deanston 12-Year-Old

Burn Stewart Distillers | www.burnstewartdistillers.com

Region and country of origin Highlands, Scotland
Distillery Deanston, near Doune, Perthshire
Alcohol content 46.3% abv
Style Single malt

Of all Scotland's distilleries, Deanston is one of the most underrated, at least by European aficionados. It also has one of the most unusual and most attractive distillery sites, but there are no visitor facilities. It is truly a hidden Highland gem, sited not far from Sterling.

Deanston distillery is actually an old cotton mill, a tall, austere, multiwindowed carbuncle of a building that wouldn't look out of place in an L. S. Lowry painting. In front of it is the fast-flowing river that powers the distillery's only electricity plant, providing enough energy not only to operate the distillery but also to light the local streets.

Most Deanston single malt is sold in the United States, but until the brand's owners changed the formula of the malt, raising the strength to 46.3 percent abv, which made chill-filtering no longer necessary, it wasn't anything much to write home about. Despite being the number three malt in the United States, it had been short on the finish and sharp on the palate. However, all that has changed, and the new version is a high-quality Highlander with improved packaging to match.

Drinkers who favor the Deanston distillery's own 12-Year-Old might like to compare it with an expression available in the Glenkeir Treasures range from the independent whisky retailing chain, the Whisky Shop. This is significantly different from both the original standard bottling and the newly improved one, being finished in oloroso sherry casks. Introduced in 2009 and with the lower alcohol content of 40 percent abv, it is a good advertisement for the distillery. **DR**

Tasting notes

Light, fresh, and fruity on the nose, with hints of cereals, honey, nuts, and orange marmalade. On the palate, it is soft, spicy, and nutty with caramel, oak, and a little saltiness. It makes a perfect entry point for blend drinkers who want to take the single-malt plunge.

Dewar's 12-Year-Old

Dewar's (Bacardi) | www.dewars.com

Region and country of origin Scotland
Distilleries Various
Alcohol content 40% abv
Style Blend

In the Dewar's story, the whisky, its namesakes, and the area of Aberfeldy are inextricably intertwined. It is a story that tests credulity, veering from the unlikely to vaudeville and ending as near legend. The career of Crofter's son John Dewar progressed from carpenter to merchant of wine and other spirits, leading to his eventual establishing of what would become the brand we know today. He always sought to keep one step ahead in his business affairs, and no doubt it was this very quality that he instilled in the two sons who came to inherit the brand. John Alexander Dewar was the offspring who had a savvy head for business, while his brother Thomas (Tommy) was the main proponent of advertising and marketing.

Tommy's advertising techniques were rarely witnessed in their day, certainly not in such an ambitious manner. In 1885 he was dispatched to London with a view to expanding the fortunes of the now-renamed John Dewar & Sons whisky. Branding and identity were paramount to the Dewars, and five years after Tommy's move to London, the family name had become well known on the restaurant scene, with Dewar's being the only supplier for distributors Spiers & Pond. This was the kind of endorsement and exposure used by Tommy to cement Dewar's fast-growing reputation for excellence.

Dewar's 12-Year-Old is double-aged, meaning that the whiskies selected for this bottling are selected and then placed in oak casks for a further six months together, during which the flavors become nuanced yet delicately balanced. **D&C**

Tasting notes

The nose is all candied fruit and traditional wedding cake, Highland toffee, oak, vanilla, and a small note of pepper. In the mouth, it is well rounded, viscous, and warm. Lighter fruit (lemon, tiniest hint of lime) and walnut come through on the palate. Lengthy finish.

Dewar's 18-Year-Old

Dewar's (Bacardi) | www.dewars.com

Region and country of origin Scotland
Distilleries Various
Alcohol content 40% abv
Style Blend

There is a famous letter from Andrew Carnegie to Dewar's recording a request from the Scottish-American businessman (not to mention industrialist, entrepreneur, and philanthropist) for "a small keg—say, nine or ten gallons—of the best Scotch Whisky you can find," with details of a shipping address—that of President Benjamin Harrison. Of course, Carnegie was an astute man with an eye for opportunity and a gut instinct for the workings of the corporate world. More interesting to us here, though, is the evident regard that Carnegie had for Messrs John Dewar & Sons. To call upon them to select a cask for a world leader was high praise indeed, and Carnegie was clearly aware that Dewar's understood the whisky it purveyed.

The significance of the occasion would not have been lost on the Dewars themselves, yet it is a testament to their refinement and taste that they did not make more of this special order, especially given their propensity for showmanship and marketing. Being given such a momentous endorsement would cloud the commercial judgement of most, and the Dewar family easily might have capitalized upon it and ultimately have appeared crass.

As it happened, the American public was outraged when it became known that President Harrison had accepted Dewar's whisky, rather than home-produced bourbon or rye. The outcry guaranteed the Dewars precious publicity, and soon requests for further shipments were flooding in. But if you excel in any field, word tends to get around. **D&C**

Tasting notes

Gorgeous nose: butterscotch and marzipan mingle with a slight trace of honey and lavender. There is light cream and a hint of vanilla. Deliciously silky on the palate; clotted cream, big oaky notes, a touch of burnt sugar, and a whisper of hazelnut. Beautiful stuff.

Grand administrative offices characterized Dewar's in its heyday.

"Why do you always insist on that particular brand of Whisky?"
"Because I believe in getting the best, and the best is

DEWAR'S "

Dewar's Signature

Dewar's (Bacardi) | www.dewars.com

Region and country of origin Scotland
Distilleries Various
Alcohol content 43% abv
Style Blend

From opening the beautiful wooden box, right up until the moment when you uncork the bottle, Dewar's Signature speaks of special occasions, treasured moments, and lasting memories. And while the packaging is exquisite, there is no doubt that the liquid inside the bottle has been carefully judged and balanced. In the short time it takes for the whisky blend's gorgeous aroma to waft from the bottleneck to your nose, you know you are assured of not just a drink but a memorable experience.

People underestimate blended whiskies, often taking them to be somewhat less than the sum of their parts. This particular bottle should go some way toward dissuading drinkers from that blinkered viewpoint. Anyone who has the chance to try their hand at blending will soon realize that mixing grain and malt, and indeed malts representing the more robust and individual characters of each whisky region, is no easy feat. To nuance a particular aspect of a blend with pinpoint accuracy takes considerable practice, knowledge, and skill, and the introduction of even the tiniest amount of whisky inappropriate for the character you are striving for can topple the blend instantly. But the experts at Dewar's undoubtedly know what they are doing, and the Signature blend clearly speaks for itself. **D&C**

Tasting notes

Berries and fudge, almond, heather honey, and fresh coffee beans. On the palate, fruitcake, butter, more fudge, a touch of dark Seville marmalade, then vanilla.

Dimple 12-Year-Old

Dewar's (Bacardi) | www.dewars.com

Region and country of origin Scotland
Distilleries Various
Alcohol content 40% abv
Style Blend

Cameronbridge (or Cameron Brig, as it is sometimes known) sits slightly inland, toward the east coast of Fife. This is the site where the Haig whisky family chose to build in the early nineteenth century. The distillery was first charged with malt, later moving to malt and grain; now, only grain runs through its stills. The quality of the grain whisky has been much lauded, both by historic authorities, such as Alfred Barnard, author of *Whisky Distilleries of the United Kingdom* (1887), and modern ones, such as the author of the renowned annual, *Jim Murray's Whisky Bible*.

In Dimple, or Pinch as it is known in some circles due to the idiosyncratic shape of the bottle, there is a significant proportion of liquid from Cameronbridge. The Dimple brand is owned by Diageo, and in the past other elements of their portfolio have gone into this blend, including Glenkinchie, Dalwhinnie, and Royal Lochnagar. Whether the proportions of these remain unchanged with each passing batch is known only to the blender.

The Dimple bottle is designed to stand out from its peers. It jumps out from the shelf, with its misshapen, trilateral footprint, all wrapped in golden wire in the manner of a traditional Rioja wine from Spain. Thankfully, just as much consideration has been invested in the creation of its contents. **D&C**

Tasting notes

Honey, cereal, oak, malt, and caramel. Light at first, then firms up on the palate, showing vanilla, toffee apple, and more oak. The finish brings back the cereal and malt.

← Rigorous logic leads to Dewar's in a stylish 1933 advertisement.

Dimple 15-Year-Old

Diageo | www.diageo.com

Region and country of origin Scotland
Distilleries Various
Alcohol content 40% abv
Style Blend

The history of Cameronbridge, and by turn Dimple, is littered with famous names: Haig, the owner; Jameson, a relation of Haig who emigrated to Dublin; and Coffey, designer of the eponymous still that would have a lasting impact on the distilling trade's economy and efficiency. The Dimple bottle itself, with its distinctive three sides, was the first of its kind to be registered as a trademark in 1919.

John Haig set up plants for blending in Markinch, around 3 miles (5 km) from Cameronbridge distillery, and the investment and reputation of the Haig family were enough to galvanize other Lowland distillers into joining him to form what would be known as the Distillers Co. Ltd. (DCL). It must be said that Haig showed an astonishing degree of vision in unifying what must have been a group of fiercely individual characters into one cohesive whole. In fact, DCL would eventually go on to secure all shares in John Haig & Co. in 1919, followed by Haig & Haig in 1925.

This same prescience must have been at play during the master blender's creation of the Dimple 15-Year-Old. To unify such individual characteristics into something so iconic is a skill and end result that the Haig name may rest proudly upon. **D&C**

Tasting notes

Light cream and nougat, followed by a touch of sherry, malt, and cereal. On the palate, a hint of meringue, oak, heather honey, and a note of cocoa. Warming finish.

Director's Tactical Selection

Douglas Laing and Co. | www.douglaslaing.com

Region and country of origin Scotland
Distillery Undisclosed
Alcohol content 50% abv
Style Single malt

Some distilleries do not deal with independent bottlers because they wish to retain full control over their products. For example, you will never see an independent bottling of a Glenfiddich or Balvenie. To ensure that a whisky cannot be sold as a single malt by an independent bottler, some distilleries will even add a drop of another distillery's whisky into its casks before releasing it (thereby making it a blended malt).

Others distilleries specify that their name is taken off any independent bottlings, to be replaced by a tantalizing pseudonym. Examples are "Speyside's Finest" and, in this case, "Director's Tactical Selection." In earlier releases of the latter, the "Ta" of Tactical was underlined, either as a hint that the letters might help to establish the whisky's identity, or, just conceivably, it was a typing error. Who knows? Hinting at provenance is now illegal, and if Douglas Laing's Director's Tactical Selection were a new release today, the consumer would have to be informed explicitly.

Distilleries inclined to write off independent bottlers as parasites would not include Douglas Laing, Gordon and MacPhail, and others that offer consumers high-quality and unique bottlings of malts otherwise unavailable to them. **PB**

Tasting notes

Gristy, sweet peat, smoke, and the sea on the nose. A big barley hit with lots of smoke and a host of warming spices. A hint of mocha and molasses into the finish.

Double Barrel: Ardbeg & Glenrothes

Douglas Laing & Co. | www.douglaslaing.com

Region and country of origin Islay and Speyside, Scotland **Distilleries** Ardbeg, Port Ellen; Glenrothes, Rothes **Alcohol content** 46% abv
Style Blended malt

The fourth (and, currently, latest) release of Douglas Laing & Co.'s Double Barrel range brings together two standout single-malt contenders from opposite ends of the whisky spectrum. If ever there were a blended malt of chalk and cheese, surely this is it.

In the red corner, the peatiest malt of them all, Ardbeg, which always punches above its weight but, despite its balance and complexity, very much in a roughhouse, bare-knuckle, brawling kind of way. In the blue corner, a true Speyside aristocrat, The Glenrothes, impeccable but never effete, with exquisite ringcraft and total adherence to the rules.

As you would expect, the assertive and direct Ardbeg comes out hitting hard, but the Glenrothes keeps away from the knockout blows and begins to impose itself with a few good jabs. Both participants give it their all, and neither will throw in the towel; they are separated at the end of the bout. All eyes turn to the judges; it is a split decision. Ardbeg wins by a point, as the more aggressive style prevails, but there is plenty of admiration and respect for how the elegant Glenrothes held its own under peaty pressure.

Good work by the promoters of this thrilling contest, Fred and Stewart Laing. **MM**

Tasting notes

Sweet and peaty on the nose at first, then vanilla and zesty citrus. The palate is fresh but smoky, like eating baklava next to a dying fire. Hay on smoldering embers.

Double Barrel: Caol Ila & Braeval

Douglas Laing & Co. | www.douglaslaing.com

Regions of origin Islay and Speyside, Scotland
Distilleries Caol Ila, Port Askaig; Braeval, Chapeltown
Alcohol content 46% abv
Style Blended malt

This was third in line in Douglas Laing & Co.'s Double Barrel series. A single cask from an Islay distillery is vatted with a single cask from a mainland (or other island) distillery to create a new blended malt.

Small distilleries such as Benrinnes or Daluiane are unlikely to be featured in this series. Whisky fanatics may recognize Caperdonich, for example, but such distilleries—in the view of the Laing brothers—do not have the commercial clout for this range. They do not underestimate the quality of the whisky from the distilleries, but see them more as blenders' malts.

It was perhaps surprising, therefore, that the third Double Barrel release should feature Braeval, originally called Braes of Glenlivet, which hardly enjoys the reputation of Highland Park or Macallan, whiskies featured in the first two editions. However, that anomaly may be allowed to pass in view of the admirable Caol Ila, a delightful single malt, both in its youth (in the form of the limited-edition Moch) and in its more mature state (as a twenty-five-year-old).

The whiskies in the Double Barrel series range from eight to twelve years old. The third edition of the Braeval and Caol Ila pairing is a ten-year-old and is limited to 654 bottles. **MM**

Tasting notes

A curiously coy nose, with some peat smoke trying to attract attention. Creamy on the palate, with more prevalent smokiness. The finish is long and drying.

Double Barrel: Highland Park & Bowmore

Douglas Laing & Co. | www.douglaslaing.com

Regions of origin Orkney and Islay, Scotland
Distilleries Highland Park, Kirkwall; Bowmore, Bowmore
Alcohol content 46% abv
Style Blended malt

The second in the Double Barrel range (which was first launched in 2008), this is, interestingly, fast outselling the original combination of Macallan and Laphroaig. Highland Park and Bowmore have already been brought together eleven times by Douglas Laing at the time of writing.

Double Barrel company director Fred Laing has said that at whisky events he is often taken to task by enthusiastic aficionados who ask him, "What is to stop me mixing together two single malts at home?" The short answer is "nothing," but his critics may be missing the point. Certainly, anyone can mix together all the single malts in their drinks cabinet, but that does not make that person a master blender, nor someone who could sell their blend commercially.

Released in mid-2009, this Double Barrel is true to form in using Islay as the fulcrum of the blend. The philosophy has been to match the Islay with another malt from the mainland or, as in this case, another island to see if the two fuse together. Bowmore will always be close to my heart—I will never forget my first visit there—and Highland Park is one of my very favorite single malts. Yet despite the distinctive character and flawless eighteenth-century pedigree of both the constituent malts, this whisky verges on a popular, easy-drinking blend.

Bottled at 46 percent and non-chill-filtered, the Double Barrel series uses mostly refill hogsheads. Sherry casks are not routinely used because Douglas Laing & Co. does not require a third influence—simply the distillery character from the two casks. **MM**

Tasting notes

Vanilla on the nose but, other than that, rather shy. A little spike of heat on the palate, then sweetness redresses the balance. Chile puffs. The finish is hot, drying, and quite long. A very pleasant blend, but one that does not do justice to its stellar components.

Double Barrel: Macallan & Laphroaig

Douglas Laing & Co. | www.douglaslaing.com

Regions of origin Speyside and Islay, Scotland
Distilleries Macallan, Craigellachie; Laphroaig, Port Ellen
Alcohol content 46% abv
Type Blended malt

This is the first release in a range from Douglas Laing in which, very simply, two single casks from two distilleries are blended together. Douglas Laing has a relaxed approach to whisky: company director Fred Laing refuses to take himself too seriously. Whisky is about enjoying yourself, and what is evident about this range is that it offers an opportunity to indulge in a whim. What if I mixed this malt with that malt?

As Fred Laing says, "We are always reactive—in a proactive way." At a Tax Free World Exhibition, a duty-free trade show, he was approached by an in-flight airline buyer who wanted to replace an existing whisky in his range. This was at a time when Douglas Laing & Co. had been looking for something unusual specifically for the Italian market: "A cask of this and a cask of that was as far as we had got. Then this meeting prompted us to start with two iconic malts for the traveler—Macallan and Laphroaig—and it immediately became a best seller for us."

Its popularity is hardly surprising: beginning with what is today the world's number one malt in value (number two in volume), Macallan, and blending it with the world's best-selling smoky whisky is a winning formula. Given time, peat softens; the objective here was to experience wafts of honey through the kicks of peat. It is feasible to appreciate honey notes through the tarry expectations of Laphroaig, once it has softened. The eighth release has been bottled as a ten-year-old. Rumor has it that a combination of Laphroaig with Mortlach is being considered: meaty and peaty. **MM**

Tasting notes

Antiseptic on the nose, then a healthy breakfast of dried apricot with Greek yogurt and honey. On the palate are peat and patisserie, smoke, and choux buns. Vanilla sweetness, then rather a dry woodiness to finish. A total knockout to the heavyweight Islay.

Dumbarton 1964

Murray McDavid (Allied Distillers)
www.murray-mcdavid.com

Region and country of origin Lowlands, Scotland
Distillery Dumbarton, Dumbarton, Dumbartonshire
(closed) **Alcohol content** 46.7% abv
Style Single grain

This forty-two-year-old Dumbarton whisky was bottled in 2007 and released by Murray McDavid Ltd. in its "Jim McEwan's Celtic Heartlands" series. That range brings together vintage bottlings from the 1960s and '70s selected by Jim McEwan, master distiller at Bruichladdich distillery on Islay, which is under the same ownership as Murray McDavid Ltd.

Now demolished, except for one building converted into apartments, Dumbarton distillery was set in the ancient town of the same name, 15 miles (24 km) northwest of Glasgow. It was built in 1937/38 by the George Ballantine & Son subsidiary of the Canadian-based Hiram Walker Gooderham & Worts organization and was intended to provide spirit for their increasingly popular Ballantine's blend.

Dumbarton was vast, the biggest distillery ever to be built in Scotland. It mirrored Hiram Walker's eponymous distillery at Walkerville in Ontario, and a small malt-whisky distillery named Inverleven was created within the complex, along with blending and bottling facilities, plus a large stock of warehousing.

Hiram Walker was taken over by Allied Breweries in 1987, and later passed to Allied Distillers Ltd. Allied eventually decided to close the Dumbarton plant in 2002, choosing to concentrate grain production at their Strathclyde distillery in Glasgow. **GS**

Tasting notes

The nose is predominantly sweet, with honey. Smooth on the palate, with vanilla pod, coconut, tropical fruit, fresh cereal notes, and developing oakiness.

Edradour 10-Year-Old

Signatory Vintage Scotch Whisky Co.
www.edradour.co.uk

Region and country of origin Highlands, Scotland
Distillery Edradour, Pitlochry, Perthshire
Alcohol content 40% abv
Style Single malt

The location and buildings of Edradour (Gaelic for "between two rivers" and pronounced "Edd-ra-dower") are among Scotland's prettiest. The distilling is usually performed by just three men, although at the time of writing, the number of workers was reduced to two. Even when fully manned, the distillery produces only twelve casks per week.

In contrast to many businesses, here there is no hankering after growth or the achievement of critical mass. The minimalist approach has stood Edradour in good stead throughout its history. Founded in 1825 as a cooperative, it was registered in 1841 as John McGlashan and Co. For the first hundred years of its existence, its products were used exclusively in premium blends, notably House of Lords and King's Ransom. It was only in 1986 that this tiny distillery first permitted the outside world to sample the joys of its single malt in its own right.

Edradour whiskies are handmade and left to mature for a minimum of ten years. The 10-Year-Old is therefore the youngster of the family. It was also the first to be marketed. Because so little of it is produced, it is not easy to find, especially in the United Kingdom; most of it is exported to Europe, although it is also available—and highly sought after—in the United States, Japan, Taiwan, and New Zealand. **GL**

Tasting notes

On the nose, dried apricot and oloroso sherry. A dry, creamy taste of almond and mint. The slightly bitter, peaty finish has spices, vanilla, caramel, and oak.

← Corks are placed by hand at the Hiram Walker distillery at Dumbarton in the 1950s.

Edradour 11-Year-Old 1996

Signatory Vintage Scotch Whisky Co.
www.edradour.co.uk

Region and country of origin Highlands, Scotland
Distillery Edradour, Pitlochry, Perthshire
Alcohol content 57.5% abv
Style Single malt

Edradour distillery, which produces only a dozen casks per week, has become famous for its many "Straight from the Cask" bottlings. These expressions, which range from ten to fifteen years old, are often finished in a unique cask. The cask is referenced on the label, and usually the label and box are the same color as the whisky, which will have taken on a vibrant shade depending upon the cask chosen for final maturation.

As the series name implies, these expressions are bottled at cask strength. The consumer is given the specific cask number, distillation date, bottling date, number of bottles produced, and specific bottle number. Some expressions are repeated.

This Edradour expression was finished in a Grand Arôme rum cask, which is presumably where the whisky obtained its chartreuse green color, as well as its unique taste. It was the first Edradour cask to be hand-selected by Brian and Bill Ciske, founders of the Maxwell Street Trading Co., a specialist distributor based in Chicago, Illinois. When the Ciske brothers first tasted it, they knew instantly it was special. They were intrigued by the abundant flavors of tropical fruit. American drinks retailer Binny's has described this Edradour as a "quirky, sweet, herbal gem." **WM**

Tasting notes

Overwhelming notes of tropical fruits, with the nose evoking lime aftershave. The complex palate is vibrant with kiwi fruit, star fruit, and lime. Rum on the finish.

Edradour 30-Year-Old

Signatory Vintage Scotch Whisky Co.
www.edradour.co.uk

Region and country of origin Highlands, Scotland
Distillery Edradour, Pitlochry, Perthshire
Alcohol content 43% abv
Style Single malt

After Pernod Ricard acquired Edradour in 1982, the business operated much as it always had. However, Edradour's takeover by Signatory (one of Scotland's three largest independent bottling companies) in 2002 was followed by a radical change in direction, from contributing malts for blends to producing own-name single malts almost exclusively.

Under Signatory, Edradour continued maturation in refill American oak hogsheads and European oak butts, but soon acquired a reputation for some innovative and idiosyncratic wood finishes. Ten varieties of first-fill wine casks were used, including ex-chardonnay, ex–Côte de Provence, and ex-Tokay.

Meanwhile, the core methods remain unchanged; Edradour gets its peated malt from Inverness, and its unpeated malt from Bairds in Edinburgh. Water for the whisky is drawn from a spring on Moulin Moor; the cooling water comes from the adjacent Edradour Burn. The rake-and-plough mash tun, installed in 1910, is made of cast iron, and the wort is cooled in Scotland's last remaning Morton refrigerator (built in 1933). This limited edition, released in 2003, is a distinctive and highly desirable single malt whose high price reflects its quality and scarcity value. **GL**

Tasting notes

The aroma is thick with honey, toffee, marzipan, and barley. The palate is full and oily, with strong suggestions of mint, sweet cereal, marzipan, and oak.

Edradour
1983 Port Wood Finish

Signatory Vintage Scotch Whisky Co.
www.edradour.co.uk

Region and country of origin Highlands, Scotland
Distillery Edradour, Pitlochry, Perthshire
Alcohol content 52.5% abv
Style Single malt

The Edradour distillery buildings were completed in 1837, after Mungo Stewart formed a cooperative with seven other farmers to lease a strip of land by the burn (mountain stream) from the Duke of Atholl. Since then, the distillery has passed through the hands of several owners, including the fascinating William Whitely (1861–1942), who took over in 1933.

A tough, straightforward Yorkshireman, Whitely was already well established as a wine and whisky merchant. One of his most important export markets was North America, and when the United States passed into law the Volstead Act, which led to Prohibition (1920–33), he took extralegal steps to protect his interests by appointing as "U.S. sales consultant" one Frank Costello. Costello—real name Francesco Castiglia (1891–1973)—was a notorious Mafia bootlegger and hood who became the Mafia *capo di tutti capi* and served as one of the models for the character of Vito Corleone in Mario Puzo's best-selling novel *The Godfather* (1969).

This remarkable single malt was released in June 2008 at natural cask strength in a limited edition of 531 bottles. It is a non-chill-filtered expression that has been finished in port pipes. **GL**

Tasting notes

The nose is perfectly balanced between smoke and fruit. The taste is comparably satisfying—full-bodied and pearlike—and the finish is warm and lingering.

Elements of Islay
Ar₂ (Ardbeg)

Speciality Drinks
www.thewhiskyexchange.com

Region and country of origin Islay, Scotland
Distillery Ardbeg, Port Ellen, Argyll
Alcohol content 60.5% abv
Style Single malt

Speciality Drinks is the independent bottling division of the Whisky Exchange, and like a lot of what owner Sukhinder Singh does, the Elements of Islay range doesn't come without its controversy but passes muster because of the high standard of the whisky.

Ardbeg distillery was closed and neglected until the late 1990s, when it was bought by Glenmorangie. Loyal fans were concerned that it would be dumbed down, so to reassure them, Glenmorangie's master distiller Bill Lumsden and his team decided to release a six-year-old version of the new whisky called Very Young. A year and a bit later, a new whisky was released called Still Young. At nine years the company released one called Almost There. Glenmorangie had been bought by luxury-goods company LVMH by then, and Ardbeg's rise has been stellar ever since. Gone are the days when you'll find Ardbeg discounted in supermarkets, and in the United Kingdom, those fledgling bottles sell for ten times the price at which they were put on sale.

Ardbeg deserves its success because every distillery bottling is a treat. The first batch, Ar₁, sold out immediately and this seems to have gone the same way. But look for it—it's young and feisty. **DR**

Tasting notes

This is the Sex Pistols in 1976: young, rough, violent, and with attitude to spare. There are bum notes aplenty—an immaturity and a lack of balance—but so what?

Elements of Islay
Bn$_1$ (Bunnahabhain)

Speciality Drinks | www.elements-of-islay.com

Region and country of origin Islay, Scotland
Distillery Bunnahabhain, Port Askaig, Argyll
Alcohol content 55.7% abv
Style Single malt

Bunnahabhain is known as the gentle malt of Islay, to the extent that some drinkers would not guess that it came from that island. However, Bunnahabhain has always made some heavily peated whisky to service its blending obligations, and in the past lucky visitors to the distillery have been treated to a wee sample from the cask. Then the distillery went legitimate and bottled a peated whisky under the name Toiteach. A big hit, it combined the fruit Highland heart of a typical Bunnahabhain with the smoky, peaty, and seaweedy elements normally associated with Islay.

This version is part of the Elements of Islay range, where the emphasis is on big, heavy hitting, cask-strength, peated whiskies. It was included in a batch that included Lagavulin, Laphroaig, Caol Ila, and Kilchoman, and, amazingly, with its sooty, industrial charcoal, it was the best sample of the bunch.

Distilleries tend to disapprove of independent bottlers putting forward atypical versions of their whiskies, but peat fans will find it hard not to take a guilty pleasure in savoring and enjoying this cracker. Now that the genie is out of the bottle, it will be interesting to see whether Bunnahabhain will be tempted to market more of this sort of thing. **DR**

Tasting notes

Big, sooty, peaty, charcoal nose, and a huge mouthfeel, with oily, peaty malt sticking to the mouth. With water, the peat still dominates, with wave after wave of smoke.

Elements of Islay
Br$_1$ (Bruichladdich)

Speciality Drinks | www.elements-of-islay.com

Region and country of origin Islay, Scotland
Distillery Bruichladdich, Bruichladdich, Argyll
Alcohol content 53.6% abv
Style Single malt

When a batch of six samples of the Elements of Islay range was sent to me for endorsement, this one stood out like a sore thumb. All the others were big, peat-dominated whiskies, but the Bruichladdich was meek in comparison. That was a surprise, really, because Bruichladdich can do smoky, phenolic whiskies with the best of them when it wants to, and smoky is what you expect from the Elements of Islay range.

Bruichladdich is a fiercely independent distillery that shoots way above its weight. Most distilleries make malts intended to be added to blended whisky, which, despite all the attention given to single malts, still accounts for more than 90 percent of the entire market. Scotland's whisky blenders all swap malts to give each a choice of flavors to choose from. And it is the unwanted whiskies from each producer that tend to end up being bottled independently.

But Bruichladdich doesn't provide stock for blending, so this product is a rarity—an independent bottling of a Bruichladdich malt. It is delivered at cask strength, and it is a surprising whisky, even for a distillery that has put out an array of malts varying from highly peated to light and fruity. This one falls at the fruity end of the spectrum. **DR**

Tasting notes

Of the 2011 Elements of Islay batch, this is the least aggressive. A rich, oily that opens out into a floral garden with water. The spice and peat elevate it.

The names of Elements of Islay bottlings are presented as chemical formulae. ➔

Elements of Islay Cl$_2$ (Caol Ila)

Specialiaty Drinks | www.islay.com

Region and country of origin Islay, Scotland
Distillery Caol Ila, Port Askaig, Argyll
Alcohol content 50.5% abv
Style Single malt whisky

ELEMENTS of ISLAY

Cl$_2$

SINGLE ISLAY MALT
SCOTCH WHISKY

DISTILLED & BOTTLED IN SCOTLAND
SPECIALITY DRINKS Ltd. NW10 7SU
www.islay.com

FULL PROOF

50cl℮   50.5%vol

It is hard to imagine a Japanese company launching a new, independent version of a Rolls-Royce, or a small Scottish rock group producing U2-based music under the name U2. Yet in the world of whisky it is perfectly possible for an independent bottler to launch and market a bottle of whisky under the name of the distillery that made it. As one might expect, the quality of whisky released by independent bottlers varies greatly, and there are whiskies bearing the name of distilleries that, frankly, should never have been released. Of course, among these are many that were never intended for single-malt status.

However, when an independent bottler gets it right, their products add color and vibrancy to the world of whisky. Often, it is through bottlers that the world of whisky gets its dynamism and excitement.

The Elements of Islay range is primarily concerned with top quality. And when you see the whisky, in a chemistry-set bottle and with the whisky described by a chemical symbol, well, you can't help but feel that Speciality Drinks is a creative and impressively professional company. Each batch of Elements is vetted by a personality in the industry.

This particular bottling is the second release of Caol Ila—hence the name Cl$_2$—and comes at cask strength. The Caol Ila distillery is the biggest on Islay and reopened in 2012 after it was extended. Much of the whisky from the distillery ends up in blends, but there are more independent bottlings from here than from most distilleries. This one certainly is worthy of the distillery name. **DR**

Tasting notes

This is truly a whisky for peat enthusiasts. It is all about oily mouthfeel, smoke, and tar: an intense, grown-up, peaty monster. There are some elements of smoky bacon and green banana skin, but wave after wave of grungy peat dominates the proceedings.

Elements of Islay Kh$_1$ (Kilchoman)

Speciality Drinks | www.elements-of-islay.com

Region and country of origin Islay, Scotland
Distillery Kilchoman, Bruichladdich, Argyll
Alcohol content 59.7% abv
Style Single malt

When Speciality Drinks, the independent bottling division of retailer the Whisky Exchange, first broached its idea for an Elements of Islay range, there was a clear understanding that the bar had to be set a lot higher than had been the case in the past. Truth be told, independent bottlers often take advantage of a distillery name by putting out poor-quality whisky that was never destined for the single-malt market.

Islay distilleries, in particular, seem to have suffered from disservices from independent bottlers. Perhaps that is because the Islay distilleries reserve all their best casks for their own official single-malt bottlings. It may also be that malts made for blending have been deliberately made to a specification different from the standard peated version, so independent bottlings of these have not been as typical of the house style as drinkers might like. But, that said, great independent bottlings do exist, and the best independent bottlers take great pride in the whisky they buy and go to great extremes to find high-quality and truly representative malts to bottle.

The Speciality Drinks cask-strength bottlings of Islay whisky are definitely all about quality. The aim is to offer drinkers a full-frontal, peat-and-smoke Islay hit. They are cleverly marketed, too. An abbreviation for the distillery name alongside the batch number gives each of the Elements of Islay its chemical symbol (geddit?). And if you doubt the quality, each batch is endorsed by an expert within the industry. The Kilchoman is fuller and bigger than the standard bottling, but it is no worse off for that. **DR**

Tasting notes

Oily, big, full, and very peaty, this is a hard-core peated Islay malt that takes no prisoners. The addition of water releases a sweet fruitiness at the heart of this whisky, but still no one could miss the mighty peat and pepper punch that it delivers to the palate.

The Famous Grouse

Edrington Group | www.thefamousgrouse.com

Region and country of origin Scotland
Distilleries Various
Alcohol content 40% abv
Style Blend

Glenturret may be Scotland's oldest working distillery, but it houses a state-of the-art visitors' center offering insights into the modern world of whisky. Visitors can dine in the award-winning restaurant, take a guided tour of the 300-year-old distillery, and participate in the Famous Grouse Experience, a tourist attraction awarded five stars by Visit Scotland, the national organization for tourism. The Famous Grouse Experience features a new interactive zone and *The Grouse*, a cutting-edge, interactive movie that takes visitors on a birds'-eye-view tour of some of Scotland's best-known landmarks.

Known generally as "Scotland's favorite whisky," the Famous Grouse takes its name from the red grouse, Scotland's national game bird. In the 1890s, when wealthy Victorians traveled to Scotland in increasing numbers to enjoy the clean air, beautiful scenery, and country sports, the Glenturret distillery saw an opportunity to introduce a special whisky for those discerning customers. It developed its own brand of blended whisky, calling it the Grouse Brand. Entrepreneur Matthew Gloag's daughter Philippa drew the red grouse that appeared on the first label. Such was the whisky's almost immediate acceptance and popularity with its well-heeled clientele that it was renamed as the Famous Grouse in 1896.

The Famous Grouse is the top-selling blended whisky in Scotland and is number two in the United Kingdom behind the Diageo-owned Bell's brand. In 2010 volume sales rose 5 percent, which amounts to more than 3 million cases being sold annually. **SR**

Tasting notes

Golden, clear, and bright. Satisfying malts like the Macallan and Highland Park married with fine grain whiskies. Oak and sherry on the nose, with a citrus note. On the palate, it is mature, easygoing, and full of bright Speyside fruit. A clean and medium-dry finish.

The Famous Grouse The Black Grouse

Edrington Group | www.thefamousgrouse.com

Region and country of origin Scotland
Distilleries Various
Alcohol content 40% abv
Style Blend

The Edrington Group has entered into a unique partnership with the Royal Society for the Protection of Birds (RSPB) to help save one of the United Kingdom's rarest birds—the black grouse—from national extinction. For every bottle of the Black Grouse sold in the United Kingdom, a donation of 50 pence goes directly to the RSPB to fund urgent conservation work in Britain. Through this partnership, the RSPB had received almost £300,000 ($470,000) by 2012, funding conservation work for the black grouse.

The black grouse is one of the most rapidly declining bird species in the United Kingdom. A survey in 2005 counted only 5,100 "lekking" (mating) males. The bird is on the IUCN Red List of species of high conservation concern on account of its serious decline. One of twenty-six bird species for which a UK Biodiversity Action Plan has been produced, it is one of the highest priorities for action.

The Black Grouse blended Scotch whisky, born out of a marriage of the Famous Grouse with Islay malt whiskies, is also a breed apart. It is a heavily peated blend that aims to tap into the new breed of younger Scotch-whisky consumers who prefer the strong, iodine flavor of Islay malts but cannot always afford them. Black Grouse was designed primarily for the Nordic market, for a group of consumers who are slightly younger than the traditional age of Scotch consumers, and who are interested in a fuller-flavored expression of Scotch whisky. The Black Grouse delivers an Islay flavor, is affordable, and carries the benchmark of the Famous Grouse. **SR**

Tasting notes

Peaty smoke, then delicate sweetness, with golden raw sugar and traces of malt and oak on the nose. Subtle, smoky-sweet tones. A silky-smooth delivery with hints of cocoa and spice. The finish is long, peaty, and aromatic. Gentle smokiness gives way to resonant oak.

Quality in an age of change.

The Famous Grouse Celebration Blend

Edrington Group
www.thefamousgrouse.com

Region and country of origin Scotland
Distillery Various
Alcohol content 43% abv
Style Blend

In recent years, one of the most exciting trends in Scotch whisky has been the tendency of big whisky producers to release special bottlings of blended whisky to reenergize the blended Scotch category.

Nobody has done this better than Edrington with its Famous Grouse brand. It is a slightly risky strategy. To release whiskies such as the Naked Grouse, with its high sherried content, or the Black Grouse, which is rich in peat, is to ask questions of the regular Famous Grouse drinker. It also takes the brand into different territory, but here it really works.

This special blend, the first totally created by new master blender Gordon Motion, marks the thirtieth anniversary of the year—1981—that the Famous Grouse became Scotland's best-selling whisky. Some of the whisky in it comes from that year. Edrington owns the Macallan and Highland Park, two of the world's greatest malts, and the whiskies are thirty years old, so you would expect the blend to deliver on the palate, and it does. Available in very limited quantities in a special Wade decanter, this deserves to join the list of great older whiskies that are good enough to drink on their own, and which you would feel guilty about mixing with anything else. **DR**

Rich, full, rounded, and smooth, with lots of honey and citrus notes, including mandarin and tangerine. Hints of smoke and oak, and a great, rounded, honeyed finish.

The Famous Grouse The Naked Grouse

Edrington Group
www.thefamousgrouse.com

Region and country of origin Scotland
Distilleries Various
Alcohol content 40% abv
Style Blend

The Famous Grouse has appeared in many forms over the years, but perhaps the most surprising, and arguably the best, is the Naked Grouse. My review bottle arrived with a note saying, "Don't mention sherry." This must be someone's attempt at a joke, for sherry is absolutely what this whisky is about.

The Naked Grouse is a big, weighty whisky dominated by sherried malt. The Edrington Group owns the Macallan, which in the past has been honored with the title of being the world's best malt whisky matured in European sherry casks, so perhaps this should not be surprising. But there is also an arguable case that the main whisky in this mix is Glenrothes, because there are some distinctly earthy notes in the mix. What makes this whisky such a surprise is the fact that it doesn't really taste like a blend at all. Indeed, you could happily sip this neat, with a dash of water or even with ice, but without any other mixer at all. In fact, it is only at the very end, when the finish dies very quickly on the palate—a good pointer to the fact that you're not drinking a single malt—that you get a clue as to what you're drinking. It is certainly like no other Famous Grouse, though, and it is impressive stuff into the bargain. **DR**

On the nose, dried apricot and oloroso sherry, with a faintly spicy smokiness. A dry, creamy taste of almond and mint recedes to a slightly bitter, peaty, spicy finish.

Wood paneling reinforces the Famous Grouse's claim to tradition in the 1990s.

The Famous Grouse The Snow Grouse

Edrington Group | www.thesnowgrouse.com

Region and country of origin Scotland
Distilleries Various
Alcohol content 40% abv
Style Blended grain

How should a whisky maker maintain the reputation of its brand but grow it at the same time? The owners of Jack Daniel's took a conservative route by stating in 2011 that the brand would not be extended into new areas. The owners of the Famous Grouse have gone a very different way. In the past they have launched several expressions, including the Famous Grouse itself released at different ages. At one time there was a range of what were then called vatted malts, but which now must be called blended malt whiskies: a mix of malts with no grain whisky. Famous Grouse owner Edrington is in a privileged position because it has at its disposal the likes of the Macallan and Highland Park, malts of the highest quality that offer an array of flavors with which to make blends.

This version, though, couldn't be farther removed from the traditional Famous Grouse. It is described as a blended grain whisky, which means it contains grain whiskies from more than one distillery. Grain whisky has long been seen as the poor relation to single malt, but in recent years it has been growing in popularity, and there is a view that it could provide a stepping stone for younger drinkers to discover malt whisky.

Grain is naturally sweet, and one of the ways drinkers are recommended to taste this is to give it some time in the freezer and then serve it chilled. Freezing makes the liquid a little bit viscous, but the taste of the grain—which they say has been "smooth-chilled"—is not destroyed; as the liquid warms in the mouth, the sweet vanilla flavors shine through. Whisky, then, but not as we normally know it. **DR**

Tasting notes

Very little nose, and the taste is uncomplicated but pleasant enough. Sweet, vanilla ice cream, honey, toffee, and not very much else. This easy-drinking whisky lends itself to cocktail making, a fact perhaps emphasized by a bottle seemingly designed for vodka.

Fettercairn 24-Year-Old

Whyte & Mackay | www.whyteandmackay.com

Region of origin Highlands, Scotland
Distillery Fettercairn, Laurencekirk, Kincardineshire
Alcohol content 44.4% abv
Type Single malt

When, in 2010, Diageo opened its superdistillery Roseisle on the very northern edge of Speyside, it unveiled a plant capable of producing two different styles of malt. One of these was is a full, meaty one that once upon a time would have been run through worm-tub condensers—flat pipes that travel through a tank of cooled water, ensuring a slow condensation and the retention of certain bolder flavors. But Diageo took the view that its new plant was a forward-thinking, environmentally friendly distillery in which worm tubs had no place—so the company installed a stainless-steel condenser.

Fettercairn distillery would have recognized this moment as ironic, because it was probably the operation of stainless-steel condensers that had caused them a lot of grief. When less copper is used in the distilling process, unwanted sulfur stays in the spirit, and if the spirit is then matured in a less-than-perfect cask, sulfur may be detected in the final product. In some cases Fettercairn had sulfur in such quantities that the spirit tasted not so much of burned match but of metal or rubber—not very pleasant.

This whisky was distilled before Fettercairn replaced its stainless-steel condenser, many years ago, but happily it has suffered no ill-effects. It has matured in good-quality wood, and while there is a meatiness, the complete malt is of good quality and flavor. This 24-Year-Old is a definitive Highland style of whisky, with an attractive mix of oak, peat, spice, and fruit. It is quaintly old-fashioned, but that is a plus. All in all, it makes a great case for this Highland giant. **SR**

Tasting notes

Full-flavored, warm, and rich. There is the merest hint of sulfur on the nose, but that is replaced by stewed fruits and freshly sliced fruit salad. On the palate, there is apple, gooseberry, kitchen-cupboard spices, and overripe, soft peach.

Fettercairn 30-Year-Old

Whyte & Mackay
www.whyteandmackay.com

Region of origin Highlands, Scotland
Distillery Fettercairn, Laurencekirk, Kincardineshire
Alcohol content 43.3% abv
Type Single malt

Some distilleries may be three hundred or more years old, and whisky production in Ireland and Scotland, in particular, is considerably older than that. Because of their huge income-earning capability and importance to the economy, their political significance is magnified. One of the slogans of the Jacobites, for example, was "No malt tax, no salt tax, no union."

Fettercairn distillery was once owned by the Gladstone family. Because British prime minister William Gladstone understood whisky, he drove through legislation that recognized the "angels' share" lost through evaporation. He adapted the law so that the final amount of whisky, and not the original spirit, was taxed, helping the distilleries to survive.

Over time, perhaps some of the whisky from Fettercairn has fallen short of the lofty standards that this sort of background might warrant, but this 30-Year-Old is not only the best of four comeback releases from Fettercairn, but a mighty warrior by any whisky standards. Highland whiskies offer up more possibility of maturing into old age than most because they are robust and rich and can withstand the effects of the wood longer. But even so, this is a remarkably vibrant whisky for its age. **SR**

Tasting notes

An enticing balance between the feistiness of younger bottlings and the delicate grapefruit marmalade of the frail 40-Year-Old. Citrus fruit meets Battenberg cake.

Fettercairn 33-Year-Old Malt Cask

Douglas Laing & Co. | www.douglaslaing.com/
www.whyteandmackay.co.uk

Region of origin Highlands, Scotland
Distillery Fettercairn, Laurencekirk, Kincardineshire
Alcohol content 50% abv
Type Single malt

Most people have attempted, at some time in their lives and with varying degrees of success, to reinvent themselves. So it is with some distilleries. For the first 150 years of its life, Fettercairn had a distinguished existence in the ownership of the political Gladstone family, among others. Since the 1970s, however, the distillery has worked under nine different company names, in part producing whisky for Whyte & Mackay and its blends. In the past ten years, there have been several attempts at rebranding and repackaging the distillery as it tries to find a niche for its malts.

The malts have changed, too, partly due to a move from stainless-steel to copper condensers, which remove some of the heavy sulfur notes. The whisky is still a bit of an oddball, however, very much with a love-it or hate-it taste. One well-known whisky writer has even questioned why it was that some distilleries fell silent while Fettercairn survived.

This particular expression from Douglas Laing and Co. was distilled in 1975 before the change to copper. It was aged in a refill hogshead, so wood has not taken over the fascinating and distinctive mix of rich flavors that can be so typical of Highland whiskies of this period. Controversial, certainly, but delicious. **AN**

Tasting notes

Midamber in color, with a nutty nose reminiscent of baker's yeast on a hot afternoon. Some fruit and dark chocolate at first, with a rich, oily feel and a little spice.

William Gladstone passed legislation in support of whisky producers. ➡

Fettercairn 40-Year-Old

Whyte & Mackay | www.whyteandmackay.com

Region of origin Highlands, Scotland
Distillery Fettercairn, Laurencekirk, Kincardineshire
Alcohol content 40% abv
Type Single malt

With very old whiskies—and very few keep going for as long as forty years, as this one has—there are three concerns. First, the strength of the whisky goes down during maturation, and if it falls below 40 percent abv it can no longer be called whisky. That means the spirit has to be carefully monitored. There is a cask of Lagavulin at the distillery on Islay that was laid down in 1969, but it has now slipped below the 40-percent-abv threshold—a calamity sufficient to break the heart of many a whisky lover.

The second factor concerns the maturation process, which also needs careful monitoring. Given too much aging time, the effects of the wood can overcome the spirit, and at that point all the efforts to enrich the flavor are reduced to nothing.

The third factor to bear in mind is that very old whisky can become frail and delicate; it can be surprisingly soft. Such whiskies require delicate handling and should be tasted without water. The reason behind this is relatively simple; a whisky is a marvel of engineering, but at this kind of age, the molecular structure is fragile and breaks apart easily. Even a little water can cause the malt to fall apart. When a whisky has cost hundreds or even thousands of dollars, that is not a good result.

This whisky is delightfully delicate and clearly has been handled extremely carefully by its makers. Rather than buy a full bottle—it will not be cheap—this might be one to seek out in one of the world's more expensive whisky bars. Go on, take the plunge—it really is rather special. **SR**

Tasting notes

This single malt talks a good game and offers a full, sherried, and sweet experience, and on the palate the chocolate orange, praline, and honeyed biscuit are delicate, sophisticated, and enjoyable. However, the finish is medium at best.

Fettercairn Fior

Whyte & Mackay | www.whyteandmackay.com

Region of origin Highlands, Scotland
Distillery Fettercairn, Laurencekirk, Kincardineshire
Alcohol content 42% abv
Type Single malt

It would be hard to think of a Scottish malt distillery that has endured more controversy than Fettercairn. For various reasons, this distillery has weathered a storm of criticism, but the local community has banded together to resolve its difficulties, and Fettercairn is moving forward once more.

In some parts of the world—Speyside, Islay, Kentucky, Tasmania—distilleries are grouped together and exist in a spirit of friendly rivalry, using their collective strength to the best advantage. However, others operate in isolation, often in some of the remotest and most challenging parts of the world. These distilleries are frequently at the heart of their communities, and they provide significant local work. Unsurprisingly, therefore, such distilleries command a great deal of loyalty, and their supporters do not take kindly to criticism. And few malts have been criticized like Fettercairn; suffice to say that the production problems of the past have been addressed.

This bottling is the first release of a new era, and is a fight back for what is both a traditional and rustic Highland distillery and an attractive and noble one. *Fior* means "pure" in Gaelic, and this release is an announcement that the distillery's traditional malt has been replaced by something altogether more of our time. It is a rugged, challenging malt, but it is unique, well made, and rewarding. It deserves rediscovery, and owner Whyte & Mackay has given it a good shot with some smart new packaging and promotion. The emphasis is placed on the new malt's quality, and its unusual strength is noteworthy, too. **SR**

Tasting notes

Not an easy ride but a worthwhile one. This comes out punching and vying for attention, with brittle nut cluster, dark coffee, intense dried fruit, and traces of smoke on both the nose and the palate. The way it evolves in the mouth is unlike any other malt.

Finlaggan Islay Single Malt Cask Strength

Vintage Malt Whisky Co. | www.vintagemaltwhisky.com

Region and country of origin Islay, Scotland
Distillery Undisclosed
Alcohol content 58% abv
Style Single malt

Venture to the northeastern corner of Islay, toward Port Askaig, and you will see a signpost for Finlaggan. Take this side road for about a mile (1.6 km) and you will find yourself at the mouth of Loch Finlaggan, surrounded by low hills. This beautiful but seemingly innocuous place belies its importance, for here was the home of the Lord of the Isles, ruler of the western part of the Scottish mainland and the islands off its west coast. Finlaggan had been occupied since very early times, probably as much for its mineral wealth as its strategic position, but, during the fourteenth and fifteenth centuries, it was occupied by the MacDonald Lord of the Isles. At one end of the loch are two islands. On one stood the chapel and hall and, on the other, the council chamber where the Lord and his councillors debated the important matters of the day. But there is no distillery here.

Finlaggan is labeled an Islay single malt, matured in a mixture of ex-bourbon casks and sherry butts, but there is no indication of the distillery that this mysterious whisky comes from. Is the name a hint that it comes from Caol Ila or perhaps even Bunnahabhain? Amazingly, even the distillers at the great peaty distilleries of the island are in disagreement as to which malt is in the bottle. From this we can conclude that it is not typical of the house style and is therefore a rogue independent bottling. But it's also possible that it changes from batch to batch. The emphasis, though, is on big, oily, smoky, and peaty whisky. Not that it matters where it comes from, because if young and prominent peat is your thing, you'll love this. **PB**

Tasting notes

Massive peat on the nose, with thrusting citrus and licorice, plus hints of ripe grape, caraway seed, and white chocolate. On the palate, it is bitter lemon, grassy, and herbal, with grilled trout skin and sweet, thumping peat. The ending is long, sweet, and ashy.

Glen Elgin 12-Year-Old

Diageo | www.malts.com

Region and country of origin Speyside, Scotland
Distillery Glen Elgin, Longmorn, Elgin, Morayshire
Alcohol content 43% abv
Style Single malt

Most distilleries in the Speyside area (and there are many of them) are easily identified from miles away thanks to their pagoda roofs or chimneys. Glen Elgin is one exception. It lies unnoticed in the small hamlet of Fogwatt on the road between Rothes and Elgin. Although it takes less than a minute to drive right through the village, it is easy to miss the small road that leads to the distillery.

Glen Elgin single malt is also easy to overlook. The main part of the production goes into various Diageo blends, White Horse in particular. The only official bottling (with the exception of a few limited releases) is the 12-Year-Old. While the owners have decided not to give Glen Elgin single malt a leading role in their range, they are obviously of the opinion that it deserves some special treatment. Instead of being released in Diageo's Flora & Fauna range, like so many others, it has its own label and own bottle design.

Glen Elgin distillery is quite small, producing only 450,000 gallons (1.7 million liters) per year. Long fermentations, lasting from fifty-six up to 120 hours, are an operational bottleneck, but are also the secret behind the character. Together with a slow distillation, they create intense and fruity flavors, but by no means a light whisky. During a second distillation, the spirit is collected down to an alcohol strength of 58 percent abv, which usually indicates an eagerness to include some heavier congeners to build the body of the spirit. Also, six wooden worm tubs outside the still house are used to cool the spirit vapors, a process that adds some robustness to the character. **IR**

Tasting notes

On the nose, honey and almond in a delightful combination, almost like a Toblerone chocolate bar but without the chocolate. It starts off quite dry on the palate, fresh and vibrant. Some fruits appear, mainly pear. The finish is well balanced and intense.

Glen Elgin
16-Year-Old

Diageo
www.malts.com

Region and country of origin Speyside, Scotland
Distillery Glen Elgin, Longmorn, Elgin, Morayshire
Alcohol content 58.5% abv
Style Single malt

Glen Elgin distillery was designed by Charles Doig (1855–1918), the architect of more than fifty Scottish distilleries, and was completed in 1898. A collapse in the market caused Glen Elgin to be sold off in 1901 for less than a third of the price it cost to build. Reopened in 1908, it was slow to modernize: it was not until 1950 that the distillery was connected to the National Grid; before then, it had been a full-time job for one man to keep all the paraffin lamps working.

The raw materials came from floor maltings until 1964, and later unpeated malt from Burghead, a small town about 8 miles (13 km) away. The soft process water comes from springs near Millbuies Loch; the cooling water is taken from the Glen Burn. The original rake-and-plough mash tun survived until 2000.

This cask-strength 16-Year-Old was distilled in 1991, matured in ex-bodega oak casks to give the whisky a strong sherry flavor, and released in 2007 in a limited edition of 9,954 bottles. Never plentiful, it soon became rare and highly prized, but the search is widely considered to be well worth the time and effort. The cost is high—this is Glen Elgin's most expensive product—but still represents excellent value for money: catch it if you can. **GL**

Tasting notes

Strong on the nose, evoking sherry and fruit, principally orange, along with vanilla fudge and almond. Oily on the palate, with fruits, spices, and notes of cedarwood.

Glen Flagler
1973

Inver House
www.inverhouse.com

Region and country of origin Lowlands , Scotland
Distillery Glen Flagler, Moffat, Airdrie, North Lanarkshire
Alcohol content 46% abv
Style Single malt

Glen Flagler is a rare single malt distilled at the Moffat distillery complex between 1965 and July 1985. Inver House was a subsidiary of Publicker Industries Ltd. of Philadelphia, who purchased the Moffat paper mill and built the Moffat distillery complex, consisting of no fewer than thirty-two warehouses, a dark grains plant, cooperage, five continuous stills producing neutral spirits and a grain whisky called Garnheath, two pairs of pot stills producing single malts Glen Flagler and Killyloch, and bottling and blending facilities. Glen Flagler stopped producing spirit in 1985, closed in 1986, and has since been demolished.

The Glen Flagler 1973 represents the last five proprietary casks, which were vatted and bottled non-chill-filtered, at natural cask strength, after twenty-nine years in oak hogsheads. Each of the 931 bottles, produced with a certificate of authenticity and tasting notes, is individually numbered.

In 1973 Glen Flagler was lightly peated, which is unusual for a lowland single malt. This was possible because the Moffat complex contained its own maltings, facilitating various peating levels. Lowland malts tend to be more delicate than this, as peat would overwhelm the typical grassy, floral notes. **WM**

Tasting notes

Hay, straw, and grass accentuated by notes of vanilla; surprisingly full-bodied. Complemented by honey, malt, and a hint of peat. Leads to a dry finish.

Glen Garioch 12-Year-Old

Morrison Bowmore Distillers (Suntory)
www.glengarioch.com

Region and country of origin Highlands, Scotland
Distillery Glen Garioch, Oldmeldrum, Aberdeenshire
Alcohol content 48% abv
Style Single malt

For many years, Glen Garioch single malt lived in the shadow of its Highland siblings, Bowmore and Auchentoshan. However, this 12-Year-Old was introduced in 2010 as part of a newly branded, upgraded range. It is made from a marriage of whiskies aged in North American ex-bourbon oak casks and European ex-oloroso sherry oak butts. The bourbon presents trademark sweet vanilla and toffee notes, while the sherry brings a floral robustness.

While the decision to bottle the range at high strength and non-chill-filtered had already been made with the launch of Founder's Reserve a year earlier, it is upon this more approachable expression that the distillery characteristics are stamped. From the start, Glen Garioch was aiming for a full-flavored, big, classic highland whisky. There was a commitment to keep close to cask-strength abv, and also a determination not to chill-filter. The intention was to keep the flavors that developed in cask. Recognizing that Glen Garioch's Highland qualities and robust spirit were of great interest to whisky enthusiasts, they decided against diluting the bottle strength to a typical 40 or 43 percent abv. If a whisky presents itself really well at a high abv, why mess with it? **IGY**

Tasting notes

Highland aromas of heather, spring flowers, and poached pear. On the palate, pear and banana, the fruitiness checked by a light, vanilla-tinged oakiness.

Glen Garioch 15-Year-Old

Morrison Bowmore Distillers (Suntory)
www.glengarioch.com

Region and country of origin Highlands, Scotland
Distillery Glen Garioch, Oldmeldrum, Aberdeenshire
Alcohol content 43% abv
Style Single malt

The Garioch—a tract of hugely fertile land—is one of Scotland's prime barley-producing areas and is known as the granary of Aberdeenshire. However, Glen Garioch, pronounced "Glen Geery," the most easterly of the Scottish distilleries, is one of the few remaining urban distilleries in Scotland. Urban distilleries have a habit of upsetting the local population because of the increased transport, noise, and smells they bring. It was objections to these that are said to have helped to close distilleries such as Rosebank and Millburn. However, the villagers of Oldmeldrum are aware that, however bad the distillery smells get, they are nothing like the hellish aromas emanating from the tannery that was once attached to the distillery.

Some writers have commented upon Glen Garioch's "hide and seek" peat levels over the years (and even between bottlings of the same expression). Prior to the distillery's closure in the mid-1990s, it was quite heavily peated; following reopening in 1997, production resumed as a nonpeated malt. Modern bottlings, however, have heralded a welcome return to the more traditional and earthy Highland style. This 15-Year-Old expression lies somewhere in between, with light peat but plenty of spice and fruit. **PB**

Tasting notes

Currant biscuits on the nose with spicy apple, ripe fruit, and light peat. On the palate, there is more ripe fruit with barley, heather, lavender, peat, and mint.

Glen Garioch 18-Year-Old

Douglas Laing & Co. | www.douglaslaing.com / www.glengarioch.com

Region and country of origin Highlands, Scotland
Distillery Glen Garioch, Oldmeldrum, Aberdeenshire
Alcohol content 57.3% abv
Style Single malt

Distilleries change hands frequently in Scotland as the owning companies merge and groupings are made and split. Usually the new owners focus their attention on one distillery in a group at a time, renovating if needed and sometimes reinventing the malt for their own purpose. A new purchase may seem to be neglected, then suddenly everything changes.

That was the fate of Glen Garioch, one of the oldest distilleries in the Highlands, with a history dating back over 200 years. Until recently, its main claim to fame was supplying malt for the VAT 69 blended whisky of its onetime owner, William Sanderson. New owners experimented with peat in the 1970s (there is the merest hint of it in this bottling), but in 1997 newest owner Suntory of Japan finally turned its focus to this traditional Highland dram.

Suntory seems to have reduced the peatiness and increased the fruit taste, partly in order to appeal to markets in East Asia, which is where the majority of this single malt is now being sold. The change in profile alienated some of the old-time Glen Garioch drinkers, and the distillery has recently relaunched a more old-fashioned, peaty, earthy bottling for them.

This Old & Rare Platinum Selection from Douglas Laing and Co., distilled in 1992 under a previous ownership, is a single-cask, cask-strength bottling. It has only a tiny whiff of smoke, rather than any heavy peat, and perfectly brings together all of the various elements that make this distillery's whiskies such a rewarding experience. Certainly enigmatic, but a delight to explore, and quite unmissable. **AN**

Tasting notes

Midgold in the glass. Malted strawberry on the nose. On the palate, spiced berry cordial at first, then the slightest hint of dry smoke in the background, which builds to complement the fruity, malted finish. With water it becomes fruitier, and the spice is less forward.

Glen Garioch 1991 Small Batch Vintage

Morrison Bowmore Distillers (Suntory) | www.glengarioch.com

Region and country of origin Highlands, Scotland
Distillery Glen Garioch, Oldmeldrum, Aberdeenshire
Alcohol content 54.7% abv
Style Single malt

In 2010, Morrison Bowmore released a small batch of 1,500 bottles of Glen Garioch that had been distilled in 1991. The distillation date on a bottle of limited-edition whisky is not always of particular significance, other than to draw attention to a degree of uniqueness, but here it is of genuine interest because the bottling came from casks that date back to a particular window of production, between 1972 and 1995. The distillery had been silent for four years due to water shortages when it finally gained access to water from a neighboring spring in 1972. Further, this whisky was distilled in the pre-1995 era, when the small Aberdeenshire distillery still had active malt barns and the whisky had a gentle, peaty note.

At that time, Glen Garioch distillery always used peat to dry its malted barley, sourcing its peat from New Pitsligo Moss, a local source about 20 miles (32 km) north of Oldmeldrum. Peating was done on a small scale, so this whisky is notably but subtly peated at a strength of approximately 8 to 10 parts per million (ppm). The peating is not on the scale of the Islay big boys, whose reputations are founded on high peating levels. Here, the peat's gentle influence is more in the nature of a condiment than a prime ingredient.

This 1991 expression is bottled at its natural cask strength of 54.7 percent abv, and it is non-chill-filtered.

Small Batch Vintage releases such as this one are set to be a regular feature from Glen Garioch. They are "handpicked, selected at the peak of their perfection" and are intended to showcase the depth of quality possible at the distillery. **IGY**

Tasting notes

The rather proud and stately, dry-humored great-aunt at the Glen Garioch family gathering. Dusty with peat smoke and lightly honeyed, with fine wafts of orange blossom, then Earl Grey tea, accompanied by a wedge of orange and ginger cake topped with marzipan.

Glen Garioch 1971

Morrison Bowmore Distillers (Suntory) | www.glengarioch.com

Region and country of origin Highlands, Scotland
Distillery Glen Garioch, Oldmeldrum, Aberdeenshire
Alcohol content 43.9% abv
Style Single malt

Glen Garioch is one of those underrated and neglected Scottish distilleries that slip under the radar but are loved by those who know them. This author once tweeted about a single-cask offering from the distillery, and the response was greater than for pretty much any other whisky ever discussed.

Glen Garioch is a tiny distillery owned by Morrison Bowmore, which in turn is owned by Japanese giant Suntory. In many ways, it is the third of three, behind Bowmore and Auchentoshan, and its cause has not been helped by the fact that its malt has changed, its packaging has changed, and its image has changed, while very little effort has been made to publicize or explain all of this to the public. The distillery, lying off the main road connecting Aberdeen with Speyside, is small and attractive, and definitely belongs in the category of Highland "hidden gems." A few years ago, a visitors' center was built for it, and this attracts a steady stream of whisky-wise tourists.

A whisky aficionado's interest in Glen Garioch, though, centers on the fact that it makes a totally uncompromising whisky. That may be changing, because the distillery owners have removed peated barley from the recipe for future bottlings. What Glen Garioch offers is lots of grungy, nutty, rustic savory malts. With very old Glen Gariochs such as this one, the drinker stumbles across sharp pepper and dry astringent notes that many would call a highly acquired taste. In fact, outside of the heavily peated whiskies from Islay, there are few that ask more questions. And that makes it a must-try whisky. **DR**

Tasting notes

The nose is not great, with some Chinese food wrapper, soy, and stewed vegetable. But the taste is like no other. Big, savory, and full, with earthy peat, old-time instant coffee mix, nuts, stewed fruits, mushrooms, and paprika. The finish is long and musty—but in a nice way.

Glen Garioch 1797 Founder's Reserve

Morrison Bowmore Distillers (Suntory) | www.glengarioch.com

Region and country of origin Highlands, Scotland
Distillery Glen Garioch, Oldmeldrum, Aberdeenshire
Alcohol content 48% abv
Style Single malt

Glen Garioch is one of Scotland's oldest distilleries and is proud of it, and the 1797 Founder's Reserve was named to commemorate that fact. It was also the first whisky of the new Glen Garioch non-chill-filtered brand to be launched.

Indeed, the launch of this flagship Glen Garioch in 2009 heralded not only significant changes in the brand, but in the whisky industry as a whole. High on a wave of increased consumer demand for better-quality whisky, the distillery moved away from traditional perceptions of the Scottish Highlands to focus on a small range of artisan, non-chill-filtered single malts. Unlike other expressions from the distillery, the 1797 Founder's Reserve does not carry an age statement on the bottle. While it is big and full of character, it is a fresher, more youthful expression than the 12-Year-Old that was launched the following year.

Creating affordable whisky can be fraught with difficulty. A young, high-strength whisky can seem insipid or spirity, and many perfectly acceptable tricks are used to achieve delicacy and complexity. Here, however, quality is achieved simply by maturing the spirit in high-quality casks. Founder's Reserve is aged in American oak casks that were previously used to age bourbon. A mix of mainly first- and second-fill casks is used, although third-fill is considered if the wood is of exceptional quality. Indeed, Morrison Bowmore is particularly proud of its very advanced wood management system, claiming to spend as much, if not more, on it as a proportion of its turnover as anyone else in the industry. **IGY**

Tasting notes

The influence of North American oak is right there in the first whiff of sweet vanilla and butterscotch, but it is done with a light touch. The palate feels cleansed by a squeeze of grapefruit, while even more refreshing green apple notes keep things zesty.

Glen Grant 10-Year-Old

Campari Group | www.glengrant.com

Region and country of origin Speyside, Scotland
Distillery Glen Grant, Rothes, Morayshire
Alcohol content 40% abv
Style Single malt

James "The Major" Grant—son of James Grant, the distillery cofounder—took over the distillery at age twenty-five after the deaths of his father and uncle. In 1872 he installed tall, slender stills with special purifiers. The latter continue in use today and impart a "fresh, malty flavor" to the "light, yet complex spirit" that The Major knew his customers would like as an alternative to the heavy, assertive whiskies of the day.

When Campari acquired Glen Grant in 2006, its whisky was being sold only as a non-age-statement bottling, except for one five-year-old expression exclusive to Italy and a ten-year-old expression only available at the distillery shop. Whisky writers Michael Jackson and Charlie MacLean were invited to discuss a rebranding and packaging of the malt. The result was Glen Grant 10-Year-Old, a mixture of ex-bourbon casks with a small percentage of ex-sherry casks and refill hogsheads. Distillery manager Dennis Malcolm thinks the result shares many qualities with other Speyside expressions, but with distinct notes of orange and tangerine among the fruit on the nose and palate.

Glen Grant 10-Year-Old is a great introduction to the distillery's single malt, showing ample fruit with a dash of spice and a lovely nuttiness on the finish. **WM**

Tasting notes

Sweet, malty, and nutty, with notes of hazelnut and almond. Full bodied with hints of vanilla and spices. A balanced combination of nuttiness, spice, and fruit.

Glen Grant 1972 Berry's Own Selection

Berry Bros. & Rudd | www.glengrant.com

Region and country of origin Speyside, Scotland
Distillery Glen Grant, Rothes, Morayshire
Alcohol content 51.8% abv
Style Single malt

Glen Grant distillery boasts beautiful gardens complete with sparkling streams and forest walks. But in recent years it started to look run-down and neglected, receiving nowhere near the attention it deserved. When Pernod Ricard bought the whisky portfolio of Allied Distillers, the French company was forced to offload Glen Grant due to monopoly concerns. It was bought by Campari, the Italian drinks giant, perhaps appropriately, because it is in Italy that Glen Grant enjoys its biggest success. Campari is serious about becoming a force in whisky. The company owns Wild Turkey, too, so expect to hear a lot more.

The problem for the new owners was that there is very little old stock, mainly because Italians like young whisky, which Glen Grant sells in volume at five and ten years old. Most remaining older stock is owned by independent bottlers such as this one; the distillery has even bought some Gordon & MacPhail twenty-five-year-old stock to fill the gap.

Old Glen Grant is a treat. This version has been selected by Doug McIvor for Berry Bros. & Rudd and is a classic example of how well this whisky stands up to old age. It is by no means the oldest whisky from the distillery, but is everything Glen Grant should be. **DR**

Tasting notes

Full, rich, and fruity, with soft toffee on ice cream and dark coffee. With water, kumquat and apricot notes appear. The oak and spice are relatively restrained.

← James "the Major" Grant enjoys the Scottish wilds with his family.

Glen Grant 170th Anniversary Edition

Campari Group | www.glengrant.com

Region and country of origin Speyside, Scotland
Distillery Glen Grant, Rothes, Morayshire
Alcohol content 46% abv
Style Single malt

Glen Grant distillery celebrated its 170th birthday in 2010, and remains on the same site where it was founded in 1840 by John Grant and his brother, James.

The 170th Anniversary bottling is a truly representative expression of Glen Grant. It contains spirit from every type of barrel used by the distillery: first- and second-fill sherry butts, sherry hogsheads, bourbon barrels, bourbon hogsheads, and more. Likewise, the expression is 50 percent composed of casks from every year between 1976 and 1982, and at least two casks from every year between 1982 and 1999. Some of the older casks are lightly peated, as that was the Speyside style twenty-five years ago. Also, spirit from the 1970s through to the mid-1980s may have a heavier, oilier flavor, because Glen Grant employed worm tubs to cool the spirit until the mid 1980s, when these were replaced by condensers.

According to Glen Grant master distiller Dennis Malcolm, "170 years on, we continue to build on the combination of tradition and innovation that the Grant brothers brought to their whisky making all those years ago. . . . We wanted to celebrate the history of the brand while translating the unique Glen Grant approach into something new and unexpected with the 170th Anniversary limited-edition whisky."

Malcolm thinks this expression is fascinating. Due to the wide variety of cask type and ages, different notes are tasted every time it is sipped. The whisky was released in August 2010 at the retail price of €100 ($130) per bottle in Europe, Taiwan, and travel retail. Worldwide, 17,000 bottles were produced. **WM**

Tasting notes

Extremely complex on the nose and palate, with a nice, slightly oily mouthfeel. Spices, nuts, and fruits are braided around an oak backbone with hints of peat. The wonderful mouthfeel and long finish make this a rewarding and thought-provoking expression.

Glen Grant Cellar Reserve 1992

Campari Group | www.glengrant.com

Region and country of origin Speyside, Scotland
Distillery Glen Grant, Rothes, Morayshire
Alcohol content 46% abv
Style Single malt

The Glen Grant Cellar Reserve 1992 was bottled in 2008 and introduced on April 2, 2009 to complement the Glen Grant 10-Year-Old. At sixteen years old, it is a more mature, complex expression of Glen Grant.

The Cellar Reserve 1992 was originally intended to be the first in a series of sixteen-year-old bottlings, to be followed by the 1993 vintage, and so on. Instead, the distillery decided to release a nonvintage sixteen-year-old, which has become its successor. It should be noted that the nonvintage expression is bottled at the lower strength of 43 percent abv. An aged expression, as opposed to a vintage release, gives the master distiller the option of utilizing older casks to add complexity to a particular vatting of the expression.

Limited to 13,542 bottles, the Cellar Reserve 1992 is a combination of bourbon and sherry casks. According to Glen Grant master distiller Dennis Malcolm, "the special bourbon and oloroso sherry casks were handpicked by myself out of our best warehouse to create a very special and limited edition of the Glen Grant single-malt Scotch whisky. Perfect in balance of flavors and bouquet—deep, rich, and fruity—whisky as it should be." The age was intended to be a contrast to the ten-year-old expression, which serves as a standard, or baseline expression.

Dennis explains that the Cellar Reserve 1992 was the first Glen Grant sixteen-year-old expression he created using a higher percentage of sherry casks. The expression also has a higher proof; it is non-chill-filtered, which amplifies the spice and nut notes and provides a more textured mouthfeel. **WM**

Tasting notes

Rich, big, and full bodied; a wonderful mélange of malt, spice, vanilla, and nuts, with hints of citrus. The malty dram has a nice oak structure, with hazelnut, pecan, and black walnut dusted with cinnamon and nutmeg. The finish is dry and lingering.

Glen Keith 21-Year-Old

Chivas Brothers (Pernod Ricard)
www.pernod-ricard.com

Region and country of origin Speyside, Scotland
Distillery Glen Keith, Keith, Banffshire
Alcohol content 43% abv
Style Single malt

Although it hasn't distilled its own spirit since the turn of the millennium, Glen Keith has avoided the fate of many closed distilleries and remains pretty much complete. Maybe owners Chivas Brothers will someday recommission it, but, until that day arrives, it still plays an active part in distilling, even if it's for someone else.

Glen Keith was built in 1957—the second distillery to be commissioned during the twentieth century—on the site of an old corn mill in the town of Keith, Banffshire. It officially opened in 1960, and right from the start they proved to be an exceptional distillery. It was a pioneer in several senses. It experimented with new yeast strains. It installed the first gas-fuelled still in Scotland and was among the first to use computers to control the distillation process. Although mothballed in 2000, its whisky is far from impossible to find, both in official and independent bottlings.

Glen Keith name was originally set up for triple-distillation in the Lowland style and would have produced a lighter, more floral, and herbal spirit. Although it later reverted to double-distillation, its later bottlings retain a grassy style that, tasted blind, could easily pass for a Lowlander. **PB**

Tasting notes

Grassy, herbal, and lemon on the nose. On the palate it's more of the same with strong, overtones of crystallized pineapple, ginger, and bitter lemon. A light citrus finish.

Glen Keith 1993 Connoisseurs Choice

Gordon & MacPhail
www.gordonandmacphail.com

Region and country of origin Speyside, Scotland
Distillery Glen Keith, Keith, Banffshire
Alcohol content 46% abv
Style Single malt

Glen Keith was deemed surplus to Seagram's requirements in 1999, at which time it boasted an annual capacity of around one million gallons (four million liters). The plant subsequently fell silent and remains mothballed, although it is structurally intact and distilling equipment remains in place. Since its closure, Glen Keith has become home to the Chivas Technical Centre, and has been used as a "testbed" for trial ingredients and processes. It also functions as a cask-filling center for Strathisla.

The distillery was formerly the "brand home" of Passport blended whisky, of which it was a significant malt component, and it was one of very few distilleries in the Highlands to practice triple-distillation. It was converted to double-distillation in 1970, when the number of stills was increased from three to five, and a sixth still was added in 1983. Glen Keith is also notable for its installation of computerization, with a microprocessor being fitted in 1980 to automate many of the production practices.

This expression from Glen Keith dates from 1993 and has been bottled in Gordon & MacPhail's popular Connoisseur's Choice range, following maturation in refill American hogsheads. **CS**

Tasting notes

Bubblegum, apple, and unripe banana on the nose. Black pepper and spice to taste, followed by sweet fruit, cedar, and oak. Medium-length, mildly herbal finish.

Glen Mhor
27-Year-Old

Signatory Vintage Scotch Whisky Co.

Region and country of origin Highlands, Scotland
Distillery Glen Mhor, Inverness (demolished)
Alcohol content 55% abv
Style Single malt

This example of Glen Mhor is a single-cask bottling in Signatory's Cask Strength Collection, and was distilled on September 1, 1982, being matured in hogshead no. 1327 before 235 bottles were filled on April 6, 2010. It represents a late distillation from the Inverness distillery, which closed in May 1983, as owners the Distillers Company Ltd. (DCL) dramatically cut back spirit output to help balance years of overproduction.

Glen Mhor was the youngest of the three distilleries operating in the "Highland capital" of Inverness, with Millburn dating from 1807 and Glen Albyn from 1846, while Glen Mhor had been established during 1892/94 by disenchanted ex-Glen Albyn manager John Birnie and Leith-based blender Charles Mackinlay & Co. However, all three were lost during DCL's 1980s rationalization program, and today the neighboring plants of Glen Mhor and Glen Albyn are lost beneath the tarmac and steel of a retail park.

Noted novelist Neil M. Gunn worked as an excise officer at the distillery from 1921 until 1937. In his seminal book *Whisky and Scotland* (1935), he writes of Glen Mhor that "until a man has had the luck to chance upon a perfectly matured, well-mannered whisky, he does not really know what whisky is." **CS**

Tasting notes

The nose is quite reticent, with developing vanilla and apple peel. The palate is resinous and fruity, with lemon, malt, and licorice. A medium-length finish.

Glen Mhor
27-Year-Old Malt Cask

Douglas Laing & Co.
www.douglaslaing.com

Region and country of origin Highlands, Scotland
Distillery Glen Mhor, Inverness (demolished)
Alcohol content 50% abv
Style Single malt

One of the mantras of the modern business world is innovation. We are constantly being told we must innovate to survive, and that the first to adopt a new innovation have an initial competitive advantage. The flip side of this is that any piece of technology is very expensive at first, so there is a risk: if you invest too much, or too soon in the wrong process, the debts begin to pile up.

So it is with the whisky industry, and we need look no further than this distillery to see what can happen. Glen Mohr (pronounced "vor") distillery was always innovative, and in 1954 it was the first to install a Saladin box. This is an enormous perforated trough with large screwlike mixing paddles, used to speed the germination of the barley without the manual turning previously required.

Rising energy costs and centralization of malt production led to its abandonment after twenty-five years. By 1983 Glen Mohr was uneconomical to operate as a distillery and was closed and subsequently demolished. This bottling by Douglas Laing dates from 1982, the last full year of operation, and is very delicate and fresh for a whisky of this age. A piece of history that must not be missed. **AN**

Tasting notes

Delicate floral nose has hints of Parma violets and an old-fashioned candy shop. Light body with spice that fades to leave a long, dry finish of apple and green fruit.

Glen Mhor Glenkeir Treasures 21-Year-Old

Glenkeir Whiskies | www.thewhiskyshop.com

Region and country of origin Highlands, Scotland
Distillery Glen Mhor, Inverness (demolished)
Alcohol content 43% abv
Style Single malt

In 2011 one of the big whisky stories was the release of the Mackinglay's "Shackleton whisky" re-creation. Ernest Shackleton had abandoned his camp in Antarctica in the early 1900s, leaving behind a whisky supply. Those bottles were found a century later and three found their way back to Scotland, where brand owner Whyte & Mackay's master blender Richard Paterson took samples and then set out to re-create the original whisky. Many wrote about the remake being a blend, but it wasn't—it was a blended malt, which means that it contains no grain whisky. What makes the story more interesting is that the original whisky was most probably all from one distillery—Glen Mhor—making the original a single malt, albeit one made of different styles of whisky from that one distillery. It says masses about Glen Mhor that the remake of Shackleton was created using malts from several different distilleries.

This bottling is part of the independent bottling range by the Whisky Shop. It's a limited edition, with only 260 bottles and, until its story gained some publicity, sat pretty much ignored. Amazingly, even then it still escaped much attention. It's also good value for a twenty-one year old. **DR**

Tasting notes

Vanilla, coconut, and oak on the nose, the taste is surprisingly gentle but enjoyable, with some smoke, but dominated by apple orchard and hints of citrus.

Glen Moray 12-Year-Old

La Martiniquaise | www.glenmoray.com

Region and country of origin Speyside, Scotland
Distillery Glen Moray, Elgin, Morayshire
Alcohol content 40% abv
Style Single malt

For many years, Glen Moray's reputation was built on producing consistent, good quality malt for blenders. Since the change of ownership from Glenmorangie to La Martiniquaise in 2009, there has been greater emphasis on producing not just standard expressions but also a range of other vintage malts. As a result, as much as 264,170 gallons (1 million liters) of the 607,600 gallons (2.3 million liters) being produced is now going into single-malt bottling.

The backbone of the single-malt maturation policy at Glen Moray is the American white oak ex-bourbon cask. Previous manager Ed Dodson worked hard to sustain a high standard of cask management—not too tricky given Glenmorangie's reputation for its American oak wood policy. Since 2005, Graham Coull has been determined to keep to that level of quality and, under La Martiniquaise, he has enjoyed enough autonomy to do so.

The spirit cut at Glen Moray is finished relatively early at 66 percent alcohol to ensure a crisp, clean, and fruity spirit. That spirit, in the case of the 12-Year-Old, is then filled into ex-bourbon casks, a large proportion of which are first-fill. These are then stored in traditional dunnage warehouses on-site. **RL**

Tasting notes

Buttery vanilla on the nose with toasted barley, lemon puffs, and cinnamon. Initial toffee and malty sweetness on the palate, followed by spice and citric zest.

The ruined cathedral at Elgin, home of Glen Moray distillery. ➡

Glen Moray Chardonnay Cask 10-Year-Old

La Martiniquaise | www.glenmoray.com

Region and country of origin Speyside, Scotland
Distillery Glen Moray, Elgin, Morayshire
Alcohol content 40% abv
Style Single malt

Glen Moray distillery was converted from a brewery by Robert Thorne and Sons of Greenock in 1897, but it was owned by Macdonald & Muir (Glenmorangie) from 1923 until 2009. In recent years, under Glenmorangie's ownership, Glen Moray had bottled a number of malts which were "mellowed in" white wine casks, notably chardonnay and chenin blanc. For these expressions, discontinued around the year 2000, "mellowed in" really meant "finished in" those wine casks; nevertheless, they had a good reputation for being fresh, fruity, sweet, and citric drams and their discontinuation was lamented by some.

This new chardonnay matured whisky is the first addition to the core range of Glen Moray for several years. This time, however, it is not merely "finished"—it has been completely matured for ten years in Chardonnay barriques of European oak (*quercus robur*). Parcels of chardonnay casks were filled with new spirit between 2001 and 2004 and a vatting of the best casks from 2001 has given rise to this expression.

It is said that the Laich of Moray enjoys forty days more summer than any other part of Scotland. These chardonnay casks have been stored in racked warehouse number five, at the highest level, where—reminiscent of bourbon "ricks" in Kentucky—the best air and most desirable ambient temperatures are found, especially in the summer months, to allow a balletic interplay between the spirit and the wood. Layers and layers of flavor coming from the spirit, the wood and the white wine have combined to create a fascinating complexity. **RL**

Tasting notes

On the nose this is sweet, fruity, floral—pineapple, orange, apricot, mango, barley sugar, buttery shortbread, gorse flowers, and orange blossom honey. Nicely balanced. On the palate the winey notes evoke dry oak and raisiny, spiced bread-and-butter pudding.

Glen Moray Port Wood Finish 1995

La Martiniquaise | www.glenmoray.com

Region and country of origin Speyside, Scotland
Distillery Glen Moray, Elgin, Morayshire
Alcohol content 56.7% abv
Style Single malt

Following the takeover of Glen Moray by La Martiniquaise in 2009, distillery manager Graham Coull was given the opportunity to develop new whiskies and to use casks from various other drinks producers within the company's portfolio, which includes Porto Cruz port. The first new bottling to emerge in 2009 was this limited-edition port wood finish whisky.

Graham selected three thirteen-year-old, second-fill bourbon hogsheads whose contents were transferred into one single port pipe, which had previously held tawny port. After about nine months, the port pipe had done its work, and the whisky was hand bottled at 56.7 percent abv. The cask yielded a scanty 725 bottles in all, making this a very limited edition and possibly a quite collectable whisky.

The Glen Moray Port Wood Finish 1995 was very much a distillery bottling, with all the decisions, from milling the malted barley through to the final bottling, being made by staff on-site. Even the label design was decided locally. The manager and his staff are very proud of this collaborative effort, which represents their first limited-edition distillery bottling. There will doubtless be many more in the months and years to come, but this one will be remembered especially fondly at Glen Moray in particular.

The contribution of the port cask adds a layer of winey complexity to the oaky vanillas of the bourbon wood, resulting in a unique and finely balanced whisky. Jim Murray scored it 95.5 in his *2010 Whisky Bible*, which qualified it for a Liquid Gold Award. **RL**

Tasting notes

Stunning. Toffee, caramel, dark barley sugars, ripe melon, candied orange, and crystallized ginger on the nose. The palate is full, rich, sweet, and very dry. Sugared almond, chocolate lime, spiced date, with a fantastic finish of angelica and soft licorice.

Hall _sculp._

Glen Ord 15-Year-Old

Diageo | www.diageo.com

Region and country of origin Highlands, Scotland
Distillery Glen Ord, Muir of Ord, Ross-shire
Alcohol content 53.3% abv
Style Single malt

Over at Glen Ord they malt their own barley on-site and also use long fermentation and slow distillation methods, meaning that the process of creation for the whisky stays pretty true to its heritage. After all, these methods have been followed since the distillery was established back in 1838. It's that old school in its approach to maintaining quality.

Set in the Black Isle of Scotland, near the village of Muir of Ord to the north of Inverness, it takes its name from the Mackenzies of Ord, who back in the thirteenth century were given plots of land by King Alexander III. Then, by 1820, Thomas Mackenzie inherited a plot of land and used it to grow barley. As such, these were the beginnings of the Glen Ord legacy and the reason we know this particular brown spirit as we do today.

It must be noted that this 15-Year-Old is pale and grassy as well as being quite sweet. The malt is from a bourbon hogshead that yielded 310 bottles, and it offers up a crisp dram filled with the scent of vanilla pods, fruit, nut, and spice. It has a short, warm finish that's also a little oily on the tongue, but then, that's just how it rolls.

Diageo has just invested millions to up the capacity and refurbish Glen Ord, so there is much to look forward to from this distillery. **AA**

Tasting notes

This is the Lolita of whiskies; a nymphet. It's all nubile fruit and sweetness balanced with a slight immaturity that just seems to work.

Glen Ord 28-Year-Old

Diageo | www.malt.com

Region and country of origin Highlands, Scotland
Distillery Glen Ord, Muir of Ord, Ross-shire
Alcohol content 58.3% abv
Style Single malt

There are no rules governing the age of a whisky. Some independents make a point of releasing whiskies at unusual ages. But there are natural parameters. Wood will eventually overcome a whisky, and the only way to recognize that point is to monitor casks carefully. Every cask reacts to spirit differently, but as a rule of thumb, whisky matured in the Highlands tends to be more robust than Lowland whisky and more likely to tastefully reach great age—that is, fifty years and more. When the wood starts to take over, you need to get your whisky out. And it's not always at an age when you might want to.

The other key concern is the strength of the whisky. In Scotland the strength of the spirit goes down during maturation and if it goes below 40 percent abv, it can no longer be called whisky. Obviously strength isn't a concern here, so why twenty-eight years? It's an oddball age, especially as Diageo has done a twenty-five-year-old. The reason is probably because, tastewise, it's at its best, a gorgeous, perfectly balanced delight. Any longer would have seen a diminishing return in taste. The only problem with this bottle is the somewhat stiff and old packaging. Twenty-eight years is an odd age for an official bottling, but Diageo has released all sorts of exciting whiskies like this in recent years. **DR**

Tasting notes

A fruity nose gives way to a preening, full-bodied, and quite delicious whisky, with wood, spice, and tannin around a rich fruit and barley heart.

← King Alexander III (1241–86), who granted lands to the Clan Mackenzie.

Glen Ord The Singleton 12-Year-Old

Diageo | www.whiskys.co.uk

Region and country of origin Highlands, Scotland
Distillery Glen Ord, Muir of Ord, Ross-shire
Alcohol content 40% abv
Style Single malt

This twelve-year-old Highland malt is part of Diageo's Singleton range, released in 2007 and joining the distilleries of Dufftown and Glendullan, who complete the lineup. Each of the three distilleries has its whiskies distributed under the Singleton banner in a different region of the world: Dufftown appears in Europe, Glendullan in the United States, and Glen Ord in Asia, with the range being very popular in travel retail.

The Singleton of Glen Ord 12-Year-Old replaces the previously available distillery expression, which was packaged in a square bottle with a large wood-topped stopper from 2004 until 2007, and was generally available in many markets worldwide. The retirement of the older 12-Year-Old and the move to distributing the Singleton solely in Asia has caused a bit of an upset for Glen Ord fans, who as of 2010, could only officially find their favorite tipple far away from its Scottish birthplace, unless they made the pilgrimage to the distillery itself. As usual, many specialist whisky retailers in other territories have managed to get their hands on a few cases of this Asian export, but the premium price that this attracts has compounded the annoyance of many Glen Ord fans.

The makeup of the Singleton of Glen Ord seems to have changed slowly since its introduction, with each batch garnering slightly different reviews as the recipe is tweaked. Generally it seems to be a combination of whiskies matured in former sherry and bourbon barrels, with the intention being to introduce single-malt whisky to the traditionally blended-whisky-loving Asian consumer. **BA**

Tasting notes

A rich and malty nose. A hint of wood sap and flowering meadows leads you in to an easy drinking whisky with a thick mouthfeel, spicy fruit, orange, and a touch of chocolate. It finishes sweet, almost cloying, and warming.

Glen Ord The Singleton 15-Year-Old

Diageo | www.malts.com

Region and country of origin Highlands, Scotland
Distillery Glen Ord, Muir of Ord, Ross-shire
Alcohol content 40% abv
Style Single malt

In the coming years, the world's leading distillers are going to have to make some smart choices about their industry—do they seek new territories for their blends and try to extend their reach to emerging markets by building new super distilleries, as Diageo seems to be doing? Or do they concentrate on looking for lucrative niche markets for their malts, to the exclusion of other markets? Do they push aged blends more than single malts in territories where there is no negative baggage? Do they keep their stock until it is very old and sell it at the super-premium end of the market? Or do they try and perfect a young but perfect-tasting unaged whisky? And most contentious of all, do they abandon some flatlining markets and move stock to where the demand is highest and the profit potential greatest?

Diageo has been doing a bit of each, and Glen Ord has become its standard-bearer in Southeast Asia, where it is very popular. The whisky has to a large extent been withdrawn from the UK market to satisfy the Asian tastes for sweet sherried whiskies. It says masses about the importance of this part of the world that while Singletons exist for Europe and America, this second older expression has been released, reflecting the increasingly mature market in Asia.

This is a designer-made malt, and it does exactly what you'd expect it to, with no uncomfortable surprises. It is an unashamedly heavy-hitting sherry whisky with more than a passing resemblance to an old-fashioned MacIllan—which happens to be the main competition in that part of the world. **DR**

Tasting notes

On the face of it, this is a classic aged sherry whisky, with kitchen-pantry aromas, red berry, orange, and fruit compote. There's a bit more, too. Some oaky depths here, and a touch of Highland earthiness. The finish is short to medium in length.

Glen Scotia 15-Year-Old Malt Cask Sherry Butt

Douglas Laing & Co.
www.douglaslaing.com

Region and country of origin Highlands, Scotland
Distillery Glen Scotia, Campbeltown, Argyll
Alcohol content 50% abv
Style Single malt

Ask anyone beginning to learn about Scottish malts to name the regions that whisky comes from and they are sure to manage three or four easily—Islay, Speyside, Highlands, Lowlands . . . but Campbeltown? Geographically closer to Belfast than to Glasgow, situated at the far end of the remote Kintyre peninsula, surely it's just a small town? Roll back the clock a hundred years, and you would find thirty-four working distilleries within a couple of miles, as well as one of the largest fishing fleets on the west coast.

The Kintyre peninsula is possibly the cradle of whisky, as it is the point at which the Scotii race came over from Ireland. Today, however, it is quite a forlorn spot, with random bursts of economic activity. But what of the whisky industry? Almost all gone now, with only three or four old names remaining, much diminished in output. Even the Scotch Whisky Association left it off their map at one point.

All of this is a pity, for those who take the trouble to find examples like this 1992 Glen Scotia, lightly peated off the still and matured in a sherry butt for fifteen years before Douglas Laing bottled it, will find it a complex and beguiling taste, coastal, salty, smoky, and yet sweet. **AN**

Tasting notes

Apple and biscuit on the nose, surprising whiffs of light smoky peat at first and a salty, dry, savory flavor. The finish manages to be fruity and smoky at the same time.

Glen Spey 12-Year-Old Flora & Fauna OB

Diageo
www.malts.com

Region and country of origin Highlands, Scotland
Distillery Glen Spey, Rothes, Aberlour, Banffshire
Alcohol content 43% abv
Style Single malt

Diageo is the world's largest spirit producer, owning twenty-eight distilleries in Scotland as well as a plethora of well-known brands. With a portfolio that includes such a wide range of whisky, it's not surprising that the company chooses to focus on a number of established single malts, while keeping back the stock of many of its distilleries such as Glen Spey for blending purposes and the occasional special release. In the Flora & Fauna series, some of these lesser-known malts are given a widely available bottling that aims to showcase the style of make produced on-site, even if most of the aforementioned spirit is destined for the blending vat.

Glen Spey is rarely sold as a single malt, even by independent bottlers, and this in part is due to the demands placed upon the distillery's output for blending. This 12-Year-Old represents the only consistently available bottling and displays the distillery's naturally light, aperitif-style malt. There have been only two other interesting official bottlings of Glen Spey released in recent years, the first a 1996 single cask in Diageo's controversial Managers' Choice series and the next, a very well received 21-Year-Old as part of their 2010 Special Releases. **StuR**

Tasting notes

A very underrated single malt, with lashings of fruit and spice, a very accessible slice of vanilla, and a good, solid, and satisfying finish.

Glenallachie 15-Year-Old

Chivas Brothers (Pernod Ricard)
www.chivas.com

Region and country of origin Speyside, Scotland
Distillery Glenallachie, Aberlour, Banffshire
Alcohol content 58% abv
Style Single malt

Whisky is enjoying a healthy boom period and much of it is to do with the fact that people are seeking out anything with genuine heritage and provenance. Buy a single-malt whisky, and you know it comes from one site. If it has an age on it, you know what general sort of quality to expect. And the words "Made in Scotland" are an assurance of quality.

Distilleries with hundreds of years behind them tell their own story. This distillery, though, has none of that pedigree. It was built in the late 1960s and has the distinction of being the last one designed by the great distillery architect Delme Evans. Its prime purpose is to make whisky for the blend market, and it is rarely released as a distillery bottling, although some of it does find its way in to the independent bottling sector. The whisky here is typical of a Speyside malt in that it is rich in sweet barley and fruit. There have been bottlings of various ages, and all of them are quite rare, but this is the pick of the bunch.

The distillery is not open to the public, but it's sited at Aberlour in the heart of the Speyside region. It has been owned since 1989 by the French drinks giant, which uses the malt in its Chivas, Royal Salute, and Ballantine's blended whiskies. **DR**

Tasting notes

Fresh and fruity, beefy ginger barley flavor on the palate, just enough peppery wood to keep the malt interesting, and a medium, fruity finish.

Glenallachie 38-Year-Old Old Malt Cask

Douglas Laing & Co.
www.douglaslaing.com

Region and country of origin Speyside, Scotland
Distillery Glenallachie, Aberlour, Banffshire
Alcohol content 50% abv
Style Single malt

Glenallachie could be called the Thomas Pynchon of whiskies. Ask people to tell you any of the finer details about the writer or distillery and the chances are, they would be completely stuck. Glenallachie must rank as one of the least-known malt distilleries in Scotland, despite having a capacity that puts it in the top thirty in terms of output.

Founded in 1967, most of its output goes into Clan Campbell blends. Like Thomas Pynchon, Glenallachie just gets on with producing work of very high quality without any of the fuss. Maybe that's the point. What does it matter if it has Oregon pine washbacks, or ones made of balsa wood or uranium? We sometimes get so caught up in the technical specifications and marketing that we fail to taste a whisky without being bombarded by context. Glenallachie never waxes lyrical about using heathery peat or rarefied water. How often do you come across a Scotch single malt with no idea of what to expect?

The Old Malt Cask version from Douglas Laing is one of only seventy-five bottles produced from a single claret wine cask, giving it a lovely reddish hue. Sure, it's full-on, so if you don't like big, sulfury whiskies, stay away and leave more for others. **PB**

Tasting notes

Slightly sulfury on the nose, with moist plum pudding, oaky spice, and coffee chocolate. On the palate it has stewed rhubarb and ginger with more sulfur.

Glencadam 10-Year-Old

Angus Dundee Distillers | www.glencadamdistillery.co.uk

Region and country of origin Highlands, Scotland
Distillery Glencadam, Brechin, Angus
Alcohol content 46% abv
Style Single malt

Glencadam distillery closed in 2000 due to a lack of cooling water, only reopening in 2003 when it was sold to the independent, family-owned company Angus Dundee. This 10-Year-Old was not launched until 2008, and it was only the second expression to be released under new ownership. The age statement here refers to the minimum time that the spirit has been aged because the three-year gap in production makes it inevitable that some batches were aged for somewhat longer than ten years.

That Glencadam's new make is light and very sweet can be attributed partly to its peculiar method of distillation. The wash still has an external heater (rather than direct fire on the still), so the wort is constantly circulating, picking up more copper and losing sulfur to produce a mellower spirit and a finer style. Another unusual feature is that the lyne arm from the still is angled upward at fifteen degrees instead of the more usual swan neck, a factor that encourages a particularly delicate and mellow spirit.

Balancing the whisky requires subtle ten-year wood treatment. The distillery management sought out bourbon casks and selected barrels that would respect the fresh, lively, clean, and crisp citrus tones. The spirit was aged in ex-bourbon casks bought from an agent in the United States who sources them from a variety of distilleries. Each of the bourbon barrels is reused up to three times and recharred when necessary. Glencadam bottles all its whisky at 46 percent abv, without chill-filtration, and with no added coloring. **IGY**

Tasting notes

At ten years old this retains much of its youthful liveliness, but the alcohol nuzzles with intent rather than bites. The clean, grassy, crisp, citrus tones and malt dough of the original new make are still in evidence, mellowed by subtle sweetness from the oak.

Glencadam 12-Year-Old Portwood Finish

Angus Dundee Distillers | www.glencadamdistillery.co.uk

Region and country of origin Highlands, Scotland
Distillery Glencadam, Brechin, Angus
Alcohol content 46% abv
Style Single malt

Glencadam 12-Year-Old Portwood Finish was added to the distillery's range in July 2010 (along with an Oloroso Cask Finish and a twenty-one-year-old).

For the first ten years of aging, the spirit is matured in ex-bourbon casks. Overseen by distillery manager Douglas Fitchett at the distillery's own warehouse, the process is no different to that of any of the other whiskies produced by a distillery. But then the casks are transferred to sister distillery Tomintoul, where they are racked into port pipes and finished under the supervision of master distiller Robert Flemming. The whisky stays in the port pipes at Tomintoul for another two years until it is bottled.

Angus Dundee is a business that was built up on blended whiskies. Its Glencadam distillery is capable of producing around 400,000 gallons (1.5 million liters) per year and has a storage capacity of approximately 20,000 casks, but the single malts form only a tiny, if lucrative, part of the business. This product's handful of port pipes would fit awkwardly in the production schedule, and they are more easily handled at Tomintoul. Also, having already established the very limited edition Tomintoul Portwood, the distillery has small-cask transfer facilities.

Even though the two distilleries both use port pipes, these are bought in tiny quantities. So, rather than source them direct from specific wine makers in Oporto, Portugal, the casks are bought locally from the Speyside Cooperage. Angus Dundee acquired a bottling site in 2011, so now Glencadam can complete the final bottling of the Portwood Finish itself. **IGY**

Tasting notes

This whisky has a beautifully seductive salmon-pink twinkle. It has lively aromas of red berry fruits and the full-on sweetness of tawny port, but not to excess. Here the once gentle Glencadam wears the mask of a rather large bear—a bear that dances *en pointe* and on ice.

Glencadam 14-Year-Old Oloroso Sherry Finish

Angus Dundee Distillers | www.glencadamdistillery.co.uk

Region and country of origin Highlands, Scotland
Distillery Glencadam, Brechin, Angus
Alcohol content 46% abv
Style Single malt

In July 2010, three new editions were added to the Glencadam range: a twelve-year-old portwood finish, a twenty-one-year-old, and this, the 14-Year-Old Oloroso Sherry Finish, which has been aged for twelve years in ex-bourbon casks and an additional two years in oloroso casks.

The first twelve years of maturation are as per the ten- and fifteen-year-olds, but then the whisky is transferred to Glencadam's sister distillery, Tomintoul. Tomintoul first used sherry butts as an experiment, and the process was expanded to Glencadam after two years. Even so, a total of just sixty casks are selected each year for use by the two distilleries.

The oloroso butts used by the two distilleries come direct from a small bodega in Jerez, Spain. The distillery owner does not divulge the identity of the cask supplier but has described how the bodega was chosen. The team first looked at each of the biggest sherry producers, but bigger distilleries such as Macallan already take thousands of casks and have developed associations with their suppliers over many years. Angus Dundee's needs were much smaller, so when they went out to Spain, they were introduced to smaller bodegas. They found a family company, sampled the sherry, looked at the casks, and have built on the relationship each year.

Glencadam's Sherry Finish is produced in small batches so each bottling tastes slightly different. The size of the operation is small enough to allow the whisky to be sampled and bottled as and when the sales team requires more stock. **IGY**

Tasting notes

An initial clue of what is to follow is the slight orangey hue, followed by sweet sherry spice on the nose. The oloroso flavors of grilled walnut and dried fig are present, and there is a pepperiness about it all that still allows the floral, vanilla oak to come through.

Glencadam 32-Year-Old

Angus Dundee Distillers | www.glencadamdistillery.co.uk

Region and country of origin Highlands, Scotland
Distillery Glencadam, Brechin, Angus
Alcohol content 46% abv
Style Single malt

Of the large stocks held at Glencadam, there are some whiskies just over thirty years old. In 2008, in addition to the core range, owner Angus Dundee began an annual release of a selection of older limited editions. Over three successive years, some of the oldest casks held at the distillery were bottled as single casks into clear-glass square decanters. This 32-Year-Old is the third in the series.

The first of the limited editions to be released was a twenty-five-year-old. It was distilled on April 22, 1983 and spent its entire maturation in a single sherry cask (no. 1002). The whisky was bottled on December 5, 2008. Only 300 bottles were produced, and these sold out quickly. The thirty-year-old that replaced it was distilled on April 6, 1978, and was also matured entirely in a single sherry cask (no. 2335); it was bottled in spring 2009, and 615 bottles were released.

This 32-Year-Old is in fact from the same batch as its predecessor, and was also distilled on April 6, 1978. This limited-edition release remained in a sherry cask (no. 2332) throughout its maturation. Then it was bottled in September 2010. Only 405 bottles of the 32-Year-Old were produced.

All three releases were bottled at 46 percent abv, without chill-filtering or added coloring. In each case, the bottle label records the cask number and the date of distillation and bottling, and each bottle has been individually numbered.

The style of these limited releases differs somewhat from younger expressions, which were all aged in ex-bourbon casks. **IGY**

Tasting notes

Great wafts of rum-and-raisin ice cream offer much encouragement to the sweet of tooth. The early promise of vanilla sweetness is delivered in scoops, but there is a light zestiness of bitter orange peel garnish that elevates it and prevents cloying on the palate.

GlenDronach 12-Year-Old Original

BenRiach Distillery Co. | www.glendronachdistillery.co.uk

Region and country of origin Speyside, Scotland
Distillery GlenDronach, Forgue, Aberdeenshire
Alcohol content 43% abv
Style Single malt

The GlenDronach distillery has a long-standing reputation for producing richly sherried single malt whiskies. Since The BenRiach Distillery Co. Ltd. purchased GlenDronach in April 2008, there has been an even greater emphasis on ex-sherry casks, with a £5 million ($7.9 million) budget allocated to keep the supply of appropriate wood flowing.

The core GlenDronach range was relaunched in 2009, led by a revamped version of the existing 12-Year-Old that was rechristened GlenDronach Original. The youngest of the trio of GlenDronach "core" expressions is matured in a combination of Spanish Pedro Ximénez and oloroso sherry casks. Managing director Billy Walker says that "the 12-Year-Old is now back to where it should be. It once again has the rich sherry wood style it used to enjoy and which works so well with the spirit's character."

Four decades ago, GlenDronach was one of the top five single malts globally, but under successive owners, the brand became somewhat neglected. The new team has made a very positive effort to reverse its fortunes, anticipating sales of 150,000 bottles in 2009 but actually passing the 300,000 mark.

Previous owner Chivas Brothers Ltd. had acquired GlenDronach as part of its takeover of Allied Domecq in 2005, and as Chivas already had something of an embarrassment of Speyside riches, the company was happy to sell the distillery and single-malt brand on to BenRiach. Just as the new owners had chosen to capitalize the central *R* in BenRiach, so they went on to capitalize the *D* in GlenDronach. **GS**

Tasting notes

The 12-Year-Old GlenDronach variant offers a sweet nose of Christmas cake fresh from the oven, with vanilla and ginger notes. Smooth and creamy on the palate, with sherry, soft oak, sultana, raisin, almond, and spice. The finish is lengthy, dry, and nutty.

GlenDronach 14-Year-Old Sauternes Finish

BenRiach Distillery Co. | www.glendronachdistillery.co.uk

Region and country of origin Speyside, Scotland
Distillery GlenDronach, Forgue, Aberdeenshire
Alcohol content 46% abv
Style Single malt

July 2010 saw an entirely new departure for the GlenDronach single-malt brand when a quartet of expressions was launched under the banner of the Wood Finish range. The distillery's new owners, who had gained considerable experience of the art of wood finishing with their BenRiach single malt, transferred their knowledge to this new acquisition.

"We've looked at what worked with BenRiach in terms of finishes and applied that knowledge and experience to GlenDronach," says Billy Walker. "People were surprised to see GlenDronach wood finishes, but we acquired some spirit which had been matured in recharred and ex-bourbon casks rather than the traditional GlenDronach sherry casks. It was a lighter style, which you could expose to other cask types.

"However, there wasn't a lot of the base spirit from recharred and ex-bourbon casks, so releases of finished GlenDronachs will be limited. In practice, all the finishes became balanced more quickly than we might have expected, given the style of GlenDronach," Walker concludes.

There are two wood-finished expressions bottled at fourteen years of age. One was finished in virgin oak, the other in casks that previously held Sauternes sweet wine from the Bordeaux region in France. The latter finish had already proved extremely popular as a finish for BenRiach. The effect of the Sauternes casks turned out to be just as positive with GlenDronach spirit. Walker notes that "the whisky spent eighteen months in the Sauternes casks. It actually worked quicker in the Sauternes wood than the BenRiach did." **GS**

Tasting notes

Fresh and fruity on the nose, with strawberry, apricot, baked apple, and dessert wine. The viscous palate is sweet, with honey barley sugar, milk chocolate, and vanilla, while a slick, winey note transfers from the nose. The finish is sweet, with raisin, fresh cream, and spice.

GlenDronach 14-Year-Old Virgin Oak Finish

BenRiach Distillery Co. | www.glendronachdistillery.co.uk

Region and country of origin Speyside, Scotland
Distillery GlenDronach, Forgue, Aberdeenshire
Alcohol content 46% abv
Style Single malt

GlenDronach 14-Year-Old Virgin Oak Finish was released in July 2010 alongside a second finish of the aged spirit, the Sauternes Finish. As with the Sauternes, positive experiences of using virgin oak casks with BenRiach encouraged the team behind the two brands to employ it with GlenDronach as well.

"We did lots of work with BenRiach and virgin oak, and people really liked it," says managing director Billy Walker. Indeed, not only was a BenRiach virgin oak wood finish released, but spirit matured in virgin oak was a component of the BenRiach twenty-five-year-old, and virgin-oak-matured single-cask bottlings were extremely well received.

Walker says that "with GlenDronach, it's a more robust experience when you use virgin oak, as Speysides like BenRiach are more delicate. The virgin casks are American oak, lightly toasted for us by the Speyside cooperage at Craigellachie. Virgin oak is great for Scotch whisky, but has been avoided in the past because it is so expensive."

When it comes to selling GlenDronach, whether "plain" or "finished," Walker outlines the same strategy as that which applies to the BenRiach brand. "We don't compete in the mass market," he declares. "Our peers would be single-malt brands such as Glengoyne. We share the same values and target the same markets." On taking over GlenDronach in 2008, Walker noted, "We have great plans for GlenDronach in the UK, Germany, USA, Belgium, Sweden, Denmark, Russia, Spain, Italy, Switzerland, France, Canada, Japan, Taiwan, Singapore, Hong Kong, and China." **GS**

Tasting notes

The nose is initially slightly smoky and even burned, quite dry, then sweetening with vanilla, banana, and cocoa powder. Very spicy in the mouth, with vanilla, cereal, hazelnut, and peanut, plus newly planed timber. The gingery finish is medium in length and drying.

GlenDronach 15-Year-Old Revival

BenRiach Distillery Co. | www.glendronachdistillery.co.uk

Region and country of origin Speyside, Scotland
Distillery GlenDronach, Forgue, Aberdeenshire
Alcohol content 46% abv
Style Single malt

GlenDronach 15-Year-Old is GlenDronach's bestseller and carries the apt name of Revival. While its twelve-year-old sibling is matured in a mix of Pedro Ximénez and oloroso sherry casks, the 15-Year-Old has been matured solely in oloroso sherry casks.

The Revival tag refers not just to the increased profile of GlenDronach as a single malt under the current regime, but also to the fact that, before the previous owner, Chivas Brothers, acquired the distillery, it had been mothballed between 1996 and 2002 by Allied Domecq, and its position in the portfolios of major distillers had never been assured.

"We only had one product when we took over," notes managing director Billy Walker, "and we have totally reinvented GlenDronach. We've brought in new wood management, extended the range, and made the whisky more 'muscular.'" The BenRiach distillery celebrates the whisky's sherry-matured provenance and the stylistic influence it has on the finished product. Previous owners, who seem to have regarded the long-standing maturation policy as a liability, had begun to reduce the role of ex-sherry casks in the GlenDronach maturation process.

However, Walker is full of praise for the condition of the distillery that he and his associates purchased from Chivas Brothers, saying that, "We knew from the way they had looked after BenRiach that GlenDronach would be in good order, and so it proved."

GlenDronach had the distinction of being the last distillery in Scotland to fire its stills with coal. Steam coils are now located within the two pairs of stills. **GS**

Tasting notes

Stronger leather and furniture polish notes than in the 12-Year-Old, with chocolate orange, and toffee. It is fuller and more luscious on the palate, with spicy leather sweetening into fruit, notably apricot, with coffee and chocolate. The lengthy finish dries to raisin.

GlenDronach 15-Year-Old Moscatel Finish

BenRiach Distillery Co.
www.glendronachdistillery.co.uk

Region and country of origin Speyside, Scotland
Distillery GlenDronach, Forgue, Aberdeenshire
Alcohol content 46% abv
Style Single malt

Moscatel is a sweet, fortified wine produced in Portugal and Spain from muscat grapes. Casks that previously held it have been used by a wide range of Scottish whisky distillers for finishing purposes, including Arran, Caol Ila, Edradour, and Tullibardine.

Along with its three wood-finished compatriots, GlenDronach 15-Year-Old Moscatel Finish has helped to extend the distillery's range away from a simple, linear, age-progression-based format. Sales director Alistair Walker says, "We needed to extend with a few wood finishes."

Having acquired an inventory of some 9,000 casks when it purchased GlenDronach, the BenRiach distillery has plenty of permutations to play with if it chooses to do so. As well as investing significantly in ex-sherry wood, sourced directly from Spain, the team at GlenDronach embarked on a program that involves reracking around 50 percent of the entire inventory into oloroso sherry casks.

Distillery manager Alan McConnochie says, "Some new make is going straight into ex-sherry casks, but we will start off a lot of our new-make spirit in bourbon wood for four or five years, and then finish it off in sherry wood." **GS**

Tasting notes

Syrup-soaked fruits on the nose, vanilla, with marzipan and a hint of nutmeg. Mouth-coating, with cinnamon, tinned pineapple, vanilla, fig, date, and a hint of nuts.

GlenDronach 15-Year-Old Tawny Port Finish

BenRiach Distillery Co.
www.glendronachdistillery.co.uk

Region and country of origin Speyside, Scotland
Distillery GlenDronach, Forgue, Aberdeenshire
Alcohol content 46% abv
Style Single malt

The initial release of GlenDronach Tawny Port Finish was a twenty-year-old expression. As sales director Alistair Walker says, "This whisky was a great success and sold out very quickly, so we decided to release a second bottling in 2011. The new 15-Year-Old Tawny Port maintains our tradition of releasing wonderful non–sherry wood finishes of the highest quality.

"We have carefully selected whisky that has been gently maturing in lighter casks, so that aficionados experience the full impact of the port. We used a very small batch of tawny port casks, which have given the final whisky its own range of idiosyncratic flavors and aromas. The very pleasing result contributes extra depth and concentrated stewed fruit flavors."

Managing director Billy Walker declares, "Port is a fantastic cask type to work with. Tawny port actually makes the GlenDronach drier, rather than richer, as you might expect. However, the GlenDronach finishes may come and go in the future because of a lack of suitable casks."

Initial maturation of the GlenDronach Tawny Port variant took place in European oak casks before the whisky was transferred into the tawny port casks for its secondary period of maturation. **GS**

Tasting notes

Musty port, plum, raisin, and cherry on the nose. Big fruit flavors on the palate, very focused red grape notes, vanilla, and fig. The finish is long, spicy, and oaky.

GlenDronach 18-Year-Old Allardice

BenRiach Distillery Co.
www.glendronachdistillery.co.uk

Region and country of origin Speyside, Scotland
Distillery GlenDronach, Forgue, Aberdeenshire
Alcohol content 46% abv
Style Single malt

GlenDronach 18-Year-Old is named Allardice, after James Allardice, who established the Glendronach Distillery Co. in 1826. This was just two years after the liberalizing Excise Act of 1824 had made legal distilling infinitely more lucrative than it was previously.

Allardice was an energetic entrepreneur. Having built his distillery, he began seeking markets for his "Guid Glendronach" whisky. He headed south to Edinburgh with a barrel and a flagon of Glendronach, but few tavern landlords showed interest. Legend relates that he was then accosted by two prostitutes who asked him to buy them a drink. Being a thrifty Highlander, Allardice declared that he had a plentiful supply of whisky in his hotel room. Later, seeing no point in carrying all his stock of Glendronach home, the distiller gave away the remainder of the flagon to his new acquaintants. Soon word of his whisky was spreading on the streets, and it was being requested by name in the city's pubs. The landlords who had previously refused to deal with Allardice now began to place orders, and the future of Glendronach distillery was secured.

Like the GlenDronach 15-Year-Old, the 18-Year-Old is matured exclusively in ex-oloroso casks. **GS**

Tasting notes

Milk chocolate, fudge, instant coffee, and glacé cherry. Stewed fruits, ripe orange, hazelnut, spice, and oak. The finish has smoke and cherry-liqueur chocolate.

GlenDronach 21-Year-Old Parliament

BenRiach Distillery Co.
www.glendronachdistillery.co.uk

Region and country of origin Speyside, Scotland
Distillery GlenDronach, Forgue, Aberdeenshire
Alcohol content 48% abv
Style Single malt

Principally due to market demand from customers, GlenDronach 21-Year-Old was introduced in 2011. The expression is named Parliament, the collective term for rooks, birds that for centuries have lived by GlenDronach distillery. Nearby flows the Dronach Burn, which provides the plant with cooling water. The surrounding trees have been home to a parliament of rooks from time immemorial. They are said to bring good fortune, and they were certainly useful in the days before legal distilling commenced at GrenDronach, when the illicit distillers in the area would be warned of the approach of strangers—and particularly excise officers—by the noise of the birds.

GlenDronach sales director Alistair Walker says, "We felt we needed something to fill the big gap between the eighteen-year-old and the thirty-year-old expressions. It's a logical place to plug the gap in the range, and it allows people to experience GlenDronach as it ages. Like the twelve-year-old GlenDronach, the 21-Year-Old is made of spirit matured in Spanish Pedro Ximénez and oloroso sherry casks, and the result is a whisky that is rich and intense, with concentrated flavors. We bottle it at 48 percent abv to set it apart from the rest of the range." **GS**

Tasting notes

Bold, sweet sherry on the nose, with soy sauce, molasses, and new leather. Caramel and lots of spicy leather, then late-developing clove and licorice.

GlenDronach 31-Year-Old Grandeur

BenRiach Distillery Co. | www.glendronachdistillery.co.uk

Region and country of origin Speyside, Scotland
Distillery GlenDronach, Forgue, Aberdeenshire
Alcohol content 45.8% abv
Style Single malt

As part of its program for extending the GlenDronach range to encompass a greater variety of "age points," the distillery released this 31-Year-Old expression in 2010, along with no fewer than eleven single-cask bottlings and four wood finishes.

Managing director Billy Walker says, "Like the fifteen- and eighteen-year-old expressions, the 31-Year-Old GlenDronach has been matured entirely in ex-oloroso sherry butts, rather than a mix of former oloroso and Pedro Ximénez casks. The style evokes chocolate and raisins. We introduced the 31-Year-Old to replace a thirty-three-year-old that had been brought in during 2005, before we bought the distillery. That was bottled at 40 percent abv. We wanted to make the 31-Year-Old our 'super-premium' expression of GlenDronach, with really good packaging, and we bottle it at the cask strength of 45.8 percent abv. Stylistically, it's quite similar to the old thirty-three-year-old, but if you compare them side by side, you definitely see the benefits of doing it at cask strength."

Like the rest of the GlenDronach bottlings, the 31-Year-Old has been given a name, in this case Grandeur, which reflects the perceived status of this flagship variant. Walker adds that "Grandeur is a classical representation of the smooth, complex, and full-bodied style that the GlenDronach distillery is famous for." It has a lot to live up to; its predecessor was described by Walker as "displaying real elegance and exuding class. A myriad of spiced fruits drizzled in bitter chocolate sauce . . . an alcoholic liquid dessert." **GS**

Tasting notes

Sweet sherry, malt, warm sugar, with underlying fresh ginger and coffee on the nose. Huge sherry and stewed fruit flavors, along with molasses and almond, but always civilized and smooth. The finish is long with hints of coal, honey, dark chocolate, and licorice.

Glendullan 1993 Connoisseurs Choice

Gordon & MacPhail | www.gordonandmacphail.com

Region and country of origin Speyside, Scotland
Distillery Glendullan, Dufftown, Keith, Banffshire
Alcohol content 43% abv
Style Single malt

In this marketing-oriented world, it is hard to imagine why any new distillery would give itself a name like Glendullan—even if, translated from Gaelic, its meaning is the rather more evocative "valley of the standing stone." In truth, the new distillery buildings do look dull and functional, replacing a very much more aesthetically pleasing late-nineteenth-century predecessor, but fortunately we can forget both name and buildings because dull this whisky is not.

It is likely that many first-time whisky drinkers around the world will never have heard of Glendullan, with the exception of those in the United States, its main market. Relatively few official bottlings are released, despite the fact that Glendullan is one of Diageo's biggest distilleries in terms of capacity: almost one million gallons (four million liters) of spirit produced annually. Glendullan's lack of fame is ironic because, with its light, elegant, and rounded taste, it firmly positions itself as a whisky for first-time drinkers.

Glendullan was previously marketed by Diageo as part of its Flora & Fauna range, where single malts that had rarely or never seen the light of day were released to the public. It is now part of Diageo's Singleton range, with its distinctive flattened bottle. Depending on where in the world you are, ordering a Singleton will yield very different single malts: a Dufftown in Europe, a Glen Ord in Asia, and a twelve-year-old Glendullan in the United States. This Connoisseurs Choice 1993 Glendullan expression from Gordon & MacPhail bears no exact indication of its age. It is matured in refill American hogsheads. **PB**

Tasting notes

Malty and creamy on the nose, with hard candy, sherbet, and hints of Parma violet. On the palate it is initially very creamy, with a burst of almond biscuit, vanilla, and coconut, and a mouth-coating, light spice. On the finish, the vanilla drifts slowly away, carried by the oak.

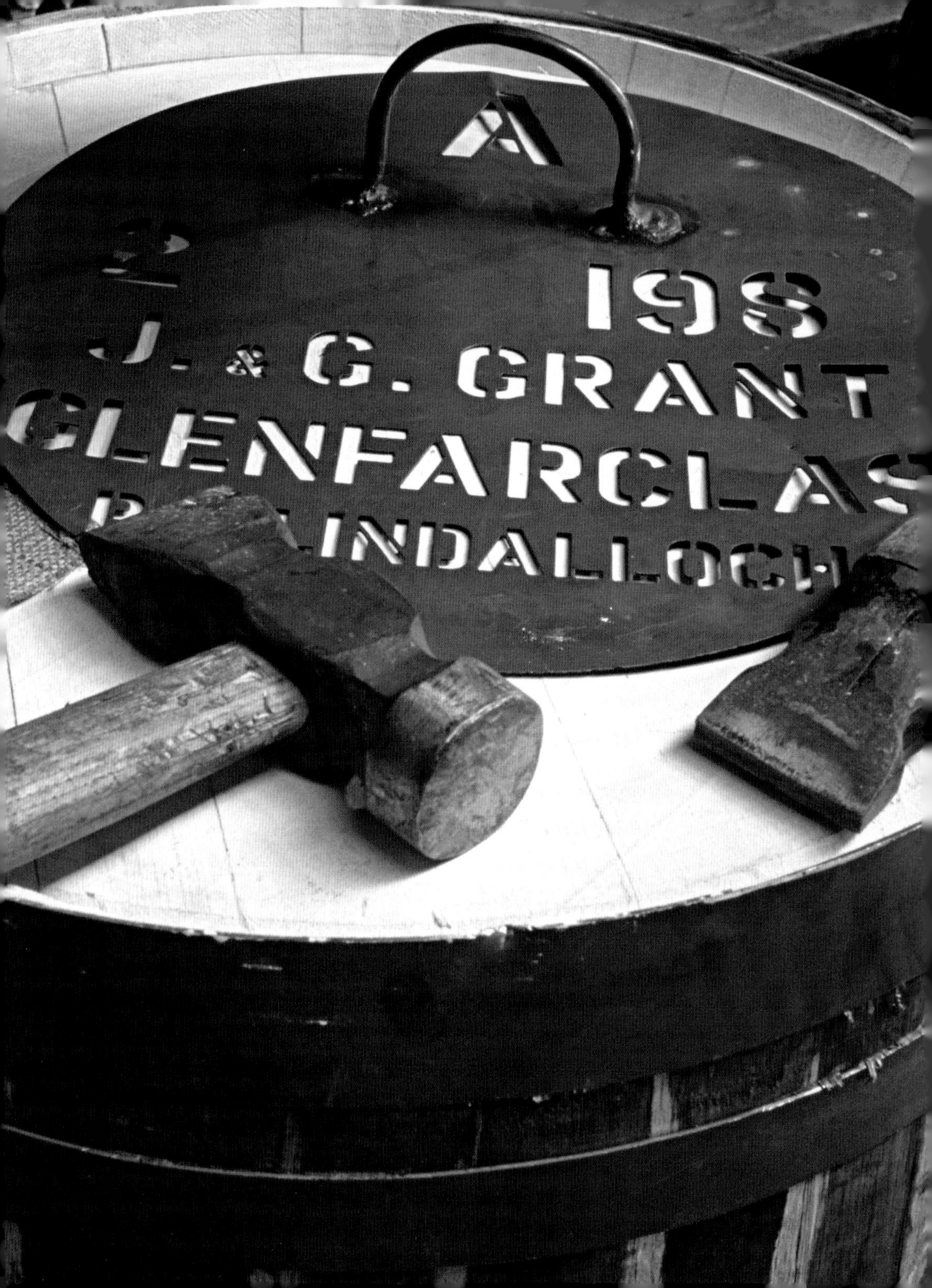
198
J. & G. GRANT
GLENFARCLAS

Glenfarclas 10-Year-Old

J & G Grant | www.glenfarclas.co.uk

Region and country of origin Speyside, Scotland
Distillery Glenfarclas, Ballindalloch, Banffshire
Alcohol content 40% abv
Style Single malt

Although Robert Hay is recorded as the founder of Glenfarclas in 1836, it is the Grant dynasty that created the worldwide success of this distillery and its distinctive whisky. Since 1865, Glenfarclas has been owned by the Grants; currently the sixth-generation Grant (George) leads the company, together with his father, John. J & G Grant is one of the very few remaining independent distilleries owned by a private family and is therefore special in the whisky world. No wonder Glenfarclas promotes its product with the slogan "The Spirit of Independence."

The Grants—who have no family ties to William Grant & Sons of Glenfiddich—are notorious for their outspokenness regarding many issues in the whisky trade, which adds to the color of this distillery and its whisky. Famous people come to visit unexpectedly—including Formula 1 hero Michael Schumacher, who arrived on his motorbike one sunny day.

Whereas Schumacher lives in the fast lane, Glenfarclas matures in an unhurried way for many years. The Grants have a preference for ex-sherry casks when it comes to maturing and don't believe in wood finishes, although they revat in another type of cask to add an extra layer of flavor. George Grant puts it this way: "We don't finish our whisky, but you can." Try the youngster in the team, this 10-Year-Old. **HO**

Tasting notes

Candied red apple, molasses, kiwi, sugared orange, cinnamon, clove, and honey finish off a whisky that is warm, round, and pleasant with lingering smoke.

Glenfarclas 12-Year-Old

J & G Grant | www.glenfarclas.co.uk

Region and country of origin Speyside, Scotland
Distillery Glenfarclas, Ballindalloch, Banffshire
Alcohol content 43% abv
Style Single malt

J & G Grant has an interesting history. Founder John Grant lived to the age of eighty-four. He was born in 1805 on a farm in the Livet valley, not too far from the current distillery's site. In those days, crops made inedible by rains could be used to make whisky; often, tenants paid their dues to the landowner in this way.

In John Grant's time, the Livet valley was littered with small copper stills run by smooth operators who skillfully avoided contact with the customs and excise man. Whisky smuggling was considered an honorable profession back then, and the system of paying dues with illicit whisky went on until 1824. In that year, a new law made acquiring a license to distill much cheaper. As a result, many Scottish distillers decided to become legitimate entrepreneurs.

By the time John Grant became the tenant of Rechlerich Farm in 1865, he had already made quite a name for himself as a cattle raiser, having bred various Aberdeen Angus champions. With the farm came a distillery called Glenfarclas, which John bought it for around £500. By entering the legal distilling world, he unknowingly became the founder of a whisky dynasty that lasts to this day. The first John Grant at Glenfarclas, therefore, is a man to remember. A liquid salute to this man seems only appropriate; this 12-Year-Old expression would serve admirably. **HO**

Tasting notes

The full fruitiness of the 10-Year-Old, but with more toffee, ripe banana, and caramel. The finish is spicy, with more than a hint of leather and a whiff of black pepper.

 A old stencil and tools for barrel making at Glenfarclas distillery.

Glenfarclas 15-Year-Old

J & G Grant | www.glenfarclas.co.uk

Region and country of origin Speyside, Scotland
Distillery Glenfarclas, Ballindalloch, Banffshire
Alcohol content 46% abv
Style Single malt

J & G Grant founder John Grant was a farmer rather than a distiller, so he sublet Glenfarclas to a relative named John Smith who was no stranger to the business. He had been a commissioning manager at the Glenlivet in 1858 and had held various positions in the industry. Son George Grant concentrated on raising cattle at Rechlerich Farm, while his father still managed the old family farm at Blairfindy. When Smith left to build his own distillery nearby (which was to become Cragganmore), George took the helm at Glenfarclas in 1870.

For twenty years, Grant father and son would jointly run the business until John died in 1889. Only a year later, George also died. The license to distill passed into the hands of his two sons, John and George, and their mother, Elsie. At the time, it was not uncommon for women to run a distillery while their menfolk were out hunting or rounding up cattle.

This 15-Year-Old expression is favored by Ishbel Grant, spouse of chairman, John. An experienced fly-fisher, she can be spotted on the banks of the Spey, catching salmon. It is rumored she has a small atomizer with some Glenfarclas 15-Year-Old to spray on the fly. That might partly explain her success in catching fish. Why not marinate your salmon in some Glenfarclas 15-Year-Old next time? **HO**

Tasting notes

Rich fruitiness unfolds in layer after layer of caramel intensity; a full, elegant body, and a faintly bitter, nutty finish: marmalade on buttered toast.

Glenfarclas 25-Year-Old

J & G Grant | www.glenfarclas.co.uk

Region and country of origin Speyside, Scotland
Distillery Glenfarclas, Ballindalloch, Banffshire
Alcohol content 43% abv
Style Single malt

John and George Grant—the grandsons of founder John Grant—were responsible for expanding the distillery in the late nineteenth century, when whisky was booming. They found business partners in the Pattison brothers of Leith, to the north of the city of Edinburgh, whisky brokers who were convicted of tampering with the books and the blended whiskies of their own company not a decade later. Glenfarclas went to the brink of bankruptcy, but the distillery survived, albeit at the cost of grandson John, who had to withdraw from the management due to ill-health precipitated by the crisis.

Grandson George must have decided never to take outside capital into the company again, since he managed to acquire the land after the lease that the Grants had taken from Ballindalloch Estate expired in 1930. From 1930 onward, the Grants were no longer paying tenants—they owned both the distillery and the land on which it stood, and were fiercely independent. They also laid down casks to mature, some for longer than the others.

Twenty-five years is an age that Glenfarclas can easily carry, being a robust spirit that holds itself well—just as the third-generation Grants did when they withstood their firm's crisis. Celebrate their perseverance with this remarkable dram. **HO**

Tasting notes

Gentle tones of bittersweet chocolate, pecan, fig jam, and baked meat float over the deep caramel and fruit tones. The finish is quiet and multifaceted.

Glenfarclas 30-Year-Old

J & G Grant | www.glenfarclas.co.uk

Region and country of origin Speyside, Scotland
Distillery Glenfarclas, Ballindalloch, Banffshire
Alcohol content 43% abv
Style Single malt

The fourth generation to take the helm at Glenfarclas distillery was George S. Grant, father of the current chairman, John. He would hold that position for more than half a century, steering the company through rough times after World War II. Visitors to Glenfarclas immediately notice the bright red doors that give access to the distillery's bonded warehouses, and the decision to paint them such a vivid color was made by George himself; red has been the signature color of Glenfarclas ever since.

Glenfarclas grew, and its product became so much in demand with blenders that George had to put his whisky on allocation, a state of affairs that would last until the start of the 1960s. Blenders were then canceling orders for the years to come, which for many distillers caused unsellable stocks to pile up. George, however, took a different and daring route. Deciding that Glenfarclas should not be jeopardized by overreliance on blending companies, he began to lay down more stock for his own single malt, letting the whisky sleep until better times came.

Thanks to the foresight of George S. Grant, we can savor old Glenfarclas whiskies, like this 30-Year-Old expression which is not even the oldest vintage. You are invited to raise a glass to independence of spirit—both in the man and the whisky. **HO**

Tasting notes

Fresh orange, raisin, and gentle oaky spiciness melt mildly and smoothly into caramel, pecan pie, and a wonderfully fruity finish.

Glenfarclas 40-Year-Old

J & G Grant | www.glenfarclas.co.uk

Region and country of origin Speyside, Scotland
Distillery Glenfarclas, Ballindalloch, Banffshire
Alcohol content 46% abv
Style Single malt

Dip into the past with this outstanding dram. Where some other single malts might turn into oak juice after so many years in the cask, Glenfarclas is remarkably fresh and fruity at this age. John Grant, the fifth generation of J & G Grant and current leader of Glenfarclas, is personally involved in selecting casks, traveling to Spain at least once a year to negotiate deals for ex-sherry casks.

John is building on the legacy of his father, George S., who laid down so many casks in previous decades. John is also responsible for selling Glenfarclas by the bottle instead of selling in bulk to brokers. Some independent bottlers still put Glenfarclas on the market, but John forbids the company name on such bottles, which go under such descriptions as "the whisky that cannot be named."

Former British prime minister Margaret Thatcher once visited Glenfarclas. John learned that she was serving cognac at 10 Downing Street and afterward decided to write her a short letter along the following lines: "Your Excellency, it has come to my attention that British industry is not supported at your dining table. You serve cognac, but whisky would be more appropriate . . ." The letter was accompanied by a fine bottle of Glenfarclas. According to John, the Iron Lady went on to serve Glenfarclas ever after. **HO**

Tasting notes

Fruit and spice lead the dance. Cedar wood, clove, cumin, and nutmeg hover above fruity caramel, apricot, and cantaloupe melon. The finish is long and complex.

Glenfarclas 105

J & G Grant | www.glenfarclas.co.uk

Region and country of origin Speyside, Scotland
Distillery Glenfarclas, Ballindalloch, Banffshire
Alcohol content Varies per batch, around 60% abv
Style Single malt

John Grant, the fifth generation of J & G Grant and current leader of Glenfarclas, pioneered the sales of cask-strength whiskies, which are undiluted when bottled. Normally, single malts are bottled at 80 to 90 proof; this whisky, at 105 proof, is around 60 percent abv. The Glenfarclas 105 was an instant success. John got the idea from his father, George S., who gave bottles filled straight from the cask to family and friends as Christmas presents.

The 105 is a powerful dram and brings back sweet memories of a special tasting at the Speyside distillery after a tour of their whiskies. The pièce de résistance was on the closing day. Early in the morning, at the Craigellachie Hotel in the eponymous village for a special tasting at Glenfarclas distillery, a "breakfast whisky" was presented—105 poured over a bowl of porridge. The latter then served as a platform to support seven more whiskies.

The tasting took place in the distillery's beautiful Ship's Room, which is fitted with the entire interior, including oak paneling and furniture, of the first-class smoking room of the ocean liner *Empress of Australia*, which started touring the oceans in 1913. The vessel, converted into a troopship during World War II, never regained its position as cruise liner, and, after seventy transports, was demolished in 1952 at Inverkeithing. John heard of this and had the grand interior transported to the distillery, where it enjoyed a new lease on life. Apparently, it is not such a big step from the waters of the ocean to the water of life. The Grants love history and tradition, and the 105 fits in well. **HO**

Tasting notes

Honey, melon, tangerine, and crisp apple lead the way into butter toffee and salted nuts. There's also big sherry notes, with spice and raisins developing and an underlying nuttiness. The finish is long, warm, and spicy. All in all, a very addictive dram.

Glenfarclas 175th Anniversary

J & G Grant | www.glenfarclas.co.uk

Region and country of origin Speyside, Scotland
Distillery Glenfarclas, Ballindalloch, Banffshire
Alcohol content 43% abv
Style Single malt

Glenfarclas is one of the last of the independent distilleries in Scotland and has achieved iconic, even legendary status. The Grant family, which owns it, has maintained a an "eyes ahead" policy and has stuck rigidly to its winning formula—excellently made whisky matured in the best sherry casks they can afford. There have been periods in the company's history when money has been tight and the standards have dipped, but in recent years the distillery has been flying.

The Glenfarclas distillery lies in the heart of the Speyside region and now has a smart reception area and shop, thorough tours, and some of the best warehouses in the entire region. But the whisky has changed not one iota. What you get is Speyside whisky of the highest order, without gimmicks or tricks. There are no special finishes or weird cask types. Just honest-to-goodness malt whisky. The policy has been a huge success, and the brand still enjoys massive loyalty and has a proportion of drinkers who will drink nothing else at a time when "portfolio" drinking is the norm.

The family has been offered the Earth to sell, but they are not interested. And in 2011 it passed another milestone when Glenfarclas reached 175 years old. This limited edition—there are just 6,000 bottles of it—was released to mark that occasion. It combines whiskies from different decades, marrying the heavier sherried style of whisky from the 1950s and 1960s with the lighter, fruity whiskies of the 1970s and 1980s. It's a perfect collector's whisky—rare and great tasting. **DR**

Tasting notes

Full-bodied, berry fruit and smoke on the nose, with fruit-and-nut chocolate bar, oak, stewed berry fruits, and orange. Surprisingly fresh and zippy. There's a peppery spice to this, softened somewhat by the fruit notes. The finish is long and delightful.

Glenfarclas Family Casks 1994, Cask 3629

J & G Grant | www.glenfarclas.co.uk

Region and country of origin Speyside, Scotland
Distillery Glenfarclas, Ballindalloch, Banffshire
Alcohol content 59.3% abv.
Style Single malt

In 1994 Glenfarclas received an intriguing letter from Mr. William Shrive in Illinois. He appeared to possess a case of Glenfarclas whisky from 1936, purchased by his father. The distillery's sales director at the time was Malcolm Greenwood. Greenwood, a real character, and John Grant bought the case. Greenwood took a plane to Illinois and then flew home with the case next to him in a reserved seat.

Greenwood recalled Mr. Shrive showing them a wooden case with twelve bottles. "We instinctively knew this was genuine. It had all the import/export markings and each bottle was wrapped in wax paper." This whisky didn't end up in the Family Cask series, but instead was put on display in 2008, in the National Museum of Scotland, Edinburgh.

Sadly, Malcolm Greenwood is no longer with us. If he were, he probably would have continued to tell this remarkable story. Over and over. What does continue is the Family Casks series and Glenfarclas. The company is beyond its 175th birthday and heading for its bicentennial. In the meantime savor this nice 1994 while raising a toast to the unforgettable Mr. Malcolm Greenwood, who managed to fly back the oldest Glenfarclas known to this day. **HO**

Tasting notes

Chocolate-covered raisin flirts with fresh spiciness, polished oak, sugared orange, pecan, fruitcake, and toffee. Full, oily body and a tight, hot, peppery finish.

Glenfarclas Family Casks 1982, Cask 633

J & G Grant | www.glenfarclas.co.uk

Region and country of origin Speyside, Scotland
Distillery Glenfarclas, Ballindalloch, Banffshire
Alcohol content 54.2% abv.
Style Single malt

The 1980s didn't start too well for the Grants. Various disasters struck, including a collapsing wash still, a spirit safe fire, and an explosion in the malt mill, all within one year. The whisky industry as a whole also didn't perform as it should. Many distilleries closed, and a couple of bottling halls went out of business. The Grants again went against the grain and increased production, laying down stock for better times, which would duly arrive in the second half of the decade.

In 1986 Glenfarclas distillery celebrated its 150th anniversary. No mean feat for a small independent distilling dynasty. The year of 1988 also marked the end of farming at and around the distillery, due to the increasing intervention of the EEC. The industry started to rock and roll again, and by the end of the decade, Glenfarclas had to fend off a hostile takeover by one of the big players in the market. They would be rewarded for their courage with many prizes, and not only for their outstanding whiskies.

In 1989 Glenfarclas won one of the weirdest trophies in the industry—the "Loo of the Year Award." One wonders, where lies your pride? Glenfarclas's pride shows in every dram, good or bad times ahead. Enjoy a good one with this 1982 dram. **HO**

Tasting notes

Lemon-vanilla custard, caramel, and gumdrops turn to white chocolate, pecan, and Christmas spices. Oily mouthfeel, yet pleasantly drying finish.

The distinctive branding of Glenfarclas bottles. ➡

Glenfarclas Family Casks 1979, Cask 11015

J & G Grant | www.glenfarclas.co.uk

Region and country of origin Speyside, Scotland
Distillery Glenfarclas, Ballindalloch, Banffshire
Alcohol content 45.2% abv
Style Single malt

On one hand, the 1970s were a good decade for Glenfarclas, who secured an important deal with Chivas Brothers to supply them with some fine whiskies for their blends. In 1973, the beautiful visitors' center—decorated with wooden paneling from the ocean liner *Empress of Australia*—was opened, one of the first of its kind.

On the other hand, there was also a lot of unrest at during this time, as the industry was in turmoil. Coal miner strikes elsewhere led to a shortage of fuel, and in 1974 a haulage drivers' strike caused problems with logistics and the delivery of goods.

It was also in 1974 that John Grant, the current chairman, joined the firm. John recalled one time, "It wasn't entirely clear what I should do. Eventually, after some discussions with my father and a period of learning the ropes, it was agreed that I should concentrate on building sales of our own bottlings." At the time, it was not common practice for distillers to bottle whisky themselves. Instead, the majority of the stock was sold to brokers and blenders. John Grant pioneered in promoting official distillery bottlings. The proof of his success is in your glass. *Sláinte Mhath!* **HO**

Tasting notes

Elegant floral tones dart between lemon meringue pie, crème brûlée, ripe melon, and honeyed cashew nuts. Creamy on the palate and with a floral honey finish.

Glenfarclas Family Casks 1969, Cask 3187

J & G Grant | www.glenfarclas.co.uk

Region and country of origin Speyside, Scotland
Distillery Glenfarclas, Ballindalloch, Banffshire
Alcohol content 56.2% abv
Style Single malt

It must be wonderful to present whiskies made by your grandfather to the world at large—and that is exactly what the current George Grant does. While his father, John, manages the company, George travels around the globe as brand ambassador, a job that might evoke some envy in many a whisky lover.

In 1968, grandfather George S. made the decision that led to the Family Casks series when he laid down extra stock because the blenders could not fulfill their promises at the time. The range starts at 1952 and remains uninterrupted up to the present day. Each year, a new twelve-year-old is added, and young George has to write a new tasting note.

Family history is important to Glenfarclas, and they pride themselves on being one of only a few Scottish distilleries to remain family owned and managed. If there is still a trade that is "father-to-son," it might be this one. So, have a dram of Glenfarclas 1969 in honor of this respected family in the world of whisky. George Grant is a hero in the Netherlands. His Dutch importer manufactured a life-size cardboard figure of him, and George is on display in various liquor stores up and down the country. Fortunately, so are his whiskies. **HO**

Tasting notes

Cinnamon and cedar spiciness, raisin, cherry, and dark chocolate mellow into hazelnut and spent fireworks, ending in a long, chocolate-covered cherry finish.

Glenfarclas Family Casks 1961, Cask 4913

J & G Grant | www.glenfarclas.co.uk

Region and country of origin Speyside, Scotland
Distillery Glenfarclas, Ballindalloch, Banffshire
Alcohol content 54.4% abv
Style Single malt

There has been a huge debate in recent years as to whether whisky should be, and indeed can be, bought as a good investment. If you know what you're doing, it can. But those who take issue with the idea of investment should bear in mind that if it hadn't been for people saving whisky, we wouldn't get the chance to taste bottlings such as this one, no matter how much they cost.

In 2007, the family-owned distillery released a whole series of whiskies covering the last fifty years as part of its Family Casks series. It made for an amazing insight into the independent distillery's history. You could taste the years when money was tight and the malt hadn't been matured in the best wood, and other eras when, for year after year, the sherried whiskies were outstanding. Best of all were the malts, which were released in the early 1960s.

This, then, and a few from around that time, can make a claim to be among the finest whiskies you will ever taste. If you win a big lump of money or save up for a really special purchase, a Glenfarclas such as this one should be on your shortlist. Yes, it's really that good. This is everything a sherried Speysider should be—with bells on. **DR**

Tasting notes

A rich, oily, fruit bowl of flavors, surprisingly fresh given their age. Orange and soft melon, with some dusty pepper. Also some oak and some tannin astringency.

Glenfarclas Family Casks 1953, Cask 1678

J & G Grant | www.glenfarclas.co.uk

Region and country of origin Speyside, Scotland
Distillery Glenfarclas, Ballindalloch, Banffshire
Alcohol content 53.7% abv
Style Single malt

Glenfarclas has always paid attention to wood management, maturation, and vintage expressions. Therefore, it is the ultimate whisky to drink at a vertical tasting—where different years can be compared head-to-head. In 2007, this idea was taken to an entirely new level, when John's son George (representing the sixth generation!) introduced the Family Casks series, bottlings from forty-something consecutive years starting with the 1952 vintage. Glenfarclas can do this because it has maintained stocks themselves, and the single malt is rarely available from independent bottlers. Hence, the Grants have nearly full control over what they bottle as a single malt and when they bottle it.

People often like to buy one of the releases as a birthday present to surprise a dear one with a whisky from his or her birth year. It is the ultimate whisky gift to a loved one. A unique one, too, since the stocks of the old whiskies will run out over time. For the purpose of a review in this book, Glenfarclas very generously donated a 1953 vintage, and it's a delightful dram with beautiful flavors from a whisky of this age. It seems history is alive and well at Glenfarclas. Come travel back in time to 1953. **HO**

Tasting notes

Caramel, clove, lemon furniture polish, and vintage car leather upholstery finish with a faint hint of wood-cured ham and mandarin orange.

Glenfiddich 12-Year-Old

William Grant & Sons | www.williamgrant.com

Region and country of origin Speyside, Scotland
Distillery Glenfiddich, Dufftown, Banffshire
Alcohol content 40% abv
Style Single malt

This is effectively the one that started the whole single-malt craze, and it is still the biggest in the world. From Kathmandu and Calgary to Cardiff, this instantly recognizable green bottle turns up in myriad far-flung bars. When the world had its head and heart filled with blends during the 1960s, the entrepreneurial Grant family started to promote its whisky as a single malt. Many scoffed at the audacity, but the stage was set for something remarkable, a wave that we are still riding today.

If you visit the distillery, as many thousands of people do each year, you can't help but be impressed at how such a comparatively small set of stills can pump out enough liquid to supply the world. Look down your nose at this so-called entry-level malt at your peril: there is a reason it occupies a lofty place in the world's affections.

One of the main elements in its success is the wood management Grant has put in place. All the American and Spanish oak casks used at the distillery are passed through the hands of the on-site coopering team to ensure consistency and quality. Another reason has to be the independence of the Grant family, which has taken a long-term view of creating its whisky. The company holds some impressive stock lists, especially of its older whiskies.

For everyday drinking, and a relatively easy malt to get your head around, the 12-Year-Old is well worth a look or even revisiting if you are well into your malt journey. This is a classic from a distiller to which the single-malt world really owes a debt. **AA**

Tasting notes

The first thing to jump out of the glass is the freshness of this youthful 12-Year-Old. Fragrant fruit, poached pear, and roast apple abound here. These follow onto the palate, which is rich and has a hint of pine. The finish is long, and the fruity sweetness lingers for a while.

Glenfiddich 15-Year-Old

William Grant & Sons | www.williamgrant.com

Region and country of origin Speyside, Scotland
Distillery Glenfiddich, Dufftown, Banffshire
Alcohol content 40% abv
Style Single malt

Glenfiddich 15-Year-Old single malt is the secret gem of the range, the one to gravitate to. If you talk to the Grant team, you'll find it is a favorite with employees, too. While the world goes crazy for super-premium, über-aged whisky, this beautiful dram should be high on any whisky explorer's list. Not simply due to price point and the complexity it delivers, but also because in drinking it, you are helping to prolong a rather unusual production method for whisky.

At one time, the 15-Year-Old carried the moniker Solera, giving away the secret that sets it apart from most other whiskies. Its creation, using the Spanish *solera* vatting technique, was fairly pioneering in the whisky world of 1998 when it was introduced by the then malt master, David Stewart. The family-owned distillery has never been afraid to experiment a little. The system involves all aspects of whisky creation and brings in a little blending expertise as well, an artisanal approach that mimics its sister distillery of Balvenie.

The vat is filled with a mix of 70 percent refill bourbon casks, 20 percent European oak, and 10 percent virgin oak. The liquid is then left to marry in the huge 700 solera vat for three to six months, before half is emptied out and bottled. The vat is then refilled to start the marrying process once more. This effectively means that some whisky in the vat dates from 1998, and even older when we look at the 40-Year-Old, which is created by the same process. Glenfiddich's solera system brings an added depth to the whisky, as well as a richer and softer texture on the palate. **AA**

Tasting notes

The nose just draws you in, slowly revealing layers of fruit, from apple and pear to more tropical flavors, such as mango. There is a touch of pie crust, too. In the mouth, more depth is discovered with malt, fruit, and oak grip. The finish is woody and fruity.

Glenfiddich 18-Year-Old

William Grant & Sons | www.williamgrant.com

Region and country of origin Speyside, Scotland
Distillery Glenfiddich, Dufftown, Banffshire
Alcohol content 40% abv
Style Single malt

The eighteen-year-old in any distillery's range is that point where people are starting to spend a little more money and are expecting more back. The general consensus is that it has to take the nearest whisky and better it. In this case, the 15-Year-Old—which, as we have already seen, is one stunning whisky.

So, what have Glenfiddich's malt masters kept maturing behind closed doors for this important age bracket? The eighteen-year-old line is still very focused on the liquid. As we hit the midpoint of the core range, we reach the turning point between the freshness of youth and the veiled secrets of maturity. The zestiness of the 12-Year-Old has mellowed into the delights of sherry and Christmas cake.

Again, the production methods differ just slightly from the usual. This is something we are going to find with most of the Glenfiddich range: each of the expressions has a slight twist, not just matured for many years and then bottled. With the 18-Year-Old, the decision was taken to bottle in small, individually numbered batches. Each combines a touch of fruity sweetness from the Spanish oloroso wood and an oakiness from the traditional American casks. The resulting liquid is left to marry together in oak casks for at least three months, where it develops a rich, mellow flavor. **AA**

Tasting notes

The nose still shows the whisky's Speyside credentials: fruity, fragrant, and very clean. The finish is rich and mellow, ending with creamy oak with a little spice kick.

Glenfiddich 21-Year-Old

William Grant & Sons | www.williamgrant.com

Region and country of origin Speyside, Scotland
Distillery Glenfiddich, Dufftown, Banffshire
Alcohol content 40% abv
Style Single malt

What's in a name? Well, that's a good question, and clearly—given the fact this expression has changed names three times—the answer is "Not much, if you have excellent liquid." The 21-Year-Old started out originally as the Havana Reserve. The Grant family worked with rum distillers from Sancti Spiritus in the heart of Cuba. The company decanted casks of Cuban rum at the distillery and refilled them with Glenfiddich 21-Year-Old to absorb the lush character lingering in the wood. It was then left to the malt master to decide the perfect time for bottling.

The Havana Reserve name and the connections with Cuba seemed to have caused a little controversy among some American consumers, given the lasting trade embargo between the island and the United States. So: name-change time and a warm welcome to the Gran Reserva. However, this did not really last very long, and the company quietly changed the name to 21-Year-Old to fit in with the core range.

The whisky is still finished in rum casks, now hand-selected bourbon barrels, although the rum is simply referred to as "Caribbean." The rum character infuses the Glenfiddich DNA and gives it a vibrant overtone and a lush toffee sweetness. One of the best ways to enjoy this malt is with a cigar—a decent Dominican really takes the flavor to a another level. **AA**

Tasting notes

The nose gives fig and toffee, with hints of banana and burnt sugar. The toffee comes through on the palate with spice and oak. A slight hint of smoke at the finish.

William Grant and his seven sons built the Glenfiddich distillery in 1886. ➡

Glenfiddich 30-Year-Old

William Grant & Sons | www.glenfiddich.com

Region and country of origin Speyside, Scotland
Distillery Glenfiddich, Dufftown, Banffshire
Alcohol content 43% abv
Style Single malt

The Glenfiddich 30-Year-Old has been tweaked in recent years, giving it new packaging and a more generous alcoholic strength. The original limited edition had bags of oak and lush sherry notes, making it quite the evening dram. It won the silver medal at the 2005 International Wine & Spirit Competition. But that change in abv gives the liquid a gorgeous coating mouthfeel, and this tweaked whisky also picked up a silver medal, this time at the 2010 International Spirits Challenge.

The new clothing for the 2010 30-Year-Old makes an impression as well. We are not in your everyday drinking drams section here. The whisky comes in a handsome thick-based bottle, sealed with a wax security tag and embossed with a brass-colored badge. For the first time, the 30 will appear in yearly batches, bearing a bottle and batch number. The oak box is decorated with brass corners inspired by detailing found on the spirit safe at the distillery. You even get a little wooden plinth, should you want to show off the latest acquisition to your whisky friends.

Inside the new bottle, single malt fans will be very pleased by this marriage of oloroso sherry and bourbon casks. The whisky has almost been mollycoddled through its thirty years of maturation. It has been nosed and tasted at least five times during this period by David Stewart (the malt master when it was laid down) and then by Brian Kinsman, the Glenfiddich malt master appointed in November 2009. Only casks that survive this close and ongoing inspection process are selected. **AA**

Tasting notes

Like standing in front of an open humidor—vibrant fresh tobacco leaf and the sweetness of aged leaves, too. Hints of citrus and preserved lemon. The palate is smooth and creamy with dark chocolate and espresso. The finish fades to leave a chocolate sweetness.

Glenfiddich 40-Year-Old Second Batch

William Grant & Sons | www.glenfiddich.com

Region and country of origin Speyside, Scotland
Distillery Glenfiddich, Dufftown, Banffshire
Alcohol content 45.8% abv
Style Single malt

With this we are heading into rarefied territory—this is not your average whisky. In its current guise, just 600 bottles of this sought-after malt will be released each year, so you can imagine how quickly it vanishes. The 40-Year-Old even reduced one of the world's greatest whisky writers to an unusual fit of ownership: "This malt has matured with elegance," wrote Michael Jackson, author of *The Malt Whisky Companion*. "It is the most urbane Glenfiddich that I have tasted . . . it tells a story a little at a time, dryly, almost teasingly. It makes such good company that I am reluctant to share it."

Previous releases of this whisky have garnered extraordinary success at international competitions. A blind tasting by seventy-five international whisky experts gave it the gold medal after independent blind tastings in Edinburgh, Kentucky, and Tokyo in 2003. Like the 15-Year-Old, this is the product of a *solera*-style system, except that some of the whiskies in the vat date back to the 1940s, and possibly the 1920s. True depth of age is apparent in every sip.

As much as these older whiskies are made to be drunk, there is more of an element of collectorship here. Sumptuous packaging is very much to the fore. The bottles are individually numbered, hand-signed, and encased in a luxury hand-stitched calf-leather case. The package also has a correspondingly numbered certificate, hand-signed by chairman Peter Gordon and four of the distillery's long-serving craftsmen, David Stewart, Don Ramsay, Eric Stephen, and Dennis McBain. **AA**

Tasting notes

A deep malt with layers of dried fruit: apricot, apple, pear, and a little coconut. Hints of roasted coffee and black cherry, subtle wood smoke, and sherry. The dried fruits continue on the palate but melt into Christmas cake, raisin, stewed apple, and chocolate.

Glenfiddich 50-Year-Old

William Grant & Sons | www.glenfiddich.com

Region and country of origin Speyside, Scotland
Distillery Glenfiddich, Dufftown, Banffshire
Alcohol content 46.1% abv
Style Single malt

There are not many distilleries that can boast a fifty-year-old; it is a rare old age for a whisky. What sets Glenfiddich apart is that it has done it twice during its history, no mean feat, given the amount of liquid that must be used to keep the 12-Year-Old at the top of its game. The first edition came in July 2009. That vatting was created from just nine casks, laid down between 1957 and 1959. Each cask represented one of founder William Grant's children, who helped their father build the Glenfiddich distillery by hand in 1886.

The second vatting, created from two casks (a 1955 and a 1957) and married for six months before bottling, was first released at a sumptuous dinner at the distillery attended by the world's whisky media in 2009. Just fifty bottles will be put on the market each year for the next ten years, from a stock of 500.

You might expect such a dinner to be packed with pomp and ceremony, and it is true there was a little, with pipers accompanying the 50-Year-Old into the dining room. But there were also moments of humility as the room listened to malt master David Stewart talk about being the custodian of such a piece of history. Then the guests were served by chairman Peter Gordon himself. It was a historic moment that will not be forgotten by those who were there.

The main market for this whisky is set to be global travel retail, with a fifth of the stock allocation headed there each year. The first bottle went on sale at Paris Charles de Gaulle Airport (T2E), with the rest following at major hubs such as London Heathrow, Dubai, Shanghai, Beijing, and Singapore Changi airports. **AA**

Tasting notes

The nose is complex, with rose and violet notes and a delicate note of drying tobacco leaf. There is a little oak and a whiff of smoke. The palate turns from sweet marmalade to layers of soft fruit and oak tannins. A gentle oak grip and a little smoke on the finish.

Glenfiddich Age of Discovery 19-Year-Old

William Grant & Sons | www.glenfiddich.com

Region and country of origin Speyside, Scotland
Distillery Glenfiddich, Dufftown, Banffshire
Alcohol content 40% abv
Style Single malt

This little beauty was released soon after Glenfiddich Snow Phoenix, and again showed off the distillery's clever and careful use of wood finishing. Madeira, like some other wine finishes, such as sassacia and Sauternes, can be difficult to work with and can result in a whisky that is either dominated by the wood or gains nothing better than a grubby vine-stalk aroma. Thankfully for Glenfiddich's first foray into Madeira, the result is pretty fantastic.

Most of Glenfiddich's Madeira casks came from the Canterio warehouse of Henrique & Henrique, a famous, family-owned Madeira company established in 1850. Here, the casks were first used to mature wine made from luscious tinta negra mole grapes. The 19-Year-Old has been dubbed the "Age of Discovery" to celebrate the whisky's link with Portugal and its fifteenth-century explorers. The theme is borne out by the packaging; the black glass bottle features a red cartouche compass, while the box is illustrated with maps tracing the travels of Portuguese explorers. Intrepid sailors in search of the sea passage to India opened sea routes from Europe to Thailand and Malaysia, discovered the islands of Porto Santo and Madeira, established the city of Macao, and gave Taiwan the name Ilha Formosa ("Beautiful Island").

The theme fits with the recent marketing campaign for Glenfiddich, which intones, "One day you will," promising that we will all experience such exciting adventures at some point in our lives. Of course, trying Glenfiddich whiskies comes under that heading, so why not begin with Age of Discovery? **AA**

Tasting notes

The Madeira finish is well integrated, the nose giving poached pear, roast apple, and bags of cinnamon and peppery spice. The palate is rich and spicy, with plenty of earthy tones, raisin, prune, and drying oak. To finish, the whisky is smooth, warming, and a little oily.

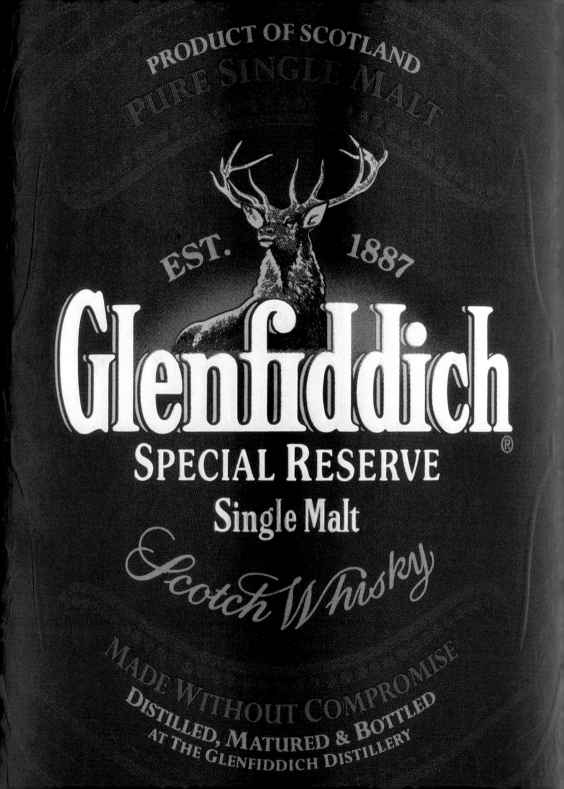

Glenfiddich Rich Oak 14-Year-Old

William Grant & Sons | www.glenfiddich.com

Region and country of origin Speyside, Scotland
Distillery Glenfiddich, Dufftown, Banffshire
Alcohol content 40% abv
Style Single malt

This expression gave the coopers and malt master at Glenfiddich the chance to show off their skills. William Grant had invested in a cooperage in Jerez, and big things were expected. Thankfully, the Glenfiddich Rich Oak 14-Year-Old delivers. The decision was taken to push the boat out and use the resources the company had been investing in, so the whisky is finished in virgin American and European oak casks.

Glenfiddich Rich Oak stands as a tribute to the skill of malt master Brian Kinsman, who had to keep an eye on the finishing whisky. As virgin wood reacts quickly with the spirit, it was important to sample the casks every couple of weeks to ensure the oak was not overpowering the final flavor balance. In the end, after its fourteen years, the whisky spent two separate twelve-week periods in new European oak and six weeks in new American oak before bottling.

The key to the flavor of this particular whisky is that the casks have held nothing before and have not been seasoned with any other spirit or wine. The American oak casks are toasted and charred in the same way as they would be for maturing bourbon. The Spanish oak casks are gently toasted rather than charred; this maximizes the rich, oaky flavor. **AA**

Tasting notes

A complex nose: a mix of fresh fruit, spice, and candy. The oak grips the palate first, then relaxes into vanillins, dried fruit, and clotted cream. Oak returns on the finish.

Glenfiddich Snow Phoenix

William Grant & Sons | www.glenfiddich.com

Region and country of origin Speyside, Scotland
Distillery Glenfiddich, Dufftown, Banffshire
Alcohol content 47.6% abv
Style Single malt

In January 2010, after weeks of heavy snow and record low temperatures, densely compacted snow covered the Glenfiddich distillery roofs and warehouses. One evening, a number of warehouse roofs collapsed under the weight of it all. In wintery conditions and temperatures of -2°F (-19°C), distillery staff worked around the clock to clear the snowfall.

Snow Phoenix was created by marrying together natural strength and non-chill-filtered casks of different ages and finishes, including American oak and oloroso sherry, aged between thirteen and thirty years. Shifting snow around the clock gave the Glenfiddich distillery team a deep admiration for those who work in extreme conditions. The distillery therefore dedicated Snow Phoenix to the Cairngorm Mountain Rescue Team (CMRT), who battle harsh conditions to save lives in the heart of Speyside, and made a special contribution to their funds.

Cynical marketing ploy? An opportunity to do something for charity? Whatever your opinion, the proof is in the tasting and the fact that it was not at all overpriced. In fact, it went so quickly, priced at less than $100 (£50) a bottle, that it may yet prove to be the bargain of the decade. **AA**

Tasting notes

A wonderfully pungent nose—sweet and fruity. There is a lovely waxiness on the palate, reminiscent of buttercream, and just a touch of oak, too.

The Glenfiddich stag speaks of both the whisky and its Scottish homeland.

Glenglassaugh 21-Year-Old

Glenglassaugh
www.glenglassaugh.com

Region and country of origin Highlands, Scotland
Distillery Glenglassaugh, Portsoy, Aberdeenshire
Alcohol content 46% abv
Style Single malt

Highlands or Speyside? We will go for the former, even though this whisky features regularly in the Spirit of Speyside festival. Also, the reopened Glenglassaugh distillery has chosen to position itself as a Highlands brand—and the way in which the term "Speyside" is applied to whiskies is fairly arbitrary anyway. Just look at the course the River Spey takes as it meanders through the countryside, collecting its tributaries from hither and thither, far and wide.

Glenglassaugh stands staunchly overlooking the unspoiled beaches that border the northeast coast of Scotland, an area rich in wildlife of all kinds, and which naturally lends itself to the production of high-quality produce and artisan foodstuffs. If you're lucky enough to stand atop the roof at Glenglassaugh in the springtime, you might easily spy a pod of dolphins off the shore of the picturesque village of Sandend. Swing around 180 degrees, squint your eyes a little, and you might just be able to pick out the lone white door that fronts the site of the Glassaugh spring, packed away among the blazing yellow gorse bushes. The distillery is gravity-fed with this hard water, which no doubt plays its part in the light character of Glenglassaugh's new-make spirit. **D&C**

Tasting notes

The nose is firstly sherry, then all sliced fruit: melon, apple, and pear. On the palate, fudge and candies appear. Peppermint on the intermediate finish.

Glenglassaugh 25-Year-Old Malt Sherry Cask

Douglas Laing & Co. | www.douglaslaing.com / www.glenglassaugh.com

Region and country of origin Highlands, Scotland
Distillery Glenglassaugh, Portsoy, Aberdeenshire
Alcohol content 50% abv
Style Single malt

In the past thirty years, many distilleries in Scotland have closed for economic reasons. A few new ones have opened to take their place, and some lucky ones, such as Glenglassaugh, have closed and reopened, with new owners, new investment, and new ideas.

The stills of Glenglassaugh have been silent for more than half of the years since its foundation in 1875. Glenglassaugh's current owners only arrived in 2008, so we will have to wait a few years yet to see what they produce. Meanwhile, there have been independent releases of stocks from before the closure in 1986, including this lovely sherry-cask 1984 example, bottled at twenty-five years.

This whisky is sure to provide much inspiration to the new team, capturing as it does a classic sherried finish on top of a feisty coastal malt base, with the saltiness of the sea air never far away but always expertly integrated. Much of the distillery's output ended up in the Famous Grouse and Cutty Sark blends at one time, but it is in the limited official bottlings and independents that the whisky really shines. No one knows whether the spirit coming off the stills today will end up as good as this in twenty years' time. Until then, this is as good as it gets. **AN**

Tasting notes

Dundee marmalade on the nose at first, with milk chocolate following. Fruitcake but with a peppery spice and some spiky tannins. Long finish, oaky and sweet.

Glenglassaugh 26-Year-Old

Glenglassaugh
www.glenglassaugh.com

Region and country of origin Highlands, Scotland
Distillery Glenglassaugh, Portsoy, Aberdeenshire
Alcohol content 46% abv
Style Single malt

Glenglassaugh distillery has stood on the outskirts of Sandend since its construction was completed in 1875. A confident building, sawtooth in profile, lights occasionally winking out into the North Sea, it has the air of knowing something we don't.

The Glenglassaugh dram itself used to be an altogether peatier prospect than the majority of expressions available for purchase today would have us believe. Whether the reason for that lies in past use of peat or sherry, coal or steam, the DNA of the distillery somehow remains intact. This is due in part to the design and construction of the building, but also to the very nature of the people who have worked there throughout the history of the distillery.

There is an intrinsic relationship between place, character, and workmanship that is borne out in the qualities of the end result, and in this era of franchises and homogenization, it would most certainly be a foolhardy person who transported the chattels of Glenglassaugh elsewhere in the vain hope of replicating what flows into barrels there now. This is a whisky that is as rich, beautiful, and welcoming as its locale. It could come from nowhere else, and has a distinguished character all its own. **D&C**

Tasting notes

Nose is huge sherry, with menthol, glacé cherry, and a touch of hard toffee. Palate is heavy fruit—currants and citrus peel soaked in brandy, with oak and pepper.

Glenglassaugh 30-plus Years Rare Cask Series

Glenglassaugh
www.glenglassaugh.com

Region and country of origin Highlands, Scotland
Distillery Glenglassaugh, Portsoy, Aberdeenshire
Alcohol content 52.3% abv
Style Single malt

This dram is beautiful to look at, a liquid gold. The label states, somewhat vaguely, that it is "aged over thirty years." In actual fact, the whisky exceeds thirty-four years old. It spent the majority of its existence taking on the character of, and being refined by, a refill hogshead. Following that, it was briefly relocated to a first-fill ex-Sauternes cask for fifteen months. This is single-cask, non-chill-filtered, cask-strength whisky that is bottled on site—about as unadulterated as a whisky of this age is ever likely to be.

Given the age of this bottle, it could be estimated that the spirit, at the time of its distillation, may well have been destined for any one of a number of blends that held Glenglassaugh in high regard. Instead, it was diverted into this particular refill hogshead. The style of spirit changed over the years, but the quality remained, and Glenglassaugh was perennially sought after. It seems sinful that a dram as fine as this would have been sent to fulfill a quota, or to balance out other dominant flavors. However, Glenglassaugh is as supportive within other whiskies as it is subtle and unique as a single malt. We should just be glad that this has made the journey of over three decades intact, and that we have a chance to savor it. **D&C**

Tasting notes

A bucket of fruit in an arboretum and a briny breeze. Palate is all cake mix and prune, before opening out into a light fruit salad of pineapple and mango.

Glenglassaugh 40-plus Years Rare Cask Series

Glenglassaugh
www.glenglassaugh.com

Region and country of origin Highlands, Scotland
Distillery Glenglassaugh, Portsoy, Aberdeenshire
Alcohol content 49.2% abv
Style Single malt

Alongside Glenglassaugh distillery is one of the most recognizable and idiosyncratic sights of the northeast coast of Scotland. "The Cup and Saucer," as it is locally known, is a stone-built windmill built by James Abercromby (1706–1781), a British Army general who returned to his Glenglassaugh estate after receiving severe criticism for his infamous and unsuccessful command at the Battle of Ticonderoga in North America in 1758.

The distillery has seen its fair share of career changes, too. Throughout each of the forty-five years (try counting them out) that this particular whisky has spent in the distillery's coastal warehouses, the one true constant in its environs was the shadow cast by the remains of Abercromby's windmill. To some, it is sad that this particular mill was not more involved in the fortunes of the distillery. Having only occasionally served as a simple storage place, it was not afforded the chance to grind barley for its neighbor.

The mill is imposing, and it is iconic—a description that could equally apply to a dram such as this. The whisky comes in its own presentation case, with certificate of ownership, and the decanter and glasses may be engraved upon request. **D&C**

Tasting notes

The nose has molasses, dried fruit, pot ale syrup, and a nutty, savory note—satay sauce. Also light mint. On the palate, it is spicy, with citrus fruit, melon, and apple.

Glenglassaugh 1978 31-Year-Old

The Whisky Exchange
www.thewhiskyexchange.com

Region and country of origin Highlands, Scotland
Distillery Glenglassaugh, Portsoy, Aberdeenshire
Alcohol content 44.6% abv
Style Single malt

Over the years distilleries have come and gone. Some will never return because they are now shopping malls, parking lots, or in the case of the last English distillery before St. George's was opened, buried under the Olympic Stadium. Others are closed down, locked up, and mothballed. You know there's a whisky boom on when distilleries start reopening or changing hands, and in recent years, whisky has been basking in one of its healthiest periods.

Some silent distilleries are easier to reopen than others. Glenglassaugh—pronounced "Glen–glassy"—was one of the more difficult ones. The distillery was effectively a shell, a work site of electricians and builders. Thieves had pretty much stripped out anything of value. And tougher still for the new owners, the buildings came without stock.

The new owners have been buying old stock from other sources, but the folk at the Whisky Exchange wisely chose this to mark the business's tenth anniversary. It's a classic example of this special East Highland distillery. Of the three expressions officially released, the 30-Year-Old was the best. So, like Brora, maybe thirty to thirty-two years is ideal for producing super-premium whisky here. **DR**

Tasting notes

The sherry influence is immediate. The palate is growly, with sharp orange savory notes and dry sherry. Camp coffee, resiny wood, and menthol. Very elegant.

Glenglassaugh distillery overlooks the rocky outcrops of Sandend Beach.

Glenglassaugh Walter Grant 1967

Glenglassaugh
www.glenglassaugh.com

Region and country of origin Highlands, Scotland
Distillery Glenglassaugh, Portsoy, Aberdeenshire
Alcohol content 40.4% abv
Style Single malt

This beautiful whisky—Glenglassaugh The Manager's Legacy Walter Grant 1967, to give it its full title—is from a refill sherry hogshead that was filled in May 1967. It has been bottled as the final installment in a series of releases that pay tribute to distillery managers who worked at Glenglassaugh between 1964 and 1986. Only 200 bottles of this particularly limited dram will ever be produced, all individually numbered and each dedicated to the work, service, and memory of Walter Grant.

The Glenglassaugh Manager's Legacy series includes vintages from the years 1986, 1974, and 1968, sourced in recognition of managers Dod Cameron, Jim Cryle, and Bert Forsyth, respectively. Walter Grant's is the oldest and final dram of the quartet. In common with the other three bottlings in this collection, it has no additional coloring and was bottled on-site at Glenglassaugh without the use of chill-filtration.

When a distillery chooses to commemorate an employee, it usually attests to their character and spirit. On these rare occasions, we may choose to raise a glass and savor the moment or, indeed, fill a couple of hundred bottles and reminisce fondly. No doubt, Mr. Grant would have been proud of this honor. **D&C**

Tasting notes

Crisp fruit and sherry, melon and apple, burnt sugar and vanilla pod. Palate is velvet soft and honeyed, with hazelnut, walnut, and more vanilla coming through.

Glengoyne 10-Year-Old

Ian Macleod Distillers
www.glengoyne.com

Region and country of origin Lowlands, Scotland
Distillery Glengoyne, Dumgoyne, Glasgow
Alcohol content 43% abv
Style Single malt

Glengoyne 10-Year-Old is the youngest member of the distillery's core range, the others being the 17-Year-Old and the 21-Year-Old. It contains at least 20 percent first-fill ex-sherry cask whisky, which helps to explain its rich, golden, natural amber color. Today, whiskies such as Glengoyne are stating "natural color" prominently on their labels to highlight the absence of the caramel coloring E150, used by some distilleries to obtain uniformity of color between batches and occasionally to suggest increased wood influence.

Glengoyne's barley is slowly air-dried and completely unpeated, like Lowland malts. As it happens, the Glengoyne warehouses, opposite the distillery, are technically in the Lowland region of Scotland—thus the whisky is uniquely Highland-distilled and Lowland-matured. It is also one of the few distilleries remaining in this part of Scotland.

The distillery claims that the "milder climate of the southern Highlands affects the maturing whisky over time and results in the fresher, lighter taste associated with this special malt." Certainly, Glengoyne 10-Year-Old's big notes of apple and accent notes of vanilla and oak give an accurate representation of what this uniquely located distillery has to offer. **WM**

Tasting notes

A very approachable whisky, bright with fruity notes of green apple and pear, which are complemented by notes of vanilla, hints of spice, and a touch of oak.

Glengoyne 12-Year-Old

Ian Macleod Distillers | www.glengoyne.com

Region and country of origin Lowlands, Scotland
Distillery Glengoyne, Dumgoyne, Glasgow
Alcohol content 43% abv
Style Single malt

Glengoyne 12-Year-Old single malt, not to be confused with Glengoyne 12-Year-Old Cask Strength, joined Glengoyne's core range in October 2009. According to marketing director Iain Weir, "The 12-Year-Old is a very welcome addition to the Glengoyne core range. The decision to introduce the 12-Year-Old is . . . in response to international demand, particularly from Western Europe, where our customers are looking for a high-quality, intermediate step between the Glengoyne 10- and 17-Year-Olds."

According to assistant blender John Glass, Glengoyne 12-Year-Old is the only expression made using some whisky aged in first-fill ex-bourbon casks. The majority of the barrels used for the 12-Year-Old are American and European refill barrels, but at least 20 percent are first-fill ex-European sherry casks, with a balance of at least 20 percent first-fill bourbon casks. This is the first time that Glengoyne has used first-fill bourbon barrels in one of its core-range expressions. The first-fill ex-bourbon barrels impart notes of vanilla and oak, and the tightly pored American oak adds a robust, tannic mouthfeel.

Glengoyne 12-Year-Old is more than simply the 10-Year-Old with an additional two years of aging. The different casks selected for the 12-Year-Old, coupled with those extra two years of maturing in oak, make it a unique expression.

Glengoyne 12-Year-Old has not been made available in the Unites States, but Ian Macleod Distillers, which owns the Glengoyne brand, plans to export it to more than sixty markets worldwide. **WM**

Tasting notes

The nose is bright, with lemon zest and a hint of coconut. On the palate these are joined by apple, toffee, honey, and a touch of cinnamon. Noticeably different from Glengoyne 12-Year-Old Cask Strength, Glengoyne 12-Year-Old single malt is softer and less spicy.

Glengoyne 12-Year-Old Cask Strength

Ian Macleod Distillers | www.glengoyne.com

Region and country of origin Lowlands, Scotland
Distillery Glengoyne, Dumgoyne, Glasgow
Alcohol content 57.2% abv
Style Single malt

Originally released in September 2004, Glengoyne 12-Year-Old Cask Strength was the distillery's first addition to its core range of whiskies since it was acquired by Ian Macleod Distillers in April 2003. The whisky was designed by distillery manager Robbie Hughes and his staff in response to increasing demand for a cask-strength product.

More than a higher-proof version of the Glengoyne 12-Year-Old single malt, Glengoyne 12-Year-Old Cask Strength contains at least 30 percent first-fill European ex-sherry casks, which is 10 percent more than the regular 12-Year-Old's quota. The Cask Strength also contains no whisky from first-fill ex-bourbon barrels; instead, the balance is provided by whisky from refill casks.

Glengoyne 12-Year-Old Cask Strength proudly asserts on the label that it is non-chill-filtered and of a natural color. As in most cask-strength expressions, the additional alcohol contributes additional flavors and a rich mouthfeel. An extra benefit is that water may be added to personal preference. It is generally recommended to add a drop of water to cask-strength whiskies, then additional water to taste.

With Glengoyne 12-Year-Old Cask Strength, water softens the nose, coaxing out notes of red fruit, red apple, grape, and plum; these flavors also become more pronounced on the palate. This whisky is no longer imported into the United States, but can still be found on retailers' shelves. Ian Macleod Distillers plans to export the expression to more than fifty other markets worldwide. **WM**

Tasting notes

Glengoyne 12-Year-Old Cask Strength is rich and spicy. Its notes of cinnamon, clove, maple syrup, and vanilla are evidence of its time in sherry butts. Black pepper, plum, and toffee emerge on the palate, with pepper lingering on the finish.

Glengoyne 14-Year-Old

Ian Macleod Distillers
www.glengoyne.com

Region and country of origin Lowlands, Scotland
Distillery Glengoyne, Dumgoyne, Glasgow
Alcohol content 43% abv
Style Single malt

Glengoyne is the only distillery in Scotland that has valid claims to making both Highland and Lowland whiskies—its stills lie just to the north of the dividing line, while its warehouses are a few feet to the south. In fact, Glengoyne is more than interregional; it is truly cosmopolitan: while the water it uses is Scottish, drawn from the adjacent Blairgar Burn, the maltings are imported from Simpson's of Berwick-upon-Tweed, which lies just over the border in England.

This 14-Year-Old cask-strength expression—a limited edition of 296 bottles—was matured in an American oak sherry hogshead (cask no. 832). The drink is made from barley that has been air-dried rather than exposed to peat smoke, which tends to produce a harsher flavor. Some claim the cask makes the finished whisky smack excessively of Spanish wine, but the overwhelming majority welcome the consequent absence of sulfur and the opportunity thus afforded for the whisky to express its essential light fruitiness without interference or interruption.

Another cask (no. 876), produced in the same year, 1993, was aged in a Pedro Ximénez hogshead: the contents have the same virtues (and, to less generous souls, the same limitations) as no. 832. These whiskies are among the distillery's most renowned creations, the equivalent of a chef's signature dishes. **GL**

Tasting notes

The nose is sherry (of course) with treacle, cedar, and a suggestion of cigar boxes. The palate is warm and mainly cherry, with overtones of spices and toffee.

Glengoyne 16-Year-Old

Ian Macleod Distillers
www.glengoyne.com

Region and country of origin Lowlands, Scotland
Distillery Glengoyne, Dumgoyne, Glasgow
Alcohol content 43% abv
Style Single malt

Glengoyne distillery lies in a part of Stirlingshire whose whisky products were classified as Lowland until the 1970s, but which have since been recategorized as Highland (South). The distillery was originally named Glen Guin (Gaelic for "glen of wild geese"), but the spelling was altered at the start of the twentieth century to make it easier for non-Scots to pronounce.

To celebrate the passing of a hundred years since that change—as well as to commemorate the fiftieth anniversary of the death of Arthur Tedder, who was born in 1890 on the distillery where his father was the excise officer and grew up to become marshal of the Royal Air Force—the current owners decided in the Fall of 2007 to create this commemorative expression. The Glengoyne 16-Year-Old was matured in twenty casks that were formerly used for shiraz wine in the Hunter Valley, New South Wales, Australia.

The casks were carefully monitored by a range of experts, including Arthur's son Robin, an Australian master of wine. Eventually only ten of them were adjudged up to the standard required for what became known as the Glengoyne Glenguin Shiraz Cask Finish 16-Year-Old, which went on sale in 2008 in a limited edition of 3,800 bottles. This product is characterized as light and fruity when young but, like all Glengoyne whiskies, gains weight with age. **GL**

Tasting notes

Toffee and popcorn, with nuts and apple. On the palate, tones of apple, grass, and licorice. The finish is sweet and malty. Water brings out linseed oil and almond.

Production—and whisky—in full flow at the Glengoyne distillery. ➡

Glengoyne 17-Year-Old

Ian Macleod Distillers | www.glengoyne.com

Region and country of origin Lowlands, Scotland
Distillery Glengoyne, Dumgoyne, Glasgow
Alcohol content 43% abv
Style Single malt

The Glengoyne 17-Year-Old is the middle child of the Glengoyne core range, with more sherry influence than the 10 but much less than the 21. At least 35 percent of the casks used are first-fill and refill sherry casks, composed of European and American oak. These Spanish sherry casks air-dry for two years, then hold maturing sherry for at least two years before being emptied and filled with Glengoyne.

According to master blender John Glass, Glengoyne 17 is the favorite of most distillery visitors, and distillery manager Robbie Hughes's favorite expression. After seventeen years, he says, "it has lost it rough edges, and the sherry has come of age."

The Glengoyne 17 is similar to the Glengoyne 10, with many of the same taste elements, but with more spice and less fruit. Hints of sulfur and clove on the nose lead one to believe there is more sherry than actually present on the palate. Although the current edition of the Glengoyne 21 is perfectly crafted for the sherry cask lover, the Glengoyne 17 carefully balances sufficient sherry cask influence to derive the desired spice notes, without sacrificing its vibrancy.

Glengoyne has dubbed itself "Scotland's unpeated malt," and the distillery emphasizes the technique of drying its barley using warm air, as opposed to the more common practice of using peat smoke to dry and flavor the barley, which imparts a smoky character to the resultant malt. The distillery believes that during the warm-air drying process "the natural flavors are allowed to freely express themselves and do not get overwhelmed." **WM**

Tasting notes

The Glengoyne 17 is rich, supple, and well integrated, with cinnamon, nutmeg, candied orange peel, raisin, and red apple. Notes of vanilla and spice are dominant, with honey and toffee intermingled and drifting off slowly, with traces of oak on the finish.

Glengoyne 21-Year-Old

Ian Macleod Distillers | www.glengoyne.com

Region and country of origin Lowlands, Scotland
Distillery Glengoyne, Dumgoyne, Glasgow
Alcohol content 43% abv
Style Single malt

Glengoyne 21-Year-Old was rereleased in February 2007 to emphasize its role as the premier expression of Glengoyne's core line. This version is matured exclusively in European oak sherry butts, evidenced by its natural rich mahogany brown color. The earlier 21-Year-Old had less sherry influence, with only around 50 percent of its casks being European oak; it was therefore of a lighter color.

According to Iain Weir, marketing director for Ian Macleod Distillers, "The 21-Year-Old is the premier product in the Glengoyne core range, and the high quality of the packaging clearly reflects this. [The whisky] is rich and elegant, with noticeably more sherry influence. By making the core range progressively more premium with age, we help customers to understand exactly what the Glengoyne single-malt whisky range has to offer."

When Glengoyne relaunched Glengoyne 21-Year-Old, the distillery's prime objective was to distinguish it as a luxury expression. Although the appearance of the bottle has remained consistent, its traditional cardboard tube has been replaced by an embossed box with a gold lining. The 100 percent sherry-matured nature of the 21-Year-Old amounts to an opulent luxury in itself, because sherry butts are considerably more expensive for distillers to buy, and typically are therefore used very sparingly.

Although the sherry influence is intense, the distillery characteristics still show through. Sweet and rich, Glengoyne 21-Year-Old is an elegant dram to share with friends, perhaps in lieu of dessert. **WM**

Tasting notes

The nose and natural brownish color betray the sherry influence. Rich cocoa, clove, cinnamon, and dark vanilla—a veritable Christmas cake, with notes of raisin, candied orange peel, and dark rum. The wonderful, oily coating mouthfeel continues on the long finish. .

Glengoyne Burnfoot

Ian Macleod Distillers
www.glengoyne.com

Region and country of origin Lowlands, Scotland
Distillery Glengoyne, Dumgoyne, Glasgow
Alcohol content 40% abv
Style Single malt

Glengoyne Burnfoot was launched in September 2007; it was made available to the duty-free and travel retail markets exclusively. The Glengoyne distillery, established by George Connell in 1833, was once called Burnfoot of Dumgoyne, a name that referred to the distillery's location at the foot of a small river (or burn). Legend suggests that the distillery is located at the very spot where outlaws once hid their illicit whisky stills. The distillery name was changed to Glengoyne in 1908.

Glengoyne Burnfoot is composed of whiskies ranging from seven to thirty-four years of age, and, while most Glengoynes are fruity in nature, the Burnfoot is rather floral. Notes of fruit are still present, including apple, banana, and citrus, among others, but Burnfoot exudes a certain dryness with notes of oak and straw, making it a unique expression. This is most likely due to the older whiskies in the vatting.

The distillery emphasizes its technique of drying the barley using warm air, as opposed to the more common practice of using peat smoke to dry and flavor it. Burnfoot is available in 0.26-gallon (1-liter) bottles depicting the local landscape and nearby Dumgoyne, a famous hill near the distillery. **WM**

Tasting notes

Burnfoot is a more reserved Glengoyne, a shy whisky with oak and spice that linger into a long finish. Granny Smith apple, banana, and a note of citrus, perhaps lime.

Glengoyne Distilled 1996

Ian Macleod Distillers
www.glengoyne.com

Region and country of origin Lowlands, Scotland
Distillery Glengoyne, Dumgoyne, Glasgow
Alcohol content 43% abv
Style Single malt

The Glengoyne 1996 is a fourteen-year-old expression bottled in 2010 from select refill American oak sherry hogsheads and butts. Only 3,000 bottles were produced, which are available for sale in the United States. Its rich, creamy palate and buttery mouthfeel is typical for Glengoyne. Many distilleries add peat bricks in lesser or greater amounts to their fires to stop the barley's germination and impart a smoky character to the malted barley, which in turn will add this flavor to the resultant whisky. Glengoyne uses warm air to dry their barley.

Glengoyne has bottled several single-cask or small-production expressions when they have an exceptional cask or group of casks. These include casks selected by various distillery personnel, and bear their name, such as Deek's Choice, and also limited-edition expressions named for the seasons, such as Summer Limited Release 19-Year-Old. Many of the limited editions are heavily sherried, likely from first-fill sherry casks, which Glengoyne takes very well. However, this Distilled 1996 expression is a great example of Glengoyne without being overpowered by the sherry. It is an interesting comparison to the Glengoyne 10- and 17-Year-Olds. **WM**

Tasting notes

Rich and buttery, with big notes of vanilla and caramel. A creamy palate with notes of toffee, star fruit, peach, and apricot. Traces of oak and a sweet nutty finish.

Glenkinchie
12-Year-Old

Diageo
www.glenkinchie.com

Region and country of origin Lowlands, Scotland
Distillery Glenkinchie, Pentcaitland, East Lothian
Alcohol content 43% abv
Style Single malt

Glenkinchie is the "Edinburgh Malt," hailing as it does from the village of Pencaitland, not far from the Scottish capital. The distillery was founded in 1825 in rolling barley country and, after an uncertain start, it found its stride producing malt that went into the Haig blends. (Most Scottish distilleries spend most of their time making components for blended Scotch.)

Today, the divide between Highland and Lowland malts is primarily viewed in terms of taste, but it was initially motivated by excise; the Wash Act of 1784 decreed that different duties should be charged on either side of the "Highland Line."

Glenkinchie 12-Year-Old is the new entry-level Glenkinchie. The distillery produces a light and very fresh malt, partly due to the size of its stills, which are among the largest in Scotland. Drinkers used to whiskies from the other side of the Highland Line will note the absence of peat. This whisky is like the landscape, soft and gentle. Part maturation in sherry brings sherry notes, but lets the floral notes sing.

Glenkinchie represents the Lowlands in bars across the world as part of Diageo's hugely successful Classic Malts range. So, wherever you are, this is probably the most easily found Lowland malt. **PM**

Tasting notes

Sweet, lightly scented with gentle licorice. There are flowers, freshly cut grass, and hay here. Try this malt straight from the freezer; it's very refreshing.

Glenkinchie
20-Year-Old 1990

Diageo
www.glenkinchie.com

Region and country of origin Lowlands, Scotland
Distillery Glenkinchie, Pentcaitland, East Lothian
Alcohol content 55.1% abv
Style Single malt

Diageo focuses on the Lowlands with this latest special release, the rare Glenkinchie 20-Year-Old, which has been matured in ex-bourbon refill casks. When maturing a whisky, there is always a balance to be maintained between the distillate and the wood. Too little maturation and the whisky will be uninteresting; too much and you might as well suck on a lollipop stick.

Twenty years is quite an age, especially for a Lowland whisky. One of the charms of Glenkinchie is its fresh and open nose, but with this whisky you have to relax and let the complex floral and cereal notes play softly on your palate. Oak can easily swamp and in the end overwhelm such a whisky, so here refill casks are used. After refills, the impact a cask has on whisky lessens, until on its third or fourth fill, it is minimal. At this point, a whisky can sit in wood for quite a while without being overwhelmed. But it is a delicate procedure, with the whisky growing more fragile as its alcohol evaporates through the wood. At 55.1 percent abv, there is still quite a wallop left in the 20-Year-Old, and Diageo has filled its 6,000 bottles in time—the nose is just on the right side of the divide between "floral" and "plank of wood." **PM**

Tasting notes

Leather and wax polish. The vanilla is slightly chewy and some of the darker fruit is turning into licorice. The rather excellent finish ends with a fennel dryness.

Glenkinchie Distillers Edition 1996

Diageo | www.glenkinchie.com

Region and country of origin Lowlands, Scotland
Distillery Glenkinchie, Pentcaitland, East Lothian
Alcohol content 43% abv
Style Single malt

For years the Glenkinchie distillery manager bred prizewinning cattle and put his success down to their diet: spent grain from the distillery. In more recent years, the cattle have gone, and instead we are getting some very interesting bespoke bottlings from the eastern Lowlands of Scotland.

Glenkinchie releases its Distillers Editions on a periodic basis, and this particular version was distilled in 1996 and bottled in 2010, making it fourteen years old. Glenkinchie has gathered many fans with its flowery nose and easy manner. Here we are given a chance to try an older and more complex malt matured in bourbon wood, but finished in Amontillado butts. This is an interesting choice of sherry styles. Darker than fino but lighter than oloroso, it oxidizes more slowly than most sherries, giving it quite a rich, round flavor. It works incredibly well here, as it picks up the floral notes on the nose, and supports the malt biscuit whisky with layers of yielding fruit.

Not surprisingly, finishing Glenkinchie in Amontillado is an old trick, and there are many releases like this on sale. Some are finer than others, some more rare. Apart from this 1996 bottling, if you see the 1986, grab it—it is particularly good, though getting hard to find. The 1991 is also excellent and more readily available. The nose on this whisky is excellent even straight from the bottle, though at 43 percent, it needs a drop of water to open it up fully. Be very careful how much water you add, as a lot of the complex flavors are lost when diluted too far. **PM**

Tasting notes

A fall pile of leaves, lemon curd, and fresh meringue— there is so much to take from just the nose. On the tongue, the spirit is soft like freshly toasted buttery fruit loaf, while the finish is sweet, with the kind of burr you got as a kid from honey-and-lemon cough medicine.

Glenkinchie The Managers' Choice 1992

Diageo | www.glenkinchie.com

Region and country of origin Lowlands, Scotland
Distillery Glenkinchie, Pentcaitland, East Lothian
Alcohol content 58.1% abv
Style Single malt

This is part of a third batch of whiskies to be released by Diageo. All are single-cask expressions of its malt whiskies and are bottled at cask strength. There are twenty-seven bottlings in each batch, one from each of its working malt distilleries. This expression of Glenkinchie comes from single cask no. 502, bottled in 2009; at seventeen years old, it is one of the oldest releases in the series. The interesting thing here is that this isn't an ex-bourbon American oak barrel, but rather a cask made from European oak, in other words the sort of wood normally used to mature sherry.

What isn't that well known is that the type of wood a cask is made from is much more important than what used to be in the cask. In other words, here it's the oak itself that will have the most impact on the maturing whisky. This bottling then is all about the wood, but finding a single cask that has the X-factor is not easy. When putting together a regular bottling, hundreds of casks may be used, so ironing out any inconsistencies is easy. Trying to match the flavor profile of Glenkinchie while at the same time offering something new is no small task.

Cask 502 was picked by a team that included the distillery manager and was chosen because it represented a unique take on Glenkinchie. Only 528 bottles of this rare expression exist, with the result that this range is aimed squarely at collectors and those who like to get personal with their favorite distillery. This is a very interesting experience, as the flavors on offer here are distinctive, yet fit firmly into the floury Glenkinchie house style. **PM**

Tasting notes

At once fruity and floury before warming up to release coconut and vanilla. There's salty toffee, chocolate orange, and mixed spice. The finish is sweet and dry, like brandy over walnuts. Try it with a drop of water to open up the flavors.

The Glenlivet 12-Year-Old

Chivas Brothers (Pernod Ricard)
www.theglenlivet.com

Region and country of origin Speyside, Scotland
Distillery Glenlivet, Ballindalloch, Banffshire
Alcohol content 40% abv
Style Single malt

The Glenlivet was the first licensed distillery in Scotland. Founder George Smith had been distilling whisky illegally, but when King George IV came to visit Scotland in 1822, he is rumored to have asked for Glenlivet by name. After the Duke of Gordon proposed the Excise Act in 1823, legalizing whisky distillation, George Smith, one of his tenant farmers, was first to apply for and be granted a license in 1824.

The Glenlivet 12-Year-Old was first introduced in 1933 after Prohibition ended. At that time, twelve was seen as the perfect age for a whisky, although originally it had no age statement. Continuing a tradition of leadership, George Smith's great-grandson went to the United States to promote his whisky. The Glenlivet's popularity continued to grow in the 1950s. Hollywood stars such as Yul Brynner and Robert Taylor insisted that it be available after filming.

The Glenlivet is a light single malt and easily overwhelmed by cask influence. For this reason the 12-Year-Old is made with roughly 99 percent ex-bourbon casks, the balance being matured in ex-sherry casks. It is extremely approachable, and well suited for introducing drinkers unfamiliar with single malts to the category. **WM**

Tasting notes

Clean and malty with notes of vanilla, spice, and nut. Medium-bodied and slightly creamy. Over time, caramel and peach emerge with a hint of cinnamon.

The Glenlivet 15-Year-Old French Oak Reserve

Chivas Brothers (Pernod Ricard)
www.theglenlivet.com

Region and country of origin Speyside, Scotland
Distillery Glenlivet, Ballindalloch, Banffshire
Alcohol content 40% abv
Style Single malt

While the Glenlivet 15-Year-Old French Oak Reserve is initially identical to the Glenlivet 12-Year-Old, between 30 and 35 percent is kept an additional three or more years in virgin Limousin white oak. This oak is traditionally used for maturing cognac and adds a soft spiciness, a dry cedarwood character, and a sweet nuttiness, along with a creamier mouthfeel.

In 2003 and 2004, responding to updated legislation, Chivas Brothers replaced the Glenlivet 12-Year-Old French Oak Finished with this whisky. The "Reserve" of its name signifies that only a portion of the casks are reracked into Limousin French oak casks; only when 100 percent of the whisky is matured in a particular wood can the term "finish" be used.

Glenlivet considers the union of single-malt Scotch whisky with new Limousin oak to be the perfect marriage, comparable to the "Auld Alliance" of France and Scotland of 1295, a treaty stipulating that, should either France or Scotland be attacked by England, the other would invade English territory.

The Glenlivet founder, George Smith, wanted to produce a whisky of such high quality that all other whiskies would be judged against it. The Glenlivet French Oak Reserve achieves that ambition. **WM**

Tasting notes

Dry and floral, with pronounced vanilla, honey, and oak. On the palate, notes of almond and apple, with hints of marzipan and citrus. A finish of cedar and nuts.

The peace is about to be shattered in this scene from an 1897 Glenlivet whisky label. ➜

Selected
Old Blended

PROPRIETORS
SHUFFLEBOTHAM
& CO.
BIRMINGHAM
& DUNDEE

GLENLIVET WHISKY

The Glenlivet 18-Year-Old

Chivas Brothers (Pernod Ricard) | www.theglenlivet.com

Region and country of origin Speyside, Scotland
Distillery Glenlivet, Ballindalloch, Banffshire
Alcohol content 43% abv
Style Single malt

Introduced in 1992, the Glenlivet 18-Year-Old quickly became the most awarded expression in the Glenlivet range. Between 12.5 and 15 percent of this expression is matured in oloroso sherry casks, then vatted with ex-bourbon and refill casks. Each cask is carefully selected from several types, which are each nosed and assessed prior to being emptied. Cask selection is extremely important; if any fails to meet the desired quality level, it is removed from consideration and production stopped until a suitable replacement can be found.

The Glenlivet 18-Year-Old is the personal favorite of master distiller Alan Winchester and most of the distillery team. It is considered "the perfect expression of age and elegance, balancing the archetypal ripe fruit notes of the Glenlivet with a drier, evocative oak influence." If it had to be described in one word, it would be "balance."

When creating new expressions, master blenders have to balance the bright, fruity exuberance of young whiskies, which can be rough and unpolished, with older whiskies that gain complexities from time in oak casks, but can become tired and woody, as well as lose their distillery characteristics. Likewise, blenders must balance the typical vanilla, toffee, caramel notes from ex-bourbon casks with the red fruit, cinnamon, and spice of ex-sherry casks. The Glenlivet 18-Year-Old achieves this balance of cask type and cask age to create a complex, flavorful, rich, fruity expression, which is noticeably fuller than either the 12-Year-Old or the 15-Year-Old French Oak Reserve. **WM**

Tasting notes

Cinnamon is prevalent, joined by nutmeg, clove, dark fruit, and additional spice. Apple from younger expressions has been baked and joined by raisin and dates, with hints of orange peel. Well integrated and balanced, the finish is short and spicy.

The Glenlivet 21-Year-Old Archive

Chivas Brothers (Pernod Ricard) | www.theglenlivet.com

Region and country of origin Speyside, Scotland
Distillery Glenlivet, Ballindalloch, Banffshire
Alcohol content 43% abv
Style Single malt

The Glenlivet 21-Year-Old Archive is the second-longest-running Glenlivet expression after the 12-Year-Old. Introduced in the 1980s, this 21-Year-Old has become an iconic expression of the Glenlivet. It is characterized by its complexity, derived from the diversity of cask types employed. Different types of casks exert different influences on maturing whisky, such as vanilla and toffee from first-fill ex-bourbon casks, and spice and fruit from ex-sherry casks. As many as seven different types of casks are used to create the Glenlivet Archive, which the distillery claims to "offer the most complete version of the Glenlivet with intense richness and depth."

The Glenlivet 21-Year-Old is created in batches, and current bottlings prominently display the batch number on both the bottle and box, so collectors and aficionados can compare notes for tasting and collecting purposes. Previously packaged in a navy-blue box and dark glass bottle, Archive is now sold in a clear bottle, contained in a handsome wood frame, prominently bearing the year 1824, a reference to when the Glenlivet was established.

When creating the Glenlivet Archive, various casks are hand-selected, nosed, sampled, emptied, and vatted together before being filled into oak casks for an additional period of maturation. This additional time allows the flavors, textures, and nuances from the various casks to integrate and harmonize prior to bottling. Consequently, each batch will show subtle taste variations, while maintaining the Glenlivet distillery profile. **WM**

Tasting notes

The nose reveals layers of complexity with various spices and hints of nuttiness melded with floral notes. The elegant palate presents spice, nut, and a hint of orange wax furniture polish. The finish is dry and spicy with cedar notes. Complex and dry.

The Glenlivet 70-Year-Old 1940 Generations

Gordon & MacPhail | www.gordanandmacphail.com

Region and country of origin Speyside, Scotland
Distillery Glenlivet, Ballindalloch, Banffshire
Alcohol content 45.9% abv
Style Single malt

With a retail price tag of round $22,000 (£13,800) per bottle, this is not a whisky that many people will have the opportunity to sample, but it is a truly great example of just how well a single malt can cope with extended aging. The Glenlivet in question was filled into a cask on February 3, 1940, and released in March 2011, making it a remarkable seventy years old. The cask was filled on the instructions of John Urquhart, grandfather of current Gordon & MacPhail joint managing directors David and Michael Urquhart.

Gordon & MacPhail was established in Elgin in 1895. It is one of the world's most renowned independent bottlers of Scotch whisky, with a depth of stock that virtually no other firm can match. It is largely due to the efforts of Gordon & MacPhail that the single-malt flame was kept alight during the decades when blended Scotch whisky was ubiquitous and very few malt distillers bottled their own produce.

The Generations series of vintage bottlings was launched in 2010 with a seventy-year-old expression of Mortlach, the oldest single malt ever bottled. This Glenlivet follows in its august footsteps. Gordon & MacPhail says, "The product epitomizes the family values of the company." The whisky was matured in a first-fill sherry butt, but unusually one made from American rather than European oak. It was stored at the Glenlivet distillery until January 10, 1980, when it was transferred to Gordon & MacPhail's own Elgin bonded warehouse. Just a hundred full-size decanters of this Glenlivet were produced, along with 175 6.8-oz (20-cl) decanters retailing at $6,000 (£3,800) each. **GS**

Tasting notes

The nose is sweet, with apple, faint vanilla, and old leather. Soft and complex. Slightly waxy in texture, with faint smoke on the fruity palate, and fruit acidity in the lengthy, well-balanced finish. Stands up nicely to the addition of water, which not all veteran whiskies do.

The Glenlivet Nàdurra 16-Year-Old

Chivas Brothers (Pernod Ricard) | www.theglenlivet.com

Region and country of origin Speyside, Scotland
Distillery Glenlivet, Ballindalloch, Banffshire
Alcohol content 57.7% abv
Style Single malt

Nàdurra is Gaelic for "natural." This sixteen-year-old expression is bottled at cask strength, at natural color, and non-chill-filtered, and is intended to replicate the experience of sampling the Glenlivet straight from the cask. According to distillery manager Jim Cryle, "Only a handful of very privileged people will ever have the opportunity to enter the private warehouses at the Glenlivet Distillery, yet alone sample whisky directly from the cask. With Nàdurra, we're able to bring this special experience here to you, and we could not be more thrilled." Originally released in travel retail at 48 percent abv in 2004, Nàdurra was issued again in the United States and United Kingdom in 2006. Both the 2004 and 2006 expressions are aged exclusively in ex-bourbon casks.

Some may find Nàdurra too hot, due to the high alcohol strength. First taste Nàdurra neat, then begin to add a few drops of water, retaste, then add more. The water will break the surface tension and release additional flavors. Few people are accustomed to drinking cask-strength whiskies, but water helps to acclimatize the palate to the higher alcohol.

In 2009 the Glenlivet introduced the limited-release Nàdurra Triumph 1991, produced from Triumph barley. Aged in a combination of ex-bourbon and ex-sherry casks, Nàdurra Triumph 1991 is bottled at age eighteen years and 48 percent abv. According to brand director Ron Zussman, "We wanted to create something new, while still incorporating the core elements that make our Nàdurra whisky so special. The result is our first-ever single varietal." **WM**

Tasting notes

The nose is light, with persimmon, freshly cut oak, and vanilla. Bursts of vanilla, cinnamon, and honey on the palate, with a strong oak backbone. A drop of water releases hints of fruit and caramel. Cinnamon and oak persist on the finish, joined by some pepper.

The Glenlivet XXV

Chivas Brothers (Pernod Ricard) | www.theglenlivet.com

Region and country of origin Speyside, Scotland
Distillery Glenlivet, Ballindalloch, Banffshire
Alcohol content 43% abv
Style Single malt

The Glenlivet XXV premiered in Asia early in 2007, but officially launched in the United States in August 2008. The oldest permanent expression in the Glenlivet portfolio, it contains spirit from hand-selected casks finished for at least twenty-four months in first-fill sherry casks. "The Glenlivet XXV was created to live up to exceptionally high standards," states master distiller Jim Cryle. Each bottle bears the batch number and signatures of the four expert whisky makers at the Glenlivet distillery who made it, and is packaged in a heavy wooden box.

Alan Winchester oversees all of the distillery, controlling the production from barley selection to spirit distillation. The Glenlivet's water is supplied by an underground spring called Josie's Well. This provides a perpetual supply of cold, mineral-rich water, which, combined with the high altitude, is deemed to aid the distillation process and "invigorate the spirit." According to Winchester, "There's no better place to make whisky."

Bill Lamb monitors the filling and warehousing of casks. He believes that "the oloroso-soaked oak imparts a nutty spiciness to the multilayered flavor of the spirit and enriches its color." David Boyd monitors the whisky, nosing and sampling from various casks to check their development. Boyd hand-selects each cask, skillfully combining the contents of different casks to ensure that the character and flavor of the whisky is consistent from one bottle to the next. Jim Cryle supervises the entire process and gives the final stamp of approval to each batch. **WM**

Tasting notes

Sherry influence with notes of leather and tobacco added to spice, dates, raisin, clove, orange peel, and vanilla. A long, spicy finish with pipe tobacco. Lovely notes of cinnamon and clove mix nicely with the orange peel and hints of dark chocolate.

Glenlochy 29-Year-Old

Signatory Vintage Scotch Whisky Co.

Region and country of origin Highlands, Scotland
Distillery Glenlochy, Fort William (closed)
Alcohol content 52.8% abv
Style Single malt

Compared to longstanding independent bottlers such as Gordon & MacPhail and Wm. Cadenhead, Signatory is a relatively new kid on the block, having been established in 1998 by Andrew and Brian Symington; however, it has grown to be one of the largest and most respected bottlers in Scotland.

Signatory markets whiskies across a number of ranges; the Glenlochy 29-Year-Old appears in the bottler's Cask Strength Collection. It was distilled on August 21, 1980, and aged for twenty-nine years in hogshead no. 649 before 265 numbered bottles were filled on June 22, 2010.

The Glenlochy distillery was located in what is now the popular West Highland vacation resort of Fort William. It made Western Highland single malts, of which only Ben Nevis and Oban remain. The Glenlochy–Fort William Distillery Co. Ltd. was formed in 1897, with production commencing in April 1901. However, Glenlochy was silent from 1917 until 1924, and had a somewhat checkered history, with several periods of closure, before ownership was transferred in 1953 to Scottish Malt Distillers, a subsidiary of Distillers Company Ltd. (DCL). When the time came for DCL to cut production during the early 1980s, the comparatively unmodernized Glenlochy was a logical contender for closure; it had just one pair of stills.

Glenlochy closed in 1983. Although some of the site was cleared after distilling ceased, a number of buildings survive, including the kiln and malt barn. The latter is now coverted to housing, and former staff cottages now serve as guest accommodation. **GS**

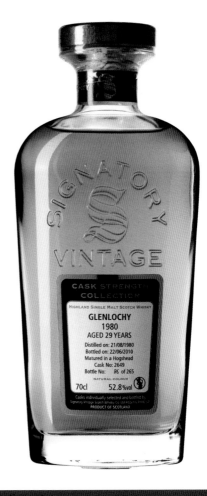

Tasting notes

Quite austere on the nose, a little waxy, with cereal, green apple, and a hint of mint. Grassy and waxy on the relatively full palate, with bitter coffee, almond, more mint, and vague citrus fruit. The finish is long, quite green, and herbal, with tannic oak notes.

Glenmorangie 18-Year-Old

Glenmorangie Co. (LVMH) | www.glenmorangie.com

Region and country of origin Highlands, Scotland
Distillery Glenmorangie, Tain, Ross-shire
Alcohol content 43% abv
Style Single malt

There is nothing wrong with an ex-bourbon or ex–Jack Daniel's cask, so why not mature the whisky longer in that type of barrel? Not every whisky can take many years in the cask, but Glenmorangie still performs well after eighteen years of maturation. The company is obsessed with wood quality and strives to secure the best oak. Its trees come from certain hillsides in the Ozark Mountains of Missouri, usually owned by private companies and especially selected for Glenmorangie.

Loggers take the oaken giants down and saw them into planks that air-dry for a specific time, after which they are taken to the Bluegrass Cooperage in Louisville, Kentucky, owned by Brown-Forman (B-F). There they are sawn into staves, raised by a cooper into a barrel, hooped, toasted, charred, and checked for leakage, after which they are sent off by truck to Lynchburg, Tennessee, to be seasoned with Jack Daniel's (also owned by B-F).

When drinking this 18-Year-Old, imagine that the cask from which this expression was drawn held American whiskey for six to eight years in its previous life, before it was broken down into staves and shipped to Scotland. When the casks are reassembled, they are usually enlarged from 53 to 66 gallons (200 to 250 liters); head and end are replaced. It takes an oak eighty years to grow before use as a barrel (the American term for cask). Add to that eight seasoning years in the United States, followed by eighteen in Scotland, and you are tasting a dram coming from wood that is more than a century old. This drink deserves some patience when savored. **HO**

Tasting notes

Clearly an older sibling of Glenmorangie the Original, with added tones of burnt sugar, buttered toast, spicy wood, sugared almond, and ripe peach. With time, floral shop aromas arrive—rose, greenery, and lily—followed by a pleasant, lingering finish.

Glenmorangie 25-Year-Old

Glenmorangie Co. (LVMH) | www.glenmorangie.com

Region and country of origin Highlands, Scotland
Distillery Glenmorangie, Tain, Ross-shire
Alcohol content 43% abv
Style Single malt

Glenmorangie—which translates from Gaelic as "valley of tranquillity"—is situated on a beautiful, quiet spot overlooking the Moray Firth, in the direct vicinity of the picturesque village of Tain. In these peaceful surroundings, whisky may sleep for a long time. So why not take the maturation period a step further? How would a twenty-five-year-old respond when interacting with wood and air for the lifespan of an entire generation?

Whiskies of this age should not only be enjoyed by savoring them, but contemplated too, preferably in good company. After all, many events happen in twenty-five years—children grow up, milestones are passed. Some of the people who helped make this expression and guarded it for so long may no longer work at the distillery or may not be with us anymore, in which case one hopes those guardians of the past had their fair angels' share of this exquisite dram.

The 25-Year-Old is the grand old lady of the house, to be revered, savored, and honored. She comes in beautiful attire, in a golden "cage." You will notice her mature, rounded figure when you release her out of her temporary prison by opening the box, since the bottle has a different shape from the rest of the Glenmorangie range. This 25-Year-Old carries her age with grace.

This is a dram for a very special occasion. What about your twenty-fifth wedding anniversary? Or, if you can't wait that long, take the twenty-fifth of the coming month and make up an excellent reason to open the bottle. **HO**

Tasting notes

Gentle and complex to the core, with honeysuckle, white chocolate, crème brûlée, and sugared slices of fresh orange. Carries hints of cedar with grace; waxy notes give way to praline pecan ice cream and a subtle, rewarding finish.

Glenmorangie Astar

Glenmorangie Co. (LVMH)
www.glenmorangie.com

Region and country of origin Highlands, Scotland
Distillery Glenmorangie, Tain, Ross-shire
Alcohol content 51.7% abv
Style Single malt

This whisky is the work of Bill Lumsden, head of distilling and whisky creation at Glenmorangie. From bonny Scotland, he traveled thousands of miles west, across the Atlantic Ocean to Missouri. There, on the northern slopes of the Ozark Mountains, he walked through the woods, personally selecting oaks that would be transformed into the casks for a new single malt he envisioned as the Astar. Does it really matter where the wood grows? Yes, it does; even the microclimate plays its part. Oak grown on northern hillsides grows more slowly, which makes the wood finer-grained. Hence, it will render more flavor to whisky during maturation.

Bill Lumsden's attention to detail is faultless. He is personally involved in every step of the making of this whisky. *Astar* is Gaelic for "journey," and, thanks to the creativity, insight, and continuous quest of a single man, we can now taste the difference it makes to go the extra mile. This is designer whisky, from the root of the oak. Take it slowly, measure by measure. It is worth the discovery. Astar is a powerful non-chill-filtered whisky, higher in alcohol than your standard Glenmorangie. And priced at around $80 (£65), it's good value, too. **HO**

Tasting notes

This whisky appreciates water, opening up into vanilla, toffee, and lemon meringue pie. Fresh sugared orange and bittersweet chocolate. Faint oak, with a long finish.

Glenmorangie The Culloden Bottle

Glenmorangie Co. (LVMH)
www.glenmorangie.com

Region and country of origin Highlands, Scotland
Distillery Glenmorangie, Tain, Ross-shire
Alcohol content 43% abv
Style Single malt

In conjunction with the National Museums of Scotland, Glenmorangie released the Culloden Bottle in 1995 to celebrate the 250th anniversary of the Battle of Culloden (April 16, 1746). The molded glass bottle is a replica of a flask once owned by Duncan Forbes, Laird of Culloden (1686–1747). It now sits in Culloden House next to the first bottle of Glenmorangie Culloden.

The Forbes family owned the Ferintosh distillery from around 1620. After 1689, in compensation for damage to their lands by James VII's supporters, they were allowed to distill Ferintosh whisky duty-free upon the payment of a trivial annual fee. The family produced large quantities of Ferintosh, which became synonymous with high-quality Highland whisky.

Glenmorangie, which stands slightly northeast of the Ferintosh site, produced 2,500 individually numbered Culloden bottles, which come in laser-etched wooden boxes with a parchment certificate, signed by then distillery manager Bill Lumsden.

Bottled on October 25, 1995, this twenty-four-year-old expression originally retailed for $195 (£125), with a portion of the proceeds donated to the National Museums of Scotland. **WM**

Tasting notes

Rich, with big notes of vanilla and pineapple, and hints of cinnamon and lemon-lime soda. Date, raisin, leather, and clove emerge. Marzipan lingers on the finish.

A nineteenth-century depiction of Culloden House.

Glenmorangie Finealta

Glenmorangie Co. (LVMH) | www.glenmorangie.com

Region and country of origin Highlands, Scotland
Distillery Glenmorangie, Tain, Ross-shire
Alcohol content 46% abv
Style Single malt

This is another release from master distiller Bill Lumsden's curiosity cabinet. Glenmorangie Finealta was released in 2010, but is re-created from an original recipe dating back to 1903. American and European at the same time, Finealta is a combination of two Glenmorangie whiskies matured separately, one in American oak, the other in ex-oloroso casks from Spain. Both whiskies were then poured into a large vat to blend into a well-balanced marriage.

To add a little bite and a tiny flavor of smoke, the malt from which the whisky was made is lightly peated. Although Glenmorangie had not used peated malt for quite some time, back in the early twentieth century, whisky-making processes were very different. In many parts of Scotland, peat was the preferred fuel for heating stoves, stills, and malting kilns. Drying green malt over a peat fire in the kiln produces distinctive smoky flavors in the eventual whisky.

When the railroads began to reach the remoter parts of the Highlands, it became easier to transport coal, which gradually replaced peat as the primary fuel for heating in the stoves at home as well as in the distillery kilns. Hence, many once-peated whiskies became virtually unpeated. Only the distilleries on the more remote islands continued to use peat for their kilns; the tradition continues, which is why those whiskies still carry the pungent aromas today.

If you want to find out what Glenmorangie might have tasted like in the early 1900s, take a sip of this one. It is a different experience altogether, but it is still Glenmorangie and as elegant as ever. **HO**

Tasting notes

A surprising combination for some: milk chocolate wrapped in wood smoke. With added water, there is a subtle reminder of seaweed on the shore, with citrus tones. Canned smoked meat mingled with campfire embers. The finish is dry and nutty.

Glenmorangie The Lasanta

Glenmorangie Co. (LVMH) | www.glenmorangie.com

Region and country of origin Highlands, Scotland
Distillery Glenmorangie, Tain, Ross-shire
Alcohol content 46% abv
Style Single malt

The necks of the pot stills at Glenmorangie are unusually slender and are the tallest in Scotland. The result is a light-bodied spirit that matures well in casks that previously contained bourbon or Jack Daniel's Tennessee whiskey. The casks deliver the creamy vanilla note that shines through in all the bottlings.

Around 1995, the whisky company decided to experiment with a process then called "wood finish." Glenmorangie ten-year-old whisky was revatted in a different type of cask to mature for an extra nine months up to a full year. The master distiller launched an extensive range, among which were Port Wood Finish, Madeira Wood Finish, Burgundy Wood Finish, and Sherry Wood Finish. The latter type of cask is common in Scotland, as various distillers like to mature their whiskies in ex-sherry casks imported from Spain. In 2007, however, LVMH decided to concentrate on fewer bottlings. They did away with the term "wood finish" and gave each expression its own name.

Glenmorangie's experiments in the 1990s kick-started a revolution. Nowadays, nearly every distillery launches one or more bottlings of whiskies that were finished in a cask other than the one they were born in. This Lasanta has spent some extra time in an ex-sherry cask, but there are many other options. In France you can occasionally find a local whisky that has spent time in a champagne cask. Some work extremely well, some less so. At Glenmorangie an interesting variation on the basic theme is achieved; an extra layer of flavor is added, but without masking the Glenmorangie whisky's original flavor profile. **HO**

Tasting notes

This has the ripened fruit and crème brûlée flavors of Glenmorangie the Original, with added raisin. Also to be detected are buttered toast with plum jam and a dusting of vanilla sugar. These give way to salted walnut and a slightly drying finish.

Glenmorangie The Nectar d'Or

Glenmorangie Co. (LVMH) | www.glenmorangie.com

Region and country of origin Highlands, Scotland
Distillery Glenmorangie, Tain, Ross-shire
Alcohol content 46% abv
Style Single malt

You are a French company, and you own a distillery in Scotland that makes excellent whisky that has slept in American oak for ten years. Is it too far-fetched to see what the spirit might do with an extra nap in a cask coming from your own country? The conclusion of Glenmorangie's master whisky maker might have been, What the heck, let's give it a try. Where to go next? Too many wines, too little time? You have to start somewhere, but the most important issue is to leave the basic flavor profile of the whisky intact.

Looking at the sweeter wines seemed an obvious thing to do. So here is a French relative in the Glenmorangie range. The Nectar d'Or is extramatured in an ex-Sauternes cask. Sauternes wine comes from the eponymous town in the Bordeaux region; its most famous vineyard is Château d'Yquem. In the United States, the word *sauterne* is used as a generic description for sweet dessert wines (the *S* at the end was deliberately dropped). Sauternes is a very sweet wine and is most often enjoyed with dessert.

The Sauternes wine casks have made the Glenmorangie Nectar d'Or a wonderful digestif. At the same time, this whisky performs well before dinner to whet the appetite. Just welcome this Frenchified variation in your glass. Take time to swirl the whisky; hold up the glass, admire the beautiful color, and pick up the subtle aromas with your olfactory protuberance—your nose. Taste the almost syrupy liquid, enjoy its full body, swallow, and welcome the quiet finish. You just found out why LVMH thinks this is the "golden drink of the gods." **HO**

Tasting notes

Floral aromas—jasmine, lily-of-the-valley—mingle with lime and honey-dressed fruit salad, then melt into nougat, toffee, and bittersweet chocolate. Well-behaved and smooth, with a sweet vanilla finish. A whisky that makes a satisfying digestif.

Glenmorangie The Original

Glenmorangie Co. (LVMH) | www.glenmorangie.com

Region and country of origin Highlands, Scotland
Distillery Glenmorangie, Tain, Ross-shire
Alcohol content 40% abv
Style Single malt

How original can you get? Well, truth be told, this is a whisky that has been around as a single malt for quite some time. Legend says that the current site hosted an illicit still as early as 1705, but it was only in 1843 that a certain William Matheson was granted a license to make whisky at a farm distillery called Morangie. With the help of his brother, Matheson built a new distillery and decided to conquer the world.

These were no shallow ambitions. By 1880 Glenmorangie could be found as far afield as San Francisco, California. Thirteen years later the distillery was taken over. The new owner, Macdonald and Muir, also purchased Glen Moray (1920), Ardbeg (1997), and the Scotch Malt Whisky Society (2004). The result was a small but handsome portfolio; this attracted Louis Vuitton Moët Hennessy, who acquired it lock, stock, and barrel at the end of that same year.

In 2007 LVMH did an extreme makeover regarding the packaging, deciding to say good-bye to the old-fashioned bottles and labeling. Instead, an entirely new range was presented in a luxurious form that resembles a crossover between a wine and a cognac bottle. Some Auld Alliance between Scotland and France echoing here? After all, LVMH is French.

Believe it or not, the Original makes a great cocktail mixed with Moët & Chandon champagne. The trick is not to overpower the champagne, but let the Glenmorangie shine through. Try this at home with various amounts of whisky in a flute, gently adding the champagne until you discover the ratio that you prefer. **HO**

Tasting notes

Produced by Scotland's tallest stills, the whisky's light citrus tones hover over its heart of sun-ripened passion fruit, white chocolate, and vanilla crème brûlée. This well-rounded dram, with its full body, finishes sweetly and smoothly with hints of orange and peach.

Glenmorangie Pride

Glenmorangie Co. (LVMH)
www.glenmorangie.com

Region and country of origin Highlands, Scotland
Distillery Glenmorangie, Tain, Ross-shire
Alcohol content 56.7% abv
Style Single malt

Glenmorangie was formally established in 1843 on a site overlooking the Dornoch Firth that had long been renowned (or, if you worked for excise and customs, notorious) for illicit distilling. It quickly reached its maximum production capacity of 20,000 gallons (75,700 liters) a year, so in 1887 the owners completely rebuilt the distillery.

By 1983, Glenmorangie had become the best-selling single malt in Scotland, and it has retained market leadership almost unbrokenly between then and the publication of this book. It currently produces around 10 million bottles per annum, of which more than 6 million are sold in the United Kingdom.

Although successful marketing increases sales, there is also a risk of a backlash. This was true for Glenmorangie, as some people were put off by all the hype. But those who do so miss out, particularly on this single malt, which was distilled from an existing 18-year-old in 1981 and then laid down for a further ten years in casks that were formerly Sauternes barriques from the French vineyards of Château d'Yquem. This has been longer in preparation than any other whisky in the history of Glenmorangie, and it is a single malt of true greatness. **GL**

Tasting notes

The aroma combines poached pear, baked pineapple sponge, nutmeg, and aniseed. On the palate, lemon vanilla madeleine and honeydew melon.

Glenmorangie The Quinta Ruban

Glenmorangie Co. (LVMH)
www.glenmorangie.com

Region and country of origin Highlands, Scotland
Distillery Glenmorangie, Tain, Ross-shire
Alcohol content 40% abv
Style Single malt

For another variation on Glenmorangie's basic theme of vanilla and crème brûlée, the distillery turned to Portugal. The Quinta Ruban is extramatured in ex-port pipes, which give this single malt a reddish hue and a winey quality. It makes a fine companion to a cheese platter after a lavish dinner, and an excellent alternative to a vintage port.

The practice of fortifying wines goes back a few centuries, when wine makers and distillers discovered that wine with a higher alcohol content does not go sour as quickly as nonfortified wine, and it also improves when maturing in the wooden barrel. Port—from Oporto—was the first wine to gain an appellation d'origine controlée (AOC, a controlled designation of origin), followed by Champagne.

Maturing whisky in different types of casks is not new. For several centuries, distilleries would try to get their hands on any type of cask available. Port, sherry, and even rum or cognac casks were used.

Glenmorangie's wood management is supervised by Bill Lumsden, who reportedly once said about wood influence, "We'll go back to the acorn if need be." The results are worth visiting and revisiting, and the proof is here in a bottle of the Quinta Ruban. **HO**

Tasting notes

Chocolate-covered cherry and port wine aromas burst into caramel and toffee with a pleasant finish. One to lure a wine enthusiast into the world of whisky.

Glenmorangie Signet

Glenmorangie Co. (LVMH)
www.glenmorangie.com

Region and country of origin Highlands, Scotland
Distillery Glenmorangie, Tain, Ross-shire
Alcohol content 46% abv
Style Single malt

Close to Glenmorangie's distillery, in a nearby field, stands a replica of the Hilton of Cadboll stone—a ninth-century standing stone intricately carved by the ancient civilization that then ruled northern Scotland—the Picts. The bottom panel of the stone has been adopted as the Glenmorangie signet, which adorns all official distillery bottlings. It is a powerful and immediately recognizable image that harks back to ancient times when distilling may not even have reached these remote lands.

Glenmorangie's Signet is considered the most richly flavored in the whole range. The whisky is a blend of the house's oldest vintage, made more than thirty years ago, and a more recently produced spirit that matured in purpose-selected "designer casks" for various periods. The malted barley—also known as chocolate barley—has been gently roasted before being processed into spirit. The resulting expression is nothing like your traditional Glenmorangie, but paradoxically is still a solid member of the family.

Should you have the opportunity to stay at Cadboll House, the Glenmorangie country home not far from the distillery, be sure to enjoy the tranquillity that is eternally locked in the name of Signet. **HO**

Tasting notes

Faintly burnt, hazelnut tones. Water brings out fig, raisin, strawberry jam, cinnamon, clove, and charred toast. Slightly astringent, complex, long finish.

Glenmorangie Sonnalta PX

Glenmorangie Co. (LVMH)
www.glenmorangie.com

Region and country of origin Highlands, Scotland
Distillery Glenmorangie, Tain, Ross-shire
Alcohol content 46% abv
Style Single malt

Glenmorangie Sonnalta PX is one step closer to the world of sherry. Spanish bodegas produce various styles of sherry, ranging from the very light and dry fino to Manzanilla, amontillado, oloroso, and palo cortado, to extremely dark and sweet sherries.

For the latter, molasses-like kind, grapes such as PX, which stands for Pedro Ximénez, are used. Where Glenmorangie Lasanta is influenced by extra maturation in ex-sherry casks, Sonnalta PX gains additional and stronger flavors from its treatment in former PX sherry butts. *Sonnalta* is Gaelic for "generous," and that is exactly what this whisky is. Sonnalta is not necessarily better than Lasanta, but it is richer in flavor, the PX butts adding an extra layer of fruity sweetness. The expression shows, once more, that sherry and single-malt whisky get along very well.

This expression is the first in a series of bottlings called the Private Edition. The output is limited and comes from master distiller Bill Lumsden's "cabinet of curiosities." These days, sherry casks are scarce and expensive, with the result that more than 90 percent of Scottish whisky matures in ex-bourbon casks. Some are bottled from those casks; others are recasked in sherry butts, just for a while—like the Sonnalta. **HO**

Tasting notes

Full, ripe raspberry, spicy cake, and ginger oakiness. Hints of cedar cigar box. Beautifully balanced. Extreme fruitiness heads for a long, deep, slightly spicy finish.

The Glenrothes 1998

Berry Bros. & Rudd | www.theglenrothes.com

Region and country of origin Speyside, Scotland
Distillery The Glenrothes, Rothes, Morayshire
Alcohol content 43% abv
Style Single malt

After the 1995, this was the second of the specifically laid-down vintages. However, in an example of why whisky continues to fascinate, the 1998 came to maturity before the 1995 and was released in 2009. This is largely because a different style was sought; the 1998 was introduced to replace the popular 1991 vintage as a conversational single malt, whereas the 1995 is more of an all-rounder, meaning that additional ripening time was required to give it more depth.

The 1998 is wonderful with desserts, in particular combining delightfully with crème brûlée and chocolate mousse. The whisky seems to tone down the sweetness and, with the amplification of so many Glenrothes flavors, creates a very satisfying match.

The Glenrothes is matured in casks of both Spanish and American oak, seasoned with either sherry or bourbon. Oak delivers up to 80 percent of whisky flavor; this singular wood policy gives the broadest possible selection of tastes and flavors from which to create each individual expression.

The 1998 vintage was created by Gordon Motion, appointed following the retirement of John Ramsay. Gordon described it as "like Carmen Miranda's hat in a bottle; tropical fruits lead with pineapple and mango, developing into sweet banana, coconut, and classic Glenrothes vanilla pod." **MM**

Tasting notes

The nose has spicy vanilla, with golden syrup and lemongrass. The palate is soft and mature, with sweet vanilla and a hint of cinnamon. Impressively long finish.

The Glenrothes 1995

Berry Bros. & Rudd | www.theglenrothes.com

Region and country of origin Speyside, Scotland
Distillery The Glenrothes, Rothes, Morayshire
Alcohol content 43% abv
Style Single malt

Released in 2011, this was the first-ever vintage of Glenrothes specifically laid down to a recipe. According to director Ronnie Cox, "We were seeking another classic after-dinner Glenrothes but as Robert Burns said, 'all the best-laid schemes o' mice an' men gang aft agley.' That is to say, it is never the case that all the casks will mature as and when expected. It is much more difficult to gauge how refill casks will turn out than new casks, and it was perhaps these which persuaded us to switch the original idea of a classic 'relaxer' style to more of an all-rounder."

Selecting casks at their very best, and to meet the flavor profile, requires the expert eye and nose of the malt master, so it is usual for a much smaller proportion of casks to be chosen than were laid down. No more than 3 percent of the distillery's production capacity eventually goes the full distance to a Glenrothes vintage bottling.

Unusually for Glenrothes, there is an evident maltiness, revealing more of the distillery character and adding intrigue on the nose. An early freshness is delivered on the palate, followed by the more familiar fruit. This zestiness adds a further layer of complexity to the whisky. Savor this expression either before or after a meal; the 1995 vintage has the freshness of a predinner drink but the richness of a digestif. **MM**

Tasting notes

Crème brûlée on the nose, with citrus, pink grapefruit, and a hint of white pepper and cedar wood. The palate is rich and sweet, with American oak and butterscotch.

The Rothes Burn, favored water source of The Glenrothes and other distilleries.

The Glenrothes 1991

Berry Bros. & Rudd | www.theglenrothes.com

Region and country of origin Speyside, Scotland
Distillery The Glenrothes, Rothes, Morayshire
Alcohol content 43% abv
Style Single malt

An approved way of keeping the gray matter functioning is to remember the passing years by their most memorable moments; thus, 1991 may forever be recalled for the collapse of the Soviet Union. An alternative is to memorize the vintages of the Glenrothes. As Boris Yeltsin was preparing for his big day, on Speyside they were distilling what the Glenrothes director Ronnie Cox calls "the intellectual conversation stimulator."

Glenrothes 1991 was first bottled in 2005, with subsequent bottlings as and when required. It is now solely available in travel retail. As with all vintages of the Glenrothes, the casks are selected and the whisky vatted together prior to being put back into "neutral" casks (those that do not affect the flavor of the vatting). Known as marrying, this process, retained by only a few distillers, encourages balance and consistency from bottle to bottle. The original cask makeup is of 40 percent American wood first-fill sherry casks, the balance being refills.

This vintage is at its most intense, unsurprisingly, when nosed and sipped neat; however, with the addition of a little water, it gradually blossoms and releases a host of intriguing and beguiling aromas. Perhaps what is most remarkable is the influence of the refill casks—second-fill sherry butts are often underrated. While the dominant vanilla butterscotch notes and flavor are heavily influenced by the American oak first-fill sherry casks, it is the Spanish oak refills that enrich the characteristic Glenrothes. This is a well-loved whisky, at once bold and soft. **GS**

Tasting notes

The nose has notes of vanilla and citrus, then a little toffee with dried apricot. Crêpe Suzette? The taste is affluent rather than super-rich, sweet and chewy, with notes of melon and dried ginger. It ends in characterful and elegantly spicy fashion—like an Alison Lurie novel.

The Glenrothes 1985

Berry Bros. & Rudd | www.theglenrothes.com

Region and country of origin Speyside, Scotland
Distillery The Glenrothes, Rothes, Morayshire
Alcohol content 43% abv
Style Single malt

This expression of the Glenrothes, like Elvis, made a very successful comeback. Initially launched in 1997, it was the second-ever Glenrothes vintage; casks had been identified, but not all of them were ready at the time of bottling. The first release (25 to 30 percent first-fill American oak sherry butts) ran to 10,646 cases.

The nose of the first release was like a Christmas treat of sherry with toasted nuts. It also had a meatiness not usually associated with the Glenrothes. However, a palate of mixed spice and mouthwatering marmalade, followed by a dry, spicy finish (with a return of the nuts), mark it out as the real deal.

By the time of the second release (some eight years later), the additional maturation time required a different tasting note and a different date of approval. Director Ronnie Cox explains, "As a matter of course, all Glenrothes labels contain the line 'Checked,' for when the spirit was first checked before delivery to cask, and an 'Approved' line, which confirms the date when the vintage makeup was given the thumbs-up. Although the Edrington Group is responsible for the distillation and wood procurement, Berry Bros. & Rudd Ltd.—the brand owner—has the initial discussions vis-à-vis the style of the eventual vintage and must give the final stamp of approval."

The second release of the whisky was smaller—only 4,846 cases—and picked up a clutch of medals, including Best in Class at the International Wine & Spirit Competition. The 1985 vintage goes perfectly with "Stolen Moments" by Oliver Nelson or "The Moontrane" by Larry Young. **MM**

Tasting notes

Second release: cinnamon, apple, and pastry—apple strudel. Then floral, leathery, and oaky and a hint of bergamot. A splendid balance of sweet and woody. Almost explosive spiciness, nutty dryness, spectacular mouthfeel, and awesome flavor development.

The Glenrothes 1979

Berry Bros. & Rudd | www.theglenrothes.com

Region and country of origin Speyside, Scotland
Distillery The Glenrothes, Rothes, Morayshire
Alcohol content 43% abv
Style Single malt

Your first taste of the 1979 vintage Glenrothes might be a revelation. The first-ever vintage whisky launched in 1995 by Berry Bros. & Rudd was entirely dependent upon a small volume of excellent stock being available (just over 3,800 cases) and the principle that a vintage-only portfolio would reflect the true nature of Scotch whisky. Director Ronnie Cox states, "We are rarely, if ever, able to produce the same batch of new make spirit twice, and it is a fact that different casks always provide slightly different flavors. Each vintage was to be a representative of the distillery character but with a different personality." So the idea was to have the freedom to create whiskies to suit every mood and every occasion; some vintages would be spring-like and some fall-like."

This whisky was distilled in the year that new stills were installed at Glenrothes. Apparently, ley lines were disturbed by the construction of the new still house, resulting in the appearance at the distillery of a popular local character, Biawa (Byeway) Makalunga. This came as something of a shock to the stillman who saw him, since Byeway had died in 1972 and was buried in Rothes cemetery, directly opposite the distillery. Since then, it has been traditional at Glenrothes to drink a toast to the ghost.

The 1979 provided a template for subsequent releases from the 1970s. Big, spicy, complex, rich, and sherried, with magnificent mouthfeel and an epic, intriguing finish, the influence of 25 percent first-fill sherry is clear. The 1979 is difficult to find these days; if you get the chance, make sure you taste it. **MM**

Tasting notes

Very clear sherry influence on the nose. Ripe and juicy with a note of orange peel—and moss. Teasing vanilla, too, and gumdrops. There is sweetness on the palate that evolves into spice with a minimum of fuss. The finish is gently drying, which makes it rather addictive.

← Ardcanny Farm, from where the distillery sources its springwater.

The Glenrothes 1978

Berry Bros. & Rudd | www.theglenrothes.com

Region and country of origin Speyside, Scotland
Distillery The Glenrothes, Rothes, Morayshire
Alcohol content 43% abv
Style Single malt

Unusually, the 1978 vintage has had two releases. Casks had been allocated for the vintage—40 percent sherry first-fill, both American and European oak—but not all were deemed ready at the time of the initial launch in 1999. An initial release of only 510 cases sold out very quickly. By the time of the second release (863 cases) in 2008, the whisky had been reracked and married for two years.

The 1978 is the last of the 1970s vintages and is as rich and complex as one could hope for, with delightfully sherried top notes. Master distiller John Ramsay's talent included the ability to create whiskies of intriguing contrasts; the 1978 is at once juicy yet dry, sweet yet spicy, but everything is in perfect balance. Truly a master class in moderation—the dryness is not overly tannic, the sweetness is never cloying. It is deep and dark without being sinister. Little wonder that the second release was awarded Best Speyside Malt at the World Whisky Awards in 2008.

Somehow, in a display of iron discipline, director Ronnie Cox manages to keep a bottle well hidden at the back of his drinks cabinet, "to prevent it from being ill-treated or abused." You have to admire the man's self-control. **MM**

Tasting notes

Second release: unsurprisingly oakier than its predecessor, with more toffee and less sherry. Spicier, too, with fruit. The finish has ginger and dried apricot.

The Glenrothes 1974

Berry Bros. & Rudd | www.theglenrothes.com

Region and country of origin Speyside, Scotland
Distillery The Glenrothes, Rothes, Morayshire
Alcohol content 43% abv
Style Single malt

Distilled in 1974—as the name might suggest—and bottled in 2003 exclusively for the growing number of discerning single-malt enthusiasts in the United States, this is one of the hardest vintages to find. As is common knowledge, one of the issues with all vintages is that they are finite, which is why the year after this release, the Glenrothes elected to change tack and create Select Reserve.

Vintages inevitably run out. They are irreplaceable and, because any vintage is restricted to a maximum of 2 percent of the distillery's yearly production capacity, the bottles are highly collectable and very hard to secure. Few more so than this vintage, which ran to only 1,582 cases.

This typically well-dressed Glenrothes takes a little time to reveal its best, but the reward of a few minutes suspense is no real surprise; it is deep and robust with notes of oak, black pepper, and brown sugar. The 1974 has perhaps the softest texture of any Glenrothes. The cask makeup has proved impossible to track down, but the whisky was reracked into sherry casks. *Wine Enthusiast* says, "The finest malt whisky that Glenrothes has ever released. Buy two [bottles]." Chance would be a fine thing. **MM**

Tasting notes

On the nose, notes of citrus and vanilla with added herbal complexity. Lemon curd and custard. The finish is lingering and full, with notes of sherry and cocoa.

The Glenrothes 1972

Berry Bros. & Rudd | www.theglenrothes.com

Region and country of origin Speyside, Scotland
Distillery The Glenrothes, Rothes, Morayshire
Alcohol content 43% abv
Style Single malt

This is possibly the finest Glenrothes of all. This vintage, the second release of the 1970s, ran to 1,989 cases and was created to satisfy the vacuum left by the short-lived 1979. It is the archetype for the Glenrothes "after-dinner style"; marmalade on the nose and then an old Jaguar car—all leather and polished walnut—with a full body and creamy mouthfeel, followed by a long, spicy, sweet finish. The cask makeup was 60 percent new Spanish sherry casks; the remainder were refills.

Adding water to venerable malts such as this can be dangerous—they seldom swim well. Alcohol forms "droplets" with water as it matures and, the longer the maturation, the bigger the droplets.

Revisiting the 1972 vintage, its deep natural red impresses as much as the viscosity. The nose has that trademark mature "Rothes nose," reminiscent of fruit gums. Older expressions of the Glenrothes take a while to open up, and this is no exception. It balances sweet notes of fudge with meatier, more savory undertones. Chocolate-covered orange peel evolves on the palate, leading into a mighty finish. Pour yourself a decent-sized measure, then put Duke Ellington's *Money Jungle* on the turntable. **MM**

Tasting notes

Belgian waffle with vanilla ice cream and mango purée on the nose. The palate is enormous and tropical; more mango with licorice, and a good amount of wood.

The Glenrothes Alba Reserve

Berry Bros. & Rudd | www.theglenrothes.com

Region and country of origin Speyside, Scotland
Distillery The Glenrothes, Rothes, Morayshire
Alcohol content 40% abv
Style Single malt

This whisky is special, not least because it is officially kosher. It was launched in 2009 in response to demand for such a whisky from American Orthodox Jewish enthusiasts, many in the New York City area.

Whiskies made by the Glenrothes are variously matured in casks of Spanish oak, American white oak, or both, a wood policy that gives the malt master the broadest possible selection of flavors from which to create distinct, individual expressions.

While the level of residual sherry in the Glenrothes Select Reserve measures less than 1,250 parts per million, the fact remains that Orthodox Jews do not regard sherry as kosher. Former master distiller John Ramsay was asked to develop a new expression that perfectly satisfied that requirement while at the same time offering the wider market a fresh Glenrothes variant. Accordingly, he selected only American oak refill bourbon casks—curiously, *Alba* is the Gaelic word for "Scotland."

The Alba Reserve single malt was authenticated by Rabbi Padwa of the London Beth Din in March 2009. A stamp certifying the whisky's kosher status appears on the back label. Its elegant style has been very well received. **MM**

Tasting notes

Coconut and vanilla on the nose, then almond, clove, and rose petal. The palate is soft, with crème brûlée and berries. The medium-length finish is sweet and creamy.

The Glenrothes John Ramsay

Berry Bros. & Rudd | www.theglenrothes.com

Region and country of origin Speyside, Scotland
Distillery The Glenrothes, Rothes, Morayshire
Alcohol content 46.7% abv
Style Single malt

John Ramsay was the Edrington Group's master blender. The man ultimately responsible for the quality of every bottle of Famous Grouse and Cutty Sark, he was also heavily involved in Macallan and Highland Park. However, Ramsay always had a particular passion for the Glenrothes, having been intimately involved in the creation and subsequent success of the brand. The very first vintage was Ramsay's work, and thereafter, in his capacity of malt master, he signed off every Glenrothes label after 2004. He began work in the whisky industry in 1966 and, having announced he was to hang up his lab coat after more than forty years, he was asked to create one last expression of his favorite single malt to mark the occasion.

Ramsay was given the whisky enthusiast's dream brief and the free run of the distillery warehouses. From the entire inventory, he selected single casks from the years 1973, 1978, 1979, 1982, 1985, 1986, and 1987, then vatted and married them. He visited his whisky and added water very gradually over a period of six months, thereby avoiding the requirement to chill-filter. Bottled at 46.7 percent, on the nose it bursts with dark chocolate, blood orange, vanilla, tiger lily, and green tea. The maturity and richness of the whisky, launched in 2009, beguiles the palate, with the signature creamy texture of the Glenrothes, before delivering a voluptuous and languorous finish.

Glenrothes's John Ramsay is everything a legacy bottling should be. Ramsay was a quiet man who let his whisky do the talking, and this is his most articulate expression. Only 1,400 bottles were released. **MM**

Tasting notes

Blood orange on the nose, with trademark vanilla notes balanced by a light spiciness. Exemplary flavor delivery with balanced oak and fruit on the palate; multilayered complexity, from fresh mango to cooked apple. The finish is elegant, long, well-developed, and tactile.

The Glenrothes Select Reserve

Berry Bros. & Rudd | www.theglenrothes.com

Region and country of origin Speyside, Scotland
Distillery The Glenrothes, Rothes, Morayshire
Alcohol content 40% abv (United States);
43% abv (rest of the world) **Style** Single malt

Launched in 2005, the Glenrothes Select Reserve was created to represent the house style of what had been until then a vintage-only portfolio; the idea was for Select Reserve to be the only product to be consistent year in, year out. It is as if the brand were built in reverse; launched as limited-edition, finite vintages, to be followed years later by the core expression.

Director Ronnie Cox explains, "The brief was developed from Berry Bros. & Rudd's 300 years of history with the top-end of London's wine business, in particular champagne. The inspiration for Select Reserve came from Krug's Grande Cuvée. By taking a portion of several vintages, Krug was able to create a product, a consistent product, in addition to the vintages being released, each of which has a distinctive personality."

Select Reserve is a whisky that can be enjoyed equally before and after dinner; it has as many uplifting and refreshing aromas as relaxing and calming flavors. It is perhaps the embodiment of the Glenrothes philosophy: that maturity matters more than age. When launched, it was seen as a bold move, as the majority of single malts were sold with age statements. Irrespective of the age of the constituents, Select Reserve delivers the same Glenrothes character. Select Reserve is naturally colored and minimally filtered to retain the maximum flavor possible. It works well with the purity of tone associated with Miles Davis—try "Freddie Freeloader" or "Summertime." Alternatively, pair it with Art Pepper's "You'd Be So Nice To Come Home To." **MM**

Tasting notes

Juicy plum, orange zest, brioche, and calvados (actually calvados Domfrontais, made with 30 percent pear) on the nose. On the palate, creamy vanilla, then mixed peel and mixed nuts. Fresh but with good depth of flavor. The finish is lightly spicy—nutty and orangey.

Glenturret 10-Year-Old

Edrington Group
www.thefamousgrouseexperience.com

Region and country of origin Highlands, Scotland
Distillery Glenturret, Crieff, Perthshire
Alcohol content 40% abv
Style Single malt

Blended Scotch whisky still accounts for well over 90 percent of all whisky sales. Whisky-loving visitors to Scotland are therefore more likely to seek out the homes of Johnnie Walker, Ballantine's, Dewar's, or Teacher's than a distillery by name. Edrington, owners of the Famous Grouse brand, understand this only too well. At Glenturret distillery, close to Crieff in Perthshire, the company has constructed the Famous Grouse Experience, one of the industry's best examples of blended whisky. However, if you are more concerned with malt whisky than popular attractions, you might think that poor old Glenturret is a little bit overshadowed by the Famous Grouse Experience.

If you go there, take time to look around one of Scotland's oldest distilleries. Glenturret is a small, solid, old-fashioned, rustic Highland distillery, and its output is rarely available in the form of single-malt whisky. Several distilleries claim to be the oldest distillery in Scotland, but this one has a history that undoubtedly stretches back to the eighteenth century. The way they make malt here clearly counters the new wave of whisky makers who argue that Scotland has sacrificed quality for quantity. This handmade, traditional whisky is very underrated and is well worth seeking out. **DR**

Tasting notes

Distinctive sweet honey notes and some oily, savory ones, with a dose of rustic charm. Tannin, spice, and green fruits battle it out for dominance, and none wins.

Glenturret 19-Year-Old Malt Cask

Douglas Laing & Co. | www.douglaslaing.com / www.thefamousgrouse.com

Region and country of origin Highlands, Scotland
Distillery Glenturret, Crieff, Perthshire
Alcohol content 50% abv
Style Single malt

The Scottish Highlands stretch from the wild remote western coasts to small glens that are Speyside in all but name. It is hard to define a particular Highlands whisky style, but the word "rustic" frequently comes up. Sometimes the whiskies are slightly peaty, but not in a heavy, in-your-face, Islay style. Sometimes, as here, they are light and zesty, with hints of acetone on the nose. Frequently, they are complex, exciting whiskies, which improve significantly into their teens. Savory and earthy flavors come and go with raw speed.

The actual distillery at Glenturret is now totally overshadowed by the Famous Grouse Experience attraction that its owners have installed next door. However, Glenturret malt is one of the core ingredients in Famous Grouse, which might lead some to think it would be unremarkable on its own. But, like a shy little sister to an older, more outgoing brother, this 19-Year-Old has come out of its sibling's shadow and developed a complex and exciting character. The refill hogshead used for maturation provided a perfect environment without dominating the flavors, allowing the regional qualities to shine through. For anyone asking for a good introduction to a typical Highland style, this would be it. **AN**

Tasting notes

Very pale straw color for a whisky of its age. The nose is also light, with tropical fruits and hints of nail-polish remover. Explodes in the mouth with zesty flavors.

The Glenturret distillery cat, Towser, has caught a recorded 20,000 mice. ➡

Grand Macnish

Macduff International | www.macduffint.co.uk

Region and country of origin Scotland
Distilleries Various
Alcohol content 40% abv
Style Blend

Distilling whisky is a craft, whereas blending whisky is considered an art. Most blends as we know them today are composed of many single-malt whiskies and one or two grain whiskies, the former being made from malted barley only, the latter from corn or wheat.

Like Lauder's, Grand Macnish is a famous old brand acquired by MacDuff International. The original recipe for Grand Macnish contained over forty single malts and was concocted by Robert Macnish, who inherited his father John's tobacco shop and grocery in Glasgow in 1863. He decided to concentrate solely on blending and selling whisky. Having carefully developed a new mixture, he invited a group of friends to taste the product. They thought it "grand," and Robert decided to call his whisky Grand Macnish.

Robert's sons, John and George, expanded the company and moved its headquarters to London. The English had been forced to change from brandy to blended whisky after a phylloxera plague in France had decimated the vineyards and cognac was hard to obtain. (The phylloxera bug sucks the sap out of every grape it finds and had been imported accidentally on an American vine in the 1850s.) During the second half of the nineteenth century, many Scottish grocers became whisky blenders and liquor merchants, profiting from the expanding export drive to England.

Many brands would come and go, and only the strong and famous seem to have survived. Grand Macnish may not be the best-known among them, but it is certainly still around, thanks to three Scottish gentlemen with a passion for history in a bottle. **HO**

Tasting notes

The nose conjures thoughts of wildflowers: lavender and gorse. The malt and floral notes are pleasingly soft. Ginger and lemon furniture polish waft over canned pear, grape jelly, sweet caramel, breakfast cereal, and pound cake. Smooth, with a quiet, friendly finish.

Grant's 12-Year-Old

William Grant & Sons | www.grantswhisky.com

Region and country of origin Scotland
Distilleries Various
Alcohol content 40% abv
Style Blend

Grant's 12-Year-Old has a history of rebranding. For many years it existed as the twelve-year-old variant of Grant's Family Reserve blend, being marketed under a variety of names. In most export markets, it was sold as Grant's Dutch Royal, and in the Far East, as Old Gold.

In the United Kingdom, it was labeled Robbie Dhu, after the spring that provides Glenfiddich distillery with water, but few people outside the Highlands could pronounce the name accurately, and it was not immediately obvious that it came from the same stable as Family Reserve. Sales dwindled from some 150,000 cases to 20,000 in just five years.

Naming the blend Grant's 12-Year-Old reversed this decline, and its membership in the Grant's family of blends was emphasized by its presentation in the same distinctive triangular bottle used for Glenfiddich and Family Reserve.

Grant's 12-Year-Old varies from Family Reserve and its older siblings by being finished for three months in first-fill bourbon casks after the blending process has been completed, the component whiskies having first been allowed to "marry" for six months in Portuguese oak tuns. The 12-Year-Old was first prepared in this manner in 2003, when it was launched as part of the Grant's Cask Selection range.

A Grant's spokesperson noted, "They were the first premium blended whiskies to be doubly matured." Also, using ex-bourbon barrels "imparts an extra flavor layer, resulting in a complex whisky where individual tastes fit together perfectly to create a full-bodied Scotch of exceptional richness." **GS**

Tasting notes

Classic Family Reserve sweet, vanilla, and malt notes, allied with black currant and spice on the nose. Notably sweet on the rich, full palate, with the influence of the bourbon finish apparent in the vanilla, honey, and spice notes. Long, smooth, balanced, and warming finish.

Grant's
18-Year-Old

William Grant & Sons
www.grantswhisky.com

Region and country of origin Scotland
Distilleries Various
Alcohol content 40% abv
Style Blend

Introduced in its current format in 2003 as part of the same Grant's Cask Selection range that saw the 12-Year-Old finished in ex-bourbon casks for the first time, Grant's 18-Year-Old undergoes a final period of several months' maturation in ex-port casks after being blended and married.

As with the other Grant's blends, the 18-Year-Old is presented in a clear, triangular bottle, first used in 1957. The idiosyncratic, three-sided, clear Standfast bottle was described as being "the first Scotch bottle to be designed specifically to fit the human hand." It soon became well known through a series of print ads featuring Sir Compton Mackenzie, author of the novel *Whisky Galore*, made into a movie in 1949.

Like the rest of the Grant's blended whisky family, the 18-Year-Old contains a total malt content of around 35 percent, with Glenfiddich, Balvenie, and Kininvie at its core, although it also contains some twenty-two other malts, including a small proportion of Laphroaig from Islay, which gives the blend additional weight and a slight wisp of peat smoke. The actual recipe remains a closely guarded secret, kept under lock and key at William Grant & Sons' center at Strathclyde Business Park, near Glasgow. **GS**

Tasting notes

The nose is rich, nutty, and spicy, with malt, peat smoke, and a hint of red wine. Nice complexity. The palate offers spicy malt, sherry, port, peat, honey, and vanilla.

Grant's
25-Year-Old

William Grant & Sons
www.grantswhisky.com

Region and country of origin Scotland
Distilleries Various
Alcohol content 40% abv
Style Blend

Grant's 25-Year-Old was launched in 2010. According to company chairman Peter Gordon, "Grant's 25-Year-Old contains twenty-five whiskies from every region of Scotland, with the most unique element being our Girvan grain—the backbone of all our blends."

Included in the blend recipe is a quantity of the first whisky ever laid down at Grant's Girvan distillery in Ayrshire when it opened in 1964, along with rare whiskies from distilleries that are no longer in existence. Girvan grain distillery was constructed from scratch in a remarkable nine months, and the first spirit flowed on Christmas Day, 1963, mirroring the first distillation at Glenfiddich on Christmas Day, 1887.

Each individually numbered batch of the 25-Year-Old is married in oak tuns for six months to enhance depth and complexity. As it was launched in 2010, Grant's 25-Year-Old was linked in promotional material to the centenary of an epic, yearlong voyage undertaken during 1909/10 by Charles Gordon, son-in-law of founder William Grant & Sons. Gordon spent a year traveling to Australia and the East Asia, appointing agents and selling whisky, thereby laying the foundations for Grant's as a global brand; the company has built on them ever since. **GS**

Tasting notes

Mellow and balanced on the nose; warm, floral, and peachy. On the palate, fresh fruits, creamy spice, discreet vanilla, and oak. A finish of ginger and oak.

Grant's Cask Editions Ale Cask Finish

William Grant & Sons
www.grantswhisky.com

Region and country of origin Scotland
Distilleries Various
Alcohol content 40% abv
Style Blend

In 2001, William Grant & Sons introduced Grant's Sherry Cask Finish and Ale Cask Finish, the first blended Scotch whiskies to be given wood "finishes." Grant's Ale Cask Finish remains the only Scotch whisky to be finished in barrels that have previously held ale.

According to a Grant's spokesperson, "Master blender Brian Kinsman fills our casks with Edinburgh Ale for thirty days, then replaces it with aged Grant's whisky. The blend then mellows for up to four months, picking up its unique crème brûlée creaminess and silky malt flavors."

While Ale Cask Finish was itself innovative, it in turn spawned a new beer category. Dougal Sharp was brewer at Edinburgh's historic Caledonian brewery when an association was formed with William Grant & Sons to supply the distillery with ale casks. Sharp formulated a malty style of beer just for this purpose, and it was eventually discovered that when the beer was disgorged from the ex-whisky casks, it was itself extremely palatable.

Accordingly, in August 2003, Innis & Gunn Oak Aged Beer was launched in association with Grant's, although, in 2008, a management buyout gave the Sharp family control of the successful brand. **GS**

Tasting notes

Cereal, ripe eating apple, a hint of lemon, and a note of hops on the nose. The palate is soft and smooth, creamy, with peaches in syrup and lots of sweet malt.

Grant's Distillery Edition

William Grant & Sons
www.grantswhisky.com

Region and country of origin Scotland
Distilleries Various
Alcohol content 50% abv
Style Blend

This wonderful blend is marketed as "100 Proof Strength." Although it is only 50 percent abv, there is no need for anyone to alert the trading standards authorities: the apparent anomaly is explained by the fact that the United States—where most of this whisky is sold, and for whose bibbers the liquor is primarily packaged—uses different measurements of alcohol from the United Kingdom.

Grant's has no shortage of awards in its trophy cabinet—remember that it is the brain trust behind Glenfiddich, the world's best-selling brand. But it is the Distillery Edition that has won some of the most coveted prizes, perhaps the most prestigious of which is the gold medal that it carried off from the International Spirits Challenge in 2008.

According to Shakespeare in *As You Like It*, good wine needs no bush, and what goes for the grape may also be applied to this particular grain: word-of-mouth has built its reputation higher than any advertising could ever have achieved. Naturally, the exact method of preparation is a closely guarded secret, but one suspects that the keys to the Distillery Edition's success are the depth of flavor and intensity of taste, which come from it being non-chill-filtered. **GL**

Tasting notes

The opening aroma is a perfectly balanced mixture of malt and vanilla that is maintained on the palate and persists into the long and lingering finish.

Grant's Family Reserve

William Grant & Sons | www.grantswhisky.com

Region and country of origin Scotland
Distilleries Various
Alcohol content 40% abv
Style Blend

William Grant & Sons first blended whisky in 1898, a dozen years after members of the Grant family had built Glenfiddich distillery on the outskirts of Dufftown. Initial progress was slow, with William Grant's son-in-law Charles Gordon famously making 181 calls before selling his first case. However, the brand gradually built up a dedicated following at home and abroad, and today in terms of market share occupies fourth place on a global basis behind Johnnie Walker, Ballantine's and J&B. The blend, which carries no age statement, sells in more than 180 countries around the world.

Having been known until the 1980s as Grant's Standfast, after the Grant clan motto, "Standfast Craigellachie!," the blend is now called Grant's Family Reserve. The "new" name reflects the fact that William Grant & Sons remains a proudly independent company in family ownership, with founder William Grant's great-great-grandson, Peter Gordon, now the company chairman, and Master Distiller Brian Kinsman maintaining the high standard of Family Reserve.

At the heart of Family Reserve is malt whisky from Grant's distilleries of Glenfiddich, Balvenie, and Kininvie. In total, around twenty-five whiskies contribute to the blend. Ailsa Bay malt whisky from the Girvan distillery complex, commissioned in 2007, is now starting to play its part. The principal grain whisky used is William Grant's own Girvan brand, which, the distillers say, is "vacuum distilled at a lower temperature to make it a lighter and more delicate spirit." **GS**

Tasting notes

Malt, gentle oak, soft fruits, sweet sherry, and a hint of smoke on the nose. A firm mouth-feel, with vanilla, malt, almonds, raisins, and a hint of peat on the palate. Extremely well balanced. Caramel, cocoa and grain in the lingering, sweet finish.

Haig Gold Label

Diageo | www.diageo.com

Region and country of origin Scotland
Distilleries Various
Alcohol content 40% abv
Style Blend

In 1827, Irish distiller Robert Stein patented a still type that was capable of distilling continuously. It was no pot still as used by the Scottish Highlanders, but a kind of column. Another Irishman, Aeneas Coffey, improved the still and registered it in 1830. The column still, also known as a "Coffey still" was born, and from that moment, it was possible to distill whisky on a grand industrial scale.

This meant a boost for blended whisky, and one of the first blenders and column distillers was John Haig, who opened the famous Cameron Bridge grain distillery in 1824. He was a cousin of Robert Stein and must have acquired a wealth of knowledge of distilling and blending. It must have helped that his relative, Margaret Haig, married John Jameson, the famous Irish whiskey distiller, who would build the foundation on which Jameson whiskey grew to be the best-selling Irish brand worldwide. This doesn't mean John Haig was a newcomer in the business. It is rumored that his forefather, Robert Haig, was banned from church in 1665 for distilling on the day of rest.

Haig is one brand that benefited hugely from a successful advertising campaign. In the 1930s, Thomas Henry Egan wrote a slogan that to this day is one of the most successful in the business: "Don't be vague, ask for Haig." He is said to have received a case of whisky and £25 ($125) for it. Pretty impressive if you consider that an unopened bottle from that period now commands up to $620 (£400) at auction. Luckily, Haig Gold is still available today, for a price that is as accessible as the taste of this whisky. **HO**

Tasting notes

Inoffensive, certainly, but unimpressive on the nose, this is a light, easy-drinking blended whisky, with some barley-sugar candy, light, sweet lemon, and grapefruit on the palate, with a nice stab of oak and spice at its heart and a warming, vanilla, soft finish.

Hankey Bannister 12-Year-Old Regency

Inver House (International Beverage)
www.hankeybannister.com

Region and country of origin Scotland
Distilleries Various
Alcohol content 40% abv
Style Blend

Together with the version with no age statement, the Hankey Bannister 12-Year-Old is the big seller of the brand. The present owner, Inver House Distillers, bought the brand in 1988, along with their first distillery, Knockdhu. Four distilleries were later acquired—namely Pulteney, Balblair, Balmenach, and Speyburn—and malt whiskies from the five are now the backbone of the Hankey Bannister blend. Whiskies from other producers are included as well.

The malt whiskies in a blend are often divided into three categories, depending on their impact on the final flavor. Core malts, or signature malts, define the overall character; top-dressing malts are high-quality whiskies intended to add depth and top notes; and packers add bulk to the final blend without adding very much flavor. Stuart Harvey, Inver House's master blender, who has been responsible for blending Hankey Bannister since 2003, has a range of thirty-eight different single malts to play with. For every expression, he decides on twelve to fifteen malts and then adds three to four different grain whiskies. The ratio between malt and grain in Hankey Bannister, including the range's older versions, is 30:70. **IR**

Tasting notes

Citrusy on the nose but with floral notes: lilac, rose, and heather. Sweet on the palate but less honey than the unaged version. More spice (red chile) and orange.

Hankey Bannister 21-Year-Old Partners Reserve

Inver House (International Beverage)
www.hankeybannister.com

Region and country of origin Scotland
Distilleries Various
Alcohol content 40% abv
Style Blend

All Scotch whisky is required by law to mature in oak casks for a period of at least three years. Almost without exception, the casks are used to mature sherry, bourbon, or other spirits before they are filled with Scotch. A cask filled for the first time with Scotch is called a first-fill cask. If whisky is allowed to mature in a first-fill cask for more than thirteen or fourteen years, there is a risk of the oak overpowering the flavor of the whisky itself; another undesirable outcome is that the end result tastes more or less bitter.

For the Hankey Bannister 21-Year-Old (and still older versions), master blender Stuart Harvey therefore uses a higher proportion of what are called refill casks. These have been used to mature whisky two to three times, and over the years, the impact of the oak has reduced. This gives the whisky a chance to develop complexity and depth without absorbing excessive resinous wood notes from the oak.

Compared to the Hankey Bannister 12-Year-Old, the 21-Year-Old provides a beautiful example of the broader spectrum of flavors that appear in an older whisky. Whether the flavors are a sign of higher quality is up to the person who drinks it to decide. **IR**

Tasting notes

An unexpected nose, with freshly cut grass and fresh clams and mussels. A little spice, and a wave of strawberry and cream, burnt sugar, and some licorice.

Hankey Bannister 25-Year-Old Partnership

Inver House (International Beverage)
www.hankeybannister.com

Region and country of origin Scotland
Distilleries Various
Alcohol content 40% abv
Style Blend

Inver House master blender Stuart Harvey chooses from thirty-eight single-malt brands, which he divides into four categories. The first is a fruity/floral group with lots of esters and often hints of citrus and oranges; of the five distilleries owned by Inver House, Knockdhu belongs to this category. Next are heavy malts, which add body and depth and include Speyburn and Balmenach. Third are those that add spicy notes to the final blend, like Balblair. Fourth are whiskies that contribute sweetness; these include malt from Pulteney distillery, but Harvey doesn't stop there. To add body and depth, he chooses a grain whisky from Invergordon, Dumbarton, or North British. If he is looking for a lighter, fruity flavor, he will go for Girvan, Strathclyde, or Cameronbridge.

When creating a blended Scotch, some producers let the different whiskies marry together for a couple of months before bottling it. However, Harvey is of the opinion that it does not add to the final quality.

The Hankey Bannister 25-Year-Old is a limited edition and is not easy to find. Harvey has plans for more special versions and is looking at releases of different Hankey Bannister vintages. **IR**

Tasting notes

Intense grass and hay, honey on buttered toast. Tropical fruits (perhaps papaya and pineapple). On the palate, it is medium sweet, with just the slightest hint of peat.

Hankey Bannister 40-Year-Old

Inver House (International Beverage)
www.hankeybannister.com

Region and country of origin Scotland
Distilleries Various
Alcohol content 43.3% abv
Style Blend

Some whiskies are hard to approach objectively, and Hankey Bannister 40-Year-Old is a good example. Its sheer age is impressive, and it has been awarded Best Scotch Blend in the world, not once but for two years in a row. And if that were not enough, the blend contains rare whiskies from distilleries that closed in the 1970s and 1980s—Garnheath, Killyloch, and Glen Flagler. This is a whisky that deserves respect.

A limited edition of 1,917 crystal decanters, it was released in 2007 to celebrate the 250th anniversary of Hankey Bannister & Co. One thing, apart from the age, that differs from the other Hankey Bannister bottlings is that the whisky has matured for the full forty years as a blend. In 2005, master blender Stuart Harvey came across five casks in a Broxburn warehouse. Consulting the ledger, he found that the sherry butts actually contained blended whisky and were the remnants of a batch of Hankey Bannister that had been bottled as a 25-year-old in 1992. Harvey decided to release them as a 40-year-old in 2007.

Harvey has already spotted a few casks containing whisky that has matured for 48 years, so brace yourselves for a Hankey Bannister 50-Year-Old. **IR**

Tasting notes

Powerful. Cooked and preserved fruit. Black currant and a little minty. On the palate, cherry pie, almond pastry, and pear. Very complex, long, and balanced finish.

Hankey Bannister Original

Inver House (International Beverage)
www.hankeybannister.com

Region and country of origin Scotland
Distilleries Various
Alcohol content 40 or 43% abv, depending on market
Style Blend

The name of this blended Scotch goes back to the mid-eighteenth century, when Beaumont Hankey and Hugh Bannister established themselves in the wine and business trade, or so the story goes. The two gentlemen are strangely anonymous, and little is known of their lives. Apparently, it did not take long before Hankey Bannister & Co. catered to the finest families of London, and from there the firm conquered the rest of the British Empire.

It should be remembered that blended Scotch (a blend of grain whisky and malt whisky) did not exist in 1757 when the company was founded. It was not until 1860 that the Spirit Act was passed, allowing grain and malt to be mixed. The first known reference to Hankey Bannister blending Scotch is dated 1882. The complete range of Hankey Bannister today consists of five different bottlings, and the Original is the only one that doesn't carry an age statement. However, the grain whisky in the bottle is typically three years old, while the malt whiskies are four to five years old.

Hankey Bannister is not in the premier league of blended Scotch. It sells around 160,000 cases per year, which is roughly 1 percent of Johnnie Walker sales. But in whisky, figures are not everything. **IR**

Tasting notes

Fresh and citrusy, with a nice maltiness. On the palate, it evolves into sweet honey and the grain notes fade away. Smooth and mouthcoating. Fairly long finish.

Harris Highland Malt

Harris Whisky Co.
www.harriswhisky.com

Region and country of origin Highlands, Scotland
Distillery Undisclosed
Alcohol content 46% abv
Style Single malt

It was while entrepreneur Mark Harris was running the bar at Green's Restaurant in Mayfair, London—where the owner had chosen to invest in quality whisky—that he was able to build on his knowledge of malts. Since then, he has developed a consultancy business for restaurants and an upmarket "secret shopper" service for restaurateurs hoping to win a few Michelin stars. He stocked the bar in London's famous landmark building, the Gherkin. And, most recently, he has started buying up casks of malt whisky to launch under his stylish Harris Whisky label. He favors gentle and light whiskies, often at unusual ages; one of his best bottlings is a sherbety Tamdhu.

Harris Highland Malt, though, is a bit of a departure for him. It is quite common for independent bottlers to avoid conflict with the whisky companies by not using the distillery name on the bottle, and there is no way of knowing where this malt comes from. Indeed, there is nothing to prevent Harris from changing the distillery for each new batch, and, should you find a Harris Highland Malt, it may well taste quite different from the one described here. Does that matter? It would if the bottling varied significantly in quality. My bet is that it won't. **DR**

Tasting notes

The nose is shy and subtle, with some red berry fruit, delicate spice, and oak. The palate is fresh and clean, with a balance between sweet barley and savory notes.

← Winston Churchill, pictured here in 1943, favored Hankey Bannister whisky.

Hazelburn 8-Year-Old

J. & A. Mitchell Co. | www.springbankdistillers.com

Region and country of origin Highlands, Scotland
Distillery Springbank, Campbeltown, Argyll
Alcohol content 46% abv
Style Single malt

Hazelburn was first bottled as a limited-edition 8-year-old in 2005, and so successful was it that the 6,000 bottles sold out within a matter of weeks. The following year, Hazelburn became a permanent feature of the Springbank distillery portfolio, and in 2009, a 12-year-old variant joined the range.

Like Longrow, the Hazelburn brand takes its name from one of Campbeltown's many "lost" distilleries. With Glengyle having been revived in 2004, there are now only three active distilleries, although in the past distilling has taken place on no fewer than thirty-four sites within the Royal Burgh.

Of Campbeltown's lost distilleries, Hazelburn in the Longrow area was ultimately the largest and most significant. The first record of its existence dates from 1825, though distilling may well have taken place earlier. In 1845, with business booming, a new, enlarged Hazelburn distillery was constructed in Millknowe Street. The new plant boasted no fewer than nine 6,000-gallon (23,000-liter) washbacks and three stills, and its 7,000-gallon (26,500-liter) wash still was the largest in Campbeltown.

The twentieth century brought a sharp decline in the fortunes of Campbeltown as a whisky-making center, and distilling ceased at Hazelburn in 1925. Two years later, the distillery was absorbed into the Distillers Company Ltd (DCL), and Hazelburn's extensive warehousing continued to be utilized for the maturation of whisky from a number of DCL distilleries until 1983. Today, only a comparatively small section of the Hazelburn complex survives. **GS**

Tasting notes

A relatively light, fruity, faintly resinous nose, with developing lemongrass and floral notes. Sherbet, malt, and vanilla on the attractive, sweet, and lively palate, which also features some flecks of brine. Spicy oak, black pepper, and a hint of smoke in the finish.

Hazelburn CV

J. & A. Mitchell Co. | www.springbankdistillers.com

Region and country of origin Highlands, Scotland
Distillery Springbank, Campbeltown, Argyll
Alcohol content 46% abv
Style Single malt

Hazelburn is one of three different single-malt whiskies produced by the family firm of J. & A. Mitchell Co. in their historic Springbank distillery, situated in the heart of the ancient port and distilling center of Campbeltown. While Springbank whisky is effectively "two-and-a-half-times" distilled, and Longrow whisky is double-distilled and heavily peated, Hazelburn differs from its stablemates by being unpeated and triple-distilled. Springbank distillery operates its own floor maltings, and the malt destined for Hazelburn is air-dried, with no peat being burned in the kiln.

According to a company spokesperson, "Instead of using the conventional double-distillation method, Springbank boasts three stills and operates a form of partial triple-distillation. The wash is pumped into a wash still, where the liquid is boiled. The resulting distillate produced, called low wines, is transferred to the low wines still, where it is boiled a second time. The product of this distillation, called feints, is then transferred to the spirit still, from which the spirit 'cut' is collected. At Springbank, the wash still is fired from the bottom by live flame, and the spirit stills are heated by steam coils from inside. It is thought Springbank is the only distillery in Scotland to do this."

Hazelburn is the youngest of the trio of malts to be made at Springbank and was first produced in 1997. The initial bottling took place in 2005, and maturation of Hazelburn spirit occurs in a mix of ex-sherry and ex-bourbon casks. The CV variant of Hazelburn carries no age statement and was introduced in 2010. **GS**

Tasting notes

Initially slightly herbal on the nose, with acetone and cigarette packet. Citrusy and malty with time. Orange, ginger, vanilla, and sherbet zest on the spicy palate. The finish is medium in length and spicy, with a slight suggestion of salt. A fresh, breezy, aperitif whisky.

Highland Park 12-Year-Old

Edrington Group | www.highlandpark.co.uk

Region and country of origin Islands, Scotland
Distillery Highland Park, Kirkwall, Orkney
Alcohol content 40% abv
Style Single malt

Highland Park is one of the truly iconic whisky distilleries, a *premier cru* malt maker producing whisky that is both wonderful to drink and lucrative to collect. The most northerly distillery in Scotland, it is situated in the middle of nowhere in the Orkneys—a series of islands that are wet, windy, and inhospitable, although warm both in terms of the climate and the people.

Making whisky here requires the investment of considerable time and effort to bring the raw ingredients to the island and to take the finished whisky and waste products away. But the owners, Edrington, does it brilliantly. For example, while other companies struggle to find sherry casks, Highland Park has them in droves. Indeed, it is thought that the company buys 95 percent of Scotland's sherry casks—not surprising when you consider the needs of The Macallan within the group.

Sherry casks are crucial to this 12-Year-Old. In fact, the percentage of first-fill sherry casks has gone up from 20 to 40 percent in recent years. But if sherry is one key ingredient in the Highland Park taste, the other is peat cut from the local Hobbister Moor. This whisky has sweet and honeyed tones, but just enough wood and smoke to keep it all interesting. **DR**

Tasting notes

Honeyed and fruity on the nose, with a hint of peat. The taste is a delightful blend of orange, red berry, rich vanilla, and honey followed by smoke and oak.

Highland Park 15-Year-Old

Edrington Group | www.highlandpark.co.uk

Region and country of origin Islands, Scotland
Distillery Highland Park, Kirkwall, Orkney
Alcohol content 40% abv
Style Single malt

It is often assumed that to make an older expression of a whisky, you simply take one version and age it for longer. But Highland Park 15-Year-Old is made in a totally different way from the 12-Year-Old. Here, the amount of American sherry oak is much higher than the European sherry oak used in the 12-Year-Old.

Highland Park's global marketing manager Gerry Tosh explains, "We often talk about whether sherry or bourbon was in the cask, but it's just as important to look at the trees that made the cask. European oak trees grow slowly and twist and turn as they try to take advantage of the sun, so the grain is looser and the spirit can get into the wood more during maturation. American oak trees go from harsh, sharp winters to boiling-hot summers, so they shoot up quickly, as straight as pencils, and the grain is much tighter. People also assume that European oak is used for sherry and American oak for bourbon, but lots of sherries are normally matured in American oak."

The result is a more citrusy, drier, and smokier style of Highland Park, making it much more of a love-it-or-hate-it whisky. Introduced in 2002, it is sold in small batches in different countries at different times, and commands great loyalty among its followers. **DR**

Tasting notes

The nose is unassertive and offers few clues about the taste, but the palate delivers grapefruity citrus, vanilla, and smoke. It's an oddball Highland Park.

← Barley germinates on the drying floor at Highland Park distillery.

Highland Park 18-Year-Old

Edrington Group | www.highlandpark.co.uk

Region and country of origin Islands, Scotland
Distillery Highland Park, Kirkwall, Orkney
Alcohol content 43% abv
Style Single malt

Seasoned rock band U2, Jamaican sprinter Usain Bolt, the New Zealand All Blacks rugby side, champion Formula 1 team Ferrari, the Australian cricket team, FC Barcelona—they all excel at what they do, but being regarded as the very best in their field takes some living up to. Heroes they may be, but inevitably there are times when even heroes let you down.

In the world of whisky, Highland Park 18-Year-Old has been described, ad nauseam, as the best whisky in the world, as well as the world's best whisky all-rounder. So is it? The latter claim is probably true, but on what grounds would it follow that it is the world's best? The problem with such tags is that they become both a blessing and a curse.

Anyone approaching this whisky and expecting a fireworks display, acrobatic act, and the Edinburgh Tattoo rolled into one will inevitably be disappointed. When all is said, the 18-Year-Old is just a whisky, and taste is highly subjective. Is it a fantastic malt? Undoubtedly. But this writer would say that, far from being the best whisky in the world, it is not even the best whisky from this distillery. That said, a very strong case may be made for the "best all-rounder" tag.

First introduced in the late 1990s, it is one of the world's best-selling 18-year-olds. It is made up of a whopping 60 percent first-fill Spanish sherry oak, and is bottled at 43 percent abv, unusual for the distillery. "It just seems to work perfectly at this strength," says global marketing manager Gerry Tosh. "It has been at that strength from the outset... at that strength everything clicks into place." **DR**

Tasting notes

If malt whisky is made up of five segments—oak, spice, peat, fruit, and honey/sweetness—then this is indeed the perfect all-rounder, with each of the share in perfect proportion to each other. This is exceptional, rich, full, and just oaky and smoky enough to satisfy the palate.

Highland Park 21-Year-Old

Edrington Group | www.highlandpark.co.uk

Region and country of origin Islands, Scotland
Distillery Highland Park, Kirkwall, Orkney
Alcohol content 47.5% abv
Style Single malt

Few businesses rely on crystal-ball gazing as much as whisky making does, and while the creation of whisky is an art, making a business out of it is a highly skilled science, and an imprecise one at that.

Apart from the obvious logistical problems caused by running a business for years on end with all the costs of high production and no immediate prospect of revenue, there are other big questions about demand and supply. For example, one distillery chose to produce spirit for one month and then shut down for the next three. Years later, it did a brilliant marketing job when it released that whisky, selling out everything it had in a day or so; it then upset everybody by being unable to supply anything for weeks. When it was able to resume supply, all media interest in the whisky had gone away.

Big questions have to be answered about how young to sell the first malt, how much to lay down for the future and for how many years, and so on. The Highland Park 21-Year-Old is a case in point. A few years ago, this author was one of the judges who voted it the best malt in the world in the World Whisky Awards—only to be told that, for complicated contractual reasons, there was not enough stock to keep it at 47.5 percent abv, so it was to be relaunched at a far less impressive 40 percent.

However, Edrington saved stock for two years and, in late 2011, restored it to its original strength. This, then, is the distillery's best bottling, and a world champion to boot. High in American sherry casks, but only 20 percent of them first-fill, it works a treat. **DR**

Tasting notes

One of the world's greatest-tasting whiskies, with perfectly weighted honey, fruit, spice, peat, and oak. The extra wood makes this preferable to the 18-Year-Old. As good as malt whisky gets—but make sure your bottle is at 47.5 percent and not 40 percent abv.

Highland Park 25-Year-Old

Edrington Group | www.highlandpark.co.uk

Region and country of origin Islands, Scotland
Distillery Highland Park, Kirkwall, Orkney
Alcohol content 48.1% abv
Style Single malt

No matter what some spokespeople within the industry might suggest, whiskies vary from batch to batch, and the smaller the batch, the more obvious the variation. At Highland Park, no one pretends that the whiskies are unvarying, but they do work hard at achieving consistency. The phenolic content of the peat, for instance, does not change, but what does change is the degree of sweetness.

"There is a difference between a European oak cask and an American oak cask," says global marketing manager Gerry Tosh. "European oak creates a sweeter whisky, so when Highland Park is matured in American oak, some think they're tasting a more peaty whisky, but they're not; it's just a less sweet one."

Tosh describes this as a "nice car mechanic" of a whisky, as opposed to the "sweet old lady" that is the distillery's 30-Year-Old. It is, he says, a proper Orcadian whisky. "When you first come to Orkney, and you've had a rough journey, and it's wet and windy, it gives you quite a fright," he says. "Get past that, though, and you will find this a remarkable place, with friendly people, and incredible in so many ways. And you fall in love with it. It's among the most incredible places on the planet. Well that's this whisky."

Made up of 60 percent first-fill sherry casks, this is the hardest Highland Park to get right because it walks a knife-edge tastewise. It changes dramatically with water, swinging rapidly from a bruising, sherried whisky to a much more delicate, grapefruity one, so you have to treat it very carefully. Lauded by many, it's another big hitter—a bruiser but a loveable one. **DR**

Tasting notes

Without water, there is an explosion of red and orange fruits, together with big, rich peat and oak. With water added, the citrusy, fresher notes come through. This is a big whisky, a point made abundantly clear by the generous oak and spice.

Highland Park 30-Year-Old

Edrington Group | www.highlandpark.co.uk

Region and country of origin Islands, Scotland
Distillery Highland Park, Kirkwall, Orkney
Alcohol content 48.1% abv
Style Single malt

It would be hard to imagine a bigger contrast than the one between this pretty and delicate whisky and the big bruising malt that is the Highland Park 25-Year-Old. Global marketing manager Gerry Tosh has described this as a sweet little old lady, whom you could talk to all day, an altogether more gentle and soft malt than its younger sibling. No two whiskies show off the difference between American oak and European oak, and first-fill and refill casks, more convincingly than these two. The 30-Year-Old has no whisky from first-fill casks and is mainly from American oak—the opposite of the 25-Year-Old's provenance.

The wood of the cask is a big influence on flavor, of course, but peat is another major factor. Just as oak varies, so does peat. In its flavor, this whisky is a long, long way from Islay. Indeed, you could say that the taste of Highland Park owes much to the Orkney wind.

Gerry Tosh explains, "If you were to take a time-travel machine and go back 3,000 years, then Orkney would not look much different to now. Because of the wind, there are very few trees, so the peat of today is made up of heather from back then. Our peat burns bright white and is sweet and smoky. Islay, on the other hand, would have been covered in trees, and in the peat there are roots, acorns, nuts, and all sorts. Burning the peat there gives the classic Islay iodine notes associated with its peaty whiskies."

This is a sophisticated and appealing gem, the easygoing, relaxed, older sister to the 18-Year-Old. Thirty years is a long time in whisky terms, but Highland Park has ensured it was worth the wait. **DR**

Tasting notes

A weird and wonderful whisky. Old oak brings an astringency and hard-hitting tannin attack, while the malt delicately travels into citrus marmalade territory. The two strands bicker and clash, but are saved from some oiliness and honey is somewhere in the mix, too.

Highland Park 40-Year-Old

Edrington Group | www.highlandpark.co.uk

Region and country of origin Islands, Scotland
Distillery Highland Park, Kirkwall, Orkney
Alcohol content 48.3% abv
Style Single malt

For its age, this is a relatively full and smoky malt, and one that shows off its region's wispy, lighter peat style. Global marketing manager Gerry Tosh argues that Orkney's ancient peat owes its light and sweet character to the absence of tree material in its makeup. The Orkneys are also subject to constant winds, but this particular expression seems to be a product of the rare windless days, when smoke gently peating the barley was not blown away and therefore imparted a bigger, smokier flavor than normal.

"In those days, we weren't making single-malt whisky at all," he says. "Everything went for blending and had to be to a tight specification. If the malt was too smoky, the blenders didn't want it, so it would have been put in casks and stored away." That's good news for us, because this is a delight. The Orkney Isles may be wet and windy, but they're in the Gulf Stream, so the temperature is quite mild. Maturation is stately and consistent—which explains why the distillery can boast so much old stock. The loss of spirit to the angels is about 1 percent—half of what it is in other parts of Scotland. So, whereas many Scottish casks have lost half their contents after twenty-five years, at Highland Park the loss is only a quarter. **DR**

Tasting notes

Honey, spice, fruit, and peat are pretty much in place even at this age, though it's oak that dominates here. This is both a fragile old man and a big-hearted bruiser.

Highland Park 50-Year-Old 1960

Edrington Group | www.edrington.co.uk

Region and country of origin Islands, Scotland
Distillery Highland Park, Kirkwall, Orkney
Alcohol content 44.8% abv
Style Single malt

It is hard to imagine how those at Highland Park must have felt when they found the casks of whisky used to create their first-ever 50-year-old. How do you "lose" five casks of whisky in the first place? Maybe Highland Park has "the dunnage warehouse time forgot."

Highland Park 50-Year-Old is the oldest whisky to be released from the renowned Orkney distiller. Its existence places it in the super elite league of distilleries that have the stock and quality of spirit to enable them to release a fifty-year-old whisky. Nowadays, with global demand for Scotch being so great, most distillers emptied their aged casks many years ago and are in no position to produce enough spirit to let it sleep in a cask for fifty years. And even if demand were not at an all-time high, many whiskies naturally reach their perfect drinking age a long time before their fiftieth birthday.

For those who haven't managed to get one of the 275 bottles from this release (or, probably the great majority of drinkers, who cannot afford one), Highland Park is expecting some 1964 casks to be ready for release in 2014. Or maybe the whisky will stay in the casks a little longer, to be released as a 52-year-old. Just how good could the whisky get? **AS**

Tasting notes

Big, deep, dark, and complex. Jamaica cake and orange liqueur. Raisin, dried prune, and sweet fig. Caramelized sugar gives way to dark chocolate, spice, and smoke.

Scottish artist Maeve Gillies designed the 50-Year-Old's silver "cage."

Highland Park 1970 Orcadian Vintage

Edrington Group | www.edrington.co.uk

Region and country of origin Islands, Scotland
Distillery Highland Park, Kirkwall, Orkney
Alcohol content 48% abv
Style Single malt

Clearly, Highland Park is trying to keep things fresh with its third Orcadian Vintage release, which hit the market in September 2010. The northernmost Scottish distiller tends to get it just right when it comes to its limited releases, and in part the success of this hugely popular distillery is a result of that.

Innovation is one of the few true cornerstones of any business. In whisky making, it is often difficult to be new and fresh because the rules governing Scotch dictate that distillers operate within very tight boundaries. But Highland Park is exceptionally good at innovation, constantly generating new interest from eager consumers while keeping an eye firmly on its existing customers and collectors, too.

The 1964 and 1968 Orcadian Vintages were successful enough for Highland Park to continue the series, and the distillery is considering another ten releases on top of the three currently available. Highland Park seems to have a knack with its limited editions, and they have become very popular. When the Earl Haakon 18-Year-Old was released, every bottle sold out within a day. They are now selling on the secondary market for anything up to $620 (£400), a healthy gain from the retail price of $250 (£160).

So, by catering to the drinkers' market, the mid-priced collectors' market (with the earlier Ambassador casks and Earl Magnus releases), as well as the top-end collectors' market (the Orcadian Vintages), Highland Park seems to have all commercial angles covered and just keeps going from strength to strength. Long may its prosperity continue! **AS**

Tasting notes

There is a sweet element of natural honey. As expected, this is lighter than the 1964. A heady mixture of resinous pine, wood notes, vanilla, and mild peat smoke, all present in varying quantities. This opens up to floral elements and a faint thread of geranium.

Highland Park 1968 Orcadian Vintage

Edrington Group | www.edrington.co.uk

Region and country of origin Islands, Scotland
Distillery Highland Park, Kirkwall, Orkney
Alcohol content 45.6% abv
Style Single malt

So, what's in a year, such as the 1968 of this bottle? The answer is that Scotch whisky with a vintage (year of distillation) always seems to become more collectable and attract more interest from buyers. When working out what makes a bottle of whisky collectable or, going even further, makes it investment-grade, the need for a vintage is right up there at the top of the list, along with getting the right distillery, whether it's natural or cask strength, and the scarcity of the bottles. So far, so good, as Highland Park 1968 Orcadian Vintage ticks all those boxes. This, the second Orcadian Vintage release from Highland Park, yielded 1,550 bottles and costs $3,500 (£2,300), a whole $2,400 (£1,540) less than the 1964 Orcadian Vintage. That's a saving of just over $590 (£380) per year of vintage. But it is still an expensive dram.

It is arguable that drinkers get a little too hung up on the year of distillation. After all, the presence of a vintage doesn't necessarily reflect a better quality of Scotch; a 1960 vintage whisky is effectively only three years old if it was released in the early 1960s. Also, whisky, unlike wine, tends not to have good years and bad years; in Scotland, the weather is fairly constant. But vintage whisky clearly tends to be older than a distillery's standard release, and with this age comes rarity, and with rarity comes an increase in cost.

So is this 1968 vintage any worse than the 1964 Orcadian release? It is just different. The Orcadian Vintage whiskies carry a high price tag, but they do represent an opportunity to try some of Highland Park's oldest and rarest whisky. **AS**

Tasting notes

Highland Park's trademark honeyed sweetness is evident, with an element of earthy freshness. A tiny ping of lime pickle. Mixed candied peel, gingersnap, and warm shortbread. Lovely, spicy, mint notes evolve into an exceptionally well-balanced whisky.

Highland Park 1964 Orcadian Vintage

Edrington Group | www.edrington.co.uk

Region and country of origin Islands, Scotland
Distillery Highland Park, Kirkwall, Orkney
Alcohol content 42.4% abv
Style Single malt

The 1964 was one of the first two Highland Park Orcadian Vintages released in 2009. It promises to be an outstanding experience for the wealthy consumer.

For both a whisky drinker and a whisky collector, Highland Park is an iconic distillery. But is the spirit worthy of the price tag? The original price of $5,950 (£3,830) for a bottle of Scotch is above most people's budgets, and clearly this should be viewed as an ultra-premium luxury item. Even an experienced whisky investor and a big Highland Park collector, who is not averse to spending a reasonable amount of cash on a bottle to drink or add to the collection, might consider this to be a step too far.

The vast majority of whisky drinkers will not purchase this bottle for the simple reason that they can't justify spending that amount of money on a bottle of Scotch to drink. And a whisky investor might see short- and medium-term potential in other bottles. The reason they might not see a good investment potential in the 1964 Orcadian Vintage could be because the price is above the market's evaluation. It hasn't sold out yet, even though only 290 bottles were yielded by two casks. it is an incredibly rare whisky that has all the right ingredients to be a collector's gem… but it's just a little costly.

Having said that, in years to come the market will catch up. Inevitably, it always does. When this happens, the bottle should start to represent a good bet as an investment. Until then, if you can afford to buy this stunning vintage old whisky, then crack it open and savor every last drop! **AS**

Tasting notes

Lusciously rich, with stewed fruits and spiced apple strudel. The oak makes a welcome appearance but does not dominate. Vanilla and mulled spices appear as the whisky reveals itself with a drop of water. Truly a whisky that dreams are made of.

Highland Park Hjärta 12-Year-Old

Edrington Group | www.edrington.co.uk

Region and country of origin Islands, Scotland
Distillery Highland Park, Kirkwall, Orkney
Alcohol content 58.1% abv
Style Single malt

Hjärta was launched in 2009 as a limited-edition (3,924 bottles) cask-strength expression by Highland Park to celebrate the opening of the Orkney distillery's newly refurbished visitor's center, and to acknowledge the brand's Scandinavian heritage.

Hjärta means "heart" in Old Norse, and the use of the name emphasizes the close historical ties between Scandinavia and the Orkney islands. Indeed, Orkney was under Nordic rule until 1468; the islands passed to Scotland when King James III of Scotland was betrothed to Margaret, daughter of King Christian I of Denmark and Norway.

Jason Craig, global controller of Highland Park at the time of Hjärta's launch, declares that, "Throughout past and present-day history, Orkney's links with Scandinavia remain strong, and this is reflected within our visitor center and this recent addition to the Highland Park product portfolio. When you make the journey to the Highland Park distillery, all that history seeps through... I believe that we have captured that through the very essence of Hjärta."

The Hjärta icon on the bottle, designed by Andy Bowman of Mountain Design in Glasgow, was inspired by ancient Viking stone carvings found on Orkney.

According to a distillery spokesperson, "The newly refurbished five-star visitor's center at the Highland Park distillery brings the integral relationship between Orkney and Scandanavia to life. The Hjärta icon is featured prominently in the visitor's center, the heart and home of this world-renowned and award-winning single malt." **GS**

Tasting notes

A sweet, buttery nose, featuring orange fondant cream, heather, and a suggestion of sweet smoke. The smoke is more overt when water is added, along with a hint of rubbery sherry. Smooth, aromatic, and spicy on the palate, with lemon, coconut, and smoke.

Highland Park
Vintage 21-Year-Old

Edrington Group
www.edrington.co.uk

Region and country of origin Islands, Scotland
Distillery Highland Park, Kirkwall, Orkney
Alcohol content 46.7% abv
Style Single malt

Highland Park has a disproportionate number of sherry casks, but its output isn't just about sherry. The Orkney distillery has casks of old, bourbon-matured malt, and has been releasing small-batch, vintage bottlings that vary massively in flavor, from light and delicate grapefruit marmalade to big, citrus and berry fruit, to monsters of oak and peat. The variation is often quite extreme, and there were rumblings a while ago when the 25-year-old changed from a big, oaky, smoky extension of the 18-year-old into a fresh, citrusy, delicate old man of a whisky.

In recent years, the owners of the Highland Park brand have released a selection of vintages from some of the older casks. At one point, the company released two whiskies at the same time: one was light and citrusy; the other was a great imitation of a bold, peaty, seaweedy, beach-barbecue malt from Islay.

This is a whisky to confront the Highland Park aficionado. From the start, it's undoubtedly a challenge to the taste buds, and it's not an easy ride. If you love Highland Park, this might be like your favorite rock band teaming up with a rapper—a bit of a shock, but in the end a total treat. It'll cost you, though; this retails at about $3,000 (£1,900) a bottle. **DR**

Tasting notes

There is a wall of tannin, chile, and peat to overcome without water. With a few drops, expect coffee, lots of sherry, hot winter punch, and some tropical fruit.

Imperial
29-Year-Old

Wm Cadenhead & Co.
www.wmcadenhead.com

Region and country of origin Speyside, Scotland
Distillery Imperial, Carron by Aberlour, Banffshire
Alcohol content 54.7% abv
Style Single malt

Like so many of Scotland's more recently "lost" distilleries, Imperial was established during the "golden decade" of Speyside whisky expansion, being constructed in 1897–98, just as the great Victorian whisky boom was coming to an end. Unusually, it was built not from stone but from Aberdeen red brick on an iron framework. It owes its unusual name to patriotism inspired by Queen Victoria's Diamond Jubilee (1897), and its maltings even boasted a large, gilded, cast-iron crown until it became badly rusted and was finally removed in 1955.

No whisky was made between 1925 and 1955. A major rebuilding program after 1955 included a doubling of the stills from two to four in 1964–65. Imperial ceased production in 1985, and four years later it was sold to Allied Distillers. Distilling recommenced in 1991, but seven years later the site was silent once again. When the Allied Distillers' empire was sold off in 2005, Imperial came under the ownership of Chivas Brothers. Although most of the plant remains intact, the future of Imperial distillery is uncertain; there are proposals to redevelop the site.

Bottled as a part of Cadenhead's Chairman's Stock series, this expression was distilled in 1977. **GS**

Tasting notes

The nose is initially quite sour, with a touch of burnt plastic and old vegetables. But on the palate, elegant and creamy, herbal, with spice, vanilla, and milky coffee.

Imperial's oblique introduction to the "velveted" whisky concept. ➡

A Bearish whiskey wouldn't be much fun!

That's why Imperial is *"velveted"*

"Velveting" takes out "gruffness"—makes IMPERIAL smooth, gentle, a real experience in enjoyment. Yes, "velveting" gives IMPERIAL the easy-to-take goodness that has made this whiskey one of America's greats, one of the most-wanted whiskies in all the land.

But like sugar and coffee, IMPERIAL is on quota—because our stills are now making war alcohol instead of whiskey.

And sometimes delivery is held up a day or so, because shipments of war materials and food naturally come first.

So if your store or tavern sometimes cannot supply you with IMPERIAL, please be patient and remember there is a mighty good reason for it.

Eighty-six proof. 70% grain neutral spirits. Copyright 1943, Hiram Walker & Sons Inc., Peoria, Illinois.

A BLENDED WHISKEY

IMPERIAL The *"velveted"* whiskey

REG. U S PAT OFF

Imperial
1997

Gordon & MacPhail
www.gordonandmacphail.com

Region and country of origin Speyside, Scotland
Distillery Imperial, Carron by Aberlour, Banffshire
Alcohol content 61.6% abv
Style Single malt

This expression of Imperial has been matured in first-fill sherry casks and bottled at cask strength in Gordon & MacPhail's Cask Strength range. It was distilled shortly after Imperial came back into production following one of its not infrequent "silent" periods. Indeed, the distillery was under threat of demolition in 2005, and only the acquisition of Allied Domecq by Chivas Brothers that year put the destruction on hold.

While several other closed distilleries have been resurrected in recent times, Imperial is less attractive to potential operators due to the sheer scale of the plant. To make decent whisky, Imperial needs to be run at full capacity, and producing bulk quantities of a single malt with no brand reputation is not an attractive option for most entrepreneurs.

This is not to say that Imperial is a poor quality dram, just that its destination was always the blending vats. According to Arthur Motley of retailer Royal Mile Whiskies, "Imperial drinks very well young, so we can drink it at affordable prices. There's loads of decent, affordable Imperial around. It's grassy, fruity, and quite robust. People are buying it because they like to consume it, rather than keep it. At ten to twenty years old, it is really good." **GS**

Tasting notes

Rounded and sweet in the mouth, with stewed fruits, creamy-smooth and quite full-bodied. Aniseed and black pepper appear in the medium-length finish.

Imperial
1997 Octave

Royal Mile Whiskies
www.royalmilewhiskies.com

Region and country of origin Speyside, Scotland
Distillery Imperial, Carron by Aberlour, Banffshire
Alcohol content 53.2% abv
Style Single malt

In 2010, Edinburgh-based retailer Royal Mile Whiskies marketed just seventy-two bottles of 1997 Imperial single malt that had spent the last three months of its maturation period in an octave-sized former sherry cask. The whisky received rave reviews.

This exclusive release was part of Huntly-based Duncan Taylor & Co. Ltd's ongoing work with octave casks, each of which holds around 13 gallons (50 liters). The theory of using such small casks is that maturation is accelerated, due to the relatively high contact between contents and oak. Duncan Taylor's managing director Euan Shand recalls, "Many years ago, I made small casks as a cooper at Glendronach distillery… I remember filling them with whatever malts I could lay my hands on from the local off license. After a few months' maturation, the resultant spirit was totally unlike what had come out of the bottle. In fact it was hugely better—it was invigorated!"

A Royal Mile Whiskies spokesperson noted that "The cask was an already very good Imperial 1997 of a light gold, almost slightly greeny color. After just three months in the octave cask it had turned a delightful toffee color and the nose and palate was transformed with this extra layer of heavy maltiness and spice." **GS**

Tasting notes

Aromas of pine, clove, and malt vie with vanilla, poached pear in cream, and freshly mown lawn. On the palate, green apple, lively oak, and dark chocolate.

Inchgower
21-Year-Old Malt Cask

Douglas Laing & Co.
www.douglaslaing.com

Region and country of origin Speyside, Scotland
Distillery Inchgower, Buckie, Banffshire
Alcohol content 50% abv
Style Single malt

In the world of wine, much store is set by the "terroir," or locality in which the wine is made and matured, and there is much debate as to how far the same effect occurs in single malts. Under particular scrutiny is the salty taste of some coastal malts, as well as the seaweedy iodine taste from Islay. Is it possible that elements present in the air can somehow permeate the oak of the cask over many years?

Inchgower is regarded by one famous whisky writer as the most attractively built distillery in the whole of Scotland. Once you are past the ranks of warehouses in front, the buildings themselves look more like a highland farmstead than an industrial plant, 99 percent of whose output goes into the Bell's, Johnnie Walker, and White Horse blends. If you seek out some of the remaining one per cent bottled as single malt, especially this whisky, distilled in 1986 and matured in a simple refill hogshead for twenty-one years, you will find some of the most attractive whisky about, pretty and beguiling. Perhaps the beauty of the buildings has found its way into the casks?

This should be good news, too, for other malts, as the extensive on-site warehousing is home to 60,000 casks brought to this spot by Diageo. **AN**

Tasting notes

Grass and fruit on the nose—a bowl of strawberries eaten in a sunny field. Sweet, buttery maple syrup at first, then an exquisitely scented tropical fruit cocktail.

Invergordon
10-Year-Old

Whyte & Mackay
www.whyteandmackay.co.uk

Region and country of origin Highlands, Scotland
Distillery Invergordon, Invergordon, Ross-shire
Alcohol content 40% abv
Style Single grain

The following might be heard in whisky shops across the world: "Good morning," says the customer, "I'm looking for a bottle of whisky, preferably something a little bit different." The assistant replies, "Might I suggest a bottle of grain whisky?" The conversation stalls, and the customer's brow furrows slightly. "Grain whisky?" he asks. "Isn't all whisky grain whisky?" Here, the sales assistant tries to explain that grain whiskies may be made with a variety of grains, including corn, wheat, rye, and unmalted barley, in a continuous process that is markedly different from malt whisky.

Grain whisky is highly misunderstood. Most customers don't really know what it is, let alone ever having tried it. But grain whisky is now being actively promoted as a whisky style of its own, helped in no small part by companies such as Compass Box and Cooley, who have released high-quality expressions of their own, such as Hedonism and Greenore. The Invergordon distillery is the only grain distillery in the Highlands. Based in the Cromarty Firth, a few miles east of the Dalmore distillery, it was commissioned in 1959 to create work after the departure of the Royal Navy from the area. This light and fruity 10-Year-Old was first released in 1990. **PB**

Tasting notes

Light, soft, and delicate on the nose. On the palate, a delightful mixture of sweetness and freshness. An unexpected burst of intensity on the finish.

Invergordon 1972 Duncan Taylor Rare Auld 38-Year-Old

Duncan Taylor & Co.
www.duncantaylor.com

Region and country of origin Highlands, Scotland
Distillery Invergordon, Invergordon, Ross-shire
Alcohol content 42.1% abv
Style Single grain

Invergordon distillery overlooks the Cromarty Firth in its native Ross-shire, and is a huge distillery capable of producing volumes of spirit that most other distilleries can only dream of. It also has its own pipe band, and a fairly prolific one at that, having released recordings since the 1960s. A skirl of bagpipes with your dram, sir? Well, don't mind if I do, thank you!

There is no doubt that Invergordon grain whisky plays a significant part in the making of Whyte & Mackay's range of blends, as the latter is the parent company of the distillery. However, Invergordon single grain is an elusive beastie to locate in its pure form. If you ever have a chance to try an independent bottler's take on it, as you do here, don't miss it.

For any spirit, the benefit of an extended slumber is an extension of character profiles that otherwise would not develop. The character is teased out by the interaction of the spirit with its particular cask. The mellowness that evolves in grain spirit after aging for this long is a thing of wonder to experience: all velvet and vanilla, it becomes an elongated ice cream cone of a drink. Try this, and you will see what I mean. **AA**

Tasting notes

Marzipan and pastry initially, but the graininess opens up to reveal butter, cream, and vanilla. On the palate, lovely and silky smooth with subtle herbal notes.

Invergordon 1966 Clan Denny 45-Year-Old

Douglas Laing & Co.
www.douglaslaing.com

Region and country of origin Highlands, Scotland
Distillery Invergordon, Invergordon, Ross-shire
Alcohol content 47.1% abv
Style Single grain

The independent bottler Douglas Laing and Co. is perhaps best known for its Old Malt Cask range. But seeing the recent upsurge in interest in single-grain whiskies, it has redeveloped an existing range to market them (grain whisky is not malt whisky, and therefore cannot be marketed as such). The Clan Denny range offers grain whiskies from distilleries such as North British, Caledonian, and Invergordon, aged between thirty-nine and forty-four years old.

Matured in ex-bourbon casks, these older grain whiskies are a delight and occupy (at least in this writer's opinion) a middle ground between bourbon and malt whisky. An aged grain whisky thus makes, for example, a special birthday present for a malt whisky drinker who enjoys something a bit different.

Grain distilleries might not ordinarily hold much interest for the malt whisky aficionado, but Invergordon might be an exception. Inside its complex was the Ben Wyvis distillery, which enjoyed a painfully short life, opening in 1965 and closing in 1977; its very few bottlings are among the most collectable and expensive malt whiskies around. **PB**

Tasting notes

A model of complexity on the nose with nuts, fruit, oak, and honey all vying for attention. The palate follows suit with mouthwatering fruit, rich chocolate, and coffee.

The Clan Denny Invergordon 1966 was released at cask strength. →

THE CLAN DENNY

SINGLE CASK

Single Grain Scotch Whisky

DISTILLED AT

INVERGORDON DISTILLERY

Vintage 1966

NATURAL STRENGTH · ALWAYS BOTTLED AT

AGED **45** YEARS

This cask reference HH 7254 - refers to a Bourbon Barrel

Lightly smoked initially-then the nose develops fabulously to an old fruit bowl of softly ripening pineapple, citrus, pears and apples - with a hint of sherbet. Palatewise - it is extremely sweet and heavy with macerated fruit (particularly pineapple) and vanilla custard. The finish is really long for a grain and carries soft mocha, spice and "fruit chews" flavour... really good with an expresso! (F)

Distilled, matured & bottled in Scotland

THE HUNTER HAMILTON COMPANY
GLASGOW G41 4NY

Hunter Hamilton

47.1% alc./vol.   700ml

Islay Mist 12-Year-Old

MacDuff International | www.macduffint.co.uk

Region and country of origin Islay, Scotland
Distilleries Various
Alcohol content 40% abv
Style Blend

Something of a paradox, Islay Mist may fairly be described as a voluptuous wallflower at the whisky ball: drinkers may not notice it at first, but they soon find it to be a captivating blend of fine, aged whiskies, all matured in oak casks for a well-rounded flavor.

Islay Mist dates from 1927, when a special whisky was commissioned to celebrate the twenty-first birthday of John Morrison, the son of the Laird of Islay House. Morrison later became the First Baron Margadale, a prominent British Conservative Member of Parliament between 1942 and 1964.

The decision to create a new and original drink was reached only after consideration of the merits of existing whiskies. The leading candidate was a Laphroaig, but eventually the laird decided that this was too heavy for all but the most catholic tastes. He ordered instead a blend with less peatiness to make it accessible to occasional whisky drinkers. The blend is produced from a selection of top-notch malts, including Glenlivet, and a range of grain whiskies. It now comes in four different expressions: Deluxe, 8-Year-Old, 12-Year-Old, and 17-Year-Old.

Connoisseurs may be able to identify some of the components, but most casual samplers will simply appreciate the overall balance and uniqueness of the finished product. One of Islay Mist's proudest achievements has been its success in introducing Islay whisky to a wider audience. Today, the charms of the Hebridean island's liquor—notably its Atlantic sea spray-soaked peat and its distinctive, peat-flavored water—are celebrated far and wide. **ST**

Tasting notes

A full-bodied whisky, dominated by peat and seaweed and oak, as you would expect of an Islay. Despite being a firm and sturdy Islay blend, it is also fairly subtle in the way it coats your mouth. Before you know it, you are seduced and wanting some more.

Islay Mist 17-Year-Old

MacDuff International | www.macduffint.co.uk

Region and country of origin Islay, Scotland
Distilleries Various
Alcohol content 40% abv
Style Blend

The Isle of Islay is known for its smoky, peaty whiskies. Initiates into these powerful single malts never forget their distinctive taste. Some like it, others find it too intense. That is where MacDuff's third famous old brand comes to the fore.

Islay Mist was created in 1928 by Laphroaig's then owner, Ian Hunter, for a special occasion: the coming-of-age party of the son of the Laird of Islay House, holding the title Lord Margadale. The straight single malt from that famous distillery on Islay was considered too overpowering for everyone's taste at the celebration. Hunter mixed Laphroaig with grain whisky and a series of outstanding single malts, among them the Glenlivet, of Speyside fame. The resulting whisky was well received and turned into a commercial blend under the name Islay Mist.

The origins of the device on the label—the Seal of the Isles—are hidden in the mists of time, but it may date from 1156, when Somerled, First Lord of the Isles, was in power. The seal depicts Somerled's brave ship conquering nine waves. The waves themselves are a symbol for victory, and that is what Somerled reputedly enjoyed against the Norsemen, who had been dominating island life for the past couple of centuries. The design was later changed by Donald I and then by Angus Mor, who left us actual proof when he sealed a document on July 7, 1292.

For sure, this is a dram whose pedigree you cannot easily beat. The inscription around the seal reads "Filii Doanaldi s'Engus de Yle." So, let us raise a glass to the Sons of Donald and Angus of Islay! **HO**

Tasting notes

This is wood smoke wrapped in a velvet cloak, breathing over fresh pear. With water, the smoke recedes, and fruit and honey come to the fore. Well balanced, oily on the palate, and finishing in doused embers. A gentler relative of the heavy peat monsters.

Isle of Jura 5-Year-Old

Speciality Drinks | www.specialitydrinks.com

Region and country of origin Islands, Scotland
Distillery Isle of Jura, Craighouse, Isle of Jura, Argyll
Alcohol content 60.6% abv
Style Single malt

Imagine that you have been invited to a huge warehouse packed with some of the finest and most expensive whiskies in the world, and that once inside the great pleasure dome, you are asked to choose any one you want. Which one would you pick? Take your time; perhaps have a flick through this book if you want a few ideas. Tough, isn't it?

Sukhinder Singh runs the UK retailer the Whisky Exchange, and when he buys whisky, he tries to set aside one bottle of each product for his own private collection. The result is that he has assembled the most wide-ranging and awe-inspiring array of liquor that you could ever hope to set eyes on. And that was the choice he offered me. "But before you start thinking of thirty-year-old and forty-year-old whiskies, or Port Ellens and other closed distilleries, let me get you something that I think you'll like," he said.

And this is what he gave me. He was wrong, though, I didn't just like it—I loved it. In fact, this is one of the best whiskies I've ever tasted. Jura isn't known for peated whisky, though in recent years it has bottled Superstition and, more recently, a significantly peated whisky called Prophecy. In musical terms, Prophecy is an Ozzy Osbourne—mean, dark, hard-hitting, and awesome. It is from a series of casks that were distilled under the tutelage of Michael Heads, an Islay native, who became manager of Ardbeg in 2007.

Some of this Jura 5-Year-Old was bottled by Matthew Forrest for the Japanese market; some of it ended up at the Whisky Exchange and is available through Sukhinder's Speciality Drinks label. **DR**

Tasting notes

Like a classroom of unruly school children all banging their desks. The peat kicks and bucks like a wild stallion, whips the oily sweet malt into a taste frenzy, and then gallops out, leaving a mountain of sooty, peppery flavor in the mouth. A stunning whisky in every way.

Isle of Jura 10-Year-Old Origin

Whyte & Mackay | www.isleofjura.com

Region and country of origin Islands, Scotland
Distillery Isle of Jura, Craighouse, Isle of Jura, Argyll
Alcohol content 40% abv
Style Single malt

To say the Isle of Jura is a special place would be a gross understatement; it is very nearly miraculous. Fewer than two hundred people live on this Hebridean island, a close-knit community whose members embody and define "salt of the earth," and blend a rugged pragmatism with a generosity of spirit and an unmatched and assured sense of self. Their practical nature is balanced by a broad artistic streak. Jura is steeped in music, metaphor, storytelling, and craft. A massively disproportionate number of musical and creative people live on the island, some raised in its inspiring landscape, others drawn to it. The island's geography, with its three "Paps," the mountain peaks that have come to symbolize it, and its almost extreme isolation—which drew author George Orwell to its northernmost tip to hide from the world and pen the novel *1984*—all have their effect on the psychology and uniqueness of the people of Jura.

Of course, in such a small place, the distillery is both the commercial and cultural focal point of the island, providing both employment and a source of local pride to the people who live there. This whisky is perhaps the purest expression of the Jura character that can be found outside its shores. It evokes the expansive wildness of the deer-populated forests, the salt air that pervades the place, the remoteness and cameraderie, and the simplicity of approach that such a life affords. It is not fancy, and yet it is rewarding. Romantic, but self-assured. But most of all, it evokes the spirit, the craft, and the creativity of the people to whom Jura is home. **D&C**

Tasting notes

On the nose, salt air and seaweed, driftwood and shells. Some hazelnut and honey. A first tasting blends these aromas with homemade fudge, licorice, and roasted coffee bean, and the finish warms and mellows, leaving a light aftertaste of peat and spice.

Isle of Jura 16-Year-Old Diurachs' Own

Whyte & Mackay
www.isleofjura.com

Region and country of origin Islands, Scotland
Distillery Isle of Jura, Craighouse, Isle of Jura, Argyll
Alcohol content 40% abv
Style Single malt

If you are from the small Hebridean island of Jura, you are known as a Diurach. The Isle of Jura 16-Year-Old is named the Diurachs' Own for the simple reason that it is far and away the most popular local dram, in part because (unlike some of the peatier whiskies) it appeals to men and women equally, but also because it is just so quaffable. The Isle of Jura 10-Year-Old is the best-known expression, and the Prophecy and Superstition perhaps the most distinctive, but the 16-Year-Old is most likely what you will be invited to share with the locals, if they think highly of you.

As a result, visitors to the island often come to consider the 16-Year-Old as the "authentic taste of Jura," and it is not unusual to find it taking pride of place in a collection, not simply because of its excellent taste and drinkability, but also because it is a great souvenir of time spent on the island.

On Jura, the locals even cook with it. At Antlers Restaurant in Craighouse, a dish of venison flame-seared in the 16-Year-Old is a highly recommended culinary treat for visitors. Venison, like whisky, is easy to come by on the island; deer outnumber people thirty to one. Cooking with the 16-Year-Old is not for the fainthearted, however: expect huge flames. **D&C**

Tasting notes

A delicate floral nose, with substantial overtones of malt extract, paprika, and cumin. Sweet with summer fruits and crème caramel. Sugared almond in the finish.

Isle of Jura 18-Year-Old Platinum Selection

Douglas Laing & Co.
www.douglaslaing.com

Region and country of origin Islands, Scotland
Distillery Isle of Jura, Craighouse, Isle of Jura, Argyll
Alcohol content 49.6% abv
Style Single malt

During the annual Islay festival, each of the island's eight distilleries holds its own celebrations; lots of whisky is drunk, friendships are renewed, and special tastings, distillery tours, and cultural events are enjoyed. The festival-goers are primarily Northern European, and the sight of many of them trying to comprehend the sometimes impenetrable local accents is worth the cost of the journey alone.

The Isle of Jura is given a kind of honorary membership to the festival, being only a mile or so away, across the Sound of Islay, so, on one of the festival's eight days, it is Jura's turn to shine. In 2011, the weather was appalling. In fact, during festival week there was said to be a wind speed recorded of 129 miles per hour (207 km/h) on Islay, and it was not much better on the other days. It was so extreme that the ferry from Islay didn't operate on the day that Jura was to hold its special events. There was no other way of getting to the island, so that was that. Festival-goers spent the afternoon at Kilchoman instead.

This Douglas Laing Platinum Selection bottling of a Jura 18-Year-Old is exclusive to the UK Whisky Shop chain. The release consisted of only 120 bottles from a single refill hogshead cask. **PB**

Tasting notes

A bit musty on the nose at first, then a peaty, vegetal character emerges. On the palate, it's sweet and lightly smoked with cucumber and a late surge of vanilla.

Isle of Jura
21-Year-Old

Whyte & Mackay
www.whyteandmackay.com

Region and country of origin Islands, Scotland
Distillery Isle of Jura, Craighouse, Isle of Jura, Argyll
Alcohol content 40% abv
Style Single malt

This sassy 21-Year-Old was a bronze medal-winner at the 2005 International Wine and Spirit Competition and is a rather rare whisky. It is deep reddish-brown in color and hails from the remote island where it was distilled in 1984 to commemorate the famous eponymous novel by George Orwell, written on that very island.

Jura distillery has four pot stills and is near a cave where illegal distilling used to take place. The buildings were established in 1810 by Laird Archibald Campbell, with the whisky maturing in beachside warehouses to give it its full flavor. The distillery went through a great many changes in ownership and renovations, and actually closed at one point. In the end, it was the need for work on the island that provided the initial push for the distillery to be reopened, not just to inject a bit of industry into island life but also as a way to reinstate the liquid's place in whisky history and remind people of its heritage.

In 1994 the Jura distillery was acquired by Whyte & Mackay. Although from 1996 (for five years or so) it was run by JBB Europe, its ownership was returned to Whyte & Mackay in 2001, from which point they have done great things with the brand. **JH**

Tasting notes

A full-bodied and toffee-scented dram, with scents of Christmas cake. This whisky has a medium finish, but a longer history. A must-try on all accounts.

Isle of Jura 21-Year-Old
200th Anniversary

Whyte & Mackay
www.whyteandmackay.com

Region and country of origin Islands, Scotland
Distillery Isle of Jura, Craighouse, Isle of Jura, Argyll
Alcohol content 44% abv
Style Single malt

Although there has been distilling on Jura since 1810, 1963 is a special year for the present distillery, for it was in this year that it was finally restored to its former glory after a rather checkered history. About four hundred people participated in its three-year reconstruction, between 1960 and 1963, virtually doubling the population of the island. According to Whyte & Mackay's master blender Richard Paterson, many of the workers came from Glasgow and were fervent soccer fanatics. The almost unparalleled ferocity of the rivalry between Glasgow's two biggest teams, Rangers and Celtic, spilled over onto Jura with regular fights between respective fans on Friday nights. To make it worse, Jura had no policeman.

Bottled to celebrate the 200th anniversary of the Isle of Jura distillery, the 21-Year-Old has been finished in a 1963 Gonzalez Byass sherry cask. This writer first tasted it in Craighouse's Jura Hotel, next to the distillery. It was on a day visit from Islay during the eight-day annual festival in May. After having chosen a peaceful lunch in the hotel bar in preference to running up the island's three famous Paps as part of the Scottish Islands Peak Race, I bought myself a glass of this and fell instantly in love with it. **PB**

Tasting notes

Clean, creamy sherry on the nose, with currant and poached pear. On the palate, it is a sublime moist fruitcake, initially spicy, then rich and fruity as well.

Isle of Jura 1996

Whyte & Mackay | www.isleofjura.com

Region and country of origin Islands, Scotland
Distillery Isle of Jura, Craighouse, Isle of Jura, Argyll
Alcohol content 43% abv
Style Single malt

Of all the Scottish distilleries, Isle of Jura is one of the most confounding. The island's remoteness means that making whisky there cannot be economic, yet this distillery defies economic gravity and carries on regardless. The owners have behaved as a reed rather than an oak, bowing to circumstances as necessary. Jura has been sold in supermarkets, but the distillery also can put out superior bottlings like this one when there is a market for them.

Perhaps the distillery is a perfect microcosm of the whisky industry in general. It is not Scotland's oldest, and at one point it seemed doomed, but Whyte & Mackay teamed up with the Riley Smith family, owners of much of Jura, to re-establish the distillery—which became Jura's main employer.

The standard Jura is a love-it-or-hate-it unpeated malt, but in recent years, the distillery has started bottling light and heavily peated whiskies along with quite sensational older stock. The whole range has been repackaged, and certain expressions have been welcomed into the premium-whisky sector. This bottling been put together from a broad range of Jura malts and is a fitting tribute to this wonderful, community-linked distillery. **DR**

Tasting notes

Sweet but not too sweet, the floral notes are offset by salt, oak, and bark. Yellow fruit, such as banana and lemon, provide a pleasant body.

Isle of Jura Boutique Barrels Bourbon JO 1995

Whyte & Mackay | www.isleofjura.com

Region and country of origin Islands, Scotland
Distillery Isle of Jura, Craighouse, Isle of Jura, Argyll
Alcohol content 56.5% abv
Style Single malt

Jura is a long, narrow island with only one road, and close proximity to water is one of the characteristics shared by its buildings. That, of course, applies to the Isle of Jura distillery, too, and its Warehouse No. 1 is close to the shoreline. It is dark inside, and, unsurprisingly, the atmosphere is markedly damp.

Distillery warehouses have a distinctive aromatic characteristic that is not shared by the other buildings nearby. It is not the spirit you notice, but a smell of old wood, dusty and musty and cool from the sea breeze and shade. The casks are steeped in liquids from their previous fills, then used to age the best of the island's produce. It is a reassuring smell, not a warm and inviting aroma but one that delights the senses nevertheless. It is the cool smell of brine and dirt floors, timber, and the slow passing of time.

The Isle of Jura Bourbon JO 1995 is a member of the distillery's Boutique Barrels range. The whisky is finished in a small-batch bourbon cask, and matured in the dark, damp, and cool conditions of Warehouse No.1. Given the place where this spirit has lain for years, it is perhaps surprising that the whisky greeting you from the bottle is such a deeply warming, freshly baked fruit-crumble dessert of a dram. **D&C**

Tasting notes

Hold this whisky on your tongue to experience rich pear drop, peach cobbler, sugar cane, and vanilla. A dash of water releases light citrus and apple.

Isle of Jura distillery nestles between hills and shoreline. ➡

Isle of Jura Elixir

Whyte & Mackay | www.isleofjura.com

Region and country of origin Islands, Scotland
Distillery Isle of Jura, Craighouse, Isle of Jura, Argyll
Alcohol content 40% abv
Style Single malt

In many ways, the world of the Internet, Facebook, Twitter, and new media would seem to be an uneasy friend to the old, traditional, and slowly evolving world of malt whisky. In actual fact, it is quite the opposite. Whisky companies have embraced bloggers, though some with more enthusiasm than others. Whole Facebook-style whisky sites exist where a new generation of whisky enthusiasts seeks the opinion of whisky buddies across the world and swaps ideas. For example, you will find any number of comments and reviews of this book online.

Press trips these days tend to include a smattering of the best bloggers, some of them "poachers turned gamekeepers" who have been employed by the whisky companies to help them understand the strange world of social media. One problem with the new media is that they are all so quick and disposable—mere hours after one whisky has been reviewed, the Web monsters are thirsty for another. However, some whisky companies have used the new media to reach out to their audience, offering competitions to visit distilleries and the like.

Isle of Jura Elixir is a new addition to the core Jura range and was launched through a competition on Twitter. Entrants had the chance to order an early sample of it and pass comment on it before it went on general sale. Their comments were posted online, creating a buzz about the whisky even before it was released. Better still, the competition and the response were tweeted countless times, creating great publicity and interest in the new expression. **DR**

Tasting notes

The Elixir's mix of bourbon and sherry casks produces nut flavors and rich fruit on the nose, then citrus fruits, overripe melon, vanilla, nutmeg, allspice, dark chocolate, and a rich, fruity nuttiness on the palate. A fresh, medium-to-long finish.

Isle of Jura Prophecy

Whyte & Mackay | www.isleofjura.com

Region and country of origin Islands, Scotland
Distillery Isle of Jura, Craighouse, Isle of Jura, Argyll
Alcohol content 46% abv
Style Single malt

According to scholars, myths are the stories that people tell themselves in order to understand the world and their place in it. Scotland is a nation steeped in narrative, and the Scots are, by heritage, singers of songs, late-night raconteurs, and tellers of tales. For that reason, it can be difficult to disentangle Scottish history from Scottish legend. In fact, the two may appear factual and fanciful in equal measure.

One story refers to the early days of the Campbell clan's ownership of the island of Jura. Having won the island from the MacDonalds of Islay, they saw fit to evict a woman who was known to be a seer. Even in Jura, a place steeped in mythology, having mystical powers was considered the mark of a bad neighbor. As she left, presumably profoundly irritated by her enforced exit, she pronounced that the last Campbell would leave the island one-eyed, transporting all his possessions to his ship in a cart pulled by a white horse. One imagines this to be accompanied by a clap of thunder. As curses go, it lacked a little panache, but her prediction was right on the money. More than two hundred years later, in 1938, Charles Campbell left for the mainland in exactly that way.

It was the seer's prophecy that inspired the name of this whisky from the Isle of Jura distillery. Just another seventy-two or so years after Charles Campbell departed, the distillery commemorated their local Nostradamus. Which is to say, they simply called the new whisky Prophecy—a far better name for it, you would surely agree, than "One-eyed with all your stuff towed behind a white horse." **D&C**

Tasting notes

Peatier than usual in a Jura whisky, but nothing too alarming. Light smoke and seaweed, like a small fire of driftwood on the beach. Some dried fruits—almost a cake mix—with a good deal of pepper and allspice on the palate. A dry, medium-to-long finish.

Isle of Jura Superstition

Whyte & Mackay | www.isleofjura.com

Region and country of origin Islands, Scotland
Distillery Isle of Jura, Craighouse, Isle of Jura, Argyll
Alcohol content 43% abv
Style Single malt

A superstition is defined as a belief that is held for reasons of tradition, not based on reason or knowledge. It also happens to be the title of a very good Stevie Wonder song. But generally speaking, the word is used in a derogatory fashion. People who believe things that other people do not are often dismissed as being superstitious, even though the people ridiculing those beliefs often have irrational beliefs of their own. Superstitions usually revolve around some symbolic item or act, and generally refer to some omen of fortune or misfortune when observed. Some superstitions are complex and intriguing; others are small matters of daily habit and frequently pass without notice.

Prominent on the middle of the bottle of Jura Superstition is the ancient Egyptian symbol known as an ankh. The people of Jura aver that good luck comes to you when you hold the ankh perfectly central in the palm of your hand as you pour this whisky. Either that, or bad luck comes to you if you don't, or some combination of the above. The important thing is that you drink it with a copper coin in your pocket, while you throw salt onto a ladder under a full moon, while a cat walks across your shadow on a crack in the pavement. Otherwise, there is no telling what might happen. When you have finished, put the cap back on tightly and send the bottle to ten friends. Good health and fortune will surely follow.

Superstition is a lightly peated and more complex malt than its ten-year-old cousin, a product not of magic but true whisky making expertise. **D&C**

Tasting notes

A lightly peated dram, so there is a bit of smoke but also, on the nose, a touch of menthol and pine, and hints of musk and yacht varnish. The taste is more akin to acid drops with honey, ripe grapefruit, and spice, and a slight aftertaste of baking soda and orange peel.

Isle of Skye 8-Year-Old

Ian Macleod Distillers | www.ianmacleod.com

Region and country of origin Isle of Skye and Speyside,
Scotland **Distilleries** Various
Alcohol content 40% abv
Style Blend

The origins of Ian Macleod Distillers go all the way
back to 1933. From that point, the company's portfolio
has expanded dramatically, building up into an
extensive and varied range, not only of single malts
and blended whiskies but of other spirit drinks also.

Isle of Skye 8-Year-Old is a blend with its roots
firmly embedded in the family name. The Clan
Macleod has seen Skye as its home for some while,
and therefore this bottle takes its name from that
same pride and heritage. The constituents of the
blend are open to conjecture, yet it is probably fair to
say that island nuances of its character that come
through on drinking are in part due to the presence of
spirit from the one distillery based in Skye itself.

That is not to say that the whisky's peaty profile is
all that there is to say about this drink. As is made quite
clear by the blender, there is also a significant degree
of Speyside malt included, which serves to temper the
occasionally overwhelming furnace that is normally
associated with Islay and neighboring island drams.
This is definitely a refined and relaxed whisky, one that
would undoubtedly be suited to gazing out toward
the horizon, watching the sky turn red over the Cuillin
Hills as dusk approaches. A drop of this in your glass
would soon chase away any chills the local climate
may inspire in the colder months.

This whisky has benefited from its eight-year
gestation in oak casks, and the results are tellingly
reminiscent of an older bottle; it does seem a great
deal more mature than its age statement asserts. A
very well-balanced dram, indeed. **D&C**

Tasting notes

The nose is honeycomb, vanilla, and creamed rice, with
the tiniest note of brine and peat beneath. Mouthfeel
is slightly oily at first, mellowing to viscous honey,
almond, and peat. The finish is sweeter, with a touch of
marmalade, almond (marzipan), and finally smoke.

Isle of Skye 21-Year-Old

Ian Macleod Distillers
www.ianmacleod.com

Region and country of origin Isle of Skye and Speyside,
Scotland **Distilleries** Various
Alcohol content 40% abv
Style Blend

A thousand of the limited, hand-numbered Wade porcelain decanters containing this particular blended whisky are out there. Each sits regally within a luxurious leather box. Such a whisky is a rare enough beast in its maturation and inner constituents, but when it is coupled with such a unique presentation, it becomes all the more special. Of course, the blue-and-gold vessels may be sought after purely for their own collectability. The Isle of Skye 21-Year-Old is not quite the dram equivalent of Shergar or Lord Lucan (there are, without question, even rarer trophies in the world of whisky), but it is not far off either.

For fans of oak, smoke, and maturity, this is a whisky that is hard to beat. It is partly matured in American oak casks and sherry butts, and it is the combination of the two types of wood that contributes and enhances the unique flavor found in this special marriage of island and Speyside whiskies. The blend has a particularly rich malt quotient of 60 percent. There is also the special magic of knowing that within the blend there are whiskies from closed distilleries. Which ones, we may never know, and the same goes for whether they are malt or grain whiskies, but it is these quirks and vagaries that no doubt contribute to the beauty of the final, hard-to-find drop that rests in your glass. **D&C**

Tasting notes

The nose is toffee apple, floral, oak, vanilla, and smoke. On the palate, it is robust sherry, giving way to caramel shortcake, vanilla, stewed fruit, and burnt sugar.

J&B Jet

Diageo
www.jbscotch.com

Region and country of origin Scotland
Distilleries Various
Alcohol content 40% abv
Style Blend

The world of travel retail and export-only whisky such as J&B Jet is in equal parts fascinating and frustrating. There are many elusive expressions out there that approach near myth in terms of availability and reputation. Who hasn't gazed in awe at the concession stands in international airport lounges, and wondered about buying new clothes at their destination in order to make room in their hand luggage for a bottle or two?

Whisky, like many consumer goods and experiences, trades off the allure of exclusivity. Few are the consumers who can resist the enjoyable sense of privilege that comes with having access to something that others do not.

But be aware that you are lucky—your good fortune is something to be treasured, not trumpeted. If you happen to be blessed by encountering a now-silent distillery's famous single-cask bottling in a bar on the opposite side of the globe from where you live, don't instantly e-mail your fellow whisky aficionados, and then post a slew of pictures on every form of social media you happen to use. The better course is to savor that rare moment, enjoy the dram, and then, on your return flight, pick up a bottle of something unique to serve upon arriving home. Whisky is, after all, best when shared among friends. **D&C**

Tasting notes

A tiny note of sherry on the nose, amid oak, vanilla, and a touch of cut grass. Mouthfeel is slick and quick to coat the tongue. Melon, apple, vanilla, and oak on the palate.

J&B Nox

Diageo
www.jbscotch.com

Region and country of origin Scotland
Distilleries Various
Alcohol content 40% abv
Style Blended malt

From the late 1950s onward, the Jet Set and the Rat Pack were rubbing shoulders in Las Vegas, a city that would become synonymous with late nights and good times. And had Sinatra, Martin, Davis Jr., and company been around in the present-day era, one could imagine J&B Nox being their dram of choice.

With any preconceived notion—cultural, historical, or otherwise—we bring our own sense of how things fit, and what is and is not possible or permissible. In defining things, we bring our own constraints and apply them through the prism of context. Should it be so with blended whisky? Without the exploration of boundaries and limits in concept, production, and marketing, there is a very real danger that a beautiful and valued part of an industry, not to mention culture, could stagnate.

After all, it was only at the end of the nineteenth century that the process of "marrying" whisky in blends was introduced. The concept was revolutionary at the time and attracted not a little skepticism, and yet now the blending process is commonplace. Without the occasional flight of fancy from whisky producers the world over, how else can this industry continue to innovate and inspire? Think about that for a second. So… a blend of malt specifically for mixing? Well, why not? **D&C**

Tasting notes

Estery, with fruity hard candy on the nose. Rounded on the palate, with traces of melon and apple, then oak and vanilla. The finish has apple mingling with oak.

J&B Rare

Diageo
www.jbscotch.com

Region and country of origin Scotland
Distilleries Various
Alcohol content 40% abv
Style Blend

The backstory of Justerini & Brooks is an amazing amalgam of romance, family secrets, and corporate takeover—the first two elements attributable to the former namesake, and the last to the latter. Giacomo Justerini followed an opera singer, the object of his desire, to London after stealing his uncle's recipes for several beverages. The beverages became immensely popular with the aristocracy, and, teaming up with George Johnson as business partner, Giacomo enjoyed huge success. The firm received a stamp of approval in the form of a royal warrant, and this attracted the attention of Albert Brooks, who bought the company in 1831 and added his initial, thus creating today's highly visible, ubiquitous brand.

Walk into any bar or club, and there is likely to be a bottle of J&B Rare on display. There are claims that two bottles of J&B Rare are opened every second; that is a phenomenal amount of whisky. Its success may stem from its well-rounded profile, making it extremely effective for use by mixologists everywhere. Numerous cocktails contain J&B Rare, and while this may offend the whisky purist, it plays no small part in guaranteeing that many a party continues into the wee small hours. The blend succeeds with a variety of mixers while retaining the balance of its forty-two constituent whiskies. No easy feat. **D&C**

Tasting notes

Incredibly light, fragrant, and delicate on the nose, with lemon, lime, pineapple, and mango. Oak and vanilla are apparent in the mouth, and a slight tannin-like quality.

J&B Reserve 15-Year-Old

Diageo | www.jbscotch.com

Region and country of origin Scotland
Distilleries Various
Alcohol content 40% abv
Style Blend

J&B Reserve 15-Year-Old is a blend with a difference, because it is unusual for a blend to have an age statement attached to it. The age statement means that no whisky in the blend may be younger than fifteen years, although the blender is free to select older whiskies to temper the more overwhelming characteristics of any one malt or grain used. Any blender providing an age statement is likely to incur higher costs of production, so this is not churned out to maximize profit; it is flagship stuff.

The aging here has been carried out in the finest barrels, in J&B's own warehouses. It would be interesting to know the component whiskies and the proportion of malt and grain whiskies in the blend. The recipe contains a few surprises, no doubt, as do most blends. Secret combinations of each Scottish whisky region—and in this case most definitely a large amount of Speyside—will have gone into making up the end result, and it is only the master blenders of this world who are privy to such information. However, when it comes down to it, there's nothing quite like sitting down with a dram and pondering these variables. Like the whisky, that's something we can all share and enjoy. **D&C**

Tasting notes

The nose has light fruit, vanilla, then tobacco notes, sherry, and marmalade. On the tongue, it is thicker, cream giving way to darker fruit, oak, and sherry again.

Johnnie Walker Black Label

Diageo | www.johnniewalker.com

Region and country of origin Scotland
Distilleries Various
Alcohol content 40% abv
Style Blend

John "Johnnie" Walker started selling whisky from his grocer's shop in Ayrshire in 1820. At a very local level, he would have sold a mixture of malts because blended whiskies weren't permitted at the time.

The Johnnie Walker success story really took off much later, though, after John Walker's death and under the stewardship of his son and grandson. Blended whisky was first legalized in 1860 and soon became globally popular. The Walkers were quick to respond to the international demand for Scotch and provided the finest whisky they could. At the same time, they presided over a series of innovations: the famous color-coded label, for instance; the square bottle that reduced the cost of breakages and allowed more bottles on the shelf; and the clever diagonal label, which permitted the whisky's name to be larger on the bottle, making it easier to identify.

Black Label is the most famous of all Johnnie Walker expressions, and is made up of perhaps forty different malts, the youngest being twelve years old. A few years back, *Whisky Magazine* asked ten blenders to name the best blend that wasn't their own. Nine named Johnnie Walker Black Label; the tenth couldn't, because he made it himself. **SR**

Tasting notes

Citrusy, fruity, and richly sweet, with hints of smoke and peat on the nose. Peat on the palate, and fruits soaked in honey and vanilla. Complex and very lovable.

Johnnie Walker's famous "Striding Man" was created by cartoonist Tom Browne. →

Born 1820 — Still going Strong

JOHN WALKER & SONS, LTD., SCOTCH WHISKY DISTILLERS, KILMARNOCK, SCOTLAND.

Johnnie Walker Blue Label

Diageo | www.johnniewalker.com

Region and country of origin Scotland
Distilleries Various
Alcohol content 43% abv
Style Blend

Increasing demand from the emerging prosperous middle classes of countries such as China, India, and Russia, coupled with growing demand in other countries across the world, makes this a healthy but challenging time for Scotch whisky.

Battling for market share and dominance, the two biggest drinks companies, Diageo and Pernod Ricard, have taken different routes. A few years ago, Pernod produced survey results showing that few people understood what an age statement on the label meant. They started a campaign stressing the importance of age to whisky, presumably to sell more old whisky at super-premium prices. Diageo, on the other hand, argues that age is just one contributor to quality, and that modern production knowledge and skills mean that quality can be delivered with no age statement at all.

The super-premium Johnnie Walker Blue Label is Diageo's proof. It contains some of the company's oldest and rarest malts, but there is some younger whisky in the mix, too. The rules state that if one drop of seven-year-old whisky is included, the whisky must be described as seven years old. That doesn't reflect the value of the other malts in the mix at all. Why is the youngster in there? Because it's like letting a toddler loose in a retirement home. It causes a stir and gets some of the old boys up and moving, giving some tired old bodies a fresh spurt of youthful energy.

Diageo has won the argument at least in part with this whisky, because it carries a big price tag but sells well because of its reputation for quality. **SR**

Tasting notes

Arguably the best all-rounder of the blended whiskies. With oak there are red, orange, yellow, and green fruits, with spice, peat, and honey. But the outstanding marriage here is that of venerable, old, and sherried whiskies and fresh, zesty, younger ones. Brilliant.

Johnnie Walker Gold Label

Diageo | www.johnniewalker.com

Region and country of origin Scotland
Distilleries Various
Alcohol content 40% abv
Style Blend

Johnnie Walker Gold Label is made of scores of whiskies, none of which is younger than eighteen years old. That raises some questions about it, the most important of which is, what do you do with it? Blended whiskies more often than not are mixed or used in cocktails. Are you really going to do that with a premium blend made up of fine malt and grain whiskies of at least eighteen years of age, and almost certainly including some that are much older? And if you conclude that you shouldn't mask a venerable and not cheap blend with ginger ale or other mixers, why would you buy the blend instead of an eighteen-year-old single malt?

The answer may be linked to water. Research shows that when England, and then the British Empire, got a taste for blended whisky, drinkers mixed it with soda water. In recent years, Japanese youngsters have done the same thing, adding ice and serving it in smart glasses as a highball. Compass Box encourages water to be taken with its Great King Street Blend. Diageo hasn't quite gone down that route, but in the past it has suggested a different way to serve its top blends. It suggested that Blue Label, the top of the Johnnie Walker range, be taken after the person drinking it has numbed the mouth with freezing water. The whisky should then be held in the mouth until the effects of the water wear off, revealing the complex flavors of the whisky.

Gold Label has also been promoted as chilled whisky, best kept in the fridge. As with Blue Label, you allow it to warm in the mouth. **SR**

Tasting notes

Floral and honeycomb notes on the nose, with some spice. The palate is sweet and soft, with a suggestion of overripe exotic fruits. The texture is rich and oily, and the flavors are wreathed by gentle smoke. A beautifully made soft cushion of a sweet malt.

Johnnie Walker Green Label

Diageo | www.johnniewalker.com

Region and country of origin Scotland
Distilleries Various
Alcohol content 43% abv
Style Blended malt

Green Label is a misfit in the Johnnie Walker portfolio because, unlike all its stablemates, it is not a blended Scotch whisky. It is actually a blended malt, which means, of course, that it doesn't contain any grain whisky, and is only made with malt whisky.

To be precise, Green Label combines single-malt whisky from four top Diageo distilleries. Two of them, Talisker and Cragganmore, are distilleries that feature in Diageo's Classic Malts range. The other two, Caol Ila (which is a core malt in all of the Johnnie Walker range) and Linkwood, are both highly respected by those who know them. The whiskies are combined with great skill to produce a phenomenal blend with depth and style. Green Label is an all-rounder.

There is something else about this whisky, too—none of its components is younger than fifteen years old. But that is why the whisky is so special. On the one hand, the fifteen-year age statement guarantees quality whisky of the highest order, but on the other, this is the most vibrant, youthful, and energetic whisky in the range. For many years Green Label was largely ignored, but it was relaunched a few years ago on a very wet and chilly day at Diageo's property in Speyside—when they insisted on making journalists play croquet in the rain.

Whether Green Label is greater than the sum of its parts is up for debate, but undoubtedly it is great value for money. Despite the age statement, you can find it on sale for less than you would expect to pay for a twelve-year-old single malt. This whisky is being discontinued in 2013, so look for it while you can. **SR**

Tasting notes

A highly impressive mix of youthful vigor with age and experience. Rich Speyside fruits bubble through the heart of the malt. Barley sweetness makes the whisky fresh and palatable, while spicy pepper and rumbling peat hold the malt in place.

Johnnie Walker Red Label

Diageo | www.johnniewalker.com

Region and country of origin Scotland
Distilleries Various
Alcohol content 40% abv
Style Blend

A whisky writer tells a good story about the opening of Diageo's super distillery, Roseisle. The distillery, capable of producing more than 2.6 million gallons (10 million liters) of spirit a year, attracted criticism from online bloggers who repeated, time and time again, unfounded allegations that the opening of Roseisle meant the imminent closure of five or six of the company's smaller distilleries. So Diageo invited a group of bloggers up to the distillery for its opening, and, over the morning, effectively castigated them for talking rubbish. The company produced chart after chart to show the massive exponential growth in the demand for whisky and the potential of many emerging whisky markets.

"We need to make more spirit to meet the demand," the Diageo bigwigs concluded. "Why would we close distilleries so that our overall output remained unchanged? If anything, we need more distilleries and more Roseisles." Compelling stuff, and this is the reason why: Diageo is a global drinks company, and it wants to sell as much whisky as it can. Single malts do not offer it the opportunity to do so, because, if a distillery only produces 500,000 gallons (1.9 million liters) of malt a year, that's your lot. It's a different story with blended whisky. The complicated mix of whiskies it contains can be cleverly tweaked and changed from market to market, allowing room for growth. Much of the groundwork has been done for Johnnie Walker. Over the last fifty years, particularly, it has built a huge reputation as a whisky of the highest quality. Few blends can touch it. **SR**

Tasting notes

The nose is very aromatic, approaching that of gin, but with rustic, peaty notes. The palate is full-bodied, robust, and lively, with ginger and spice competing with smoke, juniper, and berry fruits. A spritely, young, but very drinkable blend.

Kilchoman
100% Islay

Kilchoman | www.kilchomandistillery.com

Region and country of origin Islay, Scotland
Distillery Kilchoman, Bruichladdich, Argyll
Alcohol content 46% abv
Style Single malt

When Anthony Wills, the owner and founder of Kilchoman, presented his seventh release from the distillery in June 2011, he was back on the track of whisky matured solely in ex-bourbon barrels without any sherry influence. But that wasn't the big news about this bottling. All the previous releases had been made using malted barley from Port Ellen maltings, which lies on Islay but takes barley from the mainland. Kilchoman 100 percent Islay is made with barley grown on Islay and dried with Islay peat; it is then distilled, matured, and bottled on Islay. This three-year-old whisky is medium peated (20 to 25 parts per million); 11,300 bottles were bottled at 50 percent abv, while a special release of 1,060 bottles at 61.3 percent abv is only made available at the distillery.

Kilchoman has enjoyed a tremendous success in just a few years. All the releases so far have sold out in a short time, and increased demand has obliged Anthony to build more warehouses. In 2010 the whisky was launched on the important American market, and the distillery visitor's center is already attracting 10,000 people a year. It will be interesting to follow Kilchoman in the years to come and to see how the whisky evolves with longer maturation. **IR**

Tasting notes

Sharp and intense, with a nice maltiness. Floral, lilac note. Spicy and powerful on the palate, more floral notes and heather. Medium finish with a gristy finale.

Kilchoman
Spring 2011

Kilchoman | www.kilchomandistillery.com

Region and country of origin Islay, Scotland
Distillery Kilchoman, Bruichladdich, Argyll
Alcohol content 46% abv
Style Single malt

When Kilchoman owner Anthony Wills attended Whisky Fest in Chicago 2011 to promote his whiskies, he also accepted the award for "Artisan Whisky of the Year." In the early days, he had teamed up with Mark French, who owned Rockside Farm, a few miles from Port Charlotte on Islay. The distillery was built on the farm, and the barley grown there became a vital part of Kilchoman single malt. About a third of the malted barley used comes from the surrounding fields, and is floor-malted on-site. At first it is dried for ten hours using peat, and then for another thirty to sixty hours (depending on the season) using hot air. The phenol content is 20 to 25 parts per million.

Kilchoman Spring 2011, the distillery's sixth release, was launched in March 2011. This time it was a vatting of 70 percent three-year-old whisky and 30 percent four-year-old, both having matured in first-fill bourbon barrels. Adding to the complexity, the four-year-old spirit had also received a five-week finish in twenty-year-old oloroso sherry butts.

Kilchoman's first three releases all had a sherry finish, while the two that followed were "all bourbon." The Spring 2011 release was a return to Kilchoman single malt with a hint of sherry influence. **IR**

Tasting notes

Seashore and seaweed, autumnal notes, and suddenly Sobranie tobacco. On the palate, intense at first but more mellow with water. Red berries and spicy.

Kilchoman
Winter 2010

Kilchoman | www.kilchomandistillery.com

Region and country of origin Islay, Scotland
Distillery Kilchoman, Bruichladdich, Argyll
Alcohol content 46% abv
Style Single malt

The force behind Islay's newest whisky distillery is Anthony Wills. After a long and successful career in wine, he started Liquid Gold Enterprises, specializing in bottling single-cask whiskies. At the same time he dreamed of owning his own distillery. Because of a long family association with Islay, he decided it would be the perfect spot to settle. The distillery opened in 2005, and was the first to be built on Islay since Malt Mill opened on Lagavulin's premises in 1908.

All the releases from Kilchoman so far have been peated. The first bottling was released in September 2009 as a 3-year-old, but a few months before that, the very first bottle was sold at a charity auction for $8,500 (£5,400). Kilchoman Inaugural Release was a bourbon matured with an additional six months in oloroso sherry butts. Despite its youth, the whisky got some rave reviews, showing that, as long as the new make is well made, peated whiskies can have great charm when young.

It is the same with the Kilchoman Winter 2010. This is the fifth release from the distillery, matured in first-fill bourbon barrels from Buffalo Trace for a little more than three years. The malted barley's phenol content was an impressive 50 parts perr million. **IR**

Tasting notes

Waves of fresh clam and seaweed, briny and fresh with some sweetness. On the palate, deep-fried prawn and then mushroom, with a smoky sweetness.

Kilkerran
Work in Progress 1

J. & A. Mitchell Co. | www.kilkerran.com

Region and country of origin Highlands, Scotland
Distillery Glengyle, Campbeltown, Argyll
Alcohol content 46% abv
Style Single malt

Originally built in 1873 by William Mitchell after a falling out with his brother John at Springbank distillery, Glengyle closed in 1925. The distillery was officially reopened in 2004. Glengyle is the first distillery to open in Campbeltown in 125 years. The Glengyle trademark is owned by Loch Lomond Distillers, so the single malt has been named Kilkerran.

The stills, condensers, spirit receiver, and stainless-steel spirit safe come from Ben Wyvis, a rare single malt distilled at the Invergordon complex from 1965 to 1976. Production director Frank McHardy recalls, "We got [the Forsyth Group] to take out the purifiers and slope the lyne arms upward. They also took out the flanges and welded the body of the still to the pot and created a smooth edge. All this created smooth flow for the vapor up to the lyne arm where, because of the upward slope, some of the vapor is allowed to come back down to the pot, creating the reflux effect."

In 2009, Glengyle released 12,000 bottles of five-year-old Kilkerran Work in Progress 1. Frank saya, "On the nose there was the same sort of aroma you would get before putting dough into an oven, but also sweet malty notes. The palate was quite short but fruity, a bit of lemon zest, and sweet vanilla." **WM**

Tasting notes

A mélange of spices, jasmine, oak, vanilla, and herbs on the nose. The palate is briny, with clove, heavy spices, and a thick, oily mouthfeel. A hint of pine in the finish.

Kilkerran Work in Progress 2

J. & A. Mitchell Co. | www.kilkerran.com

Region and country of origin Highlands, Scotland
Distillery Glengyle, Campbeltown, Argyll
Alcohol content 46% abv
Style Single malt

Kilkerran is the single malt produced at the Glenglye distillery, owned by J. & A. Mitchell Co., which also owns Springbank distillery. Kilkerran Work in Progress 2 comes from the same distillation run as Work in Progress 1, and is intended to show consumers how the spirit develops. Future annual releases are planned until the 2004 distillation matures at age twelve.

According to Frank McHardy, production director at Springbank and Glengyle distilleries, Kilkerran Work in Progress 2 has "not so much spirit on the nose, dough aroma disappearing, and sweeter Parma violet notes coming through. The taste still reminds one of sweet apples and a touch of honey."

Although Kilkerran is double-distilled and lightly peated, similar to Springbank, the distillate is slightly heavier due to the still shape of the modified Ben Wyviss stills, which are slightly thinner in body. In terms of barrel selection for Kilkerran maturation, McHardy states, "We do use quite a lot of fresh bourbon casks quite intentionally, as we know that the dominant vanilla flavor will result from using this type of wood. We have produced a whisky that is as we would expect, and over the last two years, spirity notes have faded and are replaced with more pronounced fruit notes. We certainly look forward to this product developing further, but who knows? This is one of the magic things about a new product, it is like a child growing up. Kilkerran has got through the 'terrible twos' and is now much more biddable. We await the teenage years with anticipation." **WM**

Tasting notes

While not quite as heavy as Work in Progress 1, with less acetone, this still exhibits notes of spice, jasmine, and herbs on the nose, and big notes of sea brine and clove on the palate, with more herbal notes. This one is slightly more complex, with more spice on the finish.

Knockando 12-Year-Old

Diageo | www.diageo.com

Region and country of origin Speyside, Scotland
Distillery Knockando, Knockando, Morayshire
Alcohol content 40% abv
Style Single malt

"Naturally pale and lonely but fruity single seeks dominant, dark, and silent type for a long and lasting relationship on the hills of Speyside." That, at least, is how this whisky's lonely-hearts entry should have read, had it sought to encounter the perfect wooden companion in which to complete its maturation.

The creation of the Knockando 12-Year-Old involves a deliberate balance between careful control and patience. There is a mix of local malted barley, yeast, and spring water from the Cardnach spring above the distillery, along with a small proportion of oak sherry casks used to add subtle flavor to the whisky. The result is a delicate, gentle, fresh whisky with layers of fruit and nut and a slight smokiness. Each bottle of this earnest single malt will only ever include the produce of one single season, too.

The name Knockando is Gaelic for "little black hill." It refers to the site of the distillery, a little hill that overlooks the River Spey.

Everything about this whisky tastes exceptionally clean, from the whisky's character to the distillery's all-natural approach to building something wondrous. Even the quantities of peat and grain seem anything but overdone. Over time, this single malt gets a little plumper and bolder, but otherwise it is a concoction striving to be the best it can, and certainly achieving a decent mix of good balance and fresh flavors.

Indeed, if one were pressed to identify just one flaw of the Knockando 12-Year-Old, it would be that the whisky can be, at times, a little too short-lived. A longer-lasting finish would be appreciated. **JH**

Tasting notes

A short visit to a sunny town. Knockando is fresh, clean, and peachy; like a cheerleader or a school prefect, it may even be too good for you. A brief summer crush. It's good, decent, and dedicated, which always helps when introducing it to the parents.

Lagavulin 12-Year-Old Cask Strength

Diageo | www.malts.com

Region and country of origin Islay, Scotland
Distillery Lagavulin, Port Ellen, Argyll
Alcohol content 56.5% (tenth release)
Style Single malt

With the launch of its Classic Malts range in 1989, Lagavulin dropped its benchmark 12-Year-Old and introduced the 16-Year-Old. In 2002, Diageo launched a limited-edition, natural cask-strength 12-Year-Old at 58 percent abv. This became the first of a series of annual bottlings in the Special Releases range.

By the start of the following decade, there had been ten editions of the cask-strength 12-Year-Old. The tenth release was distilled in 1998. The spirit went into refill American oak casks, was aged for twelve years, and then bottled in 2012 at a cask strength of 56.5 percent abv. Details of the quantities of each batch are not published, but recent bottlings are likely to have required at least a hundred barrels married together. The 12-Year-Old expression at cask strength is much more pronounced than the 16-Year-Old. It has found a loyal audience among enthusiasts who prefer this older style of Lagavulin. Earlier expressions had a citrus acidity, but there has been a gradual evolution away from that toward greater richness.

The distillery's malting is done at Port Ellen and peated to 35 parts per million, Lagavulin's peating level since 1989. The 12-Year-Old's alcohol by volume has varied slightly year by year. **IGY**

Tasting notes

A toasty, smoky, dusty, peppery, savory dram. Old spices and herbs, mulling spices, and dried lemon. Add water to experience a beach barbecue in driving rain.

Lagavulin 12-Year-Old Special Release 2011

Diageo | www.malts.com

Region and country of origin Islay, Scotland
Distillery Lagavulin, Port Ellen, Argyll
Alcohol content 57.5% abv
Style Single malt

A few years back, drinks giant Diageo started a series of fall special releases that have become one of the highlights of the whisky year. Whoever makes the selection has managed to put together a collection of annual issues that cover a range of prices, ages, and whisky styles. And sometimes the company releases something that is a genuine surprise.

This is a case in point. Lagavulin is usually released as a sixteen-year-old, but a few years ago, stock shortages led to a younger, twelve-year-old Lagavulin being released to fill the shortfall. It was something of a bruiser, and it earned itself a loyal following.

This 2011 special release might have covered the same territory, but not at all. The start is recognizably Lagavulin, with wood smoke, phenols, and coal tar, but halfway through, and with the addition of water, it changes into a pretty, sweet, fruity delight. Imagine an American football team known for its bruising running play suddenly deciding to play a passing game instead—and then coming on for the second half of the game in pink tutus. It is amazing to see this side of one of the iconic malts. You might love this new departure, or you might feel a little short-changed, for a big peat monster it isn't. **DR**

Tasting notes

Wood smoke, tar, spice, oil, and some menthol at first. With water, sweet melon and pear come to the fore, then aniseed and menthol, followed by smoke.

← Lagavulin distillery takes advantage of distinctive local water and peat.

Lagavulin 16-Year-Old

Diageo | www.malts.com

Region and country of origin Islay, Scotland
Distillery Lagavulin, Port Ellen, Argyll
Alcohol content 43% abv
Style Single malt

Whisky from the Lagavulin distillery on Islay has been used in the Johnnie Walker and White Horse blends, but the distillery is unusual in that most of its output is released as its own single malt. The largest proportion, 608,000 gallons (2.3 million liters), of the distillery's total production goes into this expression.

The Lagavulin 16-Year-Old became available at the end of the 1980s, when Diageo launched its Classic Malts range. Until 1987, Lagavulin had been aged for twelve years (an age not to be seen again until 2002). The upgrade positioned the malt as the distillery's oldest commercial benchmark bottling. But sixteen years is a long time, and the whisky's success must have come as a surprise because the stills had only been running for a two-day week. Initially the distillery struggled to cope with the large demand. It began running seven days per week, but another sixteen years would pass before the increased production could catch up with the expression's fans.

All of the Lagavulin distillery's malting is done at Port Ellen, and the barley is peated to 35 parts per million (ppm). The distillation at Lagavulin is long, a substantial ten-and-a-half-hour run that gives the whiskies a characteristic roundness and soft, mellow edges. This heavily peated but supple spirit is then aged in American oak casks. The casks are usually second-fill, and they have a gentle impact, just enough to sweeten the already characterful new-make spirit. The spirit is left to mature for sixteen years at three locations on the island—Lagavulin, Port Ellen, and Caol Ila—as well as on the mainland. **IGY**

Tasting notes

Lapsang souchong tea and a leather armchair. Smoke, seaweed, and iodine. The scene is set. This is a distinctly peaty whisky, with an edifying touch of sweetness. The tannins are leathery and robust, and pleasingly bold. Big, sweet, smoky spice right through to the end.

Lagavulin Distillers Edition 1994

Diageo | www.malts.com

Region and country of origin Islay, Scotland
Distillery Lagavulin, Port Ellen, Argyll
Alcohol content 43% abv
Style Single malt

Diageo's Classic Malts of Scotland consists of six malts. In addition to the Lagavulin 16-Year-Old, the collection comprises malts from Dalwhinnie, Talisker, Cragganmore, Oban, and Glenkinchie. There is a Distillers Edition expression of each of these, and they are of varying quality, but none of them divides opinion more than this one.

Effectively, a Diageo Distillers Edition is the original whisky given an extra treatment. In this case, the malt is finished in Pedro Ximénez casks. You only need to look at the color of this whisky to get a sense of the sherry influence, and it is immediately evident on the palate, too, because it is extremely sweet.

The split opinion over this malt derives from the fact that some people view Lagavulin 16-Year-Old as one of the truly iconic names of whisky, believing that it is perfection in its standard 16-Year-Old form. They argue that nothing could possibly improve on its perfection, and that there is a serious danger of destroying it, by "fixing what is not broken." They say that a happy peat-and-sherry marriage is one of the toughest tricks for a whisky maker to pull off, and this doesn't manage it.

Others disagree, arguing that this takes one of the great Islay malts to a higher place. Indeed, some regard this as the finest whisky on the planet. If you have a sweet tooth, that may be the case, but if you're drawn to the holy trinity of malt distilleries—Ardbeg, Laphroaig, and Lagavulin—because of the static wall of peat they offer, then it may well be that this isn't for you. It is intriguing and well made, nevertheless. **DR**

Tasting notes

Sweet, smooth, fruity, and liqueurlike—these are not descriptors normally associated with Islay, and you have to wait a little while for the tidal wave of smoke and peat. Once that wave crashes, though, it washes over the palate forever.

Lagavulin The Managers' Choice 15-Year-Old

Diageo | www.malts.com

Region and country of origin Islay, Scotland
Distillery Lagavulin, Port Ellen, Argyll
Alcohol content 54.7% abv
Style Single malt

Of all the Scottish distillers, there are a handful that create a collective frisson of excitement every time they release a new whisky. Lagavulin is definitely one of them. A Lagavulin release is the whisky equivalent of a new offering from Kate Bush—a release from either of them is rare, but is pretty much sure to be mature, refined, esoteric, complex, and a mite mysterious. Pursuing the link with music, it should come as no surprise that the brand is the sponsor of the Islay Jazz Festival.

But there's more to Lagavulin than just mystery. The standard Lagavulin 16-Year-Old bottling is one of the truly great Scottish malts. When there were stock shortages a few years back, however, a twelve-year-old substitute was introduced, and plenty of Islay fans discovered that they preferred the youthful version. But what makes Lagavulin so special is the fact that it is able to pull off the very difficult and complex trick of marrying sherry casks with peat. Get it wrong, and the whole deck of cards comes tumbling down. Get it right, and it's the greatest trick in malt whisky. Lagavulin gets it right.

This Managers' Choice bottling is a cask in point. Bottled at cask strength, and a full-force Lagavulin whisky to boot, this is as brash and ostentatious as whisky gets. In 2011, Diageo released the most delicate of Lagavulins, and it couldn't have been more different. Both bottles are world-class. It is like watching a heavy-metal singer win a world chess championship. A frisson of excitement? No. More, much more than that. **DR**

Tasting notes

A creamy, briny, coastal, smoky, and fruity nose, then a firestorm of a palate, with a complex mix of dark berries, metallic savory notes, sweet citrus, and moody peat. Smoke wafts over the berry-fruit compote. Oily and briny with chile notes. The finish goes on forever.

Laphroaig 10-Year-Old

Beam Global | www.laphroaig.com

Region and country of origin Islay, Scotland
Distillery Laphroaig, Port Ellen, Argyll
Alcohol content 40% abv
Style Single malt

Some years ago, I spoke to someone whose job it was to persuade pubs and clubs to take gas from his utility company rather than that of the competition. He had the ultimate marketing job, he believed, because each of the rivals was supplying pretty much the same product—a colorless, odorless gas that is supplied through the same pipework as everyone else's.

But he was wrong. The ultimate marketing job is quite the opposite—selling a pungent, dark brown spirit such as Laphroaig. How many times have you heard Laphroaig—awkward name and all—called "the Marmite of the whisky world"? The owners won't thank me for saying it, but Laphroaig, which is pronounced *La-froyg*, is the Jack Daniel's of Scotch, that is, a strong-flavored whisky that has become a global phenomenon while managing to maintain a small-batch, small-scale image.

Visit the distillery and you'll see little technology and plenty of hints that the malt spirit is handmade in the traditional way. But this is a big-selling malt, and there's more to the distillery than meets the eye. You'll find it in the south of the Isle of Islay among the holy trinity of distilleries that includes Lagavulin and Ardbeg. All three produce big, growling, broody whiskies, with the medicinal, iodine, and often fishy sort of peat. Peat is like chile in curry; when you first add it, it's raw and potent, but the longer you "cook" it, the more integrated it becomes, and the more balanced the taste. Peat fans don't want that, though, they want the peat hit. So ten years is a better age for this than twelve years would be. **DR**

Tasting notes

If this whisky were a puppet act, it would have to be called Sooty and Sweet. There are phenolic, meaty, medicinal notes in attendance, too, along with a sweet, rich fruitiness. As you would expect of an Islay, there are also some seaweedy coastal notes in the mix.

Laphroaig 10-Year-Old Cask Strength

Beam Global | www.laphroaig.com

Region and country of origin Islay, Scotland
Distillery Laphroaig, Port Ellen, Argyll
Alcohol content Around 55% abv
Style Single malt

As rites of passage go, drinking Laphroaig Cask Strength isn't quite up there with sleeping naked on a mountain top in the middle of winter, or fighting an angry bear, but neither is it a stroll in the park. Which is why it was so amusing to watch a group of arrogant and inebriated London journalists order yet another drink at midnight the night before Laphroaig Day at the Feis Ile (Islay Festival). And sure enough, they looked a pretty sorry sight at nine the next morning, especially as they had to travel by small boat around the headland to the distillery and taste cask-strength Laphroaig. The water around Islay can be very choppy, and it took considerable balancing skills just to hold our glasses upright. To their credit, the journalists downed their whiskies. "Right," said our host, "that was last year's release. Now let's taste the new one." The looks on those faces were priceless.

The tasting made the point that this whisky is produced in batches, and they do vary notably from one to the next. The second release, for instance, had a beautiful, red-licorice heart. What the casks all have in common, though, are the intense seaweed, iodine, menthol, and big, big peat notes that have made this malt the Muhammad Ali of whisky. Without doubt, this is just about as close as you can get to the soul of Islay, and the whisky equivalent of visiting the British crown jewels—you have to pass through big steel doors of peat to get in, but then there is a roomful of priceless delights to enjoy. This isn't just a whisky you must try before you die; if you don't ever taste it, you will never fully know malt. **DR**

Tasting notes

A whisky with a bite much bigger than its bark. It holds back on the nose, but when you add a little water, it snaps and snarls, exploding with peaty, tarry, iodine fury. Many won't want to give it a go, but it is better than anything of its type on the market.

Turning the malted barley at the Laphroaig distillery.

Laphroaig 18-Year-Old

Beam Global | www.laphroaig.com

Region and country of origin Islay, Scotland
Distillery Laphroaig, Port Ellen, Argyll
Alcohol content 48% abv
Style Single malt

One of the trends in whisky making in recent years has been a move by some distilleries away from the style of whisky most associated with the region they operate in. Some may even move away from their established house style toward a wider portfolio of different-flavored whiskies. And why not? Why should a distillery offer only one style, when other styles might prove more popular?

Beam Global, the owner of Laphroaig, has gone the other way, however. A while back, it was decided that new expressions should focus on what made Laphroaig so famous: big, intense, peated malts, often with pronounced hickory or licorice notes. To make the point, the company scrapped its 15-Year-Old, which was to Laphroaig what an orchestra and gospel choir concert are to a Metallica gig, and they replaced it with this 18-Year-Old. It is arguably not only the best Laphroaig of them all, but also one of the top three malts in the world.

If extra years in oak usually soften the impact of peat, nobody told this teenager, just as nobody told the Lagavulin 16-Year-Old. The extra years in wood give the finished whisky a richer, fuller, fruitier flavor, and extend the reach of the full honeyed substrata. In other words, rather than being a compromise of the trademark Laphroaig qualities, the 18-Year-Old is an extension of them. At the same time, the oak has filled out the taste and enriched it, potentially opening it up to drinkers repelled by the medicinal and phenolic notes in the 10-Year-Old. However you look at, the Laphroaig 18-Year-Old is a winner all round. **DR**

Tasting notes

Readily identifiable as a Laphroaig: smoke, peat, and seaweed drifting in and out, but with vanilla and honey there too. The wave of peat grows in the mouth and coats the mouth, with nut toffee, sea spray, and rich, full, and honeyed malt at the core. Wonderful.

Laphroaig 25-Year-Old

Beam Global | www.laphroaig.com

Region and country of origin Islay, Scotland
Distillery Laphroaig, Port Ellen, Argyll
Alcohol content 40% abv
Style Single malt

Those who criticize the whisky industry for being too shy and reticent, failing to grab the marketing nettle with both hands to push its products, should have a close look at the Friends of Laphroaig scheme. It was launched in the same era as this whisky was distilled, and since then, it has grown into a global phenomenon, with thousands of members across the planet. Each year, there is a Friends of Laphroaig tasting in a different part of the world; to show the global reach of the brand, the 2011 event was staged in Sydney, Australia. Anyone can become a friend by purchasing any bottle of Laphroaig or by visiting the whisky's Web site. Membership gets you a small piece of land at the distillery. Visit your plot, and you can place your national flag on it and enjoy a landlord's dram. Clever stuff!

It is unlikely that you will be handed a glass of this particular whisky. It was first released alongside the 27-Year-Old but wasn't a success because the peat effect was subdued and arrived very late in the mix; Laphroaig fans were annoyed, and others were put off by the price. In 2010, though, and as part of the new peat policy, this bigger, fuller, and peatier version was launched. It is another fine addition to the Laphroaig squad and definitely brings something new to the party, with some oak astringency and peppery spice squeezing its way past the full-flavored malt.

All very good, although whether it justifies the investment over the 18-Year-Old would make for a good pub debate—while drinking a few different expressions of Laphroaig, of course. **DR**

Tasting notes

Mellow: sweet with a touch of wood. There is a polite battle for dominance between sherry, apple, and the classic Laphroaig peaty tang. The flavors are immediately striking, but given a chance, they develop, and the sweetness and salt complement each other.

Laphroaig 30-Year-Old

Beam Global | www.laphroaig.com

Region and country of origin Islay, Scotland
Distillery Laphroaig, Port Ellen, Argyll
Alcohol content 43% abv
Style Single malt

The idea that older whisky is better whisky may not be totally wrong, but it is simplistic and misleading. Certainly, malt spirit will pick up flavor and color from the cask it is stored in, and, up to a point, the longer it is left, the more flavor it will pick up. But then the contribution from the wood reaches a plateau, while at the same time, the wood tannins grow in strength. Without intervention, a point arrives when the spicy oak overwhelms the malt spirit and spoils it.

A robust, full, and oily Highland or island whisky is more likely to hold off the influence of wood and go the distance than a light Lowland one. Few make it to thirty years, though, and even fewer taste good at that age. Paying a lot of money for such a whisky is a calculated gamble if you intend to drink your purchase, and some examples taste like they would be better left unopened as an investment. At best, whiskies this old can become weak, frail, and delicate.

Laphroaig 30-Year-Old is an exception. Like the Brora and Talisker 30-year-olds, it successfully combines great age with delightful peat and spice. Although the age has softened the peat, this is the whisky equivalent of a pensioner in a gym—surprisingly spritely, fit, and active for its age. **DR**

Tasting notes

Peat, licorice, and aniseed dip in and out of mature barley notes and subtle, sweet oak. This is unlike any other malt for peaty, fishy, chewy oaky malt at this age.

Laphroaig 1967 Connoisseurs Choice

Gordon & Macphail | www.laphroaig.com

Region and country of origin Islay, Scotland
Distillery Laphroaig, Port Ellen, Argyll
Alcohol content 40% abv
Style Single malt

For those who seek out Scotch as a collectible or even an investment, distilleries' own bottles are generally more attractive than their independently bottled cousins. This enhanced desirability clearly puts a premium on the value of certain bottles in the secondary, or auction, market. There are, however, many exceptions to this, and the early Gordon & MacPhail Connoisseurs Choice bottles are among them. Independent bottlers should not be overlooked, because they can produce some of the rarest whiskies from long-gone distilleries at unusual ages, and sometimes with old vintages.

This 1967 Laphroaig is from the second Connoisseurs Choice release and is now a very desirable item worth up to $800 (£500) at auction. The second release is distinguished by cream and brown labels. As Connoisseurs Choice gathered a dedicated following for its ever-growing variety of rare and unusual single malts, this second series has provided collectors with some of the most desirable bottles.

The second release was followed by the widely recognized "map label" bottles, which are still current today, although the packaging and label design has recently been brought up to date. **AS**

Tasting notes

Greengage, unripe plum, and apricot. Slightly bitter tannins in the background, with a coastal up swelling of peat. Far more subtle than modern Laphroaigs.

Laphroaig 1908

Berry Bros. & Rudd | www.bbr.com

Region and country of origin Islay, Scotland
Distillery Laphroaig, Port Ellen, Argyll
Alcohol content 46% abv
Style Single malt

Berry Bros. & Rudd is best known as being the oldest surviving wine and spirit merchant in Britain, but it also has a very credible presence as an independent whisky bottler and retailer. It has been bottling Scotch for over a century and has produced some of the most valuable bottles of whisky sold at auction.

Their 1902 Highland Park and 1908 Laphroaig are not just collectibles, they are bona fide pieces of whisky history. They are something really special, bearing in mind that the oldest vintage for an official Laphroaig bottling is 1960. Don't expect them to come cheap, though, as these old bottles are now priced in thousands of dollars and have built up that momentum which iconic malts achieve when every appearance at auction attracts worldwide interest—if they ever make it to auction at all.

The 1908 Laphroaig, like all the very best investable whiskies, tastes great as well as being very rare, and there are a few people across the planet rich enough to want to pay big bucks to open and drink it. The biggest whisky retailers keep lists of high-profile customers who are contacted as soon as a bottle appears on the market, but who knows? You might still find one on a dusty shelf somewhere. **AA**

Tasting notes

Dewy, like a grassy field at dawn or seaweed strewn on a beach. With this Laphroaig, the smoke comes later, but when it does, it is big and billowy, like campfire.

Laphroaig Quarter Cask

Beam Global | www.laphroaig.com

Region and country of origin Islay, Scotland
Distillery Laphroaig, Port Ellen, Argyll
Alcohol content 48% abv
Style Single malt

Readers progressing though this book cover to cover and possessing a good memory will recall that Ardmore Traditional is matured partially in small, quarter-sized casks. That process maximizes the spirit's contact with wood, accelerating maturation and intensifying the oak flavors. This does not suit all whiskies, but if it works well with Ardmore, then it certainly works brilliantly with this whisky.

If you enjoy peat, you will want a big slab of it in your whisky. Peat impacts more when it is young. Young, peaty malts do exist, but they can be sappy, cereal, and unbalanced, and even dedicated peat fans can struggle with them. This offers a solution. Quarter casks bring out the rich, sweet, fruity flavors, making whiskies taste like they have matured for twelve years when they have been in the cask for a far shorter time. The peat, on the other hand, tastes as big and fresh as its age. The result: six-year-old peat in what seems a twelve-year-old fruity spirit. Perfect!

Some drinkers say that the standard expression of Laphroaig has been "dumbed down" over the years, and that this is how real Laphroaig should taste. It is a gem of a peated whisky, a great, roaring monster of a malt from an iconic distillery. **DR**

Tasting notes

A big, sooty, intense affair, with sweet fruits tumbling under the frothy, smoky, peat attack, with some notes of iodine, seaweed, and barbecued fish.

Laphroaig Triple Wood

Beam Global | www.laphroaig.com

Region and country of origin Islay, Scotland
Distillery Laphroaig, Port Ellen, Argyll
Alcohol content 48% abv
Style Single malt

In whisky making, one of the hardest tricks to pull off successfully is the marriage of big peated whiskies with rich sherry casks, particularly casks that previously contained big and full styles of sherry, such as oloroso. The process is like watching a particularly complicated routine by a street dancing team: lots can go wrong, and if it does, the results are confusing, messy, and risible. Get it right, though, and you occupy a platform with very few others.

A few years ago, Laphroaig released a stunning 27-year-old, one of the best whiskies this writer has ever tasted. That whisky is no more, and it was outside the budget of most of us, anyway. But to get a sense of what it was like, try this one. Without intending to be insulting, I would call this is a poor man's 27-year-old. It was initially available in travel retail only, in 33.8-ounce (1-liter) bottles, and it still represents very good value for money.

What the whisky makers have done is take the standard Quarter Cask and put it in large European oak butts that previously contained oloroso sherry. Because the butts are so big, this has the effect of decelerating maturation from fast forward in quarter casks to ultraslow in the butts. The whisky takes on a subtle depth and sherry character, nowhere near as full as the effect of the 27-year-old but noticeable nevertheless. The peat, meanwhile, holds its own. There was a period around 2010 and 2011 when everything the distillery released was gold dust, and this is another jewel in the Laphroaig crown. Let's hope the purple patch continues into the future. **DR**

Tasting notes

Bottled at 48 percent abv, with the influence of bourbon barrels, European oak butts, and quarter casks, and without chill-filtering, this has intense peat and fruit, wispy smoke, vanilla, some berry and nutty notes, and a rich, sweet, full mouthfeel.

The Last Drop 1960

The Last Drop Distillers | www.lastdropdistillers.com

Region and country of origin Scotland
Distilleries Various
Alcohol content 52% abv
Style Blend

Occasionally the world of whisky throws an oddball—a special whisky that has somehow sidestepped the system and, without planning or warning, become a charming curio or, better still, a stunning rarity. A few years back, there were three casks of rare Bowmore from the 1960s, containing spirits distilled in the same week but stored in Pedro Ximénez, oloroso, and bourbon wood, giving us the chance to see how forty-year-old whisky travels in different directions, depending on the cask. Then there's the story of Serendipity, when a batch of young Glen Moray was mistakenly added to some very old Ardbeg. The mixture created a whole new whisky, and bottles of that are rare today. Cynics question whether it is really possible for distilleries to forget their casks or make such mistakes, but there are literally millions of casks maturing all over the world.

The Last Drop is, as the name might imply, an extremely limited whisky and an amazing one. There are very few bottles of it, all from one cask that lay in a warehouse forgotten for many years before industry heavyweights Tom Jago and James Espey managed to get hold of it and bottle it. It contains seventy malts and twelve grains from 1960 or before. After some years, the whiskies were married together and recasked, and the result only saw the light of day again in 2008—a maturation period of forty-eight years.

Whisky of this age commands prices running into thousands; at under $2,400 (£1,500), this is reasonable The bottle comes with a miniature to help you decide whether to open the big bottle or keep it. **SR**

Tasting notes

Does this whisky justify its sizable price tag? Well, it is stunning stuff. Its center is rich and honeyed, with soft fruit, and it has a gossamer-light finish, with honeycomb and oak adding to the effect. If anything, the experience is most like drinking a fine Cognac.

BOTTLED IN SCOTLAND

EST'D 1834

LAUDER'S®

Finest SCOTCH *Whisky*

HIGHEST AWARDS
GOLD MEDAL
PARIS 1878

GOLD MEDALS
CHICAGO 1893
EDINBURGH 1886

BLENDED AND BOTTLED BY

Archibald Lauder & Co. Ltd.

GLASGOW, SCOTLAND

PRODUCT OF SCOTLAND

Lauder's

MacDuff International
www.macduffint.co.uk

Region and country of origin Scotland
Distilleries Various
Alcohol content 40% abv
Style Blend

In 1992, three Scottish men, Stewart MacDuff, Charles Murray, and Ted Thomson, founded the blending company MacDuff International. They purchased three famous old brands from Allied Distillers, who would later merge with Spanish Domecq and sell its portfolio to Pernod Ricard in 2005.

Lauder's was one of the brands MacDuff International bought from "Old Allied." The brand goes back to 1834, which is amazing as it is generally accepted that blending only became popular around 1850. Legend suggests that Lauder's was born in the Royal Lochnagar Vaults in Glasgow, and this immediately raises the question of whether Lochnagar is the signature malt in this blend. Lauder's took its name from a certain Archibald Lauder, a born-and-bred Glaswegian who was not only successful in blending whiskies but also fathered sixteen children.

At the turn of the nineteenth century, Lauder's was exported as far as America, Russia, and South Africa. It might have helped that this whisky was very popular with the Royal Navy; many of its legendary vessels were known to carry a bottle or two in the mess. Lauder's, first named Lauder's Royal Northern Cream Scotch Whisky, was praised for its quality at various fairs in Chicago, Edinburgh, Glasgow, Manchester, and Paris. **HO**

Tasting notes

Baked apple and stewed fruits on the nose lead into a palate of green banana, canned peach, and strawberry jam on toast. Mouth-coating, with a menthol finish.

Lauder's 12-Year-Old

MacDuff International
www.macduffint.co.uk

Region and country of origin Scotland
Distilleries Various
Alcohol content 40% abv
Style Blend

There are many cream whiskies, most notably Teacher's, but Lauder's claimed to be the first to coin this phrase, since the whisky "tickles one's palate like honey and slips over quite nicely and toothsomely." This innovative marketing approach of the late 1880s was certainly passed down to the company that acquired the brand a century later. The company's namesake, Stewart MacDuff, who unfortunately died in 2008, is remembered as a visionary who was one of the first to see the duty-free market as an excellent way to reach the customer. Nowadays, many distilleries launch special limited editions that can only be purchased at airports around the globe; in some cases, sales are even limited to four or five large airports on different continents.

So let us hail Lauder with the standard bottling, and also hail MacDuff with the 12-Year-Old. When in Scotland, you could give the whisky extra cachet by having a dram in the Royal Burgh of Lauder, a town in the Scottish Borders, about 30 miles (48 km) from Edinburgh. The chance that you will catch a glimpse of Sir Piers Dick-Lauder, the Thirteenth Baronet of the Lauder family, is slim. He is a computer specialist who lives in Australia; in 1998, he was inducted into the Australian Internet Hall of Fame. Whether he is related to Lauder's Glaswegian founder is unknown. **HO**

Tasting notes

Apricot jam spread on a shortbread cookie mingles with fresh peach and a slightly oaky spiciness. A full-bodied whisky, with a peppermint-tea finish.

◄ A Lauder's advertisement displays gold medals won by the whisky.

Ledaig 9-Year-Old Glenkeir Treasures

Glenkeir Whiskies
www.thewhiskyshop.com

Region and country of origin Islands, Scotland
Distillery Tobermory, Tobermory, Isle of Mull, Argyll
Alcohol content 40% abv
Style Single malt

Glenkeir Treasures is the Whisky Shop's independent bottling line. Glenkeir sources its whiskies from the independent bottling sector, using tasters within the company to ensure the whisky is up to close scrutiny.

Glenkeir suggests that this version of Ledaig gives Islay's finest peated whiskies a run for their money. That's slightly misleading, because it is not as peaty as the big three peated malts of Ardbeg, Lagavulin, or Laphroaig; it sits more comfortably alongside a Caol Ila or Bowmore. Accept that, and this is a fine malt.

Until Burn Stewart Distillers upped the strength of its standard Ledaig and put the whisky out non-chill-filtered, significantly improving it in the process, this was the best bottling of Ledaig in the market. It has grown up from a 7- to a 9-year-old, and still offers fans of peated whisky a stepping-stone from Bowmore to the big three down south. Ledaig is made on Mull at Tobermory, a distillery known for a slightly oddball unpeated whisky, but the distillery actually spends about half its time making peated whisky, mainly targeted for the blending sector.

At the time of writing, it remains to be seen whether Glenkeir will introduce a 10-year-old and go head-to-head with the official Ledaig bottling. **DR**

Tasting notes

A sweet, peaty, but easy-drinking whisky, with notes of grilled or barbecued fish, smoky bacon, and a distinctly coastal combination of salt and seaweed.

Ledaig 1972

Burn Stewart Distillers
www.tobermorymalt.com

Region and country of origin Islands, Scotland
Distillery Ledaig (Tobermory), Tobermory, Isle of Mull, Argyll
Alcohol content 48.5% abv
Style Single malt

The Tobermory distillery, shut since 1928, reopened in 1971 and began producing spirit in 1972, under the distillery name Ledaig. When Burn Stewart purchased the distillery in 1993, Ian MacMillan, general distilleries manager and master blender, restored the name Tobermory and painstakingly sampled all the existing stock from 1972, rating each cask and separating the peated spirit, which he called Ledaig, from the nonpeated Tobermory. Today, roughly 50 percent of the distillery's output is from peated malt.

According to MacMillan, "It was a labor of love to analyze and grade all the 1972 casks. Only the very best were selected [to be bottled as vintage expressions] and some were fantastic, a little bit of history, since some of the casks were laid down only a few months after the distillery had restarted production." When the distillery reopened in 1972, production was very inconsistent from week to week, but some production runs were simply amazing.

After reviewing all the 1972 casks, MacMillan reracked the very best in Gonzalez Byass oloroso sherry butts, bottling some as this 1972 32-year-old expression and retaining the higher-strength casks to be bottled in 2013 as a 40-year-old expression. **WM**

Tasting notes

Seaweed, fruit, and black pepper, with cinnamon, clove, cardamom, tobacco, plum, and baked red apple. The bone-dry sherry influence lingers, on with peat smoke.

Linkwood 12-Year-Old

Diageo
www.malts.com

Region and country of origin Speyside, Scotland
Distillery Linkwood, Elgin, Morayshire
Alcohol content 43% abv
Style Single malt

This Speyside single malt from a distillery on the outskirts of Elgin is definitely a hidden gem to seek out. Like so many others in the Diageo group of distilleries, Linkwood's main task is to produce malt for blending; it is also popular outside Diageo, and a third of the output is sold to other companies. The part released as single malt is really small, and the only official bottling you may find is this 12-Year-Old in the Flora & Fauna range.

A few years ago, three very limited 26- year-olds, all with their own cask finish, were released; they showed how well Linkwood single malt ages. From the early 1970s to the mid-1990s, there were actually two distilleries operating on the site, and parts of the old distillery are still being used, although not the stills. The character from pre-1970 was probably quite different from today's Linkwood, as worm tubs were used to condense the spirit vapors, creating a more robust whisky.

The distilled spirit is not collected before 30 minutes of foreshots, an unusually long time. Linkwood has a fruity character, but the light esters appearing at the start of the distillation would ruin the weight and the body of Linkwood single malt. **IR**

Tasting notes

Orange and fruit sherbet. Not as sweet on the palate as the nose suggests, but still lots of marzipan and dark chocolate. The medium finish ends in caramel.

Linkwood 13-Year-Old Douglas of Drumlanrig

Douglas Laing & Co.
www.douglaslaing.com / www.malts.com

Region and country of origin Speyside, Scotland
Distillery Linkwood, Elgin, Morayshire
Alcohol content 46% abv
Style Single malt

There has been a distillery at Linkwood since the 1820s, but the present building was constructed fifty years later and was supplemented by another self-contained unit in 1971 to increase capacity, effectively creating two distilleries on the same site. This is significant in that they use different technologies and hence can produce different-tasting spirits from the same basic ingredients. The earlier distillery uses worm-tub condensers, which impart an oiler, heavier taste in comparison to the more modern shell-and-tube systems in the later building. Worm tubs—basically a coil of pipe submerged in a tub of cold, flowing water—were used for many years but fell out of fashion by the 1970s. They require more cooling water and certainly more maintenance than newer designs, which are built more like a car radiator.

The two distilleries are known as "A" and "B," and while most of the output is now distilled in B, A was revived in 1990 on a part-time basis; the results are mixed together before casking. While this produces a more consistent spirit for blending, it does, sadly, remove the possibility of getting two different spirits from one distillery. The result, here bottled at thirteen years, is well made and easy to drink. **AN**

Tasting notes

Almost a Lowland lightness on the nose, with a fresh floral zestiness leading to a sherbet fizz in the mouth, before waves of zest take over again.

Littlemill Old Malt Cask 19-Year-Old

Douglas Laing & Co. | www.douglaslaing.com

Region and country of origin Lowlands, Scotland
Distillery Littlemill, Bowling, Dumbartonshire
Alcohol content 55.4% abv
Style Single malt

If you visit the Lowlands of Scotland today, you have to search hard to find an authentic malt, as most of the distilleries are industrial grain plants feeding into the blended whisky market. The few remaining malt whisky businesses have been reinvented often by new owners in recent years, so you may wonder what traditional Lowland malt whisky might have been like.

One way to find out is by trying this bottle of Littlemill, distilled in 1991, just three years before the distillery was closed and subsequently gutted by fire. Littlemill was a small, almost cottage-style operation, and a strong contender for the oldest distillery in Scotland—and, some claim, in the world. Althoughi it was on the north bank of the Clyde, beside the railroad from Glasgow to Loch Lomond, the distillery lay south of the Highland Boundary Fault, placing it firmly in the Lowlands. It was innovative, using triple-distillation in its early days and later installing an unusual hybrid still, partly column, partly pot still, in an effort to produce a spirit that would mature faster.

None of these experiments succeeded, though Littlemill kept changing hands, being mothballed and revived until it closed forever in 1994. It seems never to have fulfilled its potential—it was possibly a case of being in the wrong place at the wrong time.

This delicate example bottled by Douglas Laing was matured for nineteen years in an American standard barrel, slightly smaller in size than the usual hogshead, but even so, the wood does not dominate the ethereal spirit. Could this be a true taste of the authentic, old-fashioned Lowlands? **AA**

Tasting notes

A pale straw color in the glass. The fragrant nose has notes of tropical fruit and candle wax, and is light and grassy. The initial spicy hit on the palate fades to leave more clean, citrus flavors, followed by a long, warming, spicy finish that evokes a rich Christmas pudding.

Loch Dhu The Black Whisky 10-Year-Old

Diageo | www.malts.com

Region and country of origin Speyside, Scotland
Distillery Mannochmore, Elgin, Morayshire
Alcohol content 40% abv
Style Single malt

Loch Dhu could be described as one of the Scottish whisky industry's glorious failures. Deemed almost undrinkable by its critics at the time of its launch in 1996–97, bottles are now highly collectable and change hands for significant sums.

The name, meaning "black loch" in Gaelic, reflects the color of the liquid itself, which is as close to black as any whisky has ever got. It was created by United Distillers, forerunners to Diageo, at a time when the company was innovating in order to attract younger, less traditional whisky drinkers. Other experiments included premixed Bell's and Irn-Bru, and Bell's and Coke, along with Red Devil, which contained the Bell's blend plus red chile pepper and other spice, and was highly popular among distillery workers.

Loch Dhu was made by maturing spirit in double-charred casks, although the color was allegedly enhanced using large quantities of spirit caramel. The whisky was not a commercial success and was withdrawn in 2004. Undaunted, Speyside Distillers Co. decided that there was a market for a "black whisky," and subsequently launched Cu Dhub, Gaelic for "black dog," a dram for anyone who misses the old product.

Loch Dhu was produced at Mannochmore distillery, one of Diageo's lowest-profile distilleries, which dates from 1971, when it was built beside the Victorian Glenlossie plant to create extra malt-distilling capacity for United Distillers' blending activities.

In 2011, Diageo announced plans to spend some $7.8 million (£6 million) creating a bioenergy facility within the Glenlossie/Mannochmore complex. **GS**

Tasting notes

The nose is pungent, with soy sauce and something like burnt banana fritters. The palate is relatively smooth, but flavors of incinerated plastic or overused braking disks on a car are never far away. Lots of licorice, aniseed, burnt toffee, and tar in the lengthy finish.

Lochside 1981

Berry Bros. & Rudd | www.bbr.com

Region and country of origin Highlands, Scotland
Distillery Lochside (closed), Montrose, Angus (closed)
Alcohol content 46% abv
Style Single malt

Berry Bros. & Rudd has earned a great reputation for selling quality wine over the years (its shop on St James Street in London has existed at the same location since 1698), but in recent times it has started excelling at whisky, too. The company hit paydirt a few years ago by employing whisky expert Doug McIvor, who has consistently sourced exceptional whisky. Much of it is rare and special, and that, combined with outstanding quality, makes many of the bottlings exceedingly good value for money. It clearly takes a skilled buyer to ensure that an independent bottler acquires the whisky it requires for both blending (should it release blends) and single malts.

This is a case in point. Lochside is something of a curiosity as a distillery because at one time it produced both grain and malt whiskies, catering to the demands of bottlers of both blend and malt. This practice ceased in 1973, when the column still at Lochside was removed. The removal tied in with the takeover of Lochside distillery by Spanish distillers Destilerías y Crianza del Whisky (DYC).

After 1973, the vast majority of Lochside spirit was used by DYC in their various Spanish blends, with only one official bottling of a ten-year-old single malt hitting the market. Interestingly, the 10-year-old is now a collectible and sells at auction for around $235 (£150). It was with great foresight (and maybe a little luck) that Berry Bros. & Rudd purchased this spirit and laid it down to mature for more than twenty years, as this is one of the all-time great releases of this lusciously fruity Highlander. **AS**

Tasting notes

The nose is initially fruity and has an interesting freshness, with grapefruit, pineapple, and a host of other exotic fruits. A darker edge of leather and white pepper is ever present, along with a malty nuttiness. The finish is lingering and exotic.

Lochside 1964 Scott's Selection

Lochside Distillery

Region and country of origin Highlands, Scotland
Distillery Lochside (closed), Montrose, Angus
Alcohol content 47.7% abv
Style "Single blend"

Lochside was something of a unique distillery (it closed in 1992 and has since been demolished). It was among a small group of distillers that produced both grain and malt whisky under the same roof; others include Ben Wyvis (Invergordon grain distillery) and Glen Flagler (Moffat grain distillery). For a period of time, Lochside even had its own bottling plant onsite. This meant that the distillery could go from grain to bottle in the same location, not just for its very rare single malt but for its blends, too.

It is in this respect that Lochside is something of an oddity; its "single blend" is almost unique to Lochside distillery. A single blend is created when grain whisky and malt whisky are blended as new-make spirit, then put into the cask and physically matured together. Does this remove the art of the master blender? To some degree it does, but it also presents the drinker with something special. The technique of casking both grain and malt whisky has only ever been practiced by Macnab Distilleries, which owned Ben Nevis distillery at the time.

As a collectable whisky, Lochside is also starting to gather pace. There was only ever one official bottling of a 10-year-old, mainly for the Spanish market, and these bottles do occasionally appear at auction and usually sell for around $235 (£150). Well-priced bottles from the defunct distillery may also be found, such as the Connoisseurs Choice from 1991 for as little as $70 (£45). Prices are likely to increase over time. With the distillery demolished, no more Lochside can ever be produced. **DR**

Tasting notes

Freshly buttered croissant, notes of wood, oak, cedar, and some vanilla ice cream. Citrus fruit emerges subtly, complemented by mild white pepper. Tangerine and gingersnap cookies give way to a slightly tannic, leathery finish.

Longmorn 15-Year-Old

Chivas Brothers (Pernod Ricard) | www.chivasbrothers.com

Region and country of origin Speyside, Scotland
Distillery Longmorn, Elgin, Morayshire
Alcohol content 45% abv
Style Single malt

Longmorn distillery is located close to the A941 road south of Elgin, in the heart of Speyside. The distillery was established during the great 1890s Victorian Scotch whisky boom, which saw Speyside take center stage when it came to supplying malt for blending. Longmorn has been known principally as a blending whisky throughout its existence, being valued for its complexity, strong aroma, and good length.

The first spirit flowed at Longmorn in December 1894, and the distillery remained in private hands until it merged with the Glenlivet & Glen Grant Distilleries and Hill Thomson & Co. in 1970. It then passed to Seagram eight years later, coming under the control of the Canadian giant's Scottish subsidiary Chivas Brothers. Ultimately, in 2001, Longmorn became part of the Pernod Richard empire. In common with many distilleries in the northeast of Scotland, Longmorn chose to hyphenate its name with the Glenlivet suffix for several decades, though that practice has now been abandoned by virtually all Speyside distillers.

Longmorn 15-Year-Old was the only house bottling offered by Chivas Brothers, although independents Gordon & Macphail and Wm. Cadenhead also routinely bottled the single malt. It was highly regarded by whisky writers such as the late Michael Jackson, but in 2007 it was superseded by a sixteen-year-old variant. Fans of the 15-Year-Old complained that the replacement was significantly more expensive, due in part to the lavish packaging. A significant number also preferred the character of the earlier, fifteen-year-old whisky. **GS**

Tasting notes

Slightly oily on the nose, floral, and malty, with developing citrus notes. Quite big-bodied, rounded on the palate, clean, with sweet malt characteristics. The finish is long and quite dry, with initial malt, hazelnut, and a hint of dry sherry. Well balanced and elegant.

Longmorn 16-Year-Old

Chivas Brothers (Pernod Ricard) | www.chivasbrothers.com

Region and country of origin Speyside, Scotland
Distillery Longmorn, Elgin, Morayshire
Alcohol content 48% abv
Style Single malt

Longmorn is a whisky lover's whisky. The distillery has enough production capacity to cultivate a whole fleet of malts—it boasts no fewer than four pairs of stills—yet the only official distillery bottling available on general release is this 16-Year-Old. Launched in 2007, at a time when several distilleries were beginning to upgrade their benchmark bottlings, the much-loved 15-Year-Old was dropped, to be replaced by this more challenging sixteen-year-old expression.

This is an unpeated whisky; a high proportion of it is matured in first-fill American oak casks that were previously used for aging American whiskey. As with other notable contemporary releases, the distillery owners targeted the luxury connoisseur market. Accordingly, this Longmorn was bottled at a higher strength, the company eschewed the use of chill-filtration, and more elegant packaging was introduced. All the hallmarks of a successful product launch were in place but, intriguingly, the 16-Year-Old was then left to sleep off its exertions, with reviewers unaccountably failing to applaud its charms.

The reason we don't see much malt from this hidden jewel of Speyside in this era of limited editions is that the vast bulk of Longmorn is used as a highly respected top-dressing malt for blending. It is the second malt (after Strathisla) in Chivas Regal, used plentifully in Royal Salute, and is at the heart of Something Special (very popular in South America). While it is apparently every master distiller's second-favorite malt, only a tiny fraction of the spirit produced at the distillery is available as single malt. **IGY**

Tasting notes

The first hit is hot and dusty, then come smells of spice and sweet cedar wood, like an ancient wardrobe. The aromas ripen to soft, juicy, caramelized stone fruits. On the palate, spiced, honeyed almond, then cinnamon, ginger, and nutmeg, right through to the finish.

Longmorn 18-Year-Old

The Whisky Exchange
www.thewhiskyexchange.com

Region and country of origin Speyside, Scotland
Distillery Longmorn, Elgin, Morayshire
Alcohol content 57.8% abv
Style Single malt

Chivas Brothers, the owner of this malt, has some properties in Speyside where they entertain trade guests and overseas visitors. One of them, Linn House in Keith, is among those places where people dine and are then encouraged to help themselves from the whisky cabinet. There is even a Harry Potter-like "room of requirement" bar that appears in the garden at night but reverts to a brick wall in the day. Once, French writer Martine Nouet gave a journalist Longmorn with the unforgettable and very French words, "Let me introduce you to your new mistress."

Longmorn distillery is occasionally opened up to visitors, but the whisky is not as well recognized as it should be. Longmorn is the red squirrel of whisky; everyone loves it but it is very rare and hardly ever seen. The classic 15-Year-Old has been replaced by an elegant 16-Year-Old that is not quite in the same league. There are lots of independent Longmorn bottlings, of varying qualities. Berry Bros. & Rudd has sold some great ones, and there is an outstanding cask-strength bottling sold only at the distillery.

This 18-Year-Old may be the pick of the core range—more assertive than most Longmorns but excellently delivered. Whoever selected this made no mistakes at all. Be warned, though: there are better introductions to this distillery. **DR**

Tasting notes

Cask strength makes this more assertive and dominant than normal favorites, but this is very much a guilty pleasure: a big fruity Speysider, and sweet at its core.

Longmorn 1992

Berry Bros. & Rudd
www.bbr.com

Region and country of origin Speyside, Scotland
Distillery Longmorn, Elgin, Morayshire
Alcohol content 46% abv
Style Single malt

While Longmorn is not known for overly peated whisky, phenols are still present in the distillate. Peated whiskies owe their variations in taste to differences in the chemical compositions of the peats used. The difference between a Speyside peat and an Islay peat is tremendous. The local microclimate, the lie of the land, and the amount of surface vegetation all affect the makeup of an area's peat, and, ultimately, the flavor of the whisky that results from its use.

There are broadly four types of peatland in Scotland: marsh, swamp, bog, and fen. Each fosters a distinct range of plants, resulting in particular aromas and flavors in the whisky. Islay peat appears to be the most phenolic of all, which may explain Islay's status as a mecca for peat lovers.

Longmorn does have an element of smoke running through it, but if the same amount of peat were used during the malting process as for a heavily peated Islay, the whiskies would still have a lower level of phenol; they would be less peaty purely as a result of regional variances in peat composition. Longmorn's subtle phenol can be difficult to detect, but it still adds a depth and complexity of flavor to this relatively unseen 1992 whisky. Some Longmorns can be quite light, which is proof that a whisky does not have to be a sherry "bomb" to be a great Speysider. **AS**

Tasting notes

Fresh summer meadow gives way to sweet licorice and teak oil. A steely purity drizzled with limoncello. Iced green tea with a sharpness that catches the breath.

Gleaming brass and glass spirit safes at Longmorn distillery. →

Longrow 7-Year-Old Gaja Barolo Finish

J. & A. Mitchell Co. | www.springbankdistillers.com

Region and country of origin Highlands, Scotland
Distillery Springbank, Campbeltown, Argyll
Alcohol content 55.8% abv
Style Single malt

One of a trio of whiskies distilled at Springbank distillery, Longrow is a longstanding favorite of whisky collectors and investors. Although Longrow has previously been released as both a 21- and a 25-year-old, the more recent releases have tended to be relatively young whiskies with two 18-year-old batches being the most elderly.

First distilled in 1973, some of Longrow's earliest bottles are now very difficult to find and are worth a lot to collectors and investors. A "First Distillation, Last Cask" edition that was released in the old-style dumpy bottle and a wooden presentation box now sells at auction for more than $1,560 (£1,000). A specialist rare whisky retailer would probably charge in the region of $4,700 (£3,000). Other 1973 releases change hands for less than this special bottle, but still realize many hundreds of dollars at auction.

Following a number of early releases of 1973 and 1974 spirit, there is a notable gap in vintages. Longrow was distilled very sporadically between 1974 and 1992, when more regular distilling commenced. A very few independent bottlings of late-1980s vintages were released. Regular distillation has meant that "Wood Expressions" of Longrow have joined those of its Campbeltown siblings, Springbank and Hazelburn. The Wood Expressions are all limited to some degree, with some releases in the low thousands of bottles and some achieving around 12,000. The separate issues have proved very popular, as they not only demonstrate the effects of additional wood finishing but also are bottled at natural strength. **AS**

Tasting notes

Instantly right up in your face, with hot, peppered tangerine. After the initial hit, the peat surfaces and becomes more noticeable. As the dram calms a little in the glass, sweetness appears with gingerbread. Not a subtle whisky, but very enjoyable nonetheless.

Longrow 10-Year-Old

J. & A. Mitchell Co. | www.springbankdistillers.com

Region and country of origin Highlands, Scotland
Distillery Springbank, Campbeltown, Argyll
Alcohol content 46% abv
Style Single malt

The family-owned distillery of Springbank in the historic whisky-making center of Campbeltown first launched the Longrow 10-Year-Old in 1985. While Springbank single malt is effectively two-and-a-half times distilled, Longrow is double-distilled; and while Springbank has a peating level of 12 to 15 parts per million (ppm), Longrow is relatively heavily peated at 50 to 55 ppm. It is matured in a mix of ex-bourbon and former sherry casks. In 2006, a 100-proof variant of Longrow was introduced to the range.

Today, a significant number of mainland Scottish whisky distilleries have augmented their ranges with more heavily peated expressions that cater to the apparently insatiable demand, notably in northern Europe, for peaty single malts in the Islay style. Such distilleries include Benromach, Isle of Jura, and Tomintoul. No one could accuse the Mitchells of Springbank of jumping on the peaty bandwagon, however, because, in typically independent-minded fashion, they began to distill Longrow in 1973, when Islay single malts were still waiting to be discovered by most whisky drinkers.

According to a Springbank source, "The first distillation was carried out as an experiment when the Springbank chairman set out to prove that it was possible to produce an Islay-style single-malt whisky on the mainland. This experiment produced a whisky so special that Longrow was distilled again a few years later and has become an important part of the Mitchell's portfolio, with regular distillation having taken place since 1992." **GS**

Tasting notes

Full and floral on the nose, with distant wood smoke, cereal notes, and a herbal aroma. Firm and decisive on the slightly waxy palate, with lots of malt and peat. Sweet, with overripe orange and developing brine. Long in the finish with citrus, a hint of soot, and oak.

Longrow 14-Year-Old

J. & A. Mitchell Co. | www.springbankdistillers.com

Region and country of origin Highlands, Scotland
Distillery Springbank, Campbeltown, Argyll
Alcohol content 46% abv
Style Single malt

This whisky began as a bet—or rather, a challenge. The chairman of Springbank distillery, in Scotland's former premier distilling town of Campbeltown, wanted to prove that an Islay-style whisky could be produced on the mainland. Longrow was the reply to that challenge, and is a double-distilled, heavily peated, non-chill-filtered single-malt whisky. The barley used to make it is entirely peat-dried, which gives the whisky its strongly smoky, peaty character.

The original Longrow distillery closed in 1896 and was, apparently, a pretty little place where everything was done by hand. On a visit to Campbeltown during the mid-1880s, writer Alfred Barnard declared that "The Still House is one of the quaintest buildings we have seen, and contains two Pot Stills of the smuggler's pattern." One of its bonded warehouses has survived, and has been pressed into service by Springbank as a bottling hall.

These days, the Longrow 14-Year-Old is created using a combination of bourbon and sherry casks at Springbank distillery, which cleans its tanks before the richly peated malt is distilled. The whisky is subtle at the start, but then builds to become rich and smoky. It is soft and complex, with a telling whiff of the coast despite its mainland distillation. The dram is mellow, with hints of cereals and barley, but it also smells fresh and sweet—mix together pepper, spice, apple juice, and slight cigar smoke, and you get the idea. There are not many whiskies like this, with smoky embers, mint, smoke, chocolate, and cream all fighting for room on the nose and palate. Sumptuous, indeed. **JH**

Tasting notes

This may be a 14-year-old, but it tastes a lot more mature than that—in a bar, you wouldn't ask it for ID. And it is rich—actually, not so much rich as loaded, with plenty in the bank, let's say. The aging in sherry casks certainly has led to a rather satisfying single malt.

Longrow CV

J. & A. Mitchell Co. | www.springbankdistillers.com

Region and country of origin Highlands, Scotland
Distillery Springbank, Campbeltown, Argyll
Alcohol content 46% abv
Style Single malt

Not long ago, Longrow production director Frank McHardy and then distillery manager Stuart Robertson were tasked with producing a Longrow with maximum smoke and peat, yet also with balance, complexity, and maturity. The resulting whisky, introduced in 2008, along with an eighteen-year-old variant, was Longrow CV. It contains six-, ten-, and fourteen-year-old whiskies, matured in sherry, port, bourbon, and rum casks that range in capacity from 13 to 145 gallons (50 to 550 liters).

The name "CV" stands for "Curriculum Vitae," which usually means a summary of employment experience, but here refers to a blend of Longrow whiskies of various ages, matured in a variety of cask types and sizes. CV is almost a showcase for what Longrow can be. The name has also been applied to Springbank and Hazelburn expressions that are similarly released without age statements.

The Mitchells of Springbank are the "keepers of the Campbeltown flame" in a sense, as they have a passionate attachment to the town's great and under-celebrated distilling heritage. Accordingly, both the Longrow and Hazelburn single malts produced in Springbank take their names from long-lost Campbeltown distilleries. Longrow distillery was founded in 1824, when the ancient fishing port of Campbeltown was starting to see a growth in whisky-making activity as a result of the liberalizing Excise Act of the previous year. Longrow, which closed in 1896, was the third or fourth legal distillery in the borough, and was located close to the Springbank site. **GS**

Tasting notes

Slightly gummy on the nose, then brine and fat peat notes develop. Sweet vanilla and malt also emerge. The smoky palate offers lively brine and is quite dry and spicy, with background vanilla and lots of ginger. The medium finish is peaty, with persistent, oaky ginger.

The Macallan
10-Year-Old Fine Oak

Edrington Group | www.themacallan.com

Region and country of origin Speyside, Scotland
Distillery The Macallan, Craigellachie, Banffshire
Alcohol content 40% abv
Style Single malt

So we know that Macallan has a reputation for big sherry bombs, something the distillery does very well. But in 2004, the Edrington Group parent company decided to diversify into American oak as well as European, releasing a new range to complement the Sherry Oak expressions.

But why, we have to ask, would a distiller release something that could end up competing with an existing well-established range? Initially the decision sent a few shock waves through the old faithful sherry brigade, but the Fine Oak range has weathered this storm and really established itself. It provides an interesting window into another aspect of maturing whisky at Macallan.

Our starter into the range at ten years old is a complex combination of European oak seasoned with sherry and American oak casks seasoned with both sherry and bourbon. This triple-cask maturation gives a very complex malt, even at these tender years. Once again, Macallan insisted on natural color, nothing added, so all the color comes from the interaction of spirit and wood alone, combined with the timeless skill of the Macallan's master whisky maker to deliver the range's characteristics. **AA**

Tasting notes

Complex on the nose, with hints of fruit, pear, apple, and honey. Palate is soft, with malt notes, and the finish is lush, with dense fruit notes and vanilla from the oak.

The Macallan
10-Year-Old Sherry Oak

Edrington Group | www.themacallan.com

Region and country of origin Speyside, Scotland
Distillery The Macallan, Craigellachie, Banffshire
Alcohol content 40% abv
Style Single malt

Here we are delving into the upper reaches of the big three in whisky terms, Glenfiddich, Glenlivet, and the Macallan, and with the Macallan, we are into the lofty heights of a luxury brand. Everything about it, especially when you get further into the range, oozes luxury and opulence. But all big brands have to have humbler reaches, and the 10-Year-Old Sherry Oak is a great way to tap into this one without having to rob several banks.

Due care and attention is taken, as much with the 10-Year-Old as with the more expensive expressions. The spirit has spent a minimum of ten years maturing in Spanish oak casks, which are handcrafted for the Macallan and seasoned with sherry in Jerez, Spain. If ever a younger expression set a house style, it is this one—this is the benchmark for the brand.

The Macallan has also found itself entering into the political landscape. In 2001, British politician Michael Martin selected the Macallan 10-Year-Old as the official Scotch of the Speaker of the House of Commons, even though he himself does not drink. He did, however, smell whiskies to make his selection. This selection continued the tradition of the Speaker designating an official single malt. **AA**

Tasting notes

The sherry is certainly present at first on the nose, with dried fruit that follow on to the palate, where there is a big ball of sweetness and just a hint of wood smoke.

The Macallan
12-Year-Old Fine Oak

Edrington Group | www.themacallan.com

Region and country of origin Speyside, Scotland
Distillery The Macallan, Craigellachie, Banffshire
Alcohol content 43% abv
Style Single malt

If the 10-Year-Old is the introduction to the range, then the 12-Year-Old is getting closer to the heart. Again, Macallan's impressive, and expensive, wood policy comes into play here, creating a rich, round spirit that certainly stands out in comparison tastings. So let's for a moment focus in on these casks that mean so much to the brand. The story is one that moves from the heated climes of Spain to Speyside.

The trees come from the forests in the Galicia, Cantabria, and Asturias regions of northern Spain. The logs are quartersawn and then air dried. Staves are then sent to the cooperages of Jerez, where they are toasted over open fires. This helps to change the chemistry in the woods and will allow the spirit to penetrate further as it matures, picking up more of the lovely vanilla tones. To season the casks, and to draw out more of the bitter wood tannins, Macallan has the casks filled initially with a young fermenting wine; that is emptied and replaced with dry oloroso. This is then left to season for at least eighteen months.

So a lot of expense, time, and patience go into creating a bottle of Macallan, and we haven't even talked about barley and distillation yet, on which Macallan puts equal emphasis to create its malts. **AA**

Tasting notes

A smooth and mellow whisky. A very vanilla-dominated nose, with hints of ginger and dried fruits. Rich on the palate, with fruit and sherry but balanced with spice.

The Macallan
12-Year-Old Sherry Oak

Edrington Group | www.themacallan.com

Region and country of origin Speyside, Scotland
Distillery The Macallan, Craigellachie, Banffshire
Alcohol content 40% abv
Style Single malt

The Gary Barlow of whiskies. Good at what it does, sweet, but with a slightly dry side and, in some cases, too popular to be as appreciated and admired as it deserves to be. The Macallan 12-Year-Old is a very sherried whisky indeed. It is distilled in Speyside and then spends some time in sherry casks. It probably also had a period of depression, much like Mr. Barlow, but has managed to overcome this and come out on top.

Now owned by the Edrington Group, it has had its true identity revealed. Originally, even though the distillery began as family-owned way back in 1824, it has evolved into a mightily successful brand—everyone's going crazy for it. Up close, it honks of sherry, rich fruit, red berries, orange peel, and ripe plum. But go a little deeper and there's a confident, slightly smoky toffee aroma. Add a splash more water, and its true character becomes evident.

So, is it as witty or as fun as it purportedly once was? No matter. The point is that it delivers. You don't need it to be your thing to be able to appreciate it. Overlooking it purely based on obviousness and how topical it currently is would be a big mistake. Including it as a fine example of doing what it does well is by far the better assessment. **JH**

Tasting notes

Mahogany, rich, with lots of sherry notes, this could fool you into thinking it was actually going to be a sherry. Berries, plum, and a hint of smokiness on the palate.

The Macallan 15-Year-Old Fine Oak

Edrington Group | www.themacallan.com

Region and country of origin Speyside, Scotland
Distillery The Macallan, Craigellachie, Banffshire
Alcohol content 43% abv
Style Single malt

A few years ago, the Macallan owners declared that the world no longer wanted strong dark whisky in the way it had before, and they launched a range of lighter, bourbon-cask-influenced malts under the Fine Oak umbrella name. The company was wrong about the dark spirits theory—just ask Glenfarclas—but its logic for launching lighter whiskies probably had nothing to do with consumer demand and a lot more to do with the limited supply of sherry casks. Although Edrington owns a large proportion of Scotland's sherry cask inventory, much of the sherried whisky is destined for consumption in the Far East.

Whatever the reason for the release of the Fine Oak range, it has given consumers a mouthwatering choice between two totally different types of whisky. The traditionally sherried whiskies have always sent the review critics into a frenzy, but the Fine Oak range is all about the purity of the Macallan as a malt. Perhaps the age where the two are in equality is at fifteen years, where the sherried version is young enough for the sherry to show off, but the oak is in check, and the malt still has a say. In the case of the Fine Oak, the 15-Year-Old is a corker and can claim to be among the best in the range. **DR**

Tasting notes

A truly great single malt. Honey and spice on the nose, with honey continuing on to the big and rounded palate. Superb balance. The finish is lengthy, with fruit.

The Macallan 17-Year-Old Fine Oak

Edrington Group | www.themacallan.com

Region and country of origin Speyside, Scotland
Distillery The Macallan, Craigellachie, Banffshire
Alcohol content 43% abv
Style Single malt

In addition to using top-quality barley, Macallan also takes one of the finest, most restricted "cuts" of any of the distilleries (only around 16 percent of the spirit makes it to the casks), ensuring that only the best spirit is collected from its short, squat stills. For the Fine Oak range, that spirit is then matured in three different types of cask.

In addition to Spanish oak seasoned with sherry, it also uses American oak seasoned with sherry and additional American oak seasoned with premium bourbon. Each of these casks contributes something different, with the American casks offering apple, vanilla, and sweet citrus notes, and the Spanish giving dried fruit, spice, a tinge of chocolate orange, and a healthy dose of color. The result is a soft, light malt, with overtones of vanilla and fruit with a touch of oak.

Whereas the sherry maturation could be said to overpower the natural character of the Macallan spirit, the Fine Oak range allows it to shine through, offering drinkers a lighter alternative to its more robust and full-bodied expressions. This 17-Year-Old currently sits in the middle of the Fine Oak range, which is constantly evolving and, if this expression is anything to go by, constantly improving. **PB**

Tasting notes

Soft, rich, and light on the nose, with citrus and spice. Impressive but restrained oak and sherry on the palate. The finish is lightly spiced, creamy, and rounded.

← Guests of the Macallan distillery may stay at the distillery-owned Easter Elchies House.

The Macallan 18-Year-Old

Edrington Group | www.themacallan.com

Region and country of origin Speyside, Scotland
Distillery The Macallan, Craigellachie, Banffshire
Alcohol content 43% abv
Style Single malt

For those who thought that Macallan's attention was being diverted away from its renowned sherried whiskies and onto its Fine Oak range, this 18-Year-Old is evidence that sherry remains a powerful part of the Macallan psyche. This expression is matured for eighteen years in Spanish sherry oak. These aren't just sherry casks, though. Typical of the distillery's attention to detail, they have been through a painstaking series of stages in order to ensure that cask and spirit spend the eighteen years in characteristic Macallan harmony.

Even the drying of the wood is done with maximum attention to detail. Once the oak has been carved into staves, it is dried, first in the north of Spain with its inconsistent climate, where winters see typically Atlantic clouds, rain, and cool temperatures, and then in the south, which experiences high summer temperatures and an average of twelve hours of sunshine a day. It is then sent to the cooperages of Jerez to be steamed, bent, made into casks, and charred so as to change the chemistry of the wood and release favorable vanillins and tannins.

To draw out the harsher tannins, the casks are first conditioned by "mosto," a lightly fermented wine produced immediately after the grape harvest in August and September. Once this has done its job, it is replaced with dry oloroso sherry, which further conditions the cask for eighteen months. Few other distilleries have this attention to detail, which explains why the quality levels of its whisky have remained so high over the years. **PB**

Tasting notes

Rich, almost Camp-coffee-like on the nose but with lighter, buttery aromas coming through the oak. On the palate, it's ridiculously voluptuous and clean, with a touch of spice and an oaky nip. The finish, while not particularly long, is lightly spiced, rounded, and rich.

The Macallan 18-Year-Old Fine Oak

Edrington Group | www.themacallan.com

Region and country of origin Speyside, Scotland
Distillery The Macallan, Craigellachie, Banffshire
Alcohol content 43% abv
Style Single malt

Taking out a license in 1824, the Macallan became one of the first Speyside distilleries to establish itself in modern, legitimized form (an illicit still had stood on the site for generations). This single malt is thrice matured for a minimum of eighteen years in oak casks. But not ordinary oak casks: they include Spanish and American oak casks seasoned with sherry, and American oak casks seasoned with bourbon. Such attention to detail delivers a complex single malt that is both delicate and easy to drink.

Rich and light, refined and floral, the Macallan 18-Year-Old Fine Oak is a classic in anyone's terms. It is scented with spice, citrus, and wood, and suffused with smoke. This is the kind of whisky that can return a steely gaze without blinking, a confident fella, broad and steady, mature and hinting at a dramatic backstory that would grab the attention of all the guests at a dinner party. It may not linger for too long, and its finish is little more than a whisper, but that does not mean it is unmemorable. On the contrary, it makes a lasting impression, in the way that a great performer always leaves the audience wanting more.

And do not be misled by the presence of sherry, which some regard as a drink for old ladies. This whisky is testosterone-driven and gets its virility from the bourbon. If this Macallan were to assume human form, it would indubitably be male—probably a pipe-smoking male in a Barbour jacket, wearing a peppery aftershave and sporting without irony or campness a big moustache like Tom Selleck's in the 1980s television series *Magnum, P. I.* **JH**

Tasting notes

This is an elegantly masculine whisky. With its rich amber color and spiced aroma, this is one single malt that can be described as impressive and "large." While the whisky is beautifully mouth-coating, the finish unfortunately stays only for a moment or two.

Macallan 18-Year-Old Glenkeir Treasures

Glenkeir Whiskies | www.thewhiskyshop.com

Region and country of origin Speyside, Scotland
Distillery The Macallan, Craigellachie, Banffshire
Alcohol content 40% abv
Style Single malt

Glenkeir Treasures is the independent bottling arm of The Whisky Shop, which has revolutionized the way that quality whisky reaches the general public in the United Kingdom. The chain of shops combines all of the attractions of an independent liquor store with the convenience of a High Street store. The company policy is to work with the leading distillers to grow brands through its own extensive print and online magazine, *Whiskeria*. With its knowledgeable staff and comfortable environment, the group has played a major role in educating customers about the world of whisky. But it's not all entry-level stuff, and releases like this are attractive to the serious whisky fan, too, either as a drink or as an investment.

No distillery attracts as much attention from the collector as Macallan. This 18-Year-Old was particularly sought after because in the days before the Macallan Fine Oak range was launched, it was genuinely different. Its higher-than-average proportion of bourbon casks offer the drinker a chance to taste the heart of the malt, rather than the cask it has been matured in. This whisky has a loyal following and, for the age, represents very good value for money. Just enough oak to give it body, too. **DR**

Tasting notes

Apple, grapefruit, and lemongrass on the nose, with little evidence of oak. Immense blood orange and kumquat and a flurry of white pepper on the palate.

Macallan 21-Year-Old Fine Oak

Edrington Group | www.themacallan.com

Region and country of origin Speyside, Scotland
Distillery The Macallan, Craigellachie, Banffshire
Alcohol content 43% abv
Style Single malt

The importance of investing in decent wood from early on in a malt's maturing life is going to manifest itself for certain when the malt hits its teenage years. Like anything that grows up, whisky is definitely a product of its environment and upbringing as it matures. The nature–nurture argument prevails even in whisky circles.

Macallan's 21-Year-Old, in fact most of the Macallan's expressions, matures into a well rounded and balanced young adult, safe in its comfort blanket of the handcrafted casks. The spirit is kept under close observation by distiller Bob Delgarno as it matures, and it is his job to ensure that his twenty-something casks are behaving and reaching the points of perfection when they can be released into society.

To show that Macallan takes the moniker of "most luxurious single malt" very seriously, the color of the whisky is achieved wholly naturally, just through the influence of the casks, without the addition of any coloring, as has otherwise become common.

This 21-Year-Old is a master class in oak-aged whiskies—the oak is clearly present yet a plethora of other flavors are allowed to come through. A big, solid dram to savor after dinner and into the evening. **AA**

Tasting notes

Enticing citrus, vanilla, and cinnamon on the nose. The palate brings spice, clove, marmalade, and the wisps of smoke warm you gently. The finish is full, with toffee.

Macallan's Ten Pound bar at Montage Beverly Hills Hotel, California.

The Macallan 25-Year-Old Sherry Oak

Edrington Group | www.themacallan.com

Region and country of origin Speyside, Scotland
Distillery The Macallan, Craigellachie, Banffshire
Alcohol content 43% abv
Style Single malt

With the 25-Year-Old, we are reaching the top end of Macallan's sherry oak expressions, and approaching the zenith of sherried luxury. And twenty-five years in oak is no mean feat. This is the territory where the wood can overwhelm the spirit and you end up chewing a piece of balsa-wood-flavored Christmas cake: a far from pleasant experience.

Thankfully, Macallan does things with a little more aplomb than simply letting a cask have too much of its way with the maturing spirit, and this big whisky can stand up to long maturation periods in the flavorsome sherry oak. The wood does exert its influence, but what the team at the distillery has created is balance—even at this age. This expression still offers an excellent balance of oak, malt, and a little smoke that would be the envy of malts half its age. The team has also created a seriously smooth and sought-after whisky. *Sublime* is a word often attached to this expression, and if you are lucky, you can find it gracing some of the finest hotels and bars in the world.

This is where Macallan really works its luxury tag. Much sought after, precious, and very difficult to find, the 25-Year-Old fulfills the old adage that if you make it hard to get but desirable, people will want more. This is the elixir of Russian oligarchs, oil tycoons, and shipping magnates, the sort of whisky that whisky aficionados dream about having around the house just as an everyday drinking malt. We are talking an aspirational malt here, although amazingly, we're not at the peak of Macallan's offerings yet. **AA**

Tasting notes

The nose is gentle, with plenty of cooked orange mixed with cinnamon, clove, and almost a paprika hint. The palate is where all the richness is—bags of fruitcake, dried fruit, and glacé cherry. Once you swallow, it just seems to go on forever, with toffee cream and spices.

The Macallan 30-Year-Old Sherry Oak

Edrington Group | www.themacallan.com

Region and country of origin Speyside, Scotland
Distillery The Macallan, Craigellachie, Banffshire
Alcohol content 43% abv
Style Single malt

If you thought the 25-year-old was stepping into the realms of serious rarity, then the 30-Year-Old will just about blow you away—if you can find any. So rare is this bottling that most retailers will only allocate one bottle per customer, and that's when they have a bottle. Sure, there are more expensive whiskies out there, and some of them are in the Macallan's range, but nothing speaks more clearly of this distillery's sherried pedigree than this. All the other expressions are really leading to this pinnacle, like a mountain ridge you have to follow to reach your summit. But the climb is definitely worth it. The rewards for parting with your riches and seeking out this expression will be generously returned by the comforting arm of warming sherry goodness.

All the citrus, smoke, and dried fruits of previous expressions have been mellowed and matured to the point of aged perfection in the 30-Year-Old. Sometimes drinking a single malt at this age is like treasuring a relic or antique. It speaks of things that have passed, things that have made us what we are. Nature has taken its slow, gentle, but sure course of imparting spirit with cask and beautifully mellowing out the impurities.

To get a spirit to this level of perfection, without many flaws, is a testament to the sherry oak wood policy employed by the distillery, combined with the mollycoddling activities of the maturation team. Once the whisky is in the glass, you appreciate the richness of sherry maturation, and at the same time understand why Macallan is so very good at it. **AA**

Tasting notes

Seriously rich sherry hits the nose first, with cooked orange, burnt brown sugar, a hint of nutmeg spice, and a fresh humidor note. The palate reveals a smooth character full of dark fruit and spiced orange before the lavish finish brings spice, nutmeg, and cinnamon.

The Macallan Director's Edition

Edrington Group | www.themacallan.com

Region and country of origin Speyside, Scotland
Distillery The Macallan, Craigellachie, Banffshire
Alcohol content 40% abv
Style Single malt

The late, great whisky writer Michael Jackson may not have invented whisky writing, but he played a key role in bringing whisky to a wider audience, and several writers in this book owe their careers to him. One of Michael's great loves was big old-fashioned sherried Macallans, and he would have loved this expression.

Once upon a time, Macallan did little else but make big sherried whiskies, and its owners made much of the fact that they used only the finest sherry casks from Spain. In recent years, the focus of the company has been on whisky with a mix of bourbon and sherry casks, so this release in 2011 came as a bit of a shock.

The Macallan Director's Edition was originally released exclusively through the Whisky Shop, a United Kingdom retail chain, before going on general release toward the end of 2011. It has no age statement but retailed for about $60 (around £40), which is a great price for a sherried Macallan. And the taste doesn't disappoint. It is definitely worth investigating and perhaps investing in a few bottles. Michael would have agreed. **DR**

Tasting notes

Dry sherry and berry notes, treacle toffee, burnt toast, brittle toffee, praline, and blood orange. There's a lot going on here, but the main theme is definitely sherry.

The Macallan Masters of Photography 2nd Edition, Albert Watson

Edrington Group | www.themacallan.com

Region and country of origin Speyside, Scotland
Distillery The Macallan, Craigellachie, Banffshire
Alcohol content 46.5% abv
Style Single malt

In 2008 Macallan introduced the series called Masters of Photography, pairing a famous photographer with a limited-release expression. Scottish photographer Albert Watson teamed with Macallan for their second release in this series. The whisky is a vatting of two specially selected twenty-year-old first-fill oloroso sherry butts. Limited to just 1,000 bottles, each comes with ten signed portfolio prints.

According to Watson, "Macallan came to me with the incredible story of the sherry oak casks from Spain and how they are used to make their single-malt whisky and asked me to think of how I could interpret this as a photographic art project." Watson spent twelve days following the life of a cask, from the Spanish oak trees in northern Spain to the cooperages where the oak is fashioned into barrels, and on to the distillery and their long slumber.

Macallan is famous for its use of these highly prized Spanish oak sherry casks. It is believed as much as 60 percent of a whisky's flavor is derived from its cask, the remainder being a combination of the shape of the still, water, barley, and other elements. **WM**

Tasting notes

The nose explodes with dark vanilla bean, clove, coriander, nutmeg, and candied orange peel. The rich palate adds raisin, date, leather, and tobacco.

The Macallan's single malt and equally singular album of photographs. ➔

The Macallan Royal Marriage

Edrington Group | www.themacallan.co.uk

Region and country of origin Speyside, Scotland
Distillery The Macallan, Craigellachie, Banffshire
Alcohol content 46.8% abv
Style Single malt

It's unique. It's collectable. Indeed, this whisky hopes to reflect a better "marriage" than the previous one offered by the brand to celebrate the union of Prince Charles and Lady Diana Spencer in 1981. One thing it does offer is placement as a much-sought-after collectible across many countries. This limited edition of 1,000 bottles, celebrating the royal marriage of Prince William to Catherine (Kate) Middleton on April 29, 2011, features single-malt whisky taken from two casks, both filled on April 29, one from 1996 and one from 1999.

There's more than Diana's engagement ring that has featured in William and Kate's wedding—Macallan whisky maker Bob Dalgarno, who had a hand in creating the 1981 bottle for William's parents, has also been integral to the selection of casks and managing the entire process. Likewise, David Holmes, who was the creative force behind the 1981 bottle and played a big part in the Charles and Di brand's advertising campaign in the 1980s and early 1990s, has created the label and packaging design for William and Kate's edition.

This packaging is in itself a thing to behold—a duck egg blue label with interwoven monograms and silver roses is then placed in a silver-colored presentation box complete with a viewing window so that anyone can be nosy about the bottle within without compromising the item's collectability should one open the packaging. It's well thought out. It's pretty exceptional, too. If you can get your hands on one, this one is a keeper. **JH**

Tasting notes

It's all very lovely, to be honest, much like the wedding itself. Easy on the eye—golden amber, sweet on the nose—mixed spice, zesty orange peel, and barley. There's also a promisingly long finish, which is always a good sign.

Macduff 15-Year-Old Harris Bottling

Harris Whisky Co. | www.harriswhisky.com

Region and country of origin Speyside, Scotland
Distillery Macduff, Banff, Banffshire
Alcohol content 58.7% abv
Style Single malt

The towns of Macduff and Banff face each other on either side of the mouth of the River Dornoch. They have a long history of largely friendly rivalry. From the day the Banff distillery opened in 1824, residents of Macduff felt, or were made by their neighbors to feel, inferior because they had no whisky maker of their own. That all changed in 1962, when the opening of this distillery enabled them again to look people from Banff in the eye.

At the time of its construction, the Macduff distillery was very much state of the art, with several devices that have since become commonplace that then seemed extravagantly advanced, including a stainless-steel mash tun and newfangled shell-and-tube heat exchangers.

After three years in charge of the business, the original owners, Glen Deveron Distillers, sold the distillery to Block, Grey, & Block, who doubled the number of stills from two to four. In 1972, the plant changed hands again, and thereafter belonged to William Lawson, a subsidiary of the Italian firm Martini & Rossi, who rebuilt the tun room and the still house and installed a fifth still. Macduff then passed through the hands of Bacardi and Diageo, before being acquired by John Dewar & Sons, who at the time of writing are the current owners.

Whiskies that Macduff bottles itself are always marketed as Glen Deveron; those that it produces but which are bottled by other firms—such as this single malt, which is contracted out to the Harris Whisky Co.—carry the name of the distillery itself. **GL**

Tasting notes

This whisky has a sharp, summery nose of quince, pear, and lemon. It tastes of pear, too, along with smoked meat, but the effect is confined almost to the top of the palate: this whisky lacks an undercarriage. The finish is flowery and chalky in almost equal measure.

Mackinlay's Shackleton Rare Old Highland Malt

Whyte & Mackay | www.whyteandmackay.com

Region and country of origin Speyside, Islands, and Highlands, Scotland
Distillery Whyte & MacKay and Mackinlay's
Alcohol content 47.3% abv **Style** Blended malt

Mackinlay's Shackleton Rare Old Highland Malt is a special commemorative bottling and a faithful reproduction of the Mackinlay's whisky taken on explorer Ernest Shackleton's first ill-fated Antarctic expedition to the South Pole in 1907. As history tells it, Shackleton took twenty-five cases of Mackinlay's Rare Old Highland Malt on his famous expedition, but when the winter turned nasty early and the sea began to freeze, threatening their ship, Shackleton and his party were forced to make a rapid retreat.

The camp was abandoned, along with provisions, and over the coming years it was buried under ice. Among the items left behind were eleven bottles of Mackinlay's. In 2007, the cargo was discovered by the New Zealand Antarctic Heritage Trust and then, a few years later in 2011, Whyte & Mackay, who owned the original whisky, persuaded the Trust to allow some of the priceless whisky to travel to Scotland. The Trust wouldn't allow it on a regular flight so Whyte & Mackay's owner Vijay Mallya collected it in his private plane and brought it back to Scotland. Once there, the company's master blender Richard Paterson analyzed the whisky and was sufficiently impressed, even after 100 years, to set about re-creating it.

The whisky is presented in a replica bottle and wooden case similar to the way that Shackleton left it, and includes malts from Speyside, Islands, and Highlands including Glen Mhor. In all, only 50,000 bottles were produced with each bottle selling at a price of $160 (£100). Of this a donation of $8 (£5) goes to the Antarctic Heritage Trust. **JH**

Tasting notes

This pale gold whisky is soft, delicate, and elegant in aroma and has notes of caramel and nutmeg. Not only is it a gentle blend, it's also one that lingers on the palate and calls to mind a mix of vanilla, orange peel, and home baking.

A magazine reports the progress of Shackleton and his ship, *Nimrod*.

(1) HIS SHIP, (2) HIMSELF, AND (3) HIS MERRY MEN ALL

In July, 1907, Lieut. Shackleton set sail in the "Nimrod" for the South Pole. He is now on his way home, having succeeded in reaching the Southern Magnetic Pole, and actually approaching within 111 miles of the South Pole itself. In the first picture is shown the good ship "Nimrod," a forty-year old sealing ship; in the centre is a portrait of the resolute explorer himself (by Langfier, 23a, Old Bond Street); and, below, his gallant crew

Mannochmore 1991 Connoisseurs Choice

Gordon & MacPhail | www.gordonandmacphail.com

Region and country of origin Speyside, Scotland
Distillery Mannochmore, Elgin, Morayshire
Alcohol content 46% abv
Style Single malt

The 1960s were a boom time for whisky. Many new distilleries appeared, among them Tomintoul, Tormore, and Clynelish, to help slake an increasing consumer thirst. It was also the decade when consumers were able to finally lay their hands on some single malts from distilleries whose output had hitherto only been used as constituents of blends.

In 1960, George Urquhart, owner of Gordon & MacPhail, started the Connoisseurs Choice range. Rather than simply buy casks of maturing whisky as and when they became available on the open market or were deemed surplus to requirements by blenders, it sent selected casks to distilleries to have them filled with new-make spirit, bottling them only when it felt the whisky was ready. Slightly confusingly, the Connoisseurs Choice expresses the age of each whisky as a vintage (the year it was distilled), but also provides the year of bottling. Vaguely sensible, you might think, but, because there are no exact dates, it is difficult to know whether, say, a whisky distilled in 1975 and bottled in 2005 is twenty-nine or thirty years old. Does it matter? Some people might think so.

Mannochmore was built in 1971 and is situated next to the Glenlossie distillery; for years its workforce split its time between the two. It is perhaps best known for Loch Dhu, the black whisky, which was released to very mixed reviews. If you see a bottle of Loch Dhu, buy it, as it is becoming increasingly rare and collectable. Alternatively, save yourself a few dollars and pick up this lovely citrusy and crisp 1991 Connoisseurs Choice Mannochmore. **PB**

Tasting notes

Tapioca pudding, tangerine, lemongrass, and tropical fruit, herbal on the nose with a hint of light sherry. On the palate it's effervescent fruit, lime marmalade, and juicy barley with crisp green apples. The finish is sweet biscuit and vanilla.

Millburn 1978

Gordon & MacPhail | www.gordonandmacphail.com

Region and country of origin Highlands, Scotland
Distillery Millburn, Inverness, Inverness-shire
Alcohol content 46% abv
Style Single malt

The year 1988 was a dark one for the city of Inverness, the northernmost city in the United Kingdom. Having already lost its other two distilleries—Glen Mhor and Glen Albyn—two years earlier, it witnessed the dismantling of its oldest and last remaining distillery, Millburn. However, unlike Glens Albyn and Mhor, which were demolished to make room for a supermarket, not all of Millburn has disappeared; some of it remains as a steakhouse, with a lone chimney indicating its former use . . . as if that might be any consolation. Millburn's fate was sealed by its outdated equipment and the lack of room for expansion in a city that was itself expanding and didn't want a distillery in a populated area. And, as with many of the distilleries that disappeared in the 1980s, there isn't a great deal of its whisky remaining.

Millburn was founded in 1807 and was originally called the Inverness distillery. Eventually, it was renamed after the Mill Burn, a river that traverses the city, running parallel to the Caledonian Canal and River Ness. The distillery stood on the banks of the Mill Burn and used its water for cooling. The water for the whisky itself was actually piped in from 8 miles (13 km) away at Loch Duntelchaig, although the Mill Burn did originally serve that purpose, too.

The Millburn house style was said to be smoky and aromatic. This Gordon & MacPhail expression, which was distilled in 1978, matured in a refill sherry butt, and bottled in 2008 (a lack of precise dates makes it difficult to pin down an exact age), captures those elements superbly. **PB**

Tasting notes

Dusty oak, citrus, and sweet oat biscuits on the nose, with light sherry and lychees. On the palate, it is crisp green fruit, with beautifully balanced and intertwining sweet peat and oak. Quite drying on the finish, with a definite and long hit of spicy licorice.

Miltonduff 10-Year-Old

Gordon & MacPhail | www.gordonandmacphail.com

Region and country of origin Speyside, Scotland
Distillery Miltonduff, Elgin, Morayshire
Alcohol content 40% abv
Style Single malt

Considering that Miltonduff is a large distillery in terms of potential output, it is surprising the "make" has such a low profile as a single malt. This is because owners Chivas Brothers have other priority single malts on which they concentrate their marketing energies, while Miltonduff provides the malt backbone of the company's best-selling family of Ballantine's blends.

Chivas's parent company, Pernod Ricard, acquired Miltonduff—and Ballantine's—as part of the package of assets that came with the purchase of Allied Domecq in 2005, and under Allied's stewardship, Miltonduff had been bottled as a 12-year-old, though it never enjoyed wide public exposure.

Miltonduff has been key to the Ballantine's blend since the mid-1930s, but the distillery actually dates back to 1824, being situated close to historic Pluscarden Abbey. Indeed, the plant is thought to stand on the site of the abbey's meal mill. Much of the current distillery was built during the mid-1970s, and the site is also home to laboratories, technical and engineering facilities, and centralized warehousing for other Chivas distilleries in the area.

Between 1964 and 1981, Miltonduff operated a pair of Lomond stills in addition to its "standard" pot stills, producing a variant known as Mosstowie, which was used for blending purposes, though bottlings are also available from several independent bottlers.

The Gordon & MacPhail 10-Year-Old edition of Miltonduff has been matured in ex-sherry casks and is a very competitively priced single malt. **GS**

Tasting notes

Fresh and fruity on the nose, with toasted malt, some sherry and honey, and a mildly herbal note. Soft fruits, toffee, mild oak, and a hint of pepper on the relatively full and well-balanced palate. The finish is subtly drying, with a hint of ginger.

Miltonduff 15-Year-Old

Chivas Brothers (Pernod Ricard) | www.chivasbrothers.com

Region and country of origin Speyside, Scotland
Distillery Miltonduff, Elgin, Morayshire
Alcohol content 46% abv
Style Single malt

The shape and size of the copper still used in the making of a malt spirit massively affects its flavor. A tall, large still causes the evaporated spirit to pass over extra copper; the copper removes impurities, and only the lightest elements of the spirit make it to the lyne arm to be recondensed, ensuring a lighter, floral spirit. Short, wide stills allow heavier, more flavorsome, and oilier elements to get through.

It would certainly be advantageous if you could make several types of spirit in one still—and the Lomond still did just that. In the neck of the Lomond still are movable plates that may be adjusted to vary the distance the spirit has to travel. Miltonduff was one of several distilleries to have such a still, but its plates became clogged and maintaining them became costly.

For a while, malt from Miltonduff was released under a different name. Now, under the ownership of Pernod Ricard, the original name has been restored, although little of the product ends up in the single-malt market. But the distillery is sizable and can make 1.3 million gallons (5 million liters) of spirit a year.

The overall flavor here is one of fruity, sweet, and clean barley. There is no particularly big or dominant flavor, and this official bottling is not as interesting as some of the independent releases that have been produced over the years. But this bottling is a good-quality Speyside whisky that is rarely seen as a single malt. It is unusual inasmuch as it has a more savory element to it than many of the whiskies from this region. Untypically, it has a screw cap, too. **DR**

Tasting notes

On the nose, chocolate nut sundae is complemented by swirls of toffee. The palate is aromatic and floral, but savory rather than sweet with mixed herbs and sage and onion stuffing. A light and unimposing whisky that ends quietly in a gentle finish.

Monkey Shoulder

William Grant & Sons | www.monkeyshoulder.com

Region and country of origin Speyside, Scotland
Distilleries Glenfiddich, Balvenie, and Kininvie,
Dufftown **Alcohol content** 43% abv
Style Blended malt

This is one of the most important whisky releases of the last few years. It combines a modern, youthful, and even trendy approach to Scottish malt whisky with the finest traditions of good old-fashioned whisky making. It has played a key role in helping to bring Scotch malt whisky to a younger audience, and it has combined cool fashionable imagery with a no-compromise malt whisky. It is, in fact, the perfect combination of style and substance, taking all the heritage and tradition that have gone before and presenting itself in a new and exciting way.

Monkey Shoulder is a blended malt whisky and not a blended Scotch. This means it is made only with single malt whiskies and has no grain in it. In fact it is made up of three different single malts, from three different distilleries. In this case, though, the distilleries are on the same site—the Speyside plant owned by William Grant—Glenfiddich, Balvenie, and Kininvie.

The mix is light and summery, easy drinking but 100 percent all the same, and it's ideal for mixing in cocktails or serving with ice. It was launched through a series of hip events in top bars in London, and trendy outlets were encouraged to apply for Monkey Bar status. And the name? Amazingly it's as traditional as any malt whisky gets. Go to the Web site and you'll find it's all jungle music and little running monkeys. All totally irrelevant. Monkey shoulder is actually a now extinct affliction that distillery workers turning the malt by hand would get—a sort of repetitive strain injury in the upper body that caused the victim to crouch and stoop. **SR**

Tasting notes

A sweet and easy-drinking mix of fluffy apple and soft, sweet peat laced with vanilla and candy notes. It's a light summer whisky, fairly well balanced, that mixes well but tastes great on its own. Young and spritely, packaged in a good-looking bottle.

Mortlach 16-Year-Old Flora & Fauna

Diageo | www.whisky.co.uk

Region and country of origin Speyside, Scotland
Distillery Mortlach, Dufftown, Keith, Banffshire
Alcohol content 46% abv
Style Single malt

Mortlach is another one of those distilleries that doesn't seem to get much love in the world of single malt. While it's well known amongst enthusiasts, the only generally available distillery bottling is this one: a sixteen-year-old entry in Diageo's Flora & Fauna range. While it does seem criminal that Mortlach isn't more widely distributed, it does mean that there is more of it available for the ardent fans.

The 16-Year-Old sits happily as a yardstick for Mortlach releases, matured in sherry casks and selected for a rich, meaty character that has become the distillery's trademark. Along with the sherry cask influence, the spirit also has a bit of smoke to it and a hint of sulfur, a divisive flavor that is loved by some and disliked by many. This comes at least in part from the distillery's use of worm tubs to cool the distilled new spirit. These large water-filled vats contain a submerged spiral of copper tube that cools and condenses the spirit vapor into liquid after it leaves the still. The worms do not provide the spirit with as much contact with the copper as newer "shell and tube" condensers do, lessening the metal's sulfur-removing influence, leaving behind a "struck match" note that lessens during maturation. At sixteen years old, it is almost gone, but lingers on as a light flavor, complementing the smoke and sherry cask influence.

During the 2000s, there has been a slow but steady price rise for the Mortlach Flora & Fauna, as rumors have abounded that stocks are running low and that there won't be any more when they run out. One to find and try before it disappears, then. **BA**

Tasting notes

A nose of sticky maple syrup, sharp sherried fruit, mulching grass, and mint gives way to a rich taste of caramel, brittle toffee, and polished wood. Underneath there is a smoky meatiness like slow roasted beef, and it's all capped with a touch of lightly floral lavender.

Mortlach Boisdale 1991

Berry Bros. & Rudd | www.bbr.com

Region and country of origin Speyside, Scotland
Distillery Mortlach, Dufftown, Keith, Banffshire
Alcohol content 46% abv
Style Single malt

A single-cask expression with an output of 675 bottles, this whisky from the often-overlooked Speyside distillery of Mortlach was bottled for the Boisdale group by veteran wine and spirits merchant Berry Bros. & Rudd. Berry's is long established, with records dating back to 1698 showing them to be the oldest family-run wine and spirits merchant in Britain, and spirits manager Doug McIvor has had a long relationship working with the restaurant chain Boisdale, helping to choose and bottle the whiskies for their menu. Boisdale is known for their food, wine, whisky, and cigars, and they have a small but carefully selected range of whiskies bottled in their name.

This whisky continues the traditional Mortlach style, with seventeen years of maturation in a sherry butt adding layers of caramel, fruitcake, and spice. Fitting into the Boisdale menu, it is multipurpose whisky, acting equally well as a standalone dram, dessert companion, postprandial digestif, and cigar accompaniment. It achieves this by having a good base, with big fruit and spice, a rich mouthfeel, and a good slug of alcohol providing a core to hang other flavors from. It also has the distinct bonus of being very drinkable on its own. **BA**

Tasting notes

A golden syrup color, and the nose has that feel with salted caramel and a hint of smoke and lemon. To taste, it has caramel with raisins, cinnamon, and allspice.

Mortlach SMWS 76.79 Cask 7273

Diageo | www.malts.com

Region and country of origin Speyside, Scotland
Distillery Mortlach, Dufftown, Keith, Banffshire
Alcohol content 56.3% abv
Style Single malt

The Scotch Malt Whisky Society (SMWS) offers its members a unique whisky experience and a chance to taste some of the world's finest whiskies. There's something very special about going into one of the Society's two Edinburgh properties—the traditional, imposing one in Leith and the modern, stylish one in the city center, to choose a cask-strength whisky. This is the ceremony of whisky, and because the bottles bear no distillery name and only a flavor descriptor, it's fun asking the staff for help, describing what you want, and seeing how close they get to it. Pretty close normally—the staff take great pride in their work.

Mortlach distillery lies in the heart of Speyside close to Dufftown and was the first distillery in the region. It was licensed in 1823. Mortlach isn't a conventional Speyside malt, as it can swing widely in taste, from relatively conventional sherried malt to very sulfury and earthy, a taste that many purists reject out of hand but that appeals to others. This version is the latest in a long line bottled by the Society, and it falls in the middle of the two extremes, offering enough challenge for those looking for one from their Mortlach, but staying on side long enough to appeal to the more mainstream drinker. **DR**

Tasting notes

Elegant, sherried, with late gentle oak and parika, but with an apricot, rose, and peach heart, some menthol notes, grilled steak, and a hint of sulfur.

No Ordinary Whisky 16-Year-Old

Harris Whisky Co. | www.harriswhisky.com

Region and country of origin Speyside, Scotland
Distillery Undisclosed
Alcohol content 53.1% abv
Style Single malt

A love-hate relationship exists between the owners of Scotland's distilleries and the people who make a living buying up excess casks of whiskies and bottling them independently. When times are tough and whisky lakes dry up, the independents play an important role, but when whisky is plentiful, the relationship is more fractious. Some companies take steps to prevent their malts from reaching the independents, either by restricting their release, "spoiling" them by adding another malt to the mix, or threatening legal action. For this reason you get whiskies such as this one, or "A Very Special Speysider."

The full name of this is "No Ordinary Whisky, No Ordinary Distillery," and Mark Harris, the owner and a man of impeccable taste, is absolutely right about this outstanding whisky. It's from one of the great names of Speyside, known for its big, fruity and sherried whiskies, and this is bottled at cask strength to ensure that every bit of that big flavor is passed on. It's an unusual bottling because Harris tends to go for lighter, more subtle whiskies, but given the age of the malt on offer, and the fact that it's bottled at cask strength, this is very good value for money. The perfect introduction to the company and its malts. **DR**

Tasting notes

Big sherry notes, lots of red berries, some oaky tannin notes from the age, orange peel, and marmalade on the palate. Not subtle, but certainly not ordinary.

Oban 14-Year-Old

Diageo | www.diageo.com

Region and country of origin Highlands, Scotland
Distillery Oban, Oban, Argyll
Alcohol content 43% abv
Style Single malt

Oban 14, part of Diageo's Classic Malt series, is a prime example of a Western Highland malt—fruity, full-bodied, and with hints of smoke and heather. It's bold and gold. It's created traditionally at the Oban distillery in the seaside fishing village of the same name in a fairly unhurried fashion, too. This gives it an edge, and it's one of the reasons why many are endeared by it. It reminds them of the sea.

Oban is, essentially, plotted between the Scottish West Highlands and the islands where the land meets the sea. The harbor has a mild climate that is warmed a little by the Gulf Stream and misty rainfall. As such, it has a fairly briny and almost peaty waft to it. This is partly because the barley used is gently dried in a kiln where peat smoke really rounds its character.

Oban distillery in the center of Argyll looks out over the sea. It is one of the oldest in Scotland and was founded in 1794, with the town being built around it. In 1883, a chap named J. Walter Higgin bought the distillery and, over the following few years, dismantled and rebuilt it bit by bit in an effort to keep it producing Oban's malt. The stills are tiny, but have been replicated at the same size so as not to compromise on flavor or quality. **JH**

Tasting notes

Full, rich, with sea salt and smokiness playing a part on the nose. A heady mix with fig, spice, and fruit fighting for attention. Enjoy while listening to the ocean waves.

Oban 32-Year-Old

Diageo | www.diageo.com

Region and country of origin Highlands, Scotland
Distillery Oban, Oban, Argyll
Alcohol content 55.1% abv
Style Single malt

The town of Oban grew up around this distillery, one of the oldest in Scotland, which was founded in 1794 by the brothers John and Hugh Stevenson. The whisky maker remained a family concern until 1866, when it was purchased by J. Walter Higgin, who modernized the buildings in the 1890s and added a warehouse built on land dynamited out of the cliff face that backed onto the original structure. (The explosions unearthed caves in which archaeologists discovered the remains of Mesolithic humans who lived there sometime between 4500 and 3000 BC.)

The extension was completed just in time for Higgin to take advantage of the development that changed the face of this part of the West Highlands: the construction of a rail link between Oban and Crianlarich, where it joined the main line between Mallaig and Glasgow. From now on, Oban whisky had an overland route away from the formerly rather isolated port and into the wider world. On arrival there, it proved extremely popular, with the result that the distillery was soon bought by a consortium consisting of Alexander Edward (who had recently purchased the Aultmore distillery), Buchanan's, Dewar's, and Mackie's.

Oban distillery now belongs to Diageo, and it was under their auspices that this single malt was distilled in 1969 and aged for thirty-two years before being bottled at cask strength. It was released in 2002 in a limited edition of 6,000 bottles, and the chance of finding one for sale today is very slim. This huge salty sweet malt, full of fruit, is now the stuff of legend. **GL**

Tasting notes

The nose is full and conveys a range of smells: mainly nuts and dried fruit, but also peat, wood, and smoke. The palate is ripe and thick and reminiscent of marmalade. The finish is long with lots of fruit and the aftertaste is a pleasingly oily oak.

Oban Distillers Edition

Diageo | www.diageo.com

Region and country of origin Highlands, Scotland
Distillery Oban, Oban, Argyll
Alcohol content 43% abv
Style Single malt

The first Oban Distillers Edition was launched in 1998, a year after the manufacturer became part of Diageo, the global drinks company headquartered in London. The series comprises annual releases of fourteen-year-olds that have been further matured for between six and eighteen months in fresh Montilla fino sherry casks to provide extra sweetness and dryness after the liquor's initial maturation.

The main objective is to make this marriage of flavors work harmoniously. Most critics agree that it does, but there is little consensus about the exact taste: some detect spices at first, while others experience vanilla, peatiness, sea air, or ripe fruits.

In spite of such personal differences in detailed interpretation, there is little or no argument about this whisky's style and elegance. Neither is there any significant dispute about its sweetness, which is strikingly fruity and honeyed, nor yet about its complex but well-balanced synthesis of sea scents, coupled with richness and smoke that derive from the barley's time in the kiln.

Above all, the Oban Distillers Edition is a gentle dram, soft on the palate but building to become more full-bodied with every mouthful. The smoothness was one of the qualities of this multifaceted whisky to be singled out in its citation when the 2002 edition won gold in that year's International Wine & Spirit Competition. Commercially, this single malt has brought a double benefit to the makers; it has been a great success in its own right and has introduced thousands of new customers to the Oban range. **JH**

Tasting notes

This is a delicate and elegant malt, with a hint of the sea that is strong but does not overpower the accompanying light smoke and sweet sherry. The palate is much like the nose; the finish is well balanced and slightly grassy, with a hint of Spanish rum.

Octomore 3.152

Bruichladdich Distillery Co. | www.bruichladdich.com

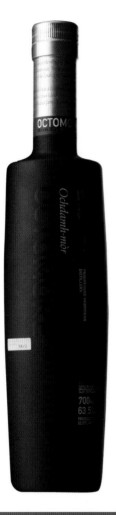

Region and country of origin Islay, Scotland
Distillery Bruichladdich, Bruichladdich, Argyll
Alcohol content 59% abv
Style Single malt

Octomore is the name of a farm just above Port Charlotte. A distillery once stood there, and the property happens to include the spring from which Bruichladdich's water flows. From the beginning, back in 2001, Bruichladdich wanted to make a peated whisky to complement the unpeated Bruichladdich style. This was the origins of the Port Charlotte whisky, peated to 40 parts per million phenolic (ppm). It was such a success that a more highly peated version seemed like a good idea—then there came the night when the Bruichladdich staff were drinking together and someone said, "What if we set out to get the peatiest whisky ever? How would that go in our stills?" Bruichladdich is the kind of company that can have these "what if?" moments and actually try them out.

The first batch of highly peated barley came in at over 80 ppm, but then the maltsters began to think how they could get it higher, by prolonging the kilning process for example, and the eventual first release of Octomore was measured at 131 ppm. The second release was 140 ppm, and this one, the third, reached 152. Octomore 4 went on to hit 167, and a note on the laddie blog in June 2011 announced that the most recent Octomore barley had practically gone off the scale at 309 ppm. That's just scary.

The high peat level and the young age (five years) make this sound a rather unattractive dram, but the truth is that it works rather well. According to Bruichladdich, it is the trickle distillation (didn't even need to use condensers) in the tall, elegant stills that does much to attenuate the raw force of the peat. **RL**

Tasting notes

A vortex of peat smoke, fire, wet seaweed, tarry pitch, and damp sailcloth on the nose. Then bog myrtle, mountain thyme, heather, and pine resin. On the palate, charred oak, chicory, dark chocolate, roasted root vegetables, ginger, and salt. Eye-watering intensity.

Octomore Orpheus

Bruichladdich Distillery Co. | www.bruichladdich.com

Region and country of origin Islay, Scotland
Distillery Bruichladdich, Bruichladdich, Argyll
Alcohol content 61% abv
Style Single malt

The second edition of Octomore had an exotic twin—Octomore Orpheus, also five years old, also 140 ppm phenolic, 61 percent abv and ACEd in Chateau Petrus red wine casks. Chateau Petrus, a fabulous Bordeaux wine from Pomerol, costs thousands of dollars a bottle. Its reputation was enhanced when Princess Elizabeth chose it to be served at her wedding to Prince Phillip in 1947. The combination of this high octane uber-peated whisky and the cream of French oak from Bordeaux shouldn't really work—but it does.

The packaging is another stunner from Jarvis—a shapely black bottle in a bright red tin. The flame red cylinder presumably represents the fires of Hades and the black glassware the color of the river Styx? Orpheus, poor lad, was just a singer-songwriter with a gift. He thought things were looking up when he got married to the beautiful Eurydice, but on their wedding day, she got jumped on by a satyr and then bitten by a snake—so off she goes to the Underworld.

Sometime later, Orpheus, who is not getting over his loss, goes down there too and, using his persuasive voice, tries to get Pluto and Persephone, who run the joint, to let Eurydice go. Because he sings even better than Frank Sinatra, they agree, but only on condition that he doesn't look back. But poor Orpheus, like old Frankie, can't help looking back, and Eurydice fades from view, inexorably hauled back to the Underworld. The only happy ending is that Orpheus eventually ends up there too after he is torn to bits by some raving female followers of Bacchus in a drunken frenzy—a common fate for rock singers. **RL**

Tasting notes

On the nose, peat and honey-glazed ham, then fruit appears from behind the smoke curtain: red berries, citrus, grape. On the palate, it is sweet, peaty, and hot with Turkish delight, barley sugar, honey, and lots of jammy cranberry, cherry, pomegranate, and kumquat.

Old Parr 12-Year-Old

Diageo | www.diageo.com

Region and country of origin Edinburgh, Scotland
Distilleries Various
Alcohol content 43% abv
Style Blend

Whisky has undergone a revolution since the turn of the millennium, and what was an old-fashioned, very male, and cliché-ridden drinks category is now bursting with color and vitality, fit and fat-free and dressing up in smart livery and even sharper marketing techniques. All very state of the art and often very necessary. But when you get to a certain age, sharp suits and fashionable shirts just won't do it, and you start to look faintly ridiculous. When you reach that point, it's time to consider growing old gracefully. And that's where we are with Old Parr.

Old Parr comes in a curious and quaintly square bottle, its outer packaging is gold and black, and the whisky logo is all old-fashioned lettering in serious and bland red and black. There's a small picture of the old boy himself, with the dates he was meant to have lived between—1483 and 1635. We're told that his name was adopted for this whisky because the original owners, Macdonald Greenlees, wanted "To communicate the enduring values of maturity and age . . . he was renowned and respected during his lifetime for his wisdom and maturity." All very traditional values and fitful for this whisky.

These days twelve years is a benchmark for premium Scotch single malts, and it's the age of Johnnie Walker Black Label, so how does Old Parr cut it? It is a refined and classy blend with less bite than Black Label but respectably soft and sophisticated—a dapper old man confident enough in its skin and dignified in its surroundings. Let's hope Diageo continues to support it. **DR**

Tasting notes

The nose is a little shy, sweet, and fruity without pressing too many buttons. On the palate, this is a restrained but class act, an almost perfect balancing act. Everything's built around the sweet grain center, and there is a fruit bowl display of citrus, orange, and red fruits.

Old Parr 15-Year-Old

Diageo | www.diageo.com

Region and country of origin Speyside, Scotland
Distillery Glendullan, Dufftown, Keith, Banffshire
Alcohol content 43% abv
Style Blend

Since the Old Parr brand was first introduced in 1909, it has developed three main variants: Grand Old Parr (a twelve-year-old), Old Parr Superior (an eighteen-year-old), and this 15-Year-Old, a blended Scotch whisky. By the start of the twenty-first century, the 15-Year-Old had carved out a lucrative niche in export markets, particularly Colombia, Japan, Mexico, and Venezuela. Its success in those countries has been based to no small degree on its striking and innovative packaging. The distinctive square brown bottle has a textured surface that is intended to represent the weathered skin of a 152-year-old man (the reputed age of the eponymous Tom Parr when he died in 1635).

However, just as you cannot judge a book by its cover, you cannot determine whether a whisky is any good simply by the way it is presented. Naturally, the only true test is to sample it, and in this regard the 15-Year-Old has been weighed carefully in the balance and not been found wanting. Devotees—and it has thousands—are unanimous in the view that this muscular heavyweight alters perceptions of whisky and raises expectations of subsequent samples, not just of blends, but of single malts as well. Indeed, some aficionados would say that experiencing Old Parr 15-Year-Old carries the penalty of a reduced enjoyment of products that previously were considered perfectly satisfactory.

Unless you happen to live in, or have access to, its main sales areas, this whisky is not easy to acquire. But it is well worth pursuing, albeit with the caveat that it may change your point of view forever. **GL**

Tasting notes

It smells of malt and linseed, like a newly oiled cricket bat. Its taste is big and full-bodied, with notes of cereal, sesame seed, sugar, honey, and raisin. The finish is long and soothing, with a growing sense of lemongrass and peat. The aftertaste is the stuff of fine memories.

Old Parr Superior 18-Year-Old

Diageo | www.diageo.com

Region and country of origin Edinburgh, Scotland
Distilleries Various
Alcohol content 43% abv
Style Blend

Although not a high-profile whisky in the portfolio of owners Diageo, Old Parr Superior is well regarded by aficionados of aged blended Scotch and is most closely associated with Glendullan distillery at Dufftown on Speyside, owned by Diageo but licensed to its Macdonald Greenlees Ltd. subsidiary.

Brothers James and Samuel Greenlees set up a whisky distilling, blending, and retailing business in 1871, establishing the deluxe Old Parr blend in London, where blended Scotch whisky was just beginning to become fashionable. The brothers named their new brand after Thomas Parr (known as "Old Parr"), who was reputedly Britain's oldest man. Legend has it he lived for 152 years and, at the age of 122, married for the second time. He died in 1635 and is buried in Westminster Abbey, London.

The Greenlees firm merged with that of Alexander and Macdonald under the ownership of Sir James Calder, who named the new firm Macdonald Greenlees and Williams (Distillers) Ltd., with William Williams & Sons Ltd. having established Glendullan at the height of the late Victorian whisky "boom" in 1896/97. The current title of Macdonald Greenlees Ltd. was adopted when James Calder & Co. was sold to the Distillers Company Ltd. in 1925.

Old Parr Superior is the oldest of the three aged variants of the brand currently available, and enjoys strong sales in Asia. It has long enjoyed a reputation in export markets rather than the United Kingdom, and this situation can be traced back to 1905 when the first consignments were sent to Brazil and Canada. **GS**

Tasting notes

Floral and nutty on the nose with summer fruits and a whiff of honey. Quite full-bodied, well balanced on the palate, relatively complex and sophisticated, with more fruit, cereal notes, vanilla, spice, and a hint of smokiness. Medium length in the finish, with sweet oak and cocoa.

Old Pulteney 12-Year-Old

International Beverage | www.oldpulteney.com

Region and country of origin Highlands, Scotland
Distillery Pulteney, Wick, Caithness
Alcohol content 40% abv
Style Single malt

Every malt whisky distiller would argue that a dram of his liquor speaks clearly of the place where it was born, but few standard expressions display that unique whisky DNA more clearly than Old Pulteney 12-Year-Old. Distilled in the very far north of the Scottish mainland in the fishing town of Wick, Old Pulteney delivers what its location promises. The spirit is intense and full of depth, with a remarkable maritime character and a propensity to surprise even the most experienced whisky connoisseur.

Imagine a summer night in the northern Highlands, where the sun dips under the horizon late at night only to set the North Sea alight again a couple of hours later. Old Pulteney 12-Year-Old is much like that at first glance, with its delightful fruity freshness on the nose. This characteristic can be partially attributed to the unusual shape of the wash still, the first of the two alembics working in a tandem to turn strong barley beer into an aromatic new-make spirit. The still features an exaggerated boil bulb that creates phenomenal amounts of reflux, leading to a bright, estery nose.

But that is not the whole story. Much like the place where it is made, Old Pulteney has a much darker, more serious side to it, too. Alcohol vapors flavored by those top-end esters rise through the stills and are led outside to condense in copper coil "worms" immersed in tubs of cold water. The setup is time-honored and technologically long surpassed, but Pulteney distillery relies on worm tubs for the heavier, slightly dirtier, leathery, and waxy notes that make it so special. **LD**

Tasting notes

Intense citrus leads the way, with vanilla custard close behind. A touch of banana adds to the complexity, while a hint of candle wax puts weight behind it. Nutty, honey flavors and a mouthwatering creamy texture on the palate. A signature salty tang on the finish.

TO COMMEMORATE THE VISIT TO PULTENEY DISTILLERY
HRH
THE PRINCE CHARLES
DUKE OF ROTHESAY
1ST AUGUST 2005

Old Pulteney 17-Year-Old

International Beverage | www.oldpulteney.com

Region and country of origin Highlands, Scotland
Distillery Pulteney, Wick, Caithness
Alcohol content 46% abv
Style Single malt

As you head up the hill along Huddart Street, nothing but a slight malty smell gives away the presence of Pulteney distillery. But as you walk through the gates into the courtyard, a whole new world opens up.

Old Pulteney 17-Year-Old is every inch the whisky you would expect from this unusual distillery in its urban but remote, coastal location. How so? Well, partly because Pulteney is one of very few distilleries in Scotland to use dry yeast. More stable in transport and storage than the liquid variety, it was initially chosen for practical reasons; all too often, land transport links in Caithness are severed by snow. Now, together with a four-water mashing regime and a long fermentation in Cor-Ten steel washbacks, the yeast contributes to the unique flavor profile of Pulteney's wash, and thus to the flavor of the whisky.

This 17-Year-Old is matured in warehouses filled with salty sea air. Second-refill American white oak casks are used for this expression, as opposed to the first-refill casks used for the 12-year-old. This understated maturation style, apart from making the whisky a shade paler than its younger brother, truly allows the spirit to shine. This Old Pulteney speaks of the process, the craftsmanship, and the place. **LD**

Tasting notes

On the nose, caramel, biscuit, and cake icing followed by orchard fruits and a whiff of sea air. Almond and ginger lead on the palate. A long, sweet finish.

Old Pulteney 21-Year-Old

International Beverage | www.oldpulteney.com

Region and country of origin Highlands, Scotland
Distillery Pulteney, Wick, Caithness
Alcohol content 46% abv
Style Single malt

Twenty-one years in casks is a long time, and to add to the complexity, two variations of seasoned oak were used in the Pulteney 21-Year-Old. The core of the spirit is matured in ex-bourbon casks made from best-quality air-dried (as opposed to kiln-dried) American white oak. This wood is used across the Old Pulteney range and is proven to work exceptionally well with the spirit. Whisky from ex-bourbon casks gives Old Pulteney 21-Year-Old its rich vanilla and honey core.

However, the 21-year-old also contains whisky matured in ex-sherry casks from Spain. Usually ex-sherry implies European red oak, which offers different maturation conditions and a different flavor profile to the American wood. But in this case, Pulteney distillery used casks made from American oak but filled previously with fino sherries. American oak and a dry, light sherry seasoning combine to make a Scotch whisky that displays spiciness plus a dark fruit and chocolate inclination, while not being too sweet.

Old Pulteney 21-Year-Old is a successful balancing act between different uses of wood and the flavor profiles they provide. It offers an insight into just how much good-quality wood can do for a whisky. A heavy, rich, and satisfying dram. **LD**

Tasting notes

Vanilla and honey, followed by black cherry, stewed apple, and orange peel. The palate is juicy and sweet with honey, spice, dark fruit, and a whiff of marzipan.

← Pulteney created a special whisky to mark a visit by Prince Charles in 2005.

Old Pulteney 30-Year-Old

International Beverage | www.oldpulteney.com

Region and country of origin Highlands, Scotland
Distillery Pulteney, Wick, Caithness
Alcohol content 44% abv
Style Single malt

There are currently nearly 20 million casks maturing in warehouses across Scotland. Most of them contain very young spirit. Within a few months of their third birthday, most of them will be emptied and the spirit, now legally called whisky, will be blended and sold around the world under famous brands.

Some of what remains will eventually be bottled as single malt, but only a small fraction of whisky stock survives the twelve-year mark. Even less will live to see twenty. At thirty years, there is hardly anything. An encounter with a whisky so rare and old is a special experience but, it has to be said, not always a pleasant one. Very old whiskies can be profoundly oaky, tart, or tannic, and, if you are not prepared for that, they may seem just a bit too much.

Old Pulteney 30-Year-Old is nothing like that. The expression, released for the first time in 2009, includes only whisky matured in ex-bourbon casks at the distillery in Wick on the Caithness coast. The low temperatures of the far north, fresh sea air, and American oak contribute to a gentle maturation process that allows this exceptional dram to express the distillery house style despite its age. After three decades in casks, this Old Pulteney shows no signs of tiredness; instead it speaks of the fruity and leathery character of the new-make spirit, and of the coastal location where it was matured. The age manifests itself in a tropical fruit burst on the nose and a creamy mouthfeel. Forget pencil shavings in a damp cellar, Old Pulteney is like a fresh mango on a beach. The only bitter thing here is the price tag. **LD**

Tasting notes

Fragrant pineapple, green banana, lemon, gooseberry, and mango on the nose. Walnut richness and white chocolate follow, giving the whisky definition and depth. On the palate, an explosive mix of canned peach, honey, and spice. A finish of coffee and cola.

Old Pulteney WK209

International Beverage | www.oldpulteney.com

Region and country of origin Highlands, Scotland
Distillery Pulteney, Wick, Caithness
Alcohol content 46% abv
Style Single malt

It is well into the evening and someone finishes a joke: "and the Scotsman says—it must have been fallout from Iceland!" People around the table burst out laughing, but you know half of them didn't get it.

Old Pulteney WK209 is like a good surreal joke. Those lucky enough to connect the first time will always like it. The rest . . . well, they won't quite know what to make of it. In 2011 Old Pulteney WK209 followed the highly successful WK499 expression as a travel retail offering from Pulteney distillery. Just like its predecessor, it carries no age statement and hasn't been colored or chill-filtered. The name comes from a boat; built in Wick in 1948, WK209 *Good Hope* was the first steam herring drifter in the area to use an echo sounder. It seems only fitting that a boat ahead of its time lent its name and image to a whisky unlike anything most people have tried from Pulteney.

In truth, WK209 is so different from the rest of the range that there is little chance of anyone linking it with Pulteney distillery in a blind tasting. Citrusy subtleties, alluring vanilla, and a gentle salty kiss are eschewed in favor of European oak's brute dark force. All whisky for this limited bottling was matured in ex-sherry casks from Spain. These turned the naturally sticky yet fragrant Pulteney spirit into what can be described as the rare steak of the whisky world, making it one of the most bold and interesting releases of recent years. So, whether you like big, sherry-driven whiskies or not, next time you're flying home, pick up one of those funky turquoise boxes. Inside is a punch line you won't want to miss. **LD**

Tasting notes

Treacle, sticky toffee pudding, plum jam, and dark chocolate, all wrapped in a heavy whiff of beef stock. The aroma is smooth, sweet, and surprisingly thick. The palate is bursting with forest fruit, hazelnut, vanilla, and blackened banana. A long, spicy finish.

Old Pulteney WK499

International Beverage | www.oldpulteney.com

Region and country of origin Highlands, Scotland
Distillery Pulteney, Wick, Caithness
Alcohol content 52% abv
Style Single malt

Pulteney distillery sits quietly near the center of Wick, a town in the northern Highlands on the east coast of Caithness. Once the busiest herring fishing port in Europe, Wick is now a surprisingly sleepy little town. Wick harbor, which at the peak of the herring boom could host as many as 1,000 vessels at a time, is now home to a few dozen. One of these is very special: *Isabella Fortuna*, registration number WK499, is the last wooden herring drifter remaining in Wick. Fishing from the port between 1890 and 1976, she was finally retired after eighty-six years of service. She was acquired by the Wick Society and later carefully refurbished with the support of Pulteney distillery.

To honor this relationship and emphasize its own maritime connections, Old Pulteney WK499 was released at the beginning of 2010. It is a no-age-statement expression bottled at a very high alcohol strength (actually not quite cask strength). WK499 was matured exclusively in ex-bourbon barrels, which gave it a sweet vanilla and spicy core. But there is more to it. Old Pulteney is sometimes referred to as the "Manzanilla of the north". The comparison of the two may seem a stretch of the imagination but in this case, it's appropriate. WK499 reveals saltiness deeper than any other Old Pulteney expression, and sea air is at the soul of this dram. Despite being crisp and zesty it is a heavyweight on the palate, making it a wonderful, bright dram with a dirty little secret. Wick once produced both barrels of silver and barrels of gold. Herring fishing may be no more, but the gold stuff is going strong. **LD**

Tasting notes

Sharply crisp and citrusy at first, the nose reveals more complexity with time and water. Vanilla cheesecake and blood-orange peel, with a hint of ginger. On the palate it starts sweet and zesty, but quickly reveals the salty side. Surprisingly mellow for such a high strength.

Pittyvaich Old Malt Cask 18-Year-Old

Douglas Laing & Co. | www.douglaslaing.com

Region and country of origin Speyside, Scotland
Distillery Pittyvaich (closed), Dufftown, Keith, Banffshire
Alcohol content 50% abv
Style Single malt

When a distillery goes to the wall and is either left to rot or, perhaps worse, flattened to make way for a supermarket, there is justifiable sadness and considerable gnashing of teeth. The kind of reverence enjoyed by lost distilleries such as Brora, Port Ellen, Rosebank, and St. Magdalene is the kind that many popes would envy. Some distilleries, though, were so short-lived as to have had hardly enough time to imprint themselves on the memory, much in the same way that His Holiness Pope John Paul I—whose reign only lasted thirty-three days—had barely enough time to make much of an impression in the Vatican before he died in his sleep. At least His Holiness can rest easily, knowing that during his short reign he never received the kind of adverse coverage that much of Pittyvaich's whisky had to endure.

Pittyvaich was opened by Bell's in the mid-1970s as a partner for the neighboring Dufftown distillery. It stopped production in 1993 and was, for a short time, used for experimentation. A brief and, let's be frank, unlamented life. When the whisky was finally released as an official bottling as part of Diageo's Flora & Fauna series, it was met with a less than enthusiastic response in some quarters. Given that, at another still-operating (and now much improved) distillery, the initial spirit was so poor that the distiller burst into tears, could not Pittyvaich have turned things around given a few more years? We'll never know—it was demolished in 2002. What we do know, ironically, is that older Pittyvaichs are actually very good, as this Old Malt Cask 18-Year-Old ably demonstrates. **PB**

Tasting notes

Pungent sherry, moist fruitcake, and dates on the nose, with a blast of sulfur. On the palate, there's a huge sweetness that coats the mouth with Seville orange and moist, rich banana cake, becoming very dry at the end. The finish is dry, with a Campari note.

Port Askaig
25-Year-Old

The Whisky Exchange | www.port-askaig.com

Region and country of origin Islay, Scotland
Distillery Undisclosed
Alcohol content 45.8% abv
Style Single malt

Some have suggested that Port Askaig is a marketing initiative rather than a pedigree whisky distiller, but the broader consensus is that this is an uncharitable criticism. While it is true that expressions produced under the label vary in detail, that is in the nature of all single malts, regardless of their provenance. What remains consistent throughout the range, however, is the overall quality, which has been widely praised on first assessment and, during the producer's first decade in business, has proved to mature over time.

To ensure that Port Askaig whiskies maintain their original flavor and character, none of them is chill-filtered, and no coloring is added. These are among the stringent requirements laid down by the owners of The Whisky Exchange, brothers Sukhinder and Raj Singh, who started as online spirit retailers in 1999.

Port Askaig whiskies are made by arrangement with Diageo and Burn Stewart, the owners of, respectively, Caol Ila and Bunnahabhain, whose distillations are the main constituents of the brand. This 25-Year-Old is the senior citizen of the range, a single malt aged in oak casks to produce a whisky designed to appeal to experienced bibbers and best appreciated with a splash of water. **GL**

Tasting notes

The nose is mainly fruity, with a hint of wood smoke, oak spice, and vanilla. The palate is elegant, with deliciously clean malt, and the finish is long and smoky.

Port Askaig
Harbour 19-Year-Old

The Whisky Exchange | www.port-askaig.com

Region and country of origin Islay, Scotland
Distillery Undisclosed
Alcohol content 45.8% abv
Style Single malt

Port Askaig is the main port of Islay, on the northeast of the island close to its nearest neighbor, Jura. It is also the name of a range of single malts marketed by the Whisky Exchange (TWE). At first, the brand name may seem confusing, given that there is no distillery in Port Askaig itself, but two of Scotland's greatest whisky producers are highly proximate: Caol Ila is less than a mile away, and Bunnahabhain is about 4 miles (6 km) distant. TWE's mission is to spread the word about them and to bring the finest whiskies of Islay to the widest possible audience.

TWE's selections are made by Sukhinder Singh, one of Britain's most respected whisky experts. He believes that his choices will meld into perfectly balanced Islay single malts that will become acknowledged classics. To date, his optimism is more than borne out by the sales figures: Port Askaig is growing in popularity by the quarter.

This expression was produced to succeed the popular 17-year-old. It is in much the same vein as its predecessor—perfectly balanced and full of the sooty, briny, lemony, single-malt goodness that typifies Islay. Its qualities are immediately apparent and will only improve with age. **GL**

Tasting notes

A striking honeyed aroma. The palate is peaty against a background of wood and brine. The lingering finish is the most satisfying part of the dram.

Islay's Port Askaig harbor, with the ferry that travels to Jura, visible beyond. ➡

Port Charlotte An Turas Mor

Bruichladdich Distillery Co. | www.bruichladdich.com

Region and country of origin Islay, Scotland
Distillery Bruichladdich, Bruichladdich, Argyll
Alcohol content 46% abv
Style Single malt

Port Charlotte is the heavily peated whisky (40 parts per million) from Bruichladdich. It was first distilled in 2001, and the distillery is so proud of its peated offspring that it has provided us with snapshots of its development every year from 2006. These releases, PC5, PC6, PC7, and PC8, all limited edition and natural strength, have become something of a cult whisky series. That's the only way to make sense of the scary prices that are now being paid for PC5.

Jim McEwan's original plan was to create a whisky that would hark back to the drams that came out of the old Port Charlotte distillery, which closed in 1929. *An Turas Mor* means "the great journey," and although we are certainly not at the end of the amazing journey of Port Charlotte whisky, we have certainly reached a milestone. For this is the first general release, no age statement, multivintage vatting of Port Charlotte, and it is bottled at the standard 46 percent abv.

The annual bottlings that have been drawn off the 2001 distillation may have depleted stocks, making a PC9 difficult to release in 2010. An Turas Mor, with its multivintage flexibility, has filled the gap. It is not a member of the PC series, and yet is heralded as achieving McEwan's original vision—a definitive statement of Bruichladdich's peaty whisky. Certainly it sits comfortably between the standard Bruichladdich and the Octomore peat monster; whether it is like the stuff produced back in Port Charlotte distillery back in 1929 is difficult to say, though one thing that makes that rather unlikely is the 100 percent abv maturation in American oak. **RL**

Tasting notes

Rich and creamy on the nose. On the palate the peat is unmistakable, with the smoke you would expect combined with a breath of briny sea air and black pepper. The finish is extra long, laced with coffee and toffee and the lingering peaty smoke.

Port Charlotte PC7 Sin An Doigh Ileach

Bruichladdich Distillery Co. | www.bruichladdich.com

Region and country of origin Islay, Scotland
Distillery Bruichladdich, Bruichladdich, Argyll
Alcohol content 61% abv
Style Single malt

The inspiration behind the Port Charlotte (PC) range was to re-create the style of whisky previously made by the defunct Port Charlotte distillery (also known as Lochindaal or Rinns distillery), which closed in 1929. Roderick Macleod, retired stillman at Bruichladdich, remembered tasting the whisky and told Jim McEwan that it was every bit as smoky as Lagavulin, so Jim set the peating level at 40 parts per million (ppm). In fact Port Charlotte was the first spirit distilled by the new regime in 2001 (May 29, to be exact).

It was first bottled in 2006 as PC5 "Evolution", a five-year-old whisky that also happened to be ACEd in sherry casks and bottled at 63.5 percent abv. It was hugely popular, probably because the tin bore a photo of the master himself, Jim McEwan. PC6 followed the year after, this time ACEd in Madeira casks (61.6 percent abv), with a series of photos of six of the distillery workers. This even more limited edition is also no longer available.

PC7 Sin An Doigh Ileach, or "unity," was the first of the limited-edition PC releases to have 100 percent bourbon-matured whisky and is bottled at 61 percent abv. The tins have photos of six members of the Islay community with some connection to Bruichladdich.

PC8 Ar Dùthchas (the name is Gaelic for "land of our heritage") has also been released. Although a small batch of PC9 is anticipated, at the time of writing, it was not yet available. The casks used to make this style of Bruichladdich whisky are stored at the warehouses in Port Charlotte that once were part of the 1929 distillery. **RL**

Tasting notes

Aromas of Islay on the nose: peat bog, gorse, pine, and birch, plus peat smoke, ash, and sea spray, hints of coffee, apple, and pear. On the palate peat smoke is king, with maritime elements, date, burnt sugar, and molasses, then licorice, chile, and ginger in the finish.

Port Charlotte PC8 Ar Dùthchas

Bruichladdich Distillery Co.
www.bruichladdich.com

Region and country of origin Islay, Scotland
Distillery Bruichladdich, Bruichladdich, Argyll
Alcohol content 60.5% abv
Style Single malt

"PC" stands for Port Charlotte, the name of the largest village close to Bruichladdich distillery on Islay and also the name of one of Islay's lost distilleries, which operated between 1829 and 1929. Parts of the old plant remain extant and are due to feature in an ongoing but delayed project by the Bruichladdich team to reinstate whisky making at Port Charlotte, utilizing the warehouse and equipment acquired from the former Innerleven distillery at Dumbarton.

To date, however, Port Charlotte single malt has been distilled at Bruichladdich and differs from the "standard" make by being significantly more heavily peated (around 40 parts per million), in line with the sort of phenol levels that would have been employed when Bruichladdich was established in 1881.

PC8 appeared in 2009 and was named Ar Duthchas, Gaelic for "land of our heritage." According to a Bruichladdich spokesperson, "The natural cask strength has fallen to 60.5 percent, the spirit becoming more compelling and complex all the time. Follow the extraordinary evolution of this heavily peated spirit's fascinating development by comparing and contrasting this bottling with the earlier PC5, PC6, and PC7." **GS**

Tasting notes

Sweet peat and malt on the nose; quite dry on the rather peppery palate; sweeter and fruitier, with barley notes when diluted. Lingering ash notes in the lengthy finish.

Port Charlotte PC9 An Ataireachd Ard

Bruichladdich Distillery Co.
www.bruichladdich.com

Region and country of origin Islay, Scotland
Distillery Bruichladdich, Bruichladdich, Argyll
Alcohol content 59.2% abv
Style Single malt

When Port Charlotte was distilled in 2001, it was the peaty antithesis to "standard" Bruichladdich, but the subsequent distillation of Octomore, with peating levels up to a record 131 parts per million, now make Port Charlotte a middle-of-the-road variant from the distillery on the western shores of Loch Indaal.

The last limited edition of Port Charlotte spirit appeared under the PC9 label during 2011, and the strength of the nine-year-old spirit had by this time dropped to 59.2 percent, compared to 60.5 percent the previous year. The output was just 6,000 bottles.

This expression was named An Ataireachd Ard, which translates from the Gaelic as "the surge of the sea," and was followed in 2012 by the graduation of Port Charlotte to the general Bruichladdich portfolio as a 10-year-old.

Production director Jim McEwan, the man behind so many of Bruichladdich's wonderful innovations, says of PC9 that "the strong pulse of Islay is unrestrained and inextinguishable. The heat, the peat, and the power are fabulous. Your heart pumps harder, your eyes light up like Roman candles, and by now your anticipation of a unique experience is about to be realized…" **GS**

Tasting notes

Unabashed peat on the nose, with black pepper, treacle toffee, and clams. Sweet and fruity in the mouth, with a hint of bourbon, while the finish is smoky and warming.

Port Charlotte lies south on the road from Bruichladdich on Islay. →

Port Dundas 20-Year-Old 1990

Diageo
www.malts.com

Region and country of origin Lowlands, Scotland
Distillery Port Dundas, Glasgow
Alcohol content 57.4% abv
Style Grain whisky

Grain whisky is often seen as the poor relation to single malt. It is whisky made with grain other than malted barley, and it is not made in batches in a pot still as single malt, but instead is produced on a continuous, or Coffey still. The resulting spirit has less distinctive flavor. Its purpose normally is to mix with malt to make blended whisky, but a small amount is bottled in its own right.

Grain whisky normally doesn't cost as much as single malt, but some insiders appreciate two things about it: one, bottlings are extremely rare, and two, over long periods of time, grain whisky can take on the characteristics of the cask, and that can make for great whisky. This 20-Year-Old is a case in point.

This grain is a big-flavored whisky that has been on a journey. Diageo has taken three casks of Port Dundas grain and matured them in refill sherry casks for three years. One has gone in to ex-sherry wood for seventeen years, one in new European charred oak, also for seventeen years, and one in ex-bourbon for seventeen years. There are just 1,920 bottles of this 20-Year-Old in existence, and this is the first time whisky from this distillery has ever been bottled at this age, so the whisky is considered very collectable. **DR**

Tasting notes

Dark chocolate, treacle toffee. Oak and spice on the nose, while the palate is a deep bourbon flavor, with oak dominating. Glacé cherry and candy in the mix.

Port Dundas 36-Year-Old

Duncan Taylor & Co.
www.duncantaylor.com

Region and country of origin Lowlands, Scotland
Distillery Port Dundas, Glasgow
Alcohol content 54.1% abv
Style Grain whisky

Distilled at Port Dundas grain distillery in January 1973, this expression from cask no. 128318 was matured for thirty-six years prior to bottling by Duncan Taylor in their Rare Auld Collection during November 2009. The cask produced just 278 bottles.

Port Dundas was equipped with Coffey stills to make grain whisky in 1845. At that time, the distillery had an annual output of 2.5 million gallons (11.6 million liters), and the scale of the plant was gradually increased. Modernization took place after World War II, and a £7 million ($15 million) upgrade was initiated in the 1970s, with a new still house—containing a pair of column stills—being built in 1976. When it fell silent in April 2010, the distillery had a capacity of some 10.5 million gallons (40 million liters).

The closure of Port Dundas by owner Diageo was announced at the same time as the cessation of bottling at the Johnnie Walker site in the blend's spiritual home of Kilmarnock, leading to widespread public opposition. However, the west of Scotland's loss was the east's gain, as Cameronbridge grain distillery in Fife was upgraded and enlarged, while the nearby Leven bottling facility was rebuilt, resulting in the creation of over 400 new jobs. **GS**

Tasting notes

Soft toffee, warm custard, cinnamon, and raisin on the nose. The palate is bold, with plenty of rich spice. The finish is long and viscous, with cream and lots of oak.

"Rare Auld" would be termed "Rare Old" south of the Scottish border. →

Port Ellen
26-Year-Old Malt Cask

Douglas Laing & Co. | www.douglaslaing.com

Region and country of origin Islay, Scotland
Distillery Port Ellen (closed), Argyll
Alcohol content 40% abv
Style Single malt

In 1983, one of the worst years in Scotland's whisky industry, almost two dozen distilleries closed in response to a downturn in demand. Port Ellen on Islay was one, and in the intervening years, the remaining stocks of its whisky have been disappearing fast in a bewildering range of independent bottlings. It seems to have achieved almost mythical status in some circles, with prices rising steadily on eBay for sought-after vintages.

This example from Douglas Laing has been matured in a refill butt, twice the capacity of the usual hogshead, which slows down the contact with the oak and hence gives a more gentle and considered maturation. Long maturation can sometimes be problematic for peated whiskies, as they can lose their characteristic flavors quickly, but this strategy helps alleviate that.

The result is a smooth, perfectly balanced example of the lighter and more approachable side of Islay without the heavier phenolic iodine notes characteristic of some its whiskies. The 26-Year-Old is a summery outdoors whisky, sitting on the beach in the evening with a barbecue glowing gently and the sound of gulls calling overhead. **AN**

Tasting notes

Sweet peat on the nose, bonfire smoke on a sunny beach. Smooth and oily in the body, with tar and polish. Lovely long finish of peppery seaweed.

Port Ellen
27-Year-Old

Douglas Laing & Co. | www.douglaslaing.com

Region and country of origin Islay, Scotland
Distillery Port Ellen (closed), Argyll
Alcohol content 40% abv
Style Single malt

Bottled by Douglas Laing & Co. Ltd. during December 2010 in its Old Malt Cask series, this expression of Port Ellen was distilled a matter of weeks before the distillery closed in May 1983. It was matured in a sherry butt, which yielded 568 bottles.

Douglas Laing & Co. Ltd. is noted for its enviable stocks of Port Ellen, partly due to the fact that the Islay malt was a favorite of Fred Laing, father of current joint managing directors, Fred and Stewart. Port Ellen is also, of course, highly prized by both consumers and collectors, and so is an assured seller for the company. However, Fred Laing points out that there is no guarantee of consistent quality from cask to cask with old whiskies.

Recalling his childhood, Fred notes that his father would usually consume a few drams of Port Ellen at work. "By the time he got home, I was usually in bed," he notes, "and I would smell this wonderful alcoholic breath! It was probably forty years later, twenty years after his death, when I was conducting a whisky tasting one day, and I got a whiff of Port Ellen, with its leathery sweep of saline, beaches, and dry ropes. It took me straight back to those days when I was a child, and it was a very emotional moment." **GS**

Tasting notes

The nose has strong spices and buttered toast. The palate is subtly peated and sweetly spiced, rich and full. Spice persists in the lengthy, sweet, and smoky finish.

Port Ellen
28-Year-Old

Signatory Vintage Scotch Whisky Co.

Region and country of origin Islay, Scotland
Distillery Port Ellen (closed), Argyll
Alcohol content 58.4% abv
Style Single malt

This twenty-eight-year-old bottling of Port Ellen in Signatory's Cask Strength Collection was distilled on May 5, 1982, and bottled on April 8, 2009. It was matured in a hogshead that yielded just 241 bottles.

Hindsight is acknowledged to be a wonderful thing, but looking back, just why did the old Distillers Company Ltd. choose to close its Port Ellen distillery on Islay in 1983? Today, whenever DCL's successor, Diageo, releases a limited bottling of Port Ellen, it sells out rapidly and commands higher prices than almost any other single malt from a "lost" distillery. Independent bottlings such as this Signatory version are equally coveted by Islay cognoscenti.

The fact is, however, that back in the 1980s, Islays did not enjoy anything like the cult status that they do today. With malt distilleries largely existing only to supply spirit for blending, a little Islay went a very long way, and at times, Islays sold for lower prices than grain whiskies. Hence the decision to sacrifice Port Ellen, which stands on the outskirts of the eponymous Islay village and ferry port, despite the fact that it had been rebuilt in the mid-1960s, having previously lain silent since 1930. Today, the old distillery maltings and a range of stone warehouses survive. **GS**

Tasting notes

Sweet and peaty on the nose, with citrus fruit. A nicely textured, medicinal palate, with pipe tobacco, smoke, malt, and ginger. The finish is quite hot and tannic.

Port Ellen 31-Year-Old
Special Release 2010

Diageo | www.malts.com

Region and country of origin Islay, Scotland
Distillery Port Ellen (closed), Argyll
Alcohol content 54.6% abv
Style Single malt

Of all the single malts offered by Diageo in its annual Special Releases program, none is more eagerly awaited or more quickly sold out than the expression of Port Ellen that is always included in the lineup. The 2010 variant—a thirty-one-year-old distilled in 1978 and matured in a mix of ex-bourbon and ex-sherry casks—was the tenth to be bottled.

The "lost" Islay malt has achieved iconic status with drinkers and collectors alike. Arthur Motley of Edinburgh and London specialist retailers Royal Mile Whiskies notes that "Port Ellen is popular partly because it's an Islay from a closed distillery, and there is not much old Islay whisky around. But it's not similar to old Laphroaig or old Ardbeg, it has a definite and distinctive character."

There are whispers that, objectively speaking, Port Ellen is not quite as good as it is claimed to be, and never really was, perhaps because of what Motley identifies as "an element of emotion, of mourning something that is lost." Thus we have Doug Johnstone in his 2011 novel *Smokeheads* describing Port Ellen as ". . . the most over-hyped Islay malt . . . wildly overrated and overpriced," though he ultimately concedes that it is ". . . a decent dram nonetheless." **GS**

Tasting notes

Dry on the nose, developing lavender notes, vanilla, and old leather. The palate offers cereal, fruity peat, and bonfire smoke. Long in the finish, with peat and oak.

Port Ellen
1982 25-Year-Old

Berry Bros. & Rudd | www.bbr.com

Region and country of origin Islay, Scotland
Distillery Port Ellen (closed), Argyll
Alcohol content 46% abv
Style Single malt

November 2011, a whisky tasting in Norfolk, and it's time for questions. A hand goes up at the back of the room. "Who thinks that the person who decided to shut Port Ellen distillery is a traitor and deserves to be hung, drawn, and quartered?" At least two-thirds of the room put their hands up. It would be hard to think of a distillery that invokes more passion. The distillery was closed and mostly demolished years ago, leaving a malting, and as the stock has dwindled, the reputation of the malt has spiralled. It's the James Dean of whisky, its reputation now almost certainly outweighing its status when it was around.

Port Ellen was shut by what is now Diageo because at the time it was considered third of three on Islay. Since then of course, peated whiskies have grown in stature and importance. This 25-Year-Old ticks all the boxes, but the stocks of Port Ellen are all but gone and the prices are rising fast. Just about any bottle is worth collecting, but when it tastes as good as this one does, it has much more appeal. This is twenty-five years old, but you can see why people are drawn to the distillery because even after that time, there is a great deal of vibrancy and character. Hung, drawn, and quartered? Far too good for them! **DR**

Tasting notes

An oily, fishy smoky nose, but the palate is refined and gentle, the peat and oak soft assertive but delivered gently. The peat grows and is dominant in to the finish.

← Port Ellen's charming distillery was closed in 1983.

Robert Burns Single Malt

Isle of Arran Distillers | www.arranwhisky.com

Region and country of origin Islands, Scotland
Distillery Arran, Lochranza, Isle of Arran
Alcohol content 40% abv
Style Single malt

Back in 2001, Isle of Arran Distillers was one of thirty-seven companies from a variety of business sectors to be invited to become patrons by the World Burns Federation, based in Kilmarnock, Ayrshire. The Federation was created on July 17, 1885, and remains dedicated to preserving the life and works of Robert Burns, "Scotland's favorite son." Because Burns had been born in Ayrshire and Arran is off the Ayrshire coast, Arran was perceived to be the local whisky for the Federation, and the one best placed to receive an official endorsement.

The Robert Burns single malt is a five-year-old Arran bottled under the Burns label, and it is targeted in particular at ex-pats, most notably in Canada, although it also sells well in Russia. As Arran Whisky managing director Euan Mitchell explains, "The Russians study Burns as a core part of their school curriculum, so there is huge brand awareness there.

"In the past, this expression has largely comprised refill casks, but we are now using more fresh bourbon barrels. We did a special edition to mark the 250th anniversary of the birth of Robert Burns in 2009. That was limited to 6,000 bottles and was a ten-year-old, made up of fifteen second-fill sherry hogsheads. As well as the Robert Burns single malt, we also produce a Burns blend that sells well in France and Russia, and we are very proud to have such an association with Robert Burns, Scotland's national bard."

The distillers describe Robert Burns single malt as being "a light, aromatic malt . . . ideal for drinking, prior to or during a meal. A whisky calvados!" **GS**

Tasting notes

Fresh and fruity on the nose in classic Arran style, with pears, toffee apple, and vanilla. Cinnamon and ginger notes develop in time. Sweet and honeyed on the palate, medium-bodied, with well-mannered background sherry lingering into the spicy finish.

Rosebank 21-Year-Old 1990

Diageo | www.malts.com

Region and country of origin Lowlands, Scotland
Distillery Rosebank (closed), Camelon, Falkirk
Alcohol content 53.8% abv
Style Single malt

From time to time, the lazy argument comes up about global drinks companies such as Diageo being bad for whisky. This is a complete load of tripe. Of course Diageo is interested in making money and wants to sell bucket loads of whisky to help it do so. But it has kept twenty-eight Scottish whisky distilleries afloat, many of them staying open in the unlikeliest of places. Let's not get too sentimental here—business is business, and many have been shut over the years, including this one, but the casualty rate would have been much higher without the company's commitment to single-malt whisky. Despite the whisky market being overwhelmingly driven by blends, Diageo bottles a single malt from each of its distilleries, and it's still making an amount of rare stock available each year so that true fans can taste great malt from another era.

Rosebank is regarded as one of the great iconic Lowland distilleries, very few of which remain in business today. The style of the Lowlands is light and floral, but when the whisky has had time to mature, as this one has, there is the potential for all sorts of complexities. And water can flip the taste of the malt completely on its head.

The Rosebank 21-Year-Old is made with some of the oldest stocks still held by the original owners and is a mix of refill American oak and refill European oak casks. Just over 5,600 bottles were released, and in many ways, this is a definitive Lowland malt, bottled at cask strength. It's not cheap, but it's a beauty and well worth pursuing. **DR**

Tasting notes

Shy at first and definitely needs water, but once that's added, rose water, raspberry blancmange, peach, and citrus notes come to the fore. On the palate, the fruit theme continues, with lemon meringue and then cracked pepper and a dry, dusty ending.

Rosebank 1991

Gordon & MacPhail
www.gordanandmacphail.com

Region and country of origin Lowlands, Scotland
Distillery Rosebank (closed), Camelon, Falkirk
Alcohol content 43% abv
Style Single malt

This bottling of Rosebank is part of Gordon & MacPhail's Connoisseurs Choice range, and has been matured in a mixture of refill sherry and bourbon casks. For many aficionados, the triple-distilled Rosebank was the most notable of all Lowland single malts, and the late Michael Jackson described Rosebank as "the finest example of a Lowland malt," considering its demise in 1993 "a grievous loss."

Although no longer a working distillery, much of Rosebank, located beside the Forth-Clyde Canal at Camelon, remains intact, and in May 2002, it was acquired from Diageo by British Waterways, which subsequently sold off some of the property for conversion into a series of apartments. A substantial number of the distillery malt stores and bonded warehouses have also been transformed into offices and a pub/restaurant to complement the existing Rosebank Beefeater restaurant and pub.

Although the Rosebank name is lost to distilling, there are plans for a new distillery venture close to the Rosebank site, with the Falkirk Distillery Company hoping to revive whisky making in the area as part of an ambitious development, which is likely to include a restaurant, visitors' center, and retail outlets. **GS**

Tasting notes

An abundance of fruit on the nose, with floral notes. Sweet citrus fruits continue on the palete, with aniseed and a trace of licorice. A long, malty finish.

Royal Brackla

Bacardi
www.bacardi.com

Region and country of origin Highlands, Scotland
Distillery Royal Brackla, Cawdor, Nairn, Nairnshire
Alcohol content 43% abv
Style Single malt

"Royal" because way back in 1835, the distillery became suppliers to the court of King William IV, and "Brackla" after its founder, Captain William Fraser of Brackla, who set up the place in 1812. Set near to Cawdor—Macbeth country—these days Royal Brackla is owned by Bacardi and happens to be its subsidiary John Dewar & Son's largest distillery, even though it's kept a relatively low profile over the years.

The one available today is the 2004 bottling of Royal Brackla, a ten-year-old single malt that is still a hard find. There have been many others before it, including Royal Brackla 1991 Connoisseurs Choice (Gordon & MacPhail), Royal Brackla 10-Year-Old 1999 Provenance (Douglas Laing), Royal Brackla 14-Year-Old 1994 (Murray McDavid), Brackla 15-Year-Old 1993 (Signatory), and Royal Brackla 10-Year-Old 1996 Provenance (Douglas Laing).

The latest release is medium bodied, crisp, and gentle. It has a fresh, grassy, leafy scent and lots of spice and fruit on the nose. The balance is well crafted and muddles barley and crumbly cake spices with warmed pear, toffee, and liquorice. It has a short, warm, dry finish, as if thumbing its nose at its rarity and beckoning you to take a second sip. **JH**

Tasting notes

This rare whisky is a adventure in time traveling through candy shops and your grandma's house, taking a brief stop at a wet fall woodland spot.

Royal Lochnagar
12-Year-Old

Diageo
www.diageo.com

Region and country of origin Highlands, Scotland
Distillery Royal Lochnagar, Ballater, Aberdeenshire
Alcohol content 40% abv
Style Single malt

It's from Queen Victoria's favorite distillery, so take note—anything that softens the facade of such a notoriously stern lady is certainly worth a look. Royal Lochnagar 12-Year-Old is light amber in color and dangerously easy to drink for such a complex whisky. Its underlying flavor hints faintly at sherry and cigars, giving it the fragrant aroma of an exclusive of members club, but this dram is far from gruff and blokey. No, it's gentler than that. Refined is what it is.

Created just a mile away from Balmoral Castle in Scotland, this whisky's grandeur is rather understated. On the mouth, it's a dry kiss tasting of vanilla and rich fruit. Like a smile from a stranger, it's noninvasive but exhilarating and ever so slightly warming.

The best thing about Royal Lochnagar 12-Year-Old is that it's not obvious. In every sense, it will always live up to expectations, even if it doesn't exceed them. It's from great stock, but it doesn't bray about it from the drinks cabinet; it just quietly exudes its regal connections. If it had a voice, it would chime like Belle and Sebastian's Isobel Campbell. If it were a film character, Kristin Scott Thomas would undoubtedly play the role, with elegant skill and an educated vernacular being the telling signs of status. **StuR**

Tasting notes

Dry and fruity with a faint smokiness. Very well-balanced, this is a complex malt that gives waves of spice and plum, with a light warm sherrylike flavor.

Royal Lochnagar
19-Year-Old Malt Cask

Douglas Laing & Co. | www.douglaslaing.com
www.discovering-distillers.com

Region and country of origin Highlands, Scotland
Distillery Royal Lochnagar, Ballater, Aberdeenshire
Alcohol content 50% abv
Style Single malt

One of the current trends in bars is a revival of cocktail making using single malts and unusual mixers. Even the ultratraditional Scotch Whisky Association lists a large selection, including ingredients as diverse as chile and kiwi fruit. One that you would probably want to miss would be red wine, particularly claret. It would seem to be murdering two lovely drinks.

Yet that is exactly the way Queen Victoria liked to take her Lochnagar. The distillery was only three years old when she moved into Balmoral, just one mile away. After an invitation to visit from the owner, she was hooked on the place and gave it a warrant, one of only three distilleries able to use the prefix "Royal."

This Douglas Laing bottling has spent nineteen years in a sherry butt that has had a strong influence on the finished product. They still use traditional worm tubs to cool the spirit, which give a fuller, heavier East Highland style. Despite its small output, some of the spirit does end up in blends, particularly VAT 69, but it is now one the Classic Malts, and distillery bottlings are widely available. A number of these are finished in sherry casks, but as yet none in claret barrels, so if you really want to re-create the Victorian taste, you're on your own. **AN**

Tasting notes

Like a full, sweet sherry on the nose with light ginger spice. Hints of coffee come through later. A warm honey cake, malty with a smooth but short and gentle finish.

Royal Lochnagar Distillers Edition

Diageo | www.diageo.com

Region and country of origin Highlands, Scotland
Distillery Royal Lochnagar, Ballater, Aberdeenshire
Alcohol content 40% abv
Style Single malt

Regal, subtle, and smooth, the Royal Lochnagar Distillers Edition exudes a devastatingly eligible edge. Not only is it sweeter than its twelve-year-old sibling, but it also offers a softer side derived from having had a second, double maturation in muscat wine casks. It is this kind of attention to detail and balance of flavor that can give a great dram such as this a truly great point of difference.

With the distillery being favored by royalty, the whisky already has some credibility, but to describe this offering with impartial fairness, it's also important to mention that it is the depth of flavor that is the real hero here and not its lofty connections. On the nose, it may be mellow and sing of wild gardens, tea, and jam, but in truth it's more complex than the scented softness it first evokes.

The Royal Lochnagar Distillers Edition has, after all, a rich and full flavor. It's a whisky with a deep voice and a booming finish. On the nose it may be all fruity cake and rice pudding, but on the palate, it's brown sugar, wood, and toasted almond wrapped in velvet.

This Distillers Edition is a dominant spirit, and it has all the protective strength of a father's embrace without being crushing. It's a whisky that laughs "so you think you know about whisky?" It's a cabinet-pleaser and a great antidote to a pause in conversation. "What do you think?" you may ask your fellow companions—each giving a moment to ponder the complexity of the dram. And to conclude, there aren't many whiskies that have a finish quite as rewarding as this one. **JH**

Tasting notes

Mix together all the ingredients for scones for what this is like on the nose. But better, because these scones are cooked by a master chef of culinary expertise. He's added mixed peel, a handful of nuts, and raw sugar to the butter along with apricot and raisin.

Lochnagar distillery in 1848; the scene is not greatly changed today. ➔

Royal Salute
21-Year-Old

Chivas Brothers (Pernod Ricard)
www.royalsalute.com

Region and country of origin Scotland
Distilleries Various
Alcohol content 40% abv
Style Blend

Royal Salute 21-Year-Old premiered on June 2, 1953, to celebrate Her Majesty Queen Elizabeth II's ascent to the throne of England. Named for the twenty-one-gun royal salute that marks special royal occasions, this expression was created to be the "pinnacle of Scotch whiskies." At the time of its release, it was the oldest certified example of blended Scotch whisky in the world, an honor now held by Royal Salute 62 Gun Salute, which is forty years old.

Royal Salute 21-Year-Old is a permanent member of the Chivas Brothers blended whisky line. Tracing its roots back to James and John Chivas, the company has a long history of laying down stocks of rare and premium Scotch whisky. Today, with over six million casks at their disposal, Chivas Brothers is uniquely situated to produce aged blends such as Royal Salute 21-Year-Old on a permanent basis.

The 21-Year-Old has delicate floral notes. Master blender Colin Scott describes it as "an armed fist in a velvet glove" with a wonderful smoky dryness in the background. Over time, different-colored flagons have been used for the blend, most recently emerald, ruby, and sapphire (the latter renamed in 2003 to pay tribute to the Queen's Golden Jubilee). **WM**

Tasting notes

An interesting nose combining dry florals and spice. The palate is very dry with smoky oak notes combining with cinnamon and vanilla. The finish is dry.

Royal Salute
Stone of Destiny

Chivas Brothers (Pernod Ricard)
www.royalsalute.com

Region and country of origin Scotland
Distilleries Various
Alcohol content 40% abv
Style Blend

Royal Salute Stone of Destiny was released in 2005 and has become a permanent expression in the Royal Salute family of blends. It is composed of significantly older whiskies, each having spent at least thirty-eight years in oak casks, and some maturing for as long as forty-four years.

The Stone of Destiny, also called the Stone of Scone, is a 336-pound (152-kg), oblong block of sandstone fitted with iron rings. Brought to Scone Abbey in the ninth century and subsequently fitted into King Edward's "coronation chair" in 1296, it has been used for centuries in coronation ceremonies for the monarchs of Scotland and England. It was last used in the coronation of Queen Elizabeth II in 1953, the day Royal Salute 21-Year-Old was launched.

According to Chivas Brothers master blender Colin Scott, Royal Salute Stone of Destiny exemplifies the power of the Royal Salute family with nice fruit, floral, and nutty notes, developing into a long finish. "Smoothness," according to Scott, "is the hallmark of the Royal Salute family." The similarities between the Royal Salute 21-Year-Old and the Stone of Destiny are apparent, but the latter is more polished, with amplified notes of dark fruit and spice. **WM**

Tasting notes

Rich, fragrant nose, with sherry spice notes of cinnamon, nutmeg, and cedar. More cedar on the palate, with dates, baked apple, toffee, and hints of orange.

← Chivas Brothers' finest, locked in the Royal Salute Vault at Strathisla distillery.

Scapa
16-Year-Old

Chivas Brothers (Pernod Ricard)
www.scapamalt.com

Region and country of origin Islands, Scotland
Distillery Scapa, Orkney
Alcohol content 40% abv
Style Single malt

A few years ago, it was said that the people of Orkney chose Scapa whisky over the whiskies of rival distillery Highland Park. In fact, Scapa was only consumed on Orkney because at the time Orkney was the only place where you could get it.

Scapa distillery, founded in 1885, was rebuilt in 1959. With views of Scapa Flow and an unusual Lomond still, it was mothballed in a ruinous state in 1994. Although essentially silent for a decade, it was reopened for a few weeks each year, ironically by workers at Highland Park, to distill a small amount of spirit for blending purposes. Owners Allied Domecq were in the process of renovating the distillery for a reopening when the company was broken up. Chivas Brothers took ownership of many of its distilleries, including this one, and restored Scapa in 2004.

Scapa whisky was originally sold as a fourteen-year-old, but after checking the inventory of their completely renovated distillery, Chivas Brothers decided to relaunch it in the form of this 16-Year-Old. The whisky itself is not as briny as the original Scapa. Despite the island location, Scapa now has more in common with sweet and fruity Speyside whiskies than with the big, peaty, island malts. **DR**

Tasting notes

The nose is fruity, sweet, and clean. On the palate, mandarin, honey, and caramel are present, but there is little real evidence of the oak. A medium-long finish.

Scapa 16-Year-Old
Distillery-only Bottling

Chivas Brothers (Pernod Ricard)
www.scapamalt.com

Region and country of origin Islands, Scotland
Distillery Scapa, Orkney
Alcohol content 60.9% abv
Style Single malt

Today, whisky is prospering worldwide, but that was not always the case. Over the years, many distilleries have been closed, mothballed, and demolished. Some owe their survival to their remoteness—on an island like Orkney, few want to replace a distillery with a parking lot or a shopping center.

So it was with Scapa. The Orkney distillery slipped into disrepair, becoming overrun by birds and animals, with its stills exposed to the elements. Now fully repaired, it has a still room with a large window overlooking Scapa Flow, where the sunken British warship *Royal Oak* lies as an official war grave. The huge Lomond still remains, distinguished by removable plates that vary the amount of contact between spirit and copper and enable the distiller to make different styles of malt. The still continues in use, although the copper plates are no longer altered.

One of the characteristics of Scapa whiskies is a maritime saltiness, which this bottling shows at its finest. The whisky is at cask strength, and is sold in a 50-cl (17-oz) bottle rather than the normal 70 cl (24 oz). As good a representation of Scapa as you will find, the whisky is sold at several Pernod Ricard distilleries and is very different from the standard 16-Year-Old. **DR**

Tasting notes

The nose is shy, but with water, this is a sweet bowl of tropical fruit—pineapple, mango, and banana—with a big mouthfeel and a long, honeyed, fruity finale.

Scapa distillery on Orkney is easily identified from the sea. →

Scottish Leader

Burn Stewart Distillers | www.scottishleader.com

Region and country of origin Scotland
Distilleries Various
Alcohol content 40% abv
Style Blend

Scottish Leader is the flagship blended Scotch whisky from Burn Stewart Distillers and is currently sold in more than sixty countries. It contains up to thirty Scotch whiskies, including five North British grain whiskies and twenty-five single malts from a wide range of distilleries, including Aberfeldy, Caol Ila, and Girvan. Some of the ingredients vary from time to time, but the heart of the blend is constant: Deanston single malt from the eighteenth-century distillery of the same name on the banks of the River Teith.

Crafted by master blender Ian MacMillan, Scottish Leader is an excellent choice for drinkers seeking high quality at an accessible price, and is a good and relatively unfamiliar alternative to other mainstream blends. It is smooth, with a honeyed flavor. Back in 1997, it won the International Spirits Challenge, an accolade that recognized its credentials as a full-bodied, well-balanced blend, all plump and sleek, with notes of gingerbread and stewed fruits.

Some people think that Scottish Leader is ostentatious, but most readily acknowledge that it has plenty to show off about—if it doesn't draw attention to itself, what else will? Its golden amber color reflects its honeyed, syrupy flavor perfectly. How best to drink it, though? Neat? With water? Mixed? And when? During festivities? After a hearty meal? Actually, what is important is not how, or when, but where. Scottish Leader is best enjoyed relaxing in the bathtub, either alone or with your chosen bathtub buddy, sipping a dram between musings while listening to the rain hammering down outside. **JH**

Tasting notes

Big, full-bodied, and well balanced, Scottish Leader is copper-amber in color and has a nose of sweet sherry, malt, and fruit pastilles. The taste is of caramel and nuts, with a hint of wine, and the finish is oaky, with some pepperiness. A whisky better savored than rushed.

Seagram's 100 Pipers

Chivas Brothers (Pernod Ricard) | www.chivasbrothers.com

Region and country of origin Scotland
Distilleries Various
Alcohol content 40% abv
Style Blend

Worldwide, blends account for around 80 percent of whisky sales. Seagram's 100 Pipers is nothing like as well known in its home market as massive players such as Johnnie Walker or its stablemate, Chivas Regal, yet it has a huge presence elsewhere. Globally it is the number seven standard blended Scotch whisky.

The blend is currently number one in Thailand and growing rapidly in many other countries, including Spain, Venezuela, Australia, and India. It is notable for doing well mostly in hot countries, where people like to add plenty of ice and turn their whisky into a long, cold, refreshing drink. That is not necessarily something drinkers in northern latitudes would want to do with their expensive single malts, a reminder that single malts have only a niche market.

A blend that sells into hot-country markets has to be a spirit embraced by everyman, a blend that is seen to be suitable for many whisky-based drinks. But once you start to look at the constituent parts of Seagram's 100 Pipers, you begin to realize why this blend in particular is garnering such a loyal following. It contains some of Scotland's finest malt whiskies, including whisky from the Chivas Brothers' Speyside distilleries of Braeval and Allt a' Bhainne.

The blend is said to be named for the men playing bagpipes who traditionally led Scottish armies into battle, inspiring the clansmen and striking terror into the hearts of the enemy. There is a "Ballad of a Hundred Pipers," commemorating Bonnie Prince Charlie's arrival at Carlyle in 1745, impressively preceded by a band of a hundred pipers. **AA**

Tasting notes

A broad, all-encompassing nose, as you might expect from a blend. Cereal and dried fruits, then furniture polish. Oily, sweet, nearly syrupy on the palate, with almond and fruit. The oak is well integrated and has a strong grip. The finish is suddenly dry and crisp.

Sheep Dip

Spencerfield Spirit Co.
www.spencerfieldspirit.com

Region and country of origin Lowlands, Scotland
Distillery Spencerfield, Inverkeithing, Fife
Alcohol content 40% abv
Style Vatted malt

Love it or hate it, it's still an interesting dram. Named because British farmers often referred to their whisky as sheep dip and also hid their home-distilled whiskies in barrels marked "sheep dip" and entered them onto their bills as such so as not to pay taxes.

This Sheep Dip is made by a small independent whisky producer called the Spencerfield Spirit Company located on an old working farm in Inverkeithing, Fife, which was first built in 1559. The range, which also includes Pig's Nose and Old Hebridean, was developed with Richard Paterson, the master blender for Whyte & Mackay. For Sheep Dip, the style is fresh, spiced, and a tad grassy, which makes for an interesting blend, but not everyone's cup of tea.

The whiskies used in the blend are aged between eight and twelve years in first-fill wood and make up a hearty and bold blend that, on the nose, suggests it's all fruit and almond as well as delicate floral tones—on the tongue, it tells a different story. The boldest notes are from the Highlands and Speyside valleys, and it's a welcome addition for anyone looking for a punchy malt that's pretty kind to the wallet. The packaging is particularly retro too and deserves some shelf space—even as a conversation starter. **JH**

Tasting notes

Golden copper in color with a refined scent on the nose and a punchy, tangy boldness on the palate. It gives both malt and toffee and ends with an impressive finish.

The Singleton of Glen Ord

Diageo
www.diageo.com

Region and country of origin Highlands, Scotland
Distillery Glen Ord, Muir of Ord, Ross-shire
Alcohol content 40% abv
Style Single malt

This gets whisky professionals as well as newcomers hot under the collar. That's because it's a dream of a dram. Tasty, yet approachable. Smooth and, more importantly, not too complex—this is easy drinking at its best. More specifically, the Asia Pacific market can't get enough of it.

The Singleton of Glen Ord manages to traverse both elite and mainstream circles rather well. It's certainly got that edge. It's mainstream, but so acceptably good that ordering one is something of which to be proud. The liquid is fermented for up to five days, which is what results in its depth, while the slow distillation in copper before it's matured in European and American oak gives it that smoothness. It's dark amber. Think polished conker in fall or a mix of maple and mahogany wood.

On the palate, there's an almost soft almondy gingerness that is reminiscent of teacakes and toffee. The finish is long, and you're hooked at one taste. To say that this is well crafted is an understatement. It's confident, without seeming cocky, nonchalant in its appeal, and its mastered underplay is perfection itself. It's friendly. It's welcoming. A straightforward malt to admire and enjoy at leisure. **JH**

Tasting notes

Best enjoyed on a battered old Chesterfield while listening to vinyl. Slightly smoky, with hints of dripping candle wax and a log fire, it feels both sweet and dry.

The Six Isles

Ian Macleod Distillers
www.ianmaclead.com

Regions and country of origin Islay and Islands, Scotland **Distilleries** Various of Islay, Jura, Skye, Mull, Orkney, and Arran **Alcohol content** 43% abv **Style** Blended malt

More than just a whisky, this is a journey in a bottle. A journey through the islands of Scotland, really. Scotland has more than 140 inhabited islands, but malt whisky is distilled on only six of them—hence the name Six Isles. The blend has been created by the team at Ian Macleod Distillers with mature single malts selected from casks drawn from just one distillery from each of those six Scottish Islands: Islay, Jura, Mull, Arran, Skye, and Orkney.

The mix of flavors ranges from the highly peaty and sea salt–scented malt of Islay to the more delicate honeyed aromas of the Orcadian malt. The Six Isles is bottled traditionally and is of natural color and non-chill-filtered too, as well as being presented in a distinctive gift tin. There are other interesting things about it. Because the whisky is slightly oily, it is prone to going cloudy in cold temperatures and is clear at room temperature. But it's the balance of peat, sweetness, and delicate creaminess that's truly fantastic. This derives from the fact that this blend combines the best of each of those six islands and what they have to offer the palate. An example of how, sometimes, blends can offer up a varied and complex mix of styles all in one dram. **JH**

Tasting notes

Clean, smoky, and sweet. Vanilla and smoke, with a balanced sweetness that continues. Good for newcomers as well as whisky enthusiasts.

Something Special

Chivas Brothers (Pernod Ricard)
www.chivasbrothers.com

Region and country of origin Scotland **Distilleries** Various **Alcohol content** 40% abv **Style** Blend

Back in the 1970s, Something Special was a notably successful "de-luxe" blend in the Seagram stable of whiskies, but today it is much more elusive in many markets. The giant Canadian Seagram Company Ltd. sold its spirits assets to Pernod Ricard and Diageo in 2001, with Pernod gaining the Chivas Brothers Scotch whisky operation, predominantly centered around Speyside distilleries. Among the blends acquired was Something Special, which has the Speyside single malt Longmorn at its heart.

Something Special is a "niche" premium blend, which has to compete for attention and resources with the big-budget, heavy-hitting Ballantine's and Chivas Regal ranges, but it performs well in a number of Latin American countries. It actually dates back to 1912, when the Edinburgh blenders and bottlers Hill, Thomson & Co. introduced it. They used to personally select casks to be filled at various distilleries in order to maintain the integrity of their creation, and today whiskies matured in both ex-bourbon American oak barrels and former-sherry European oak casks go into the blend. In 2006 the fifteen-year-old variant was introduced, which contains up to thirty-five Speyside and Islay malts in its composition. **GS**

Tasting notes

Fresh on the gently spicy nose, with vanilla, a hint of new leather, almond, and cocoa. Full-bodied, spicy, sweet, with a wisp of smoke.

Speyburn 10-Year-Old

International Beverage | www.speyburn.com

Region and country of origin Speyside, Scotland
Distillery Speyburn, Rothes, Aberlour, Morayshire
Alcohol content 40% abv
Style Single malt

"A solid dram," you may have heard said about this whisky or perhaps "they don't make them like this anymore." How very true. A bottle of Speyburn 10-Year-Old is like a 1990 Mercedes S-class: it may not be much to look at (let's be honest, you wouldn't drive one/bring a bottle to a fancy cocktail party) but the content effortlessly puts to shame most new products. And then there's the price. The value for money makes Adam Smith turn in his grave, 100 miles (160 km) south of where the whisky is made.

Speyburn was built near Rothes, Moray, in the late nineteenth century, and in 1900 it was the first distillery in Scotland to use drum maltings (also known as pneumatic maltings). The idea was simple. Instead of the labor-intensive turning of barley by hand, large cylindrical drums filled with germinating malt would do the job by slowly revolving.

Although two other Scottish distilleries (Glen Grant and St. Magdalene) also had drum maltings installed, the ones at Speyburn are the only remaining examples. They are protected by Historic Scotland and are the distillery's pride and joy. However, they went out of use in 1967 and had no part in making any of the whisky available today—all the malt is now brought in from specialist maltsters. So why talk about them? The story of drum maltings showcases the traditionally unsentimental approach to distilling at Speyburn, where innovation is always embraced. A well-tuned, one-man operation produces a heavy and fragrant spirit. All the casks destined for single-malt bottlings are stored on site. **LD**

Tasting notes

Cherry stone, tinned peach, and pear on the nose. Slightly floral and perfumed but well balanced. Haribo bears emerge with water—green ones if you're feeling geeky. The taste is creamy with notes of vanilla custard and white chocolate. Big body makes for a sticky finish.

Speyburn 25-Year-Old Solera

International Beverage | www.speyburn.com

Region and country of origin Speyside, Scotland
Distillery Speyburn, Rothes, Aberlour, Morayshire
Alcohol content 46% abv
Style Single malt

If the other Speyburn featured in this book, Solera's younger sibling, is old school heavy metal—let's say Iron Maiden—then this 25-Year-Old would be Frédéric Chopin. Exquisite, thoughtful, poetic . . . and largely misunderstood.

Speyburn Solera has a small but dedicated audience that resembles a conspiracy organization rather than a fan club. But if you happen to come across one of those elusive men and women and direct the conversation onto the right track, you will be surprised to see just how much love for the dram there actually is out there. You are likely to hear that even though the Solera is not as popular or critically acclaimed as the equivalent expressions from nearby Macallan, Aberlour, or Glenfiddich distilleries, it holds its ground well in a blind tasting while being a better value for money. And while the packaging is not exactly flashy—they would likely observe—and the marketing not geared toward a trendy young drinker, that doesn't really matter, as the Solera is all about the juice. Incredible balance, intriguing complexity, vibrant oak influence, and that little something, that sparkle that makes it a dram you remember and instantly recognize in the future.

A short explanation of the name is due. Solera is an age-old system of blending alcohol continuously by gradually topping up a vat or a cask. Some soleras are complex systems of many casks of various ages, others are simple setups with one central vat. Either way, the system is designed to ensure the highest possible consistency of the product. **LD**

Tasting notes

Slightly floral at first glance, then malty, the nose builds and reaches its fruity, chocolaty peak after some time. Elderflower, prunes, and macadamia nut. The taste is subtle, but grows and changes through a kaleidoscope of pink grapefruit, white chocolate, and marmalade.

Springbank
10-Year-Old

J. & A. Mitchell Co.
www.springbankwhisky.com

Region and country of origin Highlands, Scotland
Distillery Springbank, Campbeltown, Argyll
Alcohol content 46% abv
Style Single malt

Located on the southern Kintyre peninsula, Springbank was built in 1828 on the site of an illegal still that is thought to have been in operation since the Middle Ages. It is the only Scottish distillery to have always remained independent; it entered the second decade of the twenty-first century under the stewardship of Hedley Wright, a great-great-great grandson of the founder, William Reid.

The 10-Year-Old single malt is made from barley that is malted using local peat and fresh water from Crosshill Loch. It is distilled by means of a unique process in which around half of the low wine (the first distillation) is distilled a second time; the two halves are then mixed together and distilled for a final time. This method—by which some of the finished spirit goes through the process three times, while other parts of it are treated only twice—is known as two-and-a-half times distillation.

Springbank is then mashed in a rake-and-plough tun and matured mainly in bourbon casks. Springbank does not aim for consistency of cask selection, with the result that some of its ten-year-olds are more sherried than others; this is not considered a shortcoming but rather an added attraction. **GL**

Tasting notes

The nose is chiles and charcoal soap, with clove and a whiff of the sea. Chalky, malty, and spicy on the palate. A long, satisfying finish, with a return of the sea salt.

Springbank
15-Year-Old

J. & A. Mitchell Co.
www.springbankwhisky.com

Region and country of origin Highlands, Scotland
Distillery Springbank, Campbeltown, Argyll
Alcohol content 46% abv
Style Single malt

Springbank distillery has developed small but significant variations in preparation methods that have made it one of Scotland's most distinctive and quirky whisky makers. Take, for example, the contrast between this 15-Year-Old and its ten-year-old stable mate. The 15-Year-Old single malt is 100 percent matured in sherry casks and generally regarded as not a whisky for novices, who will most likely be confounded by its strong peatiness. It is by common consent a Scotch drinker's Scotch, one that can only be enjoyed after a meal, and, some insist, with a cigar.

The experienced palate will immediately discern that this whisky is quite unlike the 10-Year-Old: it is a much richer, more reserved, and sophisticated dram. That there should be striking differences between two such closely related drinks epitomizes the distillery's overall production values: the owners proudly claim that their whiskies are more "handmade" than any others in Scotland.

A further reflection of owner J. & A. Mitchell's versatility is that Springbank distillery is the only one in Scotland to produce three styles of single malts—Springbank, Hazelburn, and Longrow. These are not mere labels, they are radically different entities. **GL**

Tasting notes

Peat and sulfur on the nose. The palate has a silky texture that starts with pear and grape before giving way, first to oakiness, then to allspice, leather, and peat.

Springbank 16-Year-Old Rum Wood Expression

J. & A. Mitchell Co.
www.springbankwhisky.com

Region and country of origin Highlands, Scotland
Distillery Springbank, Campbeltown, Argyll
Alcohol content 55.4% abv
Style Single malt

The strange story of this magnificent single malt began in June 1991, when Jim Murray, author of the annual whisky bible that bears his name, was wandering around Springbank's bonded warehouses and came across a couple of strange-looking casks. They turned out to have been originally used for rum, and the whisky they contained was a most unusual shade of green. A tasting convinced Springbank that they were on to something, and so they set about tweaking the recipe to make it marketable.

The new formula, painstakingly applied over the next sixteen years, produced astounding results. Although by the time the second edition of the whisky was bottled in August 2007 it had lost its amazing original color, it retained all the remarkable quality. When the product went on sale in 2009 in a batch of 6,000 bottles, Springbank maintained the odd color motif by attaching a distinctive mauve label.

The brilliance of this 16-Year-Old was acclaimed at the 2010 World Whiskies Awards, where it won the award for the Best Campbeltown Malt. Its critical success has been more than matched by its popularity with seasoned bibbers: it is a prized collector's item. **GL**

Tasting notes

The nose is slightly oily and rich with sherry, angelica, and apricot. The palate is big and spicy, with hints of pepper and smoke. The finish is long, drying slowly.

Springbank 17-Year-Old Glenkeir Treasures

Glenkeir Whiskies
www.thewhiskyshop.com

Region and country of origin Highlands, Scotland
Distillery Springbank, Campbeltown, Argyll
Alcohol content 54.1% abv
Style Single malt

Springbank is a hit-or-miss distillery. It is highly traditional, small, independently owned, and capable of true greatness. Its whiskies are much sought after, and, when the expression's right, there is a delightful combination of coconut, oil, and green banana skin that cannot be matched. On the other hand, the whisky can be intense, peaty, and savory. This whisky falls into the category of "sublime" and is highly recommended as an introduction to this enigmatic but slightly unpredictable distillery.

Now a seventeen-year-old expression, it was at first bottled as a fifteen-year-old. It is part of a core group of cask-strength products in the Glenkeir Treasures range, bottled by Glenkeir Whiskies and available through the twenty-odd stores of the Whisky Shop chain in the United Kingdom. Glenkeir does a range of cask-strength whiskies, bottlings drawn from one or two casks with a yield that is often fewer than 150 bottles. The whiskies are sourced from an independent bottler rather than the distilleries themselves by someone within the Glenkeir company, and whoever it is knows exactly what they are doing. This is a good introductory whisky to one of Scotland's most distinctive distilleries. **DR**

Tasting notes

Intense, rich, and oily, with unripe banana, rustic and prickly peat, enough tannin to keep the malt in shape, and a delicious soft and sweet peach and coconut core.

Springbank 18-Year-Old

J. & A. Mitchell Co. | www.springbankwhisky.com

Region and country of origin Highlands, Scotland
Distillery Springbank, Campbeltown, Argyll
Alcohol content 46% abv
Style Single malt

Springbank, the original J. & A. Mitchell distillery in Campbeltown, retains a charming olde worlde feel. Even today, it has fewer computers than any other commercial whisky maker, but the business has moved with the times to preserve its independence: its whiskies are warehoused and bottled in modern premises on adjacent land that belonged to Longrow until that distillery's demise in 1896. Nevertheless, Springbank clings to many tried-and-trusted methods, and nowhere are these better illustrated than in its intentionally restricted volume output.

Springbank's 18-Year-Old single malt is produced annually, but each edition is strictly limited (at the time of writing to 9,000 bottles a year). Since demand dependably exceeds supply, this whisky soon becomes a rare commodity that may command surprisingly high prices in the marketplace.

The spirit is 80 percent matured in ex-sherry casks and 20 percent in ex-bourbon casks. That much is certain, but, in keeping with the finest traditions of Springbank, no vintage of this whisky is quite like any other. This variety is a consequence of the distillery's "handmade" production philosophy.

In spite of the differences between each eighteen-year-old, what unites them are the smell and the taste. In young Springbank, the former is suggestive of banana, cherry, and strawberry, but in vintages older than fifteen years, it turns into more of an assertion than a hint. Similar benefits of aging may be discerned on the palate, which becomes creamier and smokier with the passing years. **GL**

Tasting notes

The nose is slow, but gradually reveals vanilla, cereal, and dried fruit, with toasted almond and a burnt sugar smokiness. The dram is heavy and oily on the palate, with a bitter beginning and a growing sweetness. The finish is reasonably long, with a smoky aftertaste.

Springbank 25-Year-Old

J. & A. Mitchell Co. | www.springbankwhisky.com

Region and country of origin Highlands, Scotland
Distillery Springbank, Campbeltown, Argyll
Alcohol content 46% abv
Style Single malt

This special limited edition was produced in 2006 to mark the forty years in distilling of Frank McHardy, director of production at J. & A. Mitchell Co. Ltd. In fact, McHardy's ruby anniversary had fallen three years previously—he started out in 1963 sweeping the floors of the Invergordon distillery. But first McHardy himself and then everyone else who sampled the celebratory drink were quick to conclude that its quality more than compensated for this small timekeeping error.

After Invergordon, McHardy worked successively at the Tamnavulin, Bruichladdich, and Bushmills distilleries. He joined the J. & A. Mitchell in 1976, first as a distillery manager and eventually becoming production director for Springbank and Glengyle. Asked to identify the main changes to the whisky industry during his long career, McHardy identified above all "the fact that almost all the distilleries in Scotland are owned by a couple of companies."

McHardy's long-term job satisfaction derives partly from his freedom to "control all the processes in house, from malting the barley to bottling the final product." This autonomy will be preserved for as long as Springbank can remain independent in an increasingly globalized industry—and at the time of writing, even in the depths of a world recession, malt whisky sales are holding up strongly enough to raise hopes that that will be for a very long time to come.

Every one of the 610 bottles was individually signed and numbered by McHardy, and purchases were limited to one per customer. **GL**

Tasting notes

The nose is fresh with apple, lemon, and coconut. The taste is a playful mouth-filling combination of sweet and savory, with a strong tang of malt and a certain sootiness. A smoky finish, redolent of shortbread. Overall, an understated but authoritative dram.

Springbank 100 Proof

J. & A. Mitchell Co. | www.springbankwhisky.com

Region and country of origin Highlands, Scotland
Distillery Springbank, Campbeltown, Argyll
Alcohol content 57% abv
Style Single malt

This ten-year-old single malt is among Springbank's prestige products. As might be expected in view of its formidable strength—100 proof whisky contains at least 50 percent alcohol by volume—it has discernibly more power than its budget equivalent, which has an abv of 46 percent. The spirit is aged mainly in ex-sherry and American ex-bourbon casks, although rum casks may be used when the need arises: this lack of standardization in the barreling makes each bottle of Springbank unique.

Springbank 100 Proof was first released in March 2004 and is now sold as an ongoing bottling, although demand exceeds supply and it is consequently often out of stock. (Springbank is small—it currently produces around 33,000 gallons [124,90 liters] of whisky a year. It habitually closes for a part of each year, and many of the staff spend their down-time malting and distilling at Glengyle, another J. & A. Mitchell Co. distillery in Campbeltown.)

The maker's Web site proudly describes the 100 Proof as "Springbank in its purest form." Although some critics have questioned whether the 100 Proof is sufficiently different from the standard ten-year-old single malt to be worth the premium price, that does not seem an extravagant claim: most commentators and buyers seem more than satisfied—in 2004 the vintage beat a strong field to win the Loch Fyne restaurant chain's Whisky of the Year award; the judges praised its sophistication and complexity and claimed that their decision was one of the easiest they had ever had to make. **GL**

Tasting notes

The nose is roasting meats and peat, with suggestions of grass and salt. The taste is full and creamy but not sweet. The finish is medium to long and suggestive of dark almond chocolate and vanilla; water brings out a suspicion of sour cherry.

Springbank CV

J. & A. Mitchell Co. | www.springbankwhisky.com

Region and country of origin Highlands, Scotland
Distillery Springbank, Campbeltown, Argyll
Alcohol content 46% abv
Style Single malt

This single malt is a vatting of whiskies aged seven, ten, and fourteen years from different casks (bourbon, sherry, and port wine) that have all been specially selected by production director Frank McHardy and distillery manager Stuart Robertson. The intention is that each ingredient should complement the others to ensure an outstanding whisky with an abundance of flavor and the inimitable Springbank style. It is named CV (which stands for "curriculum vitae") because it aims to encompass the whole range of Springbank's capabilities within, as it were, a small space.

Springbank CV was first marketed in 2010 in cardboard carriers called "Campbeltown CV packs" containing three 20-cl (6.8-oz) bottles: the other two held the CV equivalents for Springbank's stablemates, the triple-distilled Hazelburn and the peated Longrow. Only later did the distillery make each of the malts available for purchase as single items.

The Springbank CV did not, however, meet with universal acclaim: it was described on one online forum as "lacking distillery character" and "a bit flat." Yet, to paraphrase Norman Douglas's general dictum about authors, a whisky that succeeds in satisfying everybody should have its blood pressure tested— something must be wrong with it. After all, even the most mundane single malt is an acquired taste, and Springbank products are nothing like mundane: the CV has duly acquired a reputation as an expressive and robust, if uncomplicated, whisky whose sterling qualities may be greatly enhanced by the addition of a few drops of water. **GL**

Tasting notes

Strong smoke, with a faint smell of toffee and dried fruit. There is a also a hint of sulfur and the sea. It has a good body that is big and full on the palate, evoking dark sugar, fruit, and spice with, again, a coastal feel. The long and satisfying finish is spicy and smoky.

Stewarts Cream of the Barley

Chivas Brothers (Pernod Ricard) | www.chivasbrothers.com

Region and country of origin Scotland
Distilleries Various
Alcohol content 40% abv
Style Blend

Today, the city of Dundee in the eastern central Lowlands has lost virtually all links with the Scotch whisky business, but during the late nineteenth and early twentieth centuries, the east coast port and manufacturing center, situated on the north bank of the Firth of Tay, was a major base for companies engaged in the blended whisky trade.

One such firm was Stewart & Son, which had its origins in licensed premises in Dundee's Castle Street, where Alexander Stewart ran the Glengarry Inn. Stewart was a whisky dealer by trade, and it was a logical development for the firm ultimately to produce its own "in-house" blend, using the Cream of the Barley name.

In 1969, Stewart's became part of Allied Distillers Ltd., and Cream of the Barley went on to enjoy strong sales across Scotland through Allied's on-trade business. The blend continued to be bottled in Dundee until relatively recent times, before that role was transferred to Allied's Dumbarton complex in West Dunbartonshire, to the west of Glasgow.

Under Allied Distillers' ownership, Cream of the Barley had Glencadam single malt at its core, as Allied owned the distillery, located in the town of Brechin, some 25 miles (940 km) northeast of Dundee. Since 2001, Cream of the Barley has been under the ownership of Pernod Ricard, through its Chivas Brothers Scotch whisky subsidiary. The formulation of Cream of the Barley has necessarily changed, but it still contains around fifty different malts, and the brand now enjoys strong sales in Ireland. **GS**

Initially slightly metallic, some acetone, then lemongrass, fat grain notes, and ultimately fresh peach on the nose. Sweet and quite full-bodied on the palate, rounded and maltier than the nose might suggest. Lively spices in the gingery, medium-length finish.

Strathisla 12-Year-Old

Chivas Brothers (Pernod Ricard) | www.chivasbrothers.com

Region and country of origin Speyside, Scotland
Distillery Strathisla, Keith, Banffshire
Alcohol content 43% abv
Style Single malt

Strathisla is purported to be the oldest working distillery in the Scottish Highlands. Founded in 1786 by George Taylor and Alexander Milne as the Milltown Distilling Company, the name changed to Strathisla in 1870, then to Milton, after the nearby Milton Castle, in 1890, and then back to Strathisla in 1951, when the distillery was acquired by Chivas Brothers. *Strathisla* is Gaelic for "Valley of the River Isla," and its roots date back to the thirteenth century, when Dominican monks used the nearby springs as a water source to produce their beer. The distillery is relatively small, with an annual output of only 634,000 gallons (2.4 million liters).

Strathisla whisky is considered the backbone of Chivas Regal. Most of the output is destined for the Chivas Regal and Royal Salute blends, with a small amount bottled as a single malt. Strathisla 12-Year-Old has been available since the 1970s, but has had some packaging changes over the years.

The 12-Year-Old is matured primarily in American oak casks, likely ex-bourbon barrels and hogsheads, which explains the buttery, creamy notes of vanilla and toffee. If you are a fan of Chivas Regal 12-Year-Old, you will see the similarities in this, as "it is at the heart of all the Chivas Regal blends," according to Chivas Brothers master blender Colin Scott.

According to Scott, Strathisla's "four stills are small, stout, and short, and as such they produce a full-bodied, rich new distillate." Strathisla 12-Year-Old is available in many countries and duty-free shops around the world. **WM**

Tasting notes

Strathisla 12-Year-Old shows sweet notes of fruit, honey, and vanilla on the nose. Creamy, with more vanilla, toffee, caramel, and hints of apple and pear on the palate. Dried apricot emerges over time. This expression is rich and creamy, with a peppery finish.

Strathmill 18-Year-Old Malt Cask

Douglas Laing & Co. | www.douglaslaing.com / www.malts.com

Region and country of origin Speyside, Scotland
Distillery Strathmill, Keith, Banffshire
Alcohol content 50% abv
Style Single malt

Like the instruments in an orchestra, malts made for blending often have one or other particular characteristic in nose, taste, or body that makes them a valuable component in the mix. Frequently the blender will look for a light, fresh, clean note to provide some sparkle and to counter darker, heavier spirits. Unfortunately the basic copper pot still process used in much of Scotland tends to produce more dominant flavors, and over the years, a variety of techniques have been tried to counteract this, ranging from triple-distillation and tall slender stills to a device called a purifier, which is used at Strathmill and a handful of other distilleries.

This is basically a small additional condenser that feeds back into the still before the main condenser, and it may well be partly responsible for the extremely light and fresh taste of this 18-Year-Old from Douglas Laing. The business was owned by Gilbey's (of gin fame) for almost seventy years, so it is also possible that their experience in producing a lighter spirit has been an influence as well, although the purifiers were not added until 1968.

Almost all of Strathmill's output goes for blending in Diageo's portfolio, and a select proportion of casks have been used as key components in the prestigious Alfred Dunhill Old Master blends popular in the Far East. The little that finds its way out as single malt is therefore extremely rare and is a good introduction to a totally clean and fresh tasting Speyside that feels much younger than its eighteen years and would be perfect as a weekend breakfast whisky. **AN**

Tasting notes

Extremely pale for its eighteen years. Very light, citrusy, clean nose. Taste is oily, spicy at first, fading, then waves of spice return. Some bitter lemon and green grass, with slight aniseed on adding water. Finish is scented and long, with some oakiness.

Strathmill distillery in Keith, with its twin pagoda chimneys. ➡

Stronachie
12-Year-Old

Dewar Rattray | www.stronachie.com

Region and country of origin Speyside, Scotland
Distillery Benrinnes, Aberlour, Banffshire
Alcohol content 43% abv
Style Single malt

Stronachie takes its name from a Perthshire distillery that was established during the 1890s whisky boom period and closed around 1930. It is a single malt distilled for the Ayrshire-based independent bottler Dewar Rattray Ltd. in the Diageo-owned Speyside distillery of Benrinnes. The brand was launched in 2002 and was intended to replicate the peaty, earthy character of a malt whisky as it would have been a century ago.

During 2002, a very rare bottle of the original Stronachie whisky dating from 1904 was discovered in private ownership, and a small sample was analyzed in order to find the present-day single malt that most closely matched its character. Only four bottles of "real" Stronachie are thought to exist.

Until 2010, the identity of the single malt that was bottled as Stronachie remained undisclosed by Dewar Rattray, though knowledgeable malt aficionados had already guessed that is was Benrinnes. One of Diageo's lower-profile and more idiosyncratic malts, Benrinnes is usually categorized by blenders as "First Class." The principal expression of Stronachie is this 12-Year-Old, though an eighteen-year-old variant was added to the lineup in 2010. **GS**

Tasting notes

The complex nose is fragrant and inviting, with toasted malt, stewed fruits, cream soda, honey, and a smoky, coal tar note. Caramel, oloroso sherry, poached pears.

Talisker
10-Year-Old

Diageo | www.malts.com

Region and country of origin Islands, Scotland
Distillery Talisker, Carbost, Isle of Skye
Alcohol content 45.8% abv
Style Single malt

Talisker is the only distillery on the Hebridean Isle of Skye, and its single malt has a unique style all its own. In 1988, the 10-Year-Old "entry-level" expression was selected by then owner United Distillers to be included in its new Classic Malts lineup. This replaced a previous eight-year-old "house" bottling undertaken by the predecessors of United Distillers, namely the Distillers Company Ltd.

The Classic Malts were chosen to provide a representative selection from Scotland's whisky-producing regions, and Talisker was to showcase the "Islands" category of single malts. In recent years, the Classic Malts portfolio has been extended to include a total of thirteen whiskies, but when launched, it embraced just six brands.

Talisker's traditional distilling regime features three wash and five spirit stills, rather than the balanced distillation regime of stills arranged in pairs. The bottling strength of 45.8 percent abv is unusual. Diageo's Scotch knowledge and heritage director, Dr. Nicholas Morgan, says, "our flavor experts believe that this strength is best to give Talisker its unique character. Traditionally, it was always bottled at a higher strength than other malts." **GS**

Tasting notes

Quite dense and smoky on the bold nose, with smoked fish, licorice, bladderwrack, sweet fruit and peat. Full-bodied and peaty in the mouth, with a hint of honey.

Talisker 18-Year-Old

Diageo | www.malts.com

Region and country of origin Islands, Scotland
Distillery Talisker, Carbost, Isle of Skye
Alcohol content 45.8% abv
Style Single malt

Talisker 18-Year-Old was introduced in 2004 as an older alternative to the existing 10-Year-Old.

In terms of cask selection, the 18-Year-Old follows very much in the pattern of its younger sibling, comprising principally ex-bourbon-cask-matured spirit, along with a small quantity of whisky aged in European oak ex-sherry casks. The expression is held in high regard by many aficionados, and in 2007 was pronounced Best Single Malt in the World at the World Whiskies Awards. However, there is nothing especially new about widespread appreciation of Talisker; it was highly regarded even when single-malt whisky was much more of a rarity outside the Highlands. For example, writing of whisky in his 1880 poem "The Scotsman's Return from Abroad," the novelist Robert Louis Stevenson wrote, "The king o' drinks, as I conceive it, Talisker, Isla, or Glenlivet!"

Today, Talisker is Diageo's second-best-selling single malt after Cardhu, and enjoys notably strong sales in the UK, French, and northern European markets, with many fans making the pilgrimage to the Isle of Skye and the Talisker distillery. Indeed, the visitors' center at Talisker was Diageo's busiest in 2011, with 50,550 people passing through its doors. **GS**

Tasting notes

Powerful yet mellow and sweet on the nose. The palate opens with fruity notes and hints of a smoldering peat fire. The finish is rich, with a classic Talisker peppery kick.

Talisker 25-Year-Old Cask Strength 2009

Diageo | www.malts.com

Region and country of origin Islands, Scotland
Distillery Talisker, Carbost, Isle of Skye
Alcohol content 54.8% abv
Style Single malt

Every fall, Diageo announces the latest bottlings in its annual program of eagerly awaited cask-strength Special Releases. These tend to be either unusual variants of core-range whiskies, using cask types not normally associated with specific single malts; whiskies from "lost" distilleries; or old, rare expressions of popular brands. The Special Releases range has its origins in Talisker's former Rare Malts series, initiated back in 1995, and older Taliskers have long been a firm Special Releases favorite. In 2001 just a hundred bottles of a twenty-eight-year-old, distilled in 1973, were issued, and the following year saw the appearance of a twenty-year-old from 1981. More recently, twenty-five- and thirty-year-olds have been the "norm."

This 2009 edition 25-Year-Old was the seventh Talisker to be bottled at this age. It contains whiskies matured in a mixture of European oak casks and refill American oak casks. It is the thirteenth limited release by the distillery. Diageo suggests that it is "interesting to compare with previous bottlings of this age in the same series, all of them intensely smoky, smooth, and sweet, yet still with a salty depth and a trace of Talisker's chile pepper 'catch.' [This is] Talisker, trebled. Enigmatic and charming, yet still vigorous." **GS**

Tasting notes

Soft, heathery notes on the nose, with damp tweed, sweet smoke, orange juice, and toffee. Intense, lots of black pepper, and a hint of brine. Very long in the finish.

Talisker 30-Year-Old 2009

Diageo | www.malts.com

Region and country of origin Islands, Scotland
Distillery Talisker, Carbost, Isle of Skye
Alcohol content 53.1% abv
Style Single malt

As with the Special Releases 25-Year-Old of 2009, this Talisker 30-Year-Old, the fourth such "edition" from Diageo, has been matured in refill American oak casks and European oak casks. Fewer than 3,000 bottles were marketed globally. According to Diageo, "This is the fourteenth and equal oldest limited release to be offered by the distillery. Interesting to compare with three previous bottlings of this age in the same series, all of them whiskies of great dignity, subtle nuance, and easy balance. A mild-mannered, more mature Talisker, still with plenty of personality and unmistakable character. Can Talisker be subtle? This one is an elegant, scented malt, simple in structure with all its elements easily accessible."

The whisky in this bottling dates from the 1970s. A significant change to the Talisker production regime occurred in 1972, when on-site malting ceased. Malt was subsequently produced to the Talisker specification of 18 to 20 parts per million at the Glen Ord Maltings, next to Glen Ord distillery in Ross-shire.

In the same year that the Talisker maltings closed, the stills were converted from direct firing to steam heating. The change was prompted by memories of a very serious fire in November 1960 that had caused the entire Talisker stillhouse to burn to the ground. In an event also experienced by several other distilleries, a valve on the coal-fired no. 1 spirit still was left open during distillation; spirit had escaped from the still and immediately caught fire. The entire stillhouse had been subsequently rebuilt and equipped with coal-fired stills that were exact copies of the originals. **GS**

Tasting notes

Almond, vanilla fudge, and gentle smoke on the nose. The palate is smooth and fruity, with hints of vanilla. Less blunt than the 25-Year-Old, yet retaining all of Talisker's fire in the belly, with no shortage of pepper. Big, confident, citrus and chile notes linger in the finish.

Talisker 57° North

Diageo | www.malts.com

Region and country of origin Islands, Scotland
Distillery Talisker, Carbost, Isle of Skye
Alcohol content 57% abv
Style Single malt

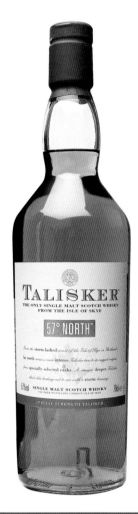

Talisker 57° North single malt was introduced in 2008. It carries no age statement, and its name refers in part to its abv, which is not the usual Talisker strength of 45.8 percent. The bottling was named in recognition of the fact that Talisker distillery on the Isle of Skye boasts a notably high latitude (the distillery's coordinates may be found on every box). Initially, Talisker 57° North was only available in travel retail outlets, although subsequently it found its way into mainstream markets.

57° North, the only regularly available "full-strength" version of the Hebridean island malt, is matured exclusively in American oak refill casks. Marketing director Nick Morgan notes, "It is almost at cask strength, and while most brands have an aged cask-strength bottling in their portfolio, Talisker 57° doesn't have an age statement. This gives us greater flexibility with it, and it's about maintaining an agreed flavor profile for the expression. Being virtually at cask strength reflects the provenance of the whisky . . . I think that it is the ultimate expression of 'Taliskerness,' with its intensity and pepper kick finale. It's a classic, intense Talisker. It's been compared to looking out to sea with a storm brewing!"

Talisker distillery has its own maritime outlook, courtesy of its location on the shores of Loch Harport in the remote northwest of Skye. The somewhat utilitarian external appearance of the distillery, which mostly dates from the early 1960s, is emphasized by the natural magnificence of its lochside setting in the shadow of the Cuillin Hills. **GS**

Tasting notes

On the nose, a blend of rich, spicy fruit and smoke from a bonfire beside the sea. The fruit fades, and spent matches appear. Full-bodied, with initially intense fruitiness followed by smoky spice and pepper notes. Long, smoky finish, with the Talisker chile flavor.

Talisker Distillers Edition 1999

Diageo | www.malts.com

Region and country of origin Islands, Scotland
Distillery Talisker, Carbost, Isle of Skye
Alcohol content 45.8% abv
Style Single malt

While some distillers have eagerly embraced the practice of cask-finishing their single malts, releasing many expressions that have undergone varying periods of secondary maturation in a wide range of cask types, Diageo has been notably restrained in its employment of the technique.

Diageo's finishing activities have centered on the Distillers Edition lineup, which began with six releases in 1997 and has subsequently been expanded to include other whiskies in the Classic Malts portfolio. Talisker was one of the initial bottlings in the Distillers Edition range. After undergoing traditional maturation in ex-bourbon barrels, the whisky was transferred to casks that had previously held amoroso sherry for an unspecified period of additional maturation. Marketing director Nick Morgan says, "Amoroso is a sweet sherry which works well with robust and maritime spirit character. The sherry matching was worked out very carefully by our flavor experts. The key was to find a cask wood finish that would complement the malt rather than overwhelm it."

In common with the rest of the Distillers Edition bottlings, Talisker Distillers Edition 1999 carries the year of distillation on each bottle, plus a unique batch number and a "bottled in" year. No age statement is presented, but the whisky is usually a minimum of twelve years old. Morgan says, "We produce around 6,000 cases per year, or less than 10 percent of the total of Talisker, which we bottle annually. The range of Distillers Editions tend to sell best in the United Kingdom and in France." **GS**

Tasting notes

Sweet-cured kipper on the nose, with orange marmalade and wood ash. Mouth-coating on the palate, with sweet, sherried peat and roasted malt notes. Long and spicy in the earthy finish, with peat, cocoa powder, stewed fruits, and a sting of ginger.

Talisker The Managers' Choice

Diageo | www.malts.com

Region and country of origin Islands, Scotland
Distillery Talisker, Carbost, Isle of Skye
Alcohol content 58.6% abv
Style Single malt

In 2009 Diageo embarked on an innovative program to offer a single-cask bottling from each of its (then) twenty-seven malt-whisky distilleries. The name of the series was born out of the fact that distillery managers were heavily involved in the final cask choices.

Talisker Managers' Choice was part of Diageo's second batch of releases, launched in January 2010. Marketing director Nick Morgan says, "The aim was to find something out of the ordinary compared to the normal bottled brand. The most obvious way to do that was by cask selection."

Diageo malt whisky specialist Craig Wallace was at the heart of the Managers' Choice initiative. He says, "I was looking for flavors that were in some way unique, and a flavor profile that was different from the normal single-bottling release from that distillery. I was looking for the distillery character and an additional 'wow factor,' but also the influence of the wood to give us something distinctive."

A bodega sherry European oak cask fill from 1997 was finally chosen as the Talisker representative, and the cask yielded just 582 bottles. Although both this bottling and the Distillers Edition have a sherry-wood input, there are significant differences between the two. "There is a more intense richness to the liquid in the Managers' Choice," explains Morgan. "It is more restrained and woodier. The whisky has been in the European oak cask from day one, which means that there have been subtractive as well as additive reactions, which is obviously not the case with the 'finished' Distillers Edition." **GS**

Tasting notes

A nose of warm, worn leather and exotic spices, plus a hint of peat. Early citrus fruits on the palate give way to sweeter apple; then characteristic Talisker peat and black pepper come through. The lengthy finish exhibits lots of peat ember and insistent spices.

Tamdhu 14-Year-Old

Ian Macleod Distillers
www.ianmacleod.com

Region and country of origin Speyside, Scotland
Distillery Tamdhu, Aberlour, Banffshire
Alcohol content 50% abv
Style Single malt

Tamdhu distillery, which opened in July 1897, was built on its present site for a reason that was common in Scotland—the site had been occupied by an illicit still that had been working well for centuries. The site was also close to the recently completed Great North of Scotland Railway, which had been extended from Aberdeen. This gave the whisky makers not only easy access to raw materials but also the most up-to-date means of distributing their finished product. By the time the distillery opened, Tamdhu even had its own railway station, which was named Dalbeallie.

Most of the products of Tamdhu distillery were used in the production of blended whiskies—among the leading blends of which it is a component are the Famous Grouse, J&B, Dunhill, and Cutty Sark. That makes this 14-Year-Old single malt an exception to the rule. It was distilled in 1990, finished in casks that had previously held Médoc red wine from Bordeaux in France, and bottled in 2004.

In 2010, Tamdhu distillery was closed by its owner, the Edrington Group. It was then sold in 2011 to independent bottler Ian MacLeod Distillers, who prioritize the continued production of single malts such as this. One of the distillery's attractions is its Saladin box, a machine used for many decades to malt the distillery's barley. **GL**

Tasting notes

Strawberry jelly and cream. The palate is lightly smoky with a suggestion of peat, but retains the fruitiness of the nose. The medium-length finish is sweet and oaky.

Tamdhu 25-Year-Old

Ian Macleod Distillers
www.ianmacleod.com

Region and country of origin Speyside, Scotland
Distillery Tamdhu, Aberlour, Banffshire
Alcohol content 43% abv
Style Single malt

There is something strange about drinking a 25-Year-Old from a distillery that was mothballed. In April 2010, the Tamdhu distillery belonging to the Highland Distillers subsidiary of the Edrington Group was closed, only to be purchased by Ian Macleod Distillers. Its Speyside malt had been used in some big-name blends, such as the Famous Grouse, J&B, Dunhill, and Cutty Sark. But for a while, only sad-looking buildings remained to greet the visitor.

However, behind the walls a tremendous production secret was hidden. Tamdhu was the last Scottish distillery to have an operational Saladin box. The Saladin is a huge trough with a perforated floor. The malting barley is poured in to a depth of about 3 feet (1 m), and heated air is blown through the perforations to control the temperature. A bank of mechanical turners, like giant Archimedean screws, turn the germinating grain, traveling slowly along the box as they do so. The screws ensure that the grain at the bottom is moved steadily to the top.

The Saladin box was a nineteenth-century French invention, named after its inventor, Charles Saladin, and it revolutionized the process of malting barley. It allowed more malt to be made than by the traditional floor method. In fact, the distillery malted barley for several distilleries in addition to its own quota. **AA**

Tasting notes

The nose is sweet with fresh fruits, melon, apple, pear, and a hint of honey. The mouthfeel is big and coating with just a hint of smoke behind the fruit notes.

The sign of the distillery-owned railway station.

Té Bheag

Pràban na Linne | www.gaelicwhisky.com

Region and country of origin Islands, Scotland
Distilleries Various
Alcohol content 40% abv
Style Blend

Té Bheag (pronounced "chay vek") comes from a very different Isle of Skye from the one most whisky drinkers are used to. Although Sleat, where it is produced, is on the same latitude as central Russia, there are no harsh unforgiving winters here. Whereas Talisker represents Skye at its most rugged and volcanic, Té Bheag stands for the part of the island that is by turns craggy, lush, soft, and rolling, caressed as it is by the Gulf Stream, earning it the title the "garden of Skye."

Té Bheag is Gaelic for "the little lady." This term is also used locally as a colloquialism for a "wee dram." It is positioned as a connoisseur's blend and has an accordingly high malt content of 40 percent. The company that produces it—Pràban na Linne—uses a combination of Island, Islay, Highland, and Speyside malts aged between eight and eleven years old. Some of these constituent whiskies are sherry matured, lending the blend a sweetness that results in a soft and rounded experience with an inner heart of fire.

Pràban na Linne is currently putting together plans for its own single malt, called Torabhaig, which will provide further employment for the islanders and double the reason for single malt drinkers to visit the Isle of Skye. We wait with bated breath. **PB**

Tasting notes

Sweet oat biscuit and a drizzle of lemon juice on the nose. Cucumber and mellow on the palate, then a slow burn and sudden explosion of pepper.

Teacher's Highland Cream

Beam Global | www.teacherswhisky.com

Region and country of origin Scotland
Distilleries Ardmore, Highlands, and others
Alcohol content 40% abv
Style Blend

Many people are under the mistaken impression that blended whiskies are by definition inferior to single-malt whiskies. However, those artisan whisky blenders who put together top grain and malt whiskies that have been aged for several years in top-quality wood can create blended whiskies that are living art and a match for even the finest malts.

Drinkers don't have to pay a lot for great blends, either. Whiskies such as this one are made by companies set up more than 180 years ago—and Teacher's has been making blended whisky ever since the category was legalized in 1865. Blenders don't stay in business for that length of time unless a lot of what they are doing is right.

That said, Teacher's isn't the easiest example of a blended whisky. The whole point of adding grain to a mix of malts is to make the whisky rounded and easier to drink. But Teacher's has a higher than normal malt content, and it is built around Ardmore, a Highland whisky that can take the form of a medium-peated malt. That makes this a gutsy, full-flavored blend that some find too much. After a few years in the wilderness, this whisky has been given a new lease on life under the Beam umbrella. It deserves it. **DR**

Tasting notes

A full and rich blend with a lot of flavor. Highland Cream offers big, rich fruitiness, a malty heart, and some satisfyingly earthy and rustic peat notes.

A seasonal 1904 advertisement for Teacher's whisky. ➡

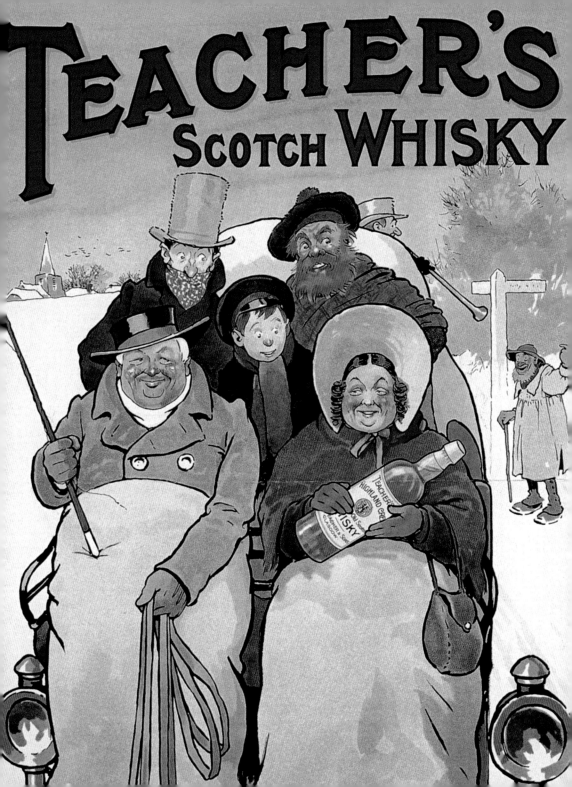

Teacher's Origin

Beam Global | www.teacherswhisky.com

Region and country of origin Scotland
Distilleries Ardmore, Highlands, and others
Alcohol content 40% abv
Style Blend

One of the main characteristics of blended whisky is its perceived consistency. Blended whisky is not meant to vary from place to place and from time to time. But, of course, in actual fact it does. It is just that nobody really wants to talk about it. As a result, there isn't much of a story behind blends, and they tend to get dismissed as boring or ignored as inferior when placed alongside sexy drinks such as single malts.

Innovation is almost unheard of, but that is what we have here. The Scotch whisky team at Beam Global had already successfully experimented with small casks with its Laphroaig and Ardmore single malts, and here it is applying some of the principles learned from that time.

There are two main aspects that make this whisky different. First, the normal way to make a blend is to take a number of matured single malts and blend them with grain whisky, letting them combine in marrying tanks before being bottled. Here, the whiskies are mixed and then returned to the cask for a further period of maturation. Not only that, but the cask is a quarter-sized one, not full-sized as is usual with whisky for blends. The second aspect is the nature of Teacher's itself. This is a gutsy, gritty, big-flavored blended whisky with a high proportion of malt in it, much of which is Ardmore. The constituent malts make for an intriguing hybrid—a Highland-style, malty whisky dressed up in the rounded and balanced finery of blended whisky. You don't see this offering around very often, and it's hard to know how it's faring, but it's definitely in a category of one. **DR**

Tasting notes

Almost a delicatessen of a whisky, with notes of olive and smoked fish joining the wispy smoke and rugged, earthy, peat base. There is plenty of butterscotch sweetness to offset the savory flavors, but this is a big, bold, and outspoken blend, all the same.

Tobermory 10-Year-Old

Burn Stewart Distillers | www.tobermory.com

Region and country of origin Islands, Scotland
Distillery Tobermory, Tobermory, Isle of Mull
Alcohol content 46.3% abv
Style Single malt

The name Tobermory is derived from the Gaelic *Tobar Mhoire*, meaning "Mary's well." In ancient times, a well dedicated to the Virgin Mary was located close to the settlement of Tobermory, which is the "capital" of the Inner Hebridean island of Mull and also gives its name to the local distillery.

Tobermory 10-Year-Old makes up the bulk of the distillery's single-malt sales, along with its peated counterpart, Ledaig. In 2010, owner Burn Stewart Distillers took the radical step of increasing the strength of its entire single-malt range to a standard 46.3 percent abv. The process of chill-filtration could then be abandoned, as it is only required to prevent cloudiness when whisky is below 46 percent abv. These changes came at the behest of master distiller Ian Macmillan, who argues that when chill-filtered, the single malts he creates become "dumbed down and lose their liveliness."

With particular regard to the Tobermory 10-Year-Old, Macmillan notes that "the change to non-chill-filtration has been quite remarkable. The aroma is richer, silkier, and livelier, while the flavor is also richer, smoother, and more buttery. Everything is enhanced. I know from comparing samples of the same whisky before and after chill-filtration just how much of a difference there really is."

The market response to the new lineup, which also includes enhanced packaging, has been overwhelmingly positive, and may well encourage other distillers to muse on the benefits of abandoning chill-filtration of their whiskies. **GS**

Tasting notes

Fresh and nutty on the nose, with citrus fruit and brittle toffee and more than a whiff of peat. Medium-bodied, nicely textured, and quite dry on the palate, with delicate peat, malt, and nuts. The finish is medium to long, with a hint of mint and a slight citrusy tang.

Tobermory 15-Year-Old

Burn Stewart Distillers | www.tobermory.com

Region and country of origin Islands, Scotland
Distillery Tobermory, Tobermory, Isle of Mull
Alcohol content 46.3% abv
Style Single malt

Tobermory 15-Year-Old was introduced in 2008 as a limited release. The whisky is accompanied by a limited-edition print of Tobermory Bay, reputedly the location on the east coast of Mull where a badly damaged galleon sank in 1588, following the defeat of the Spanish Armada. Legend has it that the vessel was carrying 30 million "pieces of eight," and treasure hunters have long sought its location.

Tobermory distillery has endured a checkered past, with several lengthy intervals of silence interspersed between its productive periods. Back in 1982, the maturation warehouse was sold off and converted into apartments. Accordingly, present owner Burn Stewart Distillers has to transport the new-make spirit either to their warehouses on the mainland at Deanston distillery or to Bunnahabhain on Islay. However, in 2007, part of a former tun room at Tobermory was converted into a small warehousing facility for the distillery.

It is in this "new" warehouse that Tobermory 15-Year-Old spends the final year or more of its maturation period, having initially been matured in former bourbon barrels before being reracked into Gonzalez Byass oloroso sherry casks and sent back to Mull, the isle of its birth. "Bringing it home lets it breathe in some sea air," declares Ian Macmillan.

Under the care of Macmillan, there has been a vast improvement in the quality of Tobermory spirit. As the distillery was acquired by Burn Stewart in 1993, all the spirit going into the 15-Year-Old bottling was distilled and matured on his watch. **GS**

Tasting notes

The rich nose offers fruit pudding, with sherry, spicy milk chocolate, and a whiff of peat smoke. Full-bodied in the mouth, with well-mannered sherry, Christmas cake, toffee, and a sprinkling of pepper. The finish is long and luxurious, with chocolate-coated raisins.

Tomatin 12-Year-Old

Tomatin (Marubeni Group) | www.tomatin.com

Region and country of origin Speyside, Scotland
Distillery Tomatin, Tomatin, Inverness-shire
Alcohol content 43% abv
Style Single malt

By 1986, when the Tomatin distillery was acquired by Takara, Shuzo and Okura, the number of its stills had been reduced from twenty-three to twelve. At the time of the Japanese takeover, the future looked bleak, and the outlook was no better for a while thereafter, but before long, the new owners managed to increase annual production to over a million gallons (3.8 million liters) of whisky a year. (This output, though less than the notional 2.6 million gallons (9.8 million liters) of which Tomatin had theoretically been capable at the time of its greatest expansion, was in fact more than it had ever produced in its history.) That level was maintained into the twenty-first century, in spite of all the uncertainties and crises in the world economy, an achievement that is greatly to the credit of both Marubeni—one of Japan's largest trading companies, which took over Tomatin from Takara in 2000—and Kokubu, a logistics firm that handled distribution after 2006.

Most of the posttakeover output was blends, but single malts were maintained, and in 2004 the Tomatin 12-Year-Old succeeded the 10-Year-Old as a component of the core range. The 12-Year-Old is matured in Spanish sherry butts before bottling. It has a distinctive golden honey color that has been likened by one online commentator to "gasoline . . . in a good way." It is sometimes described as a budget Highland Park (a premium single malt from Kirkwall, Orkney). Royal Mile Whiskies (a retailer with branches in Edinburgh and London) recommends the 12-Year-Old as a good place to start exploring single malts. **GL**

Tasting notes

The aroma is of malt, rose petal, and honeysuckle, with a hint of peat. On the palate, apple and pear, with a hint of nuttiness—the last is produced by the sherry wood. The whisky is medium-bodied, with a slightly watery beginning that is compensated by a satisfying finish.

Tomatin 18-Year-Old

Tomatin (Marubeni Group) | www.tomatin.com

Region and country of origin Speyside, Scotland
Distillery Tomatin, Tomatin, Inverness-shire
Alcohol content 43% abv
Style Single malt

Attempts to summarize the whiskies of any distillery in a single sentence can be dangerously simplistic and unjust. In particular, single malts require a lifetime's study rather than glib summary judgment. But even with that caveat in mind, it is less than normally controversial to characterize Tomatin products as medium-bodied with a faint but discernible smokiness and possessing a family nose that is aromatic with vegetal notes as a prelude to a taste that is sweet with cereals, nuts, and caramelized fruit.

Insofar as it is possible to generalize, the vintage that most strikingly conforms to that broad definition is this classy, pale gold single malt. In the opinion of many, it is Tomatin's tour de force. Introduced to the distillery's range in 2006, it has since become a firm favorite with connoisseurs. It is aged for a minimum of eighteen years and married for part of that time in Spanish oloroso sherry casks. Tomatin is one of only a few distilleries in Scotland to retain its own full-time cooper: this gives the distillery close quality control and its products an inimitable signature.

The resulting non-chill-filtered whisky is robust and packed with flavor, and has found itself a global network of loyal aficionados. *Jim Murray's Whisky Bible* is unstinting in its praise: "What a well-mannered malt. As though it grew up in a loving, caring family and behaves itself impeccably from first nose to last whimpering finale." If the 12-Year-Old is the best starting point for a study of Tomatin single malts, this 18-Year-Old stands as an advanced staging post on the way to connoisseurship. **GL**

Tasting notes

The nose is an opening chord of sherry followed by notes of apple, cinnamon, vanilla, and maple syrup, all overlaid with smoky heather. The dram tastes of honey at first, but is saved from sweetness by an oaky edge before it bites the mouth like bitter orange chocolate.

Tomatin 25-Year-Old

Tomatin (Marubeni Group) | www.tomatin.com

Region and country of origin Speyside, Scotland
Distillery Tomatin, Tomatin, Inverness-shire
Alcohol content 43% abv
Style Single malt

The first maltings of this whisky began in the late 1970s, when Tomatin was at a parlously low ebb. Throughout the decade, the distillery had expanded too much and too quickly, more than doubling the number of its stills and even building a costly dark-grains plant to process draff (the leftovers from the grain after fermentation; used as cattle feed) and pot ale (the liquor remaining in the wash still, which is made into concentrated organic fertilizer). While the distillery entered what looked like terminal decline, the adjacent village of the same name depopulated as residents moved in search of work elsewhere: at the 2001 Census, the settlement had only 183 inhabitants.

However, recovery was under way, and by the time this vintage was first bottled, the view across the Highlands was rosier than it had been for a generation. This limited expression was matured for a full quarter of a century in refill American oak bourbon casks. It first went on sale in 2005 and soon became a big hit, not only with consumers but also with critics, winning a silver medal at the 2006 International Spirits Challenge. The award of a gold medal in the same year to Tomatin's Antiquary 21-Year Old represented a double triumph for the distillery.

Among the 25-Year-Old's other laurels was a score of 93 out of 100 at the International Review of Spirits in 2006. Such accolades enabled this charming and often rather self-effacing Highland distillery to show the world that, while it was maintaining its traditional preeminence in blended whiskies, it was now easily capable of producing first-class malts as well. **GL**

Tasting notes

The nose is a malty combination of pear, black currant, gooseberry, and orange over cedar pine resins. On the palate, the initial honey sensation quickly morphs into nuttiness. Overwhelmingly dry but with a vestigial sweetness that leaves a salty aftertaste.

Tomatin 30-Year-Old

Tomatin (Marubeni Group) | www.tomatin.com

Region and country of origin Speyside, Scotland
Distillery Tomatin, Tomatin, Inverness-shire
Alcohol content 49.3% abv
Style Single malt

Tomatin 30-Year-Old single malt is a limited edition of 1,500 bottles. It was distilled on November 22, 1976, matured in oak hogsheads, and finished for three years in a pair of ex-Spanish oloroso sherry casks selected by master distiller Douglas Campbell, subsequently Tomatin's global brand ambassador. The result was bottled on October 22, 2007, and marketed at the start of the following year.

In 1961, at the age of fifteen, Douglas Campbell followed in his parents' footsteps to the distillery, where his father was a cooper and his mother secretary to the managing director. He learned the whole business by working in various parts of the distillery: "Mashing for three or four years, distilling for a couple of years, working in the warehouses, getting casks ready for dispatch." He stirred the barley in the water twice a day (a task known as turning the malt), and heated the mixture to prevent germination.

Tomatin stopped doing its own malting on-site in 1969. Some commentators regard this as a loss, but Campbell disagrees. "The distilleries that still malt themselves will tell you it makes a difference to the taste, but I don't think it really has a big impact. The water, the stills, and the casks are far more important: 70 to 80 percent of the flavor comes from the casks. That's why we still have our own cooperage." **GL**

Tasting notes

Rich, full-bodied, sherried, with a deep golden color and an aroma of leather, orange, and clove on a briny background. The taste is a creamy, orange spice.

Tomatin 40-Year-Old

Tomatin (Marubeni Group) | www.tomatin.com

Region and country of origin Speyside, Scotland
Distillery Tomatin, Tomatin, Inverness-shire
Alcohol content 42.9% abv
Style Single malt

This premium single malt is a vatting of seven oak hogsheads chosen by Tomatin's master distiller for their outstanding quality. It was distilled on May 17, 1967, and bottled on October 2, 2007. The Tomatin 40-Year-Old is a limited edition of 1,614 bottles.

The whisky is non-chill-filtered; the question of whether a whisky should be is much debated by whisky lovers. The process involves reducing the temperature of the whisky to around 32°F (0°C) so that the fatty acids and some of the proteins and esters in the grain clog together, making them easier to remove by filtration through a metal gauze. Also extracted by this method are larger particles such as coal fragments.

Opinion is divided about whether chill-filtering is worth the effort. The main reason for doing it is cosmetic: non-chill-filtered whiskies tend to develop sediment when stored in a cool place, while those subjected to the treatment retain their original golden hue almost indefinitely. Non-chill-filtered whiskies—especially those with an abv of less than 46 percent—are wont to turn cloudy when served with water or ice, an effect that misleads the uneducated into thinking the dram is "off," when there is, in fact, nothing wrong. Whether or not chill-filtering affects the taste is debatable. Decide for yourself. **GL**

Tasting notes

An aroma of beeswax and stewed fruits, including a typically Tomatin orange. The taste is complex, smooth, and creamy, with a licorice influence. The finish is long.

Tomatin 1997

Tomatin (Marubeni Group) | www.tomatin.com

Region and country of origin Speyside, Scotland
Distillery Tomatin, Tomatin, Inverness-shire
Alcohol content 57.1% abv
Style Single malt

This natural cask-strength malt was distilled in September 1997 and left to mature in a first-fill bourbon barrel before being bottled in October 2009. Production was restricted to 244 bottles, most of which were sold in western Europe and also in Japan, where Tomatin is particularly highly regarded.

Tomatin had a rather precarious and sometimes slightly shady past. The earliest whisky producer on the site was an illicit still in the fifteenth century. Cattle drovers and other travelers would stop there to replenish their canisters. The first modern limited company, the Tomatin Spey District Distillery, was established in 1897. It went bust in 1906 but was reopened three years later as New Tomatin Distillers.

The end of World War II heralded expansion: in 1956 the distillery doubled the number of its stills to four; a fifth was added in 1961. In 1974, another eighteen stills were opened, making Tomatin the largest malt whisky distillery in Scotland. But Tomatin never achieved its 2.6-million-gallon (9.8-million-liter) capacity, and eleven stills were later dismantled.

Traditionally, Tomatin did few limited editions. Most of the output still goes into the Tomatin Antiquary blend, but the present owners now want to demonstrate that the spirit is potentially versatile and works in a range of cask types. **GL**

Tasting notes

The nose is vanilla; the palate, nuts and pepper, with a touch of mint. The whisky crumbles on the tongue, with hints of gooseberry and peach, malt and smoke.

Tomatin 1991

Tomatin (Marubeni Group) | www.tomatin.com

Region and country of origin Speyside, Scotland
Distillery Tomatin, Tomatin, Inverness-shire
Alcohol content 55.9% abv
Style Single malt

Tomatin 1991 is a Highland single malt that derives its distinctive character from a variety of sources. Its topographical origins are distinctive and unusual: at 1,028 feet (313 meters) above sea level, Tomatin—from the Gaelic meaning "juniper hillock"—is one of the highest malt distilleries in Scotland.

The water used in the distillation process is drawn from the Alt-na-Frith (Gaelic for "free burn"). This pure, clear stream helps to create a malt with a rich and mellow style that provides a memorable range of delicate flavors. Alt-na-Frith runs through the Monadhliath (gray) Mountains, which extend more or less parallel to Loch Ness.

Also contributory to the quality of this single malt is the distillery's use of a stainless-steel Lauter mash tun. In 1974, Tomatin was the first Scottish whisky distillery to introduce this German device, which has rotating arms with knives that lift the malt beds to allow the worts to drain, rather than agitating the whole bed vertically and horizontally in the manner of traditional infusion vessels, with their rake-and-plough (rack-and-pinion) stirring gear. The Lauter makes for clearer worts than are possible using traditional methods. Tomatin 1991 is finished for about a year in Spanish ex-sherry casks, and the resulting dram has a large and loyal following. **GL**

Tasting notes

A dense, earthy nose evoking honey and flowers with sweet spices. On the palate, apricot seasoned in wood spices, with suspicions of pear and elderflower.

Tomatin Decades

Tomatin (Marubeni Group) | www.tomatin.com

Region and country of origin Speyside, Scotland
Distillery Tomatin, Tomatin, Inverness-shire
Alcohol content 46% abv
Style Single malt

This unique single malt was created to commemorate master distiller Douglas Campbell's fifty years at Tomatin. He started work there in 1961 and became master distiller in 2008. The malt is a blend of five whiskies, one from each of his decades in work.

From the 1960s are refill sherry hogsheads from 1967, some of the oldest Tomatin in existence. Campbell describes this component as "a sherry-influenced whisky with subtle flavors of beeswax, stewed apples, and orange peel." To represent the 1970s, Campbell chose oloroso sherry butts, distilled in 1976. They have flavors of passion fruit, blackberry, and honeydew melon to moderate the robust flavors of the younger whiskies. The 1980s component is taken from refill sherry hogsheads distilled in 1984; this is the ingredient that gives Decades much of its substantial body and depth.

The 1990s contribution comes from first-fill bourbon barrels distilled at the very start of the decade. According to Campbell, "Vanilla, raisin, and toffee are the dominant flavors here. This whisky has a big personality and wants to be noticed." Finally, the 2000s provide some first-fill bourbon barrels distilled in 2005; these peaty liquids have a youthful zest that provides a counterpoint to all four older ingredients.

Decades is a unique combination of depth of flavor and youthful charm. Tomatin CEO Robert Anderson has described this whisky as "a fitting compliment on the life and participation of Douglas in the evolution of the Tomatin style." It has been issued as a limited edition of 9,000 bottles. **GL**

Tasting notes

An initial sweet maltiness is quickly succeeded by a fruity aroma overlaid with pine and oak, flowers and smoke. The taste is of tropical fruit, Christmas cake, aniseed, cinnamon, and fudge. A rich, malty sweetness returns with a nutty edge to provide a mellow finish.

Tomintoul 10-Year-Old

Angus Dundee Distillers | www.tomintouldistillery.co.uk

Region and country of origin Speyside, Scotland
Distillery Tominoul, Ballindalloch, Banffshire
Alcohol content 40% abv
Style Single malt

Tomintoul (the name is pronounced tom-an-tail and means "hill like a barn" in Gaelic) distillery was established in 1964, with the first spirit flowing from its stills in July of the following year. The story goes that winters in the area, close to the River Avon and in the Parish of Glenlivet, were known to be so bad that during the distillery's construction, the contractors ensured that they always had two weeks' worth of materials on-site in case they became snowed in. The nearby village of Tomintoul, at 1,132 feet (345 meters) above sea level, has been identified as the highest in the Scottish Highlands.

Tomintoul's produce has been marketed as a single malt since 1973, and during the 1970s an expression bearing no age statement appeared, along with an eight-year-old. Both whiskies were offered in highly distinctive perfume-style bottles that have since become sought-after collectors' items.

A more conventionally presented ten-year-old variant followed, and this was subsequently repackaged after the family-controlled firm of Angus Dundee Distillers took over ownership of the remote Speyside distillery from JBB (Greater Europe) in 2000. "We have tried to match the existing ten-year-old style as far as possible," notes master distiller Robert Fleming, a fourth-generation Glenlivet area distiller.

In general, Tomintoul is a lightly peated malt, and much of the distillery's output has traditionally been earmarked for blending. A growing number of single-malt expressions have been developed during recent years, including this satisfying 10-Year-Old. **GS**

Tasting notes

An easy-drinking, aperitif Speyside, with a light, floral, perfumed, and pleasantly malty nose. Light-bodied, grassy, and delicate, with vanilla fudge, apple, and lemon on the palate, plus a very subtle whiff of background smoke. Honey and malt on the finish.

Tomintoul 16-Year-Old

Angus Dundee Distillers
www.tomintouldistillery.co.uk

Region and country of origin Speyside, Scotland
Distillery Tomintoul, Ballindalloch, Banffshire
Alcohol content 40% abv
Style Single malt

After buying Tomintoul distillery, the London-based Angus Dundee Distillers first released this 16-Year-Old, adding it to the portfolio in 2003. Tomintoul single malt is marketed as "The Gentle Dram," and master distiller Robert Fleming has played a major part in the expansion of the range. "The 16-Year-Old is my favorite," he notes, "because it was the first release we did, and I put a lot of effort into the selection process. It was decided that, rather than put tasting notes on the bottle, the company would use my name and say I was a fourth-generation Speyside distiller.

"The 10-Year-Old is light and floral, and I wanted to make the 16-Year-Old different, not just older, so we went for something sweeter, with heather honey notes coming through. We nosed dozens of samples of varying ages and found that the sixteen-year-olds were best for those characteristics. We are filling those types of casks on an ongoing basis and keeping them for the 16-Year-Old."

As well as the release of the 16-Year-Old, 2003 saw the construction of a blend center at the distillery, where the Tomintoul make is blended with other single malts and grain whiskies prior to bottling or bulk export. **GS**

Tasting notes

The same light and floral nose as the 10-Year-Old, but with more brittle toffee notes, orange, nuts, and mint. The medium finish offers citrus fruits and gentle spice.

Tomintoul 21-Year-Old

Angus Dundee Distillers
www.tomintouldistillery.co.uk

Region and country of origin Speyside, Scotland
Distillery Tomintoul, Ballindalloch, Banffshire
Alcohol content 40% abv
Style Single malt

Tomintoul 21-Year-Old was introduced to the brand's lineup in 2011 to fill a gap in the portfolio between the existing 16-Year-Old and 33-Year-Old. Master distiller Robert Fleming notes, "The 21-Year-Old fitted into the space between the other variants really well, and the samples were very good, too. In terms of the cask profile of this expression, we wanted to make sure the sweetness was still there, but also add more spiciness and vanilla notes. The 21-Year-Old has more of a 'tang' to it, and more vanilla spice. To help achieve that, we use more bourbon barrels than refill casks in the recipe."

Fleming adds, "Tomintoul is always light, elegant, and easy drinking, and we don't use any sherry wood for maturation, apart from the Oloroso Sherry Cask Finish edition, because we are Kosher Accredited, so cask selection is very important to get points of differentiation."

Lovers of whisky trivia might like to know that in 2009, Tomintoul single malt achieved a place in the *Guinness Book of Records* for producing the world's largest bottle of whisky. Standing almost 5 feet (1.5 m) tall, it holds the equivalent of 150 standard bottles and is on permanent display in the Clockhouse Restaurant in Tomintoul's village square. **GS**

Tasting notes

Honeydew melon, pear, warm spices, and barley sugar on the nose, with a hint of new leather. Medium-bodied, with toffee and malt notes. Spicy to the end.

Tomintoul
33-Year-Old

Angus Dundee Distillers
www.tomintouldistillery.co.uk

Region and country of origin Speyside, Scotland
Distillery Tominoul, Ballindalloch, Banffshire
Alcohol content 40% abv
Style Single malt

Tomintoul 33-Year-Old was released in 2009 to replace an existing twenty-seven-year-old expression that had been created at the request of an American customer. "We had kept casks back for that," explains master distiller Robert Fleming, "and as they got older, we didn't want to put them into [it]. When we did lots of sampling, we found that dryness seemed to go away at thirty-three years of age, and the sweetness came back. There wasn't so much vanilla and spice there, because we used more refill casks and not so many first-fill ones as in the 21-Year-Old."

The release of Tomintoul 33-Year-Old came after a limited-edition bottling of the 1976 vintage, originally introduced to the duty-free market and then given a wider release. Says Fleming, "We knew from doing this bottling that the stock existed for a thirty-three-year-old, and we thought it was very good whisky."

An independent bottling of single-cask 1966 Tomintoul in the Mackillop's Choice range revealed a whisky that had interacted notably well with its cask. "It wasn't at all woody," says Fleming. "We've nosed lots of samples from around that period, and none are overly woody. Maybe it's because of the lightness of the new spirit and good wood policy." **GS**

Tasting notes

Spicy toffee, vanilla, and a hint of caramel and cinnamon. Quite long in the finish, which dries from fruity sweetness to spicy oak. A well-balanced dram.

Tomintoul
33-Year-Old Malt Cask

Douglas Laing & Co. | www.douglaslaing.com / www.tomintouldistillery.co.uk

Region and country of origin Speyside, Scotland
Distillery Tominoul, Ballindalloch, Banffshire
Alcohol content 43.6% abv
Style Single malt

Nothing divides the world of whisky lovers like the taste of peat. It polarizes opinion: some flinch at the slightest smoky whiff; others can't get enough of the most medicinal drams. A hundred years ago, most Highland malt was peated to some degree, and in the past few years, enterprising distilleries have launched "traditional" malts that show off the lighter smoky flavors. Peat is formed from native plants and varies across Scotland. Whenever local peat is used in whisky, the local variations come through.

Speyside has built its reputation on unpeated, easy-drinking whiskies, so it comes as a real surprise to find this lightly peated and subtly smoked one from Tomintoul. The distillery was built only in the 1960s, and most of its output is blended, but owner Angus Dundee has a good range of bottlings available, as well as a few independents. They launched a peated version—Old Ballantruan—in 2005, and run peated spirit off the stills for two weeks every year.

This expression, distilled in 1975 when Whyte & Mackay owned the business, had been maturing for thirty-three years. The peat smokiness is well blended with the more expected Speyside fresh malt to make a gentle introduction to a forgotten style. **AN**

Tasting notes

A clean, malty nose with a whiff of sweet smoke. A slight rubbery taste before the peat hits. Light and fresh in the body for its age. Long, spicy, and warming finish.

Tormore 1996 Connoisseurs Choice

Gordon & MacPhail | www.gordonandmacphail.com

Region and country of origin Speyside, Scotland
Distillery Tormore, Grantown-on-Spey, Morayshire
Alcohol content 43% abv
Style Single malt

Some Scottish distillery buildings, it must be said, are exceedingly bland affairs. Fair enough; many were designed to be purely functional, their only important characteristic being the amount of spirit they produce annually. Quite a few, though, have some memorable characteristics, perhaps a pagoda roof or two or a romantic situation on the coast overlooking some hidden bay. But if someone were to suggest an award for the prettiest distillery outright, the chances are it would go to Tormore. Its splendid architectural features include a belfry, fountain, curling lake, and a musical clock that plays one of four Scottish songs every fifteen minutes. How odd, then, that this most beautiful of distilleries doesn't play the tourist game. It has no visitors' center, and there are no tours for the public, although industry tours have been known.

Tormore was the first distillery to be opened in Speyside in the twentieth century, with production starting in 1960. Since then, it has experienced several changes of ownership. There has been a limited number of official bottlings of its single malts, but most production goes into blends, including Ballantine's, Teacher's, and Long John. If you are a fan of Long John, you might want to pass the distillery in 2060, because a time capsule shaped like a pot still will be unearthed from the forecourt; inside will be a hundred-year-old half-gallon (2.25-liter) bottle of it.

Alternatively, you can save yourself a half-century wait and buy this light and fruity 1996 Connoisseurs Choice expression, matured in refill sherry hogsheads and bottled in 2007. **PB**

Tasting notes

Barley, lemon, light honey, and spice on the nose, with icing sugar, toffee apple, and tarte au citron. On the palate, there is a further lemony hit, followed by demerara sugar and an assertive seam of oak and licorice. The finish strongly evokes pear in syrup.

The Tormore distillery building was designed by Sir Albert Richardson. ➜

Tullibardine 1993

Tullibardine | www.tullibardine.com

Region and country of origin Highlands, Scotland
Distillery Tullibardine, Blackford, Perthshire
Alcohol content 40% abv
Style Single malt

Tullibardine is a recently rejuvenated distillery that is situated in the beautiful surrounds of Blackford, Perthshire. The arterial A9 road that snakes past nearby ensures that the on-site visitors' center has a steady stream of patrons. And rightly so—this is a distillery that is steeped in heritage, and distillery manager John Black is happy to share the experience he has gained during fifty-plus years in whisky.

The 1993 Tullibardine is the core expression from the distillery, which describes its dram as "eminently quaffable." The whisky does indeed have a rather addictive quality, and perhaps its lightness and easy-drinking nature are due in part to the source of the distillery's water; this is a nearby spring that supplies not only the distillery but also a well-known mineral-water company.

That the local water quality results in such a delicate spirit appears to have been appreciated for some time, and by royalty, no less. The first attempts at alcohol production on this site date back to the fifteenth century. In 1488, King James IV, recently having been crowned, purchased beer from what was, at the time, Scotland's first public brewery.

So, is this a dram fit for a king? Well, it is not an unruly malt, by any stretch of the imagination—in fact quite the opposite. It is good enough to honor any visiting dignitaries, and, should you be tempted to hold court after a few nips, it should leave you able to carry out your royal duties untroubled the next morning. Just be careful not to spill any of this on your ermine. It would be a shame to waste it. **D&C**

Tasting notes

Less of a nose on this malt and more of a floral bouquet. Plenty of energetic vanillins and oakiness in among hints of lavender and heather. The palate is light and crisp—zesty, even—with the slightest dryness at the back of the mouth. The finish is over all too soon.

Tullibardine 1988

Tullibardine | www.tullibardine.com

Region and country of origin Highlands, Scotland
Distillery Tullibardine, Blackford, Perthshire
Alcohol content 46% abv
Style Single malt

What happened in 1988? Well, um, the Seoul Olympics, for one thing. But also, far from the madding crowd, this malt spirit was being quietly placed in casks at Tullibardine in Perthshire. Whether the owners at the time, Invergordon Distillers, knew that it would be retrieved some twenty years later and bottled in celebration of the 500th anniversary of King James IV's coronation is unknown.

Perhaps they did. Perhaps that was their intention all along, and those particular casks were already earmarked to be pressed into service in order to wet the whistle of many a royalist celebrant. It would be interesting to find out the original purpose for the spirit as it was rolled into the warehouse, barrel by barrel, but unless someone is planning a particularly specialist time-travel television show, we should probably resign ourselves to being unenlightened on this score for a while yet.

No one would accuse the marketing department at Tullibardine of willful disingenuousness, but the bottling of this expression, made from stock acquired from a previous distiller, came into being a full twenty years after the actual quincentennial date.

The malt itself is straightforward, anyway, being of the non-chill-filtered variety, meaning that all the fatty acids and proteins usually removed by the filtering process remain in place. There are advocates who argue vehemently that this should be the norm. That is because chill-filtering extracts not only those elements but also the esters that contribute to the light, fruity, floral element of a dram. **D&C**

Tasting notes

Well-rounded aromas of vanilla and cream are shot through with the tartness of lemon drops. Golden syrup makes way for more cream, and the wood shows up later, warm and dry simultaneously. The finish is succinct and compact, without being abrupt.

Tullibardine 1976 Single Cask Edition

Tullibardine | www.tullibardine.com

Region and country of origin Highlands, Scotland
Distillery Tullibardine, Blackford, Perthshire
Alcohol content 54.1% abv
Style Single malt

For readers with an insatiable appetite for detail, this is bottle number 148 of 189; oh, and it is from a hogshead cask—number 3155, to be exact. This dram has lain dormant in the Tullibardine warehouse in Blackford since 1976 and was bottled in September 2008. But what does this information mean? These types of expressions are a blink-and-you'll-miss-it occurrence. There might be a number on the label and packaging that you, personally, attach significance to, but other than it being a reference for you and your associates to ensure you all get a bottle of the same particular liquid heaven, there's not much else that you can do with it.

Of course, if you were an employee, you might be privy to the knowledge that this cask was racked over a convergence of ley lines (unconfirmed), on the day that Pluto was in the Fifth House of Pain (unlikely), and that you filled the barrel while standing on one leg, one pant leg rolled up, and singing "Black Betty" (bam-ba-lam)—but would that be significant?

No. But if you worked at the distillery, you would be aware that a cask of the highest quality had been chosen, that it was checked regularly, and that a careful record was taken of samples periodically tasted and measured. Only when it was judged to be right, by the application of years of knowledge and skill, would it be bottled. Make no mistake; what we have here is pure craft, not witchcraft. There would be no shortage of willing sorcerer's apprentices if there were something as simple as a spell at the heart of the creation of such a fine drink. **D&C**

Tasting notes

The nose is refined, with almond and vanilla vying for space between plum duff and crème caramel. Mouthfeel is slick and confident. The fruit defines itself as orange marmalade; caramel becomes toffee, then butterscotch. The finish is luxurious and unhurried.

Tullibardine 1964

Tullibardine | www.tullibardine.com

Region and country of origin Highlands, Scotland
Distillery Tullibardine, Blackford, Perthshire
Alcohol content 44.6% abv
Style Single malt

Anyone who begins to get involved in whiskies of this age, regardless of whether they are blended, single-malt, or grain, has to start regarding them less as expensive social lubricants and more as definitive cultural artifacts. When this particular whisky was put down to mature, the Beach Boys and the Beatles hadn't even begun their transatlantic auditory brawl, trying to outfreak each other with *Pet Sounds* and *Sgt. Pepper's Lonely Hearts Club Band* respectively.

This masterpiece was conceived with little fanfare, but proves to be no less epiphanic to those who ingest it. It is doubtful that there ever was a Brian Wilson or a Paul McCartney at work, determined to break through to the other side, in Blackford in 1964. Instead, one might imagine a steadfast and resolute stoic workforce, turning up to work each and every day, determined to make the best spirit within their capabilities. Spirit that was made with the same tried-and-tested techniques as had been used by the generation of workers who went before them.

Sometimes the zeitgeist is overrated. Sometimes all you need is the confidence to carry on doing what you've always done, and wait for either the rest of the world to come around to your way of thinking, or for what you're working on to be just right. It may take a while—say, forty-odd years or so—but when it happens, you would be justified in sticking two thumbs aloft, and granting yourself a contented chuckle. This is whisky well made, for whisky's sake, albeit on the periphery of most people's comprehension and appreciation. Far out, indeed. **D&C**

Tasting notes

On the nose, simple notes of vanilla and oak, dry leaves, and raisin. The finish is sublime. Apple crumble folds itself into elements of heather honey, lavender, rose, and licorice, before the wood returns to package the lot into its own oaky presentation case. Spectacular.

The Tweeddale Blend

Stonedean | www.stonedean.co.uk

Region and country of origin Scotland
Distilleries Various
Alcohol content 46% abv
Style Blend

The ten-year-old Tweeddale Blend is being made by Alistair Day, founder of Stonedean Ltd., to a recipe last produced seventy years ago by his great-grandfather Richard Day, in the Borders town of Coldstream. Originally employed by local brewer and whisky blender J. & A. Davidson, Richard Day and his family subsequently took over the business and ran it on its own account. Their whisky blending had ceased by World War II, but the original cellar books survived, and in 2010, Alistair Day decided to re-create one of the old recipes, opting for the Tweeddale blend.

The Tweeddale Blend is non-chill-filtered and has a malt content of 50 percent; the malts are provided by eight distilleries. According to Day, "Each of the nine whiskies in the blend is drawn from a single cask, and in batch one the single-grain whisky is ten years old, while the eight single-malt whiskies range from ten to twenty-one years old.

"In batch two, the same single-grain whisky is fifteen years old and was matured in a sherry butt. Seven of the eight single malts are from the same casks as batch one, but are twelve to twenty-one years old. One of the malts in batch two is fourteen years old and from a different cask."

Day uses caramel spirit to add extra color to the blend, as a way of staying faithful to the recipe but with a modern slant. The original recipe specified the inclusion of 1 to 2 percent sherry or dark rum "for coloring," but the Scotch Whisky Association would take a very dim view of anyone coloring whiskies in such a way today! **GS**

Tasting notes

Robust on the nose, with malt, brittle toffee, and vanilla, becoming more floral. Fresh and zesty, lemon and lime, with the addition of water. Smooth and approachable, with peach, ripe pear, caramel, and ginger. Drying subtly in a long, satisfying, slightly spicy finish.

VAT 69

Diageo | www.diageo.com

Region and country of origin Scotland
Distilleries Various
Alcohol content 40% abv
Style Blend

Born as a blend in 1892, VAT 69 is the result of a series of trials set up by William Sanderson, a wine and spirits merchant. Sanderson produced a hundred blends in different vats and enlisted his friends to taste them blind and decide which was best. The only means of identification on each of the hundred bottles was a number. The winning whisky came, naturally enough, from the vat numbered sixty-nine.

It must have been good, because the explorer Ernest Shackleton stowed cases of the whisky aboard the ship *Endurance* for his 1914 Imperial Trans-Arctic Expedition. It was for "medicinal and celebratory purposes," and presumably also to help keep out the cold. Given how long Shackleton was trapped in the Arctic, it was probably just as well. After his ship was crushed by the ice, Shackleton and five of his men rowed 800 miles (1,300 km) to a remote island in a 26-foot (8-m) lifeboat, assisted only by rudimentary navigational equipment. How much whisky he and his men had left by that stage is anyone's guess.

Bizarrely, VAT 69 was also the nickname given to Malaysia's elite counterterrorism unit, the "Very Able Troopers" formed to fight the communist insurgency in 1969. Accordingly, you might want to resist ordering a "shot" of VAT 69 at any bar in Kuala Lumpur.

VAT 69 contains around 35 percent malt, although the versions available in the United Kingdom and those intended for export vary slightly in this regard. As with many blends, its constituent malts are kept secret, although Royal Lochnagar, Teaninich, and Glenesk have been components over the years. **PB**

Tasting notes

Smooth and light fruit and great flakes of sea salt on the nose. On the palate, it is incredibly smooth, soft, and rounded, with another hefty dose of the sea, while the oak nibbles away at the edges. The finish is medium-length, with rapidly increasing oak.

Wemyss Malts
Ginger Compote 1996

Wemyss Malts | www.wemyssmalts.com

Region and country of origin Speyside, Scotland
Distillery Benrinnes, Aberlour, Banffshire
Alcohol content 46% abv
Style Single malt

By seeking out good casks from lesser-known distilleries, independent bottlers such as Wemyss gain greater exposure for whiskies that are not marketed as single malts by the distilleries that make them—in this case Benrinnes, which markets only one single malt.

The vast majority of Scottish distilleries practice double-distillation, with just a few using triple-distillation. A few odd ones, depending on how they use their stills, practice partial triple-distillation. Benrinnes introduced partial triple-distillation in 1955, but surprisingly, abandoned it a few years ago in favor of traditional double-distillation. Partial triple-distillation has had a certain impact on flavor since 1955, and it remains to be seen in the future if the character of Benrinnes single malt has changed.

At Benrinnes, worm tubs are used instead of ordinary condensers for cooling the spirit vapors. Using worm tubs minimizes the degree to which the spirit comes into contact with copper, with the result that excess sulfur remains in the spirit; this sulfur is only eleminated by prolonged maturation. That explains why Diageo's own bottling of Benrinnes is a fifteen-year-old, just like this Ginger Compote from Wemyss, which was matured in a refill sherry butt. **IR**

Tasting notes

Definitely ginger on the nose; also slightly earthy and malty with some curious hints of salami and ham. Fiery spices. Finishes with tarte tatin. A fascinating journey.

Wemyss Malts
The Honey Pot 1996

Wemyss Malts | www.wemyssmalts.com

Region and country of origin Speyside, Scotland
Distillery Glen Moray, Elgin, Morayshire
Alcohol content 46% abv
Style Single malt

Wemyss Malts names its bottlings after a key character in the whisky, and for most of their whiskies, the description is perfect. This bottling of Glen Moray really does have strong notes of honey flying around, something that is rarely associated with the Glen Moray character, which more commonly evokes various fruits and vanilla. This is, therefore, an unusual but delightful version from this distillery.

When mashing the grist (milled barley) with hot water, there is always a decision to be made—whether to have cloudy or clear worts going on to the next step, the fermentation. A cloudy wort has a lot of remaining solids in the shape of husks from the barley, which give a malty and nutty character to the spirit. Glen Moray, however, aims for a clear wort, in order to make room for fragrant and fruity nuances.

Wemyss Malts the Honey Pot 1996 was drawn from a refill bourbon hogshead, which comes as no surprise since 99 percent of the production at Glen Moray is filled into ex-bourbon casks. Unfortunately, there will probably be far fewer releases of Glen Moray from independent bottlers ten years from now, the reason being that a couple of years ago, the owners decided to stop selling casks to others. **IR**

Tasting notes

Sweet but also fresh with lemon and orange zest, a hint of spice (maybe nutmeg), and a whiff of furniture polish. Medium-long finish with a hint of marzipan.

Wemyss Malts
Mocha Spice 1990

Wemyss Malts | www.wemyssmalts.com

Region and country of origin Highlands, Scotland
Distillery Dalmore, Alness, Ross-shire
Alcohol content 46% abv
Style Single malt

Named Mocha Spice by independent bottler Wemyss Malts, this is a Dalmore single malt. Anyone collecting every new official bottling from Dalmore would have to be a millionaire. To buy just seven of the most expensive releases would cost $250,000 (£158,000). Dalmore has the explicit aim of becoming the number one ultraluxury brand of the whisky world, but for those of us burdened by debt, there are other, more affordable Dalmores out there, such as this one.

The setup of stills at Dalmore is an exciting mix of various shapes and sizes, with the spirit stills being equipped with water jackets, peculiar and unique devices that allow for cold water to circulate between the reflux bowl and the neck of the still, thus increasing the reflux (redistillation of the spirit).

Dalmore has always been known for powerful, sherried whiskies, and master blender Richard Patterson is particular about the casks he uses. For many years, the world-famous Bodegas of Gonzalez Byass in Jerez de la Frontera in Spain has supplied Dalmore with high-quality sherry butts. Dalmore has a tendency to mature rather slowly, so kudos to Wemyss for releasing this bottling from a first-fill sherry butt at the honorable age of twenty-one. **IR**

Tasting notes

Powerful and intense. Evolves into raisin, black currant preserve, and walnut. The oak comes forward on the palate, with loads of dark chocolate and coffee beans.

Wemyss Malts
The Orange Tree 1989

Wemyss Malts | www.wemyssmalts.com

Region and country of origin Highlands, Scotland
Distillery Glen Garioch, Oldmeldrum, Aberdeenshire
Alcohol content 46% abv
Style Single malt

Glen Garioch (pronounced "Geery") is Scotland's easternmost distillery and also one of the few urban distilleries remaining. Set in the quiet hamlet of Oldmeldrum, west of Aberdeen, it is claimed to be the oldest distillery still working in Scotland—although a few other distilleries claim that, too. For most of Glen Garioch's existence, its whisky has been destined for blended Scotch, and from the end of the 1800s, it helped VAT 69 to become a bestseller.

Recently, Glen Garioch has been relaunched as a single malt. Bottles distilled before 1979 tend to be rather peaty, like neighboring distillery Ardmore's whisky. The floor maltings were closed in 1979, and the spirit produced thereafter has been unpeated, although in no way light. On the contrary, young Glen Garioch has a robustness and maltiness that is quite powerful. With age, as in this twenty-two-year-old Glen Garioch named the Orange Tree by independent bottler Wemyss Malts, the whisky softens while developing a delightful complexity. The refill bourbon hogshead that was used for this particular bottling also adds some nice vanilla notes. The vanilla comes from the American oak, and not from the bourbon that was previously in the cask. **IR**

Tasting notes

On the nose, orange marmalade, milk chocolate, crème brûlée. Quite dry and spicy on the palate, with more orange, fruit bonbon, vanilla, and a tiny hint of peat.

Wemyss Malts Peat Chimney 8-Year-Old

Wemyss Malts | www.wemyssmalts.com

Region and country of origin Islay, Scotland
Distilleries Various
Alcohol content 40% abv
Style Blended malt

Wemyss (pronounced Weems) Malts, owned by the Scottish Wemyss family, started as an independent bottler of whisky in 2005. By that time, they had already been involved in the wine industry for some years with interests in wine estates in Provence, France, and western Australia. The family had no previous experience with whisky, except for the fact that Haig's first distillery was built in the early 1800s on Wemyss land in Fife, where Wemyss Castle, home of the family since the 1300s, also stands. The family's lack of whisky experience was compensated for by engaging the world-famous whisky expert and writer Charles MacLean as head of its nosing panel, and Susan Colville, who has worked for a number of independent bottlers, as brand ambassador and key member of the nosing team.

Wemyss takes the signature malt for Peat Chimney from one of the Islay distilleries, and while Islay is famous for its often heavily peated whiskies, the Peat Chimney is definitely not a smoky attack on the palate. There are phenols, yes, but instead of dominating, they supplement all the flavors. This is a whisky full of confidence, saying, "I know I'm peated, but I can do a lot of other stuff as well!" **IR**

Tasting notes

Bacon fat smokiness, with floral notes underneath. Hint of vanilla and coconut. On the palate, charcoal paired with black pepper and licorice. Medium-long, dry finish.

Wemyss Malts Smoke Stack 1996

Wemyss Malts | www.wemyssmalts.com

Region and country of origin Islay, Scotland
Distillery Caol Ila, Port Askaig, Argyll
Alcohol content 46% abv
Style Single malt

Visitors to Islay usually head straight to the famous Kildalton Three (Ardbeg, Lagavulin, and Laphroaig) on the south part of the island. But there is one distillery in the north—Caol Ila—that produces more whisky than all the Kildalton distilleries put together.

Like most of the whiskies produced on Islay, Caol Ila single malt is about peat. Phenols give the whisky its peated character, and the phenol content of malted barley is measured in parts per million (ppm). Lagavulin and Laphroaig use the same malt specification as Caol Ila—35 to 45 ppm—and yet their peated character is completely different. This is all to do with the middle cut of the spirit run, the part saved during distillation and filled into casks for maturation.

Laphroaig and Lagavulin avoid the sweet esters of the beginning of the distillation that are thought desirable at Caol Ila. Conversely, the stillman at Caol Ila stops collecting the spirit before most of the phenolic compounds start to appear toward the end of the run; the two other distilleries collect the very last of those pungent congeners. That is why this Wemyss bottling from a Caol Ila single-refill bourbon hogshead is less phenolic, with a character more of smoked bacon than seaweed and tar. **IR**

Tasting notes

Not overly peated. Sweet, creamy texture, with a nice balance between phenols and sweetness. A long finish, with apricot and peach flavors evolving.

← Wemyss Castle, seat of the Wemyss family since the fourteenth century.

Wemyss Malts Smooth Gentleman 8-Year-Old

Wemyss Malts | www.wemyssmalts.com

Region and country of origin Speyside, Scotland
Distilleries Various
Alcohol content 40% abv
Style Blended malt

Wemyss Malts employs the effective marketing strategy of putting descriptive or evocative names on its whiskies to reflect their aromas and flavors, and therefore give customers an indication of what they might expect if they buy a bottle. Their inventive names have included Freshly Cut Grass, Ginger Treacle, and Mocha Spice.

This approach had been tried before. A few years ago, the Easy Drinking Whisky Co. (with aid from Edrington, owner of the Macallan and Highland Park) launched three whiskies that they called the Rich and Spicy One, the Smoky Peaty One, and the Smooth and Sweeter One. The company did not last more than a couple of years, so perhaps the market was not yet ready for that type of naming on the labels.

Smooth Gentleman from Wemyss is a whisky that does not require a certain occasion or mood for its enjoyment. To me, it is the perfect all-rounder; it is not demanding, but on the other hand, it is never dull. The signature malt for Smooth Gentleman comes from a distillery toward the east of Speyside. The whisky from this distillery is rarely bottled on its own, but it is popular with blenders because of its proven ability to act as the backbone of different whisky blends.

In a blender's list from 1974, all of the Scottish distilleries are ranked from a blending perspective. There are four groups, and among the twelve distilleries in the top-class category is the one that Wemyss chose to define this particular blend. It was a good choice, and Smooth Gentleman is definitely a blend I might select as my house whisky. **IR**

Tasting notes

Very estery and slightly malty on the nose, with sweet hints of green apple, pear, and crushed grape. A nice mouthfeel, with developing sweet honey and butterscotch. Chewy chocolate, mixed with citrus and heather. Easy to drink.

Wemyss Malts Spice King 8-Year-Old

Wemyss Malts | www.wemyssmalts.com

Region and country of origin Highlands, Scotland
Distillery Various
Alcohol content 40% abv
Style Blended malt

When Wemyss Malts started as a bottler back in 2005, the first products that saw the light of day were three blended malts. For whisky enthusiasts who live in the past, as I do, these are the same as vatted malts, or malts from different distilleries mixed together. This category should not be confused with blended Scotch, which contains grain whisky.

In 2005 the company released three five-year-olds: Peat Chimney, Smooth Gentleman, and Spice King. The names of the three whiskies, suggesting their tastes, would become the distinctive mark for all their subsequent bottlings. Four years later, the range was expanded with three eight-year-old versions, and in 2010, it was time to launch the twelve-year-olds, this time in selected duty-free markets only (first in India and Thailand). Each blend is composed of up to sixteen different malts.

For Spice King, a signature Highland malt was selected to give the blend the top notes that would define it. The different malts included in Spice King have not been disclosed, but some commentators claim that the signature malt could be a Talisker matured in sherry casks. Several of the other malts in the recipe come from the Speyside area, where more than forty active distilleries produce a wide variety of styles. (When you see a whisky described as a "typical Speysider," watch out, there is no such thing.) Speyside character can go from powerful and meaty to green and grassy, with much in between, so it is in the correct proportions of these varying styles that the overall Spice King character is achieved. **IR**

Tasting notes

Very fresh and herbal, with green notes, perhaps cut grass, and a hint of peat. More soft peat on the palate, after which, a few seconds later, a delightful red chile attack sets in. Toward the end, there are notes of very ripe melon. Medium-long, dry finish.

Wemyss Malts Vanilla Oak 1996

Wemyss Malts | www.wemyssmalts.com

Region and country of origin Speyside, Scotland
Distillery Mortlach, Dufftown, Keith, Banffshire
Alcohol content 46% abv
Style Single malt

Mortlach holds a place in Scottish history, for it was here in the year 1010 that the Scottish king Malcolm II defeated Danish Vikings who had succeeded in sailing their ships up the Spey river. The distillery may be situated in the very heart of the region—in fact in its very middle, the world's whisky capital of Dufftown—but the whisky itself defies any preconceived notion of what a typical Speysider should be. This is a heavyweight champion with a mighty punch.

The Mortlach character tends to be described as meaty, and since the whisky is often matured in European oak, there are strokes of firm tannins on the palate. To achieve the typical Mortlach character, the owners have always tried to minimize the spirit's contact with copper during the distillation. Copper from the stills and condensers softens the spirit and reduces its sulfur content. However, if you want to make a robust whisky, the sulfur is an intregal part of the flavor, at least in the new make.

This fifteen-year-old Wemyss bottling from a refill sherry butt is, in terms of age, in line with Mortlach's official bottling guidelines. Mortlach needs extra years to overcome its sulfury notes and achieve its potential as a great, complex whisky. **IR**

Tasting notes

Robust but floral, with notes of heather. Tropical fruits on the palate, with banana, papaya, and roasted coconut. The wood offers a slight bitterness at the end.

White Horse

Diageo | www.diageo.com

Region and country of origin Scotland
Distilleries Various
Alcohol content 40% abv
Style Blend

Lovers of bad jokes will probably know of White Horse even if they have never touched a drop of the stuff. The joke goes something like this: a horse (white, obviously) goes into a bar and orders a beer. The landlord says, "It's odd that you should order a beer when we have a whisky named after you." The horse replies, "What—Eric?"

Happily, the whisky is a whole lot better than the joke. The White Horse blend was launched in 1890 and was named after the White Horse, an inn in Edinburgh, which was the starting point for the eight-day coach trip to London. The inn itself was named after the white horse that carried the doomed Mary, Queen of Scots to and from Holyroodhouse palace.

The blend's founder, Peter Mackie, by all accounts part genius, part eccentric, and part megalomaniac, came up with the innovative idea of replacing the whisky bottle corks with screw caps. Mackie was trained at Lagavulin, said to be the spiritual home of White Horse, and Lagavulin malt has long been one of the blend's principal components, the provider of its smoky heart. Many other malts have been used over the years, including Cragganmore, Caol Ila, Talisker, and Glen Elgin. **PB**

Tasting notes

Chewy grain and peat on the nose; stewed plum and a small slice of banoffee pie. Light and nutty on the palate, with a gradual cranking up of pepper.

A 1970s advertisement for White Horse enters the realm of the surreal. ➡

You can take a White Horse anywhere

Whyte & Mackay 30-Year-Old

Whyte & Mackay | www.whyteandmackay.com

Region and country of origin Scotland
Distilleries Various
Alcohol content 40% abv
Style Blend

What immediately makes the Whyte & Mackay 30-Year-Old stand out from other thoroughbreds in the stable is its fabulous packaging. The opaque black bottle (the only one used by Whyte & Mackay) and its black box both proudly display the company's age-old logo of double lions, in bright gold instead of the usual red. The two lions represent the lion rampant from the flag of Scotland beside the lion emblem of the clan Macgregor, from which one of the founders, Whyte, claimed descent.

Sadly, the company is apparently planning to discontinue this special packaging, although probably not the rather special thirty-year-old blended whisky itself. The marrying process for the 30-Year-Old takes between one and two years—master blender Richard Paterson says that this brings out the sweetness in the blend. Only a handful of distilleries have the stocks to contribute single malts of this age, but those that exist (mostly between thirty and thirty-five years old) tend to be fantastic. Paterson says that malts matured in Missouri white oak bring elegance to the blend, while malts from oloroso sherry butts drape it in a luxurious, slinky, sable coat. Even the grain whisky contribution adds to the star quality; grain whiskies that have matured for thirty or more years are often wonderfully drinkable in their own right, but in a blend with malts, they seduce and flatter the malts, getting them to show their best sides.

This 30-Year-Old has twice been voted "best blended whisky in the world." It is surely one of the best things ever to have come out of Glasgow. **RL**

Tasting notes

Barley sugar, toffee, and marzipan on the nose are followed by pineapple, melon, tutti-frutti, and sherbet, then leather, straw, and tobacco leaf. Succulent, fruity, and surprisingly lively on the palate. The finish suggests toffee apple, with hints of tobacco and clove.

Whyte & Mackay Original 40-Year-Old

Whyte & Mackay | www.whyteandmackay.com

Region and country of origin Scotland
Distilleries Various
Alcohol content 45% abv
Style Blend

There is something about forty-year-old whisky that makes us look backward in time; it rubs the atavistic nap of our smug complacency the wrong way and awakens emotions long buried. A blend of this age is not easily assembled. Very few distilleries have stock that is old enough, and even more thought, care, and skill than usual are required of the blender. The oak influence of the aged whisky should be a strong thread in the tapestry, but it must let other textures and colors show through.

The Whyte & Mackay Original 40-Year-Old contains 70 percent malt—far more than most blends, even deluxe ones. That "seventy" has significance because it is a symbolic tribute to an important historic Whyte & Mackay figure, John McIlraith, who devoted seventy years of his life to the company, working his way from salesman to managing director over his long career. He died in 1950.

The 40-Year-Old won Best in its Class in the World Whisky Awards in 2010. The blend succeeds because of imaginative use of sherry casks—amoroso, Pedro Ximénez, and palomino fino—made possible by Whyte & Mackay's close working relationship with Gonzales Byass. The large proportion of Highland and Speyside malts in the blend provides a flavor backbone that lifts most eyes heavenward. Master blender Richard Paterson advises tasters to keep a whisky in the mouth for one second for each year of its age: that's forty seconds in this case.

This is a whisky for the most special of occasions, or to make a gift for someone highly regarded. **RL**

Tasting notes

Perfumed on the nose—you could be in a grand lady's wardrobe. Fresh mandarin and Charentais melon. Big and mouth-filling. The texture is viscous and chewy, the flavors a mingling of aromatic fruits and flickering spices. An afterglow of sweet tobacco and licorice.

Whyte & Mackay Special

Whyte & Mackay | www.whyteandmackay.com

Region and country of origin Scotland
Distilleries Various
Alcohol content 40% abv
Style Blend

Whyte & Mackay calls this blend "the Scotch the Scots drink," especially, one suspects, the discerning whisky drinkers of the company's hometown of Glasgow.

Even in this, the basic blend in the company's range, the bottle proudly announces the "double marriage" of its components. The first marriage consists of introducing the thirty-five or so single malts (all aged between four and eight years) to each other in the cosy confinement of "in situ" sherry butts for three to eight months, depending on demand. In the second marriage, six different grain whiskies (also aged between four and eight years) are introduced into the blend for at least a further two months.

Whyte & Mackay, who believes it is unique in having adopted the double-marriage process, claims that it pays dividends by producing a harmonious and consistent whisky with a soft, rounded, mellow character. The double marriage allows time for the components to integrate slowly and achieve the somewhat karmic concept of "oneness of spirit." Whyte & Mackay also hold that the double marriage is especially good at bringing out the inherent sweetness that issues from a third marriage in the whisky-making process, albeit one of a different type: the sacred union of barley and wood.

Whyte & Mackay Special is the blend that finds its way onto the optic whisky dispensers of almost every public house in Scotland. Its popularity surely confirms that the careful selection of components and their gradual harmonization is worthwhile. Master blender Richard Paterson certainly thinks so. **RL**

Tasting notes

Light honey and toffee aromas on the nose; slightly nutty, gentle grain notes waft over polished wood. On the palate, reminiscent of caramelized sugar, crème brûlée, and chocolate-coated toffee. A satisfyingly good finish—the perfect end to a hard day.

Whyte & Mackay The Thirteen

Whyte & Mackay | www.whyteandmackay.com

Region and country of origin Scotland
Distilleries Various
Alcohol content 40% abv
Style Blend

As part of a recent rebranding, Whyte & Mackay ignored common superstition and replaced their previous twelve-year-old with this offering, the Thirteen. The thirteen-year-old blend is made by the same double-marriage process used for Whyte & Mackay Special. This time, however, the result is deeper and more accentuated, for four reasons.

First, the component whiskies are all older, at least twelve years old and often older, when they are combined in the marriage of twenty-five malts.

Second, this initial marriage takes a full twelve months, which brings the malt's final age up to thirteen years. Thirteen years is a very long time for marrying component parts of a blend, but Whyte & Mackay likes to call it a "loving union." It is at this point that the six grain whiskies are introduced and the second marriage takes place.

Third, although there are fewer malts in the blend (because of the greater difficulty in accessing stock of this age from some distilleries), the malt proportion is higher than for the Special. As a general rule, the older a Whyte & Mackay blend, the higher the proportion of malts to grain.

Fourth, there is a higher proportion of sherry-matured malts; the Thirteen's malts are typically 10 to 15 percent sherry-matured (in oloroso sherry butts), while the rest has all been matured in ex-bourbon barrels of Missouri-grown American white oak.

The result of these four points of accentuation is a blend that is just a bit heavier and darker than the Special, with more weight and gravitas. **RL**

Tasting notes

The nose has an agreeable fruity elegance—dark and golden raisins, banana—also sugared almond, cornflakes, and light putty. The palate has a nice chewy feel. Iced lollipop stick along with rich, spicy ginger cake, with that spice lingering pleasantly in the finish.

IRELAND

Bushmills 10-Year-Old

Diageo | www.bushmills.com

Region and country of origin County Antrim, Ireland
Distillery Old Bushmills, Bushmills
Alcohol content 40% abv
Style Single malt

Although there is a paper trail to whiskey making in the Bushmills area going back to 1608, the current distillery most probably grew out of a company first recorded in 1784. Either way, Old Bushmills is easily the oldest working distillery in Ireland. It is also the most enigmatic. When nearly every distillery in Ireland was making pot-still whiskey, at Bushmills they were making single malt. While most Irish distilleries were enormous concerns and champions of Victorian enterprise, at Bushmills small was considered beautiful. For example, in 1825 the giant still at the Midleton distillery in Cork produced more whiskey in a day than Old Bushmills produced that entire year.

Yet at the Paris Exhibition of 1889, when the Eiffel Tower was revealed to the world, a bottle of Old Bushmills 10-Year-Old malt won the only gold medal in the competition. A single bottle of that 1889 offering is still kept under lock and key at the distillery. One day, however, curiosity got the better of master distiller Colum Egan and he hatched a plan. He got himself a syringe with a very long needle and eased it through the cork, then withdrew a sample of the precious liquid. Egan resisted the temptation to sample it and instead had it analyzed, and what he found was nothing short of amazing. The current 10-Year-Old is almost identical in every way to the sample that won in 1889, the one that put the distillery on the map. So there's no need to sneak into the distillery with a hypodermic hidden up your sleeve. If you want a taste of history, just get yourself a bottle of the current Bushmills 10-Year-Old. **PM**

Tasting notes

Pastry and honey dominate this easy-going whiskey. Whispers of chocolate and licorice with a hint of sweetness from some very elegant sherry. The 10-Year-Old is as approachable an introduction to the world of single malts as you are ever likely to taste.

← The Old Bushmills distillery was registered as a company in 1784.

Bushmills 16-Year-Old

Diageo | www.bushmills.com

Region and country of origin County Antrim, Ireland
Distillery Old Bushmills, Bushmills
Alcohol content 40% abv
Style Single malt

There is the merest whisper of a sherry influence in the Bushmills 10-Year-Old, but with that the bourbon wood is much more influential. In the Bushmills 16-Year-Old, however, three different kinds of casks are juggled with great effect, which is why this single malt is also known as "three woods."

This whiskey is created when pretty much the same quantity of sixteen-year-old bourbon and sherry-matured whiskeys are married and left for another nine or so months in port casks. However, master blender Helen Mulholland keeps a very close nose on proceedings. The role of the master blender in the world of single malts is sadly overlooked, but their skills are just as necessary here as they are when putting together a blend such as Black Bush. This all comes back to the curious nature of whiskey and how it behaves while in wood. Two casks can be filled at the same time, then left to sit next to each other in a warehouse for sixteen years and come out tasting very different. Mulholland's job is to keep the brand consistent and to iron out any wrinkles in the taste.

When it comes to knowing when this whiskey is ready for bottling, science gives way to art, as nothing can replace the nose of a master blender. For example port can be rather overpowering, and by its nature, the malt from Old Bushmills is a clean, delicate whiskey, so after just four months in the port pipes, Helen Mulholland checks the progress several times a week and it's only ready when it's ready—not a day earlier or later. So it's a real credit to all concerned that the 16-Year-Old works as well as it does. **PM**

Tasting notes

An exotic nose with a hint of marzipan and dried fruits. The taste is curiously dry at first, and there's a real buzz from the malt. The chocolate, so evident in the 10-Year-Old, is darker now, as is everything from the color of the spirit to the rumble of port pipes at the finish.

Bushmills 21-Year-Old

Diageo | www.bushmills.com

Region and country of origin County Antrim, Ireland
Distillery Old Bushmills, Bushmills
Alcohol content 40% abv
Style Single malt

All the skills that the team at Old Bushmills brings to bear on the 16-Year-Old single malt are tested to the limit when putting this extraordinary whiskey together. Following the malt's launch in 2001, this sophisticated malt has attracted a very loyal following.

Due to the influence of the Gulf Stream, Ireland is a lot warmer and damper than Scotland, so in the Emerald Isle whiskey matures a lot faster. At twenty-one years, most Irish whiskey has long been drunk, so it's not surprising that this is the oldest Irish whiskey on general release. You see whiskeys with the spine to make it this far that have been selected over the years and put aside. These are the very best casks and, after nineteen years, the house combination of equal amounts of whiskey from bourbon and sherry wood are decanted, mixed, and refilled into casks that once contained Madeira wine. They then stay in the cool warehouses at Bushmills for up to another two years.

Madeira is a fortified Portuguese wine from the islands off the west coast of Africa. Following the example of port, in the sixteenth century, small quantities of spirit were added to local wine before it was transported to the American colonies. The intense heat and movement of the vessels at sea changed the nature of the wine and gave us what we now call Madeira. This is a sweet, mellow drink with a very round and velvety feel that complements the elegant whiskey from County Antrim.

Only 900 cases of the 21-Year-Old are released each year. Production won't be expanding any time soon, as time is the one thing that can't be hurried. **PM**

Tasting notes

The most surprising thing about this is just how fresh the whiskey tastes. It's fuller and rounder than any other Bushmills malt, yet the fruity, malty notes are all present. The Madeira gives the package a wonderful toffee finish. The perfect after dinner malt?

Bushmills 1608

Diageo | www.bushmills.com

Region and country of origin County Antrim, Ireland
Distillery Old Bushmills, Bushmills
Alcohol content 46% abv
Style Blend

When it came to marking the 400th anniversary of distilling in the town of Bushmills, County Antrim, in 2008, a lot of consideration was given to what went into the bottle. The decision to go with a blend to mark such a special occasion is typical of the kind of fresh thinking to come out of Bushmills. It also shows how important innovation and experimentation are in an industry as rooted in tradition as whiskey making. Every master distiller plays around with his or her stills, but more often than not, their experiments don't amount to much. But every now and then something special happens.

Long before the 2008 anniversary, Bushmills had experimented with making whiskey from crystal malt, a kind of polished malt used by a lot of craft brewers to give their beers extra mouthfeel. It is made by adding malt to a preheated drum, then blasting it with air at 932°F (500°C). This toasts the surface sugars to create a product that's crunchier and sweeter than regular malt. But nobody had ever made a spirit with crystal malt, and as whiskey needs time to mature, it was more than a decade and a half before the Bushmills master distiller and blender realized he had a winner on his hands. But good as it was, on its own, the crystal malt whiskey wasn't quite there. This was a very special anniversary, so a tiny dash of grain was added to pull the drink together.

This whiskey is bottled at 46 percent abv and was launched in 2008. As supplies of mature crystal malt whiskey are limited by availability, if you ever see this whiskey, grab it with both hands. **PM**

Tasting notes

This is delicate, easy-to-drink whiskey that doesn't have to try very hard. The mouthfeel is exquisite, silky like cream soda. It's a gently perfumed whiskey with cereal and honey to the fore. Matured in fine bourbon barrels, the oak gently complements the spirit.

Bushmills Black Bush

Diageo | www.bushmills.com

Region and country of origin County Antrim and County Cork, Ireland **Distilleries** Old Bushmills, Bushmills, and Midleton, Midleton **Alcohol content** 40% abv **Style** Blend

For reasons unknown even to those who work in the distillery, this whiskey is known in Bushmills as "the loveable rogue." Perhaps it has something to do with the whiskey's fanatical fan base or maybe it's the quirkiness of the drink itself. Whatever the reason, Black Bush is one of the finest and most easily found Irish whiskeys.

There is a high proportion of malt in this blend, but as no grain whiskey is made at Bushmills, this component has always been sourced elsewhere. In the past the nearby Coleraine distillery used to supply it, but nowadays it comes from the far end of the island, from Midleton in County Cork.

It goes without saying that some very fine malt goes into Bushmills Black Bush, but what's really interesting are the other elements that combine to give this whiskey such character. First up is the grain. Unlike regular grain, which comes from a continuous still, this is made in a traditional copper pot still, resulting in a fuller, rounder flavor with no nasty back taste. The second element is often overlooked, and that is the huge contribution made by maturing the whiskey in expensive sherry wood.

The various components that make up Black Bush are married in a huge 23,775-gallon (90,000-liter) tank, which is never emptied. To help ensure consistency, the vat is always left more than half full, so you could say that each and every bottle of Black Bush contains elements of every bottle that went before. In our constantly changing world, connoisseurs across the globe find real comfort in that. **PM**

Tasting notes

A wonderful bouquet greets the nose: sherry, malt, and honey. The whiskey is silky in the way good milk chocolate is; expect hints of fine cocoa and buttery toast. The grain is soft as Antrim rain—this is wonderful, world-beating stuff.

Bushmills Millennium Malt

Diageo | www.bushmills.com

Region and country of origin County Antrim, Ireland
Distillery Old Bushmills, Bushmills
Alcohol content 43% abv
Style Single malt

In 1975 Bushmills laid down some whiskey for the then-coming millennium. It was released to retailers and individuals only as private casks, with Bushmills offering personalized labels if customers wished.

This was a special bottling of Bushmills, and not merely because it was laid down for the millennium, or all private cask-released. It is quite different from most Bushmills whiskeys. First, it is twenty-five years old (just a shade under, actually), quite a bit older than most Bushmills. Maybe more important, it is a single cask, non-chill-filtered whiskey. The only intervention is the addition of some spring water to dilute it to the bottling strength of 43 percent abv.

This is very much an investment-grade bottle of whiskey. Rare on its release, its rarity has undoubtedly been increased by people's natural tendency to open a bottle on the night of December 31, 1999, and, further, by reports of the excellence of the whiskey. It was a once-and-done bottling, and Bushmills has not bottled anything remotely like it since.

Amazingly, there are still some bottles out there. Some farsighted retailers bought deeply, and release a case occasionally. If you are a Bushmills fan, that will be too good an opportunity to miss. **LB**

Tasting notes

Sweet, grassy malt, a bit oily in the mouth. This is a quintessence of the Bushmills character: balanced, round, smoothly flawless with a whispering-soft finish.

Bushmills Original

Diageo | www.bushmills.com

Region and country of origin County Antrim and County Cork, Ireland **Distilleries** Old Bushmills, Bushmills, and Midleton, Midleton **Alcohol content** 40% abv
Style Blend

This blend has been called numerous things, such as White Bush, but officially it's now known as Bushmills Original. Its history is vague because record keeping at the distillery was never great, and what records that did exist were destroyed during World War II. We do know that owner Wilson Boyd bought the nearby Coleraine distillery before the war and that by 1954 he had installed a continuous still.

Old Bushmills (as it was then called) proved a hit in the United States. By the early 1970s, it had become America's bestselling Irish whiskey, but the quantities being sold were tiny. In 1975 the total sales of Irish whiskeys represented just 0.006 percent of the U.S. market. The distillery has passed through numerous hands since the Boyd family relinquished control, and when, in 1978, the owners, Irish Distillers, closed Coleraine distillery and shifted production of grain whiskey to Midleton, the brand was reformulated.

Nowadays this is a relatively young blend; the whiskeys are typically matured for five years in bourbon casks. A small quantity of the grain whiskey is specially made and comes not from a continuous still, but from a special copper pot still. This component is matured exclusively for Bushmills blends. **DR**

Tasting notes

A clean, approachable whiskey with lots of vanilla, toffee, and a curious back burr of 80 percent cocoa chocolate. The finish is crisp with a touch of spice.

← A vintage advertisement refers to "Old Bushmills" whiskey.

Connemara 12-Year-Old

Cooley | www.connemarawhiskey.com

Region and country of origin County Louth, Ireland
Distillery Cooley, Cooley Peninsula
Alcohol content 46% abv
Style Single malt

As whisky makers look for new ways to broaden the flavors of their creations while staying true to the strict rules that govern production of the spirit, the interaction of wood and peat will almost certainly come under the microscope. Already some Scottish peated malts have been matured in quarter-sized casks to intensify and accelerate maturation.

The taste of peat is the result of drying barley over peat fires, and not from peated water used in the production process. The flavor is dominant in new-make spirit, and the conventional view is that peat is at its most abrasive when young. As it matures in wood, peat flavors are softened and integrated, similar to the way chile flavors marry into meat over time.

An extensive peat tasting in *Whisky Magazine* a few years back confirmed that there are big differences between some weighty twelve-year-old peated whiskies such as Lagavulin and this, which is arguably the most intriguing of the Connemara range. Here, twelve years and an overdose of fruit have broken down the peat and smoke elements into an intriguing tapestry of flavors. Tastewise, this is a stepping stone to the Scottish mainland and one or two of the whiskeys being made at Bladnoch by Northern Irishman Raymond Armstrong—a delicate marriage of green fruit and wispy smoke. **DR**

Tasting notes

The nose is clean, with barley and a wisp of smoke, while the taste brings forward grape, gooseberry, unripe pear, and some earthiness from the peat.

Connemara Bog Oak

Cooley | www.connemarawhiskey.com

Region and country of origin County Louth, Ireland
Distillery Cooley, Cooley Peninsula
Alcohol content 57.5% abv
Style Single malt

At the turn of the millennium, whisky competitions struggled to find sufficient entrants for the Irish category. Today, there are regularly thirty or more quality entrants. Cooley distillery can be credited with a big part of that success, and it has not only expanded the category, but is also offering drinkers a broader range of drink styles. Gone are the days when Ireland could describe all its whiskeys as nonpeated, triple-distilled blends, which was how they were made to set themselves apart from Scotland.

Years ago, peated whiskey would have been the norm in Ireland—after all, the country is a huge peat bog—and scores of distilleries would have made their own malt. The distilleries were systematically put out of business by a combination of poor judgment, sour economic conditions, and some ruthless business practices from across the water in Scotland. Cooley distillery was once seen as confusing the Irish whiskey-making picture, but now many more fans are mature enough to experiment with older tastes and styles.

Connemara Bog Oak is the product of a cask partially made from oak wood lifted from peat bogs hundreds of years old. The whiskey marks a move toward innovation in Ireland, but does it make any difference? It would seem that it does, because this is a particularly delicate and sweet peat malt. **DR**

Tasting notes

A mix of late-summer orchard, with dusty dried oak, overripe and fluffy apple and pear fruit, and waves of bonfire smoke. A crescendo of peat late in the day.

← Connemara roadside peat cuttings are loaded onto transport in the 1930s.

Connemara Cask Strength

Cooley | www.connemarawhiskey.com

Region and country of origin County Louth, Ireland
Distillery Cooley, Cooley Peninsula
Alcohol content 60% abv
Style Single malt

The accepted definition of whisky is a spirit made with just grain, yeast, and water. How different countries, economic zones, and continents define those terms varies massively, but in Europe the view is that apart from these three basic ingredients (and a small amount of caramel for coloring purposes), nothing else may be added. All well and good in theory, but in practice other factors come into play. The cask, for instance, will have a strong influence on the flavor of a whisky, and therefore what that cask contained before will play a significant role in the production process. So will the type of oak used—there are big differences between Swedish, Japanese, Australian, European, and American oak.

Another major influence on flavor is peat. Not all peat is the same because it is made up of the vegetation of the country it is from, and there are huge differences between flora and fauna in different parts of the world. This is why this peated offering from Ireland is so intriguing. Here the battering ram of peat wraps itself around a traditional apple and pear sweet fruity Irish whiskey, and the result is a big, powerful, industrial single malt that tastes nothing like the whiskies coming out of Scotland. The decision to put out a double-distilled peated Irish whiskey was brave to start with. To bottle it at a whopping 60 percent, when until relatively recently few Irish whiskeys even strayed up to 43 percent, could be considered foolhardy. Or genius. Connemara Cask Strength occupies a place all its own and is a landmark release. It demands to be tasted. **DR**

Tasting notes

On the nose it's a case of calm before the storm, with burnt dust and wispy smoke, like the transformer box on a Hornby train set. On the palate there is an oily wave of smoke and peat, but it meets its match with the softer milk chocolate and soft pear and apple.

Connemara Turf Mór

Cooley | www.connemarawhiskey.com

Region and country of origin County Louth, Ireland
Distillery Cooley, Cooley Peninsula
Alcohol content 58.2% abv
Style Single malt

If ever there were a firework whiskey, this is it. Cooley distillery, a past master of shaking up the world of Irish whiskey, has come up with an incendiary device, lit the touchpaper, and casually lobbed it in our direction.

This is a heavily peated whiskey. Its whopping 58 parts per million (ppm) of peat place it above Laphroaig and Lagavulin and up there with the heaviest Ardbegs. To put this into context, the standard peated Connemara has 20 ppm.

But while the big peat punch is an unavoidable and dominant theme, the fascinating thing about this whiskey is how different it is from its Islay cousins. Turf Mór is a young whiskey, quite possibly only a few months more than the three-year legal minimum age for whiskey. It does have its detractors. One highly respected writer, citing this whiskey, called for an end of unbalanced whiskeys; focusing on its oily, rubbery notes, he described it as like an explosion in a prophylactic factory. Undoubtedly, peat, oil, and some youthful, rubbery notes play their role, but I would beg to differ with the overall conclusion. There are interesting subscripts in this whiskey, with hickory adding depth and a whizzy, fizzy aspect to it that makes it very attractive indeed.

Connemara Turf Mór is another groundbreaking malt that has not so much opened a new door but battered it down. Beyond the trademark earthy, oily surface there are still distinctive Irish notes that offer an enjoyable malt now but raise all sorts of questions about what the whiskey will be like in the future. This is very much a case of "watch this space." **DR**

Tasting notes

On the nose, the brooding dark cloud peat is offset by some sunshine fruitiness and a trace of spring meadow. It rolls across the palate with charcoal and oil to the fore. Sweet barley, traces of vanilla, and rootsy unripe fruit are also there to hold the attention.

Dungourney 1964

Cork Distilleries Company/Irish Distillers/
Pernod Ricard | www.irishdistillers.ie

Region and country of origin County Cork, Ireland
Distillery Old Midleton, Midleton
Alcohol content 40% abv
Style Single pot still

In 1994, master distiller Barry Crockett made an astonishing discovery in an old whiskey warehouse on Midleton's Dungourney Road: an uncataloged cask of whiskey that was thirty years old. The whiskey had been made by Barry's father, then master distiller in the Old Midleton distillery, way back in 1964.

The Old Midleton distillery had since been turned into a museum, so Barry had literally found the whiskey equivalent of a dinosaur. Here was a cask of pot-still whiskey made by the old Cork Distilleries Company, prior even to the forming of Irish Distillers. What's more, one of the stills used in the making of the cask remains on display in the museum.

When it came to labeling this errant child, the whiskey was named after the river that gave it life, the Dungourney, which still runs through the Old Midleton distillery and which, in the 1960s, not only supplied water for whiskey making and cooling but also powered the giant waterwheel that supplied the plant with electricity.

For us humans, life may well begin at forty, but it's a colossal age for an Irish whiskey, and this bottling does suffer a bit from an excess of wood tannins. It is also a heavier style of pot still than what we are used to nowadays. But it's a remarkable story and a fascinating window into Ireland's whiskey past. **PM**

Tasting notes

Old raincoats and leather straps. Woody, but when the spirit warms, it comes to life. Spice, chocolate, dark coffee, and enough grain to keep things interesting.

Greenore 8-Year-Old

Cooley
www.cooleywhiskey.com

Region and country of origin County Louth, Ireland
Distillery Cooley, Cooley Peninsula
Alcohol content 40% abv
Style Grain whiskey

Many believe that grain whisky is an underexplored category littered with hidden gems and capable of bringing a wave of consumers to the world of whisky. Some Scottish independent bottlers in particular have some fabulous grain whiskies stretching back more than forty years, and increasingly companies such as Whyte & Mackay are looking at the category.

Grain whisky is made with grain other than malted barley, and is made not in a pot still but in a continuous still, often called a Coffey still, named after an Irishman, Aeneas Coffey, who perfected the factory-style production of spirit distillation. Ironically, the Irish whiskey industry shunned the invention because it didn't consider the spirit it produced to be of acceptable quality to be matured as whiskey.

Greenore no longer exists as a distillery but this whiskey is an example of the sort of grain whiskey that Ireland made for its blends, and, at eight years, it is pure, fresh, and young. Grain spirit is often referred to as "grain neutral spirit" in the United States because it will pick up flavors easily from the cask. Greenore 8-Year-Old is grain spirit made from corn and matured in first-fill bourbon barrels. It is quite rare because most grain goes into blends, but nevertheless, eight years is relatively young for a single grain bottling. For this you need a sweet tooth. **DR**

Tasting notes

Sweet and clean with vanilla. The wood contribution is wispy and delicate. It would taste great on ice cream, an alcoholic butterscotch; easy drinking for dessert lovers.

The remote Cooley Peninsula, home to Cooley distillery. →

Greenore 15-Year-Old

Cooley | www.cooleywhiskey.com

Region and country of origin County Louth, Ireland
Distillery Cooley, Cooley Peninsula
Alcohol content 43% abv
Style Grain

The Greenore 15-Year-Old is a groundbreaking Irish whiskey, bringing a whole new flavor profile to the category. It has a perfect balance between grain sweetness and oaky spice.

In simplistic terms, the way to make whisky is to take a grain or grains, make a beer by adding water and yeast, and then distill the beer. But distillery beer differs from brewery beer in one essential but fundamental respect: distillery beer is not made under sterilized conditions. In the production of single-malt whisky, natural bacteria give the malt barley beer a sour taste. It is not unlike Belgian lambic beer, which is fermented by natural yeasts and is regarded as the "Champagne of beer," but which possesses a sour, challenging flavor that for many is an acquired taste.

When distillers make grain spirit from grains other than malted barley, it is usually, though not always, the case that more than one grain is used. At least some malted barley is added because it is a strong catalyst for converting sugars to alcohol. With corn as the main cereal, the distiller's beer is altogether sweeter and flabbier—like soggy cornflakes soaked in hot milk. It is the distillation of this sweet, mulchy corn mix that forms the basis of Greenore. Considering that the characteristics of white oak are vanilla, yellow fruits, and candy, it is not hard to imagine how sweet the mix may be. But Greenore 15-Year-Old has swept the board at world whiskey awards because, after this number of years, astringency, tannins, and spices come into play, so the whiskey has more balance, depth, and variety than its eight-year-old sibling. **DR**

Tasting notes

If you know the music of Isobel Campbell and Mark Lanagan, you'll understand this whiskey. The sweet grain is Campbell, angelic, pure, sweet, and charming. The oak and spice is Lanagan, bringing darker and richer qualities. Apples and oranges, working perfectly.

Greenore 18-Year-Old

Cooley | www.cooleywhiskey.com

Region and country of origin County Louth, Ireland
Distillery Cooley, Cooley Peninsula
Alcohol content 46% abv
Style Grain

The making of grain whisky has little of the romance of pot-still malt and gets far less attention, partly because the stills used to produce it are too factorylike for many observers, but also partly because the distillers themselves rarely show them off. (Cooley, for instance, is tucked away on Ireland's east coast and is so well hidden from the main road that we drove past it three times before finding it.) But grain stills are certainly impressive. They're often called column stills because that is exactly what they are. At the big producers such as Beam, they are gigantic.

After all the accolades heaped on the Greenore 15-Year-Old, there was some risk attached to introducing the Greenore 18-Year-Old in 2011. The whiskey is still comparatively young alongside some of the weighty and aged grain whiskies of Scotland, but Irish grain is lighter and more susceptible to the ravages of wood. By eighteen years, the oak has had a marked effect, cutting into the sweetness of the grain in a way that drinkers either love or hate.

What happens next depends on the wood used to mature the spirit. The Cooley distillery has always been prepared to take its whiskey into new territories, and when Greenore 18-Year-Old was first released as the oldest Irish grain whiskey ever bottled, some debate ensued. Initially it could be considered a step too far, the spice and astringency of the oak cutting through the sweet grain suddenly and harshly halfway through the drinking experience. Plenty disagreed, and it grows on you over time. Even so, it is not for the fainthearted. **DR**

Tasting notes

Starts off in typical sweet and vanilla fashion but flip-flops significantly halfway through, with rapierlike spices cutting through its heart and chunky, chewy oak notes arriving. It is a surprise, but for the prepared, it can seem intriguing and very special.

Green Spot

Mitchell & Son/Irish Distillers/Pernod Ricard | www.irishpotstill.com

Region and country of origin County Cork, Ireland
Distillery Midleton, Midleton
Alcohol content 40% abv
Style Single pot still

A single malt is a whiskey from a single distillery, made from malted barley. A single pot-still whiskey, however, is made from both malted and unmalted barley. In the nineteenth century, pot-still whiskey was unique to Ireland and—after rum—it was the world's most popular drink.

In 1887, only one of the twenty-eight distilleries in Ireland did not produce pot-still whiskey. At this time whiskey in Ireland was sold not by the distillery but by a whiskey bonder. These merchants would buy new-make spirit from local distilleries and mature it in their own warehouses, only paying excise when the spirit was sold: thus the term "bonded." Mitchell & Son, one of Ireland's most famous wine merchants, started trading on Dublin's Grafton Street back in 1805. The company is still owned by the Mitchell family and run by Jonathan (fourth generation) and Robert (fifth generation). It is the only firm of whiskey bonders left in Ireland, so Green Spot is unique.

The name Green Spot comes from the family habit of marking casks of different ages with daubs of differently colored paint. There were once a Blue Spot, Red Spot, and Black Spot, but Green Spot was always the most popular. Green Spot single pot still doesn't carry an age statement but is between seven and ten years old. It is matured in both new and refill bourbon wood, as well as some sherry casks. Only a very limited quantity of Green Spot is bottled each year, making it very hard to find outside Ireland. However, Mitchell of Dublin always has a few bottles under the counter for you if you ask nicely. **PM**

Tasting notes

The nose crackles with pot still. There is greengage, gooseberry, and a hint of sherry. The flavor is at once sharp and brittle, yet yielding and ripe with linseed and mint. The sherry is subtle. A unique and sublime experience, the whiskey equivalent of a bungee jump.

The Irishman 70

Hot Irishman | www.hotirishman.com

Region and country of origin County Cork, Ireland
Distillery Midleton, Midleton
Alcohol content 40% abv
Style Pot-still/malt blend

Innovation can take many forms and can come from the most unexpected of places. Scotland is famous, of course, for creating Scotch, a blend of malt and grain whiskies. There has never been much grain whisky in Ireland, however, so when master distiller Bernard Walsh started to dig into the history of Irish whiskey, he was interested when he found some "recipes."

In the days when bonded merchants, rather than distilleries, sold whiskey, many took to making their own brands. Bernard found that Irish merchants, using stocks at their disposal, had created their own blends of pot-still and malt whiskey. Curious as to how some of these historic curiosities might have tasted, he collected together glasses, a funnel, and a selection of bottles, and set about some kitchen-sink blending. Bernard doesn't remember how many of these recipes he tried to re-create, but he does recall the lightbulb moment he tasted a 70:30 blend of malt and pot still. To put it mildly, it tickled him nicely.

Going back to Irish Distillers, he tweaked the mix using two different styles of pot still, one light and fragrant, the other heavier and oilier. Bernard already knew his way around Midleton malt and decided that all the elements should be exclusively from first- and second-fill bourbon casks.

It is almost unfair to call the Irishman 70 a blend, as that word carries with it assumptions that just don't work here. Perhaps the term "vatting" might be more accurate. Either way, Bernard promises that the Irishman 70 will be just the first of what might yet be a series of historically inspired bottlings. **PM**

Tasting notes

Considering this is matured in bourbon wood, there is a curious dried-fruit quality to this whiskey. The malt is ripe with raisins, spiked with mixed spice. The pot still crackles in the background like a pepper firework, fizzing and popping citrus, lime, and leather.

The Irishman Single Malt

Hot Irishman | www.hotirishman.com

Region and country of origin County Cork, Ireland
Distillery Midleton, Midleton
Alcohol content 40% abv
Style Single malt

Master distiller Bernard Walsh and his wife are obsessives. For years they searched for the ultimate Irish coffee before deciding it didn't exist and creating it themselves. In 1999 they launched the blindingly obvious yet totally original Hot Irishman, a readymade Irish coffee mix. It is made from fine Colombian coffee, dark brown sugar, and Irish whiskey, actually a pot-still Irish whiskey from Midleton.

Seven years later, the Walshes decided to release an Irish single malt into a market already stuffed with them. At first this might seem like madness, but Bernard knows his whiskey. He also has a relationship with Irish Distillers, who produce malt whiskey at the Midleton distillery but keep it for blending purposes; they have never released a distillery-bottled single malt. By not going taking the obvious road to Cooley, Bernard outsmarted his rivals by securing the only available Midleton-produced single malt.

This malt doesn't carry an age statement, but it is at least ten years old and is made up of two cask types, bourbon and sherry mixed more or less 60:40. Bernard visits Midleton and tastes at least once a month but isn't too concerned about keeping each and every bottle identical. "We're not McDonalds," he says. "Slight variations are part of the craic."

The real fun here is in the glass; the massive copper stills at Midleton were designed to make single pot still, not single malt, so this is a real box of tricks. Forget about the fiddly little differences you might get between two adjacent Scottish distilleries; triple-distilled Midleton malt is a creature unto itself. **PM**

Tasting notes

The sherry is a warm handshake; the whiskey, a bear hug. This malt is big and fat and round, and totally unlike anything else. There's apricot, honey over steaming porridge, and marshmallow smoothness. You don't so much get a finish as an encore.

Jameson

Irish Distillers/Pernod Ricard | www.jamesonwhiskey.com

Region and country of origin County Cork, Ireland
Distillery Midleton, Midleton
Alcohol content 40% abv
Style Pot-still blend

What can you say about the world's most famous and best-selling Irish whiskey? You can start by looking at how it came to hold that exalted position. John Jameson founded his distillery in Smithfield in 1780, and for the best part of the next two centuries, the family-owned company didn't really change their business model. They made pot-still Irish whiskey and left the marketing and selling to someone else.

By the middle of the nineteenth century, Irish whiskey had established itself across the British Empire (and therefore most of the world) as the gentleman's tipple of choice. This comfortable status quo meant that Jameson and other Dublin distillers were slow to react to the rise of blended Scotch. By the time they realized their position in the market had been undermined, it was too late. Political upheaval in Ireland, coupled with Ireland's bloody exit from the United Kingdom, meant the empire markets dried up, while Prohibition closed down the United States.

Jameson staggered on, and in 1966 it joined Powers and the Cork Distilleries Company to form Irish Distillers. A single brand was to be chosen to carry the flag for Ireland, and thanks to Jameson's former record in export markets, it was selected. The whiskey was then reformulated; it became a blend of light pot-still and grain whiskeys, and when Pernod Ricard took over, it poured millions into sales and marketing.

Jameson may once have had a fine reputation for its whiskey, but modern Jameson is a very different drink from that of old. Nowadays it's a brand first and a whiskey second. **PM**

Tasting notes

A welcoming waft of malt and spice from the glass promises great things, but the drink somehow fails to deliver. There's some mildly interesting citrus, but not much else. This is a whiskey of very limited charm, best drunk with ice, drowned with cola, or killed with ginger.

Jameson 12-Year-Old

Irish Distillers/Pernod Ricard
www.jamesonwhiskey.com

Region and country of origin County Cork, Ireland
Distillery Midleton, Midleton
Alcohol content 40% abv
Style Blend

If you think a bottle of whiskey could have nothing in common with the early days of radio, you'd be wrong. After all this is an Irish whiskey, so anything is possible. In 1885 Marconi conducted his first outdoor tests of "wireless telegraphy." Marconi's mother was none other than Annie Jameson, which makes this Nobel Prize–winner for physics and inventor of the radio the great-grandson of John Jameson, founder of the famed distillery.

In 1995 Jameson used the centenary celebrations of the invention of radio to trial a premium whiskey, the Jameson Marconi Special Reserve. It was a success, and Irish Distillers launched a permanent addition to their range, named after the year the distillery was founded—Jameson 1780. This was renamed in 2002 to reflect the minimum age of whiskies in the blend.

Although the Jameson 12-Year-Old is the next step up from regular Jameson, the whiskeys have little in common, as this is not a straight aging. It is a different blending heavily influenced by a lot of time in sherry butts. When this blend is put together, whiskey from first-fill casks is tempered with whiskey from bourbon wood along with whiskey from sherry butts on their second or even third filling. **PM**

Tasting notes

Years spent in sherry wood are apparent. The pot still that makes up 80 percent of this blend crackles with leather and spice, while the grain is almost buttery.

Jameson 15-Year-Old Single Pot Still

Irish Distillers/Pernod Ricard
www.jamesonwhiskey.com

Region and country of origin County Cork, Ireland
Distillery Midleton, Midleton
Alcohol content 40% abv
Style Single pot still

Back in the days when handlebar mustaches were fashionable and no self-respecting country had anything but a Union Jack flying over it, pot-still Irish whiskey was the most civilized drink on the planet. But if the nineteenth century belonged to pot-still Irish, the twentieth century belonged to Scotch. It went on to dominate the world, while in Ireland the whiskey business almost went the way of the dinosaur.

So in 1984, when this pot-still whiskey was made, it seemed that only old men in tweed drank pot still, and old men in tweed have a nasty habit of dying.

As the troubled twentieth century drew to a close, this whiskey was celebrating its fifteenth birthday in a cool warehouse in East Cork. Time had transformed it into something so special that Irish Distillers decided they would embrace the new millennium by bottling it. In other words, that most stubborn of whiskey styles, the single-pot-still Irish, a whiskey from the past was used to usher in the future.

Young people who had never heard of tweed started to get very excited about this whiskey and wondered what on Earth a "single-pot-still Irish" was. A "new" star took to the stage and since then it hasn't looked back. **PM**

Tasting notes

Soft marshmallow and crisp wafers, the yin and yang of pot-still whiskey are all here, and they battle it out with pillows of choc-mint vapors. A huge mouthfeel.

A Jameson's advertisement refers to George VI's coronation in 1937.

Jameson 18-Year-Old

Irish Distillers/Pernod Ricard | www.jamesonwhiskey.com

Region and country of origin County Cork, Ireland
Distillery Midleton, Midleton
Alcohol content 43% abv
Style Blend

Jameson was the brand that saved Irish whiskey, and for many people the terms "Jameson" and "Irish" are interchangeable. In an attempt to bring loyal customers with it, Irish Distillers has introduced a bewildering range of "special reserves." Jameson 12-Year-Old is by now a classic, and after its success, it was only a matter of time before older variants came on the market. The 18-Year-Old is not a straight aging of its younger cousin; this beast is subtly different.

When Irish Distillers was formed in 1966, the three remaining whiskey families closed their separate plants and built a new distillery. Midleton Mark II was designed not to produce a new and unique style of whiskey, but rather to reproduce the output of the three plants that had to close: Jameson, Powers, and old Midleton distillery. The Victorian buildings fell cold and silent, but their whiskeys lived on.

So unlike most Scottish distilleries, which can produce just the one kind of spirit, Midleton makes a vast range of whiskey and not just pot still, malt, and grain, but numerous types of each. The alchemy of aging isn't understood, and while we get on with our lives, what happens in the cool dark warehouses on the Dungourney Road is a mystery. Casks expand and contract with the seasons, and after more than eighteen years in wood, they are ready for drinking.

In this whiskey, two different weights or styles of pot still, aged in oloroso casks for at least eighteen years, are combined with some very delicate and equally old grain whiskey. The result is a very special treat for those who like the finer things in life. **PM**

Tasting notes

Mustiness of age to this, but it's very pleasant. The years have mellowed this nicely, it's soft and round with a honeydew melon sweetness complemented by vanilla pods. But it's the spiciness that most excites, as the pot still cracks black pepper over a decent cappuccino.

Jameson Gold Reserve

Irish Distillers/Pernod Ricard | www.jamesonwhiskey.com

Region and country of origin County Cork, Ireland
Distillery Midleton, Midleton
Alcohol content 40% abv
Style Blend

Jameson Gold was one of Irish Distillers' first forays into premium whiskeys. Back in the days when air travel was exotic and duty-free shopping was the last word in chic, this whiskey was dreamed up to capture the busy executives as they rushed through some airport in the Far East. This brand also marks another first, as this is where Jameson started experimenting with finishing old whiskeys in virgin oak.

By law, all Irish whiskey has to be matured in oak. But new wood is very aggressive, releasing lots of sweet vanilla notes into the spirit. This style suits a lot of American whiskeys, but triple-distilled Irish whiskey is a delicate creature and more suited to long years in casks on their second or even third fill.

However, they found in Midleton that fully mature whiskey did quite well when finished for a few months in first-fill virgin casks. The short rush of vanilla seemed to complement the sherry notes, giving it a honey-toasted sweetness. This, then, is the flavor profile that went on to become one of the signatures of the extended Jameson family and nowadays crops up to some extent in a lot of premium offerings. Jameson Gold is where it is at its most extreme, as here it gives the whiskey an almost liqueurlike sweetness, which you either love or loathe.

In common with most of the Jameson range of whiskeys, this brand does not feature an age statement of any description. However, the pot still in Jameson Gold Reserve is usually some of the oldest available for blending and can regularly be over two decades old. **PM**

Tasting notes

Everything has been taken to an extreme. The whiskey is almost oily and sticky sweet. There is a lovely salty butter toffee thing going on, but the whiskey is eventually overpowered by vanilla ice cream, which comes from the virgin oak. An alcopop for grown-ups.

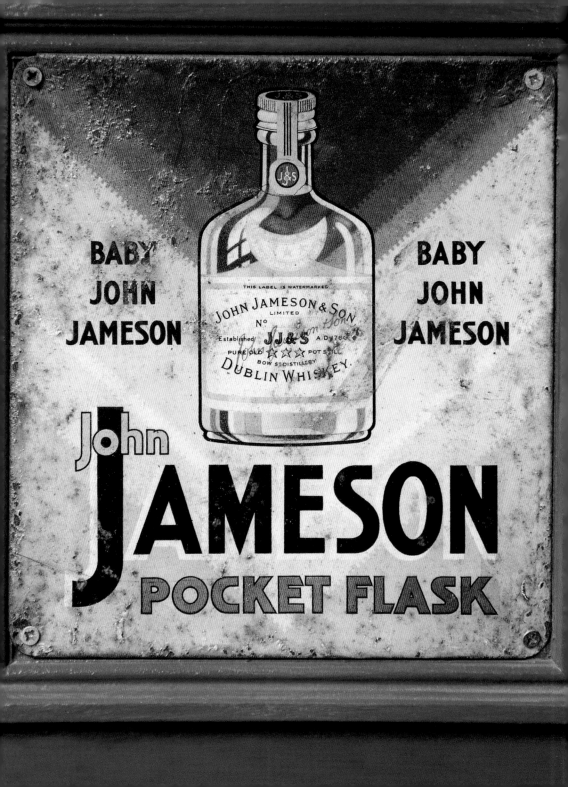

Jameson Rarest Vintage Reserve

Irish Distillers/Pernod Ricard
www.jamesonwhiskey.com

Region and country of origin County Cork, Ireland
Distillery Midleton, Midleton
Alcohol content 46% abv
Style Blend

The word *rare* gets thrown around whiskey labels a bit too freely, but in the case of this bottling it actually means something. Every year since 2007 (hence the word vintage n the name), Jameson has released a special reserve, and it contains some of the finest and oldest Midleton whiskeys available.

Because of the nature of limited release bottlings, the formula varies ever so slightly from year to year, but it is safe to expect some twenty-year-plus whiskeys, combined with an equally old second style of pot still that has been matured in port pipes. The whole thing is bottled without being chill-filtered at 46 percent abv.

With the growth of interest in rare whiskey, more and more distilleries are setting stock aside to be bottled for an elite group of fans. Every year a whiskey spends in the cask, over 2 percent of it will evaporate through the wood. Year on year this loss of volume takes it toll on both the amount of whisky in store, as well as its alcoholic content. This is what makes reserves like this more expensive and the lack of age statement on the bottle is deliberate, Irish Distillers preferring to promote what is in the bottle rather than the age on the bottle. **PM**

Tasting notes

Rich, oily, and packed with ripe fruit, port wood imparts an almost maple-syrup sweetness to the pot still, which rumbles along like a spiced vanilla milk shake.

Jameson Select Reserve—Small Batch

Irish Distillers/Pernod Ricard
www.jamesonwhiskey.com

Region and country of origin County Cork, Ireland
Distillery Midleton, Midleton
Alcohol content 43% abv
Style Blend

The almost endless interconnectivity of pot and column stills means that Midleton can and does produce a bewildering array of whiskeys and whiskey types, some of which only appear on the production schedule on a single day of the year.

At the heart of this Select Reserve is such a five-year-old grain, here making its first public appearance (hence the "small batch" status). Complementing this mysterious grain is a twelve-year-old pot-still whiskey, mostly coming from sherry wood. As for that wood, well, there are casks and there are casks, and Irish Distillers spends a considerable amount of time and money ordering and selecting its wood, so much so that cask management there is second to none and recognized as such across the industry. For this bottling, the Jameson master blender has personally selected the casks, so from the start this is a very high-quality offering.

Together, all these elements combine to make an unusual addition to the ever-expanding Jameson family. Initially released only in South Africa, which is a very hot market for all whiskey companies, success there will ensure this whiskey soon spreads to the rest of the world. **PM**

Tasting notes

The wood here is old but well behaved and gives the liquor toasty notes. There's plenty of spice too and a warm creamy underbelly, complementing the apricot.

The Jameson pocket flask—ideal for a nip while on the move.

Kilbeggan

Cooley | www.cooleywhiskey.com

Region and country of origin County Louth, Ireland
Distillery Cooley, Cooley Peninsula
Alcohol content 40% abv
Style Blend

Kilbeggan is a little town in the heart of the Irish Republic, roughly 55 miles (88 km) west of Dublin along the main road to Galway. This is a place where whiskey has been crafted for a long time. Production started in 1757 at Brusna distillery, which was renamed Locke's in 1846 after John Locke took over the business. They would hold the distillery until it closed, sadly, in 1958. The last Locke in charge, a great-granddaughter of John, was a bit of a party animal who neglected the business, favoring horse riding instead. The buildings were rented out to a German who used them as a Mercedes garage and a pigsty.

Locke's distillery seemed to have died, despite the fact that it survived the Prohibition era, with its drop in demand. But in 1982 its fate changed. A small group of enthusiasts in Kilbeggan decided to restore the old distillery. Inhabitants of the town donated time, money, and old artifacts, of which various ones are on display today in the attic of the malt barn. With love, patience, dedication, and passion, the entire complex was restored to its former glory. In 2011 Locke's started producing traditional Irish pot-still whiskey and single malts in small quantities, but the blend Kilbeggan is made at Cooley, who first became involved by maturing part of their whiskey in warehouses at Kilbeggan. After a few years, Cooley made an offer and acquired this little historical gem, which is managed by a wonderful couple—Brian and Bernadette Quinn. They took the initiative to restore the premises in the early 1980s, so a toast of Kilbeggan to them is the appropriate thing to do. **HO**

Tasting notes

This everyman's friend begins with delicate citrus notes, fresh peaches, and hot yeasty rolls, then heads into toffee and canned pears. Full body, gentle, with a medium-long finish. A permanent presence in my whiskey cabinet.

Kilbeggan 15-Year-Old

Cooley | www.cooleywhiskey.com

Region and country of origin County Louth, Ireland
Distillery Cooley, Cooley Peninsula
Alcohol content 40% abv
Style Blend

Kilbeggan is one of those sleepy rural Irish towns with a handful of shops and pubs and not a lot else. But what it also has is one of the prettiest and oldest distilleries in the world. Until a few years back, the old Kilbeggan distillery was little more than a museum, a silent and somewhat sorry symbol of Irish whiskey's decline and fall in the twentieth century.

But from the very beginning of Cooley distillery's establishment, its chairman, John Teeling, had plans for it. Many thought he was mad, others admired his chutzpah, but few thought anything would come of his intentions. That was until he moved the massive stills from nearby Tullamore Dew (which blocked the main road from Dublin to the west coast for several hours one Friday afternoon). Those stills were for show, but the next step was to get stills operating at Kilbeggan, to bring low wines from Cooley, and to finish off Kilbeggan spirit at Kilbeggan. Nothing symbolizes the change in Irish distillers' fortunes more than this reversal for the distillery. To ram home the point, some parts of the old distillery, including the waterwheel, have been brought back to life.

This particular expression of Kilbeggan was released to mark the 250th anniversary of the distillery in 2007, but it has established itself as an important core member of the Kilbeggan family. It has played a leading role in establishing premium and aged Irish whiskey. And with considerably more body and weight than the standard version, and a heavier dose of oak and spice, it is a big whiskey that has earned plaudits and medals across the world. **DR**

Tasting notes

The classic sweet green fruit associated with standard Irish blends really comes to the fore here. It's like adding a bassline to an acoustic song. The whiskey is richer, spicier, oakier, and fuller than the standard Kilbeggan and has some marzipan notes.

Kilbeggan 18-Year-Old

Cooley | www.cooleywhiskey.com

Region and country of origin County Louth, Ireland
Distillery Cooley, Cooley Peninsula
Alcohol content 40% abv
Style Blend

Irish whiskey is changing, and for the better. And while no one would argue that Irish Distillers and Bushmills don't make fine whiskeys, it's almost certainly the case that the current revolution and dynamism in the country would not have happened without the stubbornness of Cooley.

The Cooley company refused to accept that Irish whiskey had to be nonpeated and triple distilled to set it apart from Scotch. At one point, there were threats in the industry to buy the company and then close it down. That threat has gone away now, but it cannot be a coincidence that Irish Distillers has bolstered its niche premium pot-still offering and is putting out whiskey of the highest order.

Cooley subsequently installed a small working still at Kilbeggan and in 2011 started producing pot-still whiskey again, using an original recipe that includes a portion of 5 percent oats. It will, of course, be many years before we are able to taste aged versions of that. For now, though, the Kilbeggan 18-Year-Old will do. It is a blend, made in the traditional Irish way but aged for longer than most Irish whiskey. It has also spent some time in Madeira wood. The result is a fine, full, and classic whiskey. **DR**

Tasting notes

This twists and turns as sweetness, spice, and wood notes compete. Rich, full, and with a significant spice and tannin hit from the wood. An excellent whiskey.

Knappogue Castle 1951

Castle Brands | www.knappoguewhiskey.com

Region and country of origin County Offaly, Ireland
Distillery B. Daly, Tullamore
Alcohol content 40% abv
Style Single malt pot still

In the 1950s the historic but dilapidated Knappogue Castle in County Clare, Ireland, was bought by Mark Edwin Andrews, an American entrepreneur and whiskey enthusiast. Andrews collected casks of whiskey from the now-demolished B. Daly distillery in Tullamore, bottling it under his Knappogue Castle brand name when he felt it was sufficiently aged.

The last surviving B. Daly whiskey bought by Andrews is Knappogue Castle 1951. It was produced from malted barley by pot stills at the B. Daly distillery in 1951, aged for thirty-six years in sherry casks, and finally bottled in 1987. According to current chairman of the board, Mark Edwin Andrews III, "In many ways, my father's Knappogue Castle 1951 is the grandfather of today's fine Irish whiskeys. As the oldest and rarest known Irish whiskey, Knappogue Castle 1951 and the series of Knappogue Castle bottlings that it spawned, pioneered several innovative ways of presenting Irish whiskey, including the bottling of pure single malt, maturation of the whiskey in sherry casks, and bottlings with age or vintage statements. Now there are a number of other fine Irish whiskeys using these approaches." Subsequent Knappogue Castle releases have been distilled at Bushmills and Cooley. **PM**

Tasting notes

Huge notes of pear and apple, like a Calvados. Baked apple and poached pear are present, with honey, cinnamon, caramel, vanilla, and a trace of clove.

Locke's
8-Year-Old

Cooley | www.cooleywhiskey.com

Region and country of origin County Louth, Ireland
Distillery Cooley, Cooley Peninsula
Alcohol content 40% abv
Style Single malt

Irish whiskey has enjoyed some healthy trading years in the new millennium and many believe that, as it finds new markets in countries such as China and Brazil, its future is secure. If that turns out to be the case, Cooley will be able to take a great deal of credit.

A few years back, Irish whiskey was in serious trouble, and the few surviving distilleries banded together to form Irish Distillers. Turning a blind eye to the single malt from Bushmills, the new group pretty much defined how Irish whiskey would be by moving it away from Scotch, emphasizing the facts that Irish whiskey was triple distilled, nonpeated, and blended.

Cooley begged to differ. By resurrecting old Irish distillery names such as Locke's, it introduced double-distilled, peated, and single-malt whiskey and claimed history as its witness. Locke's is a single malt, and this version of it pays homage to John Locke, who took over the Kilbeggan distillery in the 1840s. The distillery still stands, and the Teeling family has started using it for limited production. This whiskey, however, is made at the Cooley distillery and sits neatly between the peated and challenging malts from Connemara and the world-class ones from Bushmills. An entry-level Irish malt, then, and none the worse for that. **DR**

Tasting notes

On the nose there are some sweet, citrus notes, predominantly orange and lemon. On the palate the citrus tends more toward lemon and lime.

Michael Collins
10-Year-Old

Cooley | www.cooleywhiskey.com

Region and country of origin County Louth, Ireland
Distillery Cooley, Cooley Peninsula
Alcohol content 40% abv
Style Blend

Cooley distillery founder John Teeling once said that the difference between a British businessman and an American one is that the former will create a product and then hope to find a market for it, whereas the latter will identify a gap and then create a product to fill it. In the drinks trade, certainly, the Americans have identified gaps in the premium spirits market and responded with multimillion-dollar success stories such as Patrón tequila and Grey Goose vodka.

The original version of this whiskey, with the same somewhat provocative Michael Collins name and fancy Champagne bottle packaging, was Cooley's attempt to find a place for premium Irish whiskey in America. It was launched early in the millennium at a time when, finding its feet, Cooley was bottling a lot of its stock for private-label and supermarket brands. Distributed through the same company as Grey Goose, it had nothing like as much impact.

This replacement contains ten-year-old whiskey and is a much stronger proposition. It is part of a vanguard of Irish whiskeys that are helping to define a new premium category. Michael Collins 10-Year-Old is aimed solidly at the U.S. market, where whisky in general is excelling. It is well worth looking for. **DR**

Tasting notes

Typically Irish and a little challenging. You will recognize the rich red and green apple notes and the honeyed, soft center. A classy, full-bodied Irish whiskey.

Midleton Barry Crockett Legacy

Irish Distillers/Pernod Ricard
www.irishpotstill.com

Region and country of origin County Cork, Ireland
Distillery Midleton, Midleton
Alcohol content 46% abv
Style Single pot still

Actually born in an Old Midleton distillery cottage, Barry Crockett is so much more than the celebrated second-generation master distiller. He is an alchemist. With just three local ingredients—water, barley, yeast—and flying the world's most complex distillery, he is able to produce a mind-boggling variety of distillates. So when it came to putting his name on a bottle, he was stuck. Which would he choose?

For a start, it had to be a single pot still, the kind of whiskey Crockett senior made when Barry was a child. The smells of his youth dictated everything—Barry wanted to capture the very essence of the area in which he had spent his life. So he chose delicate triple-distilled spirits with the grassy nose of fresh barley. He then matured the whiskey exclusively in American bourbon barrels with a top dressing of perfumed whiskey from unseasoned American wood.

Barry personally selects and tastes each and every cask that goes into Midleton Barry Crockett Legacy. This then is so much more than just another whiskey; it's the work of a lifetime—several lifetimes. As Barry says, he was only building on his father's legacy.

This is a light, delicate single pot still as gentle as the landscape around Midleton itself. **PM**

Tasting notes

A delicate fruit salad of pears and melons gives way to citrus and mashed banana. At 46 percent abv, this isn't chill-filtered, so there's subtlety to the flavors.

Midleton Single Cask 1996

Irish Distillers/Pernod Ricard
www.celticwhiskeyshop.com

Region and country of origin County Cork, Ireland
Distillery Midleton, Midleton
Alcohol content 46% abv
Style Single pot still

There was a time when the Midleton distillery was very wary of single-cask bottlings, but the good news is that the huge recent interest in Irish whiskey has made them (slightly) less cautious. This Midleton single-cask release is exclusive to the Celtic Whiskey Shop, and it is their third such offering. The shop is situated in Dublin city center, but they will be more than happy to courier you a bottle or two.

This whiskey was laid down in December 1996 and was matured in first-fill bourbon barrel 71578 until its bottling in October 2010. It is a triple-distilled sample of that unique Irish combination of malted and unmalted barley known as single-pot-still Irish. Midleton produces numerous styles of this whiskey, mostly used for blending. This, then, is a rare chance to taste a pot still on the lighter end of the spectrum. "Single pot still" shouldn't be taken as a catch-all term—these are all unique offerings and show how much potential there is in this category of whiskey.

By its nature, any single-cask offering is naturally limited, and in this case only 260 bottles were filled. The whiskey is sold at 46 percent abv and at this strength, there is no need for chill-filtering, so this whiskey is as nature intended. **PM**

Tasting notes

Lively with an almost lemongrass nose. Up front there are marshmallow and lighter dried fruits. A delicate creature, yet the pot still is still there on a whiff of linseed.

Granary openings at the old Midleton distillery. ➡

Midleton Very Rare

Irish Distillers/Pernod Ricard | www.irishdistillers.ie

Region and country of origin County Cork, Ireland
Distillery Midleton, Midleton
Alcohol content 40% abv
Style Blend

Launched in 1984, initially into the duty-free market, a new bottling of this whiskey is released annually, and it carries the year or the "vintage" in question. The industry calls this a "premium" product, and although the word *premium* has no standing in law, Irish distillers make up for that by showering this whiskey with all the trappings of exclusivity. This product is clearly aimed at those with plenty of disposable cash.

But toss aside the wooden box and the owner's scroll and what lies inside the numbered bottle? This is a pot-still-heavy blend, and like all Midleton whiskeys, it is free from the whiff of peat smoke. The vintage changes subtly every year, reflecting the stock that is available for blending at the time. As a rule all the constituent whiskies are at least twelve years old, but some of them are considerably longer in the tooth. Sometimes individual casks have been in storage for a quarter of a century. This means that earlier expressions of Midleton Very Rare contained whiskey made in the Old Midleton distillery, and although these are no longer available on the open market, they can be found if you look hard enough.

All the elements that make up Midleton Very Rare are vatted together and finished in virgin oak; that is, barrels that have not previously contained bourbon. This is a delicate process, as old whiskies can't take too much brash American wood, so at this stage casks are closely monitored. The finishing, however, gives Midleton Very Rare its trademark vanilla sweetness and helps to impose a house style on the eclectic range of whiskeys in the mix. **PM**

Tasting notes

The nose is treated to waves of dried fruits and warm spices. At first it is basically cream soda for adults, then the vanilla curtains part to reveal the show. The dance of sherry and pot still doesn't get any finer, with raisin tumbling into chocolate, which melts into honey.

Paddy

Irish Distillers/Pernod Ricard | www.paddy.ie / www.jamesonwhiskey.com

Region and country of origin County Cork, Ireland
Distillery Midleton, Midleton
Alcohol content 40% abv
Style Pot-still blend

Paddy whiskey came from the third founding arm of Irish Distillers, the Cork Distilleries Company. It gets its name from legendary salesman Paddy Flaherty, who took to the roads and lanes of Ireland in the 1920s and 1930s selling Cork Distilleries Company Old Irish Whiskey. Even then it was a bit of a mouthful, so it's not surprising that customers simply asked for Paddy Flaherty's whiskey. The name stuck, and soon Paddy's signature was attached to the bottom of every bottle.

Paddy whiskey started life in the Old Midleton distillery, which, although it is silent now, boasts an impressive visitors' center. It's also one of the world's most beautiful Victorian industrial complexes and is well worth a visit. While there, you can peek at the new Midleton distillery that was built next door. Along with Paddy, this is where Jameson and Powers are now made. However, a lot of the warehouses on site are still used, and some are even open to the public. Here the past and the present rub shoulders and although both distilleries, old and new, seem to have little in common, pot-still whiskey is still made in the same way it ever was.

Paddy whiskey is still very popular in the far south of Ireland, in the areas where Paddy Flaherty himself once plied his trade, though it is unlikely Paddy would recognize the whiskey that now bears his name.

Like Jameson and Powers, Paddy was reformulated in the late 1960s and tweaked several times since. Now it's a curious beast with a proportion of the blend being made up of Bushmills malt. The rest is a 50:50 split of grain and pot still. **PM**

Tasting notes

A ball of malt if ever there was one, with cracked black pepper over a perfume of warm cereal. A spicy aromatic nose with delicate vanilla and honey. Further background notes of honey and vanilla in the mouth with a dry and mellow finish and a tickle of pot still.

Powers
Gold Label

Irish Distillers/Pernod Ricard
www.irishpotstill.com

Region and country of origin County Cork, Ireland
Distillery Midleton, Midleton
Alcohol content 40% abv
Style Pot-still blend

When Alfred Barnard passed through Dublin in 1885 while researching his book, *The Whiskey Distilleries of the United Kingdom*, he gave Powers whiskey a glowing review: "It was as perfect in flavor, and as pronounced in the ancient aroma of Irish Whisky so dear to the hearts of connoisseurs, as one could possibly desire." In the home market, Powers was the only whiskey ever to give Jameson a run for its money; in fact, for a long time it remained the most popular Irish whiskey in Ireland. Powers Gold was, and is, darker, quirkier, and more characterful than Jameson: in short, Han Solo to Jameson's Luke Skywalker.

In the mid-1970s, the production of all Irish Distillers whiskeys was shifted to Midleton in County Cork, and the Powers plant in John's Lane, Dublin, was closed. With the move to Cork came a move in flavor. Like Jameson, Powers was reformulated as a blend, but while the former was neutered, Powers was left with about 80 percent good, old-fashioned, medium pot still, against which the grain works well. The whiskeys in Powers are typically older than those used in Jameson, with a fair amount of refill casks being used. Using refill casks minimizes the wood influence, so the flavor comes primarily from the distillate. **PM**

Tasting notes

The nose is a fireworks display of cereal, spice, and mint. The pot still grips the tongue, while the grain cracks a honeyed whip. Like nothing else on the planet.

Powers
John's Lane Release

Irish Distillers/Pernod Ricard
www.irishpotstill.com

Region and country of origin County Cork, Ireland
Distillery Midleton, Midleton
Alcohol content 46% abv
Style Single pot still

The Powers distillery in John's Lane, Dublin, was renowned the world over for the quality of its pot-still whiskey. When, in 1966, Powers merged with Jameson and the Cork Distilleries Company to form Irish Distillers, the John's Lane distillery closed and all production moved to Midleton, County Cork. In the 1970s Powers was reformulated as a blend, and, despite its high pot-still content, some of the taste that had so electrified Victorian society was lost.

So what did the whiskey from John's Lane taste like? The distillers at Midleton wondered the same thing, so they decided to build a time machine. They started by making up a special mash of malted and unmalted barley, then they fired up the stills and triple-distilled the wash, as would have been done all those years ago. Then they put the spirit into first-fill American bourbon casks, with a smaller amount going into the finest oloroso sherry butts to bring out the complex character of the whiskey. As the time machine was imaginary, they had to wait more than twelve years to see how it turned out.

The result is a fine expression of pot-still Irish, and a perfect tribute to the spiritual home of one of Ireland's most loved whiskeys. **PM**

Tasting notes

Pepper and spice, coconut, and toasted barley. With apricot, almond, and cocoa, you will find this a real old-fashioned fairground ride of a whiskey.

← Part of the large Powers distillery at John's Lane, Dublin, c.1845.

Powers Special Reserve 12-Year-Old

Irish Distillers/Pernod Ricard | www.powerswhiskey.com

Region and country of origin County Cork, Ireland
Distillery Midleton, Midleton
Alcohol content 40% abv
Style Pot-still blend

Many distilleries took the millennium celebrations as an excuse to release new and interesting bottlings. Irish Distillers have never been great at this, so when they announced Powers Special Reserve 12-Year-Old, there was much excitement. The whiskey quickly won over the public and went on to become a regular offering. However there is nothing new here.

Before distillery bottlings of Powers became the norm in the 1960s, there were as many varieties of Powers on sale as there were people selling it. Most of Dublin's whiskey bonders bought spirit hot from the still in John's Lane, filled it into their own casks, matured it in their own cellars, and sold it when they thought fit. The whiskey could only be bought from bonders, and they offered unfiltered, cask-strength whiskey at numerous ages at various prices. As this was the norm, terms such as "single cask" were meaningless. Large whiskey bonders would often experiment with their own wood finishes if they had Madeira, port, or sherry casks lying idle. However, small firms would bottle direct from a single cask, or even sell shots in a bar direct from a quarter cask.

Quarter casks, cask strength, exotic woods, age statements . . . it would seem that there is nothing new in whiskey. A lot of what was taken for granted in nineteenth-century Dublin is now seen as cutting-edge, customer-focused marketing.

This version of Powers is a straight aging of Gold Label; in other words, the whiskeys are the same as in the regular bottling, but here they are aged for at least twelve years, as opposed to four to seven years. **PM**

Tasting notes

This is Powers Gold Label with the amplifier turned up to eleven, to borrow a reference from the *Spinal Tap* movie. Everything is bigger and bolder than the younger whiskey, with the pot still in particular coming into its own and crackling with menthol and spice.

Redbreast 12-Year-Old

Irish Distillers/Pernod Ricard | www.irishpotstill.com

Region and country of origin County Cork, Ireland
Distillery Midleton, Midleton
Alcohol content 40% abv
Style Single pot still

Redbreast single pot still is one of Ireland's most celebrated whiskeys, and when it comes to gold medals, it more than holds its own against bottles costing many, many times more. It started life in 1903 when Jameson, who at the time only sold whiskey in bulk, agreed to supply the wine merchant Gilbey's with some new-make spirit. Being importers of fine sherry, Gilbey's simply filled their empty casks with Jameson that, once mature, they sold to the public. Gilbey's sold quite a range of Irish whiskeys but this whiskey was different, due to all those years in sherry wood. When held up to the light, the whiskey had what looked like a red breast, not unlike a robin's, and that's where the name came from.

Redbreast was an instant success with those who liked the finer things in life, so much so that before long it had earned itself a nickname, "the priest's tipple." So when the bonder trade came to an end in the late 1960s, instead of letting the brand die, Irish Distillers bought the well-regarded name and kept on making the whiskey.

For almost forty years, Redbreast ticked along, the only distillery-bottled single pot still in the market. Ireland's unique style of whiskey was on the edge of extinction, but refused to die. No money was spent on marketing or advertising, yet Redbreast kept, and indeed grew, a hard core of loyal drinkers. Then came the awards, then more awards, then yet more.

The formula for Redbreast is now subtly altered, being made from heavier pot-still whiskeys matured in sherry wood for at least twelve years. **PM**

Tasting notes

Like being hit in the face with a cake chock-full of raisins and prunes, all soaked in sherry and sprinkled with toasted almonds. There's pipe smoke, leather armchair, and a long, slow finish of spice, ground coffee, and licorice. A full-on assault on the senses.

Redbreast 15-Year-Old

Irish Distillers/Pernod Ricard
www.irishpotstill.com

Region and country of origin County Cork, Ireland
Distillery Midleton, Midleton
Alcohol content 46% abv
Style Blend

Redbreast has been the most consistently available single-pot-still whiskey. It has been on sale through thick and thin, even when Irish was out of fashion and hidden at the back of the bar all covered in dust. A lot has changed in the past decade, and now single-pot-still Irish is one of the most exciting categories in world whisky. This whiskey's relative, the Redbreast 12-Year-Old, has led the resurgence.

The Redbreast 15-Year-Old costs considerably more than its younger sibling, so what do you get for the extra three years, apart from a thinner wallet? For a start, it is bottled at a muscular 46 percent abv, so it isn't chill-filtered. Otherwise this is pretty much a straight aging; in other words, you are simply purchasing three extra years of maturity. Now, that may not seem like a lot, but a lot can happen in those three years, so it's all relative. Whiskeys also mature faster in Ireland than they do in Scotland, where it's colder, and—let's face it—Perth is simply nearer the North Pole than Cork.

The Redbreast 12-Year-Old is one of the world's best value buys and regularly outscores whiskies costing ten times as much. So whether the 15-Year-Old is worth a premium is up to you. **PM**

Tasting notes

A bold, assertive whiskey that redefines what whiskey should taste like. Full of chewy toffee, soft chocolate, coffee, and other delicious things that are bad for you.

Tullamore Dew

William Grant
www.tullamoredew.com

Region and country of origin County Cork, Ireland
Distillery Midleton, Midleton
Alcohol content 40% abv
Style Blend

Tullamore Dew is the wandering minstrel of the world of Irish whiskey, a brand from a long-abandoned distillery, passed from owner to owner but still playing bars across the world. Scottish distiller William Grant is the current owner; it bought Tullamore Dew because, despite decades of marketing neglect, the whiskey is second only to Jameson in U.S. sales, while in some European countries, it actually outsells Jameson.

This was the first Irish whiskey to be reformulated as a blend, and it quickly found purchase within the Irish community in America. In the 1950s, when the Tullamore distillery closed, the valuable brand was bought by Powers—which a decade later was one of the founding members of Irish Distillers. But for the next sixty years, little was done to advance the brand.

Tullamore Dew is a blend of pot-still, malt, and grain whiskeys matured for the most part in bourbon wood with a tiny fraction coming from sherry wood, and produced by Irish Distillers in Midleton. It has been done this way since the early 1970s, but William Grant's ambitious plans to take on Jameson in the United States may yet be the catalyst for a new distillery at some time in the future. Perhaps then this wandering minstrel will finally settle down. **PM**

Tasting notes

Shakes your tongue in a rather limp manner, but bracing cocoa rides in to save the day. A simple whiskey that is designed for drinking long with ice and a mixer.

Tullamore Dew 12-Year-Old

William Grant
www.tullamoredew.com

Region and country of origin County Cork, Ireland
Distillery Midleton, Midleton
Alcohol content 40% abv
Style Blend

There are many ways to keep drinkers loyal to a whiskey happy, and introducing an older version of the mother brand is not unusual. A straight aging is common in Scotland, where distilleries produce many versions of the same spirit by keeping it in various casks for different lengths of time. But when you have an orphan brand with no distillery attached, what can you do? How about inventing a whole new drink?

Jameson had already proved that you can sell premium versions with as little in common with the core brand as a racehorse has with a donkey. Irish Distillers has vast warehouses at its disposal, so it is not surprising that regular Tullamore Dew and Tullamore Dew 12-Year-Old are totally different animals.

This is a blend of triple-distilled, aged pot-still, and malt whiskeys with a dressing of grain. As is common with aged Midleton distillates, there is a huge oloroso influence at work here. In fact, the Midleton DNA is so strong that you could stick a Jameson 12½-year-old label on this product and no one would complain.

Under previous owners, this premium bottling won plenty of plaudits, but it never really got the promotion it deserved. Now this is one of the Tullamore variants singled out for greatness. **PM**

Tasting notes

Classy, spicy sherry and warm plum pudding. There is a tickle from the grain, but the aged pot-still whiskey is the real star here, bringing with it brittle almond toffee.

Tullamore Dew Black 43

William Grant
www.tullamoredew.com

Region and country of origin County Cork, Ireland
Distillery Midleton, Midleton
Alcohol content 43% abv
Style Blend

Over the past forty years, two men have done more than anyone to bring Irish whiskey back to its former glory. First is Midleton master distiller Barry Crockett. The second is the distillery's retired master blender Barry Walsh, the man who reinvented Irish whiskey. He took the traditional flavor profile of Irish and put it through the wringer, blending new combinations, experimenting with finishes, and forcing change on the world's most staid whiskey.

One of Barry Walsh's final whiskey creations was a premium offering of Tullamore Dew. The brand had long belonged to Irish Distillers, but was now owned by the Scottish distilling group William Grant. The first thing that Barry did was to pretty much start over. He did this by injecting some character—in the shape of some very spicy pot-still whiskey—into Tullamore Dew's pretty standard body, then maturing it in some high-quality oloroso casks. The result was a rebooted brand, with more than a nod in the direction of how Tullamore Dew originally tasted back in the 1950s, when it was made in the Irish midland. The whiskey was bottled at 43 percent abv; this is referred to in the name and was the strength at which a lot of Irish used to be bottled and sold. **PM**

Tasting notes

There is an intense, old-fashioned buzz to this, full of sherbet-powered sherry notes and bitter chocolate. Very well put together and great with a drop of water.

Tullamore Dew Single Malt

William Grant | www.tullamoredew.com

Region and country of origin County Louth, Ireland
Distillery Cooley, Cooley Peninsula
Alcohol content 40% abv
Style Single malt

The Tullamore distillery and its most famous master distiller, Daniel E. Williams, are long gone, but they have both gained a kind of immortality in Tullamore Dew. Without the brand, many would never have heard of the County Offaly town of Tullamore in the Irish Midlands, while on the label of every bottle, Mr. Williams lives on through his initials: DEW.

Unlike regular Tullamore Dew, which nowadays is a blend of whiskeys made by the Midleton distillery in County Cork, the whiskey in this most recent single-malt offering comes from the Cooley distillery in County Louth. Cooley makes some very fine single malts, and drunk individually, their port, sherry, and Madeira finishes are impressive. But in the case of Tullamore Dew Single Malt, all three whiskey finishes are combined. Satisfying though it would be to say that the mix is more than the sum of its parts, that is not entirely true. If distilling is the scientific part of whiskey making, then blending is the part that requires artistry. Getting any mix of whiskies right is a delicate balancing act, and, for the present writer, this blend of three finishes of the same single malt comes considerably short of the sum of its parts.

Tullamore Dew drinkers are a faithful bunch, and this all-malt offering from William Grant has been designed to give loyalists something to grow into. Some will find in it an intriguing melange of flavors, but novices who wish to learn more about Cooley whiskeys would be better off seeking out and tasting separate port, sherry, and Madeira-finished whiskeys and deciding which they prefer. **PM**

Tasting notes

The classic fruity Cooley nose of hard candy is overlaid by beguiling dried fruits, but there is an unfortunate buzz of sulfur in the background. This really makes its presence felt on the tongue, where it does battle with a confusion of dried fruits.

Tyrconnell

Cooley | www.cooley.com

Region and country of origin County Louth, Ireland
Distillery Cooley, Cooley Peninsula
Alcohol content 40% abv
Style Single malt

Tyrconnell is a beautiful, light single malt and rather rare for the Irish, since most of their whiskeys are made of malted corn and unmalted barley, and are thus blends. The Irish whiskey industry went into a serious decline around 1920, a consequence of Prohibition, since the United States had been its primary export market. The industry has yet to fully recover. Today there are only four distilleries remaining in Ireland, but combined they make over eighty different whiskeys. Cooley is the relatively new kid on the block, founded by businessman John Teeling. Displaying the Irish love for horses, tradition, and drinking, he had the Tyrconnell label redesigned to show a famous horse race. Thus a brand that had been around before Prohibition was successfully revived.

The whiskey is named after a famous racehorse. In 1876 the Watt family entered a chestnut colt named "The Tyrconnell" in an Irish classic horse race. Incredibly, it won at a hundred to one. Since the relaunch of the brand, the Tyrconnell Irish single malt has won several medals in spirits competitions.

Ireland is considered by many to be the cradle of whiskey, and once was the international market leader. Following misfortune, miscalculation, potato famine, rejecting the Coffey still, immigration, temperance, and Prohibition—sandwiched by two world wars—this changed, and Irish whiskey was dwarfed by its Scottish neighbors, who supposedly learned the trick of distilling from them in the first place. Well, the master is back and Irish whiskey is on the rise again with Tyrconnell out in front. Want to make a bet? **HO**

Tasting notes

Fresh pineapple, orange, lemon, vanilla cream, and butterscotch candy give way to cashew, linseed oil, and buttered toast. Pleasantly quiet, nutty, sweet, faintly astringent finish, which also contains malty cereal notes.

Tyrconnell Madeira Cask

Cooley | www.cooley.com

Region and country of origin County Louth, Ireland
Distillery Cooley, Cooley Peninsula
Alcohol content 46% abv
Style Single malt

Apart from its brand name, Tyrconnell has another link to the distant past. It is made in two pot stills that were acquired from the Watts distillery in Derry, Northern Ireland, and they are appropriate: Watts originally made Tyrconnell in days gone by. When looking into Irish whiskey history, dates get a little shady. A certain David Watt acquired ownership of the Abbey Street distillery in Derry in 1839, although his father had been involved with this company since 1824. At the end of the nineteenth century, Abbey Street was by far the largest distillery in Ireland.

In 1876 the Watt family's racehorse won, and they decided to launch the Tyrconnell whiskey brand to mark the occasion. Together with two other brands—Inishowen and Favourite—Tyrconnell became hugely popular in the pre-Prohibition United States, being advertised on huge posters in Yankee Stadium, New York. However, Prohibition was to spell the end of the giant distillery, which closed in 1925 and never revived. But why does the label say that Tyrconnell was established in the year 1762 instead of 1876? Well, 1762 appears to be the year that the Watt family first appeared on the Derry whiskey-making scene.

Whether or not drinkers worry about such details, it is the whiskey's taste that really matters. Raise your glass to the Madeira Tyrconnell, impregnated with a fortified wine from the archipelago of Madeira, roughly 620 miles (1,000 km) southwest of Portugal, of which country it is an autonomic region. The barrels give Tyrconnell an almost subtropical hue but leave the basic taste profile intact. **HO**

Tasting notes

A nose like someone opened the spice cabinet: cinnamon, clove, and nutmeg blend with the perfumed aromas of cedarwood, a dash of lemon, and hazelnut. The complex, long finish is reminiscent of warm apple pie.

Tyrconnell casks stored at Locke's Distillery Museum, Kilbeggan. →

Tyrconnell Port Cask

Cooley
www.cooley.com

Region and country of origin County Louth, Ireland
Distillery Cooley, Cooley Peninsula
Alcohol content 46% abv
Style Single malt

The distillery now known as Cooley was built in 1937 under another name, together with three other Irish distilleries. The foursome were owned by the state, and their purpose was to process diseased potatoes into methylated spirits—in other words, industrial alcohol. When the disease died out, the distilleries switched to molasses as base material; they remained in operation until 1985.

John Teeling and his partners bought the distillery, and Teeling single-handedly began to attack the near-monopoly of Irish Distillers, owned by the French drinks behemoth Pernod Ricard. He nearly lost the battle halfway through, but Heaven Hill Distillers in Kentucky provided backing—maybe the Irish-Americans had not forgotten their ancestral roots.

Today Cooley, a relatively small but serious player in the Irish whiskey field, is known for its innovative approach. John Teeling's business partner, Willy MacArthur, owned the rights to various old brands, one of them Tyrconnell. Both men decided to bring it back to life to underline the whiskey's pedigree. In this expression the heritage was recasked for a little while in a port pipe after having matured for ten years in ex-bourbon barrels. Enjoy the difference! **HO**

Tasting notes

Winey tones with violets and hyacinth, turning to apple, pear, mango, and a sourdough roll or scone covered in jam. Walnut and marshmallow in a medium finish.

Tyrconnell Sherry Cask

Cooley
www.cooley.com

Region and country of origin County Louth, Ireland
Distillery Cooley, Cooley Peninsula
Alcohol content 46% abv
Style Single malt

The Irish are the alleged inventors of whiskey making, but are not shy in copying successful new approaches, such as the wood finishes started by Glenmorangie in the 1990s. Cooley borrows more than that from its whisky neighbor, as most of its barley is Scottish.

Cooley distillery was the first new whiskey distillery to be set up in Ireland in more than a hundred years; it is Ireland's youngest, smallest, and—so far—only independent whiskey distillery. It started distilling in 1989 and produces malt, grain, and blended whiskeys. Inside the stillhouse are column and pot stills making not only Tyrconnell, Greenore, Kilbeggan, and Connemara, the core range of the distillery, but also a whole plethora of whiskeys made to order for supermarkets, liquor store chains, and firms requiring their own unique brand. One excellent example of the latter is a pot-still blend called Writers Tears, made for the eponymous company.

While the standard Tyrconnell whiskey has no age statement, the label on the Sherry Cask edition states ten years with a finish in sherry casks. While savoring this version of the famous Tyrconnell brand, named after a racehorse that won in 1876, appreciate a felicitous union of Ireland and Spain. **HO**

Tasting notes

Cut flowers, greenery, and floral scents mingle with candlewax and church incense layered over oranges and raisins. The finish is short, suggesting almonds.

The Wild Geese

Protégé International
www.thewildgeesecollection.com

Region County Louth **Distillery** Cooley, Cooley
Peninsula **Alcohol content** 43% abv **Style** Single malt
Full UK name The Wild Geese Irish Whiskey Collection
Full US name The Wild Geese Irish Soldiers & Heroes

The "Wild Geese" named by this whiskey were Irish soldiers who fled the country following the victory of William of Orange at the Battle of the Boyne in 1690. The men were often referred to as "the Wine Geese." Most of them settled in France, and, while some worked as soldiers of fortune, many went on to raise families and work in the drinks trade. John Lynch, for example, founded Château Lynch-Bages in Bordeaux, while Richard Hennessy's descendants now control 40 percent of the cognac distributed worldwide.

In the United States the "Wild Geese Irish Whiskey Collection" is known as the "Wild Geese Irish Soldiers and Heroes," no doubt to draw attention to the fact that most of the Wild Geese were among George Washington's principal aides—Matthew Thornton, George Taylor, and James Smith were signatories to the American Declaration of Independence. The brand promises "freedom for everyone," and, while it cannot deliver that, it is still a very tasty whiskey.

The malt in the bottle, which is not peated, comes from the feisty Cooley distillery in County Louth, so it is double-distilled, matured in bourbon casks, and does not carry an age statement. The whiskey is bottled at a spicy 43 percent abv. **PM**

Tasting notes

Comes alive on the tongue with a display of cereal and ripe berries. The finish of vanilla ice cream with a twist of oak and cracked black pepper is marvelous.

The Wild Geese Rare Irish

Protégé International
www.thewildgeesecollection.com

Region County Louth **Distillery** Cooley, Cooley
Peninsula **Alcohol content** 43% abv **Style** Blend
Full UK name The Wild Geese Irish Whiskey Collection
Full US name The Wild Geese Irish Soldiers & Heroes

The key to any good blended whiskey is choosing the right casks and striking the correct balance between consistent elements. The whiskey in the Wild Geese range comes from Cooley distillery, the smallest and newest of Ireland's three remaining plants, where both malt and grain whiskey are produced under the same roof. A lot of the young product goes into the private label trade, where price points are more important than anything, but the whiskey ages well and, having been in business for a quarter of a century, Cooley now has some excellent stocks to draw upon.

Cooley malt is light and fragrant, while the grain is firm and smooth, so the trick is to find good casks with enough stock to give consistency. In the Rare Irish blend, the grain gives real structure, supporting the malt and allowing it to hit the high notes, which it does beautifully. The vanilla in the forefront of the whiskey owes its presence to first-fill casks.

With this brand there's more blarney on display than you'd find in the Irish castle of the same name, so buyer beware: whatever the label says, there is nothing particularly "rare" about this whiskey. Instead, this is a very solid, nicely put together blend with plenty of character. And that's a fact. **PM**

Tasting notes

A fragrant nose of melon and honey. As smooth as a vanilla milk shake, with the bite of dark chocolate. The finish pulsates away on waves of pepper and spice.

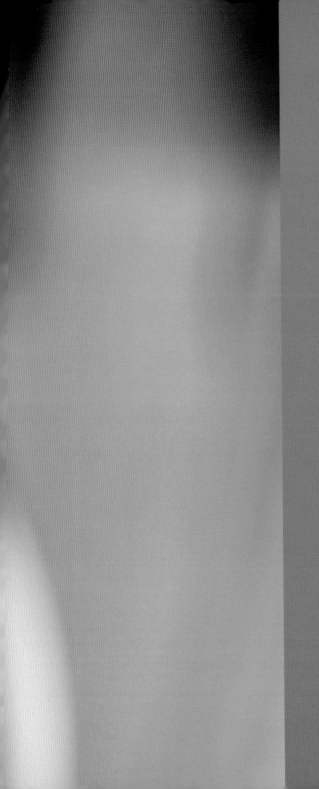

UNITED STATES

1512 Barbershop Rye

1512 Barbershop
www.1512spirits.com

Region and country of origin California, United States
Distillery 1512 Spirits, Sonoma
Alcohol content 45.5% abv
Style Unaged rye spirit

Salvatore Cimino, owner of 1512 Spirits, runs a San Francisco barbershop that became the namesake for the distillery's first release, 1512 Barbershop Rye. During Prohibition it was not uncommon for barbershops to operate as fronts for bootlegged whiskey distribution. One thing is sure—Salvatore's operation is a throwback to then. Hailing from three generations of distillers (read: moonshiners) gave him insight into the craft of whiskey making at an early age.

The 1512 involves a decidedly purist approach to whiskey making. The distillery mills (grinds) by hand the finest rye grain they can source. The grain is mashed or cooked in batches that are tiny in comparison to larger distilleries. The fermented mash is distilled in an old-fashioned copper pot still over open flames, which increases the sugar concentration in the finished distillate. The result is a fuller body or weight to the spirit.

Salvatore's goal from the start was to release 1512 as an unaged spirit. It took a great deal of honing and tweaking to retain the flavor of the rye grain. The label makes the not-so-subtle reference to this being the distillery's first "public" release. With aged whiskey coming down the pipe, it likely won't be the last. **JP**

Tasting notes

Green apple, pear, and fragrant rye grain on the nose. The palate is crisp and clean with peppery rye shining through. The finish is all rye, mild pepper, and licorice.

Ancient Ancient Age 10-Year-Old

Age International
www.greatbourbon.com/ancientage10.aspx

Region and country of origin Kentucky, United States
Distillery Buffalo Trace, Frankfort
Alcohol content 43% abv
Style Straight bourbon

Ancient Age was created shortly after the end of Prohibition by Schenley Distillers Corporation, one of the "big four" post-Prohibition spirits companies. Schenley owned many distilleries and assigned one it had in Frankfort, Kentucky, to make its new bourbon.

Since you can't make bourbon overnight, and whiskey supplies were still very tight in 1936, Schenley acquired some "bourbon style" whisky made in Canada to get things started. The name was a way to sound old at a time when most whiskey wasn't.

The new bourbon was successful. It was the principal whiskey produced at that distillery, which adopted its name informally though never officially. Today it is known as the Buffalo Trace distillery, but it still makes Ancient Age Bourbon.

For many years, the Ancient Ancient Age 10-Year-Old (yes, Ancient appears twice) has had a reputation as a great value bourbon. It was sold only in Kentucky, adding to its mystique, though now a few Chicago-area retailers carry it as well. Don't let the age statement fool you. Even at ten years, this is an old-fashioned bourbon that bites back. People expected that in the old days, just as they expected a lot of gold leaf on the label. **CKC**

Tasting notes

Spicy, with char and tannin. Licorice, light clove, butter, and plenty of sharpness and heat despite what should be the mellowing effects of age. A clean, dry finish.

Baker's 7-Year-Old

Beam Global | www.smallbatch.com/bakers

Region and country of origin Kentucky, United States
Distillery Jim Beam, Clermont
Alcohol content 53.5% abv
Style Straight bourbon

Baker's Bourbon was named after Baker Beam, who, like the bourbon that honors him, is quiet and unassuming. Baker Beam was the day-shift distiller at the main Jim Beam plant at Clermont, Kentucky, until he retired in 1992. That's the distillery his father, grandfather, and other Beam family members built after Prohibition at the site of a gravel pit the family operated during the drought.

Jim Beam was Baker's great-uncle. Baker's grandfather, Park, was Jim Beam's brother, partner, and chief whiskey maker. Baker's father, Carl "Shucks" Beam, succeeded Park and preceded Baker in the distiller's job at Clermont, which Baker shared with his brother, David, who worked the night shift. Baker and David grew up in the lovely old wood-frame house that still stands on the hill overlooking the distillery, surrounded by aging warehouses.

Baker's Bourbon was created as part of Beam's Small Batch Bourbon Collection. Although three of the four whiskeys in the collection, including Baker's, are based on the same Jim Beam mash bill, each has slightly different specifications and a different taste profile. Baker's is 53.5 percent abv and seven years old. To its fans, that is the perfect age for Beam bourbon; maturation is ended just at the point where the barrel character has developed enough to complement the clean Beam distillate and temper the sometimes foxy taste of Beam yeast.

Baker was still distiller at Clermont when Baker's Bourbon was created. It would be just like him to make his bourbon the best but not tell anyone. **CKC**

Tasting notes

Toasted almonds and dark fruit with suggestions of smoked meat and old leather, relieved by a little citrus zest, all spread over a big, fat caramel and vanilla middle. This laser-focused whiskey knows what it is and has a stiff spine.

Basil Hayden's

Beam Global | www.smallbatch.com/basilhaydens

Region and country of origin Kentucky, United States
Distillery Booker Noe, Boston
Alcohol content 40% abv
Style Straight bourbon

Basil Hayden emigrated to Kentucky from Maryland in about 1796, as part of a large group of English and Irish Catholics who settled in the area around present-day Bardstown, Kentucky. In 1882, his grandson, Raymond, established a distillery at Hobbs, Kentucky, a stop on a branch of the Louisville and Nashville Railroad.

In addition to access to the railroad, the site had two reliable springs. Hayden's distillery was large and modern, but for marketing purposes he decided to cultivate an image more typical of the previous century, the era of his grandfather, Basil, even though the era of the traditional farmer-distiller had long since passed. To foster that image, he named his whiskey Old Grand-Dad in tribute to Basil. Both the product and its marketing were highly successful, and Old Grand-Dad (with a portrait of Basil on the label) became one of the nation's leading bourbons, both before and after Prohibition.

Beam created Basil Hayden's bourbon a little while after getting Old Grand-Dad as part of its National Distillers acquisition in 1987. In addition to a venerable name and profitable price point, Old Grand-Dad had a tangible product difference, a very high rye content as compared with other bourbons, about twice as much. Basil Hayden's is that same recipe at eight years old and 40 percent abv, the relatively low abv being a concession to rye's strong flavor. Although many enthusiasts complain about the low abv, Basil Hayden's has found a market among drinkers who normally don't like bourbon, including many Scotch fans. **CKC**

Tasting notes

Sometimes unfairly dismissed as a "beginner's whiskey," this has a mild, sweet, and rye-heavy flavor with an incredibly smooth and mellow taste. Honey and mild spice on the palate, followed by a short finish—try it with just a drop of water.

Bernheim Original Kentucky Straight Wheat

Heaven Hill Distilleries | www.bardstownwhiskeysociety.com

Region and country of origin Kentucky, United States
Distillery Heaven Hill, Bardstown
Alcohol content 45% abv
Style Straight wheat whiskey

Bernheim is not the first wheat whiskey ever made; a spirit should never be described as "the first" or "the only" without checking the facts rigorously, and a long way back. Humans are wonderfully innovative at finding new ways to make alcoholic beverages. However, it is the first sold commercially since Prohibition, and while some craft distillers have made wheat whiskeys since the launch of Bernheim in 2005, it is by far the biggest, most widely available, and—at its usual five years old—the most mature.

Straight wheat whiskey is governed by the same federally regulated definitions and regulations as bourbon, except that at least 51 percent wheat is used (Bernheim is "about" 51 percent wheat, 39 percent corn, and 10 percent malt, according to the distillery). As you might expect from the smoother, less spicy character of wheated bourbons, this makes Bernheim soft, approachable, and quite friendly, even with the assertiveness of new charred-oak aging.

Bernheim is perfect for introductions. If you want your friends to drink whiskey, if only to make sure there's something good available when you visit them, Bernheim opens that door. "It's wheat whiskey" blows away any preconceived notions people might have about bourbon (or rye), and opens their minds to give it a fair chance. The smooth but flavorful whiskey—not too hot, not too woody, not too spicy—will do the rest. This is a whiskey that makes friends.

You will want to keep a bottle for yourself, of course. Take a sip in mid-afternoon and bring a smile to your face. It is a whiskey that is easy to love. **LB**

Tasting notes

Sweet and easy on the nose, with brittle mint crackling through the candy. You can feel that bit of extra proof, but the mint smooths and the spun sugar melts on the tongue. Don't be surprised to catch a quick peek of corn just before the gentle finishing coast begins.

Blanton's Single Barrel

Age International | www.blantonsbourbon.com

Region and country of origin Kentucky, United States
Distillery Buffalo Trace, Frankfort
Alcohol content 46.5% abv
Style Straight bourbon

By 1984, Americans were drinking half as much American whiskey as they had two decades earlier. Many believe it was young Japanese drinkers, rejecting the drinks of their parents' generation, who saved American whiskey from a slide into oblivion. It is certainly true that Japan was the first major market beyond North America to develop a thirst for bourbon. In 1984, the Kentucky distillery now known as Buffalo Trace, then owned by Age International, introduced the first single-barrel bourbon. Though created for Japan, it was introduced in America as well. It was named after Albert Bacon Blanton (1881–1959), who had run the distillery for thirty-one years.

Master distiller Elmer T. Lee, a Blanton protégé, was charged with creating Blanton's eponymous bourbon. Lee recalled that Blanton preferred bourbon from Warehouse H, and since 1984 every drop of Blanton's Bourbon has been aged there. Blanton's was a pioneer in providing lots of information about the whiskey's provenance. Each partially handwritten label shows the barrel number, dump date, and exact location in Warehouse H where the whiskey aged. Another feature of the packaging is the cork stopper topped with a tiny bronze sculpture of a horse and jockey in full stride. There are eight different poses. Put them all together, and they spell B-L-A-N-T-O-N-S.

Because Blanton's has been around for almost thirty years and doesn't offer any of its line extensions beyond the United States, it doesn't attract much attention, but it is nevertheless one of the finest bourbons made. **CKC**

Tasting notes

Although each barrel is slightly different, the Blanton's flavor profile is dry, subtle, and harmonious. It aims for sophistication and achieves it with an even balance of rye spice and barrel sweetness. Careful tasting teases out mint and other herbs, with just enough char.

Booker's Bourbon

Beam Global | www.smallbatch.com/bookers

Region and country of origin Kentucky, United States
Distillery Jim Beam, Clermont
Alcohol content 60.5 to 63.5% abv
Style Straight bourbon

Frederick Booker Noe Jr. (1929–2004) was the son of Frederick Booker Noe and Margaret Beam, Jim Beam's daughter. All of the descendants of Jacob Beam (1770–1834) are considered bourbon royalty, but Jim Beam's line is especially prestigious, due to the eponymous brand he launched just after Prohibition.

When Booker reached adulthood, the distiller at Beam was his second cousin, Carl Beam, son of Jim's brother, Park, who had always been the family's chief whiskey maker. Booker's mother asked Cousin Carl to train Booker alongside his own sons, Baker and David. Eventually, Baker and David succeeded their father at Beam's Clermont distillery, while Booker was put in charge of a second distillery at Boston, Kentucky.

All of the production offices were at Clermont, and Booker enjoyed being left alone. He did things his own way, forever changing a pipe here and a valve there to make the operation more efficient or flexible. Toward the end of his career, it was Booker's outgoing personality that earned him a new role as brand ambassador, both for the flagship Jim Beam Bourbon and for a new super-premium brand named after him.

A distiller has the right to tap any barrel for his personal use. Booker liked certain floors in certain warehouses and whiskey that was six to eight years old. Whiskey prepared for sale is filtered and diluted, but Booker had no use for that. The whiskey that bore his name would reflect all his preferences.

Booker received many tributes after his death. The distillery he once ran now bears his name. But there is no better reflection of the man than his bourbon. **CKC**

Tasting notes

A straightforward collection of bourbon's greatest hits—caramel, vanilla, anise, char, hints of basil and spearmint, with a corn mouthfeel almost as thick as syrup. Because the abv is so high you will taste more after you add water.

Breaking & Entering Bourbon

St. George Distillery | www.stgeorgespirits.com

Region and country of origin Kentucky, United States
Distilleries Various
Alcohol content 43% abv
Style Bourbon blend

St. George Spirits makes all of its own whiskeys, vodkas, and gins, but decided to try a different approach with Breaking & Entering bourbon. The release is the distillery's first foray into sourcing whiskeys from established distilleries and blending them into a unique finished whiskey all its own.

A large proportion of U.S. whiskey is produced by fewer than ten distilleries, many of which are based in Kentucky. With a whiskey boom currently underway, few distilleries have excess or unique product to sell to smaller operations. Some independent bottlers have managed to source whiskey from large distilleries and bottle under another label, but that is different.

St. George wanted to have an opportunity to select barrels that offered the most flexibility for their finished blend. To accomplish this, they hand-selected eighty barrels of five- to seven-year-old bourbon from some of Kentucky's largest producers. The barrels were brought back to the distillery's headquarters in a former naval aircraft hangar in Alameda, California. There, St. George's distillers Lance Winters and Dave Smith worked with a number of iterations of the blend before arriving at something unique and quite different from other bourbons on the market.

Breaking & Entering bourbon aligns well with St. George's house style of whiskeys. It has many layers of flavor and complexity, but also brightness and vibrancy. The name is a sly reference to the fact that St. George "broke in" and "stole" barrels from some of the country's biggest distilleries. The result is truly greater than the sum of its parts. **JP**

Tasting notes

Vanilla and banana cream emerge quickly on the nose with flint, dried golden fruits, and well-integrated oak. The palate is balanced with honey, toffee, white pepper, wood spices, burnt caramel, and tea. The finish is lively with corn, spice, honey, and orange peel.

Buffalo Trace

Sazerac | www.buffalotrace.com

Region and country of origin Kentucky, United States
Distillery Buffalo Trace, Frankfort
Alcohol content 45% abv
Style Straight bourbon

The way Sazerac tells it, when the company decided to change the name of its Leestown distillery in 1999, it had no intention of also creating a new bourbon using the new name. That came later, as the name became known and people started to ask where the bourbon was. By 2001, Buffalo Trace bourbon had been created and launched (from the existing whiskey stocks, obviously), and was in limited distribution. It has grown steadily ever since.

Sazerac has been a serious player in the bourbon whiskey business for only about twenty years. Most of its brands were acquired. Buffalo Trace was its first attempt to build a mainstream brand from scratch. So far, so good.

The Buffalo Trace back label says it is "the very finest bourbon created at the Buffalo Trace Distillery." That's quite a claim, considering how much bourbon is made there (a lot) and all of the different brand names under which it is sold (dozens of them). It came along at a good time, early in bourbon's modern renaissance. Buffalo Trace is crafted for modern tastes, both in its image and the whiskey itself. When you visit the distillery in Frankfort, no distinction is made between the place and the product. Buffalo Trace bourbon is the main focus, despite the company's large and diverse bourbon portfolio.

The taste of Buffalo Trace bourbon has evolved from its early days, from a good whiskey that seemed a little too young, to an outstanding and fully mature whiskey that has earned the description of "confident" that also appears on its copy-heavy back label. **CKC**

Tasting notes

A sweet first impression of concentrated caramel but finishes dry. The overall flavor is big, rich, and complex. Imagine popcorn, generously buttered and then dusted with oregano. The mash contains very little rye and puts the lie to people who say corn has no flavor.

A sculpture recalls the buffalo herds whose trace, or trail, passed the distillery site. ➡

Bulleit

Diageo | www.bulleitbourbon.com

Region and country of origin Kentucky, United States
Distillery Four Roses, Lawrenceburg
Alcohol content 45% abv
Style Bourbon

Former lawyer Tom Bulleit relaunched his family's bourbon business in 1987, and it is his personal touch that has played a large part in the success of this relatively new brand with the old-school character. Tom is on the road constantly, letting people taste his whiskey and meeting and greeting all those who express an interest. And people seem to love meeting the man whose name is on the label.

But none of that would work if there wasn't good whiskey in the bottle. Tom Bulleit says his whiskey is "frontier bourbon," old-style, rye-heavy, and unapologetic. "It's an old family recipe, passed down from my great-great-grandfather Augustus," he says. "It's a sophisticated recipe, too: two-thirds corn and one-third rye. The end, that's all. It would be hard to forget!" he laughs.

"No one was doing a high-rye bourbon. Old Fitz was a great wheated bourbon, big when I was young, but no one was doing high-rye. We tried it, and loved the taste of the white dog. Between six and eight years of age, and it's ready. Maker's has a great taste profile in wheated bourbon, and we're at the other end of the scale, a drier presentation."

Taste Bulleit next to a rye whiskey and you'll see just how much rye is in there. It's old-fashioned bourbon with a muscular, solid punch. **LB**

Tasting notes

Rye grains, mint, and a hint of warehouse wood mingle in the nose. Smooth, with corn, oak, and mint that doesn't overwhelm. The finish is tenacious and sweet.

Bulleit Rye

Diageo | www.bulleitbourbon.com

Region and country of origin Indiana, United States
Distillery Lawrenceburg, Lawrenceburg
Alcohol content 45% abv
Style Straight rye

When Bulleit announced that it was coming out with a rye whiskey, a lot of people thought, "Bulleit Rye? With all the rye smack in Bulleit Bourbon? Why bother?" Tom Bulleit chuckles when asked about it, and agrees: "It's a lot of rye. But try 'em side by side, cut back substantially—I would cut them all the way back to forty proof. I like to taste whiskeys that way. They're very different—different in taste, different in the nose. There's still a substantial corn note in the bourbon. You can't overcome that with rye."

But there was another reason for the venture: bartenders. "For years bartenders have said, 'Make a full rye for us,'" Tom claims. "A lot of the classic cocktails call for rye. So seven or eight years ago, we were saying, let's take a try. Then as we progressed with distilling and laydown, rye got bigger and bigger. We had to push back launch twice to make sure we had full supply." That's what rye whiskey's been like for the past ten years!

Bulleit Rye is made from a mash bill of 95 percent rye and 5 percent malt. It's aged around five to seven years. This one is good in a cocktail—it makes a great Manhattan. But don't deny yourself the simple pleasure of sipping it, pouring it over ice, or even building a highball in a tall glass with a lot of ice and some ginger ale. Why'd they bother? Why not! **LB**

Tasting notes

Pepper and mint in the nose, light and sweet in the mouth. There's a disconnect between big, bold Bulleit Bourbon and this drinkable rye; get over it, and enjoy.

← Bulleit bourbon is available ready-mixed with cola.

Catdaddy Carolina Moonshine (Batch 105)

Piedmont Distillers | www.catdaddymoonshine.com

Region and country of origin North Carolina, United States **Distillery** Piedmont, Madison
Alcohol content 40% abv
Style Flavored spirit

The increasing number of American distillers using the term "moonshine" is apparent to anyone who visits the whiskey section of a local liquor store. The term referring to bootleg liquor made by mountain men and outlaws is generally a marketing person's attempt to add a dose of gritty authenticity to a product. What consumers find on store shelves today couldn't be further from real moonshine. The biggest difference is summed up best by Piedmont Distillers president, Joe Michalek, "They [moonshiners] don't pay their taxes. We do!"

Piedmont's first product, Catdaddy Carolina Moonshine, was released in the fall of 2005. The packaging is reminiscent of an old clay jug that moonshiners in the southeastern United States used to reserve the best 'shine. Apart from that pesky matter of having to pay tax, the clever packaging and the crystal clear color of the spirit within invite close comparison to the illegal booze.

Piedmont Distillers stumbled across the recipe for Catdaddy while trying to duplicate the classic "American Pie" flavored moonshine, which is moonshine infused with cinnamon and other flavorings. The result wasn't exactly what they were hoping for, but it was something quite different from any other product.

Catdaddy is a heavily spice-infused corn-based liquor that has been slightly sweetened. Many try to decipher what is in the blend of spices that gives Catdaddy its one-of-a-kind flavor profile. Most fail to guess correctly, but it sure is fun trying. **JP**

Tasting notes

This spirit is as distinctive as any on the planet. Think unaged corn whiskey that's been flavored with a bold blend of baking spices. The nose erupts with nutmeg, allspice, vanilla, clove, and rock candy. The palate is sweet Christmas eggnog and vanilla taffy.

Charbay Hop Flavored Whiskey Release II

Charbay | www.charbay.com

Region and country of origin California, United States
Distillery Charbay, Napa Valley
Alcohol content 55% abv
Style Hop-flavored whiskey

Charbay's father-and-son creative team of Miles and Marko Karakasevic are the twelfth and thirteenth generations in a long line of distillers. When your family has distilled spirits for more than 250 years, the pull to step away from tradition can be strong. Having worked for his father since the age of ten, and planning for the day he would create his own style of whiskey, Marko had his "eureka!" moment in 1999.

Whiskey is distilled from a crude brew called "distiller's beer." Not exactly the stuff you'd enjoy on a hot summer day, but beer nonetheless. Taking note of this fact, the father-and-son duo wondered what would happen if Charbay used top-quality bottle-ready pilsner to distill their whiskey. They set out to determine just that, starting with 20,000 gallons (75,708 liters) of Northern California microbrewed pilsner, fortifying it further with choice hops, and then distilling it in a classic alembic Charentais pot still. This step alone took over three weeks of nearly nonstop distillation to yield 1,000 gallons (3,785 liters) of spirit. It was then placed in custom-charred, new oak barrels for aging. Strongly opposed to whiskeys that take on too much oak and wood flavor while aging, Charbay aged the whiskey for no longer than six years.

After aging, it is removed from the barrel, cut with ultrasoft purified water, and then placed into stainless-steel tanks for a whopping three years. According to Marko, this step helps the whiskey to settle as the flavors marry to the final bottling proof of 55 percent abv. Release II consists of five barrels from the initial twenty-four barrels originally distilled. **JP**

Tasting notes

The nose evolves dramatically in layers of caramel, muscat wine, raisin, and apricot. Hops provide an immense floral punch. A massive whiskey, syrupy, redolent with toffee, rum-soaked fruits, and exotic spices on the palate, closing with a hoppy beer finish.

Colonel E. H. Taylor Old Fashioned Sour Mash

Sazerac | www.buffalotrace.com

Region and country of origin Kentucky, United States
Distillery Buffalo Trace, Frankfort
Alcohol content 50% abv
Style Straight bourbon

Colonel E. H. Taylor Jr. Old Fashioned is a limited-edition sour mash, released in 2011. It was vaguely known that when Taylor himself owned the distillery, in the nineteenth century, an unconventional sour-mash technique was used. In 2002, Buffalo Trace distillery set out to rediscover it. Sour mash, used by all major American whiskey distilleries, usually involves tempering new mash with spent mash from a previous distillation. The acidic spent mash lowers the pH and creates a hospitable environment for the yeast. It also ensures consistency from batch to batch.

Souring is also accomplished by introducing lactobacillus, which produces lactic acid. Taylor's technique, re-created by Buffalo Trace master distiller Harlen Wheatley, was to let the new mash rest, allowing lactobacillus to develop naturally. Wheatley distilled the results, put it in barrels, and bottled it for sale nine years later. The experiment was a success.

Taylor himself founded and owned several distilleries in addition to Buffalo Trace. He was mayor of Frankfort and a state legislator, and helped pass the national Bottled-in-Bond Act (1897). In recognition of that last accomplishment, this whiskey is bottled in bond, hence 50 percent abv. **CKC**

Tasting notes

This sour mash has green apple tartness as one of its signature flavors. Rich with caramel, it is also earthy, with cumin and anise. Slight bitterness on the finish.

Copper Fox Rye Whiskey

Copper Fox | www.copperfox.biz

Region and country of origin Virginia, United States
Distillery Copper Fox, Sperryville
Alcohol content 45% abv
Style Straight rye

The news that rye whiskey was selling well galvanized Copper Fox distillery owner Rick Wasmund to fire up the still and create the distillery's first rye whiskey.

Copper Fox is the only distillery in North America that floor-malts its own barley. Rather than using peat to dry the malt, Copper Fox uses the smoke of cherry and apple wood. The result is a subtler, sweeter smokiness than peat produces. Rye whiskey is made with at least 51 percent rye grain mixed with other grains, typically corn and/or malted barley. Copper Fox utilizes two-thirds rye grain and one-third malted barley. After distillation, the whiskey ages for an average of twelve months in ex-bourbon barrels.

Fruitwood is also used with oak in the form of heavily toasted applewood chips. These are placed in sacks and steeped in the whiskey throughout the aging process. Wasmund says that the chips are toasted to "about a level-three char" (on a one-to-four scale, with four being the highest). He has termed this technique "chipping," and it is employed in a number of the distillery's other primary and experimental products. The finished Copper Fox Rye Whiskey is not chill-filtered, which maximizes the flavors that come from the distillery's unique processes. **JP**

Tasting notes

Cinnamon bark, dusty rye, honeysuckle, sweet smoke, flint, and burnt sugar on the nose. On the palate, hard caramel candy, youthful rye, and resinous wood.

Copper Fox
Single Malt Whiskey

Copper Fox | www.copperfox.biz

Region and country of origin Virginia, United States
Distillery Copper Fox, Sperryville
Alcohol content 48% abv
Style Single malt

According to Copper Fox owner Rick Wasmund, he opened the distillery to make a single-malt whiskey utilizing fruitwood. Wasmund left his career behind and headed for Scotland to explore the possibility, and after a six-week internship with Bowmore distillery on Islay, he put his plan into action.

The distillery's flagship product uses Wasmund's pride and joy: traditional, floor-malted barley, kiln-dried with the smoke of native apple and cherry wood. Wasmund admits that the process incurs significant expense, but declares it necessary to create his special whiskey—"the rebel offspring of bourbon and Scotch." The barley used is grown locally by a Virginia farmer and is a strain that was specially developed by Virginia Tech University, in nearby Blacksburg, to take advantage of Virginia's excellent barley-growing conditions.

Once the spirit is distilled, it ages for sixteen months on average in ex-bourbon barrels. Additional smoky wood aroma and flavor is achieved using heavily toasted apple wood and oak chips, which are placed in perforated bags and allowed to steep in the whiskey while it ages. The result is a distinctive American single-malt whiskey. **JP**

Tasting notes

On the nose, cedar and cinnamon bark. Maple syrup adds depth and sweetness. Toffee, cinnamon sugar, honey, and floral flavors, with smoky, malty back notes.

Doubled
& Twisted

Charbay Spirits | www.charbay.com

Region and country of origin California, United States
Distillery Charbay, St. Helena
Alcohol content 49.5% abv
Style Light whiskey

The term "craft" is overused these days, but there is no more fitting descriptor for the operation run by father-and-son duo Miles and Marko Karakasevic in Napa Valley, California. As the twelfth and thirteenth generations of a long line of family distillers, the Karakasevics take their work very seriously.

The Karakasevics believe that, if you start off with the best distiller's beer possible, you will end up with a better whiskey. This whiskey begins as 20,000 gallons (76,000 liters) of bottle-ready, hoppy IPA brewed by a Northern California microbrewery.

The name of Doubled & Twisted, their light whiskey, comes from days gone by when a distiller would use only his eyes to determine the proof of the clear distillate coming off the still. When a whiskey reaches 160 proof, plus or minus, it rolls and twists on itself as it streams off the still into the spirit safe.

After working with a number of proof levels, Charbay settled on 99 proof because the whiskey's aroma and flavor seemed best balanced at that level. Once off the still, the whiskey is aged for one day in barrels so old or neutral that little oak flavor and color passes to the finished whiskey. Only 135 cases were distilled, but the whiskey is worth the hunt. **JP**

Tasting notes

Floral, spicy, and herbal aromas and flavors vie with grape and muscat wine sweetness. Hop bitterness emerges with force midpalate in a long, malty finish.

Eagle Rare 17-Year-Old

Sazerac | www.greatbourbon.com/antiquecollection.aspx

Region and country of origin Kentucky, United States
Distillery Buffalo Trace, Frankfort
Alcohol content 45% abv
Style Straight bourbon

Like many rock bands, membership in the Buffalo Trace Antique Collection was fluid in the early years. The original ensemble (released in 2000) was a rye (Sazerac), a rye-recipe bourbon (Eagle Rare), and a wheat-recipe bourbon (Weller). Only Saz and Eagle have been on every record. The lineup hasn't changed since Tom Handy joined in 2006.

The Antique Collection created something bourbon never had before—a buzz about a limited-edition release. And not just a single whiskey, but a set. That first release coincided with the growth of Internet chat rooms, which allowed American whiskey enthusiasts to connect with each other like never before. The Antique Collection was a perfect focus for that. Buffalo Trace was eager to talk about it and very open about details. Eventually, Buffalo Trace began to include detailed information sheets in every case.

Once word got out, the Antiques became a quick sellout. These days they linger on the shelf a little longer (their high prices see to that), but some remain a tough find. It depends on what you like, but overall the Eagle Rare 17-Year-Old is consistently the best whiskey in the bunch. Such a claim will have plenty of detractors, including those who resent the 45 percent abv in a group with so many barrel-proofers, but this is one extra-aged specialty bottling that any whiskey fan can enjoy. It is not only for the hard core, the Speyside to their Islay. It's approachable. Sure, any high abv can easily be lowered with water, but that's the point. Bottling whiskey at a drinkable abv is a more mainstream presentation. **CKC**

Tasting notes

Here is proof that a well-made and well-cared-for bourbon can keep getting better for seventeen years or more. Look for big wood, with caramel transforming into fig and vanilla becoming pipe tobacco, and all of it balanced with a little citrus zest, mint, and anise.

Eagle Rare Single Barrel

Sazerac | www.eaglerarelife.com/eagle-rare-single-barrel

Region and country of origin Kentucky, United States
Distillery Buffalo Trace, Frankfort
Alcohol content 45% abv
Style Straight bourbon

Eagle Rare Single Barrel, aged ten years, is a whiskey you probably don't know about that deserves your attention. It is one of the best whiskeys Sazerac makes, and since they make about thirty, that's saying something. Sazerac doesn't do much marketing. No big national advertising campaigns for them. The next Jim Beam or Jack Daniel's? Not interested. But Eagle Rare has potential to be at least the next Woodford Reserve or Knob Creek, if it could just get a little juice.

They are doing a worthy cause tie-in promotion called the Rare Life Award. You can learn about the nominees and vote on their Web site. The winner gets a trophy and money to donate to a charity. Nice, but not exactly robust marketing support.

Sazerac expects their products to speak for themselves, which Eagle Rare does quite well. The name is great—very patriotic—and the packaging is superb. Ten to twelve years is the aging sweet spot for bourbon, and enthusiasts love single barrels.

The brand even has a little history, and therein lies some of its problem. Begun by Seagram in the late 1960s, it was formulated by Charlie Beam. It seems he took his inspiration from Wild Turkey, one of the few brands that held its own when bourbon sales tanked. Wild Turkey was then eight years old and 50.5 percent abv, so they made Eagle Rare ten years old and 50 percent abv. Seagram kept it going that way for about twenty years, then sold it to Sazerac, which kept it the same for another decade, until the current iteration. Many enthusiasts liked it the way it was, cheaper with a higher abv. **CKC**

Tasting notes

The Buffalo Trace earthy signature is less apparent. It has a lightness that comes from having little rye in the mash. Barrel char is apparent but not overwhelming. Allowing for barrel-to-barrel variation, it's well balanced between flavor from the distillate and the wood.

Early Times

Brown-Forman Corporation
www.earlytimes.com

Region and country of origin Kentucky, United States
Distillery Early Times, Shively
Alcohol content 40% abv
Style Straight bourbon

Early Times gets little respect from most bourbon aficionados, but then it is not made for them. The brand made a successful move away from bourbon in 1983, when U.S. bourbon sales were crashing. Hard as it is to believe today, Canadian was booming. Brand owners Brown-Forman felt a need to stem the tide.

"We had Canadian Mist," master distiller Chris Morris explains, "but there was a thought that we could capture some of the people going to the [other] lighter Canadians by lightening up one of the straight whiskeys. We couldn't change Old Forester, and Jack Daniel's was rocking. It was Early Times." So they started putting distillate in used barrels—cutting back on the full-throttle flavor of the new wood. While Early Times was a bourbon overseas, at home it became a more mild-mannered Kentucky straight whiskey, a mix of the whiskey aged in new and used cooperage.

However, this is not a blended whiskey—it is still a straight, as you can tell when you taste it. Blends contain a lot of grain spirits, and they taste watered down and a bit artificial. Early Times may not roar like a bourbon, but it is the genuine article.

Where Early Times shines is in a highball. Make it tall, with about three fingers of Early Times, plenty of ice, soda (or fresh fruit juices), and a slice of garnish. Now taste that Kentucky whiskey coming through. **LB**

Tasting notes

Sweet corn and sugar candy, fired by a boozy heat. There is a nice, sweet creaminess that hangs, then slowly fades. Smooth, sweet-tasting whiskey.

Elijah Craig 12-Year-Old

Heaven Hill Distilleries
www.heaven-hill.com

Region and country of origin Kentucky, United States
Distillery Heaven Hill, Bardstown
Alcohol content 47% abv
Style Straight bourbon

With its oversized cork and stopper, and no-neck, chubby shape, this is one of the odder bottles on the bourbon shelf. But don't be fooled by the packaging or the low price—this sadly overlooked product is one of the best bottles of bourbon to be had.

A few years ago, Elijah Craig 12-Year-Old cost about $12 (£8) a bottle and was seriously underpriced. Heaven Hill has long had a reputation for putting value in the bottle, but many thought that tag was taking things too far. As the price has slowly climbed, it has been easy to wish the old days back, yet really it is more appropriate this way. The whiskey deserves to be put in the same category as more expensive bourbons, if for no other reason than to stop making those middling-price whiskeys look bad.

It can be useful to separate bourbons into a few general characters, or types. There is the "enjoyably rough ride" (Henry McKenna or Very Old Barton), there is "lean and spicy" (Evan Williams Single Barrel or Bulleit), and then there is "juicy and luscious": Elijah Craig 12-Year-Old is in that category. It is rich and rolling, lushly sweeter than most of the bourbons master distiller Parker Beam pulls from his warehouses. It is as if he knows that some of us like a richer bourbon on certain days, and is willing to indulge us. Thanks, Parker, but just keep that price in check. **LB**

Tasting notes

Oaky heat melts through to aromatic honey-corn and brown sugar. Ride out the heat to get vanilla and deep corn; the vanilla runs with oak in the long finish.

An Early Times advertisement before its 1983 makeover.

Elijah Craig 18-Year-Old

Heaven Hill Distilleries | www.heaven-hill.com

Region and country of origin Kentucky, United States
Distillery Heaven Hill, Bardstown
Alcohol content 45% abv
Style Straight bourbon

A small number of barrels of bourbon last eighteen years. Julian Van Winkle goes farther with his Pappy's Reserve; Kentucky bourbon distillers will age some longer; and Heaven Hill itself has bottled older whiskeys. But the total number of barrels holding bourbon this old is a tiny proportion of the hundreds of thousands of barrels that are never left to mature longer than four, six, or even eight years.

Look at Elijah Craig 18-Year-Old: dark, with many seasons pushed summer-deep into the red layer, then pulled back to the center by winter's contracting chill. Smell it: spicy-hot from long contact with oak, edged with soft rims of vanilla pulled from the wood. Taste it: dry, lean, leather-laced, and vaporously keen, honed stiletto-sharp through eighteen years of oaky focus.

This isn't some Dorian Gray whiskey that somehow ducked the effects of eighteen years of aging in a hot, ironclad rickhouse, coming out "surprisingly lively" and softly sweet. This is whiskey that takes its aging head-on and brings you the results of eighteen years of proud work. Some barrels of this age are blended away: eighteen years took too much from them. A few barrels, though, possess the strength at the core, the corny guts to finish the journey.

Some people are not always in the mood for a bourbon this lean, this uncompromisingly stark, but when in relatively serious contemplation or conversation, reach for Elijah Craig 18-Year-Old, tip in a bit of water, and think about eighteen seasons in the oak and about the barrels that didn't make it. And then think about having another. **LB**

Tasting notes

The nose is full of wood, leather, and vanilla, with a hot alcohol rim around it all. Cinnamon and a glow of mace, surrounding a narrow core of corn and vanilla, fly into the mouth. Only the finish of this whiskey could be called "mellow," soothing, and just a bit sweet.

Elmer T. Lee Single Barrel

Age International | www.greatbourbon.com/elmer.asp

Region and country of origin Kentucky, United States
Distillery Buffalo Trace, Frankfort
Alcohol content 45% abv
Style Straight bourbon

At Elmer T. Lee's ninetieth birthday celebration in 2009, much fun was had involving his ubiquitous plaid newsboy cap. His peers from other distilleries honored him by wearing replicas. The cap seems to have become attached to Lee at birth, if not before, much like his attachment to the distillery. Lee began his career at what is now Buffalo Trace in 1949. He was hired by Albert Blanton, one of the distillery's many legendary figures. Lee always describes Blanton as gentlemanly in his manners, even courtly, a portrayal equally applicable to Lee himself.

The first iteration of an eponymous bourbon for him came before Sazerac, the present owner, was even in the picture. That one was replaced with the current single-barrel, gold-wax, no-age-statement, 45-percent-abv version. A picture of Lee peers at you, through the whiskey, from the back label.

The Buffalo Trace distillery makes two rye-recipe bourbon mash bills. They keep the exact proportions secret but admit that recipe #1 has more corn and, consequently, less rye, probably less than 10 percent. Recipe #2 has less corn and proportionally more rye, probably about 15 percent. Elmer T. Lee (ETL) Single Barrel uses recipe #2.

Since ETL Single Barrel is modestly priced, especially for a single-barrel bourbon, it is one of the best ways to experience that recipe. A good single barrel is usually 60 percent about consistency and 40 percent about excellence, highlighting those rare honey barrels. As such, this deserves a spot on your Buffalo Trace tasting short list. **CKC**

Tasting notes

Rye is supposed to cut corn's sweetness for a drier whiskey, but ETL Single Barrel leads with sweet. The rye presents as floridly floral—think lilacs—and spicy (think basil and oregano), but always the sweetness, flowing beneath it all, like syrup made from sour fruit.

Evan Williams 23-Year-Old

Heaven Hill Distilleries | www.heaven-hill.com

Region and country of origin Kentucky, United States
Distillery Heaven Hill, Bardstown
Alcohol content 53.5% abv
Style Straight bourbon

Heaven Hill doesn't go wild on presentation with its whiskey labels: the extra-aged Rittenhouse labels, turned sideways and capped with a cut-foil band were about as edgy as it has ever been. But the label for Evan Williams 23-Year-Old is understated even for the Shapira family: royal blue, "23 Years Old" prominently displayed, 107 proof, and that's pretty much it, except for the royal blue wax cap on the same bottle they use for Evan Williams Single Barrel.

What's the story? "It was a luxury item for Japan, initially," said master distiller Parker Beam. "We didn't have that much demand for aged whiskey, and they wanted it and would pay for it." It was a story that would be repeated in several places—Blanton's, Van Winkle, and others—as overproduction due to slowly slipping sales led to whiskey being aged past what was then considered "normal," more than eight years. But, at the time, Parker Beam and the distillery executives did not really think anything more about it.

Then Heaven Hill's Western Europe representative sent them a copy of the drinks menu from Match Bar in London. Evan Williams 23-Year-Old—not "officially" available in the United Kingdom—was selling for £400 ($650) a bottle. "Look at that!" Parker remembers yelling. So now Evan Williams 23-Year-Old is officially available in Japan and the United Kingdom . . . and at Heaven Hill's Bourbon Heritage Center in Bardstown, Kentucky. Like the tours, the tasting room, and the delicious Evan Williams orange marmalade that is on sale, it is something you can only get right there. As if you really needed another reason to visit. **LB**

Tasting notes

Dark brown, showing its age. A hit of solventlike burn turns to mint and hot corn. Surprisingly lean body, closed-up flavors. A dry finish starts early and lingers with a hint of tart berry. Water opens it up: sweet corn, even a hot grassiness, rolls into a peppery-sweet finish.

Evan Williams Black Label

Heaven Hill Distilleries | www.heaven-hill.com

Region and country of origin Kentucky, United States
Distillery Heaven Hill, Louisville
Alcohol content 43% abv
Style Straight bourbon

When you think of bourbon, the name Jim Beam immediately springs to mind, or perhaps Maker's Mark, or Wild Turkey. All good whiskeys, all familiar names. But in the South, they know another name: Evan Williams Black Label, the second-biggest selling bourbon whiskey in the United States. The name commemorates a man considered by many to be the first commercial distiller in Kentucky.

Heaven Hill president Max Shapira says that Evan Williams bourbon was "one of the great marketing projects that was doomed to failure." They came up with a solid bourbon—43 percent abv, seven years old—and put it in a specially designed bottle, with a maroon label . . . and it flopped. They were about to pull the plug when one or two retailers wrote to say, "Hold on, I'm selling some of this."

Max picks up the story. "So my dad called our label supplier and said, 'Look, we have a square bottle that we've been selling some of our other brands in. Let's go and make the cheapest label we can make for this Evan Williams brand.' Well, sir, they said, that would be a black and white label. 'Fine,' my dad says. Without much more forethought than that, the brand was developed, and all of a sudden, it became a hit. A hell of a hit. The brand just exploded into popularity all around the country."

Evan Williams is no longer a seven-year-old bourbon—though still significantly older than other whiskeys in the category—but it is still 43 percent abv, and still a very flavorful, even sophisticated whiskey for the money. Audition it as your house bourbon. **LB**

Tasting notes

Corn and oak-edginess crowd the nose, with a bit of mint around the sides. So nice to taste a flagship bourbon that doesn't tear off your head: smooth, not fiery, delivering that corn and mint without a big penalty. Hard to believe it is sippable at this price.

Evan Williams Single Barrel 2000 Vintage

Heaven Hill Distilleries | www.heaven-hill.com

Region and country of origin Kentucky, United States
Distillery Heaven Hill, Bardstown
Alcohol content 43.3% abv
Style Straight bourbon

If you want a superior whiskey at a price that makes it great for Christmas presents or stocking your liquor cabinet four bottles deep, you need to check out the Evan Williams Single Barrel Vintage series. The 2000 vintage was a great incarnation, and there's probably still some out there in backwater liquor stores.

The idea of the Single Barrel Vintage is pretty simple. Parker and Craig Beam go out into the Heaven Hill warehouses and start checking the best barrels, and you better believe master distillers know where those are. "We go back to the same warehouse floors," Parker said. "You go back to what got you there in the first place. The lower floors don't age whiskey as well. You get the premium whiskey on the upper floors. There's more air, more sun, more ventilation up there. Standard whiskey will mingle from a lot of floors. The single barrels are more focused."

Parker pulled the barrel for this vintage—Barrel 1, it says on the label—from the top floor of Warehouse X in Bardstown, Kentucky. It was at barrel proof at the Henry Clay building in Louisville at the release, and at the standard 43.3 percent from the bottle, and the bottles bring home the barrel. This is a Christmas present for aficionados of great whiskey. **LB**

Tasting notes

The corn/oak/spice hits are all there, but there's a nice, light, slippery sweetness, like sugar maple sap. The sweet mingles and swirls with dry oak in the finish.

Evan Williams Single Barrel 1994 Vintage

Heaven Hill Distilleries | www.heaven-hill.com

Region and country of origin Kentucky, United States
Distillery Heaven Hill, Bardstown
Alcohol content 43.3% abv
Style Straight bourbon

The launch of the 1994 vintage of Evan Williams Single Barrel bourbon in October 2003 was the high point of Heaven Hill's business year. While they now produce and sell many other spirits—brandy, gin, vodka, rum, and a raft of flavored spirits—"Heaven Hill is still and always will be a bourbon company," president Max Shapira stated. Evan Williams Black Label is their flagship bourbon, and the Single Barrel is the cream of that expression, several hundred barrels selected by their master distillers, Parker and Craig Beam.

When the first barrel of that series is presented to the world—and the Bardstown Whiskey Society, the most devoted fans of Heaven Hill's whiskeys—it is a special occasion indeed. In other years it has been held at the Henry Clay building or the Speed Art Museum; in 2003, it was at Kentucky Derby Museum. After the solemnities, Parker and Craig popped the bung, dipped a copper whiskey thief into Barrel No. 1, and started pouring barrel-proof samples.

The bottles are knocked down to 43.3 percent, of course, but the excitement's still there. This wasn't just another year; this was one of the exceptional ones. There is still a little bit out there—check Kentucky whiskey bars!—and it's well worth tracking down. **LB**

Tasting notes

Corn with crisp layers of oak-spice cut in around it, leaking a bit of mint at the sides. What's promised in the nose delivers in the mouth: corn, oak, mint, and vanilla.

The "Sour Mash Express," a whimsy inspired by bourbon whiskey making. ➡

Four Roses

Kirin | www.fourroses.us

Region and country of origin Kentucky, United States
Distillery Four Roses, Lawrenceburg
Alcohol content 40% abv
Style Straight bourbon

Four Roses is a very old brand with origins in the mid-nineteenth century. There are two stories about the name, the romantic one preferred by the company and the more prosaic one that's probably true. The dull version involves founder Rufus Rose, his brother, and their respective sons as the "four Roses." The official version involves Paul Jones, who brought the business to Kentucky from Georgia and told a story about a Southern belle affirmatively answering his marriage proposal by wearing a corsage of four roses on her ball gown. Better, right?

It was the Jones family that made Four Roses a player and brought it back after Prohibition before selling it to Seagram. Four Roses was the top-selling bourbon into the 1950s when Seagram, for reasons unfathomable to us now, converted it into a blended whiskey, thus beginning its long slide into obscurity. To make the story even more bizarre, Seagram continued to make Four Roses Bourbon, but only for sale outside America, where it became a leading seller.

Kirin, a brewer, had long been Seagram's partner in Japan, so when the Four Roses distillery became available because of the Seagram breakup, Kirin was the natural buyer. That began a ten-year process of relaunching Four Roses in the United States.

This, the standard Four Roses expression, is actually a blend of ten different bourbons, all made at the Lawrenceburg distillery using two mash bills and five yeasts. The whiskey is not aged at the distillery but at a separate maturation and bottling facility. All of this is unconventional but well within the rules. **CKC**

Tasting notes

Mild but not bland—more like exceptionally well balanced. The astringency of tannins and char set you up for very subtle floral and spice notes, particularly of lilacs and pepper. Here and there is a wisp of caramel. The pucker is what lasts; the rest is evanescent.

Four Roses Single Barrel

Kirin | www.fourroses.us

Region and country of origin Kentucky, United States
Distillery Four Roses, Lawrenceburg
Alcohol content 50% abv
Style Straight bourbon

Four Roses makes a lot of fuss about how its two mash bills and five yeasts produce ten different bourbons and how "mingling" them all together creates a delicious and perfectly balanced whiskey.Surely, a single-barrel whiskey would be anathema? On the contrary: when Four Roses was reintroduced into the U.S. market, its first line extension after the standard all-in version was this Single Barrel.

The decision makes sense if you think of Four Roses as a very confident producer saying, "We can do anything. Sure, we make a great whiskey by mixing ten different whiskeys together, but we're able to do that because each individual whiskey is pretty darn great, too. Here, why don't you try one?"

The standard Four Roses Single Barrel has a high-rye mash bill (35 percent) with a yeast described as "lightly fruity." It carries no age statement, but being a single barrel precludes the mixing in of younger or older whiskeys to reach a standard profile. Instead, consistency is gained through barrel selection. Some barrel-to-barrel variation is inevitable, but consumers don't like big surprises. Each barrel has to be outstanding, too, since it cannot be doctored.

Four Roses Single Barrel represents a bid to position the Four Roses brand for today's new breed of bourbon drinkers, who are unburdened by prejudices of the past. The self-described house style is "mellow." In the case of Single Barrel, "mellow" means richly flavorful but perfectly balanced.

So, with mingling, Four Roses is perfect; without mingling, it is equally perfect. That's confidence. **CKC**

Tasting notes

Plum, tobacco, table grape, licorice, char, oak, coriander, and mint. Very flavorful, and complex, "plummy" with an edge. Bold notes of char and oak keep it from being one-dimensional and render it instead a near perfect balance of smooth and sharp, sweet and bitter.

Four Roses Single Barrel Limited Editions

Kirin
www.fourroses.us

Region and country of origin Kentucky, United States
Distillery Four Roses, Lawrenceburg
Alcohol content 50 to 59.3% abv
Style Straight bourbon

Every producer that does limited editions does them a little differently. Four Roses only does them for the U.S. market, and uses its Single Barrel and Small Batch platforms for one annual limited edition release of each. So far, the Single Barrel limiteds have all been some recipe other than the high-rye (35 percent) mash bill with lightly fruity yeast that describes the standard edition. The 2011 release, for example, is the same mash bill with floral yeast, at twelve years old.

Four Roses limited editions are indeed extremely limited, comprising fewer than 4,000 bottles each, which frustrates many enthusiasts. Per-store allocation is so restricted that many believe only the retailer's friends and family have a chance. Suspicions about merchants are fanned when bottles immediately show up on eBay for several times the retail price.

A solution is to seek out the special bottlings Four Roses does for particular retailers outside of the formal limited-edition series. Although the whiskey usually is less than ten years old, all ten recipes may be represented. These sell out, too, but if one of those retailers is convenient to you (the distillery will tell you who they are), these bottles tend to stay on the shelf longer than the distillery's own limiteds. **CKC**

Tasting notes

The only consistency in this series is that all of the whiskeys are Four Roses components. All so far have been extra-aged and are, therefore, barrel-dominant.

Four Roses Small Batch

Kirin
www.fourroses.us

Region and country of origin Kentucky, United States
Distillery Four Roses, Lawrenceburg
Alcohol content 45% abv
Style Straight bourbon

Four Roses is an old brand that became one of the leading bourbons in Europe and Asia during the bourbon renaissance without being sold in America. It succeeded despite, not because of, parent company Seagram and its support. Kirin bought Four Roses when Seagram was sold for parts. Kirin had long been Seagram's partner in the Japanese market, so the company, and many consumers there, felt like Four Roses was "their bourbon" even before it, in fact, was.

Kirin immediately began to plot the brand's return to the U.S. market, a bold move championed by master distiller Jim Rutledge. At first he just urged them to sell it in Kentucky so he and the other workers could finally drink the whiskey they made.

Of the three expressions, Small Batch is in the middle in terms of the number of whiskeys used and the price. It was also the last to be introduced, and that might be the reason they made it a bit more adventurous than the other two, exposing some of the novel flavors created by the different yeasts.

"Blending" is a dirty word in American whiskey, so Four Roses calls it "mingling." It's a fine art, whatever they call it. With the diverse flavor palate their system gives them, just about anything is possible. **CKC**

Tasting notes

The other expressions are good but don't take chances. Small Batch does. You don't know what you'll find, and it might well change the next time you open the bottle.

Four Roses Small Batch Limited Editions

Kirin
www.fourroses.us

Region and country of origin Kentucky, United States
Distillery Four Roses, Lawrenceburg
Alcohol content 50% abv
Style Straight bourbon

Limited editions are a way for a producer to offer some sort of special whiskey to consumers without the trouble, risk, and expense of developing a whole new standard product. Theoretically at least, limited editions that do particularly well can be added to the portfolio. To some they are just a way to give the line news value. Limited editions, of course, are small batch by definition.

Four Roses typically releases its annual Small Batch Limited Edition in the fall; each spring it releases one in the Single Barrel guise. The idea was that each release would represent a mingling of two of the distillery's ten recipes, a limitation that was ultimately seen as too limiting.

Now it might be anything, so long as at least two recipes are in the mix. Typically both the recipes and the ages of each are disclosed. The 2010, for instance, is three recipes: (1) the high-rye mash with lightly fruity yeast at fifteen years; (2) high-rye with spicy yeast at eleven years; and (3) standard rye with spicy yeast at ten years. The proportions of each are not disclosed, but one-third each is unlikely.

If all that sounds absurdly complicated, it is, but that's what the fans love about it. **CKC**

Tasting notes

Some limited editions go for a level of consistency while others say anything goes. This is the latter, the broadest range of flavors the Four Roses system can produce.

Gentleman Jack

Brown-Forman Corporation
www.jackdaniels.com

Region and country of origin Tennessee, United States
Distillery Jack Daniel's, Lynchburg
Alcohol content 40% abv
Style Tennessee whiskey

A kinder, gentler Jack. That's the idea here, a Jack Daniel's that doesn't stomp around the room, yelling and kicking things. But how do you tame Old No. 7, and get that red-headed fire breather to settle down?

The solution turned out to be right there at the distillery, staring them in the face. The longtime head of public relations, a larger-than-life character named Roger Brashears, used to refer to the Lincoln County Process—the gradual trickle of the new make through 10 feet (3.5 m) of hardwood charcoal—as "smoothing out the hog tracks." If it worked for white dog, what might it do for red liquor? Well, that's what they do: they send aged whiskey through the charcoal again. The result, first bottled in 1988, is Gentleman Jack.

This is the sweet side of Jack Daniel's, an almost playful whiskey full of sweet corn and vanilla, shorn of any wood-aging burn. Does that mean it is a lesser whiskey? Plenty of people call Gentleman Jack "girly whiskey," which is not only a gratuitous insult to women but also suggests that the whiskey is somehow not up to snuff. That is the kind of prejudice that dismisses Canadian offerings. Just as dessert wines can be wonderful, a sweet whiskey—with the right kind of structure and quality—can be as well. **LB**

Tasting notes

Corn, sweet corn pudding, and vanilla, with a touch of oak spice. In the mouth, sweet corn pudding rolling free in a big puddle of oaky vanilla, leading to a sweet finish.

George Dickel No. 8

Diageo | www.dickel.com

Region and country of origin Tennessee, United States
Distillery George Dickel, Tullahoma
Alcohol content 40% abv
Style Tennessee whiskey

George Dickel has moved around, gone through name changes, and been the subject of an undying rumor that it was going to run out . . . but here's the old No. 8 in its distinctive bottle, still on the shelves, still the favorite whiskey of a small but staunchly loyal set of fans.

The rumors, however, persist that the George Dickel distillery has stopped making No. 8, but this is simply because they stop distilling from time to time. Lovers of No. 8 need not panic—they stop distilling because they have too much of it, so the fans actually need to drink more!

Dickel is the "other" Tennessee whiskey ("If you only know Jack, you don't know Dickel," their new advertising slogan goes) in an even smaller way than Bushmills or even Cooley is the "other" Irish whiskey. Jack Daniel's is by far the biggest American whiskey, and Dickel's sales are dwarfed by it.

This doesn't bother the folks on Cascade Hollow Road, or at least they don't let on much if it does. They make their classic whiskey, this variation on bourbon, subtly different from the way they do it over in Lynchburg. It's a bit more interesting and pleasingly smooth to drink, with caramel and a distinctive smoky finish. And despite what some say, it's not going to run out any time soon. **LB**

Tasting notes

Cocoa and cornflakes in the nose, smooth in the mouth as sugar spills out. A short, creamy run to a lingering finish. A quick whiskey, but a smooth one.

George Dickel No. 12

Diageo | www.dickel.com

Region and country of origin Tennessee, United States
Distillery George Dickel, Tullahoma
Alcohol content 45% abv
Style Tennessee whiskey

A tour of the George Dickel distillery reveals two distinctive things. First is Dickel's two twists on the Lincoln County Process. Unlike Jack Daniel's, where the whiskey trickles down through the bed of charcoal, at Dickel they close off the bottom of the vat until it's full of whiskey, and then allow it to slowly run off. The other distinctive fact is that the vats of charcoal are kept chilled. "At some point," manufacturing executive Jennings Backus explains, "someone noticed that the whiskey we made in the winter tasted better. Chilling the charcoal gave us that all year round." That has got to add some costs in a hot Tennessee summer.

One other educational thing about the distillery was a little tasting of three samples of white dog. The first was off the column still: chunky, unrefined, and burly with corn. The next was after it had been through the doubler: much cleaner, with a huge corn flavor. Finally, the spirit postcharcoal: it was clear, bright, and tasted like a corn eau-de-vie, almost ethereal. That's when you realize that the Lincoln County Process isn't marketing or filtering. It's for real, and that's why they do it at Dickel.

The No. 12 is 5 percent bigger, and blended from older whiskeys than the No. 8, and you notice it. It's bigger, and richer, but still smooth and friendly. **LB**

Tasting notes

Cornflakes and a clean heat, blowing from the glass on a sweet breeze. Dry cocoa, mint, and cinnamon fly by before a drying spice finish comes along.

← The George Dickel distillery has its own general store in Tullahoma.

United States 647

George T. Stagg

Sazerac | www.greatbourbon.com/antiquecollection.aspx

Region and country of origin Kentucky, United States
Distillery Buffalo Trace, Frankfort
Alcohol content 64.5 to 72.4% abv
Style Straight bourbon

George T. Stagg was one of the nineteenth-century proprietors of the distillery now known as Buffalo Trace. Several subsequent owners kept his name on the door long after his death. Notoriously, Stagg became sole owner by pushing out his partner, Edmund Haynes Taylor Jr., and taking legal action to prevent Taylor from using his own name on the Old Taylor brand. Taylor, admittedly, made his own bed by overextending himself financially.

Though known historically as both a distillery and brand, the Stagg name was no longer active at Buffalo Trace in 2002 when a letter from a consumer triggered the creation of what became George T. Stagg bourbon. Almost immediately, Stagg became the flagship of the then-young but already distinguished portfolio of annual limited edition releases known as the Buffalo Trace Antique Collection.

Stagg is always an uncut and unfiltered fifteen-year-old bourbon. Beautifully packaged in a tall bottle, it was an immediate hit with whiskey enthusiasts and sold out quickly, as have all subsequent releases. It is the quintessential enthusiast bourbon.

The combination of long aging and barrel proof has made Stagg's abv the highest of any U.S. whiskey sold. Many people are surprised to learn that American whiskeys often increase in abv during aging and can rise from the maximum entry proof of 62.5 percent abv to, in Stagg's case, as much as 72.4 percent. For some people, this alone is reason to buy it. Because it is bottled at whatever abv comes out of the barrel, the proof varies from year to year. **CKC**

Tasting notes

More than a tiny sip of this giant without dilution is not advised. Barrel notes predominate. After vanilla there's leather and tobacco notes, dark fruit, and smoked meat. The inevitable astringency of such long and hard aging in new charred oak makes this an acquired taste.

George Washington American Whiskey

Mount Vernon | www.discus.org/heritage/washington.asp

Region and country of origin United States
Distillery Various
Alcohol content 60.6% abv
Style Rye blend

George Washington is the single most revered figure in American history, substantially more revered than American whiskey. Yet Washington was a successful whiskey maker himself. His distillery, which added value to the grains produced on his Virginia farm, was his most financially successful enterprise.

About twenty years ago, the Mount Vernon estate approached the Distilled Spirits Council of the United States (DISCUS) about providing financial support for an excavation, study, and restoration of Washington's distillery. DISCUS, a trade association of major distilled spirits producers, agreed without hesitation; clearly, an association with Washington was just what that industry needed in its war against antialcohol forces.

One of the first events staged by DISCUS at Mount Vernon was a landing at the farm's Potomac River wharf of an eighteenth-century vessel, with a suitably attired crew, delivering to the estate one barrel of whiskey from each DISCUS member. The whiskeys represented were Jack Daniel's and George Dickel (Tennessee whiskey); Jim Beam, Wild Turkey, Very Old Barton, Virginia Gentleman, Maker's Mark, Woodford Reserve, and Rebel Yell (bourbon); and Platte Valley (corn whiskey). After aging at Mount Vernon, some of the whiskey was bottled for a fund-raiser, but not all of it. A few years later, with the remainder in danger of overaging, they decided to create a blend from it, also for the purpose of fund-raising. That blend is this whiskey. Although you won't find it in stores today, most bottles sold were never opened, so there are untasted full bottles out there. **CKC**

Tasting notes

Toffee-flavored with rich chocolate, caramel, and vanilla, and a hint of plum. Due to its very long aging, it is smoky, almost to the point of being sooty. The surprise is that, despite its many sources of flavor, the overall taste is flat, blunted, and lacking sparkle.

Georgia Moon

Heaven Hill | www.heavel-hill.com

Region and country of origin Kentucky, United States
Distillery Heaven Hill, Bardstown
Alcohol content 40% abv
Style Corn whiskey

The term "moonshine" is becoming ever more popular with whiskey company marketers. It refers to the illegal alcohol that bootlegged its way across rural parts of the southeastern United States. It would seem as though the word adds instant credibility, conjuring up smoke whispers dancing off old copper stills, or perhaps denim-clad renegades illegally distilling corn, one small batch at a time, in the foothills of the Appalachian Mountains. The reality of the present-day spirit is different, of course, but no one seems to mind.

Georgia Moon is a well-executed package, coming in moonshine's vessel of choice, a mason jar. This southern artifact is commonly used for everything from canning vegetables to holding cold glasses of southern table wine, otherwise known as sweet iced tea. Most anyone who has ever sipped the "real thing" has done so right from a jar exactly like the one that holds this whiskey.

Enough about the packaging. Inside the jar is a crystal-clear corn whiskey. U.S regulations stipulate that such a whiskey must be at least 81 percent corn. Georgia Moon further ramps up the corn quotient with a recipe that is 90 percent corn, 5 percent rye grain, and 5 percent barley malt. After distillation, the spirit spends up to thirty days aging in oak barrels.

But try not to focus too hard on the technicalities of this whiskey. After all, Georgia Moon is intended as a throwback, a showcasing of a simple corn whiskey, devoid of too much oak and sweetness, in authentic packaging. The result, a whiskey redolent of corn, is meant to be enjoyed simply. **JP**

Tasting notes

Twisting off the top of this mason-jarlike bottle is like opening a can of cooked corn. The vegetal aromas of boiled corn on the cob yield to a dusty, dry grain quality. On the sip, a hay, grain, and scant confectioner sweetness anchors this pure corn whiskey experience.

Hancock's President's Reserve

Age International | www.greatbourbon.com/hancock.asp

Region and country of origin Kentucky, United States
Distillery Buffalo Trace, Frankfort
Alcohol content 44.45% abv
Style Straight bourbon

Age International is the company that owned the Buffalo Trace distillery before Sazerac. Several of the bourbon brands made at Buffalo Trace were started by Age and are still owned by it, including Hancock's. All are single-barrel bourbons, a type Age introduced to the United States but modeled after single-cask Scottish malts.

Hancock's President's Reserve doesn't have a backstory. The name is thought to refer to Hancock McAfee, who was one of the first European settlers at the site now occupied by the Buffalo Trace distillery. He wasn't president of anything, neither did he reserve anything, so far as we know. It's just a name.

Although Hancock's is a single-barrel bourbon, there is no barrel number, rick location, or dump date written by hand on the label. The bottle is handsome, with a wide mouth and a generous, wood-topped cork stopper. Happily, the whiskey inside is excellent.

Between them, Age International and Buffalo Trace have many different bourbon brands. This gives consumers the chance to try whiskeys that differ from one another only slightly. After finding one that ideally matches their personal taste, they take ownership of it. How many people have Hancock's President's Reserve as their go-to bourbon? Not many, so you can enjoy the pleasure of introducing it to your friends.

Hancock's is made using the higher rye of Buffalo Trace's two rye-flavored bourbon mash bills, but it is not "high rye" like Bulleit or Old Grand-Dad. Although the same mash bill as Blanton's is used, it tastes very different, sweet where Blanton's is dry. **CKC**

Tasting notes

Caramel, vanilla cream, and milk chocolate, with a hot finish that detracts from what is otherwise a rich candy box of flavors. Candy notes are further tempered by hints of espresso and oregano. Mouthfeel is thick and syrupy. A very good whiskey for its type.

Heaven Hill Old Style Bourbon 6-Year-Old

Heaven Hill Distilleries | www.heaven-hill.com

Region and country of origin Kentucky, United States
Distillery Heaven Hill, Louisville
Alcohol content 50% abv
Style Straight bourbon

Never judge a book by its cover, and never judge a whiskey by its label. This whiskey bears the green-lettered white label of Heaven Hill Old Style Bourbon, and, although the distillery puts its name right on there, it's not the flagship brand; that's Evan Williams. Heaven Hill is the distillery's "value" brand.

The Heaven Hill Old Style Bourbon 6-Year-Old bonded bottling is a different breed of cat than the standard Heaven Hill Old Style, and that's why it's here. It needs no excuses, nor will it allow you any. It comes from the same mash bill as Evan Williams, Elijah Craig, and Henry McKenna—75 percent corn, 13 percent rye, and 12 percent malt—and when you pour it, you will smell and taste the earlier paths that those more mature whiskeys follow on their way to selection for their bottles. It is almost like being granted access to the warehouse to check on them.

Most obvious is the fresh, oily corn that is so different from typically aged bourbon. It's feisty, and other flavors can be a little muted, so many people enjoy this mixed with a little Coke or in a cocktail, where it excels.

This is elemental bourbon, old enough not to scorch but young enough to remember where it came from. Young bourbons sell by the carload and get dumped into cola; old bourbons are in demand by new enthusiasts, who seem to think that bourbon should emulate Scotch whisky's age. Somewhere in the middle, there's a relaxed sweet spot of rich, old-style bourbon flavor. Grab a glass, throw in some ice, and pour yourself some. **LB**

Tasting notes

Open the bottle, and you'll smell warehouse—raunchy corn spirit drooling down white oak. The corn is fresh and a bit oily: no subtlety, but without the ferocity of younger bourbon. The wood returns to crimp the corn in the finish; a quick, breathless ride.

Henry McKenna Single Barrel 10-Year-Old

Heaven Hill Distilleries | www.bardstownwhiskeysociety.com

Region and country of origin Kentucky, United States
Distillery Heaven Hill, Louisville
Alcohol content 50% abv
Style Straight bourbon

Henry McKenna is a regional bottling from Heaven Hill. It is hard to find a sample if you're not in Kentucky or Tidewater, Virginia. In that strip of coastal Virginia—essentially everything east of the I-95 superhighway, including the Eastern Shore—Henry McKenna is a cult brand. According to longtime Heaven Hill Distillery spokesman Larry Kass, "They have a fan club, and they're deathly serious."

Kass recalls that Heaven Hill bought the brand from Seagram in the early 1980s. "They had an old-time looking crock, a jug," he said. "You can still find them on eBay." That's the 80-proof bottling, though; this one is a much more burly 100 proof bottled-in-bond single-barrel whiskey. It's quite a mouthful, and it's a shame more people don't know about it.

"We came out with the single-barrel McKenna when we came out with Evan Williams and Elijah Craig single barrels," Kass said. Evan Williams is a vintage bottling, all from one year; Elijah Craig is a towering eighteen years old; but Henry McKenna is the oldest bottled-in-bond whiskey at ten years old. It's made from the same mash bill as Heaven Hill's other rye bourbons, but it's got a gripping, spicy power to it.

That's the way master distiller Parker Beam likes it: "high and dry," a whiskey that comes from the top floors of the warehouse, where the rising heat of Kentucky summers drives the whiskey deep into the oak of the barrels. None of the whiskey in Henry McKenna comes from lower than the fifth floor. When you try your first sip of this take-no-prisoners whiskey, you might want to be sitting down. **LB**

Tasting notes

The aroma leaps from the glass: fiery notes of corn and oak spice boil out. Don't expect less in your mouth—McKenna is explosive, blasting mint and pepper and hot corn across the palate, yet there's a surprisingly gentle finish. Beware: it's lulling you into a return bout.

High West 12-Year-Old Rye

High West | www.highwest.com

Region and country of origin Utah, United States
Distillery High West Distillery & Saloon, Park City
Alcohol content 46% abv
Style Straight rye

High West has built a name for itself by finding fantastic rye whiskeys. Some of its sourced whiskeys were destined to be components in whiskey blends before High West proprietor and distiller David Perkins procured them. High West has shown a penchant for good timing, whether it be releasing blended straight ryes just in time for a rye whiskey shortage in the United States, or swooping in for the rescue. Its 12-Year-Old Rye is a great example of both.

Distilled in the late 1990s at the Seagram distillery in Lawrenceburg, Indiana, this whiskey was destined for Japan as a six-year-old in 2003. Most of the whiskey made it on the shipping container except for five lonely barrels. Somehow those barrels went unaccounted for until being "found" when Pernod Ricard sold the Seagram plant five years later in 2008. David Perkins was eventually able to purchase those five barrels for bottling.

This particular whiskey is 95 percent rye mash bill (with 5 percent malted barley). It was cooked, or mashed, at a lower temperature than is customary in order to preserve the rye grain character. The result is a full-flavored rye whiskey that is bottled without chill-filtration. It is available only at the distillery. **JP**

Tasting notes

The nose is rye grain, mint, and licorice, softened by caramel and Juicy Fruit gum. Caramel and honey on the palate is spiked with rye, chile heat, and clove.

High West 21-Year-Old Rye

High West | www.highwest.com

Region and country of origin Utah, United States
Distillery High West Distillery & Saloon, Park City
Alcohol content 46% abv
Style Rye whiskey

High West's David Perkins noticed that American palates were coming around to bigger, bolder flavored whiskies, namely rye. This realization occurred around the same time that rye saw a resurgence in America, no doubt influenced by the cocktail culture. Perkins chalks it up to being in the "right place at the right time," but his penchant for finding some of the most unique, distinctive, and mature rye whiskeys available gave him an advantage.

This 21-year-old rye whiskey is another gem that Perkins was able to snatch up before it met its fate as a blending component for Canadian whisky. Distilled by Barton in Bardstown, Kentucky, its grain makeup sits right on the bubble of rye whiskey regulations, with 53 percent rye grain (rye whiskey must be at least 51 percent rye in the United States), 37 percent corn, and 10 percent malted barley.

Typically, American whiskey is aged in new charred oak barrels, but the 21-Year-Old was aged in used barrels. Perkins was never able to confirm if the barrels had previously held aged rye or bourbon whiskey, thus adding a bit of mystery to the story. Regardless, the more gentle oak interaction yields a graceful and elegant rye whiskey. **JP**

Tasting notes

Elegance and restraint that belies its age. The nose is fragrant with spearmint, rye, soft cinnamon, and vanilla. Honey, golden dried fruits, and corn on the palate.

High West Distillery is located in Park City, Utah, famous for its ski resorts. ➡

High West Bourye

High West | www.highwest.com

Region and country of origin Utah, United States
Distillery High West Distillery & Saloon, Park City
Alcohol content 46% abv
Style Bourbon and rye blend

The jackalope is a mythical creature conjured up by locals in the western and southwestern regions of the United States. Consisting of one part jackrabbit and one part antelope, with a thirst for whiskey, the creature serves as a fitting mascot of sorts on the label of High West's Bourye whiskey. Pronounced "boo-rye," the name comes from the marriage (ménage à trois, really) of components that don't normally get put together in the same bottle—straight bourbon whiskey and two rye whiskeys.

To create the blended whiskey, High West followed a model that has worked quite well for the distillery: sourcing and purchasing mature whiskey while its own whiskeys age. It is a somewhat simple concept, but one that takes tremendous work and good fortune, according to proprietor David Perkins.

Bourye starts with a ten-year-old bourbon whiskey made by Four Roses in Lawrenceburg, Kentucky. It is then mingled with the same twelve-year-old straight rye (distilled by Lawrenceburg Distillers Indiana) that is a distillery-only release at High West. Last but not least, a sixteen-year-old rye whiskey consisting of 53 percent rye grain, 37 percent corn, and 10 percent malted barley is added. This final whiskey in the mixture was distilled by Barton in Bardstown, Kentucky, for Hiram Walker in Canada.

One evening while tinkering with the whiskeys he had available, Perkins blended the bourbon and rye together. He's quick to say that it was something that "just sort of happened," but the result was far too good to ignore. **JP**

Tasting notes

The nose reveals a fruity rye character with toffee, caramel corn, and plenty of fragrant spices. There is a defined, yet harmonious, handoff from caramel sweet entry to a spicy, dry midpalate on through the finish. Proof that bourbon and rye can play nice together.

High West Double Rye!

High West | www.highwest.com

Region and country of origin Utah, United States
Distillery High West Distillery & Saloon, Park City
Alcohol content 46% abv
Style Straight rye blend

Looking to expand his lineup, distiller David Perkins wanted to create something a bit different from other High West blends, and not simply a lighter version of his acclaimed Rendezvous Rye. This one needed to be able to stand on its own. To accomplish that, High West did what it does best—sourcing hard-to-find rye whiskeys from reputable distilleries. The rye shortage was in full swing, making this task even more difficult, but High West procured a sixteen-year-old 53 percent straight rye whiskey (37 percent corn, 10 percent malted barley) from Barton in Bardstown, Kentucky. They also purchased a vivacious two-year-old 95 percent straight rye whiskey (5 percent malted barley) from Lawrenceburg Distillers Indiana. High West released this new blended straight rye whiskey in 2011, calling it Double Rye!

The name simply refers to the two straight rye whiskeys that make up the blend. While the blend is certainly harmonious, it's the two-year-old that helps to set Double Rye! apart from High West's other offerings. Perkins noticed that some of the two-year-old barrels had a pronounced green, herbal, and botanical character to them. While it is not especially uncommon for younger LDI rye whiskey, which tends to have a very fresh and bright flavor in general, these barrels had even more of this unique character.

Perkins himself hand-selected the barrels that represented this flavor profile most in order to play off against the sweeter sixteen-year-old, containing a higher percentage of corn. The result is one of the more uncommon rye whiskies on the market. **JP**

Tasting notes

One of the "greenest" noses, with gin botanicals, pine sap, evergreen, eucalyptus, and mint. The palate is alive with prickly rye, soft sweet spices (gin botanicals again, sweet red stem spearmint, and woody cinnamon), all glued together with honey and vanilla taffy sweetness.

High West Rendezvous Rye Whiskey

High West | www.highwest.com

Region and country of origin Utah, United States
Distillery High West Distillery & Saloon, Park City
Alcohol content 46% abv
Style Straight rye blend

High West is a boutique distillery and saloon based in Park City, Utah. Owner David Perkins took a completely different approach than the common new distillery model of the day, where very young whiskeys are released to generate cash flow. Perkins didn't think these youngsters tasted good enough. Fortunately, Perkins had made a smart move previously by working a stint with American whiskey icon and Four Roses master distiller, Jim Rutledge. The two were to shape the concept for High West.

While its own distilled whiskey aged, High West would source mature aged whiskeys from reputable sources to craft unique blends. But Perkins also has a love for rye whiskey and noticed consumers were shifting toward fuller-flavored spirits. Rendezvous Rye, named after the annual summer gathering of mountain men and traders in Utah, is a blend of two very distinct straight rye whiskeys. The "foundation" is a mature sixteen-year-old, 80 percent (10 percent corn, 10 percent barley) straight rye that is married to a spicy and lively six-year-old 95 percent (5 percent barley) straight rye whiskey made by Lawrenceburg Distillers Indiana. The resulting "rendezvous" yields a behemoth with intense rye-forward character. **JP**

Tasting notes

An eruption of spice (cinnamon stick, clove, rye, peppermint, and vanilla), fruit (green apple and golden fruits), and burnt chewy caramel sweetness.

High West Silver Western Oat Whiskey

High West | www.highwest.com

Region and country of origin Utah, United States
Distillery High West Distillery & Saloon, Park City
Alcohol content 40% abv
Style Oat whiskey

Rather than make another fashionable "white dog" or lightly aged whiskey, High West wanted to bring something different to the market. After working with a number of different grains in their test still, the distillery chose to release an oat whiskey. Owner David Perkins said, "I just liked the flavor from oat the best. It's an underutilized grain, and it brought such an elegant and soft flavor to the finished whiskey."

High West's Silver is made up of 85 percent oat and 15 percent barley. Technically speaking, it's a "light whiskey" by U.S. regulations. This term refers to the fact that it is distilled above 160 proof, or 80 percent alcohol, but does not exceed 190 proof (95 percent alcohol). Once it comes off the still, it is aged for a matter of minutes (about five, to be accurate) in toasted French Limousin oak, commonly used for aging cognac and wine. The aging process does very little to the spirit in terms of adding flavor and color.

High West considers the end result to be whiskey's answer to light or silver tequilas and rums, which are available in contrast to their darker and higher aged counterparts. The Silver Whiskey Western Oat is a demonstration of the delicate and interesting properties of an uncommon distiller's grain. **JP**

Tasting notes

The nose is soft and delicate with marshmallow, dried hay, and banana. On the palate, flavors of bubble gum, apple, and taffy sweetness restrain a licoricelike bite.

Hudson Baby Bourbon Whiskey

Tuthilltown | www.tuthilltown.com

Region and country of origin New York, United States
Distillery Tuthilltown Spirits, Gardiner
Alcohol content 46% abv
Style Bourbon

Tuthilltown's first release from their Gardiner, New York-based operation was New York Corn Whiskey. Made from corn sourced within ten or so miles from the distillery, it provided Tuthilltown with a good base "juice" for the distillery's second whiskey release, Baby Bourbon, the first bourbon ever distilled in New York.

Tuthilltown was one of the first distilleries to work with a number of smaller barrels rather than the typical 53-gallon (200-liter) barrels. There is a great deal of debate as to the benefits and science behind using them. Some believe the whiskey ages faster in smaller barrels. Others state the aging process isn't accelerated, but because of the larger surface area contact in the smaller barrels, the interaction with the charred oak is increased. The result is whiskey that picks up the caramel color and wood flavors quicker.

Tuthilltown uses 3-gallon (11-liter) barrels aged approximately six months and 14-gallon (53-liter) barrels aged around eighteen to twenty-four months. The barrels are agitated, which is thought to foster a speedier interaction between wood and spirit. Baby Bourbon is made from batches of the varied barrel sizes that are then blended together to achieve the desired flavor profile. **JP**

Tasting notes

Freshly splintered oak, vanilla, and floral aromas keep the corn and caramel. On the palate, corn and vanilla meld with peppermint and toasted wood.

Hudson Four Grain Bourbon Whiskey

Tuthilltown | www.tuthilltown.com

Region and country of origin New York, United States
Distillery Tuthilltown Spirits, Gardiner
Alcohol content 46% abv
Style Four-grain bourbon

Tuthilltown has demonstrated an enthusiasm for trying new things. One of Tuthilltown's early customers was Lenell's in Brooklyn, New York. Owned by Lenell Smothers, it was regarded as one of the best whiskey shops in New York, if not America, before closing in 2009. Lenell told Tuthilltown partner and distiller Ralph Erenzo that he should consider making a whiskey with four grains—corn, rye, wheat, and barley—and bring something new to the market.

The mash bill of Hudson Four Grain Whiskey consists of 60 percent corn—the same local and heirloom varieties that comprised their Corn Whiskey and Baby Bourbon. Corn is a rich, smooth grain that gives many American whiskeys backbone and structure. Rye and wheat are small flavoring grains, used to add dimension and complexity. In most cases, rye and wheat are used separately because they deliver quite different flavor characteristics. Wheat brings a soft, round sweetness, and rye adds spice and fruity character. Barley is added for additional sweetness and to help convert the grain starches into sugar for fermentation. Proportions of each grain were added to the corn to create perhaps the most balanced in the Hudson line of whiskeys. **JP**

Tasting notes

Rum-soaked dried fruits, sourdough, and teasing spice make for a semisweet nose. The palate ramps up the spice as it breaks up the corn and caramel sweetness.

Hudson Manhattan Rye Whiskey

Tuthilltown | www.tuthilltown.com

Region and country of origin New York, United States
Distillery Tuthilltown Spirits, Gardiner
Alcohol content 46% abv
Style Rye whiskey

The third release from Tuthilltown's Hudson line of whiskeys was the Manhattan Rye. The namesake paid homage to the cocktail culture that exploded in America in the early 2000s. In the late eighteenth and early nineteenth centuries, the borough of Manhattan's whiskey of choice was rye. There was even a rye-based cocktail called the Manhattan.

While bourbon is considered America's native spirit, rye whiskey deserves a place right alongside. Tuthilltown set out to create the first rye whiskey to be made in New York since Prohibition. Distillers Ralph Erenzo and Brian Lee got to work on a rye recipe by first sourcing rye grain from regional suppliers to ensure the end product was as local as possible.

One of the first steps in the whiskey-making process is to mash, or cook, the milled grain with water for converting the starch to sugar. Barley is typically used in American whiskey as an aid in this starch conversion process. In the case of Manhattan Rye, this is a single grain-only product, so enzymes were used in lieu of barley. Few grains are more frustrating to work with than rye, due to its very high gluten content. The grain has a tendency to gum up during the mashing process, making a sticky, gloppy mess. Being a microdistillery, Tuthilltown didn't have a lot of experts to call in the early days to help them overcome these obstacles.

It took months of trial and error to get the rye whiskey recipe just right. All the work and effort yielded a product to which cocktail lovers and neat whiskey freaks alike could raise their glass. **JP**

Tasting notes

Manhattan Rye is a treasure trove of spices. The nose blends sweet maple syrup, allspice, cinnamon stick, mint, dusty rye grain, and fresh oak. A resinous front entry on the sip makes way for a midpalate explosion of pepper, mint, and cinnamon through to the finish.

Single-malt whiskey fills Hudson's distinctive squat bottles. ➡

Hudson New York Corn Whiskey

Tuthilltown | www.tuthilltown.com

Region and country of origin New York, United States
Distillery Tuthilltown Spirits, Gardiner
Alcohol content 46% abv
Style Corn whiskey

Tasting notes

The transparent Hudson Corn Whiskey begins with a nose of boiled corncobs, hay, and buttered popcorn. The palate is light and dry, with mild sweetness, finishing with a nutty corn quality. It's a pure corn experience from start to finish.

In 2001, Ralph Erenzo, distiller and partner of Tuthilltown, acquired some property on 36 acres (14 ha) in Gardiner, New York. An avid hiker, Erenzo intended to use the property as a resting spot and bed-and-breakfast for hikers and climbers. And on the premises was an old gristmill and granary.

Before Prohibition, the state of New York had more than 1,000 distilleries. In the years that followed, the numbers of distilleries quickly dwindled to zero. Keen to generate some income on his property, Erenzo sought to make use of the farm, especially the historic granary. He partnered with Brian Lee, a man who knew his way around grain mills. Lee suggested they consider making whiskey, and the pair worked to convert the granary into a distillery. In order to get some cash flow, many microdistilleries release light whiskeys that have minimal age. Tuthilltown was actually one of the distilleries that started this model.

The first whiskey produced under the Hudson line was New York Corn Whiskey, and it has the distinction of being the first legal grain spirit distilled in New York in more than seventy years. The distillery makes this whiskey from 100 percent corn that is sourced from local farms. This approach to procuring raw materials would eventually become a hallmark of the distillery. Today, Tuthilltown uses a combination of 40 percent field corn and 60 percent heirloom varietals for the corn whiskey. The heirloom corn has a higher yield, less starch, and richer, bolder, "cornier" flavor. This is the whiskey that started it all for one of the most successful American microdistilleries. **JP**

Hudson Single Malt Whiskey

Tuthilltown | www.tuthilltown.com

Region and country of origin New York, United States
Distillery Tuthilltown Spirits, Gardiner
Alcohol content 46% abv
Style Single malt

Increasingly, American distilleries are producing single-grain, malted barley whiskeys, otherwise known as single malts. The trend may not have distilleries in Scotland quaking in their boots and looking to their livelihoods just yet, but the results are getting more and more impressive.

Wanting to expand the Hudson whiskey line, Tuthilltown recently developed a single-malt whiskey. Local and regional grains usually feature strongly in Tuthilltown products, but barley is one grain that does not grow well locally. Tuthilltown therefore sources two-row barley from Canada in order to make their 100 percent malted barley whiskey.

Once the single-malt spirit is distilled, Tuthilltown generally ages it in small barrels of two sizes. The single-malt distillate is placed either in 3-gallon (11-liter) or 14-gallon (53-liter) newly charred oak barrels. The barrels are charred to level four, the highest level, to ensure more oak interaction with the spirit. The Tuthilltown approach is a departure from traditional single-malt whisky aging in Scotland, where used barrels ensure a softer wood character.

Small barrels significantly increase the whiskey's contact with the oak, resulting in a quicker transfer of color and wood flavors. Aging in the 3-gallon barrels lasts for no more than six months; whiskey in the 14-gallon barrels is aged for eighteen to twenty-four months. The contents of both types are then batched together to achieve a consistent flavor. Unsurprisingly, Hudson Single Malt is one of the most spicy and wood-forward single malts on the market. **JP**

Tasting notes

The malt struggles to work its way through the thick, oily viscosity and the oak-forward flavors that result from aging in small barrels. The result is a cinnamon bomb of a whiskey, with nutmeg, black pepper, honeysuckle, scant fruitiness, and heaps of fresh oak.

Jack Daniel's Old No. 7

Brown-Forman Corporation | www.jackdaniels.com

Region and country of origin Tennessee, United States
Distillery Jack Daniel's, Lynchburg
Alcohol content 40% abv
Style Tennessee whiskey

Iconic is a word that marketers have perhaps used too heavily, but Jack Daniel's undoubtedly stands in that class. When it comes to American whiskey, it is easy to adapt Dean Martin's joking truth about Sinatra: "It's Jack's world, we just live in it." Jack Daniel's Old No. 7 Tennessee whiskey is by far the biggest-selling American whiskey, and also likely to be the first American whiskey found in bars abroad.

How iconic is it? The first time I visited the distillery in Lynchburg, I walked in on then-master distiller Jimmy Bedford as he was signing a three-quarter-gallon (3-liter) bottle of Jack. "Wow," I said, "who's that for?" "Fidel," he responded, and grinned. Well, that slightly sooty sweetness does go well with cigars.

Jack's "slightly sooty" taste comes from the Lincoln County Process, where the new-make whiskey trickles through 10 feet (3.5 m) of maple charcoal before entering the barrels for aging. That is the step that makes Tennessee whiskey different from bourbon; otherwise, it *is* bourbon. You can watch them slow-burn the wood for the charcoal. It is burned in the open air while men stand by, carefully applying water with hoses to keep the wood from igniting. The process yields barrow loads of charcoal chunks about the size of soybeans—black, like that iconic label.

Jack's is big business—the planning required to fulfill sales orders alone is highly complex. But the charcoal, the rushing water of the source spring, and Lynchburg—like having a Jack and Coke with a buddy—all still feel pretty personal. So, if you haven't tried it yet, maybe it's time you did. **LB**

Tasting notes

Hard candy and a hint of ripe watermelon, with a rippling edge of oak. Corn juice slides into the mouth. A surprisingly light and slick whiskey, with an odd, sooty cleanness coming in on its tail, dropping to a sweet corn finish. Easy for a shot, flavorful when mixed.

In Jack Daniel's advertisements, time always passes slowly. →

There Are Times At Jack Daniel's When You Can't Do Anything But Sit And Wait. So That's Exactly What We Do.

You see, every drop of Jack Daniel's is seeped for days through twelve-foot vats of finely packed charcoal. Called charcoal mellowing, this time-taking Tennessee process is the old, natural way of smoothing out whiskey... and there's nothing a man can do to speed it along.

After a sip of Jack Daniel's, we believe, you'll be glad the folks in our hollow are content to do nothing when that's what's called for.

SMOOTH SIPPIN' TENNESSEE WHISKEY

Jack Daniel's Single Barrel

Brown-Forman Corporation | www.jackdaniels.com

Region and country of origin Tennessee, United States
Distillery Jack Daniel's, Lynchburg
Alcohol content 47% abv
Style Tennessee whiskey

Look closely at a glass of Jack Daniel's Single Barrel—it is a dark whiskey, one that has done its time in the hotbox summers of the uppermost floor of a Tennessee warehouse, where all the whiskey for Single Barrel is aged. You'd think after all that time in the heat, it might be surly or squinty-eyed crazy, but there are still plenty of good intentions in this. There ought to be—they still hand-select the barrels for Single Barrel, and only about one in 100 makes it.

You get an idea of just how sweet Tennessee whiskey is when you dive into this one. It's been crucified on oak, roasting in the heat (and if you've ever been in the top floor of a rickhouse in the summer, you'll know just how hot that is) that shoves the whiskey deep into that barrel. You'll taste the wood, and there's a burly, somewhat edgy element present. Yet it retains the luscious corn, caged but not contained by the oak. It is bottled at a higher proof (47 percent abv) to keep that flavor intact in the bottle.

Single Barrel has proved popular with collectors, as there are a number of different bottlings in the range; these include commemorative, private, and sponsored casks. The bottles also come in a number of different designs with distinctive packaging.

This is one of the few American whiskeys you can purchase by the barrel. Even more singular than a bottle of Single Barrel, you get to sample and select your own. It's bottled, and each of the approximately 250 bottles will bear your name and the barrel's particulars. You get the barrel, and your name will be part of a display at the distillery. **LB**

Tasting notes

Nice and dark, with a big sweet nose, spiky with woody notes. Quite rich in corn, but slashed with milk chocolate and vanilla, and nailed firmly to a spicy oak framework. Drinkable even at 47 percent, but there's wood in the tail that brings a pop to the finish.

Jefferson's

Castle Brands | www.mclainandkyne.com

Region and country of origin Kentucky, United States
Distillery Undisclosed
Alcohol content 41.15% abv
Style Straight bourbon

The creators of Jefferson's bourbon are the Louisville-based father-and-son team of Chet and Trey Zoeller. They sold their company to Castle Brands a few years ago, but they still produce the whiskey. The Zoellers are not distillers. They buy bulk bourbon from one or several distilleries and hire a bottler to package it for them. This is not common in the United States. Few major brands are made this way, and the business is not very transparent, hence the actual distiller (or distillers) of Jefferson's bourbon is unknown.

But "maker" and "distiller" are not necessarily synonymous. Every barrel of whiskey ages a little differently, so one of the most critical parts of a whiskey maker's job is sampling barrels and making selections. That, ultimately, is how all whiskey is made, whether by a distiller or by a nondistiller producer.

Blending is not a big part of American whiskey making and is, in actual fact, considered a dirty word by some, but if you mix together several straight bourbons all made in Kentucky, you can legitimately call the result Kentucky straight bourbon whiskey. There is no age statement on Jefferson's, so all of the whiskey must be at least four years old. Some or all of it may indeed be older. Mixing together older and younger bourbon is another way to achieve a pleasing taste profile.

Understandably, distillers like to keep the best whiskey for their own brands, and it can be a challenge to maintain consistency. The Zoellers deserve recognition for maintaining the high quality of Jefferson's bourbon over the years. **CKC**

Tasting notes

There is a bit of dry cider in there, giving it a freshness that complements the darker, more tannic part. Everything is muted or restrained except the sooty char that ties it all together. The finish is long and complex, so a pause between sips is rewarded.

Jim Beam Black Label

Beam Global | www.jimbeam.com

Region and country of origin Kentucky, United States
Distilleries Jim Beam, Clermont/Booker Noe, Boston
Alcohol content 43% abv
Style Straight bourbon

For most of the twentieth century, only two products bore the Jim Beam name—Jim Beam bourbon (White Label) and Jim Beam Rye. Everything else in the portfolio was called "Beam's" something or other, such as "Beam's Black Label."

Although it was always a straight bourbon with more age and abv than the standard White Label, Black Label is one of the most fiddled-with whiskeys ever made. Time after time, the brand managers at Beam have changed the name, label, bottle, age, and abv. It has always had a black label, but that is about the only constant; everything else was changed. It went modern, it went retro; it was 45 percent abv, 40 percent abv, and 43 percent abv; it was eight years old, then it was seven years old. Eventually, it was given the full Jim Beam name, aged for eight years in wood, and released at 43 percent abv. Then, in 2010, they changed the bottle again, giving it a sleeker profile. A new slogan, "Double Aged," was introduced and included on the label.

For most of bourbon history, international markets were irrelevant because very little bourbon was exported. Now Jim Beam and other major brands get half of their sales away from home, so images have to be tweaked with a non-U.S. audience in mind. Maybe that's what they're thinking—or maybe not.

Additional age puts Jim Beam Black Label into the class of the much more expensive Booker's, Baker's, and Knob Creek, making it a good-value whiskey. If all you want to do is drink whiskey that tastes good and hits all the right notes, it is ideal. **CKC**

Tasting notes

Rich but also tannic, leading to suggestions of anise and clove. Sooty and oaky, but not too much, with a touch of citrus. Caramel is strong while vanilla is muted. The Beam yeast, so pronounced in White Label, has vanished; in its place is oak, solid as a wall.

Jim Beam links its name with an equally established star. ➡

SEAN CONNERY
The original James Bond
JIM BEAM
You can't improve on the original.
Two one-of-a-kind originals: SEAN CONNERY, the original and most famous James Bond. JIM BEAM, the world's finest Bourbon.
BEAM
SINCE 1795
THE WORLD'S FINEST BOURBON
JIM BEAM
KENTUCKY STRAIGHT BOURBON WHISKEY
Distilled and bottled by
JAMES B. BEAM DISTILLING CO.
CLERMONT · BEAM KENTUCKY
NONE GENUINE WITHOUT MY SIGNATURE
DISTILLERS SINCE 1795
86 PROOF
SINCE 1795

Jim Beam Devil's Cut

Beam Global | www.jimbeam.com

Region and country of origin Kentucky, United States
Distilleries Jim Beam, Clermont/Booker Noe, Boston
Alcohol content 45% abv
Style Straight bourbon

The name Devil's Cut plays off the term "angels' share" (whiskey lost to evaporation) and describes whiskey that has soaked deep into the oak and is not released when the barrel is dumped and rinsed in the usual way. Beam takes an additional step that combines water, heat, and agitation in a modern re-creation of a rite of passage in whiskey called "barrel sweating."

"Soakage whiskey" is very thin, tannic, and sooty on its own. What Beam has done is use it in just the right amount to flavor some of its six-year-old bourbon. The result is an impression of advanced age, the sort of barrel notes that normally only emerge after fifteen or so years of aging. Other producers recover alcohol from dumped barrels, but Beam is the first to use soakage whiskey for flavoring, too.

Beam had fun with the packaging, giving the label a look of partially burned parchment. The fanciful typography suggests horns and a tail.

Because most used bourbon barrels have a second life as Scotch barrels, Jim Beam distiller and brand ambassador Fred Noe was asked if this new process would make the used barrels less desirable for Scotch. "We don't care," was his reply, but he said it in a more colorful way and drew a big laugh. **CKC**

Tasting notes

The added tannin and char lend roughness to the usually mild Jim Beam taste profile. Good but confusing because it is like a young whiskey with an old soul.

Jim Beam Rye

Beam Global | www.jimbeam.com

Region and country of origin Kentucky, United States
Distillery Jim Beam, Clermont
Alcohol content 40% abv
Style Straight rye

Many people are confused about rye whiskey. Jim Beam, judging by its Web site, seems to think it is a type of bourbon. It is not far wrong. American straight whiskeys such as bourbon and rye have most important characteristics in common. The only difference is in the mash bill; corn predominates in bourbon, while rye predominates in rye. Both contain both grains; only the proportions change. After that, they are almost identical in how they are made and matured. New, charred-oak barrels are crucial to both.

Bourbon is the more American drink, since rye is native to the Old World and was brought by settlers, while corn is native to the Americas. The evolution of American whiskey from a base of rye to one founded on corn is symbolic of the shedding of European traditions and the formation of new American ways. The reason, of course, has less to do with heritage than with taste. Corn doesn't have much of it, rye has a lot. While a typical bourbon is 70 to 80 percent corn, a rye like Jim Beam Rye is barely legal at just 51 percent.

Jim Beam Rye has been around for as long as Jim Beam bourbon. For decades, it was the only product other than White Label bourbon to bear the full "Jim Beam" name. It is the best-selling straight rye. **CKC**

Tasting notes

Jim Beam Rye is inoffensive, yet also yeasty and grassy, expressing rye as a kind of muddiness. You can tease out some finer rye notes, like mint and cumin.

Jim Beam Signature Six Grains

Beam Global | www.jimbeam.com

Region and country of origin Kentucky, United States
Distillery Jim Beam, Clermont
Alcohol content 44.5% abv
Style Straight bourbon

Bourbon whiskey can be 100 percent corn if the maker so chooses, but typically a bourbon mash contains corn, rye, and malt. The malt is there for the enzymes that convert grain starch into fermentable sugar. The rye is there for flavor. In some bourbons, wheat is substituted for rye. Other grains can be used, as long as the mash is at least 51 percent corn.

At Jim Beam, just before distilling resumes after summer break, the distillers like to take a week to ten days to run some experiments. In 2002 and 2003 they ran several experimental batches using wheat, brown rice, and triticale (a nineteenth-century hybrid of wheat and rye) instead of rye as the flavor grain.

Beam coined the term "small-batch bourbon." It usually means a small bottling run of specially selected barrels, not a small distillation run. In this case, everything was small from the beginning. Each experimental batch was about forty barrels. By mixing several of the experiments together with some "regular" Jim Beam bourbon, they were able to bottle about 4,000 cases of Six Grains. Normal distribution would have absorbed that in an instant, so travel retail was chosen as the place to showcase both this and future Jim Beam Signature experiments. **CKC**

Tasting notes

Nuttier than most bourbon; Brazil nut, hazelnut, also granola. Mouthfeel is big, and the finish is dry. The surprise is intense notes of root beer on the nose.

Jim Beam White Label

Beam Global | www.jimbeam.com

Region and country of origin Kentucky, United States
Distilleries Jim Beam, Clermont/Booker Noe, Boston
Alcohol content 40% abv
Style Bourbon blend

White Label is the flagship product of Beam Global. All of the whiskey Beams—and there have been many—are descendants of German miller and distiller Jacob Boehm, who came to Kentucky in 1795 and reinvented himself as Jake Beam.

Jim Beam, Jake's great-grandson, co-owned a distillery business in Nelson County when Prohibition began. Until then they had been making a popular bourbon called Old Tub. When Prohibition ended, Jim built a new distillery at Clermont in Bullitt County, Kentucky. Old Tub was renamed for the family patriarch: seventy-year-old Jim. Within a few years, Jim Beam bourbon was one of the country's best-selling whiskies, and it has been ever since. The company operates two large distilleries—the one at Boston is believed to be Kentucky's largest—and about 85 percent of their combined output is sold as Jim Beam White Label four-year-old bourbon.

Although the standard Jim Beam expression is about as mass-produced as whiskey can be, what is remarkable about it is how good it is. Despite its youth, Beam is not hot or harsh, and also, despite its generous rye content, it isn't grassy or very bitter, as rye-based whiskeys can be when young. **CKC**

Tasting notes

Typical barrel notes of vanilla and caramel are balanced against nutty grain flavors and a distinctively sour yeast profile, all arranged over a backbone of sweetness.

Johnny Drum Private Stock

Kentucky Bourbon Distillers
www.kentuckybourbonwhiskey.com

Region and country of origin Kentucky, United States
Distilleries Various
Alcohol content 50.5% abv
Style Bourbon blend

Johnny Drum Private Stock is produced by Kentucky Bourbon Distillers (KBD) of Bardstown, Kentucky, one of the largest independent bottlers of whiskey in the United States. Through arrangements with a number of Kentucky's largest whiskey producers, the bottler purchases select barrels of whiskey for distribution under many private labels. Johnny Drum is one label that KBD founder Even (pronounced "Evan") Kulsveen produced in KBD's early years.

The Private Stock release is a blend of older whiskey than the entry-level Johnny Drum Bourbon. The 101-proof version was designed to have a fuller flavor while still proving to be "user friendly and medium bodied," according to KBD's Drew Kulsveen. It was previously a blend of at least fifteen-year-old whiskey, but supply issues caused KBD to reformulate in recent years, and bourbons of five to six-plus years old are now used. The contents of barrels that demonstrate a balance of sweetness, fruit, and spice are blended together in small batches of fewer than twenty barrels at a time.

The name Johnny Drum is thought to refer to the drummer boys of the American Civil War who helped soldiers keep the beat as they marched. **JP**

Tasting notes

The nose is full of pancake syrup, caramel, popcorn, and oak. Sweet with maple-glazed nuts, caramel corn, a punch of oak, and the pleasing hum of spice and heat.

J. T. S. Brown Bottled in Bond

Heaven Hill Distilleries
www.heaven-hill.com

Region and country of origin Kentucky, United States
Distillery Heaven Hill, Bardstown
Alcohol content 50% abv
Style Straight bourbon

J. T. S. Brown was made famous by Paul Newman in the 1961 movie *The Hustler*, where he name checks this bourbon. Being the whiskey of choice of a small-time pool hustler may seem incongruous today, but that's bourbon for you; in fifty years, the whole landscape has changed. The drink is nowhere near as iconic as the movie, but Heaven Hill still gets requests from pool halls for J. T. S. Brown signs.

Whiskey writer Chuck Cowdery first pointed out the bonded bottle. Standing in Toddy's Liquors, the landmark shop in Bardstown, Kentucky, he pointed to the bottom shelf and rumbled, "That's one of the best whiskeys for the price on any shelf." At $11.99 (£8), it's a fair bet for anyone with even a passing interest and an "investment" you are highly unlikely to regret.

Heaven Hill has a ton of these old brands, and most of them are sitting down there on the bottom shelf. Some of them are cooking whiskey, but some are a luscious bargain. J. T. S. Brown has been cut off from its roots, traded around the market (Heaven Hill bought it from Seagram), and mostly sells as an 80 proof. The bonded bottling hasn't seen much love lately, but it's still down there on the bottom shelf, waiting for a savvy buyer. **JP**

Tasting notes

This one rings all the bells, if faintly: corn, oak, maple, vanilla, and mint, along with 100 proof heat. Finishes with a hot wash of peppermint that's reluctant to fade.

← A fermenter is examined at the Willett distillery, a forerunner of KBD.

Kentucky Tavern Bourbon

Sazerac | www.greatbourbon.com/KentuckyTavern.aspx

Region and country of origin Kentucky, United States
Distillery Barton 1792, Bardstown
Alcohol content 40% abv
Style Straight bourbon

Kentucky Tavern was the name of both a bourbon brand and a restaurant and bar that was highly popular in the 1950s on the east side of Louisville, Kentucky. Local legend says the bourbon was named for the bar, but the reverse seems more likely, as the name was first registered as a whiskey brand in 1916.

The hostelry was on the main road between downtown and the prosperous eastern suburbs, and boasted an outdoor beer garden. Universally known by its initials, KT, it now has a modern, equally popular successor, called KT's Lounge, on the same spot.

The Kentucky Tavern bourbon, also known as KT, was long associated with the Thompson family and their Glenmore distillery, which was originally in Owensboro, Kentucky. The business itself was always based in Louisville. Glenmore was the name of a castle near the family's ancestral home in Ireland.

The KT brand was eclipsed when Glenmore bought the much bigger Yellowstone brand in 1944. Eventually the Owensboro plant was closed and all of Glenmore's bourbons, including KT, were made at Yellowstone in Shively, a suburb of Louisville. When that distillery closed, all of Glenmore's production moved back to Owensboro, but to a smaller distillery Glenmore owned there called Medley Brothers.

Glenmore was eventually acquired by what became Diageo, which closed the distillery and sold most of Glenmore's bourbon brands. KT went to Barton, where it remained until Sazerac bought the distillery in 2009. KT continues to be made at Sazerac's Barton 1792 distillery in Bardstown. **CKC**

Tasting notes

The famous back-of-the-throat burn, exorcised from most modern potions, is still available in Kentucky Tavern. Rye bitterness exactly balances corn sweetness. Sour apple in the finish recalls the bourbon's white dog roots. Otherwise, a standard rye-recipe bourbon.

Kentucky Tavern advertises both itself and war bonds in World War II. ➡

BUY THEM ★ KEEP THEM

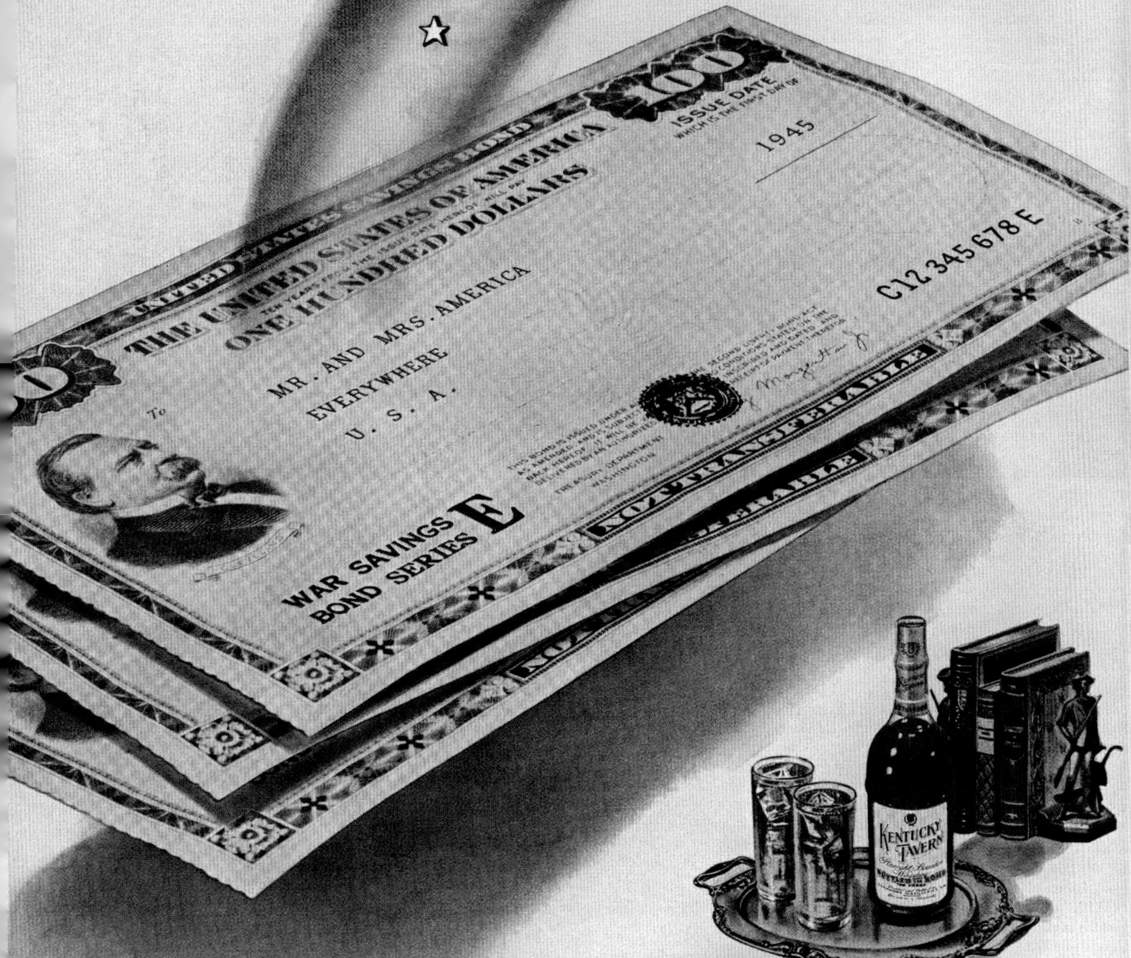

...published in the interest of the Seventh War Loan.
Glenmore Distilleries Co., Incorporated, Louisville, Kentucky.

OUR BOYS DON'T WANT THANKS ★ ★ ★ THEY WANT GUNS, SHIPS, PLANES, TANKS!

Knob Creek

Beam Global | www.knobcreek.com

Region and country of origin Kentucky, United States
Distillery Jim Beam, Clermont
Alcohol content 50% abv
Style Straight bourbon

Of the four whiskies Beam launched in 1992 as the Small Batch Bourbon Collection, Knob Creek was the longest-aged with the lowest price; it also became the company's biggest star. It now ranks third in the Beam portfolio of bourbons, directly after the heavyweights Jim Beam and Maker's Mark.

How did Knob Creek rise to such heights in less than twenty years? Was it the flask-type bottle? The evocative name? The age? The price? The higher-than-average 50 percent abv? Some or all of the above? No one can say for sure, but it worked, and Knob left its other three stablemates in the dust.

There is a real Knob Creek in Kentucky, but it does not flow past the distillery. Its significant part is near Athertonville in LaRue County, where distilleries have stood from an early date. According to local tradition, Thomas Lincoln, father of Abraham Lincoln, worked in one of them. The Lincoln farm was nearby, also on Knob Creek, and it is said that the young Lincoln once nearly drowned in the rain-swollen creek and had to be rescued by a schoolmate.

At nine years old, Knob Creek bourbon is the oldest American whiskey sold by Beam. At first it was just that, nine-year-old Jim Beam, but as it has grown, the recipe has been tweaked. Now it is tagged as Knob Creek when it enters the barrel, although it is still made from the basic Jim Beam bourbon mash bill and yeast strain. It is interesting to work your way through the Jim Beams, then Booker's, Baker's, and Knob, to see just how much the new charred-oak barrel changes the whiskey along the way. **CKC**

Tasting notes

The high alcohol content shows itself mostly on the nose and in the finish. Knock it down with water to get caramel and clove, mint and citrus. There is nothing unusual here, no sudden burst of chamomile, just bourbon flavors at high volume and in ideal balance.

Knob Creek Single Barrel

Beam Global | www.knobcreek.com

Region and country of origin Kentucky, United States
Distillery Jim Beam, Clermont
Alcohol content 60% abv
Style Straight bourbon

Several years ago, Jim Beam distiller and bourbon ambassador Fred Noe showed up at a Chicago bar for a party during Whiskey Week. The host had invited several distillers and encouraged them to "bring something special." Noe brought an unmarked Jim Beam bottle and sat by the door for most of the evening, pouring free samples from it. He would not reveal anything except that it was bourbon and they made it. "It's something we're working on," he said.

During Whiskey Week 2011, Noe revealed to a companion who had sat with him by the door that night that the mystery whiskey had been Knob Creek Single Barrel, just released that January in an uncharacteristic flurry of new product introductions. Although single-barrel bottlings are not necessarily superior to other similar whiskies, this is a special case. It is the first time a single-barrel expression has been created from an existing taste profile. Since any barrel that qualifies to be Knob Creek Single Barrel already qualifies to be Knob Creek, how do you choose? You could pick barrels at random, but why would you? The more sensible strategy is to pick only the best of the lot, the "honey barrels." That's subjective to be sure, but who better to pick than Booker Noe's son, Fred, who also is Jim Beam's great-grandson?

It is a measure of Knob Creek's success that it has earned this spin-off product, what the trade calls a line extension. In addition to selecting honey barrels, they also upped the abv to 60 percent. The company generally promotes cocktails, but both Knobs do a good shots business, too. **CKC**

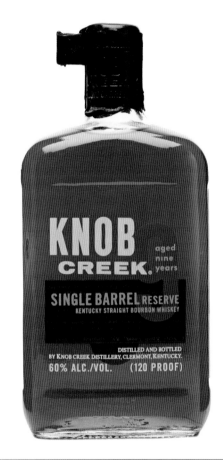

Tasting notes

Even when the abv is corrected with water, this has more sparkle than the standard version, and more Christmas cookie spices, but it finishes with olive brine. Despite the way it sounds, that is not a bad thing. The clove note is strong, with old tobacco and old leather.

Lion's Pride Dark Millet Organic Whiskey

Koval | www.koval-distillery.com

Region and country of origin Illinois, United States
Distillery Koval, Chicago
Alcohol content 40% abv
Style Millet whiskey

Koval's distiller and CEO, Robert Birnecker, is a native of Austria. His grandparents have been involved in distilling and brewing fruit and grain spirits from their family farm for more than forty years. According to Koval, among the wide variety of grain spirits used by Austrian distillers are some that are not common in other parts of the world. Koval is committed to working with the underutilized and underappreciated grains to bring something new to the whiskey market.

The distillery has taken that approach to a high level with the release of its Dark Millet Organic Whiskey under the Lion's Pride name. Since opening, Koval has become well known as a craft distiller for its light or nonaged whiskeys. The Lion's Pride range is designed to showcase grain spirits with more age and barrel flavors. Koval's Dark Millet is unique first and foremost because no other American distillery is working with the grain today.

People who have never eaten anything made with millet are probably only familiar with it in the form of birdseed. But after Robert had worked with the grain for some time, he found the results to be among his favorite whiskeys from the distillery. The whiskey is made from 100 percent single grain, which ensures that the end product is a full expression of the grain from which it was distilled. Following distillation, it is aged for less than two years in American oak barrels subjected to a level-four char, which is the highest char rating on the typical four-point scale. Lion's Pride Dark Millet is sold unfiltered to guarantee that the grain experience is an intense one. **JP**

Tasting notes

The nose is full of fresh, ripe fruit (green apple, plum, and peach), spices (ginger and anise), and caramelized nuts. The palate begins sweetly (brown sugar, canned pears in syrup) before barrel, wood spices, and licorice dry things up on through to a moderately spicy finish.

Lion's Pride Dark Oat Organic Whiskey

Koval | www.koval-distillery.com

Region and country of origin Illinois, United States
Distillery Koval, Chicago
Alcohol content 40% abv
Style Oat whiskey

When people think of oats, their first association is often with oatmeal, the "stick to your ribs" breakfast staple. Many a hardworking man or woman begins the day with this hearty porridge. Yet the craft distillers who began to experiment with distilling from oats were surprised to discover that the grain produces a most elegant, soft, and delicate whiskey.

Today, the production of oat whiskey is no more than a blip on the radar screen in the United States, but the few distilleries working with it are being rewarded for their risk taking. Koval is one such distillery that has managed to coax the essence out of this enigma of a grain. Robert Birnecker, Koval's master distiller, is a lover of the underappreciated grains for distilling whiskey. Rather than build Koval around the American whiskey staple, corn, Robert and his wife, Sonat, have focused on the road less traveled. That path has led them to work with grains like millet, wheat, rye, spelt, and of course, oat.

In November 2010, the couple introduced the distillery's newest line of whiskeys, named after their son, Lion. The Lion's Pride range features "dark" and "light" segments of each individual grain they distill. Like the other whiskeys in the lineup, Lion's Pride Dark Oat Organic Whiskey is distilled from 100 percent nonmalted oat-grain mash. It is aged for less than two years in newly charred American oak barrels with the highest char level possible. The resulting whiskey tastes as though it has been touched only lightly by the wood, a Koval distillery hallmark. The whiskey is light, clean, and vibrant, with restrained oak. **JP**

Tasting notes

This confectionery wonder has banana cream, vanilla fudge, and shortbread cookie with brown sugar syrup on the nose. The flavors on the palate are also sweet (banana bread, oatmeal cookie dough, bubble gum), but balanced by biscuity dryness and black pepper.

Lion's Pride Dark Rye Organic Whiskey

Koval | www.koval-distillery.com

Region and country of origin Illinois, United States
Distillery Koval, Chicago
Alcohol content 40% abv
Style Rye whiskey

The Koval distillery has been producing rye whiskey since it opened in 2008. Owned and operated by husband-and-wife team Robert and Sonat Birnecker, Koval began aging five types of single-grain whiskey in hopes of selling aged products as soon as they were able. In 2010 that dream was realized with the distillery's release of the Lion's Pride whiskey lineup. Consisting of five single-grain whiskeys in lighter (less aged) and darker (more aged) varieties, the Lion's Pride whiskey line uses organic grain sourced from farms in the American Midwest.

Lion's Pride Dark Rye is made from 100 percent rye grain. Rye is a notoriously difficult grain to distill due to its extremely high gluten content. This trait causes the grain to gum up like paste in the cooking or mashing process. Many distilleries circumvent the issue by adding a percentage of barley malt, which helps to convert the starch to sugars more efficiently. But Koval did not want to compromise the flavor of the rye grain with the addition of other grains. Instead, the distillery uses enzymes to aid in the starch conversion. The resulting whiskey has all the vibrant character of the grain from which it was made, coupled with Koval's lighter, cleaner, signature style. **JP**

Tasting notes

Pine sap, eucalyptus, menthol, and peppery rye grain dominate a nose that is herbal and fresh. On the palate, a wave of vibrant cinnamon, mint, licorice, and ginger.

Lion's Pride Dark Wheat Organic Whiskey

Koval | www.koval-distillery.com

Region and country of origin Illinois, United States
Distillery Koval, Chicago
Alcohol content 40% abv
Style Wheat whiskey

Robert and Sonat Birnecker are the husband-and-wife owners of Koval distillery in Chicago. Their Lion's Pride whiskey lineup is crafted from 100 percent organic single grains. This approach is not common among other American distilleries, which often use a blend of grains such as corn, rye, or wheat, and barley malt.

Robert, the master distiller, believes that a single-grain whiskey is the purest possible expression of an individual grain. His love of unusual grains has led to a Lion's Pride lineup of five neglected grains.

Lion's Pride Dark Wheat is one such example. Wheat is a small, soft grain typically used as a flavoring agent in other American whiskeys, such as Maker's Mark and Pappy Van Winkle wheated bourbons. While aged wheat whiskey is increasing in popularity, fewer than a dozen distilleries are producing it. Even fewer than that are producing 100 percent wheat whiskey.

All Lion's Pride dark whiskeys are distilled in a traditional copper pot still. The spirit is aged in 30-gallon (114-liter) new American oak barrels for no longer than two years. Robert's deft hand and focus on keeping only the best phase of the distillation yields a whisper-light wheat whiskey, in defiant contrast to heavier, sweeter whiskeys. **JP**

Tasting notes

The nose has notes of toffee, fruit-flavored chewing gum, and graham cracker. The flavors are soft and sweet with vanilla custard, sticky caramel, banana, and ginger.

A 100-percent wheat whiskey is a logical step in the state of Illinois. ➔

Low Gap

Craft Distillers | www.craftdistillers.com

Region and country of origin California, United States
Distillery Craft, Redwood Valley
Alcohol content 44.8% abv
Style Wheat whiskey

Craft Distillers, a small, boutique brandy and cognac distillery, operates at the distillery of Germain-Robin, which was started in 1982 by Ansley Coale. Coale was joined by an accomplished brandy distiller, Hubert Germain-Robin, who left France for the United States following the purchase of the distillery he worked for, Surrenne distillery in Triac. Germain-Robin's brandies are considered some of the finest in the world.

In 2003 Craft Distillers set out on a mission to create small-batch, handcrafted spirits. Distiller Crispin Cain, a former apprentice of Germain-Robin, distills the Low Gap spirit in an antique cognac still that Germain-Robin brought with him from France. Such old, hand-operated stills require a deft touch, but if controlled properly, can produce silky, elegant spirits. Cain was unsure whether the still was capable of producing a great whiskey, but decided to give it a try. The results were a surprise even to him.

Made from 100 percent malted Bavarian wheat, Low Gap is one of the very few single-grain wheat whiskeys on the market. The double-distilled whiskey is full of flavor, yet elegant and complex. The wheat mash (cooked grain and water) is fermented slowly to enhance the flavor of the grain. The distillate is then brought to Craft Distillers' desired bottling proof of 44.8 percent abv using unfiltered rainwater.

Craft Distillers has done justice to what most distilleries consider a small flavoring grain. Whether or not a longer-aged version of this product will be released remains to be seen, but with a white whiskey this good, is that even necessary? **JP**

Tasting notes

Low Gap's aroma is full of ripe fruit (pear and apple) and whole-wheat cracker. On the palate, the flavors are equally fruity, but matched with some savory buttered biscuit and a light, peppery spice. The finish is as clean and light as one of those crackers.

Maker's Mark

Beam Global | www.makersmark.com

Region and country of origin Kentucky, United States
Distillery Maker's Mark, Loretto
Alcohol content 45% abv
Style Straight wheated bourbon

Maker's Mark has had a disproportionate effect on what the U.S. market thinks of bourbon. Until recently, it was a small-production whiskey with a handmade aura to it, helped by the shape of the bottle, the hand-dipped red wax on the cork, and the deckle-edged label. Maker's Mark intrigued people and lured many into trying bourbon for the first time.

That was when they realized the real difference. Maker's Mark is a wheated bourbon, made with winter wheat instead of rye. Bill Samuels, who started the brand in the 1950s, found wheated bourbon less bitter than bourbons made with rye. Customers liked it too, and have ensured its success ever since.

Maker's Mark has been remarkably consistent, too. It is not a line of products but originally a 90-percent-proof wheated bourbon at about six years old, because that is what the Samuels family thought was best. The distillery even goes to the labor and expense of rotating barrels through the warehouses to minimize differences in whisky batches due to temperature variations on lower and higher floors.

When it was decided to expand distilling capacity, the Samuels family was determined that no changes would occur in the character of the new make, so they took the blueprints of the original distillery and built a duplicate beside it. This writer had a dipper of white dog off the still one time, and it was the smoothest conceivable. Maker's Mark is the favorite of a devoted niche of bourbon drinkers, who won't drink anything else. Bear that in mind when you try it; one sip may turn out to be a lifetime commitment. **LB**

Tasting notes

Sweet cinnamon and corn with a lacing of vanilla. This pops in the mouth like a small firework: corn, more cinnamon, then a delayed burst of oak spice, all in a beautiful balance. Sweet without being sappy or thick; the beauty of wheat.

Maker's Mark 46

Beam Global | www.makersmark.com

Region and country of origin Kentucky, United States
Distillery Maker's Mark, Loretto
Alcohol content 47% abv
Style Wheated bourbon

According to master distiller Kevin Smith, Maker's Mark 46 was initiated by distillery president Bill Samuels Jr. "Bill had a nightmare he'd died and his epitaph was 'He didn't screw it up.' He got to thinking about his legacy and asked 'What have I really done?'"

Samuels remembered consumer requests for something new and started talking to Smith. The conversation led to a desire for a bourbon with more toasted oak in the nose, without adding wood astringency in the back palate. This meant going down the road about 10 miles (16 km) to see Brad Boswell, president of Independent Stave Company, who brought in international whiskey wood expert Dr. Jim Swan to help solve Samuels's problem.

After toasting barrels, adding cubed oak or extra staves, and varying the aging—"All failures," Smith said—Boswell turned to searing French oak slats, as he had done for winemakers. Searing involved moving the slats under radiant heaters, caramelizing sugars on the surface but not charring them, and not going as deep as toasting. "I call it Profile 46," he told them. "I have no idea what it might do; the proof of what you're aging is so different from that of wine."

Smith dumps barrels of Maker's Mark into a holding tank, takes the heads off, and puts the slats in with food-grade plastic spacers. The heads are replaced and the barrels refilled from the tank. Then it's back to the warehouse for another nine weeks. "It's a pain," Smith admitted, but it is worth the trouble. Maker's Mark 46 is not only different, it is good. Time to inscribe a new tombstone, Bill. **LB**

Tasting notes

Compared to the regular Maker's Mark, the nose is deeper. The cinnamon is wrapped in thicker oak notes, and is fuller, richer. It rolls into the mouth like a wave of hot candy sugar and vanilla, checked by dry oakiness. The oak dries up the end, too. An impressive difference.

A distinctive dipped red wax seal completes Maker's Mark whiskeys.

McAFEE's

BENCHMARK

OLD № 8 BRAND

8

KENTUCKY STRAIGHT
BOURBON WHISKEY

McAfee's Benchmark Old No. 8 Brand

Sazerac
www.greatbourbon.com

Region and country of origin Kentucky, United States
Distillery Buffalo Trace, Frankfort
Alcohol content 40% abv
Style Straight bourbon

Plain Benchmark was originally a Seagram's brand, launched in the late 1960s along with Eagle Rare. The two were among the last new brands introduced before the bourbon market collapsed. In 1989, Sazerac got into the bourbon business by buying Benchmark and Eagle Rare. Both brands have been repositioned several times as the bourbon market has changed.

The McAfee name was added by Sazerac. It refers to Hancock McAfee, who is believed to have been the first European settler, in 1775, at the site where Buffalo Trace distillery stands today. (A lawyer may have told them the original name was too generic, or too much like Maker's Mark, without a modifier.)

McAfee's Benchmark is a straight bourbon, aged for at least four years. It is a rye-recipe bourbon made to Buffalo Trace's less rye-dominated mash bill, one it shares with Eagle Rare, Old Charter, Buffalo Trace, and others. Its mash bill is probably more than 80 percent corn, a characteristic it shares with Jack Daniel's.

McAfee's Benchmark offers an illustration of how whiskey matures in the barrel, and how much it can change. Some may think this a rough whiskey, but were it given a few more years in wood, it would gain the balance of Sazerac's Eagle Rare Single Barrel. **CKC**

Tasting notes

A big flavor that leads with brown-sugar sweetness, then reveals a hot finish. Rather like drinking herbal bitters. Ginger comes through as a spice note.

McCarthy's Oregon Single Malt

Clear Creek Distillery
www.clearcreekdistillery.com

Region and country of origin Oregon, United States
Distillery Clear Creek, Portland
Alcohol content 46% abv
Style Single malt

Few American distilleries were making single malt in the early 1990s when Clear Creek began producing their Islay-like, heavily peated flagship whiskey named after Clear Creek proprietor Steve McCarthy.

McCarthy's Oregon Single Malt begins with peated barley imported directly from Scotland. The barley is mashed and fermented by Widmer Brothers, a local Portland, Oregon, brewery, and Clear Creek distills the resulting peaty, smoky wash in a classic pot still to 75 percent alcohol, or 150 proof. The distillate spends time in former sherry casks before being finished in air-dried Oregon oak barrels. The Oregon wood is said to add local flavor to the whiskey.

While quite young at approximately three years, McCarthy's is known for its depth of flavor and character, resembling a long-lost cousin of some of Islay's best-known distilleries. Clear Creek says the finished whiskey most resembles a younger Lagavulin.

Clear Creek is a micro-operation, and allocations of McCarthy's Oregon Single Malt are limited to one or two small-batch releases each year. Finding it on store shelves is difficult, but Clear Creek is always willing to help enthusiasts by providing advance information on releases that might yield a bottle or two. **JP**

Tasting notes

Like a light Islay single malt. Peat smoke and brine combine with vibrant citrus rind. Malt and honey sweetness holds together an earthy, mineral quality.

← McAfee's Benchmark: another black-and-white label bourbon.

Mellow Corn

Heaven Hill | www.heaven-hill.com

Region and country of origin Kentucky, United States
Distillery Heaven Hill, Bardstown
Alcohol content 50% abv
Style Corn whiskey

The craft whiskey movement in the United States is something to behold, with new distilleries popping up all the time. Seemingly, each one of these upstarts is rediscovering and producing corn whiskey, but sadly, much of it is below standard. But Heaven Hill knows, better than most, how it should be made.

To date, the Kentucky-based distillery produces four aged corn whiskeys: Georgia Moon, J. W. Corn, Dixie Dew, and Mellow Corn. The final three are aged longer and have much in common; all are 100 proof and have a light-bodied flavor profile.

Mellow Corn may be the distillery's best product. In order for a whiskey to be called a "corn whiskey" it must be at least 81 percent corn grain. The wide availability and low cost of corn enabled corn whiskey production to predate bourbon, which requires a lower percentage of corn (51 percent minimum) and a higher percentage of flavoring grains (rye and wheat).

With Mellow Corn, Heaven Hill increases the corn component in the mash bill to 90 percent; rye and barley malt make up the remaining percentages. Corn is known to be the most efficient grain for producing alcohol, but it also serves to provide sweetness and body in a finished whiskey.

Aged less than four years in oak, Mellow Corn's rustic charm serves as a "country cottage" in comparison to bourbon's "stately manor." But whiskey enthusiasts should not ignore this category in favor of more complicated whiskeys. Variety is the spice of life, and there is just something extremely comforting about a well-made corn whiskey. **JP**

Tasting notes

Mellow Corn has a bright and brisk nose with vanilla, dried banana chip, and honeyed sweet corn. Vibrant ginger and chile emerge quickly on the palate, wrapped around a core of vanilla taffy and banana fruitiness. The finish is long and peppery.

Noah's Mill

Kentucky Bourbon Distillers | www.kentuckybourbonwhiskey.com

Region and country of origin Kentucky, United States
Distillery Undisclosed
Alcohol content 57.15% abv
Style Bourbon

Noah's Mill is a small-batch bourbon from Kentucky Bourbon Distillers (KBD), an independent aging and bottling company in Bardstown, Kentucky. KBD is renovating the old Willett distillery, but does not currently distill its own products. Instead, the company sources distilled spirits from elsewhere for aging in their own facilities. In some cases, the company purchases finished barrels from other distilleries and bottles them or ages them further. Where they get their barrels from is not disclosed.

Noah's Mill is one of KBD's barrel-strength flagship bourbons and is of exceptional quality. It is bottled at a huge 57.15 percent abv, or 114.3 proof. Early iterations of the product consisted of whiskey of at least fifteen years of age. In recent years, KBD reformulated the blend to make production more consistent and reduce some of the oak tannins that were present in the older products. Today the finished product consists of straight bourbons of between four and twenty years of age. Noah's Mill contains bourbon made to recipes with varied percentages of rye grain, blended with bourbon in which the rye grain is replaced by winter wheat. This kind of blending is not common practice.

The classification of "small-batch bourbon" can be misleading. The term has no regulations tied to it, so one distillery's "small batch" might be thousands of barrels; another's might be only a few. Noah's Mill batches consist of no more than twenty barrels. Truly a small-batch bourbon, Noah's Mill is blended and bottled one batch at a time. **JP**

Tasting notes

The nose is complex with toffee, roasted nuts, vanilla, wood, and corn. There is a nice backbone of wood spices to add some spark. The palate is full of chewy dark fruits, marmalade, almond toffee, and vanilla. The finish is long and intense with spice and charred oak.

Notch

Triple Eight Distillery | www.ciscobrewers.com

Region and country of origin Massachusetts, United States **Distillery** Triple Eight, Nantucket Island
Alcohol content 44.4% abv
Style Single malt

Triple Eight distillery began operating on Nantucket Island in 2000. Not having produced whiskey before, it enlisted the help of a former consultant to the famed Bowmore distillery on the Isle of Islay in Scotland. Affiliated with Cisco Brewers, Triple Eight called on a neighboring brewery to provide a ready-made distiller's beer crafted from Maris Otter malted barley.

The young beer is distilled in small batches in a copper pot still, which maximizes concentration of sugars and flavor. The resulting spirit is placed in ex-bourbon and American whiskey barrels purchased from noted distilleries such as Jim Beam, Jack Daniel's, Woodford Reserve, and Buffalo Trace. Once barreled, the whiskey matures in Triple Eight's bonded aging warehouse for upward of eight years. In the last few months of aging, Triple Eight transfers the whiskey to Nantucket Vineyard merlot wine barrels, which round out the whisky and lend it a red or russet hue.

Struggling for a name for its new whiskey, and knowing that the name Scotch must apply only to whiskies from Scotland, Triple Eight eventually settled on the name Notch. This was an oblique reference to the fact that the first single malt distilled on Nantucket Island was "not Scotch." It is not Scotch, certainly, but it demonstrates the ever-improving skill in the United States for creating single-malt whiskeys. **JP**

Tasting notes

On the palate, lemongrass and ginger spiciness bring zip to malty, toffee sweetness. The finish is brisk and sharp with toasted oak, cocoa, vanilla, and prickly spice.

Nantucket is self-sufficient in the drinks department. →

roducts
Nantucket

udly produced at Bartlett Farm Road, Nantucket MA.

Rudyard Kipling travels half around the world to visit Mark Twain

In the summer of 1889 young Rudyard Kipling visited Mark Twain. Of that historic meeting Twain said—
"Between us we cover all knowledge: he knows all that can be known and I know the rest."
Old Crow undoubtedly was the whiskey served. Mark Twain was so partial to Old Crow
he went to James Crow's distillery to order some for his home supply.

Taste the
Greatness
of historic
OLD CROW

Just as there are few great men—
so, too, is great whiskey a rarity.
Since Old Crow was first distilled
127 years ago, great men of every
generation have welcomed it. It set
the standards for fine Kentucky
bourbon. Today, more people buy
light, mild, 86 proof Old Crow than
any other bourbon. Try it. You can
taste its greatness.

today – lighter, milder, 86 Proof

Old Crow Reserve

Beam Global

Region and country of origin Kentucky, United States
Distillery Jim Beam, Clermont
Alcohol content 43% abv
Style Straight bourbon

James C. Crow was a Scottish physician and distiller who came to Kentucky and settled near the town of Versailles. He applied scientific methods to the usual helter-skelter of whiskey making and became one of the first to achieve consistency from batch to batch. Also rare for his time, he insisted on selling only aged whiskey and charged a two-thirds premium for it. People began to ask for Dr. Crow's whiskey by name.

When Crow died in 1856, his heirs promoted his assistant and carried on making the whiskey, eventually calling it Old Crow. It was very popular before Prohibition and became one of the best sellers for several decades after it. But when the industry's collapse began in the late 1960s, Old Crow lost its market share, in some years at a double-digit clip.

In 1987, Beam acquired Crow, closed the distillery, and produced the brand themselves. Crow languished as an undrinkable 40 percent abv, three-year-old bourbon. In 2010, Old Crow Reserve was introduced at 43 percent abv and four years old. It is quite a bit better and well worth a try. There is still a distillery on Dr. Crow's site, too. Rebuilt about twenty years after his death, it is now the Woodford Reserve distillery, owned by Beam archrival Brown-Forman. **CKC**

Tasting notes

Even after four years in new charred wood, immaturity manifests itself as heat, burn, and off flavors. Still, this four-year-old is preferable to its three-year-old sibling.

Old Fitzgerald Bottled in Bond

Heaven Hill Distilleries | www.heaven-hill.com

Region and country of origin Kentucky, United States
Distillery Heaven Hill, Bardstown
Alcohol content 50% abv
Style Wheated bourbon

Old Fitzgerald was once an iconic brand of the Stitzel-Weller distillery. The origins of the name are cloudy—there are stories of who Fitzgerald was, possibly a bourbon-loving treasury officer; while "old" is pretty much a bourbon meme. Unusually for the Stitzel-Weller distillery, this is a wheated bourbon.

Stitzel-Weller was where Julian P. "Pappy" Van Winkle put up his famous sign: "We make fine bourbon. At a profit if we can, at a loss if we must, but always fine bourbon." Pappy was not a distiller by trade, but a salesman, one of the best. When he was able to purchase the Old Fitzgerald brand after Prohibition, he made it his flagship. Pappy liked the smoother character of wheated bourbons, and hung his—and Old Fitzgerald's—hat on that by using the tagline "a whisper of wheat" to promote the whiskey.

This is one of those older brands that can still be found in bottled-in-bond form. "Bottled in bond" is used to denote "the good stuff," real bourbon for serious whiskey drinkers: 100 proof, blended from barrels of straight whiskey produced in a single season, at a single distillery, under the supervision of a single distiller. Without doubt, underpromoted bottled-in-bond bourbons like this offer superb value. **LB**

Tasting notes

A well-behaved bonded, starting with corn and light wood spice, followed by a rush of mint as the overproof heat finally shows up to briefly torch the finish.

Old Fitzgerald Very Special 12-Year-Old

Heaven Hill Distilleries | www.heaven-hill.com

Region and country of origin Kentucky, United States
Distillery Heaven Hill, Bardstown
Alcohol content 45% abv
Style Straight wheated bourbon

Bourbon enthusiasts like to guess where the spirit was distilled before it became the bourbon in the bottle in front of them. The label does not always help because many distilleries mentioned on labels do not exist. Think about it: there are fewer than ten bourbon distilleries in Kentucky, yet many more distilleries are named on labels. Is that not dishonest?

Well, before you answer that, there is more: branded bourbon is often distilled at the plant of another company altogether. Company A will mash and ferment to their own recipe and then run it through Company B's still. Capacity and schedule often work out better that way, but why they can do it is more revealing: the actual distillation in a column still has relatively little effect on flavor. Flavor really comes from the mash bill, the yeast, and, perhaps most important, the barrel-aging regimen. That, and selecting suitable barrels for a brand's profile, is how different whiskeys are made.

Why talk about this Old Fitzgerald in particular? Bardstown-based Heaven Hill bought the brand in 1999 at the same time as they bought the Bernheim distillery in Louisville for their own purposes. There is still speculation among whiskey enthusiasts about where Old Fitzgerald Very Special 12-Year-Old comes from; some opine that it is from the old Stitzel-Weller distillery where it was first made. But no: all the Old Fitz whiskey has been made at Bernheim since 1992.

Good whiskey is the result of aging and selection. Why not open a bottle of Old Fitzgerald Very Special and assess that for yourself? **LB**

Tasting notes

Sweet but fiery, crackling in the nose with oak spice and sharp mint, layered vanilla and some blackberry notes. There's heat in the first sip, with gripping layers of leather and vanilla, more of that mint, and a solid stamp of oak. A long finish of spice, vanilla, and cured tobacco.

Old Forester Birthday Bourbon 2010

Brown-Forman Corporation | www.oldforester.com

Region and country of origin Kentucky, United States
Distillery Brown-Forman, Shively
Alcohol content 47.5% abv
Style Straight bourbon

Old Forester Birthday Bourbon was released on September 2, 2010, on the birthday of Brown-Forman founder George Garvin Brown. Brown was a force in the whiskey industry and a force in his company, and this bourbon is a commemoration.

Just as significantly, it is an educational tool. Brown-Forman master distiller Chris Morris explains, "Typical bourbons [unless they are single-barrel bourbons] are batched from various dates and various warehouses, to fix the flavor profile. The latest batch of Woodford, for example, was from barrels from January 2005 back to May of 2003. The idea for Birthday Bourbon was to hold back a quarter of a day from a significant day that would otherwise be blended into standard brand profile, and follow it through. Every barrel is an individual. Batching barrels from the same day gives you a better picture of that character. There's usually something different about that day: a trial of a new malt supplier; we lost power one day; a new operator's first day on the stills; quirky things...."

What about this one? It is the wood. "It had a nice coconut note to it, really neat," Morris says. "This went back to some changes in procedure at the cooperage. Coconut indicates that the wood was left outside for quite a while, picking up some nice oak lactones."

These days, Brown-Forman is doing some very interesting things with wood and barrels, the kind of things that you can do when you have your own cooperage and the kind of money that making Jack Daniel's generates. What's next? Who knows, but Old Forester Birthdays come around every year. **LB**

Tasting notes

At first, it seems like standard oaky corn, but a swirl in the glass, and coconut notes come through. These are also in the mouth after the first hit of hot corn; a strong bottom keel to the flavor that makes this uniquely, powerfully smooth. Long, gripping finish.

Old Forester Birthday Bourbon 2007

Brown-Forman Corporation | www.oldforester.com

Region and country of origin Kentucky, United States
Distillery Brown-Forman, Shively
Alcohol content 47% abv
Style Straight bourbon

Master distiller Chris Morris met our tasting group at the door of Brown-Forman's offices in Louisville one day in 2007. We headed back to the bar to taste six glasses of whiskey, starting with Old Forester in 86 proof and 100 proof: always very fine stuff.

But then he produced a sample of the 2007 Birthday Bourbon. Whereas the regular Old Forester is a mingling of ages, from about four years to six years old, this is a vintage whiskey, usually from a single day of distillation and therefore more focused. The Birthday Bourbon is a "teaching moment," a look at something out of the ordinary involving a comparison of two variables—the length of time of the aging, and where the aging took place. The Birthday Bourbon is also more like an independent bottling: not standardized, but special.

And this one? "It's from fifty-two barrels, distilled on September 6, 1995," Chris explained. "They were all in Warehouse H, on the sixth floor. We keep them together so they'll have the variation from the different barrels, but the warehouse situation will be the same. Nothing really stood out in terms of production; we just noticed, 'Hey, this really tastes good!' Sometimes it just comes out that way. We had a couple of years in a row with mint and spearmint notes; this one had a real nice cinnamon note to it."

It arguably had both, and sure enough, the 2007 turned out to be one of the very best of the series, a multiple-award winner. Oh, and those other three whiskeys? Three candidates for 2008's Birthday Bourbon. That was a pretty good day. **LB**

Tasting notes

Big mint or spearmint nose with light fruit notes. A wave of mint floats high on sweet corn, then glides into spice and oak, with cinnamon forward, sweetening as the finish arrives. Blackberry on the palate, closing with a suggestion of leather. Exquisite.

Old Forester Classic

Brown-Forman Corporation | www.oldforester.com

Region and country of origin Kentucky, United States
Distillery Brown-Forman, Shively
Alcohol content 43% abv
Style Straight bourbon

Making Old Forester is a Brown-Forman tradition, something they are quite proud of. Bourbon used to be sold in barrels, to be dispensed by the glass or bottle at saloons and "grocery stores," a frontier euphemism for liquor sellers—Abraham Lincoln may have ran one. Old Forester is the oldest bourbon brand sold in distillery-filled bottles, a mark of how proud George Garvin Brown was of his whiskey.

It can be baffling why Old Forester's is not more popular or widely known. Admittedly, complete whisky neophytes can find their first taste of it to be an unpleasant experience, but after exploring whiskeys further they come to appreciate this as a bourbon with all the elements: corn, oak character, spicy dryness, and a long finish. It also tastes different from many others, due to the distillery's use of heat.

In Brown-Forman's brick or masonry "cycling" warehouses, steam heat is used over two weeks to slowly raise the temperature, which is held and then allowed to fall gradually. This is not about absorption of material from the wood. Master distiller Chris Morris says, "It brings in oxygen, which creates aldehydes, the fruit and spice notes. In an ironclad warehouse, that takes a long time; Mother Nature does it slow."

Heating is not about making Old Forester quickly, then. It helps to achieve "a crisp, dry flavor profile," in Morris's words. "It has those spice notes that make you think when you drink. For other bourbons to get that kind of spice and fruit, they have to age longer, and get more wood impact. Old Forester is more balanced." Whatever it is, I hope they keep it up. **LB**

Tasting notes

A fine, classic smell, and it's all there: corn, oak, rickhouse, brown sugar/maple, vanilla, and a bit of edgy spice. It's lean in the mouth: light corn, some leather, dusty cocoa hints, and a spreading warmth. It finishes with corn gripped lightly by oak and spice.

Old Forester Signature

Brown-Forman Corporation
www.oldforester.com

Region and country of origin Kentucky, United States
Distillery Brown-Forman, Shively
Alcohol content 50% abv
Style Bourbon blend

The Bottled-in-Bond Act came into force in 1897 in a bid to regulate whiskey quality. It stipulated that bonded whiskey should consist of straight whiskeys, blended from a single distilling season at a single distillery under a single master distiller—and be bottled at 100 proof. Brown-Forman master distiller Chris Morris is passionately interested in the history of the bourbon industry, and he was asked whether Old Forester Signature, which until recently was called Old Forester 100, was ever bottled in bond.

"No," he said, "it's not bottled in bond, by design. George Garvin Brown was president of two industry-wide organizations when the Bottled-in-Bond Act was debated, and he was adamantly opposed to it." Brown saw the act as interfering with a product that was already high quality. But Old Forester, previously 90 proof, became both 100 proof and a blend.

Morris was happy to explain that things had been put right. "Signature is a compromise—100 proof but blended from two seasons. We put the whiskey in the bottle, not the regulations." Signature also has more mature barrels blended in than the classic Old Forester, to achieve a more advanced wood character that accentuates the whiskey's cocoa notes. **LB**

Tasting notes

Bountiful cornbread, cinnamon, and dark chocolate; flicks of mint, young leather, and even hints of anise. The finish fades away in a breath of corn and vanilla.

Old Overholt Rye

Beam Global
www.beamglobal.com

Region and country of origin Kentucky, United States
Distillery Jim Beam, Clermont
Alcohol content 40% abv
Style Straight rye

In about 1810, Abraham Overholt and his brother shifted from general farming, with whiskey as a sideline, to making whiskey full time. Their farm was in southwestern Pennsylvania. Old Overholt didn't exist as a brand until after Abraham's death, toward the end of the century. Abraham's grandson, Henry Clay Frick (1849–1919), the great Pennsylvania railroad and steel baron, made Old Overholt the best-selling rye brand.

Prohibition closed the company, but after it ended, Old Overholt took its place in the portfolio of Seton Porter's National Distillers Products Corporation as their primary rye. Under National's stewardship, it became the top rye in the country once again, but rye whiskey never recovered the market share it had enjoyed before 1920. National eventually closed all of its Pennsylvania distilleries and shifted Old Overholt production to Kentucky, to the Forks of Elkhorn distillery outside of Frankfort, where it also made Old Grand-Dad bourbon.

Jim Beam inherited Overholt when it merged with National in 1987. When the rye whiskey made by National ran out, Beam simply used the whiskey it was already making for Jim Beam Rye. Beam has done little with it except continue to make and distribute it. **CKC**

Tasting notes

You would expect Old Overholt to taste like Jim Beam Rye, and it does. Overholt is a little older, with more tannic barrel notes, more bite, and more earthiness.

Old Potrero 18th Century Style

Anchor Distilling
www.anchorbrewing.com

Region and country of origin California, United States
Distillery Anchor, San Francisco
Alcohol content 62.55% abv
Style Rye malt whiskey

Under American rules, rye malt whiskey must be aged in new, charred oak barrels. Old Potrero 18th Century Style is not so aged, so officially it is just "whiskey." Anchor's founder, owner, and chief mythmaker, Fritz Maytag, claims that Anchor is re-creating an eighteenth-century style of whiskey, which to his mind means a 100 percent rye malt spirit lightly aged in new and used uncharred barrels.

Malting is done to produce certain enzymes, and most eighteenth-century American distillers used malted barley, as they do now, not malted rye. Since malt has always been a lot more expensive than unmalted grain, they rarely made whiskey from a 100 percent malt mash. However, the principal grain they used was unmalted rye. As their whiskey was sold and consumed within days of its manufacture, it was rarely aged on purpose; the barrels in which it sojourned ever so briefly would have been uncharred, and would have been reused. It's a mixed bag like that.

In 1977, Maytag moved his San Francisco brewery from a location it had outgrown into a new one in a nearby neighborhood called Potrero Hill. When the distillery came along in 1993, he chose Old Potrero as the brand name for his rye malt whiskeys. **CKC**

Tasting notes

Be mindful of the high abv and add water straightaway. The flavor is mostly red hot cinnamon but with other interesting layers of citrus, oak, and vanilla.

Old Potrero Hotaling's Single Malt

Anchor Distilling
www.anchorbrewing.com

Region and country of origin California, United States
Distillery Anchor, San Francisco
Alcohol content 50% abv
Style Rye malt whiskey

Like all Anchor Distilling whiskeys, Hotaling's is made from 100 percent malted rye. The name is a tribute to A. P. Hotaling & Co.'s San Francisco whiskey warehouse, which survived the 1906 earthquake.

American whiskeys are typically aged from four to six years, and the best ones are eight to twelve years old. Aging is expensive, so most microdistilleries age their whiskeys lightly, if at all. Anchor's other two whiskeys don't bear age statements, although two to four years in wood is likely.

Hotaling's is from a batch made not long after the distillery was founded, in 1993. Maybe it was reserved on purpose, maybe it was serendipity, perhaps it was a little of both. Anchor's owner, Fritz Maytag, could afford to hold back one barrel, which was charred and had been used once. When he finally decided the barrel had peaked (and while there was still enough whisky inside left to sell), it was sixteen years old.

Since only one barrel was reserved, Old Potrero Hotaling's whiskey is a limited edition, though perhaps there are a few other casks, held back in a similar way, that can be called into service when the supply of this one is exhausted. Something in the eight-to-twelve-year range would be nice. **CKC**

Tasting notes

Rye, tempered and molded in much the same way as barley is in single-malt Scotch. The predominant flavor is wintergreen, with a little char on the finish.

Old Potrero Single Malt Straight Rye

Anchor Distilling | www.anchorbrewing.com

Region and country of origin California, United States
Distillery Anchor, San Francisco
Alcohol content 45% abv
Style Straight single-malt rye

Microdistilleries are everywhere today, but for many years there was only one, at least in American whiskey. It was Fritz Maytag's Anchor Distilling, an offshoot of Anchor Brewing, located in San Francisco.

Maytag no longer owns the company, but he still looms large. An heir to the Maytag appliances fortune, and also responsible for Maytag Blue Cheese, Fritz has always been regarded as a bit of a dilettante, a rich guy whose hobbies include cheese making, brewing, and whiskey making. Actually, he works like a demon, and all three enterprises have been successful on their own merits. In all three, Maytag has been among the pioneers of a major artisan movement, as well as an evangelist. One might just as well say fabulist, too, as many of his claims for historical authenticity have their origins in his imagination.

Anchor Brewing was established in 1896. By the 1960s it was struggling to survive against the rise of national megabrews. Maytag got involved in 1966 and eventually remade the Anchor brand as a pillar of the nascent craft-brewing movement. Anchor Distilling followed in 1993.

The straight rye is the flagship of Old Potrero's line and is the most recognizable (though just barely) as a standard rye whiskey in the American style. All of the Old Potrero whiskeys are made from 100 percent malted rye, with only the maturation procedure varying. The straight rye is aged in new charred-oak barrels for at least four years (and probably not much more). Using such barrels only became common in the late nineteenth century. **CKC**

Tasting notes

Old Potrero's distillate packs a lot of flavor. Put it in a new, charred barrel, and the flavor becomes varied and intense. Mocha is forward, but the herbs and spices of rye white dog are right there too. Your first reaction might be "ouch!" but it will soon grow on you.

Old Rip Van Winkle 10-Year-Old

Old Rip Van Winkle Distillery | www.oldripvanwinkle.com

Region and country of origin Kentucky, United States
Distillery Buffalo Trace, Frankfort
Alcohol content 53.5% abv
Style Straight bourbon

Julian Proctor "Pappy" Van Winkle joined the W. L. Weller Company prior to Prohibition as a salesman. He wound up owning the place. During Prohibition he kept it going as a medicinal whiskey producer. When Prohibition ended, he merged it with its main supplier, the Stitzel distillery, with himself as president. He ran it for the next thirty-five years, until age ninety.

The company's flagship was Old Fitzgerald, but it made many different brands. One of the smallest, little more than a novelty, was Old Rip Van Winkle, a combination of the family surname with a famous character created by early American author Washington Irving. Irving's Rip famously slept for many years, a nice metaphor for well-aged bourbon.

Seven years after Pappy Van Winkle's death, the family reluctantly sold Stitzel-Weller and most of its brands, retaining only Old Rip. Van Winkle's son and namesake set up a small business producing private-label bourbon, but he also sold some under the Old Rip name. He bought most of his whiskey from Stitzel-Weller's new owners. His son, J. P. Van Winkle III, joined the business and continued it after his father's death. The fourth generation is now in place.

Stitzel-Weller distilled its last whiskey in 1992. Ten years later, with whiskey made there becoming scarce, Van Winkle formed a joint venture with Sazerac. He now bottles whiskey distilled at Buffalo Trace. The family's main contribution is their uncannily good judgment in selecting barrels from the wheated bourbon inventory Buffalo Trace makes available to them. A 45-percent-abv version is also available. **CKC**

Tasting notes

Old Rip emphasizes candy flavors like vanilla, caramel, and toffee, with a little mint, and spices like cinnamon and nutmeg. Its richness and balance are uncanny. What distinguishes Van Winkle from other wheaters is a very slight touch of citrus that leans toward orange.

Old Taylor

Sazerac

Region and country of origin Kentucky, United States
Distillery Buffalo Trace, Frankfort
Alcohol content 40% abv
Style Straight bourbon

Edmund Haynes Taylor Jr. was named for his uncle and adopted the "junior" after the uncle informally adopted him. As a banker, he observed that, although whiskey making seemed a profitable business, distilleries were often undercapitalized and went broke, despite good reputations and steady sales. In his professional capacity, he put capable distillers together with people of means and worked out sound, long-term financial plans for their businesses. He participated in the founding and ownership of at least seven distilleries in and around Frankfort, Kentucky. Near the end of his long career, he built a showplace distillery to make this bourbon.

After Taylor's death and the onset of Prohibition, Old Taylor became part of the Wathen family's American Medicinal Spirits Company, the largest part of which later became National Distillers. The Old Taylor distillery produced its last whiskey in 1972. National was bought by Jim Beam in 1987.

Old Taylor declined in the 1970s, when every bourbon with "Old" in its name suffered huge sales losses. It remained bottled in bond, thus 50 percent abv, and bore a six-year-old age statement, so it was good whiskey and good value despite its low status.

In 2009 Sazerac bought the brand and brought it back to Buffalo Trace, which Taylor had once owned. They intend to reposition it as the rye-flavored equivalent of the Van Winkle wheaters, and therefore a limited and exclusive brand, but that is long-term. The standard Old Taylor (now at 40 percent abv), a solid if unspectacular bourbon, is still available. **CKC**

Tasting notes

Old Taylor still has the traditional bourbon "bite," that little acid burn at the back of the throat, that many companies have bred out of their whiskeys. It has good body and sweetness, with a bit of tart apple sourness in the finish. Spice notes tend toward cumin and clove.

Old Weller Antique

Sazarec | www.greatbourbon.com/WellerAntique.aspx

Region and country of origin Kentucky, United States
Distillery Buffalo Trace, Frankfort
Alcohol content 53.5% abv
Style Straight wheated bourbon

Although only three major distilleries make wheated bourbon today, drinkers can, between Old Fitzgerald, Maker's Mark, W. L. Weller, and Van Winkle, taste wheated bourbons aged from four to twenty-three years, with many stops in between.

The entry-level expression of W. L. Weller is Weller Special Reserve, bottled at 45 percent abv after at least seven summers in wood. Its parallel is Old Weller Antique, which is said to be of the same age but at the higher abv of 53.5 percent. This odd abv is a carryover from Stitzel-Weller's heyday, when it was one of the few distilleries offering bourbons with extra age and higher abv; in that era, the standard abv was 50 percent. The idea of 53.5 percent was that it was very close to the actual average barrel abv when dumped, an early attempt at a "cask-strength" bottling.

Sometimes, if a product is of the same age as another but offered at a higher abv, it has the same flavor profile if water is added. In other cases, adjusting the abv will make the taste very different. The latter seems to be true of Old Weller Antique. It has more barrel character, especially char, than Special Reserve, as if it had been aged for the same length of time but on a higher floor with a more southerly exposure.

Fans were upset a few years ago when Sazarec redesigned their Weller packages and took the age statement off Old Weller Antique. Sazarec insisted that the whiskey was still seven years old; the age was removed from the label to emphasize the abv, which is its main selling point. A prominent age statement for Old Weller Antique is now on their Web site. **CKC**

Tasting notes

This wheated bourbon has an edge due to its high abv and barrel notes that emphasize char and tannin. It has the rich, candy-box flavors one would expect but also a little smokiness and bite. This is a wheater for people who normally find wheated bourbons too tame.

Pappy Van Winkle 15-Year-Old

Old Rip Van Winkle Distillery
www.oldripvanwinkle.com

Region and country of origin Kentucky, United States
Distillery Buffalo Trace, Frankfort
Alcohol content 53.5% abv
Style Straight wheated bourbon

When Julian "Pappy" Van Winkle retired in 1964, the running of the Stitzel-Weller distillery passed to his son, Julian Jr. But by 1972, the market had changed. Shareholders despaired for the future, and, predicting a fall in the company's value, they forced a sale.

Julian Jr. was not ready to give up on bourbon. In the sale, he made sure he kept all rights to the family name, and made arrangements to buy whiskey from the Stitzel-Weller distillery's new owners. He became a specialty whiskey bottler, producing private label bourbons for distributors with whom he had long relationships from the Stitzel-Weller days.

A decade or so later, Japanese consumers began to get a taste for extra-aged American whiskey, and Van Winkle was ideally positioned to source, select, and bottle small runs of high-end, extra-aged specialty whiskeys for that market. When the taste for such products returned to America, the Pappy Van Winkle's Family Reserve line was born. Created originally to bottle some of the dwindling supply of whiskey made at Stitzel-Weller, which distilled its last in 1992, the 15-Year-Old was the final launch of the three. The exact provenance of recent bottlings is uncertain, but the whiskey seems unchanged. **CKC**

Tasting notes

A full punch of char and oak but with little bitterness. A sophisticated drink that tastes like a Snickers candy bar; water opens up another full layer of flavors.

Pappy Van Winkle 20-Year-Old

Old Rip Van Winkle Distillery
www.oldripvanwinkle.com

Region and country of origin Kentucky, United States
Distillery Buffalo Trace, Frankfort
Alcohol content 45.2% abv
Style Straight wheated bourbon

The sheer scarcity of Van Winkle bourbons must contribute to the desire of bourbon enthusiasts to talk about them. Van Winkle president Julian Van Winkle III, grandson of "Pappy," admitted that most retailers keep their tiny Van Winkle allocation under the counter for their best customers. It was he who made the Van Winkle brand the principal product of the Van Winkle company and the enthusiast's darling that it is today. After years of helping other people create exclusive, expensive, extra-aged specialty whiskeys, Julian Van Winkle III decided to make some for himself. Instead of using the existing Old Rip Van Winkle trade name, he created Van Winkle Special Reserve and this Pappy Van Winkle's Family Reserve.

Since 2002, the Van Winkle brand has been a joint venture with Buffalo Trace distillery in Frankfort. All of the whiskey owned by Van Winkle is aging there, all new Van Winkle whiskey is distilled there, and all of the Van Winkle products are bottled there.

One reason for the scarcity of Van Winkle whiskeys is the family's high standards. Older sources, whose whiskeys are still in the mix, include Stitzel-Weller (which the Van Winkles once owned) and the Bernheim distillery, now owned by Heaven Hill. **CKC**

Tasting notes

This retains wheated bourbon character that is lost to the wood in older expressions. The flavors are outsized: plenty of wood, but also rich caramel and vanilla.

Old Rip Van Winkle whiskey slumbers at the distillery. ➔

Pappy Van Winkle 23-Year-Old

Old Rip Van Winkle Distillery | www.oldripvanwinkle.com

Region and country of origin Kentucky, United States
Distillery Buffalo Trace, Frankfort
Alcohol content 47.8% abv
Style Straight wheated bourbon

Pappy Van Winkle's Family Reserve 23-Year-Old bourbon is almost mythical to many whiskey lovers, who have never even seen, much less owned, a bottle. Although it will always be scarce, nowadays it promises to be a little easier to find than it once was.

The whiskey only became a standard, annual part of the Van Winkle line in 2010. The maker describes it this way: "This ultimate beverage comes from select barrels which have aged the bourbon most gracefully." That is a fancy way to say that twenty-three years in wood is often not good for bourbon, but when it is, it can be phenomenal. That is the trick: getting barrels past their twenty-third birthday in drinkable condition.

Van Winkle is not the only company to sell bourbon in this age range, but the whiskey is one of the most consistent, and it is the only wheated bourbon this old. *Fortune* magazine called Van Winkle "the ultimate cult brand," a status achieved after practicing "a strategy of scarcity." The 23-Year-Old is the brand's ultimate expression, but anyone who thinks that means it is "the best bourbon ever" is liable to be disappointed. The whiskey is not for everyone. It isn't just that few can afford it. Many just do not like it; it has too much wood for their taste. But for those who do like it, there is nothing better at any price.

Pappy 20-Year-Old and 23-Year-Old are still assumed to be Stitzel-Weller distillates. The last whiskey made there will be twenty-three years old in 2015. But the quality of younger Van Winkles that are not Stitzel-Weller whiskeys bodes well for the future. **CKC**

Tasting notes

Those who know overaged bourbons will appreciate this statement: Pappy 23-Year-Old tastes its age yet still tastes great—a difficult feat. Deep char with some soot, old leather, pipe tobacco, cured meat, dark fruit, molasses, anise, clove, and wintergreen.

Parker's Heritage Collection 10-Year-Old

Heaven Hill Distilleries | www.bardstownwhiskeysociety.com

Region and country of origin Kentucky, United States
Distillery Heaven Hill, Bardstown
Alcohol content 62.1%/63.9% abv
Style Straight wheated bourbon

For most of its history, Heaven Hill made one bourbon recipe; since 1999, it has made two. That year it bought the Old Fitzgerald brand. Old Fitzgerald is a wheated bourbon, meaning that its mash bill contains wheat instead of rye as the flavor grain. Happily, Heaven Hill that same year also bought the Louisville distillery, where this whiskey was being made.

The Parker's Heritage Collection, named for Heaven Hill master distiller Parker Beam, is Heaven Hill's high-end annual limited-edition series, launched in 2007. Its whiskeys vary but always have those dual hallmarks of limited editions: extra age and extra abv. This 10-Year-Old wheated bourbon was the 2010 release. It came to about 4,800 bottles.

Although Heaven Hill's distillery is in Louisville, it matures most of its bourbon, including this batch, at Bardstown, Kentucky. Just as every distillery has its own character, so does every warehouse, and enthusiasts thrive on detailed information about these exclusive releases. For example, this whiskey was aged entirely in Rackhouse A on the fourth, sixth, and seventh floors. Produced in two batches because some of it was judged not quite old enough, it comes in two different abvs.

Heaven Hill is the third-largest producer of American whiskey. Since special bottlings usually rely on finding something interesting and unique in existing inventory, and the two larger producers tend not to do this sort of project, the Parker's Heritage Collection is always worthy of your attention. Just don't wait too long before you start to look. **CKC**

Tasting notes

Sip it neat if you must, but a little room-temperature water brings out the rich mocha and caramel essence of this gem, which has exactly the right amount of wood and char. It is not particularly complex, just delicious, although clove and iodine are revealed in the finish.

Parker's Heritage Collection 2011 Barrel Finish

Heaven Hill
www.heavenhill.com

Region and country of origin Kentucky, United States
Distillery Heaven Hill, Bardstown
Alcohol content 50% abv
Style Straight bourbon

It has become something of an annual tradition for American whiskey that each fall a number of special bottlings are released. Over the years, the special releases, often experimental and always unusual, have helped to carve out a premium sector for the bourbon market. Whiskeys from great names such as George T. Stagg, Eagle Rare, Weller, and Evan Williams are released to the market and, because the whiskey makers don't want to price them too high and deter their loyal drinkers, they are seen as bargains. The Parker Heritage Collection, named after Heaven Hill's master distiller, Parker Beam, is part of this ritual.

This one, while still of great interest to anyone who enjoys bourbon, is matured in traditional American oak for ten years and then transferred to French Limousin oak casks previously used for cognac. The bourbon stays put for up to six months and is then bottled at natural color—a gorgeous deep russet brown. Some drinkers feel that finishing bourbon in the same way as a single malt is a step too far for a drink this powerful, and certainly this isn't standard bourbon. Is it better or worse? You decide. **DR**

Tasting notes

You expect a hammer and you get a cushion. The color suggests big oak, vanilla, and spice, but this is gentle, almost honeyed, sweet, and fruity. Light and pleasant.

Parker's Heritage Collection Golden Anniversary

Heaven Hill Distilleries
www.bardstownwhiskeysociety.com

Region and country of origin Kentucky, United States
Distillery Heaven Hill, Bardstown
Alcohol content 50% abv
Style Straight bourbon

The whiskeys in Heaven Hill's warehouses are, on average, older than those held by any other American distiller—a result of cycles in the industry, curiosity, and some barrels they just swear get lost. Now Heaven Hill is rummaging through those barrels and coming up with some real gems.

The company has been bottling the best of each year as Parker's Heritage Collection. One offering was a twenty-seven-year-old; another was Parker's first wheated bourbon; but perhaps the best is this exceptional one-off anniversary celebration of Parker Beam's fifty years in the business, bottled in 2009.

To honor those fifty years, they took whiskeys from each of Parker's five decades, beginning with an admittedly small amount from the 1960s. The blending of lively younger whiskeys with the austere power of the older ones was deft because this whiskey is anything but tired, overly woody, or bitter; it is magnificent, one of the very best. It leads to the question: is it really wise to be bottling the limited reserves of older whiskeys as straight packages, or are there amazing minglings to be made from them? **LB**

Tasting notes

Cotton candy, corn, maple, vanilla, deep oak notes. Within an oaky framework, younger whiskeys fill in with corn and mint and hints of anise and butter.

One of Heaven Hill's two spirit safes—minus its heavy padlock. ➡

Parker's Heritage Collection Wheated Mashbill

Heaven Hill Distilleries | www.bardstownwhiskeysociety.com

Region and country of origin Kentucky, United States
Distillery Heaven Hill, Bardstown
Alcohol content 63.9% abv initially, later bottlings vary
Style Straight wheated bourbon

Parker Beam has been making bourbon since the 1960s, but up until Heaven Hill bought Old Fitzgerald in 1999, he had never made wheated bourbon. Old Fitz is a wheater, though, and since Heaven Hill had also bought the Bernheim distillery in Louisville, where Old Fitz was being made (Heaven Hill lost its Bardstown distilling facility in a disastrous fire in 1996 and had to replace it), it was a pretty simple transition. "Well, I just started making it," said Parker in his plainspoken way.

What is interesting is that, while most Old Fitzgerald is sold pretty young, Parker hung on to some of those first batches, setting them back for more aging. Of course, there is Very Special Old Fitzgerald (VSOF) to be considered, but that is a tiny niche product. Parker just set himself to see what would happen, hoping for something good.

The master distiller got it, and before the twelve years VSOF takes, too. Parker's Heritage Collection of 2010 was a ten-year-old from those first runs, with the same Old Fitz mash bill of 70 percent corn, 20 percent wheat, and 10 percent malt. It was turned right into the bottle with minimal fuss: cask strength of 63.9 percent abv (dropping to 62.1 in a later dump of barrels that weren't quite ready), non-chill-filtered. It is hot at that proof, but not as hot as you would think; the wheat tames the burn. Evidently "just making it" works pretty well; at least, when you are Parker Beam.

People have asked why Heaven Hill doesn't do more with the Old Fitzgerald brand. With luck, this whiskey may represent a move in that direction. **LB**

Tasting notes

A refreshing light breeze of sweet grass and corn. A warning hint of overproof has you reaching for a splash of water for a more manageable mouthful of cornbread, oak spice, and vanilla, with a rushing slope of mint on the finish. A pretty serious dram, for wheat.

Rebel Yell

Luxco | www.rebelyellwhiskey.com

Region and country of origin Kentucky, United States
Distillery Undisclosed
Alcohol content 40% abv
Style Straight wheated bourbon

During the American Civil War (1861–65), residents and especially soldiers of the Southern states were known colloquially as "rebels," sometimes shortened to "rebs" or "Johnny Rebs." As often occurs, the label was first applied as a term of derision, only to be adopted by the rebels themselves as a badge of pride. Generally outgunned and outnumbered, the South relied on unconventional ways of fighting. Often they would shout at their enemies as they attacked, disorienting them and exaggerating their own ferocity. This war cry became known as the rebel yell.

The city of Louisville remained firmly in Union control throughout the conflict, but many of her citizens sympathized with the Southern cause, even decades later. One such was Charles Farnsley, a Louisville politician who had a family connection to the Stitzel-Weller distillery. In 1936 Farnsley contracted with Stitzel to produce a limited-edition, private-label bourbon called Rebel Yell for him to distribute to his friends and political supporters.

Rebel Yell was not a special recipe, just the standard wheated bourbon used by the company for all of its products. The name was the hook. So popular was the original release that Stitzel decided to launch it as a regular product, but only for sale south of the Mason-Dixon Line. In the 1990s, one of Diageo's predecessors tried but failed to make Rebel Yell a major international brand. Then it changed direction and sold most of its American whiskeys, including Rebel Yell. Today the brand is owned by Luxco, a small bottler and rectifier based in St. Louis. **CKC**

Tasting notes

Befitting its name and heritage, Rebel Yell was always a bit rough by design, more so since Luxco took it over. You do not often taste really green wheated bourbon, all corn husks and sweetness, like tamales without the heat. Sour on the finish, like a Granny Smith apple.

Redemption High-Rye Bourbon

Strong Spirits | www.redemptionrye.com

Region and country of origin Indiana, United States
Distillery Lawrenceburg, Lawrenceburg
Alcohol content 46% abv
Style Rye bourbon

Released in the wake of Redemption Rye whiskey, this high-rye bourbon was Strong Spirits' second product with the Redemption label. Strong Spirits wanted to produce an "in your face" rye whiskey; they succeeded.

It is quite fitting that the operation's second whiskey would be a bourbon with the highest percentage of rye grain on the market. At a whopping 38.2 percent rye, (with 60 percent corn and 1.2 percent barley malt), Redemption High-Rye Bourbon eclipses offerings from other well-known producers of high-rye bourbons, such as Four Roses. Redemption High-Rye has been aged for "at least" two years, although that is still quite young for a bourbon whiskey.

Let it be noted, Strong Spirits does not actually distill its Redemption line. That distinction belongs to Lawrenceburg Distillers Indiana (LDI). Formerly the Seagram distillery, LDI is well known for its bourbon and rye whiskeys. Today, LDI distills (and ages in many cases) products for Bulleit, Templeton, and many others, who label them independently. This practice is fairly common in the United States, where much of the whiskey produced comes from fewer than a dozen distilleries.

Having to rely on LDI, Strong Spirits had some issues in keeping pace with consumer demand for its Redemption products. With increased production and a now well-established brand name, Strong Spirits anticipates fewer problems with supply going forward. That is good news because Redemption High Rye Bourbon's youthful exuberance and brisk flavor profile are guaranteed to please rye hounds. **JP**

Tasting notes

On the nose, vibrant rye with honey, bright notes of mint and cinnamon, and a core of honeyed fruits. The palate reveals brittle caramel candy and undertones of vanilla; these serve to ground the rye's brashness on the sip before letting it go wild to a spicy finish.

Redemption Rye Whiskey

Strong Spirits | www.redemptionrye.com

Region and country of origin Indiana, United States
Distillery Lawrenceburg, Lawrenceburg
Alcohol content 46% abv
Style Rye whiskey

Over past decades, the availability of rye whiskey dwindled to only a few brands and products. Demand has recently increased, and over the last five or more years production has begun to ramp up. Various start-up distilleries and independent bottlers have turned to established distillers to provide them with rye whiskey to take to market. Redemption Rye is among the new ryes made to capitalize on America's renewed appreciation for one of its native spirits.

The Strong Spirits company does not actually distill this whiskey, but rather sources it, as do several other growing rye brands, from Lawrenceburg Distillers Indiana (LDI). This increasingly common business model can be quite confusing to consumers, but it has brought some excellent rye whiskeys to market, Redemption Rye being one of them.

A spirit must be at least 51 percent rye grain in order to be called "rye whiskey." LDI has a 95 percent rye grain mash bill—far higher than used for most other rye whiskeys on the market. Formerly owned by Seagram, LDI used whiskey made to this recipe as a component of its blended whiskey products. When Seagrams went out of business, LDI continued to produce this and a number of other whiskeys for a variety of companies.

LDI's 95 percent rye whisky is noted for its bracing rye character, which cannot hope to be duplicated by any of the more common rye whiskeys containing less than 60 percent rye grain. Whether sipped neat or at the heart of a fine cocktail, Redemption Rye, courtesy of LDI, is one distinctive whiskey. **JP**

Tasting notes

A flavor characteristic of this distillery's ryes. The nose is full of evergreen, juniper, and cinnamon bound together with wildflower honey. The palate echoes those flavors but with more anise and herbal character. The finish is softly spiced with cinnamon and licorice.

Ridgemont Reserve 1792

Sazerac | www.1792bourbon.com

Region and country of origin Kentucky, United States
Distillery Barton 1792, Bardstown
Alcohol content 46.85% abv
Style Straight bourbon

In 2003 Barton Brands made its entry into the hot, super-premium segment of the bourbon category, following the lead of successful brands such as Brown-Forman's Woodford Reserve and Jim Beam's Knob Creek. According to a Federal judge, they followed Woodford a little too closely and were forced to change the product's name from Ridgewood Reserve 1792 to Ridgemont Reserve 1792. But from the start, everyone has called it 1792, which commemorates the year of Kentucky's statehood. The brand and distillery were sold to Sazerac in 2009.

The mash bill for 1792 is unusual because it contains a higher (but secret) percentage of malt than other bourbons. Malted barley is typically about 10 percent of an American whiskey mash bill and is mostly there for its enzymes. However, master distiller Bill Friel (now retired), who developed the 1792 recipe, thought it could contribute to the taste as well.

The Barton 1792 distillery traces its origins to the Tom Moore distillery, established on the Barton site in 1889. Its rackhouses are among the most ideally situated in Kentucky. Warehouse Z, where all barrels for 1792 are aged, is considered the best of the bunch for sun exposure and air circulation. **CKC**

Tasting notes

Relatively dry with a sharp vanilla note, and a horehound and licorice edge. It has rough spots that make it interesting and satisfying to drink.

Rittenhouse Rye 10-Year-Old

Heaven Hill Distilleries | www.heaven-hill.com

Region and country of origin Kentucky, United States
Distillery Heaven Hill, Bardstown
Alcohol content 50% abv
Style Straight rye

Discovering this was a happy mistake. In 2003 I asked Heaven Hill for a sample of Rittenhouse because none could be found on store shelves—rye hadn't yet really taken off. When it arrived, there was an unlooked-for neck label saying "10 Years Old." Huh? Surely Rittenhouse has no age statement. Then I noticed something that was even more interesting: no UPC barcode, no government warning label. This looked like an export bottling (and it was, intended for Japan). Maybe I should have sent it back, but I didn't.

It turns out that a small amount of Rittenhouse Rye 10-Year-Old was released somewhat inadvertently back at this time. Cocktail writer David Wondrich, who happened to score some as well, said he would love to know who was responsible for the error; he'd put their kids through college. Other people found it on the open market and quietly scooped it up.

Is there any more out there? Not likely, in these days of rye shortages and allocations, but it is worth keeping an eye out for. I have still got about a third of my bottle. It is definitely different from the standard bottling: deeper, more rounded in some places; oakier in others. Look for it, cross your fingers, and if you do find some, share it with friends. **LB**

Tasting notes

On the nose, dark, sweet, and spicy with wood. The mouth is full of oily rye that bursts with hot mint, sun-warmed sweet grass, and a hint of vanilla.

Visitors to Heaven Hill may tour Bardstown in a vintage-style trolley. ➜

Rittenhouse Rye 23-Year-Old

Heaven Hill Distilleries | www.heaven-hill.com

Region and country of origin Kentucky, United States
Distillery Heaven Hill, Bardstown
Alcohol content 50% abv
Style Straight rye

"Old whiskey" can mean different things. It may be barrels laid down in a traditionally favorable spot in a warehouse, where master distillers know whiskey finds greatness. It may be a particular anniversary, a special batch. It may be a hopeful experiment to see just how far a whiskey can go before it begins to decline. It may be a bottling before a barrel evaporates into nothing but old tax bills.

Or it may be some barrels you forgot about. "Barrels do fall through the cracks," master distiller Parker Beam said during a discussion of three extra-aged releases of Rittenhouse Rye Single Barrel, of which this is one. "It might be a bulk customer's whiskey; they bought it, we aged it, and then they never bottled it. Rye especially; you only sold it in a couple states. You always wound up making too damned much or not enough."

Parker described the process. "It's a lot more scientific today," he said. "Years ago, we used to have a meeting just after the first of every year. Max [Shapira, president of Heaven Hill] would set numbers, and then I'd throw that out the window and make more."

This particular batch of rye was for a Missouri wholesaler. They didn't bottle all of it, and Heaven Hill bought it back. Luckily, it sat on the bottom floor of the warehouse, where it aged slowly and didn't vapor away to nothing. And twenty-three years after it went into the barrel, out came this beauty: still lively, still kicking with rye. It's almost enough to make you hope Parker's son Craig develops a bad memory for what is quietly maturing in the warehouse. **LB**

Tasting notes

Not at all shy. The nose blows teaberry, mint, a hint of warehouse raunch, and a flick of cinnamon. While you can taste the age, the whiskey is wonderfully well mannered. The wood fades on the finish, leaving mint and a crisp sweetness.

Rittenhouse Rye 25-Year-Old

Heaven Hill Distilleries | www.heaven-hill.com

Region and country of origin Kentucky, United States
Distillery Heaven Hill, Bardstown
Alcohol content 50% abv
Style Straight rye

Twenty-five years is getting toward the edge of viability for American whiskey; some would argue that this one is over that edge. Still, Parker Beam recently found a twenty-seven-year-old bourbon to add to his Parker's Heritage Collection, and he is not shy about saying a whiskey is too old to drink.

"We had to go through the warehouses," he said in a reminder that Heaven Hill has more stocks of whiskey over ten years old than any other American distiller. "We had a lot of really old barrels. Craig and I went through them and tasted them. Some of them were good . . . and some went for blending.

"We've always been pretty conservative," Parker said, thinking back over fifty-plus years with Heaven Hill. "If you had a leftover bucket of grain, well, you put it back in the mash cooker. And if you had some old whiskey, you used some in blends.

"The Rittenhouse . . . ," he continued. "We found some old barrels when we were going through, and there wasn't much whiskey in them. There were about a hundred barrels, all on the first floor." They had been distilled in 1984. Parker and Craig, his son, tanked them off in stages to stop them aging, as a third hit twenty-one years, then a third at twenty-three years, and finally a third at twenty-five years. The hot American summers can drive really old whiskey too deep into the wood, but this writer preferred the twenty-three- and twenty-five-year-old Rittenhouses to the twenty-one-year-old. Maybe it is just that first floor, or maybe it is the barrels they chose. Whatever it was, this 25-Year-Old is a very fine bottle of extra-aged rye. **LB**

Tasting notes

Oaky and sweet, hot with alcohol, and a big central wave of vanilla that comes through to temper the heat. There is caramel peeking through, with rough blocks of oak that spice things up. The finish is sweet and spicy, perhaps the best part of the whole ride.

Rittenhouse Rye Bottled in Bond

Heaven Hill Distilleries | www.bardstownwhiskeysociety.com

Region and country of origin Kentucky, United States
Distillery Heaven Hill, Bardstown
Alcohol content 50% abv
Style Straight rye

How did Rittenhouse Rye survive? You could as well ask, How did any rye whiskey survive? Rittenhouse is a classic story, repeated in a pathetically small number of cases: old Pennsylvania brand, sold off as distilleries closed, sales dropped dramatically after Prohibition and World War II, after which the brand was kept alive largely by small pockets of regular buyers, and by the low costs of making a legacy brand that needed no promotion. In their turn, Heaven Hill and Wild Turkey each mashed rye whiskey once a year (Pikesville, a Marylander, also made it.)

As Heaven Hill's Larry Kass says, "It has to do with the fact that we are a family-owned company." That family ownership implied strong relationships with family-owned wholesalers who were making money selling the whiskey, and it ensured the independence to continue making whiskey that the market had left behind. Then, unbelievably, rye came back, thanks to bartenders and whiskey writers who loved the stuff and wouldn't shut up about it. Rittenhouse led the charge, but started small—in 2005 Kass said the company had doubled its production of Rittenhouse: "We mash it twice a year now."

In 2009, though, a very relaxed Craig Beam informed whiskey journalists at the Kentucky Bourbon Festival that the Heaven Hill distillery was now making Rittenhouse for twelve days a year. A year later, with the rye whiskey still on allocation and mostly going to bars, Larry Kass was saying that new supplies were coming of age, enough to end allocation soon. Ah. Thriving . . . so much better than surviving. **LB**

Tasting notes

Spice, dry grass, and wood in the nose, with mint undergirding. Hard to believe this is 100 proof, it is so nonburningly whoosh in the mouth. Reminiscent of a green meadow in the sun; grass, mint, hot rock, flowers, all vibrantly warm. The finish fades in spice and wood.

Rock Hill Farms Single Barrel

Age International | www.greatbourbon.com/rockhill.aspx

Region and country of origin Kentucky, United States
Distillery Buffalo Trace, Frankfort
Alcohol content 50% abv
Style Straight bourbon

The major companies that make and sell American whiskey fall into two categories: they are either brand-driven or sales-driven. The brand-driven ones are the names you already know, led by Beam Global (Jim Beam, Maker's Mark, Knob Creek) and Brown-Forman (Jack Daniel's, Woodford Reserve). The sales-driven companies are the names you may not know, such as Heaven Hill and Sazerac.

Rock Hill Farms, like several of the bourbons made at Buffalo Trace distillery, is not owned by Buffalo Trace's parent company, Sazerac. It is instead the product of a partnership between Buffalo Trace and Age International. Before there was a distillery on the site of Buffalo Trace, there was a farm called Rock Hill. Buffalo Trace actually makes two different rye-recipe bourbon mash bills, one for the Sazerac bourbons and one for the Age bourbons. The Age mash bill, generally known as No. 2, has more rye in it than No. 1.

Although Rock Hill Farms Single Barrel Bourbon has been around for more than twenty years, it is not well known. So what is the company's marketing plan? Well, the product itself—quality whiskey, attractive package, high price—is the extent of its marketing. The plan is for people to "discover" it without being pushed toward it in any way, perhaps no more than a recommendation from their whiskey seller. Other bourbon brands produced by Buffalo Trace for Age International are Ancient Age, Blanton's, Hancock's Reserve, and Elmer T. Lee. All except Ancient Age are single-barrel. Each has a different abv, with Rock Hill Farms having the highest, at 50 percent. **CKC**

Tasting notes

Plenty of oaky caramel with a side order of mint, anise, and black pepper; it is easy to enjoy without water or with a splash. Evokes the beguiling gentility of Kentucky's dry-stone-fenced farms and their famous hospitality. Simply top shelf without a lot of fuss.

Rogue Dead Guy Whiskey

Rogue | www.rogue.com

Region and country of origin Oregon, United States
Distillery Rogue, Newport
Alcohol content 40% abv
Style American whiskey

Beer lovers, in particular microbrew or craft beer lovers, may recognize the name Rogue. In 1988 Rogue opened a brewery in the small town of Ashland, Oregon; they soon relocated to Newport. Today, Rogue brews some of the most critically acclaimed beers in the United States.

A very early player in the American craft beer movement, Rogue recently began a foray into the world of craft spirits to include a line of gin, rum, and, of course, whiskey. One of Rogue's most popular beers is called Dead Guy Ale and it is this very beer that is used for Rogue's Dead Guy Whiskey. Made from four barley malts (namely Northwest Harrington, Maier Munich, Klages, and Carastan), the beer is characterized by a nutty, biscuitlike, malt quality.

Rogue's operations in spirits and whiskey are headquartered at its House of Spirits on Yaquina Bay, Newport. Master distiller John Couchout crafts Dead Guy Whiskey on a Vendome copper pot still with a 150-gallon (570-liter) output. The whiskey is double-distilled and aged in new, charred American white oak barrels. The finished distillate is also filtered through charcoal in a process similar to what many associate with Tennessee whiskey.

Because the whiskey is aged for only a few months, harsh flavors that may be present in the spirit are not rounded off or removed by the wood. The charcoal filtration helps to remove any impurities from the whiskey and ensure they do not overpower its more delicate flavors. The result is a spicy and fruity whiskey worthy of the Rogue name. **JP**

Tasting notes

Fruit and Indian spices on the nose. The flavors on the palate are surprisingly sweet. A big fruitiness (maraschino cherry and pineapple) emerges quickly at the front of the palate as spice kicks in from midpalate on through the finish. A sweet, fruity, and spicy ride.

Russell's Reserve 10-Year-Old Bourbon

Gruppo Campari | www.wildturkeybourbon.com

Region and country of origin Kentucky, United States
Distillery Wild Turkey, Lawrenceburg
Alcohol content 45% abv
Style Straight bourbon

In 1954 Jimmy Russell went to work for Ernest Ripy at the distillery now known as Wild Turkey. Members of the Ripy family had operated distilleries at Lawrenceburg since 1869, and it is their heritage that Wild Turkey now claims. Russell would stay with Ernest Ripy for twenty-four years.

In 2001 Jimmy joined the growing ranks of American master distillers with their own eponymous brand. At ten years old and 50.5 percent abv, Russell's Reserve Bourbon was promoted as the profile he preferred for his own consumption. Too bad, because after a brief trial run the company pulled it in for reformulating. Staying at ten years old, it dropped to 45 percent abv, was repackaged, and even got a new Russell. Jimmy's son, Eddie, had supposedly designed it to appeal more to drinkers in their early forties.

Although whiskey makers like to pretend that nothing ever changes in their industry, taste profiles evolve as consumer preferences shift. Maker's Mark was the first to revitalize the entire bourbon market by redefining what the product should taste like. Now, many of the best-selling bourbons worldwide are new brands designed for a consumer who likes bourbon's richness but not its rough edges.

Russell's Reserve is not only different from regular Wild Turkey, it is almost its antithesis. Consequently, the company has staged it as a freestanding brand that is almost entirely separate from its peer, even though it comes from the same juice off the still. That is the magic of aging—the whiskey is all the same going in, but quite different coming out. **CKC**

Tasting notes

Russell's Reserve has a rich but mellow flavor that melds buttery caramel, vanilla, and toffee with earthy pipe tobacco and black tea. It is a fine example of a well-made, well-mannered, thoroughly modern bourbon. Dig deeper for hints of cumin, lemon, and black pepper.

Russell's Reserve Rye

Gruppo Campari
www.wildturkeybourbon.com

Region and country of origin Kentucky, United States
Distillery Wild Turkey, Lawrenceburg
Alcohol content 45% abv
Style Straight rye

Wild Turkey has always made and sold a rye whiskey, even when few in Kentucky did. Rye was America's first whiskey and the favorite type until Prohibition. Bourbon surpassed it because rye can be fiery and bitter and Americans came to like sweet and smooth better. As rye faded, so did the distillers in Pennsylvania, Maryland, and Virginia who made most of it. Rye production increasingly moved to Kentucky, where rye whiskey became more bourbonlike. More recently, distillers have tweaked their bourbon to suit modern palates, and they have done the same to rye.

Like Wild Turkey bourbon, Wild Turkey rye is made in a traditional style—some might add, "warts and all." The rye is a favorite with bartenders for its full flavor and moderate price. But for anyone who finds it to be a bit too much, the company offers Russell's Reserve Rye. It is slightly older, a little lower in abv, slightly pricier, and mellower in its flavor profile.

Although Jimmy Russell's name is embossed on the bottle, his son and associate distiller, Eddie, has taken a particular interest in both Russell's Reserve products. He sees them as ideal for younger drinkers trying American whiskey for the first time. Young drinkers, the polls suggest, want flavorful whiskey with no rough edges, and Russell's Reserve Rye has the grain's less pleasant side under control. **CKC**

Tasting notes

Some heat and bitterness, but mint, must, and pepper mellow these with plenty of corn backbone and barrel sweetness. The very sweet finish is a pleasant surprise.

Rye One [(rī)[1]]

Beam Global
ww.beamglobal.com/brands/ri1.html

Region and country of origin Kentucky, United States
Distillery Jim Beam, Clermont
Alcohol content 46% abv
Style Straight rye

Beam's main intention in producing a rye whiskey with an unusual name on the bottle—(rī)[1], expressed here for clarity's sake as Rye One—is seemingly to combine the present revival of rye whiskey with the current passion for spirits products with exotic names and packaging, although those are usually reserved for other drinks such as vodka, tequila, and liqueurs. Beam is unquestionably a whiskey company; but it is also a very successful marketing company, and the marketing department is paramount here.

Rye One is a straight rye whiskey drawn from the same warehouse stock that gives us Jim Beam Rye, the best-selling straight rye whiskey in the United States, and Old Overholt, a venerable brand from rye whiskey's pre-Prohibition heyday. Rye One, we are told, contains some older whiskey, but more than that, it is whiskey selected with modern tastes in mind.

Rye One perplexes traditional whiskey drinkers because it is supposed to be a super-premium whiskey yet it seems to be targeted at consumers for whom everything, including the distilled spirits they buy, is a fashion accessory. They may never drink it in anything but a manhattan, Sazerac, or old-fashioned, but the bottle looks good on their bar. But this is a well-mannered rye, recognizable as rye, easy to enjoy neat, and also excellent in whiskey cocktails. **CKC**

Tasting notes

This is fine whiskey, mild but well made and refined, just shorn of some of the characteristics that turned drinkers away from rye originally, in particular its burn.

← Minus their caps, bottles travel along the conveyor at Lawrenceburg.

United States 723

Sazerac 18-Year-Old Rye

Sazerac | www.greatbourbon.com/AntiqueCollection.aspx

Region and country of origin Kentucky, United States
Distillery Buffalo Trace, Frankfort
Alcohol content 45% abv
Style Straight rye

Because of the long history of the Sazerac cocktail and the modern-day Sazerac company, people assume that Sazerac Rye is an old brand. In fact it is very new, launched only in 2000 with an inaugural Buffalo Trace Antique Collection release. But it was probably inevitable—a rye-whiskey drink called the Sazerac Cocktail pretty much demands there be a Sazerac straight rye whiskey with which to make it. The no-age-statement Sazerac Rye, known popularly as "Baby Saz," came later, followed by the Antique Collection's Thomas H. Handy Sazerac Rye.

Oddly, since at least 2005, the 18-Year-Old has all been from a single batch distilled and barreled in 1985 at what is now Buffalo Trace. Reportedly, all of it was dumped and tanked at twenty years old in 2006. Although demand always exceeds supply, only the equivalent of twenty-eight barrels, down to about 43 percent of their original volume, is bottled each year. Even dealing it out so parsimoniously, the supply will run out eventually, although perhaps Sazerac is anticipating the eighteenth birthday of some of the rye made more recently at Buffalo Trace. Sazerac's fact sheets about the Buffalo Trace Antique Collection often raise more questions than they answer, such as why is there not a pipeline of Buffalo Trace–made rye whiskey, reserving something distilled in, say, 1992 or 1993, for an eighteen-year-old bottling?

As for its use in the eponymous cocktail, most enthusiasts would probably say this precious lily should be savored without gilding. Mixing with a $100 bottle of whiskey would be decadence indeed. **CKC**

Tasting notes

Whatever the exact age of this rye, it sure tastes good. Wood does not overpower the rye character, which comes through as equal parts ginger and white pepper, with dried basil and anise. Its earthiness seems equal parts rye grain and old oak, and it is just about perfect.

Sazerac Rye

Sazerac | www.greatbourbon.com/AntiqueCollection.aspx

Region and country of origin Kentucky, United States
Distillery Buffalo Trace, Frankfort
Alcohol content 45% abv
Style Straight rye

Long after New Orleans became part of the United States, its citizens still looked primarily to France for their cultural touchstones, and no spirit was considered finer than French cognac. Sazerac was a brand of cognac, specifically Sazerac de Forge et Fils, before it was ever a brand of rye whiskey, a company, a New Orleans bar, or a cocktail. The Sazerac cocktail, which came next, is usually credited to a New Orleans druggist named Antoine Amédée Peychaud Jr. (1813–76), or perhaps his father, and it was almost certainly created and promoted as a way to sell more of the cognac that was its primary ingredient. In time, as domestic whiskey began to supplant imported brandy in the hearts and minds of the city's drinkers, rye whiskey replaced cognac in the famous cocktail, whose most crucial ingredient was absinthe.

So successful was the Sazerac cocktail that the drinking establishment with which it was most associated decided to change its name to Sazerac. A third ingredient, an herbal bitters branded with the Peychaud name, became the company's new big earner. That company evolved into the present-day Sazerac, which is now a full-line distilled spirits producer best known for American whiskeys.

Sazerac Rye, then, is a fairly recent convergence of all of these threads that made its creation practically inevitable. It is often called "Baby Saz" to distinguish it from the eighteen-year-old version. The Buffalo Trace distillery, where Sazerac Rye is made, also makes Peychaud's bitters and Herbsaint, both ingredients in the "official" Sazerac cocktail. **CKC**

Tasting notes

Despite its retro packaging, Sazerac is a modern rye in the best sense. It is richly flavorful but also tempered enough to enjoy straight. The flavor is crisp and clear, with wheatgrass, ginger, and white pepper forward, solidly supported with sugar and smoke.

St. George Single Malt

St. George Spirits | www.stgeorgespirits.com

Region and country of origin California, United States
Distillery St. George, Alameda
Alcohol content 43% abv
Style Single malt

St. George distillery makes an eclectic variety of spirits, from eaux-de-vie to liqueurs and vodka. However, the owners are quick to tell you that their pride and joy is St. George single-malt whiskey.

The distillery has been making single-malt whiskey for more than fifteen years, starting long before most distilleries in the United States first took a crack at single malts. Blazing a trail is rarely easy, but one significant benefit of this early start has been the sizable reserve of older barrels of whiskey amassed by St. George over the years. This "library," as they refer to it, gives the distillery flexibility to create varied and distinct batches with each release, while still adhering to the distillery's trademark style: elegant whiskeys with complexity, depth, and lush fruitiness.

Making this whiskey begins by smoking a portion of its malted barley and roasting the remainder to a variety of levels. These processes give rise to a light, smoky backbone. St. George's recent release, Lot 10, has passed its tenth bottling of the product. The lot consists of eighteen barrels ranging from four years of age up to thirteen years. The majority of the barrels are between eight and nine years old.

Beyond simply having older whiskey stocks to pull from, St. George takes a rather diverse approach to barrel aging. They have been laying down their single malt in a variety of coopered oak, including used bourbon, French oak, and refill sherry and port barrels. St. George is quick to point out that the results can vary with each release, but Lot 10 might just be the best U.S. single malt available today. **JP**

Tasting notes

The nose opens with a ripe fruit explosion of melon, banana, pear, lemon/lime, and ginger ale, with a light, teasing smokiness in the background. The flavors on the tongue are layered with ripe orchard fruit, spiced honey, almond toffee, and gentle, smoky oak.

Stranahan's Colorado Whiskey

Stranahan's Distillery | www.stranahans.com

Region and country of origin Colorado, United States
Distillery Stranahan's, Denver
Alcohol content 47% abv
Style Single malt

The story of Stranahan's whiskey goes that Jess Graber, then a volunteer firefighter, met his neighbor, George Stranahan, while responding to his barn fire. The pair, discovering that they had a shared passion for fine whiskey, eventually developed a recipe that used only malted barley; the result was aged in newly charred oak barrels. However, knowing that, in Scotland, single malt is aged in refilled barrels to make the oak integration with the spirit less invasive, the duo took a "best of both worlds" approach to the finished product. Stranahan, who owns Flying Dog Brewery in Maryland, is no longer a minority partner, but the distillery continues to use their old recipe.

Stranahan's is the first microdistillery in Colorado and takes a great deal of pride in utilizing local products. At least 80 percent of the barley used in the whiskey is grown in Colorado and milled on the premises. The total whiskey production is small: about twelve barrels per week. It is aged for at least two years but can contain significantly older whiskey (upward of four years). The high altitude of Colorado is not without its challenges; to keep evaporation and whiskey loss to a minimum during the aging process, the barrels are aged in a temperature- and humidity-controlled warehouse.

Stranahan's takes a true small-batch approach that yields multiple differences in flavors from batch to batch. Typically, each batch of whiskey comes from around ten to twenty barrels, selected on the basis of their aroma and flavor profiles. The distillery embraces the subtle differences between the batches. **JP**

Tasting notes

The nose has ample orchard fruit (pear and apple), toffee, and fragrant charred oak and wood spices. The palate is drier than the nose suggests. An initial toffee and caramel sweetness is overcome by peppery spice, cinnamon, and a resinous, gripping oak quality.

Templeton Rye

Templeton | www.templetonrye.com

Region and country of origin Indiana, United States
Distillery Lawrenceburg, Lawrenceberg
Alcohol content 40% abv
Style Straight rye

Templeton Rye president Scott Bush hails from Iowa. He grew up hearing stories from his uncle Gus about the rye whiskey his great-grandfather and others had produced in the town of Templeton, Iowa, during Prohibition. Bush had a desire to resurrect whiskey production in Templeton, a small town of 350 residents, but he found it very difficult to locate and talk to people who had had direct connections with the Prohibition-era whiskey. Then he was introduced to Meryl Kherkoff, whose father also produced whiskey during that period. As Bush tells it, Kherkoff provided him with the missing component to the plan: the recipe of the original Templeton Rye whiskey.

Bush selected Lawrenceburg Distillers Indiana (LDI) to distill the whiskey that would pay homage to the original. As a former Seagram-owned distillery, Lawrenceburg makes whiskey for both large companies and small boutique operations. The exact mash bill of Templeton Rye whiskey could not be confirmed, but it includes at least 90 percent rye grain and has been aged for about five years (on average) in newly charred oak barrels. The resulting whiskey has a healthy dose of rye spice due to the recipe's high percentage of rye grain. Recently, Scott Bush confirmed that Templeton is now aging a portion of the barrels at their Templeton, Iowa, facility. **JP**

Tasting notes

Caramelized banana and cinnamon candy intermingled with rye and wintergreen. An early honeyed sweetness on the palate yields to rye, chile, and black pepper.

Ten High

Sazerac | www.bartonbrands.com/tenhigh.html

Region and country of origin Kentucky, United States
Distillery Barton 1792, Bardstown
Alcohol content 40% abv
Style Straight bourbon

For nearly fifty years, thousands of men and women proudly made Ten High bourbon whiskey in Peoria, Illinois. The Peoria area's first distillery was built in 1843, and every new distillery had to be the biggest in town, maybe the biggest in the world. Pre-Prohibition Peoria also had a taste for larceny, being home to the corrupt Whiskey Trust.

When Canada's Hiram Walker, makers of Canadian Club Canadian Whisky, came to town just after Prohibition, they bought the biggest distillery and enlarged it. Its main products would be Ten High, a new brand of straight bourbon, and Imperial, a blended whiskey that Walker also made and sold in Canada. The name "Ten High" is a reference to the fact that most distillers prefer the way whiskey matures on the upper floors, or ricks, of a maturation warehouse, that is, on levels higher than the tenth rick.

Peoria distillers did not survive the whiskey industry's collapse in the late 1960s, and Ten High became a Barton product, made in Bardstown, Kentucky. Always a value brand, Ten High became blended bourbon (half bourbon, half vodka) in 2008 in some markets, while it remains straight bourbon in others. Avoid the blended version, but there is nothing wrong with the bourbon. It is well made, if a bit young, and well worth its modest price. **CKC**

Tasting notes

With the heat, spice, and medicinal flavors of young bourbon, this also has rich caramel and vanilla. Good neat, it is better with ginger ale or in a cocktail.

← Distillery staff reenacted an old photograph for Templeton Rye's current label.

Thomas H. Handy Sazerac Rye

Sazerac | www.greatbourbon.com/AntiqueCollection.aspx

Region and country of origin Kentucky, United States
Distillery Buffalo Trace, Frankfort
Alcohol content 63.45–67.40% abv
Style Straight rye

Following Sazerac 18-Year-Old in Buffalo Trace's Antique Collection in 2006, Thomas H. Handy Sazerac Rye has more in common with the standard Sazerac Rye, which is probably about six years old, than it does with its fellow Antique. Thomas H. Handy is, effectively, an uncut, unfiltered, and slightly older version of the standard whiskey.

Thomas H. Handy (1830–93) was a businessman from Maryland who became a principal in some of the nineteenth-century New Orleans businesses that led to the present day Sazerac company. He worked at the Sazerac Coffee House, then took it over upon the previous owner's death. He hired Antoine Peychaud Jr. to make bitters for him and imported the Sazerac brandy from which the Sazerac cocktail got its name.

The Antique Collection is designed to give enthusiasts a chance to try expressions of common and popular whiskey types in a different and, as it turns out, more extreme form. It is not intended for beginners or as an introduction to whiskey. On its first release, therefore, many questioned how this eight-year-old whiskey (six to seven years old in later iterations) qualified for inclusion in a collection called "Antique." Customers must have been unconcerned, however, because Handy's sales have more than doubled since the whiskey's inaugural release.

The Collection samples Buffalo Trace's different mash bills in unusual ways. The distillery makes many bourbons in the six- to seven-year-old age range, but only one other rye, so having a second way to taste its rye output is definitely welcome. **CKC**

Tasting notes

Especially when sipped neat at barrel strength, Handy hits you with charcoal, caramel, vanilla, old leather, and pipe tobacco, supported by a full spice rack of other flavors. Dropped below 50 percent abv, you get even more. This is the whiskey Sazerac Rye wants to be.

Tom Moore

Sazerac | www.bartonbrands.com/tommoorebourbon.html

Region and country of origin Kentucky, United States
Distillery Barton 1792, Bardstown
Alcohol content 40% abv
Style Straight bourbon

Distiller Tom Moore was partners with J. G. Mattingly in the Mattingly and Moore distillery, founded in 1877. They made a bourbon called Belle of Nelson, an early local favorite. In 1889 Moore split from Mattingly, bought the property next door, and built his own distillery, hiring young Joe Beam, his distiller at Mattingly and Moore, to help set up the new place. More than 120 years later, the Tom Moore distillery goes by the name of the Barton 1792 distillery.

The Tom Moore distillery lasted until Prohibition, and Moore's son helped reinstate it afterward. It changed hands a couple of times in the early post-Prohibition era before being purchased in 1944 by Oscar Getz and Lester Abelson, brothers-in-law and partners in a Chicago-based whiskey business. The partners renamed it Barton, running it from Chicago with members of the Bixler family as their distillers.

Unusually, Tom Moore bourbon is a whiskey with a pre-Prohibition pedigree that has only ever been made at one place. Abelson and Getz ran Barton until their deaths in 1980 and 1982, respectively, after which the company was sold. It eventually became the distilled spirits arm of Canandaigua Wine Company, which, after it had made a few more acquisitions, became Constellation Brands. Sazarec bought most of its portfolio as well as several production facilities, including the Bardstown distillery, in 2009.

Tom Moore bourbon is available in Kentucky, and that is about it. It always has been pretty much what it is today, a solid, standard bourbon, at least four years old (no age statement), and modestly priced. **CKC**

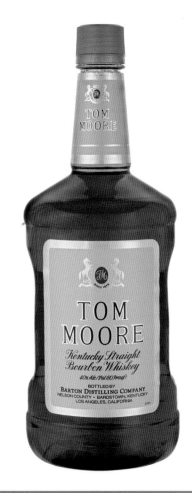

Tasting notes

There are different theories about how bourbon tasted a hundred years ago. It may well have tasted like this: sharp, hot, and pungent, with a rich, sweet spine and lots of vegetal highlights. Something to temper with soda water, simple syrup, and fresh mint.

Van Winkle Family Reserve 13-Year-Old Rye

Old Rip Van Winkle Distillery | www.oldripvanwinkle.com

Region and country of origin Kentucky, United States
Distillery Buffalo Trace, Frankfort
Alcohol content 47.8% abv
Style Straight rye

The bottling firm named Old Rip Van Winkle Distillery has built its business on wheated bourbon, a whiskey that by definition contains no rye. Yet the company's small product range also includes this 13-Year-Old straight rye whiskey. All Van Winkle whiskeys are hard to find, but, especially in recent years, this rye has become the most scarce of the bunch.

The small amounts of rye whiskey Van Winkle bottles each year are drawn from a batch Julian Van Winkle acquired more than a decade ago. This has long since been transferred to stainless-steel tanks to prevent it from aging any further.

Arguably, when rye whiskey production moved from the states of its traditional heartland—Maryland, Pennsylvania, and Virginia—to Kentucky, it became more bourbonlike. The Van Winkle rye supports that theory and that may be one key to its popularity. Bourbon fans trying it for the first time experience something that tastes largely familiar, making it easier for them to embrace the ways in which it is different.

However you choose to characterize it, what Van Winkle Family Reserve Rye has in common with the company's bourbons is impeccable balance. Julian Van Winkle's talent lies in selecting nearly flawless whiskey. He has also managed to build a successful business by keeping his products in high demand through scarcity, but there is a drawback to that approach. Arguably the rye, most of all, could have been a lot more popular with greater availability. Bars, for example, will not build featured cocktails around it because they cannot keep it in stock. **CKC**

Tasting notes

Since rye is the more common flavor grain for bourbon, Van Winkle Rye can be described as more like a very flavorful bourbon than a typical rye whiskey. It has little of rye's earthiness and fire, but instead combines a rich caramel and vanilla base with herb and spice flavors.

Van Winkle Special Reserve 12-Year-Old Lot "B"

Old Rip Van Winkle Distillery | www.oldripvanwinkle.com

Region and country of origin Kentucky, United States
Distillery Buffalo Trace, Frankfort
Alcohol content 45.2% abv
Style Straight wheated bourbon

The phenomenal rise of single malts began in the early 1970s and took about ten years to get going. Similarly, the super-premium bourbon phenomenon that began about twenty years later also took about a decade to gain serious traction.

Almost from the beginning, anything with the Van Winkle name on the label has been highly prized. For many a true devotee, the preferred Van Winkle expression is not the ancient Pappy 23-Year-Old but the more modest Van Winkle Special Reserve 12-Year-Old, known to initiates as Lot "B." While *Lot "B"* does appear on the label, it means nothing—there never was a Lot "A" and never will be a Lot "C."

Like virtually all Van Winkle releases, Lot "B" is wheated bourbon that originally came from the Van Winkle family's former distillery, the Stitzel-Weller distillery in Louisville. Even as that dwindling supply has been reserved for older Pappy expressions, the Van Winkle company has managed to maintain a generally consistent flavor profile for Lot "B," much to the relief of its faithful fans.

It has been said that the best bourbons have more in common with the brandies of France than they do with the whiskies of Scotland and Ireland, mostly due to the generous offering of oak extractives in the French distillations. Lot "B" makes that case very well, even coming in a simple wine bottle with a plain label bearing only text, like a boutique Armagnac.

Like all Van Winkles, Lot "B" is always hard to find, but stores that carry it usually can keep it in stock, unlike some of the others. **CKC**

Tasting notes

Van Winkle wheated bourbons, especially the younger ones, have an orange note, as if each bottle contains a few drops of Cointreau liqueur. Lot "B" has that and all of the other wheated bourbon attributes in ideal harmony and balance. The whiskey is close to perfect.

Very Old Barton

Sazerac
www.greatbourbon.com/VeryOldBarton100.aspx

Region and country of origin Kentucky, United States
Distillery Barton 1792, Bardstown
Alcohol content 40–50% abv
Style Straight bourbon

Although Sazerac has begun to widen its distribution, Very Old Barton has for many years been the bourbon Kentucky keeps for itself. Little known outside the commonwealths—Virginia, Kentucky, Massachusetts, and Pennsylvania—it sells like Jim Beam or Jack Daniel's within them. It is a mystery why the company has never tried to take the magic further afield.

This bourbon is unusual in many ways. It is one of only a few with a six-year-old age statement. There are other six-year-old bourbons, but usually makers only begin to brag about age at eight years. The age statement works for Very Old Barton because of its price, which would be good for a four-year-old but is a steal for a six-year-old. Very Old Barton is the only bourbon available in four different abvs: 40, 43, 45, and 50 percent (the 50 percent is bottled in bond). Many stores in Kentucky carry all four.

Very Old Barton was created after Bardstown's Tom Moore distillery was sold and renamed Barton in 1944. When bourbon enthusiasts within easy driving distance travel to Kentucky, a few handles—half-gallon (1.75-liter) bottles—of Very Old Barton always make the return trip. It is now available in Chicago, so the rest of the Midwest cannot be far behind. **CKC**

Tasting notes

Old-fashioned, meaning a lot of flavor on a solid foundation, with almost enough anise to be pastis. Oily, hot, and oaky, and caramel to butterscotch sweet.

Wasmund's Rye Spirit

Copper Fox
www.copperfox.biz

Region and country of origin Virginia, United States
Distillery Copper Fox, Sperryville
Alcohol content 62% abv
Style Non-aged rye spirit

Having introduced Copper Fox Single Malt, the first and only traditional floor-malted single-malt whiskey in the United States, master distiller Rick Wasmund wished to somehow incorporate the smoky flavors of his distillery's barley in a second product.

Rye is a notoriously tough grain to distill. Its high gluten content causes it to gum up like paste while cooking. Distillers use malted barley or enzymes to help "lubricate" the grains, making it easier to process. It was here that Wasmund found the perfect place to use Copper Fox's fruitwood-smoked barley. Smoke from apple and cherry wood in the kiln gives the malted barley a sweet, smoky quality, akin to Scottish peat-smoked barley. This decidedly American twist to a traditional process results in a rye whiskey that has a lingering smokiness unlike any other on the market.

Wasmund's Rye Spirit is simply the nonaged version of the distillery's Rye Whiskey. The mash bill consists of about two-thirds rye grain and one-third malted barley. The high barley proportion preserves Copper Fox's signature flavor profile. Wasmund's Rye Spirit is non-chill-filtered to ensure the finished product is full in flavor and retains a syrupy mouthfeel At 62 percent abv, the experience is memorable. **JP**

Tasting notes

A surprisingly intense punch of cinnamon. On the sip there is a lush, fruity quality (spiced pear) with dry spice erupting midpalate. Teasing smoke on the finish.

Wasmund's Single Malt Spirit

Copper Fox
www.copperfox.biz

Region and country of origin Virginia, United States
Distillery Copper Fox, Sperryville
Alcohol content 62% abv
Style Nonaged single-malt spirit

Copper Fox distillery owner and master distiller Rick Wasmund started as an intern with Bowmore distillery on Islay in Scotland before setting out on his own. Wasmund loved the idea of creating an Americanized version of what he saw on Islay—whisky dominated by peat-smoked single malts. Replacing peat smoke with that of apple and cherry fruitwood, Copper Fox has created something distinctive. The distillery first offered an aged version of their single malt before deciding to educate consumers with the release of the distillery's nonaged spirit.

The process starts with floor-malting the barley used to make the single malt. In this process, the barley is allowed to germinate; it is turned periodically to prevent it from clumping. Smoke from fruitwood chips then delivers a campfire smokiness, but in a much sweeter and more subtle manner than peat. Floor-malting and smoking barley in-house are time-consuming and costly, but Copper Fox believes the processes make Single Malt Spirit stand out.

This is the very same product as Wasmund's Single Malt Whiskey minus the barrel aging. At a whopping 62 percent abv, it packs a wallop of flavor conferred by the signature smoking process. **JP**

Tasting notes

Sweet malt, cereal, and spun sugar on the nose. A fruity and smoky back note then asserts itself. On the palate, big, bold, and sweet, with pepper leading to smoke.

Wild Turkey 81

Gruppo Campari
www.wildturkeybourbon.com

Region and country of origin Kentucky, United States
Distillery Wild Turkey, Lawrenceburg
Alcohol content 40.5% abv
Style Straight bourbon

Before Prohibition, 50 percent abv was the standard for U.S. whiskey, but Americans developed a taste for lighter drinks. In 1933, when Prohibition ended, producers offered lower-abv alternatives—typically 45, 43, or 40 percent—as line extensions. Lower-abv drinks were cheaper, since most taxes on spirits are based on alcohol content. Consumers abandoned the standard expressions for the new ones, and the producers followed. The standard fell to 40 percent abv, stopping there only because U.S. law required any lower abv drinks to be labeled "diluted."

The longest holdout of any major brand was Wild Turkey. Its odd 101 proof (50.5 percent abv) had become part of the brand's personality and symbolized its commitment to traditional bourbon.

In the 1990s Wild Turkey brought out several higher-end expressions, mostly at 50.5 percent abv or more, but also including Russell's Reserve bourbon and rye, at 45 percent abv. When Gruppo Campari bought Wild Turkey in 2009, they revived a stalled distillery expansion plan but made few other changes until early 2011. Their first new product was Wild Turkey 81, a vastly superior lower-proof expression. The "1" of "81" ties it to the 101-proof flagship. **CKC**

Tasting notes

Caramel and semisweet chocolate with a crystal-clear char note, supported by a little soot, so it is smoky but not acrid. Very well balanced, with just enough bite.

Wild Turkey 101

Gruppo Campari | www.wildturkeybourbon.com

Region and country of origin Kentucky, United States
Distillery Wild Turkey, Lawrenceburg
Alcohol content 50.5% abv
Style Straight bourbon

The Wild Turkey brand was born in 1940 when Tom McCarthy, an executive with a company that bought bulk whiskey and packaged it for resale, asked his warehouse manager to select some bourbon for him to take on an annual hunting trip with his buddies. Their quarry was wild turkey. The following year, his friends urged him to bring the same whiskey again because it was so good. McCarthy checked with the warehouse and discovered that it was an eight-year-old bourbon at 50.5 percent abv. Realizing its appeal, he turned it into a brand for his company.

The Wild Turkey brand has always been managed as a fine, traditional Kentucky sipping whiskey. It was kept at eight years old and 50.5 percent abv, in an old-fashioned bottle finished with a cork, not a screw cap, at a premium price, even as competitors went younger, lighter, and cheaper. However, many consumers regard it as a hard-drinking whiskey. It does, after all, have "wild" in its name, and unsolicited endorsements by Kentucky native and original "gonzo journalist" Hunter S. Thompson fueled that mystique.

Wild Turkey did not have its own distillery until 1972, when one of its suppliers was bought out. That distillery, near Lawrenceburg, Kentucky, had an association with the Ripy family dating back more than a century. It also had a long association with the Russell family. Jimmy Russell, Wild Turkey's master distiller, has worked there since 1954. His son, associate distiller Eddie Russell, started in 1980. The 101 proof (50.5 percent abv) expression has always been, and continues to be, the brand's flagship. **CKC**

Tasting notes

Deliberately rough around the edges. A traditional, full-flavored, full-bodied bourbon with plenty of wood notes, grain notes, and yeast notes. Go beneath the caramel and vanilla to where herbs and dark fruits lurk. Big and bold but also beautifully balanced.

Wild Turkey Kentucky Spirit

Gruppo Campari | www.wildturkeybourbon.com

Region and country of origin Kentucky, United States
Distillery Wild Turkey, Lawrenceburg
Alcohol content 50.5% abv
Style Straight bourbon

Kentucky Spirit is the top offering in Wild Turkey's regular portfolio and is their only single-barrel bottling. The single-barrel factor is more significant in some cases than others; most single-barrel products are freestanding one-offs, not single-barrel versions of a consistent brand.

As a result, the term "single barrel" does not necessarily mean the best of anything. In this case, however, it does. Because Kentucky Spirit is a single-barrel version of a known line, and is positioned at the pinnacle of that line, consumers are entitled to assume that the producer has selected a number of "honey barrels" that represent the very best whiskey that the distillery can make.

Kentucky Spirit was introduced in 1994 in an ornate bottle shaped to resemble a turkey's tail-feather display. The neck label provides handwritten barrel-specific information such as the barrel number and location in the warehouse maturation system.

Nothing, however, reveals the whiskey's age. For whiskey aficionados, this is a grave omission, since part of the charm of single barrels is that everything can be known about them. Since the age of the barrels is well documented, Wild Turkey's decision to withhold the information suggests that the age is something they do not want known. That is unfortunate, because it would reveal whether Kentucky Spirit's character is more a function of its age or of the finding of rare superb barrels. Perhaps both are in play more or less equally. Not knowing certainly mars an otherwise almost perfect offering. **CKC**

Tasting notes

People who like Wild Turkey for its rough spots may not like this expression, because it does not have them. All of its elements are in nearly ideal balance. It has vanilla, licorice, fig, a little mint. It brings to mind a lightly sherried malt, a comparison bourbon rarely evokes.

Wild Turkey Limited Editions

Gruppo Campari
www.wildturkeybourbon.com

Region and country of origin Kentucky, United States
Distillery Wild Turkey, Lawrenceburg
Alcohol content Various
Style Straight bourbon

Some of Wild Turkey's regular issues, such as Kentucky Spirit, rank at the very top of the super premiums. Limited-edition bottlings, therefore, are not as important a statement for Wild Turkey as they are for some other producers. Frustratingly, the limited editions are not released annually or on any other regular schedule; their timing is a mystery.

Typically age-stated and in their late teens, the limited editions are older than any of Wild Turkey's standard releases. American Spirit, for example, was fifteen years old, and so was Tribute. Freedom was a mix of seven- to thirteen-year-old bourbons. The oldest was simply called Wild Turkey 17-Year-Old. Some are released in the United States or Japan only, or in duty-free travel retail. Most are either at Wild Turkey's standard 50.5 percent abv or cask strength, which for Wild Turkey is about 53 percent abv.

If you can find a bottle of it, Wild Turkey American Spirit was particularly tasty, but it represented just 250 barrels and many of those, after fifteen years, were barely half full. To reach that milestone without becoming overwooded, an aging bourbon has to be very carefully managed. Wild Turkey invariably shows excellent judgment about what it releases. **CKC**

Tasting notes

With age, Wild Turkey becomes more subtle, not more woody. Some might find American Spirit a little thin and winey. Look for a touch of citrus sourness.

Wild Turkey Rare Breed

Gruppo Campari
www.wildturkeybourbon.com

Region and country of origin Kentucky, United States
Distillery Wild Turkey, Lawrenceburg
Alcohol content 54.1% abv
Style Straight bourbon

In the late 1980s, after years in the doldrums, exports of Kentucky bourbons were growing at a double-digit annual clip. Producers cautiously began to launch new products; some were for export only but most were introduced in the United States as well. Wild Turkey's contribution was Rare Breed.

Most American whiskey comes out of the barrel at about 65 percent abv and is diluted to 40 percent abv for bottling. Wild Turkey has a relatively low distillation and barrel entry abv of 57.5 percent, which comes out of the barrel at 54.1 percent abv. No water is added to Rare Breed, and even for the other Wild Turkey expressions very little water is used. Low distillation abv means additional flavor is retained from the fermentation, making for a more flavorful whiskey.

Many producers claim they do things the old-fashioned way, but factors such as low distillation and entry abv and heavy barrel char are genuine throwbacks. When it comes to doing things the old way, Wild Turkey is the real thing—despite a new distillery opening in 2011. Wild Turkey 101 continues to be the flagship of the brand, but many consider Rare Breed to be the best expression in the range, and most characteristic of the Wild Turkey style. **CKC**

Tasting notes

Creamy and bittersweet like cappuccino, with a sambucalike backbone, it leaves a nice tingle on the tongue with its long, slightly grassy finish.

Wild Turkey enjoys playing with its odd-sounding brand name. ➡

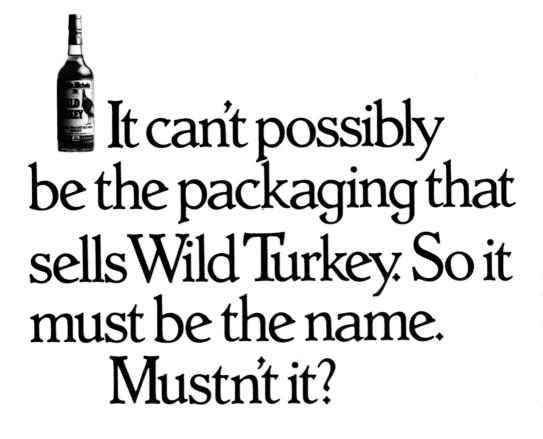

It can't possibly be the packaging that sells Wild Turkey. So it must be the name. Mustn't it?

WILD TURKEY

101 proof Kentucky straight bourbon whiskey.

Wild Turkey Rye

Gruppo Campari | www.wildturkeybourbon.com

Region and country of origin Kentucky, United States
Distillery Wild Turkey, Lawrenceburg
Alcohol content 50.5% abv
Style Straight rye

Rye was a familiar grain to European immigrants in the American colonies; they had brought it with them, as opposed to corn, used for bourbon, which they found in their new land. After the American Revolution, when whiskey began to be made in earnest, it was generally rye whiskey. Following his presidency, George Washington became a leading rye-whiskey producer. His mash bill was approximately 60 percent rye, 35 percent corn, and 5 percent malted barley. Bourbon eventually became established, but only after Prohibition did it attain dominance over rye.

Wild Turkey is a post-Prohibition brand known primarily for bourbon, but their line has always included a straight rye whiskey. Although rye sales were regional and minimal, Wild Turkey was based in New York City, which had remained, along with Philadelphia, one of the few rye strongholds.

For most of the modern era, a typical distillery's run of rye spirit was only two or three days in a year, if they made rye at all. The passion for pre-Prohibition cocktails has led to a resurgence of rye, so now a distillery will produce its quota in perhaps four. Even though rye sales have more than doubled in the last few years, they are still tiny compared to bourbon.

Wild Turkey Rye has benefited from the cocktail craze. Bartenders like it because it has an authentic flavor at a moderate price, while still seeming a little more upscale than category leaders Jim Beam Rye and Old Overholt, also made by Beam. It also beats the Beam ryes in abv, being 50.5 percent abv, the same as Wild Turkey's flagship 101 bourbon. **CKC**

Tasting notes

An earthy rye with all the expected heat, bite, mint, cumin, and black pepper. Its powerful flavors stand up to other strong flavors in drinks. Even unmixed, it benefits from some water or ice. If you are new to American straight rye, this is a great place to start.

William Larue Weller

Sazerac | www.greatbourbom.com/antiquecollection.aspx

Region and country of origin Kentucky, United States
Distillery Buffalo Trace, Frankfort
Alcohol content 58.95–67.4% abv
Style Straight wheated bourbon

Sazerac's Buffalo Trace Antique Collection is an annually updated set of aged whiskeys sourced from distilleries under Sazerac ownership. A Weller was included in the original Antique Collection; that whiskey ran out, and Weller dropped out for several years, returning in 2005 in this iteration, a barrel-strength wheated bourbon at eleven years plus. The whiskey was distilled and aged by Buffalo Trace itself, rather than originating in an acquired inventory.

In terms of the number of barrels released, William Larue Weller ranks fourth out of five in the Antique Collection. The whiskey tends to be called William Larue by enthusiasts, or by its initials, WLW, to distinguish it from other Weller expressions, especially Old Weller Antique, which is unrelated to the Buffalo Trace Antique Collection. William Larue Weller sales are about 40 percent of George T. Stagg's, even though it can be seen as Stagg's wheated bourbon equivalent; both are uncut, unfiltered, and extra-aged.

In these days of greater appreciation of older whiskeys, it is customary for barrels intended for long aging to be cosseted during their extra years. They are tucked into some cool, moist corner of a rackhouse, where they are shielded from the temperature extremes that promote barrel extraction and which can overwhelm the whiskey with wood flavors. However, barrels selected for William Larue seem not to have been treated in that gentle way. They are allowed to age as aggressively as possible, which is why harvesting them at no more than twelve years old is probably a good idea. **CKC**

Tasting notes

Char and sweetness combine to form a thick, almost viscous liquid that suggests concentrate for a cola soft drink, mixed with liquid smoke. A whiskey for lovers of extremes. Water helps, and reveals mocha and cocoa powder, dark fruit, and pipe tobacco.

W. L. Weller 12-Year-Old

Sazerac | www.greatbourbon.com/wlweller

Region and country of origin Kentucky, United States
Distillery Buffalo Trace, Frankfort
Alcohol content 45% abv
Style Straight wheated bourbon

Following Old Fitzgerald, W. L. Weller was for decades the second-best-selling bourbon in Stitzel-Weller's portfolio. Weller was arguably the more premium of the two lines—the company was called Stitzel-Weller, after all. Its various expressions were generally older and higher in alcohol than Old Fitzgerald. The whiskey found its most enthusiastic market in Texas.

All of the Stitzel-Weller bourbons were wheated, meaning that wheat was used instead of rye as the flavor grain. This difference was maintained after the company portfolio was split up in 1999 and Weller went to Sazerac. As is customary, the Weller sale included whiskey in barrels, at different ages, in sufficient volume to support that brand's sales until the new owner was able to move enough of its own spirit through the whiskey-aging pipeline.

However, Sazerac quickly created a new expression, W. L. Weller 12-Year-Old. No doubt the new owner was inspired by a careful review of the ages of its whiskey stocks. Sazerac's Buffalo Trace distillery was also short of warehouse space at the time, and twelve-year-old bourbon rarely needs to get any older. The 12-Year-Old was well accepted by Weller fans and has been in the portfolio ever since, receiving a facelift in 2007.

Sazerac does not release sales figures, but many stores ran out of some or all of the Weller expressions in 2009, and supplies have remained tight ever since. Sazerac has now shepherded the 12-Year-Old through three different distilleries and has done a good job of keeping its taste profile consistent. **CKC**

Tasting notes

Wheated bourbons are all about sweetness and no bitterness. Caramel runs through this like a river, with eddies of vanilla, mint, toast, mocha, and pancake syrup. It has nice but not overpowering char and oak, a little cinnamon, and raspberry, blackberry, and raisin.

W. L. Weller Special Reserve

Sazerac | www.greatbourbon.com/wlweller

Region and country of origin Kentucky, United States
Distillery Buffalo Trace, Frankfort
Alcohol content 45% abv
Style Straight wheated bourbon

Brothers William and Charles Weller started a wholesale liquor business in Louisville in 1849. They were later joined by another brother and William's two sons. Much of their whiskey came from the Louisville distillery of the Stitzel family. In the 1890s, Julian Van Winkle and Alex Farnsley joined the Weller company as salesmen; by Prohibition, they were running the place, selling whiskey under a medicinal permit in conjunction with the Stitzels. After Prohibition, the Stitzel and Weller companies merged under the leadership of the Van Winkle family.

The Stitzel-Weller bourbons were unique because they were wheated bourbon. Wheated bourbon is still bourbon, so mostly corn, but the flavor grain is wheat instead of rye. Stitzel-Weller sold a variety of bourbons under the Weller name, but the line's flagship has always been Special Reserve. In addition to the use of wheat, the brand is unusual because it offers nothing younger than Special Reserve's seven years.

Wheated bourbons are not necessarily lighter than rye-recipe bourbons, but the burn and bitterness of rye are eliminated. That gave Weller's "wheaters" the milder taste profile post-Prohibition drinkers seemed to prefer.

While some companies probably made wheated bourbon, there is no record of any distillery other than Stitzel-Weller making it until 1954, when Maker's Mark produced its first batch. Stitzel-Weller's motto is that the "whisper of wheat" makes the bourbon unique. W. L. Weller was always an exclusive brand, with higher-than-average age and proof. **CKC**

Tasting notes

The best Weller for experiencing Christmas cookie spices such as cinnamon, nutmeg, mint, and clove. The wood contributes vanilla, caramel, toast, and overall sweetness. Wood tannins are barely evident. Rye fans might find it cloying, but others will find it perfect.

Woodford Reserve

Brown-Forman Corporation | www.woodfordreserve.com

Region and country of origin Kentucky, United States
Distillery Woodford Reserve, Versailles
Alcohol content 45.2% abv
Style Straight bourbon

Is this whiskey Woodford Reserve? Or is it Old Forester in a fancy bottle? The story went that Woodford Reserve was to be from the distillery's three pot stills down in the hollow by Glenn's Creek, but the company needed whiskey to sell. So barrels that had been Old Forester were carefully selected for what would be the Woodford Reserve profile. And so Woodford Reserve was Old Forester in a fancy new bottle. At least, that's how most understood it.

Definitely not, says master distiller Chris Morris. "The company mishandled telling the truth on that one," he said. "It's in barrel selection; it tastes different, it's a different whiskey. They didn't know how to express that—they didn't ask me! My answer today: it never contained Old Forester and still doesn't; it was always Woodford Reserve."

Other distillers do it. A bourbon distilled from the same mash bill on the same still as another seems the same, but put it in a different warehouse, on a different floor, for a different set of years, and you have a very different whiskey.

"Old Forester is a batch of four-, five-, and six-year-old barrels," Morris explained. "Old Forester juice that was selected and held to be put in Woodford Reserve was nine years old. It was no longer Old Forester. Woodford Reserve still contains whiskey crafted at the Brown-Forman distillery that's ordered for Woodford, distilled for Woodford, and planned to age longer for Woodford." And the pot stills? "The pot-still whiskey plays a very significant role," he said. "It's hard to tell a pot-still barrel from a Brown-Forman barrel." **LB**

Tasting notes

Dry and spicy, an almost austere nose, but there is corn frolicking in the background. It all comes out on the palate: hot, sweet corn tinged with berries and a touch of apricot, a bit of leather and cinnamon, all loaded into a skyrocket that bursts into a spicy finish.

Woodford Reserve Master's Collection Four Grain

Brown-Forman Corporation | www.woodfordreserve.com

Region and country of origin Kentucky, United States
Distillery Woodford Reserve, Versailles
Alcohol content 46.2% abv
Style Straight bourbon

There are two main things to know about Woodford Reserve Master's Collection. First, its whiskeys come solely from three pot stills at Woodford Reserve. After some variation in barrel finishing, 2011 will see a 100 percent rye whiskey and master distiller Chris Morris promises, "a series of unique whiskeys coming; not really Woodford at all, just from Woodford."

Second, the collection is about experimentation. "It's part of our continuing education," Morris said, "learning about running the stills, or more flavorful tweaking influence in fermentation. We learn a lot from these experiments; we try to do a better job." The project is like a racing program for a car company.

Four Grain was inspired by the past; Morris loves distillery history. Rummaging through the old Glenmore distillery with bourbon historian Mike Veach, he found a rusty filebox full of recipes. One, from 1903, was a "four-grain recipe." Four Grain is not a re-creation—because Morris lost the file. But it stuck with him and became the first experiment.

Standard bourbons are made with corn, malt, and either rye or wheat: rye adds spice, wheat is smoother. Using both was a whiskey geek's fantasy: what would it taste like? "We played with a number of recipes," Morris said. "You can tell there's plenty of wheat and rye in it because of the nutty character. That ratio's secret; we like to keep the buzz going. Being the first, it was scary; it tasted so different. But that's why you get paid the big bucks!" Distillers such as Hudson are now making a four-grain also, so we have the chance to compare versions of this interesting whiskey. **LB**

Tasting notes

Cereal notes on the nose from the four grains. The spiciness is smooth, and the sweetness is mellow. Wheat's broad gentleness is there, but also rye's kick. This whiskey is truly educational, renewing one's appreciation of wheated bourbon character.

Woodford Reserve
Master's Collection Maple Wood Finish

Brown-Forman Corporation | www.woodfordreserve.com

Region and country of origin Kentucky, United States
Distillery Woodford Reserve, Versailles
Alcohol content 47.7% abv
Style Straight bourbon

Having its own cooperage means that, among other things, Brown-Forman can make barrels from anything. Master distiller Chris Morris says that the inspiration to make barrels from nonoak hardwoods came from working with native Kentucky hardwoods.

The team started with wood chips, toasted and charred, and soaked them in neutral spirits. If they smelled good, they would graduate to soaking in Woodford Reserve, and from there to putting whole strips of wood in barrels of mature whiskey. Ultimately, production barrels were made of four different woods: sugar maple, hickory, ash, and sassafras.

Morris said they toasted the barrels, filled them with whiskey, and "followed them along, tasting. You don't bottle an experiment; you follow it till it wrecks, and then you know when to stop."

The winner was maple (this time, anyway; Morris never actually said that the others were failures). The coopers made 120 barrels—toasted, not charred—and these were filled with fully matured Woodford Reserve at 110 proof. "You don't batch them," Morris said. "Each barrel came from an individual tree. Some took a year, some were at peak after two or three months." The result was something other than bourbon—a maple-wood-finished bourbon, or a "bourbon specialty." That is not finicky tweaking but a reflection of bourbon's tightly regulated definition.

It is good to know that the rules didn't stop Brown-Forman from having some fun. **LB**

Tasting notes

Cinnamon underpins the nose, with hints of chocolate and apricot. On the palate, the maple wood brings flavors of cedar cigar box, cinnamon, and roasted nuts. The lingering finish is best of all: maple-stewed apricot and peach, baking spices, and black tea.

Woodford Reserve
Master's Collection Seasoned Oak Finish

Brown-Forman Corporation | www.woodfordreserve.com

Region and country of origin Kentucky, United States
Distillery Woodford Reserve, Versailles
Alcohol content 50.2% abv
Style Straight bourbon

Brown-Forman has its own cooperage and has been having fun with it. The distillers have almost doubled the outdoor aging of the wood that goes into their barrels; they have introduced toasting (a lighter treatment than bourbon's traditional charring); they are playing around with different kinds of oak. More control over the wood means greater consistency in familiar whiskeys. It also has potential for additional variations, which is where this particular Woodford Reserve whiskey came from.

"This expression was inspired by our friends at Glenmorangie," says master distiller Chris Morris. "Distiller Bill Lumsden requires two-year seasoning of oak before coopering. That leaches tannins, which builds up more spice character. Cool! More spice, less tannin—let's go for as old a wood as we can. We had some three-and-a-half-year-old wood for the staves, and we had some five-year-old wood for the heads."

Mature Woodford whiskey was finished in these seasoned oak barrels. What happened? "The color was enriched," Morris said, "with very low bitterness, and the spice notes were fantastic. But because of the double-barreling, we kept the proof high going into the bottle; the more wood character you have, the more likely it is to drop out at lower proof."

There is plenty of wood in there, but also a fresh shot of busy, young whiskey. Like the Woodford Reserve Four Grain, this is an education on two aspects of bourbon in a single glass. **LB**

Tasting notes

Dark, almost chestnut. Warehouse reek puts an edge on the corn; an active mix of young and old whiskey notes. Very hot, huge oak nips the tongue, but corn and vanilla peek from underneath. Water brings out the corn from behind the wood, and a maple note.

Woodford Reserve Master's Collection Sonoma-Cutrer Finish

Brown-Forman Corporation
www.woodfordreserve.com

Region and country of origin Kentucky, United States
Distillery Woodford Reserve, Versailles
Alcohol content 43.2% abv
Style Straight bourbon

Like the other whiskeys of the Woodford Reserve Master's Collection, this one is 100 percent distilled in Woodford's three copper pot stills. Like them, it is a special project that tries something new for bourbon; in this case, additional aging in California chardonnay barrels from Sonoma-Cutrer Vineyards (also owned by Brown-Forman). Also like them, it was a limited edition in a still-shaped bottle with a wooden stopper.

Unlike the others, this one was not very well received (which means you might still find a bottle). But when sampled on a hot Kentucky summer afternoon, it seemed a perfect summertime drinking bourbon, with great fruity notes from the wine wood lifting the weight of the whiskey out of the glass. Something new, indeed.

This is exactly the kind of thing you want to see: innovation. Brand director Wayne Rose says that partly explains why the whiskeys are made in such small amounts: "We don't have to tie up a bunch of the company's money, which takes the handcuffs off. We want to make serious whiskey that tastes good, not just something experimental." Too right. **LB**

Tasting notes

A bourbon nose, sure, but with fruit on the oak tree and flowers among the corn. Much more fruit on the palate (sticky-starchy plum, fresh apple, and gooseberry).

Woodford Reserve Master's Collection Sweet Mash

Brown-Forman Corporation
www.woodfordreserve.com

Region and country of origin Kentucky, United States
Distillery Woodford Reserve, Versailles
Alcohol content 43.2% abv
Style Straight bourbon

Over the decades, the region where the pretty Woodford Reserve distillery—formerly the Labrot & Graham distillery—is sited has played a crucial role in the development of the drink we now call bourbon. Now Woodford Reserve master distiller Chris Morris and his team are experimenting with flavors and pushing bourbon into new areas. Each year sees the special release of an experimental whiskey, although not every one can be considered a bourbon.

This sweet-mash bourbon is intriguing, if not to everybody's taste. Key to the process of making regular bourbon is the addition of sour mash. That is the residue, known as backset, that is left after a bourbon run; it is sour because all its sugars have been removed and turned into alcohol. Adding backset to a new mash tun balances the acid and alkali and controls bacteria crucial to the flavor of the bourbon. By definition, the first run of distillation after any period of shutdown must be thrown away, and only its backset kept for the second run, when true bourbon spirit can be made. This release gives you an idea of what that first distillation tastes like. **DR**

Tasting notes

Big, sweet corn dominates the taste with not much to counteract or complement it. Too sweet to be exciting, but an interesting diversion nevertheless.

◄ Woodford Reserve's barrel run is used for rolling barrels by hand.

CANADA

Alberta Premium

Beam Global | www.beamglobal.com

Region and country of origin Alberta, Canada
Distillery Alberta Distillers, Calgary
Alcohol content 40% abv
Style Single-distillery rye

According to the whisky press and beaming brand ambassadors, rye whisky is in resurgence. A recent estimate using official industry figures shows that when the output of all of the U.S. distilleries is combined, worldwide sales of American rye now exceed 75,000 cases. Meanwhile, a single medium-sized Canadian distillery quietly ships 225,000 cases of 100 percent rye-grain whisky to market every year. That distillery, of course, is Alberta Distillers. Their best-known 100 percent rye whisky? Alberta Premium.

Alberta Premium is a solid, five-year-old Canadian workhorse mixing whisky. It gained worldwide fame on the whisky web—and notoriety among certain aficionados—when, for several years running, a drinks writer named it "Canadian Whisky of the Year." "Wow, just wow!" a whisky blogger gushed before awarding it no fewer than 93 points. "Imagine!" another countered, "People taste this and think it's the best Canada can do. It's not even the best that the distillery can do." But however you look at it, there is something very special about young rye whisky, a fact confirmed by a legion of loyal Alberta Premium drinkers.

Any whisky distilled from 100 percent rye grain casts a pretty long shadow to start with, especially one that outsells all American rye by an astounding three to one margin. But reluctantly we must admit that when Canadian connoisseurs want a sip of whisky they are more likely to favor the ten-year-old Alberta Springs from the same distillery. And when they're really looking for a hit of heaven? It's Alberta Premium 30-Year-Old every time. **DDK**

Tasting notes

Rich, fruity, and beautifully balanced. Hot ginger and sizzling pepper meld slowly into sweet and zesty rye spices. Soft tannins, the flintiness of 100 percent unmalted rye, and vanilla caramel tinged with maple syrup woodiness resolve in a cleansing citric pithiness.

Alberta Premium 30-Year-Old

Beam Global | www.beamglobal.com

Region and country of origin Alberta, Canada
Distillery Alberta Distillers, Calgary
Alcohol content 40% abv
Style Single-distillery rye

In Canada, rye means "whisky." For several centuries, Canadian distillers have been using a dash of rye grain to spice up their mashes. Early Canadian whisky drinkers favored corn- or wheat-based whisky with a little bit of rye in it so much that they nicknamed it "rye" to set it apart from "straight" or "common" whisky. Then along came Alberta Distillers, who made whisky mashes of nothing but rye grain. No corn, no wheat, no barley—just pure prairie rye.

A little rye, as those early Canadian distillers discovered, goes a long way. This is why Alberta Distillers distills some of its rye spirit to a very high abv until it retains just a hint of its spiciness. This causes the spirit to react differently with the wooden barrels than spirit distilled to a lower abv would, and it avoids the familiar bitterness of long-aged spirit that started out with high congener levels.

Thus, Alberta Distillers was able to age this crispy, clean rye whisky for a full thirty years, during which time it has picked up masses of woody notes without the bitter, twisted signs of old age. Instead, it has matured gracefully into a voluptuous creature "of a certain age" who shows no sign of losing the youthful twinkle in her eye.

The 1970s-style Alberta Premium bottle has become an icon on Canadian liquor store shelves, but distribution outside of Canada is limited. Perhaps it's time to start making travel plans. With just 700 cases of Alberta Premium 30-Year-Old produced, the challenge will be to actually find a bottle. But what dedicated whisky fan is not up to that challenge? **DDK**

Tasting notes

Hugely complex. Pencil shavings, dusty rye, baskets of dark fruit, overripe strawberries, and butterscotch ice cream sprinkled with bitter chocolate. Oatmeal porridge with cinnamon and brown sugar. White pepper, ginger, and cloves, black vanilla pods, cedar, and cold wet slate.

Alberta Springs 10-Year-Old

Beam Global | www.beamglobal.com

Region and country of origin Alberta, Canada
Distillery Alberta Distillers, Calgary
Alcohol content 40% abv
Style Single-distillery rye

Alberta Distillers Limited sits on 40 acres (16 ha) of industrial park in an area that was once on the outskirts of Calgary. Scenic, it is not. But travel for two hours by car and you will see the picturesque Rocky Mountains erupt out of the flat prairie like enormous white-capped molars in some gigantic jaw. Are the springs of Alberta Springs really fed by melt from those high, majestic, snow-capped mountains? They most certainly are, and one other thing is certain, too: of all the highly celebrated whiskies produced by Alberta Distillers, Alberta Springs is the cream of the crop. "It's the wood," says distillery manager Rob Tuer. He, like so many Canadians with a palate for rye, claims that Alberta Springs is his favorite.

One benefit of maturing rye whisky in barrels previously used for bourbon is that the overt primary wood notes—the vanillas, tannins, caramels—are subdued somewhat, allowing new, more subtle wood tones to emerge. Flavors that would be masked by new oak come to the fore, yielding crisp, almost exotic wood without any hint of bitterness.

There are places on the Canadian Prairies where the grain fields stretch flat to the horizon. Calgary is on the edge of these in Canada's prime rye-growing region. It is an area with blisteringly hot summers and bitterly cold winters. Such extreme changes in temperature create a natural cycle that, over ten years of aging, sees the maturing whisky penetrate deep into the oak barrels in summer, then leach flavor out of the wood and into the nascent Alberta Springs whisky as it cools in winter. **DDK**

Tasting notes

A big, bold rye nose rich in cloves, ginger, and nutmeg, with clean Canadian wood. Sweet vanilla, butterscotch, and licorice, green apple, white grape, and dried fruit. Luscious, thick, and creamy. Dry grain with hints of dry linen. Intense spicy pepper fades into a pithy citric zest.

Black Velvet Deluxe

Constellation Brands | www.blackvelvetwhisky.com

Region and country of origin Alberta, Canada
Distillery Black Velvet, Lethbridge
Alcohol content 40% abv
Style Single-distillery whisky

Every week, two tanker loads of Black Velvet whisky leave the Black Velvet distillery in Lethbridge, Alberta, heading for the United States to be bottled and sold. That's over one hundred tanker loads of Black Velvet whisky a year. Clearly, whisky fans in the United States love their Black Velvet. But what they don't know is that the whisky shipped to the United States is made to a special formula tweaked to U.S. tastes. Canada and much of the rest of the world drinks a crisper, drier whisky called Black Velvet Deluxe.

Black Velvet first came on the market in 1951 as a sideline product distilled at the Gilbey gin distillery in Toronto. It became so popular that in 1973 a dedicated distillery, named Palliser, was built in Lethbridge to produce it. A series of mergers and acquisitions followed, leading ultimately to Black Velvet becoming a kind of orphan—the only spirit facility in a global wine conglomerate called Constellation Brands.

Lethbridge sits close to the U.S. border, not far from the Milk River hoodoos—bizarre natural columns of sandstone that look like they are about to collapse into piles of sand. This is a parched land of rattlesnakes and tumbleweed. Wherever you look, there's a panorama straight out of a western. It is a beautiful place to visit, but it's not so good for growing grain. This is why the corn that goes into Black Velvet Deluxe is brought in from the American Midwest. Black Velvet Deluxe is "Blended at Birth." Once distilled, the new corn spirit is mixed with two-year-old rye-grain whisky, then poured into charred white oak barrels for a three-year sleep. **DDK**

Tasting notes

Creamy sweet butterscotch with hints of burnt sugar, then hot pepper bursting into nutmeg, cloves, and ginger. Typical Canadian fresh-sawn lumber, slightly earthy rye, and ripe black fruit are rounded out by a zippy citric zest. Fades out in a citrusy bitterness.

Black Velvet Reserve 8-Year-Old

Constellation Brands | www.blackvelvetwhisky.com

Region and country of origin Alberta, Canada
Distillery Black Velvet, Lethbridge
Alcohol content 40% abv
Style Single-distillery whisky

What do you do when you produce one of the top-selling whiskies in North America? Well, you don't mess with it, but there certainly is a temptation to build on the solid platform of an established brand by adding new expressions. This is exactly what happened in 2004 with Black Velvet Canadian whisky. In addition to the three-year-old standard Black Velvet, an eight-year-old version was introduced into the U.S. market. This new "Reserve" was not only older but had a significantly increased proportion of flavoring whisky, making it a richer and rounder dram.

At that time, Black Velvet was produced at the Schenley distillery in Valleyfield, Quebec. A cadastral survey shows it situated on a long, very narrow strip of land pointing toward the St. Lawrence River. This is typical of old Quebec. The river was the settlers' highway, and frontage was shared among as many landowners as possible. Even the fields of Black Velvet's corn and rye are long and narrow.

Today, though, Black Velvet whisky is produced some 2,200 miles (3,500 km) to the west in Lethbridge, Alberta, at the distillery to which it gave its name: Black Velvet. Unlike the fields in Quebec, those in Alberta are both long and broad, but there is not enough rain to grow corn. This is trucked in from the American Midwest to be distilled and mingled with two-year-old Alberta rye spirit, then tucked away for another eight years' maturation. The end result is a silky, upscale sipping whisky in a distinctive six-sided bottle, one that is usually reserved for the Black Velvet drinker's most special occasions. **DDK**

Tasting notes

Spicy hot pepper with dusty rye, caramel, and fresh-cut wood. Rich black fruits blanket sweet citrus tones. Caramel, blackstrap molasses, burnt sugar, and pepper dominate until washed away by undertones of grapefruit peel. Fades out on pepper and prune juice.

Bush Pilot's Private Reserve

Robert Denton & Company Limited, Bloomfield Hills, Michigan (defunct)

Region and country of origin Canada
Distillery Undisclosed
Alcohol content 43% abv
Style Single-cask whisky

These days it seems that everyone is bottling single-cask whiskies. (In bourbon country they're called "single-barrel" and even Ireland has a few single-cask whiskeys on the market now.) But as recently as the 1990s, single-cask whisky was practically unknown to connoisseurs. Perhaps the first example of these in the United States was an early 1990s release of a single-cask Canadian all-corn whisky called Bush Pilot's Private Reserve.

This started out as a lark for Marilyn Smith, whose father, Fred Johnson, was previously a successful automotive engineer who ran a hobby airline flying Detroit industrialists to an isolated fishing camp in northern Ontario. As the tale goes, when the nights grew colder, the pilots of Johnson's bush planes would warm themselves with unlabeled bottles of Canadian whisky—dubbed "the bush pilot's private reserve."

Smith's partner, Robert Denton, owned a successful wholesale liquor business and would buy blended Canadian whisky in bulk to bottle and sell in the United States. On one of his buying trips, Denton came across some barrels of mature Canadian corn whisky that had been intended for eventual blending. He was intrigued, and when the distillery manager told him there was nothing preventing him from bottling them as is, Smith and Denton decided to do just that, one myth-creating barrel at a time.

Frederick H. Johnson Jr., Smith's brother, signed the homemade paper label, but it was Smith's idea to bottle the whisky in her father's memory and name it after his adventures as the owner of a bush airline. **DDK**

Tasting notes

Richer than Scottish grain whisky, with crisp oaky notes. Sweet vanilla caramel becomes dusty, musty corn, and herbal tea touched with mint and hot white pepper spiked with baking spices. More oily than creamy, with fruity solvents and refreshing citrus pith.

Canadian 83

Diageo | www.diageo.com

Region and country of origin Quebec, Canada
Distillery Diageo Global Supply, Salaberry-de-Valleyfield
Alcohol content 40% abv
Style Blend

You're in Gimli, Manitoba, chatting with some guys from the Crown Royal plant. "So which one is your favorite?" you ask. Suddenly they're suppressing grins, waiting for your reaction. "Seagram's 83." One of them finally breaks the silence. "The best-selling whisky in Manitoba." "I guess it's Canadian 83 now," someone adds. "They dropped the 'Seagram's' when Diageo took over the plant a few years ago." "Canadian 83?" you muse. It's Canadian whisky all right, with its signature crispy wood, vibrant hot pepper, and toffee notes, but it certainly isn't Crown. "I think they would have stopped making it altogether," says one, "if it wasn't such a favorite with all the distillery workers. The Crown soaks the last of the richness out of the barrel," he explains. "All that's left for 83 is the velvet."

Joseph Seagram introduced Seagram's 83 in 1887 as the first new whisky from the Waterloo distillery since he bought it four years previously. After an illustrious career, the Waterloo distillery closed in the 1990s, and all production moved west to Gimli. But as demand for Gimli's primary product, Crown Royal, continued to grow, production of the 83 was again shifted back east, this time to Diageo's plant in Valleyfield, Quebec. **DDK**

Tasting notes

Spirity with muted rye spices, cloves and ginger, along with hot pepper. Toffee sweetness, musty sandalwood, and a zippy citrusy zing cry out for ginger ale.

Canadian Club Black Label 8-Year-Old

Beam Global | www.canadianclubwhisky.com

Region and country of origin Ontario, Canada
Distillery Hiram Walker, Walkerville
Alcohol content 40% abv
Style Single-distillery whisky

In the cruel world of the 1980s, falling sales created the "great whisky lake" that put several distilleries out of business and distillers in a funk. Meanwhile, in the warehouses, millions of barrels of whisky just kept aging. Some blenders, finding their whisky getting older and older, began blending that aged stock away into brands with younger age statements. Canadian Club was one of those brands. The label may have said six years old, but the contents of some of those 1980s bottles often crept up to eight years old and older.

North American drinkers began to notice and complained that their whisky was getting woody. But in Japan, the new, crisper bottlings were met with enthusiasm. Chagrined Canadian Club blenders quickly reverted to six-year-old stock for their North American bottlings, but the reception in Japan inspired blender Mike Booth to develop a new, wood-forward, eight-year-old version of Canadian Club, which he named "Black Label." According to Dan Tullio, brand ambassador of Canadian Club, Canadian Club Black Label is still country-specific to Japan. "This eight-year-old marque within the portfolio," he says, "has a higher ratio of rye and rye malt, which contributes a really spicy character to the whisky." **DDK**

Tasting notes

Sweet, dark fruit, rye spices, and hints of lemon. Butterscotch and vanilla resolve into citrusy pith with tingling spices, burned sugar, and fresh-cut cedar.

Canadian Club's appeal extends around the world. ➡

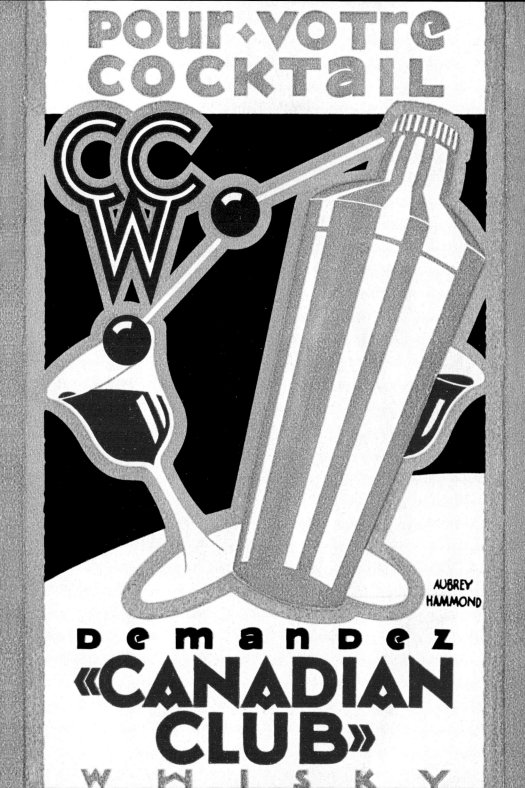

Canadian Club Reserve 10-Year-Old

Beam Global | www.canadianclubwhisky.com

Region and country of origin Ontario, Canada
Distillery Hiram Walker, Walkerville
Alcohol content 40% abv
Style Single-distillery whisky

Walk into a bar in any of more than 150 countries and ask for "rye," and chances are you'll be served six-year-old Canadian Club. Since the late nineteenth century, Canadian Club whisky has been sold in hotels, bars, and liquor stores all around the world.

In 1858 a Detroit-based American grocer named Hiram Walker built a distillery across the Detroit River in Canada, on farmland that would one day become the town of Walkerville. Success came quickly, and by the mid-1880s, when Walker introduced his Club Whisky (later dubbed Canadian Club), his reputation for making high-quality whisky had spread far.

This version of the ubiquitous "CC," as it is so fondly called, is just a little bit different from Walker's standard issue. Canadian Club Reserve is aged for an additional four years and includes a much more substantial portion of whisky made from rye grain. And not just any rye grain: CC Reserve includes whiskies made from both malted and unmalted rye.

Generally speaking, Canadian Club makes fruity, mouth-filling whiskies, and this version is true to that house style. But CC Reserve turns it up a notch. The increased rye grain used in the mash adds a classic steely edge. For those who enjoy an elegant whisky, CC Reserve is a refined sipper. For those who prefer highballs, they will practically hear CC's ginger-laden rye spices calling out for ginger ale.

Walker's distillery remains in operation to this day, making it the longest continually operating distillery in North America. It also holds the distinction of being North America's largest. **DDK**

Tasting notes

Peach pits and citrus pith balance a certain meatiness, as white pepper, ginger, and cinnamon override cream sherry and ripe black fruit. The rye begins with freshwater plants, wet soil, fragrant flowers, and a steely, hard edge. Finishes in a warming peppery glow.

Canadian Club Sherry Cask

Beam Global | www.canadianclubwhisky.com

Region and country of origin Ontario, Canada
Distillery Hiram Walker, Walkerville
Alcohol content 41.3% abv
Style Single-distillery whisky

Canadian whisky lovers watched with some dismay as Pernod–Ricard bought the Hiram Walker distillery in Walkerville, Ontario, and then let Beam Global take over its flagship brand, Canadian Club. It turns out, however, that this cloud had a silver lining in the shape of Beam's parent company, Fortune Brands, which also owns Harvey's Bristol Cream. This is a cream sherry based on the palomino grape cultivar, and blended from fino, amontillado, oloroso, and Pedro Ximénez sherries. Briefly, it's hugely flavorful, and those flavors linger on in the cask wood.

Fans of single-malt Scotch are quite familiar with sherry-finished whisky, and indeed the first impression of Canadian Club Sherry Cask is that it is one of those Scottish sherry monsters. But the label confirms that it is Canadian Club whisky that has spent an additional two years maturing in fresh sherry casks that were used to make Harvey's Bristol Cream.

Canadian Club Sherry Cask is made in batches, each with its own slight eccentricities. They start out as exactly twenty-seven Jerez sherry butts filled with fully matured, six-year-old Canadian Club whisky. This is more than a simple finish, it's a second maturation, during which the whisky assimilates some of the rich, fruity palomino flavors from the barrel.

Canadian Club whisky's ownership may have changed, but it is still made in the same Walkerville distillery where Hiram Walker himself created the original in 1882. Now a new Canadian Club benefits from its association with another venerable brand, Harvey's Bristol Cream. **DDK**

Tasting notes

A staid men's club in a *Masterpiece Theater* episode is shaken up with the youthful exuberance of *America's Got Talent*. Pencil shavings with dry oak, spicy hot pepper with rich cream sherry, old leather, and cigar smoke; rum and butter with fruity tobacco and dry tea.

Canadian Hunter

Sazerac Company | www.sazerac.com

Region and country of origin Canada
Distillery Undisclosed
Alcohol content 40% abv
Style Blend

This is not just a whisky you must try before you die; it is one you must have on your shelf. The label is nothing short of awesome. A bearded hunter stands in slushy snow, dressed in leggings and fur-collared parka, with a pair of straining huskies and a lever-action Winchester on his arm. The Canadian hunter of old movie cliché now lives on a whisky label.

The Sazerac Company of New Orleans has hundreds of thousands of barrels of Canadian whisky aging in Canadian warehouses. Sazerac uses this ready supply to blend upward of twenty brands, most of them limited to the U.S. market. Canadian Hunter, a former Seagram's brand, is one of these. The label may have recently been updated, but it remains decidedly retro and retains just enough camp to be cool.

According to the Internet, Canadian Hunter has a loyal following from one end of the United States to the other. "Allow me to introduce the liquor store's best-kept secret," enthused one Californian. The response? Someone from Alaska replied, "The logo on the bottle was what appealed to me, but it turned out to be the best whisky I have ever tasted."

Canadian whisky, yes, but unfortunately one that is not currently available in Canada. **DDK**

Tasting notes

The palate is sweet with caramel and vanilla and a wonderful peppery burn. Simple and straightforward, with rye spices and lemon rind waiting for ginger ale.

Canadian Mist Black Diamond

Brown-Forman | www.collingwoodwhisky.com

Region and country of origin Ontario, Canada
Distillery Canadian Mist, Collingwood
Alcohol content 43% abv
Style Single-distillery whisky

A famous poet once said, "A little learning is a dangerous thing." That truth was borne out at the end of the 1990s when a drinks writer visited the still room at the Canadian Mist distillery. He saw six stainless-steel columns and concluded that the whisky was made without ever contacting copper. Quite a phenomenon, as copper is necessary to remove certain off-notes in the spirit, and virtually no successful distiller makes whisky without it.

Those stainless-steel column stills were in fact packed with sacrificial copper, and after the spirit leaves those copper-packed columns it travels along copper pipes into a copper doubler. Those stills may be covered by shiny stainless-steel on the outside, but it is what's inside that really counts.

For more than forty years, Canadian Mist has quietly produced a mixing whisky that is a best seller in the United States but remains barely known in Canada. It is made for the U.S. market and is a little sweeter and fruitier as a result. Recently, however, Canadian Mist Black Diamond has hit the shelves. It's a new formulation—richer, rounder, and bigger, intended for Canadian Mist drinkers looking for something familiar but a little upscale for a special occasion. **DDK**

Tasting notes

Ripe black fruit, Concord grape, and intense white pepper. Hints of caramel, icing sugar, and chocolate-covered ginger. Slightly floral with citrusy bitters.

Distilled in Ontario using pure spring water from Georgian Bay. →

Tyee Lake, British Columbia, Canada

Canada at its best.

Enjoy the light, smooth whisky that's becoming America's favorite Canadian.
Imported Canadian Mist®

Share some tonight.

Caribou Crossing Single Barrel

Sazerac Company | www.sazerac.com

Region and country of origin Canada
Distillery Undisclosed
Alcohol content 40% abv
Style Single-barrel whisky

Caribou Crossing is the only single-barrel Canadian whisky currently on the market, making it one very special, must-have sipping whisky indeed. Although Caribou Crossing is Canadian, it is bottled (by hand) in Frankfort, Kentucky, and sold by the Sazerac Company of New Orleans. Sazerac calls Canadian whisky "the comeback category" and has put its corporate money where its trend-setting mouth is, with 220,000 barrels of Canadian whisky maturing in Canadian warehouses.

With Caribou Crossing as its flagship, Sazerac is setting out to foster a greater appreciation of Canadian whisky among U.S. consumers. They have hired Canadian master distiller Drew Mayville to lead the charge. Mayville spent twenty-three years making Canadian whisky for Seagram's, including a stint at Seagram's legendary Waterloo distillery in Ontario. Sazerac has not disclosed the particular distillery where this whisky is made, but Mayville has revealed that Caribou Crossing is made with four grains—corn, wheat, rye, and barley.

Connoisseurs of Canadian whisky know that Caribou Crossing is not the first single-barrel bottling of Canadian whisky. Bush Pilot's Special Reserve from the 1990s holds that title (Hirsch was second). The barrel number and age were clearly marked on each Bush Pilot's bottle, but this is not the case with Caribou Crossing. Some connoisseurs say they'd like to see that changed, but Canadian whisky lovers enjoy their whisky and are more likely to pour a third or fourth dram than make analytical comparisons of various barrels of the same whisky. **DDK**

Tasting notes

Soft, creamy corn, and fresh-cut firewood. Sweet rye spices poke through butterscotch, vanilla, and stewed prune, like nutmeg on rice pudding. A refreshing citrusy zing is buffeted by hot peppery spices. Velvety tannins emphasize the overall creaminess and complexity.

Artwork depicting the caribou is featured on the whisky's box. ➡

Century Reserve 15/25

Century Distillers
www.highwood-distillers.com

Region and country of origin Alberta, Canada
Distillery Highwood, High River
Alcohol content 40% abv
Style Single-distillery whisky

This is one powerhouse corn whisky with the scents of a British Columbia lumber mill wafting through it. And, as chance would have it, this whisky actually spent part of its youth in the heart of B.C.'s Okanagan Valley. As to where it was distilled, no one is certain, but until 2005 it lay maturing in the Potter's warehouse in Kelowna. Potter's did not distill whisky there, instead buying and selling whisky distilled by others. A manager who should know suspects it originally came from the long-defunct Weyburn, Saskatchewan distillery—but no one is saying for sure.

Regardless, in 2005 Highwood Distillers bought Potter's last remaining barrels. Among that stock were the barrels in which this whisky was maturing. Tasting it is slightly reminiscent of chewing on a log, but it's a fragrant, scrumptious, pleasantly aromatic log, and the creamy corn whisky coats your tongue.

Let's assume Weyburn was the source, as there's a lot of Canada in this whisky. Distilled on the flattest part of the Canadian prairie, it crossed the Rockies to the Okanagan. A return journey over Rogers Pass and through Glacier National Park brought it to Alberta's High River. Many a thirty-year-old Canadian citizen has seen far less of the country. **DDK**

Tasting notes

A complex fusion of ripe fruit, clean oak, vanilla, honey, and icing sugar. Luxurious creaminess balances hot white pepper, pencil shavings, and silky tannins.

Century Reserve 21-Year-Old

Century Distillers
www.highwood-distillers.com

Region and country of origin Alberta, Canada
Distillery Highwood, High River
Alcohol content 40% abv
Style Single-distillery whisky

If your brain's rye-drenched pleasure center requires exceptionally intense stimulation to achieve nirvana, then perhaps you should leave Century Reserve 21-Year-Old for those who find their enlightenment in nuance, suggestion, and evocation. Yes, it's a big, voluptuous, almost meaty whisky, but its many raptures take their quiet time to rise from a comfortable bed of creamy corn and silky tannin.

Century Distillers in Calgary, Alberta, is the marketing arm of Highwood distillery, a small, privately owned Canadian distillery that makes a range of Canadian rye whiskies combining wheat and rye spirits. Highwood makes several corn-based whiskies as well, although these are minglings of barrels of whisky that Century Distillers acquired when it bought Potter's Distillery in Kelowna, British Columbia. Previously based in Vancouver, also in British Columbia, Potter's had distilled whisky. Following the move to Kelowna, the company focused solely on buying and selling whisky distilled by others. However, the legend of Potter's is huge in some circles because the barrels of whisky it bought were almost always of the most outstanding quality. It is this whisky that is used for Century Reserve. **DDK**

Tasting notes

A rich, weighty body from which evolves roasted grain, teasing clean oak, dairy barn, and an intricate interplay of hot pepper and baking spices. All is nuance.

← The Okanagan Valley that birthed Century Reserve.

Chinook 5-Year-Old

MCBSW Sales Company Inc.

Region and country of origin Canada
Distillery Undisclosed
Alcohol content 40% abv
Style Single-distillery whisky

Ravinder Minhas was still a schoolboy in 1994 when the government of Alberta privatized the retail liquor industry. With the government monopoly gone, his parents moved quickly to open a liquor store. This would become the family business where Ravinder and his older sister Manjit would learn all the tricks of the spirits trade. In 1999, the siblings created a line of house-brand liquors for sale in their parents' store. Their initial bottlings included rum, Canadian rye, gin, and vodka, and soon other liquor stores were also carrying their Mountain Crest spirits.

In 2002 a poor crop of blue agave sent tequila prices skyrocketing. The Minhases, however, had negotiated locked-in supply arrangements with producers in Mexico and were able to maintain a steady supply of reasonably priced tequila. Flush with cash from this success, the siblings launched their own lines of value-priced beer. A somewhat irreverent ad campaign, featuring Ravinder as "Dr. Bubbles," helped catapult their beer to great market success.

The brother and sister team has since bought Wisconsin's Joseph Huber Brewery and renamed it the Minhas Craft Brewery. More recently they have opened their own brewery and brewpub in Calgary.

The early success of Mountain Crest liquors was due to the Minhas family's focus on cheaper "value" brands, but this time, through his own firm, MCBSW Sales Company, Ravinder has introduced Chinook Canadian whisky. A premium five-year-old Canadian whisky distilled in Calgary, it stands head and shoulders above its Mountain Crest progenitor. **DDK**

Tasting notes

Ripe orchard fruits, including peaches and pears, ripen into stewed prunes. Vanilla coconut custard is sprinkled with sweet cinnamon, candied ginger, and blistering hot pepper. Toasted bread melds into nutty breakfast cereal as rosewater and orange tail off into bitter lemon.

Collingwood

Brown-Forman | www.collingwoodwhisky.com

Region and country of origin Ontario, Canada
Distillery Canadian Mist, Collingwood
Alcohol content 40% abv
Style Single-distillery whisky

Raw, charred, or toasted, white oak barrels are the key to proper whisky flavor development. But why can't other woods be used as well? That is a question Brown-Forman's distiller Chris Morris and blender Steve Hughes set out to answer in 2008 when they came up with the concept for Collingwood whisky. Since the distinctive woody flavor of maple syrup is commonly found in Canadian whisky, what, they wondered, would happen if they added actual maple wood to whisky that had aged in white oak?

Kentucky's Brown-Forman just happens to own its own cooperage, so custom barrels were easy to come by. Brown-Forman also owns Canadian Mist, a whisky distillery located in Collingwood, Ontario. A supply of maple barrels was soon set up at Collingwood, where, instead of the barrels being charred, they were toasted inside like wine barrels. This job done, Hughes and Morris then had the barrels taken apart and shipped to the distillery as staves.

Using fully mature, oak-aged whiskies, Morris and Hughes put together a rye-rich premium blend. Then, while the whisky was still in the blending tank, they added their separated staves of toasted maple wood, letting them float on top of the blend during a prolonged marrying period. It turned out that the staves did indeed impart a unique clean spiciness to the whisky, along with sweet, almost fruity top notes. So Collingwood is not so much "finished" in maple wood as seasoned with it. Whether Brown-Forman have succeeded in producing "the smoothest whisky ever made," you must judge for yourself. **DDK**

Tasting notes

Vanilla and perhaps marzipan. Sweet, rich, almost syrupy with butterscotch, canned peaches, and musky grapes. Mouthfeel is meaty with velvet tannins and grapefruit pith, and vividly expressive. Warm with a lingering perfume character.

Crown Royal Black

Diageo | www.crownroyal.com

Region and country of origin Quebec, Canada
Distillery Diageo Global Supply, Salaberry-de-Valleyfield
Alcohol content 45% abv
Style Blend

When Canadian trade negotiators, intent on protecting the nation's identity, agreed to recognize bourbon as a distinctive product of the United States, they did so with an apparent ignorance of Canada's thriving bourbon industry. Indeed, at one time, bulk Canadian-produced bourbon was bottled in the United States and labeled with the name of a well-pedigreed American distillery. At the same time, some of this whisky was sold in Canada with the actual Canadian distillery identified on the label.

Although bureaucrats may have thought that ending this practice was for the greater good, it did not mean that Canadian bourbon stills were decommissioned or that distillers ceased to age corn-based whisky in new charred oak barrels. The upshot? The word "bourbon" has disappeared from Canada's whisky labels, and a whole assortment of its whiskies continues to display distinct elements of bourbon. Nowhere is this more obvious than in the Crown Royal family, and of these, Crown Royal Black is the most bourbonlike. And so it should be. There is still a lot of bourbon produced in Gimli, Manitoba, and Andrew MacKay—Crown Royal's master blender—took full advantage of this when developing this robust whisky.

Launched in 2010, Crown Royal Black was the most successful new entrant in the spirits market in the United States that year. Although Crown Royal has the marketing superpower of its owner Diageo behind it, staying power only comes when people enjoy the whisky enough to come back for more, and this they do in droves. **DDK**

Tasting notes

Blackstrap molasses, vanilla pods, black cherries, licorice cough drops, and fragrant lilacs. New-oak tones dominate a complex but still straight-ahead sipping whisky or mixer. Orange bitters tempers sweet fruit while cayenne reinforces hot raw ginger.

Crown Royal Limited Edition

Diageo | www.crownroyal.com

Region and country of origin Quebec, Canada
Distillery Diageo Global Supply, Salaberry-de-Valleyfield
Alcohol content 40% abv
Style Blend

For decades, Red Rose Tea was a Canadian favorite. Television commercials for Red Rose—there was a rich assortment of them—always ended with an elegant British voice opining "Only in Canada you say? Pity!" Today, Crown Royal could run those same ads with just a slight change of words. Crown Royal Limited Edition is the whisky aficionado's Red Rose—elegant, refined, and only available in Canada. Such a pity.

The inimitable Sam Bronfman created the original Crown Royal in 1939. He made a fortune during Prohibition and subsequently sought respectability. Bronfman had his new whisky placed aboard the train that carried King George VI and Queen Elizabeth, the Queen Mother, across Canada that year. There is no evidence that they tasted it, but Canadians certainly did. Sales were so brisk that Seagram's could barely keep up with demand. It took almost another twenty-five years to build up enough well-matured stocks to introduce Crown into the U.S. market. Today, Crown Royal is the world's bestselling Canadian whisky.

The tea and whisky connection can certainly be seen in international corporate boardrooms. Canada's tea, Red Rose, has become a Unilever product and is no longer limited to Canada. They may sell more units now, but where it once dominated the tea section in Canadian supermarkets, today it is adrift in a sea of brands. Similarly with whisky? Since Diageo took over Crown Royal, brand managers have resisted the urge to send Limited Edition into other markets. This is one whisky that is a lot more than just another brand. "Only in Canada you say?" Darn right! **DDK**

Tasting notes

An elegant, creamy body spiced with nutmeg, cloves, ginger, and peppermint. Crown Royal's signature bourbon notes reverberate in floral vanilla, dry grain, and bitter orange. Dusty rye meets voluptuous corn. Complex and weighty, yet balanced and restrained.

Danfield's Limited Edition 21-Year-Old

Constellation Brands | www.cbrands.com

Region and country of origin Alberta, Canada
Distillery Black Velvet, Lethbridge
Alcohol content 40% abv
Style Single-distillery whisky

According to information on the label, Danfield's whisky is made by Williams and Churchill Limited. Lists of distilleries on one whisky Web site after another record the firm as being in Valleyfield, Quebec, or Lethbridge, Alberta, but that's where the information ends. A little detective work, however, tells us Williams and Churchill is not a distillery, and instead points us to the Black Velvet family of whiskies, once distilled in Valleyfield but now based in Lethbridge, Alberta.

Indeed, Williams and Churchill is a marketing firm based at the Black Velvet distillery in Lethbridge, and set up by brand managers within the Black Velvet organization to distinguish a line of uber bottlings from their very successful international brands. New whisky is not distilled for Danfield's; rather, outstanding barrels are set aside for it as they are discovered within existing inventories. There are two Danfield's, the 10-Year-Old and the 21-Year-Old. True small-batch whiskies, they are bottled just to meet demand and are sold exclusively within Canada. Although the company gives its Danfield's line a low profile, the 21-Year-Old especially has achieved a stellar reputation among Canadian aficionados.

It is instructive to taste whisky that has matured slowly in once-used bourbon casks, for without the overt oak-vanilla tones of new wood to mask them, the individual grains—in this case rye and corn—shine clearly through. While oak still dominates, this is the crisp, clean, refill oak of well-aged Canadian rye. As they say in Canada and a few other places around the world, "*Vive la différence!*" **DDK**

Tasting notes

Fragrant oak with tannins. No hint of bitterness. A touch of pickle juice offsets fresh berries, black fruit, and slight floral notes, while zippy pepper, cinnamon, ginger, and cloves balance the creaminess of corn. Rounded out by butterscotch, burnt sugar, and bitter lemon.

Forty Creek Barrel Select

Kittling Ridge Estates Wines and Spirits | www.fortycreekwhisky.com

Region and country of origin Ontario, Canada
Distillery Kittling Ridge, Grimsby
Alcohol content 40% abv
Style Single-distillery whisky

One of Canada's most popular tourist destinations is Niagara Falls. Water drops spectacularly over the 173-foot precipice before heading into Lake Ontario and on to the Atlantic. Most people don't know that the escarpment over which Niagara plunges stretches another 450 miles, at places reaching heights of over a mile. Above the cliff, in the early days of colonization, the rich land supported farmers and home distillers. Today, below the cliff at the aptly named Forty Mile Creek some 40 miles (64 km) from the Falls, a little bit of that pioneer spirit continues to trickle from two unusual copper pot stills. And that's exactly what you can taste when you sip Forty Creek Barrel Select.

More than 350 species of birds spend at least part of their lives on the Niagara Escarpment. Among these are raptors that ride the thermals, rising up the cliffs on warm spring mornings. Climbing high into the air, these birds prepare to fly across Lake Ontario as they head north to their summer breeding grounds. This process is called "kittling" and it has lent its name to the distillery below. Kittling Ridge Estate Wine and Spirits is home to a range of whiskies called Forty Creek, and of these the most popular is the highly praised Forty Creek Barrel Select.

An experienced winemaker, John Hall spent ten years perfecting Barrel Select before releasing it, not in Canada at first, but Texas, where it was quite a hit. Kittling Ridge is the only Canadian-style distillery that allows visitors. For the luckiest, a visit includes tasting the corn, rye, and barley whiskies that Hall skillfully mingles to make Barrel Select. **DDK**

Tasting notes

Begins with rich caramel, sherry, ripe fruit, and dusty rye. Creamy, earthy sweet corn, then floral perfume, ginger, cinnamon, hot pepper, and hints of citrus peels. Zesty bitterness in the middle turns to dry grain, freshwater plants, and lingering peppery heat.

Forty Creek Confederation Oak Reserve

Kittling Ridge Estates Wines and Spirits | www.fortycreekwhisky.com

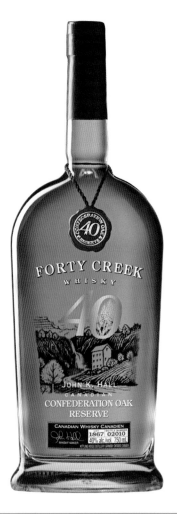

Region and country of origin Ontario, Canada
Distillery Kittling Ridge, Grimsby
Alcohol content 40% abv
Style Single-distillery whisky

Canadian whisky is experiencing a renaissance of sorts with connoisseurs, and one man who is leading the connoisseurs farther forward to an age of whisky enlightenment is John K. Hall with his Forty Creek whiskies. Of these new twenty-first-century Canadian whiskies, Confederation Oak Reserve is right at the fore and of particular interest.

Confederation Oak is blended from rye, corn, and barley whiskies in a process Hall refers to as "meritage"—a term borrowed from the wine industry in Napa Valley, California, that combines the notions of "merit" and "heritage." He matures these component whiskies separately, blends them, then rebarrels the blend for a period of marrying before bottling. Although it is common practice for distillers to allow a marrying period after blending, in the case of Confederation Oak, this period lasts for several years, an unusually long time. For Confederation Oak, the time lapse is more than a marriage and more than a finish; it is a second period of maturation.

What really sets Confederation Oak apart, though, is that this marrying process takes place in barrels made from Canadian white oak. Having grown slowly in the short Canadian summers and endured bitterly cold winters, Canadian white oak trees produce wood that is more dense than that of American oak trees of the same species. This denser wood has its own distinctive buttery vanillas and tingling spiciness. When this is added to the signature house whisky style of Forty Creek, the result is a whisky guaranteed to please the most discerning palate. **DDK**

Tasting notes

A buttery, weighty body sustains a complex, highly integrated mix of unusual flavors, including barbecue potato chips, sweet and sour sauce, and maybe bacon. Touches of bread, rye or wheat. No trace of fruit, but still not a harsh flavor.

Forty Creek John's Private Cask No. 1

Kittling Ridge Estates Wines and Spirits | www.fortycreekwhisky.com

Region and country of origin Ontario, Canada
Distillery Kittling Ridge, Grimsby
Alcohol content 40% abv
Style Single-distillery whisky

In Forty Creek John's Private Cask No. 1, the traditional flavors of Canadian rye have been concentrated into a flavor bomb that blasts the mouth with shards of spice; there are "spice flares" that simply erupt onto the palate. The sheer scale of the flavor will have you checking the alcohol content because, even though this whisky is bottled at 40 percent, the flavor level lurches wildly into cask-strength territory.

If this whisky really does come from John's Private Cask No. 1, with 9,000 bottles, it must have been quite some cask. Here is what really happened; Forty Creek whisky maker John Hall mingled the contents of twenty-three separate reserve barrels to create this robust whisky. As he goes about tasting his barrels, Hall occasionally comes across one that is, as he describes it, "over the top." He marks these with chalk for future reference. When the time came to make his 2011 special release, Hall again tasted these chalk-marked barrels and selected twenty-three with flavors that complemented one another.

Some of these barrels were filled with corn whisky; others were filled with rye or barley whisky. The creaminess of the corn is obvious in the mouthfeel, while the barley, Hall suggests, is evident in nutty cereal notes that appear right away, only to disappear into hot spices. But after that, it is the rye that takes control. Corn may provide the foundation and barley the structure, but the balance, the complexity, and the sheer exhilarating intensity come from a spiciness that only rye grain aged in toasted oak is able to yield. **DDK**

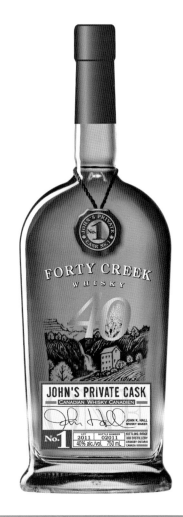

Tasting notes

Ginger, dark fruit, clean oak, and crème caramel. Sultry fruits and dusty rye spices burst like skyrockets in an ancient rain forest. Bittersweet candied orange counters surging creamy butterscotch as cedar lingers on the tongue and supple tannins pull gently at the cheeks.

Gibson's Finest 12-Year-Old

William Grant & Sons | www.gibsonsfinest.ca

Region and country of origin Ontario, Canada
Distillery Hiram Walker, Walkerville
Alcohol content 40% abv
Style Single-distillery whisky

When, in the wake of Prohibition, Lewis Rosenstiel bought John Gibson's Pennsylvania rye whiskey brands, he rescued a most prestigious whisky name from certain obscurity. Rosenstiel's Quebec-based Schenley distillery was another Pennsylvania whiskey name clutched from the ignominy of Prohibition. So when distillers at Schenley reformulated Gibson's as a Canadian whisky, they knew they had an opportunity to do something great, and the rich and creamy house style of Gibson's has become legendary among Canadian whisky enthusiasts. Gibson's 12-Year-Old has only been available in Canada, but persistent demand, particularly from the United States, has seen production stepped up in anticipation of an eventual U.S. release. It takes twelve years to make a twelve-year-old whisky, so U.S. fans of Canadian whisky will have to collect it from Canada for a little longer yet.

Although they start with the finest spirits, the key to Gibson's success is the way it manages its barrels. Using only freshly drained bourbon barrels means the whisky is imbued with barrel residues and enriched with the flavors of secondary reactions that happen very slowly, deep within the wood. These reactions are usually obscured in whisky from a newly charred oak barrel. Twelve full years of maturing allows plenty of time for these flavor-building reactions to occur.

Schenley distillery now operates as Diageo Global Supply, Valleyfield. The Gibson's brand is owned by Scotland's William Grant and Sons, who, aside from moving production, respect tradition and have not interfered with the winning formula. **DDK**

Tasting notes

Dusty rye and ripe red cherries dissolve into crème brûlée, oak, and spicy pepper. Cloves and canned pears, black fruits, citrus zip, then strawberries and cream. A cedar cigar box and a rich, weighty body with skillfully balanced and seamlessly integrated flavors.

Gibson's Finest Rare 18-Year-Old

Pernod Ricard – Corby Distilleries | www.wisers.ca

Region and country of origin Quebec, Canada
Distillery Valleyfield, Salaberry-de-Valleyfield
Alcohol content 40% abv
Style Single-distillery whisky

Among peripatetic whisky brands, Gibson's must be one of the most traveled. And to complicate matters even further, Gibson's Finest Rare 18-Year-Old is made in Valleyfield, Quebec, while its Gibson stablemates are now made in Walkerville, Ontario.

For its first ninety years, Gibson's was a renowned Monongahela rye whiskey distilled in western Pennsylvania by one John Gibson and his sons. In 1920 Prohibition brought all of that to a sudden halt. Although the distillery was eventually demolished, Louis Rosenstiel's Schenley Industries managed to salvage the Gibson's whiskey brand name.

In 1945 Schenley rebuilt an industrial alcohol distillery in Valleyfield, Quebec, and began to distill Canadian rye whiskies, giving them American brand names. In 1972 a completely reformulated Gibson's was added to the production lineup. That same Valleyfield distillery, now owned by Diageo, is where Gibson's 18-Year-Old is made. The Gibson's brand was itself purchased from Diageo by its current owner, William Grant and Sons, late in 2002. Then, in 2008, in another change, the company moved its blending and bottling of Gibson's whiskies to the Hiram Walker distillery in Walkerville, Ontario, all except Gibson's 18-Year-Old, which remained in Valleyfield.

From the outset Gibson's has stressed the importance of distilling its whiskies from locally grown corn and rye and properly aging them in once-used bourbon barrels. The crisp, clean, woody notes of Gibson's highly sought-after 18-Year-Old attest to the wisdom of that approach. **DDK**

Tasting notes

Rich and round. Sweet pine pitch and crisp, dry oak. Dark fruits, prune juice, and sour green fruits in a rich butterscotch base accented by spicy, dusty rye. Red cedar and hot pepper, kiwi, bitter lemon, and citrus zest. Clean wood, fresh-baked biscuits, and pepper.

Glen Breton Battle of the Glen

Glenora Distillery | www.glenoradistillery.com

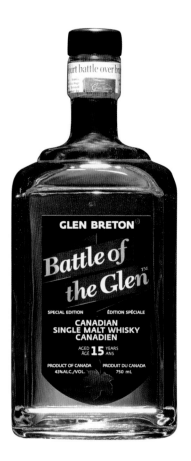

Region and country of origin Nova Scotia, Canada
Distillery Glenora, Glenville
Alcohol content 43% abv
Style Single malt

Scratch a Nova Scotian, and you'll find a Scot: feisty, friendly, loquacious, and lyrical. Since the mid-eighteenth century, when Scottish immigrants began arriving in Atlantic Canada, they have carefully nurtured their Scottishness. Scotland was heritage; Canada was home. Even today you still hear Gaelic from time to time in Nova Scotia, and in Cape Breton the road signs are in Gaelic, too. So it's something of a surprise that these Scottish expatriates took more than 200 years to begin distilling whisky here.

But in 1990, they began to do just that, in a little nook of Cape Breton called Glenville. Fine whisky it was too, so fine that the homeland was alarmed. Further, the Campbells, MacLeans, and others of the Scottish diaspora who crafted the lovely dram had the temerity to name their distillery after the nearby Glenora Falls, dubbing their gentle whisky "Glen Breton." Scottish coppersmiths at Forsythes of Rothes had been happy to sell them stills. Scottish grain brokers cheerfully sold them Scottish barley malt. Scottish consultants delighted in selling them Scottish know-how. But all of this was forgotten when the colonials used the dreaded G-word in their name.

Scottish lawyers from the Scotch Whisky Association spent nine whole years dragging them through court in an effort to make them recant their—well—Scottishness. Fortunately, at last reason prevailed and the lawsuit failed. With typical Canadian self-deprecating humor, the Campbells and the MacLeans celebrated victory with a fifteen-year-old single malt they named "Battle of the Glen." **DDK**

Tasting notes

Floral and fruity with cool crisp apples and hot roasted chestnuts. Peppery heat and dry grass, with a slightly pulling tannic oakiness that complements an otherwise creamy mouthfeel. Honey with brushes of woodland and the scent of fall.

Glen Breton Rare 10-Year-Old

Glenora Distillery | www.glenoradistillery.com

Region and country of origin Nova Scotia, Canada
Distillery Glenora, Glenville
Alcohol content 43% abv
Style Single malt

Each year Glen Breton Canadian single malt gets just that little bit tastier. The Glenora Inn and Distillery began as one man's dream. Although he lived long enough to literally taste his dream, Bruce Jardine did not see it become a reality in the marketplace. Today, people at Glenora are certain that Jardine is among the angels who visit the dunnage warehouses to slake their thirsts on the maturing spirit.

Distillery manager Donnie Campbell holds the reins on-site these days. So proud is Donnie of his domain that one year, when vacation time came, he tucked a few bottles of his flagship 10-Year-Old in a knapsack and set out on a coals-to-Newcastle distillery tour of Scotland. Following the consumer tour at each distillery, Donnie watched and listened. And then, when it was all over and all the visitors had left, he pulled out a bottle of Glen Breton Rare 10-Year-Old and sat down with the distillery manager for a dram. The comments were favorable, genuine, and most of all, eye-opening. Donnie came home with his already welcoming smile just a little bit broader.

Glen Breton 10-Year-Old is matured in traditional unheated warehouses where the frigid winters put everything into slow motion. Steady demand sees whisky withdrawn from these warehouses as quickly as new spirit is put away. Unlike large producers, Glenora does not attempt to keep the flavor profile consistent. Although the Glenora house style is clear, you can expect each batch to have a subtlety all its own. No chillfiltering here, either. As for caramel coloring, you will look for it vain. **DDK**

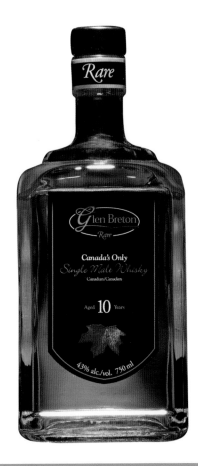

Tasting notes

Strong floral notes that fade but never disappear are tempered by vanilla, creamy caramel, and marshmallow nougat. An undefined fruitiness resolves into soft red cooking apples. Maple syrup barrel notes. Turkish delight with hints of spices fades into burnt sugar.

Grand Grizzly

MC Wine & Spirit SA de CV

Region and country of origin Canada
Distillery Undisclosed
Alcohol content 40% abv
Style Rye whisky

Great whisky is said to have one key ingredient. Is it water? No. The yeast? Not that either. How about the grain? Nothing like that at all. No, it's the story. According to the back label of Grand Grizzly, deep in the Canadian Rocky Mountains there once lived a man by the name of James Grizzly. Using traditional pot still methods, Grizzly created one of the most exceptional smooth-tasting whiskies ever known. What people did not know was that this 100 percent rye grain whisky is not only unique in body, color, and flavor, but—like a Rocky Mountain Sasquatch—it is also unique in leaving its footprint wherever it goes.

Although Grand Grizzly is distilled from nothing but rye grain, this is not the heavy straight rye of the mythical rye renaissance. No, to the nose and the palate, this is very young rye whisky with a little something extra in the mix. Yes, it has all the frolic of a Mexican hat dance, but there is also an earthiness that speaks of depth, of time, and of deliberation.

Grand Grizzly, it turns out, is the fastest growing Canadian whisky in Mexico. So that is what's lurking in the background! In the nose and on the palate, behind the crushed black pepper and the spice and the flowers is an earthy reminder of distilled blue agave. It may be all rye grain spirit—yes, indeed it is—but the earthiness of rye has been brought to the fore to tempt the Mexican palate. The distiller James Grizzly may turn out to be as mythical as the Sasquatch, but his namesake whisky is friskier than the unbridled lust of a sunburned Canadian student on the Mayan Riviera for slack week. **DDK**

Tasting notes

Prune, cereal, and sweet wood smoke. Bold and bursting with exuberance. Creaminess dissolves into caramel chocolate, while hints of spirit become menthol. Black pepper and muddy agave spirit whisper tequila, but hard and gingery rye attests to whisky.

Lot No. 40

Corby Distilleries Limited | www.corby.ca

Region and country of origin Ontario, Canada
Distillery Hiram Walker, Walkerville
Alcohol content 43% abv
Style Single-distillery rye

Every craft has its almost unattainable goals, attempted by many but achieved by only a select few. In the realm of whisky making, the black orchid, if you like, is malted rye whisky. Hiram Walker's is the only distillery in Canada to mash malted rye. Walker's is also the largest distillery in Canada and, by some counts, North America as well. But only one of its whiskies has ever pushed the possibilities of malted rye to their limit, and that whisky is Lot No. 40.

Lot No. 40 is distilled twice. First, the malted rye mash, grain, and all are run through a short column called a beer still. The spirit is then collected and distilled a second time in a large copper pot. This distillate matures for at least six years in a variety of new charred and once-used white oak barrels. The resulting whisky is stunningly exquisite. A lesser distiller would have stopped right there and released it as it was, but in the 1990s, D. Michael Booth was at the peak of his creative genius and this was to be his masterpiece. He mingled this golden elixir with judicious amounts of unmalted rye whisky and corn whisky that he had specifically tailored for the task. This, he reasoned, would broaden its tight rye palate, mellow its muscular base, and appease its potent spice and siren floral high notes of malted rye.

Lot No. 40 did not meet sales expectations. Consumers were just not ready for a Canadian whisky to be so bold. But the cognoscenti will not be denied. Patient online shoppers and dusty hunters still turn up treasured bottles in mom-and-pop liquor stores across the United States. **DDK**

Tasting notes

Rye, malted rye, and caraway rye bread. A simple blend of citrus, spice, and lilac, and a complex synthesis of vanilla, dusty grain, flint, fresh-turned earth, sweet citrus fruit with hot peppery spices, and tannic wood. A rich, robust whisky that takes an eternity to finish.

Masterson's 10-Year-Old

35 Maple Street | www.35maplestreet.com

Region and country of origin Alberta, Canada
Distillery Alberta Distillers, Calgary
Alcohol content 45% abv
Style Single-distillery straight rye

It is easy to miss the tiny pot still at Alberta Distillers in Calgary, Alberta. Unlike Scottish showpieces, this pot is shrouded in insulation, making it almost impossible to find. But the most wonderful straight ryes emerge from this still—big, robust whiskies just glistening in hard wet slate and seething with a tropical spice market of cloves, cinnamon, and nutmeg.

These unique whiskies not only meet the U.S. definition for straight rye whiskey, but they are distilled from a mash of 100 percent rye grain. So it is natural that spirits producers looking for artisans to help them create an ultrapremium straight rye whiskey would turn to Alberta Distillers.

Late in the summer of 2011, a firm called 35 Maple Street in Sonoma, California, introduced the ultra-premium Masterson's rye. The 35 Maple Street company is a subsidiary of a Sonoma winery called the Other Guys, owned by siblings Mia and August Sebastiani, whose family has made wine in the Sonoma Valley for some 110 years. Recalling earlier family forays into the spirits market with brandy and grappa, the Sebastianis launched the spirits division they call 35 Maple Street with Masterson's rye, later to be followed by other artisanal spirits, such as botanical gins, aged rums, and small-batch bourbons.

Masterson's rye is named for Canadian-born frontier lawman William "Bat" Masterson, one of the best-known American Old West personalities. Masterson gained fame as a buffalo hunter, card dealer, and U.S. marshal before retiring to New York to become a sportswriter and newspaperman. **DDK**

Tasting notes

A panorama of grassy dry grain, straw, linseed oil, damp earth, and burlap sack, along with floral vanilla pod, fragrant leather, and tobacco. Glowing white pepper succumbs to sweet but fiery ginger made sweeter by creamy toffee, then grapefruit pith refreshes the palate.

Pendleton 1910 Rye

Hood River Distillers Inc. | www.pendletonwhisky.com

Region and country of origin Canada
Distillery Undisclosed
Alcohol content 40% abv
Style Rye whisky

When Oregon's Hood River Distillers launched Pendleton 1910, their plan was to build on the burgeoning popularity of their classic Pendleton Canadian whisky. Pendleton is one of the fastest growing whisky brands in the United States. Like all Pendleton whiskies, 1910 was distilled and matured in Canada. What makes 1910 so special, though, is that it began with a mash of 100 percent rye grain and it spent twelve years maturing in charred white oak barrels in a Canadian whisky maturation house. When the whisky was fully mature, Hood River Distillers brought it to Oregon, where they blended it in glacier-fed spring water from Mt. Hood before bottling.

Since November 2010, Pendleton, which is widely known as "the Cowboy Whisky," has been the official spirit of the Professional Rodeo Cowboys Association (PRCA). The name 1910 recognizes the year of the first-ever Pendleton Round-Up. The whisky is packaged in a unique bottle, embossed with detailing reminiscent of tooling on a saddle and featuring the famous Pendleton Round-Up bucking horse. This symbol, with the "Let'er Buck" slogan that appears on most Pendleton bottles, is the logo of the rodeo itself.

Hood River Distillers believe that Pendleton 1910 delivers an exceptional, fuller-bodied flavor, but maintains the smooth finish that drinkers have come to expect of Pendleton whisky. They recommend that the whisky be served chilled or on ice for sipping and peaceful contemplation. But with twelve years of aging and 100 percent rye grain spirit, you will want to try it at least once just as it comes from the bottle. **WM**

Tasting notes

Butterscotch, maple fudge, and toasted grain with zesty limes that brace the palate for glowing hot pepper and ginger spice. Both hot and cold menthol, Canada balsam, pipe tobacco, and dark fruits. With a spicy rye kick, it finishes with peaches and pink grapefruit pith.

Pendleton Directors' Reserve 2010 20-Year-Old

Hood River Distillers Inc. | www.pendletonwhisky.com

Region and country of origin Canada
Distillery Undisclosed
Alcohol content 40% abv
Style Blend

This creamy, opulent whisky celebrates what began as a classic western story of cowboys and Indians. In 1909 three brothers named Bishop began weaving blankets for the Nez Percé people of Oregon. Blankets from their Pendleton Woolen Mills were soon viewed as a status symbol among western tribes. Within a year 7,000 people showed up when the town of Pendleton, Oregon, hosted what was billed as "a frontier exhibition of picturesque pastimes, Indian and military spectacles, cowboy racing, and bronco busting for the Championship of the Northwest." Pendleton's Round-Up hasn't missed a year since.

In 2003 Hood River Distillers launched a whisky in homage to the now legendary Pendleton Round-Up. Pendleton Canadian whisky is distilled in Canada, matured in Canada, and blended in Canada before it is shipped to Hood River in Oregon to be bottled. Pendleton whisky became an overnight sensation and was soon the fastest growing whisky in Oregon. Its success spread across the United States and spilled back into British Columbia as well.

A twenty-year-old Directors' Reserve, launched in 2006, was widely acclaimed. One local cowpoke was so impressed he paid $11,000 at the local liquor store and took home 150 bottles. When the centenary of the Pendleton Round-Up rolled around in 2010, it called for a special-edition whisky. That whisky, the 2010 Directors' Reserve, was limited to 6,000 bottles. Raising the bar for rodeo whiskies, Pendleton Directors' Reserve wins the "Whisky Championship of the Northwest" without a shadow of a doubt. **DDK**

Tasting notes

Bacon and beans on an open campfire. Hints of resin, dusty antique leather, and a complex maturity speak of age, while peppermint, lingering tingling zesty lemon, and blazing hot ginger disagree. A creamy, silky grassland crisscrossed by a dusty Oregon trail.

proof

proof brands | www.proofbrands.com

Region and country of origin Canada
Distillery Undisclosed
Alcohol content 42% abv
Style Blend

The make not only spells its name with a lowercase *p* but breaks with a few other traditions as well. This newcomer arrived on Canadian shelves in the summer of 2010. Most Canadian whiskies are best described as "single distillery" whiskies, but this sweet, citrusy liquid is blended from spirit distilled in several places across the land and brought together in Montreal. Even the package is unconventional: it's a nonstandard 500 ml bottle.

Besides playing hell with spell-checkers, small-*p* proof has no small-*p* pretensions to uppercase sippery. It is unabashedly designed for the cocktail crowd. When former LCBO corporate manager Michael Riley developed proof, he clearly had the upwardly mobile urban crowd in mind. Using trendy bars and clothing shops to launch the whisky, he soon had the trendsetters on his side, and the drink quickly developed a Toronto-based cult following.

Proof is a member of a tiny collection of Canadian whiskies: those bottled by truly independent bottlers. The company does not own a distillery and does not plan to build one. Rather, in the tradition of Scottish independent bottlers, it sources all its whisky elsewhere. Independent bottlers are scarce in Canada, making proof a true rarity, albeit a readily available one. With luck, its success will turn out to be an example to others.

Its overt citrus tenor appeals to summer quaffers, and, inspired perhaps by the molecular cocktail craze, the makers suggest mixing it with pear juice and ice. Do so, they say, and "Everything's Jake." **DDK**

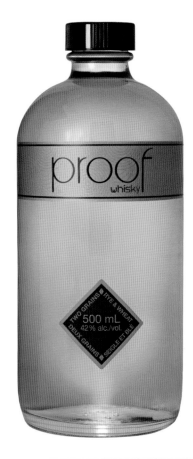

Tasting notes

Lemon drops, lilacs, and violets mingle with woody maple syrup, hot white pepper, and sweet spices. Earthy notes broaden the palate, but for a mixer it's a tad shy on the spirity side. A summer whisky for parties and barbecues rather than the connoisseur.

Revel Stoke

Phillips Distilling Company | www.revelstokewhisky.com

Region and country of origin Canada
Distillery Undisclosed
Alcohol content 45% abv
Style Spiced blend

The Columbia River flows south through British Columbia before crossing into the United States and heading west along the Washington–Oregon border to the Pacific Ocean. Along the way, it passes through Revelstoke, an isolated former mining town of 8,000 souls nestled between the Monashee and Selkirk Mountains of southern B.C. These days, Revelstoke, the town, is best known as a ski destination attracting dedicated heli-skiers from around the world. They may ski by day, but by night they drink Revel Stoke whisky.

Yes, Revelstoke has expanded its economic base, but no, it does not have a distillery. Neither does water from the Columbia River find its way into Revel Stoke whisky. So why the name? It's simple: the people at Phillips Distilling, 1,500 miles to the southeast in Minneapolis, heard of Revelstoke and liked its name so much they decided to give it to their new whisky. Revel Stoke (yes, they tweaked the spelling) is a little bit different from what whisky drinkers are used to. In the tradition of spiced rum, Revel Stoke Spiced Whisky is rich in vanilla and spices that are added during the blending process. It is one unusual whisky, for sure, and one that is better tasted than explained.

Revel Stoke has become a cult classic in the northwestern United States, and also, not surprisingly, among British Columbia ski bums. The unique advertising campaign that introduced Revel Stoke at the turn of the millennium featured urinal mats bearing the Revel Stoke name. Tens of thousands of them were stolen (and thoroughly washed, one hopes), so it must have struck a chord. **DDK**

Tasting notes

Sweet as liqueur, creamy as vanilla ice cream, and smoother than butter. Huge vanilla with black cherry, camphor oil, and bittersweet tobacco. Spicy hot pepper with cinnamon stick but not many overt "rye" notes. Simple but robust and expressive.

Rich & Rare

Sazerac Company | www.sazerac.com

Region and country of origin Canada
Distillery Undisclosed
Alcohol content 40% abv
Style Blend

The Rich & Rare name had done the rounds before New Orleans's Sazerac Company bought the brand. Originally, R&R was one of Harry Hatch's whiskies. One of the Prohibition era's most successful Canadian whisky entrepreneurs, Hatch owned the Gooderham and Worts distillery in Toronto where R&R was first produced. In the 1950s, when whisky distilling ceased in Toronto, Hatch moved his brands to another distillery that he happened to own: Hiram Walker's in Walkerville, Ontario. Although the distillery changed, the Gooderham name remained on the R&R label.

The 1980s brought an unearthly jumble of sales, takeovers, and closures that completely transformed the whisky industry worldwide. Nowhere was this felt more acutely than in Canada. When the corporate dust had settled, familiar brands had been dislocated and whisky production shifted among the surviving distilleries. One brand that came through all the turmoil tidily was the aptly named Rich & Rare.

"Rich" must be why in 2010 the judges of Chicago's International Review of Spirits awarded Rich & Rare 84 points and a bronze medal, complimenting the oily texture of its body. "Rare," however, may be a misnomer. Although virtually unheard of in Canada, it is easy to find in American liquor stores.

Where R&R is made these days is a Sazerac secret, although it would be no surprise to discover that production remains at the Hiram Walker distillery. However, once the mature whisky has been blended, it leaves Canada to be bottled in Frankfort, Kentucky, far from its Canadian home. **DDK**

Tasting notes

The vibrancy of youth with robust richness that defies its young age. Caramel, vanilla, praline, and sweet fruits with wallops of rye spices, hot pepper, and musty rye. An oily texture with smooth and peppery finish. In short, a beautifully balanced mixer.

Her age is a secret, ours isn't!

Friends of Imported O.F.C. talk a great deal about our age—and we're simply delighted. What other truly great Canadian offers you 8 year old whisky priced the same as leading Canadians two years younger? And 12 year old whisky for very little more? Taste 8 or 12 year old Imported O.F.C.—it's the Oldest, Finest Canadian. Then, you'll talk about us, too!

Schenley OFC

Constellation Brands
www.blackvelvetwhisky.com

Region and country of origin Alberta, Canada
Distillery Black Velvet, Lethbridge
Alcohol content 40% abv
Style Single-distillery whisky

In the mid-1800s, adulteration of whisky by some unscrupulous makers caused consumers to look for evidence of quality. In the western United States, which then meant Kentucky, the name "copper whisky" soon became synonymous with "fine whisky."

Copper whisky was the farm-distilled output of tiny copper pot stills. Accordingly, when E. H. Taylor bought Benjamin Blanton's Rock Hill Farm distillery near Frankfort, Kentucky, in 1870, he immediately renamed it "Old Fine Copper." In 1885 one George T. Stagg bought OFC and kept the name. The distillery prospered until Prohibition reduced production to a trickle, but at least it survived. When Prohibition ended in 1933, Lewis Rosenstiel's Schenley company acquired the distillery. OFC, the brand, drifted north to the Schenley distillery in Valleyfield, Quebec, which eventually reintroduced it as a Canadian whisky.

Although OFC has long been firmly established as a leading Canadian whisky brand, ownership of Schenley's OFC remains in American hands. Schenley itself is gone, and today OFC is owned by Constellation Brands, which produces it at the Black Velvet distillery in Lethbridge, Alberta. They have changed the name, too; today OFC means Old Fine Canadian. Descriptive, yes, but no longer evocative of the tiny copper pot from which it first flowed. **DDK**

Tasting notes

Rye nose of cloves, caramel, vanilla, and hints of bourbon. Glows with hot pepper throughout. The spirit serves to showcase the steeliness of the rye grain.

Seagram's VO

Diageo
www.diageo.com

Region and country of origin Quebec, Canada
Distillery Diageo Global Supply, Salaberry-de-Valleyfield
Alcohol content 40% abv
Style Blend

How's this for enterprise? As a young man looking for work, you hear that a local distillery has an opening. Hired, you apply yourself so much that the owner, taking an extended vacation in Europe, leaves you in charge. While he is away, you marry his sister, putting you at the head of the line when time comes to sell the distillery. This is how Joseph Seagram came to own a distillery in Waterloo, Ontario. In 1913 Seagram and his wife were preparing for the marriage of their son, and to mark the occasion Seagram developed a special whisky. Its name, VO, could stand for "very old" or "very own," but no one knows for sure.

Later, in the hands of the Bronfman family, Seagram's Waterloo distillery became the cornerstone of one of the largest distilling empires in the world, with VO as one of its leading brands. Over the years, however, the distillery began to show its age and was eventually closed. Production of VO moved to Seagram's distillery in Gimli, Manitoba. As the Crown Royal brand gained popularity, and with the sale of the Gimli plant to Diageo, production of VO was moved again, this time to Diageo's distillery in Valleyfield, where the whisky is made today. An upscale version of VO, called VO Gold, has since been released, but any list of must-have whiskies must certainly include the 1913 original. **DDK**

Tasting notes

Typical rye spices with vague flowers. Earthy, fruity, with hard white cedar, freshwater plants, and hot pepper. Caramel, citrus, ginger, sweet pickles, and cream sherry.

← A typical Schenley magazine advertisement from 1963.

Snake River Stampede 8-Year-Old

Indio Spirits | www.stampedewhisky.com

Region and country of origin Canada
Distillery Undisclosed
Alcohol content 40% abv
Style Blend

Nothing is so prototypically "Old West" as a rodeo. Broncos buck, wagons race, and steers wrestle. While today's professional cowboy is more likely to ride a pony with four wheels—and is just as likely to be a woman as a man—professional rodeo riders have stepped in to nurture the western frontier anachronisms of steer wranglin', bronco bustin', and bull ridin'. It's an irresistible image of rugged machismo, a professional sport, and Americana.

And what is more "cowboy" than sitting by a campfire telling tall tales and sipping whisky? It's a match made in marketer's heaven and has spawned a new style of whisky. They call it rodeo whisky—distilled, aged, and blended in Canada but sent to the U.S. to be bottled and labeled with the name of a popular rodeo. Probably the most colorful example is Snake River Stampede, an eight-year-old Canadian that celebrates the rodeo of the same name. Since 1911, the A-circuit Snake River Stampede rodeo has taken over Nampa, Idaho, each third week of July.

In true cowpoke fashion, the whisky found its way into the saddle when two larger-than-life characters met on a plane and got to talking. One was a distiller, the other a rodeo promoter. The men realized that their businesses could serve each other, and, on the strength of a simple handshake, they launched their own whisky. Next thing, rodeo season or not, the whole state of Idaho and half the United States was sipping Snake River Reserve. Considering how it came to take up the reins, it's a delight just how good this whisky tastes as a shooter, sipper, or highball. **DDK**

Tasting notes

Creamy, sweeter than sasparilla, dusty with rye grain that's dryer than a tumblin' tumbleweed. Hot as a campfire and fresh as a stack of newly-split firewood. Sweet ripe fruit and grippy grapefruit pith, ginger, cloves, and hints of pickle juice.

Still Waters

Still Waters | www.stillwatersdistillery.com

Region and country of origin Ontario, Canada
Distillery Still Waters, Concord
Alcohol content 40% abv
Style Single-malt vodka (white whisky)

Vodka in a book about whisky? Yes, vodka—but not just any vodka; this is Still Waters Single Malt Vodka. When Barry Stein and Barry Bernstein began distilling malt spirit in the Christian Carl pot still at their Toronto-based craft distillery, their original intention was to make single-malt whisky. And yes, there is a growing stack of barrels full of malt spirit maturing in a corner of their distillery. It comprises an assortment of new barrels coopered in Canada and first-fill bourbon barrels from the United States.

Making whisky takes a long time, though, and meanwhile there are bills to be paid. The partners therefore decided to triple-distill some of that malt spirit and bottle it as vodka. The result? A rich, creamy, and notably malty "vodka" that is only called vodka because Canadian law says it cannot be whisky until it has spent three years in oak barrels.

The U.S. border with Canada runs the full length of Canada's southern extremity, and just south of that border, distilled grain becomes whisky the minute it has spent time in wood. In the United States so-called white whisky has become a phenomenon, and some of that U.S. white whiskey is now finding its way north and onto Canadian liquor store shelves. Clearly, the market wants white whisky, but the law says that if the product is distilled in Canada, it must be called vodka. Bureaucracy has much to answer for.

So, of all the Canadian whiskies in this book, technically one of them is recognized as whisky only in the United States. In Canada it's vodka, but it's a vodka that any whisky aficionado can appreciate. **DDK**

Tasting notes

Rich, creamy, and very malty. Retains toasted barley tones and a slight barley-sugar sweetness. Hints of pepper, which are likely to develop more breadth with a few years in the barrel. Good weight and mouthfeel. Very clean new spirit.

Tangle Ridge

Beam Global | www.beamglobal.com

Region and country of origin Alberta, Canada
Distillery Alberta Distillers, Calgary
Alcohol content 40% abv
Style Single-distillery whisky

On a press junket, when the topic turned to Canadian whisky, a writer from *Wine Spectator* revealed his strong affection for Tangle Ridge. Except he didn't pronounce it like the tangle in tangled hair, but rather "tanglee." Whatever his mispronunciation, he certainly did like the whisky. And no wonder. Tangle Ridge is rich in the essences of red wine and swimming in the bourbon vanillas of Kentucky.

Alberta Distillers, which makes Tangle Ridge, is probably the best rye distillery in the world. The best in flavor, best in process, and certainly the world's largest rye distiller. What other major distillery routinely distills 100 percent rye grain whisky every working day of the year?

The house style is elegant, crisp, and well-crafted rye. Where its Alberta Premium is brittle, clean, and slatey, Tangle Ridge is round, robust, and bursting. Where its ten-year-old Alberta Springs shows notes of clean and succulent wood, Tangle Ridge, also a ten-year-old, is sweet, robust, almost mushy. This is a liqueur drinker's whisky . . . or a wine critic's.

For years Tangle Ridge came in a beautiful bottle with a long neck that guaranteed a wonderful glug-glug-glug for at least the first three pours. But it is a victim of its own success; Alberta Distillers has switched to a standard bottle that allows uninterrupted flow on the bottling line, saving production money at the expense of those glugs.

This is an unusual bold new-style whisky from a tried and true distillery, and, according to a critic from *Wine Spectator*, it's a real palate pleaser as well. **DDK**

Tasting notes

Rich, dusky overripe fruit with overtones of, can it be, gunpowder? Camphor, wine gums, dry grain with massive vanilla and subtle candy floss. And that's just the nose. Sweet, syrupy molasses, creamy fruit, and hot, hot pepper. Then, out of nowhere, bitter lemon.

WhistlePig

WhistlePig Farm | www.whistlepigwhiskey.com

Region and country of origin Canada
Distillery Undisclosed
Alcohol content 50% abv
Style Single-distillery straight rye

In the late eighteenth century, land in Vermont could be bought from U.S. state officials in both New Hampshire and New York, and also from Canadian officials in Montreal. All claimed ownership of Vermont, much to the chagrin of settlers arriving to find their land already deeded to someone else. The confusion continues today at a small farm just outside the unhurried Vermont town of Shoreham. Here, entrepreneur Raj Bhatka bought some land and named it WhistlePig Farm. The name is not a nod to the local marmots; Bhatka simply liked the word. He plans to grow organic rye there to distill into whiskey.

A field of rye grain is a wonderful sight, with tall russet stalks swaying in the breeze. Organic rye, on the other hand, is a hodgepodge of weeds producing abysmally low yields. But never mind that. Until he builds his distillery and plants his rye, Bhatka has recruited former Maker's Mark distiller Dave Pickerell to fill the gap. Pickerell sourced a stunning ten-year-old Canadian rye whisky to fill the beautiful bottles that Bhatka had fabricated. Canada, claims Pickerell, makes the very best rye whisky in the world, bar none. "Don't expect the Vermont grain to taste like its Canadian predecessor," Pickerell cautions.

WhistlePig is packaged to resemble American rye, but labeling regulations require the country of origin be listed, so there, on the back, in tiny letters, appear the words: Product of Canada. Vermont has long since been confirmed a U.S. state, but Vermont whiskey? Well, until that rye crop comes in, Vermont whiskey is 100 percent Canadian rye at 100 proof. **DDK**

Tasting notes

Massive vanilla in a huge bourbonesque overture, then toffee, blindingly hot chile, baking spices, candied orange peel, and fragrant lilac. As master distiller Dave Pickerell has expressed it, WhistlePig whiskey is "big enough to need its own postal code."

White Owl

Century Distillers | www.highwood-distillers.com

Region and country of origin Alberta, Canada
Distillery Highwood, High River
Alcohol content 40% abv
Style Whisky blanc (white whisky)

Whisky blanc was once wildly popular in the French-Canadian province of Quebec. Aged for two years in copper tanks, whisky blanc was as clear as water and had a grainy bouquet with absolutely no oaky notes. Suddenly, in the 1980s, sales of brown spirits slumped globally and production was discontinued, even though whisky blanc was actually white. Thirty years later, Alberta's Highwood Distillers reintroduced clear white whisky to Canada, but with a twist. This time it is rich in oaky barrel tones. Indeed, White Owl is the world's first fully oak-aged clear whisky.

White Owl is blended from various wheat-based whiskies that have been aged in charred white oak barrels for up to ten years, then filtered through charcoal dust to remove the color. Generous whisky flavors, however, remain untouched. Initially, distiller Glen Hopkins planned to use young whiskies to create White Owl, but it wasn't until he added substantial amounts of older whisky that he felt it tasted just right. White Owl is intended for mixing in cocktails, lending a sparkling citrus note and full whisky punch to better reflect the dramatic lighting effects commonly seen in self-consciously stylish urban bars and clubs.

The folks at Highwood Distillers thought they were onto something big when they came up with the idea for white whisky, but they had no inkling how overwhelming the response to White Owl would be. It's a popular mixer allright, but it didn't take long before people started sipping it straight as well. Since the whisky's introduction in 2010, Highwood has been racing to keep up with demand. **DDK**

Tasting notes

Cool citrus zing meets hot cayenne zip. Creamy toffee notes, sweet baking spices, and a touch of licorice root broaden the palate while Weetabix breakfast cereal, a hint of spirit, and dry lemon biscuits give a nod to the whisky's wheaty origin.

White oak barrels are crucial to the flavor of White Owl whisky.

Wiser's 18-Year-Old

Pernod Ricard – Corby Distillerie
www.wisers.ca

Region and country of origin Ontario, Canada
Distillery Hiram Walker, Walkerville
Alcohol content 40% abv
Style Single-distillery rye

When you find a whisky that seems untouched by modernity, you know you have found something truly special. Wiser's 18-Year-Old, tasted head-to-head with a 1950s Wiser's Oldest (as the whisky was then known), shows barely a hint of difference in flavor. It is a tribute to today's brand custodians that the round, dumpy bottles from the days when Wiser's was made in Corbyville, Ontario, contain essentially the same liquid as their equivalents from the Hiram Walker distillery some 340 miles (550 km) away in Walkerville, Ontario.

The packaging of Wiser's 18-Year-Old has changed several times, and older bottlings still surface occasionally online, generally selling for under $100. Today's well-known square bottle once featured a specially minted Wiser's penny on the label. The name too has varied over the years—Wiser's Oldest, Wiser's Very Old, Wiser's 18-Year-Old—but the whisky itself remains the same: deeply satisfying.

In an age of age statements disappearing from bottles, it is heartening that J. P. Wiser's successors hold firm to his original maxim that "Quality is something you just can't rush." This approach has certainly has borne fruit in Wiser's 18-Year-Old, one of a handful of whiskies that remain true to the old-time Canadian style, and one at the very top of the Canadian whisky connoisseur's "must-have" list. **DDK**

Tasting notes

Cigar box melds with burley tobacco. Butterscotch, toffee, and vanilla precede hot white pepper and ginger, followed by dried fruits and grapefruit pith.

Wiser's Legacy

Pernod Ricard – Corby Distillerie
www.wisers.ca

Region and country of origin Ontario, Canada
Distillery Hiram Walker, Walkerville
Alcohol content 45% abv
Style Single-distillery rye

Sadly, J. P. Wiser passed away in 1911 before he could put Legacy, his last whisky, into production, yet nearly a hundred years later, to the delight of connoisseurs, Wiser's successors have revived his final recipe. Shortly after it was released, Wiser's Legacy got off to a good start by winning Connoisseur Whisky of the Year (Domestic Market) in the Canadian Whisky Awards. Since then, it has garnered many awards.

While every Canadian distillery uses pot stills in addition to column stills to make whisky, Wiser's Legacy contains large amounts of pot-distilled rye-grain whisky, both malted and unmalted rye. Legacy is distilled, matured, and blended in Hiram Walker's Distillery in Walkerville, Ontario, the only one in Canada to use malted rye. Some of its succulent spices and robust creaminess may come from the large infusion of rye grain, and the floral notes are certainly enhanced by malting, but it takes more than malted rye to make such a huge whisky. The real secret is that Legacy is matured in barrels that have been toasted, rather than charred, melting the oak caramels without burning them. In turn, the toasting releases all kinds of the oak-derived spiciness that people commonly associate with rye; it also liberates a goodly shot of vanilla. Add it all up, and you have a handcrafted whisky that is both robust and complex. **DDK**

Tasting notes

Powerful cinnamon, ginger, and cloves with glowing hot pepper. Behind are stewed prunes, fresh-cut lumber, pipe tobacco, soft leather, and peppermint.

These row houses in Walkerville were built for Hiram Walker employees. ➡

JAPAN

Chichibu The First

Number One Drinks Company | www.one-drinks.com

Region and country of origin Honshu, Japan
Distillery Chichibu, Chichibu City
Alcohol content 61.8% abv
Style Single malt

The Akuto family has been in the business of making drinks for nearly 400 years. When the Hanyu distillery closed and was subsequently demolished in 2000, a chapter in Japanese distilling history seemed to end. However, Ichiro Akuto, the twenty-first generation of the drinks dynasty, had other ideas. First, he rescued the last 400 casks from the Hanyu demolition site. Then, in 2007, he built a new distillery in Chichibu. The distillery is small but excellent. The first spirit came off the still in early 2008, and Ichiro was happy to bottle a few casks as Chichibu Newborn.

The developmental releases were extraordinary because of the care and attention Ichiro had lavished on each stage of the process. The bottled whiskies belied their age. At one tasting of a heavily peated whisky (No. 451) in Scandinavia—where they know a thing or two about peated whisky—and subsequently in Paris, people were saying, "It's pretty good for a twelve-year-old," only to be astonished to learn that they had misheard: the whisky was actually only twelve weeks old.

The first release, as a three-year-old, is a parcel of thirty-one bourbon barrels yielding a total of 7,400 bottles at a natural strength of 62 percent. Half the bottles will remain in Japan for the domestic market, where Ichiro Akuto is seen as a stellar character. The remaining 3,700 bottles were reserved for export. The plan is for a regular three-year-old to come out in due course. At 46 percent, this will be in a carton rather than the Chichibu The First's presentation box. As Ichiro says, "It is very mature for its age." **MM**

Tasting notes

Deliciously rich on the nose, with vanilla and runny honey with plenty of citrus. The palate is youthfully spicy and attractively lively and the finish is medium length and with great precision. Another surprisingly mature, well-balanced bottling from Akuto-san.

Eigashima White Oak 5-Year-Old

Eigashima | www.ei-sake.jp

Region and country of origin Honshu, Japan
Distillery Eigashima, Okubo, Akashi
Alcohol content 45% abv
Style Single malt

It is often thought that Yamazaki is the oldest Japanese whisky distillery, but this statement depends on the definition of terms. The first distillery built specifically to make whisky as we know it today was, indeed, Yamazaki, constructed by Shinjiro Torii in 1923. However, the oldest distillery in Japan that produces whisky is Eigashima. Built in 1898, it has held a license for whisky production since 1919. However, the first whisky was not made until 1989, making it the first distillery in Japan to come on stream since Hakushu (until Chichibu started distilling in 2008).

As is often the case with Japan, Eigashima is highly unusual. Production is seasonal: in winter and spring, the site is dedicated to the production of sake and shochu, fall means wine bottling, and whisky distillation takes place only in the summer.

Whisky from the distillery has recently courted controversy. Perhaps surprisingly, Japanese law is relatively relaxed about what does or doesn't constitute "whisky." It was discovered that some of the blended products that had been imported into Europe contained malt whisky, grain whisky, and spirit distilled from molasses. While this can be labeled as "whisky" in Japan, it doesn't comply with EU regulations. The situation was compounded when a company representative agreed that this was indeed the case, whereas the importer denied it.

Since Akashi 5-Year-Old is a single malt, there is no doubt regarding its provenance. The whisky has its fans because it is new, unknown, and relatively distinctive. Certainly one to watch in the future. **MM**

Tasting notes

Honey, treacle, cereal, and some oak on the nose. The palate is youthful and zesty with a little spice and crisp sweetness. The finish is young with some graininess. Overall, it is young and willing. It will be intriguing to see how this develops.

Hakushu 10-Year-Old

Suntory | www.suntory.com

Region and country of origin Yamanashi, Japan
Distillery Suntory Hakushu, Matsubarakami
Alcohol content 40.5% abv
Style Single malt

Hakushu 10-Year-Old single malt was launched on May 1, 1998. It followed on from the successful launch of Hakushu 12-Year-Old some four years previously.

At the time of writing, Mike Miyamoto is laboring under the ponderous job title of general manager, quality communications, in the spirits division—when, really, he should be called something like sensei of Japanese whisky production—and he was head of Hakushu from 2001 to 2002. The distillery was only in production for three months during his eighteen-month tenure. He jokes that it that is very difficult to find a bottle of Hakushu from his time there.

Of Hakushu 10-Year-Old he says "The formula with Hakushu 10 is almost identical to that of Hakushu 12. In order to make it more characteristic, we decided to use less peating. You may get more of the freshness in the ten than in the twelve." Suntory buys both nonpeated and heavily peated malt for use at Hakushu. Nonpeated and heavily peated whiskies are then distilled and the two are blended. Mainly small white oak casks are used—bourbon barrels and hogsheads. "I see it as a daylight whisky, to enjoy at lunchtime or in the afternoon," says Miyamoto.

It's true that a glass of Hakushu 10-Year-Old before lunch won't ruin you for the evening. Not overtly characterful, it is a classic example of impeccable Japanese whisky making, flawless and discreet. Suntory's mission statement was to make Japanese whisky for Japanese people. This style of whisky is entirely in keeping with such an objective. Drink it in a highball, mizuwari style, or with Asian food. **MM**

Tasting notes

Green apple and grass aromas with refreshing fruits on the nose; a fragrant, sweet maltiness on the palate with a hint of smoke and cream. The finish is lean and sharp with a whiff of smoke. An archetypal, well-made, elegant Japanese single malt.

Hakushu 12-Year-Old

Suntory | www.suntory.com

Region and country of origin Yamanashi, Japan
Distillery Suntory Hakushu, Matsubarakami
Alcohol content 43% abv
Style Single malt

This underrated single malt, albeit one with a growing reputation, was launched on May 10, 1994. According to distiller Mike Miyamoto, "The concept of Hakushu single malt matches up to Hakushu 12-Year-Old," which means this is the defining distillery expression.

The 12-Year-Old is perhaps defined by its light smokiness, but it was not that way to start with. Suntory did not think the Japanese palate would go for smoky whisky—even if it was just slightly smoky—but the company remained interested. Experimental heavily peated malts, both at Hakushu and at Yamazaki, led to a nosing of the mature whisky a few years later with results that were, not surprisingly, very different from the nonpeated whiskies produced previously. Miyamoto continues, "We gradually expanded the experiment of Hakushu peated malt, and we came to the conclusion that the nature of the Hakushu spirit seems to go with the slightly smoky whisky. There isn't any scientific reason behind this, but it is clear on the nose and the palate. That was when we came up with the sort of style that it is now."

That style is described as refreshing but with a sweet smokiness that gives it complexity. Hakushu itself is a bit too clean and crisp, but a touch of smokiness gives it a complexity and an entirely different image. Hakushu 12-Year-Old is largely matured in white oak casks—bourbon barrels and hogsheads—but differs from the 10-Year-Old in the use of some Spanish oak sherry casks, which add fruitier characteristics. The beguiling little note of smoke makes a stunning match with smoked eel. **MM**

Tasting notes

Fresh, with pear then apple, on the nose. Refreshing, with a whiff of smoke. The palate is distinctly sweet—the fruit is forward, then relatively soft; smoky complexity follows. Attractive mouthfeel. The finish is clean and sharp with a good whiff of smoke.

Hakushu 18-Year-Old

Suntory | www.suntory.com

Region and country of origin Yamanashi, Japan
Distillery Suntory Hakushu, Matsubarakami
Alcohol content 43% abv
Style Single malt

Hakushu is mostly made in smaller casks, and whisky in smaller casks tends to mature more quickly than that in large casks. When Suntory set about creating a Hakushu 18-Year-Old, it included a greater proportion of whisky from larger sherry casks in order to balance the maturity. The 18-Year-Old has more of a sherry-matured profile than the younger whiskies, but in the past very little spirit at the Hakushu distillery was filled into sherry casks. That shortage has now been addressed but, as the whisky industry always has to wait patiently for maturation to take place, the problem persists. Launched on March 7, 2006, the 18-Year-Old was very well received, winning gold medals at the International Spirits Challenge and the International Wine & Spirits Competition.

Distiller Mike Miyamoto commented: "We would like to keep up the quality of the 18-Year-Old, but if the 18-Year-Old sells more than expected, it becomes very difficult. We didn't expect that Hakushu would be selling this much at first. It is a nice surprise, but..."

The cask makeup includes some European oak sherry casks—a mixture of first and second fill—that make a big difference. A Hakushu matured in sherry casks is different from a Yamazaki matured in sherry casks. Usually sherry casks add heaviness, making the whisky overwhelmingly robust, but Hakushu is different. This expression does have extra body, but the sherry casks somehow seem to enhance the pleasantly refreshing sweetness of Hakushu. Single malts like this illustrate perfectly how Japanese whisky has created its own identity in recent years. **MM**

Tasting notes

On the nose there are delicious fruits veering to the overripe, plus pineapple and a telltale hint of smoke. The palate is sweet yet complex. The finish is hot and smoky, but in a good way. The residual sweetness is swept away by lingering warmth.

Hakushu 25-Year-Old

Suntory | www.suntory.com

Region and country of origin Yamanashi, Japan
Distillery Suntory Hakushu, Matsubarakami
Alcohol content 43% abv
Style Single malt

Launched on February 5, 2008, Hakushu 25-Year-Old is the creation of Suntory's chief blender, Mr. Koshimizu. The story goes that he made a prototype, consisting of three different Hakushu whiskies matured in a bourbon hogshead and sherry casks, then presented it to the master blender.

According to distiller Mike Miyamoto, "The master blender didn't agree with him, so Koshimizu had to come back to him—not only once or twice but many, many times. Koshimizu was struggling, so he actually went with some prototypes to one of the leading barmen in Tokyo, Mr. Nakamura at Erika, an independent bar in the Ginza district, to see what he thought of these different whiskies. Mr. Nakamura made a very blunt comment, with no compliments at all. He said, "Koshimizu-san, what are you afraid of?" This was an experienced bartender in the late 1960s. He knew that Koshimizu-san wasn't confident in his samples. The advice the bartender gave Koshimizu is that you have to be confident in yourself, no matter what you make; otherwise, "don't bring it to me."

Koshimizu-san then knew that none of the samples would be satisfactory. He went back to create lots of new samples from scratch rather than modify those already presented. He assembled samples from a huge number of casks—"maybe a thousand of them"—and, in his research, he encountered some unusual (meaning bad) whiskies. Again according to Miyamota, Koshimizu-san had a hunch: "What if I use just a tiny bit [of unusual whisky] in my formula?" and he did. Look what happened—a superb whisky. **MM**

Tasting notes

Ripe fruits, sweet vanilla, and banana custard on the nose. Clean green forest notes. Starts quite sweet on the palate but develops with alacrity into mouth-watering overripe fruit and tobacco. To finish there is a long tussle between the smoke and the fruit.

Hanyu 1988 Single Cask No. 9501

Number One Drinks Company | www.one-drinks.com

Region and country of origin Honshu, Japan
Distillery Hanyu, Hanyu City
Alcohol content 55.6% abv
Style Single malt

Number One Drinks Co. was founded in 2005 to bring some of Japan's more obscure whiskies to an often skeptical international audience. The major distilling companies, Suntory and Nikka, were represented in Europe but many of the smaller independents were not. Number One Drinks Co. imported the first shipment of Ichiro's Malt Card series whiskies in the fall of 2005. The small firm was set up to import and distribute Japanese whisky, but also had the flexibility to act when exceptional single casks were identified during tastings; this Single Cask No. 9501 was one of them. Almost inadvertently, Number One Drinks Co. became an independent bottler of Japanese malts.

Why this cask? First, the whisky was finished in a Japanese oak cask. Although this contradicts what Yamazaki master distiller Mike Miyamoto has stated elsewhere, and I bow to his greater knowledge and understanding, there are some whiskies entirely matured in mizunara casks that seem a little overcooked, with resinous, pine notes reminiscent of some of the poorer wines endured on holidays in the Greek islands. This example, however, combined the precision of Hanyu with alluring notes of incense and sandalwood—as though the atmosphere of a Japanese temple is coming from the oak. In whisky, as in life, food, and wine, the quest is for balance.

This bottling won the Supreme Warped Cask award from the Malt Maniacs in 2007 for the best whisky finished in a special cask. Not bad for a first pick from Number One Drinks Co. In fact, the acclaim for this whisky was to influence future cask releases. **MM**

Tasting notes

There is great intensity on the nose, exotic and lightly smoky but delightfully bright with citrus and vanilla. On the palate the intensity remains, as does the smoke. This is very characterful and deep. The finish is long and satisfying with a certain darkness.

Hibiki 12-Year-Old

Suntory | www.suntory.com

Region and country of origin Honshu, Japan
Distilleries Yamazaki, Osaka, and Hakushu,
Matsubarakami **Alcohol content** 43% abv
Style Blend

Perhaps indicative of the increasing worldwide reputation of Japanese whisky, Hibiki 12-Year-Old was released initially for export. It was launched in May 2009 in Europe (primarily for the influential French market) and the United States, not being revealed domestically until September 15 of the same year.

An existing twelve-year-old blended whisky, Suntory Royal was considered too smooth for overseas markets. Instead, a different style of twelve-year-old blend was sought, and the recent international success of Hibiki as a name made it the obvious choice. Having established that, it is interesting that Hibiki 12 doesn't really share the same blend DNA as the 17-Year-Old. In the words of Distiller Mike Miyamoto, "Hibiki 12-Year-Old is an individual."

The most distinguishing feature here is the use of whisky finished in plum liquor casks. Plum liquor—umeshu—remains a popular drink in Japan; in fact sales are still growing. Suntory considered ways of differentiating their plum liquor from others on the market and hit upon the idea of curing it in American oak hogsheads for two years. The result was a great success, as the matured plum liquor, finished in oak casks, is selling for perhaps twice as much as its competitors. Casks are only used to finish the liquor once, so the opportunity arose to use the casks in whisky maturation.

Not all Hibiki 12-Year-Old is finished in this way, but the whisky does have a distinctive sweet aroma of plums with a subtle acidity, a result of the judicious use of these casks, unique in the world of whisky. **MM**

Tasting notes

Sweet notes of raspberry ripple ice cream with ripe plums on the nose. A soft, mellow taste with lots of sweetness. A lightly spicy and unusually tart finish—but in a nice way. It is said that Japanese whiskies have only recently created their own identity, and this is a case in point.

Hibiki 17-Year-Old

Suntory | www.suntory.com

Region and country of origin Honshu, Japan
Distilleries Yamazaki, Osaka, and Hakushu,
Matsubarakami **Alcohol content** 43% abv
Style Blend

This exemplary Japanese blend was launched to celebrate the ninetieth anniversary of the Suntory organization on April 3, 1989. The blend was created by the great Dr. Inatomi, Suntory's chief blender and Mike Miyamoto's boss at the time. Mike picks up the story. "He was making lots of test blends for Hibiki 17-Year-Old. I remember he just told his subordinate blenders he needed a little whisky that was very Japanese-y. That was the time we really rediscovered mizunara. One day I came to work and I went straight to the blender's lab for a tasting. I saw ten or twelve different glasses with unusually pink samples. I asked one of the blenders what they were and he replied 'mizunara.' I nosed them and found the aromas very distinctive."

Although difficult to be definitive, it is likely that the mizunara influence, which characterizes the whisky of Yamazaki, may not have been recognized as much in the earliest bottlings of that single malt as today. Yamazaki was released as a single malt in 1984, and yet it was the launch of Hibiki 17-Year-Old, five years later, that really heralded the return of mizunara.

Hibiki 17-Year-Old has a rich, fullness of style coupled with typical Japanese modesty. *Hibiki* is Japanese for "harmony"; Inatomi-san created this subtle yet expansive blend from thirty single malts (from Yamazaki and Hakushu) and a variety of grains (from Chita). He envisaged that Hibiki should be like an orchestra, with high notes and low tones harmonized by the influence of Japanese oak. This, the original Hibiki, carried no age statement at first. That only became necessary once the range expanded. **MM**

Tasting notes

A sweet nose with a rich aroma of overripe honey, mango, and crème caramel. The taste is splendidly, mouthwateringly mellow and deep. Lovely fruit from the sherry casks topped with distinctive spice from mizunara. A very rich, long, and well-balanced finish.

Hibiki 21-Year-Old

Suntory | www.suntory.com

Region and country of origin Honshu, Japan
Distilleries Yamazaki, Osaka, and Hakushu,
Matsubarakami **Alcohol content** 43% abv
Style Blend

This was the second whisky released in the Hibiki range on March 2, 1994, five years after the launch of the original Hibiki. Bearing in mind the dates and relative age statements, it would be possible to assume that the liquid in both was the same, that is to suggest that the 17-Year-Old was left to mature for a further four years. We will never know, as the information constitutes a "blender's secret."

Mike Miyamoto confirms this: "When I ask the blender for the makeup of Hibiki 17-Year-Old, it is possible to get the information. If I ask about twenty-ones and thirty-year-olds, they are much, much more secretive." Suffice to say, the plaudits are numerous, and this was awarded the accolade World's Best Blended Whisky in 2011, creating something of a unique double for Suntory as Yamazaki, 1984 was named World's Best Single Malt in 2011, too.

The pedigree of the whiskies in this blend is clear; the sherry casks deliver top-notch sweetness and dried fruit, the Japanese oak casks provide elegance and spice, while the grain whiskies add smoothness. The whole is a lesson in balance resulting in a whisky of the highest quality that is also alarmingly easy to drink. As with the very best whiskies, Hibiki 21-Year-Old is prone to evocative descriptions, in my case often involving food; the nose of this blend is like sniffing vintage marmalade in an old English car (specifically a Rover P5 Coupé or, at a push, a Jaguar Mark 2) with a worn leather bench seat and polished walnut dashboard. The whole is a master class in making the complex accessible. **MM**

Tasting notes

The nose is sweet and spicy like a box of orange peel and raisins scattered with ginger. This tastes smooth yet elegantly assertive, with spiced stewed plums and homemade vanilla ice cream. The finish is long, deep, and complex.

Hokuto
12-Year-Old

Suntory
www.suntory.com

Region and country of origin Hokkaido, Japan
Distillery Undisclosed
Alcohol content 40% abv
Style Single malt

One of the great pleasures of the world of whisky is that, beyond the reliable old distilleries, there is a largely uncharted region in which bottles come and go, whiskies turn up with labels for forgotten events or occasions, and sometimes long-lost casks reappear from nowhere. Although today computerization reduces the chances of rogue whiskies, strange drinks still turn up that have never been catalogued and are unacknowledged by their makers.

This Hokuto is a prime example of such a drink. Although it is undeniably produced by Suntory, there is no mention of it on the company's Web site. This in itself may be accounted as odd, but stranger still is the strong online suggestion that there is also a cask-strength version of the same whisky that contains malt from Suntory's Hakushu distillery. The mystery of quite what the Hokuto 12-year-old is proved beyond even the powers of Jim Murray, who classified it in his *Whisky Bible* as an unspecified malt. But unspecified does not mean inferior: this product has the most amazing flavor. It is by no means easygoing: in fact, it is like a rough ride at amusement park ride—scary while you're on it, but the kind of experience that you would not have missed for anything. **GL**

Tasting notes

Dusty wood shavings and stewed fruits on the nose, then a delicate and effeminate mix of rose petal and sherbet on the palate. A long prune and pepper finish.

Ichiro's Malt Card Series
Eight of Hearts

Number One Drinks Company
www.one-drinks.com

Region and country of origin Honshu, Japan
Distillery Hanyu, Hanyu City
Alcohol content 56.8% abv
Style Single malt

Ichiro Akuto's Card Series will comprise fifty-three or fifty-four variants, as he has earmarked a couple of jokers. Although there is no real science relating a card to a whisky, the higher-value cards are reserved for older whiskies. The Eight of Hearts, therefore, falls pretty much halfway in the distillation period of Hanyu, which ran from 1980 until it closed in 2000.

At the time of writing, Ichiro is halfway through the Malt Card series; indeed, of the 400 casks that he rescued from Hanyu (and which he refers to as "his children"), about half have been bottled. Ichiro built a brand-new distillery, Japan's newest, in November 2007 in Chichibu. Distilling began in earnest in March 2008. The distillery is very small—so small the mash is stirred by hand—and it is probably the only one with Japanese oak washbacks. Casks of young Chichibu have been released to great acclaim, and the inaugural whisky, a three-year-old, was released in 2011.

Distilled in 1991, Cask No. 9303 was bottled in 2008 as the Eight of Hearts; of 617 bottles, only 177 were exported. Initially matured in a hogshead, the whisky was finished for twelve months in a Spanish oak oloroso sherry butt. The whisky's multilayered complexity reveals itself slowly. **MM**

Tasting notes

A rich nose, reminiscent of antique leather with notes of gunpowder tea. Spicy and quite lively on the palate. A medium-length finish with raisin, ginger, and tea.

A variety of bottlings from Ichiro's alluring Malt Card series. ➡

Ichiro's Malt Card Series Five of Spades

Number One Drinks Company | www.one-drinks.com

Region and country of origin Honshu, Japan
Distillery Hanyu, Hanyu City
Alcohol content 60.5% abv
Style Single malt

The story behind Hanyu distillery will resonate with every whisky romantic. Ichiro Akuto's family has been making sake in Chichibu since 1624. The Japanese have long been interested in Western-style spirits, so Ichiro's grandfather, the nineteenth generation of the family business, built the Hanyu whisky distillery in the 1940s when Scotch became impossible to source.

It was only in 1980 that serious attempts to make single malt began with the acquisition of two pot stills. However, the business fell upon hard times and the distillery closed in 2000. As a truck was removing the last 400 casks of Hanyu single malt from the distillery, Ichiro Akuto managed to rescue his liquid legacy. The whisky was due to be poured down the drain and Ichiro wasn't prepared to allow this waste to happen. He then set about sourcing as many different kinds of cask as possible and began reracking.

A keen whisky enthusiast—and former Suntory employee—Ichiro was searching for a system to distinguish his single-cask bottlings. He felt that the distilling dates and cask numbers were a little confusing and hard to remember. The idea came to him one evening in a bar to label a series of whiskies after playing cards and so, in 2005, the highly acclaimed Malt Card series was launched.

Ichiro has a cult following, so very few bottles of the series are exported—only 177 bottles (from a total of 632) of the Five of Spades left Japan's shores. Cask No. 9601 was from the last year of distillation at Hanyu and was bottled in 2008. It was finished for twelve months in an American oak sherry butt. **MM**

Tasting notes

Sandalwood and sherry trifle on the nose. High strength but medium body, with spiced muffin and incense. Shots of sherry, then almond on the finish. Ichiro's reputation as a master of wood is illustrated in this manifestation of the Japanese pursuit of perfection.

Karuizawa 1986 Single Cask No. 7387

Number One Drinks Company | www.one-drinks.com

Region and country of origin Honshu, Japan
Distillery Karuizawa, Miyotamachi
Alcohol content 60.7% abv
Style Single malt

Not long ago, it was common for international whisky enthusiasts to underestimate Japanese whisky. There existed a preconception that, as a concept, Japanese whisky was flawed: that the Scottish, Irish, and Americans made whisk(e)y, and no one else could. How very incorrect that prejudice appears now, with worldwide acceptance of Japanese whiskies as being among the very best. Japanese malts and blends now often win major prizes at the World Whisky Awards.

It is true, of course, that some strange things happened in the relatively short history of Japanese whisky. Perhaps a few mistakes were made. We should be quick to forgive; the Japanese have been making whisky for less than a hundred years, which is one-fifth of the distilling heritage of Scotland and Ireland. But the Japanese are dedicated and relentless in their pursuit of perfection. They have learned from some of their less successful experiments, and they have learned from Scotch whisky—after all, some very famous distilleries there are owned by the Japanese. But to say that the Japanese whisky industry slavishly copies what the Scots have done is to miss the point entirely. They needed time, above all else, but encouragement and recognition would have helped.

Did Japanese whisky develop its own identity or, rather, did consumers slowly begin to understand the fundamental notion that it is not Scotch-lite? This stunning Karuizawa single cask, bottled in 2008, yielded 552 bottles. All the mysteries of the East can be accessed by enjoying a glass of whisky such as this. High-octane yes, but thrills a-plenty. **MM**

Tasting notes

Cedar, incense, and smoke on the nose. It is herbal, too, with dried fig. The palate is firm but spicy sweet, suggesting fruit compote. The finish is dusty and dry, like the last pickings in a bowl of spiced nuts. This is Karuizawa flexing its pectorals.

Karuizawa 1985 Single Cask No. 7017

Number One Drinks Company | www.one-drinks.com

Region and country of origin Honshu, Japan
Distillery Karuizawa, Miyotamachi
Alcohol content 60.8% abv
Style Single malt

Bottled in 2009, this cask yielded only 372 bottles. Everyone who has tasted whiskies from this distillery has a favorite. This cask embodies the true character of Karuizawa. It is not necessarily the best single-cask example of Karuizawa (that is the 1972 No. 7290). Nor is it the most complex (1971 No. 6878), the most aromatic (1968 No. 6955), the peatiest (1981 No. 103), the most venerable (1967 No. 6426), or the most subtle (there isn't one). However, it does encapsulate what the distillery is all about.

The strength is in excess of 60 percent, which is typical of Karuizawa and brought about by the high humidity of the region. The color is stunningly attractive—fans of sherry-matured single malts will be beguiled by its rich clarity. The nose is complex and the palate uncompromising. The whisky is muscular, reflecting the distillery's objective of making whisky "stout like a soldier." It may be politically incorrect to make this assertion, but there is something undeniably macho about this whisky.

Some casks of Karuizawa, of which this is one, define *umami*. The word, appropriately, is Japanese for a pleasant, savory taste and has been identified as one of the five primary tastes, alongside sweet, salty, bitter, and sour. Close your eyes and inhale deeply from a glass of this whisky; you can imagine a pine forest path in the fall, with lots of wood (obviously) and heady smells of wet leaves, damp moss, and even truffles. Sniff again and perhaps soy sauce will be revealed, with notes of wild mushroom risotto, aged sake (yes, there is such a thing), and tobacco. **MM**

Tasting notes

A warming early breakfast of pancakes with maple syrup and hot chocolate on the nose, while the taste is dark and faintly medicinal, with lots of sherry. The finish is long and tannic but only enough to heighten anticipation of the next sip. Very soothing.

Karuizawa 1976 Single Cask No. 6719

Number One Drinks Company | www.one-drinks.com

Region and country of origin Honshu, Japan
Distillery Karuizawa, Miyotamachi
Alcohol content 63% abv
Style Single malt

Since 2005, Number One Drinks Company has had access to some amazing Japanese single-malt whisky. Occasionally, a cask is discovered that is so unusual that it merits a distinctive presentation. Typically, the whisky embodies a Japanese style that can be tricky to define. The Noh series was created to reflect this.

Noh, one of Japan's oldest performing arts, dates back to the fourteenth century. The tradition is kept alive today by groups such as Kamiasobi, a troupe founded in 1997 by five young men whose families have been involved in Noh theater for hundreds of years. Number One Drinks Company has an exclusive arrangement for the use of the imagery. The series features stunning labels in the form of characters or masks from the ancient art form.

This particular whisky was bottled in 2009; the sherry butt yielded 486 bottles. It is one of two Noh whiskies to be awarded a gold medal by the Malt Maniacs in 2010. A particular feature of Karuizawa, apparent in this whisky, is that despite the freakishly high strengths—most are over 60 percent—they are surprisingly easy to drink unreduced. Yes, they are strong, but because the flavors are so concentrated, they taste bright. Also, the spirit is robust enough to take a lot of wood influence without being overawed. The whiskies tend, therefore, to have excellent balance with fresh fruit and spicy, woody notes. Couple this with the complexity derived from extended maturation in sherry butts, and you have a combination that is deeply spiritual. Cask No. 6719 is a very good example. **MM**

Tasting notes

A big and fragrant nose that is sweet and spicy. Vanilla and butterscotch. The palate has spicy fruit compote with a delightful, distinguished texture. The finish is very long with clear oak influence. The older Karuizawa whiskies maintain dignity at all times.

Karuizawa 1972
Single Cask No. 7290

Number One Drinks Company
www.one-drinks.com

Region and country of origin Honshu, Japan
Distillery Karuizawa, Miyotamachi
Alcohol content 65% abv
Style Single malt

Released as a follow-up to the hugely successful 1971 Single Cask No. 6878, this 1972 cask yielded 528 bottles. A Number One Drinks Co. label was used, as opposed to Karuizawa's official Vintage series labeling, to differentiate the two casks. Together, the pair of casks were instrumental in strengthening the resolve of the directors of Number One Drinks Co. to increase their investment in Karuizawa whiskies.

The directors began the process of acquiring the entire remaining inventory of Karuizawa. Less than five years before, the company had placed its very first order for 600 bottles from Hanyu; soon afterward, the directors were investing in hundreds of sherry butts, the very last stocks of Karuizawa. The casks were bought in August 2011. Immediately thereafter, a strict bottling program was put in place because all the casks were to be removed from Karuizawa by a fixed date. As many casks as possible were bottled on-site in the iconic Vintage series livery, with the remaining casks were transported to Chichibu distillery.

As there are no plans for distillation to start again at Karuizawa, this whisky is a rarity and one of the crowning glories distilled on Mount Asama. It is a piece of Japanese whisky history. **MM**

Tasting notes

The nose is rich and almost saturnine in its darkness with fig, treacle, honey, and gentle, smoky spice. Surprisingly, the high strength does not dull the senses.

Karuizawa 1971
Single Cask No. 6878

Number One Drinks Company
www.one-drinks.com

Region and country of origin Honshu, Japan
Distillery Karuizawa, Miyotamachi
Alcohol content 64.1% abv
Style Single malt

From an importer's point of view, the standard Karuizawa bottled products (12-Year-Old and 17-Year-Old) were largely uninspiring. However, the U.K. Number One Drinks Company found itself in a unique position. To generalize, an importer takes stock that is imposed upon him and has to sell it. An independent bottler buys whisky he likes and puts it in his own bottles. In this case, certain casks were specified and bottled in the official distillery livery.

For company buyers visiting Japan in November 2007, this whisky was a stand-out. It was bottled in January 2008, and the cask yielded 552 bottles at an incredible 64.1 percent abv. The atmospheric conditions at Karuizawa are ideally suited for long-term maturation of whiskies such as this. It is located at 2,788 feet (850 m) above sea level on an active volcano; the average humidity is close to 80 percent and the average temperature 46°F (8°C). A cool climate allows gentle ripening, and the high humidity encourages evaporation of water before alcohol.

The result is extremely high-strength single malts but it isn't about the alcohol level; Cask No. 6878 is proof that Karuizawa is one of the world's richest and most complex single malts. **MM**

Tasting notes

A rich and fragrant nose, from fruit tea and marmalade to leather and polish. The taste is a concentration of sherry, nuts, licorice, and smoke. The finish is exotic.

Many Karuizawa bottles feature distinctive Noh theater (classical Japanese drama) labels.

Nikka Miyagikyo 15-Year-Old

The Nikka Whisky Distilling Co Ltd | www.nikka.com

Region and country of origin Honshu, Japan
Distillery Miyagikyo, Sendai
Alcohol content 45% abv
Style Single malt

Miyagikyo distillery, also known as Sendai distillery, is located to the west of the city of Sendai in northeast Honshu. It was established in 1969 as a second distillery to Nikka's Yoichi plant, and opened some four years before chief rival Suntory's new Hakushu facility. A Nikka spokesperson explains that "after three years of research, this site was chosen for its pure air and high humidity levels, ideal for aging in barrels. The environment is similar to that of the Cairngorms region in the heart of Scotland."

There is a practical connection with Scotland, too, since the malt used at Miyagikyo is imported from Scotland as well as Australia. The distillery is largely computerized and is equipped with eight large pot stills, often likened to those at Longmorn on Speyside.

In 1998, a grain distillery with two Coffey-type stills was built on the same site as the malt distillery, which features one nineteenth-century still. The grain spirit produced in the new stillhouse is blended with Miyagikyo and Yoichi malt spirits in various combinations for Nikka's blended whisky brands.

Stylistically speaking, Miyagikyo produces malt whisky that is relatively soft, fragrant, elegant, and fruity when compared with that made in Yoichi distillery. While Yoichi's stills are direct-fired, those at Miyagikyo are heated by steam. Much of the Miyagikyo malt "make" goes for blending; single-cask bottlings have been released, and the permanent lineup includes ten-, twelve-, and fifteen-year-old expressions, though Miyagikyo single malt is not as well known as that distilled at Yoichi. **GS**

Tasting notes

Relatively light fruit notes on the soft, sweet nose, with spices, toffee, and cocoa notes. More fruit on the fleshy, smooth palate, notably tinned peaches, with honey, vanilla, nutmeg, and discreet sherry. Long in the finish, with more soft fruit and a lovely poise and balance.

Nikka Single Cask Coffey Malt

The Nikka Whisky Distilling Co Ltd | www.nikka.com

Region and country of origin Honshu, Japan
Distillery Miyagikyo, Sendai
Alcohol content 55% abv
Style Single malt

Not so long ago, the idea of Japanese whisky being compared favorably with Scotch was absurd. The Japanese made fine cars and electronic consumer items, but when it came to whisky, the attitude was one of condescension. Yet Japan has boasted a whisky industry of sorts since the 1920s and has long been adept at distillation. Given time, the Japanese would inevitably match the quality and consistency of the best Scotch whisky, just as they had more than matched Western consumer goods. Japan's receipt of many international awards in recent years has proved that the country's whisky has well and truly arrived.

It is received wisdom that malt whisky is made in a pot still and grain whisky in a Coffey or continuous still, and Japanese distillers have traditionally been quite conservative in their practice. However, in Nikka's Miyagikyo distillery a pair of Coffey stills are used to distill corn, a mix of corn and malted barley, and straight malted barley. Although innovative in modern terms, this practice was quite common in Scotland during the late nineteenth and early twentieth centuries, and has been undertaken in recent years at the Loch Lomond distillery.

In 2007 Nikka launched their single-cask Coffey Malt, a twelve-year-old whisky distilled from malted barley. However, Nikka's production of Old Rhosdhu single malt in a Coffey still led to disagreements with the Scotch Whisky Association, which claimed that whisky produced in a Coffey still could not be classified as "single-malt whisky," despite being made from malted barley. **GS**

Tasting notes

Coffee, wild berries, and new leather on the fragrant, rich, individualistic nose. Full-bodied, with a palate of vanilla, milk chocolate, ripe bananas, and Eastern spice. Even a hint of bourbon. The full, lengthy finish features more milk chocolate and spice, plus hazelnuts.

Nikka Whisky from the Barrel

The Nikka Whisky Distilling Co Ltd | www.nikka.com

Region and country of origin Hokkaido and Honshu, Japan **Distilleries** Yoichi and Miyagikyo
Alcohol content 51.4% abv
Style Blend

This tactile little bottle features a marriage of grain and malt from Miyagikyo and malt from Yoichi distilleries. It is a great introduction to Nikka whiskies, with a big bang of malt content. Beautifully presented in a squat, square bottle and with a somewhat sparse label, the contents imitate the packaging.

Whisky from the Barrel's matured grain and malts are blended and then recasked for a further period in first-fill bourbon barrels. This practice has been almost abandoned by other distillers due to cost, but the process creates a rich, full-bodied blend that should really appeal to the malt lover. An age statement is not really important here because, as the label says, the whisky is chosen cask by cask when it is ready to be bottled from the barrel—at almost marrying strength.

With no reciprocal deals existing between the main distillers in Japan, each has to produce all styles of whisky, from light to heavily peated, at each site. So walking into the Yoichi stillhouse is like entering a still maker's favorite dream; all shapes and sizes of pot stills and condensers may be found, and, in the Miyagikyo distillery, column and Coffey stills lurk as well. The distilling team also experiments with cut points, fermentation times, and wood types to gain an array of styles for the master blender to work with.

Whisky from the Barrel has started to attract the world's attention to the skills of the Japanese blenders. The whisky has garnered several prestigious awards, all of which belie its modest price point. Japan has been blending for decades now, and it's time the rest of us caught up with what is on offer. **AA**

Tasting notes

Takes a little while to open but then reveals sherry and a big smack of orange zest. There is some cedar box lurking as well. The palate continues the sweet citrus theme, with a hint of walnuts and honeyed apples. The finish is lush, rich, and impressively complex.

Taketsuru 12-Year-Old

The Nikka Whisky Distilling Co Ltd | www.nikka.com

Region and country of origin Hokkaido and Honshu,
Japan **Distilleries** Yoichi and Miyagikyo
Alcohol content 40% abv
Style Blended malt

The Taketsuru range of blended malts is named in honor of Nikka's founder, Masataka Taketsuru, the son of a prominent sake distiller. As a young man, Taketsuru enrolled as a student of organic chemistry at Glasgow University in 1918, traveling north to the Speyside "capital" of Elgin, where he undertook a crash course in practical distilling at Longmorn distillery. He later spent time at the now defunct Bo'ness distillery in West Lothian, learning the art of grain distillation in a Coffey still, before working for five months at Hazelburn distillery in Campbeltown.

Taketsuru undoubtedly deserves an honored place in Japanese distilling history, not only for his pioneering work with Suntory and the creation of Nikka, but also because his knowledge of established Scotch whisky practices, learned at firsthand, helped to determine the character and quality that would define Japanese whisky in later years.

Taketsuru whisky consists of a vatting of malts from the Miyagikyo and Yoichi distilleries. Most such whiskies are made up of a great variety of malts from different sources, but such is the flexibility and diversity of the two Nikka plants that Taketsuru actually combines the equivalent of the "make" of several individual distilleries. The Taketsuru portfolio embraces twelve-, seventeen– and twenty-one-year-old expressions. Nikka describes its Taketsuru whisky as "pure malt," a term that has been outlawed as confusing in relation to Scotch whisky. Yet Scottish legislation insists on the description "blended malt," which is no more exact than "pure malt." **GS**

Tasting notes

Fruity, perfumed nose, with apple, lemon, licorice, vanilla, and a tang of peat. Quite full-bodied and nicely balanced with honey and cream, nutmeg, gentle peat, almond, and butterscotch. Medium-length finish, with vanilla, eating apple, subtle smoke, and a hint of brine.

Taketsuru 21-Year-Old

The Nikka Whisky Distilling Co Ltd
www.nikka.com

Region and country of origin Hokkaido and Honshu, Japan **Distilleries** Yoichi and Miyagikyo
Alcohol content 43% abv
Style Blended malt

This venerable whisky is a secret weapon in Nikka's varied whisky arsenal, for in the past few years it has been stunning judges and silencing critics globally. Taketsuru 21-Year-Old has scooped the title of "World's Best Blended Malt Whisky" at *Whisky Magazine*'s World Whiskies Awards for the third time in four years.

Defying Scottish law, the bottle features the wording "pure malt," a phrase that fell out of favor with the Scotch Whisky Association, who replaced it with the term "blended malt" so as not to confuse consumers. To be clear, for Japan and Nikka, "single malt whisky" is several malt whiskies from a single distillery vatted together, while "pure malt whisky" is malt whisky from several distilleries vatted together.

Taketsuru is made up from the wonderfully oily, heavy, and mouth-coating malt from Yoichi and the fruity, spicy, and lighter style from Miyagikyo. Matured in first- and second-fill bourbon casks, the whisky has been blended to be heavy with malt yet exploding with spice. Characterized by a deep and flavorful richness and possessing excellent balance, this is a fitting whisky to bear the name of the company's founder. Taketsuru 21-Year-Old is definitely a late-night dram to be shared with a few close friends. **AA**

Tasting notes

Mint and fresh grass. Sweet notes and a deep resin tone. Oily and a little buttery with fresh fruits, sugar almond, and barley. Dried apricot and honey.

Yamazaki 10-Year-Old

Suntory
www.suntory.com

Region and country of origin Honshu, Japan
Distillery Yamazaki, Osaka
Alcohol content 40% abv
Style Single malt

A key difference between Scottish and Japanese whisky relates to the exchange of fillings. In Scotland it is common for distilling companies to provide new make spirit and, in some cases, mature whisky to other distillers on a reciprocal basis. In Japan, however, there are only two major distilling companies. The creation of whiskies for a blend therefore comes from ingenuity. At Yamazaki the six pot stills are all different sizes, and there are two types of fermentation tank. Six stills multiplied by two fermenters gives twelve different types of spirit. When these are matured in five different cask types, in effect you have sixty different whiskies. However, according to Mike Miyamoto, "The reality is not that straightforward." He explains the influence of the different washbacks. "With wooden washbacks, you get a bit more body in the wash. We believe the function of lactobacillus makes the difference. After every fermentation, we clean and we steam the washbacks to kill germs. But lactobacillus survives. Every bottle of Yamazaki will have spirit from both types of fermenter."

Yamazaki 10-Year-Old is mainly matured in white oak casks giving nuttiness and sweetness to the most accessible of Japanese single malts. **MM**

Tasting notes

The nose is laden with green apple and hazelnuts. The palate is smooth and sweet (but perhaps a little too elegant), and the finish is relatively long.

The well-stocked Yamazaki distillery. ➡

Yamazaki 12-Year-Old

Suntory | www.suntory.com

Region and country of origin Honshu, Japan
Distillery Yamazaki, Osaka
Alcohol content 43% abv
Style Single malt

Yamazaki single malt has mainly three component spirits, two of which are matured in puncheons. The first set of puncheons (130-gallon/480-liter casks) are made of American oak. The casks are not charred—their normal treatment—but, rather, toasted. While heavy charring yields vanilla flavors, toasting reveals lots of citrus and biscuit notes. In a bigger cask, whisky tends to mature quite slowly; that is an advantage of the puncheon. In this case the whisky forms a perfect base for Yamazaki 12-Year-Old.

As master distiller Mike Miyamoto explains, "There is lots of gentle sweetness from the puncheon and then we have sherry casks which give you the real sweetness and heaviness, too. You pick up different types of sweetness from the sherry cask." By combining whisky matured either in American oak puncheons or European oak sherry butts, you end up with a complex, rich, chocolate sweetness.

The third type of maturation cask at Yamazaki is the same size and shape as a puncheon and is made from *mizunara*, or Japanese oak, which gives a highly unusual aroma of aloeswood (*kyarako* in Japanese) and incense, and a spiciness not dissimilar to cinnamon. Although mizunara is subtle, its influence is felt even when present in only small proportions. As Mike Miyamoto says, "That's the beauty of the mizunara cask; it is not overwhelming, so even when the character is there, you don't get bothered by it."

Yamazaki gains the delightful character of this 12-Year-Old, launched on March 14, 1984, by combining whiskies from the three different casks. **MM**

Tasting notes

Sweet vanilla and ripe fruit aromas on the nose, with pineapple drizzled with runny honey. Layer upon layer of flavors overlap, with sherry cask and Japanese oak influence clearly apparent. The finish is richer than the 10-Year-Old, with a little bit of playful spice, too.

Yamazaki 18-Year-Old

Suntory | www.suntory.com

Region and country of origin Honshu, Japan
Distillery Yamazaki, Osaka
Alcohol content 43% abv
Style Single malt

The mizunara is a slow maturation cask. As Mike Miyamoto says, "It takes almost fifteen to twenty years to get that distinctive taste. So although we put mizunara-matured whisky in Yamazaki 12-Year-Old, it is more than twelve years old for sure. Sometimes we find whisky in the mizunara casks has matured faster than usual, but that is very rare."

It is safe to assume that some of the early-maturing mizunara-cask-aged whisky makes its way into Yamazaki 18-Year-Old. Mike continues, "We have 800,000 casks in our inventory, of which only a small percentage are mizunara casks. They are much more expensive than European oak sherry casks. We can only make 200 Japanese oak casks per year because of the scarcity of the timber. It is hard to work with—very knotty with big pores, diagonal grains, and it is easy to break. Almost everything has to be done by hand."

Obviously, as the biggest influence on flavor is wood, whisky that has matured in Japanese oak will have aromas not found in Scottish, American, or Irish whiskeys. Japanese oak is apparent in the 18-Year-Old, but the sherry influence is more immediately obvious; the same three wood types are used in its maturation as for the 12-Year-Old but, obviously, it benefits from extended maturation and a greater exposure to sherry. Launched on October 20, 1992, it has proved very popular, particularly on the U.S. market. One could imagine the sherry profile means it is not the favorite whisky of some of the production staff, but that is by the by. In Mike's words, "The consumer is the best judge and the best mentor." **MM**

Tasting notes

Sweet dried fruits and chile chocolate from the sherry cask on the nose. Mature, complex tastes due to the depth of mizunara. A distinctly spicy tannic texture. There's an excellent rum and raisin richness in the finish for a magnificently dark digestif.

Yamazaki 25-Year-Old

Suntory | www.suntory.com

Region and country of origin Honshu, Japan
Distillery Yamazaki, Osaka
Alcohol content 43% abv
Style Single malt

This was released either to celebrate the twenty-fifth anniversary of the launch of Yamazaki 12-Year-Old or to commemorate a hundred years of Suntory—or perhaps both. Either way, it was unveiled on October 5, 1999. The proposition is very straightforward: this is Yamazaki single malt matured 100 percent in sherry casks. As it is reputed to be loved by the president of Suntory, it is likely to remain in this style.

Japanese whisky afficionados are among the most dedicated to the cult of Macallan. The almost mythical status of Macallan is evident in numerous tiny Tokyo apartments, where enthusiasts display collections of Macallan whiskies probably worth several times the value of the properties. Perhaps that is why Suntory bought a significant stake in the distillery. Perhaps that is why some distilleries have tried to emulate the style of Macallan. This is a case in point; there is no Japanese oak spiciness, no puncheon sweetness, and—if one were being harsh—no distillery character. Let's put that aside, though, and concentrate on the whisky in the glass.

It is chestnut in color, as we would all be after twenty-five years in a sherry butt. It has the richness of oloroso sherry on the nose and maple syrup sweetness. The palate combines figs with chocolate-covered raisins. The finish is long, lingering, and rich. Arguably this note would apply to any single malt after maturing so long in sherry-seasoned European oak. This is a very good whisky but perhaps harks back to the days when Japanese whiskies had to pretend to be something else to gain acceptance. **MM**

Tasting notes

A lusciously sweet, mellow, and very alluring nose. The palate is complex and heavy, in a good way, but tannins are very drying. Residual sweetness is soon overcome by a bitter note. The finish is long, deep, and woody. Best enjoyed by the fireside on a winter evening.

Yamazaki 1984

Suntory | www.suntory.com

Region and country of origin Honshu, Japan
Distillery Yamazaki, Osaka
Alcohol content 63% abv
Style Single malt

This is the very best Yamazaki, according to distiller Mike Miyamoto, but, he jokes, it is a bit beyond his price range. Released on March 10, 2009, this whisky celebrates the twenty-fifth anniversary of the launch of Yamazaki single malt, which first appeared in 1984. Miyamoto says "We wanted to offer something that was different from the series of Yamazaki, so we decided to include more Japanese oak. In this expression Japanese oak is dominant, by which I mean more than half of the whisky comes from mizunara casks. You pick up real Japanese oak notes."

This whisky, more than any other Yamazaki, has those aromas of Asian spice and Japanese incense associated with mizunara. However, as before, such is the finesse of Japanese whisky making that these notes, though they are very distinctive, are extremely subtle and don't overwhelm the senses. Importantly, the other two constituent whiskies play a role. The puncheon-matured Yamazaki is always crucial in delivering notes of citrus and sweetness. The sherry cask influence is also there to give the 1984 a little more breadth and to enhance the sweetness, albeit in a very small proportion. Of course, these proportions are not set in stone.

Unlike in the world of wine, no distiller sets out expressly to win awards. Furthermore, whisky really isn't about medals. That said, Yamazaki 1984 has garnered a mightily impressive haul in the two years since its launch, including World's Best Single Malt in 2011. What more can be said? Yamazaki 1984 is a masterpiece in the art of Japanese whisky. **MM**

Tasting notes

The nose has huge intensity of sandalwood, incense, dark cherries, and darker chocolate. Cherries on the nose follow through to the palate accompanied by coconut-covered toffee. The finish is very big, hot, and peppery. Very, very big—we are talking sumo size.

Yamazaki Bourbon Barrel

Suntory | www.suntory.com

Region and country of origin Honshu, Japan
Distillery Yamazaki, Osaka
Alcohol content 59% abv
Style Single malt

No whisky nation has had to struggle as much and for so long to establish itself as a maker as Japan. Politics, generational difference, and prejudice have all at one time or another stood in the way of the country's whisky industry and hindered its advancement. Yet the country has a long and proud tradition of whisky making, and the pioneering way in which it adopted the whisky-making methods of Scotland for its own whiskies, in time adapting them to achieve their own individual twists, may well have provided the template for emerging whisky nations across the world. Considerable problems still lie ahead for Japan, not least because explosions at the Fukushima nuclear reactors following the 2011 tsunami generated levels of radioactivity that may continue to worry international buyers for years to come.

However, the country has become a victim of its own success, too. Yamazaki 18-Year-Old all but doubled in price in early 2011 as a result of being in extremely short supply. Twenty years ago, nobody could have envisaged the pile of awards that the malt would win, so no one planned for the huge demand that would follow. Simply, not enough malt spirit was laid aside for an eighteen-year maturation.

The Yamazaki Bourbon Barrel is another remarkable example of how wonderful Japanese whisky can be, and how diverse the nation's output is, despite having so few distilleries. Originally released as an exclusive to the Whisky Shop chain in the United Kingdom, it marks the start of a new trend for niche Yamazaki releases. **DR**

Tasting notes

If you are used to the monstrous sherry, intense oak, or full-frontal peat of various Japanese whiskies, this is the sweetest of treats. It is a delicious mix of soft mint toffee and banana toffee with lashings of creamy vanilla. Utterly charming and utterly irresistible.

Yoichi 10-Year-Old

The Nikka Whisky Distilling Co Ltd | www.nikka.com

Region and country of origin Hokkaido, Japan
Distillery Yoichi, Yoichi
Alcohol content 45% abv
Style Single malt

Yoichi, sometimes referred to as Hokkaido distillery, is the second-oldest in Japan, having been established in 1934. It is close to the fishing port of Yoichi on the northern Japanese island of Hokkaido, some 30 miles (50 km) west of Sapporo City. Sharing approximately the same latitude as Toronto in Canada and Vladivostok in Russia, Yoichi's location was chosen by Masataka Taketsuru, often called the "father of Japanese whisky," who worked for Torii at the time.

In the early 1920s, Taketsuru was looking for a suitable site on which to build a distillery for Torii. While he favored Hokkaido because of its excellent water supplies and similarity in environmental terms to the Scottish Highlands, a more commercially acceptable site was eventually chosen between Kyoto and Osaka. The Yamazaki distillery was built in 1923.

Torii and Taketsuru parted in 1934, and when it came to constructing his own whisky-making facility, Taketsuru was free to return to his original choice of location. Yoichi distillery is highly unusual in that it continues to use coal-fired stills rather than internal steam coils. Use of direct-firing and the presence of worm tubs rather than shell-and-tube condensers to condense the spirit give Yoichi spirit a distinctively heavy, oily style. Yoichi distillery further alters the character of its output by processing malt varying from unpeated to heavily peated, and by employing differing yeast strains, fermentation times, and distilling "cut" points. Yoichi also favors charred, new casks rather than those used previously for the maturation of bourbon or sherry. **GS**

Tasting notes

Fresh and salty on the nose, with smoke, a suggestion of chimney soot, and contrasting toffee and peaches. The palate is oily, with crisp oak, sherry, honey, apple, pineapple, and peanut. Medium-length in the finish, with enduring spice and freshly mown hay.

Yoichi 20-Year-Old

The Nikka Whisky Distilling Co Ltd
www.nikka.com

Region and country of origin Hokkaido, Japan
Distillery Yoichi, Yoichi
Alcohol content 52% abv
Style Single malt

For many years, most malt whisky produced in Japan was blended with grain spirit for the domestic market. When that market began to decline in the 1990s, distillers began to place a greater emphasis on single malts intended for the export trade. Today, Japan is the second-largest producer of single-malt whisky after Scotland.

Japanese single malts received a major boost when Yoichi 10-Year-Old won the "Best of the Best" accolade at *Whisky Magazine*'s annual World Whiskies Awards in 2001. The ultimate endorsement followed in 2008 when Yoichi 20-Year-Old landed the publication's highly coveted award for the World's Best Single Malt Whisky. At the same time, Suntory's Hibiki brand won the comparable prize for blended whisky, and the announcement of this prestigious "double" started something of a media frenzy, provoking newspaper headlines about alleged "consternation" in the Scotch whisky industry.

Scotland has survived Japan's assault on its standing as the world's top whisky producer, but there is no doubt that the Japanese alternative is now respected. Nikka promotes a wide range of Yoichi single malts in many international markets, embracing an expression with no age statement, as well as ten-, twelve-, fifteen-, and twenty-year-old variants. **GS**

Tasting notes

Seaweed and shellfish, with perfume, incense, soy sauce, a whiff of malt, and rich fruit. Oily and resinous on the palate, with lemon, leather, and peat smoke.

Yoichi 1990

The Nikka Whisky Distilling Co Ltd
www.nikka.com

Region and country of origin Hokkaido, Japan
Distillery Yoichi, Yoichi
Alcohol content 50% abv
Style Blended malt

This twenty-year-old whisky is a perfect example of what Yoichi Distillery stands for in Nikka's diverse portfolio: big, oily, and smoky, with depth and fragrance. It gets its distinct aroma and body from direct, coal-fired distillation, in which the pot stills are heated with finely powdered natural coal. Yoichi is the last distillery in the world to use this method, after Glendronach in Scotland switched to steam in 2005.

This was the first distillery that the legendary cofounder of Japanese whisky, Masataka Taketsuru, set up after leaving Suntory's Yamazaki site. The site met with Taketsuru's approval because it has an excellent water source, a climate well suited to maturation, and good communication links for barley, coal, and wood. The island also bears other striking similarities to Scotland: it is the same size, it has the same population, and its climate is closer to Scotland's than anywhere else in Japan.

The distillery is in the fishing town of Yoichi, surrounded by mountains on three sides and the sea on the other. Its proximity to the sea means that its whiskies gain a slightly salty character during maturation. This big, oily, characterful whisky will be a hit with fans of Ardbeg and Lagavulin, and there is a distinctive hint of Springbank, perhaps because Taketsuru spent time there learning the trade. **AA**

Tasting notes

A mixed nose of light smoke and clean citrus, lemon, and lime pie notes. Great mouthfeel with sherbet, citrus, spices, and honey-roast nut.

Nikka's Yoichi distillery, 31 miles (50 km) west of Sapporo on Hokkaido. ➡

EUROPE

Belgian Owl 3-Year-Old

The Owl Distillery | www.belgianwhisky.com

Region and country of origin Liège, Belgium
Distillery The Owl, Grâce Hollogne
Alcohol content 46% abv
Style Single malt

Although Belgium has a small German-speaking community that most people outside the country are unaware of, it is effectively split into two distinct cultural and linguistic groups, the French-speaking Walloons and the Flemish-speaking Flemings (Flemish is very similar to Dutch). After years of being ruled by a succession of foreign powers, including the Spanish, the Austrian Habsburg Empire, the French, and finally the Dutch, the Walloons and the Flemings rebelled and formed their own constitutional monarchy in 1830.

Unfortunately, the Walloons and Flemings have spent the past two centuries not really getting on, and there appears to be a serious movement to get them to separate once and for all. It is jokingly said that only three things hold Belgium together: the king, the beer, and the soccer. Of those, two are not doing particularly well. King Albert II isn't popular with the Flemings, and the Belgian soccer team is to success what Henry Kissinger is to stand-up comedy. Happily, the Belgians can now add another unifying factor to their beer: whisky. If you want a crisp and dangerously drinkable dram dripping with light, zesty fruit, look no further than the Belgian Owl. **PB**

Tasting notes

Sweet, sparkling white wine on the nose with Seville orange and sweet oatcake. Clean, sweet, and fresh on the palate with green banana and buttercream.

Belgian Owl 53-Month-Old Cask Strength

The Owl Distillery | www.belgianwhisky.com

Region and country of origin Liège, Belgium
Distillery The Owl, Grâce Hollogne
Alcohol content 74.1% abv
Style Single malt

Belgium, like other European countries with a brewing tradition—Germany, the Netherlands—has started to distill whisky. Judging by this example, it appears to have started off on a very strong footing indeed.

Prior to the Owl distillery's founding in 1997, distillery manager Etienne Bouillon acquired two century-old stills from a *bouilleur de cru*—an itinerant distiller. Bouillon won awards for his products, which included a pure malt distillate and Pomme d'Etienne, a combination of apple juice and eau-de-vie. Then, in 1999, the distillery ran an advertisement in a local paper announcing the bottling and sale of its first ever Belgian whisky. It stated that the first 500 callers would win a free bottle. Within seventy-two hours, 30,000 people had called. It was a hoax, but it made Bouillon realize that there would be plenty of demand should such a whisky actually exist. The distillery released Belgium's first ever single malt in 2007.

The Owl distillery's whiskies to date have been light, crisp, and fruity. Belgian Owl 53-Month-Old Cask Strength is a whopping 74.1 percent abv, and, taken neat, is not for the fainthearted. However, the addition of a little water opens out the true distillery character, revealing intense fruit and zippy spice. **PB**

Tasting notes

Marzipan and banana on the nose, with vanilla, coconut, and lemon peel. Sherbet and spice on the palate. Bitter lemon and honey on the finish.

The Owl distillery produces eaux-de-vie in addition to whiskies. →

Belgian Owl
2011

The Owl Distillery | www.belgianwhisky.com

Region and country of origin Liège, Belgium
Distillery The Owl, Grâce Hollogne
Alcohol content 46% abv
Style Single malt

Distillers in the new whisky-making countries are proving adept at taking up Scottish production methods and garnishing them with trimmings of their own history and culture. At the Owl distillery, Etienne Bouillon has taken a scientific approach to his craft, thoroughly learning the arts of distillation from Bruichladdich distillery manager Jim McEwan, who visits him in Belgium from time to time.

But as this 2011 bottling shows convincingly, the Owl distillery has found its own direction. Etienne talks passionately about the barley, which is grown on farmland next to his home, and also about the soil structure, which he says is perfect for growing rich barley for his whisky. But locally sourced ingredients are only one aspect of this delightfully .fruity, sweet, and easy-drinking malt.

The spirit comes from a portable still formerly hired out to distill brandy. The distillery operates from three small sites; Etienne would consolidate on one site, but lack of money has been an obstacle. On the strength of this bottling, he shouldn't fix what isn't broken. It is a trade-off, though, as he cannot make enough whisky to meet demand, and so the Belgian Owl is rarely seen beyond Belgium's borders. **DR**

Tasting notes

Ginger, vanilla, and honey on the nose. On the palate, clean, sweet barley, stewed pear, a little spice, and fresh meadow—a sense of summer in a glass.

Braunstein
Edition No. 2

Braunstein Distillery | www.braunstein.dk

Region and country of origin Zealand, Denmark
Distillery Braunstein, Køge
Alcohol content 63.4% abv
Style Single malt

If you are already making a beer in your brewery, you can easily take a part of the wash, distill it, and voilà: whisky. That was exactly what brothers Michael and Claus Braunstein Poulsen thought in 2007. Two years earlier they had had the chance to buy a top modern brewery, but the brewery was in Baltimore and the two brothers were in Køge, just south of Copenhagen in Denmark. That didn´t stop Michael and Claus, though, and shortly after, they found themselves established in the beer-brewing business.

When the brothers tried to decide what character their whisky should have, they found themselves in a dilemma. Michael is very much a Speyside man and loves the sherry impact from European oak in his whisky. Claus, on the other hand, is more into peated whiskies. So the only thing that seemed fair was to produce two styles. Michael had his wish when Edition No. 1 was released in March 2010, while Claus at last got his peaty whisky when Edition No. 2 followed in December 2010. Edition No. 2 was the second cask-strength expression to be released from Braunstein distillery, and it was also the second 50-gallon (190-liter) ex-bourbon cask that was filled at the Braunstein distillery back in 2007. **IR**

Tasting notes

Very fresh with lots of cereals, like muesli, with citrusy notes and apricot. A little grappalike, turning into vanilla fudge. A slight hint of peat evolves with water.

Braunstein Library Collection 10:2

Braunstein Distillery | www.braunstein.dk

Region and country of origin Zealand, Denmark
Distillery Braunstein, Køge
Alcohol content 46% abv
Style Single malt

The high regard in which brothers Claus and Michael Braunstein Poulsen hold whisky has its roots in their interest in fly-fishing. Many are the times that they found themselves standing knee-deep in the Spey river in Scotland fishing for salmon, and what better way to celebrate the day's catch than by sipping the local whisky in the evenings?

It was during these trips to Scotland that the idea of creating a Danish whisky was hatched. Despite the Scottish influence, however, Claus and Michael were determined not to imitate Scotch but to give their product its own distinctive character.

The first release from Braunstein distillery was the Edition No.1 in March 2010, which simultaneously became the first Danish single malt ever released. This was followed through 2010 by a series of expressions that the brothers called their Library Collection. The Edition No. 1 had been a cask-strength whisky, but the Library Collection were designed to be reduced in strength. The Library Collection 10:1 was released in May 2010. Next in line was Library Collection 10:2, the first Braunstein to be peated, released in September 2010 at 46 percent abv. The Library Collection 10:3 was released in December 2010 at 43 percent abv. **IR**

Tasting notes

Very malty, oatmeal crackers, and orange peel. More cereal notes on the palate, with chocolate and toffee. Slight hint of peat with a spicy (black pepper) finish.

Braunstein Library Collection 10:3

Braunstein Distillery | www.braunstein.dk

Region and country of origin Zealand, Denmark
Distillery Braunstein, Køge
Alcohol content 43% abv
Style Single malt

At the start of whisky making at Braunstein, most of the malted barley was imported from Scotland: a peated style from Port Ellen maltings on Islay and an unpeated from Simpson's in Berwick-upon-Tweed. Later, as much as 40 percent of the production was distilled from ecologically grown Danish barley. The first 100 percent "ecological" whisky from Braunstein, Edition No. 3, was released in fall 2011.

The owners of Braunstein, Claus and Michael Braunstein Poulsen, are very cautious about diluting the new-make spirit before putting it in the cask. It comes off the still at 72 percent, and to bring it down to the desired 63.4 percent they add water step by step over three weeks. According to Claus Braunstein, this is the best way to keep all the flavors intact.

When it was time for the distillery's fourth release—Library Collection 10:3 in December 2010—the brothers had started to build a reputation for their brand both within and outside Denmark. As opposed to the previous expression, Library Collection 10:2, which had matured in a bourbon cask and then married with whisky from a sherry cask, Library Collection 10:3 was bottled at 43 percent from an oloroso sherry cask and was not peated. **IR**

Tasting notes

A balanced sherry impression with pear and banana. Sherry notes on the palate, quite dry with raisin and cooked plum. Short finish. Preferable without water.

Hammer Head

The Prádlo Distillery | www.stock.cz

Region and country of origin Bohemia, Czech Republic
Distillery Prádlo, Pilsen
Alcohol content 40.7% abv
Style Single malt

The current demand for Scottish single-malt whisky from the wealthiest people in Brazil, Russia, India, and China is just the latest manifestation of a trend that stretches back many decades. Quality whisky has long been regarded as a symbol not just of wealth but of power, too. Russian journalist Erkin Touzmahamedov tells a great story about Stalin in World War II. Every year Churchill presented him with a fine bottle of Scotch, a gift that Stalin wanted to match. So he summoned one of his advisers and instructed him to go to Siberia and produce a fine whisky by the next year. Although the luckless adviser tried to explain the time issues involved with whisky production, it was to no avail, and he was shipped off into the countryside, where he lived in fear for a year. When the time came, though, there was no call from Stalin. In the following year, the turn of events in the war distracted Stalin, and he completely forgot about his whisky. So the adviser and his family lived happily undisturbed for the rest of their days.

This whisky was distilled in what was then Czechoslovakia in the late 1980s in an attempt by the Communist regime to make their own single malt. But when the wall came down, it was forgotten and lay undisturbed for twenty years. Now it is being marketed across the world. It is made with Czech barley and water from Bohemia, a region famed for the purity of its beers. The oak was also from Czechoslovakia, but its influence here is minimal. Nevertheless, an interesting addition to the whisky family and one with a good backstory. **DR**

Tasting notes

There is little evidence of twenty years in oak here, but this is an intriguing whisky, and what spice and fruit there is tastes very different from what is found elsewhere. The taste is almost tangy. It does not set the world on fire—but, like Prague, it is well worth a visit.

Dram 101 Batch No. 1

The Whisky Lounge | www.thewhiskylounge.com

Region and country of origin Yorkshire, England
Distilleries Undisclosed
Alcohol content 42.1% abv
Style Blended malt

Eddie Ludlow has worked his way through the drinks industry from managing liquor stores to being an independent whisky evangelist. His company, the Whisky Lounge, runs tasting sessions and festivals up and down the United Kingdom. For the first season of Whisky Lounge festivals, in 2010, Eddie worked with respected wine and spirit merchant Berry Brothers & Rudd to create a festival bottling, combining whiskies from all over the world. He soon decided that the next step would be to make his own.

Rather than buy a distillery and start entirely from scratch, Eddie decided to create his own blended whisky, to begin with at least. He started experimenting in his kitchen. With many contacts in the industry, he had a good stock of whisky to use in these experiments, and after months of concocting and testing different recipes on his kitchen table, he came up with his first release: Dram 101 Batch No. 1. This initial release, bottled on December 1, 2010, consisted of just 101 20-centiliter (6.8-ounce) bottles and was sold by Eddie himself at whisky shows, tasting sessions, and markets around the United Kingdom in 2011.

The composition of the whisky is a secret. The bottle is labeled as blended malt whisky, with no indication as to which countries the constituent whiskies came from. Eddie has since admitted that there are about sixty components, with a base of Speyside malt, but he insists he will take the full recipe to his grave. This is batch No. 1, the first in a series, so with luck we will be seeing others in the future. **BA**

Tasting notes

There is soft and creamy grain on the nose, with caramel, orange peel, and banana. On the palate it begins as sweet, fruity caramel, slowly souring with woody spice, cream, and sour apple. The whisky lingers on the finish with a touch of aniseed ball.

Hicks & Healey 7-Year-Old

Hicks & Healey | www.staustellbrewery.co.uk

Region and country of origin Cornwall, England
Distillery St. Austell Brewery, St. Austell, and Healey's
Cornish Cyder Farm, Truro **Alcohol content** 43% abv
Style Single malt

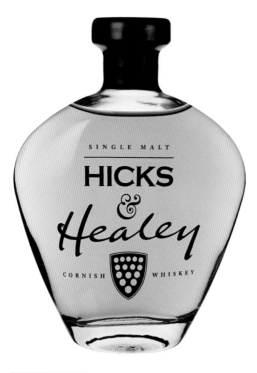

Cornwall, lying in the far southwest of England, sees itself as a distinct region. It has its own language, flag, and culture, and draws inspiration from its Celtic roots—shared with Wales and Brittany, France, rather than Scotland and Ireland.

Curiosity was aroused when the recently opened St. George's distillery in Norfolk claimed to be the first new English distillery in 300 years—by then, a Cornish enterprise had been distilling for three years. "Ah, yes, but we're not English," explained David Healey of the Cornish Cyder Farm, where the spirit was distilled. But surely you'd want to use the fact that you were first for marketing purposes alone, I asked. "Well, we are. We're the first Cornish whiskey for 300 years!"

What the distillery can certainly claim is that this is the oldest English or Cornish whiskey ever bottled, because 300 years ago, there would have been no question of a seven-year maturation. The whiskey is actually a joint venture between David Healey and St. Austell Brewery and its head brewer, Roger Ryman. An apple-brandy pot still was used to distill a batch of unhopped St. Austell beer each year from 2003. The partnership agreed that there was no commercial pressure to bottle early.

This initial batch of only 350 bottles was made available only at the farm and the distillery, and the partnership will bottle again only when the time seems right. When this was bottled in 2011, it was not the oldest whisky—an eight-year-old cask has been held back for further maturation and earmarked for potential release at ten or twelve years old. **DR**

Tasting notes

This is a beguiling marriage of fresh American oak cask and apple-tinged Cornish air, creating an apple pie and fresh cream of a whisky, with a sprinkling of sweet spice, honey and cocoa. The sweet, crisp apple dominates start, middle and finish.

Mo'land

Master of Malt | www.masterofmalt.com

Regions and country of origin Kent, England
Distilleries Undisclosed
Alcohol content 40% abv
Style Blended malt

Master of Malt is a whisky seller and independent bottler based in Kent, England, and is quite well known for producing unusual releases. This whisky was released in November 2010 in support of the Movember charity and the whisky drinking team of "Mo Bros"; it goes under the banner of "Whisky for Movember." Movember, an annual charity drive that originated in Australia in 1999, encourages its many participants to get sponsorship to grow a mustache through the month of November (*mustache* plus *November* equals *Movember*). Each November, thousands across the globe have a final shave on the last night of October before cultivating their top lips for a month. While the Movember organization does not encourage drinking, supporting men's health charities as it does, it encourages team sponsorship, and in 2009 the Whisky for Movember team was born.

Master of Malt produced an interesting "spooned" Orcadian malt (a single-malt whisky with a spoon of whisky from another distillery added) to support the team's first year, going by the name of M'Orkney, but went bigger for the second year. This time two whiskies were bottled, Smo'key (an Islay-styled blended malt) and this Mo'land (a Lowland-styled blended malt), each with five different editions, each with a label featuring a different mustachioed whisky industry notable—Dave Broom, Charlie Maclean (see right), Marcin Miller, Richard Paterson, and Serge Valentin.

The whisky itself is a blended malt designed to taste as much like a traditional Lowland Scotch whisky as possible—delicate, floral, grassy, and elegant. **BA**

Tasting notes

A nose of beeswax and malty syrup rolls into a richly woody body, with polished floor, cinnamon, and sweet vanilla pod. A drop of water loosens some fruit in the middle of the palate and draws out the spongecake finish with a jam filling.

Orbis

St. James Distillery | www.stjamesdistillery.com

Region and country of origin London, England
Distilleries Various
Alcohol content 40% abv
Style Blend

It often amazes people learning about whisky to hear that what goes into the mix does not necessarily have to come from the country that is releasing the product. It is true that, to be called Scotch, a whisky has to contain spirit that has been matured for at least three years in oak in Scotland. But there is nothing to stop a country from producing a blend that contains whisky from different countries.

Indeed, that happens a lot in Japan, out of necessity. To make a good blended whisky, blenders need a good selection of whiskies to play with. It is a brave thing to blend such distinctive and contrasting styles of whisky as Scotch, Irish, and particularly Canadian and American whiskies. While you can understand how sweet, smooth Irish whiskey might work with a fruity Speysider and an inoffensive Japanese whisky, bourbon and rye offer special challenges. That this works at all is to its credit.

This English blend contains whisky from all five traditional whisky-making countries—Scotland, Ireland, the United States, Canada, and Japan. The company putting it together operates under the name of a nonexistent distillery and does not give details as to exactly where in those countries the component whiskies come from. The whisky has been targeted at travel retail, and so perhaps the general rootlessness of it is entirely deliberate. But mixing whisky styles in this way is a strange thing to do, and Orbis is an odd-tasting drink, though nowhere near as odd as it could have been. It is definitely worth seeking out for the novelty factor alone. **DR**

Tasting notes

This is a whisky that many would expect to be much stranger than it actually is, a fact that is probably to the credit of a large grain content. Nice rather than very good, with mille-feuille, currant bun, orange-and-lemon marmalade, and a hint of oak and pepper.

St. George's Distillery Chapter 6

The English Whisky Co. | www.englishwhisky.co.uk

Region and country of origin Norfolk, England
Distillery St. George's, Norwich
Alcohol content 46% abv
Style Single malt

December 2009 saw the release of St. George's Distillery Chapter 5, the first English single-malt whisky in a hundred years. Such was the interest that people had waited in line overnight at the distillery to obtain a limited-edition decanter. Many, however, left empty-handed because much of this long-awaited first batch had been presold. Luckily for them, the whisky was soon followed by Chapter 6, St. George's unpeated three-year-old single malt, which has been in regular production ever since. Chapters 1 to 4 had been sold previously as malt spirit, not having reached the three years required by law to be called whisky.

St. George's is a whisky distillery set up by Norfolk farmers James and Andrew Nelstrop. They considered Norfolk an ideal place for a whisky distillery because of its copious supply of high-quality local barley and its relatively mild climate. They placed the distillery close to a chalk aquifer and source of good water, which required only iron filtration before it could be used. St. George's distiller David Fitt had long experience of how the mineral content of water could affect the mouthfeel and finish of beer, and knew that the same would be true of whisky.

St. George's tall stills, coupled with three years of maturation in ex-bourbon casks from Jim Beam, give Chapter 6 its light and fruity character. In addition, the water's high level of calcium contributes to the whisky's sweetness and its long finish. Each batch of Chapter 6 is a vatting of only four casks, so it is likely that drinkers will notice a slight variance in taste between batches. **PB**

Tasting notes

Mango, kiwi fruit with green fruit salad, and cream on the nose with a background of light oak. On the palate there is an immediate hit of spice that is later joined by fresh barley and citrus. The finish is of medium length with pepper and fading vanilla.

St. George's Distillery Chapter 7

The English Whisky Co.
www.englishwhisky.co.uk

Region and country of origin Norfolk, England
Distillery St. George's, Norwich
Alcohol content 46% abv
Style Single malt

Bourbon and sherry casks are obvious choices for maturing whisky, but when St. George's was offered four high-quality refill rum casks (two Jamaican and two Guyanese), it had a perfect opportunity to experiment.

Chapter 7 is initially matured in ex-bourbon Jim Beam casks for two years before being transferred to one Jamaican and one Guyanese refill cask for a further year. The rum casks are intended to impart an extra dimension to the already light and fruity St. George's whisky. The contents of both casks are then vatted together but not immediately bottled. Distiller David Fitt initially held off from releasing the whisky in May 2010 as he didn't think the rum and whisky flavors had integrated as well as they could have done. He was also determined that the rum should not overpower the whisky. Once bottled, the product was taken to various shows and proved to be the most popular whisky the distillery had yet produced, with, as he described it, hints of "vanilla and rum and raisin ice cream" that proved a major hit.

Because of the delay, Chapter 7 was actually released after Chapters 8 and 9 in a strictly limited edition of 660 bottles. **PB**

Tasting notes

Cotton candy, icing sugar, and a light grapeyness entwined around soft barley. Vanilla, fondant banana, and light spice. An exercise in subtlety.

St. George's Distillery Chapter 9

The English Whisky Co.
www.englishwhisky.co.uk

Region and country of origin Norfolk, England
Distillery St. George's, Norwich
Alcohol content 46% abv
Style Single malt

When St. George's distillery was first being set up in 2006, its owners were lucky enough to receive assistance from legendary distiller Iain Henderson, whose daughter was studying at the local university at the time. Henderson spent ten months at St. George's before handing over to his successor, David Fitt. Given his background at distilleries such as Laphroaig, it was inconceivable that Henderson would not make a peated whisky at St. George's. When Chapter 9 was released in June 2010, it was hugely successful.

Chapter 9 is essentially no different from the unpeated Chapter 6 in its production and maturation methods, except that it uses peated barley. Although eastern England's many breweries are well served by maltings, St. George's realized that the demand for peated barley in England had hitherto been negligible. They had to go a little further afield to source it, eventually settling on Simpson's Malt at Berwick-upon-Tweed on the English–Scottish border.

David Fitt's analysis? "I think it is very different from Laphroaig, but I see that as a good thing. We want our whisky to be unique, not a copy of something else— what would be the point of that?" **PB**

Tasting notes

Diesel, demerara sugar, roasted sweet corn, ginger biscuit, and stewed fruit on the nose. On the palate it is crisp apple and cream. The finish is longish and spicy.

An illustration of St. George and the Dragon appears on all St. George's bottles. ➡

EL VALEROSISIMMA TIR S GEORGE. F. ABADAL. E. M.

St. George's Distillery Chapter 10

The English Whisky Co. | www.englishwhisky.co.uk

Region and country of origin Norfolk, England
Distillery St. George's, Norwich
Alcohol content 46% abv
Style Single malt

Although it only started in 2006, St. George's distillery clearly is not going to let the grass grow under its feet. In addition to its Chapters 6 and 9 bourbon-matured casks, it has also been dabbling in casks used for Madeira, white wine, port, rum, and sherry.

The St. George's distillery house style is heavily influenced by the shape of its still, which was chosen not only for its ability to produce the required lightness of spirit but also to satisfy the aesthetic expectations of the lucrative tourist trade. The hugely popular rum-finished Chapter 7 showed that there was a market for "finished" English whiskies. Next on the agenda was Chapter 10, a sherry-matured whisky that has proved equally popular, but, unfortunately for its fans, just as elusive, with only 790 bottles produced. Chapter 10 was matured for three years in an oloroso cask that produced what distiller David Fitt refers to as an "old-fashioned style." Full maturation rather than secondary maturation gave the oloroso cask a massive influence on the otherwise light spirit and imparted a hugely rich and juicy makeover. Too many sherry-matured whiskies have been tainted (some would say ruined) by sulfur, and it is easy to see why, with a cask of this quality, it was decided to release it in limited numbers rather than marry the contents of several casks and risk a rogue butt spoiling everything.

Clearly, there is room for many other "chapters" to be released, but Fitt does not want to release too many and confuse the consumer. However, after the positive reception given to Chapter 10, he will look to release other sherry-finished whiskies in the future. **PB**

Tasting notes

Slightly vinegary on the nose at first, soon developing an intensely clean and juicy sherry, dribbling with ripe fruits and orange in jelly. On the palate there are mouth-coating and voluptuous fall fruits, date, and bitter dark chocolate. The end is long and drying.

St. George's Distillery Chapter 11

The English Whisky Co. | www.englishwhisky.co.uk

Region and country of origin Norfolk, England
Distillery St. George's, Norwich
Alcohol content 46% abv
Style Single malt

Situated some 400 miles (650 km) from the boggy ground of Islay, the dry east of England might, at first, seem an odd place to start producing peated whiskies. However, its famous leisure waterways—the Norfolk Broads—were formed when trenches left by medieval peat cutters were flooded, so it can claim just as strong an association with the fuel as anywhere in Scotland. How fitting, then, that St. George's distillery in Norfolk is starting to produce peated whiskies of renown, first Chapter 9 and now Chapter 11.

Having peat on your doorstep does not translate into a plentiful local supply of peated barley, though, and the peated barley for this still comes from Scotland. Having initially sourced it from Berwick on the English–Scottish border, St. George's now brings it from Port Gordon on Speyside, which is even farther away. The distillery has long been dabbling with peat and, in addition to the hugely popular Chapter 9, numerous experiments have taken place, including a triple-distilled peated whisky, several lightly peated wine finishes—including Burgundy, sherry, and Sassicaia—and a heavily peated rum finish.

Devotees of smoke need not despair because a three-year-old Chapter 11 was released in the summer of 2011. Its phenol level of around 52 parts per million (ppm) places it on a par with Ardbeg's 10-Year-Old (the Chapter 9 is only 35 ppm). Supplies of Chapter 11 will initially be limited because only a limited amount of peated spirit was produced at St. George's in 2008. However, by way of compensation there will also be a release of a supercharged cask-strength version. **PB**

Tasting notes

Cream and Jamaican ginger cake on the nose, with aniseed and white pepper. On the palate it is a gentle giant: creamy and clean barley at first, then the peat and pepper slowly build and fill the mouth but without overpowering. The finish is soft and lightly peppered.

St. George's Distillery Royal Marriage

The English Whisky Co. | www.englishwhisky.co.uk

Region and country of origin Norfolk, England
Distillery St. George's, Norwich
Alcohol content 46% abv
Style Single malt

To celebrate the wedding of His Royal Highness Prince William of Wales to Catherine Middleton on April 29, 2011, St. George's distillery released a special bottling produced from a complex marriage of different casks, the oldest of which was four years old. "This was a real one-off. We couldn't repeat it even if we wanted to," stated distiller David Fitt. He was not joking; it would be difficult to imagine a more tortuous marriage than was used to produce this special edition.

Fitt started with one cask of unpeated and one cask of peated St. George's, plus two Portuguese cabernet sauvignon red wine hogsheads also filled with new spirit. He then had port pipes cut down to produce four 13-gallon (50-liter) casks, in which the new spirit was matured for one year before being transferred to larger ex-Jim Beam casks for a further thirty months. The mixture from all eight casks was next vatted in a marrying tank for a short period and then run into fourteen ex-Jim Beam casks for a further two months, before vatting and bottling.

The particularly interesting technique employed was the use of cut-down port casks. Whereas small casks are normally used to speed up the maturation of the spirit before bottling, Fitt reversed this technique by transferring the resulting spirit back into larger ex-bourbon casks after a year to soften it and protect it from the onslaught of the wood. Such is the effect of the rapid maturation, this whisky seems much older than its years, possessing considerable depth of character. Its inspired creation marks something of a coming of age for St. George's distillery. **PB**

Tasting notes

Initially shortbread and citrus cream on the nose, with white chocolate, ginger spice, and raisin developing. On the palate it is at first creamy, with Seville orange and vanilla pod before finishing with a massive hit of mouth-puckering spice and faint hints of aniseed.

Old Buck

Panimoravintola Beer Hunter's | www.beerhunters.fi

Region and country of origin Satakunta, Finland
Distillery Panimoravintola Beer Hunter's, Pori
Alcohol content Varies around 69–70% abv
Style Single malt

In 1998 Panimoravintola Beer Hunter's Restaurant opened in the Finnish city of Pori on the Gulf of Bothnia. One of the eatery's main attractions was its own beer, Mufloni, produced at the microbrewery on-site and named after a local breed of sheep. Under the same ownership and next door to the restaurant is the Steak & Whisky House Galle, which serves food and also specializes in liquor and cigars. After three years in business, the proprietors made the momentous decision to start distilling their own malt, obtaining copper stills from Germany and ex-sherry casks from Spain and Portugal. It is recorded that they took the plunge at 6:00 PM on November 8, 2001.

The first batch of Old Buck is scheduled for opening to coincide with the sixtieth birthday of head distiller Mika Heikkinen. In the meantime, part of the second batch was released in December 2004 in one hundred hand-blown bottles of Estonian glass. The contents, with their Herculean strength and pure bourbon taste, had a tremendous impact. One of the whisky's effects on the industry was to inspire the Teerenpeli brewery in Lahti to diversify into whisky and make a single malt of its own.

The engagingly modest Mika Heikkinen likens his product—the first-ever Finnish single malt—to something between Laphroaig and Glenfiddich, but without their smoky aroma. However, comparisons can be restrictive, because Old Buck is a genre unto itself. *Jim Murray's Whisky Bible* named the second release in 2009 its European Whisky of the Year and was still extolling it two years later. **GL**

Tasting notes

Strong honey and licorice on the nose, with overtones of dried fruit and vanilla. The dram is medium-bodied and hits the palate with toasty honey and oak. The finish is long and multifaceted, restating the initial aromas and underscoring them with rich spices.

Teerenpeli 8-Year-Old

Teerenpeli | www.teerenpeli.com

Region and country of origin Päijänne Tavastia, Finland
Distillery Teerenpeli, Lahti
Alcohol content 43% abv
Style Single malt

Teerenpeli is one of two single malts from Finland and the only one to be made widely available so far. The distillery is part of a group that also owns four restaurants and a brewery—the latter was already established in 1995, when the first restaurant opened in Lahti. Seven years later, a distillery was added.

Even if restaurants and beer making are the main part of the business, there is no doubt that Anssi Pyysing, the founder and owner, is serious about his whisky. The two stills were ordered from Forsyth's in Scotland, suppliers to many of the major distilleries around the world. All the malted barley is obtained locally and lightly peated. The whisky is matured in both ex-bourbon and ex-sherry casks that Anssi orders from Speyside Cooperage.

The first release, in 2005, was a three-year-old that could only be bought in the restaurants. Limited bottlings for sale at Alko, the Finnish liquor monopoly, started with a five-year-old and with this 8-Year-Old. It is now possible to find Teerenpeli single malt also in Sweden and in the United Kingdom. The annual production is circa 10,000 bottles.

Having had the opportunity to sample the single malt from the very first three-year-old, I would argue that Teerenpeli has come a long way with this 8-Year-Old, a mix of both bourbon- and sherry-matured spirit, which was released in early 2011. Anssi also likes to experiment with other whiskies on the market, and in 2010 a limited edition of a vatting between Teerenpeli and an undisclosed Speyside malt was for sale at his restaurants. **IR**

Tasting notes

Very fresh nose with floral notes, coconut, and lemon. It is light but undercut with a sturdy oakiness. Sweet honey evolves on the palate, paired with vanilla from the wood. A medium long, dry finish ends up pleasingly with butterscotch.

Armorik Classic

Warenghem | www.distillerie-warenghem.com

Region and country of origin Brittany, France
Distillery Warenghem, Lannion
Alcohol content 46% abv
Style Single malt

According to Distillerie Warenghem's director general, David Roussier, the Armorik Classic represents a metaphorical blend of its Double Maturation and Édition Originale expressions. Armorik Classic has been available in the United States since the beginning of 2011 and soon will be distributed in the export markets and in French specialty shops. Aged in refill bourbon casks for between four and five years, it is then blended with some older malt whiskies from the distillery and bottled at 46 percent abv, which reveals "a lot of aromas and more character" than previous expressions. Armorik intends the Classic expression to sit at the heart of its range of whiskies.

The distillery is justly proud of its pioneering spirit. It was the first to produce a French single malt and to make use of Breton oak, but equally important is its commitment to providing work for local people and sourcing local ingredients. Emulating Kilchoman and Bruichladdich and their 100 percent Islay editions, Roussier uses Breton wheat, to be joined, in the very near future, by Breton barley.

A number of tests have been carried out to ascertain where the best Breton oaks grow. The best results for maturation, according to Roussier, are obtained "from oaks that are grown on a stony ground, on the hills," where the trees have experienced difficulties in growing and "are really tight." Compared to the more porous French Limousin oak, Breton oak allows only a very slow maturation and produces a very subtle taste, giving, as Roussier puts it, "a sort of elegance in the aromas." **PB**

Tasting notes

Ripe squashy fruit, salt and peat on the nose, with a side order of orange sorbet. On the palate it is an initial salty slap in the face, followed by a quick blitz of spice and a chunk of chocolate orange. The finish is ginger and bitter dark chocolate.

Armorik
Double Maturation

Warenghem
www.distillerie-warenghem.com

Region and country of origin Brittany, France
Distillery Warenghem, Lannion
Alcohol content 42% abv
Style Single malt

Oak is an ideal wood for maturing whisky because it is tough yet flexible, tight-grained yet porous enough to allow the cask to breathe. American and Spanish oak are commonly used, although it is not unusual to find other species employed, too. French oak, for instance, is used for selected expressions of Bruichladdich, Glenlivet, and Compass Box, among others, but with the Armorik Double Maturation, the Distillerie Warenghem has kept things that bit closer to home.

After five years in Breton oak casks, the Double Maturation is matured in sherry casks for another two years. Distillerie Warenghem's objective with this expression of Armorik is to enter the high-range markets, such as Paris's iconic La Maison du Whisky.

Director general David Roussier uses slow-growing Breton oak even though it is more expensive than American oak casks. In doing this, he may have tapped unwittingly into some of the local magic. One version of the Arthurian legend has it that Merlin the magician was bewitched by the enchantress Viviane and imprisoned in an oak tree in the ancient Breton forest of Brocéliande. All right, so Brocéliande is some distance from where the Breton oak is sourced for the Armorik whiskies, but let's not ruin a good story. **PB**

Tasting notes

A salty tang pervades an otherwise buttery, fruity, and sherried nose On the palate it is light with a pricking of woody spice and aniseed. The finish is smoky.

Armorik
Édition Originale

Warenghem
www.distillerie-warenghem.com

Region and country of origin Brittany, France
Distillery Warenghem, Lannion
Alcohol content 40% abv
Style Single malt

As one might expect, France is replete with popular tourist destinations, not least the region of Bretagne (Brittany) with its rich Celtic heritage. For the whisky lover, there are two very good reasons to visit Brittany, one of these being the Distillerie Warenghem, which has been producing whisky since 1987. When the Armorik Édition Originale was produced in 1998, it was a groundbreaking whisky. Not only was it the first Breton single-malt whisky ever produced, it was, claims the distillery, possibly the first single-malt whisky ever created in France.

Warenghem wished to create a Breton whisky that, while based on the double distillation standards of its Scottish cousins, had a light and fresh taste reminiscent of an Irish. In this latter respect they have certainly succeeded as, tasted blind, this could quite easily pass for a young Irish whiskey. The location of the distillery, a few miles from the coast, has certainly influenced the Édition Originale with definite coastal and iodine hints. This particular expression comes from 100 percent French malted barley, and is aged mainly in refilled bourbon casks for four to five years. Although distributed mainly in French supermarkets, it is also starting to appear elsewhere in Europe. **PB**

Tasting notes

Faintly salty and smoky on the nose, with caraway seed, apple hard candy. On the palate is light smoke, apple, and a sweet vanilla vein. The finish is soft and short.

Merlin and Viviane, against the Breton oak, rendered by Gustave Doré.

Armorik Single Cask for La Maison du Whisky

Warenghem | www.distillerie-warenghem.com

Region and country of origin Brittany, France
Distillery Warenghem, Lannion
Alcohol content 42% abv
Style Single malt

It hardly seems possible that the Distillerie Warenghem has been going long enough to produce an eight-year-old whisky, and yet here it is. This expression represents a milestone for the distillery in that it is their first released single-malt whisky. Distilled in June 2002, it has spent eight years in a sherry butt that previously contained fino sherry and then oloroso. Launched in October 2010 at Whisky Live in Paris, it is bottled for La Maison du Whisky.

La Maison du Whisky was started by Georges Bénitah, who had previously been a spirit merchant selling scotch and bourbons to American troops in Morocco. When things got difficult politically in his native Algeria, he moved to Paris. When La Maison du Whisky opened in 1961, single-malt whiskies were all but unknown to Parisian whisky drinkers, so Bénitah was soon traveling extensively in Scotland, visiting distilleries and distillers in order to see what treasures he could find to offer his customers. He returned with Glenfiddich, arguably the pioneer of the single-malt revolution, and he hasn't looked back since. His son, Thierry, who earned an MBA in the United States, was soon raving to his father about bourbons, insisting that they import them to France, and so they did.

If it is possible to generalize about the Distillerie Warenghem's whiskies to date, then they can be characterized by a light-bodied saltiness with a distinct tinge of apple. This, however, takes them in a new and far more complex direction, and if Distillerie Warenghem's whiskies were not on the Parisian radar before, they certainly are now. **PB**

Tasting notes

Rich sherry on the nose with licorice and salty toffee popcorn. On the palate it is hugely oily, slightly buttery, and salty with dark ginger chocolate and woody notes. The finish is chocolate-covered fruit cookie with notes of plummy red fruits and hints of coffee.

Breizh

Warenghem | www.distillerie-warenghem.com

Region and country of origin Brittany, France
Distillery Warenghem, Lannion
Alcohol content 42% abv
Style Blend

An area of France with its own identity and language (Breton), Brittany was populated during the Dark Ages by early immigrants from Wales, Ireland, and southern England. It has been a region famed for its brewing since the seventeenth century and, since the 1970s, has experienced something of a renaissance. Situated at the furthest western tip of France, Brittany enjoys a stormy but mild climate conducive to fast maturation, making it a natural place to produce whisky.

The Distillerie Warenghem, like many European whisky distilleries, had already been producing other beverages for many decades, including cider, mead, and various liqueurs. It moved into whisky production in the 1980s. According to its director-general, David Roussier, "We started producing whisky twenty-five years ago with the Whisky Breton, a blend with 25 percent malt and 75 percent grain whisky. It turned out to be a really decent blend, so we started thinking about a premium blend." The result was the Breizh, a mix of 50 percent malt and 50 percent grain. *Breizh* is Breton for "Brittany," and, although not noticeably smoky, it is made using a combination of wheat and peated, malted barley.

The water source is the nearby Rest Avel (Home of the Wind), where the water has filtered through the area's pink granite. The spirit is matured for four to five years, mainly in refill bourbon casks, although the distillery also uses local oak from the nearby Armorique Regional Nature Park. In addition to blends, Distillerie Warenghem also produces a range of single-malt whiskies. **PB**

Tasting notes

Beautifully light and fruity on the nose with some honeydew melon, grape, and ripe plum. On the palate it is light and gingery, with soft fruits, light spice, and a hint of the coast, building to an increasingly spicy woodiness at the finish.

Eddu
Grey Rock

Distillerie des Menhirs | www.distillerie.fr

Region and country of origin Brittany, France
Distillery Distillerie des Menhirs, Quimper
Alcohol content 40% abv
Style Buckwheat blend

Although some people are surprised that France has whisky at all, it really isn't that surprising. The northern regions of Brittany and Normandy are not wine-making regions, and there is a strong beer and cider culture. With cider comes Calvados, and with beer comes whisky. What is surprising in this region, though, is the excellence of the whisky, and also its diversity. Eddu, for instance, with its use of buckwheat, is a totally different animal from Kornog, a big, peaty whisky from Glann ar Mor. As this is Calvados country, so you might expect the Distillerie des Menhirs to be using apple stills, but no, the distillery has invested in proper whisky equipment.

Eddu Grey Rock is a blended whisky that echoes the Brittany region in its robust, full flavor. There is a rugged earthiness here, some smoke, the whiff of seaside salt, and, unlike many blends, its finish does not just fade away. That might be due to the fact that nearly a third of the mash bill is buckwheat, making Eddu Grey Rock a French equivalent of full-bodied Scotch blends such as Teacher's. Whatever the rights and wrongs of using buckwheat, Eddu is making a truly diverse range of impressive whiskies, and this magisterial version is well worth seeking out. **DR**

Tasting notes

A fruity nose with sea spray and smoldering embers, a rich, earthy palate with fresh apple, orange, and unripe pear, and enough salt and peat to carry it all home.

Eddu
Silver

Distillerie des Menhirs | www.distillerie.fr

Region and country of origin Brittany, France
Distillery Distillerie des Menhirs, Quimper
Alcohol content 40% abv
Style Buckwheat blend

Any comprehensive book about whiskies is bound to include some that step out of recognized definitions of what whisky is, but in such subtle ways that the differences go undetected. A number of the French whisky producers approach whisky in the same way the scrum of Les Bleus approaches rucking—they tinker on the margins. Corsica has P&M, a whisky made with chestnuts in the grist, and here we have Eddu, a whisky made not with grain but buckwheat, which is actually a pulse. It is confusing that the term "buckwheat," and also its translation into French, *blé noir*—literally "black wheat"—both suggest a grain.

The Distillerie des Menhirs does not try to downplay the fact that it is using buckwheat—far from it. Actually, the buckwheat is a big factor in their marketing. Does it matter? To a large degree, yes, because the definitions of whisky in Europe are vigorously enforced to protect the integrity of the drink and to partition it off from the cheap molasses "whisky" that is made in some countries.

Eddu Silver is a rough-and-ready, unsubtle, but big-tasting blended whisky, and that is meant to be a compliment. It is distinct, different, and, while not spectacular, pleasant and well made. **DR**

Tasting notes

A rich mix of fruit, honey, and vanilla, some sweet spice, and a touch of oak. While a bit rough around the edges, this whisky has a lot of heart.

Glann ar Mor
1 An Gwech 11

Glann ar Mor Distillery | www.glannarmor.com

Region and country of origin Brittany, France
Distillery Glann ar Mor, near Pleubian
Alcohol content 46% abv
Style Single malt

Because France is so strongly associated with wine and brandy, it is easy to underestimate its greatness as a whisky nation, too. France leads the world for Scotch consumption, and it makes great whisky of its own. The distilleries are concentrated in the Brittany region, where people are of Celtic stock and have strong links with the Cornish and Welsh, with a common language and culture. And since both Wales and Cornwall were and are whisky-producing regions, it shouldn't surprise anyone that Brittany makes fine malt.

Glann ar Mor is a relatively new distillery owned by Jean Donnay, and it makes artisanal boutique whiskies. Small quantities of whiskies are made, but slow distillation, the use of traditional worm tubs for condensation, and relaxed maturation by the coast ensure that they are of high quality. Glann ar Mor's earliest efforts were not bad at all, but the distillery has hit pay dirt with this bottling. Brittany itself is rugged, basic, and remote, and you expect something similar from the whisky, but this is as refined as European whisky gets. It is not unlike the whisky they are making at the Belgian Owl distillery. Glann ar Mor is the distillery's unpeated whisky and its delicate, almost feminine nature is a surprise and a delight. **DR**

Tasting notes

The nose is all delicate floral notes, gentle, sweet, and sherbet. On the palate there is stewed pear, apple strudel, and milk chocolate.

Kornog
Sant Ivy 2011

Glann ar Mor Distillery | www.glannarmor.com

Region and country of origin Brittany, France
Distillery Glann ar Mor, near Pleubian
Alcohol content 57.8% abv
Style Single malt

If you are not from Islay, it is a big risk putting out a big, cask-strength, peaty whisky. Comparisons with whisky's heaviest heavyweights are inevitable, and the odds are not good. But just like the big, peaty efforts of Connemara in Ireland and St. George's in England, this whisky suggests that the Scots can no longer claim a monopoly on the best smoky whiskies.

Whisky has a long history in Brittany. The developed whisky-making skills of Cornwall and Wales were certainly shared by the Bretons because there were strong links between the regions. Indeed, at one time England stopped at the Welsh border and somewhere around Plymouth, and Cornwall and Wales were linked to northwest France in an area known as Britain—hence the Brittany name.

Whisky back then would have been peated because peat was the only fuel available to dry the barley. It could be argued that Kornog is a more typically Breton-style whisky than Glann ar Mor. Previous bottlings, released at 46 percent abv, were less focused on peat. This release marks a growing confidence on the part of the distillery. It is impressive stuff, and catapults Jean Donnay and his whiskies into the top division of New World whisky. **DR**

Tasting notes

This is the most delicious honeycomb malt this side of the Blau Maus distillery. If you have ever eaten and enjoyed chile-flavored chocolate, this is for you.

P&M

Pietra Brewery | www.brasseriepietra.com

When is a whisky not a whisky? How people answer that question depends, at least in part, on whether or not they are in Europe. Corsica, home to this blend, is part of Europe, but that is not the end of the story.

While the generally accepted definition of a whisky is "a spirits drink made with grain, yeast, and water," some producers, and consumers as well, define it as "a drink that *tastes* like it was made with grain, yeast, and water." In another variant, found elsewhere in the world, a spirit may be genuinely made with grain, yeast, and water, but there may be liberal interpretations of how and with what elements distillation can take place, as well as further ingredients that may be added to the concoction.

Which brings us to P&M. A partnership exists between a Corsican brewery, the Pietra Brewery in Furiani, and a Corsican distillery, the Domaine Mavela, Aleria. The brewery makes a specific Corsican beer, which it sells to Domaine Mavela as a stand-alone product to be distilled for whisky. The resulting spirit is matured in Corsican oak barrels.

So far, all well and conventional. But a problem arises from the fact that chestnuts are used in the grist when making the beer—and strictly that means that P&M should not be called whisky, at least in Europe. There can be no doubt about the effect of the local oak and chestnut on the flavor of both the beer and the whisky. The whisky has a taste like no other in the world, an intriguing and not unpleasant one that just about slips under the defense's radar. P&M make three versions, and this one is perfectly representative. **DR**

Tasting notes

On the nose, an aroma of damp, churned-up leaves, evoking a hike through woods in late fall. On the palate the drink is intense and liqueurlike, with a rootsy earthiness. Hazelnut mousse, mahogany wood, and some citrus notes complete the experience.

Uberach

Distillerie Bertrand | www.distillerie-bertrand.com

Region and country of origin Alsace, France
Distillery Bertrand, Uberach
Alcohol content 42.2% abv
Style Single malt

The majority of people possess highly complex capabilities in sensing and recognizing smells and odors. However, it is not uncommon to have strengths and weaknesses in the realm of odor detection, and in particular circumstances, some people cannot detect any smell at all. In one pertinent example, something like one in five people cannot smell or taste sulfur.

In the world of whisky, a whiff of sulfur is generally seen as a negative factor, so those drinkers with an inability to detect it may think themselves fortunate. But a small amount of sulfur can add meatiness to a whisky, to the extent that some actually people seek it out. At the risk of stereotyping millions of people, the Germans love sulfur, which goes some way to explain why the sulfur-rich whiskies of the Mortlach distillery in Dufftown find a ready market in that country.

Uberach single malt from Alsace, a region that is now part of France but has much in common with neighboring Germany, may well have been created especially to take advantage of the German liking for sulfur. Uberach is an earthy, savory malt made by the Bertrand family, successive generations of which have been making brandy and liqueur in the region for more than 130 years, although they turned to whisky only relatively recently. Alsace has an abundance of natural resources, including rich soil, and this whisky is big and full flavored, but it is the sherry sulfur notes that define it. The distillery also bottles single casks, as well as participating in beer production.

Uberach is not for the fainthearted and not to everyone's taste, but it is very well made. **DR**

Tasting notes

Rich, full berry fruit and sherry notes, with an intense, savory earthiness, some stewed fruits, and a meaty mouthfeel. A bit of a room divider because some drinkers will particularly enjoy its underlying sulfur, while others will find the sulfur overwhelming.

BLACK HORSE

★ ★ ★ ★ ★

SCHWÄBISCHER

WHISKY

AUS DEM

AMMERTAL

MALT & GRAIN   40%VOL.

MASHED, DISTILLED & BOTTLED BY
VOLKER THEURER, DISTILLERIE
TÜBINGEN – UNTERJESINGEN
WWW.LAMM-TUEBINGEN.DE
TEL 07073/5159   BL 2009

Black Horse Original Ammertal

Hotel-Gasthof Lamm
www.lamm-tuebingen.de

Region and country of origin Baden-Württemberg,
Germany **Distillery** Hotel-Gasthof Lamm, Rot am See
Alcohol content 40% abv
Style Blend of barley, rye, and wheat

There are those who, perhaps after a negative experience with a single example of world whisky, now flatly refuse to believe that anything produced outside the traditional areas can be any good. Such drinkers need to change their mindsets and consider some of these spirits as different from Scotch. Where a tasting gets interesting is when the whisky in question slips outside the traditional definitions of whisky. For example, if you triple-distill whisky using a pot still and a traditional Irish recipe, what do you call it? And if *bourbon* is a controlled American term, what do you call a whiskey with 60 percent corn, some malted barley, and rye made using a sour-mash process?

This whisky is made at the Hotel-Gasthof Lamm in Germany, and strictly speaking, it must be described under European definitions as a blend. But that is not the whole story. Like American whiskeys, it contains three grains, but no other whisky shares this blend's recipe. The dominant grain, at 70 percent, is malted barley. The balance consists of rye and wheat, so Americans would probably call it barley whiskey. The blend is matured in a mix of ex-bourbon casks and a proportion of ex-sherry ones. All credit to them, then, for thinking outside the box. **DR**

Tasting notes

On the nose, the whisky is fruity and sweet, with some spice but not much. The dominant taste is barley. Very light, with hints of fudge and leather.

Blaue Maus Single Cask

Blaue Maus Distillery
www.fleischmann-whisky.de

Region and country of origin Bavaria, Germany
Distillery Blaue Maus, Eggolsheim
Alcohol content 40% abv
Style Single malt

A few years ago a German whisky enthusiast turned up at a distillery where he met a group of Scottish whisky experts and presented them with a sample of a whisky he said he was bottling for release. It was terrible—heavily salted and more suited to putting on fish and chips than drinking. But the group was faced with a dilemma: did they keep their opinion to themselves and risk looking stupid, or be honest and tell him the truth? Then the German burst out laughing and said, "It is called Fishky and it has been stored in a cask that was used to store herring. It is how some Scotch would once have tasted!"

This product is proof that the Germans take themselves less seriously than many other whisky nations. The Blaue Maus (Blue Mouse) distillery was the brainchild of Robert Fleischmann, and today is run by his son, Thomas. Blaue Maus is made using local grain, and the taste suggests that it is matured in bourbon casks. The distinct distillery characteristic running though the entire range of expressions is unlike anything found in Scotland, Ireland, or America. Reminiscent of a milk chocolate liqueur, it won't be to everybody's taste, but it is quite delicious and as good as anything from the distillery. **DR**

Tasting notes

The oily and berry nose gives way to praline, and hazelnut, together with honey, candy, and vanilla. Chocolate lovers will be in their element.

← The rustic charm of Ammertal whisky, complete with black horse logo.

Grüner Hund

Blaue Maus Distillery
www.fleischmann-whisky.de

Region and country of origin Bavaria, Germany
Distillery Blaue Maus, Eggolsheim
Alcohol content Varies, around 51% abv
Style Single malt

Whisky is very much in vogue now, with distilleries appearing almost daily around the world. In the 1980s, however, Robert Fleischmann's Blaue Maus distillery was a pioneering force. Blaue Maus started off as a hobby, but whisky has a habit of capturing the imagination and turning into a vocation. So when Robert let his son Thomas take control, he handed over a business of quality with a dynamic array of products.

Grüner Hund (Green Dog) is quite possibly the brightest star in a very strong lineup. The whisky has a deep, rich color that is entirely natural; nothing is added to its standard ingredients, and it is not chill-filtered. Grüner Hund is a single-cask offering, so it varies from batch to batch, but what makes it special is the fact that the spirit is matured in virgin American oak casks, making for big, bold whisky.

The Fleischmanns have also developed a distillery character, a thread of honey, caramel, chocolate, and vanilla that results directly from the casks used for aging. While there is a lot going on in this whisky, it will not be to everyone's taste. It is certainly the strangest whisky in the distillery's lineup, but at the same time it is hard not to be impressed with the high standard of the whisky making on display. An altogether softer 40 percent abv version is also available, but buy this one if you can find it. **DR**

Tasting notes

A nose that suggests nuts and a rich fruit liqueur. On the palate, a nervous walk down a dark alley; expect stewed fruit, molasses coffee, and burnt treacle.

Slyrs Bavarian

Slyrs
www.slyrs.de

Region and country of origin Bavaria, Germany
Distillery Slyrs, Schliersee-Neuhaus
Alcohol content 43% abv
Style Single malt

Of all the locations of mainland Europe, perhaps the one best suited to whisky production is Bavaria. The region has obvious similarities with Scotland, and its crisp and cold climate, plenty of mountain water, and lots of pure lake water all add up to ideal distilling conditions. However, there has never been a serious tradition of making whisky in the region.

Slyrs distillery was set up in 1999 by local beer and schnapps maker Florian Stetter, who dreamed of creating the perfect Bavarian whisky. His early efforts were unimpressive, but his present-day product has plenty to recommend it. It is obviously very well made, has an unusual and appealing taste, and combines lots of stimulating and interesting flavors.

Slyrs Bavarian single malt is made with local grain and water, and the spirit is aged in new American oak 60-gallon (225-liter) barrels for an unspecified period of time. The resulting whisky is distributed by parent company Lantenhammar, and what sets it apart from many other European distilleries is the smart way it is packaged. This standard bottle is the best the distillery has to offer, although a cask-strength version was released in 2008. The whisky is released as a new vintage each May. If you have trouble finding it, there are worse places to visit in spring. The distillery offers a tour followed by a tasting, and there is a shop. **DR**

Tasting notes

Tinned fruits, particularly pear, honey drizzled over vanilla ice cream, and caramel milk chocolate bar. There is sugar and spice interplay and a gentle finish.

Slyrs whiskies are made on the shore of Lake Schliersee, Bavaria. ➡

Spinnaker 1999

Blaue Maus Distillery | www.fleischmann-whisky.de

Region and country of origin Bavaria, Germany
Distillery Blaue Maus, Eggolsheim
Alcohol content 40% abv
Style Single malt

While Robert Fleischmann comes from a family of cigarette, drink, and food retailers with a history stretching back decades, his decision to start distilling whisky in 1980 took many by surprise. He openly admits that his first efforts were appalling, but he vowed to practice continually, and in recent years, his whiskies have been nothing short of a revelation.

These days his son, Thomas, is involved in the business. The Blaue Maus distillery produces a range of whiskies bearing such names as Grüner Hund (Green Dog) and Blaue Maus (Blue Mouse). Confusingly, though, the landlocked German distillery also has a maritime theme; in addition to a few expressions under the Spinnaker name, there is another called Schwarzer Pirat (Black Pirate).

There are plenty of people in the whisky world—including one leading German writer—who argue that the German-speaking regions of Europe should stick to distilling fruit liqueurs and leave whisky well alone. And it has to be said that there are certainly German whiskies that push the definition of whisky to its acceptable limit. However, the Spinnaker range is linked by a soft, honeyed taste, and while the nose can be oily and unbalanced, the palate is a delight over the entire range.

This vintage was bottled at around eleven years old, making it a baby in comparison to some of the expressions on offer. Robert Fleischmann seems to have perfected a method of making the whisky equivalent of eiderdown, and once you throw aside comparisons with Scotch, there is plenty to enjoy. **DR**

Tasting notes

This German whisky offers a fantastic mix of honeycomb, hot milky malt drink, and soft, milky chocolate with candy and vanilla. The finish has no length as such and no real shape, but the whisky is gloriously squidgy in the mouth nevertheless.

Spinnaker Fassstärke

Blaue Maus Distillery | www.fleischmann-whisky.de

Region and country of origin Bavaria, Germany
Distillery Blaue Maus, Eggolsheim
Alcohol content 48.2% abv
Style Single malt

Across northern Europe, there are several nations, such as Germany, the Netherlands, the Czech Republic, and Belgium, that have proud beer-making traditions and yet have seldom dabbled in whisky. Given that making beer is half the journey, so to speak, the absence of whisky is hard to account for.

In the last thirty years or so, however, that has been changing. But the really intriguing question is how have these countries, which are bound by the same strict rules as everyone else in Europe, managed to produce an array of whiskies with such radically different tastes? The answer relates partly to the type of barley used, partly to what is used to dry the barley, and partly to the kind of casks used for aging.

There are some truly immense, powerfully flavored whiskies coming from mainland Europe, and they are not to everyone's taste. The Blaue Maus distillery produces a Fassstärke version of each of its whisky expressions. Each one is stronger than the standard core offering—Fassstärke translates as "cask strength"—and they can be a challenge.

Spinnaker Fassstärke has a linseed-oil nose, evoking the oil paints supplied in paint-by-number sets. Get past that, though, and it is a chewy, schnappslike whisky unlike anything you have ever tasted. It is hard to put a finger on why it is so different, but it is quite possibly because it marries malt whisky with bourbon and then adds some local color. It definitely will take you out of your comfort zone, but stay with it and it proves something of a gem. Be sure to add some water to soften the sharpness. **DR**

Tasting notes

With this single-cask whisky you will find bourbon vanilla, honeyed malt, and ginger liqueur, with a sharp oakiness when sipped at full strength. With water added, milk chocolate comes to the fore, with intense fruit and rum and raisin. The finish is pleasant.

Telsington

Brennerei Telser | www.telsington.com

Region and country of origin Liechtenstein
Distillery Telser, Triesen
Alcohol content 42% abv
Style Single malt

There are many interesting facts about Liechtenstein. It is the sixth-smallest country in the world. It has more registered companies than it has citizens. It has had no army since 1868. It and Uzbekistan are the only two countries in the world that are double-landlocked (surrounded by countries that are themselves landlocked). And it distills whisky. Yes, Liechtenstein distills whisky, the smallest country to do so. Its Telsington single malt is three years old and has been released in two batches, each from a single cask and strictly limited in numbers. It is triple-distilled, matured in pinot noir barriques, and is not chill-filtered.

The Telser distillery that produces it has been producing high-quality distillates since 1880, and it prides itself on drawing clear mountain water from the Triesen wells, distilling over a wood fire, and maturing its various products (including schnapps and kirsch) in a protected historic site: a 500-year-old vault cellar with an earth floor. This, we are assured, allows its distillates to mature without any use of additives. And, as if to add a touch of Central European idiosyncrasy to the proceedings, Telser also produces a mixture of hot water and grist prior to undergoing fermentation. This might seem somewhat unusual, but the practice is not uncommon in neighboring Switzerland, and the distillates seem unaffected. **PB**

Tasting notes

Quite salty on the nose, with a hint of plum jam. On the palate fruit and grape dominate, without becoming oversweet. The finish is soft, with a warm glow.

Frysk Hynder 2007

Us Heit Distillery | www.usheitdistillery.nl

Region and country of origin Friesland, the Netherlands **Distillery** Us Heit, Bolsward
Alcohol content 40% abv
Style Single malt

The northernmost province of The Netherlands is called Fryslân, or Friesland. It is a country within a country, having its own language, flag, anthem, and political party. In cold winters the canals freeze, and when the ice is considered thick enough, the world-famous Eleven Cities Tour is held. Tens of thousands of ice skaters tackle a 125-mile (200-km) trial. One of the eleven cities is Bolsward, and this is where Frysk Hynder single-malt whisky is made by master distiller Aart van der Zee. He originally started a small beer brewery some thirty-odd years ago, and in 2002, he decided to combine this with distilling whisky. Aart's product was an instant hit.

The name of this single malt is Frisian for "Frisian horse," the strong, beautiful, black, and world-renowned breed. The whisky matures in a variety of casks and is bottled in batches when three years old. Due to the use of different types of barrels, the taste per batch may vary. Aart revealed that he is planning to introduce older whiskies, bottled at cask strength, in years to come. Recently a coffee liqueur was introduced, based on Frysk Hynder's whisky spirit. "After having made beer and whisky for some time, my wife asked me to make something more to her tastes, so I did," commented Aart. So now you can try a Frisian coffee instead of an Irish one for a change. **HO**

Tasting notes

The first flavor to come through is wine, probably an aged red. The fruit and barley is tangy and somewhat overpowering and comes across as sharp. Unusual.

The majestic Frisian horse is the distillery's logo.

Millstone
5-Year-Old

Zuidam | www.zuidam.eu

Region and country of origin North Brabant,
the Netherlands **Distillery** Zuidam, Baarle-Nassau
Alcohol content 40% abv
Style Single malt

Fred van Zuidam is the paterfamilias of this independent company. He earned his distilling spurs in Schiedam, where he made the traditional Dutch liqueur of genever—or jenever, as it is spelled in the Netherlands—but found a new challenge in 1975 when he built his own distillery in Baarle-Nassau, a Dutch enclave surrounded by neighboring Belgium, a country that also boasts well-crafted genever.

At first he focused on what he had been doing most of his working life: making fine Dutch genever. When his two sons came of age, Patrick, the elder, took the helm from his father and now leads the company. Gilbert became sales director, but left the domain of design to his mother. In 2007 the Zuidams surprised the whisky world when, out of the blue, they launched this five-year-old single malt. Dutch barley is milled in authentic Dutch windmills and then transported to the distillery, where it is processed into whisky by means of stills that were originally used for distilling eaux-de-vie and fruit liqueurs. The latter have become hugely successful in the United States, and are immediately recognizable on the shelves at liquor stores by their slender form and silver stopper. The whisky comes in a squat bottle. **HO**

Tasting notes

Surprisingly rich and developed taste for such a young whisky. Refined vanilla and oak and a warming baked flavor; late summer fruits and a dash of wild nature.

Millstone
5-Year-Old Peated

Zuidam | www.zuidam.eu

Region and country of origin North Brabant,
the Netherlands **Distillery** Zuidam, Baarle-Nassau
Alcohol content 40% abv
Style Single malt

Master distiller Patrick van Zuidam does not particularly like peated whisky, despite the fact that the "peaty beasties" are generally so sought after. His brother, Gilbert, differs, from a marketing and sales perspective. This peated Millstone had to develop itself into whisky over at least three years before legally it could be called a whisky.

According to Patrick, it is far easier to make a peated whisky than an unpeated one. He is convinced that the smoky character of many whiskies out there masks hidden imperfections in the whisky making. Well, this may be the talk of a whisky-making perfectionist, and it is hard to disagree with Patrick's view, but the observation does not apply to all peated whiskies. Used wisely, peat smoke can add a beautiful extra layer to the taste of a whisky.

Although the first Millstone malt was released in 2007, Patrick and Fred—the distiller's father—had been experimenting with whisky distilling since 1997. Some of the earlier whisky is still maturing, so what Zuidam has in store for us in the long run is unknown. In the meantime, whisky enthusiasts should try the smoky Dutchman and judge whether it can compete with peated whiskies from Scotland. **HO**

Tasting notes

Fruit is the leading flavor here, particularly banana, peach, and, less so, apricot. The sweetness of the fruit grows and the peat does not emerge until the end.

Millstone's packaging is designed by Hélène van Zuidam, wife of head distiller, Frank.

Millstone 8-Year-Old American Oak

Zuidam | www.zuidam.eu

Region and country of origin North Brabant, the Netherlands **Distillery** Zuidam, Baarle-Nassau
Alcohol content 40% abv
Style Single malt

Millstone has steadily gathered prizes at international competitions but is still sold in relatively small quantities, despite its international following. Master distiller Patrick van Zuidam does not want to make concessions by speeding up fermentation or distilling. Furthermore, the majority of the distillates from this tiny operation are Dutch genever, fruit liqueurs, and, since the early 1990s, vodka. Demand for the latter rose remarkably after the opening of the Russian market; company paterfamilias Fred van Zuidam, then in charge, took advantage of the market, and since then vodka has been an important part of the company portfolio.

Fred's wife, Hélène, decided to design the vodka bottle herself, convinced that she could do a better job than an outside packaging company. It is all part of the charm of the Zuidam ethos. Each of the four members, be it Fred, Hélène, or sons Patrick and Gilbert, has a distinctive say in what direction the company goes and where expansion should occur.

This Millstone single malt was matured in American oak for eight years. Zuidam sells a threesome of whiskies in a stylish set of three 20-centiliter (6.8-ounce) bottles: a delightful present for those who want to taste the trio head-to-head. The whisky can also be purchased with a set of branded tasting glasses. For lovers of golf, Hélène introduced a gift pack containing a small bottle of Millstone Malt and a leather-encased hip flask with a little bandolier of tees. The Zuidams, avid golfers themselves, clearly think that golf and whisky may be joined at the hip. **HO**

Tasting notes

Lighter than it looks, with soft touches of vanilla that slip down very easily. Paired with the vanilla is a generous helping of wild honey. Not much of a nose and not a triumphant climax, but overall pleasing and a drink to be sipped.

Millstone 8-Year-Old French Oak

Zuidam | www.zuidam.eu

Region and country of origin North Brabant, the Netherlands **Distillery** Zuidam, Baarle-Nassau
Alcohol content 40% abv
Style Single malt

The shapes of the stills at Zuidam are unusual in whisky making, being used primarily to produce a series of excellent fruit liqueurs, drunk either neat or in a cocktail. Yet pretty much identical equipment is used for all of Zuidam's distillates. The fermentation takes place in former milk tanks built in stainless steel, a common material in the whisky industry.

Master distiller Patrick van Zuidam is especially particular about maturing his whiskies. He prefers new oak barrels for the first few years, after which he recasks them in oak that has been used previously. He calls this his "teabag philosophy": the longer the bag is kept hanging in a cup of hot water, the stronger it gets. So why not use that strength a second time for the next batch of new-make spirit and recask the older spirit? After the five-year-old had been well received, it was followed by two eight-year-old expressions, one of which spent time in French oak, which is a bit unusual in the whisky world. Patrick's mother, Hélène, created a wonderful package for it, a black wooden box with gold lettering.

The bottling and packaging is done at the premises, by hand. Zuidam's headquarters is small but a delight to visit; the interior was designed by Mrs. Zuidam. She and her younger son, Gilbert, believe that the packaging for their products should match the high quality of the contents. Hélène, a frequent visitor of designer fairs in Paris, France, highlighted Patrick's choice of French oak for this expression, and he has his own ideas regarding maturation regimes. This Millstone, French in look, is still Dutch in character. **HO**

Tasting notes

Spices and fruit create a full and warming mouthfeel, making one think of wintertime. Green fruits such as apples and pears give way to mint. The French oak comes through at the end, creating a patient, beautifully crafted whisky.

Millstone Dutch Rye

Zuidam | www.zuidam.eu

Region and country of origin North Brabant, The Netherlands **Distillery** Zuidam, Baarle-Nassau
Alcohol content 40% abv
Style Rye whisky

European pioneers, among them many Dutch, brought their distilling techniques with them when they emigrated to the United States, carrying seeds of barley and rye. When the former proved difficult to cultivate in the new surroundings, rye came to the fore. Originally considered a weed, rye can grow almost anywhere, even in the poorest soil.

Rye became the primary ingredient of the first real American whiskey, called "Rye" or "Monongahela," named for the valley in Pennsylvania where many early pioneers settled. Making whiskey became an extra activity for many farmers, especially during the quiet winter months. The drink became a commodity and was used to barter clothes, food, and other items. But over time the farmers switched from growing rye to corn, the indigenous grain that the American Indians had given the first pilgrims as a welcome gift and which grows so well there.

Eventually corn replaced rye as the main ingredient in American whiskey. That remains true today, despite the small rye revival that is currently underway, causing old and nearly forgotten rye brands to reappear and prominent bourbon marques to add rye varieties to their whiskey ranges. Anyone pondering these developments over a sample of Millstone Dutch Rye might wonder whether it would not make perfect historical sense if a Dutch distiller launched a rye whisky to partake in that revival. The respected master distiller Jim Rutledge of Four Roses sampled this one and was duly impressed. Now it is your turn to see for yourself. **HO**

Tasting notes

Particularly sweet, with everything from treacle and candy, apples and marzipan making its presence known. The natural flavors such as apples and citrus are welcome here and the last minute appearance of coffee is jarring at first but somehow works.

DYC

Beam Global | www.dyc.com

Region and country of origin Castile and León, Spain
Distillery Destilerías y Crianza del Whisky, Segovia
Alcohol content 40% abv
Style Blend

There is a commendable independent streak about the Spanish, evidenced by the fact that the country has a long-established whisky distillery. Furthermore, the distillery is capable of making very good whisky.

Spain's relationship with whisky goes back to the days of General Franco. The dictator wanted to buck the world trend toward Scotch and create a Spanish-produced whisky instead. Ironically, when Franco's rule ended, DYC came to symbolize independence. It represented a new, young, vibrant, and increasingly confident Spanish consumer, and for many years it was at the cutting edge of advertising, pursuing a confident, courageous, and sometimes comical path. It continues as a favorite in Spain, but, despite a history spanning more than fifty years, it has remained unknown to most whisky drinkers outside Spain.

Who knows whether that will change, or whether this entry-level blend will be the brand to put Spanish whisky on the map. Probably not, because there is not enough going on here to differentiate it from much of the competition. In keeping with global trends, the distillery is starting to produce single malts, but DYC no longer has it all its own way in Spain: a new distillery started operating in 2010.

That said, this light, easily quaffable whisky is no slouch; it still enjoys tremendous support among young Spaniards, and it is an ideal mixing whisky. The distillery is now owned by Beam Global, and there will almost certainly be some Laphroaig and more likely unpeated malt in the blend, as well as several other ex-Allied and now Pernod Ricard whiskies. **DR**

Tasting notes

This is young whisky, dominated by grain. As a result, it is sweet and unsophisticated, but it has a delightful aspect of soft toffee on vanilla ice cream. There are some developing citrus notes, and the delivery is soft and gentle, with the merest hint of spice later on.

DYC 10-Year-Old

Beam Global | www.dyc.es

Region and country of origin Castile and León, Spain
Distillery Destilerías y Crianza del Whisky, Segovia
Alcohol content 40% abv
Style Single malt

A few years ago, anyone visiting the wonderful historic town of Segovia in central Spain would never have known that, down the road, whisky was being made. But if Elena Estoban of DYC's public relations has anything to do with it, that is set to change. She was born and raised in Segovia, seems to know everyone, and has an infectious enthusiasm for her subject. Her aim is to get Segovian whisky taken seriously by whisky fans and to use the DYC distillery to bring ever more visitors to the region.

The Segovia whisky trail links the Eras river, which passes the city and on which the distillery lies, with an incredible historic glass-making factory, from where DYC gets its bottles, and the surrounding lands, from where it sources its barley.

The DYC 10-Year-Old single malt will help with the provenance and history aspect of Sergovia whisky. After the distillery celebrated its fiftieth anniversary with a single malt, it followed up with this easy-drinking ten-year-old, matured in bourbon casks. It all bodes well for the future, and with Elena as a figurehead, you can see how DYC single malts could make a global impact. She says that some people order the whisky by asking for "a Segovian." And without doubt, she has helped to pull the local whisky into Segovia's tourism story. **DR**

Tasting notes

The apple, fresh marzipan, vanilla, and toffee themes are all in place on the nose, but there is a richer, fruitier, more Speyside theme here, too. Gentle, and pleasant.

DYC 50th Anniversary

Beam Global | www.dyc.es

Region and country of origin Castile and León, Spain
Distillery Destilerías y Crianza del Whisky, Segovia
Alcohol content 40% abv
Style Single malt

The DYC distillery in Segovia celebrated its fiftieth anniversary in 2009, but for most of the half century it had been in existence, it had done little to stretch its influence beyond Spain's borders. While DYC is the third-best-selling whisky brand in Spain, most of its sales have been in blends or mixtures of malts.

By the time the distillery reached its fiftieth birthday, big question marks had formed over the whole of Spain and its hospitality industry. Recession in the twenty-first century hit the country hard, with some commentators predicting a long-term cessation of the drinking culture. So far Maxxium, which distributes DYC, has remained in the country, and if Maxxium intends to move Spanish whisky forward and into other territories, it will be with whiskies like this one. Just 2,000 bottles of it were released, but it is the best whisky the distillery has ever produced.

DYC 50th Anniversary is a sure sign that, while Destilerías y Crianza knows exactly what it is doing, it has never had the chance to demonstrate its skills. The whisky is not challenging, but it is light and easy drinking, suits the Spanish climate, and has a great backstory. The distillery is a delight in its own right, a fact that was recognized by the local tourist authority, which used the launch of this very whisky to unveil a whisky trail in and around Segovia. **DR**

Tasting notes

The nose is light, with some floral notes. The palate is includes ginger barley, grape, suggestions of a summer meadow, and old pantry spices. The finish is addictive.

The courtyard of the DYC distillery in rural Palazuelos de Eresma. ➡

DYC Pure Malt

Beam Global | www.dyc.com

Region and country of origin Castile and León, Spain
Distillery Destilerías y Crianza del Whisky, Segovia
Alcohol content 40% abv
Style Blended malt

Ask whisky enthusiasts to name their favorite distillery and chances are you will get a wide range of answers for just as large a number of reasons, some to do with the whisky, some with the distillery, and some with location. Almost certainly no one would think of Destilerías y Crianza near Segovia, about seventy minutes' drive north of Madrid. But you could make a case for this amazing plant.

And plant it is. Now owned by Beam Global, it has a history stretching back to the 1950s, and it is unlikely that scouring the planet would yield anything else quite like it. It has a single malt distillery, grain distillery, gin distillery, and bottling plant, all under its roof; it malts its own locally produced barley in two big malting trays. It also accommodates a huge energy plant, generating heat and electricity through two Rolls-Royce engines powered by natural gas. Close by is the beautiful historical town of Segovia, with its famous fairy-tale castle, the Alcázar.

DYC Pure Malt is a blend of Segovian malt and a mix of ten Scottish malts, mainly from Speyside but also including Beam's distilleries Ardmore and Laphroaig. It marked a step outside the safety zone of the distillery, breaking free from the standard blended market, but the whisky suits the hot Spanish environment, being refreshing and easy drinking with some body. The name is out of step with the modern whisky market—"pure" is not an acceptable labeling term anymore—but this is definitely worth seeking out, a Spanish cousin for whiskies such as William Grant's Monkey Shoulder. **DR**

Tasting notes

There is fluffy apple, apple seed, raisin, vanilla, and toffee on the nose. On the palate a light fruitiness is cushioned by a soft vanilla bed, and the merest trace of earthy spice lurking beneath the surface. Very refreshing and easy drinking.

Embrujo

Destilerías Liber | www.destileriasliber.com

Region and country of origin Andalusia, Spain
Distillery Destilerías Liber, Granada
Alcohol content 40% abv
Style Single malt

What will become of Spanish whisky? Whisky drinking was hit hard by the banking crisis of 2009, mainly because prosperous Spaniards like to drink out until very late. The economic downturn hit Spanish trade hard, and whisky certainly felt the impact. But there is something more fundamental going on in Spain, too. Whisky was the drink of choice of the generation that emerged from the shadow of Franco, and traditionally it has been consumed long, over ice and often mixed with cola. Even single-malt whisky has been drunk this way. But young drinkers today are reacting against their parents and rejecting mixed whisky as the spirit of choice. Can it bounce back?

It seems that opinion is divided, and certainly in recent years the evidence has not been good. But not all hope is lost. There are whisky events in Spain, and in cities such as Barcelona there is a genuine interest in quality whisky. A few years back, Beam Global realized it had a fifty-year-old distillery in Segovia and started promoting single malts from it. Now southern Spain has its own distillery, too, the Destilerías Liber.

The interest in Embrujo whisky stems from the fact that it is always fun to see the start of a journey. Coming from a distillery nestled under Spain's tallest mountain in Granada, Embrujo is made using local barley and water from the Sierra Nevada. Oddly, the southern location does not accelerate maturation and, at five years old, the whisky is too young. That said, there are hints that good whisky will come from Destilerías Liber. Let us hope that Embrujo proves to be part of a renaissance for whisky in Spain. **DR**

Tasting notes

A Spanish dawn of a whisky, loaded with promise of a warm and exciting day ahead. There is a refreshing rich orange and lemon combination developing and some honey sweetness. But also some reedy grain notes. The start of a promising whisky-making story, though.

Mackmyra Brukswhisky

Mackmyra | www.mackmyra.com

Region and country of origin Gävleborg County, Sweden **Distillery** Mackmyra, Valbo
Alcohol content 41.4% abv
Style Single malt

Launching a whisky is always an exploration, a journey into the unknown and one fraught with pitfalls and distractions. But Mackmyra's development seems to have been almost organic, and while the whisky has ended up in a good place, to an outsider, the plans for it seem to have been made up as the owners went along. Some decisions, such as the one to use Swedish oak, barley, and peat, were entirely logical, but the decision to use an old mine for maturation seemed odd, as did the, albeit inclusive, decision to involve total strangers in the decision-making process.

Mackmyra could not have known that the Swedes would take its whisky patriotically to their hearts, but that inclusive decision is one of the reasons whenever a new bottling of Mackmyra is released through Sweden's state-controlled liquor stores, it attracts the longest lines seen since Abba last toured. The whisky has evolved from the early Privus bottling, through the Preludium bottlings, and on to the first "proper," mass-market releases. Today, the whisky is distinctly Swedish, a fruity and spicy delight that would find favor in a broad church of whisky drinkers. But it is not necessarily an easy ride, and much of the malt is bottled at cask strength.

The Brukswhisky might be Mackmyra's ideal entry level, a Mackmyra Lite or a pleasing drinking version of Mackmyra in which the fruity taste is king. Its importance in the Mackmyra canon is that it reflects the producer's growing confidence to take the whisky off in new directions. Its release followed the arrival of the first official U.S. market bottling. **DR**

Tasting notes

The nose has more green fruit than normal for a Mackmyra, with gooseberry and grape in the mix. On the palate it is far less peaky, peppery, or peaty than normal, with candylike fruits. Spices and peat sweep in late on, but first you get the heart of the malt.

Mackmyra First Edition

Mackmyra | www.mackmyra.com

Region and country of origin Gävleborg County, Sweden **Distillery** Mackmyra, Valbo
Alcohol content Varies, around 45% abv
Style Single malt

"We followed our dreams and created the first Swedish whisky," states the label of this bottling, the first to be exported to the United States. "A whisky that carries new experiences. A whisky for you who live a life less ordinary."

When the idea of a Swedish whisky first came about, a series of fortunate decisions gave the project a life of its own. The founding group decided to make one small batch of whisky to see what it would be like, giving up holidays or new cars to fund the enterprise. When the first whisky proved a big success, they decided to grow the business, but they needed more money. They found that investors were fixated with dot-com companies and would not look at them, so they invited people on the Internet to buy small shares in the business; they were inundated.

Becoming a cooperative distillery, they invited their shareholders to decide on the character of the whisky. They found a cheap property on land a couple of hours' drive from Stockholm (where one of the group had vacationed as a child), signed a supply agreement with local barley farmers, and set about giving the whisky a Swedish personality.

Peat, much of it at one time under the Baltic Sea, gives the whisky a salty, earthy element. Swedish oak—a commodity not easily found due to the depredations of Sweden's armies and navies over many generations—provides spice, as do the extreme winters and summers. Nearly half of this whisky is also matured in small casks. The end result is different, distinctively Swedish—and great. **DR**

Tasting notes

This is a sharp whisky, with big pepper, solid earthy peat, and bitter lemon fruits combining to remind you that you're not in Kansas. Or Keith or Kentucky for that matter. But it grows on you, and there is something addictive about the long spice and pepper ending.

Mackmyra
Moment Drivved

Mackmyra | www.mackmyra.com

Region and country of origin Gävleborg County, Sweden **Distillery** Mackmyra, Valbo
Alcohol content Varies, around 55.5% abv
Style Single malt

The early bottlings of Mackmyra were so peaty, spicy, and woody that the fruit heart was obscured. If you were to line up three or four Privus bottlings and three or four Preludiums, you would need a very discerning palate to define and describe them objectively. No such difficulty with more recent bottlings, though. Two of the Moment series seemed to be aimed totally at the traditional Mackmyra drinker, pulling the peat and pepper to the fore and offering a grainy, rustic, earthy drinking experience that is not necessarily to everyone's taste. This, though, is the best of the bunch. You can tell from the reedy, grainy taste that it is not particularly old whisky, but it has been brilliantly put together, it is complex and intriguing, and it pulls off the enviable feat of being both sweet and savory at the time.

The whisky consists of four hogsheads matured in a mine for seven years, mixed with spirit from an ex-bourbon cask, and finished off with malt matured in new Swedish oak. Just 1,450 bottles were released in late 2011, nearly half of which were allocated for Swedish distribution. This inevitably means it will be hard to find. It isn't cheap but may be found on international shelves waiting to be discovered. **DR**

Tasting notes

The sappy, youthful notes that you experience at first give way to a melt-in-the-mouth chocolate liqueur center. Like a syrup-covered pepper steak.

Mackmyra
Moment Jord

Mackmyra | www.mackmyra.com

Region and country of origin Gävleborg County, Sweden **Distillery** Mackmyra, Valbo
Alcohol content Varies, around 55.1% abv
Style Single malt

Mackmyra's maturation process is like no other on Earth. When the company started out, it stored all its barrels in a disused mine so large that trucks could drive into it, like the set of a James Bond movie. Within its depths, Mackmyra continues to store malt in regular casks, but also small, specially made ones. The mini-cask contents go into the regular releases but can also be purchased as single malts, and customers are encouraged to visit and taste the work in progress.

When customers at the far ends of the country complained that the mine was too far away to visit easily, Mackmyra built a warehouse on the Swedish coast at the other end of the country, thereby adding maritime maturation to its repertoire. Another maturation warehouse was built on an island close to Stockholm. Now purchasers can decide where to mature their casks.

The four bottlings that make up the Moment series are warts-and-all, small-gig whiskies with a return to the earthy peat and peppery spice of old, but with a twist. The four Moment releases followed one another quickly. Moment Jord is finished in a Bordeaux red wine cask and is worth seeking out for its quirky and unusual twist on Swedish whisky. **DR**

Tasting notes

The nose is delicate, with apricot jam, and drifting wood smoke. The palate is dominated by razor-sharp barley, and peat. This is gristy, earthy, and challenging.

The Mackmyra logo is embossed on the base of all their bottles.

Mackmyra Special 04 Double Dip

Mackmyra | www.mackmyra.com

Region and country of origin Gävleborg County, Sweden **Distillery** Mackmyra, Valbo
Alcohol content 53% abv
Style Single malt

One of the great advantages of establishing a distillery outside the areas that traditionally produce whisky is that, provided you keep within the general laws defining whisky in that part of the world, you do not have to address the historical baggage—the arcane rules, the long-established expectations of brands, the conservative harking back to past glories—that other producers are stuck with. And no distillery has turned that to its advantage quite as successfully as Mackmyra in Sweden.

From the outset, when the distillery invited members of the public to fund it by effectively buying shares in the business, gaining a say in how the whisky developed at the same time, Mackmyra has been the people's whisky. In recent years this ethos has developed further with the distillery offering customers the chance to buy small casks matured at different sites across the country.

The real masterstroke, however, has been the series of Special whiskies Mackmyra has launched to explore unusual directions for its product, without devaluing the core brand. This whisky, Special 04, has quickly established itself as the favorite Mackmyra in the hearts of many. Described by the maker as the ideal whisky for light summer nights, it is called Double Dip because it is the product of two separate maturations, the first in big bourbon barrels, the second in very small, 8-gallon (30-liter) handmade casks. The resulting whisky is less sharp, spicy, and salty than some of the company's other offerings, and is possibly the most accessible of the range. **DR**

Tasting notes

Banana, soft melon, fresh barley, and lots of candy and vanilla on the nose, then a sprinkling of sweet spices and some William pear and overripe apple. Clean and fresh, sweet and spicy. The finish returns to vanilla and oak and then fades to wood.

Säntis Malt Swiss Highlander Edition Dreifaltigkeit

Brauerei Locher | www.saentismalt.ch

Region and country of origin Appenzell, Switzerland
Distillery Brauerei Locher, Appenzell
Alcohol content 52% abv
Style Single malt

While Bruichladdich and Ardbeg are slugging it out in a battle to produce the world's most heavily peated whisky, the Brauerei Locher from Switzerland has entered stage left and produced this award-winning Säntis Malt Swiss Highlander Edition Dreifaltigkeit ("The Trinity"), named for a local mountain peak. Neither an age nor an official peating level is given, but this cask-strength version is, in its own way, as intense as anything produced on Islay.

The intensity is not only due to macho peating levels, though. The malt is smoked in three different ways: beech-smoked, oak-smoked, and peat-smoked. This is done in two stages. The barley, having already been smoked over the two woods, is then resmoked using peat from the local Appenzell Highmoor. The Dreifaltigkeit is actually said to be a "lightly peated" whisky, which suggests that the intense flavors come not just from a one-dimensional blast of peat but from the trinity of smoke sources, in addition to toasted oak casks and the dark beer they previously contained.

Situated in Appenzell in northeast Switzerland, Brauerei Locher has been brewing beer for more than a hundred years. It has put the oak beer casks at its disposal to excellent use. These are not merely casks made from century-old trees, but have been used to mature beer for a century in the process known as lagering. Such uniqueness has its price, as the oaken casks are clearly not an inexhaustible commodity. Consequently, the output is limited to a couple of thousand bottles per year. But if you like smoke in abundance, you won't want to miss this Swiss. **PB**

Tasting notes

Heavily smoked cheese, yeast extract, and cured bacon on the nose, with a layer of cream underpinning the savoriness. On the palate there is citrus with smoked wood and slightly burnt butterscotch. The finish is long and pungent with charcoal and grapefruit peel.

Säntis Malt Swiss Highlander Edition Säntis

Brauerei Locher | www.saentismalt.ch

Region and country of origin Appenzell, Switzerland
Distillery Brauerei Locher, Appenzell
Alcohol content 40% abv
Style Single malt

The family-owned Brauerei Locher is situated at the foot of the Swiss Alps, surrounded by the peaks after which its whiskies have been named. In addition to a huge selection of beers, including the delightfully named Quöllfrisch and Lager Hell, three single malts are produced. This Edition Säntis is named after the tallest mountain in the Alpstein mountain range, from whose peak, on a clear day, one can see Liechtenstein, Italy, Germany, Austria, France and—unless the weather is particularly bad—Switzerland.

Brauerei Locher claims to have produced the first Swiss single malt after the 1998 repeal of the law banning spirits from being distilled from grain—a holdover from World War II when food was in short supply and the Swiss government decreed that food production was more important than the production of grain-based spirits.

From this delicious and creamy Edition Säntis, reminiscent in its flavors of an explosion in a Swiss pastry shop, one can move into more aromatic territory with its triple-distilled Edition Sigel, matured in smaller oak beer barrels, and then on to the supercharged smoke-fest that is the cask strength Edition Dreifaltigkeit. Given the Brauerei Locher's impressive range of beers, the distillery has a considerable range of barrels with potential flavors for maturing its whisky. Unlike the Dreifaltigkeit, which uses barrels previously used to mature dark beer, the Säntis is matured in ex-lager beer casks, giving it a lighter, smoother, and far less smoky demeanor, although smoke is still detectable on the nose. **PB**

Tasting notes

Sweet pastry and walnut on the nose, with light smoke and hints of clove. On the palate it is vanilla ice cream with apple, kiwi fruit, pepper, and toasted almonds. The finish is long, creamy, and spicy with marzipan, ending with echoes of cucumber and mint.

Säntis Malt Swiss Highlander Edition Sigel

Brauerei Locher | www.saentismalt.ch

Region and country of origin Appenzell, Switzerland
Distillery Brauerei Locher, Appenzell
Alcohol content 40% abv
Style Single malt

The Swiss food and drink scene is packed with surprises. Of course we know about the chocolate, but Swiss wine is also considered of excellent quality—some of it is world-class—although less than 1 percent of it leaves Switzerland. Swiss cheeses and cakes are also highly regarded, not least *biberli*, the spicy honey cake that must mature for six to eight weeks before consumption. So, despite being miles from any ancient spice route, Switzerland knows a thing or two about spiciness, as anyone who has ever tasted Swiss Highlander whisky will tell you.

Like the Edition Säntis, this distinctive whisky has been matured in oak casks previously used by specialist brewers Brauerei Locher to make their award-winning beer. The whisky is cold fermented, triple-distilled, and then hot-filled into the carefully selected small beer casks for maturation in Brauerei Locher's cool, dark cellars. The wood delivers rich vanilla and plenty of spice, with more peppery spice continuing on to the palate. This is a smooth and gentle whisky with dominant incense notes. It is very well balanced and very drinkable, aromatic with plenty of fruit—grape, in particular, leads the way.

The Säntis Malt Swiss Highlander Edition Sigel might not be as intensely smoky as their Dreifaltigkeit, but it is dripping with grape, spice, and incense. Like the Swiss wine mentioned above, it can be hard to track down, but encouraged by strong sales, the distillery is building up its international presence. Try contacting Säntis through their Web site to find out about availability where you are. **PB**

Tasting notes

Massive grape and church incense on the nose with toasted cinnamon. On the palate the incense, while slightly reduced, dominates initially but gradually recedes, leaving a creamy, lightly wooded spiciness. The finish is long, with marzipan and spicy butter.

Whisky Castle
Castle Hill Doublewood

Käsers Schloss
www.whisky-castle.com

Region and country of origin Aargau, Switzerland
Distillery Käsers Schloss, Elfingen
Alcohol content 43% abv
Style Single malt

Whisky Castle proprietor Rudi Käser specialized in making a variety of other distillates before turning to whisky. They included schnapps in 130 different flavors, such as thyme, basil, garlic, and, bizarrely enough, geranium. The latter started as something of a novelty but actually turned out to be rather good. By his own admission, Käser is not interested in making whisky in an Irish or Scottish style, but instead wants to develop a uniquely Swiss style. He freely admits that Scotland might not approve his methods.

By using a variety of different grains, including barley, rye, spelt, oats, and one called triticale—a high-yield, disease-tolerant hybrid of wheat and rye devised more than a hundred years ago—he has certainly created whiskies that are far removed from average Scottish or Irish malts. As its name suggests, the three-year-old Doublewood expression is matured in two different woods, rather than two oak casks that happen to have been filled with different wines or spirits in the past. After an initial period in an oak cask, it is transferred to a cask made of chestnut wood, which gives the whisky a real sweetness, particularly on the nose. The resulting whisky is an intriguing mix of rich, sweet, and savory flavors. **PB**

Tasting notes

Lightly smoked cheese, raisin, and Danish pastry spices on the nose, with caramel chocolate. On the palate, black pepper, followed by fresh raisin and dried fruit.

Whisky Castle
Port Cask Smoke Barley

Käsers Schloss
www.whisky-castle.com

Region and country of origin Aargau, Switzerland
Distillery Käsers Schloss, Elfingen
Alcohol content 50% abv
Style Single malt

Compared to the average Scottish distillery, the output from the Whisky Castle distillery is tiny (25,000 bottles annually). Situated in Elfingen in the canton of Aargau, it clings to a slope on the Frick Valley in northern Switzerland; the semicircular gallery jutting over its doorway makes it look like a combination of an American farmhouse brewery and a wooden church.

Käser sources his lightly smoked malted barley from Germany, where the barley is dried over beech wood, and his barrels from places as diverse as Hungary, the United States, France, and Belarus. The whiskies are distilled in small pot stills whose appearance is immediately reminiscent of the robot in the children's television program *Lost in Space*.

The Port Cask Smoke Barley expression is exactly what is suggested by the label, but the whisky is far from an Islay wannabe. Instead of evoking thumping peat and crashing waves in a Hebridean winter, the experience of sipping it is more akin to eating a smoky and slightly crispy Christmas cake. Other available smoked expressions employ a range of grains, including Smoke Rye and Smoke Spelt, plus a version of Smoke Barley of lower strength that was somewhat provocatively dubbed Girls Choice. **PB**

Tasting notes

Currant and cranberry on the nose. On the palate it is spicy, smoky, with a helping of almond biscuit and rich port. A thin veil of smoke, spice, and grape on the finish.

Zürcher Lakeland Single Malt

Daniel and Ursula Zürcher
www.lakeland-whisky.ch

Region and country of origin Bern, Switzerland
Distillery Zürcher, Port
Alcohol content 42% abv
Style Single malt

In 1999 the Swiss government repealed an eighty-year-old law forbidding distillation from grain. Numerous distilleries have sprung up in Switzerland since the lifting of the ban, including the Spezialitätenbrennerei Zürcher, based near the lake of Bielersee in western Switzerland, which had already been producing fruit liqueurs and, somewhat incongruously, sausages.

It is usual for distilleries to take care of the entire production process, from mashing right through to maturation, but at Zürcher, whisky distillation is something of a sideline. The wash for the whisky is actually brought from a nearby brewery to be distilled in small pot stills on-site. A certain percentage of Zürcher's spirit is returned to the brewery to be matured in bourbon casks under the brewery's own label. Maturation for the Lakeland Single Malt takes place in oloroso sherry casks at the distillery.

Zürcher distillery started producing whisky in 2000, and in 2003 the first 1,000 bottles of Lakeland were released by Heinz Zürcher. In 2004 Heinz's nephew Daniel took over the operation; Zürcher has released further small batches ever since. Although this is only a three-year-old whisky, there are plans to release older expressions in the future. **PB**

Tasting notes

Ripe pear, vanilla, and treacle on the nose. On the palate, rounded with salt, fresh fruit, and a hint of peppermint. The finish is short and lightly gingery.

Penderyn 2002 Cask 10895

Penderyn
www.welsh-whisky.co.uk

Region and country of origin Rhondda Cynon Taf, Wales **Distillery** The Scotch Malt Whisky Society
Alcohol content 60.4% abv
Style Single malt

The Scotch Malt Whisky Society is a club that sources and sells whiskies as cask-strength, single-cask offerings. The bottles do not bear the name of the distillery on them but instead have a reference number and a teasing descriptor on the label. The Society is not above breaking out from the Scottish borders, either, as this Welsh example shows.

Penderyn whisky is produced on a unique still and matured in three different styles of casks, giving it a distinctive floral nose and a sweet flavor. But this expression has been matured entirely in port pipes and has taken on a much weightier, fuller, and more distinctive flavor than usual. The cask strength of 60.4 percent abv adds to the gravitas of the liquid.

Because this is a single-cask offering and the society has members spread across the world, the chances of finding this particular example are not great. However, the Society index number of 10895 gives a clue to the number of casks the Society has bottled; it is quite a few now, and more will be on the way. Also, Welsh whisky is not the most requested bottling from the Society, so you might be fortunate. Regardless of availability, cask-strength Penderyn finished in port is a revelation. **DR**

Tasting notes

Weird, musty old apple on the nose. Liqueurlike intensity and date, raisin, and sweet apple on the palate. Big, rich, and with a very full and long finish.

Penderyn Cask 11/200

Penderyn | www.welsh-whisky.co.uk

Region and country of origin Rhondda Cynon Taf, Wales **Distillery** Penderyn, Penderyn
Alcohol content 61.2% abv
Style Single malt

Penderyn's regular whiskies have one thing in common—they are all whiskies with a cask finish. After an initial maturation in one type of cask (in Penderyn's case these are former bourbon casks sourced from the Buffalo Trace distillery in Kentucky), they are transferred to a different kind of cask for further maturation. In general, secondary maturation takes less time than the initial one, although there are tales of whiskies that have been "finishing" for decades and still have not left the warehouse. At Penderyn, wine casks are used for the Madeira and Portwood expressions, and casks from the island of Islay for the Peated. This whisky, however, is different in that it is matured only in one type of cask.

Not only is it unfinished, it is also a single-cask bottling taken from a single ex-bourbon cask, bottled at cask strength, a hefty 61.2 percent abv. Penderyn distills its spirit in a unique still—designed by Dr. David Faraday, a descendant of eighteenth-century scientist Michael Faraday—to a high 92 to 96 percent abv, then dilutes it to an industry-standard strength before filling the casks. Even so, 61.2 percent abv is quite impressive for a whisky after ten years of evaporation and maturation.

Penderyn Cask 11/200 was distilled in 2000, the year that the distillery opened, and was one of the few remaining casks from that year when bottled. A total of 210 bottles were made available in celebration of the Welsh Whisky Company's tenth anniversary in September 2010, making the whisky the oldest that the company had bottled at that time. **BA**

Tasting notes

A nose of apple and pear upside-down cake, with some sweet dessert wine and bourbon vanilla, leads on to a spicy and alcoholic body that softens to cream, cinnamon, and perfumed wood. Adding a few drops of water will present this whisky at its best.

A dancing Welshman happily recommends his local whisky. ➡

Why? with capers so many?
John Jones, gay, you are,
" Welsh Whisky," dear Jenny,
From Bala; "*bur ddha.*"

Penderyn Madeira

Penderyn | www.welsh-whisky.co.uk

Region and country of origin Rhondda Cynon Taf, Wales **Distillery** Penderyn, Penderyn
Alcohol content 46% abv
Style Single malt

This whisky has the honor of being the flagship release from the first legal whisky distillery to be established in Wales since the nineteenth century. Released on March 1, 2004, the feast day of St. David, Wales's patron saint, this was the Penderyn distillery's first foray into the world of single-malt whisky. Starting right from scratch, Penderyn decided to produce a uniquely Welsh style of whisky to complement the longstanding traditions of Scottish and Irish whiskies, and the similarly newly reemerging English whisky.

As the initial release in Penderyn's small standard range, this whisky set the benchmark for the rest. It initiated the distillery's now routine approach of combining spirit matured in first- and second-fill bourbon casks (the first-fills all coming from Buffalo Trace distillery in Kentucky), then finishing the whisky for a few months in a different kind of wood. The Madeira barriques used are much less common for finishing than the sherry and port casks tried by many other distilleries. The barriques are sourced from Portugese cooperage J. Dias & Ca., based just south of the port production center of Porto in Portugal and known for supplying high-quality casks across the wine and spirits industries since their founding in 1935.

During finishing, the bourbon cask-matured spirit goes on to soak up the rich, dark flavors of the Madeira that the barriques previously contained. These flavors join the vanilla, coconut, and lighter notes that the spirit has already picked up from its initial maturation. The resulting rounded and complex whisky is a fitting lead product for this pioneering Welsh distillery. **BA**

Tasting notes

At the start, a savory meatiness is studded with raisin and spread with sugary royal icing that wafts out of the glass. On the palate there is a big, tannic middle surrounded by a light sugary sweetness that leads to a long finish of perfumed fruit and dry wood.

Penderyn Peated

Penderyn | www.welsh-whisky.co.uk

Region and country of origin Rhondda Cynon Taf,
Wales **Distillery** Penderyn, Penderyn
Alcohol content 46% abv
Style Single malt

Considering that the use of peat as a heat source for malting barley goes back centuries, the notion that whisky can be peaty is far from uncommon. But Penderyn distillery takes a slightly different approach: avoiding the use of peat itself, it uses previously peated casks to mature its whisky.

Penderyn Peated is made up of spirit matured in two different types of wood: first, in the ex-bourbon casks from Buffalo Trace, Kentucky, that feature in Penderyn's other expressions, and then in second-fill casks that previously held Scottish whisky. Some of the Scotch casks are from distilleries that make peaty whiskies, and so the light new-make spirit at the heart of Penderyn's style picks up some of the smoky flavors that have been soaked up by the wood while the former peaty contents of the cask were maturing.

The Scotch casks used by Penderyn will have been used at least twice before, as almost all Scotch casks have been filled with some kind of alcohol before they get to Scotland. Consequently, many of the traditional flavors, as well as colors, that such casks impart will already have been sucked out of the wood, leading to a more lightly flavored and colored Welsh whisky, although still with a hint of smoky peat.

Penderyn Peated is a very different prospect from a traditional peated whisky, and one that has been explored by other distillers. The Scotch casks impart a light smokiness that mingles with the flavors of the Penderyn spirit rather than overwhelming them. To release more of the muddy peat flavor, rather than that of peat smoke, just add a drop of water. **BA**

Tasting notes

A predominantly sweet nose has a hint of something savory hiding behind it, with sugared lemon and vanilla on a bed of light wood smoke. On the palate it has charcoal mixed in with apple, lime, and green wood, finishing with smoke tinged with sugar and stone dust.

Penderyn Portwood

Penderyn | www.welsh-whisky.co.uk

Region and country of origin Rhondda Cynon Taf,
Wales **Distillery** Penderyn, Penderyn
Alcohol content 41% abv
Style Single malt

A young distillery, Penderyn has spent a lot of time experimenting with different casks and finishes to perfect its core range. Experiments in the use of port casks to finish their whisky have led to a number of very popular single-cask releases, including one released in 2009 that Jim Murray named as the European Single Cask Whisky of the Year. However, some considered the whiskies a bit extreme, with high alcoholic strengths due to having been bottled straight from the cask. The experiments continued.

This expression, released in 2011, builds on the previous port cask-finished bottlings but is very much intended for the wider market. It is a vatting of a number of casks, rather than a single cask, and is designed to be much more accessible than the earlier experiments. The abv is diluted to 41 percent, a mere roar compared to the jet-engine blast of the earlier releases, and it has a rich but not overpowering palate. Despite the dilution, and in common with the other Penderyn bottlings, it is not chill-filtered, so it retains all of the spirit's flavor and oily mouthfeel. But appearance may suffer—at lower strengths, unfiltered whisky can become cloudy when cool or diluted.

Penderyn Portwood was originally produced to be distributed mainly in France, but fortunately it has also made available at the distillery. **BA**

Tasting notes

A fantastic mix of milk chocolate, orange, and marzipan leads into a rich body of black currant and polished wood. It finishes with blackberry, licorice, and vanilla.

Penderyn Sherrywood

Penderyn | www.welsh-whisky.co.uk

Region and country of origin Rhondda Cynon Taf,
Wales **Distillery** Penderyn, Penderyn
Alcohol content 46% abv
Style Single malt

Rather than play it safe and take a traditional Scottish or Irish approach to distilling, maturation, and finishing, the Penderyn distillery set out to build a new Welsh style of whisky. Distilling to a much higher abv than either Scottish or Irish malt whisky producers, and cutting from the still at between 86 and 92 percent abv, Penderyn achieves new-make spirit with fewer impurities—the elements that give the spirit flavor—and so the wood has a stronger influence. Penderyn claims that the initial high cut allows the whisky to mature faster; after this, the new make is diluted to an industry-standard 63.4 percent abv and is transferred to ex-sherry casks.

For the Sherrywood, Penderyn applies its normal maturation method by starting off with first- and second-fill bourbon barrels before decanting the liquid into finishing casks, in this case dry oloroso barrels. Oloroso casks are commonly used in the whisky industry because an understanding of the wood's profile makes it relatively easy to predict the effects of the casks on the maturing spirit.

Flavorwise, the whisky is different from its Scottish sherried counterparts. It veers more toward an Irish style, with a lighter body and a noticeable extraction of the sweetness of the sherry wood, against the heavier fruit often characteristic of Scottish whiskies. **BA**

Tasting notes

Nail-polish remover and pear drop on the nose, moving to glacé cherry, sponge cake, and cream. Buttered malt loaf adds earthy sweetness, softening the tannic finish.

Oak barrels in the Penderyn distillery, situated in Brecon Beacons National Park.

REST OF THE WORLD

Bakery Hill
2011

Bakery Hill | www.bakeryhilldistillery.com.au

Region and country of origin Victoria, Australia
Distillery Bakery Hill, Balwyn North
Alcohol content 46% abv
Style Single malt

With an owner by the name of David Baker, you might think that the Bakery Hill distillery is named after him. It's not, and a glance at the company emblem and the crossed shovel and pickax gives a clue why.

Bakery Hill is the smallest suburb of Ballarat, Victoria, and refers to a local hill, the site of the town's original bakery. (The distillery lies about 80 miles (130 km) to the east, at Balwyn North.) In 1854 a dispute between local miners and their British bosses came to a head here. Poor working conditions, high prices for equipment, and a system forcing workers to purchase tiny plots of land that were useless for mining led to a rebellion. Miners erected the Eureka Stockade to confront troops, and more than thirty died when the uprising was brutally put down. But the incident lit a flame, and in some quarters it is seen as the launching point for Australian democracy.

It is this sort of tenacity and national pride that has driven the Bakery Hill distillery here to succeed. David has been producing consistent, good-quality whisky for some time, cleverly combining it with a traditional, historical, and very Australian image. The whisky is still very hard to get hold of, but in 2011 there were signs that he was set to start exporting. **DR**

Tasting notes

A sweet, honeyed, uncomplicated malt both on nose and palate, and the taste brings to mind a spring orchard, with floral notes and a dose of apple and pear.

Bakery Hill
Cask Strength Peated

Bakery Hill | www.bakeryhilldistillery.com.au

Region and country of origin Victoria, Australia
Distillery Bakery Hill, Balwyn North
Alcohol content 60% abv
Style Single malt

On a recent visit to Buffalo Trace in Lexington, Kentucky, our guide explained why the barrel is so important to bourbon maturation. Someone asked if this wasn't the case in Scotland. "Oh, no," said the guide. "The barrel isn't important at all. The flavor of Scotch whisky comes from the peat. That's why the tastes vary from region to region. Each region has different flowers and trees, and they eventually die and get crushed down to become peat. So each region has different-flavored peat." Unfortunately, our guide was mistaken—the barrel is just as important in the making of Scotch as it is in the making of bourbon.

Where the guide did have a point, however, was that different flora and fauna produce different-flavored peat. In Tasmania, what they dig up in the bogs has a totally different character from the peats of Islay or Ireland. How distillers on different continents will pursue these regional differences in the future remains to be seen, but we're at the start of a journey.

Early Bakery Hill peated whisky was made with imported Scottish malt, although it was already on a different taste path. Locally peated whisky is now in play, and it's set to take Bakery Hill farther. Try this, and you will discover the difference for yourself. **DR**

Tasting notes

The nose is shy and wispy but the peat delivers on the palate. Some stewed fruit, exotic fruit, and full smoky peat. The peatiness lingers in the medium finish.

 Engraving by W.J. Smedley depicting the Eureka Stockade at Bakery Hill.

Bakery Hill Classic

Bakery Hill | www.bakeryhilldistillery.com.au

Region and country of origin Victoria, Australia
Distillery Bakery Hill, Balwyn North
Alcohol content 46% abv
Style Single malt

The development of Australian whisky has been rapid and varied, and it will be some years before it settles down and we get a good picture of the form it will take. From early on, though, it became clear that there would be a divide between the relatively bunched Tasmanian collective and the rest. Australia is a vast country, and mainland distilleries can be thousands of miles apart from each other. That can make it hard to establish any real national identity.

David Baker is without doubt among Australia's finest whisky makers. He is one of the longest-established distillers and a vocal supporter of the move to maintain high distilling standards so that Australia would be taken seriously across the world. His response to Australian whisky's issue with identity has been to seek out advice and to travel to distilleries to further his knowledge and to develop what he can offer. His hard work has paid off. For proof, just check out the Bakery Hill Web site and read the comments about why the distillery doesn't use caramel.

If Baker has a problem, however, it is that he operates out on a limb; as Tasmania bands together, it would seem that distilleries such as Bakery Hill have been cast adrift a bit. No matter, because the distiller has been in the game long enough to have alerted the opinion formers in Europe that his whisky more than stands up to scrutiny. This entry-level malt whisky is made using local Australian barley and is the culmination of an eight-hour distillation run. The new-make spirit is casked at 46 percent abv in American ex-bourbon casks. **DR**

Tasting notes

Delightfully clean and fresh, with spritely sweet cereal notes and some green apple and pear notes. It is not particularly complicated, but the balance of freshness and honeyed notes makes it just as it should be—an easy-drinking summer malt.

Bakery Hill Classic Cask Strength

Bakery Hill | www.bakeryhilldistillery.com.au

Region and country of origin Victoria, Australia
Distillery Bakery Hill, Balwyn North
Alcohol content 60% abv
Style Single malt

At the risk of making some appalling generalizations, Australians have long held a reputation for enterprise and endeavor, and these qualities can be found throughout the country's fledgling whisky industry. Bill Lark, owner of Lark distillery, won the support of Tasmania's law officers and politicians to change the outdated prohibition laws so that distilling could once again take place. Now he's shaping a Tasmanian whisky industry that capitalizes on the island's splendid abundance of clean and healthy resources. And he's not the only one.

When the government sought to help the country's struggling spirits business by scrapping minimum maturation times, serious whisky makers opposed the idea and insisted on a two-year maturation period before a malt spirit could be called whisky, thereby ensuring that all-important medium- to long-term credibility around the world.

The Bakery Hill distillery clearly has this credibility in abundance. David Baker, a former biochemist, opened it in 1998, and his first single-malt whisky was made available in the fall of 2003. He has slowly but surely established a solid reputation in Australia and beyond since those early days, but it was the Classic Cask Strength release that successfully helped the distillery make the leap from the bottom of the world to the attention of whisky experts in Europe. Smaller 13-gallon (50-liter) casks as well as 26-gallon (100-liter) ones are used in production to accelerate maturation, and, at this higher strength, there are some intense flavors not present in the standard bottling. **DR**

Tasting notes

The whisky is still sweet and cerealy on the nose, but the relatively high strength allows orange and other citrus flavors to find their way into the mix. On the palate it is rich, dense, and intense, with a mouth-coating oiliness that is dominated by fruity notes.

Bakery Hill Classic Peated

Bakery Hill | www.bakeryhilldistillery.com.au

Region and country of origin Victoria, Australia
Distillery Bakery Hill, Balwyn North
Alcohol content 46% abv
Style Single malt

As more and more countries produce whisky, it seems inevitable that the industry will be challenged by upstarts, and some long-standing truisms will be questioned. It's already happening. Because whisky can be ridiculously complicated, it's been explained away in a sort of industry shorthand. Some of the newer producers argue that the shorthand could be misleading and even detrimental to their businesses. What's the point of declaring an age statement on a bottle if you don't consider cask size and type, and climactic issues that affect maturation such as heat, heat extremes, humidity, and barometric pressure, they argue? And who's to say you need twelve years' maturation to make a premium whisky? Australia illustrates the last point on its own. It's such a vast country that there will be maturation differences even between Tasmania and the mainland.

This is a young whisky, but those maturation issues and the fact that peat can enhance and complement youthful barley combine to make this a big hitter that shouts very loudly indeed. It has to, of course, because David Baker can call on few resources with which to market and promote his whisky, and has nowhere near enough money to build his brands in the way they deserve. There are no economies of scale, either, so the whisky is at premium boutique bottle level. And yet, despite every hurdle, David's still in the game. This is arguably in Australia's front line with Lark and Sullivans Cove. In 2011 David spoke about having enough stock to start modest exports to Europe. If you get the chance to try this, take it. **DR**

Tasting notes

Gooseberry, green apples, and banana skin over a gritty, earthy peat base. A very natural bouquet. There's some sweetness, but it's held in place, stopping it from becoming sickly. The whisky has a medium finish. A second sip is guaranteed to follow quickly.

Bakery Hill Double Wood

Bakery Hill | www.bakeryhilldistillery.com.au

Region and country of origin Victoria, Australia
Distillery Bakery Hill, Balwyn North
Alcohol content 46% abv
Style Single malt

The biggest problems facing distilleries located on the peripheries of recognized whisky markets are, first, how to get their whisky to those markets; second, how to transport it at a cost that the consumer is willing to pay, albeit indirectly; and third, how to create a product that is interesting enough to tempt someone to buy it instead of a recognized Scottish, Irish, or American world-beater. Australia has long experience and form here. Its wine producers have stormed the Old World and competed at every level with the finest wine makers. Can whisky makers follow suit?

Truth be told, it has a long way to go. A substantial number of Scottish distilleries are older than Australia is, and, of course, Scottish whisky making goes back hundreds of years beyond that. Australian whisky is in its infancy, and, as time goes by, it may decide its future isn't in the Old World at all but in the emerging markets of Asia, India, and Africa. For some years now, it has increasingly recognized its Southeast Asian markets. If it does attempt to "take coals to Newcastle," it will do so by stressing the high-quality boutique and artisanal nature of its spirit over the large-scale malt production in Scotland.

If so, the Double Wood is the sort of whisky that will be in the vanguard. This is arguably Bakery Hill's most ambitious and gutsy release so far. The name refers to casks of American bourbon and French oak, in both 13-gallon (50-liter) and 26-gallon (100-liter) sizes. You sense it will get better with time, and already it is proving to be a well-made whisky, and one that is bubbling with character. **DR**

Tasting notes

The fruitiest and juiciest of the Bakery Hill whiskies, with some syrupy exotic fruit and sweet spice on the nose, and chewy orange, plum, and honey on the palate. Just enough oak and spice in the mix to keep it all honest. A medium and sweet conclusion.

Belgrove White Rye

Belgrove
www.belgrovedistillery.com.au

Region and country of origin Tasmania, Australia
Distillery Belgrove, near Kempton
Alcohol content 40% abv
Style White rye whisky

Many assume that Australian whisky is all single malt made in the Scottish way. But on Tasmania they're trying lots of different methods and styles, including a triple-distilled Irish-style whisky and a corn mash recipe not unlike the whiskies of Kentucky. And then there's this one, made by farmer Peter Bignell on a small still built in an old stable, with the still and fermenting vessels in one horse stall and the maturing barrels in another. Like several others in Tasmania, he took up whisky making as a hobby but has sought out the advice of Bill Lark from Lark distillery.

Bignell wanted to do something different, so he decided to make use of the plentiful supply of rye he grows on his farm. He also decided to build his own stills and fermenting vessels, and he's come up with a system in which there is no wastage. His copper pot still is fired with biodiesel produced from waste cooking oil, which makes Peter's minidistillery quite possibly the most environmentally friendly in the world. He only distills once a week or so, and he only started in 2011, so his efforts are at the very earliest stage. Spirit matured for a few months tastes understandably sappy and linseedy, which is why this white rye, bottled at 40 percent, is such a revelation. Its taste is gentle and less spicy taste than American ryes, making for very easy aperitif-style drinking. **DR**

Tasting notes

The nose of this clear rye spirit is gentle and rounded, but the taste has more in common with pastis. Toffee, licorice, and aniseed blend with the gentlest of spices.

Hellyers Road Original

Hellyers Road
www.hellyersroaddistillery.com.au

Region and country of origin Tasmania, Australia
Distillery Hellyers Road, near Burnie
Alcohol content 46.2% abv
Style Single malt

Hellyers Road distillery is situated near Burnie, some 200 miles (320 km) northwest of Hobart. It lies not far from Chasm and Sulphur creeks and west of Prospect Bay. The distillery is named after Henry Hellyer, who worked for the Van Dieman's Land Company. In 1825 Hellyer was given the task of building a pioneering road through the rugged wilderness of northwest Tasmania. The aim was to provide an artery for the growing town of Emu Bay, now known as Burnie. Actually named the Old Surrey Road, his road will always be known by many as Hellyer's Road.

When it was decided to make whisky here, the distillery owners chose to recognize Hellyer's determination. "We've been inspired by Henry's spirit to create a product that captures the very taste and character of Tasmania," they say. "Henry's life was his work—a life we think is worth celebrating."

Peated, lightly peated, and pinot-noir finished versions are made in addition to this standard bottling, but this is the first one I have tried. It is a rapidly evolving malt, throwing off its grainy and cerealy youthfulness and developing a richer, sweeter, and fuller taste as it benefits from increased maturity. Hellyers Road Original is made with local barley and water, and matured in American oak casks. It is bottled at the unusual strength of 46.2 percent abv. **DR**

Tasting notes

The nose shows fresh fruit on cereal and vanilla notes. The warming palate is creamy in texture and delivers the generous, malty flavors promised by the nose.

Belgrove distillery labels are completed by hand during bottling.

Hellyers Road Single Malt Whisky

Hellyers Road | www.hellyersroaddistillery.com.au

Region and country of origin Tasmania, Australia
Distillery Hellyers Road, near Burnie
Alcohol content 43.6% abv
Style Single malt

Tasmania's whisky industry is only two decades old, but it has already been on a remarkable journey. The process of making malt spirit is a relatively straightforward one, and it can be done on a very small scale indeed. While we tend to view the world of whisky through the lens of the five big whisky-making nations, there are some distilleries that make spirit in small batches for their own communities, do not need or want publicity and so don't seek it out, and are content with their lot as very small batch producers. There are even a couple of fully functional model distilleries in existence that produce barely a cupful of spirit on each run.

Hellyers Road isn't small, but it seems content to stay outside the recognized whisky world. You rarely find it beyond Australia, but it is one of the older and, indeed, bigger distilleries. In the past it made the common but regrettable mistake of bottling its spirit too young. It overproduced, so it has had periods when it didn't operate, prompting rumors that it had shut down. And yet here it is with a perfectly acceptable malt that it's telling nobody about.

Hellyers Road had an unusual whisky story to tell. It was set up by a consortium from Tasmania's milk producers in response to a threat from fierce competition in the dairy industry from mainland Australia. Should their milk business crash, the producers decided, whisky would provide a future for them. The milk business has survived but somebody at the company is still making an effort with the whisky, too. **DR**

Tasting notes

Sweet but vegetal nose, with hay and summer meadow notes. On the palate there are gooseberry, gentle spice, briars, and cut grass. Quite dry and aperitif-like, with some late pepper and a touch of fruit in the finish.

Hellyers Road barrels portray surveyor Henry Hellyer and his dog. ➜

Lark
Distiller's Selection

Lark | www.larkdistillery.com.au

Region and country of origin Tasmania, Australia
Distillery Lark, Hobart
Alcohol content 46% abv
Style Single malt

Perhaps the greatest task faced by Australian distillers has been to persuade the rest of the world to take Australian whisky seriously. Neighbors who seek to profit by taking shortcuts do not help—one guy in New Zealand uses stainless-steel vats to make neutral spirit, to which he adds flavor and color by dipping in a "teabag" containing oak shavings and flavorings.

At one point the amount of imitation and poor-quality whisky in Australia far outweighed the amount of good whisky available. Then the Australian government offered to make life easier for spirits producers by removing restrictions on minimum maturation times. Horrified, the more respectable whisky makers asked for the minimum periods to be maintained so that they could distance themselves from the cowboys and sharks in the eyes of the world.

The ratio of bad to good is changing rapidly now. A few more bottlings like this, and the Australians won't have anything to prove when it comes to premium malt. This mix of different casks from Lark was an early indicator that some of its malts were coming of age. This is a whisky that isn't just matured to a sufficient age—it consists of well-made spirit, and it has been excellently put together. **DR**

Tasting notes

Chewier than a bag of soft toffee. Lots going on here—a subtle mix of orange, mint, intense cocoa, and in the finish, milk chocolate, wood, and toffee.

Lark
Para Single Malt

Lark | www.larkdistillery.com.au

Region and country of origin Tasmania, Australia
Distillery Lark, Hobart
Alcohol content 43% abv
Style Single malt

The Lark distillery occupies two sites. One is in the wine-growing region of Tasmania and is the site of the distillery itself. The other is called the Cellar Door and has a central Hobart location with a shop and a bar. And here, should you be lucky enough to make the trip, you will get the chance to experience versions of Lark whisky unavailable anywhere else.

That's because up at the distillery they're very much into experimentation. They do everything manually, tasting and nosing the spirit run to judge when to make the cut. What Lark has discovered is that its whisky works best in small quarter casks, and particularly ones that had previously contained port.

This version of Lark is a malt that has been aged in casks made with wood that was previously used to mature vintage Para port, some of it a hundred years old. Bill Lark says that he had to go to great lengths to secure the casks, but it was worth it because it has brought a special dimension to his whiskies, and certainly you sense a certain coming of age. This is a fully grown malt with no nods to the sappy, rootsy notes that suggest youth. It is an example of fine quality distilling and marks the moment when Lark stepped into the premier league. **DR**

Tasting notes

Rich and fruity on the nose with overripe apple and cherry cough drop on the palate, and some stewed red and black berry fruits. Almost liqueurlike and intense.

Lark Single Cask

Lark | www.larkdistillery.com.au

Region and country of origin Tasmania, Australia
Distillery Lark, Hobart
Alcohol content 43% abv
Style Single malt

Bill Lark started producing small batches of this flagship whisky in 1992, and his pioneering efforts have been emulated ever since then. Like many distillers across the world, he has made mistakes, such as bottling immature spirit too early. But overall his efforts have resulted in quality Tasmanian whisky, and he has been generous with his time when asked for help by would-be distillers. Tasmania is growing into a major whisky hub, and Bill Lark has been at the center of the story. The island has ten or so distilleries, and most have the hand of Lark on them somewhere.

The core malt for Lark Single Cask originates as local Franklin barley from the Cascade Brewery, and the whisky is lightly peated. About 50 percent of the grain used is peated. The spirit is matured in 26-gallon (100-liter) casks, and some of it is now eight years old, but this is only a guide as to maturity and quality—the climate and humidity in Tasmania is markedly different from Scotland, and the maturation is accelerated significantly. That fact also means that a higher proportion of spirit is lost to the angels and, as with all distilleries in this part of the world, production and transport costs put the distillery at a disadvantage. But the whisky is excellent and well worth a try. **DR**

Tasting notes

Pepper and peat on the nose. The palate is oily, chunky, and intense with bright grain and green fruits dancing over an earthy, dusty, and polished oak and peat carpet.

Lark Single Malt Cask Strength

Lark | www.larkdistillery.com.au

Region and country of origin Tasmania, Australia
Distillery Lark, Hobart
Alcohol content 58% abv
Style Single malt

The success of Bill Lark's whiskies has meant that he has had to choose between distilling, being an ambassador worldwide for his brand, dealing with sales and marketing, or focusing on business and finance. Some former blenders and distillers live on the road, talking and teaching about their whiskies, while others shun the spotlight. These days Bill's daughter Kirsty does the whisky making and his wife handles the business, while Bill focuses on the growing international nature of his firm. He works with the Tasmanian authorities to showcase the tourist potential of the island, and, strangely, many visitors want to see the source of his distillery's peat.

There's an irony in the fact that an island noted for its clean air, beautiful shorelines, and stunning scenery should attract so much attention for its peat bogs, but that has indeed been the case. Because of the island's unique flora and fauna, the peat is very different from that found in Scotland. The effects of peat on this version of Lark are astounding. The combination of sweet peat, chewy and gristy cereal, and longer maturation times—which give the whisky weight and depth—results in a delightful whisky worthy of a place in any whisky cabinet. **DR**

Tasting notes

Three flavors pull in different directions but result in a balanced and easy-drinking malt. Sweet, gingerish barley; earthy, spicy peat; and soft, clean, green fruits.

Limeburners Barrel Bottlings

Great Southern Distilling Company
www.distillery.com.au

Region and country of origin Western Australia
Distillery Great Southern Distilling Co., Albany
Alcohol content Varies around 60% abv
Style Single malt

Great Southern Distilling Company started making whisky in 2004 in Western Australia, and its malt whisky, Limeburners, is now both established and at the forefront of the whisky explosion.

Although Australian distillers have historically stood together and presented a united front to the world, the formation of the Tasmanian Distillers and Allied Industry Group has ring-fenced the island's distillers from the likes of Limeburners on the mainland. But it is a vast country, and having a diverse and fractured whisky industry may be a sign of its growing confidence and maturity.

Limeburners is made at a small distillery that has a history of spirit and liqueur production. The driving force behind the distillery is company director Cameron Syme, whose aim is to provide Australia with a quality single malt that will be embraced by his country's enthusiasts and connoisseurs. He produces small-batch bottlings at cask strength. The whisky is not cheap, but it is beautifully presented, and it has been making major strides forward after a shaky start. On the strength of this release, Syme's well on the way to achieving his goal—a genuinely different but impressive Australian malt. **DR**

Tasting notes

This is a big, oily, and complex whisky. With water it explodes into life, with notes of ginger, eucalyptus, and allspice pepping up green fruits.

Limeburners Barrel M23

Great Southern Distilling Company
www.distillery.com.au

Region and country of origin Western Australia
Distillery Great Southern Distilling Co., Albany
Alcohol content 61% abv
Style Single malt

Whisky lovers dream of setting up a distillery, but the reality is often more like a nightmare. A year of outlay building and equipping a distillery often takes its toll, not helped by a minimum of three years paying overheads without any income. At age three, when the spirit becomes whisky, the accountants want to see some cash, but bottling an immature and inferior spirit, often at a high price due to the boutique nature of the distillery, is fraught with risk. If the whisky is poor, unbalanced, and unpalatable, a reputation can be fatally damaged right at the outset.

Many distillers cringe when they recall their earliest efforts; in Australia, pioneers Patrick Maguire at Sullivans Cove and Bill Lark at Lark have both distanced themselves from their first bottlings. On the strength of this whisky and recent bottlings, it is probable that Limeburners are already feeling the same way. But the tentative bottlings from before 2010 have turned into graceful swan whiskies, big, bright, and confident. Most important, perhaps, they demonstrate a distinctive character of their own.

This is the start of a journey into the whisky outback. Where Limeburners will end up is unknown, but it is likely be a very exciting place indeed. **DR**

Tasting notes

Rich and liqueurlike. Red berries, peach, and plum surf over a gloopy, rich, and full grain heart. Sweet and intense, underpinned by nail polish and new wood.

Limeburners are the only single malts made in Western Australia. ➡

Limeburners
Hand Distilled
western australian
Single Malt Whisky
BARREL STRENGTH
Barrel M23
BOTTLE
021
PRODUCT OF AUSTRALIA

Nant Port

Nant | www.nantdistillery.com

Region and country of origin Tasmania, Australia
Distillery Nant, Bothwell
Alcohol content 43% abv
Style Single malt

The Nant distillery stands at the heart of the Tasmanian Central Highlands, a region settled in the 1820s. The whisky distillery is relatively new, however. A plentiful supply of pure water and good-quality barley make it a natural home for malt production. Bottling only started in 2010 in relatively small quantities. Perhaps learning from the likes of Tasmania distillery's Patrick Maguire and Lark's Bill Lark, the distillery seems to have hit the ground running, picking up critical acclaim for its malts. Respected whisky writer Jim Murray scored the inaugural malt 91.5 and described it as "a statement of intent."

The distillery is about an hour from Hobart in a part of the country that is sparse, rugged, and down-to-earth. Make the effort to get there, though, and a unique tourist experience awaits, with tours of both the Nant distillery and the historic watermill—in commercial use since 1823, the mill still grinds flour. A Highland cottage on the site sleeps nine people and is available for hire, should you so wish, and the region offers shooting, fishing, and golf. Whisky enthusiasts have the opportunity to buy their own cask of Nant.

If you cannot make it all the way to Tasmania, never fear. Despite the small quantity of whisky made, Nant has secured export deals in France and Canada as well as mainland Australia. **DR**

Tasting notes

Slightly oily and sappy barley taste of a young whisky—it's little more than three years old—but pleasant red berry and citrus notes and an attractive sweetness to it.

Nant Sherry

Nant | www.nantdistillery.com

Region and country of origin Tasmania, Australia
Distillery Nant, Bothwell
Alcohol content 43% abv
Style Single malt

Tasmanian whisky is still in its relative infancy. Lark and Tasmania distilleries are the island's longest established ones, but six or seven others are following behind. Some of them are in old sheds and tiny; others, such as Nant, are properly established. What is certainly the case, though, is that the island is starting to establish a unique identity. Much of the whisky is matured in port casks, for instance. The island style of malt tends to be rich in green and red fruits, and a number of the distilleries, including Nant, use the same style of boutique copper still made by an Australian company. The stills are small, so it's a bit like seeing a Scottish distillery in miniature.

Nant distillery is a delight. It has been set up to take advantage of the Tasmanian tourist boom, and it's properly geared up for visitors. The distillery boasts both wood and stainless-steel washbacks, giving a rare chance to compare the two, and they can do small runs of spirit for experimentation.

This particular version of its whisky, finished in sherry casks, is proving to be the island's lightest and sweetest and has attracted a substantial following, particularly among women. On summer evenings there are far worse places to sit than in the stylish bar terrace with a glass of this and a large lump of locally produced Tasmanian goat cheese. **DR**

Tasting notes

Young, sweet, and not particularly sophisticated but with a soft, rounded sweet malt flavor set off by some peach and apricot notes. Very drinkable.

← Nant distillery prides itself on its pristine Central Highlands water.

Old Hobart Overeem Port Cask Single Malt

Old Hobart
www.oldhobartdistillery.com

Region and country of origin Tasmania, Australia
Distillery Old Hobart, Hobart
Alcohol content 43% abv and cask strength
Style Single malt

Casey Overeem's interest in distilling stems from the 1980s, when he traveled to visit relatives in Finland and became fascinated with the microdistilleries that many families had in their cellars. He now oversees operations at Old Hobart distillery, which received its license in 2005. At the time of writing, no whisky had been bottled, but four-year-old samples of the sherry cask and this, the port cask version—both at cask strength—confirmed that, six months before it was to be bottled, the whisky was already extremely good.

Tasmanian distilling took a definite step forward in 2011. Lark and Tasmania have whisky that would be considered premium-aged even in central Europe, even without the maturation advantages the Tasmanian climate offers. But younger whiskies such as these are making a mockery of the traditional understanding of age statement. To mark their growing confidence, the distillers of Tasmania formed their own "appellation contrôlée" with the launch of the Tasmanian Distillers and Allied Industry Group. Old Hobart will bottle normal- and cask-strength versions of sherry, bourbon, and port casks, and a Distiller's Edition that will mix all three cask-strength styles, making a total of seven Old Hobart expressions. **DR**

Tasting notes

Spice and mint on the nose, with further spice on the palate accompanied by licorice and fruit notes. Deliciously creamy with a superb clean finish.

Old Hobart Overeem Sherry Cask Single Malt

Old Hobart
www.oldhobartdistillery.com

Region and country of origin Tasmania, Australia
Distillery Old Hobart, Hobart
Alcohol content 43% abv and cask strength
Style Single malt

The distillery name of Old Hobart is a historic reference to Tasmania's original distilling industry. The first whisky from Tasmania was distilled in 1822 by Thomas Haigh Midwood in what was then Van Diemen's Land. By 1824, the island had a grand total of sixteen distilleries, but fifteen years later, Governor John Franklin outlawed all distilling, and that was that for legal whisky on the island for more than 150 years.

With the opening of Old Hobart in 2005, Tasmania passed the halfway mark in returning to those heady days of sixteen distilleries. In a very short space of time, Tasmania has become one of the biggest whisky-making regions in the world, now possessing more distilleries than Islay, the whole of Canada, the whole of Japan, or the whole of Ireland.

Whether Old Hobart's whisky tastes anything like the pioneering spirit cannot be ascertained, but Casey Overeem's knowledge and understanding of stills would suggest that the new liquid will be much more refined than its ancestor. At the time of writing, the whisky had reached four years old and was due for bottling. Overeem and his team plan a total of seven Old Hobart expressions in all, four of which will be bottled at cask strength. **DR**

Tasting notes

Intense, almost overwhelming flavor, incredibly rich and vibrant. Sherry to the fore, backed by plenty of fruit. Very well made, this will get even better with age.

Raymond B. Whiskey

The Hoochery
www.hoochery.com.au

Region and country of origin Kimberley, Western Australia **Distillery** Hoochery, Kununurra
Alcohol content 40% abv
Style Corn mash

There is an assumption that when a new country enters the world of whisky, its distilleries will look to Scotland for inspiration and its output will attempt to emulate single malt from there. But why should it? Bourbon and Irish whiskey are both distinctively different in both production and taste, and there are no rules in Asia, South America, or Australia saying that whisky must be made in a particular way.

Australia has a long and proud record of entrepreneurship, so if there's a gap in the market, someone will fill it. Pose the question, "Is Tasmania Australia's Islay?" and the honest answer is, "No, the island's whiskies are far too diverse for that."

This product of the Hoochery distillery is an American-style corn mash whisky filtered through charcoal in the manner of Tennessee whiskeys such as Jack Daniel's. The distillery is best known for its rum, for which it has established a strong reputation in the locality. The whisky, it would seem, is a labor of love. The people at the Hoochery promise an honest-to-goodness genuine taste experience. "With the Hoochery you get no gimmicks, no fancy labels, just bloody-good-dinky-di Kimberley spirit!" they claim. You can't say fairer than that. **DR**

Tasting notes

Smooth, rounded, and sweet, but undoubtedly young, Raymond B. has more in common with moonshine corn whiskey than Tennessee whiskey or bourbon.

Sullivans Cove Cask Strength 10-Year-Old

Tasmania
www.tasmaniadistillery.com

Region and country of origin Tasmania, Australia
Distillery Tasmania, Cambridge, Hobart
Alcohol content 60% abv
Style Single malt

Tasmania distillery wasn't Tasmania's very first, but its story stretches back to the earliest days. Like several others, it can claim credibility by turning to history. Tasmania was occupied by the British and used as a penal colony in the early part of the nineteenth century, and the island has a long history of distilling from those days. The distillery was established in 1994 on the banks of the River Derwent at Sullivans Cove, the site where the British planted their flag and began to build Hobart, Australia's second-oldest city.

The distillations of the Sullivans Cove brand began in 1995 on a single pot still. However, the modern era only began in earnest with a change in ownership in 2003 and a move to a new site at Cambridge, a quiet village on the outskirts of Hobart. The original pot still, all the equipment, and the maturing casks were moved there, and the original still is now capable of producing 6,340 gallons (24,000 liters) of spirit each year. This 10-Year-Old stretches back to before the change of ownership but is benefiting from its long time in casks, the equivalent of up to eighteen years in Scotland. After a shaky start, the Tasmania distillery is making full, fruity, and pleasant whiskies. **DR**

Tasting notes

A well-made and above-average malt, with soft yellow and green fruit, some vanilla, and sweet spice. This would not look out of place among some Speysiders.

Sullivans Cove Cask Strength 11-Year-Old

Tasmania | www.tasmaniadistillery.com

Region and country of origin Tasmania, Australia
Distillery Tasmania, Cambridge, Hobart
Alcohol content 60% abv
Style Single malt

Tasmania distillery is neither the largest nor the oldest distillery in Tasmania, but it was the one that achieved the greatest distribution early on. Its Sullivans Cove brand, probably the most famous name in Australian whisky, has been at the forefront of an Australian drive for international recognition. More than most, however, it suffered from "too-early syndrome." Having to return some of the initial investment in year three, and the temptation to bottle immature whisky to meet an unexpectedly high demand meant that some drinkers were put off by sappy, cereal whisky. Or, to put it another way, its early bottlings were, to borrow a phrase from Australian cricketing great Ricky Ponting, "a bit ordinary." Once you have earned a reputation, good or bad, it is hard to change it. It is harder still if you are far away from your markets, and Tasmania is certainly that.

Distillery manager Patrick Maguire talks of three categories of Sullivans Cove whisky: the poor, very early efforts; a middle, average, and unexceptional period; and the most recent, top-quality spirit. This bottling is almost certainly the oldest Australian whisky ever, and presumably it comes from the second, average period, but it rises above the norm because it has spent extra years in good-quality American oak, gaining a fuller and richer flavor.

If you were put off by Sullivans Cove in the past, now is the time to revisit it. The big questions are how much older can Tasmanian whisky go, and how good will the eleven- and twelve-year-olds distilled in 2006 and after turn out to be? We watch with interest. **DR**

Tasting notes

Gold color and fairly clear. Filled with rich notes of chocolate and nuts, with a strain of fruit that adds longevity to the mouth taste. A hint of spice emerges and blends beautifully. This is a meaty, long whisky that needs to be savored.

Sullivans Cove Cask Strength French Oak Port Cask

Tasmania | www.tasmaniadistillery.com

Region and country of origin Tasmania, Australia
Distillery Tasmania, Cambridge, Hobart
Alcohol content 60% abv
Style Single malt

Hear the words "Sullivans Cove" and what is the picture you get in your mind? Craggy shores, deep blue waters, and waves crashing on to a beach perhaps? This whisky—the richest, fullest, and most exotic of the Sullivans Cove range due to the fact that it has been matured in French oak casks previously used to mature port—suggests a product from a lavish and stylish distillery. But nothing could be further from the reality.

The distillery is among the oldest on the island, but it has gone through distinct stages and is currently under the ownership of Patrick Maguire. It has matured into a good-quality whisky, as this particular bottling illustrates, and has outgrown its home. In the coming years, the distillery will move to a new site, where it can start living up to its name and take full advantage of the growing whisky tourism that Tasmania is attracting.

Where Maguire will take this is anyone's guess, but he doesn't shy away from the island's past as a penal colony—he has even used it for advertising purposes. Indeed, whisky is intrinsically linked to the island's past. So widespread was the production of malt spirit among prisoners on the island that it started to threaten food supplies, even though Tasmania is richly endowed with natural resources. Eventually distillation was prohibited altogether, a ban that lasted some one hundred years, until the late 1990s, when Bill Lark successfully lobbied for the law to be changed. Patrick Maguire worked for Lark originally and is now proving himself with whiskies like this. **DR**

Tasting notes

Rich, full, fruity, and liqueurlike, with a bouncing, strutting, loud, and oily mouthfeel, but not a battering ram by any means. There is a great deal going on here, and Sullivans Cove is certainly playing in the big boys' league these days.

Sullivans Cove Double Cask

Tasmania | www.tasmaniadistillery.com

Region and country of origin Tasmania, Australia
Distillery Tasmania, Cambridge, Hobart
Alcohol content 40% abv
Style Single malt

Australians have never been slow to spot an opportunity and turn it to their advantage. And just as the country's wine producers have traded on their informality, approachability, and modernity at the expense of their sometimes staid and aloof Old World counterparts, so too are Australian distillers increasingly stressing their small-batch, handcrafted, and boutique approach to whisky making, in contrast to the high-volume methods of big distilleries owned by global drinks giants—Scotland comes to mind.

Take this puff from the Tasmania distillery's Web site: "As has been the case with Australia's wine producers over the last two decades, the whisky producers from Down Under are now breaking down barriers and traditions with a no nonsense 'can do' approach and bringing the pleasures of single malt whisky to more people than ever before."

Not so very long ago, such a confident statement might have rung hollow. Even as recently as 2008, Australian whiskies were unpredictably hit or miss—and mainly miss. No one could claim that there existed a small lake of world-class whisky, but things have changed and a new era is dawning. Sample after sample of whisky from Australia is clearing the bar with ease, this one included.

"Double cask" refers to the fact that the spirit is matured in top-quality casks made of American white oak and used originally to mature bourbon on the one hand, and French oak casks from wine and port production on the other. This is a confident whisky and one that deserves acclaim. **DR**

Tasting notes

A mix of whisky matured in bourbon and French oak casks, this is a delight. Handcrafted, naturally colored, and non-chill-filtered, this is gutsy, oily, and powerful whisky with a nice mix of fruit and spice held together by mouth-coating oils.

Ships on the Derwent River in 1916, with Sullivans Cove and Hobart beyond. ➜

Timboon Single Malt

Timboon Railway Shed | www.timboondistillery.com

Region and country of origin Victoria, Australia
Distillery Timboon Railway Shed, Timboon
Alcohol content 40% abv
Style Single malt

This splendidly named distillery is in the southwest of Victoria, an area known for illicit distilling and the legendary exploits of the great pioneers who built the railways. Timboon is close to the site where notorious distiller Tom Delaney made illicit mountain dew whisky throughout the 1880s and 1890s, to the chagrin of the local police. If you are familiar with the classic album *Born Sandy Devotional* by Australian cult band the Triffids, the nearby Great Ocean Road will no doubt stir up evocative images.

The distillery does, indeed, occupy an old railway shed, built to store provisions in about 1910, when Australia was still being discovered. The shed also incorporates a restaurant that has earned itself a strong reputation by specializing in locally sourced and seasonal food. Southwest Victoria has received a considerable boost from the tourist authorities and is a visitor's dream. There is a 21-mile (34-km) rail trail that offers a chance to enjoy great scenery and spot Australian wildlife. Visitors daunted by that distance should know that the trail is flat for the first 1¾ miles (3 km). The distillery is small and compact, and visitors are permitted to come and watch the spirit being made from behind a specially installed glass panel.

The whisky at Timboon distillery is produced in the traditional Scottish way and looks to the great Scottish distilleries for inspiration. But the finished product is markedly different from anything in Scotland, with unusual, almost European, fruity liqueur notes. It is an odd dram, then, but interesting, and part of a delightful Australian whisky story. **DR**

Tasting notes

A weird and wonderful mix of youthful sweet barley, cocoa, and eucalyptus on the nose and ginger barley, green apple, vanilla, orange liqueur, and menthol notes on the palate. Spice and chocolate notes in the finish.

Trapper's Hut Single Cask

Trapper's Hut | www.trappershut.com.au

Region and country of origin Tasmania, Australia
Distillery Tasmania, Cambridge, Hobart
Alcohol content 45% abv
Style Single malt

Such is the speed of change and development in Australian whisky that plotting it accurately is a little like trying to plant a flag in quicksand. The picture's evolving at such a pace that by the time you read this, another three distilleries will have opened and three more will have bottled whisky for the first time. Much of the whisky will be sold only locally, and you won't get to taste it. Furthermore, a lack of clear information and the tendency for some companies, such as this one, to source their whisky from other distilleries, makes for a complex and confusing picture.

Nevertheless, watch for bottles from the new wave of distilleries that, at the time of writing, were on the point of releasing their first whiskies. These include Triptych distillery, located in the wine-producing region of Yarra Valley, and the Valley distillery, Essendon Fields, both in Victoria; The Wild Swan Distilling Company, located in Swan Valley, Western Australia, which was established in 2002; and Mackeys, an Irish-style triple-distilled whiskey in Tasmania. Trapper's Hut doesn't distill—it bottles single casks from Tasmania distillery—and finding it will require some effort. But as Tasmania is bottling clean, rich, and fully matured whisky these days, the Trapper's Hut releases provide a fascinating snapshot into whisky evolution. Matured for at least eight years in bourbon casks, the whisky doesn't sell in big quantities, but the distillery bottles in a variety of sizes. Typically, the malt is sweet, cereal, and unpeated, although in tasting notes for the first cask released the distillery mentioned a faint whiff of peat. **DR**

Tasting notes

A young, grainy nose, but the palate is fuller, with a smooth, rounded, fruity, vanilla, Speyside-style delivery. There is some sweetness with apple notes, but overall it's a clean, fruity, and easy-drinking whisky with a smooth finish.

Amrut 100

Amrut | www.amrutdistilleries.com

Region and country of origin Karnataka, India
Distillery Amrut, Bangalore
Alcohol content 57.1% abv
Style Single malt

From anyone else but Amrut, this particular whisky might face the charge of being a marketing gimmick. Indeed, if it did not taste so good, you would dismiss it as a victory of style over substance. But it actually represents a determined attempt to continue to break new ground, and if that seems contrived and convoluted, put it down to overenthusiasm. As Amrut managing director Neelakanta Rao Jagdale has admitted, "Getting established is one thing, but staying up there is going to be a tough task."

If the Amrut company continues to come up with whiskies such as this, its future is assured. The name references elements of its production process; it's all about 100. The whisky is matured in 100-liter (26-gallon) virgin oak casks and is bottled in 100-centiliter (33.8-ounce) bottles. Only a hundred bottles were dispatched to each sales territory. It is also bottled at 100 British proof, the equivalent of 57.1 percent alcohol by volume (abv), or 114.2 American proof. Confused? The abv measure means that in any hundred units there are 57.1 units of pure alcohol. The British proof system is based on a historic measure; 100 proof measures the exact strength of alcohol where gunpowder soaked in it would ignite when lit by a match; this happens at 57.1 percent abv. The American proof system is simply double the abv.

Because of the limited availability of this whisky, you are likely to struggle to find it—it was released in the wake of the hysteria over Amrut Fusion, and the bottles were snapped up quickly. But it is well worth the effort to seek it out. **DR**

Tasting notes

Amrut has moved a long way from its entry-level malts in a relatively short period of time, and the sharp chile pepper, nutmeg, and cardamom spice hit is intense, complex, and aggressive, with berry and green fruit notes in the mix. The finish is long.

Amrut Cask Strength

Amrut | www.amrutdistilleries.com

Region and country of origin Karnataka, India
Distillery Amrut, Bangalore
Alcohol content 61.8% abv
Style Single malt

Amrut Cask Strength was a major breakthrough for the company. The decision to release the original whiskies at cask strength was akin to someone turning up their amplifier from six to eleven and demanding that people pay attention to the music.

At around the time the whisky was released, two landmark moments occurred. The first was the decision by the late whisky lover and Glaswegian public house licensee Ken Storrie to slip Amrut unannounced into a whisky tasting at his pub, the Pot Still. It went down a storm, was hailed by surprised Scottish whisky enthusiasts, and sent a wave of electricity through the world of whisky.

The second event was a decision by Amrut's management to attend Whisky Live London, and to risk trial by expert in the company of some of the world's finest whiskies. The word went around the show quickly. This author remembers being dragged to the stand to taste the whisky by the Scotch Malt Whisky Society's Annabel Meikle, who described it as being like a ten- or twelve-year-old Bruichladdich. That was a good marker. Amrut's management always believed that it would take recognition from outside India for its whiskies to be accepted at home. What those prescient men probably hadn't anticipated was the speed at which that would happen.

"When people started to compare Amrut to twelve-year-old Scottish malt, we knew we had a product that could win international acclaim," says executive director Rick Jagdale. "It gave us the motivation to keep going forward." **DR**

Tasting notes

With a little water added, this explodes into life. An oral delight, it is something of a roller-coaster ride, with a lemon citrus nose and an intense, bittersweet taste on the palate. Honey, dusty spice notes, and sweet rich barley all jostle for pole position.

Amrut Cask Strength Peated

Amrut | www.amrutdistilleries.com

Region and country of origin Karnataka, India
Distillery Amrut, Bangalore
Alcohol content 62.8% abv
Style Single malt

Given the amount of whisky consumed in India and the long-standing British love affair with Indian food—often consumed in Indian restaurants with pints of Indian Kingfisher or Cobra beer—it is perhaps surprising that no Indian company before Amrut had tried to establish an Indian whisky in the United Kingdom. Perhaps Amrut's rival whisky producers were content with their healthy domestic sales figures in India, or perhaps they made no effort because they assumed that Scotland and Ireland had divided the market between themselves. Another obvious factor was that a sizable number of leading whisky brands already established in the United Kingdom were produced by global drinks giants. If you are already a presence in a market with your own established brands, you have no incentive to bring in Indian brands and compete against yourself.

Nevertheless, the decision to target Indian restaurants was a logical one. Although the subject of whisky and food pairing is still relatively new, from the outset it was felt that strong whiskies, particularly spicy or peaty ones, offered a perfect partnership with highly flavored curries. However, it didn't quite work out like that. Groups of young men and women who enjoy a curry washed down by copious amounts of lager resisted the idea of changing to cask-strength quality whisky. Not all promotions succeed.

Amrut Cask Strength Peated needs some water, but once unlocked, the malt combines complex flavors with an assertive, earthy, and distinctive peat. The whisky is extremely well made indeed. **DR**

Tasting notes

Without water, this is no great shakes. With water, it becomes a different beast altogether, the intense peaty notes reminiscent of peppered smoked fish. Sweetness and fruit remain, however, performing a captivating danse macabre with the grouchy smoke.

Amrut Double Cask

Amrut | www.amrutdistilleries.com

Region and country of origin Karnataka, India
Distillery Amrut, Bangalore
Alcohol content 46% abv
Style Single malt

As more countries enter the world of whisky, each with its unique climate, humidity, and temperature range, unusual-tasting whiskies are likely to become more common. Amrut Double Cask indicates one direction in which whiskies can travel.

Double Cask is a rare whisky, unfortunately, because just over 300 bottles of it were released. It is made up of just two casks of Amrut, but they were among the oldest the distiller had, stretching back seven years. Doesn't sound very old, does it? But in Bangalore's microclimate, a staggering 60 percent of the liquid is lost to the angels. One of oak's mysteries is the way it allows liquid vapor to pass out.

Scotland has a very gentle evaporation of two percent liquid a year, the majority of which is alcohol, so the strength of the whisky goes down. In Kentucky, the warehouses are high. On the top floors, intense dry summer heat means that water is the dominant vapor leaving the cask, so the strength goes up; on the lower floors, the reverse is true, and on the damp, dark, basement floors, the bourbon follows Scotland. In Bangalore, the maturation is dramatic and violent; the strength of the whisky goes up from the casking strength of 62.5 percent abv to about 70 percent.

Amrut Double Cask may be compared to another Amrut whisky, the Intermediate Sherry. This begins in virgin oak or ex-bourbon casks, is transferred to sherry casks for a time, and then returned to bourbon casks. There is nothing particularly new about combining sherry cask malt and bourbon cask malt, but fusing them in this manner is a stroke of brilliance. **DR**

Tasting notes

Amrut Double Cask is liqueurlike in character—fruity, delightful, rich, sweet, and intense. By comparison, the Intermediate Sherry is a delicious mix of red berries and rich stewed fruits and sweet vanilla ice cream, with sherry flavors in the ascendency.

Amrut Fusion

Amrut | www.amrutdistilleries.com

Region and country of origin Karnataka, India
Distillery Amrut, Bangalore
Alcohol content 50% abv
Style Single malt

Amrut Fusion is the whisky that took the company into the whisky equivalent of the World Series. It won a bucketload of awards, including high praise from global whisky expert Jim Murray and malt overlords the Malt Maniacs, who declared it Best Natural Cask Whisky in the Daily Drams Category at the Malt Maniacs Awards 2009.

All expressions of Amrut are made with homegrown unpeated barley and peated barley from Scotland, which are distilled and matured in the tropical garden city of Bangalore at 3,000 feet (914 m). The trick here was to bring the two barley types together in the original grist. The innovation did not end there, though. For its homegrown barley, the distillery buys in crops from the Punjab, Rajasthan, and Delhi, to the north of India. The country's extremely hot summers and ferociously cold winters produce different types of barley within India itself, and certain barley strains are very different from the ones produced in Scotland. The variations within the Indian barley contribute to the complexity of the whisky.

Further, it was decided to bottle Fusion at 50 percent abv, a strength that brings out the big flavors of the whisky but at the same time allows the drinker to explore and enjoy the complex marriage between the Indian and Scottish grains. **DR**

Tasting notes

Big, bitter, and challenging dark chocolate notes bouncing off a fiery, feisty center. Lashings of fruit, oak, and smoke with a peaty underlay in the Highlands style.

Amrut Kadhambam

Amrut | www.amrutdistilleries.com

Region and country of origin Karnataka, India
Distillery Amrut, Bangalore
Alcohol content 50% abv
Style Single malt

The word *kadhambam* translates roughly as "mixture" in Tamil, and refers to the variety of wood casks used in the aging process: ex-oloroso sherry butts, ex-Bangalore Blue Brandy casks, and ex-rum casks. Quite a unique wood profile for this single malt. Whether Kadhambam is set to become a permanent brand extension to the Amrut range is not confirmed at the time of writing, but the whisky marks the first foray by the company into the territory of wood finishing. After its tough early years, Amrut has not only completed a rapid learning curve in terms of making whisky, but it is starting to benefit from possession of older whiskies and access to finer quality casks used previously to make not only sherry and bourbon but also port and other spirits.

After Kadhambam is finished in the rum and brandy casks, it is bottled at the unusual strength of 50 percent. It works well, and the rich sweetness of the cask mingles nicely with the core malt.

Managing director Neelakanta Rao Jagdale is confident about the company's direction: "I think our future holds everything that was never there in the past. It holds things not even conceived by previous generations or by those who were brought up to think that India could only produce inferior whiskies. We have the chance to go on a new and exciting journey." **DR**

Tasting notes

A complex, sweet, and fragrant nose with delicate wood notes. Almond and a lingering suggestion of fruit. Excellent mouthfeel with pepper and spice.

← Amrut Fusion: a product of barleys from the East and West.

Amrut Kadhambam No.2

Amrut | www.amrutdistilleries.com

Region and country of origin Karnataka, India
Distillery Amrut, Bangalore
Alcohol content 50% abv
Style Single malt

The growing confidence of Amrut was summed up late in 2011 when the distillery released four new whiskies: new batches of Kadhambam and Two Continents, and two very different new expressions, Herald and Portonova. Of the four, the two most dissimilar were Herald and Kadhambam. With only 213 bottles issued to start with, Herald was a rarity. It was a delightfully creamy single-cask bottling, straight from the cask, very sweet with vanilla and toffee. It is a brave thing to put out a single-cask bottling because imperfections have nowhere to hide, but Herald was a note-perfect, world-class whisky.

If Herald was a solo acoustic performance of a malt, Kadhambam Batch No. 2 is an altogether different beast: the whisky equivalent of a rock concert. The whisky here is big, bold, and aggressive, with a small portion of peated barley adding a solid earthiness. A mix of peated and unpeated malts matured in rum, brandy, and more conventional oloroso sherry casks produces a rich, full, and sweet whisky. Unfortunately for Amrut fans, it is a U.S.-only release, reflecting the distillery's continuing but diminishing problems in matching demand with supply. But if you can find it, this second batch of Kadhambam is another talking point of a malt, one that some would deem their favorite Amrut. **DR**

Tasting notes

Sweetness from the rum casks, berry notes from the sherry, and liqueurlike blood orange, glacé cherry, and clementine. Also paprika and sooty peat.

Amrut Nonpeated

Amrut | www.amrutdistilleries.com

Region and country of origin Karnataka, India
Distillery Amrut, Bangalore
Alcohol content 46% abv
Style Single malt

One subject for debate over a dram or two is whether China or India will become the next superpower. Both are developing at a phenomenal rate, but in different ways. And they both have a growing thirst for the very best premium Scotch whiskies. China has no grain whisky history, so the country's nouveau riche are importing a drink that is largely unknown to them. India has a long history of whisky consumption dating from the days of the British Empire, but for every genuine Scotch, there are ninety-nine imitators, many of them not whisky at all but made from molasses. The Indian whisky producer faces a choice. Does he or she go for quality or for mass appeal?

Amrut has been making whisky for three decades now, and has always focused on quality. However, punitive import duties have made buying single malt from Scotland prohibitive, so it started producing its own single malt for use in its blends. This is a straightforward, fruity whisky, and as an entry-level malt, it is perfectly acceptable. But one of the burdens an emerging whisky nation must bear is comparison with the motherland, and the whisky's Speysidelike properties don't provide compelling enough reason to choose it over Scotland's finest. It is well made, though, and worth trying just to see where the amazing Amrut whisky journey started. **DR**

Tasting notes

This is a young whisky, but balanced and built around a clean and sweet barley core, with toffee and vanilla at its center. Some developing oak and spice in the finish.

Amrut Peated

Amrut | www.amrutdistilleries.com

Region and country of origin Karnataka, India
Distillery Amrut, Bangalore
Alcohol content 46% abv
Style Single malt

Wary of fakes, Indian whisky drinkers tend to view the age of a whisky as a sign of quality. There is, of course, a direct link between the quality of a whisky and the length of time it is in the cask, but that is not the only factor involved by a long way. As technology improves, and whisky comes to be shipped from an increasingly diverse range of countries with varying temperatures and humidities, a growing number of younger but excellently made whiskies are turning the focus of drinkers from a whisky's age to its taste.

Given Amrut's heritage, its decision to bottle its Peated without an age statement was a brave one. But it could merely reflect the facts that the whisky is very young and that the early releases were targeted not at the Indian market at all, but the British one.

Of the two original Amrut releases—Nonpeated and Peated—this is the better one. The nonpeated component of the mix is Indian, but the peated barley is imported from Scotland. The peating levels are not heavy, but are sufficient to flesh out the malt and give body and character. Neither one of the original whiskies was particularly successful, but the company ascribed this to the garish original packaging. Certainly, there is nothing wrong with the whisky. This release's importance lies in its interpretation of peat—distinctly different from anything made in Scotland. **DR**

Tasting notes

Fruit notes hold their own against the peat. The smoky peat tastes like barbecued trout and drifts in and out, making smoke rings round the sweet, malty heart.

Amrut Portonova

Amrut | www.amrutdistilleries.com

Region and country of origin Karnataka, India
Distillery Amrut, Bangalore
Alcohol content 62.1% abv
Style Single malt

The Amrut story is all things to all people: a chance punt at a business idea that turned into a golden chalice; a struggle against the odds that repaid the effort; an amateurish, ugly duckling that grew into a beautiful swan; and, perhaps best of all, a dramatic and quick conversion from Scotch wannabes to entrepreneurial pacesetters leading from the front. The owners talk about the mistakes they made and how close they came to giving up, but they wanted to show off Indian ingenuity and know-how, so they stuck at it. And, boy, have they succeeded.

Time and time again the Amrut distillery has turned simplicity into genius. Portonova is a port pipe version of the Amrut Intermediate Sherry—a sort of port sandwich. The spirit is initially matured for a few years in virgin oak or white American oak. Then it spends a few months in a port pipe. Finally it is returned to American oak for a few months to finish off. The result is a huge, fruity, and complex malt that further enhances the distillery's reputation.

The whisky was originally released for distribution in the United States, Canada, Europe, and Taiwan late in 2011, and, as so often with special Amrut releases, it was not expected to last for long. But hopes are high that its popularity will secure it a spot in the core range, and that further releases will go forward. **DR**

Tasting notes

Dynamic, vibrant, fruity nose, with black currant, damson, and blueberry, dark chocolate, fruit liqueur, traces of aniseed, and lots of spice and pepper.

Amrut Two Continents

Amrut | www.amrutdistilleries.com

Region and country of origin Karnataka, India
Distillery Amrut, Bangalore
Alcohol content 46% abv
Style Single malt

Amrut Indian whisky is not so much a case of trying to sell coal to Newcastle as selling malt to Newcastle. The idea of launching an Indian whisky was born at Newcastle University in the north of England, and among the first "guinea pigs" for the malt were the Indian restaurateurs in that city. Amrut single malt had been produced for some years in India for inclusion in Indian blended whisky, but its journey to the bars and shop shelves of the United Kingdom was the result of a thesis by Rick Jagdale, son of the distillery's owner, while at university.

Rick's feasibility study on the subject of launching Indian whisky in the United Kingdom was to become the distillery's blueprint. However, the Amrut team quickly found that the practice was far more difficult than the theory and that it would take more than just good whisky to win over the whisky world. Amrut Two Continents was part of the innovative solution.

Two Continents is matured partly in Europe and partly in India, with the separate malts traveling in different directions while converting from spirit to whisky. Maturation in India takes place in Bangalore, which has its own microclimate. The city, inland in the south of India, stands about 3,000 feet (914 m) above sea level and has a varying humidity and generally mild climate. Maturation is accelerated without the scalding and freezing extremes that speed up the process elsewhere. This spirit is mixed in Bangalore with spirit matured in the traditional stately fashion of Scotland. The method of production may explain this whisky's mellow, cushionlike foundations. **DR**

Tasting notes

Velvety, rich, and chewy, this is still young with some sappiness and a delightful grainy sweetness, but it is distinguished by an exquisite double whammy of yellow, green, and red fruits on a spiky, smoldering peat base. The finish is medium and full flavored.

New Zealand's 1987 24-Year-Old

Greg Ramsay

Region and country of origin South Island, New Zealand **Distillery** Wilson's, Dunedin (closed 2000)
Alcohol content 53.3% abv
Style Single malt

New Zealand hasn't really covered itself in glory in recent years when it comes to whisky. While the rest of the world has been making new and exciting spirits, New Zealand has all but fallen off the whisky map. This is all the more surprising when you consider the sizable Scottish community there. Or maybe that's part of the problem. What whisky industry there was seems to have nearly fizzled out, save for one or two very small enterprises. Talk of new distilleries has, as yet, come to nothing, though in late 2011 there were signs that a new wave of whisky entrepreneurs was going to give it another shot.

New Zealand's problem has been that too many poor whiskies were bottled, and what remains from closed distilleries has been average. This bottling comes from the demolished Wilson's distillery in Dunedin—the second-largest city on the South Island, also known as the "Edinburgh of the South." It is part of the remaining stock now stored at Omaru, and is owned by Greg Ramsey, an Australian entrepreneur living in Tasmania. A distillation from 1987—the most recent year in which the All Blacks were declared world champions—it was released for the 2011 Rugby World Cup. There is little information on the bottle, but the rugby link is made very clear, and we are told that, at 53.3 percent abv, it's a cask-strength bottling.

The man behind the release has a big reputation and promises more carefully selected releases from his inventory. All of which means that the whisky flame in New Zealand is still just about burning, and there's hope for the country yet. **DR**

Tasting notes

Surprisingly clean and vibrant, with citrus on the nose followed by lemon and lime rind marmalade, a big chile hit, some dark chocolate and raisin, and a sharp woody but not unpleasant conclusion. It has a particularly smooth and elegant finish.

Murree's 12-Year-Old Millennium Reserve

Murree Brewery Company | www.murreebrewery.com

Region and country of origin Rawalpindi, Pakistan
Distillery Murree, Hattar
Alcohol content 43% abv
Style Single malt

Of all the odd places where whisky is made, this might well be the oddest. The idea of a whisky distillery in a Muslim country might seem highly unlikely, and yet Murree is a company that makes a wide range of alcoholic drinks. It could be argued that the presence of the Murree distillery and brewery testifies to tolerance in a country that lies on the front line of two religions, between religious and secular cultures.

Murree's 12-Year-Old has the appearance of a single-malt Scotch whisky, and its label is in English. The format and descriptors are aimed at premium malt whisky drinkers, although perhaps the brewery bites off more than it can chew. "We claim that the Millennium compares with some of the most celebrated malt whiskies available anywhere in the world of equal age," say the owners on the packaging. "Murree Millennium is a whisky for the connoisseur and we invite connoisseurs to test this claim. Sip without a dilutant to fully savor the warm, smooth, rich, and unforgettable flavor of Murree's Millennium."

Well, that is the challenge, and the comparison is aimed squarely at the Scotch whisky market. In truth, the whisky cannot be said to taste better than any other twelve-year-old single-malt whisky. That said, this whisky is worth seeking out because it is a genuine original. It is matured at a low temperature in underground cellars, and American, Spanish, and—oddly—Australian casks are used. It does not taste like Scotch, so Murree would be better advised to follow the world trend away from such comparisons and plow its own furrow instead. **DR**

Tasting notes

The whisky's color indicates that its underground maturation has been slow. That maturation is reflected in the taste, which has a grapey, sappy, almost rootsy core with a liqueurlike tobacco-leaf note and a soft, peppery finish that is short and inoffensive.

Bain's Cape Mountain Whisky

Distell Group Ltd. | www.bainscapemountainwhisky.co.za

Region and country of origin Western Cape, South Africa **Distillery** James Sedgwick, Wellington
Alcohol content 43% abv
Style Single grain

Bain's Cape Mountain Whisky is made at the James Sedgwick distillery by the leading South African wine and spirits producer, Distell Group Ltd. The distillery dates back to 1886 and is located near the foothills of the Bain's Kloof Pass, close to the Berg River in Wellington. Bain's Cape Mountain Whisky is named after Scottish-born Andrew Geddes Bain, who was responsible for constructing the pass, opened in 1853, which connected Wellington to the interior.

Although whisky was first distilled in South Africa in the late nineteenth century, the country's favored spirit has traditionally been brandy. Whisky has subsequently found a market in the black middle class that has emerged in recent years. In addition to Bain's Cape Mountain Whisky, Distell produces a number of different blends of imported Scotch malt whisky and domestically distilled grain spirit, including members of the Three Ships range.

The year 2009 saw a radical departure from the creation of blended whiskies when Distell launched this single-grain expression, distilled from locally grown corn. The venture came partly in response to an increase in the number of women drinking whisky in South Africa; their palates were expected to be receptive to the sweet, smooth qualities of a single grain. Distell has remarked, "Our whisky is quite uniquely double matured in specially selected first-fill bourbon casks. After the initial three years of maturation, the whisky is transferred to a second set of first-fill bourbon casks to age for a further two years while continuing to extract further flavor." **DR**

Tasting notes

The nose offers delicate floral aromas, along with vanilla and brittle toffee. Sweet and spicy on the palate, with bourbon influences of honey and vanilla, plus developing citrus fruit notes. The finish features cinnamon and lively oak. Smooth and appealing.

Drayman's Single Malt Whisky

Drayman's Brewery | www.draymans.com

Region and country of origin Pretoria, South Africa
Distillery Drayman's Brewery, Silverton
Alcohol content 43% abv
Style Single malt

Drayman's Brewery has built a strong reputation in South Africa for the boutique high-quality beer from its microbrewery in the heart of Pretoria on the high plateau region of Highveld. Owner Moritz Kallmeyer is regarded as a beer maestro, and for him it was a logical step to start making whisky. He looked to Scotland for inspiration, and although he says that he could never reach Scotland's lofty standards, he has definitely made something unique and special.

Kallmeyer's first bottlings are only five years old, but this is not obvious. The spirit is matured in French oak casks previously used for brandy and wine. The high altitude and climate of the Highveld—the whisky is matured 5,250 feet (1,600 m) above sea level—have had a profound effect on maturation, and although there are cereal notes to be found, there is a richness not normally associated with whisky this young. Indeed, it is another classic example of why attitudes to maturation should be reconsidered as more whisky from around the world is released.

The operation is lean. Fourth- and fifth-fill wine and brandy casks are regenerated by shaving and recharring. They have been known to be filled with the brewery's beer for seasoning. Mainly, though, French red wine is the influence. Whisky has never been made in Pretoria before, but Kallmeyer has taken to the skills of distilling with ease. Drayman's is a welcome example of another distiller adopting an innovative approach to whisky making, and whisky lovers are anticipating great things from this distillery in the future. For now, this single malt will do just fine. **DR**

Tasting notes

A fruity, liqueurlike nose is reflected on the palate, with rich juicy raisins, peach melba covered in whipped cream, and apricot rumtopf. It is big and bold with spice and oak. Some youthful notes are buried in there, too, but it matters not a jot. Different and a real grower.

Drayman's Solera

Drayman's Brewery | www.draymans.com

Region and country of origin Pretoria, South Africa
Distillery Drayman's Brewery, Silverton
Alcohol content 43% abv
Style Blend

Solera is the process of fractional blending that results in a whisky of a mixed ages. The word *solera* refers to the set of various casks and barrels used in this process. Drayman's Solera is made from a variety of imported Scotch and South African whiskies, and includes aged single malt and younger blends. The oldest component in the mix is eighteen years, the youngest just three years. Distiller and owner Moritz Kallmeyer estimates that up to fifty different whiskies are used in the solera process, with a Laphroaig ten-year-old being the most prominent.

A total of eight French oak casks are used in the solera aging process. In 2006 the first four were filled with the Scotch and South African blend, and over the next four years the remaining four casks were filled at six-month intervals. The first Drayman's Solera release was bottled in 2009 when the "mothercask" was tapped; the cask was then topped up with whisky from the next oldest cask, which in turn was topped up from the next, and so on.

While Drayman's Solera is bottled at 43 percent abv, whisky enthusiasts have the option of buying a unique 1-gallon (4.5 liter) cask of Solera direct from the distillery. Kept at home, the whisky continuously increases in alcoholic strength as water evaporates through the wood. After a few months, the whisky can be enjoyed at cask strength, around 47 percent abv, or it can be diluted with spring water to the standard 43 percent abv. Purchasers may also top up the cask when it is half-empty by adding whiskies of their choice; the flavors change and evolve accordingly. **DR**

Tasting notes

The very nature of this whisky goes beyond normal tasting notes because it is an organic, evolving creature that changes with time. Suffice to say that it is not timid on the taste buds, though, and is very much in keeping with what you might expect from South Africa.

Three Ships 5-Year-Old

James Sedgwick | www.threeshipswhisky.co.za

Region and country of origin Western Cape, South Africa **Distillery** James Sedgwick, Wellington
Alcohol content 43% abv
Style Blend

Just as there will always be people who can't accept that anywhere but France can make great wine, so too does an inherent prejudice exist against any whisky that is not single malt from Scotland. This is pure ignorance, as any number of blends and whiskies from the other big four territories—the United States, Ireland, Japan, and Canada—have demonstrated time and time again. There is also an irony that, as whisky becomes fashionable again and international demand encourages a new wave of distillers across the world, a handful, such as James Sedgwick in South Africa, may be perceived as a bit passé. In truth, distilleries such as this one, Tasmania distillery in Australia, and the likes of Amrut in India and Mackmyra in Sweden, have all fine-tuned their offerings and are now making whisky that is excellent by anyone's standards.

The history of the James Sedgwick distillery stretches back more than 150 years. Captain James Sedgwick first sailed into the Cape, South Africa, as the master of the clipper *Undine* in 1850, and soon after established a business supplying quality liquor, tobacco, and cigars. The distillery in Wellington, Western Cape, was purchased in 1886.

The company's standard blend was first launched in 1977. The 5-Year-Old marks the point where the James Sedgwick distillery joined premier whisky ranks. Launched in 1991, it is a blend of South African and Scotch whiskies and is deceptively robust and full flavored. The blend has performed successfully in blind tastings in competitions across the world, picking up medals and plaudits along the way. **DR**

Tasting notes

Buckets of personality as the zappy youthfulness gives it a fizz, fruit provides a big heart, and some impressive earthy peat casts a glance to the Scottish Highlands. Very well balanced with a long, smooth finish. Impressive stuff.

Three Ships 10-Year-Old

James Sedgwick | www.threeshipswhisky.co.za

Region and country of origin Western Cape, South Africa **Distillery** James Sedgwick, Wellington
Alcohol content 43% abv
Style Single malt

Why does this South African distillery have a penchant for maritime references, including its Three Ships whisky trade name? Certainly, James Sedgwick was a sea captain who sailed to South Africa before becoming involved in distilling. However, the squadron depicted on all Three Ships whisky labels consists of Bartholomew Diaz's two lateen-rigged caravel ships and a square-rigged support ship that set out from Portugal in 1487 on an exploratory expedition. Their task was to sail around the tip of Africa and plot a route that would open up the lucrative trading potential of India and Asia.

It was a journey fraught with danger. Early on, it went well; the squadron kept close to the African coastline and made good progress. But then a thirteen-day storm blew them out to the South Atlantic. The crew mutinied, and Diaz was forced to return, but not before seeing the tip of Africa and naming it the Cape of Storms—it was later renamed the Cape of Good Hope by King John II of Portugal.

This single-malt whisky is made with only South African ingredients, and its age of ten years marks a step forward for the distillery. The whisky is a limited edition and is available in three different tins, the pick of which is a stylish blue illustrated with the three ships negotiating choppy waters off the African coast. But best of all, from a whisky drinker's point of view, the whisky is excellently made and put together, and its quality marks a true advance for Three Ships. This is a whisky that wouldn't look out of place alongside many quality Scottish single malts. **DR**

Tasting notes

While you might expect this South African malt to be a big bruiser of a whisky, it is actually less assertive than the 5-Year-Old. With savory salt and pepper and an earthy, peaty underlay, this is not unlike a Glen Garioch or Benromach.

Three Ships Bourbon Cask Finish

James Sedgwick | www.threeshipswhisky.co.za

Region and country of origin Western Cape, South Africa **Distillery** James Sedgwick, Wellington
Alcohol content 43% abv
Style Blend

The town of Wellington, forty-five minutes from Cape Town, lies in the heartland of South Africa's wine production. It is home to the current, ultra-modern James Sedgwick distillery, which is designed to produce new expressions of premium whisky in quantity. Just as with much else in South Africa, greater national self-confidence has produced development in the interest and understanding of whisky of all types. An emerging black middle class, in particular, has sought out premium Scotch single malts, and the major cities boast hotel bars where whisky is showcased in a way that few other countries, except perhaps Japan, can match.

This Bourbon Cask Finish, launched in 2005, was a milestone in the story of James Sedgwick and South African whisky. The special release was notable as South Africa's very first 100 percent homegrown blended whisky; both the malt and grain components were distilled and matured in the country. The name is a little confusing and misleading, however; all whisky has to be matured entirely in oak casks, and more often than not, those casks previously contained bourbon. The name actually refers to the marrying period. After its initial maturation, the blend is returned for a further marrying period in specially imported first-fill American bourbon casks.

The whisky has picked up international medals and has been honored every year since it was first released. In addition, it scored a highly impressive 90 points in the reliable *Jim Murray's Whisky Bible*, where it was also described as "brilliant." **DR**

Tasting notes

On the palate there's gentle honey sweetness underpinned with subtle spice. The extra six months' marrying period results in a sweeter flavor while still maintaining notes of vanilla. A long finish with whispers from the bourbon cask.

Kavalan Concertmaster Port Cask Finish

King Car Company | www.kavalanwhisky.com

Region and country of origin Yilan County, Taiwan
Distillery Kavalan, Yuanshan
Alcohol content 40% abv
Style Single malt

No debut whisky has ever created the sort of stir that Kavalan did when it first came on the scene in 2009. Of course, there have been major world whisky success stories—Amrut, Mackmyra, and Penderyn among them. But Kavalan was different; it did not so much raise eyebrows as take a blowtorch to them.

This writer's first encounter with Kavalan was at the World Whisky Awards, when two of its versions turned up in a box of samples in the opening round of the "Rest of the World" category. One was straw blond, the other chestnut brown. Both were marked "China"—and both were sensational. When it was later announced that the samples were just two years old—and therefore legally could not be called whisky in Europe—you could hear the industry's collective intake of breath.

Kavalan whisky went global when a Scottish newspaper put English whisky up against young Scottish malt in a blind tasting in the hope of tricking some whisky experts. It worked, but it was Kavalan, put in to make up numbers, that really fooled the connoisseurs. By the time it reached four years old, it was already winning awards and challenging the likes of Amrut in world whisky terms.

Concertmaster Port Cask Finish is packaged in a garish bright green bottle more reminiscent of gin. Its main flavor comes from a second maturing in Portuguese ruby, tawny, and vintage port casks that give delicate woody notes on the palate. Kavalan deservedly earned its silver medal at the 2011 San Francisco World Spirits Competition with this one. **PB**

Tasting notes

A big, sweet, and rich malt absolutely bursting with flavor. It is a tropical fruit bowl, with mango, pineapple, guava, and kiwi fruit, and it is a total delight. Only one nitpicking criticism: its youthfulness means that the finish is a little too soft and sweet.

Kavalan Solist Fino

King Car Company | www.kavalanwhisky.com

Region and country of origin Yilan County, Taiwan
Distillery Kavalan, Yuanshan
Alcohol content Varies around 57–58% abv
Style Single malt

Whisky consultant Dr. Jim Swan is an unsung hero. Although you wouldn't necessarily know it, he has influenced distilleries across the world and not just those that make whisky. Wherever you visit, chances are he has been there before you. If you are thinking of setting up a distillery, you go to him for confirmation that it is feasible. He will shoot your dreams down in flames if you have not thought things through properly, but you will thank him for it in the long term. And if he does think that your bird can fly, you can bank on him doing all he can to make it happen.

Dr. Swan believes that technological advances in whisky making have meant that the old necessity of aging spirit is no longer the obstacle it once was in the creation of good whisky. From his experience of working with the Kavalan distillery in Taiwan, he would argue that, for whisky makers working in the humidity of the island—as high as that of Speyside—as well as its heat—about 20°F (6°C) higher than Aberdeen—maturation is on fast forward. In fact, his biggest obstacle in Taiwan was keeping water cool enough to condense the spirit.

Dr. Swan is immensely proud of what Kavalan is achieving and has no doubt about the validity of its output. The range in the Solist series is remarkable, a selection of big, cask-strength whiskies from a variety of casks. This one is fino sherry, and it's a monster. The only clue to the fact that it isn't a sherried eighteen-year-old from Scotland is a lack of astringency and spice. It is a little boy doing an impression of an old man. In a word, stunning. **PB**

Tasting notes

Dry sherry and sweet barley batter against and bounce off each other with startling effect. The experience could be described as the oral equivalent of putting metal in a microwave. Oddly, it tastes both old and venerable and young and vulnerable at the same time.

King Car Whisky

King Car Company | www.kavalanwhisky.com

Region and country of origin Yilan County, Taiwan
Distillery Kavalan, Yuanshan
Alcohol content 46% abv
Style Single malt

At the risk of promoting stereotypes, it could be said that there are big parallels between how the Japanese and Taiwanese have approached car manufacture and how each has approached making whisky.

Japanese whisky has a history stretching back a hundred years. Just as with its car manufacture, where Japanese engineers studied American and European models exhaustively, the whisky makers studied long and hard how Scotland made malts and then set out with painstaking accuracy to re-create them. They have done so well that few whisky lovers fail to acknowledge the remarkable quality of Japanese whisky. But if there is one pronounced difference between Japan's approach to its cars and its whisky, it is that, while Japanese cars are very often technically outstanding and extremely well made but without character, the whiskies are excellently made and packed full of personality.

Taiwan, on the other hand, has proved adept at creating impressive replicas in the shortest possible time. This alacrity has caused some commentators to become suspicious of the Taiwanese whisky industry. Is it really laying the foundations of a new whisky dynasty, or is it merely doing a passable impression? In the final analysis, is it just an impersonator of something greater? Time will tell, of course, but the Kavalan distillery definitely deserves the benefit of the doubt. It has invested heavily in good equipment and sought the advice of, among others, the distillery consultant and sharpshooter Dr. Jim Swan. This whisky offers a strong case for the defense. **PB**

Tasting notes

Tasted blind, this seems to be a Speysider at the outset, and perhaps a Highlander at the finish. There are sweet, plum, and prune notes at the start, but halfway through hot chile pepper cuts through. Better suited to the Western palate than other Kavalan bottlings.

Whisky-Producing Nations

SWEDEN

NETHERLANDS

DENMARK

BELGIUM

SCOTLAND

CANADA

IRELAND

WALES

ENGLAND

FRANCE

SPAIN

UNITED STATES

SWITZERLAND

LIECHTENSTEIN

SOUTH AFRICA

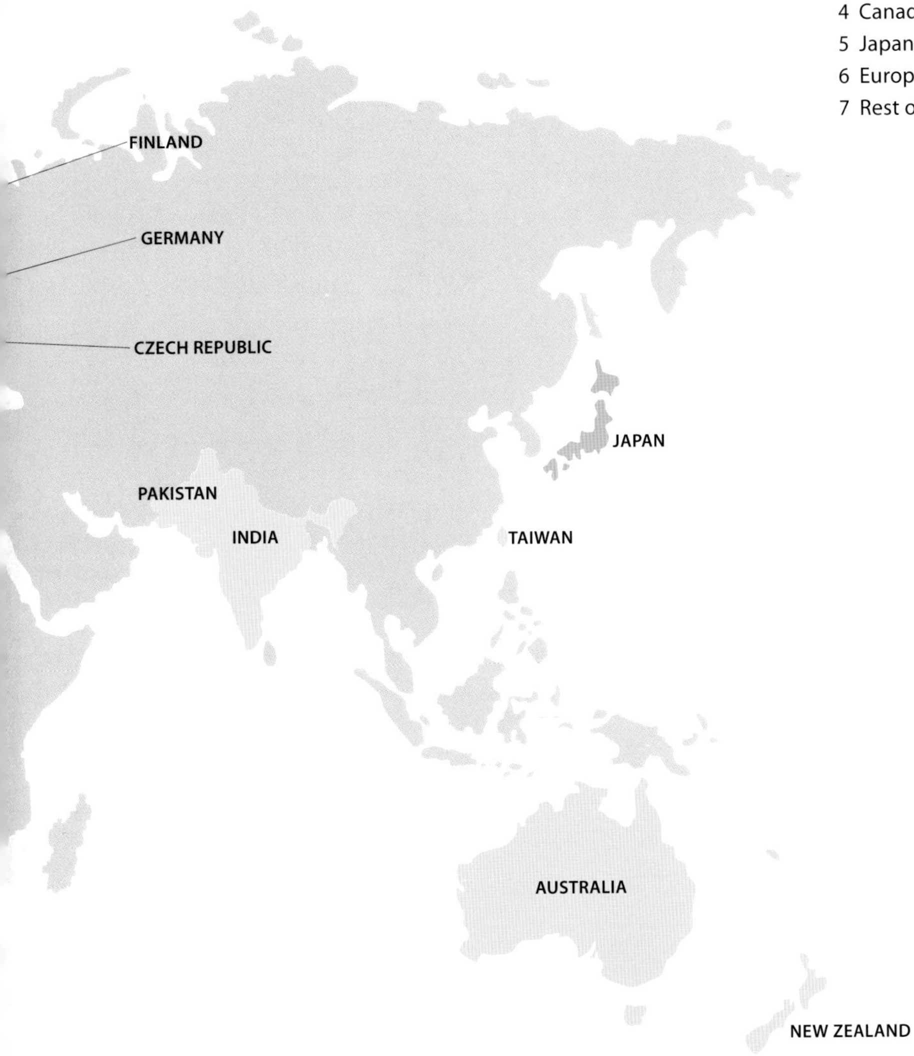
FINLAND
GERMANY
CZECH REPUBLIC
JAPAN
PAKISTAN
INDIA
TAIWAN
AUSTRALIA
NEW ZEALAND

CHAPTERS

1 Scotland
2 Ireland
3 United States
4 Canada
5 Japan
6 Europe
7 Rest of the World

Glossary

Abv
Short for alcohol by volume, used to denote the percentage of alcohol in a spirit.

ACE'd
Short for Additional Cask Enhancement. This process involves a final maturation period, often in an exotic wood, to add taste and color.

Alembic
An early still, dating from ancient Greece. The name is from the Arabic: al-inbīq, meaning "still."

Amontillado
A type of sherry, named after the Montilla region of Spain where the style originated.

Amoroso
A dark, rich, and sweet sherry.

"Angels' share"
A small volume of whiskey that is lost to evaporation during the maturation process.

Bonded warehouse
A place where whisky is stored "under bond" before duty is paid on it.

Butt
A wine or sherry cask that contains around two hogsheads (about 125 to 126 gallons, or 475 to 480 liters) of liquid.

Caramel
A dark brown sugar-based confectionery used by some whisky makers as a basis for a coloring agent.

Cask strength
The level of alcohol-by-volume (abv) strength after maturation, which is typically 60 to 65 percent abv, and before dilution.

Charring
Part of the barrel-making process, whereby the inside is toasted with flame. This releases flavors in the wood that change the taste of the whisky as it matures in the barrel.

Chill-filtered
A method of removing residue and cloudiness from a whisky by cooling and filtering it for cosmetic reasons.

Coffey still
An improved version of the column still, patented in 1831 by Irishman Aeneas Coffey.

Column still
Also known as a patent or continuous still, this two column distillation apparatus was invented in 1826 by Scotsman Robert Stein.

Congeners
Chemical compounds formed during fermentation, distillation, and maturation of whisky that affect its taste and smell.

Continuous still
See column still.

Cooper
The person who makes casks and barrels for the maturation of wine and spirits.

Dram
Scottish term for a measure of whisky, typically around 25 ml.

Dunnage
A traditional warehouse where whisky is matured, typically low-rise stone buildings that have optimum conditions for the maturation process. See also racked warehouse.

Fermentation
The process of turning sugar in to alcohol.

Finish
The flavors of a whisky that remain after it has been swallowed. Finish is measured in length—a long finish is usually perceived as better.

Fino
A dry and pale Spanish sherry.

First-fill cask
Term used for an oak cask filled for the first time with new-make whisky, after it has been emptied of its previous contents.

Graff
The husks and bits of grain that are left after mashing. This residue is often dried and compressed into anima feed.

Grist
A course flour of malt and other grains used to make a whisky.

Hogshead ("hoggie")
A cask holding approximately 55 gallons (208 liters) of liquid.

Madeira
A fortified Portuguese wine made in the Madeira islands in a number of different styles.

Marsala
A wine produced in the area surrounding the Italian city of Marsala in Sicily.

Mash bill
The different grains that go into a whisky. A whisky's mash bill is essentially its list of ingredients.

Mashing
The process whereby grain(s) and water is combined and heated.

Mashman
The person who oversees the mash tun.

Mash tun
The large vessel used for mashing. It typically features a stirring mechanism, known as a mash rake, and a heating device.

Mouth-coating
Moving the whisky around the mouth to coat the four taste receptors to help release flavors.

Mouthfeel
A way of assessing a whiskey's intensity by holding it on the center of the tongue for a few seconds.

New make
The spirit produced by a distillery, prior to maturation.

Nose
A whisky's individual fragrance.

Oloroso
A dark and nutty variety of sherry produced by oxidative aging.

Pedro Ximénez
A type of white grape grown in certain parts of Spain.

Phenols
Chemical compounds introduced to a whisky through a peat-heated fire. Phenols add a smoky aroma and flavor to the spirit.

Pot still
Commonly used in whisky production, this type of still directly heats the vessel holding the wash.

Port pipe
A large oak barrel used in the maturation process.

Racked warehouse
Large, commercial premises for the maturation of whisky. "Racked" refers to the way the whisky is stacked one on top of another, sometimes up to 12 barrels high. See also dunnage.

Saladin box
A nineteenth-century French invention in which barley germinates while being mechanically turned.

Solera
A process for aging liquids by fractional blending in such a way that the finished product is a mixture of ages.

Spirit safe
This locked glass box allowed the makers to check the progress of the whisky in the still without actually coming into contact with it. It was securely locked to prevent distillers from siphoning off the spirit to avoid paying duty; keys to the safe were held by Customs & Excise officers.

Staves
Individual strips of wood that are used to form a barrel.

Wash
The liquid produced at the end of the fermentation of the wort, after the yeast has been added.

Washback
A large vat, usually made of wood, in which distillers ferment the wort to form wash.

Wash still
Large vessels, typically made of copper, for distilling malt whisky.

Worm
A coiled copper tube, usually submerged in water, used to condense the alcohol vapors coming out of the still.

Wort
The sugary liquid obtained from the mashing process. The sugars will ferment to form alcohol.

Contributors

Billy Abbott (BA), a self-confessed whisky obsessive and cocktail snob, is a drinks blogger tempted away from his career as a software engineer in the financial services world to work as a writer for the Whisky Exchange. A booze generalist, whisky remains his first love.

Pat Barrow (PB) lives on the Norfolk-Suffolk border in England and is a director of the Whisky Tasting Club, taking part in both regional tastings and the annual Independent Bottlers' Challenge. He loves all whisky, particularly Rosebank, Springbank, and Balvenie.

Lew Bryson (LB) has been managing editor of *Whisky Advocate* magazine since 1996, and writes the publication's "American Spirit" column. His passion is American whiskey: bourbon, rye, Tennessee, and the craft distillers. He also writes about beer and brewing.

Charles K. Cowdery (CKC) is the author of *Bourbon, Straight: The Uncut and Unfiltered Story of American Whiskey* and producer/director of the "Made and Bottled in Kentucky" DVD. He writes about American whiskey for *The Malt Advocate*, *Whisky Magazine,* and other publications.

Clutch Daisy (D&C) is a composer, singer, and guitarist as well as a reformed scenic carpenter. He holds regular online tasting sessions with Andrew Dubber (below), where the whiskies they review are published in advance so others can take part. Follow @Twhisky to find out more.

Andrew Dubber (D&C) is founder of New Music Strategies. Although a New Zealander, his father was born in Glasgow, so Andrew is genetically predisposed to an appreciation of single malt Scotch. Together with Clutch Daisy (above) he runs dubberandclutch.com, a web site dedicated to whisky.

Lukasz Dynowiak (LD) gained popularity as a tongue-in-cheek drinks blogger and subsequently took the industry by storm to become an acclaimed brand ambassador and whisky competition judge in 2010.

Isabel Graham-Yooll (IGY) is the associate director of London-based whisky specialists Milroy's of Soho, where she is responsible for the shop and the brand. She was a former manager of Selfridges' wine and spirits department, where she first discovered an interest in fine and rare whisky.

Jessica Harvey (JH) is a drinks journalist who writes for magazines including pub trade title *The Publican's Morning Advertiser*, where she is deputy features editor, duty-free show guide *The TFWA Daily*, and style magazine *SuperSuper*. She has a degree in English, a post-graduate degree in business journalism, a penchant for dark spirits, and an appreciation for good pubs and bars.

Davin de Kergommeaux (DDK) is the author of *Canadian Whisky: The Portable Expert* and co-author of three other whisky titles. He is contributing editor of *Whisky Magazine*, writes for *Whisky Advocate Magazine*, and he publishes the web site canadianwhisky.org.

Robin Laing (RL) has written four whisky books, including *Whisky Legends of Islay* (Luath Press), and writes tasting notes for the Scotch Malt Whisky Society. He is also a singer/songwriter who has released four CDs of whisky songs.

George Lewis (GL) is the nom de plume of a London-based style commentator and mystery diner who has reported on restaurants throughout North America and Eurasia, from Carmel, California, to Kazan, Tatarstan.

William C. Meyers (WM) co-authored Michael Jackson's *Complete Guide to Single Malt Scotch*, 6th Ed. (known in the United States as *The Complete Guide to Single Malt Scotch*), and writes for the *Chicago Tribune*, the *St. Louis Post-Dispatch*, and other publications. He is renowned for his knowledge and passion for whisky.

Marcin Miller (MM), a former editor of *Whisky Magazine*, runs a UK drinks marketing consultancy and a Japanese whisky distribution business. He also developed the Whisky Live! series of events and has become an industry icon for both Scotch and Japanese whisky.

Peter Mulryan (PM) is the author of four whisky-related books and has also written for *Whisky Magazine* and *Whisky Advocate*. When he isn't writing, he works as a TV producer specializing in food and drink, and recently hosted a series of films on pot still Irish whiskey.

Andrew Naylor (AN) became interested in whisky while living in western Scotland twenty years ago. Since moving to Norfolk in 2007 he has enjoyed evenings with Dominic Roskrow's tasting groups and has contributed to *Whiskeria* magazine.

Hans Offringa (HO) has written twenty books on whisky, three novels, and nine non-fiction books ranging from golf and champagne to submarines and historic buildings. Together with his wife Becky he conducts whisky nosing and tasting sessions for restaurants and business clubs under the name The Whisky Couple.

Jason Pyle (JP) edits and oversees one of the more popular whiskey-related web sites, which can be found at www.SourMashManifesto.com. Based in Franklin, Tennessee, Jason is an acclaimed American whiskey expert, but declares himself a foodie at heart.

Sally Rasmussen (SR) is relatively new to whisky but she represents a new generation of malt-curious young women. She has written about the hospitality industry for more than fifteen years, most recently in a marketing and public relations capacity.

Stuart Robson (StuR) is a whisky (and chocolate) enthusiast and resident blogger for Whisky Marketplace. He is passionate about the traditional craft of distilling whisky, and has a particular interest in independent distilleries and bottlers.

Ingvar Ronde (IR) took the initiative to publish the first edition of *The Malt Whisky Yearbook* in 2005, and since then he has written, edited, and published another six editions of this world famous bible for the whisky aficionado. A Swedish writer and publisher, he currently spends much of his time visiting distilleries around the world.

Dominic Roskrow (DR), this book's general editor, is an award-winning drinks writer. He edits *Whiskeria*—the world's biggest whisky magazine— and writes regularly for *Whisky Magazine* (of which he was editor for four years), *Harpers*, *Drinks International*, *Malt Advocate*, as well as others. In 2007 he received the Scotch whisky industry's highest honor when he was made a Keeper of the Quaich, and in 2010 he was made a Kentucky Colonel.

Gavin D. Smith (GS) is a specialist whisky writer and the author of more than twenty books, including *The A–Z of Whisky*, *Worts, Worms & Washbacks*, *Whisky Wit & Wisdom*, and *Whisky: A Brief History*, to name just a few. He is proud to be a Keeper of the Quaich, and he lives on the Fife coast in Scotland.

Resources

FURTHER READING

Malt Whisky Companion (6th Edition)
Michael Jackson (Dorling Kindersley)

Malt Whisky Yearbook 2012
Ingvar Ronde (MagDig Media Ltd)

The Whiskies of Scotland:
Encounters of a Connoisseur
Michael Jackson (Duncan Baird Publishers)

200 Years of Tradition:
The Story of Canadian Whisky
Lorraine Brown (Fitzhenry & Whiteside)

MacLean's Whiskypedia
Charles MacLean (Birlinn Ltd)

Scotch Whisky: Its Past and Present
David Daiches (Birlinn Ltd)

Bourbon: The Evolution of Kentucky Whiskey
Sam K. Cecil (Turner Publishing Company)

The Whiskeys of Ireland
Peter Mulryan (O'Brien Press Ltd)

Whiskey: A Global History
Kevin R. Kosar (Reaktion Books)

The Little Book of Whisky Tips
Andrew Langley (Absolute Press)

A-Z of Whisky
Gavin D. Smith (Angel's Share)

Whisky: The Definitive World Guide
Michael Jackson, Dave Broom, Ian Wisniewski,
and Jürgen Deibel (Dorling Kindersley)

The Whisky Trails
Gordon Brown (Prion Books Ltd)

Bourbon Whiskey Our Native Spirit
Bernie Lubbers (Blue River Press)

The Book of Classic American Whiskeys
Mark H. Waymack (Open Court Publishing Co.)

Scotch Missed: Lost Distilleries of Scotland
Brian Townsend (Angel's Share)

The Art of Distilling Whiskey and Other Spirits
Bill Owens and Alan Dikty (Quarry Books)

Classic Bourbon, Tennessee, and Rye Whiskey
Jim Murray (Prion Books Ltd)

Japanese Whisky—Facts, Figures, and Taste
Ulf Buxrud (DataAnalys Scandinavia AB)

The Classic Whisky Handbook
Ian Wisniewski (Lorenz Books)

Irish Whiskey Almanac
James Murray (Prion Books Ltd)

Jim Murray's Whisky Bible
Jim Murray (Dram Good Books Ltd)

Malt Whisky Almanac: A Taster's Guide
Wallace Milroy (Neil Wilson Publishing)

The Malt Whisky File
John D. Lamond and Robin Tucek (Canongate Books)

Whisk(e)y
Stefan Gabanyi (Abbeville Press)

MAGAZINES

Whiskeria
(Whisky Shop Publications)

Whisky Magazine
(Paragraph Publishing)

Drinks International
(Agile Media)

Whisky Advocate
(M. Shanken Communications)

WEB SITES

www.whiskymag.com
www.ralfy.com
www.whiskylive.com
www.whiskyadvocate.com
www.whiskyfestblog.com
www.scotchwhisky.net
www.whisky-distilleries.info
www.whisky-pages.com
www.maltmadness.com
www.whiskyfun.com
www.maltmaniacs.org
www.worldwhiskyindex.com
www.drinksint.com
www.whisky-pages.com
www.whiskyfinder.eu
www. awardrobeofwhisky.com

ONLINE COMMUNITIES

www.connosr.com
www.whiskywhiskywhisky.com/forum
www.whiskymag.com/forum
www.whisky.com/forum

ONLINE SHOPS

www.whiskyshopusa.com
www.parkaveliquor.com
www.masterofmalt.com
www.whiskyshop.com
www.thewhiskyexchange.com
www.gordonandmacphail.com
www.milroys.co.uk
www.lovescotch.com
www.celticwhiskeyshop.com
www.whiskys.co.uk

FESTIVALS

Spirit of Speyside Whisky Festival
May, Glasgow, Scotland
www.spiritofspeyside.com

Kentucky Bourbon Festival
September, Bardstown, Kentucky
www.kybourbonfestival.com

International Whisky Festival
November, Leiden, The Netherlands
www.whiskyfestival.nl

AWARDS

San Francisco World Spirits Competition
www.sfspiritscomp.com

World Whiskies Awards
www.whiskymag.com/awards

Jim Murray's Whisky Bible Awards
www.whiskybible.com

www.maltmaniacs.org
Malt Maniacs Awards

Index of Whiskies by Country

Armorik Édition Originale 853
Armorik Single Cask for La Maison
	du Whisky 854
Breizh 855
Eddu Grey Rock 856
Eddu Silver 856
Glann ar Mor 1 An Gwech 11 857
Kornog Sant Ivy 2011 857
P&M 858
Uberach 859

Germany

Black Horse Original Ammertal
	861
Blaue Maus Single Cask 861
Grüner Hund 862
Slyrs Bavarian 862
Spinnaker 1999 864
Spinnaker Fassstärke 865

India

Amrut 100 920
Amrut Cask Strength 921
Amrut Cask Strength Peated
	922
Amrut Double Cask 923
Amrut Fusion 925
Amrut Kadhambam 925
Amrut Kadhambam No. 2 926
Amrut Nonpeated 926
Amrut Peated 927
Amrut Portonova 927
Amrut Two Continents 928

Ireland

Bushmills 10-Year-Old 569
Bushmills 16-Year-Old 570
Bushmills 21-Year-Old 571
Bushmills 1608 572
Bushmills Black Bush 573
Bushmills Millennium Malt 575
Bushmills Original 575
Connemara 12-Year-Old 577
Connemara Bog Oak 577
Connemara Cask Strength 578
Connemara Turf Mór 579

Dungourney 1964 580
Greenore 8-Year-Old 580
Greenore 15-Year-Old 582
Greenore 18-Year-Old 583
Green Spot 584
Irishman, The 70 585
Irishman, The Single Malt 586
Jameson 587
Jameson 12-Year-Old 588
Jameson 15-Year-Old Single Pot
	Still 588
Jameson 18-Year-Old 590
Jameson Gold Reserve 591
Jameson Rarest Vintage Reserve
	593
Jameson Select Reserve—Small
	Batch 593
Kilbeggan 594
Kilbeggan 15-Year-Old 595
Kilbeggan 18-Year-Old 596
Knappogue Castle 1951 596
Locke's 8-Year-Old 597
Michael Collins 10-Year-Old
	597
Midleton Barry Crockett
	Legacy 598
Midleton Single Cask 1996 598
Midleton Very Rare 600
Paddy 601
Powers Gold Label 603
Powers John's Lane Release
	603
Powers Special Reserve
	12-Year-Old 604
Redbreast 12-Year-Old 605
Redbreast 15-Year-Old 606
Tullamore Dew 606
Tullamore Dew 12-Year-Old 607
Tullamore Dew Black 43 607
Tullamore Dew Single Malt 608
Tyrconnell 609
Tyrconnell Madeira Cask 610
Tyrconnell Port Cask 612
Tyrconnell Sherry Cask 612
Wild Geese, The 613
Wild Geese, The Rare Irish 613

Japan

Chichibu The First 800
Eigashima White Oak 5-Year-
	Old 801
Hakushu 10-Year-Old 802
Hakushu 12-Year-Old 803
Hakushu 18-Year-Old 804
Hakushu 25-Year-Old 805
Hanyu 1988 Single Cask
	No.9501 806
Hibiki 12-Year-Old 807
Hibiki 17-Year-Old 808
Hibiki 21-Year-Old 809
Hokuto 12-Year-Old 810
Ichiro's Malt Card Series
	Eight of Hearts 810
Ichiro's Malt Card Series
	Five of Spades 812
Karuizawa 1971 Single Cask
	No. 6878 817
Karuizawa 1972 Single Cask
	No. 7290 817
Karuizawa 1976 Single Cask
	No. 6919 815
Karuizawa 1985 Single Cask
	No. 7017 814
Karuizawa 1986 Single Cask
	No. 7387 813
Nikka Miyagikyo 15-Year-
	Old 818
Nikka Single Cask Coffey
	Malt 819
Nikka Whisky from the
	Barrel 820
Taketsuru 12-Year-Old
	821
Taketsuru 21-Year-Old 822
Yamazaki 10-Year-Old 822
Yamazaki 12-Year-Old 824
Yamazaki 18-Year-Old 825
Yamazaki 25-Year-Old 826
Yamazaki 1984 827
Yamazaki Bourbon Barrel 828
Yoichi 10-Year-Old 829
Yoichi 20-Year-Old 830
Yoichi 1990 830

2 © Trinity Mirror / Mirrorpix / Alamy 20-21 © CBW / Alamy 22 SSPL via Getty Images 24 Dewar's 25 Dewar's 26 Chivas Brothers 27 Chivas Brothers 28 Chivas Brothers 29 Chivas Brothers 32 International Beverage 33 International Beverage 35 © 19th era / Alamy 36 The Whisky Exchange 37 The Whisky Exchange 38 The Whisky Exchange 39 The Whisky Exchange 42 © Peter L. Hardy / Alamy 44 The Whisky Exchange 45 Private Collection 46 The Whisky Exchange 47 The Whisky Exchange 49 2006 Getty Images 50 Beam Global 51 The Whisky Exchange 52 Beam Global 53 Beam Global 54 Isle of Arran Distillers 55 Isle of Arran Distillers 56 © Matthew Hart / Alamy 57 Isle of Arran Distillers 58 Isle of Arran Distillers 59 The Whisky Exchange 60 Isle of Arran Distillers 61 Isle of Arran Distillers 64 © David Gordon / Alamy 66 The Whisky Exchange 67 The Whisky Exchange 70 The Whisky Exchange 71 The Whisky Exchange 72 The Whisky Exchange 73 Douglas Laing & Co. 74 Simon Pask 75 Inver House 78 Inver House 80 Chivas Brothers 81 The Advertising Archives 82 Chivas Brothers 83 Chivas Brothers 84 Chivas Brothers 86 William Grant & Sons 87 William Grant & Sons 89 © Corbis 90 The Whisky Exchange 91 William Grant & Sons 94 The Whisky Exchange 95 Simon Pask 96 Private Collection 97 © Corbis 100 The BenRiach Distillery Co. 101 The BenRiach Distillery Co. 104 The BenRiach Distillery Co. 105 The BenRiach Distillery Co. 107 © David Gowans / Alamy 108 The BenRiach Distillery Co. 109 The BenRiach Distillery Co. 110 © SuperStock / Alamy 112 The BenRiach Distillery Co. 113 The BenRiach Distillery Co. 116 Gordon & MacPhail 117 Gordon & MacPhail 118 Benromach Distillery 119 Gordon & MacPhail 121 © John Macpherson / Alamy 122 Gordon & MacPhail 123 Douglas Laing & Co. 124 Duncan Taylor & Co. 125 Duncan Taylor & Co. 126 © Gordon Langsbury / Alamy 128 Private Collection 129 Duncan Taylor & Co. 131 © South West Images Scotland / Alamy 134 © David Osborn / Alamy 136 Berry Bros. & Rudd 137 Berry Bros. & Rudd 138 Berry Bros. & Rudd 139 Berry Bros. & Rudd 140 © David Robertson / Alamy 142 The Whisky Exchange 143 The Whisky Exchange 147 © Corbis 148 The Whisky Exchange 149 A Wardrobe of Whisky 152 © Mary Evans Picture Library 2010 154 Bruichladdich Distillery Co. 155 Bruichladdich Distillery Co. 156 Bruichladdich Distillery Co. 157 Bruichladdich Distillery Co. 158 Bruichladdich Distillery Co. 159 © Les Gibbon / Alamy 160 Bruichladdich Distillery Co. 161 Bruichladdich Distillery Co. 164 Bruichladdich Distillery Co. 165 Bruichladdich Distillery Co. 166 Bruichladdich Distillery Co. 167 Private Collection 168 Private Collection 170 Bruichladdich Distillery Co. 171 Bruichladdich Distillery Co. 172 Mary Evans Picture Library 174 Burn Stewart Distillers 175 Burn Stewart Distillers 176 Burn Stewart Distillers 177 Burn Stewart Distillers 178 Burn Stewart Distillers 180 Diageo 181 Simon Pask 182 Diageo 183 Simon Pask 185 © Jeremy Sutton-Hibbert / Alamy 186 © David Gowans / Alamy 190 The Whisky Exchange 191 Chivas Brothers 192 Chivas Brothers 193 The Advertising Archives 194 Chivas Brothers 195 Pernod Ricard 196 Douglas Laing & Co. 197 Douglas Laing & Co. 199 © Neil McAllister / Alamy 200 © Worldwide Picture Library / Alamy 202 The Whisky Exchange 203 Simon Pask 204 The Whisky Exchange 205 Compass Box 206 Compass Box 207 Compass Box 208 Compass Box 209 Compass Box 212 Compass Box 214 Simon Pask 215 © ilian food & drink / Alamy 216 Edrington Group 217 © dieKleinert / Alamy 218 Edrington Group 219 Edrington Group 220 © Tegestology / Alamy 224 Whyte & Mackay 225 Whyte & Mackay 226 Whyte & Mackay 227 Whyte & Mackay 228 Simon Pask 232 Whyte & Mackay 234 Simon Pask 235 Dewar's (Bacardi) 236 Dewar's (Bacardi) 237 © Beryl Peters Collection / Alamy 238 © Illustrated London News Ltd/Mary Evans 242 Douglas Laing & Co. 243 Douglas Laing & Co. 244 Gamma-Keystone via Getty Images 249 Elements of Islay 250 The Whisky Exchange 251 The Whisky Exchange 252 Edrington Group 253 Edrington Group 254 Image Courtesy of The Advertising Archives 256 Edrington Group 257 Whyte & Mackay 259 Getty Images 260 Whyte & Mackay 261 Whyte & Mackay 262 The Whisky Exchange 263 Diageo 266 Douglas Laing & Co. 267 The Whisky Exchange 268 The Whisky Exchange 269 Simon Pask 270 Campari Group 272 Campari Group 273 Campari Group 277 © International Photobank / Alamy 278 Private Collection 279 La Martiniquaise 280 © Mary Evans Picture Library / Alamy 282 Diageo 283 Diageo 286 Angus Dundee Distillers 287 Angus Dundee Distillers 288 Angus Dundee Distillers 289 Angus Dundee Distillers 290 BenRiach Distillery Co. 291 BenRiach Distillery Co. 292 BenRiach Distillery Co. 293 BenRiach Distillery Co. 296 BenRiach Distillery Co. 297 Gordan & Macphail 298 © Scottish Viewpoint / Alamy 302 The Whisky Exchange 303 J & G Grant 305 J & G Grant 308 William Grant & Sons 309 William Grant & Sons 311 © World Pictures/Photoshot 312 William Grant & Sons 313 William Grant & Sons 314 William Grant & Sons 315 Private Collection 316 © drink Alan King / Alamy 320 © David Gowans / Alamy 323 © David Gordon / Alamy 324 Ian Macleod Distillers 325 Ian Macleod Distillers 327 © Photoshot 328 Ian Macleod Distillers 329 Ian Macleod Distillers 332 The Whisky Exchange 333 The Whisky Exchange 335 Mary Evans / The National Archives, London, England 336 Chivas Brothers (Pernod Ricard) 337 Chivas Brothers (Pernod Ricard) 338 Private Collection 339 The Whisky Exchange 340 The Whisky Exchange 341 Signatory Vintage Scotch Whisky Co. 342 Simon Pask 343 The Whisky Exchange 345 © 19th era

Spirits **713** Strong Spirits **715** Heaven Hill Distilleries **716** The Whisky Exchange **717** Heaven Hill Distilleries **718** Heaven Hill Distilleries **719** Age International **720** Rogue **721** Gruppo Campari **722** Gruppo Campari **724** Sazerac **725** Sazerac **726** St George Spirits **727** Stranahan's Distillery **728** Templeton **730** Sazerac **731** Sazerac **732** Old Rip Van Winkle Distillery **733** Old Rip Van Winkle Distillery **736** Gruppo Campari **737** Gruppo Campari **739** Image Courtesy of The Advertising Archives **740** Gruppo Campari **741** Sazerac **742** Sazerac **743** Sazerac **744** Brown-Forman Corporation **745** Brown-Forman Corporation **746** Brown-Forman Corporation **747** Brown-Forman Corporation **748** © Blaine Harrington III / Alamy **750-751** © Tom Gardner / Alamy **752** Beam Global **753** Beam Global **754** Beam Global **755** Constellation Brands **756** Constellation Brands **757** Private Collection **759** © Lordprice Collection / Alamy **760** Beam Global **761** Beam Global **763** Private Collection **764** Sazerac Company **765** Sazerac Company **766** Mary Evans Picture Library **768** MCBSW Sales Company Inc. **769** Brown-Forman **770** Private Collection **771** Private Collection **772** Constellation Brands **773** Kittling Ridge Estates Wines and Spirits **774** Kittling Ridge Estates Wines and Spirits **775** Kittling Ridge Estates Wines and Spirits **776** William Grant & Sons **777** Pernod Ricard—Corby Distilleries **778** Glenora Distillery **779** Glenora Distillery **780** Private Collection **781** Private Collection **782** 35 Maple Street **783** Hood River Distillers Inc. **784** Hood River Distillers Inc. **785** proof brands **786** Phillips Distilling Company **787** Sazerac Company **788** Image Courtesy of The Advertising Archives **790** Indio Spirits **791** Still Waters **792** Beam Global **793** Private Collection **794** Century Distillers **795** © Paul Bock / Alamy **797** Cosmin Nahaiciuc **798-799** © Jeremy Sutton-Hibbert / Alamy **800** Number One Drinks Company **801** Eigashima **802** Private Collection **803** Suntory **804** Suntory **805** Suntory **806** Number One Drinks Company **807** Suntory **808** Suntory **809** Suntory **811** © Jeremy Sutton-Hibbert / Alamy **812** Number One Drinks Company **813** Number One Drinks Company **814** Number One Drinks Company **815** Number One Drinks Company **816** © Swim Ink/Corbis **818** The Nikka Whisky Distilling Co. Ltd **819** The Nikka Whisky Distilling Co. Ltd **820** The Nikka Whisky Distilling Co. Ltd **821** The Nikka Whisky Distilling Co. Ltd **823** © Jeremy Sutton-Hibbert / Alamy **824** Suntory **825** Suntory **826** Suntory **827** Suntory **828** Suntory **829** The Nikka Whisky Distilling Co. Ltd **831** The Nikka Whisky Distilling Co. Ltd **832-833** © Foodfolio / Alamy **835** The Owl Distillery **838** The Prádlo Distillery **839** The Whisky Lounge **840** Hicks & Healey **841** Master of Malt **842** St James Distillery **843** Simon Pask **845** © Lebrecht Authors / Lebrecht Music & Arts / Corbis **846** The English Whisky Co. **847** The English Whisky Co. **848** Simon Pask **849** Panimoravintola Beer Hunter's **850** A Wardrobe of Whisky **851** Warenghem **852** © Leonard de Selva/Corbis **854** Warenghem **855** Warenghem **858** A Wardrobe of Whisky **859** A Wardrobe of Whisky **860** Hotel-Gasthof Lamm **863** © imagebroker / Alamy **864** Blaue Maus Distillery **865** Blaue Maus Distillery **867** Us Heit Distillery **868** Zuidam **870** Zuidam **871** Zuidam **872** Zuidam **873** Beam Global **875** Beam Global **876** Beam Global **877** Destilerías Liber **878** Mackmyra **879** Mackmyra **881** Mackmyra **882** Mackmyra **883** Brauerei Locher **884** Brauerei Locher **885** Brauerei Locher **888** Penderyn **889** Penderyn **890** Penderyn **891** Penderyn **892** Penderyn **894-895** AFP / Getty Images **896** © The Print Collector / Alamy **898** Bakery Hill **899** Bakery Hill **900** Bakery Hill **901** Bakery Hill **902** Belgrove **904** Hellyers Road **905** © Alex Hinds / Alamy **909** Great Southern Distilling Company **910** Nant **914** Tasmania **915** Tasmania **916** Tasmania **917** © National Geographic Society / Corbis **918** Timboon Railway Shed **919** Trapper's Hut **920** Private Collection **921** Simon Pask **922** Amrut **923** A Wardrobe of Whisky **924** Amrut **928** A Wardrobe of Whisky **929** Greg Ramsay **930** Murree Brewery Company **931** Distell Group Ltd **932** Drayman's Brewery **933** Drayman's Brewery **934** James Sedgwick **935** James Sedgwick **936** James Sedgwick **937** King Car Company **938** King Car Company **939** King Car Company **944-945** Volina / Shutterstock

Acknowledgments

Dominic Roskrow and Quintessence would like to thank the following individuals and organizations for their assistance in the creation of this book:

Philip Contos

Sebastian Peyer, for Pat Barrow's German translations

Miguel Angel Blanch Lardin, for images. Please visit www.awardrobeofwhisky.com.

Pat Barrow and William Myers for images

Billy Abbot at Whisky Exchange

Simon Pask photography

Milroys of Soho

All the distilleries who were kind enough to provide images and information.